Credit, Intermediation, and the M

Credit, Intermediation, and the Macroeconomy

Readings and Perspectives in Modern Financial Theory

EDITED BY
Sudipto Bhattacharya
Arnoud W. A. Boot
and Anjan V. Thakor

OXFORD
UNIVERSITY PRESS

OXFORD

UNIVERSITY PRESS

Great Clarendon Street, Oxford OX2 6DP

Oxford University Press is a department of the University of Oxford.

It furthers the University's objective of excellence in research, scholarship, and education by publishing worldwide in

Oxford New York

Auckland Bangkok Buenos Aires Cape Town Chennai
Dar es Salaam Delhi Hong Kong Istanbul Karachi Kolkata
Kuala Lumpur Madrid Melbourne Mexico City Mumbai Nairobi
São Paulo Shanghai Taipei Tokyo Toronto

Oxford is a registered trade mark of Oxford University Press
in the UK and in certain other countries

Published in the United States
by Oxford University Press Inc., New York

British Library Cataloguing in Publication Data
Data available

Library of Congress Cataloging in Publication Data
Data available

ISBN 0-19-924294-1 (hbk.)
ISBN 0-19-924306-9 (pbk.)

10 9 8 7 6 5 4 3 2 1

Typeset by Newgen Imaging Systems (P) Ltd., Chennai, India
Printed in Great Britain
on acid-free paper by
Antony Rowe Ltd, Chippenham, Wiltshire

CONTENTS

Contents

ACKNOWLEDGMENTS

Part I Monitoring by and of Banks

1. Boyd, J. H., and Prescott, E. C. (1986). "Financial intermediary-coalitions." *Journal of Economic Theory*, 38: 211–32.
2. Calomiris, C. W., and Kahn, C. M. (1991). "The role of demandable debt in structuring optimal banking arrangements." *American Economic Review*, 81: 497–513.
3. Repullo, R., and Suarez, J. (1998). "Monitoring, liquidation, and security design." *Review of Economic Studies*, 11: 163–87.
4. Hellwig, M.F. (2000). "Financial intermediation with risk aversion." *Review of Economic Studies*, 67: 719–42.

Part II Liquidity Provision via Banks and Markets

5. Diamond, D. W. (1997). "Liquidity, banks, and markets." *Journal of Political Economy*, 105: 928–56.
6. Holmström, B., and Tirole, J. (1998). "Private and public supply of liquidity." *Journal of Political Economy*, 106: 1–40.
7. Bhattacharya, S., Fulghieri, P., and Rovelli, R. (1998). "Financial intermediation versus stock markets in a dynamic intertemporal model." *Journal of Institutional and Theoretical Economics*, 154: 291–319.
8. Hart, O., and Hardman-Moore, J. (1996). "The governance of exchanges: Members' cooperatives versus outside ownership." *Oxford Review of Economic Policy*, 12: 53–69.

Part III Bank Runs and Financial Crises

9. Chari, V. V., and Jagannathan, R. (1988). "Banking panics, information, and rational expectations equilibrium." *Journal of Finance*, 43: 749–61.
10. Morris, S. and Shin, H.-S., (1998). "Unique equilibrium in a model of self-fulfilling currency attacks." *American Economic Review*, 88: 587–97.
11. Freixas, X., and Parigi, B. (1998). "Contagion and efficiency in gross and net interbank payment systems." *Journal of Financial Intermediation*, 7: 3–31.

Part IV Regulation of Financial Intermediaries

12. Rochet, J.-C. (1992). "Capital requirements and the behaviour of commercial banks." *European Economic Review*, 36: 1137–78.

13. Kroszner, R.S., and Rajan, R.G. (1994). "Is the Glass–Steagall act justified? A study of the U.S. experience with universal banking before 1933." *American Economic Review*, 84: 810–32.
14. Aghion, P., Bolton, P., and Fries, S. (1999). "Optimal design of bank bailouts: The case of transition economies." *Journal of Institutional and Theoretical Economics*, 155: 51–70.

Part V Financial Contracting and Interbank Competition

15. Boot, A. W. A., Greenbaum, S. I., and Thakor, A. V. (1993). "Reputation and discretion in financial contracting." *American Economic Review*, 83: 1165–83.
16. Petersen, M. A., and Rajan, R. G. (1995). "The effect of credit market competition on lending relationships." *Quarterly Journal of Economics*, 110: 407–43.
17. von Thadden, E.-L. (1995). "Long-term contracts, short-term investment, and monitoring." *Review of Economic Studies*, 62: 557–75.
18. Winton, A. (1997). "Competition among financial intermediaries when diversification matters." *Journal of Financial Intermediation*, 6: 307–46.

Part VI Comparative Financial Systems: A Survey

19. Dewatripont, M., and Maskin, E. (1995). "Credit and efficiency in centralized and decentralized economies." *Review of Economic Studies*, 62: 541–55.
20. Bhattacharya, S., and Chiesa, G. (1995). "Proprietary information, financial intermediation, and research incentives." *Journal of Financial Intermediation*, 4: 328–57.
21. Boot, A. W. A., and Thakor, A. V. (1997). "Financial system architecture." *Review of Financial Studies*, 10: 693–733.
22. Allen, F., and Gale, D. (1997). "Financial markets, intermediaries, and intertemporal smoothing." *Journal of Political Economy*, 105: 523–46.

Part VII Credit Markets, Intermediation, and the Macroeconomy

23. Holmström, B., and Tirole, J. (1997). "Financial intermediation, loanable funds, and the real sector." *Quarterly Journal of Economics*, 52: 663–91.
24. Kiyotaki, N., and Hardman-Moore, J. (1997). "Credit cycles." *Journal of Political Economy*, 105 (2): 211–49.
25. Suarez, J., and Sussman, O. (1997). "Endogenous cycles in a Stiglitz–Weiss economy." *Journal of Economic Theory*, 76: 47–71.

LIST OF CONTRIBUTORS

Aghion, Philippe Harvard University, Cambridge, UK

Allen, Franklin University of Pennsylvania, Philadelphia

Bhattacharya, Sudipto W. P. Carey School of Business, Arizona State University, USA, London School of Economics and Political Science, London, UK, Centre for Economic Policy Research (CEPR), UK

Bolton, Patrick Princeton University, Princeton

Boot, Arnoud W. A. University of Amsterdam, Amsterdam, The Netherlands

Boyd, John H. University of Minnesota, Minneapolis

Calomiris, Charles W. Columbia University, New York

Chari, V. V. University of Minnesota, Minneapolis

Chiesa, Gabriella Università di Bologna, Bologna, Italy

Dewatripont, Mathias Université Libre de Bruxelles, Bruxelles, Belgium

Diamond, Douglas W. University of Chicago, Chicago

Freixas, Xavier Universitat Pompeu Fabra, Barcelona, Spain

Fries, Steven European Bank for Reconstruction and Development, London, UK

Fulghieri, Paolo University of North Carolina, Chapel Hill

Gale, Douglas New York University, New York

Greenbaum, Stuart I. Washington University, St Louis

Hardman-Moore, John University of Edinburgh, Edinburgh, UK

Hart, Oliver Harvard University, Boston

Hellwig, Martin F. University of Mannheim, Mannheim, Germany

Holmström, Bengt Massachusetts Institute of Technology, Boston

Jagannathan, Ravi Northwestern University, Evanston

Kahn, Charles M. University of Illinois, Urbana

Kiyotaki, Nobuhiro London School of Economics and Political Science, London, UK

Kroszner, Randall S. University of Chicago, Chicago

Maskin, Eric Princeton University, Princeton

Morris, Stephen Yale University, New Haven

Parigi, Bruno Università di Padova, Padova, Italy

Peterson, Mitchell A. Northwestern University, Evanston

Prescott, Edward C.   Federal Reserve Bank, Minneapolis, Minnesota
  Another address: Arizona State University, Tempe
Rajan, Raghuram G.   University of Chicago, Chicago
Reichlin, Pietro   University of Rome La Sapienza, Rome, Italy
Repullo, Rafael   CEMFI, Madrid, Spain
Rochet, Jean-Charles   Université Toulouse, Toulouse, France
Rovelli, Ricardo   Università di Bologna, Bologna, Italy
Santomero, Anthony M.   Federal Reserve Bank of Philadelphia,
  Philadelphia
Shin, Hyun-Song   University of Oxford, Oxford, UK
Suarez, Javier   CEMFI, Madrid, Spain
Sussman, Oren   University of Oxford, Oxford, UK
Thakor, Anjan V.   Washington University, St Louis
Tirole, Jean   Institut D'Economie Industrielle (IDEI), Toulouse, France
von Thadden, Ernst-Ludwig   University of Lausanne, Lausanne,
  Switzerland
Winton, Andrew   University of Minnesota, Minneapolis

Introduction

Sudipto Bhattacharya, Arnoud W. A. Boot, and Anjan V. Thakor

For little more than a quarter of a century, a flourishing literature on modeling imperfect capital markets with informational asymmetries and moral hazard regarding agents' choices has yielded many insights regarding the nature of market equilibrium, corporate financial policies, and the roles of ownership and control rights in characterizing institutions in these settings; see, for example, Rothschild and Stiglitz (1976), Jensen and Meckling (1976), Stiglitz and Weiss (1981), and Grossman and Hart (1986). In particular, our understanding of quantity-constrained financial (cum insurance) contracts, of managerial incentive schemes, and of signaling (Spence 1973) via choices of financing and payout policies were vastly improved and helped refine explanations of phenomena such as dividend payments (Bhattacharya 1979), "under-pricing" of new equity issues (Rock 1986) and complex capital structures (Constantinides and Grundy 1989). Alongside these developments, two early and important papers, by Leland and Pyle (1977) and by Bryant (1980), provided models and suggestions for a theory of the roles of *financial intermediaries* as institutions which might facilitate the resolution of these problems of informational asymmetry and corporate governance, and laid the foundations for a burgeoning sub-field of financial economics grounded in recent developments in information economics and the theory of contracts. A review of these developments was provided by Bhattacharya and Thakor (1993). In this collection of selected readings and commentaries (perspectives) provided by several prominent scholars working in this area, we go a step beyond that review paper to encompass in depth most of the key aspects of this sub-field, including its implications for optimal regulatory policies and the macro-behavior of the real economy.

We begin with a brief description of the overarching logic that underlies the selection of the topics in this book and their sequence. The first question in any examination of financial intermediation is: Why do financial intermediaries (FIs) exist? The answer is that they provide two fundamental economic services: (i) monitoring and screening, and (ii) liquidity provision. However, the provision of liquidity creates the possibility of bank runs and financial crises. This necessitates regulation of FIs. Regulation, in turn, affects the kinds of contracts FIs can write and interbank competition. However, FI regulation cannot be contemplated in isolation of the other components of the financial system because of the interaction between FIs and financial markets. This interaction has both complementary and competitive aspects. Thus, a careful consideration of comparative financial systems is necessary.

The "big-picture" questions this book confronts are thus the following:

(1) Why do FIs exist and how do they provide screening and monitoring outcomes that are more efficient than what is possible in non-intermediated settings?
(2) How do FIs provide liquidity?
(3) What is the mechanism by which liquidity provision by FIs leads to bank runs and financial crises?
(4) How should FIs be regulated?
(5) What are the attributes of the financial contracts FIs use and how do these financial contracts affect the nature of the services provided by FIs?
(6) What is the role of FIs in the overall financial system and how do different financial systems compare in terms of the flow of services they provide for the real sector of the economy?
(7) What is the impact of the financial system on the functioning of credit markets and the macroeconomy?

The first question, which is addressed in Part I, was first examined by Leland and Pyle (1977), who modeled the role of non-diversified insider equity holdings as signals of their project qualities (mean returns) by asymmetrically informed risk-averse entrepreneurs. This paper noted that internal diversification within coalitions of such entrepreneurs may reduce the dead-weight costs of such a signal for each of them. Diamond (1984) and Ramakrishnan and Thakor (1984) added the important alternative technology of (external) monitoring—with results verifiable only to monitors—for resolving informational asymmetries, and showed that in some circumstances monitoring by an intermediary coupled with its "diversifying" over many investments (by pooling the funds of many investors) could reduce per-project costs of resolving informational asymmetry to that of unduplicated monitoring.

These contributions are discussed at length in our introduction to Part I, which also contains chapters in which the above themes of monitoring cum diversification by intermediaries have been further developed. These chapters are the early work of Boyd and Prescott (1986), which deals with finite information-processing coalitions, the Calomiris and Kahn (1991) analysis, which considers a multiperiod model in which demandable debt liability contracts serve to discipline intermediary agents, and Repullo and Suarez's (1998) model, which focuses on an intermediary that controls entrepreneurs' moral hazard via a credible threat of interim liquidation, which may require the coexistence of bank debt and non-monitoring public market financing. The fourth chapter in this part, that of Hellwig (2000), extends the model of Diamond (1984) in which the financial intermediary is a single agent carrying out delegated monitoring and bearing the residual risks of an increasing sequence of the sums of independent risks, to examine when the claimed superiority of such intermediated financing holds when such agents are strictly risk-averse.

The answer to Question 2 was first suggested by Bryant (1980), who focused on the liability side of bank-type intermediaries. That paper proposed a rationale for the bank deposit or demandable debt contract as being the optimal solution in a setting where investors' ex post intertemporal preferences for consumption are random with privately observed realizations, and the technologies for investment by a bank yield higher rates of return over longer maturities. The problem of bank runs could then arise from such demandable deposit contracting, especially when some agents might receive private information concerning the prospective returns on their bank's long-term investments. Diamond and Dybvig (1983) further developed these themes, and noted that runs could arise as Pareto-dominated Nash equilibria even when banks' asset returns are certain. They considered remedies such as suspension of convertibility in a setting where the aggregate demand for early consumption (liquidity) is certain, and deposit insurance combined with injection of nominal liquidity in a setting where the aggregate liquidity demand is random.

These models, set in a "representative intermediary" context, did not consider the alternative of markets for trading the long-term investments at the interim date to generate liquidity. Jacklin (1987) showed that, given ex ante optimal choices of investment portfolios, markets could do as well as deposits—without any fear of runs—in the Diamond–Dybvig model with agents having ex post corner preferences over their consumptions (from savings) at two different time points, but this was not the case more generally; deposit contracts could then provide agents with greater ex ante risk-sharing. Bhattacharya and Gale (1987) noted that if agents, or intermediaries, sought liquidity via unfettered interim trading of their long-term investments, the consequence would be sub-optimal ex ante investment allocations over long- and short-term investments. The reason for this is the incompleteness of insurance markets with respect to the agents' private intertemporal preference shocks. They suggested key roles for a pre-committed Central Bank Discount Window, as well as for regulatory constraints (floors) on banks vis-à-vis the observable components of their short-term investments (liquid reserves).

In Part II, we have included two recent models of liquidity provision in intertemporal models via interim markets, via pre-committed credit lines, and via governmental bonds backed by the power of taxation. These are Diamond's (1997) work, which considers limited market participation, and Holmstrom and Tirole's (1998) research, which considers interim liquidity shocks (random investment requirements) for their project originators. We have also included Bhattacharya et al. (1998) on an extended Bryant–Diamond–Dybvig model of liquidity risk-sharing in an overlapping generations (OLG) setting—in which the long-term investments of prior generations can provide liquidity for "early diers" of subsequent generations—where successive generations of agents may disagree over a stock market ("vested") versus a contractual transfer-based ("pay as you go") mechanisms. These and some other related papers, including his own key contributions to these themes, are discussed by von Thadden. We conclude this section on liquidity provision with a chapter that focuses on trading exchanges rather than on intermediary contracts, by Hart and Moore (1996), which illustrates the scope of the emerging methodology of the literature on incomplete contracts and ownership rights, that is germane also to some of the later parts of our collection.

Question 3 is taken up in Part III. Here we deal with post Bryant–Diamond–Dybvig contributions to the issues concerning bank runs including their alleged systemic risk features such as Contagion (of runs spreading across banks). The first such contribution by Chari and Jagannathan (1988) (Chapter nine) goes beyond Bryant, Diamond and Dybvig, and Jacklin and Bhattacharya (1988) to consider a model in which there is a possibility of both a large liquidity demand shock and a negative shock to a bank's prospective long-term asset returns, which some depositors know in advance. Less informed depositors can react based on the size of the early-withdrawals queue. And they may panic and run (demand early withdrawal) even when in truth it is only a high liquidity (consumption demand) shock that their bank can cope with, because of it being confounded with bad returns prospects. This provides a natural framework for building a model of contagious runs at other banks as well, if their asset portfolio returns are highly correlated across these banks. A run, when it occurs, is a unique equilibrium in the Chari and Jagannathan model. Morris and Shin (1998) obtain a similar unique-equilibrium result, by considering an environment in which agents have dispersed items of private information about the true state of nature. Although it is cast in the context of exchange rate crises, extending the idea of the paper to bank runs has been proven to be fruitful (Goldstein and Pauzner 2002).

The final contribution to this part, by Freixas and Parigi, considers the relative ex ante efficiency of Gross versus Net interbank settlement systems for their customers' transfers. They show that (the equilibrium set of) a Net system dominates, by economizing on liquid (short-term) asset reserves, in the absence of local information about future asset returns. However, when uninsured depositors do have adverse information about their bank's returns prospect, they try to transfer their future withdrawal rights to the other bank, thus creating externalities for the depositors of the other bank. They do so instead of starting a run in their own bank—which would have led to allocationally efficient liquidation of its long-term assets, a key assumption—and hence the contagion in this chapter is one of inefficient continuation, not liquidation. In contrast, Allen and Gale (2000) have recently considered contagion in the form of inefficient (negative-sum) early liquidation of long-term investments spreading across the banking system, owing to the demandable nature of the deposit contract and bilateral interbank ties in a multiple banks system. In their model, a run arises from a sufficiently high liquidity-demand shock at only one bank which causes enough losses to its related banks' interbank deposits to start runs by their depositors as well, and these in turn spread to their depositor banks. Rochet discusses these chapters and other related literature, including his own recent research in this area.

Part IV takes up the issue of FI regulation, thereby tackling Question 4. There are at least three major issues in regulation. The first is that if the liquidity-provision function of FIs causes an inherent fragility in the system due to runs and panics, then what regulatory initiatives can help reduce this fragility? The literature on this subject has exhaustively examined capital requirements, deposit insurance, regulatory auditing, and bank–asset–portfolio restrictions as components of optimal regulation. The Rochet (1992) paper (Chapter twelve) included in Part IV, is part of this very extensive literature and focuses on the incentive effects of bank capital regulation.

The second major issue has to do with optimal regulatory policies with respect to bailouts of financially troubled FIs. The Aghion and Bolton (1999) chapter (Chapter fourteen) in this part examines this issue in the context of transitional economies; a general analysis of optimal closure policy is provided by Mailath and Mester (1994). These papers assume that regulators act in the best interests of tax payers and thus ignore the complication of regulatory career concerns that cause their self-interested closure decisions to diverge from the socially optimal closure policy; this is the focus in Boot and Thakor (1993).

The third issue is how much freedom regulated institutions should be allowed in their asset portfolio choices, given the runs-related negative externality associated with partially insured institutions choosing excessive risk and their risk-seeking propensity, due to the perverse incentive effects of deposit insurance. The now-defunct Glass–Steagall Act in the U.S., which proscribed investment banking and insurance for commercial banks, was intended to provide the desired portfolio restrictions. Whether this separation between different types of FIs was empirically justified is what Kroszner and Rajan (1994) examine in their chapter, which is also included in this section. The discussion by Freixas and Santomero concludes Part IV.

The structure of the contracts designed and deployed by FIs has a potentially profound impact on the nature of the financial services provided by FIs. It is therefore important to understand the determinants of these contracts and the effects they produce. This issue, embedded in Question 5, is the subject of Part V. The integrating overview for this part is provided by Winton. The three key factors that affect the design of contracts by FIs are: Reputational rents, the relationship-based nature of bank credit, and interbank competition.

Boot et al. (1993), included in this part, develop a model in which banks' incentives to honor previously sold loan commitments are affected by their reputational rents. Banks trade off reputational capital against financial capital when deciding whether or not to honor their commitments. The amount of discretion permitted the bank in deciding whether to honor its contracts then depends on its reputation in honoring them, which then explains not only observed relationships between the types of contracts that are used by FIs and the attributes of these FIs, but also predicts when FIs will go beyond their binding legal obligations in honoring contracts.

Petersen and Rajan (1995), also included in this part, take a different approach. They apply and build on Rajan's (1992) and Sharpe's (1990) work on the benefits of relationship-based lending. Petersen and Rajan argue that relationship lending facilitates the smoothing of lending rates, which could be beneficial for de novo borrowers who would get initially lower lending rates provided that the bank can recoup these subsidies later on in the relationship. These benefits need to be weighted against distortions related to potential hold-up problems. Similar issues are examined in a model with a clear structure by von Thadden (1995), also included in this part. Like Petersen and Rajan's contribution, von Thadden's analysis illuminates the ways in which bank finance differs from less relationship-oriented debt and when one will be preferred over the other.

The final chapter in this part is Winton (1997), which seeks to explain why we do not observe economies dominated by one or two very large, (almost) perfectly diversified FIs, if the incentive costs of contracting decline with FI size, as in the models of Diamond (1984) and Ramakrishnan and Thakor (1984). The key to Winton's analysis is that when FIs are delegated monitors and compete with each other, "adoption externalities" arise as borrowers' beliefs about which FIs investors will use will determine the equilibrium size and structure of FIs, which may lead to an equilibrium in which the industry is highly fragmented.

While much of the financial intermediation literature has focused on banks, there has recently been increasing recognition that a broader theoretical perspective needs to be developed that views banks, other FIs and capital markets as parts of an overall financial system. This is the motivation for Part VI, and is embedded in Question 6. Allen and Gale provide the introduction to and a thorough overview of the chapters in this part and the related literature. The major theme of this part is that the principal issue in financial system design is that of determining the relative roles of institutions and markets. This determination hinges on four key factors analyzed in the four chapters included in this part: The tradeoff between information aggregation benefits and the benefits of resolving moral hazard, the desire to protect the privacy of proprietary information, the need to avoid soft budget-constraint problems, and risk sharing.

The Allen and Gale (1997) paper (Chapter twenty-two) included in this part focuses on the risk-sharing aspect. It argues that FIs have an advantage over markets in providing agents with optimal intertemporal and inter-generational risk-sharing, whereas markets facilitate more competitive outcomes, albeit with less insurance.

The Boot and Thakor (1997) paper (Chapter twenty-one), also included in this part, examines the second tradeoff. Their theory shows that FIs are preferred when (asset-substitution) moral hazard problems are severe among those seeking external finance, which intermediaries can mitigate via monitoring, whereas financial markets are preferred when many disparate information signals need to be aggregated via traded asset prices and this information has value for real decisions.

Whereas Boot and Thakor construct a setting in which the market *collectively* knows more about the firm's future prospects than its manager does, the more "standard" approach is to assume that the manager knows more. Bhattacharya and Chiesa (1995), whose chapter is the second in this part, make this more standard assumption in the context of a model of research incentives. This allows them to focus on the third tradeoff in financial system design, namely that a borrower may prefer to go to an FI when it can be more assured that sensitive proprietary information that it shares with the lender will not be disclosed to its competitors, which is a very real possibility in a financial market due to the "two-audience" signaling problem of information leakage to the firm's competitors as well as its investors. However, from an ex ante perspective, firms may sometimes welcome such leakages, unless it impedes their research incentives, and the trade-off between these two effects may depend on stages of their life cycle, which would affect the degree to which their knowledge is patentable and their efforts are monitorable.

Finally, the fourth chapter in this part, Dewatripont and Maskin (1995), suggests yet another factor differentiating FIs and markets. When a borrower must obtain credit in multiple periods, an FI can suffer from a "soft-budget-constraint" problem in that it may have an incentive to "throw good money after bad" and lend to a bad borrower simply to protect the value of the debt claim it had purchased earlier from the borrower. In contrast, because of the free-rider problem among many small (uncoordinated) bondholders, the financial market will typically be better at sticking to its commitment to not extend further credit to such borrowers.

All of this interest in comparing financial system is overdue; it has been shown, both theoretically and empirically, shown that financial system design affects the real economy (see Levine 1999, for example). Part VII, which addresses Question 7, seeks to examine several issues on this topic. The overview here is provided by Pietro Reichlin. The first of the chapters in this part is by Holmstrom and Tirole (1997). This chapter explains the determination of a firm's optimal debt capacity, derives the equilibrium composition of firms' liabilities and characterizes the impact of FI liabilities on the degree of moral hazard and firms' investment activity.

The second chapter included in this part, by Kiyotaki and Hardman-Moore (1997), examines the effect of the financial sector on the real sector by explicitly recognizing the effects of collateral on borrowers' incentives to repay. Since reputational concerns are excluded, it is only the threat of losing collateral that induces borrowers to repay. This chapter assigns two roles to collateral. One is to determine the economy's aggregate output through the use of collateralizable assets in the production process. The other is that the need for collateral in credit contracts creates binding credit limits on borrowers. Thus, when the economy experiences a negative productivity shock, borrowers will cut back on their investment spending, which diminishes their demand for collateral and causes its price to fall, intertemporally propagating the effect of the initial productivity shock. This is a way to understand the persistence of exogenous shocks to the economy through credit–market interactions.

A different propagation mechanism for shock persistence is considered in Suarez and Sussman (1997), the final chapter in this part. Instead of collateral or financial fragility leading to the amplification of exogenous shocks, it is liquidity that does the trick. An increase in borrowers' production generates excess supply and price deflation, which then reduces borrowers' cash flows and liquidity. This exacerbates moral hazard by weakening borrowers' incentives to improve project outcomes. Thus, endogenous cycles are obtained by creating a link between liquidity effects and relative price movements.

References

Allen, F., and Gale, D. (2000). *Comparing Financial Systems*. Cambridge, MA: MIT Press.

Bhattacharya, S. (1979). "Imperfect information, dividend policy, and the 'bird in the hand' fallacy." *Bell Journal of Economics*, 10: 259–70.

——, and Gale, D. (1987). "Preference shocks, liquidity, and central bank policy," in W. A. Barnett and K. J. Singleton (eds.), *New Approaches to Monetary Economics* (Cambridge: Cambridge University Press).

——, and Thakor, A. V. (1993). "Contemporary banking theory." *Journal of Financial Intermediation*, 3-1: 2–50.

Boot, A. W. A., and Thakor, A. V. (1993). "Self-interested bank regulation." *American Economic Review*, 83-2: 206–12.

Bryant, J. (1980). "A model of reserves, bank runs, and deposit insurance." *Journal of Banking and Finance*, 4: 335–44.

Constantinides, G., and Grundy, B. (1989). "Optimal investment with stock repurchase and financing as signals." *Review of Financial Studies*, 2: 445–66.

Diamond, D. (1984). "Financial intermediation and delegated monitoring." *Review of Economic Studies*, 51: 393–414.

——, and Dybvig, P. (1983). "Bank runs, deposit insurance, and liquidity." *Journal of Political Economy*, 91: 401–19.

Goldstein, I., and Pauzner, A. (2002). "Demand deposit contracts and the probability of bank runs." Working paper, February.

Grossman, S. J., and Hart, O. D. (1986). "The costs and benefits of ownership: a theory of vertical and lateral integration." *Journal of Political Economy*, 94: 691–719.

Jacklin, C. J. (1987). "Demand deposits, trading restrictions, and risk-sharing," in E. C. Prescott and N. Wallace (eds.), *Contractual Arrangements for Intertemporal Trade* (University of Minnesota Press).

——, and Bhattacharya, S. (1988). "Distinguishing panics and information-based bank runs: welfare and policy implications." *Journal of Political Economy*, 96: 568–92.

Jensen, M. C., and Meckling, W. H. (1976). "Theory of the firm: Managerial behavior, agency costs and capital structure." *J. Finan. Econ.*, 3: 305–60.

Leland, H., and Pyle, D. (1977). "Informational asymmetries, financial structure, and financial intermediation." *Journal of Finance*, 32: 371–87.

Levine, R. (1999). "Law, finance, and economic growth." *Journal of Financial Intermediation*, 8-1/2, 36–67.

Mailath, G., and Mester, L. (1994). "A positive analysis of bank closure." *Journal of Financial Intermediation*, 3: 272–99.

Rajan, R. (1992). "Insiders and outsiders: The choice between Informed and arm's-length debt." *Journal of Finance*, 47: 1367–400.

Ramakrishnan, R. T. S., and Thakor, A. V. (1984). "Information reliability and a theory of financial intermediation." *Review of Economic Studies*, 51: 415–32.

Rock, K. (1986). "Why new issues are underpriced." *Journal of Financial Economics*, 13: 187–212.

Rothschild, M., and Stiglitz, J. (1976). "Equilibrium in competitive insurance markets: An essay on the economics of imperfect information." *Quarterly Journal of Economics*, 90.

Sharpe, S. (1990). "Asymmetric information, bank lending, and implicit contracts: A
stylized model of customer relationships." *Journal of Finance*, 45: 1069–87.

Spence, M. (1973). "Job market signalling." *Quarterly Journal of Economics*, 87:
355–74.

Stiglitz, J., and Weiss, A. (1981). "Credit rationing in markets with imperfect
information." *American Economic Review*, 71: 393–410.

Part I

Monitoring by and of Banks

Financial Intermediary-Coalitions

John H. Boyd and Edward C. Prescott

1. Introduction

Five facts concerning real-world financial intermediaries are as follows:

(i) Financial intermediaries borrow from one subset of agents in the economy and lend to another.

(ii) Both subsets—borrowers and lenders—are typically large. Thus, to the extent that numbers represent diversification, financial intermediaries are generally well diversified on both sides of their balance sheets.

(iii) Financial intermediaries deal with borrowers whose information set may be different from theirs. In practical terms, this means that would-be borrowers often have better information concerning their own credit risk than do the intermediaries.

(iv) Financial intermediaries produce costly information on the attributes of would-be borrowers. This information is used to allocate loans and set terms.

(v) Financial intermediaries issue claims that have state contingent payoffs different from claims issued by ultimate borrowers.

This chapter analyzes a primitive environment in which financial intermediaries endogenously emerge and exhibit these five characteristics. In the environment studied, all equilibrium arrangements display these five

We thank Jack Kareken for interesting us in this project and providing insightful comments. We also thank workshop participants at Carnegie–Mellon University, the University of Chicago, the University of Pennsylvania, and the Federal Reserve Bank of Minneapolis—in particular, Douglas W. Diamond, Edward J. Green, Bruce D. Smith, Michael J. Stutzer, Robert M. Townsend, and Oliver E. Williamson. We gratefully acknowledge financial support from the National Science Foundation.

The views expressed herein are our own and not necessarily those of the Federal Reserve Bank of Minneapolis or the Federal Reserve System.

features, except for one special case, in which diversification is unnecessary.[1]

Much has been written about financial intermediaries, and there is general agreement that these firms, which account for about 8% of U.S. gross national product, are somehow important. Despite the volume of past studies, however, research on this topic remains at a relatively primitive stage. This is primarily so because in Arrow–Debreu economies such organizations are unneeded. Until quite recently, serious analysis of intermediaries was therefore hindered by the lack of convincing general equilibrium theories that give rise to trading frictions.

An economy in which intermediaries endogenously emerge was described by Townsend [12, 13]. In this economy, intermediary-coalitions trade off gains from risk-sharing against per capita connecting (transaction) costs. If this structure has a weakness, it is that transaction costs are assumed to exist and are not explicitly related to exchange technologies nor differentiated between types of trades. Even so, our work is significantly indebted to Townsend and, following his example, we have adopted a core equilibrium concept as the most appropriate for studying intermediated environments.

Another group of studies has exploited recent advances in information economics, applying them to the study of intermediation. These are too numerous to review in detail. (See, for example, Diamond and Dybvig [3], Diamond [2], Haubrich and King [7], Ramakrishnan and Thakor [10], Smith [11], and Williamson [15].) However, their similarities to and differences from our own work should become apparent as we proceed.

In some respects, Diamond [2] is close to this study. He investigates an environment in which lenders delegate the costly monitoring of borrowers to an agent called a financial intermediary. He shows that as the intermediary agent deals with an increasing number of borrowers and lenders, contracting costs decline monotonically. Thus, the intermediary agent will contract with as many individuals as possible. This result, or at least a similar incentive to deal with many borrowers and lenders, is obtained in several of the other studies (for example, Ramakrishnan and Thakor [10] and Williamson [15]), as well as in our own. And like Diamond [2] and Williamson [15], we obtain this result in an environment in which all agents are risk-neutral.

There are, however, a number of important differences between our work and Diamond's. For example, our assumptions concerning information differ from his. In our analysis, there are informational asymmetries prior to contracting; thus, adverse selection is a crucial problem. Moreover, the production of

---

[1] By financial intermediaries, we mean commercial banks, thrift institutions, loan companies, consumer finance companies, and so forth—the so-called asset transformers (Gurley and Shaw [5]). We do not include security brokers, dealers, and exchanges. These are perhaps better described as an arrangement for executing security transactions by providing payment, delivery, and accounting, as well as a system for arriving at a price.

information in our model is public and there are no nonpecuniary penalties. The equilibrium definitions used are different as well: following Townsend [12, 13], we employ a core equilibrium concept, whereas Diamond uses a partial equilibrium market construct. And finally, in equilibrium our intermediaries are coalitions of many agents, whereas his are single agents.

In one important respect, our environment differs from those assumed in previous studies and leads to very different conclusions. Our environment has (endowed) informational asymmetries prior to contracting and *also* the possibility of producing additional information after contracting. Only in the general case with both "sources" of information open do intermediary-coalitions emerge endogenously. That is, if either information "source" is closed (for example, by assuming all agents are identically endowed or by prohibiting information production after contracting), financial intermediaries are unnecessary, in the sense that the same allocations can be achieved with simpler market type arrangements. Thus, financial intermediary-coalitions arise to efficiently produce information in environments in which project owners have private information concerning their investment opportunities.

We hope this study also contributes to the general understanding of equilibrium in economies with private information prior to contracting, and thus is of interest beyond the study of intermediation per se. The equilibrium concept defined and employed here is related to that of the core, but there are two important differences necessitated by private information considerations: First, we assume that coalitions have access to a contracting technology which can preclude subsequent recontracting. Second, we assume that agents cannot be excluded from coalitions based upon private information about agents' types. For our economy, core equilibrium allocations exist and are essentially unique. Like large, pure exchange economies, the distributions of the gains from trade depend upon the relative numbers of different agent types.

Briefly, the chapter proceeds as follows. In Section 2 we describe the economy. In Section 3, we define a core equilibrium concept for this class of economy. In Section 4, we conjecture that a particular Pareto-optimal allocation is the core equilibrium allocation for this environment. In Section 5, prove that it is, and that it is essentially unique. In Section 6, this allocation is supported with competitive intermediary-coalitions. Then, we show that it *cannot* be supported with a securities market. In Section 7, three special cases are examined. In the first two, intermediary-coalitions prove to be unnecessary when agents are identically endowed (there is no adverse selection) or when information production is not possible. In both cases, the core equilibrium allocation can be supported with a securities market. The third special case is one in which intermediary-coalitions are needed to support the core equilibrium, but they need not borrow from and lend to a large number of agents. Section 8 summarizes and concludes the paper.

2. The Economy

There is a countable infinity of agents who live for two periods. In the initial period, they are endowed with one unit of time and an investment project of either a good type, $i = g$, or a bad type, $i = b$. In the first period, agents can use their endowment of time either to produce one unit of the investment good or to evaluate a project. Agents' preferences are ordered by expected consumption in the second and final period. Thus, $E\{c\}$ orders the distribution of consumption outcomes where $E\{\cdot\}$ is the expectation operator. Consumption is necessarily nonnegative—an assumption which plays an important role in the analysis.

The rate of return per unit of investment in a project is either $r = b$ or $r = g$, where $g > b$ for investments x in the range $0 \leqslant x \leqslant \chi$. Here χ is the maximum investment in a project, and it is assumed that χ is large relative to an individual's one-unit endowment of the investment good. If a project is evaluated, a signal $e = b$ or $e = g$ is observed. This signal provides information about the rate of return on the project, which may be better or worse than the information provided by the project type. This concept will now be made precise.

Project, or agent, types (i, e, r) are identical and independent draws with $\pi(i, e, r)$ denoting the probability of type $(i, e, r) \in \{g, b\} \times \{g, b\} \times \{g, b\}$. Since there is a countable infinity of agents, throughout this analysis we consider the fractions of the various types, which are just the $\pi(i, e, r)$, and write resource constraints in per capita terms. For a rigorous justification of this procedure, see Green [4].

Agents know their own type $i = g$ or $i = b$ and, of course, the probabilities $\pi(i, e, r)$. They do not have the opportunity to enter into contracts before observing their i. Throughout this paper, expectations are with respect to the probability distribution defined by the $\pi(i, e, r)$. Agent type i is the only private information. The actions of evaluating and investing are publicly observed, and also publicly observed are realized project returns r, consumption outcomes c, evaluation results e, and terms of all contracts. No important result would be affected if e were private, however, since it is assumed that there exists a contracting technology whereby any agent's consumption can be made independent of the e that agent reports.

It is further assumed that $i = g$ and/or $e = g$ signals that the return on the project will be high, or that $r = g$. That is,

$$\pi\{r = g | i = g\} > \pi\{r = g | i = b\}$$

and

$$\pi\{r = g | i, e = g\} > \pi\{r = g | i, e = b\}, \qquad \text{for} \quad i \in \{b, g\}.$$

In addition, all the $\pi(i, e, r)$ are strictly positive, so signals are imperfect; it is impossible to deduce i given the evaluation e and the return r.

The following assumptions are made to restrict the analysis to the "interesting" cases—those in which there is evaluation in equilibrium and trade between classes of agents.

$$\chi E\{r|i = g, e = g\}\pi\{e = g|i = g\} + \chi E\{r|i = g\}\pi\{e = b|i = g\}$$
$$> (\chi + 1)E\{r|i = g\}. \tag{2.1}$$

The left-hand side of (2.1) is the return for a group of agents who have $\chi + 1$ units of the investment good and at least two type $i = g$ projects, and who adopt the strategy of evaluating and fully funding one of their $i = g$ projects, if and only if $e = g$. Otherwise, they will fully fund another type $i = g$ project. This strategy dominates the no-evaluation strategy of unconditionally allocating the full $\chi + 1$ units of the investment good to type $i = g$ projects, the expected return of which is the right-hand side of (2.1). In other words, without the privateness of project type i, it always pays to evaluate type $i = g$ projects.

$$\chi E\{r|i = b, e = g\}\pi\{e = g|i = b\} + \chi E\{r|i = b\}\pi\{e = b|i = b\}$$
$$< (\chi + 1)E\{r|i = b\}. \tag{2.2}$$

By the same logic as above, (2.2) implies that the cost of evaluating type $i = b$ projects exceeds the expected return to doing so. Without the privateness of i, it would never pay to evaluate type $i = b$ projects.

$$E\{r|i = g, e = b\} < E\{r|i = b\}. \tag{2.3}$$

The implication of (2.3) is that it is better to invest unconditionally in a type $i = b$ project than to invest in a type $i = g$ one with a bad evaluation.

$$\chi\pi\{i = g, e = g\} < 1 - \pi\{i = g\}. \tag{2.4}$$

With assumption (2.4), if all type $i = g$ projects are evaluated and all those that obtain a good evaluation are fully funded, some of the investment good will still remain. And given assumptions (2.2) and (2.3), without privateness the remainder will be unconditionally invested in type $i = b$ projects. Thus type $i = b$ will always be the "marginal" projects that may or may not be funded.

The timing of various events and actions during the two periods is shown in Table 1.

Resource constraints are that per capita investment in projects plus the fraction of the projects evaluated is constrained by per capita endowment and that per capita consumption is constrained by per capita production of the

Table 1.

Event or Action
During Period 1
All agents know whether their project type is $i = g$ or $i = b$ prior to any contracting opportunities.
Agents can enter into contracts. Agents can evaluate.
Agents make investments.
During Period 2
Projects' returns are realized.
Consumption occurs.

consumption good:

Total investment per capita + Total number of evaluations per capita

$\leqslant$ Total endowment per capita. $\qquad(2.5)$

Per capita consumption $\leqslant$ Per capita production of the consumption good.

$\qquad(2.6)$

DEFINITION. An intermediary-coalition is a group of $n \geqslant 1$ agents which publicly announces rules for its members. These rules specify each member's actions, including investing, evaluating, and contracting with nonmembers, as well as members' consumption outcomes. A large coalition is one with n infinite.

Discussion. It may be helpful to think of an intermediary-coalition as first announcing group rules and then contracting with nonmembers according to those rules. The rules themselves may be viewed as complex contracts involving many agents. As will be demonstrated, the optimal rules condition the consumption outcomes of coalition members on *group* experience as well as on observables for individual members—something that cannot be done with bilateral (two-agent) contracts.

An intermediary-coalition is therefore a group of agents that jointly evaluate projects, invest in projects, and share project returns. They might be called "firms," "joint ventures," or "cooperatives," for in this primitive environment there is little to distinguish among these organizational forms. They are not, however, "firms" in the Arrow–Debreu sense of a technology specified as a subset of the commodity space.[2]

Throughout this chapter, no intermediary-coalition has any monopoly power. In the economies described later—those with competing intermediary-coalitions—this is accomplished by having a countable infinity of agents and by

---

[2] Our intermediary-coalitions could also be viewed as a nexus of contracts (Coase [1]) or as an arrangement to economize on transaction costs (Williamson [14]).

intermediaries being "small" in the sense that the fraction of all agents that deals with any intermediary is zero. At the same time, intermediaries are "large" in the sense that each has a countable infinity of borrowers and lenders.

3. Definition of Equilibrium

In this section, j denotes what type an agent reports himself to be, while i denotes the agent's true type. Attention is restricted to those arrangements in which it is never in the agent's interest to misrepresent his type, the so-called simple direct mechanisms. Our justification for this restriction is the revelation principle, which ensures, for a class of economies including ours, that if a particular arrangement entails dishonesty in equilibrium, then there exists another arrangement which does not and which has the same equilibrium allocation.[3]

It is necessary to introduce some additional notation to specify the direct mechanisms. This notation is:

z_i = fraction of type-i projects evaluated

x_i = amount invested in each type-i project not evaluated

x_{ie} = amount invested in each evaluated type-i project with evaluation e

c_{ir} = consumption of a type-i project with return r, not evaluated

c_{ier} = consumption of a type-i project with evaluation e and return r.

In addition, z denotes the pair of z_i, x the set of two x_i and four x_{ie}, and c the set of four c_{ir} and eight c_{ier}. Finally, $u_i(c, z, j)$ is the expected consumption of a type-i agent who reports to be a type j; thus,

$$u_i(c, z, j) = z_j E_{e,r}\{c_{jer} \mid i\} + (1 - z_j)E_r\{c_{jr} \mid i\}.$$

The subscripts on the E operator are the random variables over which the expectation, or averaging, operator is taken.

DEFINITION. An allocation (c^o, x^o, z^o) is an equilibrium if no large coalition of agents, with fractions $\pi^d(i)$ of agent types i, can achieve a *different* allocation (c^d, x^d, z^d) which satisfies (3.1)–(3.3) below.

[We shall refer to this subset of agents, indicated with the d-superscript, as a "deviant," or breaking, coalition. Note that because the coalition is large (that is,

---

[3] See Harris and Townsend [6]. If agents were not risk-neutral, it would be necessary to consider consumption lotteries contingent upon the observables, as in Prescott and Townsend [8, 9]. If it were not part of the technology to precommit to evaluation subsequent to the report of type, the revelation principle would fail and the analysis would be more difficult.

$n = \infty$), $\pi^d(e, r|i) = \pi^d(i)\pi(e, r|i)$; or conditional on i, the coalition's population fractions are representative of the entire population.]

$$u_i^d > u_i^o, \text{ for some type } i. \text{ (Here, } u_i^a \text{ denotes the utility}$$
$$\text{of a type-}i \text{ agent resulting from allocation } a.) \tag{3.1}$$

$$\text{If } u_i^d < u_i^o, \quad \text{then } \pi^d(i) = 0, \tag{3.2a}$$

$$\text{if } u_i^d = u_i^o, \quad \text{then } \pi^d(i) \leqslant \pi(i), \tag{3.2b}$$

and

$$\text{if } u_i^d > u_i^o, \quad \text{then } \pi^d(i) \geqslant \pi(i). \tag{3.2c}$$

Investment good resource constraint:

$$\sum_e \sum_i \pi^d(i)\pi(e|i)[z_i(x_{ie} + 1) + (1 - z_i)x_i] \leqslant 1. \tag{3.3a}$$

Consumption good constraint:

$$\sum_i \pi^d(i)[u_i(c, z, j = i)] \leqslant \sum_i \pi^d(i)[z_i E_{e,r}\{rx_{ie}|i\} + (1 - z_i)E_r\{rx_i|i\}]. \tag{3.3b}$$

Incentive constraints:

$$u_i(c, z, j = i) \geqslant u_i(c, z, j \neq i) \quad \text{for all } i$$
$$u_i(c, z, j = i) \geqslant E_r\{r|i\} \quad\quad\quad \text{for all } i. \tag{3.3c}$$

Other constraints:

$$z_i \leqslant 1 \quad \text{for all } i$$

$$x_i \leqslant \chi \quad \text{for all } i$$

$$x_{ie} \leqslant \chi \quad \text{for all } i, e. \tag{3.3d}$$

Discussion. Conditions (3.1) and (3.2a) require that, to attract members, a deviant coalition must make at least some of its members better off and none worse off. Condition (3.2b) deals with ties. It states that when agents of type i are indifferent between an O-allocation and a d-allocation, some of them may go to the deviant coalition. However, as indicated by (3.2c), the deviant coalition cannot attract higher-than-population proportions of type-i agents unless it makes them strictly better off. Conditions (3.3a)–(3.3d) are resource, incentive, and nonnegativity constraints, respectively. It is important to note that in the resource constraints (3.3a) and (3.3b), the average is with respect to the type-i population fractions in the deviant coalition.

4. A Conjectured Equilibrium Allocation

In this section, we conjecture that a particular Pareto-optimal allocation is an equilibrium allocation as defined above.[4] It is the feasible allocation which maximizes the utility of type $i = g$ agents, subject to the constraint that it is in the interest of type $i = b$ to participate. (In Section 5, we prove the conjecture and also prove that the equilibrium allocation is essentially unique.)

Our candidate for an equilibrium allocation is the solution to the program

$$\max_{x,c,z \geq 0} u_g(c, z, j = g), \tag{4.1}$$

subject to the investment good resource constraint

$$E_{i,e}\{z_i(x_{ie} + 1) + (1 - z_i)x_i\} \leq 1; \tag{4.2}$$

the consumption good constraint

$$E_i\{u_i(c, z, j = i)\} \leq E_i\{z_i E_{e,r}\{rx_{ie}|i\} + (1 - z_i)E_r\{rx_i|i\}\}; \tag{4.3}$$

the incentive constraints

$$u_i(c, z, j = i) \geq u_i(c, z, j \neq i) \quad \text{for all } i \tag{4.4}$$

$$u_i(c, z, j = i) \geq E_r\{r|i\} \qquad \text{for all } i; \tag{4.5}$$

and the other constraints

$$z_i \leq 1 \quad \text{for all } i \tag{4.6}$$

$$x_i \leq \chi \quad \text{for all } i \tag{4.7}$$

$$x_{ie} \leq \chi \quad \text{for all } i, e. \tag{4.8}$$

Although not a linear program, it can be transformed into one by changing variables as follows: substitute v_{ie} for $z_i x_{ie}$, v_i for $(1 - z_i)x_i$, w_{ier} for $z_i c_{ier}$, and w_{ir} for $(1 - z_i)c_{ir}$. Note that (4.7) becomes $v_i \leq \chi(1 - z_i)$ and (4.8) becomes $v_{ie} \leq \chi z_i$. It is now a linear program in z, v, and w. Solution values are denoted with an asterisk.

If we use assumptions (2.1)–(2.4), this program is interesting and not so formidable. First, all good projects are evaluated and are fully funded if and only if $e = g$. Further, $c_{ger}^* = 0$, unless both $e = g$ and $r = g$. If this were not the case, slack could be introduced into the binding incentive constraint—the

---

[4] Here and throughout this chapter, by "Pareto-optimal" we mean optimal subject to incentive and resource constraints.

one which ensures it is not in the interest of type $i = b$ to claim to be of type $i = g$. This slack could be produced without affecting the objective function or any other constraints. Evaluating projects with $i = b$ is wasteful of resources and does not help with respect to the key incentive constraints. Consequently, no projects of type $i = b$ are evaluated at an optimum.

Using these facts, $z_g^* = 1$ and $z_b^* = 0$ while $x_{gg}^* = \chi$. At the optimum, all other variables are zero except for $x_b^*, c_{ggg}^*, c_{bg}^*$, and c_{bb}^*. The solution to the problem is not unique. Given any solution, changes in c_{bg}^* and c_{bb}^* which do not alter the expected consumption of type $i = b$ agents yield alternative optimal allocations. Consequently, only $c_b^* \equiv E_r\{c_{ir}^*|i = b\}$ is uniquely determined. It, along with c_{ggg}^* and x_b^*, remains to be determined.

These three elements can be deduced from knowledge of the binding constraints. First, constraint (4.2) is binding, so

$$\chi \pi(i = g, e = g) + x_b^* \pi(i = b) = 1 - \pi(i = g). \tag{4.9}$$

Second, incentive constraint (4.4) with $i = b$ and $j = g$, or constraint (4.5) with $i = b$, is binding, so

$$c_b^* = \max\{E\{r|i = b\}, c_{ggg}^* \pi(e = g, r = g|i = b)\}, \tag{4.10}$$

as is resource constraint (4.3), or

$$c_{ggg}^* \pi(i = g, e = g, r = g) + c_b^* \pi(i = b)$$
$$= x_b^* E\{r|i = b\} \pi(i = b) + E\{\chi r|i = g, e = g\} \pi(i = g, e = g). \tag{4.11}$$

Equations (4.9)–(4.11) have a unique solution which is nonnegative. We are particularly interested in parameter values for which $c_b^* > E\{r|i = b\}$, for then, as shown in Section 6, securities markets cannot be used to support this allocation. If χ is sufficiently large, if e provides sufficiently little information concerning r for type $i = b$, and if $\pi(i = g)$ is sufficiently small, then $c_b^* > E\{r|i = b\}$. An example in Section 6 establishes that the set of parameters for which this holds is nonempty.

5. Proof That the Candidate Allocation is the (Essentially) Unique Core Equilibrium Allocation

PROPOSITION 1. *The allocation defined by the solution to the program (4.1)–(4.8) it is an equilibrium allocation. [Following our notational convention, this is called a *-allocation and $u_i^* \equiv u_i(c^*, z^*, j = i)$.]*

Proof. By construction, both types of agents weakly prefer the *-allocation to autarky. Thus, to attract any agents, a d-coalition must attract some agents of both types. This, in turn, requires that some agents be made better off, by condition (3.1), and no agents be made worse off, by (3.2a). Since the *-allocation is itself a Pareto optimum, the d-coalition must therefore attract higher-than-population proportions in the sense that $\pi^d(g) > \pi(g)$. From (3.2b) and (3.2c), to attract higher-than-population proportions requires that $u_g^d > u_g^*$ and $u_b^d = u_b^* = c_b^*$. However, these expected consumptions are not incentive feasible. If the expected consumption of a type-g agent is higher in the d-coalition than in the *-coalition, then by (4.10), $u_b(c^d, z^d, j = g) > c_b^*$. Every type-$b$ agent would want to join the d-coalition and misrepresent project type. Thus, a d-coalition cannot simultaneously satisfy (3.1)–(3.3), and Proposition 1 is proved.

PROPOSITION 2. *The *-allocations are the only equilibrium allocations.*

Proof. Any allocation that is not a Pareto optimum could be broken by a deviant coalition of the whole. Thus, without loss of generality, we restrict our attention to Pareto-optimal allocations. Now consider any Pareto-optimal allocation *other than* a *-allocation. We call this a "p-allocation." If some Pareto-optimal allocation results in utilities u_b^p and u_g^p, then there exists an allocation which also results in these utilities with $c_{br}^p = u_b^p$, for all r; $c_{gb}^p = 0$; and $c_{ger}^p = 0$, unless $e = g$ and $r = g$. Further, c_{gg}^p and c_{ggg}^p may be set so that the expected utility of type $i = g$ agents is the same, whether or not they are evaluated. Note that $z_b^p = 0$, since Pareto optimality requires that no type $i = b$ projects are evaluated and, of course, that $x_{gg}^p = \chi$ and $x_{gb}^p = 0$.

To break any p-allocation, we construct a deviant coalition with the following properties: The fraction of type $i = g$ agents is increased until it is just high enough that investment in type $i = b$ projects is driven to zero. This will occur when

$$\pi^d(i = g) = \left[1 - \pi(i = g, e = g)z_{gg}^p\right] / \left[1 + \chi - \pi(i = g, e = g)\left(z_{gg}^p + \chi\right)\right]. \quad (5.1)$$

All incremental type $i = g$ projects (those in excess of population proportions) are evaluated and, if $e = g$, funded at level χ. Owners of these projects are assigned the same consumptions as other type $i = g$ agents whose projects are evaluated. By adding and evaluating type $i = g$ projects, investment funds can be reallocated from projects with low expected returns to ones with high expected returns. Production of the consumption good increases by an amount that exceeds the consumption of the incremental type $i = g$ agents. Consequently, there will be slack, say $\delta > 0$, in the consumption good constraint—that is, constraint (4.3) with $\pi^d(\cdot)$ fractions of agent types.

Now, let $c^\theta = \theta c^p + (1 - \theta)c^*$ for $0 < \theta < 1$. Next, increase every component of c^θ by $\varepsilon > 0$ where

$$\varepsilon = \theta\left(u_b^p - u_b^*\right). \quad (5.2)$$

Choose a θ such that $\varepsilon < \delta$. The resulting consumption contract (which is a 12-tuple) is denoted c^d. Other elements of contract d are $x_{gg}^d = \chi$, $x_{gb}^d = 0$, $x_b^d = 0$, $z_b^d = 0$, and

$$z_{gg}^d = \left[1 + \pi(i = g, e = g)\left(\chi z_{gg}^p - z_{gg}^p - \chi\right)\right] \Big/ \left[1 - \pi(i = g, e = g)z_{gg}^p\right] \quad (5.3)$$

where z_{gg}^d is the value of z_{gg} which solves the investment resource constraint, given that $\pi^d(i = g)$ satisfies (5.1) and all other variables in the d contract are set as specified.

The c^θ contract satisfies incentive constraints (4.4) and (4.5) because the constraints are linear in c, and c^θ is a convex combination of c^p and c^*, which both satisfy these constraints. Adding ε to all elements of c increases both sides of (4.4) by ε and cannot violate the inequality. It adds ε to the left-hand side of (4.5) and cannot violate that inequality either. Contract d is resource and incentive feasible with $\pi^d(\cdot)$ fractions of agent types. As $u_b^d = u_b^p$, $u_g^d > u_g^p$, $\pi^d(i = g) > \pi(i = g)$, and $\pi^d(i = b) < \pi(i = b)$, requirements (3.1) and (3.2) for a blocking group are satisfied as well. Thus, the p-allocation is broken by the d-allocation, and Proposition 2 is proved.

6. The Core Equilibrium Allocation Can be Supported with Large Intermediary-Coalitions, But not with a Securities Market

An institutional arrangement that supports the core allocation is one with large coalitions of type $i = b$ agents. In period one, each coalition commits to the following policy:

— Each coalition member will evaluate one project.
— For each unit of the investment good deposited with it, the coalition agrees to deliver c_b^* units of the consumption good in the second period. These depositors give the coalition the right to invest in their project and to receive the entire output if the coalition chooses to invest. Total deposits are limited to $n[\chi \pi(i = g, e = g) + x_b^* \pi(i = b)]$.
— The coalition agrees to evaluate n projects, whose owners must deliver a unit of the investment good prior to investing. Coalition members use their endowments for evaluation. The coalition agrees to fund each of the $n\pi(e = g | i = g)$ projects with good evaluations. (Recall that this activity is publicly observable.) Project owners (entrepreneurs) are promised c_{ggg}^* units of the consumption good in the next period if the project has evaluation $e = g$ and return $r = g$, and zero units if otherwise.

— After it has fully invested in all the type $i = g, e = g$ projects it obtains, the coalition invests any remaining funds in type $i = b$ projects of depositors (or coalition members).

— Members of the coalition are residual claimants and share equally in profits.

The fraction of type $i = b$ agents that become coalition members is $\pi(i = g)/\pi(i = b)$. This ensures that there are just enough of them to evaluate all type $i = g$ projects. The remaining type $i = b$ agents become depositors, and all type $i = g$ agents contract with a coalition. This arrangement is incentive and resource feasible, and the core allocation results. Consequently, it is a core equilibrium and there can be no blocking coalitions.

We do not claim that this is the only institutional arrangement that could support the core-equilibrium allocation. For example, coalitions could be composed of agents who act as depositors and hire other type $i = b$ agents to do the evaluations. It does appear, however, that small (finite-sized) intermediary-coalitions cannot support the core. For reasons of technical efficiency, it is essential that the actual fraction of type $i = g, e = g$ projects obtained by *each* coalition not be too large; for if any coalition obtains too many good projects, not all of them can be fully funded. And with small coalitions this problem occurs with positive probability. Further, the problem cannot be circumvented by evaluating prior to contracting (and thus perfectly sorting so as to obtain exact population proportions at each coalition). With that arrangement, there is an incentive for some type $i = b$ agents to misrepresent their type and "mimic" the type $i = g$. (Such mimicking will be discussed in detail shortly.) Nor can the problem be overcome by permitting individual agents to recontract after initial coalition formation—say, by having some of them split off and form new coalitions. Every type $i = b$ agent who becomes a coalition member or depositor publicly reveals his type and cannot expect to obtain expected consumption exceeding $E\{r \mid i = b\}$ if recontracting is necessary.

Admittedly, if there are separate organizations which provide insurance to small intermediary-coalitions (insurance against obtaining other-than-population proportions of project types), the core equilibrium allocation can be supported with small intermediary-coalitions. However, the insurers themselves must necessarily be large, and thus this arrangement is hardly different than one with large intermediary-coalitions.[5]

---

[5] If there were a legal or technological constraint limiting the maximum value of n, then the equilibrium would be one in which that constraint was binding for all intermediary-coalitions. The constraint would be costly, since not all type $i = g, e = g$ projects could be fully funded. Period two consumption of coalition members and/or depositors would also be uncertain. An interesting question posed by Douglas Diamond is, Can the core allocation be supported by an arrangement with nondiversified (that is, finite-sized) coalitions, along with a post-evaluation credit market in which only coalitions can participate? The answer is no. The law of one price dictates that the deposit

A securities market arrangement cannot support the core equilibrium allocation

Another possible arrangement is a decentralized one in which some agents become "entrepreneurs," issue securities to other agents called "investors," and use the proceeds to fund their projects. We now consider such an arrangement. First, we define a security. Next, we describe the securities market equilibrium allocation, one that is Pareto-inferior to the core equilibrium allocation. Finally, we show that the core equilibrium allocation cannot be supported with a securities market.

DEFINITION. A security is a contract which in period one specifies the following:

— An amount $x \in [0, \chi]$ to be invested in a particular project indexed $e \in \{0, g, b\}$, where $e = 0$ corresponds to no evaluation.
— The consumption of the project's owner in period two. This could be contingent on the owner investing some amount in the project and on the project's return realization $r \in \{g, b\}$.
— Some share of the project's output, net of the owner's compensation, if any, that the security holder will receive in period two.

With a securities market arrangement, any agent can become an entrepreneur and issue securities in order to fund his project. A constraint on the contract offered investors is that the expected return must be at least the market rate of interest r^*. The expected return is conditional upon the investor's information set, and the key element in that information set is the offered contract. For example, if only type $i = g$ agents issue a particular security, then investors will assume that an agent offering that security is of type $i = g$. Less obvious, if the fraction of all agents that are of type i and that offer a particular security is θ_i, then investors' conditional probability of an agent being type i is $\theta_i/(\theta_g + \theta_b)$, for $i \in \{g, b\}$. In other words, it is assumed that agents use equilibrium population proportions in forming probability assessments.

If a security of type s is issued by a type-i agent, the issuer's resulting expected utility is denoted $u_i(s)$. Market equilibrium requires that each issuer of a security select from the set of offered securities one which maximizes his expected utility. Let the u_i^* be the maximum utilities. A final condition for a securities market equilibrium is that it not be in the interest of any agent to offer a security not in

interest rate c_b^* and the interest rate in the post-evaluation credit market r^* be the same. But this is not possible in equilibrium, because if $r^* = c_b^*$, evaluating agents could realize a higher utility than c_b^*, which is the core utility for type $i = b$ agents. They could do so by following a strategy of accepting no depositors. If a coalition of size n evaluated n projects and at least one obtained an $e = g$ evaluation, the evaluating agents' post-evaluation utility would exceed c_b^*. If no evaluations with $e = g$ were obtained, they could still lend their n units of the investment good at the post-evaluation market rate r^* and realize utility c_b^*. Thus, with this strategy, their pre-evaluation expected utility would strictly exceed c_b^* if $r = c_b^*$. This contradiction shows that the post-evaluation markets cannot overcome the need for diversified (i.e., large) coalitions to support the core allocation.

the offered set. More formally, no (i, s) exists for which $u_i(s) > u_i^*, u_j(s) \leqslant u_j^*$ for $j \neq i$, and for which the expected return to investors (who assume the issuer is of type i) is at least r^*.

A securities market equilibrium exists for this economy and has the following characteristics:

— All type $i = g$ agents evaluate their projects and, if $e = g$, issue securities, each of which provides share $1/\chi$ of the project's return, less the return-contingent compensation of the entrepreneur. The entrepreneur's compensation is zero if $r = b$ and c_g^* if $r = g$.

— Some type $i = b$ agents mimic the type $i = g$; that is, they evaluate their projects and, if $e = g$, issue shares. The other type $i = b$ agents become investors. Let m_b^* be the fraction of type $i = b$ agents that choose to mimic and to evaluate their projects.

Then r^*, m_b^*, and c_g^* are determined by the following equilibrium conditions, which have straightforward economic interpretations. Mimicking type $i = b$ agents receive the same expected return as investors:

$$r^* = \pi(e = g, r = g | i = b)c_g^*. \tag{6.1}$$

The demand for the investment good equals the supply:

$$\chi[\pi(i = g, e = g) + m_b^*\pi(i = b, e = g)] = 1 - \pi(i = g) - m_b^*\pi(i = b). \tag{6.2}$$

Per capita consumption equals per capita output:

$$r^*\pi(i = b) + c_g^*\pi(i = g, e = g, r = g) = \pi(i = g, e = g)E\{\chi r | i = g, e = g\}$$
$$+ m_b^*\pi(i = b, e = g)E\{\chi r | i = b, e = g\}. \tag{6.3}$$

These linear equations have a unique solution in the three variables.

As the following numerical examples will demonstrate, the market allocation can be different than, and inferior to, the core equilibrium allocation in the interesting cases in which the core equilibrium utility level of type $i = b$ agents exceeds $E\{r | i = b\}$. In the core allocation, fraction x_b^* of type $i = b$ projects are funded without evaluation. Given assumption (2.2), this is required for technical efficiency. In the market allocation, however, some type $i = b$ projects are evaluated. This results in a misallocation of resources, at least relative to the core.

The question is, Could a securities market arrangement support an allocation in which there is positive investment in type $i = b$ projects without evaluation? The answer is no, for the interesting cases. For this to occur, some type $i = b$ agents would have to issue securities without evaluation. But given assumptions (2.1) and (2.2), "no evaluation" is a perfect signal of (bad) type. Potential investors would know with certainty that these projects had expected return $E\{r|i = b\} < r^*$, and there would be no demand for their securities. It follows that intermediary-coalitions are "needed" to support the core allocation, an allocation which Pareto-dominates the decentralized securities market equilibrium allocation.

Numerical examples

Figure 1 sets out the parametric assumptions for some numerical examples. With these parameters, which satisfy (2.1)–(2.4), the core equilibrium allocation, which is the solution to (4.1)–(4.8), is $x_b^* = 0.818$, $c_b^* = 1.441$, $c_{ggg}^* = 14.407$, and $u_g^* = 10.373$. The expected consumption of type $i = g$ agents is 10.373, and the expected consumption of type $i = b$ is 1.441. Since $E\{r|i = g\} = 3.7$ and $E\{r|i = b\} = 1$, both classes of agents prefer this allocation to autarky.

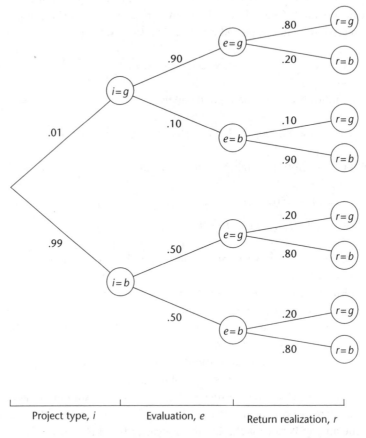

Figure 1. Parameters for the numerical examples. The parameters are $\chi = 20$, $r_g = 5$, $r_b = 0$, and the probabilities shown above.

The securities market equilibrium allocation, which satisfies (6.1)–(6.3), is $m_b^* = 0.0744$, $r^* = 1.372$, $c_g^* = 13.72$, and $u_g^* = 9.878$. The expected consumption of type $i = g$ agents is now 9.878 and of type $i = b$ agents is 1.372. Both classes would prefer this allocation to autarky, but both are worse off than in the core allocation. This is due to the 7.44% of type $i = b$ agents who evaluate their projects even though, by assumption, $\pi(r = g | i = b, e = g) = \pi(r = g | i = b, e = b)$. This diverts resources from productive investment and reduces the equilibrium consumption of all.

7. Three Special Cases

Three special cases merit brief discussion. The first is when all agents are initially alike or, equivalently, when i is independent of (e, r). In this case, information may be produced through evaluation but is, of course, public. Since i is suppressed, there is no private information whatsoever. Assumptions (2.2), (2.3), and (2.4) are necessarily dropped, but assumption (2.1)—with i suppressed—is maintained. The Pareto-optimal equilibrium allocation is still the solution to (4.1)–(4.8), but is much simplified when the i index is suppressed. Slightly redefining z^* to be the fraction of all projects evaluated, the solution is now characterized by two conditions which have simple economic interpretations.

The demand for the investment good equals the supply:

$$z^* \chi \pi(e = g) = 1 - z^*. \tag{7.1}$$

Per capita consumption equals per capita output:

$$c^* = z^* \chi \pi(e = g) E\{r | e = g\}. \tag{7.2}$$

In equilibrium, fraction z^* of projects are evaluated and fully funded if $e = g$, and all agents obtain expected consumption of c^*. With no private information, this allocation can obviously be supported by a securities market or a number of other arrangements. Intermediary-coalitions are not needed.

Second, consider the case in which evaluation is prohibited or, equivalently, e is independent of (i, r). Assumptions (2.1)–(2.3) are dropped, but (2.4)—with e suppressed—is maintained. The solution to (4.1)–(4.8) now defines a different Pareto-optimal core equilibrium allocation, characterized by three equations similar to (6.1)–(6.3).[6]

Type $i = b$ agents who mimic receive the same expected return as investors:

$$r^* = \pi(r = g | i = b)c_g^*. \tag{7.3}$$

---

[6] Note that m_b^* was defined slightly differently in (6.1)–(6.3), since there, mimicking required evaluation. Here it requires only an (incorrect) statement of type.

The demand for the investment good equals the supply:

$$\chi [\pi(i=g) + m_b^*\pi(i=b)] = 1 - \pi(i=g) - m_b^*\pi(i=b). \tag{7.4}$$

Per capita consumption equals per capita output:

$$r^*\pi(i=b) + c_g^*\pi(i=g,r=g)$$
$$= \pi(i=g)E\{\chi r|i=g\} + \pi(i=b)m_b^*E\{\chi r|i=b\}. \tag{7.5}$$

This is another "mimicking" equilibrium in which some fraction m_b^* of type $i=b$ agents misrepresents type. All type $i=g$ projects are fully funded, as is fraction m_b^* of type $i=b$. Expected utility of type $i=g$ agents is maximized by having zero consumption when $r=b$ (that is, $c_b^*=0$) and maximum resource-feasible consumption when $r=g$ (that is, $c_g=c_g^*$). This minimizes the incentive to mimic. But with evaluation suppressed, this is *all* the type $i=g$ agents can do to differentiate themselves. The allocation satisfying (7.3)–(7.5) can be supported with a securities market arrangement similar to that for (6.1)–(6.3) and again, intermediary-coalitions are unneeded.

The third special case is an intermediate one in which agents are differently endowed and evaluation is possible, but observations on e provide no additional information about a project's return other than the information contained in i. Formally, this means that i is sufficient relative to the pair (i, e) in forecasting r, or

$$\pi(r|i,e) = \pi(r|i) \quad \text{for all } (i,e,r). \tag{7.6}$$

This violates assumptions (2.1) and (2.3), but assumptions (2.2) and (2.4) are maintained. Unlike the case just considered, however, e does provide information about i, in the sense that

$$\pi(i=g|e=g) > \pi(i=g). \tag{7.7}$$

With these assumptions, the securities market equilibrium entails mimicking and is the same as that described by (6.1)–(6.3). The core equilibrium allocation is slightly different than in Section 4, however. In particular, (4.9) becomes

$$\chi\pi(i=g) + x_b^*\pi(i=b) = 1 - \pi(i=g) \tag{7.8}$$

and (4.11) becomes

$$c_{ggg}^*\pi(i=g,e=g,r=g) + c_b^*\pi(i=b)$$
$$= x_b^*E\{r|i=b\}\pi(i=b) + \pi(i=g)E\{\chi r|i=g\}. \tag{7.9}$$

The key change in the core equilibrium allocation is that, since r is independent of e, investment allocations are no longer conditioned upon e. However, i is not independent of the realization of e, and the decision to evaluate is, in effect, a dissipative signal of type. Thus, consumption allocations are still conditioned on (i, e, r) as they were in Section 6. And, as earlier, this allocation can be supported with competitive intermediary-coalitions.[7]

However, there are two important differences. In the present case, even in the core there is some dissipative signaling due to the evaluation of type $i = g$ projects. It is important that intermediary-coalitions can commit in advance to evaluate the projects of those agents who claim to be of type $i = g$. Only those who actually have promising projects will so claim in equilibrium, and as a result, monitoring is unnecessary and wasteful *ex post*. This *ex post* inefficiency, however, is a necessary part of the *ex ante* efficient arrangement. If it were not part of the technology to commit in advance, this arrangement would not constitute an equilibrium.

The second important difference between this case and the one in Section 6 is that although intermediary-coalitions are still needed to support the core equilibrium, it is no longer necessary that the coalitions be large. Recall that, in the previous case, it was essential that each intermediary-coalition not obtain more type $i = g, e = g$ projects than it could fund at level χ. Since e is a random variable observed after contracting, this could only be achieved with certainty by committing to evaluate a large number of projects. In the present environment, though, investment decisions are not conditional upon e, and size is unimportant. An intermediary-coalition can be composed of any number n of type $i = b$ agents, as long as it evaluates n projects and contracts with $n(\chi - 1)$ depositors. It is still essential, however, that the intermediary-coalition can commit in advance to evaluate projects of those agents who claim to be of type $i = g$. Otherwise, some type $i = b$ agents would have an incentive to mimic, as they do with the securities market arrangement.

8. Summary

The intermediary-coalitions which endogenously emerge in the environment studied exhibit all five of the stylized facts listed in the introduction. And

---

[7] A numerical example may help clarify the last case. Assume the parameters in Fig. 1 are changed so that $\pi(e = g|i = g) = 0.75, \pi(r = g|i = g, e = g) = \pi(r = g|i = g, e = b) = 0.8$. With these changes, e provides no information about r additional to that provided by i. Observation of e does give information about i, however. The core equilibrium allocation is now $x_b^* = 0.798, c_b^* = 1.514,$ $c_{ggg}^* = 15.143,$ and $u_g^* = 9.086$. The securities market equilibrium allocation is $m_b^* = 0.0771, r^* = 1.298, c_g^* = 12.984,$ and $u_g^* = 7.790$. Both types of agents again prefer the core equilibrium to the securities market equilibrium. But even in the core, some type $i = g$ projects are evaluated, and this is ex post inefficient.

although, for brevity, we will not reiterate them here, each characteristic is necessary in supporting the equilibrium allocation. This is only true, however, in the most general case studied—the one in which we allow for *both* adverse selection and information production via evaluation. If either "source" of information is closed, intermediary-coalitions are unnecessary, in the sense that the same allocation can be supported with a (simpler) securities market arrangement. We know of no other study that has considered this class of environment or has obtained these results.

It seems logically straightforward, albeit not necessarily mathematically simple, to construct richer and more complex environments in which both intermediary-coalitions and securities markets exist side by side to support the equilibrium. (This could be done, for example, by having some, but not all, agents endowed with private information at the beginning of period one.) Similarly, it seems very likely that we could construct environments in which some intermediary-coalitions are necessarily diversified and others are not. Although we shall not pursue the matter here, it is interesting that in this general environment, when we change assumptions concerning the structure of information, endowments, and so forth, the optimal supporting arrangement also changes. In principle, one could generate testable hypotheses concerning the environmental characteristics that lead to the emergence of different intermediation arrangements. That task will be left for future research.

Some extensions of this work appear to be straightforward. For example, allowing for more than two evaluation outcomes would not be difficult. Nor would it be difficult to introduce systemic risk into the environment, in which case residual claims against intermediary-coalitions could be risky and, in that sense, more like the equity shares issued by their real-world counterparts. Diamond [2] has touched on this issue and, for present purposes, it seemed a needless complication. An extension which is not so easy, however, is to allow for more than two agent (or project) types.

References

1. Coase, R. H. (1937). "The nature of the firm." *Economica, n.s.* 4: 386–405. (Reprinted in G. J. Stigler and K. E. Bouldings et al. (1952). *Readings in Price Theory* (Homewood, IL: Irwin).)
2. Diamond, D. W. (1984). "Financial intermediation and delegated monitoring." *Rev. Econ. Stud.* 51: 393–414.
3. ——, and Dybvig, P. H. (1983). "Bank runs, deposit insurance, and liquidity." *J. Polit. Econ.*, 91: 401–19.
4. Green, E. J. (1984). "Continuum and finite-player noncooperative models of competition." *Econometrica*, 52: 975–94.

5. Gurley, J. G., and Shaw, E. S. (1956). "Financial intermediaries and the savings–investment process." *J. Finance*, 11: 259–75.

6. Harris, M., and Townsend, R. M. (1981). "Resource allocation under asymmetric information." *Econometrica*, 49: 33–64.

7. Haubrich, J. G., and King, R. G. (1984). "Banking and Insurance." Working Paper, *Nat. Bur. Econ. Res.*, Washington, D.C.

8. Prescott, E. C., and Townsend, R. M. (1984). "Pareto optima and competitive equilibria with adverse selection and moral hazard." *Econometrica*, 52: 2–46.

9. ——, and —— (1984). "General competitive analysis in an economy with private information." *Int. Econ. Rev.*, 25: 1–20.

10. Ramakrishnan, T. S., and Thakor, A. V. (1984). "Information reliability and a theory of financial intermediation." *Rev. Econ. Stud.*, 51: 415–32.

11. Smith, B. D. (1984). "Private information, deposit interest rates, and the 'stability' of the banking system." *J. Monet. Econ.*, 14: 293–318.

12. Townsend, R. M. (1979). "Optimal contracts and competitive markets with costly state verification." *J. Econ. Theory*, 21: 265–93.

13. —— (1983). "Theories of intermediated structures," in *Carnegie–Rochester Conference Series on Public Policy*, Vol. 18, pp. 221–72.

14. Williamson, O. E. (1975). *Markets and Hierarchies: Analysis and Antitrust Implications: A Study in the Economics of Internal Organization*. New York: Free Press.

15. Williamson, S. D. (1985). "Costly monitoring, financial intermediation, and equilibrium credit rationing." Working Paper, Department of Economics, Queen's University, Kingston, Ontario.

2

The Role of Demandable Debt in Structuring Optimal Banking Arrangements

Charles W. Calomiris and Charles M. Kahn

For centuries, the vast majority of externally financed investments have been funded by banks, for which demandable-debt instruments (bank notes and checking accounts) have been the principal source of funds. The goal of this chapter is to explain the emergence of demandable-debt banking historically as the primary means of external finance in the economy.

Demandable debt warrants explanation because, in several respects, it appears more costly than available alternative contracting structures. By issuing demandable debt, banks created a mismatch between the maturity of assets and liabilities. This mismatch left them exposed to the possibility that depositors would attempt to withdraw more funds than a bank could supply on short notice. When this occurred, the consequences were costly. Individual banks that did not meet their obligations were forced into expensive procedures (liquidation or receivership) that would not have arisen in an equity-based or maturity-matched contracting structure.[1] If depositors en masse attempted to withdraw funds from the entire banking system, banks as a group were forced to suspend convertibility of their liabilities into specie on demand. Such suspension was also disruptive and costly. To defend against either of these undesirable consequences, banks had to hold a proportion of their assets in idle reserves to insulate themselves from excessive withdrawals.

We thank Lee Alston, Herbert Baer, Kyle Bagwell, Ben Bernanke, Sudipto Bhattacharya, Doug Diamond, Gary Gorton, Monica Hargraves, Charlie Jacklin, Dick Jefferis, and participants in the joint Northwestern-University of Chicago theory seminar and seminars at the Federal Reserve Bank of Chicago, Purdue University, SUNY Stony Brook, the University of Illinois, the National Bureau of Economic Research, and the Garn Institute for helpful comments. The initial work was partially funded by the National Science Foundation under grant SES-8511137. We are grateful to the Garn Institute of Finance and the Herbert V. Prochnow Educational Foundation of the Graduate School of Banking, Madison, WI, for additional support.

[1] Kenneth R. Cone (1983) shows that, in a world of full information, the risk of depositor liquidation under demandable debt is absent, provided that financial intermediaries are maturity-matched.

Given these costs, demandable debt seems inferior to both maturity-matched debt and equity contracting. However, in this chapter, we show that demandable debt has an important advantage as part of an incentive scheme for disciplining the banker. In effect, demandable debt permits depositors to "vote with their feet"; withdrawal of funds is a vote of no-confidence in the activities of the banker. Without the ability to make early withdrawals, depositors would have little incentive to monitor the bank.

This account gives a natural rationale for two important institutional features of banking. The so-called "sequential service constraint," by which payments were made to demanders on a first-come, first-served basis, becomes intelligible as a way to make monitoring depositors interested in registering their no-confidence votes at the first opportunity. The ease with which banks may be forced into liquidation, far from being an unfortunate consequence of the contracting structure, turns out to be central to the structure: we show that, by submitting to the threat of liquidation under appropriate circumstances, the banker can reduce his cost of capital.

In addition, our account may have wider applicability. Features of modern capital structures of nonfinancial institutions bear important similarities to the historical role of demandable debt. Modern-day firms often have multilayered debt structures, in which certain debt-holders have priority of claim for repayment. Claimants to short-term senior debt in modern firms may play a similar role to that of the monitoring depositors in our model.

The chapter is organized as follows: In Section I, we contrast our explanation of demandable debt with the literature based on desire for flexibility of consumption. The model in Section II demonstrates the value of a demandable-debt contract in the case of a single investor contracting with the banker monopolist. Here, a run corresponds to a demand by the investor for liquidation of the bank. Section III examines the case in which different monitors receive different (independent and identically distributed) signals. In this case, it pays to have more than one depositor monitoring the bank, because the quality of signals in the aggregate improves with the number of monitors. Banks find it advantageous to hold reserves to provide a buffer that reduces the likelihood of unwarranted liquidation. An optimal threshold of withdrawal orders is chosen at which the bank is liquidated, and relative payoffs ensure that the optimal number of monitors invest in receiving signals.

At the end of Section III, we briefly and informally indicate how solving the incentive problem facing the banker will also make the banker's liabilities more transactable. Formal models combining the incentive problem and liquidity are an important field for further research.[2] Section IV summarizes and indicates important limitations of our results.

---

[2] See Gary Gorton and George Pennacchi (1988), Charles J. Jacklin (1988), and A. P. Villamil (1988) for various approaches to combining the liquidity and incentive arguments.

I. Explanations for Demandable Debt

Recent theoretical work on the role of banks has tended to divide into two categories. Theory in one category emphasizes the role of banks as providing flexibility for depositors in the timing of consumption. Theory in the other category, to which our chapter belongs, emphasizes the *incentive* problem inherent in the divergence of interest between a bank's depositors and its managers.[3] For reasons indicated below, we believe that accounts which ignore the incentive problem facing the banker do not adequately explain why banks historically settled on demandable debt.

A. Consumption flexibility and demandable debt

In the past several years, the preeminent theoretical analyses of banks, bank runs, and bank regulation have assumed that the economic role of demandable debt is to provide flexibility to risk-averse depositors who are uncertain about the timing of their future consumption demand.[4] In this category of models, bank runs, when they occur, are an unfortunate and undesirable side-effect of a contract whose whole purpose is to provide consumption flexibility.

Although these models provide both a concise formalization of the fact that banks provide consumption flexibility and a coherent account of bank runs, they are unable to account for several important institutional features of demandable debt. First, in the absence of incentive constraints on the part of the banker, the optimal arrangement in liquidity-based accounts always involves suspension of convertibility, rather than expensive liquidation. However, suspension was not an option available to individual banks; it was only an alternative for the financial system as a whole, in the face of system-wide panics. Individual banks that could not satisfy creditors' fears about solvency were not permitted to suspend; they were forced to close.[5]

Second, studies of actual bank failures give fraud a prominent place in the list of causes. Studies of 19th- and 20th-century banking indicate that fraud and

---

[3] Jacklin and Sudipto Bhattacharya (1988) give a concise but useful review of these approaches.

[4] Fundamental papers that utilize this approach are by John Bryant (1980), Douglas W. Diamond and Philip Dybvig (1983), and Jacklin (1987). For a model emphasizing the costs to depositors of delay in liquidation, see Merwan Engineer (1987).

[5] See Calomiris and Larry Schweikart (1988) for a discussion of suspension rules during the early U.S. experience. Kevin Dowd (1988) argues that individual-bank suspension of debt redemption would have been beneficial but was prevented by legal prohibitions. We argue that the prohibition-of-suspension option clauses simply reflected the learned desirability of placing the decision regarding whether suspension was "justified" outside the control of the individual banker. The legal prohibition of option clauses on notes may have been perceived as necessary to protect some unsophisticated note-holders, while no such law was deemed necessary for relatively sophisticated depositors.

conflicts of interest characterize the vast majority of bank failures for state and nationally chartered banks.[6]

Third, receivership resulted from a critical mass of depositor withdrawal orders and was invoked because of information about bank asset values, not because of exogenous liquidity needs of individual depositors. In cases of massive exogenous demand for an individual bank's assets by small depositors, banks avoided failure by appealing to other banks for loans of reserves; however, when large informed depositors (including other bankers) concluded that a bank was in trouble, they would precipitate a run, depleting the bank's reserves and forcing it to be placed in receivership.[7]

These considerations make it apparent that the liquidation of banks—which was part and parcel of demandable-debt contracts—was designed to place the assets of banks beyond the reach of the banker. The rationale for prohibiting banks from suspending at their own discretion may have been the discipline that it imposed on the behavior of the banker. Thus, a model of demandable debt with bank liquidation through receivership should account for the desirability of taking control of the bank away from the banker at the option of depositors.

Fourth, the "sequential-service constraint" (first-come, first-served rule) for bank withdrawals, which allowed informed depositors to receive repayment before banks were placed into receivership, also warrants explanation. In cases other than banking, payments from bankrupt firms to creditors in anticipation of bankruptcy are not allowed, and creditors may be forced to relinquish such payments during the bankruptcy proceeding. Why in the case of banking should those who run the bank receive preferential treatment in liquidation states?

---

6 For example, E. L. Smead (1928) found that three of the nine most common causes of bank failure in the 1920s involved fraudulent or questionable activities by the banker: loans to officers and directors, outright defalcation, and loans to enterprises in which officers and directors were interested. For discussions of the role of fraud in earlier eras, see Carter H. Golembe and Clark Warburton (1958), George J. Bentson and George G. Kaufman (1986), and Calomiris and Schweikart (1988). Data on national bank failures, by cause, can be found in the Annual Report of the Comptroller of the Currency (1920 pp. 56–79). For information on the importance of fraud in more recent bank failures, see Comptroller of the Currency (1988).

7 Henry C. Nicholas (1907 p. 26) dismissed the importance of withdrawals by uninformed depositors in causing bank liquidation. He wrote, "If a bank is actually in bad shape there is far more likelihood of its initial condition being discovered by other banking institutions than by the individual depositors of the bank.... A run is sometimes started in this manner... and continues until it has practically wiped out the reserves of the suspected institution, the ordinary depositors receiving their first information regarding the position of the bank when that institution is finally forced to close its doors and formally apply for a receiver." This discussion makes important points about bank runs which appear in our model: some depositors are informed, while others are not. Runs by informed depositors end in liquidation. Informed depositors are able to exercise their withdrawal option before uninformed depositors are able to observe the bank's difficulty (or the run).

B. Demandable debt as an incentive scheme

Models in the second category of theory on the role of banks begin with the assumption that bankers have an informational advantage in determining which projects are most worthy of financing. Therefore, the banker has a comparative advantage in allocating funds for investment, but he also may have the ability to act against the interests of uninformed depositors.[8]

We show that demandable debt can provide an incentive-compatible solution to this problem in the presence of costly information. The right to take one's money out of the bank if one becomes suspicious that realized returns are low makes it in the depositor's interest to keep an eye on the bank. If enough depositors agree with this negative assessment of the bank's future, liquidation will be called for, and the bank will close. The demandable-debt contract allows the banker to precommit to a set of payoffs he otherwise would not be able to offer depositors.

Not all depositors need to monitor the banker. We argue that the first-come, first-served (sequential service) rule of demandable debt provides compensation for those who choose to invest in information and thus avoids free-riding. We view bank intermediation, therefore, as a three-sided relationship. The monitors pay the costs of vigilance but receive the benefit of knowing that they will be "first in line" (and thereby receive a higher payment than other depositors) should it become necessary to withdraw their funds from the bank. The depositors who do not monitor are willing to pay the price of being last in line in "bad" states, because they receive a benefit in return: the active monitors keep the banker in line and thereby provide a benefit to the passive depositors. Depositors need not reveal whether they are active or passive; the same contract works for both types.

The physical structure we assume includes the following important features. (1) The bank is operated by a monopolist with special access to a profitable investment opportunity which yields either a good or a bad realization. (2) There is potential for cheating by the banker which takes the form of his absconding with a proportion of the bank's assets after the investment realization. (One can think of this more generally as costly ex post fraudulent behavior which the banker undertakes whenever it is more profitable to do so than to make the promised

---

[8] This point is emphasized by Diamond (1984) and Ben Bernanke and Mark Gertler (1987). For an overview of the relation between agency costs and the structure of financial contracts, see Eugene F. Fama (1988). Diamond's solution to the delegated-monitoring problem of financial intermediation relies on two assumptions that are absent in our framework: the existence of an ex post nonpecuniary penalty that can be imposed on the banker and the ability of the banker to construct a riskless portfolio through diversification. The second assumption permits enforcement of the penalty, even if cheating is costly to observe directly, whenever the banker fails to meet his obligations. Bernanke and Gertler provide a simple macroeconomic model in which bankers are subject to moral hazard and depositors desire liquidity. They explicitly assume that costly monitoring and punishment of defaulting bankers are not possible. For them, demandable debt is desirable solely for its liquidity. In our model, demandable debt is desirable although liquidity demand is absent.

payments to depositors.) (3) Depositors face different costs of obtaining a signal that allows them to predict profitability. (4) An authority exists who will enforce contracts (some of which may stipulate conditions for bank liquidation) and who can act as receiver for liquidated banks. (5) Depositors have a reservation level of return on their endowments below which they will not invest funds with the banker.

The profit-maximizing banker will act to maximize social gain by selecting a contract that achieves beneficial intermediation (investment in profitable enterprises), while avoiding as much as possible the costs associated with absconding or liquidating. We find that the demandable-debt contract is optimal for a range of parameter values. The potential for costly liquidation may be more than offset by the social gain that comes from enhanced investment opportunities.[9]

II. The Model with a Single Depositor

A. Physical structure

A banker has an investment opportunity, but he lacks sufficient capital to take advantage of it. The investment opportunity costs one dollar. Each potential depositor has one dollar to invest. We will let S represent the total expected return available for a dollar's investment elsewhere in the economy. We assume that all agents are risk-neutral; thus, any scheme the banker develops will have to yield a depositor that same expected return.

The investment opportunity yields an uncertain payoff which may take one of two values, T_1 or T_2, with $T_2 > T_1$. The probability of the high outcome is γ. The realization is unknown to all parties at the outset and is observable ex post only by the banker. Thus, there is no way to make a contract tied directly to the value of T_i.[10]

---

[9] V. Chari and Ravi Jagannathan (1988) provide an example of an information-based run for a model that has many features in common with ours. A key difference is that they assume an (exogeneously imposed) negative externality from liquidation of the bank's assets. In their model, the creation of a liquidation technology is not efficient. In our model, there is a *positive* externality from running the bank: when the depositor observes a bad signal, he calls for liquidation, thereby salvaging some of the bank's value. The bank's structure is designed to internalize this positive externality and allows nonmonitoring depositors to compensate monitors for the benefits they provide.

Our model can also be interpreted as allowing depositors to exercise a put option based on the information they receive. However, unlike the usual "inside-trading" scenario, the uninformed depositors also benefit at the expense of the bank. While the uninformed depositors receive a lower payoff than the informed depositors, they benefit because the bank is prevented from cheating. In the usual scenario (e.g., Albert S. Kyle, 1981), the uninformed either lose or the informed cannot successfully earn a return on their information-production because of free-riding, as in Sanford J. Grossman and Joseph E. Stiglitz (1980). We thank an anonymous referee for suggesting this comparison to us.

[10] We assume that the banker is not able to trade in equity shares. This conforms with the relative illiquidity of equity trade in the period under examination. It could also be generated as a conclusion

Let period 3 be the date at which the payoff is realized and the loan is to be repaid. We assume that in period 3, immediately before repayment, the banker has the opportunity to abscond with the funds. Absconding is socially wasteful; for concreteness, we will assume that it reduces the realization T_i by the proportion A, where A is between 0 and 1.

Although the act of absconding reduces the size of the pie that is divided between the banker and the depositor, it places the banker beyond the reach of the law. Therefore, he is no longer constrained to repay the loan as initially promised. Thus, any promise to pay the depositor an amount P is actually an option of the banker either to pay P or to leave town with his assets diminished by the proportion A.

The losses from absconding may be interpreted in a variety of ways. They may represent the cost of engaging in fraud (payments to coconspirators) or the costs (forgone earnings) of placing the bank's resources in a form that allows theft. The latter interpretation requires a richer, multiperiod model than the one we provide, in which bankers' allocation decisions depend on last-period earnings.[11]

It should be readily apparent that the temptation to abscond will be greater with lower realizations of T_i. In deciding whether to abscond, the banker compares the "tax" on absconding, AT_i, with the promised funds due the depositor. If the absconding tax is less, then absconding is more profitable than paying up. Historical evidence confirms the greater prevalence of fraud in times of low returns to bank investments.[12]

Because of the threat that the banker will abscond—a threat against which he cannot commit himself—it will generally be necessary for the banker to increase the payment offered to a depositor by a "default premium" as protection against those states in which the depositor will, in fact, receive nothing.

Note that the addition of a default premium can, in turn, increase the probability of default, by making it desirable for the banker to abscond in good states as well. For example, suppose

$$S > AT_1$$

so that any payment promised to the depositor must be sufficiently large to incur absconding in the low realization; that is, a promise to pay P will only be honored

in a model in which bankers possess specialized information about investment projects of borrowers. Robert M. Townsend (1979) notes that in circumstances when only one party has access to information, debt contracts (i.e., contracts not contingent on the private information) will often be the only feasible alternative.

[11] The plausibility of our "leaky bucket" assumption and possible multiperiod reinterpretations are discussed further in the final section of this chapter. For an initial generalization of the absconding assumption see Calomiris et al. (1990).

[12] The concentration of bank fraud during times of regional or national economic decline is pronounced in national bank-failure data. See the Annual Report of the U.S. Comptroller of the Currency (1920 pp. 56–79).

a fraction γ of the time. Suppose also that

$$\gamma T_2 + (1 - \gamma)(1 - A)T_1 > S$$

so that the investment would be socially desirable (even taking into account the loss from absconding in the low realization). Then, if

$$S > \gamma A T_2$$

there is no way to promise the depositor enough expected payment to make him willing to invest, despite the social desirability of the project; the promised payment would have to exceed AT_2, making it desirable for the banker to abscond all the time.

Because of the loss of socially desirable opportunities, it is useful to have a method of thwarting absconding. One such method is the liquidation of the bank in period 2. Liquidation means that the bank's assets are taken over by a receiver, controlled by a court. This is an expensive process, not the least because the court-appointed and court-controlled receiver is likely to be less able to realize the full potential of the assets. On the other hand, the fact that the assets are no longer in the banker's control preempts any decision by him to abscond with the funds.

We assume that liquidation reduces the value of the assets by the proportion L, so that L can be regarded as the tax due to liquidation. For a complete characterization of the process of liquidation, it is necessary to take some stand as to the maximum that can be feasibly paid to the depositor in the case of liquidation. We call this value M, and we assume that[13]

$$AT_2 > M > AT_1 \tag{1}$$

so that the amount that can be guaranteed to the depositor in a liquidating contract is greater than the maximum amount that can be guaranteed in a nonliquidating contract. We also assume that

$$L > A \tag{2}$$

so that liquidation is less wasteful socially than is absconding.[14]

---

[13] There are several ways we can approach the question of the maximum to be paid once the court has control. For simplicity, we assume that M does not vary with the realization of T_i. One argument is that the value of the firm might be determined by the court, but at a very high cost.

[14] Actual liquidation costs in the United States varied historically, depending on time, location, and bank size but seem to have been small relative to potential social losses from absconding, as our model assumes. Bankruptcy expenses averaged between 3 percent and 6 percent of total collections for national banks between 1872 and 1904 (Brian C. Gendreau and Scott S. Prince, 1986).

In some cases, it may be desirable *always* to put the assets of the bank into liquidation rather than risk the banker's absconding. We call such an agreement a "simple liquidation contract," as opposed to a "simple nonliquidation contract," which states a promised repayment and leaves it to the banker whether to abscond or not.

The more interesting case, however, is one in which the depositor, based on his own information, is given the option of demanding liquidation or not. Specifically, suppose that by paying a cost I the depositor is able to receive a signal σ in period 1 as to the likelihood of a high (T_2) or low (T_1) realization. The action of investing in the signal and the result of this action are private. The signal σ works as follows. It takes on one of two values $\{g, b\}$ (for "good" and "bad").[15] The probability of a high realization, contingent on the signal, is ρ_σ:

$$\rho_g > \gamma > \rho_b. \tag{3}$$

We will use the indicator variable $e \in \{0, 1\}$ to represent the depositor's choice: $e = 1$ if there was an investment in the signal, 0 otherwise.

In summary, the physical structure of our model is as follows. There are three periods. In period 1, the depositor may invest in receiving a signal. In period 2, the bank may be liquidated. In period 3, the loan is repaid to the depositor, unless the banker decides to abscond (which he can only do if the bank has not been liquidated).

B. The contracting structure

Contracts are arranged in period 0. The monopolist banker offers the profit-maximizing contract among those which yield the depositor at least S in expected returns. (If no such contract exists or the best such contract yields negative profits, then none is offered.)

The universe of contracts in this structure is as follows. A contract is a function from a space of announcements Σ into *outcomes*. An outcome is a pair (P, Λ), where $\Lambda \in \{0, 1\}$ is an indicator variable equaling 1 if liquidation is mandated and 0 otherwise. P is the mandated repayment. (Of course P will only be received if the banker does not abscond.)[16]

[15] In the single-depositor case, the assumption that the signal takes only two values is not restrictive. In fact, the multidepositor model of the subsequent section can be reinterpreted as a single-depositor model with multivalued signals.

[16] As it stands, the specification of the contract is incomplete in two technical respects. First, the specification of the outcome should include a specification of the banker's response (i.e., whether he chooses to abscond) as a function of the announcement $\hat{\sigma}$ and of the realization T_i. However, in almost all contracts, the banker's response is easily discerned: he absconds if $P_{\hat{\sigma}} > gAT_i$, and does not abscond if $P_{\hat{\sigma}} > AT_i$. Only in the case of indifference would it be necessary to specify his response in detail. Second, the contract does not include the possibility of randomized outcomes. These can be shown never to dominate deterministic outcomes.

If the contract only specifies one outcome, we call it a "simple contract"; otherwise we call it a "compound contract." We have already described the two kinds of simple contracts: the simple liquidating contract and the simple nonliquidating contract. A straightforward application of the revelation principle demonstrates that, for the single depositor case, contracts need never contain more than two outcomes, because the signal the depositor may observe has only two values. We can identify the announcements in a compound contract with assertions by the depositor that he has observed one or the other signal. Thus, a compound contract consists of a quartet $(P_b, \Lambda_b, P_g, \Lambda_g)$.

Each contract generates a sequential game in which the depositor chooses the level of investment in information-gathering (e) and the announcement he makes as a function of the signal he receives. The banker chooses whether to abscond as a function of the announcement made by the depositor and the realization on the investment. An *optimal* contract is one for which there is a sequential equilibrium that generates maximum profits consistent with the depositor's receiving expected returns equal to the amount S.

THEOREM 1.[17] *The optimal contract in the problem takes one of the following four forms*:

(a) *a simple nonliquidating contract*
(b) *a simple liquidating contract; in this case,*

$$AT_1 < P \le M$$

(c) *a compound contract composed of two simple nonliquidating contracts* ($\Lambda_b = \Lambda_g = 0$); *in this case,*

$$P_b \le AT_1 \quad and \quad AT_1 < P_g \le AT_2$$

(d) *a compound contract composed of one simple liquidating contract and one simple nonliquidating contract* ($\Lambda_b = 1, \Lambda_g = 0$); *in this case,*

$$AT_1 < P_b < P_g \le AT_2.$$

If the optimal contract is a compound contract, then the depositor invests in the signal; if it is a simple contract, he does not. In the case of compound contracts, absconding occurs if and only if the signal was g but the low-value outcome T_1 was realized.

We call contract d "demandable debt." It works as follows: after making the deposit, the depositor invests in learning what the likely outcome will be. If he receives the bad signal, he opts for liquidating the bank. This delivers a payment with certainty. If he receives the good signal, he opts for not liquidating the bank. This promises a higher payment but runs the risk of the banker's absconding.

[17] Proofs of theorems are outlined in the Appendix.

Contract c works in virtually the same way. The only difference is that the guaranteed payment in the case of a bad signal is sufficiently low that the banker will never wish to abscond and so it is not necessary to use liquidation to hold him in place. Since liquidation always involves social costs, it is not difficult to demonstrate that in any case where contract c is feasible, it dominates contract d. We will (with prejudice) describe contract c as a "nuisance contract."

Next, we provide a characterization of when the various contracts will be observed. We do so under the assumption that the signal is "accurate" (i.e., ρ_g is high and ρ_b is low, so that the signal is a good predictor of the state) and the signal is "cheap" (so that I is small). It is easily demonstrated that, if the signal is sufficiently inaccurate or sufficiently expensive, a compound contract is not useful.

THEOREM 2. *If the signal is sufficiently cheap and accurate, then there exist values S^* and $\hat{S}$, such that the optimal contract depends on the required returns S in the following way: for $S \leq AT_1$ the simple, nonliquidating contract is optimal; for $S \in (AT_1, S^*]$, the nuisance contract is optimal; for $S \in (S^*, \hat{S}]$, demandable debt is optimal; and for $S > \hat{S}$, no contract is feasible.*

In other words, demandable debt will be observed when the returns that depositors can receive in alternate investments are relatively high.

III. Multiple Depositors with Independent Signals

In this section, we develop a model for the case in which a number of depositors enter into contracts with the banker. As before, each depositor has one dollar to invest, and the banker has one "project" he can pursue. The project costs Y and yields a total return of YT_i, which takes one of two values. Any deposits the banker receives in excess of Y can be used to yield the same competitive return S that depositors have available to them on their own. Deposits in excess of Y will be identified with "reserves."

We make the following natural assumptions about the difference between the two forms of bank assets, "project" and "reserves." If the bank is liquidated, the value of the project decreases by L; the value of the reserves is unchanged.[18] If the banker absconds, then he takes the projects with him and receives $(1-A)YT_i$. The depositors retain the entirety of the reserves.[19] We strengthen assumption (2) as follows:

$$L < A(T_1/T_2). \tag{4}$$

---

[18] This assumption is natural, given that we regard the project as requiring the banker's expertise and regard the reserves as invested in publicly available technologies.

[19] An alternative assumption is that, if the banker absconds, he takes the entirety of the reserves as well. The assumption in the text is natural if we regard absconding as occurring by siphoning a project into a less desirable project whose returns accrue directly to the banker. The assumption in this footnote is natural if we regard absconding as occurring when the banker piles the loot into the stagecoach and heads out of town.

Table 1. Payoffs on Each of the Three Nodes of the Game Tree

Contract	Banker receives	Depositors receive
Liquidation	$(1 - L)T_i Y + (Z - Y)S - P$	P
No liquidation		
Banker absconds	$(1 - A)T_i Y$	$(Z - Y)S$
Banker does not abscond	$T_i Y + (Z - Y)S - P$	P

There are Z individuals available to enter into a contract with the bank. Of these individuals, K can receive signals by investing at a cost I; for the remainder, the cost of receiving a signal is prohibitive.[20] Signals are independent and identically distributed (i.i.d.) conditional on T_i. For any individual, a "bad" signal is associated with reduced likelihood of the high-productivity state T_2, so $\rho_b > \rho_g$, as before.

Supposing that all K individuals have invested in the signal, let N be the number who receive the "bad" realization. Given the i.i.d. structure, N is a sufficient statistic for T_i, and the probability that the realization is T_2 decreases with N.

A. The contract from the banker's viewpoint

We start by examining only the incentive problem for the banker, taking the behavior of all depositors as given. We will return to the individual depositors' incentives in the succeeding subsection. For now, we assume that all K individuals who can invest in obtaining the information do so and report it truthfully.[21] A *contract* specifies an aggregate payment P and a liquidation decision Λ as functions of the number of depositors who announce observations of the bad signal. (In the succeeding subsection, we will investigate a scheme for dividing aggregate payments among the depositors.) Note therefore that the contract is the direct generalization of the contract in the previous section to a case of multiple signals.

After the announcement of the signals, the game tree is as before: if a liquidation is not mandated, the banker makes a decision whether to abscond. Table 1 describes the payoffs on each of the three nodes of the game tree.

The *optimal contract* maximizes the banker's expected profits subject to three restrictions.

(1) The expected payments to the depositors equal their aggregate reservation level:

$$SZ + KI.$$

[20] This is the simplest structure of supply of signals; it can be generalized. Alternatively, the cost of investing in a signal could be determined in a general equilibrium model.

[21] It will be clear that, as long as the cost of investing in the signal is sufficiently low, it is optimal to have all individuals with cost I make the investment.

That is, all depositors must be compensated for the opportunity cost of their funds; in addition, any monitors must be compensated for the cost of monitoring.

(2) In the case of liquidation, actual payment cannot exceed what is assumed feasible; as before, we suppose that a liquidated investment Y pays off at most MY to the depositors. Thus, the total payment to depositors out of the project and the reserves is

$$P \leq MY + (Z - Y)S \quad \text{if } \Lambda = 1.$$

(3) Finally we must consider the banker's incentive to abscond. If liquidation does not occur, then the banker will prefer to abscond whenever

$$AT_i Y < P - (Z - Y)S.$$

If the inequality is reversed the banker prefers not to abscond.

As before, we define $\hat{S}$ to be the least upper bound of feasible expected returns to depositors from the project; if the required rate of return exceeds $\hat{S}$, no contract is feasible. $\hat{S}$ can be calculated explicitly.

Our first result is that, for required returns which are sufficiently high (but less than $\hat{S}$), the optimal contract calls for liquidation when the number of bad signals is high, and not when the number of bad signals is low. When the number of bad signals is low, there is a positive (but small) probability that the banker will abscond.

THEOREM 3. *For an interval of values of S, $(\underline{S}, \hat{S}]$, the optimal contract has the following form: there exists $\underline{N}$ such that:*

$$\text{If} \quad N > \underline{N},$$
$$\Lambda(N) = 1 \quad \text{and} \quad P(N) = MY + (Z - Y)S;$$
$$\text{If} \quad N < \underline{N},$$
$$\Lambda(N) = 0 \quad \text{and} \quad P(N) = AT_2 Y + (Z - Y)S.$$

In other words, the contract has informed agents announce whether their signal was bad. If more than a critical number $\underline{N}$ announce bad signals, the bank is liquidated. If fewer than $\underline{N}$ announce bad signals, the bank is not liquidated, and the banker chooses to abscond if the productivity draw was low.[22]

---

[22] If exactly $\underline{N}$ announce bad signals, the optimal contract has a randomization between liquidation and nonliquidation. We omit the details.

It can be shown that, for values of S below this range, it will be useful to have two thresholds rather than one. For a range of values of bad signals received, it will be optimal to reduce the promised payment, rather than liquidate the bank. This is analogous to the nuisance contract discussed previously, and as before, it can be precluded by sufficiently high reservation levels of return.

Note that Z is arbitrary in this contract. As Z increases, the optimal P increases one-for-one: additional deposits beyond those invested in the project are held in reserves and returned to the depositors with certainty.[23]

B. Depositor incentives

It remains to be shown that the total aggregate payment to depositors specified in the previous section can be divided among depositors in such a way as to maintain the incentives for low-cost-information depositors to invest in the signal and to report it truthfully. In this section, we derive a demandable-debt contract that achieves this goal.

We make the following assumptions about the population of monitors and the signals:

ASSUMPTIONS. *There are large numbers of potential depositors (Z) and potential monitors (K). The cost of monitoring (I) is small. The probability of any one monitor receiving a bad signal is small. The probability of a bad realization of T is small (although the losses can be large).*

In modeling a bank, each of these assumptions seems natural to us. The assumptions allow us to model the distribution of the number of bad signals as a Poisson distribution. More precise criteria for "small enough" or "large enough" are indicated in the complete appendix. Note that as long as I is sufficiently small, it is always optimal to have all the potential monitors engage in investment.

The contract for all depositors is identical. Ex post depositors will pick one of two announcements within the contract. Since there are three information possibilities (observing g, observing b, or not making an investment), there will have to be some pooling in the outcomes. We will build a contract in which it is incentive-compatible for the depositors who have made no investment to pool with those who have observed the good draw.

Each depositor's payoff depends on his announcement and the signal (if any) he observes. We let the symbol $EU(\hat{\sigma}, \sigma)$ denote the expected return for a depositor who observes signal σ and announces signal $\hat{\sigma}$.

Individual depositors are subject to two sorts of constraints: participation constraints (i.e., the contract must give expected returns that are sufficient for depositors to participate) and incentive constraints. From the point of view of the individual depositors, the contract must satisfy the following requirements.

(1) Always announcing g gives an expected return of S, which exceeds the expected return from always announcing b. This means that depositors

---

[23] Here, reserves are used solely for redistributing payouts between monitors and nonmonitors in an incentive-compatible way. In a richer model, banks would choose between holding reserves and investing more in higher-earning projects.

with high costs of gathering information will be willing to participate in the contract in the manner specified.

(2) Announcing the observation truthfully gives a return of $S + I$, which exceeds the return from lying. If conditions in requirement 1 are satisfied as well, then individuals with a cost of I for investing are willing to make the investment in monitoring and report truthfully.

These constraints for individual depositors can be written as follows:

$$\lambda EU(\hat{g}, g) + (1 - \lambda)EU(\hat{g}, b) = S \geq \lambda EU(\hat{b}, g) + (1 - \lambda)EU(\hat{b}, b)$$

$$\lambda EU(\hat{g}, g) + (1 - \lambda)EU(\hat{b}, b) = S + I \geq \lambda EU(\hat{b}, g) + (1 - \lambda)EU(\hat{g}, b)$$

where λ is the prior probability of signal g.

The scheme we consider has payments of a particularly simple form: any depositor announcing b receives the payment R with certainty. We can call an announcement b a "withdrawal of funds." If more than $\underline{N}$ depositors announce b, the bank is liquidated; otherwise, it is not, and the banker has the option of absconding. In any event, those depositors who do not announce b evenly split the aggregate payment to depositors described in the previous section, less the funds withdrawn. We call this scheme a "standard demandable-debt contract."

Under a standard demandable-debt contract, of course,

$$EU(\hat{b}, b) = EU(\hat{b}, g) = R.$$

However, for depositors who do not withdraw their funds, the payment depends on the number of depositors N who do withdraw, and on whether the banker absconds. Table 2 describes the payments for a depositor who announces g.

For example, if more than $\underline{N}$ depositors withdraw funds, then the bank is liquidated, and according to the contract, the total payment to depositors P is $MY + (Z - Y)S$; that quantity, less the withdrawn deposits RN is split among the

Table 2. Payoff to Depositor Who Announces g

Project realization	Payoff to depositor announcing g	
	Number of depositors announcing b < $\underline{N}$	Number of depositors announcing b > $\underline{N}$
T_1	$\dfrac{(Z - Y)S - RN}{Z - N}$	$\dfrac{MY + (Z - Y)S - RN}{Z - N}$
T_2	$\dfrac{AT_2 + (Z - Y)S - RN}{Z - N}$	$\dfrac{MY + (Z - Y)S - RN}{Z - N}$

remaining depositors $Z - N$, yielding the quantity in the right-most column of the table. The remaining numbers are calculated in a similar fashion.

Given the probabilities of the realizations of T_i and the probability of each signal contingent on T_i, it is a straightforward matter to calculate $EU(\hat{g}, b)$ and $EU(\hat{g}, g)$. For this scheme, the incentive and participation constraints reduce to the following:[24]

$$EU(\hat{g}, b) = R - I/(1 - \lambda)$$

$$S > R.$$

When an aggregate contract of the sort described in the previous section is optimal, it can always be implemented with a demandable-debt scheme, as stated in the following theorem.

THEOREM 4. *Under the distributional assumptions and the conditions of the previous theorem, the optimal outcome can be achieved with a simple demandable-debt contract.*

The role of reserves in our model warrants discussion. By holding reserves, the bank is able to guarantee early payment to a small number of monitors (those who receive bad signals) without forcing the bank to be placed into receivership. Reserves allow the bank to commit to the sequential-service constraint (early withdrawals by those who run the bank), which supports the implementation of the contract between bankers and depositors. More familiar justifications for bank reserve holding include the usefulness of reserves in meeting stochastic demands for conversion into gold (say, due to foreign-transactions needs of depositors) or the contribution of reserves to an optimally diversified portfolio of bank assets. Our model adds to these transactions and portfolio motivations for holding reserves an "incentive-compatibility" demand for reserves.

C. Transactability and demandable debt

Thus far, we have argued that demandable-debt intermediation may arise in order to permit profitable investment opportunities to be realized. In our models, there is no demand for transactability; therefore, assets are valued entirely based on expected return. Historically, however, an important feature of demandable-debt instruments has been their use as a medium of exchange. In this subsection, we briefly consider the implications of our model for the liquidity of demandable debt.

---

[24] The constraints initially have two equalities that must be satisfied. However, given the fact that the total expected payments equal $SZ + KI$, as they do by construction of the demandable-debt contract, one of the equations is redundant: if the informed depositors are each receiving $S + I$, then the uninformed depositors are automatically receiving the remainder, or S per depositor.

It is important to note from the outset that transactable instruments need not be demandable. Postdated bills of exchange and postdated bank notes were physically transactable instruments that existed in the 19th century in the United States (Davis R. Dewey, 1910). Their primary difference from demandable debt was that they could be redeemed, not on demand, but only on the date of maturity. Since such instruments could be maturity-matched, they would seem to have none of the disadvantages of demandable debt. Nonetheless, demandable debt outcompeted these as a medium of exchange.

In order to explain the relative liquidity of demandable debt, one must explain why the ability to redeem a bank note or deposit on demand makes people more willing to accept it as a means of payment. We argue that, under demandable debt, monitors and nonmonitors alike are better informed of the market value of the debt instrument at all times.[25]

The fact that "the bank is open" (that monitors have not called for a liquidation) is revealing to nonmonitors. In the simplest, one-monitor case, the fact that the bank is open is fully revealing, because the signal that the monitor receives takes one of two values. In the multimonitor case, the fact that the bank is open is not fully revealing; it only indicates that fewer than the threshold number of bad signals have been announced. Even this information, however, places a lower bound on the value of the bank's liability.[26] If the liquidity of an asset depends on the extent to which information about its value is shared, then one would expect demandable debt to have been more liquid than other contracts with which it competed (see George Akerlof, 1970; Benjamin Klein, 1974). Thus, it may be possible to view the liquidity of bank claims as a by-product of the solution to the agency problem.

While we argue that the transactability of demandable debt enhanced its attractiveness, it is interesting to note that demandable-debt banking predates the transactability of demandable debt.[27] Thus, the desirability of demandable-debt contracting does not seem to have depended crucially on the transactability of the instruments.

[25] In a different context, Gorton and Pennacchi (1990) also employ this definition of liquidity. They show that debt instruments may be more liquid than equity because debt instruments reduce the potential gains insiders can receive from trading. Their model does not, however, explain the special liquidity of demandable debt.

[26] Historically, specie prices of bank notes published in bank-note "reporters" confirm the view that nonmonitors faced little price uncertainty for notes of banks that were open. Discounts on antebellum bank notes convertible on demand into specie traded in the home city at par; in distant locations, the discounts for notes mainly reflected the risk due to the time it would take to reach the city of issue. Typically, one could know the value of a bank's notes in New York by knowing the state in which the bank was located. These discounts typically remained small (between $\frac{1}{8}$ percent and 2 percent) and were subject to little variation. Discounts of notes for failed banks were not quoted in bank note reporters or were subject to extreme variations across banks in the same locale and over time (see Calomiris and Schweikart, 1988).

[27] For example, Roman banks issued demandable claims which were not transactable (A. W. Ferrin, 1908).

The "liquidity premium" that demandable debt enjoys can be included in our framework by reducing the level of the required return S on demandable debt by the amount of the liquidity premium. In other words, demandable debt would face a lower threshold reservation level to satisfy than the nonliquidating compound contract. This implies an expansion of the parameter values for which demandable debt is preferred over the "nuisance" contract.

IV. Summary

We have argued that historical demandable-debt banking can be understood as the optimal means of incentive-compatible intermediation in an environment of asymmetric information with potential for fraudulent behavior on the part of the banker. Monitoring by some depositors and runs by monitors who receive bad signals ensure sufficiently high payoffs to depositors in states of the world that would otherwise lead to malfeasance by the banker.

Agency problems are inherent in banking. Depositors entrust their endowments to bankers, who decide how to invest them and have essentially unfettered immediate control over the depositors' funds. We capture this agency problem in a simple way by allowing the potential for "absconding" by the banker. The banker has the ability to remove funds from the bank. Absconding is socially wasteful; if the banker steals funds from the bank, he uses a "leaky bucket," so that the amount he actually receives is less than the amount stolen.

If the required return for depositors is sufficiently high, then the banker may find it attractive to abscond, rather than make the promised payment to depositors. Anticipating this, depositors will be unwilling to entrust their funds to the banker, and efficient intermediation will not take place. In other words, the possibility for a banker to abscond may make it difficult for him to attract depositors to his bank.

We introduce a liquidation technology that allows depositors, at a cost, to prevent the banker from absconding and makes it possible for the banker to attract depositors. We show that, under some circumstances, the optimal arrangement has the depositor choose whether to liquidate the bank, contingent on a costly signal he receives. In good states, it will pay for the banker not to abscond and to pay the depositor as promised; in bad states, in absence of a liquidation announcement, the banker will abscond rather than pay as promised. Thus, when monitors receive bad signals, they call for liquidation.

If the signal is perfect and costless to the depositor, liquidation will occur only when there are bad loan-investment realizations. If the signal is imperfect and costly, but not prohibitively so, it still makes sense to use the contingent liquidation contract, even though on occasion monitoring depositors may make errors in judging when to "run the bank" and force the bank to liquidate unnecessarily. Banks can fail either because the banker absconds or because the depositor initiates a run on the bank. The purpose of a run is to prevent absconding from taking place.

In the case of multiple depositors, the bank uses reserves to offer guaranteed payments to early withdrawers and to insulate itself from a few bad idiosyncratic signals. At the same time, under circumstances that probably would lead to costly absconding, depositors as a group are likely to order liquidation preemptively. The number of monitors and the threshold at which a bank liquidation is called for will be chosen optimally to minimize total expected costs of liquidation, absconding, and monitoring.

Limitations and suggested extensions

Our analysis has several important limitations. First, our goal is to explain the *historical* importance of demandable debt in banking. In today's more regulated environment, where for example, regulations on clearing through the Federal Reserve System have favored demandable-debt instruments and where deposit insurance makes depositor monitoring less important, demandable debt may persist simply as an artifact of regulation.

Second, our framework does not consider the possibility of trade in bank shares. Unlike the historical context in which demandable debt arose, in today's more sophisticated financial markets, shares of financial intermediaries are actively traded. In this richer context, equity trading could conceivably provide a superior disciplinary alternative to demandable debt and contingent liquidation. For example, leveraged buy-outs offer a possible alternative means to prevent managerial misconduct and provide rewards that make monitoring incentive-compatible.

Third, our account is one of individual banks and individual bank liquidations, not of systems of banks or economy-wide bank panics. We are only attempting to model the operation of demandable debt in normal times, when the rules require banks to pay on demand. In historical practice, the provisions of demandable debt, including liquidation, were suspended during crises (see James G. Cannon, 1910; Calomiris and Schweikart, 1988). That is to say, demandable debt was a contingent rule; it required banks to meet the threat of runs in response to idiosyncratic problems, but it allowed banks to escape convertibility on demand in the face of systemic disturbances. Only individual bank difficulties led to placing a bank in receivership. Suspension and interbank relations during panics are important as well, but doing this topic justice requires a larger analysis than the one we have undertaken in this paper (see Calomiris and Kahn, 1989; Gorton, 1989; Calomiris and Gorton, 1990).

Fourth, our model relies on a crude and extremely stylized incentive problem characterized by the "leaky bucket" with which the banker can abscond. This leaky-bucket assumption is useful, because it allows us to model the problem in an extremely simple way, but it raises natural questions as to whether the degree of leakiness necessary to generate the results is at all realistic. After all, if the banker's own stake is less than 1 percent of the value of the assets, then it would be necessary that more than 99 percent of the value of the assets leak from the bucket in good times in order to keep the banker from absconding.

A more reasonable interpretation of our story is as a simplification of a multi-period account, in which the banker is in fact choosing whether to engage in malfeasance today, when the decision not to engage in malfeasance always leaves the option open for tomorrow. Suppose that the returns to a bank's investments are intertemporally correlated. Then, in a good realization, the banker may be unwilling to engage in malfeasance because it will destroy the prospects for future returns (including the possibility of future malfeasance), even without assuming the bucket implausibly leaky.[28] Thus, it is important to investigate multiperiod versions of our model to determine whether a consistent account can be generated with plausible parameter values.

Finally, our model does not include any demand for liquidity. We have inten-tionally limited the model in order to emphasize the difference between our account and those accounts that depend on liquidity demand. Nonetheless, this limitation means that the model is not adequate to investigate the rela-tion between demandable debt and transactions demand. Although we have briefly and informally considered the links, formal models combining the consumption-flexibility and monitoring accounts of banking are an important goal for future research.

APPENDIX

To make the proofs more concise, we will make the following modifications to the structure without loss of generality. First we can treat the choice of $e = 0$ as generating a "signal" which is pure noise. Let $\rho(\sigma, e)$ be the posterior probability of the high realization given an investment e and the receipt of signal σ. Then

$$\rho(\sigma, e) = \rho_\sigma \quad \text{if } e = 1,$$
$$= \gamma \quad \text{if } e = 0.$$

From this, we can generate expectations as functions of σ and e.

A *contract* is a quartet $(\Lambda_b, P_b, \Lambda_g, P_g)$ with the restriction that $P_\sigma \leq M$ if $\Lambda_\sigma = 1$. We can identify simple contracts with quartets $(\Lambda_b, P_b, \Lambda_g, P_g)$ in which $\Lambda_b = \Lambda_g$ and $P_b = P_g$. Finally, by the revelation principle, we can restrict attention to contracts in which the announcement $\hat{\sigma}(\sigma) = \sigma$ in equilibrium.

---

[28] We are grateful to an anonymous referee for suggesting this interpretation.

The choice of a contract generates a game in which the depositor picks a strategy consisting of investment and announcement $\{e, \hat{\sigma}(\sigma)\}$ and the banker picks a probability of absconding as a function of the depositor's announcement and the realization of T_i: $\alpha(\hat{\sigma}, T_i)$. (Let $\alpha = 1$ indicate absconding, and $\alpha = 0$ indicate no absconding.)

The banker's equilibrium strategy can be described simply:

$$\alpha = 1 \quad \text{if } \Lambda_\sigma = 0 \quad \text{and} \quad P_\sigma > AT_i,$$

$$= 0 \quad \text{if } \Lambda_\sigma = 0 \quad \text{and} \quad P_\sigma < AT_i.$$

Let the function $U(\hat{\sigma}, \sigma)$ represent the expected profits of the depositor conditional on his observation σ and on his announcement $\hat{\sigma}$. Then

$$U(\hat{\sigma}, \sigma) = P_{\hat{\sigma}} \qquad\qquad\qquad \text{if } \Lambda_{\hat{\sigma}} = 1,$$

$$= P_{\hat{\sigma}}(1 - E\{\alpha(P_\sigma, T_i)|\sigma, e\}) \quad \text{if } \Lambda_{\hat{\sigma}} = 0.$$

LEMMA. *An optimal contract generates an equilibrium with $e = 0$ if and only if the contract is a simple contract.*

Proof. If $e = 0$ in equilibrium, then

$$U(\hat{\sigma}, g) = U(\hat{\sigma}, b)$$

because the signal conveys no information. Thus

$$U(g, g) = U(b, g) = U(g, b) = U(b, b);$$

otherwise, the contract would not induce truth-telling. If the depositor is indifferent between announcements, but the banker is not, then the contract is sub-optimal, because banker profits could be improved by having the depositor always make the announcement the banker prefers.

Thus, both depositor and banker must be indifferent between the stated outcomes for the two announcements. This requires the outcomes themselves to be identical.

The converse follows from the next lemma. Define λ to be the probability of observing the signal g, so that

$$\lambda = (\gamma - \rho_b)/(\rho_g - \rho_b)$$

LEMMA. *A contract generates an equilibrium with $e = 1$ if and only if*

$$U(\hat{b}, b) - U(\hat{g}, b) \geq I/(1 - \lambda), \qquad (A.1)$$

$$U(\hat{g}, g) - U(\hat{b}, g) \geq I/\lambda. \qquad (A.2)$$

Proof. If the depositor does not make the investment in the signal, he has the following options: he could always report that the signal was g; he could always report that the signal was b; or he could make a randomization. In equilibrium, $e = 1$ if and only if all of these strategies are dominated by the strategy in which the depositor makes the investment and reports the signal truthfully, that is, if and only if

$$\lambda U(\hat{g}, g) + (1 - \lambda)U(\hat{b}, b) - I \geq \lambda U(\hat{g}, g) + (1 - \lambda)U(\hat{g}, b),$$

$$\lambda U(\hat{g}, g) + (1 - \lambda)U(\hat{b}, b) - I \geq \lambda U(\hat{b}, g) + (1 - \lambda)U(\hat{b}, b).$$

These two inequalities simplify to those in the statement of the lemma.

Note that these inequalities imply that if $e = 1$ the contract is not a simple contract. Note also that these inequalities automatically imply that truth-telling is preferred:

$$U(\hat{b}, b) - U(\hat{g}, b) \geq 0,$$

$$U(\hat{g}, g) - U(\hat{b}, g) \geq 0.$$

For reference Figure A1 depicts $U(\hat{\sigma}, g)$ and $U(\hat{\sigma}, b)$ as functions of $P_{\hat{\sigma}}$ in the case where $\Lambda_{\hat{\sigma}} = 0$ and $e = 1$. Note that

$$U(\hat{\sigma}, g) \geq U(\hat{\sigma}, b) \quad \text{for all } P_{\hat{\sigma}}. \qquad (A.3)$$

As payment promised in the contract increases up to the level AT_1, the expected payoff to the depositor increases one-for-one. From AT_1 to AT_2, it increases less than one-for-one, since the depositor knows he will receive the payment only in the good realization which happens with probability ρ_{σ}. Promised payments above AT_2 are irrelevant, since the depositor knows he will never receive them. Note also that there is a unique equilibrium value of the banker's response α, except when the contracted repayment equals AT_1 or AT_2. In this case, the banker is indifferent among absconding, not absconding, and any randomization of those two responses. In this case, U is a correspondence, where the particular value depends on the choice of banker's strategy in the equilibrium.

Proof of Theorem 1. The claim that an optimal contract must conform to one of the four cases listed in the theorem is equivalent to the following claims:

a: If $P_\sigma \leq AT_1$ in an optimal contract, then $\Lambda_\sigma = 0$.
b: If the optimal contract is a compound contract, then $\Lambda_g = 0$ and $P_g \in (AT_1, AT_2]$.
c: If the optimal contract has $e = 1$, then $P_g > P_b$.

Claim a is fairly immediate: If a contract has liquidation with a promised price less than or equal to AT_1, it is obviously suboptimal. The depositor can be guaranteed the same amount without liquidation, since the banker will never desire to abscond. And if there is no liquidation, the banker's profits are greater.

Most of claim b is derived from the following lemma:

LEMMA. *If an optimal feasible contract has* $e = 1$, *then* $\Lambda_g = 0$, *and* $P_g \in [AT_1, AT_2]$.

Proof. If $\Lambda_g = 1$, then the return the depositor receives if he says g is independent of the true signal. If $\Lambda_g = 0$ but P_g is not in the specified interval, then the return is also independent of the signal (see Figure A1). In either case, that is,

$$U(g, b) = U(g, g).$$

But by the incentive conditions (A.1)–(A.2), this implies

$$U(\hat{b}, b) > U(\hat{b}, g)$$

contradicting (A.3).

Claim c follows by noting first that P_b is certainly less than AT_2 (if it is equal to or greater than AT_2, then there is a lower price for which all incentive constraints are satisfied for the depositor, and which gives greater profits to the banker). If this is the case, then $P_b < P_g$.

The final step in demonstrating claim b is to verify that any feasible compound contract in which $P_g = AT_1$ is dominated by a simple contract with P_g less than or equal to AT_1.

Proof of Theorem 2. If $S \leq AT_1$, it is immediate that the optimal contract is a simple non-liquidating contract. Such a contract entails no social waste, since the required payback is so low that the banker never has an incentive to abscond. Therefore, assume $S > AT_1$.

It is straightforward to show that whenever a contract is feasible and optimal, the depositor receives a return equal to his outside return plus compensation for any investment he has made. If the nonliquidation contract is chosen, then profits are

$$\lambda(\rho_g T_2 + (1 - \rho_g)(1 - A)T_1) + (1 - \lambda)(\rho_b T_2 + (1 - \rho_b)(1 - A)T_1) - S. \quad \text{(A.4a)}$$

If the simple liquidation contract is chosen, then profits are

$$\lambda(1-L)(\rho_g T_2 + (1-\rho_g)T_1) + (1-\lambda)(1-L)(\rho_b T_2 + (1-\rho_b)T_1) - S. \qquad \text{(A.4b)}$$

If the nuisance contract is chosen then profits are

$$\lambda(\rho_g T_2 + (1-\rho_g)(1-A)T_1) + (1-\lambda)(\rho_b T_2 + (1-\rho_b)T_1) - S - I. \qquad \text{(A.4c)}$$

If the demandable debt contract is chosen, then profits are

$$\lambda(\rho_g T_2 + (1-\rho_g)(1-A)T_1) + (1-\lambda)(\rho_b(1-L)T_2 + (1-\rho_b)(1-L)T_1) - S - I. \qquad \text{(A.4d)}$$

Profits in a nuisance contract are greater than profits in a demandable debt contract. If

$$\rho_g > (A-L)T_1/[(A-L)T_1 + LT_2] > \rho_b, \qquad \text{(A.5)}$$

then the demandable debt contract dominates any simple contract for I sufficiently small.

Assuming (A.5), the optimal contract is the nuisance contract if there exists an incentive compatible one which yields the depositor a return equal to $S+I$. If there exists no such contract, the optimal contract is a demandable debt contract if there exists an incentive compatible one which yields the depositor a return equal to $S+I$. If neither of these contracts exist, the optimal contract is a simple contract if one is feasible.

In any feasible complex contract, the return to the depositor must exceed $S+I$:

$$\lambda P_g \rho_g + (1-\lambda)P_b \geq S+I. \qquad \text{(A.6)}$$

A nuisance contract satisfying Theorem 1 (one with $\Lambda_b = \Lambda_g = 0$ and P_b not equal to P_g) exists if and only if there are a pair of payments P_b and P_g satisfying restriction (c) of Theorem 1, (A.6), and the incentive compatibility restrictions (A.1) and (A.2). (The last two reduce to)

$$P_g \rho_g \geq P_b + I/\lambda, \qquad \text{(A.7)}$$

$$P_b \geq P_g \rho_b + I/(1-\lambda). \qquad \text{(A.8)}$$

The following five inequalities are necessary and sufficient for the existence of such a P_g and P_b

$$
\begin{aligned}
S + I &\le \lambda A T_2 \rho_g + (1 - \lambda) A T_1 &\text{(a)} \\
S + I &\le A T_1 \left(1 + \lambda \frac{\rho_g - \rho_b}{\rho_b} \right) - \lambda \frac{\rho_g}{\rho_b} \frac{I}{1 - \lambda} &\text{(b)} \\
S + I &\le A T_2 \rho_g - \frac{1 - \lambda}{\lambda} I &\text{(c)} \\
\frac{I}{\rho_g - \rho_b} \left(\frac{1}{\lambda} + \frac{1}{1 - \lambda} \right) &\le A T_2 &\text{(d)} \\
\frac{I}{\rho_g - \rho_b} \left(\frac{\rho_g}{\lambda} + \frac{\rho_b}{1 - \lambda} \right) &\le A T_1 &\text{(e)}
\end{aligned}
\qquad \text{(A.9)}
$$

For each I sufficiently small, there exists $S^* > A T_1$ such that these inequalities are satisfied by all S less than S^*. In the interval $(A T_1, S^*]$ the nuisance contract is optimal.

The demandable debt contract is feasible if there exist payments P_g and P_b satisfying (A.1) and (A.2), condition (d) of Theorem 1, (A.6), and the feasibility restriction that $P_b \le M$. Necessary and sufficient conditions for such payments to exist are

$$
\begin{aligned}
S + I &\le \lambda A T_2 \rho_g + (1 - \lambda) M &\text{(a)} \\
S + I &\le M \left(1 + \lambda \frac{\rho_g - \rho_b}{\rho_b} \right) - \lambda \frac{\rho_g}{\rho_b} \frac{I}{1 - \lambda} &\text{(b)} \\
S + I &\le A T_2 \rho_g - \frac{1 - \lambda}{\lambda} I &\text{(c)} \\
\frac{I}{\rho_g - \rho_b} \left(\frac{1}{\lambda} + \frac{1}{1 - \lambda} \right) &\le A T_2 &\text{(d)} \\
\frac{I}{\rho_g - \rho_b} \left(\frac{\rho_g}{\lambda} + \frac{\rho_b}{1 - \lambda} \right) &\le M &\text{(e)}
\end{aligned}
\qquad \text{(A.10)}
$$

Note that these conditions are identical to the five conditions in (A.9) with M substituted for $A T_1$. For I sufficiently small, the conditions are satisfied by all S less than or equal to some critical value S^{**}, where $S^{**} > S^*$. In the interval $(S^*, S^{**}]$ demandable debt is the optimal contract.

Provided that

$$
\rho_g > M / A T_2 > \rho_b \qquad \text{(A.11)}
$$

for I sufficiently small,

$$
S^{**} = \lambda A T_2 \rho_g + (1 - \lambda) M - I,
$$

which exceeds the maximum possible payout to the depositor under any simple contract. Thus for required returns beyond S^{**}, no contract is feasible.

Thus, the theorem is proved provided that the signal is sufficiently accurate in the sense that inequalities (A.5) and (A.11) hold and provided that I is small enough—that is, if it satisfies the following eight requirements: Expression (A.4d) exceeds (A.4a) and (A.4b); inequalities (A.9d) and (A.9e) hold; the right sides of (A.9b) and (A.9c) exceed AT_1; the right sides of (A.10b) and (A.10c) exceed the right side of (A.10a). Given (A.5) and (A.11), these eight inequalities hold strictly for $I = 0$; therefore, they hold in an interval of I small but positive.

Proof of Theorem 3. We begin by determining the optimal contract in general.

LEMMA. *The optimal contract in general involves three regions. For high values of N, the contract mandates liquidation. For intermediate values of N, liquidation is not mandated, but aggregate payment is set sufficiently low that absconding never occurs. For low values of N, payment is set sufficiently high that absconding takes place in low productivity outcomes.*

Proof. In this proof, we explicitly include the possibility of randomized outcomes for various realizations of N. Recall that Λ is the indicator variable for a liquidation and α is the indicator variable for absconding. Let N_α, N_Λ, N_o be any triple of integers t such that,

$$\Pr\{\Lambda = 1 \,|\, N_\Lambda\} > 0$$

$$\Pr\{\alpha = 1, \Lambda = 0 \,|\, N_\alpha\} > 0$$

$$\Pr\{\alpha = 1 \,|\, N_0\}\, 0 \quad \text{and Pr} \quad \{\Lambda = 0 \,|\, N_0\} > 0.$$

(Thus, N_Λ is an N for which liquidation can occur, N_α is an N for which absconding can occur, N_o is an N for which absconding does not occur and for which liquidation need not occur.) Let

$$X_\Lambda \text{ be a subset of the event } \{\Lambda = 1 \cap N = N_\Lambda\}$$

$$X_\alpha \text{ be a subset of the event } \{\Lambda = 0 \cap N = N_\alpha\}$$

$$X_0 \text{ be a subset of the event } \{\Lambda = 0 \cap N = N_0\}$$

each with identical probability ϵ, and independent of T. Suppose $N_\Lambda > N_0$. Then by reversing behavior on X_Λ and X_0 (i.e., setting $\Lambda = 0$, $\alpha = 0$ on X_Λ and $\Lambda = 1$ on X_0 and reversing the payoffs between the two), we do not affect the distribution of aggregate payoffs to the depositors, but since the good outcome is more likely for N_0 we increase the expectation of the banker's profits.

Suppose $N_0 < N_\alpha$. Then the distribution of $T_i|N_0$ stochastically dominates the distribution $T_i|N_\alpha$. Reverse the payoffs on X_α and X_0 and let α be determined by the incentive compatibility condition. This change reduces the likelihood of absconding; it increases both depositors' expected payments and the banker's profits.

If liquidation occurs, P can be no greater than

$$MY + (Z - Y)S$$

If absconding occurs with zero probability, P can be no greater than

$$AT_1 + (Z - Y)S$$

If absconding occurs with less than probability 1, P can be no greater than

$$AT_2 + (Z - Y)S$$

Next we show that in each of the three regions described in the previous lemma, these maximal payoffs are binding. It is clear that for a maximum, constraint (3.6) is binding. If $S > AT_1$ the total payoff to depositors must be greater than AT_1 in some state, and this implies that either liquidation or the possibility of absconding must have positive probability in some state. Both liquidation and the possibility of absconding reduce social benefits. In other words, for a given required aggregate expected payment to the depositors, profits are maximized by making the region of no liquidation and no absconding (the intermediate region described in the lemma) as large as possible. If in some state, the payoff is not at its maximum, then by increasing the payoff to the maximum in that state we could expand the intermediate region.

Next we determine the boundaries of the three regions. In our calculations, we will treat the variable N as if it had a continuous distribution. The calculation with N a discrete random variable is analogous and the resultant conditions are identical, but the complete description in that case consumes considerable notation and is therefore omitted.

Let $F(N)$ be the distribution of N, and let $\rho(N)$ be the probability that $T_i = T_2$ conditional on N bad realizations. Given the results so far, the choice of an optimal contract can be reduced to a choice of two numbers, $\underline{N}$ and $\bar{N}$, to maximize

$$\int_0^{\underline{N}} [\rho(N)T_2 + (1 - \rho(N))\,(1 - A)T_1]\,dF(N)$$

$$+ \int_{\underline{N}}^{\overline{N}} [\rho(N)T_2 + (1 - \rho(N))T_1]\,dF(N)$$

$$+ \int_{\overline{N}}^{K} [(1 - L)\rho(N)T_2 + (1 - L)(1 - \rho(N))T_1]\,dF(N) \qquad \text{(A2.0)}$$

subject to

$$\int_0^{\underline{N}} \rho(N)AT_2Y\,dF(N) + \int_{\underline{N}}^{\overline{N}} AT_1Y\,dF(N) + \int_{\overline{N}}^{K} MY\,dF(N) \geq YS + KI \qquad \text{(A2.1)}$$

and

$$\underline{N} \leq \overline{N}. \qquad \text{(A2.2)}$$

The maximand is basically the sum of the firm profits and the expected payments to the depositors. Constraint (A2.1) is essentially a transformation of the aggregate participation constraint; the righthand side is a transformation of the aggregate reservation payment for all depositors.

Define $\underline{\rho} = \rho(\underline{N})$ and $\overline{\rho} = \rho(\overline{N})$. Then the first order conditions for this maximization problem are as below:

$$[\overline{\rho}T_2 + (1 - \overline{\rho})T_1] - [\overline{\rho}(1 - L)T_2 + (1 - \overline{\rho})(1 - L)T_1] - \sigma[M - AT_1] = 0$$

$$- [\underline{\rho}T_2 + (1 - \underline{\rho})T_1] + [\underline{\rho}T_2 + (1 - \underline{\rho})(1 - A)T_1] - \sigma(AT_1 - \underline{\rho}AT_2) = 0$$

where $\overline{\rho} < \underline{\rho}$ and σ is the Lagrange multiplier attached to constraint (A2.1). As the right side increases from AT_1Y in constraint (A2.1), σ increases from zero, $\overline{\rho}$ rises, and $\underline{\rho}$ falls—in other words, the region in which there is no absconding and no liquidation shrinks. Finally, there is a critical level such that for σ greater than the critical level constraint (A2.2) becomes binding. From this point, the solution is defined by constraints (A2.1) and (A2.2) holding with equality. For $YS + KI$ above this level, the middle region is degenerate, and the contract takes the form described in the text. When the middle region is degenerate the right side of (A2.2) is calculated from the following formula

$$W(\underline{N}) = \int_0^{\underline{N}} \rho(N)AT_2Y\,dF(N) + \int_{\underline{N}}^{K} MY\,dF(N)$$

where $\underline{N}$ is the boundary between the remaining two regions.

The remaining portion of the proof demonstrates that given $LT_2 > AT_1$, the set of values $W = YS + KI$ for which the optimum has a degenerate middle region is a closed interval $[\underline{W}, \overline{W}]$ with $\underline{W} > \overline{W}$.

The lower end of the interval is found as follows: Combine the above first order conditions as follows:

$$\frac{L(T_2\bar{\rho} + T_1(1 - \bar{\rho}))}{AT_1} = \frac{M - AT_1}{\rho AT_2 - AT_1}. \tag{A2.3}$$

Solve when $\bar{\rho} = \rho$ for the unique positive root. (Call it ρ^*.) Then

$$\underline{W} = W(N^{-1}(\rho^*)).$$

Provided $LT_2 < AT_1$, as W increases beyond the critical point, the optimum is achieved by reducing the region in which liquidation occurs and increasing the region in which absconding becomes a possibility. In other words, as W increases it takes more and more individuals to call for a liquidation.

The upper end of the interval is found by determining the maximum feasible amount for $W(\underline{N})$. The maximum occurs at $N^{-1}(M/AT_2)$. By using the equation (A2.3) it is possible to verify that

$$\rho^* > M/AT_2$$

Finally, we note that $\hat{S}$ as described in the text is equal to $\overline{W}/Y$. If S exceeds this amount, no matter how small I is there is no way to pay the depositors the required amount in aggregate.

Proof of Theorem 4. Given the payoff structure we can explicitly write $EU(\hat{g}, b)$ as follows:

$$EU(\hat{g}, b) = \rho_b \left[\sum_{N=0}^{K} \Pr\{N|T_2\} \frac{S(Z - Y) - NR}{Z - N} + \sum_{N=0}^{N} \Pr\{N|T_2\} \frac{AT_2 Y}{Z - N} \right.$$

$$\left. + \sum_{N=\underline{N}+1}^{K} \Pr\{N|T_2\} \frac{YM}{Z - N} \right]$$

$$+ (1 - \rho_b) \left[\sum_{N=0}^{K} \Pr\{N|T_1\} \frac{S(Z - Y) - NR}{Z - N} + \sum_{N=\underline{N}+1}^{K} \Pr\{N|T_1\} \frac{YM}{Z - N} \right]$$

where $\Pr\{N|T_i\}$ is the probability of N individuals out of K receiving bad signals conditional on the productivity draw being T_i and individual 1 already having received a bad signal. (Recall that ρ_b is the probability of T_2 conditional on an individual's observing a bad realization of the signal.)

From the incentive conditions we know that for sufficiently small I, the structure satisfies the conditions if and only if we can find Z and R such that

$$EU(\hat{g}, b) = R,$$

$$S > R.$$

By combining these two conditions with the formula for $EU(\hat{g}, b)$, and simplifying the expressions, we see that the following condition is equivalent:

$$S\left[\sum_{N=0}^{K} \Pr\{N|b\}\frac{1}{Z-N}\right] > AT_2\rho_b\left[\sum_{N=0}^{\underline{N}} \Pr\{N|T_2\}\frac{1}{Z-N}\right] + M\left[\sum_{N=\underline{N}+1}^{K} \Pr\{N|b\}\frac{1}{Z-N}\right]$$

where $\Pr\{N|b\} = \rho_b\Pr\{N|T_2\} + (1 - \rho_b)\Pr\{N|T_1\}$

If Z is very large, this inequality can be approximated by

$$S > AT_2 \Pr\{T_2 \text{ and } N \leq \underline{N} \mid b\} + M \Pr\{N \geq \underline{N} \mid b\}.$$

(Note also that Z must be greater than N and greater than $Y + RK/S$ so that all payments specified for all individuals are non negative in our contract.)

It remains only to show that for $S = \hat{S}$, calculated at the end of the previous proof, this strict inequality holds. But using the same approximation for large Z, the definition of $\hat{S}$ implies that

$$\hat{S} > AT_2 \Pr\{T_2 \text{ and } N \leq \underline{N}\} + M \Pr\{N > \underline{N}\}$$

It is, therefore, sufficient to demonstrate that

$$AT_2\Pr\{T_2 \text{ and } N \leq \underline{N}|g\} + M \Pr\{N > \underline{N}|g\}$$

$$\geq AT_2 \Pr\{T_2 \text{ and } N \leq \underline{N}|b\} + M \Pr\{N > \underline{N}|b\}.$$

Given that $AT_2 > M$, we only need to demonstrate that

$$\Pr\{T_2|N \leq \underline{N}, b\} \leq \Pr\{T_2|N \leq \underline{N}, g\}$$

which in turn is equivalent to

$$\frac{\Pr\{N \leq \underline{N} - 1|T_2\} \Pr\{b|T_2\}}{\Pr\{N \leq \underline{N}|T_2\} \Pr\{b|T_2\}} \leq \frac{\Pr\{N \leq \underline{N} - 1|T_1\} \Pr\{b|T_1\}}{\Pr\{N \leq \underline{N}|T_1\} \Pr\{b|T_1\}}.$$

Using the Poisson distribution, the ratio in the above inequality for a given T_i can be approximated by

$$\frac{\sum_{x=0}^{\underline{N}-1} f(x; \mu_i)}{\sum_{x=0}^{\underline{N}} f(x; \mu_i)}\mu_i$$

where

$$f(x, \mu) = \mu^x e^{-\mu}/x!.$$

For $\underline{N}$ sufficiently large, this quantity is decreasing in μ. From the previous theorem, increases in S increase the cutoff level of $\underline{N}$. It is therefore only necessary to determine that $\underline{N}$ can be sufficiently large without rendering the contract infeasible, that is, without allowing the quantity $\rho(\underline{N})$ to fall below M/AT_2. Direct calculation reveals that if $\underline{N}$ satisfies the following inequality, then the contract remains feasible:

$$(\mu_2/\mu_1)^{\underline{N}} \geq \frac{M}{AT_2 - M} e^{-(\mu_1 - \mu_2)} \frac{1 - \gamma}{\gamma}.$$

By setting γ, the probability of the good outcome, sufficiently large, we can make the maximum feasible $\underline{N}$ arbitrarily large, thereby guaranteeing that the incentive constraint is satisfied without the contract becoming infeasible.

References

Akerlof, G. (1970). "The market for 'lemons': Qualitative uncertainty and the market mechanism." *Quarterly Journal of Economics*, 89: 488–500.

Benston, G. J., and Kaufman, G. G. (1986). "Risks and failures in banking: Overview, history and evaluation." Federal Reserve Bank of Chicago, Staff Memorandum SM 86-1.

Bernanke, B., and Gertler, M. (1987). "Banking and macroeconomic equilibrium," in William Barnett, and Kenneth J. Singleton (eds.), *New Approaches to Monetary Economics, Proceedings of the Second International Symposium in Economic Theory and Econometrics* (Cambridge: Cambridge University Press), 89–111.

Bryant, J. (1980). "A model of reserves, bank runs and deposit insurance." *Journal of Banking and Finance*, 4: 335–44.

Calomiris, C. W., and Gorton, G. (1990). "The origins of banking panics: Models, facts, and bank regulation." Working Paper, Northwestern University, November.

——, and Kahn, C. M. (1989). "A theoretical framework for analyzing self-regulation of banks." Working Paper, University of Illinois, Urbana, June.

——, Kahn, C. M., and Krasa, S. (1990). "Optimal contingent bank liquidation under moral hazard." Working Paper, University of Illinois, Urbana, January.

——, and Schweikart, L. (1988). "Was the south backward?: North–South differences in antebellum banking during crisis and normalcy." Working Paper, Federal Reserve Bank of Chicago.

Cannon, J. G. (1910). "Clearing Houses," in National Monetary Commission, *Senate Document No. 491, 61st Congress, 2nd Session*, Washington, DC: U.S. Government Printing Office, pp. 1–335.

Chari, V. V., and Jagannathan, R. (1988). "Banking panics, information, and rational expectations equilibrium." *Journal of Finance*, 43: 749–63.

Cone, K. R. (1983). "The Regulation of depository institutions." Ph.D. dissertation, Stanford University, 1983.

Dewey D. R. (1910). "State banking before the civil war," in National Monetary Commission, *Senate Document No. 581, 61st Congress; 2nd Session*, Washington, DC: U.S. Government Printing Office, pp. 1–226.

Diamond, D. W. (1984). "Financial intermediation and delegated monitoring." *Review of Economic Studies*, 51: 393–414.

——, and Dybvig, P. (1983). "Bank runs, deposit insurance, and liquidity." *Journal of Political Economy*, 91: 401–19.

Dowd, K. (1988). "Option clauses and the stability of a Laissez Faire monetary system." *Journal of Financial Services Research*, 1: 319–33.

Engineer, M. (1987). "Bank runs and the suspension of demand deposit withdrawals." Unpublished Manuscript, Queen's University, July.

Fama, E. F. (1988). "Contract costs and financing decisions." Working Paper 145, Center for Research in Security Prices, University of Chicago, July.

Ferrin, A. W. (1908). "The business panic of A.D. 33." *Moody's Magazine*, 6: 81–2.

Gendreau, B. C., and Prince, S. S. (1986). "The private costs of bank failures: Some historical evidence." *Federal Reserve Bank of Philadelphia Business Review*, 3–14.

Golembe, C. H., and Warburton, C. (1958). "Insurance of bank obligations in six states during the period 1829–1866." Unpublished Manuscript, Federal Deposit Insurance Corporation, 1958.

Gorton, G. (1989). "Self-regulating banking coalitions." Working Paper, Finance Department, The Wharton School, University of Pennsylvania, June.

——, and Pennacchi, G. (1988). "Transactions contracts," paper presented at the Garn Institute of Finance Academic Symposium (August 18–20, 1988), Finance Department, The Wharton School, University of Pennsylvania.

——, and Pennacchi, G. (1990). "Financial intermediaries and liquidity creation." *Journal of Finance*, 45: 49–72.

Grossman, S. J., and Stiglitz, J. E. (1980). "On the impossibility of informationally efficient markets." *American Economic Review*, 70: 393–408.

Jacklin, C. J. (1987). "Demand deposits, trading restrictions, and risk sharing," in E. C. Prescott and N. Wallace (eds.), *Contractual Arrangements for Intertemporal Trade, Minnesota Studies in Macroeconomics*, Vol. 1 (Minneapolis: University of Minnesota Press), 1987.

—— (1988). "Demand equity and deposit insurance," paper presented at the Garn Institute of Finance Academic Symposium (August 18–20, 1988), Stanford University Graduate School of Business.

——, and Bhattacharya, S. (1988). "Distinguishing panics and information-based bank runs: Welfare and policy implications." *Journal of Political Economy*, 96: 568–92.

Klein, B. (1974). "The competitive supply of money." *Journal of Money, Credit and Banking*, 6: 423–53.

Kyle, A. S. (1981). "An equilibrium model of speculation and hedging." Ph.D. dissertation, University of Chicago.

Nicholas, H. C. (1907). "Runs on banks." *Moody's Magazine*, 5: 23–6.

Smead, E. L. (1928). "Bank suspensions in 1927 and during 1921–1927." Unpublished Memorandum, Federal Reserve Board of Governors, 11 April.

Townsend, R. M. (1979). "Optimal contracts and competitive markets with costly state verification." *Journal of Economic Theory*, 21: 265–93.

Villamil, A. P. (1988). "Demand deposit contracts, suspension of convertibility, and optimal financial intermediation." Unpublished Manuscript, University of Illinois, Urbana, 1988; *Economic Theory*, forthcoming.

Comptroller of the Currency (1920). *Annual Report*, Washington, DC: U.S. Government Printing Office, 1920.

—— (1988). "An evaluation of the factors contributing to the failure of national banks." Unpublished Memorandum, January 1988.

3

Monitoring, Liquidation, and Security Design

Rafael Repullo and Javier Suarez

This chapter develops a model of how entrepreneurial firms source their financing needs. There are three alternatives for raising finance: uninformed, informed, and a mixture of both. Under informed finance the lender observes at a certain cost the entrepreneur's level of effort, which determines the probability of success of his project. Although this information cannot be used to enforce a contingent contract, it enables the lender to liquidate the project (and recover part of the investment) if the observed effort does not guarantee her a sufficient continuation payoff. When liquidation values are large enough, a credible threat of liquidation leads the entrepreneur to choose first-best effort. Otherwise it is impossible to ensure a sufficiently tough liquidation policy without compromising the lender's participation constraint.

The conflict between preserving the credibility of the liquidation threat and compensating the lender provides a rationale for mixed finance: adding a passive uninformed lender allows a reduction in the funds contributed by the informed lender and hence restores the credibility of the threat. Our analysis shows that, for some entrepreneurs, mixed finance can improve upon both uninformed and informed finance. Thus it may explain why many firms are not exclusively funded by informed lenders (such as banks) or uninformed lenders (such as small bondholders), but by a mixture of both.

The effectiveness of mixed finance may be impaired by the possibility of collusion between the entrepreneur and the informed lender (to the detriment of the uninformed lender). In particular, if these informed parties can renegotiate their share of continuation proceeds after the effort decision has been made, first-best effort is no longer attainable. This renegotiation possibility determines the form of the optimal three-party contracts. Our results predict that, in order to give the informed lender the right incentives to liquidate, informed debt will be, in case of liquidation, secured and senior to uninformed debt. Moreover, in

We would like to thank Leonardo Felli, Julian Franks, Paolo Fulghieri, Denis Gromb, John Moore, and David Webb for helpful comments and discussions. This chapter also greatly benefited from the comments of Franklin Allen.

the optimal renegotiation-proof contract informed debt capacity (the maximum informed debt compatible with a credible liquidation threat) will always be exhausted.

We aim to offer a testable theory of the choice of the mix of informed and uninformed finance. Given the active role assigned to informed lenders under the optimal contracts, we will argue that private debt such as bank loans can be considered informed finance, whereas public debt such as corporate bonds or outside equity can be considered uninformed finance. We identify two key determinants of the optimal mode of finance: the level of entrepreneurial wealth (or the firm's net worth) and the liquidation value of the investment project. We predict that investments which involve nonspecific liquid and tangible assets are more likely to be funded exclusively by banks or large active investors, while as we move to projects involving less and less redeployable assets we will observe increasing reliance on arm's-length finance.

This chapter is related to the literature on debt contracts that has stressed the disciplinary role of liquidation. Hart and Moore (1989) and Bolton and Scharfstein (1990) consider models in which cash flows are unverifiable, showing that in this context it is optimal to give liquidation rights to the lenders in order to discourage strategic default. Berglöf and von Thadden (1994) analyze the rationale for multiple lenders in a similar setting. They show that if liquidation values are low, it is optimal that short-term and long-term claims be held by separate investors, and short-term claims be secured. This arrangement strengthens the ex post bargaining position of the short-term lenders and diminishes the firm's incentives to default strategically. Our article transmutes into a moral hazard context the insight that a second lender may be useful to ensure the credibility of liquidation threats.[1]

In Diamond (1993a, 1993b), short-term debt forces borrowers to renegotiate their contracts after some signal about their quality is publicly observed. So depending on the signal, firms are either liquidated or refinanced on terms more closely related to their actual prospects. The liquidation rights associated with short-term debt are important for dealing with the adverse selection problem. However, refinancing short-term debt entails a risk of inefficient liquidation due to the loss of control rents. He shows that introducing junior long-term debt and allowing the issue of additional senior debt in the future reduces this risk. In contrast to our chapter, the second lender comes in to prevent excessive liquidation rather than to restore the credibility of the liquidation threat. From an empirical viewpoint. Diamond highlights bank priority over cash flows in a context where

---

[1] Rajan (1992) studies the trade-off between bank and arm's-length debt in a moral hazard model similar to ours. He examines the impact of bank lenders ex post bargaining power on the efficiency of the entrepreneur's effort decision. He stresses the importance of the *hold-up* problem as a cost of bank debt, suggesting (unlike us) that arm's-length debt should have priority over bank debt. An alternative moral hazard setting is explored in Gorton and Kahn (1993).

control rents and refinancing risk are important, whereas we stress bank priority over liquidated assets when moral hazard problems are pervasive.

Finally, other articles derive implications for the design of the priority structure and covenants of different classes of debt in settings where the emphasis shifts from the discipline associated with liquidation threats to the idea that different classes of lenders have different abilities to renegotiate [Detragiache (1994)], different reputations for monitoring well [Chemmanur and Fulghieri (1994)], of different incentives to monitor [Rajan and Winton (1995)]. In most respects, their results and ours can be thought of as complementary.

This chapter is organized as follows. Section 1 describes the model. Sections 2 and 3 characterize the optimal contracts under uninformed and informed finance, respectively. Section 4 presents our results on mixed finance. Section 5 analyzes the optimal choice between these modes of finance. Section 6 contains a discussion of the implications of the model. Section 7 concludes.

1. The Model

Consider a model with four dates ($t = 0, 1, 2, 3$) and a continuum of risk-neutral entrepreneurs. Each entrepreneur has the opportunity of undertaking an *indivisible project* that requires an investment at $t = 0$ which is normalized to one. The entrepreneur can affect the outcome of the project through the amount of *costly effort*, $p \in [0, 1]$, expended at $t = 1$. At $t = 2$ the project can be liquidated. The indicator variable ℓ will take the value 1 if liquidation occurs and 0 otherwise. Contingent on p and ℓ, the project yields verifiable returns at $t = 3$. The timing of events is depicted in Figure 1.

If the project is undertaken and liquidation does not take place ($\ell = 0$), with probability p the project is successful and the return is $Y > 0$, whereas with probability $1 - p$ the project fails and the return is 0. If the project is liquidated ($\ell = 1$), a certain return $L > 0$ is obtained, irrespective of p. The cost of effort $\phi(p)$ is incurred regardless of the outcome of the project.

Each entrepreneur is characterized by his initial wealth w and the liquidation value of his project L. We will restrict attention to the case where $w < 1$, so entrepreneurs require external finance in order to undertake their projects.

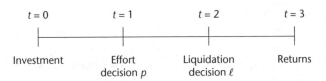

Figure 1. Timing of events.

We make the following assumptions.

ASSUMPTION 1. *The function $\phi(p)$ is increasing and strictly convex, and satisfies $\phi(0) = \phi'(0) = 0$ and $\lim_{p \to 1} \phi'(p) = +\infty$.*

ASSUMPTION 2. *There exists a perfectly elastic supply of funds at an expected rate of return which is normalized to zero.*

ASSUMPTION 3. $\max\{pY - \phi(p)\} \equiv \bar{p}Y - \phi(\bar{p}) > 1.$

ASSUMPTION 4. $L < 1.$

ASSUMPTION 5. *The entrepreneur's effort decision p is not contractible.*

Assumption 1 is standard and is made to ensure that the entrepreneur's maximization problem is convex and has a unique interior solution. Assumption 2 is used to close the model in a very simple manner, normalizing the expected rate of return required by lenders to zero. Assumption 3 (together with Assumption 2) ensures that the net present value of the project when the entrepreneur chooses the first-best level of effort $\bar{p}$ is positive. Notice that, by Assumption 1, $\bar{p} \in (0, 1)$ and is characterized by the first-order condition

$$Y = \phi'(\bar{p}). \tag{1}$$

which equates the marginal benefit of effort to its marginal cost. Assumption 4 (together with Assumption 2) states that investing in order to liquidate is not profitable. Finally, Assumption 5 introduces a moral hazard problem. In particular, if an entrepreneur with wealth w borrows $1 - w$ in exchange for a promise to repay $R \in [0, Y]$, and the project is never liquidated, he will choose p in order to maximize $p(Y - R) - \phi(p)$. The solution to this problem is characterized by the first-order condition

$$Y - R = \phi'(p). \tag{2}$$

which implicitly defines the entrepreneurial choice of p as a function of R. Comparing Equations (1) and (2), and using the assumption that $\phi'' > 0$, one obtains that the solution for p in Equation (2) is smaller than the first-best level of effort $\bar{p}$.

In what follows, we examine the disciplinary role of liquidation threats by lenders in this moral hazard setup. The relationship between an entrepreneur and his lender is assumed to be governed by a contract, signed at $t = 0$, that specifies how the parties agree to share the funding and the verifiable returns of the project under both liquidation and no liquidation.

Formally, a contract between an entrepreneur and a lender is described by a vector (I, Q, R) that specifies (i) the funds I invested by the lender in the project, (ii) the part Q of the liquidation proceeds L which go to the lender if she decides to liquidate, and (iii) the part R of the success return Y that is paid to the lender if she does not liquidate.

For expositional convenience, we will assume that each entrepreneur invests his entire wealth w in the project, showing later that this is indeed optimal. Sections 2 and 3 study the optimal contracts between lenders and entrepreneurs under uninformed and informed finance, respectively. Under uninformed finance, the choice of p by the entrepreneur is not only noncontractible but also unobservable to the lender. Under informed finance, a costly technology is used by the lender to observe p.

2. Uninformed Finance

Under uninformed finance, given a contract (I, Q, R), the interaction between an entrepreneur and his lender can be modeled as a game with imperfect information. In this game, the entrepreneur first chooses the level of effort $p \in [0, 1]$, and then the lender, without observing the entrepreneur's decision (thus the imperfect information), takes the liquidation decision $\ell \in \{0, 1\}$. The payoff to the entrepreneur is $L - Q - \phi(p)$ if the project is liquidated, and $p(Y - R) - \phi(p)$ otherwise. The payoff to the lender is Q if she liquidates the project and pR otherwise.

A contract (I, Q, R) for an entrepreneur with wealth w is said to be feasible under uninformed finance if there exists a (pure strategy) Nash equilibrium (p^*, ℓ^*) such that

$$(1 - \ell^*)p^*R + \ell^*Q \geq I = 1 - w, \tag{3}$$

and

$$(1 - \ell^*)p^*(Y - R) + \ell^*(L - Q) - \phi(p^*) \geq w. \tag{4}$$

Equations (3) and (4) are participation constraints for the lender and the entrepreneur, respectively. A feasible contract has to provide enough funds to undertake the project, it has to guarantee the lender the required expected rate of return, and it has to provide the entrepreneur with an expected utility greater than (or equal to) the value of his initial wealth.

A feasible contract (I, Q, R) for an entrepreneur with wealth w is said to be optimal under uninformed finance if it maximizes the equilibrium expected utility of the entrepreneur in the class of all feasible contracts.[2]

[2] In the definitions of feasible and optimal contracts we have restricted attention to pure strategy equilibria. This is done without loss of generality, because allowing for mixed strategy equilibria does not change the sets of feasible and optimal contracts. To sketch why this is so, notice first that for any given probability of liquidation chosen by the lender, the payoff to the entrepreneur is strictly concave in the level of effort p, so the entrepreneur never mixes. Moreover, the value of p chosen by the entrepreneur is decreasing in the probability of liquidation. With regard to the lender, there might be equilibria in which she randomizes her choice of ℓ, while the participation constraints [Equations (3) and (4)] are satisfied. Nevertheless, liquidating with positive probability is inefficient, since it worsens the entrepreneur's incentives and (given $L < 1$) reduces the overall surplus. Therefore the mixed strategy equilibria associated with feasible contracts (if they exist) are always Pareto dominated by the unique pure strategy equilibrium of the game.

The following result characterizes the optimal contracts under uninformed finance.

PROPOSITION 1. *There exists a critical value $\overline{w}_u \in [0, 1)$ such that, for any entrepreneur with wealth $w \geq \overline{w}_u$, the optimal contracts under uninformed finance are given by*

$$I_u(w) = 1 - w, \quad Q_u(w) \in [0, \min\{L, 1 - w\}], \ and$$
$$R_u(w) = (1 - w)/p_u(w), \tag{5}$$

where $p_u(w)$ is the largest value of p that solves the equation

$$p[Y - \phi'(p)] = 1 - w. \tag{6}$$

For $w < \overline{w}_u$ there is no feasible contract under uninformed finance.

Proof. The Nash equilibrium (p^*, ℓ^*) of the game defined by any feasible contract has to satisfy $\ell^* = 0$; otherwise adding up the participation constraints [Equations (3) and (4)] we would get $L - \phi(p^*) \geq 1$, which contradicts Assumption 4. But then the threat of liquidation cannot play any role in the optimal contract. Since $\ell^* = 1$ and the definition of equilibrium implies $Q \leq p^*R$, we can pick any $Q \in [0, \min\{L, p^*R\}]$, and focus on the optimal choice of R.

This requires finding the best solution for the entrepreneur to the system of equations formed by the entrepreneur's first-order condition [Equation (2)] and the lender's (binding) participation constraint $pR = 1 - w$. Substituting $R = (1 - w)/p$ into Equation (2) gives the equation $f(p) \equiv p[Y - \phi'(p)] = 1 - w$. Under Assumption 1, the function $f(p)$ is continuous and satisfies $f(0) = f(\overline{p}) = 0$. Moreover, it is positive for $p \in (0, \overline{p})$ and negative for $p \in (\overline{p}, 1)$. Then it is clear that the equation $f(p) = 1 - w$ has at least one solution if $\hat{f} \equiv \max f(p) \geq 1 - w$, and any solution will be smaller than $\overline{p}$ (since by assumption $1 - w > 0$). Now substituting $pR = 1 - w$ into the entrepreneur's payoff function gives the function $U(w, p) \equiv w + pY - \phi(p) - 1$. Since $U(w, p)$ is increasing in p for $p < \overline{p}$, it follows that the value of p corresponding to the optimal contract is the largest solution $p_u(w)$ to the equation $f(p) = 1 - w$, and $R_u(w) = (1 - w)/p_u(w)$.[3]

The entrepreneur's participation constraint requires $V_u(w) \equiv U(w, p_u(w)) \geq w$. The function $p_u(w)$ is increasing, continuous from the right, and satisfies $\lim_{w \to 1} p_u(w) = p$. Since $U(w, p)$ is increasing in w and in p for $p < \overline{p}$, it follows that $V_u(w)$ is increasing and, by Assumption 3, satisfies $\lim_{w \to 1} V_u(w) > w$, so for large values of w the participation constraint will be satisfied. Now let $\hat{w} \equiv \max\{1 - \hat{f}, 0\}$. Then if $V_u(\hat{w}) \geq \hat{w}$, the critical value $\overline{w}_u$ is given by $\hat{w}$. If,

---

[3] It should be noticed that the first-order condition [Equation (2)] implies $Y - R_u(w) = \phi'(p_u(w)) > 0$, so the payment promised to the lender is always smaller than Y.

on the other hand, $V_u(\hat{w}) < \hat{w}$, $\overline{w}_u$ is defined by the conditions $V_u(w) \geq w$ for $w \geq \overline{w}_u$, and $V_u(w) < w$ for $w < \overline{w}_u$. ∎

It should be noted that since $pY - \phi(p)$ is increasing in p for $p < \overline{p}$, and $p_u(w)$ is smaller than $\overline{p}$ and increasing in w, the equilibrium expected utility under uninformed finance $V_u(w) \equiv w + p_u(w)Y - \phi(p_u(w)) - 1$ satisfies $V_u(w + \varepsilon) > V_u(w) + \varepsilon$ for all $w \geq \overline{w}_u$ and $\varepsilon > 0$. Hence it is optimal for the entrepreneur to invest all his wealth in the project.

Proposition 1 shows that under uninformed finance the option to liquidate has no value to the lender. There exists a critical level of wealth $\overline{w}_u$ such that only those entrepreneurs with wealth above $\overline{w}_u$ are able to fund their projects (whatever their value of L). When $w \geq \overline{w}_u$ the optimal contract is characterized by a promised payment to the lender $R_u(w) = I_u(w)/p_u(w)$. The term $1/p_u(w)$ can be interpreted as a default premium. As w goes down (increasing the reliance on external financing) the moral hazard problem becomes more severe, and so the default premium rises until the cutoff point $\overline{w}_u$ is reached. For $w < \overline{w}_u$ the moral hazard problem is so severe that uninformed finance is not feasible.

3. Informed Finance

In this section we introduce an alternative mode of financing the investment projects, which will be called informed finance. Specifically, we assume that the lender can (contractually) commit to use a monitoring technology that, at a cost $c > 0$ per project, reveals to her the value of p chosen by the entrepreneur. By Assumption 5 this information cannot be included in the contract between the lender and the entrepreneur, but it may be useful to the lender when deciding on liquidation.

The assumption that the lender can commit to monitor the entrepreneur is restrictive but fairly standard [see, e.g., Diamond (1991) and Rajan (1992)]. The information obtained by the lender in this mode of finance can be interpreted as the result of a continuous close relationship with the borrower along which the entrepreneur exerts his effort under the surveillance of the lender. This may involve, for example, regular interviews with the firm's executives and main customers, visits to the firm's premises, as well as (in the case of informed bank finance) observing the movements in the firm's bank accounts.[4]

---

[4] In an attempt to endogenize the informed lender's monitoring decision (in the context of a simplified version of the model with two levels of effort), we came to the conclusion that, although many of our results are robust to this change, such a setup would make the intuition behind them less transparent. In particular, situations in which monitoring takes place are associated with equilibria in which both the entrepreneur and the (potentially) informed lender play mixed strategies. The lender is indifferent between monitoring and not monitoring precisely because the entrepreneur mixes between high and low effort in such a way that the expected gain to the lender upon detection of low effort exactly compensates the monitoring cost.

Under informed finance, given a contract (I, Q, R), the interaction between an entrepreneur and his lender can be modeled as a sequential game in which the entrepreneur first chooses the level of effort p, and then the lender, after observing the entrepreneur's decision, takes the liquidation decision ℓ. The payoffs to the entrepreneur and the lender are the same as those for the case of uninformed finance.

A contract (I, Q, R) for an entrepreneur with wealth w is said to be feasible under informed finance if there exists a subgame perfect equilibrium $(p^*, \ell^*(p))$ such that

$$[1 - \ell^*(p^*)]p^*R + \ell^*(p^*)Q \geq I = 1 - w + c, \tag{7}$$

and

$$[1 - \ell^*(p^*)]p^*(Y - R) + \ell^*(p^*)(L - Q) - \phi(p^*) \geq w. \tag{8}$$

This definition of feasibility differs from that corresponding to uninformed finance in two respects. First, given the different nature of the game—which becomes genuinely sequential when the lender is informed—it refers to subgame perfect instead of Nash equilibrium. Second, it includes the monitoring cost c in the right-hand side of the lender's participation constraint [Equation (7)]. An equilibrium strategy of the lender specifies not only her reaction to the equilibrium strategy of the entrepreneur, $\ell^*(p^*)$, but also her reaction to entrepreneurial decisions off the equilibrium path, $\ell^*(p)$ for all $p \neq p^*$. However, the definition of feasibility only takes into account the players' decisions on the equilibrium path. As under uninformed finance, a feasible contract has to guarantee the lender the required expected rate of return on her initial investment (now including the monitoring cost c), and it has to provide the entrepreneur with an expected utility greater than (or equal to) the value of his initial wealth.

In order to make informed finance feasible, we will strengthen Assumption 3 to

ASSUMPTION 3'. $\max\{pY - \phi(p)\} \equiv \bar{p}Y - \phi(\bar{p}) > 1 + c$.

A feasible contract (I, Q, R) for an entrepreneur with wealth w is said to be optimal under informed finance if it maximizes the equilibrium expected utility of the entrepreneur in the class of all feasible contracts.

The following proposition characterizes optimal contracts under informed finance when the sum of the initial wealth of the entrepreneur w and the liquidation value of his project L is sufficiently large.

PROPOSITION 2. *For any entrepreneur with $w + L \geq 1 + c$, the optimal contract under informed finance is given by*

$$I_i(w) = Q_i(w) = 1 - w + c \quad and \quad R_i(w) = (1 - w + c)/\bar{p}. \tag{9}$$

Proof. We first show that under this contract, a subgame perfect equilibrium of the game between the entrepreneur and the informed lender is given by

$$p^* = \bar{p} \quad \text{and} \quad \ell^*(p) = \begin{cases} 0, & \text{if } p \geq \bar{p} \\ 1, & \text{otherwise.} \end{cases} \tag{10}$$

To prove this, note that if $p < \bar{p}$ we have $pR_i(w) = p(1 - w + c)/\bar{p} < Q_i(w)$, so the lender will choose $\ell^*(p) = 1$. On the other hand, if $p > \bar{p}$ by the same argument she will choose $\ell^*(p) = 0$. Finally, if $p = \bar{p}$ the lender is indifferent between $\ell = 0$ and $\ell = 1$. Setting $\ell^*(\bar{p}) = 0$, the entrepreneur will choose $p^* = \bar{p}$ in the first stage of the game. This is because, by Assumption 1 and the definition of $\bar{p}$, $p[Y - R_i(w)] - \phi(p)$ is decreasing in p for $p \geq \bar{p}$, and we have

$$L - Q_i(w) - \phi(p) \leq L - Q_i(w) < w < w + \bar{p}Y - (1 + c) - \phi(\bar{p})$$
$$= \bar{p}[Y - R_i(w)] - \phi(\bar{p}).$$

The first inequality follows from the fact that $\phi(p) \geq 0$, the second from Assumption 4 and the definition of $Q_i(w)$, and the third from Assumption 3'. Since the equilibrium payoff of the lender is $1 - w + c$, and the equilibrium payoff of the entrepreneur is greater than w, Equation (9) is feasible. To prove that it is optimal it suffices to note that the equilibrium expected utility of the entrepreneur coincides with the maximum that he could achieve in the first-best world in which p was verifiable (but the costs of the project were $1 + c$). ∎

According to Proposition 2, informed finance leads to the first-best choice of effort for those entrepreneurs with wealth $w + L \geq 1 + c$. This reflects the nature of the disciplinary device that operates under informed finance: the threat of liquidation. When liquidation proceeds are greater than the funds invested by the lender in the project ($L \geq 1 - w + c$), a contract that triggers liquidation whenever the entrepreneur chooses $p < \bar{p}$ can be signed at $t = 0$. The threat of liquidation is credible because the contractual value of Q can be chosen large enough to give proper incentives to the lender. On the equilibrium path, however, liquidation does not take place.

By Proposition 2, the equilibrium expected utility under informed finance for an entrepreneur with $w + L \geq 1 + c$ is $V_i(w) \equiv w + \bar{p}Y - \phi(\bar{p}) - (1 + c)$. As the slope of this function is equal to 1, investing all his wealth in the project is weakly optimal (he should invest at least $1 + c - L$).

Next we consider what happens when $w + L < 1 + c$. Since feasible contracts cannot lead to liquidation on the equilibrium path (otherwise adding up the participation constraints of Equations (7) and (8) we would contradict Assumption 4), it must be the case that $p^*R \geq 1 - w + c > L \geq Q$. From here it follows that p^* is strictly greater than the critical $\hat{p}$ that triggers liquidation (i.e. that solves $\hat{p}R = Q$), so liquidation threats are not effective. Given this, we can prove a result similar to Proposition 1 characterizing the optimal contracts under informed finance for entrepreneurs with $w + L < 1 + c$. Since in this case the lenders have to recover the monitoring cost c, it is clear that these contracts are dominated by the corresponding optimal contracts under uninformed finance.[5]

Summing up, under informed finance the lender observes the effort put by the entrepreneur at a certain cost. This information may be used by the lender to decide on the liquidation of the project, but this is not always valuable. The threat of liquidation is effective in disciplining entrepreneurs with $w + L \geq 1 + c$. When this condition is not satisfied, the threat of liquidation cannot be credible, and so (given the monitoring cost) informed finance is dominated by uninformed finance.

4. Mixed Finance

In Sections 2 and 3 we analyzed the problem of designing optimal two-party contracts between lenders and entrepreneurs under informed and uninformed finance. Somewhat surprisingly, informed finance leads to the first-best level of effort $\bar{p}$ for those entrepreneurs with wealth $w + L \geq 1 + c$, whereas it does not allow an improvement compared to uninformed finance when $w + L < 1 + c$. The reason for this is that low values of L in relation to the funds $1 - w + c$ the informed lender has to invest in the project impede the effective use of the threat of liquidation. There is a conflict between providing the lender with incentives to liquidate if a deviation from $\bar{p}$ occurs (that is, setting Q and R such that $\bar{p}R = Q \leq L$) and compensating her for her investment in the project (that is, setting R such that $\bar{p}R \geq 1 - w + c$). If $w + L \geq 1 + c$ there exist Q and R such that $\bar{p}R = 1 - w + c = Q \leq L$; otherwise the liquidation threat cannot be binding, and the information acquired by the lender at a cost c is completely worthless.

The nature of this conflict provides a prima facie case for mixed finance, the coexistence of an informed active lender whose contribution to the project is reduced to a level which provides her the right incentives to liquidate (if the entrepreneur deviates from $\bar{p}$), and an uninformed passive lender who contributes the rest. Such a possibility is explored in this section.

Under mixed finance, the relationship between an entrepreneur and two lenders, one informed and another uninformed, is assumed to be governed by a contract, signed at $t = 0$, that specifies how the parties agree to share the

---

[5] By the same argument as in the proof of Proposition 1, the effort chosen by the entrepreneur in the optimal contract under informed finance, $p_i(w)$, is the largest solution to the equation $f(p) \equiv p[Y - \phi'(p)] = 1 - w + c$. Using Equation (6) together with the properties of the function $f(p)$ it is immediate that $p_i(w) < p_u(w)$, which implies $V_i(w) < V_u(w)$.

funding and the verifiable returns of the project under both liquidation and no liquidation.

Formally, a contract between an entrepreneur, an informed, and an uninformed lender is a vector $(I_i, I_u, Q_i, Q_u, R_i, R_u)$ that specifies (i) the funds I_i and I_u invested in the project by the informed and the uninformed lender; (ii) the parts Q_i and Q_u of the liquidation proceeds L which go to the informed and the uninformed lender if the former decides to liquidate; and (iii) the parts R_i and R_u of the success return Y that are paid to the informed and the uninformed lender if the former does not liquidate.

In what follows, we first analyze the optimal three-party contracts in the absence of any renegotiation. These contracts are, however, not robust to the possibility of collusion (and renegotiation) between the entrepreneur and the informed lender at the date when the option to liquidate has to be exercised. The optimal renegotiation-proof contracts are then derived.

4.1 Mixed finance without renegotiation

For the same reasons as in the case of pure uninformed finance, under mixed finance the uninformed lender is a passive player in the game between the three parties to the contract. The interaction between the entrepreneur and the informed lender can then be modeled as a sequential game in which the entrepreneur first chooses the level of effort p, and then the informed lender takes the liquidation decision ℓ. The payoff to the entrepreneur is $L - Q_i - Q_u - \phi(p)$ if the project is liquidated, and $p(Y - R_i - R_u) - \phi(p)$ otherwise. The payoff to the informed lender is Q_i if she liquidates the project and pR_i otherwise. Finally, the payoff to the uninformed lender is Q_u if the project is liquidated and pR_u if it is not.

Our earlier definitions of feasible and optimal contracts can be easily extended to the mixed finance case, so for the sake of brevity we skip their formal statement.

For entrepreneurs with $w + L \geq 1 + c$, the equilibrium expected utility under informed finance is already at its highest possible level under mixed finance (corresponding to the first-best with costs $1 + c$). For this reason we focus on the case of entrepreneurs with $w + L < 1 + c$. The following proposition characterizes the optimal contracts under mixed finance when there is no renegotiation at $t = 2$.

PROPOSITION 3. *For any entrepreneur with $w + L < 1 + c$, there is a family of optimal contracts under mixed finance, parameterized by $x \in (0, L]$, which is given by*

$$I_i(w, x) = Q_i(w, x) = x, \quad R_i(w, x) = x/\overline{p},$$

$$I_u(w, x) = (1 - w + c) - x, \quad Q_u(w, x) = L - x, \quad and \tag{11}$$

$$R_u(w, x) = [(1 - w + c) - x]/\overline{p}.$$

Proof. We first show that for any $x \in (0, L]$, a subgame perfect equilibrium of the game between the entrepreneur and the informed lender is given by Equation (10). To prove this, note that if $p < \bar{p}$ we have $pR_i(w, x) = px/\bar{p} < Q_i(w, x)$, so the lender will choose $\ell^*(p) = 1$. On the other hand, if $p > \bar{p}$ by the same argument she will choose $\ell^*(p) = 0$. Finally, if $p = \bar{p}$ the lender is indifferent between $\ell = 0$ and $\ell = 1$. Setting $\ell^*(\bar{p}) = 0$, the entrepreneur will choose $p^* = \bar{p}$ in the first stage of the game. This is because, by Assumption 1 and the definition of $\bar{p}$, $p[Y - R_i(w, x) - R_u(w, x)] - \phi(p)$ is decreasing in p for $p \geq \bar{p}$, and we have

$$L - Q_i(w, x) - Q_u(w, x) - \phi(p) \leq 0 < w + \bar{p}Y - (1 + c) - \phi(\bar{p})$$

$$= \bar{p}[Y - R_i(w, x) - R_u(w, x)] - \phi(\bar{p}).$$

The first inequality follows from the definitions of $Q_i(w, x)$ and $Q_u(w, x)$ and the fact that $\phi(p) \geq 0$, and the second from Assumption 3'.[6] Moreover, the players' participation constraints are satisfied, so the family of contracts described in Equation (11) is feasible. To prove that they are optimal it suffices to note that the equilibrium expected utility of the entrepreneur coincides with the maximum that he could achieve in the first-best world in which p was verifiable (but the costs of the project were $1 + c$). ∎

According to Proposition 3, mixed finance leads to the first-best choice of effort even for entrepreneurs with $w + L < 1 + c$. The explanation for this result is simple: the presence of an uninformed lender allows a reduction in the contribution of the informed lender to $I_i \leq L$, so we can set $\bar{p}R_i = Q_i = I_i$, thereby restoring her incentives to liquidate if the entrepreneur deviates from $\bar{p}$ while compensating her for her investment in the project.

It is interesting to note that in these optimal three-party contracts the informed lender is fully secured in the case of liquidation, that is, $Q_i(w, x) = I_i(w, x)$, while the uninformed lender is not, that is, $Q_u(w, x) < I_u(w, x)$. This feature of the optimal contracts, which will be further discussed below, may be interpreted as the seniority of informed debt, which arises endogenously in order to restore the credibility of the liquidation threat.

4.2 The effects of renegotiation between the informed parties

The results obtained so far on mixed finance do not take into account the possibility of renegotiation between the entrepreneur and the informed lender after the former has made his effort decision but before the latter decides on liquidation. Given the presence of a third party (the uninformed lender), renegotiation

---

[6] Notice that $Q_u(w, x)$ could be chosen to be smaller than $L - x$, as long as the entrepreneur does not prefer liquidation to continuation (with $p = \bar{p}$), that is, provided that $L - x - Q_u(w, x) \leq w + \bar{p}Y - (1 + c) - \phi(\bar{p})$.

in this context should be understood in terms of an additional contract between the two informed parties that changes the payment promised to the informed lender, if she does not liquidate the project, to R'_i.

The exclusion of the uninformed lender from this renegotiation is explained by the fact that she is not informed about p. This may seem restrictive since, with two informed agents (and no constraints on contractibility), it is generally possible to design a mechanism that truthfully reveals this information to a third, uninformed, agent. However, the introduction of such a mechanism is impeded by the noncontractibility of p (that is, the impossibility of describing the level of effort in a way suitable for enforcing contracts contingent upon it).[7]

In what follows we first show that the contracts described in Proposition 3 are not robust to renegotiation between the informed parties. We then characterize the optimal renegotiation-proof contracts under mixed finance.

In the renegotiation game, the status quo payoffs of the entrepreneur and the informed lender are $p(Y - R_i - R_u) - \phi(p)$ and pR_i, respectively, and in addition the lender has an *outside option* (the option to liquidate) which is worth Q_i to her. If $p(Y - R_u) < Q_i$, the informed lender would liquidate the project, since the maximum expected payment under continuation is smaller than what she can get upon liquidation. On the other hand, if $p(Y - R_u) \geq Q_i$, by the "outside option principle"[8] the equilibrium outcome of the renegotiation game is

$$R'_i(p) = \begin{cases} R_i, & \text{if } pR_i \geq Q_i \\ Q_i/p, & \text{otherwise.} \end{cases}$$

Thus the initial contract will be renegotiated if the probability of success p chosen by the entrepreneur satisfies $Q_i/(Y - R_u) \leq p < Q_i/R_i$,[9] in which case the informed lender's payoff $pR'_i(p)$ will be equal to her liquidation payoff Q_i. Anticipating this outcome, the entrepreneur will choose $p \geq Q_i/(Y - R_u)$ in order

---

[7] If, nevertheless, the uninformed lender became informed and participated in the renegotiation, mixed finance would not improve on pure informed finance: assuming efficient renegotiation, the critical $\hat{p}$ that triggers liquidation would solve $\hat{p}Y = Q_i + Q_u \leq L$, whilst feasibility would require $p^*Y \geq I_i + I_u = 1 - w + c > L$. Hence p^* would be strictly greater than $\hat{p}$, so liquidation threats would not be effective.

[8] This principle is formulated in the context of a noncooperative bargaining model with alternating offers in which one of the players (say player 1) can quit the negotiations to take up an outside option [see Sutton (1986) and Osborne and Rubinstein (1990)]. In general, it states that if the value of this option is smaller than the equilibrium payoff of player 1 in the game with no outside option, then the option has no effect on the equilibrium outcome. Otherwise the equilibrium payoff of player 1 is equal to the value of his option.

[9] Note that $R_i + R_u \leq Y$ implies $Q_i/(Y - R_u) \leq Q_i/R_i$. Moreover, for the contracts described in Proposition 3, these inequalities are strict.

to maximize

$$p[Y - R'_i(p) - R_u] - \phi(p) = \begin{cases} p(Y - R_i - R_u) - \phi(p), & \text{if } pR_i \geq Q_i \\ p(Y - R_u) - \phi(p) - Q_i, & \text{otherwise.} \end{cases}$$

For the contract in Proposition 3, the condition $pR_i \geq Q_i$ reduces to $p \geq \bar{p}$. But then given that, by Assumption 1 and the definition of $\bar{p}$, $p[Y - R_i - R_u] - \phi(p)$ is decreasing in p for $p \geq \bar{p}$, and we also have $(Y - R_u) - \phi'(\bar{p}) < Y - \phi'(\bar{p}) = 0$, the entrepreneur has an incentive to choose $p^* < \bar{p}$ and subsequently bribe the informed lender in order to avoid liquidation. The uninformed lender will then get $p^* R_u < \bar{p} R_u = I_u$, so anticipating this outcome she will not be willing to participate in the funding of the project.[10]

Given this negative result, the following proposition characterizes the optimal renegotiation-proof contracts under mixed finance.

PROPOSITION 4. *There exists a critical value $\bar{w}_m \in [\bar{w}_u, 1 + c)$ such that, for any entrepreneur with $w + L \in [\bar{w}_m, 1 + c)$, the optimal renegotiation-proof contract is given by*

$$I_i(w, L) = Q_i(w, L) = L, \quad R_i(w, L) = L/p_m(w, L),$$

$$I_u(w, L) = (1 - w + c) - L, \quad Q_u(w, L) = 0, \quad and \qquad (12)$$

$$R_u(w, L) = [(1 - w + c) - L]/p_m(w, L),$$

where $p_m(w, L)$ is the largest value of p that solves the equation

$$p[Y - \phi'(p)] = 1 - w + c - L. \qquad (13)$$

For $w + L < \bar{w}_m$ there is no feasible contract under mixed finance.

Proof. See the Appendix.

The result in Proposition 4 can be explained as follows. Mixed finance without renegotiation leads to liquidation by the informed lender if the entrepreneur deviates from the first-best level of effort $\bar{p}$. However, if we allow for renegotiation, entrepreneurial deviations are not necessarily followed by liquidation because the informed parties will bargain over the sharing of the continuation surplus: the liquidation threat enters as an outside option for the informed lender that provides a lower bound to her expected payoff. Since the uninformed lender is an outsider to this renegotiation, her stake will not be considered as a component of the expected continuation surplus to be bargained between the informed parties. By the "outside option principle," the equilibrium renegotiation payoffs

---

[10] Note that in the case of pure informed finance $R_u = 0$ implies $p^* = \bar{p}$, so the contract in Proposition 2 is robust to renegotiation.

of the entrepreneur and the informed lender will be $p(Y - R_u) - \phi(p) - Q_i$ and Q_i, respectively. Given this outcome, the solution to the entrepreneur's maximization problem will be a decreasing function of R_u that approaches the first-best level of effort $\bar{p}$ as R_u tends to zero. From here it follows that the entrepreneur will be interested in signing a contract in which the contribution I_u of the uninformed lender, and so the (irrevocable) payment R_u promised to her under continuation, are minimized.

Comparing Equations (6) and (13), we can see that the probability of success $p_m(w, L)$ chosen by the entrepreneur under this contract is equal to $p_u(w + L - c)$, that is the probability of success chosen by an entrepreneur with wealth $w + L - c$ under uninformed finance. This means that, under mixed finance, the liquidation value of the project plays the role of additional wealth that helps improve entrepreneurial incentives, since as noted in Section 2 the function $p_u(w)$ is increasing.

Using this result, the equilibrium expected utility under mixed finance for an entrepreneur with $w + L \in [\bar{w}_m, 1 + c)$ can be written as $V_m(w, L) \equiv w + p_u(w + L - c)Y - \phi(p_u(w + L - c)) - (1 + c)$. Hence, by our previous argument, it is again optimal for him to invest all his wealth in the project.

Two final comments are in place. First, although the possibility of collusion between the informed parties reduces the efficiency of mixed finance (given that $p_m(w, L) < \bar{p}$), some entrepreneurs can obtain funds that they could not get under pure informed or uninformed finance (in particular, those with $w + L \in [\bar{w}_m, 1 + c)$ and $w < \bar{w}_u$). Second, in the optimal renegotiation-proof contract, informed debt is, in the case of liquidation, fully secured and senior to uninformed debt.

5. The Choice Between Informed, Uninformed, and Mixed Finance

This section brings together the results of the previous sections in order to analyze the optimal choice between informed, uninformed, and mixed finance. We begin by summarizing in Figure 2 our results on the regions of the $w - L$ space where these modes of finance are feasible.

According to Proposition 1, uninformed finance is feasible for all $w \geq \bar{w}_u$. By Proposition 2, informed finance is feasible for all pairs (w, L) above or on the line $w + L = 1 + c$; informed finance is also feasible for some pairs (w, L) below this line, but in these cases it is strictly dominated by uninformed finance. Finally, by Proposition 4, mixed finance (with renegotiation between the informed parties) is feasible for pairs (w, L) with $w + L \in [\bar{w}_m, 1 + c)$, where $\bar{w}_m \geq \bar{w}_u$.[11]

---

[11] This inequality is strict except in the limiting case where $\bar{w}_m = \bar{w}_u = 0$.

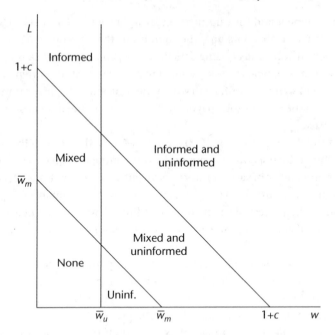

Figure 2. Feasible modes of finance. The entrepreneur's initial wealth *(w)* and the liquidation value of his project *(L)* determine the modes of finance that are feasible. The feasibility of uninformed finance only depends on *w*, whereas that of informed and mixed finance depends on the sum of *w* and *L*.

Since two modes of finance are feasible in two of the regions in Figure 2, we next consider which one dominates in each of them.

PROPOSITION 5. *In the region where both uninformed and informed finance are feasible, there exists a unique $w^* \in [\bar{w}_u, 1)$ such that the former dominates the latter for $w \geq w^*$.*

Proof. The entrepreneurs' equilibrium expected utility under uninformed finance is $V_u(w) \equiv w + p_u(w)Y - \phi(p_u(w)) - 1$, whereas his expected utility under informed finance is $V_i(w) \equiv w + pY - \phi(\bar{p}) - (1 + c)$. Since $\lim_{w \to 1} p_u(w) = \bar{p}$, we have $\lim_{w \to 1}[V_u(w) - V_i(w)] = c > 0$. But then using the fact that $p_u(w)Y - \phi(p_u(w))$ is increasing in w, the result follows. ∎

It is immediate to show that the critical value w^* is decreasing in the monitoring cost c, reaching the value $\bar{w}_u$ for large c.

PROPOSITION 6. *In the region where both uninformed and mixed finance are feasible, there exists a function $L(w) \in [\max\{\bar{w}_m - w, 0\}, 1 - w + c]$ such that the former dominates the latter for those pairs (w, L) with $L < L(w)$. Moreover, $L(w) = 1 - w + c$ for $w \geq w^*$.*

Proof. The entrepreneur's equilibrium expected utility under mixed finance is $V_m(w, L) \equiv w + p_u(w + L - c)Y - \phi(p_u(w + L - c)) - (1 + c)$. Given that $\lim_{L \to 1-w+c} p_u(w + L - c) = \bar{p}$, we have $\lim_{L \to 1-w+c} V_m(w, L) = V_i(w)$. But by the definition of w^* in Proposition 5 we have $V_i(w) \leq V_u(w)$ if and only if $w \geq w^*$. Since $V_m(w, L)$ is increasing in L, the result follows.   ∎

Figure 3 summarizes our results on the characterization of the optimal modes of finance. Informed finance is optimal for high liquidation values and low entrepreneurial wealth. Uninformed finance is optimal for either high wealth or intermediate wealth and low liquidation values. Mixed finance is optimal for low entrepreneurial wealth and intermediate liquidation values. Finally, no mode of finance is feasible for low wealth and low liquidation values.

Finally, we comment on the behavior of equilibrium interest rates for the different regions of Figure 3. According to Proposition 1, in the region where

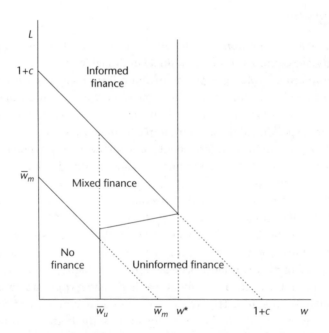

Figure 3. Optimal modes of finance. This figure shows the modes of finance that are optimal for different values of the entrepreneur's initial wealth *(w)* and the liquidation value of his project *(L)*. In the region where informed and uninformed finance are both feasible, decreasing *w* worsens the moral hazard problem under uninformed finance, but does not affect informed finance, so informed finance is optimal for low *w*. In the region where mixed and uninformed finance are both feasible, decreasing *w* and increasing *L* so as to keep *w + L* constant worsens the moral hazard problem under uninformed finance but does not affect mixed finance, so mixed finance is optimal for low *w* and high *L*.

uninformed finance is optimal, equilibrium interest rates $R_u(w)/(1 - w) = 1/p_u(w)$ are decreasing in the level of entrepreneurial wealth w, because reducing the external financing requirement ameliorates the moral hazard problem. In the limit when w tends to 1, this problem disappears, and $1/p_u(w)$ approaches the value $1/\bar{p}$. By the reasons explained in Section 3, in the region where informed finance is optimal, the threat of liquidation eliminates the moral hazard problem, so equilibrium interest rates are constant and equal to $1/\bar{p}$. Finally, in the region where mixed finance is optimal, the moral hazard problem reappears due to the possibility of collusion between the informed parties. By Proposition 4, equilibrium interest rates $1/p_m(w, L)$ are in this case decreasing in both the level of entrepreneurial wealth w and the liquidation value of the project L. Moreover, $1/p_m(w, L)$ tends to $1/\bar{p}$ as $w + L$ approaches the value $1 + c$.

6. Discussion

The need for active monitoring under informed and mixed finance suggests the desirability of assigning this task to a single informed lender. It will save on the cost of monitoring (avoiding duplication) and will eliminate potential free-rider problems as well as conflicts over the exercise of the liquidation option. On the contrary, the passive role of uninformed lenders in uninformed or mixed finance can be performed by one or multiple lenders. These differences provide a rationale for identifying uninformed finance with the placing of publicly traded securities in the market (arm's-length finance) and informed finance with either bank lending or the issuance of tightly held (private) securities.[12]

With this interpretation, our model offers an explanation of the characteristics and coexistence of financial contracts such as typical bank loans and corporate bonds. In particular, our characterization of the securities associated with informed and uninformed finance, respectively, seems broadly consistent with the description of these contracts made by Gorton and Kahn (1993, p. 1): "A typical bank loan contract with a firm involves a single lender who is a secured senior debt claimant on the firm. The contract contains a large number of covenants which effectively give the lender the right to force the borrower to repay the loan early if demanded. In contrast, corporate bonds typically involve multiple lenders who are not secured, may not be senior, have less detailed covenants, and have no option to force the borrower to repay."

There are various real-world counterparts of the liquidation option which characterize our optimal contracts under both informed and mixed finance.

---

[12] Whether informed finance can be identified with *intermediated finance* is a question beyond the scope of this chapter: further specification of the relative sizes of investors' financial resources and entrepreneurs' financial needs, the stochastic dependence of the returns of the different investment projects, and the nature of the intermediaries would be required to address this issue.

If the entrepreneur's bargaining power is large, the optimal contract under informed finance can be approximately implemented by a sequence of short-term contracts.[13] Similarly, the optimal contract under mixed finance can be approximately implemented by a sequence of short-term contracts (with the informed lender) plus a long-term contract (with the uninformed lender), with the interesting property that short-term claims would be secured (and effectively senior to long-term claims) if they were not rolled over and subsequently the firm went into liquidation. Therefore, having the entrepreneur tied up with securities that mature before the project yields sufficient cash flows may be a way of granting an informed lender the option to liquidate. A similar effect could be achieved if the project were (totally or partially) financed (as commonly done by banks) through a line of credit callable at the option of the lender under "materially adverse circumstances": these vaguely specified circumstances would correspond, in terms of our model, to the observation of an unsatisfactory level of effort.

In order to derive the empirical implications of the results summarized in Figure 3, we can associate the variable w with the firm's net worth (relative to the size of its investment opportunities) and the variable L with some measure of the redeployable value of the investments. Then, among highly capitalized firms we would expect to observe a preference for the use of arm's-length securities, such as public debt or outside equity. In contrast, banks or large active security holders would have a prominent role among poorly capitalized firms: either as the only financiers (for high liquidation values) or in conjunction with some form of arm's-length finance (for lower liquidation values). The richest variety of modes of finance would be observed for firms in the middle range of net worth values. Among them, investments which involve nonspecific liquid and tangible assets (for example, those in basic industrial activities) would be funded exclusively by banks or large active investors (informed finance). As we move to projects involving more and more specific illiquid or intangible assets (for example, those in high-tech and service activities) we would observe increasing (and finally total) reliance on arm's-length finance.

Some of these predictions are consistent with recent empirical findings. In particular, Alderson and Betker (1995) analyze a survey of firms reorganized under Chapter 11 for which there is information on the liquidation value of their assets. They show that firms in the lowest quartile of the distribution of liquidation costs (inversely related to our variable L) have a postbankruptcy financial structure with an average ratio of private debt to total debt of 0.816, whereas for those in the highest quartile (low L) the ratio is 0.531. Similarly, the average ratios

---

[13] If the entrepreneur had all the bargaining power [as, for example, in Berglöf and von Thadden (1994)], the two alternatives would be equivalent.

of secured debt to total debt for the same groups of firms are 0.845 and 0.630, respectively.

From our results concerning the characteristics of contracts under each mode of finance, we would expect a lower dispersion of the implicit default premia for firms that borrow exclusively from banks (pure informed finance) than for firms that borrow from both banks and the market (mixed finance) or exclusively from the market (pure uninformed finance). We would also expect that a credit rating agency involved in assessing the quality of a public issue of corporate bonds would focus on the valuation of the firm's net worth rather than the specificity or liquidity of the assets involved in the new investments. In contrast, a bank or a large corporate lender would also pay attention to the redeployable value of the investments, trying to ensure that the threat of "pulling the plug" is effective.

7. Conclusion

This article discusses optimal security design in the context of a model of entrepreneurial firms' financing. We consider three alternatives for raising finance: uninformed, informed, and a mixture of both. We show that the key role of informed finance is to impose a credible threat of liquidation. However, the credibility of this threat fails when liquidation values are low, in which case a mixture of informed and uninformed finance may be optimal, and informed debt will be secured and senior to uninformed debt.

We argue that uninformed finance may be identified with the placing of pub- licly traded securities in the market and informed finance with either bank lending or the issuance of tightly held securities. With this interpretation, the model provides a number of predictions on the influence of observable vari- ables, such as the firms' net worth and assets' liquidity, on the choice between modes of finance. Our results suggest the desirability of multivariate approaches in empirical studies on firms' financing decisions.

APPENDIX

Proof of Proposition 4. The optimal contract under mixed finance with renegoti- ation between the informed parties is a solution to the problem:

$$\max_{(I_i, I_u, Q_i, Q_u, R_i, R_u)} [\hat{p}(Y - R_u) - \max\{\hat{p}R_i, Q_i\} - \phi(\hat{p})] \tag{1}$$

subject to the constraints

$$\hat{p} \equiv \operatorname*{argmax}_{p \geq Q_i/(Y-R_u)} [p(Y - R_u) - \max\{pR_i, Q_i\} - \phi(p)], \tag{2}$$

$$I_i + I_u = 1 - w + c, \quad Q_i + Q_u \le L, \quad R_i + R_u \le Y, \tag{3}$$

$$\max\{\hat{p}R_i, Q_i\} = I_i, \quad \hat{p}R_u = I_u,^{14} \tag{4}$$

and

$$\hat{p}(Y - R_u) - \max\{\hat{p}R_i, Q_i\} - \phi(\hat{p}) \ge w. \tag{5}$$

Let $\overline{w}_m$ be defined as $\overline{w}_u$ in Proposition 1, but for a case in which the lender's participation constraint is $pR = 1 - w + c$. To prove the result we first show that if $w + L \in [\overline{w}_m, 1+c)$ the contract stated in the proposition satisfies Equations (15)–(18). By construction, $p_m(w, L)[Y - \phi'(p_m(w, L))] = 1 - w + c - L = p_m(w, L)R_u(w, L)$, which implies $[Y - R_u(w, L)] - \phi'(p_m(w, L)) = 0$, so $p_m(w, L) = \text{argmax}[p(Y - R_u(w, L)) - \phi(p)]$. But since $p_m(w, L)R_i(w, L) = Q_i(w, L)$, we also have

$$p_m(w, L) = \text{argmax}[p(Y - R_u(w, L)) - \max\{pR_i(w, L), Q_i(w, L)\} - \phi(p)].$$

Now, by construction, $p_m(w, L)[Y - R_i(w, L) - R_u(w, L)] = p_m(w, L)Y - (1 - w + c)$, and if $w + L \ge \overline{w}_m$ we have $p_m(w, L)Y - (1 - w + c) \ge w + \phi(p_m(w, L))$, so we conclude

$$p_m(w, L)[Y - R_i(w, L) - R_u(w, L)] \ge w + \phi(p_m(w, L)) > 0. \tag{6}$$

This implies $p_m(w, L)[Y - R_u(w, L)] > p_m(w, L)R_i(w, L) = Q_i(w, L)$, so $p_m(w, L) > Q_i(w, L)/[Y - R_u(w, L)]$, and the proposed contract satisfies Equation (15). As for the other constraints, they are either trivially satisfied or follow immediately from Equation (19).

Next consider an arbitrary contract $(I_i, I_u, Q_i, Q_u, R_i, R_u)$ for an entrepreneur with wealth w that satisfies the constraints of Equations (15)–(18). We are going to prove that this contract is dominated by the contract stated in the proposition. Substituting Equation (17) into Equation (14), and using the constraint $I_i + I_u = 1 - w + c$, it suffices to show that $w + L \ge \overline{w}_m$ and

$$p_m(w, L)Y - \phi(p_m(w, L)) \ge \hat{p}Y - \phi(\hat{p}). \tag{7}$$

For this, we first note that since the function in Equation (15) is concave (because $\phi''(p) > 0$ and for $p = Q_i/R_i$ we have $(Y - R_u) - \phi'(p) > (Y - R_i - R_u) - \phi'(p))$, and $Q_i/(Y - R_u) \le Q_i/R_i$ (because $R_i + R_u \le Y$), $\hat{p}$ must satisfy one of the following conditions: (i) $\hat{p} \ge Q_i/R_i$ and $(Y - R_i - R_u) - \phi'(\hat{p}) = 0$; (ii) $\hat{p} = Q_i/R_i$, $(Y - R_u) - \phi'(\hat{p}) > 0$ and $(Y - R_i - R_u) - \phi'(\hat{p}) < 0$; or (iii) $\hat{p} \le Q_i/R_i$ and $(Y - R_u) - \phi'(\hat{p}) \le 0$ (with strict inequality only if $\hat{p} = Q_i/(Y - R_u)$).

If $\hat{p}$ satisfies condition (i), then using Equations (16) and (17) we can write $[Y - (1 - w + c)/\hat{p}] - \phi'(\hat{p}) = 0$, that is $\hat{p}[Y - \phi'(\hat{p})] = 1 - w + c$. But then using

---

[14] We are assuming, without loss of generality, that the lenders' participation constraints are satisfied with equality.

the properties of the function $f(p) \equiv p[Y - \phi'(p)]$, noted in the proof of Proposition 1, together with the definition of $p_m(w, L)$, we conclude that $w > \bar{w}_i$ and $\hat{p} < p_m(w, L) < \bar{p}$. But since $pY - \phi(p)$ is increasing for $p < \bar{p}$, this implies that Equation (20) holds.

Suppose next that $\hat{p}$ satisfies condition (ii). Then using Equations (16) and (17) we have $(Y - I_u/\hat{p}) - \phi'(\hat{p}) > 0$ and $[Y - (1 - w + c)/\hat{p}] - \phi'(\hat{p}) < 0$, which implies $I_u < \hat{p}[Y - \phi'(\hat{p})] < 1 - w + c$. Moreover, $I_i = Q_i < L$ together with Equation (16) implies $1 - w + c - L \leq I_u$. Hence we have $1 - w + c - L < \hat{p}[Y - \phi'(\hat{p})] < 1 - w + c$. But then by the properties of the function $f(p)$ and the definition of $p_m(w, L)$, we conclude that $\hat{p} < p_m(w, L) < \bar{p}$ and $w > \bar{w}_m$, so Equation (20) also holds.

Finally if $\hat{p}$ satisfies condition (iii), we, first note that if $\hat{p} = Q_i/(Y - R_u)$, then using the fact that $Q_i/(Y - R_u) \leq Q_i/R_i$ we would have

$$\hat{p}(Y - R_u) - \max\{\hat{p}R_i, Q_i\} = \hat{p}(Y - R_u) - Q_i = 0,$$

which contradicts Equation (18). Hence it must be $(Y - R_u) - \phi'(p) = 0$, so using Equation (17) we have $(Y - I_u/\bar{p}) - \phi'(\hat{p}) = 0$, that is $\hat{p}[Y - \phi'(\hat{p})] = I_u$. Moreover, $I_i = Q_i < L$ together with Equation (16) implies $1 - w + c - L \leq I_u < 1 - w + c$. Hence we have $1 - w + c - L \leq \hat{p}[Y - \phi'(\hat{p})] < 1 - w + c$. But then by the properties of the function $f(p)$ and the definition of $p_m(w, L)$ it must be the case that $\hat{p} \leq p_m(w, L) < \bar{p}$ and $w \geq \bar{w}_m$, so Equation (20) holds.   ∎

References

Alderson, M. J., and Betker, B. L. (1995). "Liquidation costs and capital structure." *Journal of Financial Economics*, 39: 45–69.

Berglöf. E., and von Thadden, E.-L. (1994). "Short-term versus long-term interests: Capital structure with multiple investors." *Quarterly Journal of Economics*, 109: 1055–84.

Bolton, P., and Scharfstein, D. S. (1990). "A theory of predation based on agency problems in financial contracting." *American Economic Review*, 80: 93–106.

Chemmanur, T. J., and Fulghieri, P. (1994). "Reputation, renegotiation, and the choice between bank loans and publicly traded debt." *Review of Financial Studies*, 7: 475–506.

Detragiache, E. (1994). "Public versus private borrowing: A theory with implications for bankruptcy reform." *Journal of Financial Intermediation*, 3: 327–54.

Diamond, D. W. (1991). "Monitoring and reputation: The choice between bank loans and directly placed debt." *Journal of Political Economy*, 99: 689–721.

—— (1993a). "Bank loan maturity and priority when borrowers can refinance," in C. Mayer and X. Vives (eds.), *Capital Markets and Financial Intermediation* (Cambridge, MA: Cambridge University Press), 46–68.

Diamond, D. W. (1993*b*). "Seniority and maturity of debt contracts." *Journal of Financial Economics*, 33: 341–68.

Gorton, G., and Kahn, J. (1993). "The design of bank loan contracts, collateral, and renegotiation." Working Paper 4273, National Bureau of Economic Research.

Hart, O., and Moore, J. H. (1989). "Default and renegotiation: A dynamic model of debt." Working Paper 520, Department of Economics, Massachusetts Institute of Technology.

Osborne, M. J., and Rubinstein, A. (1990). *Bargaining and Markets*. San Diego: Academic Press.

Rajan, R. G. (1992). "Insiders and outsiders: The choice between informed and arm's-length debt." *Journal of Finance*, 47: 1367–400.

Rajan, R., and Winton, A. (1995). "Covenants and collateral as incentives to monitor." *Journal of Finance*, 50: 1113–46.

Sutton, J. (1986). "Non-cooperative bargaining theory: An introduction." *Review of Economic Studies*, 53: 709–24.

4

Financial Intermediation with Risk Aversion

Martin F. Hellwig

1. Introduction

The purpose of this chapter is to study the impact of risk aversion on financial intermediation in the agency cost approach to financial relations. Two questions will be addressed: First, what is the impact of risk aversion on the *viability of financial intermediation*? Second, what is the impact of risk aversion on the *allocation of risks* in a financial system based on intermediation?

As pointed out by Diamond (1984), viability of financial intermediation is an issue because intermediation lengthens the chain of transactions in the provision of finance. This may widen the scope for moral hazard. Intermediated finance involves agency costs of having households provide funds to intermediaries as well as agency costs of intermediaries providing funds to firms. The viability of financial intermediation then depends on how the *overall* agency costs of intermediated finance compares to the agency costs of direct finance.[1]

For a complete assessment of this issue, one must look at financial intermediation as a relation involving intermediaries, firms, *and* households, paying attention to *both*, the relation between intermediaries and firms *and* the relation between intermediaries and households. Much of the recent literature has tended to focus on *either* the relation between intermediaries and firms *or* the relation between intermediaries and households.[2] Strictly speaking, in terms of model mechanics, it is not always clear that this work is about financial intermediation at all. What is labelled as "bank finance of firms", tends to be *exclusive* finance by one financier; this financier is called "the bank". For strategic as well as technical

---

[1] In this chapter, the question of viability of financial intermediation is addressed solely in terms of relative efficiency. I neglect the question raised by Yanelle (1997) of what this means in terms of strategic interactions in the markets for funds.

[2] See, e.g. Diamond (1991), Fischer (1990), Sharpe (1990), Calomiris and Kahn (1991), Rajan (1992), Hellwig (1994), von Thadden (1992, 1995). In contrast, Besanko and Kanatas (1993) as well as Bolton and Freixas (1998) do consider intermediation as a whole; however, they take for granted that the law of large numbers can be relied upon.

reasons, there may be advantages to having exclusivity in finance.[3] However to interpret exclusive finance as "bank finance", one must presume that (i) the provision of exclusive finance to firms requires the intervention of an intermediary, and (ii) the provision of funds from households *to* the intermediary involves no further difficulties. Given the underlying view that *all* financing relations are beset by agency problems, the latter presumption requires some justification.

The prototype for such a justification has been developed by Diamond (1984), see also Krasa and Villamil (1992). As I have discussed elsewhere (Hellwig (1991)), the reasoning of these papers can be adapted quite mechanically to turn any model of exclusive finance into a model of intermediated finance. The present chapter shows that one does not even have to consider whether the intermediaries in question might be risk averse; this is remarkable because the argument given relied on risk neutrality of the intermediary in an essential way.

Assuming risk neutrality of the intermediary and using a large-numbers argument, Diamond (1984) as well as Krasa and Villamil (1992) showed that the agency costs of having households provide funds to an intermediary may be relatively small if the intermediary in turn provides funds to many entrepreneurs with stochastically independent returns. Lending to many entrepreneurs with independent returns provides the intermediary himself with a relatively riskless return pattern. This enables him to incur a return-independent payment obligation to his own financiers without much of a default risk. The agency cost of his own external finance is then negligible[4] and the assessment of intermediated finance depends solely on the agency costs associated with the intermediary's *lending* operations. The main results of Diamond (1984) or Krasa and Villamil (1992) showed that *if* the intermediary is financing and monitoring sufficiently many independent entrepreneurs, then the efficiency of intermediated finance relative to direct finance depends *only* on how the agency costs associated with the intermediary's lending operations compare to the agency costs of direct finance for the same entrepreneurs. If there is enough diversification across borrowers, a nonzero cost advantage of the intermediary in lending will outweigh the disadvantage that the intermediary's own external finance involves

---

[3] Technical effects of exclusivity in the provision of finance arise from economies of scale in monitoring, see, e.g. Diamond (1984), Krasa and Villamil (1992), or von Thadden (1995). Strategic effects concern bargaining power and bargaining costs in renegotiations, see, e.g. Fischer (1990), Sharpe (1990), or Bolton and Freixas (1998). Negative effects of bargaining power from exclusivity are stressed by Rajan (1992) and von Thadden (1992). The main arguments are surveyed in Hellwig (1991).

[4] This assumes that moral hazard is limited to problems of state verification and effort choice and that there is no concern about risk choices (Hellwig (1998a)). If the intermediary has discretion over the extent of diversification in his lending policy, the well known phenomenon of "excessive risk taking" induced by debt finance may preclude the intermediary's making efficient use of available diversification opportunities; Diamond's large-numbers argument may then be altogether moot (Hellwig (1998b)).

additional agency costs, the large-numbers argument implying that the latter are relatively negligible.

In this reasoning, the assumption of risk neutrality of the financial intermediary is used to normalize the intermediary's total return by the number of projects he finances. Whereas the intermediary's actual return corresponds to a simple sum of random returns in his dealings with entrepreneurs $i = 1, \ldots, N$, the law of large numbers is a statement about sums of random variables *normalized* by the number of terms in the sum. If the intermediary is risk neutral, there is no problem about formulating the intermediary's choice over lending policies in terms of normalized rather than actual sums of returns from different entrepreneurs: As his von Neumann–Morgenstern utility function $u(\cdot)$ is only defined up to a monotone, affine transformation one can for any N replace it by $u(\cdot)/N$, and if $u(\cdot)$ itself is linear, this poses the problem of choosing a lending policy in terms of normalized rather than actual sums of returns over the different potential borrowers. If the intermediary is risk averse, $u(\cdot)$ is *nonlinear*, this device is not available, and the large-numbers arguments used by Diamond (1984) as well as Krasa and Villamil (1992) cannot be applied.

From the general theory of decisions under uncertainty, it is well known that when risks are added rather than subdivided risk-averse agents assessing large compounds of independent random variables may not pay much attention to the law of large numbers. Given the nonlinearities in their utility functions, they may be assigning so much weight to the losses from large negative deviations from the mean or so little weight to the gains from large positive deviations from the mean that considerations of risk affect their choices even in situations in which the law of large numbers might be expected to come into play (Samuelson (1963)). As Diamond (1984) himself pointed out, this raises the question how robust his result is to the introduction of risk aversion.

The chapter settles this question, showing that *the main conclusion about the viability of financial intermediation is valid even when the intermediary is risk averse*. The paper relies on arguments used by Nielsen (1985) and Hellwig (1995) to show that *if* a decision maker's von Neumann–Morgenstern utility function satisfies certain additional conditions at large negative and large positive wealth levels, then the law of large numbers will be relevant for the choice between large sums of independent random variables, and the choice between such sums will be guided by expected values if the number of summands in the compounds is sufficiently large. In the present context, the additional conditions on von Neumann–Morgenstern utility functions may not even be needed; in some circumstances, the contracts used by intermediaries to obtain their own finance already defuse the effects of large deviations that were stressed by Samuelson (1963).[5]

---

[5] Whereas Diamond (1984) relied on Chebyshev's inequality, the argument here relies on Bernstein's inequality (Rényi (1979), p. 324) providing for exponential convergence in the law of

Going a step further, the chapter also shows that if there are many entrepreneurs with stochastically independent returns, an optimal intermediation policy requires the intermediary to assume approximately all risks of the entrepreneurs and, depending on his own risk preferences, to keep them or to shift them on to final investors (in an incentive-compatible way). This contrasts with the case of risk neutrality in which it is optimal for entrepreneurs to be financed by standard debt contracts, retaining as much of their return risk as is compatible with their consumption being nonnegative (Krasa (1988)). *With risk aversion, optimal intermediation policies provide final borrowers with insurance as well as finance.*

The analysis uses the original model of Diamond (1984) of financial contracting with *intermediation as delegated monitoring*. In this model, financiers do not automatically observe the return realizations of the people they finance, so ex post they are vulnerable to fraudulent claims that no returns have been realized and therefore no debt service payments can be made. To mitigate this problem, two devices are available: (i) Nonpecuniary penalties can be used to penalize low debt service payments, and (ii) a costly monitoring system set up in advance can provide the person who invested in it with independent information about the true return realizations. Monitoring is assumed to be too expensive to be used by the many households required to finance a firm or an intermediary. However direct finance of firms based on nonpecuniary penalties may be dominated by intermediated finance with monitoring of firms by an intermediary who in turn obtains funds from households through contracts involving nonpecuniary penalties.

In the following, Section 2 sketches the basic model of incentive contracting with nonpecuniary penalties under the assumption that borrowers are risk averse with respect to consumption and risk neutral with respect to penalties. The presentation is based on a more systematic analysis given in Hellwig (1998c). Whereas Diamond (1984) had found that under risk neutrality, an optimal finance contract takes the form of *debt* with a return-independent repayment obligation, with risk aversion unfortunately no robust and simple characterization of optimal finance contracts is available. Luckily, for this chapter this is not so important because the main results about intermediation can be proved with reference to intermediaries being financed by debt (even though debt is typically not the optimal contract). Following an explanation of why optimal incentive contracting with risk aversion is rather messy, Section 2 therefore concludes with a characterization of incentive-compatible debt contracts in the present setting.

The core of the analysis is contained in Sections 3 and 4. Section 3 extends Diamond's result on the viability of intermediated finance to the case of risk aversion, showing that if the intermediary's cost of monitoring any one

---

large numbers. Exponential convergence was also used by Krasa and Villami (1992) in their analysis of intermediation in a costly-state-verification framework.

entrepreneur is less than the agency cost of direct finance and if the number of entrepreneurs with mutually independent project returns is sufficiently large, then the agency cost of intermediated finance is less than that of direct finance; the agency cost of the intermediary's own external finance is relatively negligible. Section 4 moves on to show that an optimal intermediation policy will involve the assumption of *all* return risks by the intermediary who relies on the law of large numbers to provide enough diversification of these risks.

Section 5 considers the robustness of the analysis to the possibility that agents exhibit risk aversion with respect to nonpecuniary penalties as well as consumption. The conclusions of Sections 3 and 4 are again obtained when the intermediary's von Neumann–Morgenstern utility function satisfies the additional conditions of Nielsen (1985) and Hellwig (1995) about the behaviour of risk preferences at large levels of nonpecuniary penalties or consumption.

Another robustness issue concerns the specification of the monitoring technology. In the discussion paper (Hellwig (1999)), the conclusions of Sections 3 and 4 are also shown to hold for the Krasa–Villamil (1992) model of intermediation based on *outcome-contingent* monitoring, with households monitoring the intermediary (and bearing the costs) when he defaults as well as the intermediary monitoring entrepreneurs when they default.[6] Here, as in Sections 3 and 4, the additional conditions of Nielsen (1985) and Hellwig (1995) are *not* needed. If the entrepreneurs' projects are sufficiently profitable to be worth undertaking when funds are provided by a single fictitious risk neutral financier, then if the number of entrepreneurs with mutually independent projects is sufficiently large, intermediation is viable, and an optimal intermediation policy will provide entrepreneurs with contracts that are close to what they would get in contracting with a fictitious risk neutral, non-wealth-constrained financier.[7]

2. Incentive Contracting with Nonlinear Utility

As in Diamond (1984), a representative entrepreneur has a venture that requires a fixed investment $I > 0$ and bears a random return $\tilde{y}$. The random variable $\tilde{y}$ has a probability distribution G with a density g, which is continuous and strictly

---

[6] There is no inherent necessity to introduce outcome-contingent monitoring of entrepreneurs by the intermediary and outcome-contingent monitoring of the intermediary by final investors jointly. One might also consider the possibility that (i) the intermediary employs outcome-contingent monitoring of entrepreneurs and (ii) the final investors are protected by nonpecuniary penalties imposed on the borrower when he reports low return realizations. It is easy to check that this specification again supports the main conclusions of the chapter.

[7] As discussed in Townsend (1979), this does not usually provide the entrepreneur with full insurance of his return risks. It usually is preferable to have fixed payments to the financier and no monitoring at high return realization. This worsens the allocation of return risks, but saves on monitoring costs. See also Gale and Hellwig (1985).

positive on the interval $[0, Y]$. The expected return $\bar{y} = \int y \, dG(y)$ of the venture is strictly greater than the cost I, i.e.

$$\bar{y} > I. \tag{1}$$

The owner/manager of the venture, with own funds $w_E \geq 0$, wants to raise external finance, either because his own funds are too small and he needs additional funds to undertake the investment at all, or because he wants to avoid committing all of his own funds to the venture and he prefers to share the risk of the venture with others.

Outside financiers know the return distribution G, but in contrast to the entrepreneur they are unable to observe the realizations of the return random variable $\tilde{y}$. The agency problems caused by this information asymmetry can be reduced by the use of nonpecuniary penalties as a device to discourage misreporting of return realizations. The entrepreneur who has earned a positive return will refrain from claiming that he has not earned anything and therefore cannot pay anything if such a claim induces an appropriate penalty. As in Diamond (1984), the penalties are determined endogenously as part of the finance contract.

A finance contract is represented by a number L indicating the funds provided by outside financiers and by two functions $r(\cdot)$ and $p(\cdot)$ such that for any $z \in [0, Y]$, $r(z)$ is the payment to financiers and $p(z) \geq 0$ is the nonpecuniary penalty the entrepreneur suffers when he reports that his return realization is equal to z. With outside funds L, his own financial contribution to his project is $E = I - L \leq w_E$. Any excess of w_E over E is invested in an alternative asset, which bears a safe return at a gross rate of return equal to one.

Given a finance contract $(L, r(\cdot), p(\cdot))$, the entrepreneur's consumption is $w_E + L - I + y - r(z)$ if the true return realization is y and the reported return realization is z; the corresponding payoff realization is $u(w_E + L - I + y - r(z)) - p(z)$. A contract $(L, r(\cdot), p(\cdot))$ is said to be *feasible* if $w_E + L - I \geq 0$ and

$$w_E + L - I + y - r(y) \geq 0, \tag{2}$$

for all $y \in [0, Y]$, so the entrepreneur's consumption is never negative; it is *incentive compatible* if it is feasible and moreover

$$u_E(w_E + L - I + y - r(y)) - p(y) \geq u_E(w_E + L - I + y - r(z)) - p(z), \tag{3}$$

for all $y \in [0, Y]$ and all $z \in [0, Y]$ such that $w_E + L - I + y \geq r(z)$.

The utility function $u_E(\cdot)$ is assumed to be strictly increasing and strictly concave as well as twice continuously differentiable on $\Re_{++}$; moreover, $u_E(0) = \lim_{c \to 0} u_E(c)$, with the usual conventions when $\lim_{c \to 0} u_E(c) = -\infty$. Given these assumptions, standard arguments from incentive theory yield:

PROPOSITION 1. *A finance contract* $(L, r(\cdot), p(\cdot))$ *satisfying* (2) *for all* $y \in [0, Y]$ *is incentive compatible if and only if (i) the function* $r(\cdot)$ *is nondecreasing on* $[0, Y]$ *and (ii) for all* $y \in [0, Y]$,

$$p(y) = p(Y) + \int_y^Y u_E'(w_E + L - I + x - r(x)) \, dr(x). \tag{4}$$

A proof of Proposition 1 is given in Hellwig (1998c). The proposition shows that up to a constant of integration, $p(Y)$, the penalty function $p(\cdot)$ is entirely determined by the amount of funds L that are raised and the repayment function $r(\cdot)$. This makes it easy to compute expected payoffs. The entrepreneur's expected payoff from an incentive-compatible contract is equal to:

$$\int_0^Y u_E(w_E + L - I + y - r(y)) \, dG(y) - \int_0^Y p(y) \, dG(y). \tag{5}$$

Upon using (4) to substitute for $p(y)$ and integrating the resulting double integral by parts, one finds that this is equal to

$$\int_0^Y u_E(w_E + L - I + y - r(y)) \, dG(y)$$

$$- \int_0^Y u_E'(w_E + L - I + y - r(y)) G(y) \, dr(y) - p(Y). \tag{6}$$

Funds are provided by households. For simplicity, all households are taken to have the same characteristics, an initial wealth $w_H > 0$, and a von Neumann–Morgenstern utility function $u_H(\cdot)$. The utility function $u_H(\cdot)$ is assumed to be strictly increasing and concave as well as twice continuously differentiable on $\Re_{++}$. Direct finance of an entrepreneur through a finance contract $(L, r(\cdot), p(\cdot))$ involves household h providing a share α_h of the loan L and receiving a share α_h of the repayment $r(\tilde{y})$; households are unaffected by the penalty $p(\tilde{y})$. Given that households are identical, there is no loss of generality in assuming that the shares α_H are all the same, i.e. that $\alpha_h = 1/H$ for all h, where H is the overall number of households. If the entrepreneur in question is the only one receiving funds and there is also a safe asset with a rate of return equal to one, the household's expected utility from providing finance through an incentive-compatible contract $(L, r(\cdot), p(\cdot))$ is equal to $E u_H(w_H - L/H + r(\tilde{y})/H)$. If the household's alternative is to invest the entire wealth w_H in the safe asset, he will consider the finance contract $(L, r(\cdot), p(\cdot))$ to be *acceptable* if and only if it satisfies the inequality

$$\int_0^Y u_H \left(w_H - \frac{1}{H}(L - r(y)) \right) dG(y) \geq u_H(w_H). \tag{7}$$

An acceptable incentive-compatible finance contract $(L, r(\cdot), p(\cdot))$ is called *optimal* if it maximizes the entrepreneur's expected payoff (6) over the set of all acceptable incentive-compatible contracts.

As discussed in Hellwig (1998c) for the case when households are risk neutral, optimal finance contracts do not seem to have any significant qualitative properties that are robust to changes in the specification of risk preferences and/or the distribution function G. Formally the problem of choosing an optimal incentive-compatible finance contract can be treated as an optimum-control problem in which the entrepreneur's consumption

$$c(y) := w_E + L - I + y - r(y), \tag{8}$$

is the state variable and the slope of $c(\cdot)$ the control. The problem of maximizing (6) over the set of acceptable incentive-compatible finance contracts $(L, r(\cdot), p(\cdot))$ is equivalent to the problem of choosing a constant $p(Y)$ and a function $c(\cdot)$ so as to maximize

$$\int_0^Y u_E(c(y))\, dG(y) - \int_0^Y u_E'(c(y))G(y)\, dr(y) - p(Y) \tag{9}$$

$$= u_E(c(Y)) - \int_0^Y u_E'(c(y))G(y)\, dy - p(Y), \tag{10}$$

under the constraints that

$$\int_0^Y u_H \left(w_H + \frac{1}{H}(w_E + y - I - c(y)) \right) dG(y) \geq u_H(w_H), \tag{11}$$

$$c(y) \geq 0, \tag{12}$$

and

$$c(y) - c(z) \leq y - z, \tag{13}$$

for all $y \in [0, Y]$ and all $z \in [0, y]$.

Without going into details, I note the following:

- Given condition (one), if H is sufficiently large, the set of acceptable contracts is nonempty, containing in particular the contract generating the consumption pattern $c(\cdot)$ such that $c(y) \equiv w_E$.
- If the set of acceptable contracts is nonempty, an optimal incentive compatible contract exists. If $u_E''(\cdot)$ is a strictly increasing function, e.g. if the entrepreneur exhibits nonincreasing absolute risk aversion, the optimal contract is unique in the sense that consumption patterns corresponding to different optimal contracts all coincide on $(0, Y]$.
- An optimal incentive-compatible contract satisfies $p(Y) = 0$. The constant of integration in (4) and (10) hurts the entrepreneur without helping his financiers.

- The consumption pattern $c(\cdot)$ under an optimal incentive-compatible contract must satisfy a suitable analogue of Pontryagin's conditions for the given control problem. Specifically, there exist a Lagrange multiplier μ for the constraint (11) and a costate variable $\psi(\cdot)$ such that for any $y \in [0, Y]$,

$$\frac{d\psi}{dy} \leq u_E''(c(y))G(y) + \mu u_H'(w_H + (w_E + y - I - c(y))/H)g(y),$$

with equality if $c(y) > 0$, $\qquad(14)$

$$\psi(y) \geq 0, \quad \text{with equality unless in a neighbourhood of } y, \qquad(15)$$

$c(\cdot)$ is continuously differentiable with $\dfrac{dc}{dy} = 1,$

$$\psi(Y) = u_E'(c(Y)) \quad \text{and} \quad \psi(0) = 0. \qquad(16)$$

If $u_E''(\cdot)$ is a strictly increasing function, these conditions, together with the constraints (11)–(13) are sufficient as well as necessary for $c(\cdot)$ to be maximizing (10) under the given constraints.

Optimal incentive-compatible contracts are difficult to characterize because risk sharing and incentive compatibility considerations interact in intricate ways: Risk sharing considerations suggest that risks should be shifted away from the entrepreneur, e.g. by having the payment $r(y)$ be high when y is high and low when y is low, so that $c(y)$ would be somewhat insulated from variation in y. Such risk shifting though requires nonpecuniary penalties; as indicated by the second term in (6) and (9) the size of these penalties depends on $u_E'(c(y))$, which means that, at the margin, risk shifting may be undesirable and $c(y)$ may be chosen to be *sensitive* to y when $u_E'(c(y))$ is large. The tradeoff between risk sharing effects and penalties may actually give rise to interior solutions with $c(y) > 0$ and $dc/dy < 1$; as indicated by (14) and (15), this entails $u_E''(c(y))G(y) + \mu u_H''g(y) = 0$, showing that optimal consumption patterns will be quite sensitive to the specification of $u_E(\cdot)$, $u_H(\cdot)$, and G.

Fortunately, the analysis of this chapter does not have to rely on any detailed knowledge of optimal contracts. Where *direct finance* is concerned, it will be enough to know that optimal incentive-compatible contracts exist, and that, because of the imperfectness of risk sharing and/or the use of nonpecuniary penalties, the certainty equivalents $\hat{w}_E^H$ of these contracts for the entrepreneur are strictly less than and bounded away from the sum of the entrepreneur's own initial wealth and the expected surplus generated by the project,

$$K := w_E + \bar{y} - I. \qquad(17)$$

To see this, note that (11) implies

$$\int_0^Y c(y)\, dG(y) \leq K, \qquad(18)$$

so for any H, $\hat{w}_E^H$ is less than the certainty equivalent $\hat{w}_E$ of the solution to the problem of maximizing (10) subject to (18), (12), and (13); because of imperfect risk sharing and/or the use of nonpecuniary penalties, $\hat{w}_E$ is certainly less than K. The difference $K - \hat{w}_E$ in turn provides a measure of the *agency cost of direct finance* in an economy with many households ($H \to \infty$) where under symmetric information the entrepreneur would obtain with perfect insurance as well as finance.

Where *indirect finance* is concerned, I shall be interested in the scope for intermediation when intermediaries are financed by optimal incentive-compatible contracts. This scope is certainly no smaller than the scope for intermediation when intermediaries are financed by simpler contracts which are not necessarily optimal. In this spirit, the formal arguments that I use will rely on contracts taking the form of *debt*.

By a *standard debt contract with minimum living allowance* ε I will understand an incentive-compatible contract $(L, r(\cdot), p(\cdot))$ such that for some fixed $\varepsilon \geq 0$ and $\hat{y} \in (0, Y)$, one has

$$r(y) = w_E + L - I + \min(y, \hat{y}) - \varepsilon, \tag{19}$$

for all $y \in [0, Y]$. In this contract, the amount $w_E + L - I + \hat{y} - \varepsilon$ represents a return-independent debt service obligation. If the entrepreneur can meet this obligation, he does so and retains the excess of his actual return y over the critical return level $\hat{y}$ as well as the living allowance ε. If he cannot meet his obligation, he defaults and retains just the living allowance ε. For $y < \hat{y}$, incentive compatibility requires that he bear a penalty which is equialent to the amount of money that he saves by paying $r(y)$ rather than $r(\hat{y})$. Indeed, when $r(\cdot)$ is given by (19), the incentive compatibility condition (4), with $p(Y) = 0$, reduces to

$$p(y) = u_E'(\varepsilon) \max(0, \hat{y} - y). \tag{20}$$

The ex ante expected payoff of the entrepreneur (6) is then equal to

$$\int_0^Y u_E(\varepsilon + \max(0, y - \hat{y})) \, dG(y) - u_E'(\varepsilon) \int_0^Y G(y) \, dy. \tag{21}$$

In Diamond (1984), standard debt contracts with a *zero* living allowance are shown to be optimal when the entrepreneur is risk neutral. For a given return distribution $G(\cdot)$ whose density g is bounded away from zero, this result can be extended to the case where the entrepreneur's risk aversion is everywhere sufficiently low; however, it no longer holds when the entrepreneur's absolute risk aversion is (locally) unbounded, e.g. if $u'(0) = \infty$ (Hellwig (1998c)).

3. Intermediated Finance

To study the scope for intermediated finance, I assume that there are N entrepreneurs of the sort considered so far and $H_N = NM$ households. For simplicity, the characteristics of the entrepreneurs are taken to be all identical *ex ante*. Every entrepreneur has the same initial wealth level $w_E \geq 0$, the same von Neumann–Morgenstern utility function $u_E(\cdot)$, and an investment project with the same investment cost I and the same return distribution $G(\cdot)$. The return random variables $\tilde{y}_1, \ldots, \tilde{y}_N$ of the different entrepreneurs are assumed to be mutually independent.

In the absence of financial intermediation, each entrepreneur i will receive direct finance through an incentive-compatible contract $(L_i, r_i(\cdot), p_i(\cdot))$ as discussed in the preceding section. Assuming that for $i = 1, 2, \ldots, N$, these contracts are shared evenly between households, any one household with initial wealth w_H and von Neumann–Morgenstern utility function $u_H(\cdot)$ will obtain the expected payoff $Eu_H(w_H + \sum_{j=1}^{N}(r_j(\tilde{y}_j) - L_j))/NM)$, and is willing to accept his share of the contract $(L_i, r_i(\cdot), p_i(\cdot))$ for entrepreneur i if and only if

$$\int u_H\left(w_H + \frac{1}{NM}\sum_{j=1}^{N}(r_j(y_j) - L_j)\right) dG(y_1)\ldots dG(y_N)$$

$$\geq \int u_H\left(w_H + \frac{1}{NM}\sum_{j=1,j\neq i}^{N}(r_j(y_j) - L_j)\right) dG(y_1)\ldots dG(y_N). \qquad (22)$$

Taking Taylor expansions and using the independence of returns across entrepreneurs, one can rewrite (22) in the form

$$\int_0^Y r_i(y_i)\, dG(y_i) \geq L_i + o(1/NM), \qquad (23)$$

where $o(1/NM)$ is a term that goes to zero as NM goes out of bounds. Thus if there are many households providing funds to the entrepreneur, condition (22) is slightly stronger than the requirement that $\int_0^Y r_i(y_i)\, dG(y_i) \geq L_i$, i.e. that the expected debt service covers the opportunity cost of the loan L_i. In view of (8), this in turn is equivalent to condition (18), the condition that the entrepreneur's expected consumption be no greater than $K = w_E + \bar{y} - I$. When the number of households is large, the certainty equivalent of an optimal incentive-compatible direct-finance contract will therefore be approximately equal to, but slightly less than $\hat{w}_E$, the certainty equivalent of a consumption pattern that maximizes (10) subject to (18), (12), and (13). As discussed above, $\hat{w}_E$ is strictly less than K; here as in Section 2, the difference $K - \hat{w}_E > 0$ provides a measure of the agency cost of direct finance when there are many households.

As an alternative to direct finance, I consider the possibility that any one entrepreneur i obtains a loan L_i from an intermediary, whom he promises to repay an amount $\pi_i(\tilde{y}_i) \leq w_E + L_i - I + \tilde{y}_i$ when returns are realized. The intermediary monitors the entrepreneur's returns so incentive compatibility is not an issue in choosing the repayment specification. However, to monitor entrepreneur i, the intermediary must spend A units of money.[8] These resources must be committed at the time of the initial investment, i.e. before the return $\tilde{y}_i$ is actually realized. They comprise the costs of making the information about $\tilde{y}_i$ verifiable to the courts if this should be necessary for contract enforcement.

Given that ex ante the entrepreneurs are all alike, there is no loss of generality in assuming that loans and repayment obligations will be the same for all of them. A *lending policy* of the intermediary is then given by a pair $(L, \pi(\cdot))$ such that L is the loan offered to any one entrepreneur and $\pi(\cdot)$ is the repayment function. Given a lending policy $(L, \pi(\cdot))$, the intermediary himself earns the gross return $\tilde{z} = \sum_{i=1}^{N} \pi(\tilde{y}_i)$. This is assumed to be unobservable by outside financiers.[9] The intermediary's own financing problem is therefore a special case of the financing problem under asymmetric information that was studied in Section 2, with $\tilde{y}$ replaced by $\tilde{z} = \sum_{i=1}^{N} \pi(\tilde{y}_i)$ and the investment I replaced by the intermediary's expenditures $NL + NA$ for finance and for monitoring. A *finance contract for the intermediary* will be a triple $(D, r_I(\cdot), p_I(\cdot))$ such that D is the total deposit of final investors with the intermediary, $r_I(\cdot)$ is a function indicating the dependence of the intermediary's repayment on his own return $\tilde{z}$, and $p_I(\cdot)$ is a function indicating the nonpecuniary penalties suffered by the intermediary in order to establish incentive compatibility of the contract. The combination of a lending policy $(L, \pi(\cdot))$ and a finance contract $(D, r_I(\cdot), p_I(\cdot))$ for the intermediary will be referred to as an *intermediation policy*.

An intermediation policy $(L, \pi(\cdot), D, r_I(\cdot), p_I(\cdot))$ will be called *feasible* if the lending policy $(L, \pi(\cdot))$ satisfies $w + L - I \geq 0$ and

$$w + L - I + y - \pi(y) \geq 0, \tag{24}$$

for all $y \in [0, Y]$, and if moreover the finance contract $(D, r_I(\cdot), p_I(\cdot))$ of the intermediary is feasible; an intermediation policy $(L, \pi(\cdot), D, r_I(\cdot), p_I(\cdot))$ is called *incentive-compatible* if it is feasible, and moreover the intermediary's finance contract $(D, r_I(\cdot), p_I(\cdot))$ is incentive-compatible, i.e. if and only if for all z and

---

[8] The assumption that monitoring costs are expended in the form of money rather than effort is not essential for the analysis. Indeed since monitoring costs in the form of money add to the intermediary's financing requirements, this assumption makes it more difficult to establish the viability of intermediation. If monitoring costs were expended in the form of effort, Proposition 2 would be that much easier to establish.

[9] Given the assumption that monitoring provides information about $\tilde{y}_i$ that is verifiable by the courts, this assumption may seem problematic. As in Diamond (1984), the underlying notion here is that w_H is on the order of $1/M$, so on the order of M households are needed to finance one entrepreneur's investment I. If M is a large number, making the result of monitoring $\tilde{y}_i$ verifiable by M investors may be prohibitively costly, much costlier than making it verifiable by just the courts.

$\bar{z}$ in the range of the random variable $\tilde{z} = \sum_{i=1}^{N} \pi(\tilde{y}_i)$, one has either

$$u_I(w_I + D - NL - NA + z - r_I(z)) - p_I(z)$$

$$\geq u_I(w_I + D - NL - NA + z - r_I(\bar{z})) - p_I(\bar{z}), \tag{25}$$

or $w_I + D - NL - NA + z < r_I(\bar{z})$; here $u_I(\cdot)$ is the intermediary's von Neumann–Morgenstern utility function and w_I is his own initial wealth.

The utility function $u_I(\cdot)$ is assumed to have the same properties as the entrepreneurs' utility function $u_E(\cdot)$, i.e. it is strictly increasing and strictly concave as well as twice continuously differentiable on $\Re_{++}$; moreover, $u_I(0) = \lim_{c \to 0} u_I(c)$, with the usual conventions when $\lim_{c \to 0} u_I(c) = -\infty$.

Given these assumptions, Proposition 1 implies that an intermediation policy $(L, \pi(\cdot), D, r_I(\cdot), p_I(\cdot))$ for the intermediary is incentive-compatible if and only if the function $r_I(\cdot)$ is nondecreasing and moreover for all z and $\bar{z}$ in the range of the random variable $\tilde{z} = \sum_{i=1}^{N} \pi(\tilde{y}_i)$, one has

$$p_I(z) = p_I(\bar{z}) + \int_z^{\bar{z}} u_I'(w_I + D - NL - NA + x - r_I(x)) \, dr_I(x). \tag{26}$$

An incentive-compatible intermediation policy $(L, \pi(\cdot), D, r_I(\cdot), p_I(\cdot))$ generates the expected payoffs

$$\int u_E(w_E + L - I + y - \pi(y)) \, dG(y), \tag{27}$$

for entrepreneurs $i = 1, 2, \ldots, N$,

$$\int \left[u_I \left(w_I + D - NL - NA + \sum_{i=1}^{N} \pi(y_i) - r_I \left(\sum_{i=1}^{N} \pi(y_i) \right) \right) \right.$$

$$\left. - p_I \left(\sum_{i=1}^{N} \pi(y_i) \right) \right] dG(y_1) \ldots dG(y_N), \tag{28}$$

for the intermediary, and

$$\int u_H \left(w_H + \frac{1}{NM} \left(r_I \left(\sum_{i=1}^{N} \pi(y_i) \right) - D \right) \right) dG(y_1) \ldots dG(y_N). \tag{29}$$

for households as the final investors. The intermediation policy $(L, \pi(\cdot), D, r_I(\cdot), p_I(\cdot))$ is said to be *acceptable to the intermediary*, if his expected payoff (28) is at least as great as $u_I(w_I)$, his payoff in the absence of intermediation; the policy is *acceptable to final investors* if their expected payoff (29) is at least as great as $u_H(w_H)$. An incentive-compatible intermediation policy that is acceptable to both, households and the intermediary, is called *viable*.

The first major result of this paper is now stated as:

PROPOSITION 2. *Assume that the cost A of monitoring an entrepreneur is strictly less than the agency cost* $K - \hat{w}_E$ *of direct finance when there are many households. Then for any sufficiently large N, there exists a viable incentive-compatible intermediation policy* $L^N, \pi^N(\cdot), D^N, r_I^N(\cdot), p_I^N(\cdot))$ *which makes entrepreneurs strictly better off than any incentive-compatible contract for direct finance that is acceptable to households.*

Proof. It will be useful to sketch the basic idea before giving any details. The desired intermediation policies will be specified as policies under which for some sufficiently small $\varepsilon > 0$, (i) the entrepreneurs are left with the safe consumption $\hat{w}_E + \varepsilon$, and (ii) the intermediary obtains the funds he needs to finance his lending and monitoring through a *debt contract* with a minimum living allowance $w_I + \varepsilon$ and a debt service obligation $\hat{y}^N = N(\bar{y} - \varepsilon)$. Under these intermediation policies, entrepreneurs are trivially better off than under direct finance, so the only question is whether these policies are viable. The intermediary defaults on the obligation $N(\bar{y} - \varepsilon)$ to final investors if and only if $\sum \tilde{y}_i < N(\bar{y} - \varepsilon)$ or, equivalently,

$$\frac{1}{N} \sum_{i=1}^{N} \tilde{y}_i < \bar{y} - \varepsilon. \tag{30}$$

By Bernstein's inequality (see, e.g. Rényi (1979), p. 324), the probability of this event goes to zero, *exponentially* in N, as N becomes large. From (20), with $u_I(\cdot)$ in the place of $u_E(\cdot)$ and the given living allowance and debt service obligation, one also sees that the intermediary's penalty in the event of default is bounded above by $u_I'(w_I + \varepsilon)\hat{y}^N = u_I'(w_I + \varepsilon)N(\bar{y} - \varepsilon)$, which increases just linearly in N.[10] Therefore, as N goes out of bounds, the expected value of the intermediary's nonpecuniary penalty must go to zero and must eventually be outweighed by the fact that the given intermediation policy provides him with the consumption $w_I + \varepsilon + \max[0, \sum \tilde{y}_i - N(\bar{y} - \varepsilon)] > w_I$. As for the final investors, as N goes out of bounds and the probability of default vanishes, their receipts, normalized by N, converge almost surely to $\bar{y} - \varepsilon$. Given that the monitoring cost A is less than the agency cost of direct finance, this turns out to be enough to cover the opportunity cost of their funds provided that $\varepsilon > 0$ is sufficiently small.

To make the argument precise, let $\Delta := K - \hat{w}_E - A$ denote the difference between the agency cost of direct finance when there are many households and the monitoring cost A, and set $\varepsilon := \Delta/5$. For any N, consider the intermediation

---

[10] This argument parallels the one underlying Proposition 1, p. 467, of Nielsen (1985) or Theorem 2, p. 305, of Hellwig (1995), see also Section 5 below. Whereas those papers start from a given von Neumann–Morgenstern utility function that is defined on all of $\mathfrak{R}$, the analysis here has the intermediary's consumption restricted to $\mathfrak{R}$, and uses nonpecuniary penalties to define the intermediary's attitudes to large shortfalls of his returns from his debt service obligations.

policy $(L^N, \pi^N(\cdot), D^N, r_I^N(\cdot), p_I^N(\cdot))$ where

$$L^N = I - w_E + \hat{w}_E + \varepsilon, \tag{31}$$

$$\pi^N(y) \equiv y, \tag{32}$$

$$D^N = NL^N + NA + \varepsilon, \tag{33}$$

$$r_I^N(z) \equiv \min[z, N(\bar{y} - \varepsilon)], \tag{34}$$

$$p_I^N(z) \equiv u_I'(w_I + \varepsilon) \max[0, N(\bar{y} - \varepsilon) - z]. \tag{35}$$

As mentioned above, this involves a standard debt contract for the intermediary with minimum living allowance $w_I + \varepsilon$ and debt service obligation $N(\bar{y} - \varepsilon)$. By Proposition 1, this contract is incentive-compatible: (34) ensures that $r_I^N(\cdot)$ is nondecreasing, and (35) ensures that $p_I^N(\cdot)$ and $r_I^N(\cdot)$ satisfy (4). A final investor's expected payoff from the given intermediation policy is

$$\int u_H\left(w_H + \frac{1}{NM}\left(r_I\left(\sum_{i=1}^{N}\pi(y_i)\right) - D^N\right)\right) dG(y_1)\dots dG(y_N)$$

$$\geq \int u_H\left(w_H + \frac{1}{M}\left(\min\left[\frac{1}{N}\sum_{i=1}^{N}y_i, \bar{y} - \varepsilon\right] - L^N - A - \varepsilon\right)\right) dG(y_1)\dots dG(y_N).$$

By the law of large numbers, in combination with Lebesgue's bounded-convergence theorem, for any sufficiently large N, this is at least as great as

$$u_H\left(w_H + \frac{1}{M}(\bar{y} - 2\varepsilon - L^N - A - \varepsilon)\right) = u_H\left(w_H + \frac{1}{M}(\bar{y} - I + w_E - \hat{w}_E - A - 4\varepsilon)\right)$$

$$= u_H\left(w_H + \frac{1}{M}(\Delta - 4\varepsilon)\right) > u_H(w_H), \tag{36}$$

and the intermediation policy is acceptable to final investors.

As for the financial intermediary, his expected payoff from the intermediation policy $(L^N, \pi^N(\cdot), D^N, r_I^N(\cdot), p_I^N(\cdot))$ is

$$\int \left[u_I\left(w_I + D^N - NL^N - NA + \sum_{i=1}^{N}\pi(y_i) - r_I\left(\sum_{i=1}^{N}\pi(y_i)\right)\right)\right.$$

$$\left. - p_I\left(\sum_{i=1}^{N}\pi(y_i)\right)\right] dG(y_1)\dots dG(y_N)$$

$$= \int u_I \left(w_I + \varepsilon + N \max \left[\sum_{i=1}^{N} y_i/N - \bar{y} + \varepsilon, 0 \right] \right) dG(y_1) \dots dG(y_N)$$

$$- \int_0^{N(\bar{y}-\varepsilon)} u_I'(w_I + \varepsilon) \Pr \left\{ \sum_{i=1}^{N} \tilde{y}_i \leq z \right\} dz$$

$$\geq u_I(w_I + \varepsilon) - u_I'(w_I + \varepsilon)N(\bar{y} - \varepsilon) \Pr \left\{ \sum_{i=1}^{N} \tilde{y}_i/N \leq \bar{y} - \varepsilon \right\}. \tag{37}$$

By Bernstein's inequality, there exists a constant $A(\varepsilon) > 0$ such that for any N

$$\Pr \left\{ \sum_{i=1}^{N} \tilde{y}_i/N \leq \bar{y} - \varepsilon \right\} \leq 2e^{-NA(\varepsilon)}. \tag{38}$$

Hence (37) implies that the intermediary's expected payoff from the intermediation policy $(L^N, \pi^N(\cdot), D^N, r_I^N(\cdot), p_I^N(\cdot))$ is no less than

$$u_I(w_I + \varepsilon) - 2u_I'(w_I + \varepsilon)N(\bar{y} - \varepsilon)e^{-NA(\varepsilon)}. \tag{39}$$

Since $\lim_{N \to \infty} Ne^{-NA(\varepsilon)} = 0$, it follows that for any sufficiently large N, this is larger than $u_I(w_I)$, the intermediary's payoff if he remains inactive. In combination with (36), this shows that for any sufficiently large N the policy $(L^N, \pi^N(\cdot), D^N, r_I^N(\cdot), p_I^N(\cdot))$ is viable.

Finally, an entrepreneur's payoff from the given intermediation policy is

$$\int u_E(w_E + L^N - I + y - \pi^N(y)) dG(y) = u_E(\hat{w}_E + \varepsilon). \tag{40}$$

As discussed above, the acceptability condition (22) for an incentive-compatible contract for direct finance is somewhat stronger than the break-even condition (23), so by definition of $\hat{w}_E$, the entrepreneur's expected payoff from any incentive-compatible and acceptable contract for direct finance cannot be greater than $u_E(\hat{w}_E)$. Since $u_E(\hat{w}_E) < u_E(\hat{w}_E + \varepsilon)$, the intermediation policy $(L^N, \pi^N(\cdot), D^N, r_I^N(\cdot), p_I^N(\cdot))$ fulfils the claim made in the proposition. ∥

Proposition 2 is exactly Diamond's result, generalized to allow for risk aversion of the entrepreneurs and the intermediary. With risk aversion, as with risk neutrality, delegation costs, i.e. the agency costs associated with the intermediary's own finance contract, are negligible if the number of independent projects financed by the intermediary is sufficiently large. Therefore, as in Diamond (1984), *the relative assessment of intermediated finance and direct finance hinges only on the comparison of the intermediary's monitoring costs with the agency costs of direct finance when there are many final investors.*

4. Intermediation and Risk Sharing

In the preceding analysis, intermediation provides for insurance as well as finance. The intermediation policy considered in (31)–(35) shifts all return risks from entrepreneurs to the intermediary. This suggests that intermediated finance may be advantageous because it provides for risk sharing, so the entrepreneurs may profit from intermediation even in situations where w exceeds I and it would be feasible to do without external finance altogether. The entrepreneurs want somebody else to share their risks; as a way to achieve this, intermediation with monitoring may be more effective or cheaper than direct finance with incentive contracting.

Following up on this observation, the present section looks at the allocation of risks under optimal intermediation policies. Given that different classes of agents are involved, "optimality" here is ambiguous and depends on whose interests one is concerned with. I will consider two classes of Pareto-optimal policies, entrepreneur-oriented policies and intermediary-oriented policies. An *optimal entrepreneur-oriented intermediation policy* will be one that maximizes the entrepreneurs' expected payoff subject to the condition that the policy be viable, i.e. that the intermediary's and the final investors' expected payoffs be at least equal to their payoffs in the absence of intermediation. An *optimal intermediary-oriented intermediation policy* will be one that maximizes the intermediary's expected payoff subject to the condition that the entrepreneurs and the final investors be at least as well off as they are in the absence of intermediation.

Under either notion of optimality, a detailed characterization of optimal intermediation policies seems out of the question. Optimality of an intermediation policy requires that the finance contract $(D, r_I(\cdot), p_I(\cdot))$ for the intermediary be an optimal incentive-compatible contract when the intermediary's own return from the entrepreneurs he finances is given by the random variable $\tilde{z} = \sum_{i=1}^{N} \pi(\tilde{y}_i)$. As discussed in Section 2, this implies that the form of the aggregate claim $r_I(\tilde{z})$ of the household sector on the intermediary depends on the distribution of $\tilde{z} = \sum_{i=1}^{N} \pi(\tilde{y}_i)$ as well as the participants' risk preferences. Even if the distribution of the intermediary's claim $\pi(\tilde{y}_i)$ on an individual entrepreneur has a simple form, such structure is lost as one looks at the sums $\sum_{i=1}^{N} \pi(\tilde{y}_i)$ for different N.

Even without a detailed characterization of optimal policies it is however possible to show that *any optimal intermediation policy must provide entrepreneurs with approximately full insurance of their return risks if the number of entrepreneurs N is large.* Equivalently, if $(\hat{L}, \hat{\pi}(\cdot))$ is a lending policy that does *not* provide the borrower with full insurance, any intermediation policy involving this lending policy will be dominated if N is sufficiently large.

The argument does not just rely on the intermediary's passing return risks on to the final investors. The intermediation policies that will be used to show that intermediation policies involving the lending policy $(\hat{L}, \hat{\pi}(\cdot))$ are dominated actually involve *debt finance* of the intermediary, with default probabilities of the intermediary going to zero as N becomes large. Asymptotically, under these policies, the intermediary will be bearing all risk in the economy as diversification across entrepreneurs makes him able and willing to assume all return risks even though he is risk averse and indeed his risk aversion may be bounded away from zero.

PROPOSITION 3. *Assume that if c is sufficiently large, the intermediary's absolute risk aversion, $-u_I''(c)/u_I'(c)$, is bounded above. Assume further that $w_E + \bar{y} - I - A > \overline{w}_E$ where $\overline{w}_E = \max(w_E, \overline{w}_E)$ is the best the entrepreneur can do in the absence of intermediation. For any N that is large enough so that there exists a viable intermediation policy which provides entrepreneurs with expected payoffs greater than or equal to $\overline{w}$, let $(L^{*N}, \pi^{*N}(\cdot), D^{*N}, r_I^{*N}(\cdot), p_I^{*N}(\cdot))$ be an optimal intermediary-oriented intermediation policy and consider the induced consumption pattern $c^{*N}(\tilde{y}_i)$ of entrepreneur i, where, for any $y \in [0, Y]$,*

$$c_E^{*N}(y) = w_E + L^{*N} - I + y - \pi^{*N}(y). \tag{41}$$

As N goes out of bounds, $c_E^{*N}(\tilde{y}_i)$ converges in distribution to the nonrandom constant $\overline{w}_E$.

Proof. In the first step of the proof I give an upper bound on the intermediary's expected payoff under the policy $(L^{*N}, \pi^{*N}(\cdot), D^{*N}, r_I^{*N}(\cdot), p_I^{*N}(\cdot))$. Let

$$\tilde{c}_I^{*N} := w_I + D^{*N} - NL^{*N} - NA + \sum_{i=1}^{N} \pi^{*N}(\tilde{y}_i) - r_I^{*N}\left(\sum_{i=1}^{N} \pi^{*N}(\tilde{y}_i)\right), \tag{42}$$

be the intermediary's consumption random variable under this policy. Given that the intermediary is risk averse, by inspection of (28), one finds that for any N, his expected payoff under the policy $(L^{*N}, \pi^{*N}(\cdot), D^{*N}, r_I^{*N}(\cdot), p_I^{*N}(\cdot))$ is bounded above by $u_I(E\tilde{c}_I^{*N})$, the payoff he would obtain if he got $E\tilde{c}_I^{*N}$ for sure, without any nonpecuniary penalties. Given that the final investors' utility function is also concave, by inspection of (29), one also finds that acceptability of the policy $(L^{*N}, \pi^{*N}(\cdot), D^{*N}, r_I^{*N}(\cdot), p_I^{*N}(\cdot))$ to final investors requires

$$D^{*N} - Er_I^{*N}\left(\sum_{i=1}^{N} \pi^{*N}(\tilde{y})\right) \leq 0. \tag{43}$$

Upon combining (42) with (43) and (41), one therefore obtains

$$E\tilde{c}_I^{*N} \leq E\left[w_I - NL^{*N} - NA + \sum_{i=1}^{N} \pi^{*N}(\tilde{y}_i)\right]$$

$$= w_I + N(w_E + \bar{y} - I - A) - \sum_{i=1}^{N} Ec_E^{*N}(\tilde{y}_i)$$

$$= w_I + N\left(K - A - \int_0^Y c_E^{*N}(y)\, dG(y)\right). \tag{44}$$

For any N, the intermediary's expected payoff from the optimal intermediary-oriented policy $(L^{*N}, \pi^{*N}(\cdot), D^{*N}, r_I^{*N}(\cdot), p_I^{*N}(\cdot))$ is thus no larger than $u_I(w_I + N(K - A - \int_0^Y c_E^{*N}(y)\,dG(y)))$.

Now suppose that the proposition is false. Then for any i, there exists a subsequence $\{c_E^{*N'}(\tilde{y}_i)\}$ of consumption patterns that fails to converge to $\bar{w}$ in distribution. Given the strict concavity of $u_E(\cdot)$ and the entrepreneurs' participation constraint

$$\int_0^Y u_E(c_E^{*N}(y))\,dG(y) \geq u_E(\bar{w}_E), \tag{45}$$

this implies that for some $\eta > 0$ one has

$$\int_0^Y c_E^{*N'}(y)\,dG(y) \geq \bar{w}_E + \eta, \tag{46}$$

and hence, from (44),

$$E\tilde{c}_I^{*N'} \leq \bar{c}_I^{N'} := w_I + N'(K - A - \bar{w}_E - \eta), \tag{47}$$

for all N'. The intermediary's expected payoff from the optimal policies $(L^{*N'}, \pi^{*N'}(\cdot), D^{*N'}, r_I^{*N'}(\cdot), p_I^{*N'}(\cdot))$ is thus bounded above by $u_I(\bar{c}_I^{N'}) = u_I(w_I + N'(K - A - \bar{w}_E - \eta))$, for any N'. I will show that this is not compatible with the presumed optimality of the intermediation policies $(L^{*N'}, \pi^{*N'}(\cdot), D^{*N'}, r_I^{*N'}(\cdot), p_I^{*N'}(\cdot))$ when N' is large.

For any N', consider an alternative intermediation policy such that

$$L^{N'} = I - w_E + \bar{w}_E, \tag{48}$$

$$\pi^{N'}(y) \equiv y, \tag{49}$$

$$D^{N'} = N'(L^{N'} + K - \bar{w}_E - \eta), \tag{50}$$

$$r_I^{N'}(z) \equiv \min[z, N'(\bar{y} - \eta/2)], \tag{51}$$

$$p_I^{N'}(z) \equiv u_I'(\bar{c}_I^{N'})\max[0, N'(\bar{y} - \eta/2) - z]. \tag{52}$$

Under this alternative intermediation policy, the intermediary finances entrepreneurs and provides them with a safe consumption equal to $\bar{w}_E$. The intermediary itself is financed by a debt contract with a debt service obligation equal to $N'(\bar{y} - \eta/2)$ and a minimum living allowance equal to the upper bound $\bar{c}_I^{N'}$ on his expected consumption under the presumed optimal policy $(L^{*N'}, \pi^{*N'}(\cdot), D^{*N'}, r_I^{*N'}(\cdot), p_I^{*N'}(\cdot))$.

By construction, the alternative policy $(L^{N'}, \pi^{N'}(\cdot), D^{N'}, r_I^{N'}(\cdot), p_I^{N'}(\cdot))$ provides entrepreneurs with the payoff $u_E(\bar{w}_E)$, so it satisfies their participation constraint.

As for the final investors, their expected payoff is

$$\int u_H \left(w_H + \frac{1}{N'M} \left(r_I^{N'} \left(\sum_{i=1}^{N'} \pi^{N'}(y_i) \right) - D^{N'} \right) \right) dG(y_1) \ldots dG(y_{N'})$$

$$= \int u_H \left(w_H + \frac{1}{M} \left(\min \left[\frac{1}{N'} \sum_{i=1}^{N'} y_i, \bar{y} - \frac{\eta}{2} \right] - \frac{D^{N'}}{N'} \right) \right) dG(y_1) \ldots dG(y_{N'}).$$

The law of large numbers in combination with Lebesgue's bounded convergence theorem ensures that for any sufficiently large N', this is no less than

$$u_H \left(w_H + \frac{1}{M} \left(\bar{y} - \frac{3\eta}{4} - (L^{N'} + K - \bar{w}_E - \eta) \right) \right)$$

$$= u_H \left(w_H + \frac{1}{M} \left(I - w_E - L^{N'} + \bar{w}_E + \frac{\eta}{4} \right) \right) > u_H(w_H), \qquad (53)$$

as required for acceptability to final investors.

Finally, the intermediary's expected payoff from the intermediation policy (48)–(52) is

$$\int \left[u_I \left(w_I + D^{N'} - N'L^{N'} - N'A + \sum_{i=1}^{N'} \pi^{N'}(y_i) - r_I^{N'} \left(\sum_{i=1}^{N'} \pi^{N'}(y_i) \right) \right) \right.$$

$$\left. -p_I^{N'} \left(\sum_{i=1}^{N'} \pi^{N'}(y_i) \right) \right] dG(y_1) \ldots dG(y_{N'})$$

$$= \int u_I \left(\bar{c}_I^{N'} + \max \left[\sum_{i=1}^{N} y_i - N'(\bar{y} - \eta/2), 0 \right] \right) dG(y_1) \ldots dG(y_{N'})$$

$$- \int_0^{N'(\bar{y}-\eta/2)} u_I'(\bar{c}_I^{N'}) \Pr \left\{ \sum_{i=1}^{N'} \tilde{y}_i \leq z \right\} dz$$

$$\geq u_I(\bar{c}_I^{N'}) + [u_I(\bar{c}_I^{N'} + N'\eta/4) - u_I(\bar{c}_I^{N'})] \Pr \left\{ \sum_{i=1}^{N'} \tilde{y}_i/N' \geq \bar{y} - \eta/4 \right\}$$

$$- u_I'(\bar{c}_I^{N'}) N'(\bar{y} - \eta/2) \Pr \left\{ \sum_{i=1}^{N'} \tilde{y}_i/N' \leq \bar{y} - \eta/2 \right\}. \qquad (54)$$

The assumption on the intermediary's risk aversion implies that for some $\sigma > 0$, one has $-u_I''(c)/u_I'(c) \leq \sigma$ for any sufficiently large c. By a straightforward integration, it follows that

$$u_I(\bar{c}_I^{N'} + N'\eta/4) \geq u_I(\bar{c}_I^{N'}) + u_I'(\bar{c}_I^{N'}) \frac{1 - e^{-\sigma \eta N'/4}}{\sigma}, \qquad (55)$$

for any sufficiently large N', at which point (54) implies that the intermediary's expected payoff under the alternative intermediation policy $(L^{N'}, \pi^{N'}(\cdot), D^{N'}, r_I^{N'}(\cdot), p_I^{N'}(\cdot))$ is bounded below by

$$u_I\left(\bar{c}_I^{N'}\right) + u_I'\left(\bar{c}_I^{N'}\right) \frac{1 - e^{-\sigma \eta N'/4}}{\sigma} \Pr\left\{\frac{1}{N'}\sum_{i=1}^{N'}\tilde{y}_i \geq \bar{y} - \frac{\eta}{4}\right\}$$

$$- u_I'\left(\bar{c}_I^{N'}\right) N'\left(\bar{y} - \frac{\eta}{2}\right) \Pr\left\{\frac{1}{N'}\sum_{i=1}^{N'}\tilde{y}_i \leq \bar{y} - \frac{\eta}{2}\right\}. \tag{56}$$

Now the law of large numbers implies that $\Pr\{\sum_{i=1}^{N'}\tilde{y}_i/N' \geq \bar{y} - \eta/4\}$ converges to one as N' becomes large. Moreover, Bernstein's inequality (Rényi (1979), p. 324) implies that $\Pr\{\sum_{i=1}^{N'}\tilde{y}_i/N' \leq \bar{y} - \eta/2\}$ converges to zero, exponentially in N', and

$$N'(\bar{y} - \eta/2) \Pr\left\{\sum_{i=1}^{N'}\tilde{y}_i/N' \leq \bar{y} - \eta/2\right\}$$

converges to zero as N' becomes large. But then for any sufficiently large N', (56) must exceed $u_I(\bar{c}_I^{N'}) + u_I'(\bar{c}_I^{N'})/2\sigma$, and the intermediary's expected payoff from the policy $(L^{N'}, \pi^{N'}(\cdot), D^{N'}, r_I^{N'}(\cdot), p_I^{N'}(\cdot))$ must be strictly greater than $u_I(\bar{c}_I^{N'})$. Given that $u_I(\bar{c}_I^{N'})$ has been shown to be an upper bound on his expected payoff from the policy $(L^{*N'}, \pi^{*N'}(\cdot), D^{*N'}, r_I^{*N'}(\cdot), p_I^{*N'}(\cdot))$, it follows that the policy $(L^{*N'}, \pi^{*N'}(\cdot), D^{*N'}, r_I^{*N'}(\cdot), p_I^{*N'}(\cdot))$ cannot be optimal. The assumption that $c_E^{*N}(\tilde{y}_i)$ fails to converge in distribution to $\bar{w}$ has thus led to a contradiction and must be false. ‖

A key element in the proof of Proposition 3 is the endogeneity of the intermediary's minimum living allowance. As indicated by (52) and (54), in the alternative intermediation policies $(L^{N'}, \pi^{N'}(\cdot), D^{N'}, r_I^{N'}(\cdot), p_I^{N'}(\cdot))$, the intermediary's living allowance is equal to $\bar{c}_I^{N'}$, which goes out of bounds with N'. This is important because it implies that the marginal-utility weights in the nonpecuniary default penalties go to zero as N' becomes large. As indicated by (56), this in turn is crucial for the assessment that nonpecuniary default penalties are negligible relative to the consumption gains from the alternative intermediation policies. If the marginal-utility weights in the nonpecuniary default penalties were independent of the number of entrepreneurs the intermediary finances, this assessment would not be valid any more. Although the consumption gains from the alternative intermediation policies would be large, their effects on the intermediary's utility might be small relative to their effects on penalty costs as, e.g. with absolute risk aversion bounded away from zero, his utility itself would be bounded above. If the intermediary were constrained to finance himself by debt contracts with an exogenously given living allowance, the conclusion of Proposition 3 would therefore not generally be true.[11]

Interestingly, the analogous result for optimal entrepreneur-oriented intermediation policies does not require these endogenous living allowances. Like the proof of Proposition 2, the proof of the following proposition relies on intermediation policies that involve debt finance of the intermediary with a fixed minimum living allowance that is independent of the number of entrepreneurs.

PROPOSITION 4. *For any N that is large enough so that a viable intermediation policy exists, let* $(L^{*N}, \pi^{*N}(\cdot), D^{*N}, r_I^{*N}(\cdot), p_I^{*N}(\cdot))$ *be an optimal entrepreneur-oriented intermediation policy, and consider the induced consumption pattern* $c_E^{*N}(\tilde{y}_i)$ *of entrepreneur i, where, for any* $y \in [0, Y]$, $c_E^{*N}(y) \equiv w_E + L^{*N} - I + y - \pi^{*N}(y)$, *in (41). As N goes out of bounds,* $c_E^{*N}(\tilde{y}_i)$ *converges in distribution to the nonrandom constant* $K - A$.
Proof. I first show that for any N, one has

$$\int_0^Y c_E^{*N}(y)\, dG(y) \leqq K - A. \tag{57}$$

As discussed in the proof of Proposition 3, for any N, the intermediary's expected payoff from the policy $(L^{*N}, \pi^{*N}(\cdot), D^{*N}, r_I^{*N}(\cdot), p_I^{*N}(\cdot))$ is bounded above by $u_I(E\tilde{c}_I^{*N})$ where $\tilde{c}_I^{*N}$ is given by (42) and is the intermediary's consumption random variable under the given optimal intermediation policy. Therefore the intermediary's participation constraint requires $E_{\tilde{c}_I}^{*N} \geqq w_I$, and hence, by (42),

$$D^{*N} + \sum_{i=1}^N E\pi^{*N}(\tilde{y}_i) \geq N(L^{*N} + A) + Er_I^{*N}\left(\sum_{i=1}^N \pi^{*N}(\tilde{y}_i)\right). \tag{58}$$

Given that, as discussed in the proof of Proposition 3, the final investors' participation constraint implies $Er_I^{*N}\left(\sum_{i=1}^N \pi^{*N}(\tilde{y}_i)\right) \leq D^{*N}$, (58) yields

$$\sum_{i=1}^N E\pi^{*N}(\tilde{y}_i) = NE\pi^{*N}(\tilde{y}_1) \geqq N(L^{*N} + A). \tag{59}$$

Therefore (41) implies

$$Ec_E^{*N}(\tilde{y}_i) = w_E + L^{*N} - I + \bar{y} - E\pi^{*N}(\tilde{y}_i)$$
$$\leqq w_E + L^{*N} - I + \bar{y} - L^{*N} - A$$
$$= K - A, \tag{60}$$

as claimed.

---

[11] For a systematic discussion of this issue, see Hellwig (1995), Section 3, as well as Section 5 below.

Now consider the entrepreneurs' expected payoff, $\int u(c^{*N}(y))\, dG(y)$, from the intermediation policy $(L^{*N}, \pi^{*N}(\cdot), D^{*N}, r_I^{*N}(\cdot), p_I^{*N}(\cdot))$. From (57) and the concavity of $u_E(\cdot)$, one has

$$\int_0^Y u_E(c^{*N}(y))\, dG(y) \lessgtr u_E(K - A),\qquad (61)$$

for all N. Moreover the argument in the proof of Proposition 2, with $\hat{w}$ replaced by $K - A - \eta$, shows that for any $\eta > 0$ and any sufficiently large N, there exists a viable intermediation policy $(L^N, \pi^N(\cdot), D^N, r_I^N(\cdot), p_I^N(\cdot))$ that satisfies

$$\int_0^Y u_E(c^N(y))\, dG(y) \geqq K - A - \eta.$$

This in turn implies that the optimal entrepreneur-oriented intermediation policy $(L^{*N}, \pi^{*N}(\cdot), D^{*N}, r_I^{*N}(\cdot), p_I^{*N}(\cdot))$ must satisfy

$$\int_0^Y u_E(c^{*N}(y))\, dG(y) \geqq K - A - \eta,\qquad (62)$$

for any $\eta > 0$ and any sufficiently large N. From (61) and (62), it follows that $\int_0^Y u_E(c^{*N}(y))\, dG(y)$ converges to $u_E(K - A)$ as N goes out of bounds. In view of (57) and the strict concavity of $u_E(\cdot)$, this is only possible if the consumption patterns $c_E^{*N}(\tilde{y}_i)$ converge in distribution to the constant $K - A$ as N goes out of bounds. $\|$

Proposition 4 should be compared to a result of Krasa (1988) showing that *under risk neutrality* an optimal entrepreneur-oriented intermediation policy will necessarily involve *debt finance* of entrepreneurs with repayment functions $\hat{\pi}^N(\cdot)$ of the form

$$\hat{\pi}^N(y) = w_E + \hat{L}^N - I + \min(y, \hat{y}^N),\qquad (63)$$

without any living allowance and corresponding consumption patterns $\hat{c}^N(\cdot)$ of the form

$$\hat{c}^N(y) = \max(0, y - \hat{y}^N).\qquad (64)$$

Krasa's result is based on the observation that nonpecuniary penalties in the intermediary's own finance contract induce a kind of quasi risk aversion on the side of the financial intermediary. A mean-preserving spread in the returns available to the intermediary will put more weight on the tails of the intermediary's return distribution, including the lower tail where bankruptcy penalties are needed to preserve incentive compatibility of the contract. A mean-preserving spread in the returns available to the intermediary will therefore raise expected nonpecuniary penalties in the intermediary's own finance contract and, other things being equal, lower the intermediary's expected net payoff. Given this quasi risk aversion of the intermediary and given the risk neutrality of entrepreneurs, an optimal intermediation policy will leave as much risk with the entrepreneurs as possible. Given the feasibility constraint (24), this criterion singles out the consumption pattern (64) which corresponds to debt finance of the entrepreneurs without any living allowance.[12]

In contrast, Proposition 4 shows that when the entrepreneurs as well as the intermediary are risk averse the risk allocation may be reversed. If there are enough entrepreneurs for the law of large numbers to come into play, an optimal entrepreneur-oriented intermediation policy leaves little risk with the entrepreneurs and instead places all risks with the intermediary and/or the final investors. Because of the large-numbers effect, the intermediary's concern for the lower tail of the distribution, which is at the heart of Krasa's argument, is outweighed by the entrepreneurs' desire to get rid of risk altogether.

5. Risk Aversion with Respect to Default Penalties

In this section, I consider to what extent the preceding results depend on the specification of nonpecuniary penalties. In Sections 3 and 4 payoffs were assumed to be additively separable in default penalties and consumption. This assumption is quite special. It is to some extent justified if one can identify nonpecuniary default penalties with losses of future opportunities that are due to adverse interventions of creditors. With intertemporal additive separability of utility, one can then interpret $p_I(z)$ as a conditional expectation of the present value of these losses when the intermediary reports the return realization z. This conditional expectation depends on the final investors' reactions to the report z, namely, the (conditional) probability with which they intervene to impose those future opportunity losses on the intermediary as well as the actual losses when they do intervene (see, e.g. Povel and Raith (1999)).

However, if one thinks of default penalties in terms of debtor's prison, loss of social standing, and the like, it is no longer clear that additive separability is a suitable assumption, nor even what a suitable assumption might be. Additive separability has the awkward implication that the debtor is risk neutral with respect to the penalty. For a given pair $(\tilde{c}, \tilde{p})$ of state-contingent consumption and nonpecuniary penalty, the expected utility $Eu_I(\tilde{c}) - E\tilde{p}$ depends on $\tilde{p}$ *only* through its expected value. One may therefore wonder what happens to the results of Sections 3 and 4 if the intermediary exhibits risk aversion with respect to nonpecuniary penalties as well as consumption.

---

[12] That debt is the optimal financial contract for a risk neutral entrepreneur and a risk averse financier under perfect information had also been shown by Freixas, see Freixas and Rochet (1997), p. 92.

Without any pretense of generality, I investigate this question for the case when the intermediary's von Neumann–Morgenstern utility function $u_I(\cdot)$ is defined on the entire real line rather than just $\Re_+$ and his expected payoff from a given pair $(\tilde{c}, \tilde{p})$ of state-contingent consumption and nonpecuniary penalty is equal to $Eu_I(\tilde{c} - \tilde{p})$. In this specification the nonpecuniary penalty is defined in terms of equivalent units of consumption losses, and the intermediary's risk aversion affects his assessment of the penalty just as it affects his assessment of his consumption. Special though it is, this formulation turns out to be convenient for illustrating when and why the specification of default penalties may make a difference to the analysis of financial intermediation with risk aversion.

Given the utility specification $u_I(c - p)$, the intermediary's payoff expectation (28) from an intermediation policy $(L, \pi(\cdot), D, r_I(\cdot), p_I(\cdot))$ (with monitoring committed *ex ante*) is replaced by

$$\int u_I \left[w_I + D - NL - NA + \sum_{i=1}^{N} \pi(y_i) - r_I \left(\sum_{i=1}^{N} \pi(y_i) \right) - p_I \left(\sum_{i=1}^{N} \pi(y_i) \right) \right]$$

$$\times \, dG(y_1) \dots dG(y_N). \tag{65}$$

The question is how this modification affects the viability of intermediation and the comparative assessment of intermediation policies by the intermediary.

To answer this question, I note that with the utility specification $u_I(c - p)$ a standard debt contract with bankruptcy point $\hat{z}$ for the intermediary is incentive-compatible if the penalty function satisfies

$$p_I(z) = \max(0, \hat{z} - z), \tag{66}$$

for all realizations z of the intermediary's gross return.[13] Thus the intermediation policy $(L, \pi(\cdot), D, r_I(\cdot), p_I(\cdot))$ that is given by (31)–(34) and (66) with $\bar{z} = N(\tilde{y} - \epsilon)$ is incentive-compatible in this setting. The intermediary's expected payoff from this policy is equal to

$$\int u_I \left(w_I + \varepsilon + \sum_{i=1}^{N} y_i - r_I \left(\sum_{i=1}^{N} y_i \right) - p_I \left(\sum_{i=1}^{N} y_i \right) \right) dG(y_1) \dots dG(y_N)$$

$$= \int u_I \left(w_I + \varepsilon + \sum_{i=1}^{N} y_i - N(\bar{y} - \varepsilon) \right) dG(y_1) \dots dG(y_N), \tag{67}$$

since obviously $r_I(z) + p_I(z) = N(\bar{y} - \epsilon)$ for all z.

---

[13] As in Diamond (1984), one can actually show that regardless of the specification of the intermediary's lending policy, it is optimal for him to be financed by a standard debt contract with a zero living allowance and penalty function (66).

The question of whether in this setting the intermediation policy $(L, \pi(\cdot), D, r_I(\cdot), p_I(\cdot))$ is acceptable to the intermediary is thus equivalent to the question of whether an expected-utility maximizer with von Neumann–Morgenstern utility function $u_I(\cdot)$ defined on the entire real line is willing to accept any sufficiently large compound of the independent, identically distributed gambles $\tilde{y}_i - \bar{y} + \varepsilon, i = 1, 2, \ldots$, with the common expected value $\varepsilon > 0$. This is precisely the question treated by Nielsen (1985). According to his main result (Proposition 1, p. 467, see also Theorem 2, p. 305, in Hellwig (1995)), the acceptability of any sufficiently large compound of the independent, identically distributed gambles $\tilde{y}_i - \bar{y} + \varepsilon, i = 1, 2, \ldots$, can be affirmed regardless of other properties of the distribution of $\tilde{y}_i - \bar{y} + \varepsilon$ if and only if $u_I(\cdot)$ satisfies the following:

Condition 5. For any $\lambda > 0$, there exists $c \in \Re$ such that for any $c - p < c, u_I(c - p) \geq -e^{\lambda c}$, i.e. as $c - p$ goes to $-\infty, u_I(c - p)$ does not go exponentially fast to $-\infty$.

To understand the role of this condition, recall that the analysis of the viability of financial intermediation rests on Bernstein's inequality implying that in an N-fold compound of independent, identically distributed random variables, the probability of an outlier of order of magnitude N is small, exponentially in N. If the negative weights assigned to negative outliers of order of magnitude N grow less than exponentially with N, any effect of these outliers on the decision maker's assessment of the compound will be swamped by the mean $N\varepsilon$ going out of bounds as N becomes large. In contrast, if the negative weights assigned to negative outliers of order of magnitude N are exponentially large, these outliers need not become negligible as N goes out of bounds. The decision maker's assessment of any large compound of the gambles $\tilde{y}_i - \bar{y} + \varepsilon$ will then depend on the details of the "tradeoff" of probabilities becoming exponentially small and negative weights becoming exponentially large as N becomes large.

If the intermediary's utility function $u_I(\cdot)$ satisfies Nielsen's condition, the conclusions of this chapter about the viability of intermediation and about optimal entrepreneur-oriented intermediation policies remain valid without change, i.e. if monitoring is committed ex ante and monitoring costs are less than the agency costs of direct finance, then for large N, intermediation is viable (Proposition 2) and optimal entrepreneur-oriented intermediation policies provide entrepreneurs with approximately full insurance of their return risks (Proposition 4). If monitoring is chosen ex ante, but can be made contingent on returns, a similar conclusion is obtained, namely, when N is large, optimal entrepreneur-oriented intermediation policies provide entrepreneurs with approximately the optimal incentive-compatible contracts that they would obtain in contracting with a risk neutral non-wealth-constrained financier.

In contrast, the asymptotic characterization of optimal *intermediary-oriented* intermediation policies in Proposition 3 does not carry over to the present setting *unless* the intermediary's utility function $u_I(\cdot)$ satisfies a further condition.

The choice of an intermediation policy to maximize the intermediary's payoff expectation under participation constraints for entrepreneurs and households goes beyond the question of acceptability, i.e. the comparison of a given intermediation policy with the initial position of the intermediary. This choice requires a comparison of different policies all of which provide the intermediary with positive net benefits. As the number of entrepreneurs N increases, the base on which the intermediary collects this benefit is increased and the intermediary experiences a positive income effect. This income effect in turn will influence his attitude towards the risks inherent in different lending policies. In consequence, even if Nielsen's condition holds, it is *not* generally true that if only there are enough entrepreneurs, his relative assessment of two lending policies will *only* depend on the expected net returns per borrower. Risk considerations may drive his choice between lending policies regardless of how large the number of loan clients may be.

For the abstract decision problem of an expected-utility maximizer with von Neumann–Morgenstern utility function $u_I(\cdot)$ choosing between two compounds of independent, identically distributed gambles, Hellwig (1995) introduces the additional.

Condition 6. For any $v > 0$ and any $\alpha \in (0, 1)$, there exists $\hat{c} \in \Re_+$ such that $u_I(c) - u_I(\alpha c) \geq -e^{-vc} + e^{-\alpha vc}$ for all $c \leq \hat{c}$.

In combination with Condition 5 and concavity of $u_I(\cdot)$ on $\Re_+$, Condition 6 is necessary and sufficient to ensure that in choosing between the two compounds $\sum \tilde{X}_i, \sum \tilde{Y}_i$, the decision maker will exhibit a preference for the one with the higher mean, regardless of other properties of the distribution of $\tilde{X}_i$ and $\tilde{Y}_i$, if only the number of gambles N in each compound is sufficiently large (see Theorems 4, p. 310, and 5, p. 312, in Hellwig (1995)). Given this result, it is easy to see that the asymptotic characterization of optimal intermediary-oriented intermediation policies in Proposition 3 will remain valid in the present setting, with (65) rather than (28) determining the intermediary's assessment of intermediation policies, *if and only if* the intermediary's utility function $u_I(\cdot)$ satisfies Condition 6 as well as Condition 5.

Condition 6 is just slightly weaker than the assumption that the intermediary's degree of absolute risk aversion, $-u_I''(c - p)/u_I'(c - p)$, goes to zero as $c - p$ goes out of bounds.[14] As the number of loan clients becomes large, any intermediation policy that enables him to earn a strictly positive expected return per loan client will eventually make his final consumption exceed any given bound with a probability arbitrarily close to one. If his risk aversion goes to zero as his

---

[14] Similarly, Nielsen's condition is just slightly weaker than the condition that the intermediary's degree of absolute risk aversion go to zero as c converges to $-\infty$. Both Nielsen's condition and Hellwig's condition are violated if absolute risk aversion is everywhere bounded away from zero.

consumption goes out of bounds, this means that his evaluation of such intermediation policies involves almost exclusively that part of the domain of his utility function where his risk aversion is small. Asymptotically his choices between intermediation policies are then driven *only* by the means of returns per loan client that the policies generate; being "risk neutral in the limit", he is willing to avail himself of any risk premium that risk averse entrepreneurs are willing to provide in return for being delivered from return risks.

In summary, if the utility specification $u_I(c) - p$ is replaced by the specification $u_I(c-p)$, which allows for risk aversion with respect to the penalty p as well as the level of consumption c, all the major results of this paper remain valid provided that (i) the behaviour of $u_I(\cdot)$ at large negative values of $c - p$ does not induce the decision maker to attach exponentially large weight to extreme negative outliers, and (ii) the behaviour of $u_I(\cdot)$ at large positive values of $c - p$ does not induce the decision maker to attach exponentially small weight to large positive gains from following the intermediation policy that maximizes his expected return. It seems reasonable to conjecture that suitable adaptations of these conditions will be necessary and sufficient to ensure the validity of analogous results under other utility specifications as well, i.e. to ensure that if monitoring costs are less than the agency costs of direct finance, then asymptotically, as the number of entrepreneurs to be financed goes out of bounds, intermediation becomes viable and optimal intermediation policies involve the assumption of all return risks by the intermediary.

In Sections 2–4, there was no need to impose the analogues of Conditions 5 and 6 as explicit assumptions. An analogue of Condition 5 was implicit in the fact that the specifications (34), (35) and (51), (52) of debt contracts used in the proof of Propositions 2–4 involve nonpecuniary penalties growing *linearly* with shortfalls of returns from debt service obligations. A substitute for Condition 6 was implicit in the specification (51), (52) of debt contracts involving living allowances that are large and nonpecuniary penalties that are small if the number of entrepreneurs financed by the intermediary is large; this neutralizes the income effects of the intermediary's financing many entrepreneurs and earning positive expected returns from all of them. Indeed if living allowances in debt contracts were taken to be exogenous, the conclusion of Proposition 3 would not in general be true; in this case, Condition 6 would again be necessary (and, with Condition 5, sufficient) for optimal intermediary-oriented intermediation policies to be asymptotically assuming all risks from entrepreneurs.

The preceding discussion raises the intriguing possibility that for certain specifications of the intermediary's preferences the asymptotic characterization of risk sharing under optimal intermediation policies may depend on the relative bargaining strengths of entrepreneurs and the intermediary. In those cases where Condition 5 is satisfied, but Condition 6 is not, optimal intermediation policies will asymptotically involve a full transfer of return risks from entrepreneurs to the intermediary if the bargaining power lies with the entrepreneurs, but *not* if it lies with the intermediary. The characterization of optimal intermediary-oriented intermediation policies in such cases is an intriguing topic for further research.

References

Besanko, D., and Kanatas, G. (1993). "Credit market equilibrium with bank monitoring and moral hazard." *Review of Financial Studies*, 6: 212–32.

Bolton, P., and Freixas, X. (1998). "A dilution cost approach to financial intermediation and securities markets." Discussion Paper No. 305, Financial Markets Group, London School of Economics.

Calomiris, C., and Kahn, C. (1991). "The role of demandable debt in structuring optimal banking arrangements." *American Economic Review*, 81: 497–513.

——(1984). "Financial intermediation and delegated monitoring." *Review of Economic Studies*, 51: 393–414.

Diamond, D. (1991). "Monitoring and reputation: The choice between bank loans and directly placed debt." *Journal of Political Economy*, 99: 689–721.

Fischer, K. (1990). "Hausbankbeziehungen als Instrument der Bindung zwischen Banken und Unternehmen: Eine theoretische und empirische Analyse." Doctoral Dissertation, University of Bonn.

Freixas, X., and Rochet, J. C. (1997). *Microeconomics of Banking*. Cambridge: MIT Press.

Gale, D., and Hellwig, M. F. (1985). "Incentive-compatible debt contracts: The one-period problem." *Review of Economic Studies*, 52: 647–63.

Goldman, M. B. (1974). "A negative report on the 'near optimality' of the max-expected-log policy as applied to bounded utilities for long-lived programs." *Journal of Financial Economics*, 1: 97–163.

Hellwig, M. F. (1991). "Banking, financial intermediation and corporate finance," in A. Giovannini and C. Mayer (eds.), *European Financial Integration* (Cambridge: Cambridge University Press), 35–63.

——(1994). "Liquidity provision, banking, and the allocation of interest rate risk." *European Economic Review*, 38: 1363–89.

——(1995). "The assessment of large compounds of independent gambles." *Journal of Economic Theory*, 67: 299–326.

——(1998a). "Banks, markets and the allocation of risks." *Journal of Institutional and Theoretical Economics*, 154: 328–45.

——(1998b). "Allowing for risk choices in diamond's 'financial intermediation as delegated monitoring'." Discussion Paper No. 98-04, Sonderforschungsbereich 504, University of Mannheim.

——(1998c). "Risk aversion and incentive compatibility with *ex post* information asymmetry." *Economic Theory* (forthcoming).

——(1999). "Financial intermediation with risk aversion." Discussion Paper No. 98-39 (rev.), Sonderforschungsbereich 504, University of Mannheim.

Krasa, S. (1988). "Optimality of debt contracts for financial intermediaries." Research Paper No. 1041, Graduate School of Business, Stanford University.

——, and Villamil, A. P. (1992). "Monitoring the monitor: An incentive structure for a financial intermediary." *Journal of Economic Theory*, 57: 197–221.

Nielsen, L. T. (1985). "Attractive compounds of unattractive investments and gambles." *Scandinavian Journal of Economics*, 87: 463–73.

Povel, P., and Raith, M. (1999). "Endogenous debt contracts with undistorted incentives." Discussion Paper No. 99-61, Sonderforschungsbereich 504, University of Mannheim.

Rajan, R. (1992). "Insiders and outsiders: The choice between relationship and arm's length debt." *Journal of Finance*, 47: 1367–400.

Rényi, A. (1979). *Wahrscheinlichkeitsrechnung*, VEB Deutscher Verlag der Wissenschaften, Berlin.

Samuelson, P. A. (1963). "Risk and uncertainty: A fallacy of large numbers." *Scientia*, 6th Series, 57th Year, 1–6.

Sharpe, S. (1990). "Asymmetric information, bank lending, and implicit contracts: A stylized model of customer relationships." *Journal of Finance*, 45: 1069–87.

Townsend, R. M. (1979). "Optimal contracts and competitive markets with costly state verification." *Journal of Economic Theory*, 21: 1–29.

von Thadden, E. L. (1992). "The commitment of finance, duplicated monitoring and the investment horizon." WWZ Discussion Paper, University of Basel.

——(1995). "Long-term contracts, short-term investments and monitoring." *Review of Economic Studies*, 62: 557–75.

Yanelle, M. O. (1997). "Banking competition and market efficiency." *Review of Economic Studies*, 64: 215–39.

Monitoring by and of Banks: A Discussion

Sudipto Bhattacharya, Arnoud W. A. Boot, and Anjan V. Thakor

1. Introduction

A key paradigm in the modern literature on financial intermediation is that informational asymmetries and moral hazard across borrowers and investors are central to understanding the role of financial intermediaries (FIs). This literature has shown that FIs attenuate information-related problems more efficaciously than is possible with direct (non-intermediated) financing transactions in financial markets, because of free-rider problems, coordination failures and duplicated monitoring costs among dispersed investors. The role of FIs is then to provide delegated monitoring and/or screening services on behalf of investors.

In important papers in this literature, Leland and Pyle (1977), Diamond (1984), Ramakrishnan and Thakor (1984), and Boyd and Prescott (1986; see Chapter One) rationalize the existence of FIs on these grounds. The primary question addressed in these papers is how an FI can be incented to perform its monitoring or screening role on behalf of investors. More specifically, in its role as a delegated monitor/screener, the FI "resolves" the agency problem between the borrower and those who invest in the borrower through the FI, but a new agency problem emerges now between the FI and its investors. An important contribution of the Diamond and Ramakrishnan–Thakor papers is to show that well-diversified FIs represent the cost-efficient solution to this delegation/agency problem between the FI and its investors.

The types of intermediaries that emerge in these papers are, however, quite different. Diamond (1984) rationalizes depository FIs that provide on-balance-sheet funding to borrowers, financed through deposits from investors. The FI in this framework provides post-financing monitoring of borrowers and engages in *asset transformation*, that is, the claims of investors on the FI differ in risk from those that the FI has on its borrowers. By contrast, Ramakrishnan and Thakor (1984) rationalize non-depository FIs—essentially coalitions of information sellers like credit rating agencies—that provide pre-financing screening services *without* engaging in funding. This coalitional view is also present in the paper of Boyd and Prescott (1986), included in this part (Chapter One), which we will discuss here as well.

It is interesting that even in this early literature, part of the focus was on FIs that emerge as pure information sellers that eschew borrower funding; this role of FIs as information sellers has been explored in later research as well (e.g. Allen 1990). Innovations like securitization, which has been growing rapidly in banking since the 1980s, provide a somewhat mixed role for FIs, where a FI initially provides funding and then takes these assets off its books, transferring funding to the capital market. The complementarity and substitutability between bank and financial market funding is an important topic in various parts in this book (see Parts V and VI). For now, we will focus on the role of FIs as delegated monitors/screeners.

2. Formalization of FIs as Delegated Monitors/Screeners: Monitoring by Banks and Monitoring of Banks

In this section, we first explain the types of informational problems that lead to the emergence of FIs. We begin with an examination of non-intermediated outcomes, and then continue with an examination of how FIs improve on such outcomes. The key insight is that, on the one hand, FIs arise to monitor/screen borrowers, and on the other hand, they must themselves be credibly monitored/screened by the investors who provide them funding. Much of the discussion in what follows is based on Bhattacharya and Thakor (1993).

2.1 Non-intermediated Outcome

Consider an economy with n investment projects, each having uncertain returns and $N > n$ primary investors. Each investor has one unit of endowment of the single commodity to invest, and each project requires $I > 1$ units of investment. Projects are initiated by entrepreneurs who are privately informed about either (i) the ex ante prospects of their projects, as in Ramakrishnan and Thakor (1984) and Boyd and Prescott (1986; Chapter One), or (ii) the realized (ex post) payoffs on their projects, as in Diamond (1984). The economy lasts for only these two periods and all consumption takes place in the second period. Cash flows are imperfectly correlated across projects; for simplicity, in scenario (ii), these are assumed to be independently, identically distributed (i.i.d.) random variables. Outside (non-entrepreneur) investors have two means of eliciting information about projects:

(a) In scenario (i), investors can acquire information either directly by incurring a monitoring (observation/auditing) cost of K per project or indirectly by inferring it from the undiversified project holdings of strictly risk-averse entrepreneurs (Leland and Pyle 1977). That is, the project holding of the entrepreneur acts as a signal, with a per-project signaling cost of s, and a total cost of ns for n projects. The total monitoring cost M for N investors and n projects is $M \in [NK, NnK]$, where the cost NK is incurred if there is no diversification by investors (and hence little duplication) who invest all of their wealth in a single project and NnK is the cost incurred with full diversification involving all investors spreading their wealth across all n projects.

(b) In scenario (ii), each investor can obtain this information either directly by incurring a monitoring/auditing cost of K per project, leading to a total cost of NK, or indirectly by inferring it from the entrepreneur's decision to repay investors the amount D initially borrowed from them. If repayment occurs, investors can infer that the project payoff exceeded D; if the entrepreneur fails to make the payment, he or she suffers a non-pecuniary penalty P which is sufficiently great to ensure that D is paid whenever the realized payoff allows it, so investors can infer that the realized payoff was below D in the event of default.[1] The probability that the penalty P will be

---

[1] The penalty P must be a dissipative cost. Moreover, it is not an exogenous bankruptcy cost; it is determined *endogenously* by the lender to ensure that the entrepreneur pays the debt obligation to the extent permitted by cash flow. These restrictions make it difficult to relate the model to debt contracting in practice. Diamond (1984) states that P could be interpreted either as the entrepreneur's loss in reputation due to default or as physical punishment. The reputational interpretation is strained, however, since the (competitive) lender would not be able to calibrate the damage to the borrower's reputation in order to guarantee repayment. Note also that: "monitoring" refers to ex post cash flow auditing rather than pre-cash-flow-realization scrutiny of the borrower's actions in order to alter the cash flow distribution.

Table 1. Resolutions of Information Asymmetries in the Non-intermediated Case

Scenario	Cost of information acquisition through direct monitoring	Indirect information acquisition via entrepreneurial shareholding or payout commitment
(i) Ex ante informational asymmetry, risk-averse agents	$M \in [NK, NnK]$, where the monitoring cost M depends on extent of diversification desired by the risk-averse investor (M increases with the desired degree of diversification)	ns
(ii) Ex post informational asymmetry, risk-neutral agents	$M = NK$	$n \times P \times \pi(D)$

incurred is $\pi(D)$, so that the per-project expected penalty is $P \times \pi(D)$, and the total expected penalty over n projects is $n \times P \times \pi(D)$.

Assuming that all projects are funded ($nI = N$), the cost of resolving informational asymmetries by the two methods outlined above, neither involving intermediaries, are summarized in Table 1.

2.2 Diversified intermediaries

Now, suppose that a single FI monitors or audits the (ex ante) quality of the (ex post) outcome of each project, resulting in a cost of nK, which is less than the direct monitoring cost, M, in the nonintermediated outcome in either scenario (i) or (ii). However, the FI must now credibly communicate to its primary investors the value of its assets. This may require that the FI incur a signaling cost of S in scenario (i), or suffer nonpecuniary penalties of nP with probability $\pi^n(D)$ in scenario (ii); the penalty must increase in proportion to scale to ensure incentive compatibility in the ex post reporting of the n-fold larger cash flows. Therefore, intermediation is Pareto-improving if

$$\min[M, ns] > [nK + S] \quad \text{(Scenario (i))} \tag{1A}$$
$$\min[M, nP\pi(D)] > [nK + nP\pi^n(D)] \quad \text{(Scenario (ii))} \tag{1B}$$

Diamond (1984) examines whether (1A) and (1B) will be satisfied under plausible conditions, if only asymptotically as n becomes large (holding N/n constant).

In scenario (ii), with risk-neutral agents, the answer is transparently yes. Since $\pi^n(D)$ is the probability that the sample average of cash flows across n i.i.d. projects will be less than D, the weak law of large numbers implies that (1B) holds for n sufficiently large, with a fixed $N/n > 1$ along the limiting sequence, if D is strictly less than the population mean of the n i.i.d. project cash flows.

What about scenario (i)? In the exponential-utility-and-normal-distributions model of Leland and Pyle (1977)—where entrepreneurs possess private information about mean cash flows which they signal through undiversified insider holdings—feasibility is unclear. If the FIs have the same exponential utility as the entrepreneurs, each of whom is monitored at cost K, then $S = ns$. The reason is that, with (negative) exponential utility, the certainty equivalent of the sum of two independent risks $(\tilde{A} + \tilde{B})$ is simply the sum of the certainty equivalents of $\tilde{A}$ and $\tilde{B}$. Hence, with $S = ns$, (1A) cannot be satisfied with $K > 0$. However, if the FIs are *coalitions of agents* who can ensure each other's monitoring efforts and jointly signal the value of the diversified package of n projects, say with observable insider holdings, then $S < ns$. Hence, for n sufficiently large, so that the signaling costs of excessive insider holdings are lowered sufficiently, and a given $N/n > 1$, (1A) would ultimately be satisfied. Ramakrishnan and Thakor (1984) show that intermediation is beneficial because cooperation among the risk-averse agents comprising the intermediary results in two positive externalities. One is improved risk sharing, attainable because the prospects of individual agents are imperfectly correlated. The second and less obvious gain comes from the amelioration of moral hazard since the effort of each agent stochastically increases that agent's direct payoff as well as the total payoff of the intermediary, a share of which accrues to that agent.[2]

If in the ex post informational asymmetry environment of scenario (ii), if agents who individually intermediate "diversified" aggregates of projects are assumed to be risk averse, intermediation may arise only under somewhat restrictive conditions. In Diamond (1984), the restrictions noted on

---

[2] The result that an intermediary consisting of numerous agents who *cooperate*—in the sense that they allocate aggregate effort as a team—can improve upon the outcome attainable through bilateral contracting is a special case of the result that cooperation is of value under fairly general conditions. See Ramakrishnan and Thakor (1991) and Itoh (1991).

agents' utility functions which ensure that such intermediation is viable imply that the intermediating agent is strictly risk-loving for sufficiently high wealth levels.[3]

Two notions of diversification are germane, one involving "sharing risks" and the other of "adding risks." With sharing risks, n risk-averse agents invest in n (imperfectly correlated) gambles, and each agent spreads his or her investment across the n gambles (see Ramakrishnan and Thakor 1984). With adding risks, a single agent bears all of the n independent risks, and promises fixed payouts to primary investors. Both Diamond (1984) and Ramakrishnan and Thakor (1984) show that with sharing of risks an intermediary provides risk-reduction benefits for each agent in its coalition, whereas Diamond (1984) shows that with adding risk (scenario ii) intermediation is Pareto improving provided his utility function restrictions are satisfied. The recent paper of Hellwig (2000) (see Chapter Four), included in this section, extends his analysis in important ways, showing that Diamond's result on the asymptotic viability of intermediation with many projects extends to scenarios in which (a) the intermediary agent is risk-averse with respect to wealth but risk-neutral with respect to non-pecuniary default penalties, or (b) the utility agent's function, considering possibly negative wealth net of non-pecuniary penalties has, an absolute risk-aversion coefficient that has no strictly positive lower bound.

Ramakrishnan and Thakor (1984) also show that an infinitely large FI attains the first best, even though the effort contribution of each agent within the FI coalition is unobservable to outsiders. As in Diamond (1984), therefore, the optimal size of the FI is infinite. These theories therefore present a puzzle since we do not observe infinitely large intermediaries. However, Millon and Thakor (1985) show that the Ramakrishnan and Thakor (1984) finding is sensitive to the assumption that cooperating agents within the FI can monitor each other costlessly. Millon and Thakor (1985) thus assume that internal monitoring is impossible, and agents' information has systematic elements that provide scale economies via cross-sectional information reusability gains. Their intermediary is no longer a natural monopoly and its optimal size is finite because intrafirm incentive problems arise for the FI as individual agents attempt to free ride on each other's efforts. As the FI grows larger, these incentive problems

---

[3] However, these restrictions that the third and fourth derivatives of the agents' utility functions be strictly positive, imply *risk-loving* behavior for sufficiently high wealth. This restriction is unappealing because expression (1B) is assumed to hold asymptotically, so that agents prefer risk under the very conditions that ensure that expression (1B) holds.

increase, at some point offsetting the information-sharing gains that increase with size.

Diamond's (1984) FI is an asset transformer because it provides depositors a riskless claim while lending to risky entrepreneurs. Given the monitoring services, the FI is not simply a mutual fund. By contrast, the FI of Ramakrishnan and Thakor (1984) and Millon and Thakor (1985) is a pure broker because it merely produces information for resale (see also, Allen 1990).[4] A second distinction between the two FIs lies in the contractual relationship between the agent being screened/monitored and the FI. In the case of the broker, this relationship is constrained only by the restriction of no collusion/bribes. In the case of the asset transformer, however, the Diamond (1984) model generates a non-traded debt contract as the optimal arrangement between his intermediary and primary investors (depositors). Townsend (1979) first provided an economic rationale for a debt contract when state realizations can be observed (monitored) ex post only at a cost by the providers of capital (see also, Gale and Hellwig 1985). A similar justification was provided in a banking context by Diamond (1984), but like Townsend only with *deterministic* monitoring.[5]

Boyd and Prescott (1986), included in this part (Chapter One), extend this literature by combining some of the features of Diamond's (1984) and Ramakrishnan and Thakor's (1984) analyzes. Like Diamond, the FI in Boyd and Prescott is an asset transformer that issues deposits and invests these in the projects of the entrepreneurs. In the spirit of Ramakrishnan and Thakor, the FI produces information on project quality and the FI—as a coalition of agents—can (perfectly) mitigate the misinterpretation problems that arise with individual agents. More specifically, in Boyd and Prescott (1986), entrepreneurs with bad projects form an intermediary (the FI), and devote themselves to monitoring. These agents are granted a residual claim on the FI which funds a large pool of projects.

3. Recent Advances in Monitoring of Banks and by Banks

In our discussion so far, we have emphasized that FIs could serve as delegated screeners/monitors. In these models, the task of monitoring

---

[4] This distinction between the two types of FIs is significant because it leads to different resolutions of the moral hazard from the FI's propensity to underinvest in screening/monitoring.

[5] Mookherjee and P'ng (1989) analyze optimal costly monitoring schemes with a risk-neutral principal and risk-averse agent and show that in any optimal scheme that provides positive consumption in every state, all monitoring must be *random*. Moreover, given optimal monitoring, the optimal contract is *never* a debt contract. The usual justification for assuming deterministic monitoring is the difficulty in ensuring implementation of randomized schemes.

borrowers is performed by the FI, while diversification of the FI helps resolve the agency problem between the FI and its primary investors. Following these pioneering papers, a subsequent literature has devoted considerable attention to the agency problem between the FI and its primary investors, that is, the problem of monitoring the bank itself, and has also provided fresh insights into how FIs monitor their borrowers, as well their role in the context of other financing channels.

The papers by Calomiris and Kahn (1991) and Repullo and Suarez (1998), both included in this part (Chapters Two, and Three, respectively), add important perspectives on these issues. Calomiris and Kahn (1991) study the problem of the bank being monitored by its depositors. They focus on an asset-substitution moral hazard problem, involving the bank expropriating wealth from its depositors. This agency problem, they argue, could be overcome by designing the deposit contract to have a sequential service constraint (SSC) feature, that is, for it to be a demand deposit contract. Depositors who smell trouble can thus withdraw their deposits instantly (on demand), forcing the bank to liquidate assets. This threat of liquidation keeps the bank's management honest. In his discussion in Part VI, Winton elaborates on this by noting the key linkages between the funding structure of FIs and how they are monitored by investors.

Repullo and Suarez (1998) examine *how* banks monitor their borrowers. In particular, they ask: what is the nature of control provided by a bank that lends to a borrower? Their insight is that funding by a bank can be accompanied by a credible threat of early liquidation on borrowers subject to moral hazard, which, when combined with (subordinated) nonbank market funding, enhances welfare. Such nonbank financing may be required to preserve the credibility of the threat of liquidation by the bank. Thus, juxtaposing Calomiris and Kahn's (1991) contribution with that of Repullo and Suarez (1998), we see that borrowers are provided their appropriate behavioral incentives in pretty much the same way that banks are provided these incentives, namely through a credible threat of costly asset liquidation. In both these two chapters, the intermediary agent is treated as a singular entity rather than a coalition with internal (team) effort-incentives problems, a topic on which further research is needed.

4. Conclusions

To summarize, intermediation is a response to the inability of market-mediated mechanisms to efficiently resolve informational problems. The models discussed in this chapter consider different types of informational frictions and rationalize different types of FIs (banks, venture capitalists, financial newsletters, investment banks, and bond-rating agencies, among others). But informational frictions represent the common thread among all these papers. Informational frictions raise the questions of monitoring of borrowers by FIs and monitoring of FIs by their primary investors. The nature of the FI's loan contracts with its borrowers affects the first type of monitoring (Repullo and Suarez 1998), whereas its liability structure affects the second type of monitoring (Calomiris and Kahn 1991). Winton's discussion in Part V notes other progress that has been made on these issues.

Our understanding is far less advanced on two other distinct sets of issues that deserve careful further study. One concerns the optimal size and diversification of financial institutions in light of competitive pressures. The other concerns bank stability. These issues are also related to the almost exclusive obsession with the lending function of FIs in the theoretical work, although more recent research has also encompassed the choice between bank borrowing and capital market funding (see also Part VI on comparative financial systems). The richness of financial institutions, including the provision of transactions, safekeeping and risk management services, suggests that more theoretical work is needed to understand the economic rationale for these functions and their interactions. This suggests the need to explore a rather fundamental question: where is the true value added in banking?

This brings us quite naturally to the second set of yet-to-be-explored questions, those about bank stability. Issues of diversification and competition are intrinsically linked to bank stability. Parts III and IV address these stability issues, including regulatory concerns. However, while stability issues have been examined quite extensively, particularly in the context of bank runs, our rather incomplete understanding of the complex nature of banking, especially in terms of the provision of risk-management and transactions services, impedes our ability to conduct a thorough analysis of stability issues. In particular, an FI's role in risk management exposes it to possibly substantial systemic risk. Are counterparty risk and macro shocks unavoidable in banking, or could they be off-loaded by banks to the capital market? How should regulation, including risk-based capital controls, attempt to cope with these risks (see Gordy, forthcoming) if they are inherent to banking? Important questions such as these await further research.

References

Allen, F. (1990). "The market for information and the origin of financial intermediation." *Journal of Financial Intermediation*, 1-1: 3–30.

Bhattacharya, S., and Thakor, A. V. (1993). "Contemporary banking theory." *Journal of Financial Intermediation*, 3-1: 2–50.

Diamond, D. (1984). "Financial intermediation and delegated monitoring." *Review of Economic Studies*, 51: 393–414.

Gale, D. and Hellwig, M. (1985). "Incentive-compatible debt contracts: The one-period problem." *Review of Economic Studies*, 52: 647–63.

Gordy, M. B. (2003). "Risk-factor model foundations for ratings-based capital rules." *Journal of Financial Intermediation*, 12: 199–232.

Hellwig, M. (1998). "Banks, markets, and the allocation of risks in an economy." *Journal of Institutional and Theoretical Economics*, 154(1): 328–45.

Itoh, H. (1991). "Incentives to help in multi-agent situations." *Econometrica*, 59: 611–36.

Leland, H., and Pyle, D. (1977). "Informational asymmetries, financial structure, and financial intermediation." *Journal of Finance*, 32: 371–87.

Millon, M., and Thakor, A. V. (1985). "Moral hazard and information sharing: A model of financial information gathering agencies." *Journal of Finance*, 40: 1403–22.

Mookherjee, D., and P'ng, I. (1989). "Optimal auditing, insurance and redistribution." *Quarterly Journal of Economics*, 104: 399–415.

Ramakrishnan, R. T. S., and Thakor, A. V. (1984). "Information reliability and a theory of financial intermediation." *Review of Economic Studies*, 51: 415–32.

——, and —— (1991). "Cooperation versus competition in agency." *Journal of Law and Economic Organization*, 7: 248–83.

Townsend, R. M. (1979). "Optimal contracts and competitive markets with costly state verification." *Journal of Economic Theory*, 21: 1–29.

Part II

Liquidity Provision via Banks and Markets

5

Liquidity, Banks, and Markets

Douglas W. Diamond

I. Introduction

Financial markets and banks are competing mechanisms that provide investors with liquidity by providing access to their capital, at good terms, on short notice. This chapter examines the impact of banks on the liquidity provided to investors and, in addition, on the liquidity provided by markets. Markets can provide too little liquidity when some potential investors are not continuously available for trade. If there is this limited participation in the market, banks lower the cost of giving investors rapid access to their capital. Banks hold assets to finance demand deposits offered to those who deposit, and they divert some demand for liquidity away from markets. This chapter characterizes the effects of increased participation in financial markets on the structure of banks, the maturity structure of real and financial assets, and the fraction of capital invested through banks.

Investors are concerned about the return they can obtain on short notice because they are uncertain when they will need their funds. The activities of banks provide liquid investment opportunities through two channels. First, bank deposits offer an option to obtain funds on short notice at a lower opportunity cost than is available with markets alone. Second, banks improve the liquidity of markets. The liquidity of markets is enhanced because long-term assets can be sold before maturity at higher prices than would prevail without banks.

The model can most clearly be applied to effects of financial development in developing economies. The optimal financial mechanism, which includes a banking sector, adapts as market participation increases. The maturity of both financial assets and real investments increases when market participation increases. In addition, the scale of the banking sector falls (more capital is

I gratefully acknowledge helpful comments from Patrick Bolton, John Boyd, Jerry Caprio, Mike Dotsey, Phil Dybvig, Gary Gorton, Lars Hansen, Bengt Holmström, Pete Kyle, Jeff Lacker, Matthew Rothman, Bruce Smith, Lars Stole, Jean Tirole, Neil Wallace, John Weinberg, and seminar participants at Chicago, Duke, Massachusetts Institute of Technology, the Federal Reserve Bank of Richmond, and the World Bank. This chapter was presented at the Nobel Symposium on Law and Finance in Stockholm in August 1995.

invested in marketable assets), and the maturity of assets held by banks falls. Some evidence consistent with these predictions is discussed in Section V.

The model also resolves some theoretical issues about the roles of banks and markets in Diamond and Dybvig's (1983) model. The model differs from the Diamond–Dybvig model by adding a financial market with limited participation and endogenizing the liquidity of assets. The Diamond–Dybvig model, where asset liquidity is not linked to the operations of markets, has been interpreted as inconsistent with active markets. Jacklin (1987) introduces a secondary market in which bank deposits trade for other financial assets and shows that this implies that banks are not important.[1] Haubrich and King (1990), von Thadden (1997), and Hellwig (1994) also present models that question the liquidity role of banks when there is a financial market. Wallace (1988) argues that the Diamond–Dybvig model can usefully be interpreted as a model in which there are no financial markets because investors are physically separated, and none participates in financial markets. This paper examines the roles of banks and markets when there is a financial market with limited participation. Such a market has an impact on bank activities, but banks remain important. Banks and markets coexist and influence each other's activities.

Limited market participation is introduced by assumption. I argue below that the most plausible interpretation is that participation is limited because of private information about the value of assets. The model has limited participation, but no explicit private information about the value of assets: assets are riskless. Private information possessed by others can lead investors to avoid trading in markets (Akerlof 1970). It is possible to interpret increases in participation in markets as equivalent to better access to information by less informed investors. A full analysis of the effects of changes in information structure on markets and banks is beyond the scope of this chapter.

A sketch of the model and its results

The key elements of the analysis are a demand for liquidity by investors and costs of obtaining liquidity. There is a demand for liquidity because investors are uncertain about the date on which they need their funds, as in Bryant (1980) and Diamond and Dybvig (1983). Liquidity is costly for an individual to obtain because short-term, self-liquidating real assets have a lower rate of return than long-term assets (which are not self-liquidating). Either trade in a market or a bank contract that offers an option to withdraw is needed to provide liquidity without investing primarily in short-term assets.

Investors in the model are ex ante identical and risk averse. Some will turn out to need all of their wealth for consumption soon thereafter, whereas the others

---

[1] The Jacklin result drops the Diamond–Dybvig assumption that consumption is observable and that those who withdraw use the proceeds for consumption.

will be in no rush to liquidate. How do markets perform without banks when some investors need to liquidate? Those who must consume their wealth immediately will sell their assets and will participate in markets. The other investors, who do not need to liquidate immediately, have no need to participate in financial markets. A fraction is assumed not to participate, but this is best interpreted that a fraction will turn out to have a high opportunity cost of participating. Plausibly, this cost is the expense of obtaining information to value the assets offered for sale. Limited participation has the following implications for markets. First, assets offered for sale in the market will not attract bids from all possible buyers, which will depress the selling price. Consequently, anticipation of a low resale price will depress the investment in long-term assets that mature after an investor might need liquidity. Investors will increase their investment in shorter-term assets that are self-liquidating. Second, investors who turn out not to need immediate liquidity (potential buyers), but do not participate in the market for buying assets offered for sale, will reinvest the proceeds from their shorter-term assets to obtain a lower return than they could obtain in the market. Excessive investment in self-liquidating assets is doubly inefficient: it yields a low immediate return that is sometimes reinvested in low-return assets. In short, limited participation in markets causes overinvestment in short-term real assets that are valued for their ability to self-liquidate.

Banks (or other financial institutions) can substitute for illiquid markets. Banks economize on liquid assets by avoiding the possibility that a nonparticipating potential buyer holds excessive liquidity. An individual will turn out to need liquidity on a single date. A bank is a coalition of individuals that has predictable liquidity needs on each date. When financial markets by themselves perform poorly, the bank as a coalition can manage the maturity of its assets to avoid the need to trade, while offering the option to withdraw on short notice to the members of its coalition. This holding of assets based on the anticipated timing of liquidity needed by a bank is often called *asset management of liquidity*. Besides avoiding the need to use markets, this asset management diverts some demand for liquidity from markets, which can improve the performance of markets.

It is also possible that, besides managing asset maturity better than an individual, financial institutions can participate in markets for investors. Given the informational motivation for limited participation, economies of scale or scope could allow institutions to have better access to information. Liquidity management based on superior access to markets is closely related to the other traditional approach to bank liquidity management: *liability management of liquidity*. Both roles for financial institutions are examined.

At the outset, I impose no constraints on financial institutions' participation in markets and determine how much of their participation is required. Later, I analyze the effects of restricted market participation by financial institutions. In the interest of simplicity, no costs of operating financial institutions are introduced. The existence of variable costs, however, would lead to the smallest scale of the banking industry that implements a given set of liquid consumption opportunities. Analyzing the smallest feasible scale of banks allows the model to examine the effects of increased market participation on the scale, structure, and activities of the banking sector.

Related models that use limited participation to understand financial markets are Merton (1987), which examines the effect on the relative prices of risky assets, and Allen and Gale (1994), which examines the volatility of asset prices. The most closely related study relating banks to the demand for liquidity is Holmström and Tirole (1996). It studies the impact of managerial moral hazard in firms on the ability of markets to allocate liquidity efficiently. The ex ante amount of liquidity that a firm should have available to it can differ from what spot markets would provide, as in Diamond (1991, 1993). Uncertainty about the amount of liquidity a firm needs is similar to the uncertain timing of consumption in this paper. Also related is Gorton and Pennacchi (1990), which examines the ability of intermediaries or firms to create riskless (and thus easy to value) securities when private information causes problems in risky asset markets. Bhattacharya and Gale (1987) examines the effects of a market for bank reserves on the liquid asset holdings of banks. These papers do not have limited participation in markets, but their results have a related focus.

Section II describes the model and characterizes the total amount of liquidity optimally created by the combination of the financial markets and the banking system. Section III describes the implications of optimal liquidity creation for the scale of the banking industry, the contracts the banking system offers, the assets that banks fund with those deposits, and the maturity structure of financial and real assets. Section IV discusses ways in which the analysis might be generalized and gives some more general interpretations of the existing results. Section V concludes the chapter.

II. The Model

There are three dates, 0, 1, and 2. All investors are small: there is a continuum of investors. Each is endowed with one unit of date 0 capital. Investors find out their need for liquidity and their participation in the market on date 1, and each investor's type is his or her private information. As of date 0, all investors are identical, but each is uncertain on which date he or she will need to consume and need liquidity. There are three types of agents as of date 1: type 1, type 2A, and type 2B. Type 1 investors will need liquidity at date 1: they need to consume at date 1 and place no value on date 2 consumption. Types 2A and 2B do not need liquidity on date 1 and place no value on date 1 consumption. The only

difference between types 2A and 2B is their participation in a secondary market
for assets on date 1. Type 2A agents are active in the secondary market, and type
2B agents are not. As of date 0, an investor is of type τ on date 1 with probability
q_τ. Assume that $q_1 > 0$, and some investors will need to consume at date 1.
Whenever $q_{2B} > 0$, there is limited participation in markets.

Define $c_{t\tau}$ as the consumption on date t of a type τ investor. Investors are risk
averse, and the date on which they prefer to consume depends on their type.
The form of the utility function of investor j, who consumes c_1 at date 1 and c_2
at date 2, is

$$u_j(c_1, c_2) = \begin{cases} U(c_1) & \text{if } j \text{ is of type 1} \\ U(c_2) & \text{if } j \text{ is of type 2A or 2B,} \end{cases}$$

where $U : R_{++} \to R$ is twice continuously differentiable, increasing, and strictly
concave and satisfies the Inada conditions $U'(0) = \infty$ and $U'(\infty) = 0$. Also,
the relative risk aversion coefficient $-cU''(c)/U'(c) \geq 1$ everywhere. Investors
maximize expected utility. These preferences are identical to those assumed in
Diamond–Dybvig, except here types 2A and 2B are distinguished. Diamond–
Dybvig allows no secondary market, which essentially assumes that there are
only investor types 1 and 2B.

The date 0 objective function of each investor is given by

$$\max_{c_{11}, c_{22A}, c_{22B}} \Psi = q_1 U(c_{11}) + q_{2A} U(c_{22A}) + q_{2B} U(c_{22B}),$$

subject to resource and incentive constraints specified below.

There are two real assets. The first is a short-term asset that yields a one-period-
ahead cash flow of $R \leq 1$ per unit invested (with constant returns to scale). The
second real asset is a long-term asset that yields a two-period-ahead cash flow of
$X > R^2$ (with constant returns to scale) and nothing in one period. This implies
that liquidity is difficult to obtain, because repeated investment in real assets that
pay quickly is less profitable than long-term investments. In addition, limited
participation limits the ability of markets to allocate available liquidity to its best
use. Table 1 summarizes the timing of events.

In the Diamond–Dybvig model, there are no secondary markets, but long-
term assets can be physically liquidated for a return that weakly exceeds the
return on short-term assets, implying that all investment should be long-term.[2]
In the current model, long-term assets cannot be physically liquidated. This
implies a nontrivial decision on how to allocate investment between short- and
long-term assets.

---

[2] Diamond–Dybvig also assumes that the return on one-period assets is $R = 1$ and that date
2 utility is discounted by a factor $\rho \leq 1$. The minor differences here of $R \leq 1$ and $\rho = 1$ are not
significant.

Table 1. Timing of Events

Date 0	Date 1	Date 2
Identical investors receive endowment of one to allocate between one-period assets, two-period assets, and bank deposit claims, if available	Investors learn their type and choose their withdrawal from bank, and some may trade	
	Type 1 investors sell any date 2 claims held directly or withdrawn from the bank and consume all wealth	Type 1 investors do nothing
	Type 2A investors sell any date 1 claims held directly or withdrawn from the bank to buy date 2 claims or fund new one-period investment	Type 2A investors consume all wealth
	Type 2B investors take any date 1 claims held directly or withdrawn from the bank to fund new one-period investment	Type 2B investors consume all wealth

The performance of markets when all assets are held directly

Suppose that there are no banks. This means that all investors must hold assets directly, with the possibility of trade between those who turn out to be of type 1 or 2A. Each investor has one unit to invest at date 0. Let each investor put α into one-period assets and $1 - \alpha$ into two-period assets. Before any trade, each investor holds date 1 claims of αR and date 2 claims of $(1 - \alpha)X$. Type 2B investors have no access to the market and take their maturing date 1 claim of αR and invest it in a new one-period asset, yielding αR_2 of date 2 consumption, in addition to their original date 2 holding of $(1 - \alpha)X$. Trade at date 1 would lead the type 1 investors to trade their date 2 claims for date 1 claims of type 2A investors. Markets clear when the date 1 value of date 2 claims offered by type 1 investors is equal to the date 1 claims offered by type 2A investors. Let the date 1 price of a unit claim on date 2 consumption be b_1. Investors are price takers because each is small. Trade with all assets held directly leads to the outcome described in lemma 1.

LEMMA 1. *When all assets are held directly, the date* 1 *price of a unit claim on date* 2 *consumption,* b_1, *is less than or equal to* R/X. *Investors place a fraction greater than or equal to* q_1 *of date* 0 *wealth in one-period assets* ($\alpha \geq q_1$), *and type* 1 *consumption,* c_{11}, *is less than or equal to* R. *With limited participation* ($q_{2B} > 0$), *all inequalities are strict* ($b_1 < R/X$, $\alpha > q_1$, *and* $c_{11} < R$). *With full participation, the price is* $b_1 = R/X$, *the fraction of short-term investment is* $\alpha = q_1$, *and type* 1 *consumption is* $c_{11} = R$.

Proof. Each investor on date 0 allocates an endowment of one, choosing to put α into short-term assets and $1 - \alpha$ into long-term assets to maximize expected utility. Expected utility is

$$\Phi = q_1 U(c_{11}) + q_{2A} U(c_{22A}) + q_{2B} U(c_{22B}),$$

where consumption of each type is given by $c_{11} = \alpha R + (1 - \alpha) b_1 X$, $c_{22A} = \alpha(R/b_1) + (1 - \alpha)X$, and $c_{22B} = \alpha R^2 + (1 - \alpha)X$. The first-order condition for an interior optimum with $\alpha \in (0, 1)$ is $d\Phi/d\alpha = 0$, or

$$q_1 U'(c_{11})(R - b_1 X) + q_{2A} U'(c_{22A}) \left(\frac{R}{b_1} - X \right)$$

$$+ q_{2B} U'(c_{22B})(R^2 - X) = 0.$$

The date 1 price b_1 will be positive (and c_{11} will be positive) only if there is some date 0 investment in short-term assets (only if $\alpha > 0$). There is short-term investment as long as $q_{2B} < 1$, because otherwise $U'(c_{11}) = \infty$ and $R/b_1 = \infty$. If investors are to choose to invest anything in short-term assets at date 0, the date 1 price of a unit claim on date 2 consumption, b_1, must be less than or equal to R/X. Otherwise, decreasing α will increase the consumption of all types (increasing expected utility). The date 1 price, b_1, is therefore less than or equal to R/X. The price is strictly less than R/X when $q_{2B} > 0$ (limited participation) because c_{22B} is decreasing in α. In addition, one can show that $b_1 < 1/R$, and trading one unit of a date 1 claim in the market will buy more than R units of date 2 consumption. It follows because $X > R^2$, implying $R/X < R/R^2 = 1/R$, which implies $b_1 < 1/R$. As a result, only type 2B investors will reinvest in short-term investments at date 1. In aggregate, type 1 investors trade all their date 2 claims for all the date 1 claims of type 2A investors. This leads to a market-clearing price of $b_1 = q_{2A}\alpha R/q_1(1-\alpha)X$. In summary, this discussion implies that the consumption levels are given by

$$c_{11} = \frac{q_1 + q_{2A}}{q_1} \alpha R,$$

$$c_{22A} = \frac{q_1 + q_{2A}}{q_{2A}} (1 - \alpha)X,$$

$$c_{22B} = \alpha R^2 + (1 - \alpha)X.$$

The date 1 price of a claim of one unit maturing on date 2 is

$$b_1 = \frac{q_{2A}\alpha R}{q_1(1 - \alpha)X}.$$

To show that $\alpha \geq q_1$, with strict inequality when there is limited participation ($q_{2B} > 0$), substitute $\alpha = q_1 > 0$ into the equation for the price b_1, yielding

$$b_1 = \frac{q_{2A}q_1 R}{q_1(1 - q_1)X} = \frac{q_{2A}R}{(q_{2A} + q_{2B})X}.$$

The price $b_1 < R/X$ if $q_{2B} > 0$, implying that expected utility is increasing in α. When there is full participation and $q_{2B} = 0, \alpha = q_1$ is the equilibrium value because expected utility is strictly increasing in α for all lower values and strictly decreasing in α for all higher values of α. Q.E.D.

Lemma 1 characterizes the liquidity that financial markets provide and the real investment decisions implied by this level of market liquidity. Markets with limited participation lead to lower liquidity than full-participation markets because the secondary market price, b_1, is lower, and the consumption of those who turn out to need liquidity, c_{11}, is lower than when all investors participate in the market. In addition, there is less investment in high-return illiquid real assets when there is limited participation. One can show that increased participation increases all these quantities toward the full-participation values. Lemma 1 is primarily used as a benchmark with which to compare the outcomes when banks are formed. When there is limited participation, investors put more capital into short-term liquid assets and obtain lower date 1 consumption than when banks are formed. The next subsection characterizes the optimal allocations when investors form banks.

Banks and optimal mechanisms

Financial institutions such as banks can improve access to liquidity in two ways. First, by centralizing the holding of liquid assets, the institution reduces the opportunity cost of excess date 1 liquidity held by investors who do not participate in the market. Second, financial institutions possess some ability to cross-subsidize investors. Investors who need to consume unexpectedly at date 1 (type 1) can receive higher returns at the expense of those who cannot trade in the market (type 2B).

To characterize the role of intermediaries and markets in providing the optimal amount of liquidity, I solve for the optimal set of incentive-compatible consumption opportunities that a coalition of investors can choose at date 0, and later determine how they are related to markets and intermediaries. The standard method for characterizing the optimal consumption is to examine direct mechanisms in which each investor reveals his or her type and is given type-contingent consumption on each date, subject to the constraint that each investor is willing to make an honest report. It turns out that the report of an investor's type corresponds to a choice of which withdrawal option to select from those offered by a bank.

The optimal financial mechanism solves the date 0 maximization problem described above:

$$\max_{c_{11}, c_{22A}, c_{22B}} \Psi = q_1 U(c_{11}) + q_{2A} U(c_{22A}) + q_{2B} U(c_{22B}),$$

subject to resource and incentive constraints. As of date 0, one unit of date 1 consumption costs $1/R$ and one unit of date 2 consumption costs $1/X$. There is one unit of endowment per capita on date 1, and as a result, the resource constraint is given by

$$\frac{q_1 c_{11}}{R} + \frac{q_{2A} c_{22A} + q_{2B} c_{22B}}{X} \leq 1.$$

Consumption on the "wrong" date (by a type who assigns no value to consumption on that date) is never optimal, and at the optimum, $c_{21} = c_{12A} = c_{12B} = 0$. There are several incentive constraints as well, which may not be binding. If only the resource constraint is imposed, the first-order condition for optimal consumption levels is given by

$$U'(c_{11}) = U'(c_{22A}) \frac{X}{R} = U'(c_{22B}) \frac{X}{R}.$$

This equates the ratio of marginal utility of consumption of the two periods with the marginal rate of transformation across periods and equates the date 2 consumption of types 2A and 2B: $c_{22B} = c_{22A}$. Investors who are sufficiently risk averse would choose cross-subsidization to allow them to hold liquid claims with high one-period returns (high $c_{11} > R$) at the expense of lower two-period returns (lower $c_{22A} = c_{22B} < X$). This allows increased consumption when they have low consumption, due to forced liquidation of assets, and is financed by reduced consumption when they have high consumption. Consider the base case without cross-subsidization. This occurs when each investor receives consumption equal to the value of investing all of his or her date 0 endowment in a real asset that matures on the date on which he or she needs to consume: R at date 1 or X at date 2. A bank could achieve this because it knows the timing of the aggregate consumption of all depositors. If there is no cross-subsidization, then $c_{11} = R$ and $c_{22A} = c_{22B} = X$. The first-order condition holds with no cross-subsidization if and only if each investor's relative risk aversion equals one, and $U(c) = \log(c)$. For risk aversion greater than one, the empirically relevant case, $U'(R) > U'(X) \times (X/R)$, implying that liquidity is increased: there is cross-subsidization with $c_{11} > R$ and $c_{22A} = c_{22B} < X$.[3]

The cross-subsidized optimal consumption levels may not be incentive-compatible. Each investor's type is private information, and in addition types 1 and 2A can trade anonymously at date 1. The incentive constraints that trade implies are analyzed in the next subsection. It turns out that there is scope for a beneficial subsidy to type 1 agents.

---

[3] If risk aversion is below one, then optimal risk sharing leads to cross-subsidization to reduce liquidity ($c_{11} < R$ and $c_{22B} > X$) if type is observable and there is no possibility of trade.

Date 1 incentive constraints imposed by a limited participation market

On date 1, an agent who joins a financial mechanism at date 0 will be given a choice of claims on date 1 and date 2 consumption. Type 1 and 2A agents can trade anonymously at date 1 and privately consume the proceeds from those trades. As a result, they can choose claims on both dates' consumption without wasting goods. Let $W_{t\tau}$ denote the pretrade date 1 holding of date t claims by a type τ investor. After choosing these claims, type 1 and 2A investors have the ability to trade at date 1. Let b_1 denote the date 1 price of a claim on one unit of date 2 consumption. Type 2B investors cannot trade, but if a type 2B investor has a claim maturing on date 1, he or she can earn a return R per unit by initiating a new one-period asset at date 1. Consumption of each type is given by

$$c_{11} = W_{11} + W_{21}b_1,$$

$$c_{22A} = \frac{W_{12A}}{b_1} + W_{22A},$$

$$c_{22B} = W_{12B}R + W_{22B}.$$

The date 1 market value of the claims selected by type 1 agents is c_{11}, and the date 2 market value of claims selected by type 2A agents is c_{22A}. The price, b_1, on date 1 of claims on a unit of date 2 consumption must be c_{11}/c_{22A}; otherwise $c_{11} \neq b_1 c_{22A}$, and the claims intended for one type will have a higher market value than the other. If the market values differ, the ability to trade at date 1 implies that it is not incentive-compatible for one type to select the correct claims. The date 1 incentive constraint for types 1 and 2A not to prefer the claims intended for the other is $b_1 = c_{11}/c_{22A}$: the rate of return from taking the claims intended for one's type must equal the rate of return from taking the claims intended for the other type and then trading them. If trade allows a return higher than c_{22A}/c_{11}, type 2A investors will take the withdrawal intended for type 1. If trade offers a return lower than c_{22A}/c_{11}, type 1 investors will take the withdrawal intended for type 2A.

A type 2B investor does not have access to the financial market. A type 2B investor can use the proceeds of date 1 claims to invest in new short-term investments that mature on date 2. He or she must not have incentives to take the wrong claims for the purpose of initiating a new one-period investment at date 1. It is feasible to give types 1 and 2A claims only on date 1 consumption, which a type 2A uses to buy date 2 claims (supplied by the bank) in the financial market. As a result, a type 2B can be induced to choose the proper claim as long as $c_{22B} \geq c_{11}R$. This constraint is not binding. Finally, the date 1 incentive constraint that type 2A investors not prefer the date 2 claims intended for type 2B investors is $c_{22A} \geq c_{22B}$. Lemma 2 summarizes the date 1 incentive constraints in a limited participation market.

LEMMA 2. *The date 1 incentive-compatibility constraints are satisfied if and only if* $b_1 = c_{11}/c_{22A}$, $c_{22A} \geq c_{22B}$, *and* $c_{22B} \geq c_{11}R$.

Proof. See the Appendix.

In addition to these constraints that each type be willing to withdraw the proper amount, there are date 0 constraints. These constraints are imposed by the possibility that investors invest directly at date 1, or that they join a competing bank. These constraints are described in the next subsection.

Date 0 incentive constraints: competing banks and voluntary deposits

Individuals can form alternative mechanisms ("competing banks") at date 0, realizing that the members of all banks who turn out to be of type 1 or 2A will be able to trade in the same anonymous market at date 1. This ability imposes coalition incentive-compatibility constraints, because trade in the market allows investors to form coalitions at date 1. For investors to choose to join a financial coalition (deposit in the bank), each must get type-contingent consumption as desirable as can be obtained from joining another coalition (bank) or from investing directly. Because there are no costs of establishing banks, any individual asset holdings can be replicated by those of a competing bank. The ability to form competing banks imposes coalition incentive constraints at date 1. The importance of competing banks in models of this type was first identified by von Thadden (1997).

The constraint imposed by date 0 coalition formation is that the return from trading assets must equal the physical returns offered by the real assets. If these returns are not equal, a competing bank coalition can offer claims that allow its members who participate in markets to consume more. Real assets allow a date 0 cost of $1/R$ per unit of date 1 consumption and $1/X$ per unit of date 2 consumption. If the market price on date 1 of one unit of date 2 consumption is not R/X, then offering the option for depositors to withdraw and trade at that price will allow higher consumption. If some depositors can trade, then the date 0 marginal rate of transformation of date 1 to date 2 consumption must be equal to the ratio of prices that will prevail on date 1 of claims on unit claims maturing on those dates. Lemma 3 describes the incentive constraints.

LEMMA 3. *A dominating competing bank coalition exists unless* $b_1 = R/X$ *and prices are in line with marginal productivity. Combined with the date 1 incentive constraints in lemma 1, this implies that the date 1 and date 0 incentive constraints are* $c_{22A} = c_{11}(X/R)$, $c_{22B} \geq c_{11}R$, *and* $c_{22A} \geq c_{22B}$. *The resource constraint then reduces to*

$$(1 - q_1 - q_{2A})c_{22B} = \left[1 - (q_1 + q_{2A})\frac{c_{11}}{R}\right]X.$$

Proof. See the Appendix.

Combining lemma 2 and lemma 3 implies that the subsidy provided to type 1 investors must also be provided to type 2A investors. The ratio of consumptions c_{11}/c_{22A} must be constant. If not, one type can get a higher market value of proceeds by choosing the wrong withdrawal, or a competing bank can be set up that offers its depositors better returns. Cross-subsidy of both types 1 and 2A is possible, with the subsidy of liquidity provided by type 2B investors who cannot trade.

The banking system creates more liquidity than there would be without a banking system or secondary markets. The banking system also makes the secondary market more liquid: secondary markets will offer the amount of liquidity implied by the short-term physical return on capital. I assume that interbank deposits are identifiable as such (if only by their size). This prevents a competing bank from obtaining the liquidity subsidy provided by another bank by simply investing directly in the one-period deposits of the bank.[4] Some benefits of liquidity creation can be focused on the individual bank's depositors. However, the effect of banks' liquidity creation on market liquidity is available to all competitors because of free entry into trades in the anonymous secondary market.

The condition for banks to create more liquidity than secondary markets is that risk aversion exceed one (so cross-subsidy is valuable) and that not too many investors participate in the secondary market (so much of the subsidy goes to type 1 investors who need liquidity). Proposition 1 states this result.

PROPOSITION 1. *If the coefficient of relative risk aversion is above one and a sufficient fraction of investors do not participate, $q_{2B} > \hat{q}_{2B} > 0$, then banks provide more liquidity than the secondary market and set $c_{11} > R$ and $c_{22B} < X$. If the coefficient of relative risk aversion is less than or equal to one, the banks increase the liquidity of the market but provide no more liquidity than the market and set $c_{11} = R$ and $c_{22A} = c_{22B} = X$.*

The proof is in the Appendix, but it is useful here to describe the key first-order condition. If relative risk aversion is greater than one, the first-order condition for optimal consumption is

$$q_1 U'(c_{11}) \leq \{q_1 U'(c_{22B}) + q_{2A}[U'(c_{22B}) - U'(c_{22A})]\}\frac{X}{R},$$

with equality whenever $c_{11} > R$, which occurs for q_{2A} not too large. If relative risk aversion is less than or equal to one, $c_{11} = R$ and $c_{22A} = c_{22B} = X$, because $c_{22A} = c_{11}(X/R) \geq c_{22B}$ is binding and there is no potential for

---

[4] If interbank deposits could not be identified, an argument similar to the one above shows that not only must $b_1 = R/X$, but also $c_{11} = R$ and $c_{22A} = c_{22B} = X$.

a cross-subsidy provided to type 1 investors (with none desirable if risk aversion equals one).

The next proposition shows the effect of increased secondary market liquidity (increased q_{2A}) on the amount of liquidity created by banks.

PROPOSITION 2. *Increasing individual participation in the secondary market (increasing q_{2A} by reducing q_{2B}) weakly reduces the liquidity that banks create relative to secondary markets ($c_{11} - R$) and reduces c_{11} (strictly if $c_{11} > R$), the short-term return available to investors.*

Proof. See the Appendix.

Increased market participation reduces the cross-subsidy that banks provide to short-term holders, because it increases the fraction of the benefit that goes to those who profit from trading (type 2A investors who have high consumption) rather than to those who need liquidity for consumption (type 1 investors who have low consumption). The consumption of those who do not need liquidity and do not participate in the secondary market can increase or decrease (c_{22B} can rise or fall), but $c_{22B} - c_1$ rises as participation increases: there is less risk sharing between those who turn out to need liquidity and those who do not participate in secondary markets.

The Diamond–Dybvig and Jacklin models

The Diamond–Dybvig model characterizes the optimal amount of liquidity cross-subsidization to provide when the option for an increased short-holding period return is financed by a lower long-holding period return. Jacklin (1987), Haubrich and King (1990), von Thadden (1997), and Hellwig (1994) examine the effects of competitive financial markets and reach largely negative conclusions about the viability of bank liquidity created by cross-subsidy. The results in the two propositions show that these results follow not from the existence of a financial market, but from a market in which all investors participate continuously. Increased participation in markets reduces the subsidy that short-term holders receive from long-term holders of bank deposits. In addition, even when banks provide no cross-subsidy, banks are important and changes in market participation have interesting effects.

The polar cases of propositions deliver the Diamond–Dybvig and Jacklin (1987) models. Proposition 1 delivers the Diamond–Dybvig result when $q_{2A} = 0$. If trade between agents is impossible ($q_{2A} = 0$ and no type 2A's exist), then investors with relative risk aversion above one choose cross-subsidization to allow them to hold liquid claims with high one-period returns (high $c_{11} > R$) at the expense of lower two-period returns (lower $c_{22B} < X$). Banks must offer a demand deposit in which each depositor is offered a choice between c_{11} at date 1 and c_{22B} at date 2 because no trade is possible, and because $c_{11} > Rc_{22B}$, all investors will self-select.

Proposition 1 delivers the Jacklin (1987) result when $q_{2B} = 0$. Jacklin shows that the ability of banking mechanisms to cross-subsidize investors is eliminated when there exists a full-participation secondary market for bank assets. In this case, cross-subsidization is impossible, and $c_{11} = R$ and $c_{22A} = X$ is the only feasible compatible consumption pair (there are no type 2B investors). The reason is the date 0 constraint: investors will prefer not to join the bank at date 0 if $c_{11}/c_{22A} \neq R/X$, because they then would prefer to trade in the market (no competing banks are required when there is full participation). In this case, $c_{22A} = c_{11}(X/R)$ combines with the resource constraint to yield $c_{11} = R$ and $c_{22A} = X$.

With a full-participation secondary market, there is not only no scope for cross-subsidization but no beneficial role for banks. If each investor holds a fraction q_1 in short-term assets and $q_{2A} = 1 - q_1$ in long-term assets, then $c_{11} = R$ and $c_{22A} = X$, without using banks. Jacklin's result has been interpreted as meaning that banks and markets cannot coexist, and if liquidity is enhanced ($c_{11} > R$), either markets or the direct holding of assets must be prohibited.

When there is a limited-participation market, there is a role for banks even without cross-subsidization. Unless q_{2A} is very high, there is cross-subsidization. The existence of a limited-participation market reduces but does not eliminate cross-subsidization. In addition, there is an interaction between the amount of cross-subsidization, the scale of the banking sector, and the degree of market participation. This is explored in the next section.

III. Direct Holdings and Bank Claims: The Scale of the Banking Sector

The contracts that banks write with investors influence the performance of financial markets. If there is limited participation in markets and all claims are held directly, financial markets will provide too little liquidity. Investing a fraction of wealth through banks diverts some demand for liquidity away from markets. This allows the limited supply of liquidity in the market to be better matched with demand. Not all the financial claims need to be held by banks at date 0 for banks and markets to provide increased liquidity to investors. If there are variable costs associated with running wealth through intermediaries, the scale of the banking sector is the minimum needed to implement the desired amount of liquidity. The scope for direct holdings arises because the optimal mechanism leads to a set of tradable claims held by investors before trade at date 1 that can be separated into two components: one is a holding that is identical for all investors (and thus not type-specific), and the other is a type-specific choice selected from the options offered by the bank at date 1. The total claim, $W_{t\tau}$, on date t consumption held by investor type τ on date 1 (before any trade) is decomposed into two parts: $W_{t\tau} = d_t + w_{t\tau}$, where d_t is the component that is not type-specific and $w_{t\tau}$ is type-specific. Each investor can directly hold assets that constitute the claims that are not type-specific. The claim $w_{t\tau}$ is the claim on date t consumption withdrawn by a type τ investor at date $t \in \{1, 2\}$.

The holding of short-term liquidity must be centralized to avoid inefficient reinvestment in short-term assets at date 1 by type 2B investors. This requires that no date 1 claims be held by type 2B investors ($W_{12B} = 0$), which requires that individuals hold no short-term assets directly ($d_1 = 0$). All directly held claims are long-term. If investors hold a fraction β of their date 0 wealth as bank claims, they invest $1 - \beta$ in long-term claims, and this gives each a direct holding of date 2 claims of $d_2 = (1 - \beta)X$. A lower bound on the date 0 scale of banks is the amount of assets needed to finance short-term investment. This lower bound on date 0 investment in banks is

$$\beta \geq \frac{q_1 c_{11}}{R} \equiv \beta_1$$

(scale of banks when they hold just all the short-term assets), because total date 1 consumption is c_{11} by a fraction q_1 of investors. If this minimal fraction of assets were invested in banks, the banking system would hold only short-term assets. All long-term assets would be held directly, and each investor would hold date 2 claims of $(1 - \beta_1)X$.

Incentive-compatible bank withdrawals

Too large a direct holding of long-term assets can be inconsistent with self-selection of the proper type-specific withdrawals at date 1. The problem arises when banks cross-subsidize short-term holders, because the high short-term return (c_{11} in excess of R) is not reflected in the market prices of directly held assets. Positive holdings of date 2 claims by all types tighten the incentive constraint that type 2B investors choose to leave their funds in the bank until date 2. This constraint is loosest when all claims selected by types 1 and 2A are date 1 claims, because trade allows them a higher return at date 1 than is available to nonparticipating type 2B investors. When investors all directly hold a fraction $1 - \beta$ of date 2 claims, the bank claims selected by both types 1 and 2A are $w_{11} = w_{12A} = c_{11} - (1 - \beta)R$ and $w_{21} = w_{22A} = 0$. The value of the date 2 bank withdrawal intended for type 2B investors is $w_{22B} = c_{22B} - (1 - \beta)X$. It is incentive-compatible for type 2B investors to choose w_{22B} instead of taking w_{22} and investing it in a short-term investment at date 1 only if $w_{22B} > Rw_{11}$, which is equivalent to

$$\beta \geq 1 - \frac{c_{22B} - Rc_{11}}{X - R^2} \equiv \beta_{IC}.$$

This incentive constraint need not be binding because β_{IC} can be less than $\beta_1 = q_1 c_{11}/R$. For sufficiently low risk aversion or for sufficiently high participation ($q_{2A} \to 1 - q_1$), cross-subsidization is low, and $\beta_{IC} \to 0$ (and is less than β_1), because $c_{22B} - Rc_{11} \to X - R^2$. In this case, the banking system does not hold long-term assets. For sufficiently high risk aversion and sufficiently low market participation, $\beta_{IC} > \beta_1$, and the banking system holds a fraction $\beta_{IC} - \beta_1$ of long-term assets. Increasing market participation (q_{2A} increases for fixed q_1) reduces β_{IC}, reducing the banks' holdings of long-term assets, eventually to zero as $q_{2A} \to 1 - q_1$.

Market clearing and bank trades

Up to this point, no constraint has been imposed on bank trades in markets. Given total pretrade holdings $W_{t\tau}$, individual traders' supply of short-term claims to the market is $q_{2A} W_{12A}$, and the date 1 value of the date 2 claims offered by individuals is $q_1 W_{21}(R/X)$. For individuals, the date 1 excess supply of date 1 claims is $q_{2A} W_{12A} - (R/X)q_1 W_{21} \equiv m_1$. Market clearing implies that the bank buys (with date 2 claims) date 1 claims of m_1 on date 1 (sells date 1 claims of $-m_1$ when $m_1 < 0$). Setting a small value of β can require $m_1 < 0$, which requires that the bank sell short-term claims to buy existing long-term assets in the market at date 1. Factors such as limited information that constrain type 2B agents' ability to value existing long-term assets might plausibly also prevent banks from valuing those assets and require that $m_1 \geq 0$. The impact of requiring $m_1 \geq 0$ is analyzed in the next subsection. Note that a date 1 market is required whenever there is cross-subsidization ($c_{22A} > c_{22B}$), because some date 1 claims must be selected by type 2A agents to allow type 2A investors to choose high consumption not available to nontrading type 2B investors.

Scale of the banking sector and banks' ability to trade assets

To determine the link between bank trades in the market and the implied scale of the banking sector, begin with the benchmark in which banks do not trade in the financial market and $m_1 = 0$. If the bank makes no trades, it must hold sufficient assets to provide type 1 agents with consumption c_{11}, plus provide enough date 2 assets to provide the excess of type 2B's consumption over that obtained from their direct holdings of assets. If the bank holds more assets, it must sell some date 2 assets at date 1 or give date 2 claims to types 1 and 2A for them to trade. If the bank holds fewer assets, it must buy some date 2 claims in the market at date 1. When $m_1 = 0$, the date 2 assets held directly by type 1 and 2A investors will finance the consumption of type 2A investors, and those held directly by type 2B investors will finance the part of their own consumption that does not come from bank deposits.

All investors will choose the same direct holding on date 0, when their liquidity need and type are unknown. Without trading with the bank, consumption of type 2A investors can come from holdings of date 2 claims by type 1 and 2A agents. The date 2 value of date 2 claims held by types 1 and 2A must be $q_{2A}c_{22A}$. Date 0 direct holdings of long-term claims must equal $q_{2A}c_{22A}/(q_1 + q_{2A})X$, because a fraction $q_1 + q_{2A}$ of direct claims are held by types 1 and 2A. Because type 2A consumption is $c_{22A} = c_{11}X/R$, the date 0 value of direct holding when banks do not trade is $1 - \beta = q_{2A}c_{11}X/(q_1 + q_{2A})R$. This implies that the balance of date 0 capital is invested by the bank, and if $m_1 = 0$, the scale of the banking sector is

$$\beta = 1 - \frac{q_{2A}c_{11}X}{(q_1 + q_{2A})R} \equiv \beta_{MC}$$

(scale of banks with no trade by banks). The minimum scale of banking when there is no bank trade weakly exceeds the minimum scale q_1c_{11}/R of holding only short-term assets, because the market-clearing condition requires that the bank hold some long-term assets when $c_{11} > R$.

The scale of the banking sector at date 0 is $\beta_{MC} + (m_1/R)$. If the bank cannot value others' long-term assets and $m_1 \geq 0$, then the minimum scale of the banking industry is $\max\{\beta_{MC}, \beta_{IC}\}$. The value of β_{MC} decreases with increased market participation, and β_{MC} goes from one to q_1 as q_{2A} goes from zero to $1 - q_1$. If $\beta_{MC} < \beta_{IC}$, then the bank holds more long-term assets at date 0 than needed and sells them to type 2A depositors at date 1. An alternative explanation of this is that the bank must raise some deposits at date 1 from type 2A investors by paying market rates of interest.

In summary, if the bank participates fully in markets, $\beta = \max\{\beta_{IC}, q_1c_{11}/R\}$. If the banks face the market participation constraint equal to that of type 2B investors, the scale of banking is

$$\beta = \max\left\{\beta_{IC}, \frac{q_1c_{11}}{R}, \frac{q_{2A}c_{11}X}{(q_1 + q_{2A})R}\right\}.$$

Whether or not the bank can participate in markets on behalf of investors, the banking sector shrinks as financial market participation increases. There are other interesting interpretations of this result. Because the banking system issues liabilities with an option to withdraw at date 1 and the remaining assets held by investors are long-term, the scale of the banking system measures the proportion of financial assets that are short-term. Whenever the scale of the banking sector exceeds that implied by the minimal liquidity needs of the economy (its scale exceeds $\beta_1 = q_1 c_{11}/R$), the banks hold long-term assets as well. An increase in the amount of long-term assets held by banks is an increase in the mismatch between the maturities of real and financial assets in the economy. Proposition 3 summarizes the results in this section.

PROPOSITION 3. *The scale of the banking sector, the fraction of financial assets that are short-term, the fraction of real assets that are short-term, and the gap between the maturities of financial and real assets all decrease as direct market participation increases (q_{2A} increases and q_{2B} decreases).*

IV. Alternative Interpretations and Possible Extensions

Several of the assumptions of the model can be generalized without qualitatively changing the results and implications. This section describes alternative assumptions and alternative interpretations of what has been assumed. Some open questions for future work are also identified.

The key exogenous variable in the model is the amount of direct participation in financial markets. Exploration of the factors that limit participation, and the impact of these factors on banks and markets, is beyond the scope of this chapter. It is useful to outline some additional motivation for the specification used here. A motivation for limited participation based on asymmetry of information follows. Suppose that evaluating existing assets offered for resale in the market is costly, and they cannot be distinguished from less valuable assets. Investors with low costs will trade in the market for existing assets, and those with high costs will not (see Akerlof 1970). One could imagine that there is a continuous cost of information and that the informed are those whose cost is below a given level. For simplicity imagine that there are informed investors who get information at no cost and uninformed investors who get it only at a prohibitive cost. Only the informed investors (type 2A) and those who are in need of liquidity (type 1) are active in the secondary market. Increased disclosure of public information or a reduction in the amount of private information would increase the fraction of traders active in the secondary market, by transferring some traders from the uninformed group to the informed group. As a result, one can interpret an increase in direct participation as a reduction in the cost of acquiring information.

Explicit study of private information would also be useful in motivating the limits to arbitrage by competing banks. The current model assumes that a bank cannot borrow at date 1 from the type 2B customers of another bank by issuing deposits backed by the bank's existing long-term assets. The information-based motivation is that retaining a claim in an existing bank that does not buy others' long-term assets gives investors the unconditional mean return from those assets. Because of the potential for adverse selection, this exceeds the anticipated return from switching to another bank that chooses to raise additional funds from uninformed type 2B investors rather than informed 2A investors in the market. The alternative assumption that the other bank can always borrow from type 2B investors at date 1 would imply that having assets held by a bank allows full participation in the market for all claims that are derivatives of the underlying real assets in the economy. This would yield the same consumption levels as a full-participation market in the underlying assets. There would be no cross-subsidization, but banks would still be needed to hold assets. It is possible that some of these issues could be clarified by embedding the analysis in an overlapping generations model, such as that in Qi (1994).

The model can easily accommodate costs of financial intermediation (e.g. a proportional cost of banks' holding assets), but the analysis is much more complicated with very few new insights. The effects of these costs can be seen by comparing the case in which there are no intermediation costs, analyzed here, with that in which the costs are so large that all assets are held directly. When intermediation costs are so high that all assets are held directly, each investor invests more in short-term assets. Yet the consumption of those who need liquidity (c_{11}) is lower, and the secondary market price of long-term assets (b_1) is lower than it is when banks face low intermediation costs. Reduced intermediation costs make financial markets more liquid and lower the opportunity cost of liquidity. In addition, in the case in which banks can participate in the market, the reduction of intermediation costs also increases the volume of trade in the financial market. Reduced bank costs can increase the volume of trade even when banks cannot access the secondary market, because of the increased holding of long-term assets by individuals due to the higher secondary market prices of long-term assets. This suggests that improvements in banking, through reduced costs or less oppressive regulation, will be conducive to the liquidity of financial markets and to financial market development. Improvements in access to financial markets (increased disclosure and transparency) that make the market more liquid will diminish the role of banks but will also reduce banks' costs if the improvements provide increased bank access to the market. This two-way causality suggests that empirical study of the roles of banks and markets must use structural information to disentangle the effects. The line of empirical research started by Demirgüç-Kunt and Levine (1996) on banks, markets, and development has documented that banks and markets tend to develop together. Future work should attempt to disentangle the conflicting effects of banks and markets on each other.

Finally, this analysis abstracts from important problems with enforcement of property rights over collateral and other bankruptcy/ enforcement issues that are also present in many developing countries. Explicit analysis of information and incentives could allow these issues to be integrated into the analysis of participation in markets.

V. Conclusion

With limited participation in markets, the banking system creates liquidity in two ways. First, banks fill the liquidity gap in markets by diverting demand for liquidity from markets. This improves the market's liquidity, increasing the price of illiquid assets above what it is when all assets are held directly. Second, if investors are sufficiently risk averse and enough do not participate in markets, bank deposits provide higher short-term returns than the market. The short-term assets held by individuals are bank liabilities, and the short-term real "reserve assets" are held only by banks. In this case, banks provide a cross-subsidy to those who withdraw early that is financed by those who hold bank claims for many periods.

The model can be most clearly applied to the understanding of financial markets and institutions in developing economies. Limited participation in secondary markets implies that the maturity structure of financial claims will adjust to fill the gap by allowing individuals to hold self-liquidating financial claims. As the financial markets develop, one should expect to see increased use of longer-term claims such as long-term debt or equity. The analysis implies that there will be a small supply of long-term direct claims in economies in which few participate in financial markets. The banking system will have a large role in the allocation of capital and the provision of liquidity.

More participation in markets leads to less cross-subsidization of short-term returns by banks, a smaller banking sector, and a longer average maturity of financial assets. More participation also leads to longer-maturity physical investment and a smaller gap between the maturity of financial assets and physical investments. In addition, as more liquid markets force the banking system to shrink, the banks' holdings of long-term assets (term loans) will shrink more rapidly than their holdings of shorter-term loans. The empirical study by Hoshi, Kashyap, and Scharfstein (1990) documents the effects of market development on banks and their structure. Regulatory changes opened access to the Japanese bond market. The effects were broadly in line with the implications of this model. Banks' market share was reduced, and their holdings of long-term assets fell more rapidly than their holdings of short-term assets.

The analysis also has implications for the effect of development of the banking sector on financial markets. Adding banks, or reducing their costs of operation, makes liquidity cheaper to obtain, and this makes markets more liquid. Because investors then choose to hold more long-term assets, the development of a banking system will lead to increased turnover and volume in financial markets. These links between banks and markets are worthy of further study. The current model of the link between liquidity provided by financial institutions and liquidity provided by markets is quite rudimentary, but I hope that further study of this link will provide more insight into these issues in financial structure and development.

APPENDIX

Proof of Lemma 2. Let $W_{t\tau}$ denote the pretrade date 1 holding of date t claims by a type τ investor. After choosing these claims, type 1 and 2A investors have the ability to trade anonymously at date 1 and to privately consume the proceeds from those trades. Let b_1 denote the date 1 price of a claim on one unit of date 2 consumption. A type 2B investor does not have access to the financial market. As a result, the only way that a type 2B investor can convert date 1 consumption into date 2 consumption is to use the proceeds of date 1 claims and invest in new short-term investments that pay off on date 2. This implies that the final consumption levels of each type of agent are given by

$$c_{11} = W_{11} + W_{21}b_1,$$

$$c_{22A} = \frac{W_{12A}}{b_1} + W_{22A},$$

$$c_{22B} = W_{12B}R + W_{22B}.$$

The type-contingent consumption offered on date 1 is incentive-compatible if and only if no investor prefers the consumption implied by the claims $W_{t\tau}$ intended for another type of investor. Let $c_{t\tau}^{\bar{\tau}}$ denote the consumption on date t of a type τ investor who misrepresents himself or herself as a type $\bar{\tau}$ investor, choosing the claims $W_{1\bar{\tau}}, W_{2\bar{\tau}}$ and trading at the market price b_1 if of type 1 or 2A. With this definition and the definitions of individual consumption, $c_{t\tau}$, given above, the following are the date 1 constraints on incentive-compatible consumption (IC $\tau, \bar{\tau}$):

$$c_{11} = W_{11} + b_1 W_{21} \geq W_{12A} + b_1 W_{22A} \equiv c_{11}^{2A} = c_{22A}b_1, \qquad \text{(IC 1, 2A)}$$

$$c_{11} = W_{11} + b_1 W_{21} \geq W_{12B} + b_1 W_{22B} \equiv c_{11}^{2B} = c_{22B}b_1, \qquad \text{(IC 1, 2B)}$$

$$c_{22A} = \frac{W_{12A}}{b_1} + W_{22A} \geq \frac{W_{11}}{b_1} + W_{21} \equiv c_{22A}^{1} = \frac{c_{11}}{b_1}, \qquad \text{(IC 2A, 1)}$$

$$c_{22A} = \frac{W_{12A}}{b_1} + W_{22A} \geq \frac{W_{12B}}{b_1} + W_{22B} \equiv c_{22A}^{2B} \geq c_{22B}, \qquad \text{(IC 2A, 2B)}$$

$$c_{22B} = W_{12B}R + W_{22B} \geq W_{11}R + W_{21} \equiv c_{22B}^{1}, \qquad \text{(IC 2B, 1)}$$

$$c_{22B} = W_{12B}R + W_{22B} \geq W_{12A}R + W_{22A} \equiv c_{22B}^{2A}. \qquad \text{(IC 2B, 2A)}$$

The constraints (IC 1, 2A) and (IC 2A, 1) together imply that $c_{11} = c_{22A}b_1$ and $b_1 = c_{11}/c_{22A}$. If the relative price of date 2 consumption in terms of date 1 consumption were not c_{11}/c_{22A}, either type 1 or type 2A would prefer to take and then sell the claim withdrawn by the other type of investor, because the date 1 market value of the claims would differ. The market value of the amount withdrawn by type 1 investors must equal that of type 2A investors; otherwise both will take the one with higher market value and trade to get higher consumption on the desired date.

This implies that types 1 and 2A are indifferent about taking the claims intended for either of the two types. One feasible allocation is $W_{11} = W_{12A} = c_{11}$, $W_{21} = W_{22A} = W_{12A} = 0$, and $W_{22B} = c_{22B}$. In this case, the consumption of type 2B's must exceed $c_{11}R$, which is not binding. The date 1 market clears as follows. All wealth is deposited in the bank at date 0. Type 1 depositors take and consume W_{11}, and type 2A's take W_{12A} and sell in the market to the bank in exchange for $c_{22A} = W_{12A}(X/R)$. In this allocation, the bank holds all assets at date 0 and is the only seller of date 2 claims at date 1, when type 2A agents are the only buyers. The type 2B's do not withdraw at date 1, but take $W_{22B} = c_{22B}$ at date 2. The bank need not hold all assets, and individuals can both buy and sell assets at date 1. This has implications for the equilibrium scale of the banking sector when banks and markets coexist. These implications are developed in Section III. Q.E.D.

Proof of Lemma 3. Suppose that at date 0, a competing bank contract can be proposed by "bank II." Bank II accepts deposits at date 0 and offers date 1 and date 2 type-contingent payments and a portfolio policy. A contract offered by bank I is date 0 coalition incentive-compatible if no dominating contract can be proposed on date 0 by bank II. A contract offered by bank II can offer its members claims on date 1 and date 2 consumption that its type 1 or type 2A members can use to trade on date 1 in the anonymous market that includes members of bank I. The constraint imposed by the possibility of trade after withdrawing from an individual bank is that the price $b_1 = c_{11}/c_{22A}$. The constraint that a competing bank not propose a dominating contract is $b_1 = R/X$. If this does not hold, then a competing bank can give tradable claims to its members that lead to superior consumption opportunities for its members who can trade at price b_1.

Suppose that bank I proposes a contract that, if no competing contract were proposed, would lead to type-contingent consumptions $(c_{11}^I, c_{22A}^I,$ and $c_{22B}^I)$, with $c_{11}^I/c_{22A}^I > R/X$. If no competing contract is proposed, then b_1, the date 1 price of date 2 claims, will be high: $b_1^I = c_{11}^I/c_{22A}^I > R/X$. This allows bank II to propose a dominating contract. Suppose that bank II proposes a contract that gives the same c_{22B} as bank I $(c_{22B}^{II} = c_{22B}^I)$ but invests more of the remaining capital in long-term assets (and less in short-term) to give types 1 and 2A tradable claims slightly biased toward date 2 consumption. Investing one unit more in long-term assets and one fewer in short-term claims allows an R decrease in date 1 and an X-unit increase in date 2 claims. Choose $\epsilon > 0$ such that

$$W_{11}^{II} = W_{12A}^{II} = W_1^{II} = \frac{q_1 c_{11}^I}{q_1 + q_{2A}} - \epsilon,$$

$$W_{21}^{II} = W_{22A}^{II} = W_2^{II} = \frac{q_{2A} c_{22A}^I}{q_1 + q_{2A}} + \frac{\epsilon X}{R}$$

such that

$$\frac{R}{X} \leq \frac{q_1 W_1^{II}}{q_{2A} W_2^{II}} < \frac{c_{11}^I}{c_{22A}^I}. {}^5$$

This implies that

$$c_{11}^{II} = \frac{q_1 c_{11}^I}{q_1 + q_{2A}} - \epsilon + \left(\frac{q_{2A} c_{22A}^I}{q_1 + q_{2A}} + \frac{\epsilon X}{R} \right) b_1$$

$$= \frac{q_1 c_{11}^I}{q_1 + q_{2A}} - \epsilon + \left(\frac{q_{2A} c_{22A}^I}{q_1 + q_{2A}} + \frac{\epsilon X}{R} \right) \frac{c_{11}^I}{c_{22A}^I}$$

$$= c_{11}^I + \epsilon \left(\frac{c_{11}^I X}{c_{22A}^I R} - 1 \right) > c_{11}^I.$$

Similarly, for type 2A agents,

$$c_{22A}^{II} = \left(\frac{q_1 c_{11}^I}{q_1 + q_{2A}} - \epsilon \right) \frac{1}{b_1} + \frac{q_{2A} c_{22A}^I}{q_1 + q_{2A}} + \frac{\epsilon X}{R}$$

$$= \left(\frac{q_1 c_{11}^I}{q_1 + q_{2A}} - \epsilon \right) \frac{c_{22A}^I}{c_{11}^I} + \frac{q_{2A} c_{22A}^I}{q_1 + q_{2A}} + \frac{\epsilon X}{R}$$

$$= c_{22A}^I + \epsilon \left(\frac{c_{11}^I X}{c_{22A}^I R} - 1 \right) > c_{22A}^I.$$

Trade with members of bank I at price b_1^I would allow members of bank II to get date 1 consumption at date 0 cost $(b_1^I X)^{-1} < 1/R$, which is less than the actual date 0 cost of date 1 consumption. If the price ratio, b_1, of date 1 to date 2 consumption is not in line with marginal productivity, R/X, a competing bank can offer a dominating contract. A symmetric argument rules out $b_1 < R/X$. If, and only if, $b_1 = R/X$, is there no dominating contract possible for a competing bank.

---

[5] As an alternative to increasing W_2^{II}, bank II could directly sell long-term assets at date 1.

Proof of Propositions 1 and 2.   When we substitute in the resource constraint, the objective function, Φ, becomes

$$\Phi = q_1 U(c_{11}) + q_{2A} U\left(\frac{c_{11}X}{R}\right)$$

$$+ q_{2B} U\left(\frac{[1 - q_1(c_{11}/R) - q_{2A}(c_{11}/R)]X}{q_{2B}}\right),$$

$$\Phi'(c_{11}) = q_1 U'(c_{11}) + q_{2A} U'\left(\frac{c_{11}X}{R}\right)\frac{X}{R}$$

$$- (q_1 + q_{2A})U'\left(\frac{[1 - q_1(c_{11}/R) - q_{2A}(c_{11}/R)]X}{q_{2B}}\right)\frac{X}{R}.$$

At $c_{11} \leq R$, the resource constraint implies that

$$c_{22B} = \frac{[1 - q_1(c_{11}/R) - q_{2A}(c_{11}/R)]X}{q_{2B}} \geq X$$

and

$$c_{22A} \leq X.$$

The function $U(c)$ is more risk averse than log (c), and $U'(c) > ZU'(cZ)$ for $Z > 1$, implying that $U'(c_{11}) > U'(c_{11}(X/R))(X/R)$. Risk aversion implies that

$$U'\left(\frac{c_{11}X}{R}\right)\frac{X}{R} \geq U'\left(\frac{[1 - q_1(c_{11}/R) - q_{2A}(c_{11}/R)]X}{q_{2B}}\right)\frac{X}{R}.$$

These two results imply that $\Phi'(c_{11}) > 0$ for $c_{11} \leq R$. Because $\Phi(c_{11})$ is continuous but not differentiable at $c_{11} = R$, the optimal value of $c_{11} \geq R$.
    The function Φ is concave:

$$\Phi''(c_{11}) = q_1 U''(c_{11}) + q_{2A} U''\left(c_{11}\frac{X}{R}\right)\frac{X^2}{R^2} + \frac{(q_1 + q_{2A})^2}{q_{2B}}$$

$$\times U''\left(\frac{[1 - q_1(c_{11}/R) - q_{2A}(c_{11}/R)]X}{q_{2B}}\right)\frac{X^2}{R^2} < 0,$$

because $U''(c) < 0$.

Proof That the Right Derivative at $c_{11} = R$ Is Negative if q_{2B} Is Small

Set $c_{11} = R + \epsilon$ for $\epsilon > 0$. From $q_{2B} = 1 - q_1 - q_{2A}$,

$$\Phi'(R + \epsilon) = q_1 U'(R + \epsilon) + q_{2A} U' \left(\frac{(R + \epsilon)X}{R} \right) \frac{X}{R}$$

$$- (q_1 + q_{2A}) U' \left(\frac{\{1 - (q_1 + q_{2A})[(R + \epsilon)/R]\}X}{1 - q_1 - q_{2A}} \right) \frac{X}{R}$$

$$= q_1 U'(R + \epsilon) + q_{2A} U' \left(\left(1 + \frac{\epsilon}{R} \right) X \right) X$$

$$- (q_1 + q_{2A}) U' \left(\frac{\{1 - (q_1 + q_{2A})[1 + (\epsilon/R)]\}X}{1 - q_1 - q_{2A}} \right) \frac{X}{R}$$

$$= q_1 \left[U'(R + \epsilon) - U' \left(X - \frac{(q_1 + q_{2A})\epsilon X}{1 - q_1 - q_{2A}} \right) \frac{X}{R} \right]$$

$$+ q_{2A} \frac{X}{R} \left[U' \left(X + \frac{\epsilon X}{R} \right) X - U' \left(X - \frac{(q_1 + q_{2A})\epsilon X}{1 - q_1 - q_{2A}} \right) \right].$$

For any fixed $\epsilon > 0$ (and for all smaller values of ϵ), one can choose $q_{2B} = 1 - q_1 - q_{2A} > 0$ such that

$$q_{2A} \frac{X}{R} \left[U' \left(X + \frac{\epsilon X}{R} \right) - U' \left(X - \frac{(q_1 + q_{2A})\epsilon X}{1 - q_1 - q_{2A}} \right) \right]$$

is arbitrarily negative; in particular, is less than

$$-q_1 \left[U'(R + \epsilon) - U' \left(X - \frac{(q_1 + q_{2A})\epsilon X}{1 - q_1 - q_{2A}} \right) \frac{X}{R} \right],$$

implying that the right derivative at $c_{11} = R$ is negative if $q_{2B} > 0$ is sufficiently small.

By a similar argument, if q_{2A} is sufficiently small, then there exists $\epsilon > 0$ such that $\Phi'(R + \epsilon) > 0$; because $\Phi(c_{11})$ is concave, the right derivative at $c_{11} = R$ is positive, and the optimal value of c_{11} exceeds R.

As to proposition 2, increasing liquidity implies that more type 2 agents participate and that q_{2B} decreases as q_{2A} increases. If the solution is not at the kink at $c_{11} = R$, then $c_{11} > R$, and $c_{22A} > c_{22B}$. If $c_{11} > R$, then $c_{22A} = c_{11}X/R > c_{22B}$, from concavity of $U(\cdot)$. We have $U'(c_{11})(X/R) > U'(c_{22B})(X/R)$, and as a result, $\Phi'(c_{11})$ is strictly decreasing in q_{2A}.

The expression

$$\frac{\partial \Phi'(c_{11})}{\partial q_{2A}} = \frac{X}{R} \left[U'(c_{22A}) - U'(c_{22B}) - \frac{q_1 + q_{2A}}{q_{2B}} (c_{22B} - c_{22A}) U''(c_{22B}) \right]$$

is less than zero because at the optimum $c_{22A} > c_{22B}$, and concavity of $U(\cdot)$ implies both $U'(c_{22A}) < U'(c_{22B})$ and $U''(c_{22B}) < 0$.

Combined with the previous result that $\Phi''(c_{11}) < 0$, this implies that

$$\frac{\partial c_{11}}{\partial q_{2A}} = -\frac{\partial \Phi'(c_{11})}{\partial q_{2A}}\Phi''(c_{11}) < 0,$$

and the optimal value of c_{11} is decreasing in q_{2A}. This proves proposition 2.

References

Akerlof, G. A. (1970). "The market for 'lemons': Quality uncertainty and the market mechanism." *Q.J.E.*, 84: 488–500.

Allen, F., and Gale, D. (1994). "Limited market participation and volatility of asset prices." *A.E.R.*, 84: 933–55.

Bhattacharya, S., and Gale, D. M. (1987). "Preference shocks, liquidity, and central bank policy," in William A. Barnett and Kenneth J. Singleton (eds.), *New Approaches to Monetary Economics* (New York: Cambridge Univ. Press).

Bryant, J. (1980). "A model of reserves, bank runs, and deposit insurance." *J. Banking and Finance*, 4: 335–44.

Demirgüç-Kunt, A., and Levine, R. (1996). "Stock Market Development and Financial Intermediaries: Stylized Facts." *World Bank Econ. Rev.*, 10: 291–321.

Diamond, D. W. (1991)."Debt maturity structure and liquidity risk." *Q.J.E.*, 106: 709–37.

——(1993). "Seniority and maturity of debt contracts." *J. Financial Econ.*, 33: 341–68.

——, and Dybvig, P. H. (1993). "Bank runs, deposit insurance, and liquidity." *J.P.E.*, 91: 401–19.

Gorton, G., and Pennacchi, G. (1990). "Financial intermediaries and liquidity creation." *J. Finance*, 45: 49–71.

Haubrich, J. G., and King, R. G. (1990) "Banking and insurance." *J. Monetary Econ.*, 26: 361–86.

Hellwig, M. (1994). "Liquidity provision, banking, and the allocation of interest rate risk." *European Econ. Rev.*, 38: 1363–89.

Holmström, B., and Tirole, J. (1996). "Private and Public Supply of Liquidity." Working paper. Cambridge: Massachusetts Inst. Tech., Dept. Econ., 1996.

Hoshi, T., Kashyap, A. K., and Scharfstein, D. S. (1990). "Bank monitoring and investment: Evidence from the changing structure of Japanese corporate banking relationships," in G. Hubbard (ed.), *Asymmetric Information, Corporate Finance, and Investment* (Chicago: Univ. Chicago Press (for NBER)).

Jacklin, C. J. (1987). "Demand deposits, trading restrictions, and risk sharing," in Edward C. Prescott and N. Wallace (eds.), *Contractual Arrangements for International Trade* (Minneapolis: Univ. Minnesota Press).

Merton, R. C. (1987). "A simple model of capital market equilibrium with incomplete information." *J. Finance*, 42: 483–510.

Qi, J. (1994). "Bank Liquidity and stability in a overlapping generation model." *Rev. Financial Studies*, 7: 389–417.

von Thadden, E.-L. (1997). "The term structure of investment and the banks' insurance function." *European Econ. Rev.*, 41.

Wallace, N. (1988). "Another attempt to explain an illiquid banking system: the diamond and dybvig model with sequential service taken seriously." *Fed. Reserve Bank Minneapolis Q. Rev.*, 12: 3–16.

6

Private and Public Supply of Liquidity

Bengt Holmström and Jean Tirole

I. Introduction

This chapter addresses a basic, yet unresolved, question: Do private assets provide sufficient liquidity for the efficient functioning of the productive sector? Or does the state have a role in supplying additional liquidity and regulating it through adjustments in the stock of government securities or by other means?

These questions presume a demand for liquidity, where liquidity refers to the availability of instruments (market and nonmarket) that can be used to transfer wealth across periods.[1] Part of this demand will, of course, come from consumers who want to implement their optimal intertemporal consumption plans. Indeed, papers that have addressed the sufficiency of liquidity have typically focused on the consumer sector (see Section V). We are interested in the production side of the economy. Theoretically, it is less clear why producers demand liquidity. Indeed, in the standard theory of finance (based on the Arrow–Debreu model of general equilibrium) there is no such demand. Since at any time firms can issue claims up to the full value of their expected returns, they have no reason to hold liquid reserves in order to meet future financing needs. As long as firms use their funds to finance positive net present value projects, they will never encounter liquidity problems.

The first step in our analysis then is to build a model in which firms have a demand for liquidity; that is, they need advance financing. For this purpose we use an entrepreneurial model of moral hazard in which the value of external claims on the firm is strictly less than the full value of the firm for the standard

We thank Daron Acemoglu, Sudipto Bhattacharya, Olivier Blanchard, Ricardo Caballero, Peter Diamond, Mark Gertler, Oliver Hart, Peter Howitt, Arvind Krishnamurthy, Robert Marquez, Rafael Repullo, Jean-Charles Rochet, Julio Rotemberg, Andrei Shleifer, Jeremy Stein, Robert Wilson, and Michael Woodford for many helpful discussions and comments. This research was supported by a grant from the National Science Foundation.

[1] Liquidity can be given many other interpretations. For instance, the liquidity of an asset is often measured by how quickly it can be sold without a price discount. The role of liquidity in atemporal exchange leads to an entirely different set of issues that our model does not address (see, e.g., Banerjee and Maskin 1996).

reason that the entrepreneur must be given a minimum share in order to be motivated. The wedge between the full value of the firm and the external value of the firm prevents it from financing all projects that have positive net present value. In a dynamic setting, this feature implies that liquidity shocks could force the firm to terminate a project midstream even though the project has a positive continuation value. To protect itself against such risks, the firm wants to hold liquid reserves in the form of marketed assets that can be readily sold or by arranging in advance for a line of credit (a long-term loan).

The second step in our analysis links the firm's financing problem with the market supply of liquidity. The key observation here is that the same agency problem that limits the amount of financing that firms can raise ex post also limits the amount of liquid assets that are available in the market to back up long-term financial commitments by outside investors. When firms can sell outsiders only a small fraction of their expected returns, the security market as a whole has a very limited capacity to transfer wealth from one period to the next. It is this interplay between the ex post agency problem of the individual firm and the ex ante commitment problem of the market investor that is the central and novel feature of our analysis.

After this brief tour of the main plot, let us describe the paper in some more detail.

We study the determinants of the firm's liquidity demand in a simple, dynamic moral hazard model. There are three periods. At date 0, the firm raises funds to invest in a variable-sized project that pays off at date 2. At date 1, the firm experiences a liquidity shock. The shock is a random fraction of the date 0 investment and represents the amount of additional investment that must be made to continue the project.[2] If the necessary funds can be raised, the project proceeds, delivering a stochastic date 2 return that depends on the entrepreneur's effort.

We show that the optimal date 0 contract between the firm and the outside investors limits both the initial investment level and the amount that the firm is allowed to spend on the liquidity shock, both constraints being proportional to the firm's initial assets. Because the firm is credit-constrained, the second-best solution trades off the benefits of a higher initial investment against the increased likelihood of having to terminate the project early and see it all go to waste. This solution can be implemented in several ways. One is to give the firm all the necessary funds in advance but add a *liquidity covenant* in which the firm promises to set aside a certain amount of funds to cover future liquidity

---

[2] The liquidity shock admits several interpretations. It can be a cost overrun on the initial investment. Alternatively, it can represent a shortfall in the date 1 revenue, which could have been used to finance date 1 operating expenses. Or the shock might simply be information about the firm's date 2 returns. The central feature in all these cases is that the shock affects the firm's net worth, which determines its financing capacity.

needs. Alternatively, intermediaries could fund future liquidity needs via a *credit line.*[3]

Having established a demand for liquidity, we move on to study its supply by embedding the model of the firm in a general equilibrium setting with a large number of similar firms. Each firm (or intermediary) can issue arbitrary claims contingent on its date 2 financial position, and these claims can be freely traded in the market.[4] The government can also supply liquidity by selling securities such as Treasury bonds. There are no other assets that firms and intermediaries can use to transfer wealth from one period to the next.[5] Thus a firm can meet liquidity needs in four ways: by issuing claims on its own productive assets, by holding claims on other firms, by holding government-issued claims, or by using a credit line.

We are mainly interested in understanding the government's role in supplying and managing liquidity as a function of the severity and nature of the liquidity shocks. We consider two polar cases: one in which the firms' liquidity shocks are independent, so that there is no aggregate uncertainty; and the opposite case in which the firms' liquidity shocks are identical.

In the absence of aggregate uncertainty, we show that government securities do not add useful liquidity beyond that provided by private claims; nor does the government have any role in managing aggregate liquidity.[6] There is a simple intuition behind the self-sufficiency of the private sector: The date 1 continuation value of the private sector, which is deterministic, must exceed its date 0 value; else it could not have invested at date 0. Therefore, the private sector can raise sufficient funds at date 1 by diluting its shareholdings or, equivalently, by leveraging itself up with new debt.

However, even though the private sector is self-sufficient in the aggregate, we show that individual firms will in general be unable to satisfy their liquidity needs by holding only private market instruments. One might have thought that it would suffice for each firm to hold a share of the market portfolio, which it could sell when the liquidity shock hits. But this market solution is, in general, not efficient because lucky firms with low liquidity shocks end up holding excess liquidity. Thus scarce liquidity is wasted.

We show that an optimal allocation can be achieved by introducing intermediaries that hold all corporate claims and simultaneously grant credit lines to firms. These intermediaries take into account the fact that some firms (namely,

---

[3] Our theory is too sparse to distinguish between different financial institutions. When we use language that suggests an institutional interpretation (intermediary, bank, etc.), it should be interpreted merely as illustrative of many similar arrangements.

[4] In contrast to much of the literature, we do not restrict the set of claims that firms can issue. This is to avoid a spurious demand for publicly supplied liquidity.

[5] We can allow other assets, such as real estate, as long as their value does not fulfill the private sector's liquidity needs. See Section VI.

[6] If issued, government securities will carry no liquidity premium.

those with low liquidity needs) will not exhaust their credit lines at date 1. Intermediaries can therefore redistribute excess liquidity to firms that do need extra funds. They act like *liquidity pools* or insurers in preventing a wasteful accumulation of liquidity in the firms that end up being lucky at date 1. Thus *intermediation may strictly dominate financial markets that trade in individually issued claims.*[7]

In the presence of pure aggregate uncertainty, the preceding argument for self-sufficiency breaks down. Now there can be no cross-subsidization, because each firm faces trouble exactly when the other firms do. As the private sector is unable to provide insurance, there will be a liquidity shortage whenever the reinvestment need exceeds the date 1 value of corporate claims. This creates a potential demand for government-provided liquidity. We show that the government can achieve a Pareto improvement by issuing Treasury bonds and that these bonds can be sold at a *liquidity premium*. The productive sector is willing to purchase low-yielding securities because they serve as an input into the production process. Despite identical, risk-neutral consumers, securities with different rates of return can coexist in equilibrium.

It is important to point out what the government can achieve that the private sector cannot. In our model, investors are assumed unable to commit their future endowments, unless these commitments are backed up by marketable assets (wealth). Unsecured credit, including short selling, is not available to individuals. This assumption is both theoretically and empirically reasonable. In practice, individuals can borrow very limited amounts without pledging collateral (as in the case of a mortgage). Because the private sector has no power to audit income and levy taxes, it is unable to check who is lying about endowments at date 1. By contrast, the government has the power to audit incomes and impose nonfinancial penalties (such as jail) to enforce tax payments. It can therefore commit funds on behalf of the consumers at date 1.[8] This is what Treasury bonds issued at date 0 achieve.

When the government issues securities at a premium and when firms are constrained to issue a single security (equity), a problem of free-riding emerges. Firms can get liquidity more cheaply by buying shares of those firms that purchase government securities. We show that firms have an incentive to eliminate free-riding by issuing multiple securities in order to price-discriminate between the investors who value liquidity services (producers) and those who do not (consumers). Corporate debt then sells at a premium relative to equity.

Issuing multiple securities is better than issuing single securities, but the solution still falls short of achieving the socially efficient outcome. Since bonds sell at

---

[7] The critical feature of the credit line that yields a productive optimum is that it allows negative net present value investments at date 1. Such commitments may be possible in markets as well if we allow put options on mutual funds. We shall discuss this in more detail later.

[8] If our model included overlapping generations, the government could commit the incomes of future consumers as well.

a premium, the productive sector will try to economize on their use by distorting its investment policy. In particular, firms (or intermediaries) will resort to partial liquidations at date 1, a practice that is socially inefficient. The source of the problem is that the private sector often ends up paying for bonds that it does not need ex post. We show that it is more efficient to have the government issue state-contingent bonds, which supply liquidity only as needed by the private sector. Such bonds have a high value when liquidity needs are high and a low (zero) value when liquidity needs are low. We interpret state-contingent bonds as a metaphor for an active government policy in which liquidity is tightened when the aggregate liquidity shock is favorable (low) and loosened when the aggregate shock is unfavorable (high). Thus the model offers a potential rationale not only for government-supplied liquidity but also for the active management of liquidity by the government.

The chapter is organized as follows. Section II studies the partial equilibrium problem of a single firm. Section III analyzes the general equilibrium model under the assumption of independent liquidity shocks. Section IV considers the case of aggregate uncertainty and analyzes the demand for and supply of government securities, including the optimal use of state-contingent bonds. Section V relates our results to the literatures on credit rationing, intermediation, and government debt. Section VI discusses the robustness of the results and potential extensions.

II. Exogenous Liquidity Supply

A. The model

This section studies the investment decision of an individual firm.

There are three periods, $t = 0, 1, 2$, and two types of agents, firms (entrepreneurs) and investors (consumers). There is one (universal) good used for both consumption and investment. All agents are risk-neutral with an additively separable utility function over undiscounted consumption streams: $u(c_1, c_1, c_2) = c_0 + c_1 + c_2$. For the moment we assume that the good can be stored at a zero rate of return and simply refer to it as "cash." This guarantees that there is no shortage of liquidity. In later sections we shall drop this assumption since we are interested in the endogenous supply of liquidity, that is, in how well financial assets can service the liquidity needs of firms.

The firm has access to a stochastic constant-returns-to-scale technology, which for an initial investment I returns RI if the project succeeds and zero if it fails. The scale of the investment I can be varied freely, subject only to financial constraints. The investment is made at date 0. At date 1, an additional, uncertain amount $\rho I > 0$ of financing is needed to cover operating expenditures and other cash needs. The liquidity shock ρ is distributed according to the cumulative

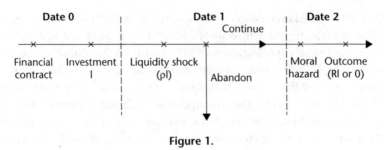

Figure 1.

distribution function F, with a density function f. If ρI is paid, the project continues and a final payoff is realized at date 2. If ρI is not paid, the project terminates and yields nothing (partial liquidation will be considered later).

Investment is subject to moral hazard in that the firm (entrepreneur) privately chooses the probability p that the project succeeds. The firm can either "behave" or "shirk." If the firm behaves, the probability of success is p_H (high); if it shirks, the probability of success is p_L (low), where $p_H - p_L \equiv \Delta p > 0$. If the firm shirks, it enjoys a private benefit, $BI > 0$, proportional to the level of its investment I. The firm makes the decision on p after the continuation decision. The timing of events is described in figure 1.

The firm has a date 0 endowment of cash, $A > 0$, and no endowments at dates 1 and 2.[9] It can raise additional funds from outside investors. For the moment, we assume that the initial investment level, the project outcome, and the liquidity shock are all verifiable (as we shall see, nothing changes if only the entrepreneur observes the liquidity shock). A contract with outside investors specifies the amount that the investors will contribute, the initial scale of the project, the contingencies in which the project is continued at date 1, and the distribution of the proceeds from the investment. The contract has to offer the investors a nonnegative expected return. A key constraint is that the firm cannot pay out more funds than it has: there is *limited liability*.

The net present value of the investment is maximized by continuing the project if and only if $\rho \leq \rho_1 \equiv p_H R$, that is, whenever the expected return $p_H R$ from continuation exceeds the cost ρ. We shall refer to ρ_1 as the *first-best cutoff*. To make the problem interesting, we assume that the project's net present value is positive if the firm is diligent (chooses p_H) but not if it shirks (chooses p_L):

$$\int \max\{p_H R - \rho, 0\} f(\rho)\, d\rho - 1 > 0 > \int \max\{p_L R + B - \rho, 0\} f(\rho)\, d\rho - 1. \quad (1)$$

---

[9] There is no loss of generality in assuming zero endowments as long as cash is available. In the presence of a random date 1 revenue stream, the liquidity shock should be thought of as the *net* cash flow at date 1.

Given (1), we need to consider only contracts that implement the action p_H. Let $C = \{I, \lambda(\rho), R_f(\rho)\}$ be a generic contract, where I is the level of investment, $\lambda(\rho)$ is a state-contingent continuation policy (1 = continue, 0 = abandon), and $R_f(\rho)$ is the amount the firm is paid if the project succeeds (given a liquidity shock ρ). Investors are left with $R - R_f(\rho)$. If the project fails or is abandoned, we assume that both sides receive zero. This assumption is made without loss of generality since any feasible contract in which transfers are made despite a zero outcome can be replaced by a payoff-equivalent (or superior) contract in which payments are made only when the project succeeds. An optimal contract can be found by choosing $\{I, \lambda(\rho), R_f(\rho)\}$ to solve the following *second-best program*:

$$\max I \int p_H R_f(\rho) \lambda(\rho) f(\rho) f(\rho) \, d\rho - A \tag{2a}$$

$$\text{subject to} \quad I \int \{p_H[R - R_f(\rho)] - \rho\} \lambda(\rho) f(\rho) \, d\rho \geq I - A \tag{2b}$$

$$\text{and} \quad R_f(\rho) \Delta p \geq B \quad \text{for every } \rho. \tag{2c}$$

Program (2) maximizes the firm's net return subject to the investors' break-even constraint (2b) and the firm's incentive compatibility constraint (2c).

Program (2) is linear in I, so it will have a finite solution only if constraint (2b) binds. For the moment, assume that this is the case; we shall provide precise conditions below. Solving (2), one finds that the optimal continuation policy is a cutoff rule of the form "continue if and only if $\rho \leq \hat{p}$." Substituting (2b) into (2a), we can then write the firm's objective in the form

$$U_f(\hat{\rho}) = m(\hat{\rho}) I, \tag{3}$$

where

$$m(\hat{\rho}) = \int_0^{\hat{\rho}} (\rho_1 - \rho) f(\rho) \, d\rho - 1 \tag{4}$$

is the *marginal net social return* on investment. Writing the firm's payoff in the form (3) underscores the fact that, as a residual claimant, the firm receives the full social surplus.

It is easily verified that $m(\hat{\rho})$ is quasi-concave and achieves its maximum at the first-best cutoff $\hat{\rho} = \rho_1$. Because the net present value of the project is positive by assumption (1), we have $m(\rho_1) > 0$. But then the marginal return $m(\hat{\rho})$ for the second-best policy must also be strictly positive because the first-best cutoff rule $\hat{\rho} = \rho_1$ is feasible in (2) (for small enough I). Given $m(\hat{\rho}) > 0$, it follows from (3) that the firm will choose payments $R_f(\rho)$ to maximize I. This is achieved by setting $R_f(\rho) = R_b \equiv B/\Delta p$, the minimum payment necessary to keep the entrepreneur diligent.[10] By taking out as little as possible, the firm maximizes

---

[10] The minimum payment to the entrepreneur can more broadly be interpreted as a rent shared by all employees of the firm. Without such rents, employees will not work as efficiently.

the amount that it can pay to outside investors, which (per unit invested) is $\rho_0 \equiv p_H[R - (B/\Delta p)]$. We shall refer to ρ_0 as the *date 1 pledgeable unit return* from investment.

The fact that outside investors can be promised only an expected return $\rho_0 I$ at date 1 rather than the full social value $\rho_1 I$ plays a key role in our analysis.[11] Without a positive wedge $\rho_1 - \rho_0 > 0$, investments would be self-financing and there would be no demand for liquidity (as will become clear later). In fact, the firm would be free to invest arbitrary large amounts at date 0, making the second-best problem unconstrained. To see this, return to the break-even constraint (2b). The left-hand side is maximized by following the cutoff policy $\hat{\rho} = \rho_0$ and promising investors ρ_0 in each contingency ρ. To eliminate self-financing, we must assume that such a policy does not provide investors an expected marginal return that is larger than the marginal cost of their date 0 investment, which means that

$$\int_0^{\rho_0} (\rho_0 - \rho) f(\rho) \, d\rho < 1. \tag{5}$$

Note that if $\rho_0 = \rho_1 (B = 0)$, assumption (5) is inconsistent with assumption (1). A positive wedge $\rho_1 - \rho_0 > 0$ is therefore essential for ruling out self-financing.

Condition (5) is necessary and sufficient for the break-even constraint (2b) to be binding and for the second-best solution to be finite. It follows from (2b) that the firm's *investment capacity*, the maximum amount it can invest at date 0 given the cutoff rule $\hat{\rho}$, is

$$I = k(\hat{\rho})A, \tag{6}$$

where

$$k(\hat{\rho}) \equiv \frac{1}{1 + \int_0^{\hat{\rho}} \rho f(\rho) \, d\rho - F(\hat{\rho})\rho_0} \tag{7}$$

is the *equity multiplier*. The denominator of the equity multiplier specifies the amount of internal funds that the firm has to put in per unit invested in order to make up for the shortfall implied by (5).

It is easy to verify that $k(\hat{\rho})$ is quasi-concave, achieves its maximum at $\hat{\rho} = \rho_0$, and has $k(\rho_0) > 1$. The equity multiplier can be less than one if the cutoff $\hat{\rho}$ is set sufficiently high. This may be optimal if the expected liquidity demand at date 1 is large. In that case $I - A < 0$. (The total investment, the initial investment plus the expected liquidity payments, will of course exceed the firm's initial cash A; else the firm would not go outside for funding.) Unless otherwise specified, we shall assume that $I - A > 0$, since it seems natural to have the firm a net borrower at date 0.[12]

---

[11] We could have created a wedge between the social value ρ_1 and the pledgeable value ρ_0 more expediently, but less realistically, by assuming that the entrepreneur can steal the difference.

[12] A sufficient condition for $I - A > 0$ is that $k(\rho_1) > 1$.

It remains to determine the second-best continuation threshold ρ^*. If we substitute (6) into (3), the firm's net payoff becomes

$$U_f(\hat{\rho}) = m(\hat{\rho})k(\hat{\rho})A. \tag{8}$$

The second-best threshold is chosen to maximize (8). Because m and k are both quasi-concave functions, with m reaching a maximum at ρ_1 and k reaching a maximum at ρ_0, the second-best threshold ρ^*, must fall in the interval $[\rho_0, \rho_1]$. Economically, this can be understood by noting that if $\rho < \rho_0$, both the firm and the investors prefer to continue ex post; if $\rho < \rho_1$, the net present value of continuing is negative, and hence it is Pareto-optimal to abandon the project. (Since transfers from investors to the firm are not constrained by incentive compatibility, investors can always pay the firm to abandon an inefficient project.)

Within the interval $[\rho_0, \rho_1]$ the firm faces a trade-off. It can raise $\hat{\rho}$ in order to be able to withstand higher liquidity shocks, thereby raising the marginal return $m(\hat{\rho})$ on its date 0 investment, or it can lower $\hat{\rho}$ to expand on the date 0 level of investment $k(\hat{\rho})A$. It cannot do both, because the investors' break-even constraint places a limit on its overall spending. Because m is strictly increasing at ρ_0 and k is strictly decreasing at ρ_1, the firm resolves this trade-off by choosing ρ^* so that

$$\rho_0 < p^* < p_1. \tag{9}$$

Faced with credit rationing, the firm lets itself be rationed both ex ante and ex post.

This choice of ρ^* can also be interpreted as the outcome of (second-best) risk sharing. Because the firm cannot raise more than $\rho_0 I$ at date 1 even though the social value of continuation is $\rho_1 I$, it purchases insurance from investors at date 0. If the liquidity shock ρ falls below ρ_0, the investors win (the firm would not have needed insurance). If ρ falls above ρ_0, the firm wins (the investors participate in a deal that gives them a negative expected return). With limited resources the second-best policy is to buy some, but not full, insurance.

To characterize ρ^*, we can write out the firm's net payoff $U_f(\hat{\rho})$ using (4) and (7) and then divide through by $F(\hat{\rho})$. This shows that

$$\rho^* \text{ minimizes } \frac{1 + \int_0^{\hat{\rho}} \rho f(\rho)\, d\rho}{F(\hat{\rho})}. \tag{10}$$

Stated verbally, the second-best threshold minimizes the expected unit cost of total expected investment. The first-order condition for (10) is simply

$$\int_0^{\rho^*} F(\rho)\, d\rho = 1. \tag{11}$$

It is a bit surprising that the second-best cutoff ρ^* does not depend either on ρ_0 or on ρ_1 as long as it falls between these two values.[13] Thus the additional funding that becomes available when ρ_0 goes up will all be used to expand scale rather than to add liquidity. The result is driven by the linear structure, which implies that marginal rates of substitution across states and periods are independent of the level of investment.

With (11), the firm's net return can be written in the compact form

$$U_f(\rho^*) = \frac{\rho_1 - \rho^*}{\rho^* - \rho_0} A. \tag{12}$$

Equations (11) and (12) have the following interesting consequence. Suppose that the liquidity shock becomes riskier in the sense of a mean-preserving spread in the distribution F. Then (11) shows that the cutoff ρ^* goes down; the firm buys less insurance, because it costs more in reduced date 0 investment. At the same time, (12) shows that the firm's net return $U_f(\rho^*)$ is higher when the liquidity shock has a riskier distribution. The explanation for this slightly counterintuitive result is that the option to terminate the project makes a riskier distribution more valuable. Indeed, if the liquidity shock had a degenerate distribution, assumption (5) would imply that the firm could never invest.

We close this subsection with two remarks.

Remark 1. The results above are unaffected if we allow for partial liquidation. This can be seen by letting $\lambda(\rho)$ vary freely between zero and one in program (2). The second-best $\lambda(\rho)$ would still be zero or one, with no change in the optimal cutoff. As we shall see later, this result will not hold when the firm has to pay a premium for liquidity services.

Remark 2. For future reference we note that the firm's expected output, $F(\hat{\rho})\rho_1 k(\hat{\rho})A$, and the value of the investors' claims on this output, $F(\hat{\rho})\rho_0 k(\hat{\rho})A$, are quasi-concave in $\hat{\rho}$ and reach their maximum at the second-best optimum $\hat{\rho} = \rho^*$.

B. Implementation of the optimal policy

Suppose that the decision to continue the project is left to be negotiated at date 1. In that case, investors would be willing to inject more cash into the project if $\rho \leq \rho_0$, but not if $\rho > \rho_0$. In the latter case, even if the firm were allowed to dilute the claims of the initial investors by issuing senior securities at date 1, it could not raise enough cash because the most the firm can promise outside investors at date 1 is $\rho_0 I$. Thus, to cover liquidity shocks up to the second-best cutoff $\rho^* > \rho_0$, one must find a way for outside investors to commit funds at date 0.

---

[13] If ρ^*, as determined by (11), falls below ρ_0, the firm's investment capacity is infinite. If it falls above ρ_1, the firm cannot profitably raise external funds.

One solution is to give the firm $I - A$ at date 0 and extend it an *irrevocable line of credit* in the amount $\rho^* I$, which the firm can use to meet liquidity needs at date 1. Since the firm cannot consume funds and since it always prefers to continue the project whenever it can, this credit line will implement the second-best solution.[14] Equivalently, the investors can extend an irrevocable credit line in the amount $(\rho^* - \rho_0)I$ and grant the firm the right to dilute outside claims as needed to cover the liquidity shock.

In practice, individuals do not grant credit lines to firms. One reason is that individuals have difficulties committing their future income or endowments. They can too easily avoid payment by claiming that they have no funds. The limited amount of nonsecured, personal borrowing that takes place testifies to these problems. In practice, credit lines are granted by intermediaries such as banks, which can make commitments, assuming of course that they have enough funds to meet later credit needs. This raises the question, How do intermediaries guarantee that their own liquidity needs can be met? In the next section, we show that they can do so by issuing shares that pay off only at date 2.

An alternative solution is to give the firm $I(1 + \rho^*) - A$ at date 0 and require that $\rho^* I$ of this amount is kept in liquid assets. In other words, investors demand that the firm maintains a *liquidity ratio* equal to $\rho^*/(1 + \rho^*)$, at least up to date 1. Indeed, a minimum liquidity ratio is a commonly observed debt covenant. As in the case of credit lines, an intermediary is the natural party for overseeing the compliance of such a covenant. It is worth stressing that the partial equilibrium model with "cash" does not distinguish between a credit line and the hoarding of liquid assets by the firm. But as the next section shows, these two methods of providing reserves are no longer equivalent once general equilibrium aspects (implying that liquid assets sell at a premium) are brought into consideration.

Remark 1. We assumed that the liquidity shock is verifiable. Nothing is altered if only the firm observes the liquidity shock as long as the firm cannot use part of the credit line or its financial assets for consumption at date 1. Given the firm's reserves, it can continue whenever $\rho < \rho^*$. If $\rho > \rho^*$, it cannot continue, since no outsider can be induced to invest in the firm. A rational investor would infer that a firm that tries to raise new funds does so because it has exceeded its reserves and therefore has experienced a shock $\rho > \rho^* > \rho_0$.

Remark 2. If investors cannot control the firm's initial allocation of funds, one can show that the firm does not want to distribute the funds between date 0 investment and date 1 investment in accordance with the second-best solution.

---

[14] Could the line of credit be renegotiated for mutual advantage once ρ is realized? The answer is no. If $\rho \leq \rho^*$, then $\rho < p_H R$ and it is ex post efficient to continue, so there is no scope for renegotiation. Nor can both parties benefit from an increase in the line of credit when $\rho^* < \rho \leq p_H R$. Even though this increase raises total surplus, there is no way to distribute the surplus in a manner that satisfies the investors.

Either the firm wants to invest less initially in order to be able to continue in more states at date 1; or the firm wants to invest excessively at date 0, relying partly on being bailed out by the investors when $\rho < \rho_0$ and there is a cash shortfall. To illustrate the latter possibility, suppose that the firm invests the full amount $I(1 + \rho^*) \equiv I^*$ at date 0 rather than saving ρ^*I for date 1. Despite no cash for reinvestment, the project will often be continued since the investors have an incentive to rescue the firm whenever $\rho \leq \rho_0$. Of course, the investors might want to claim initially that they will not put any more money into the venture, but this is not a credible commitment. Anticipating a "soft budget constraint," the firm may overinvest. Indeed the firm prefers investing I^* rather than I if $F(\rho^*)p_H R_b I < F(\rho_0)p_H R_b I^*$, or $F(\rho^*) < F(\rho_0)(1+\rho^*)$. This condition can be satisfied by adjusting B so that ρ_0 falls just below ρ^*.

We summarize the results of this section in the following proposition.

PROPOSITION 1. *In the second-best allocation, the following are true: (i) A firm with initial capital A invests $I = k(\rho^*)A$, where the equity multiplier $k(\cdot)$ is given by (7). (ii) The project is continued if and only if the liquidity shock falls below the cutoff ρ^*. The cutoff ρ^* lies strictly between the (per unit of investment) pledgeable expected return $\rho_0 = p_H[R - (B/\Delta p)]$ and the expected return $\rho_1 = p_H R$. (iii) Neither party is paid anything if the project is terminated or fails. If the project succeeds, the firm is paid $(B/\Delta p)I$ and the investors $[R - (B/\Delta p)]I$. (iv) The second-best allocation can be implemented by raising $I - A$ in external funds for the initial investment and by extending the firm a line of credit in the amount ρ^*I to be used for reinvestment. Alternatively, the firm can be given $(1 + \rho^*)I$ at date 0 with the covenant that it keeps ρ^*I in reserve for reinvestments.*

III. Endogenous Liquidity Supply without Aggregate Uncertainty

A. The economy

Next we embed our model in a general equilibrium framework. Our objective is to analyze the endogenous supply of liquidity. To focus on the problem of creating assets that can meet the demand for liquidity at date 1, we drop the assumption that there is an exogenously given storage technology. The single consumption good cannot be stored (there is no longer cash), nor are there any other private assets (such as real estate) that can be used to transfer wealth from one period to the next. The only way to transfer wealth across periods is to buy claims issued by firms. Later on, we shall introduce government bonds.

There is a continuum of firms with unit mass. Each firm is endowed with the stochastic technology described in Section II. Because of constant returns to scale, there is no loss in assuming that firms have identical endowments; the representative firm is endowed with A units of the good at date 0 and none at dates 1 and 2.

As before, consumers and entrepreneurs are risk-neutral and do not care about the timing of consumption. Consumers receive endowments per period that collectively are large enough to finance all required investments and taxes that may be levied. Consumers cannot sell claims on (or borrow against) their future endowments because they can default with impunity. Only promises that are backed up by marketable assets (claims on firms) can be made. This is a key assumption. Without it, there would be no shortage of liquid instruments, nor any role for government intervention.

Any assets purchased by the consumers must yield a zero expected return given that their collective endowments exceed investment demand. By contrast, firms may be willing to purchase assets at a premium (a negative return) as long as those assets help them to meet their liquidity needs. Thus rates of return, to the extent that they deviate from zero, will be entirely determined by the productive sector. This is the convenience afforded by a linear preference structure.

In this section we shall consider the case in which liquidity shocks are independent. Because there is a continuum of firms, there is no aggregate uncertainty; and $F(\rho)$ denotes both the ex ante probability that a given firm faces a liquidity shock below ρ and the realized fraction of firms with liquidity shock below ρ. The independence assumption and the analysis in Section II imply that the date 1 funds needed by the productive sector to achieve the productive optimum are the deterministic amount

$$D \equiv I \int_0^{\rho^*} \rho f(\rho)\, d\rho, \tag{13}$$

where I is the representative firm's investment.

The two ways of implementing the productive optimum discussed in Section II, an irrevocable credit line and a liquidity requirement, both relied on an exogenously supplied liquid asset, cash. With cash no longer available, we are led to investigate whether firms can finance their liquidity needs D by using available market instruments, that is, by issuing additional claims at date 1 or by holding stakes in other firms.

B. Financial markets

For the time being, assume that there are no intermediaries. There is only a financial market for individual claims issued by firms or composite securities such as mutual funds. We exclude put options. In our interpretation, puts on mutual funds fall in the category of intermediation.

We first compute the maximum amount that a firm can raise by selling new (senior) securities at date 1. If the firm is able to continue with the amount thus raised, its market value at date 1 is $p_H(R - R_b)I = \rho_0 I$. This value reflects the fact that the firm must retain a minimum stake $R_b I$ as an inside claim in order to behave. Since date 0 investors, those who bought the firm's initial securities, get nothing if the firm cannot meet its liquidity needs, they are willing (ex post) to dilute their claims up to the full amount $\rho_0 I$ in order to salvage some of their initial investment. Of course, initial investors take the possibility of dilution into account in the pricing of initial claims.

A firm is unable to meet its liquidity needs by issuing new claims whenever the realized liquidity shock ρ falls in the interval $(\rho_0, \rho^*]$. Can a firm cover the potential shortfall by buying, at date 0, claims issued by other firms and selling these claims at date 1? That is, can the firm assure itself enough liquidity through the financial market? The answer is, in general, negative.

To develop an intuition for why the financial market may be unable to serve the firms' liquidity needs efficiently, let us assume (for illustration only) that all external claims are equity claims and that, to the extent that firms buy these claims to meet liquidity needs, they all end up with the same share of the market portfolio (because firms are identical).[15] The absence of aggregate shocks implies that S_1, the value of the market portfolio at date 1, is deterministic. Suppose that the productive optimum of Section II obtains: a firm with liquidity shock ρ continues if and only if $\rho \leq \rho^*$. Then a fraction $F(\rho^*)$ of firms will continue at date 1. The total value of external claims on the productive sector at date 1 is therefore

$$V_1 = F(\rho^*)\rho_0 I. \tag{14}$$

In the absence of credit lines, these external claims need to be diluted by the amount D defined in (13), so the value S_1, of the market portfolio at date 1 is

$$S_1 = V_1 - D$$

$$= \left[F(\rho^*)\rho_0 - \int_0^{\rho^*} \rho f(\rho)\, d\rho \right] I = I - A. \tag{15}$$

The value of the market portfolio is positive, since we assumed that $I - A > 0$.

Let us conduct the following thought experiment: Suppose that a fraction $\alpha \in (0, 1)$ of the market portfolio is held by the firms. At date 1, each firm can then withstand liquidity shocks ρ satisfying

$$\rho I \leq \rho_0 I + \alpha S_1. \tag{16}$$

For the right-hand side of (16) to equal $\rho^* I$ for some $\alpha < 1$, one must have

$$\rho^* + \int_0^{\rho^*} \rho f(\rho) d\rho < [1 + F(\rho^*)]\rho_0. \tag{17}$$

---

[15] Assuming that firms are identical is not significant for the argument.

Recalling that ρ^* is independent of the extent of moral hazard as measured by B (see [11]), we conclude that, for B large enough, ρ_0 is so small that condition (17) is violated. In that case, firms are unable to withstand liquidity shocks up to ρ^* by holding a share of the market portfolio. Intuitively, when B is large, the firm's minimum inside share R_b must be large, and therefore the firm cannot raise much capital by diluting claims at date 1. Concurrently, and for the same reason, the market portfolio has a low value, so the firm cannot raise much by selling its shares in the other firms.

Actually, as the next section demonstrates, the issue is not that the stock market delivers too little liquidity *in the aggregate*. Rather, the ex post *distribution* of liquid assets is inefficient. Lucky firms (those with liquidity shocks $\rho < \rho_0$) end up holding shares they do not need, whereas unlucky firms with large liquidity shocks cannot continue because the average share of the market portfolio offers insufficient liquidity.

It is clear that the previous reasoning does not rely on the particular securities issued by individual firms. The difference between the total value of external claims and the aggregate reinvestment cost when the threshold is ρ^*, S_1, is an upper bound on the combined value of *all* external date 0 claims on the productive sector. Hence, in the aggregate, the value of the financial claims held by the firms cannot exceed S_1. Given that dilution cannot raise more than $\rho_0 I$ per firm, some firms (all firms, if financial claims are uniformly distributed among firms) cannot withstand shocks exceeding $\rho_0 I + S_1$.

To conclude, financial markets in which only "pure plays" (claims on individual firms) are traded cannot in general implement the productive optimum.

C. Intermediation

When the financial market fails to supply enough liquidity, the productive optimum can be implemented by introducing an intermediary that offers insurance against liquidity needs by pooling firm risks. In accordance with Section II, optimal insurance entails subsidizing firms with a high liquidity demand by allowing them to draw on the market value of firms that experience a low liquidity demand.

We first check that there is enough liquidity in the aggregate to implement the second-best policy. Let all individual firms be pooled together into a single firm, an economywide conglomerate. If the conglomerate follows the second-best policy, where individual firms continue if and only if $\rho \le \rho^*$, the conglomerate can be sold at date 1 (gross of reinvestments) for the value $F(\rho^*)\rho_0 I$. The conglomerate needs to raise D (see [13]) to cover its liquidity needs. Since $F(\rho^*)\rho_0 I - D = S_1$, which is positive, the conglomerate can raise the necessary funds to implement the second-best policy.

It remains to show that an intermediary can make full use of the potential market value of the private sector. There are many ways in which this can be done. The simplest is to let the intermediary replicate the conglomerate solution as follows.[16] At date 0, it issues shares to investors. These shares are claims on the intermediary's financial position at date 2.[17] The intermediary uses the proceeds from its share issue to buy up all the external claims on firms. Firms are priced so that the intermediary breaks even on each firm issue (ex ante). Similarly, the shares of the intermediary are so priced that investors break even. If the intermediary succeeds in implementing the second-best policy, its shares will now sell for the amount S_1, since its market value equals the value of its investment portfolio. The intermediary's net "cash flow" at date 0 is zero, guaranteeing that the arrangement is financially feasible.

The intermediary proceeds to grant each firm a credit line equal to ρ^*I. Attached to the credit line is the covenant that a firm cannot issue new claims at date 1. A firm can use all or just a portion of its credit line at date 1. There is no charge for using credit (we shall return to this point below). However, the firm has no use for excess credit since the entrepreneur cannot consume funds, and any returns from market assets that the firm might purchase at date 1 will go to the intermediary (except for the portion R_bI, which goes to the entrepreneur if the project succeeds). Given the credit line, a firm can continue whenever $\rho \leq \rho^*$.

The only remaining issue is whether the intermediary can raise enough funds at date 1 to meet its (deterministic) credit obligations D. But this follows immediately from the fact, argued above, that the private sector in the aggregate can raise $S_1 + D = (I - A) + D > D$. Since we assumed that firms raise a positive amount ex ante ($I - A > 0$) and the ex ante calculation includes the expected cost of covering the liquidity shock, firms must be able to raise a positive amount also ex post when the liquidity shock is not part of the valuation.

Remark 1. There are many variations on intermediation that are equivalent to the one described above. For instance, the intermediary could be made to resemble a bank by letting firms issue shares directly to investors and having the intermediary hold only firm debt (claims senior to equity). The intermediary could also charge the firm according to the amount of credit used rather than just an upfront fixed fee. To illustrate, a credit arrangement could call for a repayment of $(\rho/\rho^*)(R - R_b)I$ at date 2 (which can be met, of course, only if the project succeeds) if the firm uses ρI ($\leq \rho^*I$) of credit at date 1. Note that the implied price for credit is below par since the expected repayment equals $(\rho\rho_0/\rho^*)I$, which is less than ρI, the amount of credit used. In

---

[16] In our model, the number of intermediaries is indeterminate. We shall describe the implementation of the second-best solution as though there were a single intermediary.

[17] As in Jacklin (1987), it is important to avoid claims that can be redeemed at date 1, since such claims can lead to "bank runs."

fact, because firms are fully diluted when $\rho > \rho_0$, there is no credit contract that charges an actuarially fair price for all realizations of ρ. An additional up-front fee must be imposed to cover the intermediary's expected loss. In reality, such fees are common, suggesting that use of credit is indeed underpriced ex post.

Variations like these influence only how surplus is redistributed among external claim holders and how initial claims are priced, but they have no effect on real outcomes. Therefore, we can proceed without pinning down these contractual details.[18]

Remark 2. One may wonder what it is that an intermediary can do that the financial market cannot do. We argued in Section IIIA that the financial market fails to provide adequate liquidity because the value of the market claims that the firm holds cannot be made contingent on the firm's idiosyncratic liquidity shock. By contrast, the value of the credit line does depend on the firm's realized need for liquidity. Even when the intermediary is unable to observe ρ, the firm reveals the liquidity shock voluntarily. Thus intermediation does not necessarily require more information than the market has. This feature is of course quite dependent on our assumption that the firm cannot spend credit on anything other than the liquidity shock. Without that assumption, the self-revelation mechanism implied by the credit line would break down.

If the intermediary is just a passive coordinator of contracts, one would think that a complex market instrument could replace it. Indeed, we could interpret our intermediary solution as a put option on a mutual fund that holds the market portfolio. Puts would function just like credit lines, assuming that the firms could not use the puts for anything other than to cover their liquidity shocks. On the other hand, if one assumes that anonymous markets cannot impose constraints on how investors use the proceeds from their market trades, then an intermediary that can put such constraints on firms will dominate the market. To the extent that such constraints require monitoring, our intermediary solution does require more information than the market has.

PROPOSITION 2. *In the absence of aggregate uncertainty, the following are true: (i) The productive optimum cannot always be achieved through an (anonymous) financial market. Ex post, liquidity may be misallocated. (ii) The productive optimum can be implemented (if $I - A > 0$) by relying on private intermediation of credit. Intermediaries act like insurers against liquidity shocks, cross-subsidizing firms. Intermediaries need not observe individual liquidity shocks in order to implement the optimum. (iii) There is no liquidity role for government securities. If issued, such securities must be offered at par (yielding zero interest) and do not affect real allocations.*

---

[18] Monitoring and control right considerations could be introduced to reduce contractual ambiguity, but the implications of such embellishments must await further research.

IV. Endogenous Liquidity Supply with Pure Aggregate Uncertainty

A. The demand for government bonds

In the previous section liquidity shocks were independent. We now shift to the other extreme, the case in which there is only aggregate uncertainty. All firms experience the same liquidity shock.

It is clear that in this case the private sector cannot be self-sufficient. With pure aggregate uncertainty, every firm needs to raise ρI at the same time. Since a firm is worth at most $\rho_0 I$ to outsiders at date 1, the aggregate demand for liquidity will exceed the aggregate value of the private sector whenever $\rho_0 < \rho \leq \rho^*$. Intermediation cannot overcome the problem, because at best it can realize the net ex post value of the productive sector, which in this event is zero.

This creates a demand for government-supplied liquidity. The government can meet the demand thanks to its assumed ability to commit future consumer endowments via taxation. Suppose that the government issues one-period bonds in the amount $(\rho^* - \rho_0)I$ at date 0 and sells them at par. We are then back to the environment analyzed in Section II, with government bonds providing a storage facility equivalent to cash. The productive optimum can be achieved by having investors invest $(1 + \rho^*)I - A$ in each firm at date 0, with the requirement that firms spend $(\rho^* - \rho_0)I$ of this amount on the purchase of bonds.[19]

Since government bonds, issued at par, lead to the productive optimum, we know from the analysis in Section II that the introduction of bonds raises total output and expected aggregate investment (the date 0 investment plus the expected value of date 1 reinvestments). Recall, however, that the initial level of investment I decreases as firms save more of their resources to cover date 1 liquidity needs. Thus issuing government bonds crowds out productive investments at date 0 but increases (expected) reinvestments at date 1.

PROPOSITION 3. *In the presence of aggregate uncertainty, the following are true: (i) The private sector is not self-sufficient with regard to the supply of liquidity. (ii) If the net social cost of taxation is zero, the government can ensure the productive optimum by issuing enough bonds at the market rate of interest (here, zero), in which case there is no demand for intermediation. (iii) The introduction of government bonds reduces date 0 investments and increases date 1 reinvestments (reduces liquidations). Expected output, aggregate investment, and the value of firms all increase.*

---

[19] Alternatively, an intermediary can offer each firm a credit line $(\rho^* - \rho_0)I$, backed by the purchase of an equal amount of government bonds. Firms can raise the missing $\rho_0 I$ by issuing new shares.

B. The government's objective and liquidity premia

By restricting attention to government securities that yield the market rate of interest, Section IVA made two implicit assumptions. First, there is no deadweight loss of taxation.[20] Otherwise, the gain in productive efficiency brought about by the bond issue must be traded off against the change in the deadweight loss of taxation. Second, the government maximizes the firms' profit subject to the consumers' breaking even. If either assumption is violated, the government may want to issue securities at a price q above par ($q > 1$) per unit of expected return. We refer to $q - 1$ as the *liquidity premium*. Note that since consumers have no liquidity needs, they will not buy bonds (or any other assets) that sell at a premium. They would like to go short on bonds, but this is excluded by our assumption that individual consumers cannot make financial commitments without backing them up with marketable assets.[21] For small premia, there is still a demand for government securities since the private sector uses them as complementary inputs into the production process.

As is well known, credit rationing models raise some conceptual difficulties for a welfare analysis. A government that aims at maximizing total surplus (consumers' plus producers') would redistribute all endowments to entrepreneurs since one unit of net worth creates more than one unit of output. On the other hand, a government that represents only consumers might confiscate some or all of the entrepreneurs' initial wealth A. Because these conceptual problems are not specific to our model and lie beyond the limited scope of this paper, we shall not investigate the effects of alternative assumptions on the government's objective function. Instead, we simply assume that the government arranges the financing of bonds so that firms bear the net cost of supplying liquidity, leaving consumers as well off as without government intervention (see, however, the upcoming remark on seigniorage). The overall tax effect includes the benefit of distributing the proceeds from the bond issue at date 0 (or reducing date 0 taxes) and the deadweight loss from taxing consumers to redeem the bonds at date 1. It is apparent that at the social optimum the marginal deadweight loss of taxation must be time-increasing. Suppose that the marginal deadweight loss were higher at date 0 than at date 1, say. The government could then issue at date 0 additional one-period bonds at par (at a zero rate of interest). Taxpayers would strictly gain and firms would be made (at least weakly) better off by the increased supply of liquidity. We conclude that, for the optimal debt policy, $q \geq 1$.[22]

---

[20] Or, more generally, the marginal deadweight loss of taxation is the same at all dates; so the date 0 deadweight loss due to the income received by issuing government securities is equal to the date 1 (or date 2) deadweight loss associated with the reimbursement of the public debt.

[21] Claims on firms will not do as collateral because they do not span the bond return.

[22] The government cannot gain by reimbursing public debt at date 2 because the deadweight loss of taxation is higher at date 2 than at date 1 by the same reasoning.

C. The demand for government bonds

Let us temporarily rule out cross-shareholdings and intermediation, and run through the analysis of Section II A to see how firms respond to the presence of a liquidity premium $q-1 > 0$. We continue to assume that a firm cannot partially liquidate its investment. Given a cutoff $\hat{\rho}$, the investors' participation constraint becomes

$$F(\hat{\rho})\rho_0 I \geq I - A + \left[\int_0^{\hat{\rho}} \rho f(\rho) d\rho \right] I + (q-1)(\hat{\rho} - \rho_0)I, \qquad (18)$$

where use is made of the fact that the maximum dilution at date 1 is $\rho_0 I$, so that $(\hat{\rho} - \rho_0)I$ in government securities is needed to reach the threshold $\hat{\rho}$.

The firm's net utility is now

$$U_f(\hat{\rho}, q) \equiv m(\hat{\rho}, q)k(\hat{\rho}, q)A,$$

where

$$m(\hat{\rho}, q) \equiv F(\hat{\rho})\rho_1 - 1 - \int_0^{\hat{\rho}} \rho f(\rho)d\rho - (q-1)(\hat{\rho} - \rho_0)$$

is the modified margin per unit of investment profit, and

$$k(\hat{\rho}, q) \equiv \frac{1}{1 + \int_0^{\hat{\rho}} \rho f(\rho)\, d\rho + (q-1)(\hat{\rho} - \rho_0) - F(\hat{\rho})\rho_0} \qquad (19)$$

is the modified equity multiplier. The firm chooses the threshold $\rho^*(q)$ to minimize the expected unit cost of effective investment:

$$\rho^*(q) \text{ minimizes } \frac{1 + \int_0^{\hat{\rho}} \rho f(\rho)d\rho + (q-1)(\hat{\rho} - \rho_0)}{F(\hat{\rho})}$$

over $\hat{\rho} > \rho_0$. As a generalization of condition (9) we get

$$\rho_0 < p^*(q) + \frac{q-1}{f(\rho^*(q))} < \rho_1.$$

We next ask whether this allocation remains an equilibrium when firms are allowed to issue and trade claims in a financial market. First we argue that if firms are constrained to issue a *single security* (equity), the equilibrium described above unravels because of free-riding. Suppose that all firms issue shares at date 0. Suppose to the contrary that the opening of the financial market does not affect the equilibrium. Shares must then trade at par; else investors would not want to buy them. But then an individual firm could satisfy its liquidity needs more cheaply by buying shares rather than government bonds. To see this, note that the representative firm in the equilibrium without a financial market has an ex post value equal to $[\rho^*(q) - \rho]I > 0$ when the liquidity shock ρ falls in the interval $(\rho_0, \rho^*(q))$. This value stems from the excess amount of bonds it holds. Hence, by holding enough shares in the other firms, an individual firm can accommodate shocks arbitrarily close to $\rho^*(q)$ without paying any liquidity premium. Thus the equilibrium without cross-shareholdings must unravel once firms are allowed to buy each other's shares.

The intuition why the equilibrium breaks down is clear: *Liquidity is a public good if the government charges a premium.* Each firm therefore wants to free-ride on those firms that purchase government bonds. Of course, all firms cannot follow the free-rider strategy, since then no firm would buy government bonds and there would be no protection at all against liquidity shocks above ρ_0.

D. An analysis of the private sector's optimal policy

This subsection derives the private sector's optimal policy when the government charges a premium. The next subsection will analyze the implementation of this policy, in particular the private sector's response to the possibility of free-riding.

Suppose that the private sector buys $(\hat{\rho} - \rho_0)I$ bonds (where I is the investment level of the representative firm) and allocates the funds efficiently at date 1. All firms can withstand the liquidity shock if $\rho \leq \hat{\rho}$; but if $\rho > \hat{\rho}$, some firms must shut down. Instead of shutting down all firms, however, the private sector can resort to *partial liquidation* at the industry level, allowing a fraction $(\hat{\rho} - \rho_0)/(\rho - \rho_0)$ of firms to continue (we can assume that firms that continue are drawn randomly). Whether this is optimal depends on how high the liquidity shock is. If ρ is high enough, it may be better to return the bonds to the investors rather than to use the funds for reinvestment.

To determine the private sector's optimal policy, let zI be the face value of the bonds that the private sector buys and let $\lambda(\rho, z)$ be the fraction of firms allowed to continue when the aggregate shock is ρ. Since entrepreneurs get paid $p_H R_b = \rho_1 - \rho_0$ per unit invested if the project continues, an optimal strategy can be found by solving the following program:

$$\max_{I,\lambda(\cdot)} I \int_0^\infty \lambda(\rho, z)(\rho_1 - \rho_0)f(\rho)\,d\rho$$

$$\text{subject to (i)} \quad I \int_0^\infty \lambda(\rho, z)(\rho_0 - \rho)f(\rho)\,d\rho - I(q-1)z \geq I - A, \quad (20)$$

$$\text{(ii)} \quad 0 \leq \lambda(\rho, z) \leq \min\left\{1, \frac{z}{\rho - \rho_0}\right\}.$$

Let δ be the Lagrangian multiplier for the budget constraint. Then the optimal choice of λ is

$$\lambda(\rho, z) = \begin{cases} \min\left\{1, \dfrac{z}{\rho - \rho_0}\right\} & \text{if } \rho \leq \bar{\rho} \equiv \dfrac{\rho_1 + (\delta - 1)\rho_0}{\delta} \\ 0 & \text{if } \rho > \bar{\rho}. \end{cases} \quad (21)$$

The choice of z is governed by the first-order condition

$$\int_{\rho_0^+z}^{\bar{\rho}} \frac{\partial \lambda(\rho, z)}{\partial z}[(\rho_1 - \rho_0) + \delta(\rho_0 - \rho)]f(\rho)\,d\rho - \delta(q - 1) = 0. \tag{22}$$

Note that the lower integration bound is $\rho_0 + z$ because of (21). Also, by (21), the term in brackets in the integrand is nonnegative. Therefore, (22) implies that $\partial \lambda(\delta, z)/\partial z > 0$ for some values of ρ as δ and $q - 1 > 0$. In particular, $z < \bar{\rho} - \rho_0$, so that whenever $z + \rho_0 \equiv \hat{\rho} < \rho \leq \bar{\rho}$, we have $0 < \lambda(\rho, z) < 1$, implying that the private sector uses the option of partial liquidation for these ρ-values.

The reason the private sector resorts to partial liquidation is suggested by this analysis. If the private sector bought enough bonds to allow all firms to continue whenever $\rho \leq \bar{\rho}$, the choice of λ would be unconstrained (λ would equal zero or one). The first-order cost of a reduction in z would then be zero, whereas the first-order benefit would be $q - 1 > 0$; it would be better to reduce z. Partial liquidation allows the private sector to economize on the use of bonds. Only when bonds carry no opportunity cost ex post ($q = 1$) will the private sector buy full coverage against liquidity shocks.

PROPOSITION 4. *If $q > 1$, that is, if the net deadweight loss of taxation (which must be nonnegative) is strictly positive, the private sector's optimal solution is characterized by two thresholds, $\hat{\rho}$ and $\bar{\rho}$, such that (i) $\rho_0 < \hat{\rho} < \bar{\rho} < \rho_1$; (ii) the private sector buys $zI = (\hat{\rho} - \rho_0)I > 0$ government bonds; and (iii) all firms continue if $\rho \leq \hat{\rho}$; the fraction $(\hat{\rho} - \rho_0)/(\rho - \rho_0) < 1$ of firms continue if $\hat{\rho} < \rho \leq \bar{\rho}$, and no firms continue if $\rho \geq \bar{\rho}$. This solution is more efficient, privately and socially, than when firms act independently.*

The last inequality in part i follows because δ represents the marginal value of firm wealth and therefore must be greater than one. The integrated solution of Proposition 4 is better than what individual firms could obtain on their own (as described in Section IVC) because partial liquidation is feasible at the aggregate level, but not at the firm level. The outcome is also socially more efficient because consumers are as well off whether firms act alone or collectively. In both cases, all the social surplus goes to the entrepreneurs.[23] If partial liquidation at the firm level were feasible, the analysis of Section IVC would of course coincide with the analysis in this subsection.

---

[23] It is worth noting that the established social value of the private optimum depends on the government's objective function. If the government, instead of letting all the surplus go to the entrepreneurs, chose to maximize its net revenue from selling bonds (i.e., consumer surplus), it might well be that restrictions on private arrangements would lead to a higher social utility. The private sector's optimal policy just described has two effects. On the one hand, it makes bonds more valuable to firms, increasing their demand; on the other hand, it allows firms to bypass the government's markup, reducing the demand for bonds. This situation is reminiscent of a government trying to maximize seigniorage in a monetary model. Seigniorage may be higher if private liquidity creation by way of intermediation and cross-shareholdings is restricted.

E. Implementing the optimal policy: A rationale for multiple securities

We turn to the implementation of the optimal policy described in Proposition 4. There are two issues to discuss.

The first one concerns the role of intermediation in coordinating the use of liquidity. If partial liquidation is impossible at the firm level, it must be carried out by intermediaries operating on an industry or economy level. Intermediation reduces the cost of liquidity by allowing firms to economize on the purchase of expensive government bonds. Intermediaries can buy fewer bonds without increasing the average extent of liquidation. This function of intermediation is closely related to, though distinct from, the insurance role that intermediation played in an environment without aggregate shocks. In the independent risk case, liquid claims command no premium, and the function of intermediation is to dispatch liquidity efficiently across a heterogeneous set of firms. This function remains even if firms could liquidate partially. By contrast, *with purely aggregate risk, intermediation is unnecessary if partial liquidation at the firm level is feasible*. As we mentioned earlier, firms then solve the same program and achieve the same outcome as in Proposition 4.

The second, and more interesting, implementation issue to discuss is free-riding. We argued earlier that if bonds sell at a premium and if firms that buy bonds issue a single type of security (equity), there will be an opportunity to free-ride. Equity will provide valuable liquidity without charge because it has to be priced to attract consumers, who do not care about liquidity. Free-riding becomes an issue whether intermediation is used or not. We conclude that if firms or intermediaries issue only one kind of security, the optimum in Section IV*D* cannot be achieved.

The problem has a simple solution. Firms can issue multiple securities, allowing them to price-discriminate among investors who value liquidity services differently.[24] To illustrate this idea in the simplest way, let us eliminate the role of intermediation by allowing *partial liquidation at the firm level*. We shall construct an industry equilibrium that implements the allocation described in Proposition 4. In this equilibrium, all firms invest I (the level given in Proposition 4) and all have a capital structure designed to withstand liquidity shocks up to $\bar{\rho}$. A fraction α of the firms, the *type 1 firms*, purchase $(\bar{\rho} - \rho_0)I$ bonds at price q and hold no shares in other firms. At date 0 they issue two kinds of claims: (i) equity, sold at par, and (ii) short-term debt (maturing at date 1) with face value $(\bar{\rho} - \rho_0)I$, sold at price q'. The debt issue comes with the covenant that the firm will dilute its equity before selling any bonds. This implies that equity in type 1 firms carries no liquidity premium, since it becomes valueless when the aggregate shock exceeds ρ_0. Once the liquidity shock exceeds ρ_0, the firm is

---

[24] This clientele rationale is reminiscent of, but distinct from, the argument in Gorton and Pennacchi (1990).

allowed to sell up to $(\rho - \rho_0)I$ of bonds before servicing its short-term debt. This covenant makes the short-term debt worth $(\overline{\rho} - \rho)I$ at date 1 if the liquidity shock ρ belongs to the interval $[\rho_0, \overline{\rho}]$.

The remaining fraction $1 - \alpha$ of the firms, the *type 2 firms*, do not purchase bonds, but buy all the short-term debt of type 1 firms. Let α be given by

$$\alpha(\overline{\rho} - \hat{\rho}) = (1 - \alpha)(\hat{\rho} - \rho_0). \tag{23}$$

There is no liquidation in either type of firm when $\rho \leq \hat{\rho}$. Suppose that $\rho_0 \leq \rho \leq \hat{\rho}$. Then the value of short-term debt (of a type 1 firm) held by a representative type 2 firm is equal to $\alpha(\overline{\rho} - \rho)I/(1 - \alpha) \geq (\rho - \rho_0)I$; thus by selling these debt claims and by diluting their initial equity (to obtain $\rho_0 I$), type 2 firms can withstand their liquidity shock, ρI. On the other hand, when $\rho \in [\hat{\rho}, \overline{\rho}]$, type 2 firms will partially liquidate but type 1 firms will not. Type 2 firms can continue to operate a fraction λ_2 of their assets, where

$$\lambda_2 \rho I = \lambda_2 \rho_0 I + \frac{\alpha}{1 - \alpha}(\overline{\rho} - \rho)I.$$

That is, they can pledge $\lambda_2 \rho_0$ to new investors in addition to the income from their short-term debt in type 1 firms. The aggregate fraction λ of assets (from both types of firms) that are not liquidated is therefore

$$\lambda = \alpha + (1 - \alpha)\lambda_2 = \alpha + (1 - \alpha)\left(\frac{\alpha}{1 - \alpha}\frac{\overline{\rho} - \rho_0}{\rho - \rho_0}\right)$$

$$= \frac{\hat{\rho} - \rho_0}{\rho - \rho_0}$$

and coincides with the fraction specified in Proposition 4. Note also that the aggregate demand for bonds is the same as in part ii of Proposition 4, because (23) implies that

$$\alpha(\overline{\rho} - \rho_0)I = (\hat{\rho} - \rho_0)I.$$

Finally, set the price of short-term senior debt, q', so that firms are indifferent between being a type 1 and a type 2 firm. Then α can be chosen as specified in (23).

We conclude that the optimal policy can be implemented by issuing multiple corporate securities in the case in which partial liquidation at the firm level is feasible. When it is infeasible, the optimal policy can be implemented by intermediaries that act like the firms described above, issuing multiple securities in order to price-discriminate and avoid free-riding.

F. State-contingent bonds

While partial liquidation reduces the deadweight loss of taxation and is efficient for the private sector given that the government issues noncontingent bonds at a premium, this is not the socially most efficient solution. In this subsection we show how the government can achieve a better outcome by issuing state-contingent bonds. We begin by characterizing the social optimum when general state-contingent transfers between consumers and producers are allowed.

A social plan is defined by (i) the initial level of investment I per firm and (ii) a state-contingent continuation policy $\lambda(\rho) \in [0, 1]$ that determines the fraction of firms that continue when the aggregate liquidity shock is ρ.

The social program is identical to the program studied in Section IVD, with the exception that the transfers are not constrained by an initial purchase of bonds. Formally, the social program solves

$$\max_{I, \lambda(\cdot)} I \int_0^\infty \lambda(\rho)(\rho_1 - \rho_0) f(\rho) d\rho$$

$$\text{subject to (i)} \quad Iq \int_0^\infty \lambda(\rho)(\rho_0 - \rho) f(\rho) d\rho \geq I - A, \tag{24}$$

$$\text{(ii)} \quad 0 \leq \lambda(\rho) \leq 1.$$

The budget constraint takes into account that the consumer cost of date 1 tax transfers expressed in date 0 units is $q > 1$. Let δ be the Lagrangian multiplier of the budget constraint. Then the solution to this program is

$$\lambda^*(\rho) = \begin{cases} 1 & \text{if } \rho \leq \rho^{\#} \\ 0 & \text{if } \rho > \rho^{\#}, \end{cases}$$

where $\rho^{\#}$ is defined by

$$\rho^{\#} - \rho_0 = \frac{\rho_1 - \rho_0}{\delta q} \tag{25}$$

In contrast to the solution in Section IVD, the social optimum specifies either that all firms continue or that no firm continues; there is never partial liquidation. The explanation for this is that in the social program bonds do not have to be purchased in advance to guarantee liquidity; rather, ex post transfers can be provided as needed.[25] Furthermore, since $q > 1$ and $\delta > 1$ (it is the shadow price on entrepreneurial wealth), we see that the socially optimal cutoff $\rho^{\#}$ satisfies $\rho_0 < \rho^{\#} < \rho_1$.

The social optimum $\lambda^*(\rho)$ can be implemented using state-contingent bonds, which pay the holder an amount $x(\rho)$ as a function of the aggregate shock ρ. Let the bonds have the following date 1 payoff:

$$x(\rho) = \begin{cases} 0 & \text{if } \rho \leq \rho_0 \text{ or } \rho > \rho^{\#} \\ \rho - \rho_0 & \text{if } \rho_0 < \rho \leq \rho^{\#}. \end{cases}$$

---

[25] Partial liquidation would become relevant only if investors or entrepreneurs were risk-averse or if the government could not use state-contingent transfers.

Set their date 0 price equal to

$$\int_{\rho_0}^{\rho^{\#}} q(\rho - \rho_0) f(\rho)\, d\rho.$$

Priced this way, bond revenues exactly compensate consumers for the dead-weight loss of taxation associated with the policy $\lambda^*(\rho)$.

It is straightforward to check that with these payoffs and prices, firms can replicate the social optimum, if they so desire, by buying I bonds, where I is the socially optimal level of investment. This amount of bonds enables a firm to continue exactly when the social plan calls for continuation. Also, the firm's budget constraint coincides with the social budget constraint so that the firm can attract the required funds from investors at date 0.

Can the firm do better by deviating from the socially optimal plan? Suppose that there is a better plan for the firm. In this plan, let $\tilde{I}$ be the date 0 investment level, let $\tilde{z}\tilde{I}$ be the amount of state-contingent bonds the firm purchases, and let $\tilde{\lambda}(\rho)$ be the continuation policy. To be feasible, the plan must satisfy both an ex ante and an ex post budget constraint. The ex ante constraint is

$$\tilde{I} \int_0^{\infty} \tilde{\lambda}(\rho)(\rho_0 - \rho) f(\rho)\, d\rho \tag{26}$$

$$-\tilde{I}\tilde{z} \int_0^{\infty} \lambda^*(\rho)(q - 1)(\rho - \rho_0) f(\rho)\, d\rho \geq \tilde{I} - A. \tag{27}$$

The ex post constraint is

$$0 \leq \tilde{\lambda}(\rho) \leq \min\{1, \tilde{z}\lambda^*(\rho)\}. \tag{28}$$

Substituting the ex post constraint into the ex ante constraint, we see that it would be feasible for a social planner to replicate the firm's plan. Given that the social objective function coincides with the firm's, the firm's plan cannot be better than the social optimum.

Finally, note that the government need not concern itself with the possibility of free-riding because, used correctly, state-contingent bonds never leave any extra liquidity in firms.

Remark on seigniorage.—As an alternative objective, suppose that the government aims at maximizing net revenue from issuing government securities, ignoring costs of taxation. Let us compute an upper bound R on the government's net revenue. Let $\overline{U}(= m(\rho_0)k(\rho_0)A)$ denote the "autarky utility" of an entrepreneur with assets A, that is, the utility she gets when holding no reserves. Clearly, $\overline{U}$ is a lower bound on entrepreneurial utility. Consider the following program:

$$\max_{I,\lambda(\cdot)} R$$

subject to

$$\text{(i)} \quad I \int_0^\infty \lambda(\rho)(\rho_1 - \rho_0) f(\rho) d\rho \geq \overline{U},$$

$$\text{(ii)} \quad -R + I \int_0^\infty \lambda(\rho)(\rho_0 - \rho) f(\rho) d\rho \geq I - A, \qquad (29)$$

$$\text{(iii)} \quad 0 \leq \lambda(\rho) \leq 1.$$

Constraint ii reflects the fact that investors must break even. Substituting constraint ii (which obviously holds with equality) into the objective function, we see that program (28) is the dual of program (24). That is, the social optimum has the same characterization whether the government maximizes entrepreneurial welfare subject to a deadweight loss of taxation or maximizes seigniorage.

G. An interpretation of state-contingent bonds

The economic rationale for using state-contingent bonds is simple. Bonds that pay a fixed amount will provide excess liquidity in most states at date 1. Firms (or intermediaries) will cash in the bonds that they do not need for reinvestment, forcing the government to tax consumers and implement a wealth transfer that is unnecessary and socially costly (in the interpretation of the deadweight loss of taxation). While partial liquidation reduces the tax burden, it still leaves slack and also distorts investment and liquidation decisions. The solution that attacks the root cause of the problem is a state-contingent bond, which dispenses liquidity exactly as needed and eliminates all wasteful wealth transfers.

Of course, this solution works ideally only in our idealized model. In reality, state-contingent bonds are not used. The most obvious reason why such bonds are not used is that there is no aggregate, measurable state that unequivocally identifies times when firms should be provided more liquidity. Rather than the use of bonds that are contingent on a few foreseeable and verifiable variables, a discretionary policy may be more effective (when commitment and credibility problems associated with such a policy are ignored). Thus we view the use of state-contingent bonds as a metaphor for an active government policy rather than as a serious policy instrument in its own right.[26] Their value shows that, besides *creating* liquidity, the government has a potential role in actively *managing* liquidity. This is true even if private contracts could be indexed on government actions or on the aggregate shock. However, it is important to recognize that our model does not rationalize continuous intervention and fine tuning in the bond market. Quite the opposite. In our model, *optimal liquidity management entails increasing the value of government bonds only in times when liquidity needs are high.*

[26] Pagano (1988) and Gale (1990) offer the same interpretation in their analysis of state-contingent bonds.

Since we have assumed that bonds mature at date 1, redemption of bonds is accompanied by a corresponding immediate increase in taxes. It may seem odd that taxes are being raised in adverse liquidity states (recessions), as consumers could simultaneously be experiencing negative demand shocks. But this just underscores the importance of considering multiple shocks, as mentioned above. Our specific result is clearly sensitive to the assumption that there is a single liquidity shock with consumers experiencing no shocks at all. If consumers experience an adverse demand shock that requires resources to be shifted to consumption, then taxation might need to be shifted to date 2 or reduced overall rather than increased. This does not negate the general logic that an active policy can improve the allocation of resources through wealth transfers between consumers and producers.

We cannot associate state-contingent bonds with monetary policy, since our model does not distinguish between nominal and real claims. But certain analogies can be drawn between the effects of state-contingent bonds in the model and the alleged effects of monetary policy in reality. One aspect of monetary policy suggested by our analysis is that the government should attempt to inflate the value of the corporate sector's liquid claims in recessions.[27] In particular, in a more realistic model in which there is still a demand for liquid assets at date 1, the government can control the date 1 price of long-term bonds issued at date 0 by early redemptions (purchases) of these bonds or by issuing new bonds. For instance, purchases raise the price of existing bonds (lower the rate of interest) at date 1 and help the corporate sector to withstand the liquidity shock at date 1. Such state-contingent debt management is akin to our state-contingent bonds.

Of course, one should endogenize the date 1 demand for bonds. So, imagine a second generation of entrepreneurs entering at date 1, facing liquidity shocks at date 2, and producing at date 3. Then tighter liquidity (lower bond prices) at date 1 would *decrease* date 1 investments and increase date 2 reinvestments (Proposition 3), since the cost of carrying liquidity into date 2 would become relatively less expensive. In other words, tighter liquidity at date 1 reduces both reinvestments (of date 0 entrepreneurs) and initial investments (of date 1 entrepreneurs), moving aggregate investment unambiguously down at date 1. Again, this conforms with standard views on policy effects.

V. Relationship to the Literature

Several papers have relevance for our work, although they do not address in a unified way the main questions we are interested in, namely corporate liquidity

---

[27] For instance, consider the recent collapse of the Eastern Bloc. In several European countries no attempt was initially made to accommodate this shock (or, if one wants to interpret the central banks' stubborn stance on exchange rates as an active policy, money was made very tight). The result was a big reduction in entrepreneurial wealth as interest rates soared and asset values plunged. Our analysis supports those who argued that governments should have responded to the shock with looser money that would have transferred some wealth back to the entrepreneurs.

needs, the partial self-sufficiency of the private sector, and the foundations for liquidity supply and management by the government. Let us take up these themes in order.

A. Corporate liquidity demand

By now, there is a very large literature on credit rationing, making the point that investment will be constrained by the firm's net worth. Much of this literature is focused on the implications of credit rationing on aggregate investment, consumption, and other macro-economic phenomena (for a survey, see Bernanke, Gertler, and Gilchrist [1994]). These models rarely address the demand for liquidity because they work out of a single-period agency framework. The demand for liquidity is inherently tied to the need for long-term financing. Recently, there has been a surge of multiperiod agency models in corporate finance in which long-term contracts are essential for implementing second-best investment plans (see, e.g., Hart and Moore 1989; Diamond 1991; Berglof and von Thadden 1994). Any one of these models could have been used as the basic building block for our analysis. The virtue of our model is that it is very simple and lends itself readily to a characterization of the second-best solution. For this reason, it has some independent interest. Also, the result that the implementation of the optimal contract limits the firm to maintain a minimum liquidity ratio and a maximum leverage is, to the best of our knowledge, new.[28]

That real assets serve a dual purpose, as productive inputs as well as collateral for debt, has been exploited in recent papers by Shleifer and Vishny (1992) and Kiyotaki and Moore (1997). Both models are concerned with the general equilibrium implications of wealth-constrained financing. Shleifer and Vishny's model, in particular, shares some features with our model. It has two firms, each facing an idiosyncratic demand shock. If the demand shocks are not perfectly correlated (so that firms are not in default simultaneously), the firms can offer each other partial insurance, not directly through security purchases, as we have it, but rather by offering a viable resale market for liquidated assets. In effect, the model describes a market mediated (albeit imperfect) way of enhancing firm liquidity.

B. Private liquidity supply and intermediation

The study of the demand for consumer liquidity was originated by Bryant (1980) and Diamond and Dybvig (1983); see also Ramakrishnan and Thakor (1984), Williamson (1986), and von Thadden (1994). Diamond and Dybvig demonstrate

---

[28] Our model is also related to a smaller literature that focuses specifically on loan commitments and how they can be kept in light of the temptation to renege on promises to finance projects with a negative ex post value (see, e.g., Boot, Thakor, and Udell 1991). The suggested solutions to these commitment problems are much more elaborate than what we offer.

that intermediaries can provide limited insurance by subsidizing consumers that are experiencing high liquidity needs. Jacklin (1987), however, shows that the associated cross-subsidy is infeasible in the presence of financial markets, since those consumers with low liquidity needs can pretend to have high liquidity needs, pocket the subsidy, and reinvest it in financial markets.[29] Thus financial markets in the Diamond–Dybvig framework are detrimental to welfare since they undermine the insurance role of intermediation. In our model, intermediaries bring strict improvements despite the existence of financial markets; indeed, the ability to issue and sell securities in the date 1 market is essential for implementing the second-best outcome. One reason for the difference in conclusions is that our firms cannot abuse credit lines. Entrepreneurs cannot divert corporate funds for their own use other than in the limited fashion captured by the opportunity cost B (the alternative project).

The prescription in Section IV on how the government should manage liquidity is also quite different from that in Diamond and Dybvig. In their model, government policy can be made contingent on the macroeconomic shock (the number of withdrawing depositors), whereas bank contracts with depositors cannot be made contingent on this macroeconomic shock.[30] In our model, government policies do not use more aggregate information than private contracts.

Boyd and Prescott (1986), in a related effort to understand the role of intermediation, construct a model in which financial markets cannot duplicate the services provided by intermediaries. Their model is not about the provision of liquidity as such but rather about the efficient organization of monitoring. Financial markets are inefficient relative to intermediation because financial contracts are assumed to be contingent on whether projects are evaluated and also on the outcome of the evaluation. Intermediaries, on the other hand, can offer contracts before an evaluation is made, avoiding the problem of premature information revelation. This seems to be an ad hoc limitation in favor of intermediation.

Bhattacharya and Gale (1987) look at a variation of the Diamond–Dybvig model that is closer in structure to ours. In their model there are several banks (corresponding to our firms), which experience idiosyncratic, sectoral liquidity shocks that cancel out in the aggregate. The paper characterizes the socially optimal mechanism for sharing risks across banks, noting that this mechanism cannot be implemented through an interbank lending market. Whether a market in bank shares or some other institution could implement the social optimum is

---

[29] Diamond (1997) shows that intermediaries have a role to play as long as some consumers have imperfect access to financial markets.

[30] The subsequent literature on bank runs for the most part assumes independent shocks, as we do in Section III. Hellwig (1994) introduces macroeconomic uncertainty through a date 1 shock on the short-term interest rate between date 1 and date 2 and shows that depositors who withdraw at date 1 must bear some of the aggregate risk.

left open. The authors suggest that a central bank might be the right institution for carrying out interbank risk sharing.

C. Government-supplied liquidity

The first paper to argue that government debt can improve the intertemporal allocation of investment is Diamond (1965). In an overlapping generations model, he showed that government debt can improve welfare by crowding out real investments that in the absence of government debt may be excessive. In our model, public debt facilitates private investment. Another difference is that in Diamond's model, government bonds provide no liquidity services and are sold at par. Models of intergenerational insurance (Fischer 1983; Pagano 1988; Gale 1990) and of asynchronized investment opportunities (Woodford 1990) are expressly concerned with the role of government debt as a medium of transfer across periods. Woodford's paper is perhaps closest to ours. In one version of his model, individuals periodically receive investment opportunities, which they cannot take advantage of without storing wealth from one period to the next. Government debt is a vehicle for storing wealth. He shows that in a stationary state, the optimal level of government debt should be positive. He interprets government debt as a liquidity-enhancing instrument the way we do and shows that bonds will sell at a premium. However, he does not consider the possibility that a private market in claims on output could accomplish the same as government debt, something it may well do, since there are no agency costs to limit how much can be pledged to outsiders.

Gale (1990) studies the efficient design of public debt, using various overlapping generations models in which asset markets are incomplete. In his models, the purpose of government debt is to improve intergenerational risk sharing. He shows that noncontingent debt can enhance welfare if the asset market is sufficiently sparse and that debt of longer maturity can be particularly valuable when productivity shocks are serially correlated, since then bond prices will vary negatively with asset returns. Gale also considers contingent debt, concluding that this instrument, while valuable as a mechanism for transferring wealth between generations, cannot in general implement the optimal state-contingent transfer policy. These results resemble ours, but it is difficult to draw exact parallels since the style of modeling is quite different. A key distinction is that Gale, following the tradition of a large literature on incomplete markets, simply takes the imperfect market structure as exogenously given (something he fully recognizes and discusses at length).[31] In principle, the government or even a private, long-lived institution could complete the market and get to the first-best. In our model the informational constraints that limit first-best are explicitly spelled out.

---

[31] Elul (1995) has recently shown that generically one can add an asset to such a market structure and make everyone better off.

Finally, there are some points of contact with the literature on money. The most closely connected may be the paper by Williamson (1992), who demonstrates the benefits of fiat money in a model in which adverse selection prevents entrepreneurs from pledging their entire future income.[32] Fiat money plays the role of a store of value (which is the counterpart of government securities in our model and may have value because Williamson's model is one of overlapping generations). Williamson's focus is distinct from ours: he argues in favor of government securities (in the form of fiat money) and against the trading of private claims. Indeed, Williamson concludes that fiat money has no value if private claims are traded and that there exists an equilibrium with fiat money that Pareto dominates the purely private equilibrium as long as agents are prevented from trading private claims.

VI. Concluding Remarks

We view our model as a preliminary investigation into the logical link between wealth-constrained financing and the liquidity services offered by financial markets. A large literature has emphasized the importance of an individual firm's or an entrepreneur's net worth for the ability to invest and grow, but little attention has been paid to the fact that, to the extent that net worth constrains capital formation, it will also reduce market liquidity and restrict the financing options for all market participants. Highlighting the close connection between liquidity and capital formation has been one of the main objectives of this chapter.

How significant this connection is depends, as we have emphasized, on how correlated the firms' liquidity needs are. If the shocks are independent, wealth constraints do not limit aggregate liquidity; if the shocks are identical, the market offers no additional liquidity support. While we have not analyzed the case extensively, it is evident that a shortage of liquidity will lead firms to invest in technologies that place lesser demands on long-term financing. Firms will move in the direction of self-supplied liquidity by investing in self-financing projects. A proper welfare analysis of the government's role in managing liquidity would have to assess the costs of distorted investments in the private sector with the costs associated with distortionary consumer taxes. Liquidity premia on government debt should provide the right starting point for such calculations.

In our model, the only source of private liquidity is the very projects that seek financing and demand liquidity. One may wonder how the analysis would change if we were to introduce real estate or other real assets, which could be

---

[32] On the adverse selection problem and related issues, see also Banerjee and Maskin (1996) and the references in Williamson (1992). For other models on money and government debt, see, e.g., Bewley (1980) and Levine (1991).

used to transfer wealth from one period to the next.[33] Our initial investigations suggest the following conclusions. If there are enough real assets and the values of these assets are constant, then liquidity problems would disappear and with them the need to issue government bonds. But there is reason to believe that neither assumption holds. First, the empirical evidence suggests that there are liquidity premia. Such premia can emerge only when there is a shortage of liquid instruments. Second, if real estate and other similar assets are held for liquidity purposes, then their prices are likely to be negatively correlated with liquidity shocks, because the assets will be sold off when firms need liquidity and bought when firms want to store liquidity. The negative correlation will make the assets less desirable as sources of liquidity (see Holmström and Tirole 1997b). A potential role for government-supplied liquidity will remain, and part of that role may entail maintaining stable asset prices.

A related question concerns the realism of the investment/capital ratio. Our model implies that government intervention is needed only when the aggregate demand for liquidity exceeds the value of the private sector. This seems grossly at odds with the empirical fact that the market value of the corporate sector is large relative to investment. Part of the explanation has to do with the inter-pretation of investment. In our model, reinvestments include all the cash outlays (wages and working capital, for instance) needed to continue the firm, not just investments in physical capital. This figure is surely an order of magnitude larger than measured aggregate investment.

Nevertheless, it remains true that the private sector can continue on its own as long as $\rho \leq \rho_0$, that is, as long as the value of the initial claim holders' investment has not been driven down to zero. Only when their investment has lost all its value need the government step in. This is an unrealistic feature of the model. It is driven by the equally unrealistic feature that external claims are fully liquid. To the extent that new issues of equity and debt are costly, because of difficulties in valuing these claims correctly, the private sector will run into reinvestment problems before the initial claim holders have lost all their investment. Similarly, the holdings of monitors (large shareholder, bank, venture capitalist, etc.) cannot be diluted without generating further incentive problems.[34] Thus we think of ρ_0 as the point at which the private sector hits a serious debt capacity constraint, a point that is likely to be encountered well before the initial investors have been cleaned out.

Finally, let us suggest some extensions of our model. The presence of liquidity constraints suggests that this type of analysis can be used to develop a model

[33] A reduction in the net funding needs of a firm at date 1 corresponds to adding real assets to the model. Note that the value of an additional unit of funds at date 1 is higher than the value of a unit of funds at date 0, if there is a liquidity premium.

[34] It is straightforward to add monitors into our model, along the lines of Holmström and Tirole (1997a).

of asset pricing based on liquidity premia. In Holmström and Tirole (1997*b*), we describe a simple version of such a liquidity-based asset pricing model. There are several reasons for our interest in this model. One is that the demand for assets is not uniform across agents; rather, different groups demand different types of assets. Such heterogeneity has implications for the empirical evaluation and estimation of Euler equations and may help to explain such phenomena as the equity premium puzzle. A second potential application is the term structure of interest rates. It is often suggested that the term structure is driven in part by the "preferred habitats" of institutional investors. Such preferences are hard to explain without reference to liquidity constraints that vary depending on the nature of investments in the corporate sector.

Currently, the link between the producer and the consumer sector is very stark and uninteresting. In reality, consumer and producer shocks affect the overall economy and feed back on each other. A general equilibrium extension provides a more realistic picture of the need for transferring wealth in one direction or the other and therefore on how the government should manage liquidity. In this context, one would also want to be more careful about the deadweight losses caused by taxation and the role played by individual time preferences and risk aversion. A related extension would introduce more periods into our model. The government could then issue long-term as well as short-term bonds, which would allow one to address questions about the optimal maturity structure of government debt.

While intermediaries play a role in our model, it is a passive one. Intermediaries are merely conduits for forming contracts that are unavailable in the financial market. This is an artifact of assuming that firms have no use for extra credit and therefore never abuse their credit lines. In reality, intermediaries play a more active role, monitoring investments and liquidity needs. A more advanced model of liquidity would recognize the importance of intermediaries in generating information and in creating local pools of liquidity. How these pools should be linked to each other and what effect this information hierarchy has on the management of liquidity are among the most interesting research questions that lie ahead.

References

Banerjee, A. V., and Maskin, E. S. (1996). "A Walrasian theory of money and barter." *Q.J.E.*, 111: 955–1005.

Berglof, E., and von Thadden, E.-L. (1994). "Short-term versus long-term interests: Capital structure with multiple investors." *Q.J.E.*, 109: 1055–84.

Bernanke, B., Gertler, M., and Gilchrist, S. (1994). "The financial accelerator and the flight to quality." Working Paper no. 4789. Cambridge, Mass.: NBER, July.

Bewley, T. (1980). "The optimum quantity of money," in J. H. Kareken and N. Wallace (eds.), *Models of Monetary Economies* (Minneapolis: Fed. Reserve Bank).

Bhattacharya, S., and Gale, D. (1987). "Preference shocks, liquidity, and central bank Policy," in W. A. Barnett and K. J. Singleton (eds.), *New Approaches to Monetary Economics* (Cambridge: Cambridge Univ. Press).

Boot, A. W. A., Thakor, A. V., and Udell, G. F. (1991). "Credible commitments, contract enforcement problems and banks: Intermediation as credibility assurance." *J. Banking and Finance*, 15: 605–32.

Boyd, J. H., and Prescott, E. C. (1986). "Financial intermediary coalitions." *J. Econ. Theory*, 38: 211–32.

Bryant, J. (1980). "A model of reserves, bank runs, and deposit insurance." *J. Banking and Finance*, 4: 335–44.

Diamond, D. W. (1991). "Debt maturity structure and liquidity risk." *Q.J.E.*, 106: 709–37.

—— (1997). "Liquidity, banks, and markets." *J.P.E.*, 105: 928–56.

——, and Dybvig, P. H. (1993). "Bank runs, deposit insurance, and liquidity." *J.P.E.*, 91: 401–19.

Diamond, P. A. (1965). "National debt in a neoclassical growth model." *A.E.R.*, 55: 1126–50.

Elul, R. (1995). "Welfare effects of financial innovation in incomplete markets economies with several consumption goods." *J. Econ. Theory*, 65: 43–78.

Fischer, S. (1983). "Welfare aspects of government issue of indexed bonds," in R. Dornbusch and M. H. Simonsen (eds.), *Inflation, Debt, and Indexation* (Cambridge, Mass.: MIT Press).

Gale, D. (1990). "The efficient design of public debt," in R. Dornbusch and M. Draghi (eds.), *Public Debt Management: Theory and History* (Cambridge: Cambridge Univ. Press).

Gorton, G., and Pennacchi, G. (1990). "Financial intermediaries and liquidity creation." *J. Finance*, 45: 49–71.

Hart, O. D., and Moore, J. (1989). "Default and renegotiation: A dynamic model of debt." Working Paper no. 89–069. Boston: Harvard Bus. School.

Hellwig, M. (1994). "Liquidity provision, banking, and the allocation of interest rate risk." *European Econ. Rev.*, 38: 1363–89.

Holmström, B., and Tirole, J. (1997a). "Financial intermediation, loanable funds, and the real sector." *Q.J.E.*, 112: 663–92.

—— (1997b). "LAPM: A liquidity-based asset pricing model." Manuscript. Cambridge: Massachusetts Inst. Tech., March.

Jacklin, C. J. (1987). "Demand deposits, trading restrictions, and risk sharing," in Edward C. Prescott and Neil Wallace (eds.), *Contractual Arrangements for Intertemporal Trade* (Minneapolis: Univ. Minnesota Press).

Kiyotaki, N., and Moore, J. (1991). "Credit cycles." *J.P.E.*, 105: 211–48.

Levine, D. K. (1991). "Asset trading mechanisms and expansionary policy." *J. Econ. Theory*, 54: 148–64.

Pagano, M. (1988). "The management of public debt and financial markets," in F. Giavazzi and L. Spaventa (eds.), *High Public Debt: The Italian Experience* (Cambridge: Cambridge Univ. Press).

Ramakrishnan, R. T. S., and Thakor, A. V. (1984). "Information reliability and a theory of financial intermediation." *Rev. Econ. Studies*, 51: 415–32.

Shleifer, A., and Vishny, R. W. (1992). "Liquidation values and debt capacity: A market equilibrium approach." *J. Finance*, 47: 1343–66.

von Thadden, E.-L. (1994). "Optimal liquidity provision and dynamic incentive compatibility." Manuscript. Basel: Univ. Basel.

Williamson, S. D. (1986). "Costly monitoring, financial intermediation, and equilibrium credit rationing." *J. Monetary Econ.*, 18: 159–79.

—— (1992). "Laissez-faire banking and circulating media of exchange." *J. Financial Intermediation*, 2: 134–67.

Woodford, M. (1990). "Public debt as private liquidity." *A.E.R. Papers and Proc.*, 80: 382–8.

7

Financial Intermediation versus Stock Markets in a Dynamic Intertemporal Model

Sudipto Bhattacharya, Paolo Fulghieri, and Riccardo Rovelli

1. Introduction and Summary

Models of intertemporal liquidity risks, or "preference shocks'—developed in Bryant [1980] and further examined in the works of Diamond and Dybvig [1983]. Bhattacharya and Gale [1987], and Jacklin [1987] among others—have recently been extended to the realm of ongoing dynamic overlapping generations (OLG) economies (see Bencivenga and Smith [1991], Qi [1994], Fulghieri and Rovelli [1993], and Dutta and Kapur [1994]). These models may be used to evaluate the essential tradeoffs which arise in two distinct areas of current debate. The first is on the evaluation of alternative (or possibly complementary) arrangements for the monetary system, for example the relative merits of a market-value-based versus an intermediated banking system. The second interpretation, clearly requiring a considerably longer definition of the time unit, pertains to the debate on the viability and desirability of differing social security (pension) systems, and in particular the choice between pay-as-you-go (PAYG) versus funded or capital reserve systems (e.g. Boldrin and Rustichini [1994]). Our paper considers the latter set of tradeoffs in an OLG model outside of long-run steady states.

In our chapter, agents choose among intertemporal liquidity sharing or insurance mechanisms, in an OLG economy in which the *capital stock is possibly longer-lived than agents' lives*. We focus on the comparisons between "banking"

We are grateful to CEMFI (Madrid, Spain), CEPR (London, UK), ICER (Torino, Italy), IGIER (Milano, Italy) and the Studienzentrum Gerzensee (Switzerland) for research and financial support. Discussions with Patrick Bolton, John Boyd, Ed Green, Martin Hellwig, Jorge Padilla, Ailsa Roell, Bruce Smith, and Elu von Thadden have been helpful. We are grateful for the comments of the discussants. Thorsten Hens and Christian Keuschnigg, at the 15th International Seminar on the New Institutional Economics held in Wallerfangen Saar, Germany, June 4–6, 1997. Alessandro Secchi made several useful suggestions. Giacomo Elena and Wim Deblauwe provided excellent research assistance. All errors remain our responsibility. A previous version of this chapter was circulated as "Turnpike Banking: Only the Meek Shall Inherit the Earth."

or PAYG systems, of both an *intra-* and *inter*generational nature, versus stock-market-based *inter*generational financial systems. The essential tradeoffs across these institutional mechanisms arise from the need for financial contracting to provide agents with liquidity insurance, related to the uncertainty regarding their preferences for their intertemporal allocation of consumption.[1] Such preference shocks, coupled with real investment opportunities that are long-lived and technologically illiquid, create a demand for interim stock markets, or financial intermediaries and contracts such as deposits withdrawable (fully or partially) on demand.

In dynamic OLG economies, there is in addition the possibility of designing contracts (or mechanisms) for sharing such liquidity risk *across generations*, taking advantage of the "life-cycle" structure to the demand for savings of each generation. With the long horizons envisioned, one may think of events such as uncertain workers' disability as a source of early withdrawal demand. In recent papers of Qi [1994], Fulghieri and Rovelli [1993], and Dutta and Kapur [1994], alternative institutional arrangements for such intertemporal consumption smoothing and liquidity risk sharing mechanisms, within and across generations, have been examined and compared.

Under some assumptions, in particular the restriction of the analysis to steady states only, both Qi [1994] and Fulghieri and Rovelli [1993] show that there exist intergenerational financial intermediation contracts that can attain the "Golden Rule" (Phelps [1961]) levels of investment and consumption smoothing. The paper by Fulghieri and Rovelli, and the later work by Bhattacharya and Padilla [1996], also focuses on the comparison of intergenerational *banks versus stock markets* for investments that are long-lived in nature. In contrast to the earlier models, which focus either on a static economy (Bhattacharya and Gale [1987]) or on *intra*generational mechanisms only (Bencivenga and Smith [1991]), Fulghieri and Rovelli find that stock markets result (in steady state) in *under*investment in the long-lived technology, relative to the Golden Rule optimum, without any investment in short-term liquid technologies or early liquidation.[2] This occurs essentially owing to the incompleteness of contracts for resource transfers across generations, which in a stock market economy can

---

[1] The background assumption is that there are many small uninsurable risks to endowments, to health or family size, for which it is extremely costly to develop separate insurance markets, in part due to private observability of outcomes, which could be monitored by insurers only at a prohibitive cost. The lack of such markets gives rise to uncertain indirect utility functions for agents over their intertemporal withdrawal patterns from their invested savings.

[2] In Bhattacharya and Gale [1987] it is shown that the opening of an *interim* stock market in the Diamond and Dybvig [1983] model leads to *over*investment, relative to the ex ante optimal level, in the long-term technology, when agents have relative risk aversion greater than unity and they make investment choices individually. See Bhattacharya and Padilla [1996] for a further discussion of these contrasting results, which arise from the dominance of different incomplete markets effects within and across generations.

take place only through real investments in long-lived technologies and bilateral trading at their interim market valuations.

In all of the above mentioned papers, the analysis of the functioning of intermediaries and stock markets is confined to steady states, in which the inheritance of a stationary level of investment by prior generations is taken as given. However, given the endowment structure in these models, this is a restrict- ive assumption, especially vis-à-vis the *first* generation which only has its initial endowment to start a resource transfer *cum* liquidity insurance scheme. While Qi [1994] briefly examines this issue (see his propositions 5 and 6), his analysis is focused on PAYG systems only, rather than on the choices among *alternative risk sharing mechanisms*.

More specifically, the following questions remain unanswered: Given initial conditions, is it possible to predict which allocational mechanisms would be chosen by the generations present, and would the same choice be repeated by the subsequent generations, i.e. be intergenerationally stable or self-sustaining? For example, consider the three institutional mechanisms which we shall ana- lyze below: *intra*generational banking (B), *inter*generational banking (IB), and *inter*generational stock market (SM). Suppose these may be ranked in a particular way by the steady state welfare criterion. Then, is it necessarily true that, when the issues related to transition to the steady state on the one hand, and non- cooperative intergenerational choices on the other hand are taken into account, the most efficient steady state allocational mechanism would indeed be chosen and be intergenerationally self-sustaining? We seek to address these questions in this chapter.

In defining our notions of intergenerational choices over mechanisms for financing of investment and consumption smoothing, we shall not be employ- ing notions such as the "core," whose applicability to the OLG setting is dubious at best. As Esteban [1986] and Esteban and Millan [1990] have shown, even when the Golden Rule allocation *does* improve the welfare of the first generation (the Samuelson [1958] case of Gale [1973]), it is *not* in the intergenerational core (never for a single commodity setting).[3] Fortunately, as Esteban and Sakovics [1993] have emphasized, negative results like those mentioned above do not imply that intergenerational transfer mechanisms become infeasible. Society may cope with such a conundrum, created by the "not in the core" result, by *restricting the language* or *strategy space of intergenerational proposals* for choosing its institutional mechanisms for intergenerational reallocations. In the context of the Esteban–Sakovics model, of a pure exchange OLG environment with agents' endowments tilted to the early period(s) of life, they argue that in a time–stationary model the appropriate notion of an institutional proposal is that

---

[3] The obvious reason is that each subcoalition of current and future generations has an incentive to deviate from the Golden Rule allocation by denying the anticipated positive old age transfer to the immediately prior generation, when each generation's endowment pattern is tilted towards its youth.

of a time–stationary transfer scheme, from *each* current and future generation when young to its preceding generation when old. Institutions survive if and only if they constitute subgame perfect equilibria (Selten [1975]) in such an intergenerational proposal game. A similar restriction is employed by Boldrin and Rustichini [1994], in their modeling of *inter*generational social security schemes versus *intra*generational accumulation of short-lived investments.

In our model below, we define the concept of a *self-sustaining* investment and consumption allocation *mechanism*, using restrictions motivated by analogous considerations. The spirit of these is that proposals that make *later* generations strictly worse off than the proposing one are not allowed. Such a restriction may arise spontaneously for market-based mechanisms, or be a result of societal norms embodied in a *legislated* PAYG mechanisms such as IB. In particular, we restrict the set of proposals by each generation to be one of the three institutions that were indicated above: transition to steady state of *inter*generational banking (TIB), *inter*generational stock market (SM), and *intra*generational banking (B). (The first of these takes into account the lack of inherited prior capital investments for the first generation.) Some of these proposals may require that an older and a younger generation agree on the "sharing" of the inherited capital stock plus the endowment of the young. Hence, each stage game in our model is one of proposals and counter-proposals by the two overlapping generations, unlike in Esteban and Sakovics [1993] where only the young propose transfers to the currently old.

Our chapter is organized as follows: In section 2, we set out the basic model and delineate the Golden Rule and other steady state allocations under the three alternative institutional arrangements of B, IB, and SM. The dynamics of transition to these steady states, and the ranking of welfare levels attainable under each alternative institutional mechanism (TIB, SM, and B), taking transition into account, are the *foci* of section 3. Intergenerational proposal games over these (transition) institutions and their subgame perfect equilibria, which we term intergenerationally *self-sustaining mechanisms*, are described and characterized in section 4. In section 5, we conclude with a discussion of our results in the context of recent literature and with suggestions for further research.

The major results that emerge from the analysis in the paper are the following: First, we point out that there exists a feasible stationary consumption path (TIB) such that capital accumulation along that path will lead, within a finite horizon, to the Golden Rule steady state optimal allocation; furthermore, the consumption levels attained along this path ensure that the welfare of each generation involved in the transition *strictly* exceeds that attainable from *any* *intra*generational mechanism.[4] Second, we show that there exists a faster oneshot transition to the steady state SM allocation (Fulghieri and Rovelli [1993]).[5] Third,

---

[4] Hence, the reliance on *intra*generational mechanisms in an OLG context, as in Bencivenga and Smith [1991] and others, appears to be not very well justified.

[5] In addition, we also show the existence of a steady state periodic stock market equilibrium.

we prove that a transition to the SM that benefits the proposing current young, which exists unless they are *extremely* risk-averse, *must* involve strictly rationing the participation of the concurrent preceding generation in the initial market (only). Fourth, we prove that under reasonable parameter values, there exists an *intergenerational conflict* in any stage game; specifically, at any time, the currently young may stand to gain by proposing a (rationed and immediate) transition to the stationary SM allocation, whereas the currently middle-aged are made strictly worse off, relative to the "slowest turnpike" allocation (TIB), from accepting such a proposal. Finally, in the last step we delineate how this conflict may be resolved, in the sequence of equilibria of the intergenerational proposal games across overlapping generations.

The equilibrium outcome of the intergenerational proposal games depends *crucially* on the relative expected utility payoff(s) of the middle-aged generation(s) from their rationed transition to the SM, versus their *fallback option* of doing *intra*generational liquidity risk sharing (B), based on their inherited endowment net of prior payout obligations. It turns out that the currently middle-aged generation(s) are better off from their fallback option, relative to the constrained (for them only) transition to the SM proposed by their "children," if and only if the proportion of the generation requiring *early liquidity* (withdrawal) is *small*, and agents in the generation are ex ante *highly risk-averse* (or averse to unsmoothed consumption profiles). If *either* of these conditions on agents' ex ante characteristics is *not* satisfied then, and only then, the SM institutional arrangement (which is always suboptimal relative to IB in the steady state) becomes the unique subgame, and "trembling-hand" (Selten [1975]), perfect equilibrium of the intergenerational proposal games.[6]

2. The Model and Stationary Allocations

2.1 Optimal allocations and intermediated outcomes

We consider an extended version of the OLG model of Samuelson [1958], that was first advanced by Bryant [1980]. Time is indexed by $t = 0, 1, 2, \ldots, \infty$. Each generation consists of a continuum of agents of unit measure. An agent born at time point $t \geq 0$ is alive at $(t + 1)$, and possibly also at $(t + 2)$. Each generation is endowed with one unit of the single commodity, spread equally across its members, at birth; this may be thought of as labor income or prior savings. To simplify matters, we assume that an agent born at t only wishes to consume from his savings at $(t+1)$ if he is an *early dier*, or at $(t+2)$ if he is a *late dier*. Such simple

---

[6] Hence, our results differ from those of Esteban and Sakovics [1993] in their simpler "transfer games" context (with no endogenous real investments), in which—as the cost of making new proposals goes to zero—they obtain nearly efficient steady state outcomes as unique equilibria.

ex post corner preferences, introduced by Diamond and Dybvig [1983], imply that the allocations produced by *intra*generational stock markets and banking systems coincide, provided market participation is suitably restricted (see Jacklin [1987], and Bhattacharya and Gale [1987]).

Agents become early or late diers with probabilities ε and $(1 - \varepsilon)$ respectively. These events are independent across the continuum of agents in each generation, so that a proportion $(1 - \varepsilon)$ of agents born at t is alive at $(t + 2)$, when they die. Thus, the ex ante expected utility of a representative agent of generation t is given by

$$V_t = \varepsilon U(C_{t,1}) + (1 - \varepsilon)U(C_{t,2}), \tag{1}$$

where $\{C_{t,1}, C_{t,2}\}$ are the certain allocations of consumption to early and late diers of generation t, respectively. The utility function $U(\cdot)$ is assumed to be strictly increasing and concave, with $U'(0) = \infty$.

There are two investment technologies in the model. The first is long-lived with constant returns to scale: Investment of I_t at time t returns $RI_t, R > 1$, at $(t+2)$. The second technology is that of storage, without any loss or depreciation, between t and $(t+1)$. The long-lived investment I_t can also be liquidated at $(t+1)$ to yield $Q L_{t+1}$, where $0 \le Q \le 1$, and $0 \le L_{t+1} \le I_t$. We assume $Q = 1$, so that early liquidation and storage technologies are equivalent.[7]

The Golden Rule stationary optimal *inter*generational investment and consumption plan thus solves the problem

$$V^* \equiv \underset{\{I_t, L_t, C_{t,1}, C_{t,2}\}}{\text{Max}} [\varepsilon U(C_{t,1}) + (1 - \varepsilon)U(C_{t,2})], \quad \text{s.t.} \tag{2}$$

$$\varepsilon C_{t-1,1} + (1 - \varepsilon) C_{t-2,2} \le 1 + R(I_{t-2} - L_{t-1}) + L_t - I_t, \forall t, \quad \text{and} \tag{2a}$$

$$0 \le L_{t+1} \le I_t \le 1. \tag{2b}$$

As shown, for example, in Fulghieri and Rovelli [1993, proposition 1], the solution of this problem is characterized by full investment of the initial endowment of each new generation, no liquidation of invested capital, and a level of consumption for early and late diers which is constant and equal to R. Furthermore, Qi [1994], Fulghieri and Rovelli [1993], and Dutta and Kapur [1994] give the conditions under which the Golden Rule allocation may be implemented by an IB system. These results are summarized in the following proposition.

PROPOSITION 1. *(a) The Golden Rule stationary optimal intergenerational allocation rule, which maximizes (2) subject to (2a) and (2b), is given by $I_t^* = 1, L_t^* = 0, C_{t,1}^* = C_{t,2}^* = R, \forall t$.*

---

[7] The assumption that $Q = 1$ is used by Diamond and Dybvig [1983] to prove the existence of panic bank runs of early withdrawals for storage at $(t + 1)$ by agents who do not wish to consume from savings until $(t + 2)$. However, simple measures, such as suspension of convertibility, can eliminate such runs, so we ignore this problem. This assumption considerably simplifies the analysis of *transition* to optimal steady state allocations.

(b) *If agents depositors can be subject to a no redepositing condition within (and across) banks, then a single welfare maximizing bank (or equivalently, many representative competing banks) would, in equilibrium, offer each generation the deposit contract "I_t in deposits leads to withdrawal rights RI_t at $(t + 1)$ or $(t + 2)$, at the choice of the depositor." Furthermore, all agents born at t would deposit all their initial endowment in banks, which would invest it ($I_t = 1$) in long-lived investments only, without early liquidation. Thus IB would implement the Golden Rule optimum. Hence in particular: $C_{t,i}^{IB} = C_{t,i}^{*} = R, i \in \{1, 2\}, \forall t$.*

(c) *If redepositing after early withdrawal by agents is not monitorable (indistinguishable from an initial deposit), especially if done across banks, but depositing at one bank by another can be prohibited, then ex ante Bertrand competition among banks would lead to the following outcome: Depositing $I_t = 1$ by each depositor of each generation t confers him with withdrawal rights C_1^U at $(t + 1)$ or C_2^U at $(t + 2)$, where these (suppressing the t-subscript) satisfy*

$$C_1^U < R < C_2^U, \tag{4a}$$

$$(C_1^U)^2 \le C_2^U, \quad \text{and} \tag{4b}$$

$$\varepsilon C_1^U + (1 - \varepsilon)C_2^U = R. \tag{4c}$$

Proof. See either Qi [1994], Fulghieri and Rovelli [1993], or Dutta and Kapur [1994].

Remark. The Golden Rule optimum is, of course, strictly valid as a solution concept only when $t \in \{-\infty, \ldots, -1, 0, 1, \ldots, \infty\}$ since, for example, if $t \in \{0, 1, \ldots, \infty\}$, and $I_1 = 1$ and $L_1 = 0$, then the early diers of generation 0 will obtain consumption $C_{0,1} = 0$. These issues raise questions about the *transition* to these stationary optimal allocations, which we discuss in the next section. The notion of a competitive banking system is also not unambiguous in an OLG setting, and one may think instead of the resulting allocations as arising from a legislated allocation mechanism.

In contrast, the constrained optimal *intra*generational allocation solves the problem

$$\overline{V} \equiv \underset{\{I, L, C_1, C_2\}}{\text{Max}} [\varepsilon U(C_1) + (1 - \varepsilon)U(C_2)], \quad \text{s.t.} \tag{3}$$

$$0 \le \varepsilon C_1 \le L, \tag{3a}$$

$$0 \le (1 - \varepsilon) C_2 \le R(I - L), \quad \text{and} \tag{3b}$$

$$0 \le I \le 1. \tag{3c}$$

The solution to this problem is characterized by Diamond and Dybvig [1993], who also show that this allocation may be implemented with a single welfare maximizing bank or several (representative) competing banks, which are

Bertrand competitors and obtain clienteles of strictly positive measure (restated in proposition 2 below). The latter result assumes *no interim trading of assets across competing banks* at the interim period (see Bhattacharya and Gale [1987]).

PROPOSITION 2. *The optimal intragenerational allocation rule, which maximizes* (3) *subject to* (3a)–(3c), *is given by* $\bar{I} = 1, U'(\bar{C}_1) = RU'(\bar{C}_2), \bar{C}_1 = \bar{L}/\varepsilon, \bar{C}_2 = R(1 - \bar{L})/(1 - \varepsilon)$. *Furthermore, in a competitive B system equilibrium, deposit contracts of the form "deposit I at time t implies withdrawal rights* $C_1^B = \bar{C}_1 I$ *or* $C_2^B = \bar{C}_2 I$, *at* $(t + 1)$ *or* $(t + 2)$ *respectively" would prevail leading to expected utility* $V^B = \bar{V}$, *and each depositor would deposit* $I = 1$ *at one (or many) bank(s), and each bank would invest its deposits in short-term (early liquidation) and long-term investments, in the proportions* $\bar{L}$ *and* $1 - \bar{L}$ *respectively.*

Proof. See Diamond and Dybvig [1983].[8]

The following implications of proposition 2 are straightforward.

COROLLARY 1. *For all* $\varepsilon > 0$, *the expected utility* V^B *of an agent in the optimal intragenerational allocation is strictly less than its level* V^* *at the Golden Rule intergenerational optimum.*

Proof. Since $\{\bar{C}_1, \bar{C}_2\} > 0$ and hence $\bar{L} \in (0, 1)$, given $U'(0) = \infty$, we have $1 < \varepsilon \bar{C}_1 + (1 - \varepsilon) \bar{C}_2 = \bar{L} + R(1 - \bar{L}) < R$, whereas $C_1^* = C_2^* = R$, from which the conclusion follows using Jensen's inequality.   Q.E.D.

COROLLARY 2. *If* $U(C_i), i \in \{1, 2\}$, *has its relative risk aversion coefficient uniformly strictly greater than unity (that for logarithmic utility), then* $1 < \bar{C}_1 < \bar{C}_2 < R$, *implying* $\varepsilon < \bar{L} < 1$.

Proof. See Diamond and Dybvig [1983].

We should briefly mention the *alternatives* to the existence of bank type intermediaries (and "unconditional" withdrawal rights) in this setting. The extreme one is that of intra- and intergenerational autarky, under which each agent would invest $I = 1$ when young, and consume $C_1^A = 1$ if he is an early dier, and $C_2^A = R$ if he is a late dier, and with expected utility

$$V^A \equiv \varepsilon U(C_1^A) + (1 - \varepsilon)U(C_2^A). \tag{5}$$

It is obvious that $V^A \leq \bar{V} < V^*$, with the first inequality also strict unless $U(C) = \log(C)$, since $\{L = \varepsilon, C_1 = 1, C_2 = R\}$ is always feasible under B.

A less extreme comparison is with an institution often analyzed in "standard" financial modeling: the intragenerational stock market. If individuals still invest

---

[8] This intragenerational optimal allocation B is the unique equilibrium outcome of such a contract if banks can suspend early withdrawal rights once a proportion ε of their depositors has withdrawn (that is, a fraction $\bar{L}$ of their investments has been liquidated). All agents would then deposit all their initial endowments in such banks, and not invest in real investments on their own. They would also withdraw early if and only if they are early diers.

on their own, but can sell their long-term investments I_t at a linear price $P_{t-1}I_t$ at $(t + 1)$, then it turns out that the *interim value maximizing* investment and consumption outcome will be the *same* under intragenerational stock markets as under autarky (see Bhattacharya and Gale [1987]). The reason is that, under the interim value wealth maximization criterion used to choose liquidation L_{t+1} from I_t, subject to $0 \leq L_{t+1} \leq I_t$, $L_{t+1} \in (0, I_t)$ will be chosen by individuals if and only if $p_{t+1} = 1$. With the ex post corner preferences assumed, this will be the case if and only if $\{C_{t,1} = 1, C_{t,2} = R\}$, as shown by Bhattacharya and Gale [1987].

Bencivenga and Smith [1991] and others have emphasized *this difference* between banking and stock market allocations, suggesting that it should apply even when the setting is *inter*generational in nature. However, with *intra*generational stock markets, as argued in Bhattacharya and Gale [1987] and Bhattacharya and Padilla [1996], investment decisions would be made by *firms*, or mutual funds, which consist of *coalitions* of agents of strictly positive measure (to pool their liquidity risks). Such a coalition, if it plans to invest I and liquidate $L \leq I$ next period, will issue a dividend stream $\{L, R(I - L)\}$ at the two consecutive points, and early diers would sell their ex first dividend shares to late diers of the *same* fund. However, the appropriate choice criterion for such mutual funds, if interim trading of ex first dividend shares is *restricted* to the members of a fund, would be to maximize the ex ante expected utility V of their members, and not the interim market value of the $\{I, L\}$-tuple. Hence $L = \overline{L}$ would be chosen, leading to $C_1 = \overline{C}_1, C_2 = \overline{C}_2$, $V^B = \overline{V}$. As this is the *same* allocation which occurs under B (intragenerational Diamond–Dybvig banking), we will disregard *intra*generational stock markets in the analysis to follow.

We now proceed to consider alternative institutions in an intergenerational setting.

2.2 Intergenerational stock markets (SM)

We consider a situation in which the generation born at time t invests $0 \leq I_t \leq 1$ in new real investments, creating I_t new firms, and $(1 - I_t)$ is invested by the newborn in the shares of existing firms. The price of ongoing (one-period old) firms per unit of real investment at any point of time t is given by p_t, with the price of completed technologies being R. These prices must satisfy the perfect foresight no arbitrage conditions, where q_t is the unit price of *new* investments at time t:

$$\frac{p_{t+1}}{q_t} = \frac{R}{p_t}, \quad \text{and} \tag{6a}$$

$$\frac{p_{t+1}}{q_t} \frac{p_{t+2}}{q_{t+1}} = \frac{R}{q_t}. \tag{6b}$$

The RHS of (6b) represents the gross rate of returns from the "two-period invest and hold" strategy, while the LHS of (6b) represents the rate of return from holding a share of a new firm for one period, selling it, and then reinvesting in a share of a new firm at $(t+1)$. In contrast, the criterion in (6a) results from equating the contemporaneous rates of return on holding the shares of new firms, with that on holding one-period old firms.

If agents can short-sell existing firms' shares to obtain additional resources (beyond their endowments) for new real investment, or they can sequentially create, sell, and then create new investments, value maximizing investment equilibrium requires that, for $I_t \in (0, 1]$ to be optimal:

$$q_t = 1, \quad \forall t. \tag{6c}$$

Also, substituting back from (6c) into (6b), we see that both (6a) and (6b) imply that, if the chosen investment levels are interior and finite, then for all $t \geq 1$ the following intertemporal equilibrium condition must hold:

$$p_t p_{t+1} = R, \quad \forall t \geq 1. \tag{6d}$$

Let $\{I_t\} \in (0, 1], t = 0, 2, \ldots, \infty$, with $\{L_t\} = 0$, be the levels of new real investments in the economy above, in an SM equilibrium (so that $q_t = 1, \forall t$). Denote $0_{t,1}$ and $0_{t-1,t}$, for $t \geq 1$, as the *per capita proportions* of one-period old capital stock, I_{t-1}, held at time t by a representative agent of generation t and a late dier of generation $(t-1)$, respectively. Then, agents' budget constraints at different points of their lives together with stock market clearing imply that

$$I_t + \theta_{t,t} p_t I_{t-1} = 1, \quad \forall t \geq 1, \tag{7a}$$

$$\theta_{t,t} p_t I_{t-1} = \varepsilon p_t I_{t-1}, t = 1, \tag{7b}$$

$$\theta_{t,t} p_t I_{t-1} + (1 - \varepsilon)\theta_{t-1,t-1} R I_{t-2} = \varepsilon p_t I_{t-1}, \quad \forall t \geq 2, \tag{7c}$$

$$\theta_{t,t} + (1 - \varepsilon)\theta_{t-1,t} = 1, \quad \forall t \geq 1, \quad \text{with} \tag{7d}$$

$$I_0 = 1 \quad \text{and} \quad \theta_{0,0} = 0. \tag{7e}$$

Equation (7a) results from the fact the newborn will invest all their endowment in either new real investments, or in buying the shares of one-period old firms from early diers of the previous generation. (7b) states that the $(t = 1)$-sales of early diers of the 0th generation must be wholly absorbed by purchases by the members from the 1st generation. (7c) states that at all time points $t \geq 2$, the dividends which survivors (late diers) from generation $(t-1)$ obtain from maturing technologies are used to purchase the difference between sales by early diers of the same generation minus purchases of one-period old technologies by the newborn. Finally, (7d) represents the fact that total shareholdings of one-period old investments must add up to unity.

These stock market equilibrium conditions also have implications for the consumption allocations of early and late diers. For early diers, it is straightforward to see, by updating (7a), that

$$C_{t,1} = p_{t+1}I_t + R\theta_{t,t}I_{t-1}, \quad \forall t \geq 0. \tag{7f}$$

For late diers, multiply (7d) by $p_t I_{t-1}$ and substitute in (7c) to obtain, after dividing by $(1 - \varepsilon)$:

$$\theta_{t-1,t} p_t I_{t-1} = p_t I_{t-1} \theta_{t-1,t-1} R I_{t-2}. \tag{7g}$$

In other words, their per capita portfolio value, after rebalancing at t(LHS), equals the value of their old real investment made at $(t-1)$, plus the dividends currently received on maturing financial investments (in ongoing technology), which they had made at $(t-1)$. Updating the RHS of (7g) we obtain

$$C_{t,2} = \theta_{t,t+1} R I_t, \quad \forall t \geq 0. \tag{7h}$$

In an SM equilibrium with perfect foresight agents of generation t therefore maximize to solve

$$V^{SM} \equiv \max_{\{I_t, \theta_{t,t}, \theta_{t-1,t}\}} [\varepsilon U(C_{t,1}) + (1 - \varepsilon)U(C_{t,2})], \tag{8}$$

subject to the constraints embodied in (7a) and (7f)–(7h). Furthermore, prices and quantities satisfy the perfect foresight no arbitrage and market clearing conditions of (6d) and (7b)–(7e). We show the existence of such equilibria *constructively* below.

LEMMA 1. *The characteristic dynamic equilibrium equation of the SM, relating interim age (secondary market) real investment prices and levels over time, can be written as*

$$(1 - I_{t+1}) = p_{t+1}[\varepsilon - (1 - I_t)], \quad \forall t \geq \tau, \tag{9}$$

where $(\tau + 1)$ is the time of the first unconstrained transaction on the SM.

Proof. To characterize the set of SM equilibria, it is useful to first simplify (7g), by dividing both sides by p_{t+1}. Then, using (6d) and (7a) successively, one obtains

$$\theta_{t,t+1}I_t = I_t + \theta_{t,t} p_t I_{t-1} = I_t + (1 - I_t) = 1, \quad \forall t \geq 1. \tag{9a}$$

Next, letting $\tau \equiv (t - 1)$ in (7d) only, we obtain, on multiplying by I_τ, that $\theta_{\tau+1,\tau+1}I_\tau + (1 - \varepsilon)[\theta_{\tau,\tau+1}I_\tau] = I_\tau, \forall \tau \geq 1$, which on using (9a) implies

$$1 - I_\tau = \varepsilon - \theta_{\tau+1,\tau+1}I_\tau, \quad \forall \tau \geq 1. \tag{9b}$$

Finally, using (7a) again in (9b) to substitute for $\theta_{\tau+1,\tau+1}$, we get our desired result that $p_{\tau+1}(1 - I_\tau) = \varepsilon p_{\tau+1} - \theta_{\tau+1,\tau+1} p_{\tau+1} I_\tau = \varepsilon p_{\tau+1} - (1 - I_{\tau+1})$; or:

$$(1 - I_{\tau+1}) = p_{\tau+1}[\varepsilon - (1 - I_\tau)], \quad \forall \tau \geq 1. \tag{9c}$$

which is equivalent to (9). Notice though that since $I_0 = 1$ and (from (7a) and (7b)) $I_1 = 1 - \varepsilon p_1 I_0$, if the early diers of generation 0 can sell *all* their shares to the next young, then *in that eventuality*, (9c) is also satisfied for $\tau = 0$. Q.E.D.

As we show in proposition 3 below, the characteristic equation (9), reflecting perfect foresight, absence of intertemporal arbitrage, and market clearing, has only *two* consistent solutions. The first, due to Fulghieri and Rovelli [1993], and Dutta and Kapur [1994], satisfies $p_{\tau+\kappa} = \sqrt{R}, \forall \kappa \geq 0$. But, as we shall see in the next section, it also requires *rationing* of the very first generation to sell in such a market at τ. The second solution is a *two-periodic* one: with $p_{\tau+\kappa} = 1$, for $\kappa \geq 1$ and odd; and $p_{\tau+\kappa} = R$, for $\kappa \geq 2$ and even; where τ is the first generation to trade in such a market. To simplify notation (only) in the following steady state result, we assume $\tau = 0$, although that is inconsistent with the 0th generation having no prior investments to buy in the secondary market.

PROPOSITION 3. *The set of stationary and periodic steady state SM equilibria, satisfying (7a)–(7h) and (8), is isolated, being one of the two following, assuming the anticipation of stock market trading commencing at some $t = 0$. The respective consumption allocations are given by using (8a) and (8b).*

(a) Stationary *equilibrium:*

$$\{p_t\} = \sqrt{R}, t = 1, 2, \ldots, \infty; \tag{6e}$$

implying $\{I_t\} = I^{SM}, t = 1, 2, \ldots, \infty$, *which from (9) satisfies* $1 - I^{SM} = \sqrt{R}[\varepsilon - (1 - I^{SM})]$. *Rearranging yields*

$$I^{SM} = 1 - \varepsilon\sqrt{R}/(1 + \sqrt{R}). \tag{10}$$

The consumption allocation is

$$C_{t,1} = \sqrt{R} \quad and \quad C_{t,2} = R, \quad \forall t \geq 0. \tag{12}$$

(b) Periodic *equilibrium:*

$$\{p_t\} = 1, \quad for\ t = 1, 3, 5, \ldots, odd; \tag{6f}$$
$$\{p_t\} = R, \quad for\ t = 2, 4, 6, \ldots, even; \tag{6g}$$

with

$$I_t = 1, \quad for\ t \geq 0\ and\ even; \tag{11a}$$
$$I_t = 1 - \varepsilon, \quad for\ t \geq 1\ and\ odd; \tag{11b}$$

which clearly satisfies equation (9). The consumption allocation is

$$C_{t,1} = 1 \quad and \quad C_{t,2} = R, \quad for\ t \geq 0\ and\ even; \tag{13a}$$

$$C_{t,1} = R \quad and \quad C_{t,2} = R, \quad for\ t \geq 0\ and\ odd; \tag{13b}$$

Proof. For part (a), see Fulghieri and Rovelli [1993] or Dutta and Kapur [1994]. For part (b), it suffices to note that equation (6f), (6g), (11a), (11b), and (13) satisfy (9). Q.E.D.

Remarks. If stock market equilibrium commences at $t = 0$, with $I_{t-1} = 0$, then given (7a) the *only* SM equilibrium consistent with the initial condition is the *periodic* one. Also note that, since iterating (6d) implies that $p_t = p_{t+2}, \forall t \geq 1$, *no other* periodic stock market equilibrium with periodicity $k > 2$ exists.

We now move on to consider the *dynamics of transition* to the steady state intergenerational allocation and risk sharing mechanisms described above.

3. Transitions and Comparative Payoffs

3.1 The "slowest turnpike" path to intergenerational banking (IB)

The first question we ask is the following: If the very first generation, born at $t = 0$, wishes to announce a feasible program of transition to the steady state *IB* outcome, then what is the maximum expected utility (consumption levels of early and late diers) that can be guaranteed on *a feasible and stationary* transition path to the steady state level of full investment of all new endowments in real long-lived technologies? We have the following result, which identifies the "slowest turnpike" transition path (*TIP*) to *IB*.

PROPOSITION 4. *A stationary (along the path) and finite transition path of consumption and long-lived investment (possibly coupled with partial early liquidation) to the Golden Rule optimal allocation exists, and it can support any interim consumption pair* $\{C_1^{TIB}, C_2^{TIB}\}$ *for early diers and late diers, satisfying*

$$(1 + R)\varepsilon C_1^{TIB} + 2(1 - \varepsilon)C_2^{TIB} < 2R. \tag{14}$$

Sketch of Proof. The proof is closely related to Qi [1994, proposition 5]. Consider the transition path described in table 1, which ensures a constant level of expected utility to all members of all generations alongside the path. Given $I_0 = 1$, it is easily shown that the investment sequence along this path is described

Table 1. Intergenerational Banking: Transition to the Golden Rule

Time	Resources*	Aggregate consumption	Investment
$t = 0$	1	0	1
1	1	εC_1	$1 - \varepsilon C_1$
2	$1 + R$	$\varepsilon C_1 + (1 - \varepsilon) C_2$	$1 + \delta$
		$\equiv R - \delta$	
3	$1 + R - R\varepsilon C_1$	$R - \delta$	$1 + \delta - R\varepsilon C_1$
4	$1 + R + \delta R$	$R - \delta$	$1 + \delta(1 + R)$
5	$1 + R + \delta R - R^2 \varepsilon C_1$	$R - \delta$	$1 + \delta(1 + R) - R^2 \varepsilon C_1$
6	$1 + R + \delta R + \delta R^2$	$R - \delta$	$1 + \delta(1 + R + R^2)$
7	$1 + R + \delta(R + R^2) - R^3 \varepsilon C_1$	$R - \delta$	$1 + \delta(1 + R + R^2) - R^3 \varepsilon C_1$

*Resources = endowment + maturing investment.

by

$$I_t = 1 + \delta \sum_{k=0}^{\frac{t}{2}-1} R^k = 1 + \delta \frac{R^{t/2} - 1}{R - 1}, \quad \text{for } t \text{ even;} \tag{15a}$$

$$I_{t+1} = 1 + \delta \sum_{k=0}^{\frac{t}{2}-1} R^k - R^{t/2} \varepsilon C_1 = 1 + \delta \frac{R^{t/2} - 1}{R - 1} - R^{t/2} \varepsilon C_1, \quad \text{for } (t+1) \text{ odd;}$$

$$\tag{15b}$$

where

$$\delta \equiv R - \varepsilon C_1 - (1 - \varepsilon) C_2 > 0. \tag{15c}$$

For this transition path to reach the steady state optimal allocation from some finite time point on, it is necessary that, for some τ sufficiently large:

$$I_\tau + I_{\tau+1} \geq 2, \quad \text{for } \tau \text{ even,} \tag{16}$$

so that at $(\tau + 1)$ a level of investment $(I_\tau - 1)$ can be liquidated and $(1 - I_{\tau+1})$ can be reinvested in the long-term technology, thus having $I_t \geq \tau + 1$. Using (15a)–(15c), condition (16) is equivalent, for τ sufficiently large, to

$$R^{\tau/2}[2\delta - (R - 1)\varepsilon C_1] \geq 2\delta. \tag{17a}$$

For $0 < \delta \leq R$, a τ sufficiently large satisfying (17a) exists if

$$2\delta - (R - 1)\varepsilon C_1 > 0. \tag{17b}$$

which, using the definition (15c) of δ, yields inequality (14).

Note that a feasible transition path to the Golden Rule steady state allocation must also ensure that all interim investment levels along the path are non-negative. To satisfy this non-negativity constraint it may become necessary to liquidate in odd periods some of the investment made during the previous even period. In Qi [1994] it is shown that, if condition (17b) is satisfied, these additional non-negativity constraints are also satisfied.   Q.E.D.

Remarks. First, consider the following program $\{C_1^{TIB}, C_2^{TIB}\}$, which a transitional generation may advance as a proposal:

$$V^{TIB} \equiv \max_{\{C_1, C_2\}} [\varepsilon U(C_1) + (1 - \varepsilon)U(C_2)], \tag{18}$$

subject to a *weak* inequality in (14), leading to $[I_t + I_{t+1} = 2 - \varepsilon C_1]$, for all t even. This is the maximum stationary sustainable utility profile of Qi [1994, proposition 5]. With the slightest altruism towards future generations, or discreteness in consumption and/or investment choices, (14) will hold *strictly*, and hence the Golden Rule steady state of proposition 1 will be attained by generations born at time τ and afterwards.

Second, if the transition path of table 1 is continued past period τ, as defined in (16), then — instead of moving on to the Golden Rule steady state — the accumulation of inherited capital could proceed *beyond* the steady state level of unity, eventually allowing even higher levels of consumption for some future generations. We do not consider such schemes, as the $\{C_1^{TIB}, C_2^{TIB}\}$-proposal is motivated by the concerns of *not* making future generations worse off than earlier ones, as in Esteban and Sakovics [1993], with generational self-concern subject to this constraint.

We can now prove the following.

COROLLARY 3. *The optimal consumption plan* $\{C_1^{TIB}, C_2^{TIB}\}$ *available on the TIB to the Golden Rule steady state strictly dominates the consumption plan* $\{C_1^B, C_2^B\}$ *available with intragenerational banking* (B); *that is:*

$$V^{TIB} > V^B. \tag{19}$$

Proof. From proposition 2, the consumption plan available with B must satisfy the constraint, obtained by eliminating L between equations (3a) and (3b), that $\{C_1^B, C_2^B\} \in S^B \equiv [\{C_1, C_2\} | R\varepsilon C_1 + (1 - \varepsilon)C_2 \leq R]$. Conversely from proposition 4, the consumption plan under TIB must satisfy $\{C_1^{TIB}, C_2^{TIB}\} \in S^{TIB} \equiv [\{C_1, C_2\} | ((1 + R)/2)\varepsilon C_1 + (1 - \varepsilon)C_2 < R]$. The desired result now follows from the fact that $S^B \subset S^{TIB}$, for $R > 1$.   Q.E.D.

3.2 Transitions to and payoffs from stock markets

The next question we pose relates to the concern that a transition path to the IB steady state might be "upset" (see below for details) by an alternative proposal to establish an SM. We thus prove the following extension to the results in proposition 3, delineating feasible transitions to the stationary SM equilibria.

PROPOSITION 5. *A proposed transition to an SM equilibrium at time t by the young must result in either of the following two cases.*

(a) *If the generation prior to t is* not *allowed to trade in the stock market at t:*

$$p_{t+i} = 1, \quad \text{for } i \geq 1 \text{ and odd}; \qquad p_{t+i} = R, \qquad \text{for } i \geq 2 \text{ and even};$$
$$I_{t+k} = 1, \quad \text{for } k \geq 0 \text{ and even}; \qquad I_{t+k} = 1 - \varepsilon, \quad \text{for } k \geq 1 \text{ and odd}.$$

(b) *If early diers of generation* $(t - 1)$ *are* allowed to do a quantity-constrained *trading with the newborn generation t of* $1/(1 + \sqrt{R})$ *of their one-period old investment per capita at t:*

$$p_{t+i} = \sqrt{R}, \quad \forall i \geq 0;$$
$$I_{t+k} = 1 - \varepsilon\sqrt{R}/(1 + \sqrt{R}), \quad \forall k \geq 0;$$

with no rationing for subsequent generations.

No other transition path of interim investment prices and levels exists, that is consistent with perfect foresight, no arbitrage and stock market clearing at all times $\tau \geq t + 1.$

Proof. See Bhattacharya, Fulghieri and Rovelli [1998].

Remarks. Since the transition to the periodic equilibrium in part (a) of proposition 5 leads to the consumption profile $C_{t,1} = 1$ and $C_{t,2} = R$ (as in part (b) of proposition 3) for the proposing generation t, it follows from corollary 3 that *no generation* when young can gain relatively to TIB (nor, for that matters, to B) from such a transition. Hence it will never be proposed. Thus, in what follows, we restrict attention to the immediate transition to the *non-periodic* SM equilibrium. In doing so, we assume that the strictly positive but quantity-constrained participation in this market by the middle-aged generation at t is feasible to implement. In particular, only sell orders by the currently middle-aged generation will be acceptable, and rationed *pro rata*.

At this point it is useful to ask how the proposed quantity-constrained (for the middle-aged generation) transition to the SM compares in expected utility, for the two transitional generations, with that resulting from the TIB to the Golden Rule steady state optimal allocation. We have the following result, applicable to the initial generation born at $t = 0$.

PROPOSITION 6. *If the currently middle-aged generation at t have inherited one-period old real investments of unity, and no other financial maturing investments (as is the case with generation 0, for example), then the constrained transition to the non-periodic and stationary SM equilibrium path results in expected utilities of V^{SM} (MA) for the currently middle-aged, and V^{SM} (NB) for the newborn starting the stock market, such that*

$$V^{SM}(MA) < V^{TIB}, \quad and \tag{a}$$

$$V^{SM}(NB) \gtrless V^{TIB}, \tag{b}$$

with V^{SM} (NB) > V^{TIB} if the agents' ex post corner utility functions for consumptions $U(C_i), i \in \{1,2\}$, has globally a relative risk aversion coefficient ρ in some open neighborhood of the closed interval $1 \leq \rho \leq (2\log((1+R)/2))/\log(R) \leq 2$.

Proof. Concerning part (a), we know from the characterization in part (b) of proposition 5, that the early diers of generation $(t-1)$ are able to sell at t, per capita, $1/(1+\sqrt{R})$ units of real investments made at $(t-1)$ at price $\sqrt{R}$ to the newborn of generation t. Hence, they must physically *liquidate* their remaining real investments, since late diers of their own generation have no dividends from maturing investments to buy shares with. Thus, the expected consumption level of the early diers of generation $(t-1)$ is

$$C_{t-1,1}^{SM(MA)} = \frac{\sqrt{R}}{1+\sqrt{R}} + \left[1\frac{1}{1+\sqrt{R}}\right] = \frac{2\sqrt{R}}{1+\sqrt{R}}, \tag{20a}$$

whereas the consumption level of its late diers is

$$C_{t-1,2}^{SM(MA)} = R. \tag{20b}$$

Comparing the allocation tuple in (20a) and (20b) with that resulting from the TIB, we see from proposition 4 and inequality (14) that, if C_2^{TIB} is set at R, then

$$C_1^{TIB} < \frac{2R}{1+R}, \tag{21}$$

with the inequality holding with arbitrarily small slack (see the first remark to proposition 4). The result then follows from noting that $2R/(1+R) > 2\sqrt{R}/(1+\sqrt{R})$ for $R > 1$, and that $U(C_i), i \in 1,2$, is assumed to be strictly increasing.

For part (b), see Bhattacharya, Fulghieri, and Rovelli [1998].   Q.E.D.

Remarks. In Figure 1, we have drawn the graph of numerical simulations of the inequality $V^{TIB} \gtrless V^{SM}$ (NB), for ε in discrete grids of 0.1 over $\{0.1, 0.9\}$, constant ρ in discrete grids of 0.5 over $\{0.6, 5.6\}$, and R in discrete grids of 0.5 over $\{1.5, 5\}$, where $R = 5$ corresponds to a real rate of return of 4.1 percent over 40 years, the

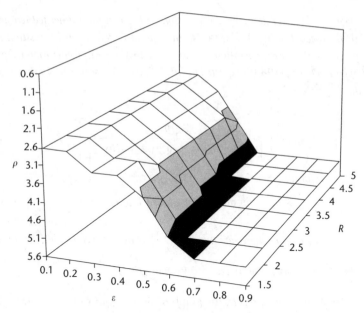

Figure 1. Comparison of $V^{SM}(NB)$ With V^{TIB}.

Note: On or above the surface, $V^{SM}(NB) > V^{TIB}$.

half-life of a generation.[9] *On or above* the drawn surface, $V^{SM}(NB) > V^{TIB}$. The graph shows that $V^{SM}(NB) \leq V^{TIB}$ is indeed possible, but only for relatively *high* levels of risk aversion. With $\varepsilon = 0.3$ and $R \geq 1.5$ for instance, $\rho > 3.6$ is necessary for $V^{SM}(NB) \leq V^{TIB}$, so that the newborn are *not* tempted to propose a transition to SM away from TIB.

3.3 The stand-alone option and its payoff

In this subsection we compare $V^{SM}(MA)$ with V^{B}, the expected utility arising from a constrained transition to the SM and that from *intra*generational banking (B), the latter being also the *stand-alone option* of the currently middle-aged when faced with any proposal by the younger generation.[10] In the next section, we shall in fact analyze a class of *intergenerational proposal games* over liquidity sharing mechanisms, across the infinite sequence of overlapping generations at times $t = 1, 2, 3, \ldots, \infty$. As a preliminary to that discussion, we have here the following result, which relies on comparisons analogous to those made in proposition 6, and is applicable also to the initial generation born at $t = 0$.

---

[9] One may think of a 40 year period as made up of ages 40 to 80, so that a (disabled) individual may take early retirement at the age of 60, or continue working until 80 and then enjoy an increased level of consumption, with both dying soon after retirement.

[10] In thinking of V^{B} as the outside option of the currently middle-aged, when the next generation proposes a transition to SM, we are implicitly assuming that *intragenerational solidarity* among the middle-aged is present (or, more plausibly, that times of death are unresolved for them), when the next generation proposes.

PROPOSITION 7. *For a middle-aged generation with one unit of inherited real invest-ments, their expected utility. $V^{SM}(MA)$, from a quantity-constrained transition to the SM proposed by the next generation, compares with their intragenerational optimal (Diamond and Dybvig [1983]) expected utility, V^B, as follows. If either of the following holds, then $V^{SM}(MA) > V^B$:*

$$1 \le \rho \le \left[\frac{\log(R)}{\left\{ \log(1 + \sqrt{R}) - \log(2) + \log(R)/2 \right\}} \right] \le 2, \qquad (22a)$$

for all $R \ge 1$ and $\varepsilon \in [0, 1]$;

$$\varepsilon \to 1^-, \quad \text{for all} \ \rho \ge 1 \quad \text{and} \quad R \ge 1. \qquad (22b)$$

If neither of the conditions above are met, then $V^{SM}(MA) \le V^B$ for ε sufficiently small.

Proof. See Bhattacharya, Fulghieri, and Rovelli [1998].

Remarks. In Figure 2, we present the graph of simulations of the $(V^{SM}(MA), V^B)$-comparison, in the ε-ρ-R-space, using the same grid as that underlying figure 1. *On or above* the drawn surface, the middle-aged generation is found to prefer a constrained transition to the SM, relative to their stand-alone option of B. This is generally the case if their risk aversion is low, or if the proportion of early diers is high. However, for say $\varepsilon = 0.3$, $V^B \ge V^{SM}(MA)$ for all $\rho \ge 2.1$ for $R \ge 3.5$, which corresponds to an annual real rate of return of 3.18 percent over 40 years. The reason is that, for sufficient curvature in $U(C)$, the "intertemporally inflexible" allocation of SM *plus* the selling constraint that the early diers among the initial transitional middle-aged are subjected to, lowers $V^{SM}(MA)$ sufficiently relative to V^B, if ε is low or moderate. For sufficiently high ε however ($\varepsilon \ge 0.6$ in our simulations), the effect of the tighter *intra*generational resource constraint of the B allocation dominates, and we get $V^{SM}(MA) > V^B$ for all ρ and R in the range simulated.

   Note that, in these simulations, for $\varepsilon = 0.3, R \ge 3.5$ and $\rho \in [2.1, 3.6]$, $V^{SM}(NB) > V^{TIB}$ but at the same time $V^{SM}(MA) < V^B$. As we shall see below, this implies that the middle-aged would be credibly able to resist a self-interested proposal by the young to switch to SM from TIB.[11] These considerations suggest the theme and anticipate the results of the following section: Given an inter-generational proposal game over choices among {B, TIB, SM}, agents could be

---

[11] In contemplating these transitions, we are not allowing the middle-aged generation to do *both* the constrained trading with the young, and also further within-generation risk sharing as in B; otherwise, $V^{SM}(MA)$ would always exceed V^B. Our rationale is that we think of the SM-mechanism as being more individually decentralized than either B or TIB, which require intragenerational coordination at least. If, on the other hand, the middle-aged could renegotiate B among themselves, the economy would shift to SM (following a proposal from the newborn) whenever $V^{SM}(NB) > V^{TIB}$.

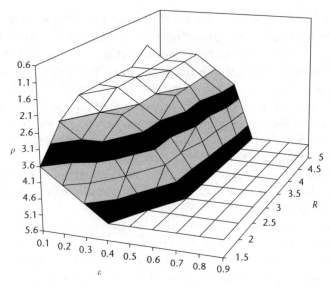

Figure 2. Comparison of $V^{SM}(MA)$ with V^B.

Note: On or above the surface, $V^{SM}(MA) > V^B$.

so risk-averse that *all* (middle-aged and young) prefer TIB (which dominates B) to SM, or sufficiently risk-averse that $V^{SM}(MA) < V^B$, so SM is *blocked* by the middle-aged generation in favor of TIB. If however *neither* of these conditions holds, then an SM-proposal by the young will *prevail* and move the economy to what is, in the steady state perspective, a worse equilibrium.

4. Intergenerational Proposal Games and Equilibria

4.1 Self-sustaining mechanisms

We now move on to define and analyze a class of non-cooperative intergenerational proposal games, across the sequence of overlapping generations in our model. Each *stage game* of the proposal game, at times $t = 1, 2, \ldots, \infty$, is modeled as a proposal *cum* counter-proposal game between the two generations, born at $(t - 1)$, the middle-aged, and at t, the newborn, which at t are in a position to make (real or financial) investment decisions. This represents an extension of the "transfer game" across generations analyzed by Esteban and Sakovics [1993], in which the authors allow only the young at any time t to make proposals for changing the previously agreed upon transfers to the old of the immediately prior generation. Our *two-sided* proposal/counter-proposal game is necessary, because two of the allowed proposals involve either the access to the initial endowment of the newborn by the currently middle-aged (TIB), or the utilization (acquisition at some price) of the inherited intermediate maturity capital stock of the middle-aged by the young (the non-periodic, quantity-constrained SM transition of part (b) of proposition 5). Hence, because of this change relative to Esteban and Sakovics, we must specify not only the payoffs to agents taking into account *subsequent* stage games at $t+1, t+2, \ldots$, but also their payoffs in the events of both *agreement* (regarding the allocational mechanism to be continued or switched to) as well as *disagreement* among the overlapping generations at any time t. We do so below assuming, firstly, that in the event of an *agreement* at t, this is *binding* until $(t+1)$ at least, and secondly, that in the event of *disagreement* on proposals at t the currently middle-aged obtain their autarkic payoff given their endowment, and the newborn at t can always *revise* both their proposal/program at t and their planned proposal at $(t+1)$.

We restrict the pure strategy set of each overlapping generation in the stage games at times $t = 1, 2, \ldots, \infty$, to be the 3-tuple of allocation mechanisms (or institutions, in the terminology of Esteban and Sakovics) {B, TIB, SM}, that were characterized in sections 2 and 3 above. We do so for the following reasons: First, as we have suggested earlier, the TIB and SM intergenerational allocation mechanisms have the feature that, if at t a current agreed upon mechanism is started and is continued through $t, t+1, t+2, \ldots$, then generations *subsequent* to the newborn at t are never worse off than the generation t. We postulate that reasonable proposal processes (e.g. in a legislature) satisfy this "minimal degree of fairness" property, even though the resulting mechanism need not guarantee, say, ultimate attainment of the Golden Rule optimum in the long run. The spirit of this restriction is identical to that underlying the transfer institutions or proposals described in Esteban and Sakovics [1993] or Boldrin and Rustichini [1994]. Second, while we have *not* proved that the three institutions/mechanisms, which each generation is allowed to propose, are the *only* ones that are, on the one hand, intergenerationally *stationary* for *future* generations on their continuation paths, and viable on the other hand, they do represent the set of major significant alternatives in many aggregate (macroeconomic) settings, such as generationally autarkic, PAYG, and market-based *pension plan systems*. Once we step outside the class of these three mechanisms, we essentially open a Pandora's Box of proposals that satisfy the second criterion (viability) but not the first (intergenerational stationarity), that we deem desirable to impose.[12]

The stage games, at each time point of the infinite horizon intergenerational proposal game, could themselves involve at least the following three alternative

---

[12] For example, generation 1 could offer to buy ε units of real one-period old investments from generation 0 at $t = 1$, *at unit price*, and invest the remainder of its endowment $(1 - \varepsilon)$ in real investments, thus guaranteeing *its* early and late diers consumption levels of $\{C_{1,1} = R, C_{1,2} = R\}$. Generation 0 would not have a better outside option (as this would involve physical liquidation) and generation 2 would be strictly worse off than generation 1.

extensive forms: Case (A), the middle-aged moving first and proposing, and the young counter-proposing. Case (B), the newborn moving first and proposing, and the middle-aged counter-proposing. Case (C), simultaneous moves and proposals by the two generations overlapping at any point in time.

Of these alternatives, cases (B) and (C) are relatively more in accordance with the spirit of the transfer proposal game of Esteban and Sakovics. Furthermore, the equilibrium outcome in case (A) is also somewhat obvious, given that *always* $V^{TIB} > V^B$ (corollary 3) and $V^{TIB} > V^{SM}(MA)$ (part (a) of proposition 6). It turns out, on the other hand, that the equilibrium outcomes in cases (B) and (C), suitably defined, generically *coincide* with each other, and furthermore that they depend on the *relative* magnitude of V^{TIB} versus $V^{SM}(NB)$, as well as on that of $V^{SM}(MA)$ versus V^B. We now proceed to describe the agents' strategies and payoffs more precisely, and also to define the notion of *self-sustaining mechanisms* arising from these proposal games across current and future generations.

In Table 2, we describe the pure strategy payoffs in case (C) of the proposal stage scheme, across generations 0 and 1, postponing the discussion of subsequent stage games until the subsequent result (proposition 8 below). Notice that the *continuation payoff*, $V(c)$ or $V(c')$ of the newborn in the event of disagreement takes into account the optimal reswitching strategy of these agents. It is easy, using table 2, to write the payoffs in the extensive form game trees of the stage games in cases (A) and (B). Mixtures of stage game pure strategies (uncorrelated) by players are allowed in all the cases.

We define the continuation payoff for the newborn, at any stage game at t, as

$$V(c) = [V^{TIB}], \quad \text{if } \{TIB, TIB\} \text{ is in } [SSM(t+1)|H_t+1 = (1,0)]; \tag{23a}$$

$$V(c) = [V^{SM}(MA)|H_{t+1} = (1,0)], \quad \text{otherwise;} \tag{23b}$$

where H_{t+1} is the vector of real capital stock (one-period old and maturing) which the current (as of time t) newborn generation will be holding at $(t+1)$; and $SSM(.)$ represents the notion of self-sustaining mechanisms, to be defined below. The payoff $V(c')$ is analogously defined, with H_{t+1} now equaling the *inherited* capital stock vector along the TIB, starting at $t = 0$.

Table 2. Payoffs in the First Stage Proposal Game

Newborn	Middle-aged		
	B	TIB	SM
B	$\{V^B, V^B\}$	$\{V(c), V^B\}$	$\{V(c), V^B\}$
TIB	$\{V(c), V^B\}$	$\{V(c'), V^{TIB}\}$	$\{V(c), V^B\}$
SM	$\{V(c), V^B\}$	$\{V(c), V^B\}$	$\{V^{SM}(NB), V^{SM}(MA)\}$

We conclude this subsection with the following definition of equilibrium outcomes in the proposal game.

DEFINITION. *A self-sustaining mechanism is a sequence of outcomes of the inter-generational stage games at $t = 1, 2, \ldots, \infty$, such that the outcomes and equilibrium strategies (given H_t) at each t, $\{SSM(t)\}$, satisfy the criteria that, $\forall t \geq 1$:*

(a) $\{SSM(t)\} \in NE(t)$,   *Nash equilibrium in the stage game at t;*
(b) $\{SSM(\tau)\}_{\tau=t}^{\infty} \in NE(\tau)$, *subgame perfect equilibrium across stages;*
(c) $\{SSM(t)\} \in SPE(t)$,   *subgame perfect equilibrium in the stage game at t, in cases (A) and (B); or*

$\{SSM(t)\} \in TPE(t)$,   *trembling-hand perfect equilibrium in the stage game at t, in case (C).*

4.2 Equilibrium outcomes: Only the meek shall inherit the earth

We can now state and prove the result suggested in the previous section (propositions 6 and 7). We do so assuming that $V(c) = V(c')$. While this assumption on $V(c)$ is critical for a unique outcome in a subset of case (C), and it may appear to be unduly restrictive, in proposition 8 below we shall prove that, under reasonable conditions, it is naturally satisfied.[13]

THEOREM 1. *Self-sustaining mechanisms in the* first *stage intergenerational proposal game are characterized as follows.*

(a) *In case (A): $SSM(t) = \{TIB, TIB\}$.*
(b) *In case (B), either of the following three equilibria may result:*
   (b1) *$SSM(t) = \{TIB, TIB\}$, if either $V^{SM}(NB) < V^{TIB}$, or $V^{SM}(NB) \geq V^{TIB}$ and $V^{SM}(MA) < V^B$;*
   (b2) *$SSM(t) = \{SM, SM\}$, if $V^{SM}(NB) > V^{TIB}$ and $V^{SM}(MA) \geq V^B$;*
   (b3) *both $\{SM, SM\}$ and $\{TIB, TIB\} \in SSM(t)$, if $V^{SM}(NB) = V^{TIB}$ and $V^{SM}(MA) \geq V^B$.*
(c) *In case (C), either of the following three equilibria may result:*
   (c1) *$SSM(t) = \{TIB, TIB\}$, if either $V^{SM}(NB) < V^{TIB}$, or $V^{SM}(MA) < V^B$;*
   (c2) *$SSM(t) = \{SM, SM\}$, if $V^{SM}(NB) > V^{TIB}$ and $V^{SM}(MA) \geq V^B$;*
   (c3) *both $\{SM, SM\}$ and $\{TIB, TIB\} \in SSM(t)$, if $V^{SM}(NB) = V^{TIB}$ and $V^{SM}(MA) \geq V^B$.*

Proof. Part (a) follows from corollary 3 and proposition 6. In part (c2), the fact that $\{SM, SM\}$ is uniquely in $SSM(t)$ follows from using the trembling-hand perfect equilibrium concept and from the maintained hypothesis that $V(c) = V(c')$ (see the discussion concerning proposition 8 below). The remainder of parts (b) and (c) are obvious, on examination of table 2 and equations (23).   Q.E.D.

---

[13] In other words, we are analyzing cases in which the newborn at t do not "go along with" the middle-aged, on $\{TIB, TIB\}$, *just* to acquire $H_{t+1} > 1$ to do better in a move to SM, i.e. for $[V^{SM}(MA)|H_{t+1}]$ at the *next* stage game at $(t + 1)$.

Remarks. In *economic terms*, theorem 1—together with propositions 4, 5 and 6 — implies the following: First, the very first generation will never start a stock market in long-lived capital (SM), nor an intragenerationally autarkic bank (B). Second, the TIB to Golden Rule steady state IB would survive (continue) at time *t*, if *either* it is a dominant strategy for both the newborn and middle-aged at *t* or, at least, the middle-aged at *t* can *credibly resist* a switch to the steady state non-periodic SM at *t*, by *threatening* to revert to their autarkic B allocation. Third, in particular, the most desirable steady state outcome (the Golden Rule supported by IB) will be reached when people are *sufficiently risk-averse* and are *not too likely to require early utilization* of their savings (or liquidity).

For the TIB to be maintained, we must have that it is *also* an equilibrium outcome of the intergenerational proposal games at all dates along the accumulation path, until the switch to the Golden Rule steady state can actually take place. We conclude this section by showing that if {SM, SM} is *not* a Nash equilibrium outcome in the initial stage game, it will continue not to be so for all intergenerational stage games along the accumulation path in a wide class of cases. We do this in the following proposition 8, which serves to justify the assumption that $V(c) = V(c')$, which was used in the proof of theorem 1. Then, given $V(c) = V(c')$, the proof of theorem 1 also applies in *all* stage games. Furthermore, the *same* equilibrium outcome would arise in all current and subsequent stages.

The thrust of our argument is the following: Assume TIB to be the unique Nash equilibrium outcome in the first stage intergenerational proposal game. Then, in the first cases of part (b1) and (c1) of theorem 1, it will clearly continue to be the chosen equilibrium over time, since the terms of choice between TIB and competing mechanisms will be invariant across stage games, even as capital accumulation proceeds along the transition path. In the other cases, where the newborn might prefer a move to SM, but the middle-aged can credibly resist such a proposal *in the first stage* of the game by credibly threatening to revert to the autarkic B allocation, then the terms of this choice will change as capital accumulation proceeds along TIB. We can still prove, for the class of *homothetic* (instantaneous) *utility functions*, that this credible threat to revert to B will persist along the accumulation path. We can thus state the following.

PROPOSITION 8. *If TIB is a (Nash, and subgame perfect or trembling-hand perfect) equilibrium allocation in the first stage of the intergenerational proposal game, it will continue to be an equilibrium allocation in all subsequent stage games, for all homothetic $U(C) = C^{1-\rho}/(1 - \rho)$ with $\rho > 0$.*

Sketch of Proof. In Bhattacharya, Fulghieri and Rovelli [1998] we show that if, as used in theorem 1, at the first stage game

$$V_{t-1}^{SM}(MA) < V_{t-1}^{B}, \quad \text{for } t = 1,$$

then in all subsequent stage games

$$V_{t-1}^{SM}(MA) < V_{t-1}^B, \quad \forall t \geq 2.$$

To prove this, we note that the inherited endowment level at time t,

$$Z_t \equiv [RI_{t-2} + I_{t-1} - (1 - \varepsilon)C_2^{TIB}].$$

net of contractual obligations to the generation born at $(t - 2)$, and constituting the maximum liquidable resources of the $(t - 1)$th middle-aged generation at t, satisfies the feature that

$$Z_t \geq Z_1, \quad \forall t \geq 2.$$

Given this, we then show that

$$C_{t-1,1}^{SM}(MA) = \left[Z_t + \frac{\sqrt{R} - 1}{(1 + \sqrt{R})} \right] \quad \text{and}$$

$$C_{t-1,2}^{SM}(MA) = \begin{cases} RZ_t, & \text{if } RI_{t-2} \leq (1 - \varepsilon)C_2^{TIB} \\ Z_t + (R - 1)I_{t-1}, & \text{otherwise} \end{cases}$$

From this, it follows by defining

$$M_{1t} \equiv \frac{C_{t-1,1}^{SM}(MA)}{C_{0,1}^{SM}(MA)} \quad \text{and} \quad M_{2t} \equiv \frac{C_{t-1,2}^{SM}(MA)}{C_{0,2}^{SM}(MA)},$$

that it is also *feasible* to have, under the *intragenerational* mechanism B for the $(t - 1)$th generation:

$$B_{1t} \equiv \frac{C_{t-1,1}^B}{C_{0,1}^B} = M_{1t} \quad \text{and} \quad B_{2t} \equiv \frac{C_{t-1,2}^B}{C_{0,2}^B} \geq M_{2t}.$$

Hence, for all homothetic $U(C_i), i = 1$, if $V_0^{SM}(MA) < V_0^B$, then also $V_{t-1}^{SM}(MA) < V_{t-1}^B$, at the time of the proposed transition to SM by generation t.   Q.E.D.

Remark. Given proposition 8, our main theorem, and definitions (23a) and (23b), $V(c') = V(c)$ holds true for the continuation payoffs if $[V^B|H_1 = (1, 0)] > [V^{SM}(MA)|H_1 = (1, 0)]$. Alternatively, suppose $[V^B|H_1 = (1, 0)] < [V^{SM}(MA)|H_1 = (1, 0)]$, *but* still {SM, SM} is not the unique trembling-hand perfect self-sustaining mechanism at $t = 1$ in case (C) because, by hypothesis, $V(c') > V(c)$. But then {TIB, TIB} must also be in $SSM(t + 1)$ because $V(c') > V(c)$ will continue to hold also at $t = 2$, in light of the proof of proposition 8. But then it contradicts the definition of $V(c)$ in (23a), (23b) to assume that $V(c') \neq V(c)$ at $t = 1$.

5. Concluding Remarks

In this chapter we have attempted to extend and synthesize the extant and emerging theoretical frameworks pertaining to static liquidity sharing (consumption smoothing) mechanisms, intergenerational (OLG) tradeoffs and modifications to these (in and out of steady states), and non-cooperative intergenerational proposal games related to sustainable mechanisms or institutions in these settings. Our results show that, if currently young generations are constrained to be "minimally altruistic" towards their descendants (i.e. not to do relative harm to them) in their "feasible" (allowed) proposals, then transition to the long-run optimal Golden Rule (Phelps [1961]) outcome may be obtained as the unique non-cooperative equilibrium outcome among generations, but only if the agents involved have preferences embodying a significant degree of relative risk aversion, or curvature in the (additive) utility functions for consumption at different points of their stochastic life-spans, and also a relatively low likelihood of liquidity or early withdrawal needs. By embodying such a reasonably restricted notion of intergenerational "autonomy," we have improved on the essentially planning-theoretic modeling of, for example, Allen and Gale [1995], and also enriched (in context) the methodology of Esteban and Sakovics [1993], obtaining quite different results vis-à-vis the universality of long-run efficiency attainment.

Our model may also be usefully compared to that of Boldrin and Rustichini [1994]: With no long-lived capital and, hence, no transfer of property rights to capital *across* generations taking place, they find that whether or not PAYG social security (intergenerational transfer) systems are voted into existence (and maintained), depends on the return to capital and the dynamics of stochastic population growth (a high rate of growth will favor the adoption of a PAYG system).[14] Keeping in mind that both our transition path to intergenerational banking (TIB) and also the intergenerational banking steady state (IB) share an essential similarity with PAYG systems, our results point to the fact that whether or not a PAYG outcome will be chosen, in an environment with *long-lived capital stock and stochastic lifetimes*, may also depend on the extent of agents' aversion to risk and random needs for early withdrawal or liquidity. A synthesis of these two types of modeling, with roles for both endogenous trade or exchange of property rights to capital *and* for aggregate shocks to state variables pertaining to agents' (preference) characteristics, demographic changes, and return to capital, should help provide important and policy-relevant answers to intriguing economic questions regarding the nature and efficiency of equilibrium financial intermediation *and* social security systems.

---

[14] In common with our model and Esteban and Sakovics [1993], Boldrin and Rustichini [1994] also assume that a proposed social security transfer to the old embodies in it the same proportional transfers to the current young when they would be old (unless this is then modified by a new proposal by the then young agents).

References

Allen, F., and Gale, D. (1995). "A welfare comparison of intermediaries and financial markets in Germany and the US." *European Economic Review*, 39: 179–209.

Bencivenga, V., and Smith, B. (1991). "Financial intermediation and endogenous growth." *Review of Economic Studies*, 58: 195–209.

Bhattacharya, S., Fulghieri, P., and Rovelli, R. (1998). "Financial intermediation versus stock markets in a dynamic intertemporal model." Working Paper Series No. 9807 FIN, INSEAD, Fontainebleau, France.

——, and Gale, D. (1987). "Preference shocks, liquidity, and central bank policy," in W. A. Barnett and K. J. Singleton (eds.), *New Approaches to Monetary Economics* (Cambridge: Cambridge Univ. Press), 69–88.

——, and Padilla, J. (1996). "Dynamic banking: A reconsideration." *Review of Financial Studies*, 9: 1003–32.

Boldrin, M., and Rustichini, A. (1994). "Equilibria with social security." CORE Discussion Paper No. 9460, Université Catholique de Louvain, Belgium.

Bryant, J. (1980). "A model of reserves, bank runs, and deposit insurance." *Journal of Banking and Finance*, 4: 335–44.

Diamond, D. W., and Dybvig, P. H. (1983). "Bank runs, deposit insurance, and liquidity." *Journal of Political Economy*, 91: 401–19.

Dutta, J., and Kapur, S. (1994). "Liquidity preference and financial intermediation." Discussion Paper in Economics No. 17, Birkbeck College, London.

Esteban, J. (1986). "A characterization of the core in overlapping-generations economies." *Journal of Economic Theory*, 39: 439–56.

——, and Millan, T. M. (1990). "Competitive equilibria and the core of overlapping generations economies." *Journal of Economic Theory*, 50: 155–74.

——, and Sakovics, J. (1993). "Intertemporal transfer institutions." *Journal of Economic Theory*, 61: 189–205.

Fulghieri, P., and Rovelli, R. (1993). "Capital markets, financial intermediaries, and the supply of liquidity in a dynamic economy." Working Paper No. FB-93-04, Graduate School of Business, Columbia University, New York.

Gale, D. (1973). "Pure exchange equilibrium of dynamic economic models." *Journal of Economic Theory*, 6: 12–36.

Jacklin, C. J. (1987). "Demand deposits, trading restrictions, and risk sharing," in E. C. Prescott and N. Wallace (eds.), *Contractual Arrangements for Intertemporal Trade* (Minneapolis: Univ. of Minnesota Press), 26–47.

Phelps, E. S. (1961). "The golden rule of accumulation: A fable for growthmen." *American Economic Review*, 51: 638–43.

Qi, J. (1994). "Bank liquidity and stability in an overlapping generations model." *Review of Financial Studies*, 7: 389–417.

Samuelson, P. A. (1958). "An exact consumption-loan model of interest with or without the social contrivance of money." *Journal of Political Economy*, 66: 467–82.

Selten, R. (1975). "Re-examination of the perfectness concept for equilibrium points in extensive games." *International Journal of Game Theory*, 4: 25–55.

8

The Governance of Exchanges: Members' Cooperatives versus Outside Ownership

Oliver Hart and John Hardman-Moore

I. Introduction

In all countries, securities exchanges face a number of important new challenges. First, exchanges compete increasingly with each other. This is in large part a result of the reduced cost of communications, which has allowed exchanges to gain access to a geographically dispersed set of customers. The impact of this changing technology was initially felt by regional exchanges, which lost their local franchises and in many cases were forced out of business. However, national exchanges are now also to a large extent in competition internationally. Competition has been heightened by the fact that quite similar economic attributes may often be shared by apparently different securities.

Second, the product mix of exchanges is changing. Traditionally exchanges have performed a variety of functions, such as providing a trading mechanism, disseminating information, acting as a clearing house, settling trades, etc. But exchanges no longer need to be vertically integrated in this way. Many of these functions are offered by specialist service providers and, in many cases, exchanges have hived off particular functions. Thus, competition occurs both horizontally between exchanges and vertically between exchanges and service providers.

Third, the development of technology has meant that exchanges have become more capital intensive. Periodically exchanges need to finance substantial

This is an abbreviated version of our 1995 Discussion Paper, which also appeared as a City Research Project Subject Report (No. XXII). We thank Roger Barton, David Burton, Noel Lawson, Philip Lynch, Herschel Post, and Peter Rawlins for their time, and for providing us with background information. However, the views expressed here are our own. We also grateful to Eric Bergloff, Richard Brealey, Jenny Ireland, Kevin Roberts, Ailsa Roell, and a number of colleagues for useful discussions. Richard Brealey was extremely generous in redrafting the early sections of the chapter; we are greatly indebted to him.

investment programmes. Since the pay-off may often occur several years after the investment, a structure is needed which ensures that those who provided the initial capital also receive the pay-off from the investment.

Fourth, membership of exchanges has become more open and, as a result, more diverse. Members not only perform different roles within the exchange, but they may have other activities outside the exchange (such as over-the-counter business) which in effect make them competitors of the exchange.

These rapid and fundamental changes in the economics of exchanges suggest that it is important to consider whether the governance structures that have evolved in the past are likely to remain appropriate for the future. The success of exchanges in responding to change is likely to depend in large measure on their organizational structure. It is possible to point to a number of instances where reforms have been hindered by an exchange's difficulty in securing consensus among its members. For example, the speed with which the New York Stock Exchange has been able to implement new technologies has been in part determined by the reluctance of floor traders to accept changes that primarily benefited larger brokerage houses.[1] In Germany the divergent interests of the *kursmakler*, the *freimakler*, and the banks led for a time to the development of competing trading systems and threatened to fragment further an already fragmented market-place. In Chicago conflicts between agricultural and financial futures traders have impeded the proposals by the Chicago Board of Trade to expand the financial futures pit. And so on.

Exchanges differ from most commercial organizations in a number of ways. In particular, a common feature of most major exchanges is that they are run as *cooperatives*. In other words, broadly speaking they are run on behalf of their members, the people who use the exchange (market-makers, brokers, and so on). In London, the Stock Exchange has operated as a cooperative, as has Lloyd's and four futures exchanges (the International Financial Futures Exchange, the Metal Exchange, the Commodity Exchange, and the International Petroleum Exchange). In other countries, too, the major exchanges operate as cooperatives. For example, in the USA, the New York Stock Exchange, the American Stock Exchange, the futures and derivatives exchanges, and the regional stock exchanges are all organized in this way.

There are, of course, wide differences in the details of how these various exchanges are run. For example, they differ in the balance of power given to different types of user, and voting structures differ. Exchanges differ in terms of the role of the board, the delegated powers of the chief executive, and the composition and power of exchange committees. There are different degrees of outside involvement by public-interest representatives. Regulatory environments vary.

---

[1] For a discussion of this issue see Blume et al. (1993).

Many exchanges are non-profit organizations. Membership may be open to newcomers who satisfy certain minimum requirements, or membership may be closed. When the number of seats on the exchange is fixed, changes in membership may or may not be permitted through the trading of seats. There are many other differences besides these among exchanges. But their differences are of less significance than their similarity, namely that they all have a cooperative structure of governance.

In essence, an exchange can be viewed as simply a particular kind of firm, offering a particular kind of service to its users. And so it is striking that, although exchanges are run as members' cooperatives, most commercial organizations do not operate in this way. Certainly, some consumer and worker cooperatives exist; and we see other kinds of cooperatives, such as partnerships, particularly among professional groups (lawyers, consultants, and accountants, for example). Also, many non-commercial organizations act as cooperatives, ranging from sports clubs to religious groups. Nevertheless, measured as a percentage of national product, cooperatives are the exception rather than the rule (Bonin et al., 1993).

The more common form of governance structure is *outside ownership*. This is a very broad category: it ranges from owner-managed businesses to widely held public corporations. Under outside ownership, the people who have control over the firm, and take decisions on the firm's behalf, are typically not the same people who buy and use the firm's product. That is, in contrast to a members' cooperative, ownership is not bundled with the right to consume.

There are some indications that exchanges are radically rethinking their structure. For example, in October 1990 the Stockholm Stock Exchange took the unusual step of writing to the Swedish Ministry of Finance recommending that the Exchange should be transformed into a limited liability company. Two years later the Exchange made an issue of shares which (after a short interval) could be freely traded.

The Stockholm Exchange is a relatively small exchange, but in 1994 two much larger exchanges announced that they were developing proposals to transform themselves into public companies. These were the Chicago Mercantile Exchange and the New York Mercantile Exchange. A decision by either of these exchanges to change their structure would almost certainly affect their strategy and prompt considerable debate on the governance of exchanges.

Another development that is likely to stimulate interest in exchange structure is the increasing competition between traditional exchanges and limited companies. In some cases, the latter offer trading systems, such as Reuter's Instinet system and Crossing Network for stock trading or Globex for futures trading. In other cases, public companies are competing with exchanges in related activities such as information dissemination or settlement.

II. The Distinction Between a Cooperative Structure and Outside Ownership

To draw a distinction between a cooperative governance structure and outside ownership, one first needs to define what is meant by a 'firm'. We have developed a theory of the firm based on the key notion of *residual rights of control over nonhuman assets* (Grossman and Hart, 1986; Hart and Moore, 1990; Hart, 1995). According to this framework, a firm is defined by its non-human assets. In particular, for an exchange, the relevant assets are tangible assets, such as its physical location and its facilities, and intangible assets, such as its rules and its reputation for honesty. Perhaps above all, the key asset of an exchange is market depth: the fact that traders know that they can deal with many other traders at the exchange (i.e. there is an agglomeration effect). As a measure of how important are the assets of an exchange, just imagine how difficult it would be—or at least how difficult it would have been in the past, before the advent of new technologies—for an entrepreneur to duplicate the assets of, say, the London Stock Exchange in order to start up a rival exchange. In the past, these assets afforded an exchange a considerable monopoly advantage, and to an extent still do.

The question then arises: where does authority rest to make decisions concerning the assets? In an ideal world, in which the indefinite future can be anticipated and planned for, all these decisions could be specified in an initial, enforceable contract written by members of the exchange when it is first set up. In such a world, since contracts cover all future contingencies, authority is irrelevant: given that everything has been specified contractually, there is nothing left to decide. In reality, transactions costs prevent the writing of comprehensive contracts, and so actual contracts are highly incomplete. Under these conditions, the allocation of authority and control rights matters, since those in authority determine decisions with respect to which the initial contract is silent.

Our central idea is that the authority to make decisions lies with the *owner(s)* of the exchange. More precisely, the owner has *residual rights of control*—that is, the right to make all decisions except those that have been specified contractually. Decisions, such as: Who should have access to the exchange? What should be traded and how? What are the rules and the fee structure? What facilities should the exchange provide and what investments should be undertaken?

(In passing, note that control rights might not be the attribute one would first associate with ownership. One might instead think that an owner is someone with the right to the residual income stream, or profit, of the assets. The difficulty with this profit-based view of ownership is that it does not take us very far in discovering what is distinctive about cooperatives. After all, many cooperatives are non-profit organizations, and so the ownership of residual income is a non-issue.)

The advantage of a control-based view of ownership is that it enables us to define a cooperative rather naturally. We offer the following rudimentary model of an exchange run as a cooperative:

Members' cooperative: the assets of the exchange are controlled by the members, who take decisions democratically, on a one-member, one-vote basis.

This model of cooperatives is, of course, a drastic simplification.[2] It hides many real-world complications—not least that, in practice, there are often different classes of membership enjoying different voting rights. We will return to the matter of equal versus unequal treatment of different types of member in section VIII. But for the moment we strip away any complexity, and consider a plain voting system, with the rule that a decision is passed if it attracts a simple majority of the members' votes. Even when the decision-making procedure is this simple, we will see that important effects are in evidence.

We will compare the performance of this cooperative structure with the performance of the more conventional governance structure:

Outside ownership: the assets of the exchange are controlled by an outside owner (who maximizes profit).

Here, too, we are simplifying a lot. For example, we do not distinguish between, on the one hand, ownership by an outside corporation which itself has many shareholders, and, on the other hand, ownership by an individual who personally manages the exchange. In effect, we are abstracting from agency problems. We return to this matter in section VIII.

III. A Brief Summary of our Findings

We show that both forms of governance, outside ownership and a members' cooperative, are inefficient—but for different reasons and in different ways. Since an outside owner is typically interested only in maximizing profit, he or she has a tendency to make inefficient decisions, tailored to the marginal user. (This is a generalization of the familiar idea that a monopolist inefficiently restricts supply in order to raise price and increase profits.) In a cooperative, collective decision-making is inefficient because in a vote the views of the decisive voter are not necessarily those of the membership as a whole.

We find that two factors critically determine the relative performance of a members' cooperative and outside ownership: the *variation* in membership of the exchange, in terms of the size or nature of the members' business; and the *degree of competition* the exchange faces, either from other exchanges, or from

---

[2] For a recent survey and discussion of the literature on cooperatives, see Hansmann (1994).

direct trading. In particular, we make two claims:

Claim 1: Outside ownership becomes relatively more efficient than a members' cooperative as the variation across the membership becomes more skewed.[3]

Claim 2: Outside ownership becomes relatively more efficient than a members' cooperative as the exchange faces more competition.

Here, we use 'efficient' as a formal term. We say that outcome X is more efficient than outcome Y if the total pie (that is, total benefits minus total costs) enjoyed by the users and owners (added together) is larger under X than it is under Y.[4]

A propos claim 1, it is interesting that the diversity of interests between members has emerged as an important issue in the debate over the structure of the Chicago Mercantile Exchange and the New York Mercantile Exchange. For example, *Euromoney* quoted one member of the Chicago Mercantile Exchange as saying:[5]

For the FCMs [futures commission merchants] to bring all the capital and those customers and then to have relatively little say in how the exchange operates is very frustrating. The locals' view is exactly the opposite. Their attitude is: 'We used to run this place. Now we have all these big firms, we have less and less say, we're making less and less money.' The biggest threat to the exchanges is that they may very well not have the right structure to succeed.

Euromoney concluded that tensions between members

lead pessimists to speculate that the governance of the exchanges may pose the biggest threat to their future, with the interests of the institutional side, embodied in the futures commission merchants…diverging ever more sharply from those of the locals.

And, with regard to Claim 2, both the Stockholm Exchange and US futures exchanges operate in a particularly competitive environment and this competition appears to have been influential in the debate over the structure of the exchanges. For example, although the Stockholm Exchange had a legal

---

[3] By 'skewed' we mean that the median is not equal to the mean.

[4] Note that this is not as strong as saying that everyone is better off under X than under Y (the Pareto criterion)—although of course they could all be made better off if there were a suitable redistribution. The great merit of the definition of efficiency given in the text (which is the one commonly used in antitrust cases, and in the area of law and economics) is that it is *distribution-free*: the same outcome will be efficient, regardless of how income and profit are distributed. Of course, in many areas of public policy, it could well be argued that our definition of efficiency is unacceptable as a criterion for making welfare judgements. However, in the present context, where the players are companies and financiers, issues to do with fairness and equity seem less pressing.

[5] 'Confidence Soars as Exchanges' Business Hits Fresh Peaks', *Euromoney*, June 1994, 180–4. See also Smith (1994).

monopoly within Sweden, it analysed its position in 1990 as follows:

During the 1980s, the monopoly position...became increasingly overwhelmed by external developments. The internationalization of stock trading meant increased competition from international stock exchanges. The development in the data communications area also facilitated cross-border trading. In addition, the Stock Exchange's form of organization was not sufficiently market-adjusted and made generation of capital for risk investments impossible.[6]

Claims 1 and 2 cast light on the issue of whether it is still sensible to operate exchanges as cooperatives. We believe that the balance of the argument is shifting towards outside ownership; and this seems to be supported by the actions of the Chicago Mercantile Exchange, the New York Mercantile Exchange, and the Stockholm Exchange. However, exchanges differ in the degree of competition that they face and the diversity of interests that they must accommodate. We do not evaluate the case for individual exchanges to change their structure.

IV. This Chapter

Our purpose in this chapter is to provide a framework for thinking about the governance of exchanges, and to show how the relative merits of a cooperative structure and outside ownership depend on the level of competition and the diversity of interests. We should stress that we make no attempt to model the richness of real-world governance structures. To do so would not only result in an intractable model, but would also rob our analysis of any generality.

The chapter is written to be accessible to non-economists as well as economists, at least for the most part. Section V presents an extended analogy: that of a golf club. We pose the question: should a golf club be run as a cooperative by its members, or should it be run by an outside owner? Although the parallel with an exchange is not exact, the golf club analogy has the virtue that it conveys our ideas without requiring numbers or algebra. (Economists may find the golf club analogy frustrating *because* it does not contain numbers or algebra, in which case they may prefer to skim section V, and go on to section VI.)

Section VI presents a model which confirms the intuitions provided by the golfing analogy. It is a simple model of an exchange in which the only decision to be made is what *price* to charge its users. It is unavoidable that we use algebra here, given that the questions are intrinsically too hard for a purely verbal treatment.

In section VII we take a broader look at how and why cooperatives operate inefficiently. Section VIII briefly discusses some other issues.

[6] Stockholm Stock Exchange, *Annual Report* 1990.

V. A Golfing Analogy

To help understand the economic logic behind our ideas, and in particular Claims 1 and 2, consider the analogy of a golf club. In our imaginary club, members divide into two groups: those who seriously concentrate on golf, the *playing members*; and those who get more benefit from the social facilities, the *social members*. The distinction between the two groups is quite marked. However, within each group there is also some variation in preferences. The most fanatical players may never darken the door of the clubhouse, and perhaps some of the socializers have never been seen on the course. But these are the outliers. Almost everyone else has less extreme tastes, and enjoys both golf and socializing, at least to some degree.

For the analogy to succeed, we need to keep it simple, even at the expense of realism. We shall assume that it is infeasible to charge different fees to different types of member. That is, there is no objective way of discriminating between playing members and social members. Also, there is no point in asking people to self-select: the story is that, since almost everyone wants access to both the course and the clubhouse, and it is difficult to monitor the frequency with which different people use one or the other, it isn't sensible to try to impose differential fees. The only kind of fee is an annual membership fee, common to all who wish to stay members.

The other simplification we make is to assume that the membership cannot rise above current levels: there are no potential newcomers interested in joining. However, people may choose to leave. (Like all analogies, this one is imperfect. The prize for spotting all eighteen holes in our argument is a drink at the nineteenth.)

It happens that the membership of our club is somewhat skewed towards the social members. That is, in a ballot the social members could muster a few more votes than the playing members. Imagine, hypothetically, that one were to line up the membership in the order of their preferences, starting from the most extreme socializer at one end (the left-hand end, say) and working along to the most fanatical player at the other (the right-hand end). Then, in a head count, one would find that the person who is half way along this line would be a social member—albeit a social member with moderate tastes (he enjoys golf, as well as socializing). We will see that this median person has a pivotal role, and so for future reference it helps to give him a name, George. The fact that George is a social member rather than a playing member simply reflects our assumption that the distribution of membership is skewed towards the social members.

We suppose the playing members are really much more devoted to their golf than the social members are to socializing. In fact, we will assume that if required to do so, the playing members would each be prepared to pay more than twice as much in membership fee as each of the social members. (The reason might be that there are pubs nearby to which the socializers can repair, should they wish to. But this golf course is the only one in the area, and so the playing members have much more at stake in the club.)

The parallel with an exchange should be reasonably clear. The assets of the golf club (the course and clubhouse) correspond to the assets of the exchange. The playing members correspond, say, to large financial institutions; the social members correspond, say, to smaller brokers. In money terms, the large financial institutions have much more at stake in the exchange than have the smaller brokers.

One could draw a different parallel: the playing members might correspond to dealers in, say, financial futures; the social members might correspond to dealers in, say, agricultural commodities. The important point is that there are conflicts of interest.

To return to golf, a decision needs to be taken about investment in the club's future. There are three basic options available:

Option A: Leave the clubhouse alone, but invest heavily in the course: better greens and improved bunkering.

Option B: Make only modest investments in both the course and the clubhouse: better greens and plusher bar.

Option C: Leave the course alone, but invest heavily in the clubhouse: plusher bar and new restaurant.

These three options are in descending order of preference for the playing members, but in ascending order for the social members.

There is also a fourth, more radical option that is on the agenda:

Option D: Sell off the back nine holes, and use the money to build a lavish new clubhouse, with bar, restaurant, business facilities, etc.

Option D is actually the favourite option for the majority of social members; but some of the more moderate social members, including George, prefer Option C to D. (That is, for George, Option C is the best of the four options: he enjoys the facilities of the clubhouse, but he also likes an eighteen-hole round of golf.) Needless to say, the playing members think Option D is terrible.

Incidentally, whichever investment choice is taken, we continue to suppose that the maximum willingness-to-pay of the playing members is still more than twice that of the social members.

We assume that, on efficiency grounds, the options are ranked in the following order:

Option B (the most efficient),
Option C
Option A
Option D (the least efficient).

Recall that we are measuring efficiency by the size of the total pie: the sum of everyone's benefits minus the cost of investment. (We assume that running costs are negligible.)

Of course, in addition to choosing among the four investment options, the club also needs to set the annual fee. This only affects distribution, and so does not have any efficiency implications—unless the fee is set so high that the social members choose to leave, which in itself would be an efficiency loss.

In these circumstances, what governance structure should the club adopt? Should it be run by an outside owner? Or should it be run as a members' cooperative, on a one-member, one-vote basis?

An *outside owner* is only interested in profit. Since the playing members are willing to pay more than twice as much to use the club as are the social members, the profit-maximizing strategy is to focus exclusively on the playing members, and to charge them a high fee—even though this means losing just over half the membership (because the social members will leave). The point is that, in terms of overall revenue, halving one's market is worthwhile if one can more than double one's price.

The outside owner tailors his investment decision to suit his chosen market niche, hence he chooses the option the playing members most want: Option A (that is, he will invest heavily in the course).[7] Notice that, by assumption, this outcome is inefficient: it would be more efficient to make modest improvements to both the course and the clubhouse (Option B). The reason for this distortion is that, in making his investment choice, the outside owner does not take into account the preferences of the social members, since he is pricing them out anyway.

In fact, the outside owner's actions are doubly inefficient. Not only is his investment decision inefficient, but, on top of that, he introduces a second inefficiency when he squeezes the social members out of the club.

Now consider how a *members' cooperative* acts. They have to vote on the investment decision. One might be tempted to think that since Option B yields the biggest total pie, the members will vote for it. After all, they do not have to contend with an outsider who is only interested in profit. Moreover, Option B offers something for everyone: better greens for the playing members and a plusher bar for the social members.

However this simple logic misses the point that, in a democracy, real decision-making power rests with the pivotal voter, who in this case is George. Recall our hypothetical line-up, with George in the middle, each person to the left of him even more of a socializer than he is, and each person to the right more of a player. We argue that because George prefers Option C to the other options, Option C will win (that is, the club will invest heavily in the clubhouse). To see

---

[7] We suppose that it *is* worth making the investment, even though the market is halved.

why, suppose there were a contest between Options C and B. George prefers C to B—as does everyone to the left of him. Hence Option C commands more than 50 per cent of the vote, and must win. The same would happen in a contest between Options C and A. Lastly, suppose there were a contest between Options C and D. George prefers C (he doesn't want a lavish new clubhouse if it means selling off the back nine holes)—as does everyone to the right of him. And so, again, Option C commands more than 50 per cent of the vote and wins.

Thus the cooperative votes for an inefficient outcome, Option C. The reason for this is that the pivotal voter, George, a social member, does not represent average opinion. Average opinion would be a suitably weighted mix of the social members' and the playing members' preferences. The discrepancy between the pivotal voter's preferences and average preferences can be explained by the fact that the distribution of opinion is skewed, in this case towards the social members. This is a subtle, but crucial idea: the shape of the distribution of opinion matters.[8]

One rough way to think about it is that the majority of the electorate comprises social members, who know that they will be the main beneficiaries of the new bar and restaurant (Option C), and yet the cost is borne by everyone, including the playing members. Relative to the most efficient alternative (Option B), we therefore have over-investment in what the majority enjoys (the clubhouse) and under-investment in what the minority enjoys (the course).

To sum up what our analogy has taught us so far: both governance structures, outside ownership and a members' cooperative, yield inefficient outcomes. An outside owner would go for Option A, where too much is spent on the course, and nothing on the clubhouse. He would also price out the social members. A members' cooperative would vote for Option C, where nothing is spent on the course, and too much on the clubhouse.[9]

---

[8] Political scientists have for a long time been thinking about such issues in the context of voting theory. Economists have applied the ideas, particularly to questions of public choice. A notable paper is Roberts (1977), who considers how a society might vote over taxation schedules. In the same Chapter, Roberts proves a powerful version of the Median Voter Theorem, to which we appeal throughout the chapter.

[9] The automatic reaction of economists to an inefficiency is always to ask: why don't the agents concerned bargain their way round it? That is, given that Option B is more efficient than Option C, why don't the gainers (the playing members) bribe the losers (the social members) to switch from Option C to Option B?

Here, and throughout the chapter, we assume that there are large numbers of agents, and each agent's characteristics—e.g. how keen he is on golf versus socializing—is private information. Given this, every agent—taking the point of view that he is too small to affect the final outcome—will have an incentive to claim that he is one of those who will be hurt by a proposed change and that he therefore should be compensated. The problem is that if everyone does this, there is no one to do the compensating, and so the bargaining breaks down. (Thus Option C is chosen by the members' cooperative, rather than Option B.) For a formalization of the idea that free-rider problems combined with large numbers and (only a little) asymmetric information leads to bargaining failure, see Mailath and Postlewaite (1990).

But recall that, in terms of *relative* efficiency, Option C is ranked higher than Option A, and therefore a members' cooperative is the lesser of two evils. (This is true even without taking into account the fact that an outside owner introduces a second inefficiency when he squeezes the social members out of the club.)

At this point, it is worth drawing the parallel with an exchange. Recall that the playing members might correspond to dealers in, say, financial futures; the social members might correspond to dealers in, say, agricultural commodities. Option A could be investing heavily in the financial trading floor. Option C could be investing heavily in the agricultural trading floor. On the one hand, if the exchange were to be owned by an outsider, he might choose to squeeze out the (smaller) agricultural dealers, and invest heavily on behalf of the financial dealers. On the other hand, if the exchange were to operate as a members' cooperative, everyone would be kept in, but investment would benefit only the agricultural dealers. Both outcomes are inefficient. But the members' cooperative may be relatively more efficient than outside ownership. In a nutshell, the distortions an outside owner would create because he is only concerned with extracting rent from the users of the exchange can be reduced (but not eliminated) if the users run the exchange themselves. The root problem with either governance structure is the conflict of interest between different groups of user.

It is time to check out Claims 1 and 2, in the golfing context.

Take Claim 1 first. Suppose the distribution of club members skews even further towards the social members. For example, suppose one or two of the former playing members are injured and, because they cannot play golf any longer, they take up socializing in earnest. However, the shift in composition is not so drastic as to change the efficiency ranking of the four options, which is still Option B, followed by C, then A, and finally D.

Not much has changed for the profit-maximizing outside owner. Although he has lost one or two of his playing members, let us suppose that this isn't enough to cause him to switch from his high-fee strategy. This means that he still has the incentive to tailor his investment decision to suit his chosen market, which comprises the playing members. Hence he continues to choose Option A.

The small change in the distribution of preferences may have a big impact on the members' cooperative, however. In the hypothetical lineup, there are now one or two people who have shifted position, from the right of George to the left of him. As a result, George is no longer pivotal. It is now someone else, to the left of him, who occupies the median position. This new person is more of a socializer than George, and, unlike George, he may well prefer Option D to Option C: i.e. he may prefer to sell off the back nine holes to pay for a lavish new clubhouse. As a result, Option D may now win—an outcome which is even less efficient than Option C. The extra skew in preferences means that the performance of the members' cooperative has deteriorated.

On the face of it, the members' cooperative may now appear to be less efficient than outside ownership, given that Option A is ranked above Option D. But this is not taking into account the second inefficiency an outside owner introduces: viz, that he squeezes the social members out of the club. Overall, the efficiency comparison may go either way. However, what is true is that, as the distribution of preferences becomes more skewed, so outside ownership becomes relatively more efficient than a members' cooperative. That is, Claim 1 is borne out.

Next, take Claim 2. Suppose a new golf club opens up nearby, offering a membership fee well below the fee which an outside owner of our club would charge in the absence of competition—in fact, low enough to attract both groups, playing and social members.

However, the new club's fees are well above what a members' cooperative at our club would charge themselves. (The reason for this may be that the new club has to cover the interest payments on its fixed costs; whereas the land and buildings of the old club were paid for years ago.)

Increased competition has an immediate effect on the outside owner of our club. He can no longer get away with charging a high fee. Instead, he will charge a sufficiently low fee that both playing and social members are deterred from moving to the new club. There is, therefore, no longer any gain from tailoring his investment to suit just the playing members (Option A). He finds Option B more profitable, since it offers something for everyone.[10] On efficiency grounds, this is all to the good: Option B is the best of all the options, and the social members are no longer being squeezed out. In the case of an outside owner, then, competition increases efficiency.

Meantime, a members' cooperative is shielded from the competition. Since they can afford to charge themselves a low membership fee, none of the members is near the point of leaving, even though the new club has now opened up. Thus nothing changes. The cooperative continues to vote for the same option, Option C or D, depending on the skewness of the distribution of preferences. In the case of a members' cooperative, then, competition does not improve efficiency.

This means that, in response to competitive pressure, outside ownership becomes relatively more efficient than a members' cooperative—which bears out Claim 2.

The overall message our analogy offers to an exchange currently operating as a members' cooperative is that, *as the population of traders becomes more uneven (which is what has happened in many cases) and/or as the environment becomes more competitive (which it certainly has done recently), so, on efficiency grounds, there may be more of a case for selling off the exchange to an outside owner.*

Before leaving the golfing analogy, we should tease out one final point. Consider a club that is currently run as a members' cooperative. (Ignore competition.)

---

[10] The analysis here is actually complicated, and the text rather hides this fact.

In principle, the members could always vote to sell the club, distributing the proceeds equally. They know that if they do this, control of the club's assets would be given to a new owner who would take Option A. Moreover, he would charge a high membership fee, which the social members wouldn't want to pay.

Notice that a sale is in effect a variant on Option A, in which those people who want access to the club's facilities have to pay a high fee, but a dividend is paid to everyone. There are similar variants on Options B, C, and D. Earlier, when we were considering how a members' cooperative would vote, we implicitly assumed that these 'sale' options would not be attractive enough to get a majority. Instead, we assumed that the cooperative would vote either for Option C or for Option D, depending on the skewness of preferences.

The import of this is that a situation can arise where outside ownership is the superior structure of governance for an exchange (in the sense of maximizing the total pie)—that is, Option A is more efficient than Option D—but a members' cooperative may fail to adopt outside ownership. In such a situation, a degree of outside coercion may be needed for an efficiency-enhancing change in governance structure to occur.[11] The reason is that even though outside ownership leads to a bigger pie, there is no feasible way for the gainers to bribe the losers (see also footnote 9 on this).

We must stress that we would not necessarily advocate coercion under these conditions. Any change which causes some people to lose—even if others gain more—must be viewed with caution. The purpose of our analysis is to point out that changes in circumstances can change the relative desirability of a members' cooperative and outside ownership. We have little to say about the mechanism for moving from one governance structure to another.

VI. A Simple Pricing Model

We need to confirm that the intuitions from our golfing analogy can be established rigorously. In this section we look at a simple model of pricing.

We consider a (very!) stylized exchange. There are three components to our model: the people, the costs, and the benefits.

First, the people. There are $2N - 1$ people, $i = 1, 2, \ldots, 2N - 1$, who use the exchange, and we simply call them all traders. (We don't need to distinguish between market-makers, brokers, and so on.)

Second, the costs. We suppose that the exchange's services can be measured in terms of 'units supplied'—akin to the units of product that a firm supplies. Let us assume that the cost of supplying a unit to a trader equals c, a constant.

---

[11] If necessary, the non-profit status of exchanges may also need changing, so that former members can be compensated for their loss of membership.

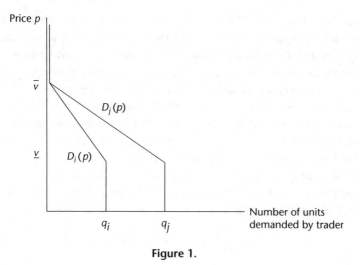

Figure 1.

Third, the benefits. We suppose that the benefit trader i derives from a marginal unit of exchange services is captured by the demand curve $D_i(p)$ in Figure 1. (It doesn't matter whether these benefits are profit he gets from trading on his own behalf, or profit he gets from commission for trading on some outsider's behalf.) Also drawn is the demand curve $D_j(p)$ of some larger trader, j.

As the figure shows, each trader demands nothing at a price above some cut-off level $\bar{v}$, and demand stops rising for prices below some cutoff level $\underline{v}$. Traders are distinguished by the amount demanded at price $\underline{v}$: trader i demands q_i; the larger trader j demands $q_j > q_i$. Between prices $\bar{v}$ and $\underline{v}$, demand is linear. Assume that $\underline{v} < c < \bar{v}$.

These restrictions on demand are obviously strong, but are made solely for ease of computation.

The aggregate demand curve, $D(p)$, has the same shape as the demand curve of an individual trader i, except that the intercept on the horizontal axis is at

$$Q = \sum_{i=1}^{2N-1} q_i,$$

rather than at q_i.

We order the traders according to their size:

$$q_1 < q_2 < \cdots < q_i < \cdots < q_{2N-1}.$$

Given this ordering, it is not surprising that trader N will turn out to be the pivotal voter in a members' cooperative. (N is the median of $1, 2, \ldots, 2N - 1$.)

We will confine our attention to *uniform-pricing* policies, even though, in principle, multi-part tariffs would be useful. There are arguments as to why multi-part tariffs may not work—e.g. that secondhand markets develop, or that traders are able to trade through one another. Notwithstanding these arguments, we think that our broad findings would remain intact even if multi-part tariffs were feasible. (For models which do not make the *ad hoc* restriction that pricing policies are uniform, see Sections III and IV of Hart and Moore, 1995.)

Before we analyse what happens under outside ownership or in a members' cooperative, we should establish the efficient bench-mark. First-best efficiency is attained by setting the price, p, equal to the cost, c. We will be able to judge the extent of inefficiency by how far p deviates from c.

Let us start with an *outside owner*, facing the aggregate demand curve $D(p) = Q(\bar{v} - p)/(\bar{v} - \underline{v})$, for $\underline{v} \leq p \leq \bar{v}$. (Notice that this expression for $D(p)$ reflects the fact that demand is linear between $\underline{v}$ and $\bar{v}$.) His profit function is

$$\Pi(p) = \{[Q(\bar{v} - p)]/(\bar{v} - \underline{v})\} \times (p - c) \quad \text{for } \underline{v} \leq p \leq \bar{v}.$$

Differentiating $\Pi(p)$ with respect to p, we find that profit is maximized by setting price equal to

$$p^m = (1/2)(c + \bar{v}).$$

That is, price is higher than cost: there is inefficiency. In choosing the price p^m, the outside owner balances the conflicting goals of maximizing sales and extracting rent from the most valuable trades.

What of a *members' cooperative*? Consider trader i. If the cooperative sets a price of p, he will trade $[q_i(\bar{v} - p)]/(\bar{v} - \underline{v})$ units. From this he gets a consumer surplus of

$$q_i \int_p^{\bar{v}} [(v - p)\, dv]/(\bar{v} - \underline{v}) = q_i(1/2)(\bar{v} - p)^2/(\bar{v} - \underline{v}).$$

In addition, he receives a dividend of $[1/(2N - 1)] \times \Pi(p)$. That is, all $2N - 1$ members receive an equal share of the exchange's profit $\Pi(p)$. Notice that $\Pi(p)$ will be negative if $p < c$—in which case the exchange charges its members a per capita membership fee (over and above the price p per unit traded) to cover its trading losses. Overall, trader i gets a pay-off:

$$U_i(p) \equiv q_i(1/2)(\bar{v} - p)^2/(\bar{v} - \underline{v})$$

$$+ [1/(2N - 1)] \times Q(\bar{v} - p)(p - c)/(\bar{v} - \underline{v}).$$

Differentiating $U_i(p)$ with respect to p, we find that trade i's pay-off is maximized when $p = p_i$, say, where

$$p_i = \theta_i c + (1 - \theta_i)\bar{v},$$

and

$$\theta_i = Q/[2Q - (2N - 1)q_i].$$

Notice that trader i's preferred price is a weighted sum of c and $\bar{v}$. The weighting θ_i on c is always greater than half, so that his preferred price is never as high as p^m (the average of c and $\bar{v}$). Also notice that θ_i is an increasing function of q_i; and if q_i is greater than the mean, $Q/(2N-1)$, then θ_i is greater than 1. That is, as a trader gets bigger, he prefers a lower price; and if he is larger than average then his preferred price is less than the cost.

These formulae are very intuitive. Each member of the cooperative faces a trade-off. On the one hand, he would like the price to be low, so as to gain as much as possible on his own trades. On the other hand, he would like the price to be high, so as to extract rent from his colleagues. Naturally, the bigger the trader, the more the consumption effect kicks in, and so the lower is his preferred price.

The median trader N's preferred choice of price, $P_N = p^c$, say, will dictate the outcome of the vote. Bigger traders, whose $q > q_N$, will push for a lower price than p^c; smaller traders, whose $q < q_N$, will push for a higher price.[12] That is, the cooperative will vote for a price

$$p^c = \theta_N c + (1 - \theta_N)\bar{v}.$$

The interesting point here is that p^c may be greater than or less than the cost c—depending on whether θ_N is less than or greater than 1, respectively.[13] This in turn depends on whether the median, q_N, is less than or greater than the mean, $Q/(2N-1)$, respectively. Only in the knife-edge case where the median exactly equals the mean, will the cooperative vote to set price equal to cost and avoid inefficiency. (In section VII we prove a general proposition to this effect.)

In a members' cooperative, then, the nature of the distortion in price depends on the skewness of the distribution. If the size distribution of members is symmetric, a cooperative works efficiently: price is set equal to cost. However, if a disproportionate number of members are small (so that the median size is less than the mean), then price will be set higher than cost. And vice versa.[14]

[12] We have not been specific about the precise order of moves that lead to a price of p^c. One possibility is to suppose that anyone is free to put up a proposal or counter-proposal, but it costs a small amount to do so. Given the cost, no one will put up a proposal that can be beaten. In equilibrium, the only proposal which is put up is the winning price of p^c.

[13] In the case where price is less than cost ($p^c < c$), readers may be wondering why a small trader—e.g. trader 1—doesn't quit the cooperative, given that he has to pay a membership fee to cover the exchange's trading losses, and he gets only a small consumption benefit to compensate.

Our model can be amended to deal with this problem. Suppose that, in addition to all its other assets, the exchange has liquid assets whose return more than covers the trading losses. Then there will be a dividend paid out, and no membership fee. Everyone will be better off staying on as a member rather than quitting—even the small traders.

[14] Intuitively, in the case where the smaller members are more numerous, they are more concerned with extracting rent from the larger members than they are with getting down the trading cost to themselves. This is, perhaps, the leading case, insofar as one thinks that in practice votes are, in proportionate terms, more concentrated in the hands of smaller traders. In this case, as with

We end by confirming that Claims 1 and 2 from section III hold in this model.

An increase in the skewness of the size distribution of members—so that the median size is further from the mean—increases the difference between p^c and c, and so increases the inefficiency of a members' cooperative. However, it has no effect on the outside owner's price, p^m. This bears out Claim 1: outside owner-ship becomes relatively more efficient as the variation across the membership becomes more skewed.

To confirm Claim 2, consider the effect of introducing competition from another, equivalent exchange. Suppose the second exchange charges a fee of p^*, where p^* lies between c and p^m.

The presence of the second exchange has an obvious effect on all of our earlier calculations: *any price above p^* is no longer relevant*, since for prices above p^* all traders would elect to trade on the second exchange.

For an outside owner, the new profit-maximizing strategy is to charge as high a price as he can get away with, namely p^*.

For the members' cooperative, however, nothing need change as a result of competition. Previously, we showed that any price up to p^m would be outvoted by a price of p^c. This continues to hold true, except that now the menu of potential prices is restricted to those below p^*. Thus, *a fortiori*, p^c continues to win—unless $p^c > p^*$, in which case it is straightforward to show that the cooperative will vote for p^*.[15]

This bears out Claim 2: outside ownership becomes relatively more efficient than a members' cooperative as the exchange faces more competition.

VII. A Broader Perspective on Voting in Members' Cooperatives

At this point, it may help to give a broader economic perspective on why a members' cooperative typically votes for an inefficient outcome; and to discover under what circumstances it will be efficient.

In any market, total surplus (or total pie, as we have called it), $TS(p)$ say, is made up of the sum of total producer surplus (or total profit), $TPS(p)$ say, and total consumer surplus, $TCS(p)$:

$$TS(p) \equiv TPS(p) + TCS(p).$$

an outside owner, price is set too high. But price is not set as high as it would be by an outside owner—since, recall, p_i is never as large as p^m, for any i (including the decisive median voter, $i = N$).

[15] We assume that resale is impossible—otherwise a member of the cooperative could buy at the low price of p^c, and make a profit by selling to an outsider at the competing exchange for p^*. In the context of exchanges, it is very reasonable to assume away the possibility of resale, given that, unlike apples, exchange services are hard to transport.

Here p refers to price. However, the argument is much more general: it could be any scalar variable (such as quality or investment).[16]

The first-best outcome is attained at a price where total surplus is maximized; let this efficient price be p^0:

$$p = p^0 \text{ maximizes } TPS(p) + TCS(p). \tag{0}$$

In the pricing model of section VI, p^0 equals the cost, c.

Were price to be set unilaterally by the producer(s), he (they) would choose a price p^1, say, which maximizes $TPS(p)$ alone:

$$p = p^1 \text{ maximizes } TPS(p). \tag{1}$$

Typically, p^1 is higher than the efficient price p^0—because (1) omits the $TCS(p)$ term from (0), and $TCS(p)$ is decreasing in p near p^0. In the pricing model, (1) corresponds to an outside owner charging p^1 equal to p^m.

Now consider a cooperative of the $2N - 1$ (say) consumers. Total consumer surplus is the sum of each of their individual surpluses, $cs_i(p)$ say, where $i = 1, 2, \ldots, 2N - 1$:

$$TCS(p) \equiv cs_1(p) + cs_2(p) + \cdots$$
$$+ cs_i(p) + \cdots + cs_{2N-1}(p).$$

As we have seen in both the golfing analogy and the pricing model, decisions will in effect be taken by the median consumer, $i = N$, say. Given that everyone receives a $1/(2N - 1)$ share of the total profit $TPS(p)$, this consumer votes for a price p^2, say, which maximizes his overall pay-off:

$$p = p^2 \text{ maximizes } cs_N(p) + [1/(2N - 1)] \times TPS(p). \tag{2}$$

The first term is his personal consumer surplus; the second term is his dividend (i.e. his share of total profit). In the pricing model, (2) corresponds to the members' cooperative voting for price p^2 equal to p^c.

It is revealing to multiply (2) by the factor $(2N - 1)$:

$$p = p^2 \text{ maximizes } TPS(p) + (2N - 1) \times cs_N(p), \tag{2'}$$

and to contrast this with (0). Clearly, in general p^2 will *not* equal p^0.

---

[16] The great difficulty in analyzing a cooperative when *more* than one decision has to be taken is that we have no equivalent of the Median Voter Theorem. In more than one dimension, there is typically no equilibrium in a simple-majority voting game. One may be able to make progress by appealing to the results in Caplin and Nalebuff (1988) on super-majority voting rules.

However, there is an important exception. Suppose it happens to be the case that

$$(2N - 1) \times cs_N(p) \equiv TCS(p),$$

or, equivalently,

$$cs_N(p) \equiv [1/(2N - 1)] \times TPS(p). \tag{3}$$

Then (2′) coincides with (0), and p^2 equals p^0. In this special case, a members' cooperative chooses the first-best outcome.

Equation (3) simply says that the consumer surplus of the median consumer equals the average consumer surplus. Thus we have:

PROPOSITION. *A members' cooperative is first-best efficient if, and only if, the median voter has average preferences.*[17]

In the golfing analogy of Section V, the median member, George, did not have average preferences, since he was a social member. As a result, the voting tilted away from the first-best outcome (Option B) towards George's preferred outcome (Option C).

In the pricing model of section VI, the median trader was not necessarily average: $p^c = c$ if and only if $q_N = Q/(2N - 1)$.

VIII. Further Considerations

We are aware that, in the interests of clearly presenting our own views, we have trodden a rather narrow path through the forest of questions that naturally arises in connection with cooperatives. To close the Chapter, then, we will touch upon some of the issues that we side-stepped earlier on. Unfortunately, we do not have space to do them justice.

(i) Expanding and changing the membership

We have assumed throughout that the membership of the exchange—that is, the set of potential users—is fixed. (In our models, we assumed that there was no inward trade.) By making such an assumption, we have avoided one of the major preoccupations of the literature on cooperatives—viz, to what extent will a cooperative choose to expand its membership?

The answer critically depends on whether new members pay their way in; i.e. whether they pay an entry fee to cover any future rents they may subsequently earn. If they do not pay their way in, there is an obvious incentive for existing members to limit the number of new members, so as to avoid dilution. Our view

---

[17] This result presupposes that the median voter is pivotal, which is not always the case. See Roberts (1977) for a general result showing when the so-called Median Voter Theorem holds.

is that this so-called *common pool* problem is an artifact. Economic logic points to the conclusion that entry fees should be allowed for.

Even with entry fees, the question still remains: how far to expand? But notice that this decision is faced both by a members' cooperative and by an outside owner. The expansion decision is very like any other decision—pricing, quality, or investment. As before, the difference in outcome between a members' co-operative and outside ownership derives from the fact that the right to make such decisions rests with different people. We believe that the conclusions from our earlier analysis should, in a broad sense, carry over.

However, there is one special, and very intriguing, new issue that arises. If the membership expands, the composition of the *future* electorate changes. When today's members vote for expansion, they have to take into account the impact on tomorrow's vote. This is difficult territory.[18] And the question is begged: why give any voting rights to new members? Why not sell them non-voting membership instead? We leave such tantalizing issues to future research.

First cousin to the question of expansion is the question of changing the membership. Should individual members be allowed to sell their places?

There is a strong argument for allowing them to do so. If a member cannot sell their place, then they will be much less willing to vote for and contribute to some long-term investment project, given that their horizon may be shorter than the length of the project. (Why invest in someone else's future?) Our view is that by allowing members to sell their places, a cooperative can largely overcome such horizon problems.

(ii) Free entry

In practice, although certain exchanges are run as members' cooperatives, they operate within a regulatory environment which obliges them to let new members in free. (The London Stock Exchange is a case in point.) New members may have to meet certain requirements—for example to pass a test of financial fitness—but there is no price of entry *per se*. How does this affect the efficiency of the cooperative relative to outside ownership?

On the face of it, free entry of new members is bad for a cooperative, for the reasons alluded to earlier. There is a serious *horizon problem*: existing members are less willing to invest in the exchange since they anticipate that new members will enjoy the benefits later on, and as a result there is too little investment. Here, 'investment' can be financial, or it can be in the less tangible form of becoming involved in running the exchange and planning for its future. Under-investment problems are exacerbated by the fact that if existing members ever have to leave the cooperative they will not be able to sell their place.

---

[18] Two interesting papers which address dynamic voting issues are Roberts (1989), which considers dynamic voting in the context of a trade union; and Dewatripont and Roland (1992), which looks at a dynamic political-economy model of transition.

Despite these serious drawbacks, a free-entry rule may nevertheless have some advantages to a cooperative. Recall the analysis of voting over price given in Section VI. We learned that a cooperative will typically not price efficiently. In some cases, it will price above cost—just as an outside owner overprices. The question arises: How does the cooperative distribute surplus back to the membership? Surplus is typically not paid out as a dividend (many exchanges operate on a non-profit basis). Rather, it is used to improve facilities, which takes time. Since new members will enjoy these improvements for free, the existing members may choose not to generate any surplus in the first instance. That is, free entry encourages the membership to adopt a policy of pricing at cost—which is more efficient. This argument does not apply to an outside owner, of course, since he retains his profit. And so the free-entry rule may make a members' cooperative relatively more efficient.

We must also not lose sight of the potential social welfare gains from a free entry rule. The regulatory authorities may insist on such a rule in order to increase competition in the market: members will be less able to keep their commission rates high if outsiders can come into the exchange. So far in the paper, we have ignored these antitrust considerations, and focused on the narrower question of which organizational form is more efficient from the viewpoint of the members themselves.

(iii) Raising capital

Related to the issue of membership is the question: does a members' cooperative have a peculiar difficulty in raising new capital?

A cooperative can raise money in a number of ways. Clearly, it can use retained earnings, or raise the membership fee. It can also issue debt or non-voting equity. Of course, all these methods can also be used by an outside owner.

What a cooperative cannot do is to sell standard voting equity ('standard' in the sense that the equity is not bundled with other rights—e.g. the right to trade on the exchange). Here, an outside owner is at an advantage, because he can issue voting equity. In this sense, the cost of capital to a cooperative will be higher than for an outside owner.

(iv) Agency problems

Another respect in which a members' cooperative suffers relative to, say, a public corporation, is that for a cooperative there is typically no effective market for corporate control.

Exchanges are large businesses, run on a day-to-day basis by managers. Normally, an individual member of a cooperative cannot buy up the votes of his colleagues, because unbundling votes from membership is not permitted. Nor is he permitted to acquire power by buying up lots of seats for his own use.

Hence it is difficult for an individual to exert pressure on management, except through the democratic process, which we know suffers from severe free-rider problems. (Why put in a lot of work running a campaign, if one does not reap much by way of personal benefit?) In a cooperative, then, managers may be more entrenched than they would be in a public corporation.

There is another, related, kind of agency problem. What instructions (or incentive scheme) should a cooperative give to its manager? An outside owner has a relatively simple task: he instructs his manager to maximize profit. (Of course, this does not guarantee that the manager *will* maximize profit.) Profit-maximization has the merit of being (at least in principle) a clear-cut objective. A cooperative has a more complex objective: to maximize the pay-off of the median voter, say. But what, in day-to-day terms, does this mean?

To offset these two agency costs peculiar to a members' cooperative, there is an agency cost associated with an outside owner. It is important that the members have an incentive to work hard. The difficulty with an outside owner is that he may be in a position to expropriate more rent from an individual member (and thereby reduce the latter's incentives) than are the fellow members of a cooperative.

(v) Unequal treatment

Throughout the chapter, we have assumed there is only one type of member in a cooperative. However, there may be good reasons for trying to introduce different classes of membership.

In the context of our golf club, one can imagine allowing people to choose between playing or social membership. Different classes of membership might bundle different levels of service with different voting rights and different membership fees. Barzel and Sass (1990) have written an interesting paper in which they discuss how voting rights and membership obligations are allocated in condominia. Tenants' voting rights and obligations can be assessed in a number of different ways: for example, they can be made to depend on floor area, or on the number of people in the household. Among other things, Barzel and Sass find that in practice these assessments are made so as keep costs and benefits in proportion to each other—thus minimizing conflicts of interest between different classes of tenant.

Presumably, similar efficiency gains can be obtained from introducing different membership classes in the case of exchanges.[19] However, there are also costs. Clear, fixed arrangements such as one member/one vote may have the drawback

---

[19] Indeed, we see different membership classes in practice. For example, the London International Financial Futures Exchange has five different classes of member: Class A membership has 20 votes (per share); Class B has five votes; and so on down to Class E, with just one vote. Different classes come bundled with different rights to trade.

of leading to inefficient outcomes in the voting; but they have the merit of not being open to abuse. A policy of equal treatment makes it less likely that one class of member will gang up on another—for example, by raising the membership fee of the other class.

References

Barzel, Y., and Sass, T. (1990). "The allocation of resources by voting." *Quarterly Journal of Economics*, 105: 745–71.

Blume, M., Siegel, J., and Rottenberg, D. (1993). *Revolution on Wall Street: The Rise and Decline of the New York Stock Exchange*. W. W. Norton.

Bonin, J., Jones, D., and Putterman, L. (1993). "Theoretical and empirical studies of producer cooperatives: Will the twain meet?." *Journal of Economic Literature*, 31: 1290–320.

Caplin, A., and Nalebuff, B. (1988). "On 64%-Majority Rule." *Econometrica*, 56: 787–815.

Dewatripont, M., and Roland, G. (1992). "Economic reform and dynamic political constraints." *Review of Economic Studies*, 59: 703–30.

Grossman, S., and Hart, O. (1986). "The costs and benefits of ownership: A theory of vertical and lateral integration." *Journal of Political Economy*, 94: 691–719.

Hansmann, H. (1994). *The Ownership of Enterprise*. New Haven, CT: Yale University Press.

Hart, O. (1995). *Firms, Contracts and Financial Structure*, Oxford: Clarendon Press.

——, and Moore, J. (1990). "Property Rights and the Nature of the Firm." *Journal of Political Economy*, 98: 1119–58.

——, and —— (1995). "The governance of exchanges: Members' cooperatives versus outside ownership." Financial Markets Group Discussion Paper No. 229, London School of Economics. Also appeared as City Research Project Subject Report, No. XXII.

Mailath, G., and Postlewaite, A. (1990). "Asymmetric information bargaining problems with many agents." *Review of Economic Studies*, 57: 351–67.

Roberts, K. (1977). "Voting over income tax schedules." *Journal of Public Economics*, 8: 329–40.

Liquidity Provision via Banks and Markets: A Discussion

Ernst-Ludwig von Thadden

Liquidity provision is usually considered to be one of the main macroeconomic functions of the banking system. Yet, while this notion is old and can be traced back at least to Adam Smith, precise definitions and analyses of the role of banks for liquidity provision date only from the early 1980s. In this survey, I will briefly review this earlier literature, thus paving the way for some of the work of the 1990s that is collected in the main part of this section.

To begin with, it is useful to define what is meant by liquidity, because this term is used in different contexts and with varying meanings. The core of the different notions of liquidity used in finance is similar: Liquidity allows agents to transact when they most want it at low costs. Yet, the definitions begin to differ when it comes to the institutional setting, with two broad directions standing out. In one view, concerned mainly with market structure and marketability, "an asset is liquid if it can be bought or sold quickly at low transaction costs and a reasonable price" (Biais et al. 1997). In the other perspective, grounded more in security design and financial engineering, "liquidity refers to the availability of instruments (market and nonmarket) that can be used to transfer wealth across periods" (Holmström and Tirole 1998 and in this volume, Chapter Six), where wealth transfers are gauged by the intertemporal substitution preferences of the agents in question.

The first and the second type of definition are largely complementary, as they refer to different institutional settings. However, the two definitions can be in conflict, if the institutional settings are mixed up. For example, the existence of a market that is highly liquid according to the first definition may adversely affect the liquidity of an asset according to the second definition. Among the chapters in the present volume, this issue arises in the work of Diamond (1997) and Bhattacharya et al. (1998), and is still a subject of ongoing research.

In the sense of the second of the two definitions above, banks can provide liquidity through operations on their asset side and on their liability side. The work on banking and liquidity of the early 1980s is concerned with the liability side and mainly associated with the names of Bryant, Diamond, Dybvig, Haubrich, King, Bhattacharya, Gale, and Jacklin. For brevity, this is what I will mostly focus on, and turn to the liability side at the end of these notes.

As a basis for this discussion, I will present a simple model along the lines of Bryant (1980) and Diamond and Dybvig (1983). This model assumes an economy with three dates, $t = 0, 1, 2$, one (physical) good, and a continuum of agents $a \in [0, 1]$ who each have identical endowments of 1 at date 0, nothing thereafter, and identical preferences over future consumption at date 0, given by

$$U(c_1, c_2) = \begin{cases} u(c_1) & \text{with probability } q \\ u(c_2) & \text{with probability } 1 - q. \end{cases}$$

The individual consumption shocks of different agents are realized at date 1, are identically distributed and satisfy the Law of Large Numbers. Hence, there is no uncertainty about aggregate consumption needs. This utility is extreme in the sense that agents only consume once in their lives (they are either extremely "impatient" or "patient"), but the analysis can be extended to more general preferences. Individual consumption needs are private information. Therefore, if agents interact, type-dependent consumption allocations must be incentive-compatible.

In this model, preferences for liquidity arise from uncertainty over future utility, given fixed endowments. The alternative modelling approach is to assume that utility is fixed and certain, but future endowments are uncertain. This approach has been proposed by Haubrich and King (1990), but not been followed in most of the literature.

The final ingredient of our model is one (real) investment opportunity, which has constant returns to scale, is arbitrarily divisible, is available to everybody, and yields a gross return per unit invested at date t of either R_1 in $t + 1$ or R_2 in $t + 2$, where $R_1^2 \leq R_2$ and $R_2 > 1$. Hence, if investment takes place at time 0 it can either be "left in place to mature", or it can be "liquidated early."

The assumption that $R_2 > 1$ means that the economy is not shrinking and is made for notational convenience. The assumption that $R_1^2 \leq R_2$ simply means that the option of leaving the asset in place is meaningful, that is, not dominated by liquidating early and reinvesting. If $R_1^2 < R_2$, the investment has an "irreversibility, or goods-in-process, feature" (Wallace 1988): Leaving the investment in place for two periods yields strictly higher returns than a sequence of short-term investments.

The model describes a situation in which agents are facing a liquidity problem, in the sense that they may be forced to consume their investments when these have not yet matured. This will be the case under autarky, where the consumption path of each agent is given by $(c_1, c_2) = (R_1, R_2)$ (note that an agent consumes either c_1 or c_2). By definition, an allocation is said to provide liquidity if it insures the agent against such an outcome. Optimal liquidity is then defined as first-best intertemporal insurance, that is, as the allocation agents would like best at date 0 if there were no informational constraints ex post. Formally, this amounts to maximizing expected utility subject only to the constraint that consumption is feasible in the aggregate:

$$\max qu(c_1) + (1 - q)u(c_2)$$

$$\text{subject to } (R_1 - qc_1)\frac{R_2}{R_1} = (1 - q)c_2$$

$$\Leftrightarrow \quad q\frac{c_1}{R_1} + (1 - q)\frac{c_2}{R_2} = 1$$

The second version of the resource constraint shows that $1/R_t$ can be interpreted as the state-price density in a standard dynamic consumption problem. The solution to this problem will then depend on the relative magnitude of the intertemporal income and substitution effects for the representative agent. Formally, it is given by the following first-order condition, which equates state-price weighted marginal utilities:

$$R_1 u'(c_1) = R_2 u'(c_2).$$

The first-best solution has the following qualitative features. If the income effect compensates exactly the substitution effect (logarithmic utility), then $c_t^* = R_t$ and autarky is optimal. If the substitution effect dominates, then $c_1^* < R_1 < R_2 < c_2^*$, and if the income effect dominates, then $R_1 < c_1^* < c_2^* < R_2$. For liquidity concerns to play a role, the literature typically assumes that the elasticity of instantaneous marginal utility with respect to consumption ("intertemporal relative risk aversion") is larger than 1. In this case, the income effect dominates and agents want to consume more in the short run than they have under autarky, hence need "liquidity."

Having discussed the first-best, let us return to the informationally constrained problem and suppose that there exist competitive markets for intertemporal trade in $t = 0$ and $t = 1$, in which agents can take market clearing prices as given. Obviously, in $t = 0$ there is no trade because everybody is identical, and everybody invests 1 unit into the (real) asset.

In $t = 1$, agents differ and can trade the asset (or equivalently, date 2 consumption). Let p denote the price (at date 1) of 1 unit of the asset (i.e. of R_2 units of date 2 consumption). In principle, each agent now has five possibilities: (i) liquidate the asset and consume the proceeds, (ii) liquidate the asset and use the proceeds to buy the asset in the market, (iii) sell the asset in the market and consume the proceeds, (iv) sell the asset in the market and invest the proceeds in new units of the asset, and (v) hold on to the asset. Note that impatient agents will choose between (i) and (iii) and patient agents between (ii),(iv), and (v).

Comparing the returns from (i) and (iii) yields the following asset excess demand by impatient agents:

$$D^I(p) = \begin{cases} -q & \text{if } p > R_1 \\ [-q, 0] & \text{if } p = R_1 \\ 0 & \text{if } p < R_1 \end{cases}$$

Similarly, patient agents' excess demand correspondence is:

$$D^P(p) = \begin{cases} -(1-q) & \text{if } p > R_2/R_1 \\ [-(1-q), 0] & \text{if } p = R_2/R_1 \\ 0 & \text{if } R_1 < p < R_2/R_1 \\ [0, (1-q)R_1/p] & \text{if } p = R_1 \\ (1-q)R_1/p & \text{if } p < R_1 \end{cases}$$

Not surprisingly, patient agents sell when the price is high, hold when it is intermediate, and buy when it is low. Setting aggregate excess demand equal to zero shows that in equilibrium patient agents must be indifferent between holding and buying. More precisely, we have:

PROPOSITION 1. (Diamond and Dybvig, 1983): *In a competitive market for intertemporal trade, the unique equilibrium price is $p = R_1$, and the resulting consumption path is the autarkic one, $(c_1, c_2) = (R_1, R_2)$.*

Note that there may be trivial trades in equilibrium, of patient agents who liquidate their asset holdings with impatient ones who do not. But the resulting allocation is no improvement over autarky. This proposition also shows that the definition of liquidity used here is very different from the first notion of liquidity introduced earlier: Because of the price-taking assumption, the competitive market is perfectly "liquid" (according to the market-microstructure definition), but it does not provide "liquidity" as defined here.

Let us now consider, as an alternative to the Walrasian market of Proposition 1, a simple model of demand deposit contracts (offered by "the banking system"), which collect the agents' funds at date 0, invest them, and pay back a prespecified amount at either time 1 or 2. Formally, a demand deposit outcome is a list $(d_1, d_2, \alpha, A_1, A_2)$, where A_1 and A_2 are a partition of the set of all agents, such that

(1) each agent invests the fraction α of her funds in the real asset and deposits $1 - \alpha$ with the bank in $t = 0$,
(2) depositors $a \in A_1$ withdraw $(1-\alpha)d_1$ at date 1 and nothing at date 2,
(3) depositors $a \in A_2$ withdraw $(1-\alpha)d_2$ at date 2 and nothing at date 1,
(4) each depositor prefers her withdrawal date over the alternative one,
(5) the repayments satisfy $\lambda(d_1/R_1) + (1 - \lambda)(d_2/R_2) \leq 1$, where λ is the measure of A_1.

In this definition, d_1 and d_2 are the gross interest rates paid on deposits over one, two periods respectively, and $1 - \alpha$ can be interpreted as the size of the banking system. Note that we have imposed symmetry ex ante (which is reasonable because all agents are identical ex ante).

PROPOSITION 2. (Diamond and Dybvig, 1983): *Suppose that $R_1 = 1$ and that no markets for intertemporal trade exist. Then the first-best consumption path can be implemented as a demand deposit outcome $(d_1, d_2, \alpha, A_1, A_2) = (c_1^*, c_2^*, 0, \{impatients\}, \{patients\})$. The implementation is unique if the deposit contract suspends convertibility in case of excess withdrawal.*

Suspension of convertibility is a mechanism which has historically been used as a "circuit breaker" in banking panics. In the present model it states that the bank pays out significantly less than d_1 to at least some depositors at date 1 if more than λ depositors demand their money back. The proposition then simply states that, in the absence of markets, banks can provide optimal liquidity, and that optimal liquidity provision cannot be upset by bank runs if suspension of convertibility is imposed.

Propositions 1 and 2 study markets and banks separately. In important papers, Jacklin (1987) and Haubrich and King (1990) have asked the following question, which in hindsight is obvious: What is the role of deposit contracts if a market for intertemporal trade exists in the model introduced above? In fact, in his paper, Jacklin made three important contributions, which should be kept apart. First, he showed that other institutional arrangements than deposit contracts (market based ones) can provide liquidity in the Diamond–Dybvig model. Second, he generalized the model to less extreme, smooth preferences. His third contribution, the "Jacklin critique" discussed here, however, was less convincing as it stood, because it considered individual deviations from the banking contract at date 0, without modelling trading at date 1 (if every agent but one invests in the bank, there is no market!).

The following argument corrects this lacuna, by integrating the concept of (Walrasian) market equilibrium used earlier with that of demand deposits. Again, we assume that all agents behave identically at date 0, which is plausible and standard, given that they are identical. Hence, market activity only takes place at date 1. We can then define a market equilibrium with banking as a demand deposit outcome $(d_1, d_2, \alpha, A_1, A_2)$ with $\alpha < 1$ and an asset price p, together with net trades for each agent at date 1, such that all agents maximize their utility from trading and the asset market clears.

In market equilibria with banking, the trading possibilities at date 1 are richer than in the situation of Proposition 1. Without going into the details, however, one can derive the following proposition.

PROPOSITION 3. *Suppose the bank offers a deposit contract (d_1, d_2) at date 0 and a perfect asset market exists at date 1. At a market equilibrium with banking one has $d_1 = R_1$, and*

- *either all agents withdraw their deposit at date 1, and the patient agents buy the impatients' asset holdings with the proceeds from the withdrawal,*
- *or all impatients withdraw their deposits at date 1, patients are indifferent between withdrawing and not, and withdraw just enough to buy the impatients' asset holdings.*

Both of these two types of equilibria yield the autarkic consumption path (R_1, R_2) to each agent, and in both banking is degenerate. In each type of equilibrium, the return path from banking is identical to the one from investing directly into the asset (taking into account trading in the first type of equilibrium), and hence, agents are indifferent ex ante between investing in the asset or the bank. The proposition, therefore, is nothing but a new version of the famous insight that "banks are useless in the Arrow–Debreu world" (Freixas and Rochet 1997).

Although this finding comes as no surprise to anybody brought up on general equilibrium theory, it still constitutes a basic conceptual problem for banking theory: A market that is perfectly liquid according to the first definition given at the beginning of this chapter, makes liquidity provision in the sense of the second definition impossible. Since the mid-1980s, the literature has developed in several directions in response to this dilemma, some of which I will briefly review in the sequel.

In a pragmatic approach, Wallace (1988) simply proposed to interpret the Diamond–Dybvig model differently. In his interpretation, the three dates of the model are periods during which the agents live without inter-acting with each other. Banking then is a substitute for market activity in a world where agents are isolated. In practice, this means that demand deposits either concern only those financial activities for which markets do not form, such as minor transactions services, or are used only by agents who do not have access to existing markets, such as unsophisticated savers.

Yet, as von Thadden (1998, 2002) has pointed out in a model that generalizes the preceding model to many periods, even in Wallace's (1988) isolated world, a basic incentive constraint must be taken into account: Agents can withdraw and re-invest deposits privately. This point does not concern the original model of Diamond and Dybvig (1983), where $R_1 = 1$. It only becomes relevant in the more general model above when $R_1 > 1$, where it can be shown that the scope for liquidity provision through demand deposits depends on the degree of irreversibility of the market investment opportunity. If the latter is fully reversible, no liquidity provision is possible at all.

On the other hand, the less the investment opportunity is reversible, the more liquidity can be provided through demand deposits. In complement-ary work, building on Haubrich and King (1990) and Bhattacharya and Gale (1987), von Thadden (1997) identified another element facilitating liquidity provision, by extending the above base model to include a second investment opportunity with a different intertemporal return structure. In such a model, any autarkic portfolio has the additional downside that whenever an agent consumes, she consumes one asset whose yield is not optimal at the time of consumption. Hence, in addition to the "liquidity risk" discussed until now, there is "maturity risk." Von Thadden (1997) showed that in the model with two assets, demand deposit contracts can fully eliminate maturity risk and provide partial insurance against liquidity risk. Even more, in a multi-period setting, demand deposit contracts can provide first-best insurance if intertemporal risk aversion is sufficiently large. Insurance against maturity risk therefore stabilises insurance against liquidity risk in the sense that the latter becomes incentive compatible if the former is provided in conjunction with it.

Diamond (1997, and in this volume, Chapter Five), in work building on Wallace (1988), also considered a model with two assets and addressed the Jacklin critique head on. Weakening Wallace's isolation assumption, he assumes that at date 1 there exists a Walrasian market as introduced above, but that a certain fraction of all agents learns at time 1 that they will not have access to the market. The size of this group is known at date 0, but not its composition, so agents are exposed to the risk of individual exclusion, but can provide for it collectively. Banks now do exactly that: Diamond (1997) shows that all short-term asset holding is optimally done through banks (agents at date 0 only hold deposits and the long-term asset), and that banks typically trade at date 1 in order to reallocate deposits among patient and impatient agents. The first feature is that of maturity insurance discussed above, the second feature shows how markets can actually be complements rather than substitutes for banks in the creation of liquidity.

Diamond's (1997) work takes up the general insight that interim trading among bank clients must be restricted in order for banks to have a role. In the one-asset case, this is the theme of Proposition 3, in the case of assets with different maturities, the problem lies in the fact that investment in the more liquid assets may be sub-optimal because of the free-rider problem in the use of ex-post liquidity. Limited market participation is, therefore, an important feature of bank liquidity models.

Another line of research, proposed mainly by Jacklin and Bhattacharya (1988), Jacklin (1993), Gorton and Pennacchi (1990), and De Nicoló (1993), introduces information asymmetries into the problem, in order to make collective contracting more attractive than market interaction. This line of work starts from the insight that trading can impose costs on market participants stemming from informational asymmetries, and argues that demand deposits are an institutional reaction to this deficiency of markets. For such a theory to work, the base model is generalized in two directions. First, the long-term return, R_2, is assumed to be uncertain and agents have different information about the realization of R_2 when they contemplate trading at date 1. Second, agents differ with respect to their expected liquidity preference q (which, therefore, also becomes a random variable, whose values are realized at date 1). Under this type of two-dimensional uncertainty, market prices at date 1 typically fail to be fully revealing and cannot achieve social optimality. Now there is room for institutions to offer deposit or debt-like contracts, precisely to help avoid the costs of market trading. Some individuals will prefer to hold deposits, which are less information sensitive and, therefore, have low individual risk, others will hold tradable assets and incur the informational risk related to the lemons problem in this market. Again, banks and markets naturally coexist, but for reasons very different from those in Diamond (1997).

The final line of research concerning banks and markets to be reviewed here has been mainly pioneered by Bernanke and Gertler (1987), Bencivenga and Smith (1991), Qi (1994), and Fulghieri and Rovelli (1993). This literature takes a fully dynamic view on the interaction between banks and investors, by embedding the base model above in an overlapping-generations framework. Much of this literature has been concerned with steady-state allocations $(\bar{c}_1, \bar{c}_2)$ obtainable through demand deposit contracts, where $\bar{c}_1$ and $\bar{c}_2$ denote gross returns (i.e. consumption) of middle-aged, old-aged agents respectively, who have deposited their one unit of endowments with the bank when young.

A basic insight of this type of work has been that due to the open-endedness of the horizon and the possibility of intergenerational transfers through the banking system, higher steady-state payoffs can be realized in the OLG-model than in the three-period base model. In particular, a steady-state (R_2, R_2) would be technically feasible. However, an incentive constraint similar to the one discussed by von Thadden (1998) makes these payoffs impossible: Under such an interest rate path, a patient middle-aged depositor has an incentive to withdraw and redeposit elsewhere in the banking system, to obtain a payoff of $(R_2)^2$ when old. Taking this constraint into account, the optimal steady-state banking path has the feature that $\bar{c}_2 > R_2 > \bar{c}_1 > R_1$ and can be shown to yield higher ex-ante utility than the infinitely repeated solution (c_1^*, c_2^*) of the base model.

Even the basic OLG-model allows several other interesting insights. First, as in the case of Proposition 1 above, the optimal steady state cannot be realized as a decentralized Walrasian equilibrium outcome. Interestingly, this holds even if fiat money is introduced as an additional store of value into the model. Second, and differently from the static base model, at the steady state, no side-payments among depositors can upset the banking contract. This is because $\bar{c}_2 > R_2$: The rewards of staying with the bank until old age are sufficiently high to make it attractive to forego even the individual long-term return. And third, suspension of convertibility is no longer sufficient (as in Proposition 2) to rule out bank runs. The reason for this important result is that an intergenerational bank will typically rely on new deposits to (partly) pay off existing depositors. In case of a run, then, suspension of convertibility can prevent existing deposits from flowing out of the bank, but it cannot force new deposits into the bank.

Building on these insights, the literature has then addressed several farther reaching questions, most notably the explicit comparison of stock market and banking environments and the transition to steady states (see, in particular, Bhattacharya et al. 1998, and this volume, Chapter Seven).

After this extensive discussion of bank liquidity provision on the liability side of the balance sheet, I now turn briefly to the asset side. Although it had long been claimed that banks serve to provide liquidity to firms, a precise description of the relationship between corporate liquidity needs and banking, analogous to that of the Diamond–Dybvig model for the household sector described earlier, was lacking. The problem quickly becomes clear if one tries to set up such a model.

Suppose a firm has an investment project that needs initial finance I at date 0 and continuation finance I_1 at date 1 to generate a return of R at date 2. If the lending relationship is subject to uncertainty and borrower moral hazard, I_1 is stochastic, and the firm earns insufficient short-term returns, then full ex-ante financing of I_1 is typically impossible, I_1 can be interpreted as a liquidity shock, and the lending of the necessary additional funds as liquidity provision. Such sequential lending models are useful in their own right, but they fail to address the basic question—the analog of Proposition 1 above for the corporate sector—of why banks are needed to provide the liquidity.

One possible route to an answer is the theory of relationship banking, based on informational asymmetries, reviewed in Part 6 of this volume. Another, ingenious solution has been proposed by Holmström and Tirole (1998, and in this volume, Chapter Six) who shed light not only on the liquidity problem, but also on the working of financial intermediation in general equilibrium and on possible policy concerns.

Their work embeds a version of the above lending problem into a simple general equilibrium model with a continuum of ex ante identical firms and (in its first part) no aggregate uncertainty (note the similarity in structure to the household model described earlier). In principle, therefore, it seems that firms could insure themselves against liquidity problems by holding diversified portfolios of each others' shares (the market solution), because aggregate refinancing needs are certain. However, such redistribution of aggregate liquidity ex post is not sufficient to satisfy all liquidity demand for one simple reason: Under this mechanism firms with low refinancing needs obtain liquidity that they do not need and that they cannot pass on because of borrower moral hazard. Hence, the market "wastes" liquidity. In this situation, banks can play a useful role in redistributing liquidity very much as in the model of household liquidity demand discussed earlier. In fact, banks can commit to liquidity redistribution through credit lines or liquidity covenants in short-term loans, because with these instruments, the unused liquidity of firms with low refinancing needs does not belong to these firms, but to the banks.

Having discussed liquidity provision on the liability and on the asset side of banks' balance sheets, the last question I should briefly raise in the perspective of this survey is that of the relationship between the two sides. Put differently: Is there an economic rational for liquidity provision to households and to firms to be undertaken by the same institution? The literature here is still relatively young, but the existing theory in this area—most prominently Calomiris and Kahn (1991), Diamond and Rajan (2001), Kashyap et al. (2002), and Webb (2000)—all suggest that there exist synergies between the banks' special short-term lending function and the fragile structure of banks' liabilities created by their liquidity role for households.

Kashyap et al. (2002) make this point in a simple model, which again relies on the basic assumption of limited market access discussed earlier. They consider two hypothetically separated institutions, one providing liquidity to households through demand deposits and one providing liquidity to firms through loan commitments. If these institutions cannot trade funds immediately and costlessly on the market when needed and if the liquidity shocks affecting households and firms are not perfectly correlated, the two institutions can improve efficiency by pooling their ressources. The empirical part of their work provides evidence supporting this theory: Commercial banks provide more short-term liquidity to firms—especially through unsecured credit lines—than all other types of lending intermediaries.

References

Allen, F., and Gale, D. (1994). "Limited market participation and volatility of asset prices." *American Economic Review*, 84: 933–55.

Bencivenga, V., and Smith, B. (1991). "Financial intermediation and endogenous growth." *Review of Economic Studies*, 58: 195–209.

Bernanke, B., and Gertler, M. (1987). "Banking and macroeconomic equilibrium," in W. A. Barnett and K. J. Singleton (eds.), *New Approaches to Monetary Economics* (Cambridge: Cambridge Univ. Press).

Bhattacharya, S., and Gale, D. (1987). "Preference shocks, liquidity, and central bank policy," in W. A. Barnett and K. J. Singleton (eds.), *New Approaches to Monetary Economics* (Cambridge: Cambridge Univ. Press).

——, Fulghieri, P., and Rovelli, R. (1998). "Financial intermediation versus stock markets in a dynamic intertemporal model." *Journal of Institutional and Theoretical Economics*, 154: 291–319.

Biais, B., Foucault, T., and Hillion, P. (1997). Microstructure des Marchés Financiers: Institutions, Modèles et Tests. Paris: Presses Universitaires de France.

Bolton, P., and Freixas, X. (2000). "Equity, bonds, and bank debt: Capital structure and financial market equilibrium under asymmetric information." *Journal of Political Economy*, 108: 324–51.

——, and von Thadden, E.-L. (1998). "Blocks, liquidity and corporate control." *Journal of Finance*, 53: 1–25.

Bryant, J. (1980). "A model of reserves, bank runs, and deposit insurance." *Journal of Banking and Finance*, 4: 335–44.

Calomiris, C., and Kahn, C. (1991). "The role of demandable debt in structuring optimal banking arrangements." *American Economic Review*, 81: 497–513.

De Nicoló, G. (1993). "ε-Efficient banking without suspension or deposit insurance." Manuscript, University of Minnesota.

Diamond, D. (1997). "Liquidity, banks, and markets." *Journal of Political Economy*, 105: 928–56.

——, and Dybvig, P. (1983). "Bank runs, deposit insurance, and liquidity." *Journal of Political Economy*, 91: 401–19.

——, and Rajan, R. (2001). "Liquidity risk, liquidity creation, and financial fragility: A theory of banking." *Journal of Political Economy*, 109: 287–327.

Freixas, X., and Rochet, J. C. (1997). *The Microeconomic Theory of Banking*. Cambridge, MA: MIT Press.

Fudenberg, D., Holmström, B., and Milgrom, P. (1990). "Short-term contracts and long-term agency relationships." *Journal of Economic Theory*, 51: 1–31.

Fulghieri, P., and Rovelli, R. (1993). "Capital markets, financial intermediaries, and the supply of liquidity in a dynamic economy." Manuscript, Columbia University.

Gorton, G., and Pennacchi, G. (1990). "Financial intermediaries and liquidity creation." *Journal of Finance*, 45: 49–71.

——, and Winton, A. (1999). "Liquidity provision, the cost of bank capital, and the macroeconomy." Manuscript, University of Minnesota.

Haubrich, J., and King, R. (1990). "Banking and insurance." *Journal of Monetary Economics*, 26: 361–86.

Hellwig, M. (1994). "Liquidity provision, banking, and the allocation of interest rate risk." *European Economic Review*, 38: 1363–90.

Holmström, B., and Tirole, J. (1998). "Private and public supply of liquidity." *Journal of Political Economy*, 106: 1–40.

Holmström, B., and Tirole, J. (2001). "LAPM: A liquidity-based asset pricing model." *Journal of Finance*, 56: 1837–67.

Jacklin, C. (1987). "Demand deposits, trading restrictions, and risk sharing," in E. C. Prescott and N. Wallace (eds.), *Contractual Arrangements for Intertemporal Trade* (Minneapolis: University of Minnesota Press), 26–47.

—— (1993). "Market rate versus fixed rate demand deposits." *Journal of Monetary Economics*, 32: 237–58.

——, and Bhattacharya, S. (1988). "Distinguishing panics and information-based bank runs: Welfare and policy implications." *Journal of Political Economy*, 96: 568–92.

Kashyap, A., Rajan, R., and Stein, J. (2002). "Banks as liquidity providers: An explanation for the co-existence of lending and deposit-taking." *Journal of Finance*, 57: 33–73.

Qi, J. (1994). "Bank liquidity and stability in an overlapping generations model." *Review of Financial Studies*, 7: 389–417.

Samuelson, P. (1958). "An exact consumption-loan model with or without the social contrivance of money." *Journal of Political Economy*, 66: 467–82.

von Thadden, E.-L. (1997). "The term-structure of investment and the banks' insurance function." *European Economic Review*, 41: 1355–74.

—— (1998). "Intermediated versus direct investment: Optimal liquidity provision and dynamic incentive compatibility." *Journal of Financial Intermediation*, 7: 177–97.

—— (1999). "Liquidity creation through banks and markets: Multiple insurance and limited market access." *European Economic Review*, 43: 991–1006.

—— (2002). "An incentive problem in the dynamic theory of banking." *Journal of Mathematical Economics*, 38: 271–92.

Wallace, N. (1988). "Another attempt to explain an illiquid banking system: The Diamond and Dybvig model with sequential service taken seriously." *Quarterly Review, Federal Reserve Bank of Minneapolis*, 3–16.

Webb, D. (2000). "The impact of liquidity constraints on bank lending policy." *Economic Journal*, 110: 69–91.

Part III

Bank Runs and Financial Crises

Part III

Bank Rules and Financial Crises

9

Banking Panics, Information, and Rational Expectations Equilibrium

V. V. Chari and Ravi Jagannathan

Banking panics were a recurrent phenomenon in the United States until the 1930s. They have re-emerged as a source of public concern and much theoretical research recently. In this paper, we provide an information-theoretic rationale for bank runs. The traditional "story" is that contagion is an important aspect of bank runs. The idea seems to be that when the general public observes large withdrawals from the banking system, fears of insolvency grow resulting in even larger withdrawals of deposits.

In our model, some individuals withdraw because they get information that future returns are likely to be low. Uninformed individuals observing this also have an incentive to liquidate their investments. In addition, some individuals need to withdraw deposits for other than information based reasons. Thus, if the random realization of such a group of individuals is unusually large, then the uninformed individuals will be misled and will precipitate a run on the bank. The technology is such that a large volume of withdrawals involves liquidation costs. Consequently, runs on the bank do impose social costs.

A mechanism that may reduce these costs in our model is to suspend convertibility if withdrawals are high. However, those individuals who need to withdraw their assets for liquidity reasons are worse off ex post. Our model provides a rationalization for restrictions in demand deposits that were widespread prior to 1929. Friedman and Schwartz [7] suggest that restrictions of payments ensured

The authors are deeply indebted to Larry E. Jones. We also wish to thank the seminar participants at Northwestern University, the University of Chicago, and the Twentieth Annual Conference of the Western Finance Association. Chari's research was supported by the Banking Research Center, Northwestern University. Jagannathan's research was supported by a grant from the McKnight foundation to the University of Minnesota. The views expressed herein are those of the authors and not necessarily those of the Federal Reserve Bank of Minneapolis or the Federal Reserve System.

that "the panic(s) had a reasonably small effect on the banking structure ... and gave time for the immediate panic to wear off." However, "they were regarded as anything but a satisfactory solution by those who experienced them, which is why they produced such strong pressure for monetary and banking reform" (ibid., p. 329).

Our model is closely related to Diamond and Dybvig [5]. They model banks as providing insurance for individuals who are uncertain about their liquidity needs. Investment in assets with long maturities yields higher return than in short maturities. The optimal contract yields a higher level of consumption for those who withdraw early than the technological return. Consequently bank runs occur when every agent believes that all other agents will withdraw early. Essential to this story is that the bank must honor a sequential service constraint. We do not impose such a constraint. Jacklin [10] in a very similar framework to ours addresses the question of the choice between deposit and equity contracts given that individuals may get information about future returns. Again, a key characteristic is that banks are not allowed to make deposit contracts contingent upon the number of people who desire to withdraw.

Gorton [8] models bank runs as precipitated by the perception on the part of depositors that the return on currency exceeds that on deposits. Banks are better informed about the state of their investments. The driving feature of the model is the assumption that interest rates on deposits cannot be raised or lowered by the banks. Thus, the optimal ex ante agreement specifies that when depositors' expectations about future returns are wrong, the bank suspends convertibility. This occurs only because the bank is assumed not to be able to change the interest payments on deposits in the interim period when information about the state of the bank's investments is revealed (fully to the banks, imperfectly to the depositors).

Bhattacharya and Gale [3] consider a variant of the Diamond–Dybvig model in which there are many intermediaries, each of which has access to information only about the proportion of the population who withdraw from it at the interior stage. They demonstrate that there are welfare gains from setting up an institution such as a central bank or, at any rate, a market for intermediaries to trade in the interim period.

Bhattacharya and Jacklin [4] in a paper similar in some ways to ours consider the choice between deposit and equity contracts in an environment in which some agents receive superior information about future expected returns in the interim period. Their interest is primarily in characterizing the relationship between the riskiness of the underlying stream of returns and the desirability of equity contracts over deposit contracts. Our interest is in developing a model of the information revealed to depositors by the withdrawal decision of *other* depositors.

I. The Model

We consider an environment where people live for three periods: a planning period, time 1, and time 2. There is a single commodity. An investment decision is made during the planning period that yields a sure return at time 1. If resources are reinvested in period 1 they generate a random return at time 2. If resources are not reinvested, there is a liquidation cost that depends upon the level of consumption. There are a large number of individuals (technically, a continuum on the interval [0, 1] on which the Lebesque measure is induced), each of whom has access to the blueprint technology.

A. Technology

The idea behind the technology specified here is straightforward. Individuals invest in the planning period. They receive a random but high expected return in period 2 if the investment is not liquidated in period 1. The return in period 1 is affected by an *exogenously* imposed externality. If many individuals wish to consume in period 1, then each individual's consumption is low. If only a few individuals wish to consume in period 1, then the total return on investment is 1—i.e., a unit invested in period 0 will yield one unit of output in period 1. Our attempt here is to capture some notion of liquidity. The idea is that investments are, at least in part, illiquid but they can be transformed into consumption goods at a cost that depends upon aggregate amount of consumption.

An investment plan for an individual is a pair of numbers (k_0, k) representing investment in periods 0 and 1, respectively. Realized output is a pair of numbers (y_1, y_2) in periods 1 and 2, respectively. Investment decisions are costly to liquidate in period 1. In particular, the cost of liquidation depends upon the aggregate investment decisions made in the economy. Let K represent the aggregate volume of investment. Then, output for any individual's technology is

$$y_1 = k_0 - k \qquad \text{if} \quad K \geq \overline{K}$$
$$y_1 = (1 - \alpha)(k_0 - k) \quad \text{otherwise} \tag{1}$$

where $0 \leq \alpha \leq 1$ and $\overline{K}$ are exogenously specified. Output in period 2 is random and is given by

$$y_2 = \tilde{R}k, \tag{2}$$

where R is a random variable which takes the value H with probability p and L with probability $(1 - p)$, with $H > L$. For convenience, we set $L = 0$.

B. Preferences

All agents in this economy are risk neutral and maximize expected utility of consumption. There are two types of individuals in the economy. Type-1 agents care only about consumption in period 1. Type-2 agents derive utility from consumption in both periods 1 and 2. The utility functions of the respective types are given by

$$U^1(c_1, c_2) = c_1 + \beta c_2$$
$$U^2(c_1, c_2) = c_1 + c_2 \tag{3}$$

where the pair (c_1, c_2) represents consumption levels of the commodity in periods 1 and 2, respectively, and β, the discount factor, is positive and arbitrarily close to zero.

No individual knows his or her type at the planning period. A random fraction $\tilde{t}$ of individuals are of type 1. The random variable $\tilde{t}$ can take on only finitely many values. For ease of exposition we assume that $\tilde{t}$ can take on one of three values, $t\epsilon\{0, t_1, t_2\}$ with probabilities r_0, r_1, and r_2, respectively. Setting the first element to zero is without loss of generality.

C. Endowments

All agents are endowed with one unit of the good at the planning period.

D. Information

At the beginning of time 1, a random fraction $\tilde{\alpha}$ of type-2 agents receive information about prospective time-2 returns. We will assume that this information is perfect. The fact that individuals are risk neutral implies that this assumption is innocuous. The fraction $\tilde{\alpha}$ of type-2 individuals who receive this information can take on two values, $\alpha\epsilon\{0, \bar{\alpha}\}$. The probability that $\tilde{\alpha} = \bar{\alpha}$ is q and the probability that $\tilde{\alpha} = 0$ is $(1 - q)$.

We will assume that the random variables $\tilde{t}, \tilde{R}$ and $\tilde{\alpha}$ are indepenent of each other. Let $\theta \equiv (t, R, \alpha)$, the triplet that represents the state of the world. We will denote the set of all possible values for θ by $\ominus$.

No individual at the planning period knows whether he or she will be informed or not. Furthermore, the realization of $\tilde{t}, \tilde{\alpha}$ and the information received by the informed agents (if any) of the economy are not observable by other agents in the economy. The only information that is public is the aggregate investment decision. To put it differently, what is observed is the fraction of the population that chooses to continue investing, rather than the reasons for doing so.

E. Parameter Restrictions

In order to ensure that individuals have a nontrivial signal-extraction problem upon observing the bank's balance sheet, we clearly need "confounding." Assume that

$$t_1 = \bar{\alpha} \tag{4}$$

$$t_2 = t_1 + \bar{\alpha}(1 - t_1). \tag{5}$$

Further, assume that, absent any information, it is desirable to continue the investment. Thus:

$$pH + (1 - p)L > 1. \tag{6}$$

In some of what follows, results do depend upon the magnitude of $\bar{K}$. In general, any concave transformation of investment into consumption will suffice for the results. It will be assumed, for reasons that will become apparent, that

$$\bar{K} = 1 - t_2. \tag{7}$$

II. Equilibrium

The decision problem in the planning period is trivial since no individual cares about period-0 consumption. All individuals therefore choose to invest one unit in period 0. The decision problem at time 1 of type-1 agents is also trivial. They consume all their resources by liquidating all their investment. The sequencing of the decisions of other agents is as follows. At time 1, t is first realized and every individual knows his or her own type. A random fraction $\alpha \epsilon \{0, \bar{\alpha}\}$ of type-2 agents receive the informative signal. Agents then decide how much of their investment to liquidate. The decision problem of type-2 agents who get the informative signal is also trivial. Given the fact that $H > 1$ (see equation (6)), they will liquidate their investment only if they get information that the return on the project will be low, i.e., $\tilde{R} = L$. Before making the investment decision, agents observe K, the aggregate investment level at date 1. All uninformed type-2 agents will realize that the equilibrium level of K is correlated with the signal received by the informed agents and hence "reveal," albeit imperfectly, their signal. It is important to realize that the aggregate investment could be low *either* because the value of t is high *or* because some type-2 agents have received information that prospective returns are low. It is this confounding that is crucial to our results. Agents take this into account in their decisions.

The problem faced by the representative type-2 uninformed agents is:

$$\max_k c_1 + \int c_2 \, dF(\theta \mid K) \tag{8}$$

subject to

$$c_1 = (1 - \alpha)(1 - k) \quad \text{if } K < \overline{K} \text{ and } 1 - k \text{ otherwise}$$

$$c_2 = w + kR$$

where w is the period-2 endowment and $F(\theta \mid K)$ denotes the distribution of θ conditional on knowing the aggregate investment level K at time 1.

Let the solution to this problem be denoted by $k = k(K)$. As pointed out earlier, for the informed type-2 agent $k = 1$ if $\tilde{R} = H$ and $k = 0$ if $\tilde{R} = L$. We will denote the informed agent's investment at time 1 as $k^1(R)$.

The aggregate demand for investment at time 1, K_D, for any level of observed aggregate investment, K, can now be defined.

$$K_D = \alpha(1 - t)k^I(R) + (1 - \alpha)(1 - t)k(K). \tag{9}$$

Of course, in equilibrium $K_D = K$. The first term on the right-hand side is the aggregate investment decision of the informed type-2 agents. The second term on the right is the aggregate investment decision of the uninformed type-2 agents. Recall that type-1 agents have no desire to invest and that the informed type-2 agents will liquidate their investment at time 1 if and only if their signal is $\tilde{R} = L$. Table 1 gives K_D for every state of the world θ.

DEFINITION 1. Rational-Expectations Equilibrium. A *rational-expectations equilibrium* is: (i) an aggregate investment function $K(\theta)$ that specifies the aggregate investment K for each state of nature θ; (ii) an investment demand function $k(K)$ for each uninformed type-2 agent such that:

(a) $K(\theta) = \alpha(1 - t)k^I(R) + (1 - \alpha)(1 - t)k(K(\theta))$, for all θ,
(b) $k(K)$ solves the maximization problem in equation (8),
(c) if $\alpha(1 - t)k^I(R) + (1 - \alpha)(1 - t)k(\cdot) = \alpha'(1 - t')k^I(R) + (1 - \alpha')(1 - t')k(\cdot)$ for any two states $\theta \equiv \{t, R, \alpha\}$ and $\theta' \equiv \{t', R', \alpha'\}$, for all functions $k(\cdot)$, then $K(\theta) = K(\theta')$.

Condition (a) is a consistency requirement that is analogous to the familiar market-clearing condition. It merely requires that aggregate outcome be the same as the sum of individual decisions. It is trivial to verify that the assumed symmetry of individual decisions is in fact the outcome of optimizing behavior on the part of agents. Condition (b) needs no explanation. Condition (c) requires some explanation. The analogue of this condition is found in rational-expectations equilibria in competitive markets. In such a case several authors have found it necessary to impose a condition that essentially states that the price function must be measurable with respect to the market excess-demand function of agents.[1] In order to see the need for such a condition as the one we have imposed,

---

[1] See Admati [1], Anderson and Sonnenschein [2], and Diamond and Verrecchia [6].

Table 1. Aggregate Demand Function for Investment

State of nature		The aggregate investment demand function $K_D(\cdot)$ defined in equation (9)
No.	$\theta \equiv [t, R \cdot \alpha]$	
1	$(0, R, 0)$	$k(K)$
2	$(0, H, \bar{\alpha})$	$\bar{\alpha} + (1 - \bar{\alpha})k(K)$
3	$(0, L, \bar{\alpha})$	$(1 - \tilde{\alpha})k(K)$
4	$(t_1, R, 0)$	$(1 - t_1)k(K)$
5	$(t_1, H, \bar{\alpha})$	$(1 - t_1)[\bar{\alpha} + (1 - \bar{\alpha}k(K)]$
6	$(t_1, L, \bar{\alpha})$	$(1 - t_1)(1 - \bar{\alpha})k(K)$
7	$(t_2, R, 0)$	$(1 - t_2)k(K)$
8	$(t_2, H, \bar{\alpha})$	$(1 - t_2)[\bar{\alpha} + (1 - \bar{\alpha})k(K)]$
9	$(t_2, L, \bar{\alpha})$	$(1 - t_2)(1 - \bar{\alpha})k(K)$

note that without this condition, the market could reveal more information than anybody in the economy possesses. For example, $K = 0$ whenever $\tilde{R} = L$ and $K = 1 - t$ whenever $\tilde{R} = H$, regardless of the value of α, is consistent with conditions (a) and (b) of the definition of the equilibrium. This is obviously absurd and reflects the fact that there is no mechanism in conditions (a) and (b) alone describing *how* information is aggregated in a competitive environment. We could alternatively impose the requirement that equilibrium outcomes be measurable with respect to the join of all the information possessed by all the agents in the economy. What we seek to capture in this model, however, is the notion that equilibrium outcomes reflect the information that individuals possess *through their decisions* rather than through some arbitrary process. It is appropriate to view the right side of equation (9) as an aggregate excess-demand function for investment. With this interpretation, it seems appropriate that if the aggregate excess-demand functions are the same for two states of the world, then the equilibrium outcomes should also be the same.

DEFINITION 2. Panic Equilibrium. A rational-expectations equilibrium is a *panic equilibrium* if the equilibrium aggregate investment is zero for at least one state in which $\alpha = 0$, i.e., $\theta = \{t, R, 0\}$.

In other words, in a panic equilibrium every one liquidates his or her investment at date 1 even though no one has any information about the return next period.

It is worthwhile to contrast the panic-equilibrium outcome with the full-information outcome. In this case, given that $pH + (1 - p)L > 1$, it follows that individuals would want to continue investing when no one receives the informative signal. Hence the panic–equilibrium outcome can occur only if there is confounding between a large number of individuals unexpectedly desiring to liquidate their investments for "transactions" reasons and the possibility that some individuals have received information that returns are expected to be poor. Theorem 1 below establishes sufficient conditions for all rational-expectations equilibria to be panic equilibria.

THEOREM 1. *A. Given restriction (6), if the following conditions hold, there exists a rational-expectations equilibrium that is also a panic equilibrium:*

$$\frac{r_1(1-q)pH}{r_0(1-p)q + r_1(1-q)} > 1 \tag{10}$$

$$\frac{r_2pH}{r_1(1-p)q + r_2(1-q) + r_2pq} < (1-\alpha). \tag{11}$$

B. In this economy, every rational-expectations equilibrium is also a panic equilibrium.

Proof. See the Appendix. Q.E.D.

Remark 1. In a rational-expectations equilibrium a panic (i.e., $K = 0$ even when no one has any adverse information) can never occur in states in which some agents receive the informative signal (i.e., $\alpha = \bar{\alpha}$) and $R = H$. Hence any panic equilibrium must involve $K = 0$ in some subsets of states from the collection $\{1, 4, 7\}$ in Table 1. Using the fact that $K(3) = K(4)$ and $K(6) = K(7)$ to satisfy the measurability condition (c), it can be verified that the only other equilibria in this economy are those in which either (a) $K = 0$ in states 1, 3, 4, 6, 7, and 9; or (b) $K = 0$ in states 1, 6, 7, or 9; or (c) $K = 0$ in states 3, 4, 6, 7, and 9. In a sense there is "minimal" panic in the equilibrium we have described in Table 2. For this reason if extra market arrangements like "suspension of convertibility" improve on the allocations of the equilibrium described in Table 2, they will also improve on the allocations obtained in the other equilibria in this economy.

Remark 2. The most serious problem with the model presented here is the absence of markets for trading in asset claims.[2] It is possible to show that the rational-expectations equilibrium allocations can be supported as a competitive equilibrium in asset markets where short sales and forward contracts are prohibited.

The model presented above has no apparent role for a bank or other financial intermediary. A few comments are appropriate about our modeling choices. Our intent here has been to develop an explicit model where the observed decisions of *other* agents are relevant for the decision making of uninformed agents. Obviously, banks play many roles other than providing insurance to depositors.

---

[2] We are indebted to Sandy Grossman for pointing this out to us.

Table 2. A "Minimal" Panic Equilibrium for the Economy Described in the Text

	State			Probability	Investment K in a rational expectations equilibrium	
No.	t	R	α		Without suspension of convertibility	With suspension of convertibility
1	0	no	info	π_1	1	1
2	0	H	$\bar{\alpha}$	π_2	1	1
3	0	L	$\bar{\alpha}$	π_3	$1 - t_1$	$1 - t_1$
4	t_1	no	info	π_4	$1 - t_1$	$1 - t_1$
5	t_1	H	$\bar{\alpha}$	π_5	$1 - t_1$	$1 - t_1$
6	t_1	L	$\bar{\alpha}$	π_6	0	$1 - t_1$
7	t_2	no	info	π_7	0	$1 - t_1$
8	t_2	HG	$\bar{\alpha}$	π_8	$1 - t_2$	$1 - t_1$
9	t_2	L	$\bar{\alpha}$	π_9	0	$1 - t_1$

Notes:

(a) $t_2 = t_1 + (1 - t_1)\bar{\alpha}$.

(b) $\pi_1 = r_0(1 - g)$; $\pi_2 = r_0 pq$; $\pi_3 = r_0(1 - p)q$; $\pi_4 = r_1(1 - q)$;
$\pi_5 = r_1 pq$; $\pi_6 = r_1(1 - p)q$; $\pi_7 = r_2(1 - q)$; $\pi_8 = r_2 pq$; $\pi_9 = r_2(1 - p)q$.

(c) K is the equilibrium aggregate investment in the economy in time 1.

Among other things, they monitor the actions of their debtors and provide means of payments. For our purposes, therefore, we think that it is misleading to focus on the liquidity services that banks provide. Instead, we chose to focus on the information content of the "line length" and the withdrawal decisions of other depositors. From that perspective, also, risk aversion on the part of depositors would have caused us to focus on the optimal insurance contract. Since these issues have been addressed extensively in the literature we chose a framework that would focus on issues of information.

The most troublesome (to us) issue is the fact that liquidation costs are exogenously imposed rather than generated from deeper elements of technology and preferences. Obviously, a richer model would have many intermediaries, perhaps geographically isolated, and would generate liquidation costs from the difficulties of monitoring a particular intermediary's portfolio choice. One interpretation of our model is that we focus on runs on a particular bank. Our preferred interpretation is that this is a first step in modeling information-based bank runs. The obvious extension is to consider interbank trades in the interim stage.

The relationship between the equilibria discussed in this section and observed banking panics is discussed in Section III below.

III. Equilibria with Suspension of Convertibility

The model described in Section II is best thought of as a production economy with no apparent role for a financial intermediary. We describe below a mechanism that can, under appropriate circumstances, yield allocations that are superior in terms of ex ante expected utility to the allocations associated with the rational-expectations equilibrium and the market equilibrium discussed in Section II. The tradeoff for the equilibrium in Section II is between the fact that liquidation costs are sometimes incurred, while at the full-information optimum these costs would not have been incurred (see row 7, Table 2). A mechanism is described below that can dominate the equilibrium allocations. This mechanism is closely linked to "suspension of convertibility."

The idea is that individuals pool their resources and entrust them to a "bank" at the planning period. The observable magnitude is the assets of the bank. These assets correspond to K at date 1. At date 1, individuals "queue" up at the bank to make their withdrawals. The bank is permitted to ration depositors at date 1. We assume that the conditions of Theorem 1 hold. Given the results in Theorem 1 and the remarks following the theorem, suspension of convertibility is meaningful only if no more than the first t_1 investors are permitted to withdraw at will at time 1 but every one else must wait. Suspending convertibility at a level of withdrawal higher than t_1 will be of no help in preventing panic in state 7.

It is then readily verified that the only equilibrium with suspension of convertibility, when the bank suspends convertibility whenever withdrawals reach a level of t_1, will be the one described in Table 2.

Clearly, there is gain in the state when there is no information available (state 7), but a loss because either (a) investments are made even though prospective returns are low (states 6 and 9), or (b) some type-1 agents who get little utility from time-2 consumption are prevented from withdrawing when the return is known to be high (state 8).

Suspension of convertibility will improve ex ante expected utility if

$$\sum_{j=I}^{9} \pi_j[U_s(j) - U_e(j)] > 0, \tag{12}$$

where π_j denotes the probability that the event described by state $j, j = 1, 2, \ldots, 9$ will occur, and U_s and U_e denote utilities with and without suspension of convertibility, respectively. Substituting the expressions for $\pi_j, j = 1, 2, \ldots, 9$, we get

$$r_2(1 - q)[t_1 + \beta(t_2 - t_1)pH + (1 - t_1)pH - (1 - \alpha)]$$
$$> r_1(1 - p)q[(1 - \alpha) - t_1] + r_2(1 - p)[(1 - \alpha) - t_1]$$
$$+ (t_2 - t_1)(I - \beta H)r_2pq. \tag{13}$$

Inequality (13) has been written so as to highlight the potential conflict between the possibility that suspension of convertibility can gain in ex ante terms and the fact that, in order for the equilibrium to involve runs on banks without suspension of convertibility the conditions of Theorem 1 must hold. This establishes Theorem 2.

THEOREM 2. *If inequalities (10), (11), and (13) hold, the equilibrium with suspension of convertibility yields higher ex ante utility than the rational-expectations equilibrium[3] of Section II.*

It is important to note that suspension of convertibility improves upon the rational-expectations equilibrium outcomes primarily because of the specification of the liquidation technology. The liquidation costs have been set up so that sudden or large-scale withdrawals are costly.

Of course, such suspension of convertibility accompanied by random assignment of withdrawal rights leaves some individuals worse off than others who are identically situated. In a sense, therefore, the fact that suspension of convertibility was consistently practiced in every bank run but that there were many ex post complaints about this state of affairs is explained by this model.

The assumption that individuals are risk neutral also plays a role in our evaluation of the welfare consequences, since consumption is different across otherwise identical individuals with suspension.

The role of a financial intermediary in the model we consider is solely to allow agents to coordinate their strategies. Intermediaries clearly perform many other functions, so our description of the role of a bank must be viewed primarily as a means of focusing attention on one issue. Within this perspective, it is optimal to ration consumption at date 1. One means of rationing consumption is to form a "mutual fund" that is required as part of the rules of the game to suspend convertibilty under certain circumstances. This policy inevitably carries ex post regret. Those who are rationed out get less consumption than their lucky colleagues.

IV. Conclusion

In a sense this chapter is an extended example. Expanding the number of states yields no major changes in the results, so we have chosen to restrict the number of states in order to make the results more transparent. We have established that bank runs can be modeled as an equilibrium phenomenon in a model in which all equilibria have bank runs. Previous work (Diamond and Dybvig) generates bank runs as one of a series of possible multiple equilibria. Multiple-equilibria

---

[3] It is possible to show that the set of parameters that satisfy the conditions of Theorem 2 are nonempty. For example, for the parameter values given in the Appendix, the left side of inequality (13) is 0.02229 and the right side of the inequality is 0.01887.

models in which only some of the equilibria involve bank runs of course suffer from the problem that they have limited predictive power. We have demonstrated that some aspects of the intuitive "story" that bank runs start with fears of insolvency of particular banks and then spread to other sectors can be rigorously modeled. The essence of our model is that if individuals observe long "lines" at banks, they correctly infer that there is a possibility that the bank is about to fail and precipitate a bank run. Bank runs occur *even if* no one has any adverse information about future returns.

In making explicit this "story," it has been necessary to abstract from the important issues of what exactly banks do. Instead, our focus is on a particular signal-extraction problem in which agents reasonably infer poor prospects for a bank from the withdrawal decisions of other depositors. Obviously, this model can be embedded in a framework where insurance is desirable and the choice between equity and deposit contracts studied (as, for example, in Jacklin [10] and in Bhattacharya and Jacklin [4]). Our focus has been to argue that runs can occur even in environments where banks provide services other than insurance.

We have also argued that suspension of convertibility can improve upon the equilibrium allocations. This occurs because in the model considered here there are two sources of social costs in bank runs. One is the cost involved in liquidating fixed investments, the other is the fact that bank runs occur in some states even though returns are high and are known by some individuals to be high. Essentially, the fear induced by a large number of withdrawers, even though their withdrawals are not informationally based, causes a run on the bank.

The conditions required to ensure that there are bank runs are not crucially dependent upon risk neutrality. It is quite possible, however, that suspension of convertibility might no longer lead to an improvement of ex ante welfare. An important direction in which this model needs to be extended is to incorporate the linkage between failures of particular banks and runs on the banking system as a whole. We have imposed a liquidation cost on the technology to capture the idea that failures of many banks are more costly than failures of a few. It is not clear to us why this might be so. In addition, the aggregate risks in this model are exogenously imposed. The interaction between bank runs and business cycles needs to be modeled explicitly.

APPENDIX

Proof of Theorem 1, Part A. For convenience, we denote states by the row numbers in Table 2. For example, state 1 will refer to the state described in row 1 of Table 2, i.e., $\theta = \{0, R, \alpha\}$. (The reader will find it useful to refer to Table 2 at this stage.)

The outcomes in Table 2 can be thought of as follows. All uninformed type-2 agents continue to invest unless they see an aggregate investment of zero. The information partitions of uninformed type-2 agents in the conjectured equilibrium are:

$$
\begin{aligned}
K &= 1 & &\text{implies } \theta \in \{1,2\} \\
K &= 1 - t_1 & &\text{implies } \theta \in \{3,4,5\} \\
K &= 1 - t_2 & &\text{implies } \theta \in \{8\} \\
K &= 0 & &\text{implies } \theta \in \{6,7,9\}.
\end{aligned}
$$

Since $pH + (1 - p)L > 1$, it is optimal for the uninformed agent not to liquidate if he or she observes $K=1$, i.e., in states 1 and 2.

The left side of inequality (10) is the expected future consumption from maintaining the investment when $\theta = \{3,4\}$. Since $R = H$ in state 5, the expected future consumption conditional on $\theta \in \{3,4,5\}$ is greater than the left side of inequality (10). Since the left side of inequality (10) is greater than 1, it is optimal not to liquidate if the agent observed $K = 1 - t_1$, because this implies $\theta = \{3,4,5\}$.

The left side of inequality (11) is the expected future consumption from maintaining the investment when $\theta \in \{6,7,8\}$. Since the aggregate investment $K = 0$ in states 6, 7, and 9, the agent will only get $(1 - \alpha)$ units if he or she liquidates his or her investment whenever the agent observes $K = 0$. However, since the left side of inequality (11) is less than $(1 - \alpha)$, it is still optimal to liquidate if the agent observed $K = 0$, i.e., $\theta \in \{6,7,9\}$, since $\tilde{R} = L$ in state 9 while state 8 has $\tilde{R} = H$. Hence the outcomes described in Table 2 constitute an equilibrium. Since all agents liquidate in state 7, which is a state in which no one has any adverse information about the next-period return, it is a panic equilibrium.

Proof of Theorem 1, Part B

Recall that $\bar{\alpha} = t_1$ and $(1 - t_1)(1 - \bar{\alpha}) = (1 - t_2)$. The measurability condition (c) in our definition of the equilibrium together with the definition of the function $K_D(\cdot)$ given in equation (9) and Table 1 then immediately implies that the equilibrium investment must be the same in states 3 and 4 and states 6 and 7.

Suppose that the equilibrium involves no panic. In such a case (by definition) it must be that $K(t, R, 0) > 0$ for all t, i.e., the aggregate investment should be strictly positive in states 1, 4, and 7. However, the argument above then implies that $K(t, L, \bar{\alpha}) > 0$ if $t = 0$ or $t = t_1$. In other words, the aggregate investment should be strictly positive in states 3 and 6 as well. Let $K(i)$ denote the value of K in each state $i, i = 1, 2, \ldots, 9$. We have already argued that in any equilibrium with no panics $k(K(6)) = k(K(7))$. Since there are no panics, $k(K(6)) = k(K(7)) > 0$. It follows from Table 1 that $K(j) \neq K(6), j = 1, 2, 3, 4, 5,$ and 9. To see why this is true, suppose $K(6) = K(1)$. This would imply from the definition of equilibrium that $(1 - t_1)(1 - \bar{\alpha})k(K) = k(K)$. This yields an obvious contradiction since $(1 - t_1)(1 - \bar{\alpha}) = (1 - t_2) > 0$. A similar argument holds for the other cases. It is possible that $K(6) = K(7) = K(8)$. This will be true if $k(K(6)) = 1$. In such a case if an uninformed agent observes $K = K(6) = 1 - t_2$, he or she will infer that the only possible states are 6, 7, and 8. However, in this case, the expected consumption from continuing to invest is given by the left side of inequality (11). This is less than the right side of inequality (11), which is the utility that can be attained by liquidating the investment. Hence all uninformed agents will wish to consume in period 1 in the event that $K = 1 - t_2$. Therefore $k(K(6)) = 1$ cannot be an equilibrium.

If $0 < k(K(6)) < 1$, the only confusion is between states 6 and 7. But recall that $R = H$ in state 8. Hence the expected future consumption conditional on $\theta \in \{6, 7\}$ must be less than the expected future consumption conditional on $\theta \in \{6, 7, 8\}$. We have already shown that individuals will wish to liquidate if $\theta \in \{6, 7, 8\}$. Therefore $k(K(6)) > 0$ cannot be optimal.

It follows that *any* equilibrium must involve panic in the sense that agents choose to liquidate even though *nobody* has any information.[4] Q.E.D.

References

1. Admati, A. R. (1985). "A noisy rational expectations equilibrium for multi-asset securities markets." *Econometrica*, 53: 629–57.
2. Anderson, R. M., and Sonnenschein, H. (1982). "On the existence of rational expectations equilibrium." *Journal of Economic Theory*, 26: 261–78.
3. Bhattacharya, S., and Gale, D. (1985). "Preference shocks, liquidity and central bank policy." Working paper, University of California, Berkeley.
4. ——, and Jacklin, C. (1986). "Distinguishing panics and information based bank runs: Welfare and policy implications." Working paper, University of Chicago.
5. Diamond, D. W., and Dybvig, P. (1983). "Bank runs, deposit insurance and liquidity." *Journal of Political Economy*, 91: 401–19.
6. ——, and Verrecchia, R. E. (1981). "Information in a noisy rational expectations economy." *Journal of Financial Economics*, 9: 221–35.
7. Friedman, M., and Schwartz, A. J. (1963). *A Monetary History of the United States and the United Kingdom*. Chicago: University of Chicago Press.

---

[4] The reader can verify that there are parameter values satisfying the restrictions imposed in Theorem I. An example is $\beta = 0.0000001; H = 2.31; p = q = 0.5; r_0 = 0.1875; r_1 = 0.75; r_2 = 0.0625; \bar{\alpha} = 0.05; t_1 = 0.25; t_2 = t_1 + \bar{\alpha}(1 - t_1) = 0.2875; \alpha = 0.66$. The value of the left side of inequality (11) is $1.026 > 1$, and the left side of inequality (12) is $0.308 < (1 - \alpha) = 0.34$.

8. Gorton, G. (1985). "Bank suspension of convertibility." *Journal of Monetary Economics*, 15: 177–93.

9. Grossman, S. J., and Stiglitz, J. E. (1983). "On the impossibility of informationally efficient markets." *The American Economic Review*, 70: 393–408.

10. Jacklin, C. A. (1983). "Information and the choice between deposit and equity contracts." Mimeo, Stanford University.

10

Unique Equilibrium in a Model of Self-Fulfilling Currency Attacks

Stephen Morris and Hyun-Song Shin

Speculative attacks are sometimes triggered without warning, and without any apparent change in the economic fundamentals. Commentators who have attempted to explain episodes of speculative crises have pointed to the self-fulfilling nature of the belief in an imminent speculative attack. If speculators believe that a currency will come under attack, their actions in anticipation of this precipitate the crisis itself, while if they believe that a currency is not in danger of imminent attack, their inaction spares the currency from attack, thereby vindicating their initial beliefs.[1]

However, merely pointing to the self-fulfilling nature of beliefs leaves open a number of crucial questions. First, such an account leaves unexplained the actual *onset* of an attack when it occurs. By most accounts, both the European Exchange Rate Mechanism (ERM) and the Mexican peso were "ripe" for attack for some time before the crises that brought them down in the early 1990s—at least two years in Europe and perhaps a year in Mexico (Barry Eichengreen and Charles Wyplosz, 1993; Rudiger Dornbusch and Alejandro M. Werner, 1994). At any point in those periods, concerted selling by speculators would have raised the costs of maintaining the exchange rate sufficiently high that the monetary authorities would have been forced to abandon the parity. Why did the attacks happen when they did? Conventional accounts resort to forces that operate outside the theoretical model in trying to explain the shift of expectations that precipitated the attack. Some of these informal accounts are more persuasive

We are grateful to Marcus Miller for encouraging us to pursue this topic and to Stephen Coate and John Driffill for advice during the preparation of this paper. We thank Anne Sibert for her comments as discussant at the CEPR conference on "Origins and Management of Financial Crises." The first author acknowledges the support of the Alfred P. Sloan Foundation. The second author acknowledges the support of the U.K. Economic and Social Research Council under Grant No. R000221556.

[1] This theme is explored in Robert P. Flood and Peter M. Garber (1984) and Maurice Obstfeld (1986, 1994, 1996). A closely related literature explores self-fulfilling debt crises; see Guillermo A. Calvo (1988), Jonathan Eaton and Raquel Fernandez (1995), and Harold L. Cole and Timothy J. Kehoe (1996).

than others, but none can be fully compelling as a theoretical model of the onset of a currency crisis.

Secondly, merely pointing to the self-fulfilling nature of beliefs leaves open the policy issues associated with curbing speculative attacks. For example, it is often argued that increased capital mobility induced by lower transaction costs increases the likelihood of currency crises, and that judicious "throwing of sand" into the excessively well-oiled wheels of international finance will play a role in curbing speculative attacks (Eichengreen et al., 1995). However, an account that merely points to the self-fulfilling nature of belief cannot contribute to this debate, since the question of how the beliefs are determined is beyond the scope of such an account. Any argument for or against the proposal has to resort to forces outside the formal theory.

We argue here that the apparent multiplicity of equilibria associated with self-fulfilling beliefs is the consequence of assuming too simple a picture of the role played by information in a speculative episode. Although market participants each have a window on to the world, the imperfect nature of such a vantage point generates a failure of common knowledge of the fundamentals. Thus, everyone may know that the fundamentals are sound, but it may not be that everyone knows that everyone knows this. Still higher orders of such uncertainty may be relevant. Uncertainty about other participants' beliefs is crucial to a speculative episode, since the onset of a speculative attack relies to a large extent on coordinated behavior of speculators. We propose a more realistic modelling of the information structure underlying speculative situations that enables us to pinpoint the forces which determine the onset of a speculative attack. When speculators observe an independent noisy signal of the state of fundamentals, common knowledge of the fundamentals no longer holds. This is enough to induce a unique equilibrium of the model, in which there is a critical state below which attack always occurs and above which attack never occurs.[2] The value of this critical state depends on financial variables such as the mass of speculators and the transaction costs associated with attacking the currency. As a consequence, we can say something about how this unique outcome depends on the parameters of the problem, such as the costs of speculation, the underlying strength of the economy, and the size of the pool of hot money in circulation.

Information plays a subtle role in speculative crises. What is important is not the amount of information, per se, but rather how public and transparent this information is. If market participants are well informed about the fundamentals, but they are unsure of the information received by other participants, and hence unsure of the beliefs held by others, speculative attacks may be triggered even

---

[2] Andrew Postlewaite and Xavier Vives (1987) discuss the role of information in selecting among multiple equilibria in the closely related context of bank runs. Our analysis builds on and extends the earlier incomplete information game analysis of Hans Carlsson and Eric E. van Damme (1993) and Morris et al. (1995).

though everyone knows that the fundamentals are sound. Our analysis high-lights the importance of the transparency of the conduct of monetary policy and its dissemination to the public.

I. Model

Our model is concerned with the strategic interaction between the government and a group of speculators in the foreign exchange market that takes place against the backdrop of a competitive market for foreign exchange. The economy is characterized by a state of fundamentals θ, which we assume to be uniformly distributed over the unit interval $[0, 1]$. The exchange rate in the absence of government intervention is a function of θ, and is given by $f(\theta)$. We assume that f is strictly increasing in θ, so that higher values of θ correspond to "stronger fundamentals."

The exchange rate is initially pegged by the government at e^*, where $e^* \geq f(\theta)$ for all θ. Facing the government is a continuum of speculators who may take one of two actions. A speculator may either attack the currency by selling short one unit of the currency, or refrain from doing so. There is a cost $t > 0$ associated with short-selling. If a speculator short-sells the currency and the government abandons the exchange rate peg, then the payoff at state θ by attacking the currency is given by the fall in the exchange rate minus the transaction cost. Thus the speculator's payoff is $e^* - f(\theta) - t$. If the government defends the peg, then the speculator pays the transaction cost, but has no capital gain. Thus his payoff is $-t$. If the speculator chooses not to attack the currency, his payoff is zero.

The government derives a value $v > 0$ from defending the exchange rate at the pegged level, but also faces costs of doing so. The cost of defending the peg depends on the state of the fundamentals, as well as the proportion of specula-tors who attack the currency. We denote by $c(\alpha, \theta)$ the cost of defending the peg if proportion α of the speculators attack the currency at the state θ. The govern-ment's payoff to abandoning the exchange rate is thus zero while the payoff to defending the exchange rate is

$$v - c(\alpha, \theta).$$

We assume that c is continuous and is increasing in α while decreasing in θ. In particular, to make the problem economically interesting we will impose the following assumptions on the cost function and the floating exchange rate $f(\theta)$.

- $c(0, 0) > v$. In the worst state of fundamentals, the cost of defending the currency is so high that it exceeds the value v even if no speculators attack.

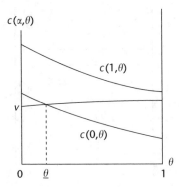

Figure 1. Cost and benefit to the government in maintaining the currency peg.

- $c(1, 1) > v$. If all the speculators attack the currency, then even in the best state of the fundamentals, the cost of defending the currency exceeds the value.
- $e^* - f(1) < t$. In the best state of the fundamentals, the floating exchange rate $f(1)$ is sufficiently close to the pegged level e^* such that any profit from the depreciation of the currency is outweighed by the transactions cost t.

Let us denote by $\underline{\theta}$ the value of θ which solves $c(0, \theta) = v$. In other words, $\underline{\theta}$ is the value of θ at which the government is indifferent between defending the peg and abandoning it in the absence of any speculative selling. When $\theta < \underline{\theta}$, the cost of defending the currency exceeds the value, even if no speculators attack the currency (see Figure 1). At the other end, denote by $\bar{\theta}$ the value of θ at which $f(\theta) = e^* - t$, so that the floating exchange rate is below the peg by the amount of the cost of attack. When $\theta > \bar{\theta}$, then the floating exchange rate is sufficiently close to the peg that a speculator cannot obtain a positive payoff by attacking the currency (see Figure 2). Using the two benchmark levels of the state of fundamentals $\underline{\theta}$ and $\bar{\theta}$, we can classify the state of fundamentals under three headings, according to the underlying strategic situation.

A. *Tripartite classification of fundamentals*

Assuming that $\underline{\theta} < \bar{\theta}$, we can partition the space of fundamentals into three intervals,[3] emphasized by Maurice Obstfeld (1996).

- In the interval $[0, \underline{\theta}]$, the value of defending the peg is outweighed by its cost irrespective of the actions of the speculators. The government then has no reason to defend the currency. For this reason, we say that the currency is *unstable* if $\theta \in [0, \underline{\theta}]$.

---

[3] This assumption will hold if v is large and t is small.

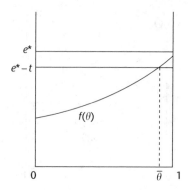

Figure 2. The managed exchange rate and the exchange rate in the absence of intervention as a function of the state of fundamentals.

- In the interval $(\underline{\theta}, \overline{\theta})$, the value of defending the currency is greater than the cost, provided that sufficiently few speculators attack the currency. In particular, if none of the speculators attacks, then the value of defending the currency is greater than the cost, and so the government will maintain the peg, which in turn justifies the decision not to attack. However, it is also the case that if all the speculators attack the currency, then the cost of defending the currency is too high, and the government will abandon the peg. Moreover, since $\overline{\theta}$ is the right end point of this interval, a speculator will make a positive profit if the government were to abandon the peg at any state θ in the interval $(\underline{\theta}, \overline{\theta})$, so that if a speculator believes that the currency peg will be abandoned, then attacking the currency is the rational action. For this reason, we say that the currency is *ripe for attack* if $\theta \in (\underline{\theta}, \overline{\theta})$.
- Finally, in the interval $[\overline{\theta}, 1]$, although the speculators can force the government to abandon the peg, the resulting depreciation of the currency is so small that they cannot recoup the cost of attacking the currency. Thus, even if a speculator were to believe that the currency will fall, the rational action is to refrain from attacking it. In other words, it is a dominant action not to attack. For this reason, we say that the currency is *stable* if $\theta \in [\overline{\theta}, 1]$.

The interesting range is the "ripe for attack" region. Suppose that the government's decision on whether or not to defend the currency is determined purely by weighing up the costs and benefits, and that it makes its decision once all the speculators have made their decisions. Then, if all the speculators have perfect information concerning the realization of θ, the "ripe for attack" region gives rise to the standard case of multiple equilibria due to the self-fulfilling nature of the speculators' beliefs. If the speculators believe that the currency peg will be maintained, then it is optimal not to attack, which in turn induces the government to defend the currency, thereby vindicating the speculators' decisions not to attack the currency. On the other hand, if the speculators believe that the currency peg will be abandoned, the rational action is to attack the currency, which in turn induces the government to abandon the peg, vindicating the decision to attack. Given this multiplicity of equilibria, no definitive prediction can be made as to whether the currency will come under attack or not. We will now see, however, that the situation is very different when the speculators face a small amount of uncertainty concerning the fundamentals. Each state of fundamentals gives rise to a unique outcome.

B. *Game with imperfect information of fundamentals*

Suppose that the speculators each have a signal concerning the state of fundamentals, as in the following game.

- Nature chooses the state of fundamentals θ according to the uniform density over the unit interval.
- When the true state is θ, a speculator observes a signal x which is drawn uniformly from the interval $[\theta - \varepsilon, \theta + \varepsilon]$, for some small[4] $\varepsilon > 0$. Conditional on θ, the signals are identical and independent across individuals. Based on the signal observed, a speculator decides whether or not to attack the currency.
- The government observes the realized proportion of speculators who attack the currency, α, and observes θ.

The payoffs of the game follow from the description of the model above. We assume that if a speculator is indifferent between attacking and not attacking, he will refrain from attacking and that if the government is indifferent between defending the peg and abandoning it, it will choose to abandon it.[5]

An equilibrium for this game consists of strategies for government and for the continuum of speculators such that no player has an incentive to deviate. We can solve out the government's strategy at the final stage of the game, to define a reduced-form game between the speculators only. To do this, consider the critical proportion of speculators needed to trigger the government to abandon the peg at state θ. Let $a(\theta)$ denote this critical mass. In the "unstable" region $a(\theta) = 0$, while elsewhere $a(\theta)$ is the value of α which solves $c(\alpha, \theta) = v$. Figure 3 depicts this function, which is continuous and strictly increasing in θ where it takes a positive value, and is bounded above by 1.

The unique optimal strategy for the government is then to abandon the exchange rate only if the observed fraction of deviators, α, is greater than or equal to the critical mass $a(\theta)$ in the prevailing state θ.

---

[4] In particular, we assume that $2\varepsilon < \min\{\underline{\theta}, 1 - \bar{\theta}\}$.
[5] Nothing substantial hinges on these assumptions, which are made for purposes of simplifying the statement of our results.

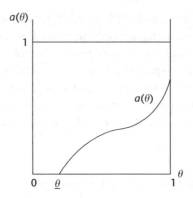

Figure 3. The proportion of speculators whose short sales are sufficient to induce depreciation, expressed as a function of the fundamentals.

Taking as given this optimal strategy for the government, we can characterize the payoffs in the reduced-form game between the speculators. For a given profile of strategies of the speculators, we denote by

$$\pi(x)$$

the proportion of speculators who attack the currency when the value of the signal is x. We denote by $s(\theta, \pi)$ the proportion of speculators who end up attacking the currency when the state of fundamentals is θ, given aggregate selling strategy π. Since signals are uniformly distributed over $[\theta - \varepsilon, \theta + \varepsilon]$ at θ, we have[6]

$$s(\theta, \pi) = \frac{1}{2\varepsilon} \int_{\theta-\varepsilon}^{\theta+\varepsilon} \pi(x) \, dx. \tag{1}$$

Denote by $A(\pi)$ the event where the government abandons the currency peg if the speculators follow strategy π:

$$A(\pi) = \{\theta \mid s(\theta, \pi) \geq a(\theta)\}. \tag{2}$$

We can then define the payoffs of a reduced-form game between the speculators. The payoff to a speculator of attacking the currency at state θ when aggregate short sales are given by π is

$$h(\theta, \pi) \equiv \begin{cases} e^* - f(\theta) - t & \text{if } \theta \in A(\pi) \\ -t & \text{if } \theta \notin A(\pi). \end{cases} \tag{3}$$

---

[6] The following formula is for $\theta \in [\varepsilon, 1 - \varepsilon]$.

However, a speculator does not observe θ directly. The payoff to attacking the currency must be calculated from the posterior distribution over the states conditional on the signal x. The expected payoff to attacking the currency conditional on the signal x is given by the expectation of (3) conditional on x. Denoting this by $u(x, \pi)$, we have

$$
u(x, \pi) = \frac{1}{2\varepsilon} \int_{x-\varepsilon}^{x+\varepsilon} h(\theta, \pi) \, d\theta
$$

$$
= \frac{1}{2\varepsilon} \left[\int_{***} (e^* - f(\theta)) \, d\theta \right] - t. \tag{4}
$$

Since a speculator can guarantee a payoff of zero by refraining from attacking the currency, the rational decision conditional on signal x depends on whether $u(x, \pi)$ is positive or negative. Thus if the government follows its unique optimal strategy, π is an equilibrium of the first period game if $\pi(x) = 1$ whenever $u(x, \pi) > 0$ and $\pi(x) = 0$ whenever $u(x, \pi) \leq 0$.

II. Unique Equilibrium

We now state the main result of our paper, noting the contrast between the multiplicity of possible outcomes when there is perfect information of the fundamentals against the uniqueness of outcome when there is a small amount of noise.

THEOREM 1. *There is a unique θ^* such that, in any equilibrium of the game with imperfect information, the government abandons the currency peg if and only if $\theta \leq \theta^*$.*

The argument for our result can be presented in three steps.

LEMMA 1. *If $\pi(x) \geq \pi'(x)$ for all x, then $u(x, \pi) \geq u(x, \pi')$ for all x.*

In other words, if we compare two strategy profiles π and π', where π entails a greater proportion of speculators who attack for any message x, then the payoff to attacking the currency is greater given π than when it is given by π'. Thus speculators' decisions to attack the currency are strategic complements.

Proof of Lemma 1. Since $\pi(x) \geq \pi'(x)$, we have $s(\theta, \pi) \geq s(\theta, \pi')$ for every θ, from the definition of s given by (1). Thus, from (2),

$$
A(\pi) \supseteq A(\pi').
$$

In other words, the event in which the currency peg is abandoned is strictly larger under π. Then, from (4) and the fact that $e^* - f(\theta)$ is nonnegative,

$$u(x, \pi) = \frac{1}{2\varepsilon} \left[\int_{A(\pi) \cap [x-\varepsilon, x+\varepsilon]} (e^* - f(\theta)) \, d\theta \right] - t$$

$$\geq \frac{1}{2\varepsilon} \left[\int_{A(\pi') \cap [x-\varepsilon, x+\varepsilon]} (e^* - f(\theta)) \, d\theta \right] - t$$

$$= u(x, \pi'),$$

which proves the lemma.

For the next step, consider the strategy profile where every speculator attacks the currency if and only if the message x is less than some fixed number k. Then, aggregate short sales π will be given by the indicator function I_k, defined as

$$I_k(x) = \begin{cases} 1 & \text{if } x < k \\ 0 & \text{if } x \geq k \end{cases} \tag{5}$$

When speculators follow this simple rule of action, the expected payoff to attacking the currency satisfies the following property.

LEMMA 2. $u(k, I_k)$ *is continuous and strictly decreasing in* k.

In other words, when aggregate short sales are governed by I_k, and we consider the payoff to attacking the currency given the marginal message k, this payoff is decreasing as the fundamentals of the economy become stronger. Put another way, when the fundamentals of the economy are stronger, the payoff to attacking the currency is lower for a speculator on the margin of switching from attacking to not attacking. Such a property would be a reasonable feature of any model of currency attacks where the government is able to resist speculators better when the fundamentals are stronger.

The proof of Lemma 2 is simple but involves some algebraic manipulation, and hence is presented separately in the Appendix. Taking Lemma 2 as given, we can then prove the following result.

LEMMA 3. *There is a unique* x^* *such that, in any equilibrium of the game with imperfect information of the fundamentals, a speculator with signal* x *attacks the currency if and only if* $x < x^*$.

To prove this, we begin by establishing that there is a unique value of k at which

$$u(k, I_k) = 0.$$

From Lemma 2, we know that $u(k, I_k)$ is continuous and strictly decreasing in k. If we can show that it is positive for small values of k and negative for large values, then we can guarantee that $u(k, I_k) = 0$ for some k. When k is sufficiently small (i.e., $k \leq \underline{\theta} - \varepsilon$), the marginal speculator with message k knows that the true state of fundamentals is in the "unstable" region, since such a message is consistent only with a realization of θ in the interval $[0, \underline{\theta}]$. Since the payoff to attacking the currency is positive at any θ in this interval, we have $u(k, I_k) > 0$. Similarly, when k is sufficiently large (i.e., $k \geq \overline{\theta} + \varepsilon$), the marginal speculator with message k knows that the true state of fundamentals is in the "stable" region. Since the payoff to attacking is negative at every state in this region, we have $u(k, I_k) < 0$. Hence, there is a unique value of k for which $u(k, I_k) = 0$, and we define the value x^* as this unique solution to $u(k, I_k) = 0$.

Now, consider any equilibrium of the game, and denote by $\pi(x)$ the proportion of speculators who attack the currency given message x. Define the numbers $\underline{x}$ and $\overline{x}$ as

$$\underline{x} = \inf\{x | \pi(x) < 1\}$$

$$\text{and } \overline{x} = \sup\{x | \pi(x) > 0\}.$$

Since $\overline{x} \geq \sup\{x | 0 < \pi(x) < 1\} \geq \inf\{x | 0 < \pi(x) < 1\} \geq \underline{x}$,

$$\underline{x} \leq \overline{x}. \tag{6}$$

When $\pi(x) < 1$, there are some speculators who are not attacking the currency. This is only consistent with equilibrium behavior if the payoff to not attacking is at least as high as the payoff to attacking given message x. By continuity, this is true at $\underline{x}$ also. In other words,

$$u(\underline{x}, \pi) \leq 0. \tag{7}$$

Now, consider the payoff $u(\underline{x}, I_{\underline{x}})$. Clearly, $I_{\underline{x}} \leq \pi$, so that Lemma 1 and (7) imply $u(\underline{x}, I_{\underline{x}}) \leq u(\underline{x}, \pi) \leq 0$. Thus, $u(\underline{x}, I_{\underline{x}}) \leq 0$. Since we know from Lemma 2 that $u(k, I_k)$ is decreasing in k and x^* is the unique value of k which solves $u(k, I_k) = 0$, we have

$$\underline{x} \geq x^*. \tag{8}$$

A symmetric argument establishes that

$$\overline{x} \leq x^*. \tag{9}$$

Thus, from (8) and (9), we have $\underline{x} \geq x^* \geq \overline{x}$. However, we know from (6) that this implies

$$\underline{x} = x^* = \overline{x}.$$

Thus, the equilibrium π is given by the step function I_{x^*}, which is what Lemma 3 states. Hence, this proves Lemma 3.

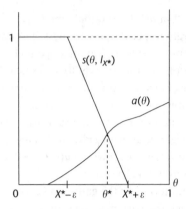

Figure 4. The derivation of the cutoff point for the state of
fundamentals at which the equilibrium short sales are equal to
the short sales which induce depreciation.

From this, it is a short step to the proof of our main theorem itself. Given that equilibrium π is given by the step function I_{x^*}, the aggregate short sales at the state θ are given by

$$s(\theta, I_{x^*}) = \begin{cases} 1 & \text{if } \theta < x^* - \varepsilon \\ \dfrac{1}{2} - \dfrac{1}{2\varepsilon}(\theta - x^*) & \text{if } x^* - \varepsilon \leq \theta < x^* + \varepsilon \\ 0 & \text{if } \theta \geq x^* + \varepsilon. \end{cases}$$

Aggregate short sales $s(\theta, I_{x^*})$ are decreasing in θ when its value is strictly between 0 and 1, while $a(\theta)$ is increasing in θ for this range. See Figure 4, which illustrates the derivation of the cutoff point for the state of fundamentals at which the equilibrium short sales are equal to the short sales which induce depreciation.

We know that $x^* > \underline{\theta} - \varepsilon$, since otherwise attacking the currency is a strictly better action, contradicting the fact that x^* is a switching point. Thus, $s(\theta, I_{x^*})$ and $a(\theta)$ cross precisely once. Define θ^* to be the value of θ at which these two curves cross. Then, $s(\theta, I_{x^*}) \geq a(\theta)$ if and only if $\theta \leq \theta^*$, so that the government abandons the currency peg if and only if $\theta \leq \theta^*$. This is the claim of our main theorem.

III. Comparative Statics and Policy Implications

A. *Changes in the information structure*

When there is no noise, there are multiple equilibria throughout the "ripe for attack" region of fundamentals. But when there is positive noise, there is a unique equilibrium with critical value θ^*. The value of θ^* in the limit as ε tends to zero has a particularly simple characterization.

THEOREM 2. *In the limit as ε tends to zero, θ^* is given by the unique solution to the equation $f(\theta^*) = e^* - 2t$.*

The proof is in the Appendix. Intuition is gained by considering the marginal speculator who observes message $x = \theta^*$. With ε small, this tells the speculator that the true θ is close to θ^*. Since the government abandons the peg if and only if θ is less than θ^*, he attaches equal probability to the currency being abandoned and defended. So, the expected payoff to attacking is $1/2(e^* - f(\theta^*))$, while the cost is t. For the marginal speculator, these are equal, leading to the equation in Theorem 2.

Information plays a subtle role in the model. What matters is not the amount of information, per se, but whether there is common knowledge. With noise, it is never common knowledge that the fundamentals are consistent with the government maintaining the currency Peg, i.e., that $\theta \geq \underline{\theta}$. If you observe a signal greater than $\underline{\theta} + \varepsilon$, then you can claim to *know* that $\theta \geq \underline{\theta}$, since your message has the margin of error of ε. When do you know that *everyone* knows that $\theta \geq \underline{\theta}$? In other words, when do you know that everyone has observed a signal greater than $\underline{\theta} + \varepsilon$? Since others' signals can differ from yours by at most 2ε, this will be true if you observe a signal greater than $\underline{\theta} + 3\varepsilon$. Proceeding in this way, there is "nth order knowledge" that $\theta \geq \underline{\theta}$ (i.e., everyone knows that everyone knows ... (n times) that everyone knows it) exactly if everyone has observed a signal greater than or equal to $\underline{\theta} + (2n - 1)\varepsilon$. But, by definition, there is common knowledge that $\theta \geq \underline{\theta}$ if and only if there is nth order knowledge for every n. But for any fixed ε and signal x, there will be some level n at which nth order iterated knowledge fails. Thus it is never common knowledge that θ is not in the unstable region.

One interpretation we may put on noisy information is that the recipients of the differential information learn of the true underlying fundamentals of the economy with little error, but that there are small discrepancies in how these messages are interpreted by the recipients. When looking for a cause or a trigger for a currency attack, we should look for the arrival of noisy information, i.e., news events that are not interpreted in exactly the same way by different speculators. The informational events that matter may be quite subtle. A "grain of doubt," allowing that others may believe that the economy is, in fact, unstable, will lead to a currency crises even if everyone knows that the economy is not unstable. In predicting when crises will occur, average opinion or even extreme opinion need not precipitate a crisis. Rather, what matters is the higher order beliefs of some participants who are apprehensive about the beliefs of others, concerning the beliefs of yet further individuals, on these extreme opinions. This interpretation may shed light on some accounts of recent currency crises. Rumors of political trouble in Chiapas Province were widely cited as a cause of the 1994 Mexico crisis

(*New York Times*, 1994); uncertainty about Maastricht, German unification, and Bundesbank pronouncements were argued to be important in the 1992 European Monetary System crises. Our analysis suggests that such "informational events" might precipitate a crisis even if no investor thought they conveyed real information about fundamentals themselves. It is enough that the announcements remove common knowledge that the fundamentals were sustainable.

Above all, our analysis suggests an important role for public announcements by the monetary authorities, and more generally, the transparency of the conduct of monetary policy and its dissemination to the public. If it is the case that the onset of currency crises may be precipitated by higher-order beliefs, even though participants believe that the fundamentals are sound, then the policy instruments which will stabilize the market are those which aim to restore transparency to the situation, in an attempt to restore common knowledge of the fundamentals. The most effective means towards this would be a prominent public announcement which is commonly known to convey information to all relevant participants. The canonical case of a communication arrangement which would be conducive to achieving common knowledge is the "town hall meeting" in which an announcement is made to an audience gathered in a single room, where everyone can observe that all other participants are in an identical position. In contrast, if the audience is fragmented, and must communicate in small groups, common knowledge is extremely difficult to achieve.[7] The Clinton administration's announcement of the $40 billion dollar rescue package for the Mexican peso can be seen as an attempt to restore the sort of transparency referred to above. Its effectiveness derived more from its very public nature, rather than the actual sum of money involved. This suggests a crucial role for the timely and effective dissemination of information on the part of policy makers, and the smooth functioning of a reliable and transparent set of communication channels between market participants and the policy makers, as well as between the market participants themselves.

B. *Changes in transaction costs*

We next examine shifts in t. Drawing on Theorem 2, which determines θ^* in the limit are ε becomes small, we can totally differentiate the equation $f(\theta^*) = e^* - 2t$ to obtain

$$\frac{d\theta^*}{dt} = -\frac{2}{f'(\theta^*)}.$$

Thus increasing transaction costs prevents currency crises, since it reduces the range of fundamentals where an attack occurs. The size of this effect depends

---

[7] Ariel Rubinstein's (1989) e-mail game is a case in point, and Michael S.-Y. Chwe (1996) has suggested some of the relevant factors which would allow us to address this issue in a more general context.

on the slope of f: when the f' is small, an increase in the cost of speculation has a large effect on the switching point θ^*. This suggests that the imposition of small transactions costs as advocated by several commentators will have a large impact on the prevalence of speculation precisely when the *consequences* of such speculative attacks are small. If speculative attacks are predicted to lead to drastic effects (i.e., when $f(\theta)$ is a steep function of θ), then the imposition of a small additional cost is unlikely to have a large effect on the incidence of currency attacks.

C. Changes in aggregate wealth

Now consider how our analysis is affected when aggregate wealth varies. The international flow of so-called "hot money" would be one factor in determining this aggregate wealth, as well as changes in the numbers of speculators themselves. The main effect of a change in aggregate wealth of the speculators is a change in the function $a(\theta)$, which indicates the critical proportion of speculators needed to attack the currency in order to induce the government to abandon the currency peg. When the aggregate wealth of the speculators increases, then this critical proportion of speculators falls, since the government's decision is based on the absolute *level* of short sales.

As can be seen from Figure 4, a downward shift in the $a(\theta)$ function has the effect of enlarging the set of states at which the government abandons the exchange rate peg. In other words the event $A(\pi) = \{\theta | s(\theta, \pi) > a(\theta)\}$ is strictly larger with a lower $a(\cdot)$ function. Since the payoff to speculation is given by

$$\int_{A(\pi) \cap [x-\varepsilon, x+\varepsilon]} (e^* - f(\theta))\, d\theta - t,$$

the enlargement of the event $A(\pi)$ has an unambiguous effect in increasing the payoff to attacking the currency at any value of the signal x. Thus, the benchmark value θ^* is shifted to the right, and the incidence of speculative attacks increases.

Note, however, from Figure 4 that the effect of an increase in the $a(\cdot)$ function depends on the size of the noise ε. The effect is largest when ε is also large. In the limiting case when ε tends to zero, the equilibrium $s(\theta, I_{x^*})$ becomes the step function I_{x^*}, so that a shift in the $a(\cdot)$ function has no effect on the switching point θ^*. Thus, our analysis suggests that changes in the aggregate wealth of speculators need not have a large impact on the incidence of currency attacks when the speculators have fairly precise information concerning the fundamentals. It is when the noise is large that shifts in wealth have a big impact.

This suggests that the imposition of direct capital controls work best when there is a lack of "transparency" of the economic fundamentals, in the sense that observers differ widely in their interpretation of the economic fundamentals. When the fundamentals are relatively transparent to all (corresponding to a small ε), direct capital controls seem far less effective. Under such circumstances, strategic considerations dominate any uncertainty concerning the fundamentals.

IV. Conclusion

Existing models of currency attacks that focus on fundamentals ignore the role of speculators' beliefs about other speculators' behavior. Existing self-fulfilling beliefs models of currency attacks assume that speculators *know* (in equilibrium) exactly what other speculators will do. Neither feature is realistic. Our model takes neither extreme. Because there is some uncertainty about equilibrium, speculators are uncertain as to exactly what other speculators will do; but their behavior depends nontrivially on what they believe they will do. Because our model of self-fulfilling currency attacks is consistent with unique equilibrium, we are able to analyze the impact of alternative policies.

APPENDIX

Proof of Lemma 2. Consider the function $s(\theta, I_k)$, which gives the proportion of speculators who attack the currency at θ when the aggregate short sales is given by the step function I_k. Since x is uniformly distributed over $[\theta - \varepsilon, \theta + \varepsilon]$, we have

$$s(\theta, I_k) = \begin{cases} 1 & \text{if } \theta \leq k - \varepsilon \\ \frac{1}{2} - \frac{1}{2\varepsilon}(\theta - k) & \text{if } k - \varepsilon \leq \theta \leq k + \varepsilon \\ 0 & \text{if } \theta \geq k + \varepsilon. \end{cases} \tag{A1}$$

If aggregate short sales are given by I_k, there is a unique θ (which depends on k) where the mass of speculators attacking equals the mass of speculators necessary to cause the government to abandon the exchange rate [where $s(\theta, I_k) = a(\theta)$]. Write $\psi(k)$ for the amount that θ must exceed k in order for this to be true. In other words, $\psi(k)$ is the unique value of ψ solving $s(k + \psi, I_k) = a(k + \psi)$. Observe that $\psi(k) = \varepsilon$ if $k \leq \underline{\theta} - \varepsilon$, while if $k > \underline{\theta} - \varepsilon$, then $-\varepsilon < \psi(k) < \varepsilon$ and is the value of ψ solving $(1/2 - \psi/2\varepsilon) = a(k + \psi)$.

Since the government abandons the currency peg if and only if θ lies in the interval $[0, k + \psi(k)]$, the payoff function $u(k, I_k)$ is given by

$$\frac{1}{2\varepsilon} \int_{k-\varepsilon}^{k+\psi(k)} (e^* - f(\theta)) \, d\theta - t. \tag{A2}$$

Since $e^* - f(\theta)$ is strictly decreasing in θ, if we can show that $\psi(k)$ is weakly decreasing in k, this will be sufficient to show that $u(k, I_k)$ is strictly decreasing in k. To see that $\psi(k)$ is weakly decreasing in k, totally differentiate the equation

$(1/2-\psi/2\varepsilon) = a(k+\psi)$ with respect to k, to obtain $-(1/2\varepsilon)\psi'(k) = a'(\theta)(1+\psi'(k))$. Hence,

$$\psi'(k) = -\frac{a'(\theta)}{a'(\theta) + (1/2\varepsilon)} \leq 0,$$

which is sufficient for $u(k, I_k)$ to be strictly decreasing in k. Finally, the continuity of $u(k, I_k)$ follows immediately from the fact that it is an integral in which the limits of integration are themselves continuous in k. This completes the proof of Lemma 2.

Proof of Theorem 2. Consider the switching point x^*, which is the solution to the equation $u(x^*, I_{x^*}) = 0$. Then, writing $F(\varepsilon) = \int_{A(I_{x^*}) \cap [x^*-\varepsilon, x^*+\varepsilon]} (e^* - f(\theta)) \, d\theta$, we can express this equation as $(F(\varepsilon)/2\varepsilon) - t = 0$. By using L'Hôpital's rule,

$$\lim_{\varepsilon \to 0} \frac{F(\varepsilon)}{2\varepsilon} = \frac{F'(0)}{2} = \frac{e^* - f(x^*)}{2}. \tag{A3}$$

Thus, in the limit as $\varepsilon \to 0$, equation (A3) yields $f(x^*) = e^* - 2t$. Finally, we note that x^* converges to θ^* when ε tends to zero, since in the limit, $s(\theta, I_{x^*}) = I_{x^*}$.

Authors' Note

There is a mistake in the limiting result of Theorem 2: this is discussed in Heinemann (2000) and in section 2.3 of Morris and Shin (2002). Morris and Shin (2002) also review more recent work using similar methods, describe a general methodology (with weaker assumptions) for the class of continuum player "global game" models in this paper, and discuss the theoretical background for this work.

References

Calvo, Guillermo A. (1988). "Servicing the public debt: The role of expectations." *American Economic Review*, 78(4): 647–61.

Carrison, H., and van Damme, E. E. (1993). "Global games and equilibrium selection." *Econometrica*, 61(5): 989–1018.

Chwe, M. S.-Y. (1996). "Structure and strategy in collective action: Communication and co-ordination in social networks." Mimeo, University of Chicago.

Cole, Harold L., and Kehoe, T. J. (1996). "Self-fulfilling debt crises." Federal Reserve Bank of Minneapolis Research Department Staff Report No. 211.

Dornbusch, R., and Werner, A. M. (1994). "Mexico: Stabilization, Reform and No Growth." *Brookings Papers on Economic Activity*, 253–315.

Eaton, J., and Fernandez, R. (1995). "Sovereign debt," in G. M. Grossman and K. Rogoff (eds.), *Handbook of International Economics*, Vol. III (Amsterdam: North-Holland), 2031–71.

Eichengreen, B., Tobin, J., and Wyplosz, C. (1995). "Two cases for sand in the wheels of international finance." *Economic Journal*, 105(428): 162–72.

——, and Wyplosz, C. (1993). "The unstable EMS." *Brookings Papers on Economic Activity*, 51–143.

Flood, R. P., and Garber, P. M. (1984). "Gold monetization and gold discipline." *Journal of Political Economy*, 92(1): 90–107.

Heinemann, F. (2000). "Unique equilibrium in a model of self-fulfilling currency attacks: A comment." *American Economic Review*, 90: 316–18.

Morris, S., Rob, R., and Shin, H. S. (1995). "*p*-Dominance and belief potential," *Econometrica*, 63(1): 145–57.

——, and Shin, H. S. "Global games, theory and applications," in Mathias Dewatripont, Lars Peter Hansen, and Stephen J. Turnovsky (eds.), *Advances in Economics and Econometrics: Theory and Applications*, Eighth World Congress, Cambridge: Cambridge Univ. Press (forthcoming 2002).

The New York Times. (1994). December 20–23, various articles.

Obstfeld, M. (1986). "Rational and self-fulfilling balance-of-payments crises." *American Economic Review*, 76(1): 72–81.

——(1994). "The logic of currency crises." *Cahiers Economiques et Monetaires (Banque de France)*, 43: 189–213.

——(1996). "Models of currency crises with self-fulfilling features." *European Economic Review*, 40(3–5): 1037–47.

Postlewaite, A., and Vives, X. (1987). "Bank runs as an equilibrium phenomenon." *Journal of Political Economy*, 95(3): 485–91.

Rubinstein, A. (1989). "The electronic mail game: Strategic behavior under 'almost common knowledge'." *American Economic Review*, 79(3): 385–91.

11

Contagion and Efficiency in Gross and Net Interbank Payment Systems

Xavier Freixas and Bruno Parigi

1. Introduction

The impressive growth in the value of daily interbank payments[1] has raised concerns about the potential systemic risk induced by contagion. This effect, also known as the domino effect, occurs if the failure of a large financial institution to settle payment obligations triggers a chain reaction that threatens the stability of the financial system. (See, among others, Brimmer (1989).) The two main types of large-value interbank payment systems, "net" and "gross," differ sharply in their exposure to contagion risk. In the former, netting the positions of the different banks through compensation of their claims only at the end of the day implies intraday credit from one bank to another, and exposes banks to contagion.[2] In the latter, transactions are typically settled irrevocably on a one-to-one basis in central bank money, so that banks have to hold large reserve balances in order to execute their payment orders.

We thank Jane Marrinan, Marco Pagano, Jean-Charles Rochet, Anthony Santomero, Jean Tirole, Ernest Ludwig von Thadden, and audiences at the University of Venice. Cattolica Milano, I.G.I.E.R. Bocconi, I.D.E.I. Toulouse, the E.E.A. meeting in Istanbul, the V Financial Conference at the University of Rome Tor Vergata, the Regulatory Incentives Conference at the Bank of England, and the European Finance Association meeting in Vienna for useful comments. Financial support from I.D.E.I. and I.N.R.A. at the University of Toulouse, DGICYT Grant PB93–0388 at Universitat Pompeu Fabra, and Consiglio Nazionale delle Ricerche Grant 97.01390. CT10 at the University of Venice is acknowledged. The usual disclaimers apply.

[1] The average daily transactions on the U.S. payment systems C.H.I.P.S. and FEDWIRE have grown from $148 and $192 billion, respectively, in 1980 to $885 and $796 billion in 1990. (See Rochet and Tirole (1996b).)

[2] Average payments made by large banks can be tenfold the capital of smaller banks in the netting process. Because of this difference in size the failure of a single large participant, even if its own net credit position does not threaten the settlement system, could lead small banks to have settlement obligations greater than the amount of their capital. See the simulations by Humphrey (1986). Similar simulations by Angelini *et al.* (1996) for the Italian system yield a much smaller impact of systemic risk.

Technological improvements in data transmission have substantially lowered the transaction cost of settling in gross payment systems, but netting still significantly economizes on the liquidity that banks have to transfer. Thus an important question is: how do gross and net interbank payment systems compare from a cost–benefit standpoint? In particular, how do the characteristics of these systems compare under different environments? Our objective in this paper is to address these questions.

A number of factors must be taken into account when the trade-offs between alternative settlement mechanisms are evaluated: collateral needs, use of information about bank solvability, and above all liquidity needs and contagion risk.[3] Our aim is to address what happens when we derive the liquidity costs and the contagion costs endogenously from the liquidation of long-term projects.

To tackle these issues we construct a general equilibrium model based on Diamond and Dybvig (1983) (D–D). Unlike D–D, where consumers' uncertainty arises only from the time of consumption, in our model consumers are also uncertain about the location of their consumption. Consumers' geographic mobility generates payment needs across space. Financial intermediaries mediaries are justified on two accounts: their insurance role, as in D–D, and their role in transferring property rights, as in Fama (1980). Payments across locations can be made by transferring either liquid assets (gross system) or claims against the intermediary in the location of destination (net system). The choice of a net or gross payment system affects equilibrium consumption, and we can compare the two systems by measuring ex ante expected utility.

A key assumption in our analysis is that investment returns are uncertain and some depositors have better information on returns. If investment returns were certain, there would be only speculative bank runs, as in D–D. In this case, which we examine only as a benchmark, we show that netting dominates. But in a setting with asymmetric information and uncertain returns, information-based (or fundamental) runs can occur, as in Chari and Jagannathan (1988) and Jacklin and Bhattacharya (1988). In this richer and more realistic setting, the issue of the trade-off between gross and net systems arises.[4]

A first contribution of this paper is to identify the equilibria under gross and net systems. Since under the gross system banks are not linked to each other, the equilibria simply correspond to those of isolated islands. Under netting, on the other hand, since banks are linked through intraday credits, the failure of one bank may affect the payoff of depositors in another. This feature of netting generates two equilibria, both inefficient. In the first there are no bank runs; banks net their claims, and are therefore exposed to contagion. We call this the *potential contagion equilibrium*. Because with netting each bank has claims on

---

[3] See, e.g., Rochet and Tirole (1996b).

[4] Using data from the national banking era (1863–1914). Gorton (1988) shows that the majority of bank panics were in fact information-based.

the assets of the other banks, when one goes bankrupt others are affected. In the second equilibrium, consumers rationally anticipate the potential effect of contagion on future consumption and optimally decide to run on their bank. We call this the *contagion-triggered bank run equilibrium*.

The main contribution of the chapter is the analysis of the trade-off between gross and net systems. Our results are consistent with the intuition that a gross system is not exposed to contagion but makes intensive use of liquidity, while a net system economizes on liquidity but exposes banks to contagion. We show when, depending on the values of model parameters, a particular system is preferred. A gross payment system is preferred if the probability of banks having a low return is high, if the opportunity cost of holding reserves is low, and if the proportion of consumers that have to consume in another location is low. Otherwise a net system dominates.

There is an incipient literature on payment systems which helped us derive our modeling framework. McAndrews and Roberds (1995) model bank payment risk using the D–D framework of speculative runs. They focus on the banks' demand for reserve provisions and consider a multilateral net settlement system where claims on a bank are valid only if reserves are transferred to the recipient bank. Kahn and Roberds (1996a) analyze a gross settlement system where adverse selection gives rise to the Akerlof effect because banks with above average assets prefer cash settlements to debt settlements. Using an inventory-theoretic framework to model the trade-off between safety and efficiency, Kahn and Roberds (1996b) find that netting economizes on reserves but increases moral hazard because it gives the banks additional incentives to default. Rochet and Tirole (1996a) model interbank lending to address the issue of contagion and the "too–big–to–fail" policy.

The chapter is organized as follows. Section 2 reviews the main institutional aspects of the payment systems. Section 3 sets up a benchmark model of the payment system without investment return uncertainty. In Sections 4 and 5, which are the core of our analysis, we introduce private information on future uncertain returns and compare the equilibria under the different mechanisms. Section 6 discusses some policy implications. Section 7 suggests extensions. Section 8 concludes.

2. Institutional Aspects of the Interbank Payment System

Time dimension of settlement

The organization of interbank payment systems revolves around the time dimension of the final settlement of transactions. It is convenient to begin our discussion by introducing two stylized alternative mechanisms, gross and net, both with settlement in central bank money. The risk and liquidity characteristics of the two mechanisms are the object of our analysis.

The gross mechanism achieves immediate finality of payment at the cost of intensive use of central bank money. Bilateral and multilateral netting economize on the use of central bank money, essentially by substituting explicit or implicit interbank intraday credit for central bank money. A difference between a net settlement system and an interbank money market is that risk is priced in an interbank market and rationing of a particular bank may occur, triggered by bad news on its solvency. This does not happen under netting, where implicit credit lines are automatically granted.

The very fact that netting economizes on central bank money allows a participant both to accumulate large debt positions during the day, perhaps exceeding its balances in central bank money, and to accumulate claims on other banks that may exceed its own capital. In fact, if no incoming payment decreases a bank's exposure, the interbank market will usually provide the necessary central bank money. A *settlement risk* arises when a participant has insufficient funds to settle its obligations when they are due. In this case different procedures are followed in the various systems, ranging from deleting the orders with insufficient funds and recalculating the balances (unwinding), to queuing them.[5] As a result of settlement risk, netting also increases *systemic risk*, because of the possible contagion effects. Contagion is possible when unwinding of orders takes place, because participants that had been net creditors of the failed institution may have sent order payments on the basis of the expected funds that are not forthcoming.[6]

Settlement risk also arises when commercial bank money is used to settle, as the finality of the transaction is then delayed by definition.

Before the widespread diffusion of telematic technology, the systems most often encountered were gross mechanisms settled in commercial bank money and net mechanisms settled in central bank money. Due to its high liquidity cost, gross settlement in central bank money was practically never used (Padoa-Schioppa (1992)). The advent of telematics has made possible another mechanism, namely real-time gross settlement in central bank money. The innovation stems from the real-time feature, which dramatically increases the velocity of circulation of deposits at the central bank and thus reduces the opportunity cost of using central bank money. The net systems have also been influenced by telematics as recent technological developments that increase the amount that can be netted per unit of reserve increase both settlement and systemic risk. To this it must be added that multilateral netting is subject to moral hazard since

---

[5] In the Swiss system, when there are insufficient funds in the originator's account, orders are queued until sufficient funds have accumulated in that account and may be canceled at any time by the originator. Orders still in queue at a prespecified time are cancelled automatically.

[6] For a detailed analysis of systemic risk see Van den Berg and Veale (1993) and for estimates of the consequences of unwinding see Humphrey (1986) and Angelini and Giannini (1994).

banks perceive that the central bank will prevent systemic collapses. In balance, telematics has altered the trade-off between cost and risk, making real-time gross settlement systems relatively cheaper. In fact, its use is now encouraged by several central banks.

Models of interbank payment systems

The large-value interbank payment systems currently operational can be grouped into three general models (Horii and Summers (1993)): (i) Gross settlement operated by central bank with explicit intraday credit (e.g., FEDWIRE); (ii) Gross settlement operated by central bank without intraday credit (e.g., Swiss Interbank Clearing System (S.I.C.)); (iii) Deferred net multilateral settlement (e.g., Bank of Japan Network, B.O.J.; and Clearing House Interbank Payment System, C.H.I.P.S). See Table 1 for a synthesis of the main features of payment systems.

Table 1. Main Payment Systems, 1992

	USA		Japan	Switzerland
	FEDWIRE	C.H.I.P.S.	B.O.J.-NET	S.I.C.
Starting year	1918	1971	1988	1987
Gross vs net settlement	Gross	Net	Net[a]	Gross
Privately vs publicly managed	Public: FED	Private: NYCHA	Public: Bank of Japan	Public: Swiss national bank
Intraday central bank credit	Yes	No	No	No
Payment volume per year in million	68	40		64
Payment value per year in trillion $	199	240		50
Average payment in million $	3	6.1	33.4[b]	0.4
Daily payment value in billion $	797	942	1,198	93
Number of participants	11,453 banks	20 settling banks 119 nonsettling banks	461 banks, securities firms, and brokers	163 banks
Procedures in case of failure to settle	If overdraft exceeds cap transaction is rejected or queued	Loss shared among participants; settlement is guaranteed	Ordering bank borrows from central bank	Order queued

[a] BOJ-NET offers also a gross settlement system.

[b] Only for the Clearing component.

Source: Summers (1994).

In the FEDWIRE model, the central bank settles orders payment-by-payment and irrevocably. Insufficient funds in the ordering bank's accounts result in an extension of explicit intraday credit from the central bank. Credit is provided with the expectation that funds will be deposited in the account before the end of the business day. Meanwhile the central bank bears the settlement risk.

The S.I.C. model is a no-overdraft system in which payment orders are processed on a first-in first-out principle as long as they are fully funded from accounts at the Central Bank. It thus implies real-time computing facilities to execute payments, to prevent the use of intraday credit, and to handle orders with insufficient funds.

In the C.H.I.P.S. model, at designated times during the day payments are multi-laterally netted, resulting in one net obligation for each debtor due at settlement time. Implicit intraday credit is extended by the participants, not by the operator of the system, which may be either a private clearinghouse or the central bank. Limits are set for intraday credits, both in this and in the FEDWIRE model. Loss-sharing arrangements govern the distribution of losses from settling failures among the members. Regardless of who operates the system, deferred obligations are finally settled in accounts at the central bank.

In what follows, we will mainly focus on gross vs. net payment systems.[7]

3. Setup of the Model

Basic model

We consider two identical island-economies, $J = A, B$, with D–D features. Consumers, whose total measure is 1 at each island, are located at A or at B. There is one good and there are three periods: 0, 1, 2. The good can be either stored at no cost from one period to the next or invested. In each island there is a risk-neutral perfectly competitive bank (which can be interpreted as a mutual bank) with access to the investment technology. Each consumer is endowed with 1 unit of the good at time 0. Consumers cannot invest directly but can deposit their endowment in the bank in their island which stores it or invests it for their future consumption. The investment of 1 unit at time 0 returns R at time 2, with $R > 1$, if not liquidated at time 1. If a fraction α of the investment is liquidated at time 1, the return is α at time 1 and $(1 - \alpha)R$ at time 2.

The bank offers depositors a contract that allows them to choose when to withdraw.[8] To finance withdrawals at time 1 the bank liquidates L units so that it receives $R(1 - L)$ at time 2.

---

[7] Since we take a general equilibrium standpoint, the case where central bankers bear the risk (as in FEDWIRE) is left out because it means that the central bank has to levy taxes to fund its rescue operation. Hence, up to a redistribution, we are facing the same issues as in a netting payment system.

[8] As is usual in this literature, deposits cannot be traded at time 1.

As in D–D, consumers are of two types, early diers and late diers. A fraction t die in the first period and $(1 - t)$ die in the second period. However, we modify the D–D model by introducing the additional complexity that late diers face uncertainty at time 1 as to the island in which they will be able to consume at time 2. A fraction $(1 - \lambda)$ of the late diers (the *compulsive travelers*) can consume only in the other island. The remaining fraction λ (the *strategic travelers*) can consume in either island interchangeably. Nature determines at time 1 which consumers are early diers and which of the late diers are compulsive travelers or strategic travelers. This information is revealed privately to consumers.

To analyze how individuals can consume at time 2 in the other island we introduce two payment mechanisms: gross and net.[9]

In a gross mechanism, to satisfy the travelers' demand for the good at time 1 the banks liquidate a fraction of the investment. Then the travelers transfer the good costlessly from A to B or vice versa. The implicit cost of transferring the good across space is the foregone investment return. Since liquidation occurs before the arrival of incoming travelers, their deposits cannot be used to replace those of the departing travelers. In our model a gross system does not allow trade among banks.

The attempt to replace the deposits of the departing travelers with those of the incoming travelers is the rationale behind a netting system. In a netting system, banks are linked by a contract. Under the terms of this contract, member banks extend credit lines to each other to finance the future consumption of the travelers without having to make the corresponding liquidation of investment. The claims on the banks' assets arising from these credit lines are accepted by all banks in the system. Thus in a net mechanism, the late diers, besides liquidating the investment and transferring the good across islands by themselves, have the additional possibility of having their claims to future consumption directly transferred to the bank in the other island. At time 2 the banks compensate their claims and transfer the corresponding amount of the good across space. The technology to transfer the good at time 2 is available for trades only between banks. Under certainty about investment returns, the claims just offset each other and in a netting system no liquidation takes place to satisfy the travelers' consumption needs.

To summarize, early diers withdraw and consume at time 1. Compulsive travelers consume at time 2 but, under netting, also have the choice between withdrawing early and transferring the good themselves to the other island or transferring their bank accounts to the other island. Strategic travelers have the same options as the compulsive travelers along with the additional possibility

---

[9] To be consistent with Section 2, in terms of the previous classification of interbank payment systems, models (i) as FEDWIRE and (iii) as B.O.J. are "net" because there is no need to liquidate the investment, while (ii) as S.I.C. is "gross."

to have their account untouched and to consume at time 2 at their own island.

Consumers have utility functions

$$
\begin{aligned}
U(C_1, C_2, \hat{C}_2) = & U(C_1) & & \text{with probability } t \\
& U(\hat{C}_2) & & \text{with probability } (1-t)(1-\lambda) \\
& U(C_2 + \hat{C}_2) & & \text{with probability } (1-t)\lambda \text{ with } C_2 \cdot \hat{C}_2 = 0,
\end{aligned}
$$

where C_2 denotes consumption at time 2 in the home island and $\hat{C}_2$ denotes consumption at time 2 at the other island, U is a state-dependent utility function such that $U' > 0, U'' < 0, U'(0) = +\infty$ and with a relative risk aversion coefficient greater than or equal to one.[10] The condition $C_2 \cdot \hat{C}_2 = 0$ forbids consumption in both islands.

The structure of the economy and the agents' ex ante utility functions are common knowledge.

Strategies

Denote by Ψ the set of late diers' types; i.e., $\Psi = \{ST, CT\}$, where ST stands for strategic traveler, and CT for compulsive traveler. In any given candidate equilibrium, the deposit contract offers a consumption profile at time 1 and time 2 which is a function of the actions of the depositors in both islands (Run, Travel, or Wait). Early diers withdraw at time 1 and do not act strategically. Late diers behave strategically, playing a simultaneous game at time 1. We now introduce some notation we use for the rest of the chapter. The strategic travelers' set of actions is $S = \{W, T, R\}$, where W stands for waiting and withdrawing at time 2, T for traveling and having your claims transferred to the other island, and R for running, that is, withdrawing at time 1 and storing the good if necessary. The compulsive travelers' set of actions is $S' = \{T, R\}$. Since $S' \subset S$, whenever the strategic travelers choose an action in S', the compulsive travelers will do the same. A strategy S_ψ is an element of the set of functions from Ψ into S for the strategic travelers, and into S' for the compulsive travelers.

It is worth pointing out a difference in the interpretation of the time horizon between our model and that of D–D. In our model, the three periods of the D–D timing all take place within 24 h, when all transactions are executed. The costs associated with the liquidation of the investment can be interpreted as the interest differential between reserves and interest-bearing money market instruments.

As a benchmark, we now compare net and gross payment systems.

[10] We will drop the superscript "^" whenever this does not create ambiguity.

PROPOSITION 1. *Under certainty about investment returns,*

   (i) *gross and net settlement systems yield the same allocations as two D–D economies with different fractions of early diers, $t + (1 - t)(1 - \lambda)$ for the former, and t for the latter;*

   (ii) *net settlement dominates gross settlement.*

Proof. Point (i) is obvious from the above discussion. As for (ii), the fact that in a D–D economy the expected welfare decreases with the proportion of early diers is proved in the Appendix, although it is quite intuitive.   ■

Since in a gross system, more consumers withdraw at time 1, a higher proportion of the investment is liquidated than under netting. Since the investment returns more than 1, a netting system dominates a gross system. As liquidation is costless, a higher proportion of liquidation is equivalent to a higher proportion of reserves in the banks' portfolio. Proposition 1 is tantamount to saying that with certain investment returns, in a gross system banks would have to hold more reserves.

The intuition for our result is similar to that of the related papers by Bhattacharya and Gale (1987) and by Bhattacharya and Fulghieri (1994). Both papers study modified versions of D–D economies. Bhattacharya and Gale consider several banks with i.i.d. liquidity shocks in the sense that their proportion of early diers is random. Bhattacharya and Fulghieri consider banks with i.i.d. shocks in the timing of the realized returns of the short term technology. A common theme of both papers is that if the shocks are observable and contractible, in the aggregate, liquidity shocks and timing uncertainty are completely diversifiable. Thus an interbank market (which in our model can be interpreted as a netting system) can improve upon the allocation with no trade between banks (in our model a gross system). The additional location risk we introduce with respect to D–D is also fully diversifiable. If it was not, the optimal allocation would be contingent on the aggregate risks, as Hellwig (1994) has shown for interest rate risk.

4. Stochastic Returns and Informed Depositors

The preceding analysis offers a benchmark to compare gross and net settlement systems. We now extend the basic setup to introduce contagion risk.

The investment return $\tilde{R}$ at time 2 is random, $\tilde{R} \in \{R_L, R_H\}$, where L and H stand for low and high respectively, p_L denotes the probability of the low return (which we assume is "sufficiently" low in a sense to be defined precisely later), and $R_L < 1 < R_H, E\tilde{R} = p_L R_L + p_H R_H > 1$. At time 1 the late diers in each island privately observe a signal $y_K \in Y = \{y_L, y_H\}, K = L, H$, uncorrelated across islands, which fully reveals $\tilde{R}$. Ex ante the two banks offer the same contract.

Strategies

With stochastic returns, late diers choose their actions as functions of the signal in both islands. A strategy $s_\psi(y_K)$ is an element of the set of functions from $\Psi \times Y$ into S for the ST, and into S' for the CT.

A strategy profile is a set of strategies for each type of late dier and for each signal-island pair. For example, in the strategy profile $[(W_{ST}(y_H), T_{CT}(y_H))$ $(T_{ST}(y_L), T_{CT}(y_L))]$ (which we will denote simply $[(W, T), (T, T)]$ whenever this is unambiguous), if the high signal is observed, the strategic travelers wait and withdraw at time 2 and the compulsive travelers travel: (W, T). If the low signal is observed, all late diers travel: (T, T).

Notice that with interim information, withdrawal at time 1 by late diers might be socially optimal (as in the model of information-based runs of Jacklin and Bhattacharya (1988) or Chari and Jagannathan (1988)), while it was never so in the deterministic case. Hence, runs have a disciplinary role because they trigger the closure of inefficient banks.[11]

For a given settlement system we can summarize the timing as follows. At time 0 a deposit contract is offered by the banks to consumers in the same island and the banks invest. At time 1 time preference shocks occur and are privately revealed to depositors; the realization of the investment return on each island is revealed to its residents; the late diers in the two islands then play a *simultaneous game* acting on the basis of this information; in each island the bank liquidates a fraction of the investment to reimburse the depositors withdrawing at time 1. At time 2 the investment matures and the proceeds are distributed according to the contracts.

Gross settlement

In a gross system the banks are isolated, and thus contagion is absent. Hence, except for the bank run equilibrium in a high-signal bank, all outcomes are efficient. That is, investment in the low-signal bank is liquidated and investment in the high-signal bank is allowed to mature, so that the efficient decision regarding bank closure is always taken.

Net settlement

An analysis of the net settlement is more complex and requires several additional assumptions that make explicit how claims are settled in case of bankruptcy.

---

[11] One criticism made to models of this type is to question why managers acting on behalf of their depositors would keep the bank operating when it is worth more dead than alive. In our model the answer relies on the fact that bad banks have an incentive to stay in business to free ride on the assets of the good ones through the payment system.

A bankruptcy occurs when a bank is not able to fulfill its time 1 or time 2 obligations from the deposit contract. We will use two simplifying rules.

Bankruptcy Rule 1.   This rule defines the assets to be divided among claim holders. Claim holders have a right to all the banks asset's, including those brought by incoming travelers at time 2. Under this rule a bankrupt bank at time 1 stays in business simply to receive assets brought by the incoming travelers at time 2 and to pay the late diers.

Bankruptcy Rule 2.   This rule, which defines how to divide the assets among the claim holders, establishes the equal treatment of claim holders (no seniority or discrimination of any kind).

Bankruptcy at time 2 is solved by dividing the assets at time 2 using Rule 2. However, bankruptcy at time 1 is far more involved. We have to determine how to treat agents that pretend to be early diers. Under Bankruptcy Rule 1, late diers are allowed to postpone their consumption and benefit from the high-return assets the incoming travelers might bring with them. But a low return at time 2 for the other bank will diminish the payments the incoming travelers bring. The above rules capture the notion that banks participating in a netting scheme agree to honor the other members' liabilities arising from automatic intraday credit lines due to netting.[12]

Equilibrium analysis

A strategy profile is an equilibrium if there is no unilateral incentive to deviate. We characterize the equilibria in a net system in the following proposition.

PROPOSITION 2. *Under netting there are two equilibria.*

Equilibrium 1. [(W, T), (T, T)] occurs if and only if the equilibrium expected pay-off for a strategic traveler in the low-signal bank exceeds that from running, i.e., if and only if $p_H U(C_A) + p_L U(C_L) > U(C_1)$, where C_1 denotes first period consumption,

$$C_L \equiv \frac{(1 - tC_1)R_L}{1 - t}$$

denotes second period consumption when both banks experience the low signal and

$$C_A = \frac{(1 - tC_1)(R_H(2 - \lambda) + R_L)}{(1 - t)(3 - \lambda)}$$

denotes second period consumption in the high-signal island when the other island experiences the low signal.

Equilibrium 2. ([(R, R), (R, R)]). Regardless of the signal observed, it is optimal for all late diers to run.

---

[12] A similar loss-sharing rule is adopted in C.H.I.P.S. when a participant fails to settle its obligations.

Furthermore there are two efficient outcomes, [(W, T), (R, R)] and [(T, T), (R, R)], which cannot be supported as equilibria.

For sufficiently low values of p_L equilibrium 1 dominates equilibrium 2.

Proof. See Appendix.

Proposition 2 is the central proposition of this paper. Both equilibria exhibit contagion, in the sense that the signal received in one island affects the behavior and hence the consumption of depositors in the other. In the first equilibrium contagion arises when the two islands receive different signals.[13] Payoffs to the depositors are an average of the two banks' returns, so that the bank with a high return pays its depositors less than it would in isolation. This is analogous to the domino effect whereby the low return of a bankrupt bank lowers the return of an otherwise solvent bank (potential contagion equilibrium).

The inefficiency stems from a loss of the disciplinary role of bank runs under net settlement. Depositors in the low-signal bank expect to free ride on the other bank. Hence, when the low signal is observed, all late diers travel instead of running. When both banks receive a low signal, both keep operating. The reason banks are not liquidated when both islands observe a low signal, is that each late dier, ignoring the signal of the other island, prefers the expected utility from traveling to a high- (low-) signal bank with probability $p_H(p_L)$ to the certain utility from withdrawing.

There are two ways in which contagion may trigger bank runs in equilibrium 2. First, for some parameter values equilibrium 1 fails to exist. The potential free riding of the late diers in the low-signal island destroys equilibrium 1 and makes it optimal to run in the high-signal island. In this case runs occur in both islands. The run that occurs in the high-signal island is induced by the mere fear of what can happen at the settlement stage. Second, even for the parameter values for which equilibrium 1 exists, given a speculative run in the high-signal island, it is optimal to run in the low-signal island as well. Notice that no similar argument applies under a gross system.

In what follows we will mainly focus on equilibrium 1, assuming that p_L is sufficiently low so that equilibrium 1 is preferred.

The effect of different bank sizes

Proposition 2 allows us to compare payment systems when banks have the same size. Still, it is interesting to have some insight on the type of equilibrium we obtain when banks have different sizes. This can be captured assuming a different depositors' measure in the islands, with the ratio between the two sizes

---

[13] Notice that this is the outcome of an insurance mechanism and not a swap of agents' spending patterns.

going to infinity in the limit. The strategy space is now more complex because the strategies are conditioned not only on the signal, but also on the size. Still the analysis of the limit case is straightforward and revealing. The outcome is determined by the signal the large bank receives. The analog of equilibrium 1 in the asymmetric bank case in the limit is given by the following strategies: for the large bank [(W, T), (R, R)] and for the small bank [(W, T), (T, T)]. The intuition for this is that in the limit case the consumption levels in case of different signals in the two islands are equal to the consumption level in the large bank, which is either C_H or 1 depending on the signal there. Hence, the signal observed by the late diers in the small island have a negligible effect on their consumption. Under the maintained assumptions what they obtain in equilibrium, $p_H U(C_H)+p_L U(1)$, exceeds what they obtain by withdrawing, which is $U(C_1)$. This justifies the strategy of the small bank compulsive travelers regardless of their signal and the strategy of the strategic travelers in the low signal bank. As for the strategic travelers receiving a high signal in a small bank, by waiting they obtain C_H with certainty against C_H with probability p_H and 1 with probability p_L.

For the large bank, the effect of the small bank is negligible. Therefore, the outcome is similar to what would occur with only one bank in the system. When the low signal is received, running is optimal because there is no possibility to free ride on the other bank's high return. When the high signal is received, it is optimal not to withdraw, because $U(C_H)$ is obtained.[14]

5. The Trade-off Between Gross and Net Payment Systems

The previous results demonstrate that the benefits from netting stem both from the possibility to invest more and from allowing the travelers to share the high expected return of time 2. Its cost stems from the continued operation of inefficient banks, those that receive a low signal. It is therefore possible to analyze the trade off between gross and net payment systems in terms of their allocative efficiency and study how this trade off is altered when the characteristics of the economy change.

[14] Between the symmetric case of Proposition 2 and the zero/infinite size case we consider, the equilibrium may be far more involved because pure strategy equilibria may fail to exist. To understand this, consider a sufficiently large bank for which it is no longer optimal to play the strategy of equilibrium 1, [(W, T), (T, T)], because in case of low signal the return would be too low. The alternative equilibrium in the limit case, [(W, T), (R, R)], is not a Nash equilibrium either. Once all depositors of the large bank observing a low signal are running, a zero measure of depositors of the large bank observing the low signal will prefer to travel thus obtaining $p_H U(C_H) + p_L U(1)$, which is superior to the bank run outcome, $U(1)$. As a consequence, the equilibrium is characterized by mixed strategies on behalf of large banks' depositors facing a low signal. A proportion of these depositors will travel thus lowering the return from traveling until we obtain $C_A = 1$, which is the indifferent point.

Let the superscripts G and N denote gross and net, respectively. Since with gross settlement there is no contagion or wealth transfers between banks, expected utility is

$$EU^G(\cdot) = p_H \left\{ [t + (1-t)(1-\lambda)]U(C_1^G) \right.$$

$$\left. + (1-t)\lambda U\left(\frac{1 - C_1^G[t + (1-t)(1-\lambda)]}{(1-t)\lambda} R_H \right) \right\} + p_L U(1),$$

where C_1^G is the optimal ex ante time 1 consumption under gross. With net settlement expected utility is

$$EU^N(\cdot) = tU\left(C_1^{II} \right) + (1-t)\left\{ p_H^2 U\left(C_H^{II} \right)] + p_H p_L[U(C_A) + U(C_B)] \right.$$

$$\left. + p_L^2 U\left(C_L^{II} \right) \right\}$$

where C_1^{II} is the optimal ex ante time 1 consumption under netting, C_H^{II} and C_L^{II} are the values of consumption when both banks receive a high or low signal, respectively, and C_A and C_B are, respectively, the values of consumption at islands A and B when the bank at A experienced a high signal and that at B a low signal.

To compare gross and net settlement systems we construct the difference in their expected utility, $\Delta \equiv EU^G(\cdot) - EU^N(\cdot)$. We establish the following results.

PROPOSITION 3. *A gross settlement system is preferred ($\Delta > 0$) when there is (i) a high expected cost of keeping an inefficient bank open (low R_L), (ii) a small fraction of compulsive travelers (low $1 - \lambda$), (iii) a low probability that the state of nature is high (low p_H).*

Proof. See Appendix.

We now illustrate these trade-offs for the particular case of logarithmic utility. In this case, it is easily proved that the optimal contract for an isolated bank is $C_1^* = 1, C_2^* = \tilde{R}_K, K = L, H$, and therefore speculative bank runs never occur. [15] With gross settlement, expected utility is

$$EU^G(\cdot) = (1-t)\lambda p_H \ln(R_H).$$

---

[15] The fact that $C_1^* = 1$ (contrary to the D–D model, where there is no role for intermediation when $C_1^* = 1$) does not constitute a limitation of our analysis since we focus on information-based bank runs rather than speculative bank runs as in D–D.

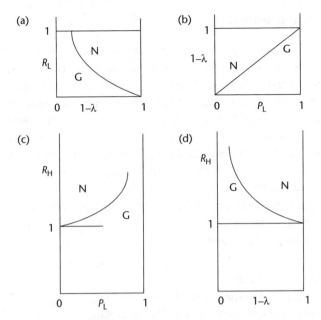

Figure 1. Main tradeoffs between gross and net payment systems.
G: gross settlement is preferred: N: net settlement is preferred.

With net settlement expected utility is

$$EU^N(\cdot) = (1-t)\left\{p_H^2\ln(R_H) + p_H p_L[\ln(C_A) + \ln(C_B)] + p_L^2\ln(R_L)\right\}$$

$$= (1-t)\left\{p_H^2\ln(R_H) + p_H p_L\left[\ln\left(\frac{(1 - tC_1^{II})(R_H(2-\lambda) + R_L)}{(1-t)(3-\lambda)}\right)\right.\right.$$

$$\left.\left. + \ln\left(\frac{(1 - tC_1^{II})(2R_L + (1-\lambda)R_H)}{(1-t)(3-\lambda)}\right)\right] + p_L^2\ln(R_L)\right\}$$

$$= (1-t)\left\{p_H^2\ln(R_H)\right.$$

$$\left. + p_H p_L\ln\left(\frac{[(2-\lambda)R_H + R_H + R_L][2R_L + (1-\lambda)R_H]}{(3-\lambda)^2}\right) + p_L^2\ln(R_L)\right\}.^{16}$$

Assuming $\lambda < p_H$, it is straightforward to show that $\partial\Delta/\partial R_H < 0, \partial\Delta/\partial R_L < 0, \partial\Delta/\partial\lambda > 0, \partial\Delta/\partial p_H < 0$. Figure 1 presents the limiting frontier $\Delta = 0$ which separates the values of $p_L, \lambda, R_L,$ and R_H for which each system is preferred.

---

[16] This corresponds to equilibrium (1) in Proposition 2. Since $C_1^* = 1$, equilibrium (2) will only occur if the necessary condition of equilibrium (1) is not fulfilled.

6. Policy Implications

Although our model simplifies many aspects of the payment systems, it is useful to evaluate the payment system design policy. In many countries, gross real-time payment systems have proliferated, largely due to reduced operating costs for the data processing technology. While this aspect is important, disregarding the opportunity costs of holding liquid assets leaves out an essential dimension of payment systems and results in inefficient system design. Because of the trade-off between liquidity costs and contagion risk highlighted in the model, efficiency effects depend on a full constellation of parameters in addition to the technological dimension.

From that perspective it is helpful to list the main features that have changed in the banking industry in recent years. These trends are well-documented facts in the main industrialized countries.

(1) Diminished costs of information processing and transferring;
(2) Increased probability of failure;
(3) Increased concentration in the banking industry;
(4) Increased number of transactions due to mobility;
(5) Improved liquidity management.

The implications of our model for these observations are straightforward. The first three observations favor a gross payment system, while the final two favor a net system. In our model we have deliberately abstracted from the reduction in the cost of information processing and simply assumed that it was zero. Given this, the model predicts that a gross payment system is efficient when the probability of bank failure is high. Were this probability to decline sufficiently in the future, a net system might again become more attractive.

Regarding concentration, in our model a larger concentration in the banking industry implies that there are fewer compulsive travelers since the probability of traveling to another branch of the same bank is larger. With fewer compulsive travelers, a gross system is preferred. Hence, increased concentration favors a gross payment system.

On the other hand, the enormous growth in the volume of transactions that the payment system now handles, as well as improved liquidity management techniques that increase the opportunity cost of holding reserves, makes a net system more attractive.

The fact that we have observed such extensive development of gross systems suggests that Central Banks weigh the absence of contagion more heavily in their objective functions than the opportunity cost of holding reserves.[17] Whether this

---

[17] The central banker's preference for gross settlement is clearly stated by Greenspan (1996, p. 691): "Obviously a fully real-time electronic transaction, clearing and settlement system, for example one with no float that approximates the currency model, would represent, other things equal, the ultimate in payment system efficiency."

weighting scheme is socially optimal deserves further consideration. If managers were given sufficient incentives to close the inefficient banks, then netting would always dominate gross payments. Moreover, were payments to be backed by a portfolio of high quality loans as collateral, efficiency would be improved by providing a substitute for the loss of bank-run discipline. Finally, a gross system might encourage good banks to create clubs which netted among themselves in order to economize on liquidity. Entry into those clubs would be difficult since it would confer a competitive advantage on members.[18] This final result is a matter of deep concern about the market structure of the banking industry in the next century.

7. Extensions

Our basic framework can be extended in various directions. First, one could examine how bank capital can be used to mitigate contagion risk. Since equity capital reduces risk-taking, regulatory theory has suggested imposing minimum capital requirements. In our model this would lead to two potential benefits. On the one hand, since, once we introduce capital, the set of contracts equity holders can offer managers is enriched, they can provide managers with a sufficient stake in bank capital to compensate for their private benefits from keeping an inefficient bank open. On the other hand, capital requirements reduce the probability of bank failure and this might decrease the cost of contagion for depositors. The benefits of these two effects must be weighed against the cost of raising bank capital.

Second, *interbank suspension* of convertibility might mitigate contagion risk in a net settlement system. Suppose the suspension mechanism is defined in such a way that the banks refuse to serve travelers from the other bank in excess of the proportion of compulsive travelers, $(1 - t)(1 - \lambda)$. This notion of suspension can be interpreted as *bilateral credit limits* (as in C.H.I.P.S.). Suspension does not affect the strategies of the travelers from the high-signal bank, but it affects those of the travelers from the low-signal bank. In fact it would ration the travelers from the low-signal bank and might force some of them to withdraw at time 1. Since this forces liquidation of some low-signal bank assets, it improves efficiency. This could support the efficient outcome, [(W, T), (R, R)], as an equilibrium. If in addition to interbank suspension, we introduce *intrabank suspension* conditional on the good state as in Gorton (1985), we also eliminate any speculative bank run in the high-signal island.

---

[18] Private clearinghouses are emerging in the foreign exchange market. Examples include Echo in London, MultiNet in the U.S., and the global clearing bank called Group of Twenty, which comprises 17 of the world's largest banks and plans to create a 24-hr organization for foreign exchange settlements within the next few years. (See *The Economist* (1996a, p. 83) and *The Economist* (1996b, p. 18).)

Third, changes in bilateral credit limits could replace the lost disciplinary effect of bank runs if they resulted from peer monitoring (see Rochet and Tirole (1996a) for a theoretical discussion). In our model this extension is straightforward if we view monitoring as allowing a bank to observe the signal of the other bank. When monitoring costs are not "too high," a disciplinary effect is introduced. A bank observing a bad signal on its counterpart will reduce its bilateral credit assessment to zero and force its counterpart to liquidate its assets. Inefficient banks disappear. Thus, absent asymmetric information about investment returns, a netting system dominates gross, as in Proposition 1.[19]

Fourth, we can analyze the role of collateral in securing payments in a net system. Notice that if cash is the only collateral asset, netting provides no gains over a gross payment system. Moreover, if we allow a portfolio of loans to be used as collateral, if valued at their nominal value, the effect is the same in the two systems because ex post the collateral value is insufficient. On the other hand, if the bank portfolio of loans could be used as collateral once the number of its traveling depositors was known, then the inefficiency of netting would be resolved. A bank in which every depositor travels will not find sufficient collateral and will therefore be forced to default. Since this happens only in the case of low returns, inefficient banks disappear.

Fifth, we can also analyze the coexistence of net and gross payment systems, a standard feature in most industrialized countries. Our model implies that by combining the two systems in the right proportions it is possible to improve efficiency. The source of inefficiency under netting is the lack of the disciplinary role of runs. Consequently, by combining the two systems, it is possible to preserve information-based runs (although with fewer agents or smaller payments) while economizing on liquid assets. Our model does not, however, predict that large-value transactions will be executed through the gross settlement, a feature commonly observed. Only if we make the ad hoc assumption that informed depositors make large transactions would we conclude that it is efficient to channel them through the gross payment system and net the small amounts.

8. Conclusions

In this chapter we have modeled the impact of the payment system on the risks and the returns in the banking industry. Our analysis establishes the trade-off between real-time gross settlement (RTGS) and netting in terms of the necessary reserves and contagion risk. Second, it points out that the disciplinary effect of

---

[19] If bilateral credit limits could be changed costlessly, the functions of the settlement system could be taken over by the interbank lending market. The difference from the interbank market resides in the existence of implicit automatic credit lines in a settlement scheme.

bank runs may be lost in a netting system. Finally, it allows to establish how regulation may improve upon both RTGS and netting.

In this conclusion we discuss one final potential extension by focusing on a particular application of our results to the analysis of the European Monetary Union. The trade-off between risk and liquidity in gross and net payment systems is one of the key factors in the design of the TARGET (Trans-European Automated Real-Time Gross Settlement Express Transfer) system for transactions in Euro.[20] As a liquidity-intensive but safe RTGS international system, TARGET has been designed to minimize the systemic risk due to cross-border transactions. Our framework makes it possible to analyze this issue from the point of view of resource allocation and risk sharing. According to our model, where we reinterpret each bank as a National Central Bank, the choice of gross versus net depends on the comparison between the cost of holding reserves in accounts at the National Central Banks and the cost of losing the disciplinary effect of bank runs. It is reasonable to assume that the cost of holding reserves is low because the Euro is expected to be a hard currency with low interest rates. The cost due to the loss of disciplinary role is here more difficult to interpret. One possible interpretation is that one country in the Euro area is affected by a negative productivity shock and that, as a result, deposits fly to other countries. In this case the cost of the loss of disciplinary effect is high because, in addition to the cost of forbearance, there is a high political cost of transferring wealth from the supranational central bank (the European Central Bank) to a particular country. Furthermore, domestic banking authorities might have an additional incentive to keep a domestic bank open to free ride on sound foreign banks.

Finally, our model shows that an unintended consequence of weighing more safety than liquidity cost in TARGET might be that low-risk banks will benefit from developing their own private unsecured, reputation-based netting system to reduce the level of reserves they need. This may lead to an extension of the

---

[20] The architecture of the payment systems in the Euro area will be composed of the European System of Central Banks (the European Central Bank and its regional offices corresponding to the current national central banks) and of TARGET. TARGET establishes the linkages between national RTGS systems. In TARGET each payment order is immediately and irrevocably settled in central bank money by debiting and crediting the banks' accounts with the national central bank, as, e.g., in FEDWIRE. The novelty of the mechanism, however, is that in TARGET when a bank from country A sends a payment message to a bank in country B, bank A's account with its national central bank will be debited and bank B's account with its national central bank will be credited. Thus the two national central banks will net their positions bilaterally each day. Intraday credit has a limited role in TARGET. In fact, on the one hand, the national central banks will provide intraday credit to participants in TARGET only by making use of two facilities, fully collateralized intraday overdrafts and intraday repurchase agreements, which is essentially equivalent to the first. On the other hand, banks of European Union countries which are not part of the Euro area are excluded from the European Central Bank's overdraft on the ground that an overdraft collateralized by assets denominated in a non-Euro currency entails an exchange rate risk. For an analysis of the main features of TARGET see European Monetary Institute (1996).

correspondence system if higher risk banks are short in the collateral required to obtain Central Bank overdrafts.

APPENDIX

Proof of Proposition 1. Assume first that the strategic travelers choose to consume at their home island. In a gross system the bank at a given island solves

$$\max tU(C_1) + (1-t)[\lambda U(C_2) + (1-\lambda)U(\hat{C}_2)] \text{ w.r.t. } \{C_1, C_2, \hat{C}_2, L\}$$

s.t.

$$tC_1 + (1-t)(1-\lambda)\hat{C}_2 = L \tag{A.1}$$

and

$$(1-t)\lambda C_2 = R(1-L), \tag{A.1'}$$

which yields $tU'(C_1) = \theta t$ and $(1-t)(1-\lambda)U'(\hat{C}_2) = \theta(1-t)(1-\lambda)$, where θ is the Lagrange multiplier of the constraint (A.1), from which $C_1 = \hat{C}_2$. Notice that $C_2 > \hat{C}_2$. Therefore consuming at home is preferred by the strategic travelers.

In a net system consumption contracts in each island are C_1^* and C_2^*, and banks store L^* and leave $1 - L^*$ in the long-run technology, with $tC_1^* = L^*$, $(1-t)C_2^* = R(1-L^*)$. From the first order condition $U'(C_1^*) = RU'(C_2^*)$ it follows that

$$U'(L^*(t)/t) = R \cdot U'((1-L^*(t))R/(1-t)). \tag{A.2}$$

Differentiating (A.2) w.r.t. t, we have

$$U''(C_1)\left[\frac{-L^* + tdL^*/dt}{t^2}\right] = R^2 \cdot U''(C_2)\left[\frac{(-dL^*/dt)(1-t) + (1-L^*)}{(1-t)^2}\right]$$

from which

$$[dL^*/dt]\left[\frac{U''(C_1)}{t} + \frac{R^2}{1-t}U''(C_2)\right] = U''(C_1)\frac{L^*}{t} + R^2 \cdot \frac{(1-L^*)}{(1-t)^2}U''(C_2).$$

Since

$$\left[\frac{U''(C_1)}{t} + \frac{R^2}{1-t}U''(C_2)\right] < 0 \text{ and } U''(C_1)\frac{L^*}{t} + R^2\frac{(1-L^*)}{(1-t)^2} \cdot U''(C_2) < 0.$$

then $dL^*/dt > 0$. Since $R(1-L^*)$ is the return from the proportion of investment not liquidated, it follows that it declines with L^*. Thus total welfare is reduced and consumption levels in both states are reduced. ∎

Proof of Proposition 2. We sketch here the main argument. The rest of the proof follows exactly the same lines, so we have not detailed it. A complete proof is available from the authors upon request.

Strategy profiles and candidate equilibria. Since the compulsive travelers' strategy space is a subset of that of the strategic travelers, for each signal it must be the case that if the ST run, so must the CT and if the ST travel, so must the CT. As a result 16 strategy profiles are possible candidate equilibria that we label conjectures. The home island is A unless otherwise specified. We use the following convention and notation.

Number of conjecture	Signals		
	y_H	y_L	
I	[W, T]	[R, R]	Equilibrium 1
II	"	[T, T]	
III	"	[W, R]	
IV	"	[W, T]	
V	[W, R]	[R, R]	
VI	"	[T, T]	
VII	"	[W, R]	
VIII	"	[W, T]	
IX	[R, R]	[R, R]	Equilibrium 2
X	"	[T, T]	
XI	"	[W, R]	
XII	"	[W, T]	
XIII	[T, T]	[R, R]	
XIV	"	[T, T]	
XV	"	[W, R]	
XVI	"	[W, T]	

where, for example, conjecture I must be read as follows:

(W, T) means that when y_H occurs it is optimal for strategic travelers to wait and for compulsive travelers to travel;

(R, R) means that when y_L occurs it is optimal both for strategic travelers and for compulsive travelers to run;

and so on for the other conjectures.

Deposit contracts Consumption at the two times is a function of the strategies of the late diers in both islands, which are in turn a function of the signals in both islands. Let C_1^i denote time 1 consumption under the candidate equilibrium corresponding to the strategy profile of conjecture $i = 1, \ldots, XVI$. Define second period consumption when both banks receive the same signal K, under conjecture i, as

$$C_K^i \equiv \frac{\left(1 - tC_1^i\right)R_K}{1 - t}, K = L, H.$$

We will drop the superscript i whenever this does not create ambiguity. As in D–D, we assume parameter values such that $C_1^i > 1$.

Equilibrium analysis. We now check the incentive to deviate unilaterally from the two equilibria which do exist (which correspond to conjectures II and IX) and the two efficient outcomes that cannot be supported as equilibria (conjectures I and XIII) for a zero measure of late diers.

Conjecture I ([(W, T), (R, R)]). We will show that $R_{ST}(y_L)$ (that is, running for a strategic traveler that has received signal y_L) is not the optimal strategy. Assume y_L is observed at A. If a low signal is observed at island B and all the late diers run, the return will be 1. With probability p_H, a high signal is observed at island B, the strategic travelers at B wait and the compulsive travelers at B travel to A bringing assets $(1 - t)(1 - \lambda)C_H$. The expected payoff from a run is $p_L U(1) + p_H U(C_R)$, where

$$C_R = \frac{1 + (1 - t)(1 - \lambda)C_H}{1 + (1 - t)(1 - \lambda)}.$$

When a zero measure of strategic travelers deviate to travel to island B they obtain $p_H U(C_H) + p_L U(1)$. With probability p_H they end up in a high-signal bank at B and with probability p_L they end up at a low-signal bank at B where all the late diers run returning 1. Since $p_L U(1) + p_H U(C_R) < p_L U(1) + p_H U(C_H)$, conjecture I is not an equilibrium, because late diers are better off deviating.

Conjecture II ([(W, T), (T, T)] is an equilibrium). Period 2 consumption may take the following values:

$$C_K^{II} \equiv \frac{\left(1 - tC_1^H\right)R_K}{1 - t}$$

are the values if the banks at both islands experience the same signal $K = L, H$; C_A and C_B are the values at islands A and B, respectively, if the bank at A experienced a high signal and that at B a low signal. To compute C_A and C_B consider the time 2 balance sheets of bank A with a high signal and of bank B with a low signal:

$A(y_H)$	
Assets	Liabilities
$(1 - tC_1^{II})R_H$	$(1 - t)\lambda C_A(\text{ST})$
$(1 - t)C_B$	$(1 - t)(1 - \lambda)C_A(\text{CT})$
	$(1 - t)C_A$ (Late diers from B)
$(1 - tC_1^{II})R_H + (1 - t)C_B$	$2(1 - t)C_A$

$B(\gamma_L)$	
Assets	Liabilities
$(1 - tC_1^{II})R_L$	$(1 - t)C_B$
$(1 - t)(1 - \lambda)C_A$	$(1 - t)(1 - \lambda)C_B(CT)$
$(1 - tC_1^{II})R_L + (1 - t)(1 - \lambda)C_A$	$(1 - t)(2 - \lambda)C_B$

From the above balance sheets we obtain two equations,

$$\left(1 - tC_1^{II}\right) R_H + (1 - t)C_B = 2(1 - t)C_A \quad \text{and}$$

$$\left(1 - tC_1^{II}\right) R_L + (1 - t)(1 - \lambda)C_A = (1 - t)(2 - \lambda)C_B,$$

whose solutions are

$$C_B = \frac{\left(1 - tC_1^{II}\right)((1 - \lambda)R_H + 2R_L)}{(1 - t)(3 - \lambda)} < C_A = \frac{\left(1 - tC_1^{II}\right)((2 - \lambda)R_H + R_L)}{(1 - t)(3 - \lambda)}$$

since $R_L < R_H$, where $C_J, J = A, B$, are the claims of each depositor on bank J's assets.

Finally to compute the optimal deposit contract one has to choose $\{C_1^{II}, C_A, C_B, C_L^{II}, C_H^{II}\}$ to

$$\max tU\left(C_1^{II}\right) + (1 - t)\left\{p_H^2 U\left(C_H^{II}\right) + p_L^2 U\left(C_L^{II}\right) + p_H p_L[U(C_A) + U(C_B)]\right\} \text{ s.t.}$$

$$C_K^{II} \equiv \frac{\left(1 - tC_1^{II}\right) R_K}{1 - t}; \quad C_B = \frac{\left(1 - tC_1^{II}\right)((1 - \lambda)R_H + 2R_L)}{(1 - t)(3 - \lambda)};$$

$$C_A = \frac{\left(1 - tC_1^{II}\right)((2 - \lambda)R_H + R_L)}{(1 - t)(3 - \lambda)}$$

which yields

$$U'\left(C_1^{II}\right) = p_H^2 U'\left(C_H^{II}\right) R_H + p_L^2 U'\left(C_L^{II}\right) R_L$$

$$+ p_H p_L \left[U'(C_B)\frac{(1 - \lambda)R_H + 2R_L}{3 - \lambda} + U'(C_A)\frac{(2 - \lambda)R_H + R_L}{3 - \lambda}\right].$$

We want to prove that equilibrium 1 exists if and only if the condition we state in proposition 2 holds, namely

$$p_H U(C_A) + p_L U\left(C_L^{II}\right) > U\left(C_1^{II}\right). \tag{A.3}$$

Notice first that if (A3) holds, we also have

$$p_H U\left(C_H^{II}\right) + p_L U(C_A) > U\left(C_I^{II}\right) \tag{A.4}$$

and

$$p_H U\left(C_H^{II}\right) + p_L U(C_B) > U\left(C_I^{II}\right). \tag{A.5}$$

To check the optimality of $W_{ST}(Y_H)$ we first compute the payoffs from the different strategies:

— The expected payoff from waiting is $p_H U\left(C_H^{II}\right) + p_L U(C_A)$. Either the bank at island B has received a high signal and its late diers do not withdraw or it has received a low signal so that the return is C_A.
— Similarly, the expected payoff for a strategic traveler from a deviation to travel is $p_H U\left(C_H^{II}\right) + p_L U(C_B)$. Therefore, for the strategy $W_{ST}(y_H)$ to be optimal, the expected payoff from waiting must exceed that from traveling, which is satisfied since $C_A \geq C_B$.
— The expected payoff for a strategic traveler from a deviation to running is $U(C_I^{II})$. The necessary condition for $W_{ST}(y_H)$ to be optimal is (A.4).

To check the optimality of $T_{ST}(y_L)$ notice first that the expected payoff from traveling is $p_H U(C_A) + p_L U(C_L^{II})$, which exceeds that from waiting $p_H U(C_B) + p_L U\left(C_L^{II}\right)$ since $C_A > C_B$. Since the expected payoff from running is $U(C_I^{II})$, the necessary and sufficient condition for $T_{ST}(y_L)$ to be optimal is (A.3). Notice that if (A.3) is satisfied, both $T_{ST}(y_L)$ and $W_{ST}(y_H)$ are optimal.

To check the optimality of $T_{CT}(y_H)$ notice that it is the optimal strategy if (A.3) holds. Recalling that (A.3) implies (A.5) and observing that $C_B > C_L^{II}$, the expected payoff from traveling for a compulsive traveler, $p_H U\left(C_H^{II}\right) + p_L U(C_B)$, exceeds that from a deviation to running, $U(C_I^{II})$.

To check the optimality of $T_{CT}(y_L)$, remark that the same conditions of $T_{ST}(y_L)$ apply because the compulsive travelers' strategy set is a proper subset of the strategic travelers' under y_L.

Conjecture IX ([(R, R), (R, R)] is an equilibrium). The proof is obvious. It corresponds to a speculative run in each island.

Conjecture XIII ([(T, T), (R, R)] is not an equilibrium). To show that $T_{ST}(y_H)$ is not the optimal strategy, notice that because of the bankruptcy procedure, in equilibrium the strategic travelers in the high-signal island receive less than C_H in expected value. By waiting they receive C_H.

Using the same procedure one can show that the other conjectures cannot be supported as Nash equilibria, as there exist profitable deviations.

Finally we show that equilibrium 1 dominates equilibrium 2 for sufficiently low values of p_L.

Since

$$tU\left(C_1^{II}\right) + (1-t)\left[p_H^2 U\left(C_H\right) + p_L^2 U(C_L) + p_H p_L(U(C_A) + U(C_B))\right]$$

$$> tU(1) + (1-t)\left[p_H^2 U\left(R_H\right) + p_L^2 U(R_L) + p_H p_L\left(U\left(\frac{(1-\lambda)R_H + 2R_L}{3-\lambda}\right)\right.\right.$$

$$\left.\left. +U\left(\frac{(2-\lambda)R_H + R_L}{3-\lambda}\right)\right)\right]$$

we have that a sufficient condition for equilibrium 1 to dominate equilibrium 2 is that $p_L < p_L^*$, where p_L^* solves

$$\left[(1-p_L^*)^2 U(R_H) + (p_L^*)^2 (R_L) + (1-p_L^*)p_L^*\left(U\left(\frac{(1-\lambda)R_H + 2R_L}{3-\lambda}\right)\right.\right.$$

$$\left.\left. +U\left(\frac{(2-\lambda)(R_H + R_L)}{3-\lambda}\right)\right)\right] = U(1). \qquad \blacksquare$$

Proof of Proposition 3. Using the envelope theorem we consider changes in Δ close to the point $\Delta = 0$. (i) To show $\partial\Delta/\partial R_L < 0$ notice that $EU^G(\cdot)$ does not depend on R_L and that $EU^N(\cdot)$ is increasing in R_L. (ii) To show $\partial\Delta/\partial\lambda > 0$ notice that from the FOC we have $U'\left(C_1^G\right) = U'\left(C_H^G\right)R_H$, where C_H^G is the optimal time 2 consumption in a gross system. Hence, from the assumption of relative risk aversion coefficient superior or equal to 1, it follows that $C_1^G \geq 1$. Notice that

$$\frac{\partial EU^G(\cdot)}{\partial\lambda} = p_H(1-t)\left\{U\left(C_H^G\right) - U\left(C_1^G\right) + U'\left(C_H^G\right)R_H\right.$$

$$\cdot \frac{-1 + tC_1^G + (1-t)C_1^G[\lambda + (1-\lambda)]}{(1-t)\lambda}\right\}$$

$$= p_H(1-t)\left\{U\left(C_H^G\right) - U\left(C_1^G\right) + U'\left(C_H^G\right)R_H\frac{C_1^G - 1}{(1-t)\lambda}\right\} > 0.$$

On the other hand, since

$$\frac{dC_A}{d\lambda} = \frac{(1 - tC_1^{II})(R_L - R_H)}{[(1-t)(3-\lambda)]^2} < 0$$

and

$$\frac{dC_B}{d\lambda} = \frac{2(1 - tC_1^{II})(R_L - R_H)}{[(1-t)(3-\lambda)]^2} < 0,$$

then

$$\frac{\partial EU^{N}(\cdot)}{\partial \lambda} = p_{H}p_{L}(1-t)\left[U'(C_A)\frac{dC_A}{d\lambda} + U'(C_B)\frac{dC_B}{d\lambda}\right] < 0.$$

Hence $\partial\Delta/\partial\lambda > 0$. (iii) To show $\partial\Delta/\partial p_H < 0$ is sufficient to observe that in the high-return state, expected utility is higher under the net system as shown in Proposition 1.

References

Angelini, P., and Giannini, C. (1994). "On the economics of the interbank payment systems." *Economic Notes*, 23: 194–215.

——, Maresca, G., and Russo, D. (1996). "Systemic risk in the netting systems." *Banking Finance*, 20: 853–68.

Bhattacharya, S., and Fulghieri, P. (1994). Uncertain liquidity and interbank contracting, *Econ. Lett.*, 44: 287–94.

——, and Gale, D. (1987). "Preference shocks, liquidity, and central bank policy," in W. Barnett and K. Singleton (eds.), *New Approaches to Monetary Economics* (Cambridge: Cambridge Univ. Press), 69–88.

Brimmer, A. F. (1989). "Distinguished Lecture on Economics in Government: Central banking and systemic risks in capital markets." *J. Econ. Perspect*, 3: 3–16.

Chari, V. V., and Jagannathan, R. (1988). "Banking panics, information, and rational expectations equilibrium." *J. Finance*, 43: 749–61.

Diamond, D., and Dybvig, P. (1983). "Bank runs, deposit insurance, and liquidity". *J. Polit. Economy*, 91: 401–19.

Economist, (The) (1996a). "Foreign exchange. Ghostbusters?," March 16th.

—— (1996b). "International banking survey," April 27th.

European Monetary Institute (1996). "First Progress Report on the TARGET Project," Frankfurt, August.

Fama, E. (1980). "Banking in the theory of finance." *J. Monet. Economics*, 6: 39–57.

Gorton, G. (1985). "Bank suspension of convertibility." *J. Monet. Economics*, 15: 177–93.

—— (1988). "Banking panics and business cycles." *Oxford Econ. Pap.*, 40: 751–81.

Greenspan, A. (1996). "Remarks on evolving payment system issues." *J. Money Credit Banking*, 28: 689–95.

Hellwig, M. (1994). "Liquidity provision, banking, and the allocation of interest rate risk." *Eur. Econ. Rev.*, 38: 1363–9.

Horii, A., and Summers, B. J. (1994). "Large-value transfer systems," in B. J. Summers (ed.), *The Payment System, Design, Management, and Supervision* (Washington, DC: International Monetary Fund), 73–88.

Humphrey, D. B. (1986). "Payments finality and risk of settlement failure." in A. S. Saunders and L. J. White (eds.), *Technology and Regulation of Financial Markets: Securities, Futures and Banking* (Lexington, MA: Lexington Books), 97–120.

Jacklin, C., and Bhattacharya, S. (1988). "Distinguishing panics and information-based bank runs: Welfare and policy implications." *J. Pol. Econ.*, 96: 568–92.

Kahn, C., and Roberds, W. (1996a). "On The role of bank coalitions in the provisions of liquidity." Federal Reserve Bank of Atlanta, working paper, June.

——, and —— (1996b). "Payment system settlement and bank incentives," Federal Reserve Bank of Atlanta, working paper, September.

McAndrews, J., and Roberds, W. (1995). "Banks, payments and coordination." *J. Finan. Intermed.*, 4: 305–27.

Padoa-Schioppa, T. (1992). "Le Risque dans les systems de paiment de gros montants." National Westminster Bank, working paper, February.

Rochet, J. C., and Tirole, J. (1996a). "Interbank lending and systemic risk." *J. Money Credit Banking*, 28(2): 733–62.

——, and —— (1996b). "Controlling risk in payment systems." *J. Money Credit Banking*, 28(2): 832–62.

Summers, B. J. (ed.) (1994). *The Payment System, Design, Management, and Supervision* (Washington, DC: International Monetary Fund).

Van den Berg, P., and Veale, J. M. (1994). "Payment system risk and risk management." in B. J. Summers (ed.), *The Payment System, Design, Management, and Supervision* (Washington, DC: International Monetary Fund).

Bank Runs and Financial Crises: A Discussion

Jean-Charles Rochet

1. Introduction

The last three decades have witnessed an impressive wave of banking and financial crises, hitting a very large number of countries. For example, Lindgren et al. (1996) report that roughly three-quarters (130 out of 180) of IMF member countries experienced serious banking problems between 1980 and 1995. The cumulative output loss of these crises was huge: A recent study by the IMF (1998) evaluates the average loss per country to 11.6 percent of GDP. Even more impressive, the same study evaluates the cost of more recent crises in 1998 to more than 40 percent of GDP in Argentina, Indonesia, Korea, and Malaysia.

Starting with the U.S. Savings and Loans debacle in the early 1980s, these crises have initiated a renewal of economic research on the sources of fragility of banks and the possible remedies to it. This chapter aims at synthesizing recent theoretical research on this topic. We start by examining the most plausible explanations for the fragility of individual banks (Section 2). In Section 3, we will discuss the impact of aggregate shocks and financial crises on the banking sector. Finally we turn to the question of contagion, an important concern of banking supervisory authorities. Contagion can be defined as the propagation to the whole banking and financial sector of solvency problems encountered by one or a small number of financial institutions. Economists still disagree about the frequency and extent of such contagion episodes. In Section 4, we present some of their arguments and discuss the possible channels of such propagations.

2. Sources of Fragility for Individual Banks

Even though there is still a lot of controversy about the causes of global banking crises, there is now some consensus concerning the main source of fragility for individual banks, namely the fractional reserve system, under which long term, illiquid, loans or investments are financed by demandable deposits. The early literature on bank runs (Bryant 1980; Diamond and Dybvig 1983) has insisted on the presence of a coordination problem between these depositors, even in the case where the bank's assets are perfectly safe. Indeed, whenever a large enough fraction of depositors decide to withdraw, it is individually rational for others to do the same, thus provoking an inefficient bank run. Notice that this happens only when the bank under attack is forced to liquidate prematurely its assets (as it was the case before the development of interbank markets) or more realistically today, because the bank can only borrow (on interbank markets) less than 100 percent of the value of its assets (this is what Central Bankers sometimes call a "haircut"), presumably for reasons of adverse selection (see, for instance, Flannery 1996) or moral hazard (see, for instance, Holmström and Tirole 1997, 1998).

This cost of liquidity generates strategic complementarity between depositors' actions (the more depositors withdraw, the more it is profitable to do so for any other depositor), which creates the potential for multiple equilibria. However, creation of a deposit insurance system is a simple way to get rid of inefficient bank runs. Indeed, provided this insurance is sufficiently generous and credible, each depositor does not have to pay attention anymore to other depositors' behavior and withdraws his money only when he needs it. This is not the only possible institutional response to bank runs. Indeed, when there is no doubt about the bank's solvency, Diamond and Dybvig (1983) suggest two other, equivalent, means of eliminating inefficient bank runs: Suspension of convertibility, or emergency liquidity assistance by the Central Bank, acting as a Lender of Last Resort.

However, when there is doubt about the solvency of the bank, bank runs can sometimes be efficient: They can indeed provide an appropriate way to liquidate insolvent banks (Gorton 1985; Postewaite and Vives 1987). The difficulty is to eliminate inefficient bank runs, while preserving efficient ones (see the analysis of Jacklin and Bhattacharya 1988). In the absence of information asymmetries, this can be obtained by creating a coordinating institution that decides on a bank's closure on behalf of its depositors. This is the position defended by Dewatripont and Tirole (1994) who view the role of supervisory authorities as that of representing the collective interest of dispersed depositors. In a world of symmetric information and complete contracts, efficiency and stability of the banking system could thus be obtained by a combination of deposit insurance and banking supervision, interpreted as a complete contract between the banker and the deposit insurance corporation.

However, when information about banks' solvency is asymmetric and/or contracts are incomplete, things become more intricate. In such a framework, Gorton (1985) suggests that suspension of convertibility during liquidity crises may still be a good system whenever banks have the possibility to credibly disclose the value of their assets, against the payment of a certification cost. Postlewaite and Vives (1987) and Chari and Jagannathan (1988) study what happens in the Diamond and Dybvig model when some of the patient depositors may have superior information on the return on banks' assets. Postlewaite and Vives (1987) show that in some cases, the presence of these informed depositors may allow to get rid of the multiplicity of equilibria. Chari and Jagannathan (1988) assume that uninformed depositors can observe the length of the "lines" of depositors (however they cannot differentiate informed depositors from uninformed ones) who want to withdraw early and infer from it the likelihood of bad returns on the bank's assets. This generates efficient bank runs when returns on the bank's assets are low but also inefficient runs (that they call panics) since uninformed depositors cannot always tell whether other depositors want to withdraw for fundamental (low returns on the bank's assets) or idiosyncratic reasons (liquidity shocks). Suspension of convertibility may sometimes help, when the cost of inefficient bail outs of insolvent banks is more than outweighted by the benefit of avoiding panics.

Of course, a fundamental issue remains to be clarified, given the consensus that the fractional reserve system is the ultimate cause of fragility of individual banks. Specifically, is it a good idea to let commercial banks finance illiquid loans by demand deposits, instead of equity or other securities? Diamond and Dybvig (1983) justify it by the provision of liquidity insurance for risk-averse depositors who are uncertain about their future liquidity needs. However, this argument seems to be less convincing in the presence of financial markets. For example, Jacklin (1987) shows that bank equity can sometimes provide a better instrument for risk sharing than bank deposits. Also, in a continuous-time extension of the Bryant–Diamond–Dybvig model, von Thadden (1998) shows that the possibility of depositors to withdraw early and invest on financial markets severely limits the possibilities for a fractional reserve system to provide liquidity insurance. However, within this liquidity insurance paradigm, the fractional reserve system dominates the narrow banking solution (Wallace 1988) whereby banks would be forced to invest all their demandable deposits into riskless assets. It also dominates the modern form of narrow banks, the monetary service companies (Gorton and Pennacchi 1993), which are allowed to invest demand deposits into risky assets, but provided these assets are "marked-to-market" on a continuous basis.

To summarize, the liquidity insurance paradigm only provides a good theoretical foundation for the fractional reserve system in the absence of financial markets. In order to understand whether such a system can still be useful in the presence of sophisticated financial markets, other paradigms have to be explored further, all being related to asymmetric information problems:

- The disciplining role of demandable debt (Calomiris and Kahn 1991; Rey and Stiglitz 1994; Qi 1998; Diamond and Rajan 2000; Carletti 1999), whereby early withdrawals are viewed as a credible punishment for the case where banks' managers could be tempted not to properly monitor their loans (ex ante moral hazard) or even fraudulently appropriate the assets of the bank.
- Insuring firms against liquidity shocks (Holmström and Tirole 1998): If there is interim moral hazard on the choice of investments, firms cannot obtain enough liquidity on financial markets at the interim date. Banks have a role to play in this context, by granting credit lines to the firms, thus avoiding inefficient liquidations of these firms.
- Limiting the impact of insider trading (Gorton and Pennacchi 1990): If some investors are more informed than others on the future profitability of banks' assets, the adverse effects of asymmetric information can be limited by differentiating the liabilities held by these investors: Less informed investors will tend to hold deposits (which are not very sensitive to the banks' returns) while more informed depositors will hold stocks (which are more sensitive to banks' return).
- Economies of scope between taking deposits and lending (Kashyap et al. 1999): If deposits withdrawals and credit lines takedowns are imperfectly correlated, the total cost of holding reserves is decreased by simultaneously undertaking deposit and lending activities.

After exploring the causes of fragility of individual banks, we now analyze the sources of systemic risks, broadly defined as including all the risks that affect the banking and financial system as a whole. We will start by discussing aggregate shocks and financial crises, and then focus on the possibilities of contagion, that is the propagation to the whole banking system of solvency problems encountered by a limited number of financial institutions.

3. Aggregate Shocks and Financial Crises

Our broad definition of systemic risk includes those forms of risks that simultaneously affect a large number of financial institutions or even all the agents in an economy (albeit to different extents). For example, Gorton (1988) shows the existence of a strong correlation between business cycles and banking panics in the U.S., prior to the creation of the Federal Reserve. These shocks are usually referred to as systematic or macroeconomic shocks in the financial literature. Some are clearly exogenous like natural catastrophes, bad crops, wars. Some are somewhat endogenous, in the sense that they might be amplified or even provoked by ill-designed organizational features of the financial system. For example, Friedman and Schwartz (1963) argue that the peculiarities of the U.S. banking system in the nineteenth century (unit banks, with a pyramiding of reserves in New York) were responsible for the frequency of bank panics. Similarly, Schwartz (1986) argues that the severe consequences of the Great Depression (1929–1933) in the U.S. could have been considerably limited had the Fed properly conducted lender of last resort operations. More recently, Allen and Gale (2000b) provide a theoretical model explaining how asset prices bubbles (like the Japanese real-estate bubble in the 1980s) may actually be provoked by the speculative behavior of undercapitalized banks who gamble with their depositors' money.

Elaborating on the ideas introduced by Carlsson and Van Damme (1993) for selecting a unique equilibrium in a certain class of games, Morris and Shin (1998) construct a model of currency crises whereby investors are influenced not only by their own opinion on fundamentals, but also by what they think of the opinion of other investors and so on and so forth (higher order beliefs). Whereas under symmetric information (when all investors observe the same signal) there would be several equilibria of the game between investors, the introduction of a small amount of asymmetric information (or diversity of opinions) is enough to select a unique equilibrium. This equilibrium is characterized by a threshold on fundamentals below which a currency crisis occurs, this threshold being above the efficient level. The uniqueness of this equilibrium allows Morris and Shin (1998) to derive testable implications on currency crises. Several applications of the same methodology have recently been proposed:

- Morris and Shin (2004) obtain reasonable estimates of spreads on corporate bonds, by adding to the classical default premium an additional premium, which they call the coordination risk premium.
- Rochet and Vives (2000) (see also Goldstein and Pauzner 2000) adapt the Morris and Shin model to banking crises, and provide a theoretical fondation for the controversial notion of "solvent but illiquid bank", central to the classical doctrine of the lender of last resort.

It is usually considered that the adverse consequences of aggregate shocks can be limited by two types of public policies:

- Adopting proper organization and regulation of financial institutions so that real shocks are dampened (and not amplified) by the financial sector. The importance of this question justifies the recent interest of the academic world for understanding in depth the mechanisms by which financial cycles appear and develop.
- Intertemporal smoothing of aggregate shocks by use of stabilizing monetary and/or fiscal policies. Central Banks are supposed to participate in these policies, since they are traditionally assigned the dual mission of maintaining the stability of the payments system and implementing monetary policy (even though the official objectives of monetary policy are often nowadays limited to the control of inflation and do not include anymore output stabilization as they did some decades ago).

4. The Channels of Contagion

We now set aside aggregate shocks, and turn to the core notion of systemic risk, which has to do with *contagion*, or propagation of solvency problems encountered by *a single* financial institution to a group of other banks. Although some authors (e.g. Kaufman 1994) argue that these contagion phenomena are equally damaging in the non-financial sector, central bankers (e.g. Corrigan 1989) view them on the contrary as highly specific to the banking industry, and as the main rationale for public intervention in the banking industry (see, for example the discussion about the LTCM bailout in Edwards 1999). This public intervention takes three main forms: Deposit insurance, prudential regulations, and lender of last resort interventions. It is fair to say, however, that the mechanisms of propagation are not fully understood: We are now going to review the main theoretical scenarios that have been proposed so far.

4.1 Wealth effects

A first possible vehicle for financial contagion are wealth effects (see for instance Kyle and Xiong 2001). If investors suffer severe losses on one financial market, they may decide to downsize their positions on other financial markets (either because their risk-bearing capacity decreases for regulatory reasons or internal risk-management practices, or simply because their risk-aversion increases) which provokes declining prices, decreased market depth and liquidity and increased volatility. Thus even in the absence of correlation of fundamentals, asset prices and volatilities may be correlated across markets. Relatedly, Chiuri et al. (2001) show that the enforcement of banks capital adequacy requirements (Basel 1988) in emerging economies could have contributed to the propagation of recent banking crises.

4.2 Informational externalities

Several types of models have been proposed to explain systemic risk by informational externalities. In these models, the closure of a particular bank may, or may not, bring new information to depositors and provoke their decision to switch to the "panic" equilibrium. Often, this new information comes from a Bayesian revision process: Either a re-evaluation of the quality of banks' assets (assuming positive correlation of asset returns across banks,the failure of one bank is bad news for the other banks) or re-evaluation of the willingness of banking authorities to let a bank fail. For example, Aharony and Swary (1983) study the market reactions to the failures of big U.S. banks. Park (1991) looks at bank panics in U.S. history and shows that most of them are due to a lack of bank specific information. He argues that contagion can be stopped by provision of detailed financial information on banks. More recently, Chen (1999) models banking panics as the outcome of information-based herding behavior by depositors. In these models, systemic risk may occur in the absence of any interbank relations. More recently, two strands of the literature have focused on the contrary on the fragility created by those interbank relations, through two alternative channels: Interbank markets, on the one hand, and payment systems on the other hand. I will now review these two strands of the literature.

4.3 Interbank markets

Bhattacharya and Gale (1987) have clearly established the role played by interbank markets in a fractional reserve system. By allowing banks to trade their reserves at an interim date, interbank markets insure banks against idiosyncratic liquidity shocks, very much in the way that the banks themselves provide liquidity insurance to depositors. The counterpart is that the banking system becomes more fragile, again in the same way that fractional reserves make individual banks more fragile. This idea is modelled by Donaldson (1992) who studies the influence of interbank relations on the probability of a bank run. Similarly, Aghion et al. (1999) and Allen and Gale (2000a) build models of the banking industry where the introduction of interbank markets has two contrasting effects:

- The probability of individual bank failures decreases,
- But the probability of a collapse of the entire banking system increases.

A natural way to avoid this systemic risk would be to have interbank deposits insured by the Central Bank, in the same way that individual deposits are insured by the Deposit Insurance system. The counterpart would be increased moral hazard, since the disciplining power of short term interbank loans would be lost. Calomiris (1999) criticizes the IMF for having implicitly provided such an insurance against credit losses of international banks on their loans to the domestic banks of the Asian countries affected by the recent crisis. Calomiris advocates in favor of a "peer monitoring system" whereby IMF loans could be granted only if sufficiently many commercial banks also participate, and incur the risk of losing money if the investments reveal bad. This would provide incentives for commercial banks to monitor each other in their lending activities. For the same reason, Calomiris (1999) also advocates the use of Subordinated Debt as part of the capital requirement that regulators impose on banks.

In fact, Rochet and Tirole (1996) have studied the properties of such a peer monitoring system, whereby commercial banks have to be given proper incentives not only to monitor their own borrowers, but also the lending activity of other banks. Rochet and Tirole show that peer monitoring generates economies of scope between commercial lending and interbank lending: It is less costly to provide incentives for a single bank to monitor simultaneously its own borrowers and other banks, rather than having two different banks specialized, respectively, in interbank loans and commercial loans. On the other hand, these scope economies are precisely the source of systemic risk: In the absence of peer monitoring, the failure of any individual bank can be completely disconnected from the rest of the banking system, either if the Central Bank insures interbank loans of if it provides emergency liquidity assistance to the banks temporarily affected by the failure. However, in the presence of peer monitoring, the decision to close a bank (say, bank 1) or not can be modified by the closure of another bank (say, bank 2) if bank 1 has lent money to bank 2 (which implies that bank 1 is supposed to monitor bank 2). For some realizations of the returns of banks' assets, it may be optimal to bail out bank 1 *only* when bank 2 is itself bailed out, because should bank 2 be closed, the benefit of having it monitored by bank 1 would disappear. This externality may generate "efficient" propagation, in the sense that if the Central Bank could commit perfectly on its closure policy, there are cases in which the (ex ante) efficient regulatory system would involve propagating closure decisions. Indeed, Rochet and Tirole solve for the optimal regulatory system (in the case where full commitment is possible by the Central Bank) and give an example where a small negative shock on the portfolio of a single bank is enough to justify the closure of a large number of banks. Of course, this extreme solution is not credible ex post, which seriously limits the practical relevance of the peer monitoring solution: Proper incentives for peer monitoring could only be given if the Central Bank was potentially ready to close a large number of banks, which is not very likely.

4.4 Payment systems

Banking authorities of many countries have recently reformed the organization of large value interbank payments systems, transforming them from "Net" systems (where payment orders become irrevocable only at the end of the day, after compensation of interbank flows, and settlements of the net positions of each bank have taken place) into Real Time Gross Systems (RTGS) where each individual payment order becomes irrevocable in real time, provided the sending bank has enough cash on its account with the Central Bank. The move to such gross systems, which obviously creates an increased need for liquidity, is motivated by the fear that, in a net system, the illiquidity of a large bank might propagate to a large number of other banks. For example, Humphrey (1986) simulates the impact of a settlement failure of a major participant in the U.S. interbank payment system CHIPS and shows that it could lead to a significant number of further failures. The reason is that, in a net system, banks typically incur large intraday overdrafts, given that their positions are only checked at the end of the day. Should a default occur in a net system, it could involve very large amounts, whereas in a RTGS, default is by construction detected instantaneously. Moreover, in a net system, other banks never know for sure whether a given bank will be able to settle its debt at the end of the day, and whether the payment orders it has sent will not ultimately be revoked.

Freixas and Parigi (1998) compare the performances of the two types of payment systems. They construct a model where several banks à la Diamond–Dybvig send each other payment orders motivated by exogenous transactions needs of their customers. They characterize the equilibrium behavior of depositors in the two systems and study the trade-offs between safety and efficiency. They are able to provide an explanation for the recent move from net to gross systems by showing that gross payment systems are preferable when the probability of bank failure increases, when transactions volumes increase and when the opportunity cost of liquid reserves increases.

Using a similar model, Freixas et al. (2000) study the externalities generated by the functioning of interbank payment systems. In "normal" conditions, all banks are solvent and depositors use the payment system to transfer their money to the location where they need it. However, if they do not trust in the solvency of the corresponding bank, they can decide to withdraw their deposits from their home bank, which may oblige this bank to fire sell some of its assets. This captures a fundamental externality present in a net payment system: In the model of Freixas et al. (2000), depositors force their home bank to liquidate some of its assets not because they do not trust in the quality of these assets, but because they do not trust in the quality of the assets of their destination bank.

Freixas et al. (2000) study the fragility of the banking system when confronted with two types of intraday events:

- "Bad news" about the solvency of one bank, taking the form of a public signal that reveals that one bank is likely to be insolvent at the final date.

- Closure of one bank by banking authorities, provoking the cancellation of all payment orders headed from and towards this particular bank.

Freixas et al. (2000) show that the ability of a given banking system to absorb these two kinds of shocks (without provoking a gridlock of the payments system) depends on the shape of the (exogenous) matrix of payment orders (what Freixas et al. call the "architecture" of the payment system). They compare different architectures (what they call, respectively, diversified lending, credit chains, and a pyramidal system with money center banks). Surprisingly, an isotropic architecture (diversified lending) is not very stable with respect to "bad news", even though it performs well in front of the closure of a particular bank. They also compute the total volume of liquidity that the Central Bank may have to inject in the system in order to prevent a panic after the closure of a particular bank. This amount varies with the position occupied by this bank within the payment system. In particular, in a pyramidal system, it is much bigger for a money center bank than for a pyramidal bank, which may give a rationale for a "too-big-to-fail" policy.

References

Aghion, P., Bolton, P., and Dewatripont, M. (1999). "Contagious bank failures." Mimeo, University College London, Princeton University and ECARE, Harvard University, Cambridge, Mass.; and Université Libre de Bruxelles, mimeograph.

Aharony, J., and Swary, I. (1983). "Contagion effects of bank failures: Evidence from capital markets." *Journal of Business*, 56: 305–32.

Allen, F., and Gale, D. (2000a). "Financial contagion." *Journal of Political Economy*, 110: 460, 256–72.

——, and Gale, D. (2000b). "Bubbles and crises." *Economic Journal*, 108: 1–33.

Basel Committee on Banking Supervision (1988). "International convergence of capital measurement and capital standards." BCBS, BASEL, Switzerland.

Bhattacharya, S., and Gale, D. (1987). "Preference shocks, liquidity and central bank policy," in W. Barnett and K. Singleton (eds.), *New Approaches to Monetary Economics* (Cambridge: Cambridge University Press).

Bryant, J. (1980). "A model of reserves, banks runs, and deposit insurance." *Journal of Banking and Finance*, 4: 335–44.

Calomiris, C. (1999). "Building an incentive-compatible safety net." *Journal of Banking and Finance*, 23: 1499–519.

——, and Kahn, C. (1991). "The role of demandable debt in structuring optimal banking arrangements." *American Economic Review*, 81: 497–513.

Carletti, E. (1999). "Bank moral hazard and market discipline." Unpublished article, FMG, LSE, London, UK.

Carlsson, H., and Van Damme, E. (1993). "Global games and equilibrium selection." *Econometrica*, 61: 989–1018.

Chari, V. V., and Jagannathan, R. (1988). "Banking panics, information and rational expectations equilibrium." *Journal of Finance*, 43(3): 749–61.

Chen, Y. (1999). "Banking panics: The role of the first-come, first-served rule and information externalities." *Journal of Political Economy*, 107(5): 946–86.

Chiuri, M. C., Ferri, G., and Majnoni, G. (2001). "The macroeconomic impact of bank capital requirements in emerging countries." World Bank, Washington D.C., U.S.A.

Corrigan, G. (1989). "A perspective on recent financial disruptions." *Federal Reserve Bank of New York Quarterly Review*, 14: 8–15.

Dewatripont, M., and Tirole, J. (1994). *The Prudential Regulation of Banks*. MIT Press: Cambridge, MA.

Diamond, D. W., and Dybvig, P. H. (1983). "Bank runs, deposit insurance, and liquidity." *Journal of Political Economy*, 91(3): 401–19.

——, and Rajan, R. (2000). "A theory of bank capital." *Journal of Finance*, LV: 2431–65.

Donaldson, R. G. (1992). "Costly liquidation, interbank trade, bank runs and panics." *Journal of Financial Intermediation*, 2: 59–82.

Edwards, F. (1999). "Hedge funds and the collapse of LTCM." *Journal of Economic Perspectives*, 13: 189–210.

Freixas, X., and Parigi, B. (1998). "Contagion and efficiency in gross and net payment system." *Journal of Financial Intermediation*, 7: 3–31.

——, Parigi, B., and Rochet, J. C. (2000). "Systemic risk, interbank relations and liquidity provision by the central bank." *Journal of Money, Credit and Banking*, 32: 611–38.

Friedman, M., and Schwartz, A. (1963). *A Monetary History of the United States, 1867–1960*, Princeton N.J., Princeton University Press.

Goldstein, I., and Pauzner, A. (2000). "Demand deposit contracts and the probability of bank runs." Mimeo, Tel Aviv University, Israel.

Gorton, G. (1985). "Banks' suspension of convertibility." *Journal of Monetary Economics*, 15: 177–93.

—— (1988). "Banking panics and business cycles." *Oxford Economic Papers*, 40: 741–81.

——, and Pennacchi, G. (1990). "Financial intermediaries and liquidity creation." *Journal of Finance*, 45(1): 49–71.

——, and Pennacchi, G. (1993). "Money market funds and finance companies: Are they the banks of the Future?" in M. Klausner and L. White (eds.), *Structural Change in Banking* (New York: New York University).

Holmström, B., and Tirole, J. (1997). "Financial intermediation, loanable funds and the real sector." *Quarterly Journal of Economics*, 112(3): 663–91.

——, and —— (1998). "Private and public supply of liquidity." *Journal of Political Economy*, 106: 1–40.

Humphrey, D. (1986). "Payments finality and risk of settlement failure," in Saunders and White (eds.), *Technology and the Regulation of Financial Markets* (Lexington MA: Lexington Books), 97–120.

Jacklin, C. J. (1987). "Demand deposits, trading restrictions and risk-sharing," in E. C. Prescott and N. Wallace (eds.), *Contractual Arrangements for Intertemporal Trade* (Minneapolis, MN: University of Minnesota Press).

Jacklin, C. J., and Bhattacharya, S. (1988). "Distinguishing panics and information-based bank-runs: Welfare and policy implications." *Journal of Political Economy*, 96(3): 568–92.

Kashyap, A., Rajan, R., and Stein, J. (1999). "Banks as liquidity providers: An explanation for the co-existence of lending and deposit taking." NBER working paper 6962.

Kaufman, G. G. (1994). "Bank contagion: A review of the theory and the evidence." *Journal of Financial Services Research*, 8(2): 123–50.

Kyle, A., and Xiong, W. (2001). "Contagion as a wealth effect." *JOF*, 56: 1401–40.

Lindgren, C., Garcia, G., and Saal, M. (1996). *Bank Soundness and Macroeconomic Policy*. Washington, D.C.: IMF.

IMF International Monetary Fund (1998). *World Economic Outlook*. Washington D.C.: IMF.

Morris, S., and Shin, H. (1998). "Unique equilibrium in a model of self-fulfilling currency attacks." *American Economic Review*, 88: 587–97.

——, and —— (2004). "Coordination risk and the price of debt." *European Economic Review*, forthcoming.

Park, S. (1991). "Bank failure contagion in historical perspective." *Journal of Monetary Economics*, 28: 271–86.

Postlewaite, A., and Vives, X. (1987). "Banks run as an equilibrium phenomenon." *Journal of Political Economy*, 95(3): 485–91.

Qi, J. (1998). "Deposit liquidity and bank monitoring." *Journal of Financial Intermediation*, 7(2): 198–218.

Rey, P., and Stiglitz, J. (1994). "Short-term contracts as a monitoring device." INSEE discussion paper 9446, Malakoff, France.

Rochet, J. C., and Tirole, J. (1996). "Interbank lending and systemic risk." *Journal of Money, Credit and Banking*, 28(4): 733–62.

——, and Vives, X. (2000). "Coordination failures and the lender of last resort: Was Bagehot right after all?" Unpublished manuscript, Toulouse University, France.

Schwartz, A. (1986). "Real and pseudo-financial crises," in F. Capie and G. Wood (eds.), *Financial Crises and the World Banking System* (New York: St. Martin Press).

von Thadden, E. L. (1998). "Intermediated vs direct investment: Optimal liquidity provision and dynamic incentive compatibility." *Journal of Financial Intermediation*, 7: 2.

Wallace, N. (1988). "Another attempt to explain an illiquid banking system: The Diamond–Dybvig model with sequential service taken seriously." *Quarterly Review of the FRB of Minneapolis*, 12(4): 3–16.

Part IV

Regulation of Financial Intermediaries

12

Capital Requirements and the Behavior of Commercial Banks

Jean-Charles Rochet

1. Introduction

This chapter is motivated by the adoption at the EEC level of a new capital requirement for commercial banks. This reform (fully effective from January 1993) is in fact closely inspired by a similar regulation (the so-called Cooke ratio) adopted earlier (December 1987) by the Bank of International Settlements.

I try to examine here what Economic Theory can tell us about such regulations, and more specifically:

— why do they exist in the first place?
— are they indeed a good way to limit the failure risk of commercial banks?
— what consequences can be expected on the behavior of these banks?

In fact, the above questions have already been examined, notably by U.S. economists, who used essentially two competing sets of assumptions. In the first setup, financial markets are supposed to be complete and depositors are perfectly informed about the failure risks of banks. Then the Modigliani–Miller indeterminacy principle applies and the market values of banks are independent of the structure of their assets portfolio, as well as their capital to assets ratio. However, when a bankruptcy cost is introduced as in Kareken and Wallace (1978), it is found that unregulated banks would spontaneously choose their assets portfolio in such a way that failure does not occur. The reason is market discipline: since capital markets are supposed to be efficient and banks' creditors (including depositors) are supposed to be perfectly informed, any increase in the bank riskiness would immediately reflect in the rates of return demanded by stockholders and depositors. It is only when a deposit insurance scheme is introduced that this market discipline is corrupted and the banks' decisions become distorted. This is a classical 'moral-hazard' argument: depositors have no more incentives to

I have benefited from helpful comments by participants of ISOM 91, Madrid, and in particular Colin Mayer and Rafael Repullo. All errors are mine.

monitor the investment behavior of their banks, since they are (a priori) insured against failures.

However, all this comes from the mispricing of deposit insurance: even when it is provided by a formal insurance company, like the FDIC in the U.S.A., its price is not computed on an actuarial basis. Indeed the insurance premia only depend on the volume of deposits, and not on assets composition or capital ratios. As a consequence these premia are not related to the failure probabilities of banks. But if we accept the assumption of complete, efficient capital markets there is no need for regulating banks' capital:

— if depositors are fully informed, banks choose spontaneously efficient portfolios and deposit insurance is useless,
— if depositors are not fully informed (but the Regulator is), they should be protected by a deposit insurance scheme funded by actuarially fair premia. The only remaining difficulty is then technical: we have to find a reasonably simple way to compute these premia [a solution to this problem is offered in a companion paper, Kerfriden and Rochet (1991)].

On the other hand, it is hard to believe that a deep understanding of the banking sector can be obtained within the set-up of complete contingent markets, essentially because of the already mentioned Modigliani–Miller indeterminacy principle. This principle implies that, except for bankruptcy costs considerations, banks are completely indifferent about their assets portfolio and capital ratios. Therefore, we have to turn to an incomplete markets setting. The problem then comes from the absence of a theoretically sound objective function for firms in general, and banks in particular. Consequently, an alternative set of assumptions has been adopted by a second strand of the literature, notably Koehn and Santomero (1980) and Kim and Santomero (1988). It is adapted from the portfolio model of Pyle (1971) and Hart and Jaffee (1974). Banks are supposed to behave as competitive portfolio managers, in the sense that first they take prices (and yields) as given, and second that they choose the composition of their balance sheets (including liabilities) so as to maximize the expectation of some (ad hoc) utility function of the bank's financial net worth. The results obtained by Koehn and Santomero (1980) and Kim and Santomero (1988) are essentially the following:

— Imposing a capital regulation will in general lead banks not only to reduce the total volume of their risky portfolio but also to recompose it, in such a way that their assets allocation becomes inefficient.
— As a consequence it is quite possible that the failure probability of some banks may increase (!) when the capital regulation is imposed.
— Nevertheless, it is possible to compute 'theoretically correct risk weights' such that these adverse effects are eliminated.

However, there are two features of the Pyle–Hart–Jaffee model which are difficult to justify here:

— First, equity capital is treated in the same way as other securities: banks are assumed to be able to buy and sell their own stocks at a given exogenous price, which is in particular independent of the investment behaviour of the bank. This is hard to reconcile with the fact that the returns to the bank's stockholders clearly depend on the bank's investment policy.
— Secondly, banks behave as if they were fully liable! In other words, although the regulation under study is precisely motivated by the default risk of commercial banks, this is not taken into account by the banks themselves.

Thus I do essentially two things in this chapter:

— I re-examine the conclusions of Koehn and Santomero (1980) and Kim and Santomero (1988) in a model where bank's equity capital is fixed, at least in the short run. Their main result, namely that adoption of a capital requirement will not necessarily entail a diminution of the banks' risk of default, is shown to be also valid in our context, where it is simpler to understand. I also provide a very simple recommendation for computing 'correct' risk weights: to make them proportional to the systematic risks (the betas) of the assets.
— I take into account limited liability and I show that it modifies in a substantial way the banks' behavior towards risk. Under certain circumstances, banks may become risk-lovers. Imposing a minimum capital is then necessary to prevent them from choosing very inefficient portfolios. A solvency ratio alone, even with correct risk weights, would not be sufficient.

The Chapter is organized as follows: the model is presented in section 2; section 3 is dedicated to the behavior of banks in the complete markets setup. The portfolio model is introduced in section 4, and the behavior of banks without capital requirements is examined in section 5. Capital requirements are introduced in section 6, and limited liability in section 7. Section 8 contains some concluding remarks, and mathematical proofs are gathered in two appendices.

2. The Model

It is a static model with only two dates: $t = 0$, where the bank chooses the composition of its portfolio; and $t = 1$ where all assets and liabilities are liquidated. There are only two liabilities: equity capital K_0 and deposits D. In most of the paper, K_0 is exogenously fixed but D is chosen by the bank, taking into account the total cost (operating costs + interest paid to depositors + possibly deposit insurance premia) $C(D)$ of these deposits. This cost function depends on the institutional framework (which will be discussed below) as well as on the competitive position of the bank on the deposit market (existence or size of a branch network...) The marginal cost of deposits, $C'(D)$ is supposed to be strictly increasing, continuous, with $C'(+\infty) = +\infty$. On the asset side, the bank is allowed to invest any amount x_i on security $i(i = 0, \dots, N)$, taking as given the random returns $\tilde{R}_i$ on these securities. Security zero is supposed to be riskless (R_0 is deterministic). The accounting equations giving the total of the balance sheet are easily obtained:

$$\sum_{i=0}^{N} x_i = D + K_0 \qquad\qquad (\text{at } t = 0),$$

$$\sum_{i=0}^{N} x_i(1 + \tilde{R}_i) = D + C(D) + \tilde{K}_1 \quad (\text{at } t = 1).$$

$\tilde{K}_1$, the final net worth of the bank can easily be expressed in terms of the risky portfolio $x = (x_1, \dots, x_N)$ and D, which we will take as decision variables:

$$\tilde{K}_1 = \sum_{j=1}^{N} x_i \tilde{\rho}_i + (R_0 D - C(D)) + K_0(1 + R_0), \qquad\qquad (1)$$

where $\tilde{\rho}_i = \tilde{R}_i - R_0$ denotes the excess return on security i.

For the moment, we assume that financial markets are complete in the Arrow–Debreu sense, and equally accessible to all agents. Thus it is possible to compute the equilibrium price S_0 at date 0 of any security S, characterized by its random liquidation value $S(\omega)$, where ω represents the state of the world at date 1, and belongs to some probability space $(\Omega, \mathcal{A}, \pi)$. In order to avoid technicalities we assume for the moment that Ω is finite and we denote by $(p(\omega))_{\omega \in \Omega}$ the vector of Arrow–Debreu contingent prices. We have then

$$S_0 = \sum_{\omega \in \Omega} p(\omega) \tilde{S}(\omega).$$

In particular, for all $i = 0, \dots, N$, we have

$$1 = \sum_{\omega \in \Omega} p(\omega)(1 + \tilde{R}_i(\omega)) \qquad\qquad (2)$$

and notably

$$\frac{1}{1 + R_0} = \sum_{\omega \in \Omega} p(\omega). \qquad\qquad (3)$$

Thus, for all $i = 1, \dots, N$,

$$0 = \sum_{\omega \in \Omega} p(\omega) \tilde{\rho}_i(\omega). \qquad\qquad (4)$$

We are now in a position to compare the decisions of banks under different institutional arrangements, assuming that each bank tries to maximize its market value $\mathcal{V}$:

$$\mathcal{V} = \sum_{\omega \in \Omega} p(\omega) \max(0, \tilde{K}_1(\omega)) \qquad (5)$$

[where $\max(0, \cdot)$ appears because of limited liability],

$$\tilde{K}_1(\omega) = \sum_{i=1}^{N} x_i \tilde{\rho}_i(\omega) + [R_0 D - C(D)] + K_0(1 + R_0).$$

3. The Behavior of Banks in the Complete Markets Set-Up

Following Merton (1977) several authors (among whom Kareken and Wallace (1978), Sharpe (1978), Dothan and Williams (1980)) have used option pricing formulas for computing the net present value of the subsidy implicitly provided by the Deposit Insurance system to commercial banks. The two crucial assumptions of this approach (namely that option prices can always be computed and that banks maximize the net present value of their capital) can only be justified when financial markets are complete. The purpose of this section is to analyze directly the behavior of banks in such a complete markets setup. This will illustrate the limits of this approach for modeling the banking system. We now characterize this behavior of banks under alternative institutional arrangements.

3.1 Without deposit insurance

If depositors are fully informed, they will require an interest rate R_D that takes into account the possibility of failure. Therefore, there is no need for a deposit insurance scheme. If we neglect for a moment the payments services provided by deposits, we must have

$$D = \sum_{\omega \in \Omega} p(\omega) \min \left[D(1 + R_D), (D + K_0)(1 + R_0) + \sum_{i=1}^{N} x_i \tilde{\rho}_i(\omega) \right]. \qquad (6)$$

It is clear in particular that R_D depends on $x = (x_1, \ldots, x_N)$, D and K_0. Moreover, $C(D)$ is just equal to $R_D D$ and we can rearrange eq. (5) to get

$$\mathcal{V} + D \frac{1 + R_D}{1 + R_0}$$

$$= \sum_{\omega \in \Omega} p(\omega) \max \left[D(1 + R_D), (D + K_0)(1 + R_0) + \sum_{i=1}^{N} x_i \tilde{\rho}_i(\omega) \right].$$

Adding this to (6), we obtain

$$V + D\left(1 + \frac{1 + R_D}{1 + R_0}\right)$$

$$= \sum_{\omega \in \Omega} p(\omega)\left[D(1 + R_D) + (D + K_0)(1 + R_0) + \sum_{i=1}^{N} x_i \tilde{\rho}_i(\omega)\right].$$

Using eq. (2) we get

$$V + D\left(1 + \frac{1 + R_D}{1 + R_0}\right) = D\left(1 + \frac{1 + R_D}{1 + R_0}\right) + K_0.$$

Finally

$$V = K_0 \tag{7}$$

and we are back to the Modigliani–Miller indeterminacy principle: the market value of the bank is completely independent of any of its actions. If we introduce a reorganization cost g supported by the bank in case of failure, as in Kareken and Wallace (1978), then (7) becomes

$$V = K_0 - \left(\sum_{\omega \in \Omega_F} p(\omega)\right) g,$$

where Ω_F denotes the set of states of nature in which the bank fails. V is then maximum for any choice of x and D that prevents this failure, i.e. such that $\Omega_F = \varnothing$.

3.2 With deposit insurance, but no capital requirement

From now on, depositors are assumed to be imperfectly informed on the banks' activities, which justifies implementation of a deposit insurance scheme. We will suppose that this scheme provides full insurance for all deposits, and is funded through proportional insurance premia:

$$P = kD, \quad k > 0.$$

We also take into account the payments services provided by the banks in association with deposits. They have a unit cost γ but in counterpart, depositors are ready to accept interest rates R_D lower than R_0. More specifically, there is an (inverse) supply function $R_D(D)$ [with $R_D' > 0$ and $R_D(+\infty) = R_0$] and the bank is supposed to behave as a (local) monopoly on the deposit market. The cost function is then

$$C(D) = (R_D(D) + \gamma + k)D.$$

Again, the market value of the bank can be written as

$$V = \sum_{\omega \in \Omega} p(\omega) \max(0, K_0(1 + R_0) + DR_0 - C(D) + < x, \tilde{\rho}(\omega) >). \tag{8}$$

But in contrast with case no. 1, $C(D)$ is now independent of x and K_0. We have to solve

$$(P_1) \begin{cases} \max_{x,D} V, \\ x_i \geq 0, \quad i = 1, \ldots, N, \\ \sum_{i=1}^{N} x_i \leq K_0 + D. \end{cases}$$

PROPOSITION 1. *We assume complete contingent markets, full deposit insurance with premia depending only on deposits and no capital requirement. Then the bank specializes on a unique, risky, asset.*

Proof. It is a straightforward consequence of the remark that formula (5) implies that V is a *convex* function of x. Thus, D being fixed, P_1 amounts to maximize a convex function on a convex polytope. Its solution is obtained for one of its extreme points $x^0, x^1, \ldots, x^N$ characterized by

$$x^0 = 0, \quad \text{and} \quad \begin{cases} x_i^j = 0 & \text{if } i \neq j, \quad i = 1, \ldots, N \\ x_j^i = K_0 + D & (\text{or } x_0^j = 0). \end{cases}$$

Each of these extreme points corresponds to a specialization of the bank's portfolio on a unique asset j. It remains to prove that this cannot be the riskless asset $j = 0$. For that purpose, it is enough to remark that

$$\frac{\partial V}{\partial x_i}(x^0) = \sum_{\omega \in \Omega} p(\omega) \tilde{\rho}_i(\omega) = 0, \quad i = 1, \ldots, N.$$

Therefore x^0 corresponds to the *minimum* of V on the feasible set.

Let us remark in passing that, as soon as the probability of failure is positive, the volume of deposits chosen by the bank is also inefficient. The bank attracts more deposits than a full liability bank would. $\square$

In this set-up, it is also easy to study the decision of increasing the bank's capital. For that purpose, we need to define two new variables: a retention coefficient τ (i.e. the proportion of the stock that remains in the hands of initial stockholders) and the amount ΔK collected at $t = 0$ from new stockholders. Because of our complete markets assumptions, these two variables are linked by the following equation:

$$\Delta K = (1 - \tau) \sum_{\omega \in \Omega} p(\omega) \max(0, \tilde{K}_1(\omega)), \tag{9}$$

where the new expression of the final net worth of the bank, $\tilde{K}_1(\omega)$, is:

$$\tilde{K}_1(\omega) = \sum_{i=1}^{N} x_i \tilde{\rho}_i(\omega) + (R_0 D - C(D)) + (K_0 + \Delta K)(1 + R_0). \tag{10}$$

The objective function of the initial stockholders is

$$V = \tau \sum_{\omega \in \Omega} p(\omega) \max(0, \tilde{K}_1(\omega)).$$

Because of (9) it can also be written as

$$V = \sum_{\omega \in \Omega} p(\omega) \max(0, \tilde{K}_1(\omega)) - \Delta K.$$

The program to be solved is now:

$$(\mathcal{P}_2) \begin{cases} \max V, \\ x \in \mathbb{R}_+^N, \quad \Delta K \geq 0, \\ \sum_{i=1}^{N} x_i \leq D + K_0 + \Delta K. \end{cases}$$

See Figure 1.

PROPOSITION 2. *Under the assumptions of Proposition 1, the bank will not choose to increase its capital: $\Delta K^* = 0$. The solutions of $\mathcal{P}_2$ and $\mathcal{P}_1$ are the same: specialization on a unique, risky, asset.*

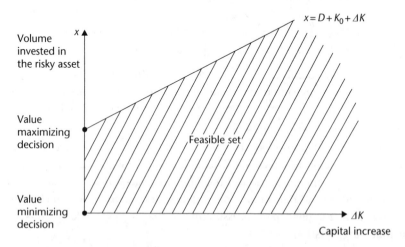

Figure 1. The feasible set and the bank's optimal decision with value maximizing banks, fixed-rate deposit insurance and no capital requirement (case $N=1$).

Proof. Again, V is convex with respect to $(x, \Delta K)$. Moreover it is non-increasing with respect to ΔK:

$$\frac{\partial V}{\partial(\Delta K)} = \sum_{\omega \in \Omega_{NF}} p(\omega)(1 + R_0) - 1 \leq 0 \quad \text{[because of (3)],}$$

where Ω_{NF} is the set of 'no–failure' states.

Since the solution of $\mathcal{P}_2$ is an extreme point of the feasible set only two cases are possible:

- $\Delta K = 0$, and we are back to problem $\mathcal{P}_1$;
- $\Delta K > 0$ and all other constraints are binding, which is impossible since $D + K_0 > 0$. $\square$

3.3 With deposit insurance and capital requirements

Now we introduce a capital requirement, taking the following form:

$$\langle \alpha, x \rangle = \sum_{i=1}^{N} \alpha_i x_i \leq K_0 + \Delta K,$$

where $\alpha_i > 0$ is to be interpreted as the 'risk weight' of security i. The decision problem of the bank becomes

$$(\mathcal{P}_3) \begin{cases} \max V \\ x \in \mathbb{R}_+^N, \quad \Delta K \geq 0, \\ \sum_{i=1}^{N} x_i \leq D + K_0 + \Delta K, \\ \sum_{i=1}^{N} \alpha_i x_i \leq K_0 + \Delta K. \end{cases}$$

See Figure 2.

PROPOSITION 3. *Under the assumptions of Proposition 1, except that a capital requirement is introduced, three cases are possible for the bank's optimal behaviour:*

(1) *No increase of capital ($\Delta K = 0$): Maximum investment on a unique risky asset [$x_i^* = 0$ for $i \neq j, x_j^* = \min(D + K_0, K_0/\alpha_j)$], the rest (if any) being invested in the riskless asset.*

(2) *Complete specialization on a unique, risky, asset: ($x_i^* = 0$ for $i \neq j, x_j^* = D + K_0 + \Delta K$); capital increase just sufficient for meeting the capital requirement.*

(3) *No increase of capital ($\Delta K = 0$): Specialization on two risky assets $j, k(x_i^* = 0$ for $i \neq j, k$) in such a way that the capital requirement binds.*

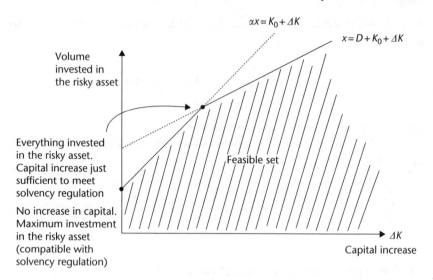

Figure 2. The feasible set and two possible optimal decisions when a solvency ratio is introduced (case $N = 1$).

Proof. Again, it is a straightforward consequence of the convexity of $\mathcal{V}$ with respect to $(x, \Delta K)$ and the fact that $\mathcal{V}$ is non-decreasing in ΔK. Three cases are possible:

— $\Delta K = 0$, and there exists j such that:

$$\begin{cases} x_i^* = 0 \quad \text{for } i \neq j \\ x_j^* = \min\left(D + K_0, \dfrac{K_0}{\alpha_j}\right). \end{cases}$$

— $\Delta K = 0, x_i^* = 0$ for $i \neq j, k$:

$$\begin{cases} x_j^* + x_k^* = D + K_0 \\ \alpha_j x_j^* + \alpha_k x_k^* = K_0. \end{cases}$$

— $\Delta K > 0$: Then there exists j such that:

$$\begin{cases} x_i^* = 0 \quad \text{for } i \neq j \\ x_j^* = D + K_0 + \Delta K = \dfrac{K_0 + \Delta K}{\alpha_j}. \end{cases} \qquad \square$$

It is clear then that if we believe in the complete markets assumption, a capital requirement is a very inefficient tool for limiting the risk taken by banks. Moreover, it entails severe reallocations of assets since in most cases it is optimal for banks to specialize in at most two risky assets. On the other hand, there is a very simple solution to our problem (if we assume that the Regulator is able to monitor the investment decisions of the bank), namely to charge a 'actuarially fair' premium for deposit insurance. This premium is defined by

$$P^* = \sum_{\omega \in \Omega} p(\omega) \max(0, -\tilde{K}_1(\omega)). \tag{11}$$

Instead of adding the insurance premium to the cost of deposits, we are going now to subtract it from the objective function of the bank, which becomes

$$V = \sum_{\omega \in \Omega} p(\omega) \max(0, \tilde{K}_1(\omega)) - \Delta K - P^*.$$

Because of eq. (11), we have also

$$V = \sum_{\omega \in \Omega} p(\omega) \tilde{K}_1(\omega) - \Delta K,$$

$$V = \sum_{\omega \in \Omega} p(\omega) [\langle x, \tilde{\rho}(\omega) \rangle + R_0 D - C(D) + (K_0 + \Delta K)(1 + R_0)] - \Delta K.$$

Finally, using (3) and (4), this simplifies into

$$V = K_0 + \frac{R_0 D - C(D)}{1 + R_0}. \tag{12}$$

PROPOSITION 4. *Under the assumptions of Proposition 1, except that insurance premia are computed in an actuarial basis, the bank is indifferent on its asset portfolio x and capital increases ΔK. As a consequence, capital requirements are useless.*

Proof. (Obvious from eq. (12)). □

4. The Portfolio Model

Since the complete market set-up is rather disappointing for studying capital regulations, we turn to the incomplete markets case. However, things become extremely intricate, unless we adopt several stringent assumptions:

ASSUMPTION 1. *The bank behaves as a portfolio manager, i.e., it tries to maximize the expectations of $u(\tilde{K}_1)$ where u is a (Von Neumann–Morgenstern) utility function (with $u' > 0, u'' < 0$).*

The justification of this assumption is the well-known difficulty of defining a theoretically sound objective function for firms in an incomplete markets setting.

ASSUMPTION 2. *Equity capital is fixed ($\Delta K = 0$).*

This is a departure from previous papers on the subject [Kahane (1977), Koehn and Santomero (1980), Kim and Santomero (1988)], who made the same assumption as Hart and Jaffee (1974): There is an exogenous price for equity capital, and the bank chooses ΔK in a competitive fashion. Since we are concerned with failure possibilities, it does not seem reasonable to assume that the price of capital is independent of the investment policy of the bank. However, again because of our incomplete markets assumption, it is not easy to specify a reasonable way in which the price of capital depends on x, ΔK and D. Therefore, we were forced to adopt Assumption 2.

In order to simplify the analysis we are finally going to make a technical assumption:

ASSUMPTION 3. *The vector* $\tilde{\rho} = (\tilde{\rho}_i, \ldots, \tilde{\rho}_N)$ *is Gaussian, with mean* $\rho = (\rho_i, \ldots, \rho_N)$ *and non-singular variance–covariance matrix* V.

A well-known consequence of this assumption is that we can restrict ourselves to a mean–variance analysis:

PROPOSITION 5. *Under Assumptions* 1, 2, 3, *the objective function and the default probability of the bank only depend on*

$$\mu = E(\tilde{K}_1) = \langle x, \rho \rangle + R_0 D - C(D) + K_0(1 + R_0),$$

$$\sigma^2 = \langle x, Vx \rangle.$$

More specifically,

$$Eu(\tilde{K}_1) = U(\mu, \sigma)$$

where U *is concave in* (μ, σ), *increasing in* μ, *decreasing in* σ.

$$\text{Prob}[\tilde{K}_1 < 0] = N\left(-\frac{\mu}{\sigma}\right)$$

where N *denotes the standard Gaussian cumulative.*

Proof. Assumption 3 implies that $\tilde{K}_1$ is Gaussian of mean μ and variance σ^2. Therefore:

$$Eu(\tilde{K}_1) = \int u(\sigma y + \mu)\, dN(y) = U(\mu, \sigma);$$

u being increasing, so is the mapping $\mu \to u(\mu + \sigma y)$ (for all y), which implies that U is increasing in μ; u being concave, so is the mapping $(\mu, \sigma) \to u(\mu + \sigma y)$ (for all y), which implies that U is concave in (μ, σ). Finally, by symmetry of N, we can write

$$U(\mu, \sigma) = \int_0^{+\infty} \{u(-\sigma y + \mu) + u(\sigma y + \mu)\}\, dN(y);$$

u being concave, the mapping $\sigma \to u(\mu + \sigma y) + u(\mu - \sigma y)$ is decreasing (for all $y > 0$), and thus U is decreasing in σ.

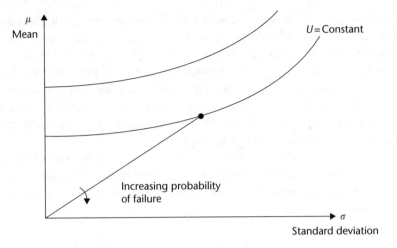

Figure 3. Indifference curves and failure probability of a full liability bank in the portfolio model.

Finally:

$$P(\tilde{K}_1 < 0) = P\left[\frac{\tilde{K}_1 - \mu}{\sigma} < -\frac{\mu}{\sigma}\right] = N\left(-\frac{\mu}{\sigma}\right),$$

which is a decreasing function of μ and an increasing function of σ. ☐

See Figure 3.

5. The Behaviour of Banks in the Portfolio Model without Capital Requirements

In order to solve the bank's decision problem, we are going to use Proposition 5 and first characterize the feasible set in terms of means and variances. Before that, let us determine the optimal quantity of deposits D^*. Since we have evacuated liquidity considerations (i.e. we assumed deterministic deposits) and since U is increasing in μ, D^* is simply determined by the condition

$$C'(D^*) = R_0.$$

In the case where the bank would only invest in the riskless asset (and choose $x = 0$), its final net worth would be non-random, and equal to

$$K = R_0 D^* - C(D^*) + K_0(1 + R_0).$$

This quantity, which we call 'corrected net worth', incorporates the intermediation margin obtained by the bank in the deposit activity. The magnitude of this margin may be very different across countries, because it depends in particular on the (possible) regulations of deposit rates and the degrees of competition for deposits. Similarly, the magnitude of this term may be very different across banks in the same country, because different banks may have very different cost functions. In some countries, it is clearly non-negligible. Let us remark incidentally that this intermediation margin introduces a relation between the deposit and assets activities of the bank, even though the riskless asset is inelastic. This has to be contrasted with Klein (1971).

Let us turn now to the portfolio choice, by characterizing first the 'feasible set' (in terms of means and variances) for an unregulated bank of corrected net worth K. For the sake of simplicity, we will suppose that the 'borrowing constraint' ($x_0 \geq 0$) is not binding.

$$A_0(K) = (\text{def.}) \left\{ (\sigma, \mu), \exists x \in \mathbb{R}_+^N, \begin{array}{l} \mu = K + \langle x, \rho \rangle \\ \sigma^2 = \langle x, Vx \rangle \end{array} \right\}.$$

By Proposition 5, Our problem is equivalent to

$$(\mathcal{P}') \begin{cases} \max U(\mu, \sigma) \\ (\sigma, \mu) \in A_0(K) \end{cases}.$$

Since U is increasing in μ, the solution of $(\mathcal{P}')$ will always belong to the 'efficient set':

$$A_0^+(K) = \{(\sigma, \mu) \in A_0(K), \forall \mu' > \mu(\sigma, \mu') \notin A_0(K)\}.$$

As is well known, $A_0^+(K)$ is a straight line.

LEMMA 1. $A_0^+(K) = \{(\sigma, \mu), \mu - K = \lambda \sigma\}$ where λ is a positive constant.

Proof. See Appendix A.

Remark. Thus the no-short-sales requirement ($x \in \mathbb{R}_+^N$) does not modify the traditional results of the CAPM: all banks choose portfolios collinear to x^*. At equilibrium, x^* is thus proportional to the market portfolio x^M. If the same no-short-sales requirements apply to all investors in the economy, then $x_i^M > 0$ for all i (otherwise security i is not traded). Ex post, the no-short-sales requirements are non-binding and we are back to the CAPM:

$$x^* = \frac{V^{-1}\rho}{\langle \rho, V^{-1}\rho \rangle} \quad \text{and} \quad \lambda = \langle \rho, V^{-1}\rho \rangle^{1/2}.$$

In particular the vector ρ of mean excess return is proportional to the vector $\beta = Vx$ of the covariances with the market portfolio return.

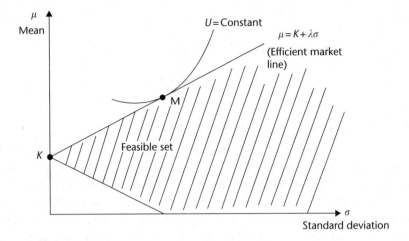

Figure 4. The feasible set and the optimal decision of a utility maximizing bank, with full liability and no capital requirement.

In this very simple mean-variance world, a good indicator of default risk is given by the following 'adjusted' capital ratio:

$$CR = \frac{K}{\langle \alpha, x \rangle}.$$

This is indeed a consequence of the following proposition:

PROPOSITION 6. *Under Assumptions* 1, 2, 3 *and when capital is not regulated, the default probability of a bank is a decreasing function of its adjusted capital ratio.*

Proof. It is easily deduced from the fact that all banks choose risky portfolios with the same composition. Let $x(K)$ be the optimal risky portfolio for a bank having an 'adjusted net worth' equal to K. By the arguments above we know that

$$x(K) = \sigma(K)x^M,$$

where x^M is the market portfolio, normalized in such a way that it has a unit variance (i.e. $x^M = V^{-1}\rho/\lambda$). $\sigma(K)$ is a non-negative constant, equal to the standard deviation of the argument maximum of $\mathcal{P}$. It is the maximum of $\sigma \to U(K+\lambda\sigma, \sigma)$ and in particular, the mean return on $x(K)$ equals

$$\mu(K) = K + \lambda\sigma(K).$$

As a consequence

$$CR(K)^{-1} = \frac{\langle \alpha, x(K) \rangle}{K} = \frac{\sigma(K)}{K}\langle \alpha, x_M \rangle$$

and

$$\mathrm{Prob}(\tilde{K}_1 < 0) = N\left(-\frac{\mu(K)}{K}\right) = N\left(-1 - \lambda\frac{\sigma(K)}{K}\right)$$
$$= N\left(-1 - \frac{\lambda\langle\alpha, x_{\mathrm{M}}\rangle}{CR(K)}\right).$$

Since $\lambda > 0$, and N increasing, the proof is completed. $\quad\square$

Proposition 6 may seem a good justification of capital requirements. *Independently* of the choice of risk weights $\alpha_1, \ldots, \alpha_N$, but provided that the numerator of the ratio is adjusted to incorporate intermediation profits on deposits, the capital ratio is an increasing function of the default risk. The trouble is that as soon as the capital requirement is imposed, the banks' behavior changes and Proposition 6 ceases to be true. This will be the subject of the next section.

As a conclusion to the present section, we examine the dependence of the default risk of an unregulated bank on its (corrected) net worth. Is $CR(K)$ a monotonic function of K? In other words, if no capital regulation was imposed, would the more capitalized banks be more or less risky than the less capitalized ones? It turns out that the answer to this question depends on the properties of the utility function u. More specifically:

PROPOSITION 7. *If the Arrow–Pratt relative index of risk aversion* $-xu''(x)/u'(x)$ *is decreasing (resp. increasing), then the default probability of an unregulated bank is an increasing (resp. decreasing) function of its 'adjusted' net worth K.*

Proof. By Proposition 6, the default probability of an unregulated bank is an increasing function of

$$\tau(K) = \frac{\sigma(K)}{K},$$

where $\tau(K)$ is the solution to $\max_{\tau} E u[K(1 + \tau\tilde{R}_{\mathrm{M}})]$ and $\tilde{R}_{\mathrm{M}}$ is the random return of the market portfolio. By well-known results of Arrow (1974) and Pratt (1964), if $-(xu''(x))/(u'(x))$ is monotonic, then $\tau(K)$ is monotonic in the other direction.

As a consequence of Proposition 7, the most frequently used specifications of VNM utility functions, namely exponential and isoelastic functions, lead to a default probability that is, respectively, a decreasing and a constant function of K.

6. Introducing Capital Requirements in the Portfolio Model

In order to concentrate on one distortion at a time, we will assume that the capital regulation requires the *adjusted* capital ratio to be less than 1. Or equivalently, we neglect the intermediation margin $K - K_0$. The new feasible set is now restricted to:

$$A_1(K) = \left\{ (\sigma, \mu), \exists x \in \mathbb{R}_+^N, \begin{array}{l} \mu - K = \langle x, \rho \rangle \\ \langle x, Vx \rangle = \sigma^2, \langle \alpha, x \rangle \leqq K \end{array} \right\}.$$

As before, let us denote by $A_1^+(K)$ the 'efficient set under regulation' i.e. the upper contour of $A_1(K)$.

PROPOSITION 8. *In general the efficient set under regulation is composed of a subset of the 'market line' $A_0^+(K)$ and a non-decreasing curve (a portion of hyperbola). In the particular case when the risk weights α_i are proportional to the systematic risks β_i or to the mean excess returns ρ_i, this portion of hyperbola degenerates into a horizontal line.*

Proof. See Appendix A.

Proposition 8 shows that the consequences of imposing a capital requirement are very different according to the value of the risk weights α_i. If these weights are 'market-based', in the sense that the vector α is proportional to the vector β of systematic risks, then the new efficient set is a strict subset of the market line. All banks continue to choose an efficient portfolio. Those which are constrained by the regulation choose a less risky portfolio than before. As a consequence, their default probability decreases.

On the other hand, if the risk weights are not 'market-based', the adoption of the capital regulation has two consequences: for those banks which are constrained, the total 'size' of the risky portfolio (as measured by $< \alpha, x \rangle$) decreases, but the portfolio is reshuffled, by investing more in those assets i for which ρ_i/α_i is highest, and investing less in the other assets. The total effect on the failure probability is ambiguous. As shown by the example given in Appendix B, it may very well increase in some cases, the reshuffling effect dominating the 'size' effect. A similar result has been obtained before in Kim and Santomero (1988).

As a conclusion to this section, let us examine the following question: which banks are going to be constrained by the capital regulation? The answer is again related to the monotonicity of the relative index of risk aversion.

PROPOSITION 9. *If the relative index of risk aversion $-(xu''(x))/(u'(x))$ is decreasing (increasing), the banks with the highest (lowest) net worth will be constrained by the capital regulation.*

Proof. A bank is constrained by the capital regulation if and only if the portfolio chosen in the unregulated case has a variance greater than $\bar{\sigma}^2 = \langle \rho, V^{-1}\rho \rangle / \langle \alpha, V^{-1}\rho \rangle^2$. The result follows then from Proposition 7. □

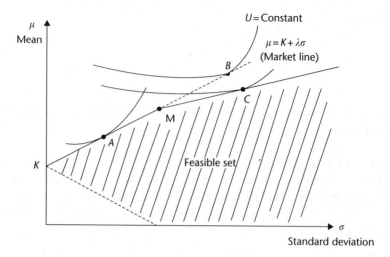

Figure 5. The feasible set and the optimal decisions of utility maximizing banks (with full liability) when there is a capital requirement with a arbitrary risk weights. *A*: choice of an unconstrained bank; *B*: previous choice of a constrained bank; *C*: new choice of the same bank. In this example the failure probability of the constrained bank has increased after the imposition of the capital requirement.

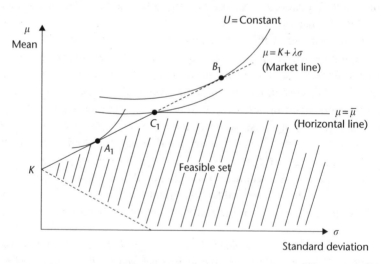

Figure 6. The feasible set and the optimal decisions of utility maximizing banks (with full liability) when there is a capital requirement with *correct* risk weight. *A₁*: choice of an inconstrained bank; *B₁*: previous choice of a constrained bank; *C₁*: new choice of the same bank. Notice that the failure probability of the constrained bank has decreased and that it still chooses an efficient portfolio.

7. Introducing Limited Liability in the Portfolio Model

As remarked by Keeley and Furlong (1990), it is ironical that the very source of the problem under study, namely the limited liability of banks, has been neglected so far in the portfolio model. When it is taken into account, the objective function of the bank becomes

$$W(\mu,\sigma) = \int_{-\mu/\sigma}^{\infty} u(\mu + \sigma y)\, dN(y) - CN\left(-\frac{\mu}{\sigma}\right),$$

where $C \geq 0$ represents a (fixed) bankruptcy cost, and u has been normalized in such a way that

$$u(0) = 0.$$

Let us remark that our normality assumption implies that the bank's utility still depends on (μ,σ) and not on the truncated moments of $\tilde{K}$. However, the properties of W will differ markedly from the utility function under full liability, given by

$$U(\mu,\sigma) = \int_{-\infty}^{+\infty} u(\mu + \sigma y)\, dN(y).$$

It is easy to see that, the U, W is an increasing function of μ. However, unlike U, W is neither necessarily increasing nor concave with respect to σ.

In fact, our first result asserts that if the absolute index of risk aversion is bounded above, then:

— for small μ and large σ, W is increasing in σ (the bank exhibits locally a risk-loving behavior !);
— W is not everywhere quasi-concave.

PROPOSITION 10. *We assume that*

$$-\frac{u''(x)}{u'(x)} \leq a$$

for all x. Then, if

$$\mu a\left[1 + \frac{aC}{u'(\mu)}\right] < 1,$$

we have

$$\lim_{\sigma \to +\infty} \frac{\partial W}{\partial \sigma}(\mu,\sigma) = 0^+.$$

As a consequence, for σ large enough, W is increasing in σ. Moreover, W is not everywhere quasi concave.

Proof. See Appendix A.

The shape of indifference curves in the (μ,σ) plane is given by Figure 7.

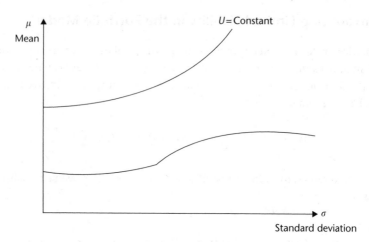

Figure 7. The shape of the bank's indifference curves under limited liability.

We are now in a position to study the portfolio choice of a limited liability bank. For simplicity we are going to take from now on $C = 0$. Let us begin with the unregulated case. Since W is increasing in μ, we can limit ourselves to $A_0^+(K) = \{(\mu, \sigma)/\mu = K + \lambda\sigma\}$. In order to find the maximum of W on $A_0^+(K)$, we have to study the auxiliary function

$$\omega(\sigma) = W(K + \lambda\sigma, \sigma).$$

PROPOSITION 11. *We assume that* $-(u''(x))/(u'(x)) \leqq a$ *for all* x *and that* $C = 0$. *For all* $K < 1/a$, $\omega(\sigma)$ *is increasing with* σ. *Therefore its supremum is attained for* $\sigma = +\infty$.

Proof. See Appendix A.

Of course, Proposition 11 does not mean that a bank with small enough own funds would choose a 'infinitely risky portfolio'. Indeed, we have neglected non-negativity constraints on asset choices. Therefore, even in the unregulated case, only a portion of the market line is in fact attainable. When non-negativity constraints start to be binding, the efficient set becomes a hyperbola similar to the one we found in the regulated case. The correct interpretation of Proposition 11 is that for $K < 1/a$, the bank will choose a very 'extreme' portfolio with (at least partial) specialization on some assets. The convexity of preferences due to limited liability eventually dominates risk aversion.

Although we do not provide a full characterization of the behaviour of a limited liability bank, Propositions 10 and 11 have together an interesting consequence. Even with correct risk weights, a capital ratio may not be enough to induce an efficient portfolio choice of the bank. This is explained by Figure 8.

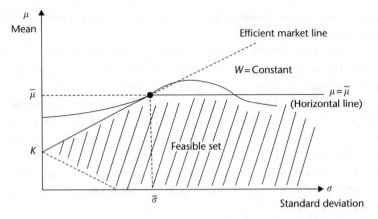

Figure 8. Portfolio choice with limited liability and 'correctly weighted' solvency ratio but no minimum capital.

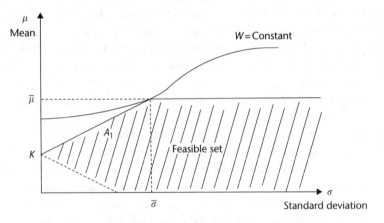

Figure 9. Portfolio choice with limited liability, 'correctly weighted' solvency ratio and minimum capital $\overline{K}$.

When K is small enough, W is increasing on the efficient market line but it may happen that $W(\overline{\mu}, \sigma)$ becomes larger than $W(\overline{\mu}, \overline{\sigma})$ for σ large enough. Consequently, and in contra-distinction with the full liability case, the bank would not choose $(\overline{\mu}, \overline{\sigma})$. As a consequence it may be necessary to impose an additional regulation, in the form of a minimal capital level $\overline{K}$, as suggested by Figure 9.

8. Conclusion

Of course one should not take too literally all the conclusions of the very abstract and reducing model presented in the paper. However, we have clarified several elements of the polemic between value maximizing models and utility maximizing models.

If we accept the assumption of complete contingent markets (the only correct way to justify value maximizing behavior), then it is true that under fixed-rate deposit insurance, absence of capital regulations would lead to a very risky behavior of commercial banks. However, capital regulations (at least of the usual type) are a very poor instrument for controlling the risk of banks: they give incentives for choosing 'extreme' asset allocations, and are relatively inefficient for reducing the risk of bank failures. The correct instrument consists in using 'actuarial' pricing of deposit insurance which implies computing risk-related premia. A pricing formula incorporating interest rate risk is obtained in a companion paper [Kerfriden–Rochet (1991)].

On the other hand, if we take into account incompleteness of financial markets and adopt the portfolio model (utility maximizing banks), the correct choice of risk-weights in the solvency ratio becomes crucial. If these risk-weights are related to credit risk alone (as is the case for the Cooke ratio and its twin brother, the EEC ratio), this may induce again very inefficient asset allocations by banks. We suggest instead to adopt 'market-based' risk-weights, i.e. weights proportional to the systematic risks of these assets, measured by their market betas. However, contrarily to previous papers using the portfolio model, we do not neglect the limited liability of the banks under study. We show that it implies that insufficiently capitalized banks may exhibit risk loving behaviors. As a consequence it may be necessary to impose a minimum capital level as an additional regulation.

It may seem unrealistic to suggest the adoption of 'market-based' risk-weights for bank loans, which constitute a large proportion of banks' assets and are a priori non-marketable. However, the success of the securitization activity in the U.S.A. has shifted the border between marketable and non-marketable assets. Moreover, once non-systematic risk has been diversified there is not much of a difference between a pool of loans and a government bond. However, further research is needed to correctly account for the asymmetic information aspects of the banking activity.

APPENDIX A

A.1. Proof of Lemma 1 By the projection theorem, the function $\langle x, Vx \rangle$ (which equals $\|Bx\|^2$, where B denotes the 'square-root' of V, i.e., the unique symmetric positive definite matrix such that ${}^tBB = V$) has a unique minimum x^* on the convex set

$$C = \{x \in \mathbb{R}^N_+, \langle x, \rho \rangle = 1\}.$$

Thus

$$A_0^+(K) \cap \{\mu = 1\} = \{(\lambda, 1)\},$$

where

$$\lambda = \langle x^*, Vx^* \rangle > 0.$$

By homogeneity of the definition of $A_0(K)$, we obtain:

$$A_0^+(K) = \{(\sigma, \mu), \mu - K = \lambda\sigma\}.$$

A.2. Proof of Proposition 8 For arbitrary $\mu \geq K$ we have to solve

$$(\mathcal{P}'') \quad \begin{cases} \min \langle x, Vx \rangle \\ \text{for} \quad x \in \mathbb{R}_+^N \quad \text{such that} \quad \begin{array}{l} \langle \rho, x \rangle = \mu - K, \\ \langle \alpha, x \rangle \leq K. \end{array} \end{cases}$$

When the second constraint is not binding, we are back to our initial problem. The solution of $\mathcal{P}''$ is

$$x = (\mu - K)x^* \quad \text{where } x^* = \frac{V^{-1}\rho}{\langle \rho, V^{-1}\rho \rangle}.$$

This is feasible if and only if

$$\langle \alpha, x \rangle = (\mu - K)\frac{\langle \alpha, V^{-1}\rho \rangle}{\langle p, V^{-1}\rho \rangle} \leq K. \tag{A.1}$$

In that case

$$\sigma = \langle x, Vx \rangle^{1/2} = \frac{\mu - K}{\langle \rho, V^{-1}\rho \rangle^{1/2}} = \frac{\mu - K}{\lambda}.$$

In particular if $\langle \alpha, V^{-1}\rho \rangle \leq 0$, condition (A.1) is always satisfied for $\mu \geq K$ and the capital requirement is ineffective. This case is completely uninteresting. Therefore we may assume that $\langle \alpha, V^{-1}\rho \rangle > 0$.

When the second constraint is binding, we have to distinguish between two cases:

Case 1: $\exists h > 0, \alpha = h\rho$

Then the feasible set of problem $\mathcal{P}''$ is non-empty only when condition (2) is satisfied, that is when

$$\mu - K \leq K/h.$$

As a consequence

$$A_1^+(K) \subset \left\{ (\sigma, \mu), \mu - K = \min\left(\lambda\sigma, \frac{K}{h}\right) \right\}.$$

When α is positive, $A_1(K)$ is in fact a triangle.

Case 2: α and ρ are linearly independent

The Lagrangian of $(\mathcal{P}'')$ can be written as

$$\mathcal{L} = \langle x, Vx \rangle - 2v_1 \langle \rho, x \rangle - 2v_2 \langle \alpha, x \rangle,$$

and the first-order condition gives

$$Vx = v_1\rho + v_2\alpha,$$

where v_1, v_2 are determined by

$$\langle \rho, x \rangle = \mu - K \quad \text{and} \quad \langle \alpha, x \rangle = K.$$

In other words,

$$v = \begin{pmatrix} v_1 \\ v_2 \end{pmatrix} = M^{-1} \begin{pmatrix} \mu - K \\ K \end{pmatrix},$$

where

$$M = \begin{pmatrix} \langle \rho, V^{-1}\rho \rangle & \langle \rho, V^{-1}\alpha \rangle \\ \langle \alpha, V^{-1}\rho \rangle & \langle \alpha, V^{-1}\alpha \rangle \end{pmatrix} \text{ is positive definite,}$$

consequently,

$$\sigma^2 = \langle x, Vx \rangle = v_1 \langle \rho, x \rangle + v_2 \langle \alpha, x \rangle = (\mu - K)v_1 + v_2 K,$$
$$\sigma^2 = (\mu - K)^2 r + 2(\mu - K)Ks + tK^2, \tag{A.2}$$

where

$$M^{-1} = \begin{pmatrix} r & s \\ s & t \end{pmatrix} \text{ is such that } \Delta = rt - s^2 > 0, \text{ and } s < 0$$

(because $\langle \alpha, V^{-1}\rho \rangle > 0$).

Since M^{-1} is positive definitive, (A.2) is the equation of an hyperbola. x is indeed the solution to $\mathcal{P}''$ if and only of $v_2 \leq 0$, which is equivalent to

$$\mu - K \geq -\frac{tK}{s} = \frac{\langle \rho, V^{-1}\rho \rangle}{\langle \alpha, V^{-1}\rho \rangle} K.$$

Finally, we obtain

$$
A_1^+(K) \subset \left\{ (\sigma, \mu), \quad
\begin{array}{ll}
\mu - K = \lambda \sigma & \sigma \leqq \bar{\sigma} K \\[2mm]
\mu - K = \dfrac{K}{r}\left[-s + \sqrt{\dfrac{r\sigma^2}{K^2} - \Delta}\right] & \sigma > \bar{\sigma} K
\end{array}
\right\}
$$

where

$$
\bar{\sigma} = -\frac{t}{s\lambda} = \frac{(\rho, V^{-1}\rho)^{1/2}}{\langle \alpha, V^{-1}\rho \rangle}.
$$

A.3. Proof of Proposition 10

$$
\frac{\partial W}{\partial \sigma}(\mu, \sigma) = \int_{-\mu/\sigma}^{+\infty} y u'(\mu + y\sigma)\, dN(y) - \frac{C\mu}{\sigma^2} f\left(\frac{\mu}{\sigma}\right).
$$

Since

$$
-\frac{u''(x)}{u'(x)} \leq a,
$$

$e^{ax}u'(x)$ is an increasing function of x, which implies

$$
\forall y \quad y u'(\mu + y\sigma) \geqq y u'(\mu) e^{-ay\sigma}.
$$

Thus,

$$
\frac{\partial W}{\partial \sigma}(\mu, \sigma) \geq y u'(\mu) \int_{-\mu/\sigma}^{+\infty} y e^{-ay\sigma} f(y)\, dy - \frac{C\mu}{\sigma^2} f\left(\frac{\mu}{\sigma}\right).
$$

After straightforward computations the right-hand side can be transformed as follows:

$$
\frac{\partial W}{\partial \sigma}(\mu, \sigma) \geq f\left(\frac{\mu}{\sigma}\right)\left[\left\{1 - a\sigma A\left(\frac{\mu}{\sigma} - a\sigma\right)\right\} u'(\mu) - \frac{C\mu}{\sigma^2}\right],
$$

where we have introduced the auxiliary function

$$
A(t) = \frac{N(t)}{f(t)},
$$

which is such that

$$
A'(t) = 1 + tA(t).
$$

Similarly,

$$
f'(t) = -tf(t).
$$

We need a technical lemma:

LEMMA A.1. $\forall t\ A(t) \leqq -1/t + 1/t^3$; *moreover when* $t \to -\infty$, *these two functions are equivalent.*

Using this lemma, we obtain

$$\frac{\partial W}{\partial \sigma} \geq f\left(\frac{\mu}{\sigma}\right) u'(\mu) \left[1 - \frac{C\mu}{u'(\mu)\sigma^2} + \frac{1}{(\mu/a\sigma^2) - 1} - \frac{(1/a\sigma)^2}{((\mu/a\sigma^2) - 1)^3}\right].$$

Denoting $\psi(\sigma)$ the term between brackets we have

$$\psi(\sigma) = 1 - \frac{1}{1 - (\mu/a\sigma^2)} - \frac{C\mu}{u'(\mu)\sigma^2} + \frac{1}{a^2\sigma^2(1 - (\mu/a\sigma^2))^3}$$

$$= \frac{1}{\sigma^2}\left[-\frac{\mu/a}{1 - \mu/a\sigma^2} - \frac{C\mu}{u'(\mu)} + \frac{1}{a^2(1 - (\mu/a\sigma^2))^3}\right]$$

and

$$\lim_{\sigma \to +\infty} \sigma^2 \psi(\sigma) = \frac{1}{a^2} - \frac{\mu}{a} - \frac{C\mu}{u'(\mu)}.$$

Thus if $\mu a(1 + (aC/u'(\mu))) < 1$, $\partial W/\partial \sigma$ is positive for σ large enough. Since $\partial W/\partial \sigma$ is negative for σ small enough, W cannot be quasiconcave with respect to σ.

Proof of Lemma A.1

$$A(t) = \int_{-\infty}^{t} \exp \tfrac{1}{2}(t^2 - x^2)\,dt.$$

Let

$$s = \exp \tfrac{1}{2}(t^2 - x^2) \quad \text{or} \quad x = -\sqrt{t^2 - 2\ln s},$$

$$A(t) = \int_{0}^{1} \frac{ds}{\sqrt{t^2 - 2\ln s}}.$$

Let $B(t) = t^2(tA(t) + 1)$ and

$$\phi(s,t) = \frac{-2\ln s}{(1 - (2\ln s)/t^2) + \sqrt{1 - (2\ln s)/t^2}},$$

$$B(t) = \int_{0}^{1} t^2 \left\{1 - \frac{1}{\sqrt{1 - (2\ln s)/t^2}}\right\} ds,$$

$$B(t) = \int_{0}^{1} \phi(s,t)\,ds.$$

For all s in $[0,1]$, $t \to \phi(s,t)$ is increasing. Moreover,

$$\lim_{t \to +\infty} \phi(s,t) = -\ln s.$$

By Lebesgue's monotone convergence theorem

$$\inf_{t} B(t) = \lim_{t \to -\infty} B(t) = -\int_{0}^{1} \ln s\,ds = 1$$

and the proof is completed.

A.4. Proof of Proposition 11

$$w'(\sigma) = \lambda \frac{\partial W}{\partial \mu} + \frac{\partial W}{\partial \sigma}$$

$$= \int_{-\mu/\sigma}^{+\infty} (\lambda + y) u'(\mu + \sigma y) \, dN(y).$$

Using the fact that $x \to e^{ax} u'(x)$ is increasing we have

$$\forall y \quad (\lambda + y) u'(\mu + \sigma y) \geq (\lambda + y) u'(\mu - \sigma \lambda) e^{-a\sigma(y+\lambda)}.$$

Thus

$$w'(\sigma) \geq u'(\mu - \sigma \lambda) e^{+a(\mu - \sigma \lambda)} \int_{-\mu/\sigma}^{+\infty} (\lambda + y) e^{-a(\mu + \sigma y)} \, dN(y).$$

After straightforward computations the right-hand side can be expressed as follows:

$$w'(\sigma) \geq u'(\mu - \sigma \lambda) e^{+a(\mu - \sigma \lambda)} f\left(\lambda + \frac{K}{\sigma}\right) \left[1 + (\lambda - a\sigma) A\left(\mu + \frac{K}{\sigma} - a\sigma\right)\right].$$

Let us consider the auxiliary function

$$H(\sigma) = 1 + (\lambda - a\sigma) A\left(\lambda + \frac{K}{\sigma} - a\sigma\right).$$

We have

$$\lim_{\sigma \to +\infty} H(\sigma) = +\infty.$$

We are going to prove that the graph of H crosses the horizontal axis at most once, by showing that

$$\forall \sigma > 0 \quad H(\sigma) = 0 \Rightarrow H'(\sigma) < 0.$$

A straightforward computation gives indeed

$$H'(\sigma) = -A\left(\lambda + \frac{K}{\sigma} - a\sigma\right)\left[a + \left(a + \frac{K}{\sigma^2}\right)(\lambda - a\sigma)\left(\lambda + \frac{K}{\sigma} - a\sigma\right)\right]$$
$$- (\lambda - a\sigma)\left(a + \frac{K}{\sigma^2}\right).$$

Thus

$$H(\sigma) = 0 \Rightarrow -A\left(\lambda + \frac{K}{\sigma} - a\sigma\right) = \frac{1}{\lambda - a\sigma} < 0$$

$$\Rightarrow H'(\sigma) = \frac{1}{\lambda - a\sigma}\left[a + \frac{K}{\sigma}\left(a + \frac{K}{\sigma^2}\right)\right] < 0.$$

By the technical lemma already used in the proof of proposition 10, we know that

$$\lim_{t \to -\infty} (t^2 + t^3 A(t)) = 1;$$

consequently,

$$\lim_{t \to +\infty} \sigma^2 H(\sigma) = \lim_{t \to -\infty} \frac{\sigma^2(t)}{t^2} \left[t^2 + \left(t - \frac{K}{\sigma(t)} \right) t^2 A(t) \right],$$

where

$$\sigma(t) = \sigma \quad \Leftrightarrow \quad t = \lambda + \frac{K}{\sigma} - a\sigma.$$

In particular

$$\lim_{t \to +\infty} \frac{\sigma^2(t)}{t^2} = \frac{1}{a^2}.$$

Thus

$$\lim_{\sigma \to +\infty} \sigma^2 H(\sigma) = \frac{1}{a^2} \left[1 + aK \lim_{t \to -\infty} t A(t) \right] = \frac{1 - aK}{a^2}.$$

Thus, when $K < 1/a$, $\lim \inf_{\sigma \to +\infty} w'(\sigma) \geq 0$ and w is increasing.

APPENDIX B

An Example of an Increase in the Default Probability Consecutive to the Adoption of the Capital Requirement

We take an exponential specification: $u(x) = (1/a)(1 - e^{-ax})$ where $a > 0$. In that case we have

$$U(\mu, \sigma) = u \left(\mu - \tfrac{1}{2} a\sigma^2 \right).$$

The portfolio chosen in the unregulated case is such that

$$\mu_0 = K + \lambda \sigma_0,$$

where σ_0 solves

$$\max_{\sigma} \left(\lambda \sigma - \tfrac{1}{2} a\sigma^2 \right).$$

That is

$$\sigma_0 = \frac{\lambda}{a} \quad \text{and} \quad \mu_0 = K + \frac{\lambda^2}{a}.$$

When the capital requirement is introduced, and the bank is indeed constrained, the portfolio it chooses has a mean return μ_1 that maximizes

$$\mu - \tfrac{1}{2} a[(\mu - K)^2 r + 2(\mu - K)Ks + tK^2],$$

that is

$$\mu_1 = K + \frac{1}{r}\left[\frac{1}{a} - Ks\right]$$

and

$$\sigma_1^2 = tK^2 + \frac{1}{r}\left[\frac{1}{a^2} - K^2 s^2\right].$$

When a tends to zero we have

$$\frac{\mu_0}{\sigma_0} \sim \lambda \quad \text{and} \quad \frac{\mu_1}{\sigma_1} \sim \frac{1}{\sqrt{r}}.$$

But

$$\lambda^2 = \langle \rho, V^{-1}\rho \rangle = \frac{t}{\Delta} = \frac{t}{rt - s^2} > \frac{1}{r}.$$

Consequently, when the parameter a is small enough, $\mu_1/\sigma_1 < \mu_0/\sigma_0$ and the failure probability of the bank increases when the capital requirement is adopted.

References

Arrow, K. J. (1974). Essays in the Theory of Risk-Bearing, Amsterdam: North-Holland.

Dothan, U., and Williams, J. (1980). "Banks, bankruptcy and public regulation." *Journal of Banking and Finance*, 4: 65–88.

Hart, O. D., and Jaffee, D. M. (1974). "On the application of portfolio theory to depository financial intermediaries." *Review of Economic Studies*, 41: 129–47.

Kahane, Y. (1977). "Capital adequacy and the regulation of financial intermediaries." *Journal of Banking and Finance*, 2: 207–17.

Kareken, J. H., and Wallace, N. (1978). "Deposit insurance and bank regulation: A partial equilibrium exposition." *Journal of Business*, 51: 413–38.

Keeley, M. C., and Furlong, F. T. (1990). "A reexamination of mean-variance analysis of bank capital regulation." *Journal of Banking and Finance*, 14: 69–84.

Kerfriden, C., and Rochet, J. C. (1991). "Measuring interest rate risk of financial institutions." Unpublished manuscript, GREMAQ, University of Toulouse, Toulouse.

Kim, D., and Santomero, A. M. (1988). "Risk in banking and capital regulation." *Journal of Finance*, 43: 1219–33.

Klein, M. A. (1971). "A theory of the banking firm." *Journal of Money, Credit and Banking*, 3: 205–18.

Koehn, H. and Santomero, A. M. (1980). "Regulation of bank capital and portfolio risk." *Journal of Finance*, 35: 1235–44.

Merton, R. C. (1977). "An analytical derivation of the cost of deposit insurance and loan guarantees: An application of modern option theory." *Journal of Banking and Finance*, 1: 3–11.

Pratt, J. "Risk aversion in the small and in the large." *Econometrica*, 2: 122–36.

Pyle, D. (1971). "On the theory of financial intermediation." *Journal of Finance*, 26: 734–47.

Sharpe, W. F. (1978). "Bank capital adequacy, deposit insurance and security values." *Journal of Financial and Quantitative Analysis*, 701–18.

Comments by Colin Mayer

The determination of capital requirements for European banks has become a subject of particular concern to regulators involved in the integration of financial markets and the creation of a single European currency. Different forms of bank regulation conflict in a single market in which banks can freely trade and establish branches across borders. Problems of coordination of regulation have been addressed through international negotiation; a greater degree of consensus has emerged in the imposition of solvency ratios for banks than in most areas of financial regulation. The Basle Accord specified risk based solvency ratio requirements that have in large part been followed by the European Community.

This chapter is concerned with the reasons for and the effects of capital requirements. It has the commendable feature of bringing rigorous theoretical analysis to bear on an important policy area without resorting to the ad hoc assumptions that have afflicted most of the literature.

The analysis is in three stages. In the first stage, the chapter discusses a 'complete markets' model of banks with the possibility of bankruptcy occurring. The second stage is a portfolio model without bankruptcy and the third stage combines the first two in a portfolio model with bankruptcy.

Stage One—the complete markets model

For bankruptcy to have any effect on bank behaviour in a complete markets model, it is necessary to assume that interest rates fail to reflect fully risks of bankruptcy. Bankruptcy makes the bank's pay-off function convex. As a consequence, for investments of given mean return, the equity value of banks is greater the higher is the level of risks of a bank's assets.

Capital requirements are neither necessary nor sufficient for reducing risk taking by banks in a complete markets model. They are not sufficient because increasing capital does not alter bank behavior: it is always optimal for a bank to choose the highest risk investments. They are not necessary because properly priced insurance internalizes the externality associated with returns in bankrupt states.

Stage Two—a portfolio model without bankruptcy

Relaxing the complete markets assumption, it is necessary to consider the relation between risk and return. Since the model takes net worth as given, this can be done in the context of an asset pricing model. Applying a Capital Asset Pricing Model, for example, the effect of a capital requirement can be viewed as a shift of the bank's chosen portfolio along the efficient market line (KM in Figure 4 of the chapter) towards the riskless asset (K).

Provided that the chosen portfolio remains on the market line, there is an unequivocal reduction in the risk return ratio as measured by the ratio of standard deviation to mean returns. However, if by imposing capital requirements the relative price of different risky assets is changed then the risk return ratio may increase, as shown by the move from B to C in Figure 5 of the chapter. Whether this happens depends on the balance between income and substitution effects: with increasing relative risk aversion the default probability of low net worth banks is higher. The chapter therefore correctly concludes that it is important to ensure that risk weights in capital requirements are 'market based'.

The solvency ratios that are specified in the Basle Accord have gone someway towards imposing risk based capital requirements. However, they only account for credit risk and not for market risk arising, for example, from interest and exchange rate fluctuations. Furthermore, the credit risk requirements do not come close to approximating true market risk measures.

A major obstacle to imposition of market based risk requirements is the information which is required. Market values of assets of mutual funds, brokers and dealers can in general be measured. However, information theories suggest that a primary rationale for the existence of banks is that they can acquire information and monitor firms at lower cost than outside investors. The market values of bank assets are not therefore readily observable. Thus while risk based capital requirements can be imposed on some *non*banks, they cannot readily be determined for banks. Indeed, market based capital requirements are imposed on brokers and dealers in the U.K. but not on banks. This recommendation is therefore more applicable to nonbanks than banks.

Stage Three—a portfolio model with bankruptcy

With bankruptcy, the relation between utility of shareholders and asset returns is no longer uniformly convex or concave. For low values of capital requirements, banks will tend to choose risky investments for the reasons described in Stage One. However, this will be deterred at higher values of capital requirements because of risk aversion.

Combining this with the results of Stage Two suggests a rule that capital requirements should be set according to market risk weights and at a sufficiently high level to deter choice of risky assets. However, as Stiglitz and Weiss have noted in the context of credit rationing, in the presence of diminishing risk aversion, the imposition of high capital requirements may lead to the selection of agents with lower levels of risk aversion and therefore preferences for higher risk investments.

The above description makes clear that capital requirements are viewed in this analysis as playing an incentive role. Recent literature on capital structure suggests that it is difficult to consider firm financial policy in this way. The reason is that incentives can be provided in other forms without any implication for chosen financial structure.

Another way of putting this is that this model does not appear to have much to do with banks. It could be applied to any firm where there is a risk of default and debt may not be correctly priced. It does not address the issues that are most commonly considered in the context of bank regulation, namely risks of runs and contagion.

In that respect, the complete markets analysis is curious. If there were complete markets, then there would be no risk of runs: liquidity demands could be specified and liquidity withdrawals could be distinguished from insolvency. A complete markets assumption is not attractive in the context of a model of bank runs and contagion.

Justification for the imposition of capital requirements usually comes from a combination of externalities across banks through risks of contagious bank failures and the fact that banks play important functions in offering payments services and maturity transformation of short-term deposits into long-term loans. Widespread bank failures are therefore unacceptable.

Provided that they have adequate financial resources, banks have incentives to avoid contagious failures by rescuing failing banks themselves. Where they are unable to do so then liquidity may have to be injected through lender of last resort facilities and bail-outs. The former has monetary and the latter fiscal consequences. A desire to avoid the monetary and fiscal consequences of bank failures leads to the imposition of liquidity and capital requirements on banks.

Capital requirements are therefore determined by considerations of systemic rather than individual bank risk. This single bank model is therefore unable to take account of factors which appear most relevant to the determination of optimal capital requirements.

To summarize, this is a careful analysis of the risk reducing function of capital requirements. However, both the structure of the model and the recommendations suggest that it is more relevant to the regulation of non-banks than banks.

Comments by Rafael Repullo

The purpose of Jean-Charles Rochet's chapter is to contribute to the recent academic debate on the effects of capital regulation on risk-taking behaviour by banks. The chapter considers a simple static model of bank behaviour under two alternative assumptions about the underlying market structure, namely complete and incomplete markets.

The complete contingent markets assumption poses immediately the question of why should there be any financial intermediaries (such as banks) in the first place. Since this issue is not addressed in the chapter, I am not sure about how should one take Propositions 1–4. For this reason, I am going to focus my comments on the second part of the chapter.

Of course, the incomplete markets model is not without problems, since in this case banks' profits in different states of nature cannot be aggregated into a single index, and so profit maximization is not well defined. Thus, the chapter asumes that the bank's objective function is to maximize the expectation of a von Neumann–Morgenstern utility function $u(.)$ that describes the preferences of the risk-averse owner-manager.

The argument of this utility function is the bank's final net worth, a random variable given by

$$\tilde{K}_1(x) \equiv \tilde{\rho} \cdot x + [R_0 D - C(D)] + K_0(1 + R_0),$$

where $x \in \mathbb{R}^N$ is the portfolio of the N risky securities, $\tilde{\rho} \equiv \tilde{R}-1$. R_0 is the (random) vector of excess returns of the risky securities, $R_0 D - C(D)$ are the profits obtained by investing the bank's deposits D, which cost $C(D)$, in the riskless asset, and $K_0(1+R_0)$ are the profits from the bank's capital K_0. Assuming that the marginal cost of deposits $C'(D)$ is increasing, one can immediately determine the optimal amount of deposits D^*, which leads to the definition of 'corrected net worth' $K \equiv R_0 D^* - C(D^*) + K_0(1 + R_0)$. Lastly, assuming $\tilde{p} \sim N(\rho, V)$ one can write

$$\tilde{K}_1(x) \equiv \mu(x) + \sigma(x)\tilde{y},$$

where $\tilde{y} \sim N(0, 1)$, $\mu(x) = \rho.x + K$, and $\sigma(x) = (x'Vx)^{1/2}$.

Given this set-up, most of the second part of the Chapter is devoted to the analysis of bank behaviour under both unlimited liability and no short-selling restrictions. Under these assumptions, the bank's problem is to choose $x \in \mathbb{R}^N$ to maximize

$$E[u(\tilde{K}_1(x))] = E[u(\mu(x) + \sigma(x)\tilde{y})] \equiv U(\mu(x), \sigma(x)).$$

This problem is solved in two stages. First, the bank's portfolio frontier in the $\mu - \sigma$ space is obtained (by solving the standard portfolio choice problem with a riskless asset), and then $U(\mu, \sigma)$ is maximized over this frontier.

What can one say in the (rather more realistic) case of limited liability? Clearly, one should start by specifying what happens to the bank's creditors in the bankruptcy states [i.e. when $\tilde{K}_1(x) < 0$], so that their behaviour ex ante can be properly modeled. Unfortunately, the chapter does not discuss this issue. This is not very serious for depositors, provided there is a deposit insurance system in place. But it seems quite unreasonable to suppose that limited liability banks could short-sell the existing securities at their given rates of return. Thus, either short-selling is prohibited or one has to add an endogenous bankruptcy risk premium to the cost of short-sold securities. Computing the latter is obviously a difficult task, so there seems to be no alternative but to restrict short-selling.

Table 1. Results When Short-Selling is Allowed

	Risk neutrality	Risk aversion
Unlimited liability	No solution	Interior solution
Limited liability	No solution	Indeterminate

However, to continue with the line of argument in the paper, let us suppose for the time being that short-selling of all the securities (including) the riskless asset were allowed. Then the objective function of the limited liability bank could be written as follows [ignoring bankruptcy costs and assuming $u(0) = 0$]:

$$E[u(\max\{\tilde{K}_1(x), 0\})] = \int_{-\mu(x)/\sigma(x)}^{+\infty} u(\mu(x) + \sigma(x)y)\mathrm{d}N(y) \equiv W(\mu(x), \sigma(x)).$$

It should be noted that in this expression $\mu(x)$ and $\sigma(x)$ are the mean and standard deviation of the distribution of $\tilde{K}_1(x)$, and *not* the moments of the distribution of $\tilde{K}_1^+(x) \equiv \max\{\tilde{K}_1(x), 0\}$. This means that we can use the same portfolio frontier as for the unlimited liability bank, maximizing $W(\mu, \sigma)$ over this frontier.

What properties does the function $W(\mu, \sigma)$ have? In this respect the analysis in the paper is somewhat incomplete, considering only the sign of $\partial W/\partial \sigma$ when σ tends to infinity under the assumption of bounded absolute risk aversion (see Proposition 10). In fact, one can go further than this for particular utility functions. For example, in the limit case of risk neutrality $(u(K_1) = K_1)$ one can show that

$$W(\mu/\sigma) = \mu N(\mu/\sigma) + \sigma f(\mu/\sigma),$$

where $f(.)$ is the normal density funtion. Also, for CARA utility functions $(u(K_1) = 1 - \exp[-aK_1])$ one gets

$$W(\mu, \sigma) = N(\mu/\sigma) - \exp[-a(\mu - (a\sigma^2/2))]N((\mu/\sigma) - a\sigma).$$

Thus, at least for these two particular cases one can draw the corresponding indifference curves in the $\mu - \sigma$ space. Then it can be shown that even with risk aversion the bank's maximization problem may have no solution (i.e. the bank would like to choose an infinitely risky portfolio).

The results commented up to this point can be summarized in Table 1.

Introducing a capital requirement of the form $\alpha.x \leq K$ in the model with no short-selling restrictions is quite straightforward, since it only changes the portfolio frontier leaving the indifference curves unchanged. In particular, it should be noted that if the capital constraint is binding, the bank's portfolio problem is formally identical to the standard portfolio choice problem without a riskless asset, yielding the usual hyperbola except when the risk weights are proportional to the mean excess returns (i.e. when $\alpha = \delta\rho$ for some

Table 2. Results When Short-Selling is Prohibited

	Risk neutrality	Risk aversion
Unlimited liability	Corner solution	Interior or corner solution
Limited liability	Corner solution	Interior or corner solution

scalar $\delta > 0$), in which case the hyperbola collapses to a horizontal line (see Figures 5 and 6).

From our previous discussion, it is clear that capital requirements do not change the results in Table 1. In particular, with limited liabiity the bank's maximization problem may not have a solution (even with risk-aversion and market-based risk weights). Thus, it appears that something important must have been overlooked. In this respect, I want to argue that the capital constraint $\alpha \cdot x \leq K$ makes little sense with unrestricted short-selling, since it implies that banks can arbitrarily relax the constraint by shorting any security i with $\alpha_i > 0$. I would either consider a constraint of the form $\alpha.x^+ \leq K$, where $x_i^+ = \max\{x_i, 0\}$, or (even better for the earlier reason) introduce the constraints $x \geq 0$ and $x_0 = D + K_0 - x \cdot 1 \geq 0$.

What happens to the model when we introduce these short-selling constraints? Again we only have to worry about the change in the portfolio frontier. But this is not a trivial task, unless we are willing to restrict attention to specific examples. Nevertheless, we can be sure of one thing, namely the fact that the portfolio frontier now has to be bounded. Hence one gets the results summarized in Table 2.

Although corner solutions are in principle not very appealing, one can at least pose the question of what are the consequences of introducing capital requirements in this model. I will not attempt to answer here this rather difficult question. Let me just say that I think that one should consider not only the effect of capital requirements on the probability of bankruptcy $N(-\mu/\sigma)$ (the main focus of Rochet's Chapter), but also on the expected cost for the deposit insurance system, which is given by

$$E[-\min\{\tilde{K}_1, 0\}] = -\int_{-\infty}^{-\mu/\sigma} (\mu + \sigma y)\, dN(y) = \sigma f(\mu/\sigma) - \mu N(-\mu/\sigma).$$

(Interestingly, the slope of the isocost curves in the $\mu - \sigma$ space equals the hazard rate $H(\mu/\sigma) \equiv f(\mu/\sigma)/[1 - N(\mu/\sigma)]$.)

To conclude my comments, I want to emphasize that the analysis of the effects of capital regulation on bank behaviour is just a first step, to be followed by an analysis of the market implications of these regulations. The final aim would be to construct simple equilibrium models of the banking sector in which the effects of capital (and other) regulations could be properly assessed.

13

Is the Glass–Steagall Act Justified?
A Study of the U.S. Experience with
Universal Banking Before 1933

Randall S. Kroszner and Raghuram G. Rajan

The Glass–Steagall Act of 1933 prohibits commercial banks from underwriting, holding, or dealing in corporate securities, either directly or through securities affiliates.[1] The driving force behind the Act was Senator Carter Glass, who strongly believed that direct commerical-bank involvement with corporate securities was detrimental to the stability of the financial system. The commingling of investment and commercial banking functions, Glass and others argued, creates significant conflicts of interest. This view gained popular support after the Pecora Committee investigations (U.S. Senate Committee on Banking and Currency, 1933–1934) into the potentially conflict-laden and putatively abusive practices at securities affiliates of the two most prominent national banks, National City Company and Chase Securities Company.

We thank David Brown, Charles Calomiris, Tyler Cowen, Andrew Dick, Douglas Diamond, Gene Fama, Mark Flood, Ken French, Steve Kaplan, George Kaufman, Daniel Klein, Geoffrey Miller, Mitchell Petersen, Ellis Tallman, Rob Vishny, Larry Wall, David Wheelock, and seminar participants at the University of Chicago, the University of Florida, the University of Illinois, the University of Southern California, the Universities of California at Los Angeles and Irvine, Northwestern University, the Federal Reserve Banks of Chicago, Kansas City, and St. Louis, the Federal Trade Commission, the Securities and Exchange Commission, the NBER Summer Workshop in Corporate Finance, the NBER Conference on Financial Structure and Macroeconomic Instability, and the Western Financial Association for helpful comments. We are indebted to an enthusiastic and committed group of research assistants—especially Brian Tyler—who helped collect and organize the data. This research is supported by National Science Foundation grant no. SES-9211231 and the William S. Fishman Faculty Research Fund at the Graduate School of Business of the University of Chicago.

[1] Technically speaking, the Act applies only to national banks and state-chartered banks that are members of the Federal Reserve System and permits limited holdings of investment-grade corporate bonds and even equity under certain conditions. For a thorough legal exposition of Glass–Steagall and its subsequent interpretation, see Jonathan Macey and Geoffrey Miller (1992 pp. 175–78, 496–97, 543–57).

The case of the Fox Motion Picture Company is often cited as a chilling illustration of the alleged defects of universal banking (Barrie Wigmore 1985: 171–5). The acquisition of the financially distressed Fox by General Theaters and Equipment (GTE) in 1929 was financed in part with a $15 million loan from Chase National Bank. In early 1930, Chase Securities Company underwrote $23 million of common stock and $30 million of debentures for GTE, which used part of the proceeds to repay the bank loan from Chase. GTE was in financial distress the following year and turned to Chase for further assistance. At that time, Chase Securities held both equity and debt in GTE, and it decided to underwrite another $30 million in debentures. Two years later GTE was bankrupt. Wigmore (1985 p. 175) argues that the Pecora Committee investigations show that the conflict of interests at Chase caused it to underwrite "poor securities to pay off its own loans, [and] information was concealed or misrepresented" about the quality of securities Chase was attempting to sell.[2]

A second issue of concern to the framers of Glass–Steagall was whether direct involvement of commercial banks in the securities business increases the riskiness of banks and the financial system. Our empirical study focuses primarily on the conflict-of-interest argument, not because risk is unimportant, but because earlier work by Eugene White (1986) already addresses the risk issue.[3] With this exception, however, we have been unable to find any work since World War II which systematically analyzes the union of commercial and investment banking functions in the United States before Glass–Steagall.[4]

---

[2] Since Chase ended up owning most of the issues (because it could not convince the public to purchase them) and taking losses of over $70 million, the Fox "escapade" could be interpreted as an example of bad business judgment rather than an "abuse" (see also George J. Benston, 1990 pp. 96, 103). Benston's (1990) recent book examines many of the specific cases from the Pecora hearings cited as examples of abusive practices and argues that few stand up to close scrutiny.

[3] White (1986) finds that securities operations of commercial banks did not impair their stability prior to Glass–Steagall. Banks engaged in the securities business had no higher earning variance or lower capital ratios than banks without such operations. In addition, those banks with securities operations were less likely to fail. Although 5,000 banks failed during the 1920s, virtually none were the city banks, which were the most likely to have securities affiliates (Vincent P. Carosso, 1970: 242; see also White 1983). In the bank crises between 1930 and 1933, more than a quarter of all national banks failed, but less than 10 percent of those with large securities operations closed (White 1986 p. 40). Since banks with securities affiliates tended to be larger than average-size banks and larger banks failed less often than smaller ones, this evidence must be interpreted cautiously.

[4] We have been able to discover only two early works, Terris Moore (1934) and George W. Edwards (1942), which attempt to examine systematically the relative performance of the securities underwritten by the two types of houses. These studies suffer from serious sample-selection problems and do not benefit from a modern understanding of financial economics. After completing this paper, we became aware of the work of James S. Ang and Terry Richardson (1993), which compares the activities of the two types of houses.

Again today, the appropriate degree of separation between commercial and investment banking is being debated in Washington.[5] As in the 1920s, corporations are increasingly bypassing commercial banks and approaching the financial markets directly. Faced with disintermediation, commercial banks have lobbied regulators to expand the spectrum of permissible financial activities, and regulators have responded by eroding the barriers separating the functions. Theoretical research is ambiguous about the merit of such changes. Rajan (1992), for example, finds a trade-off between the informational economies banks realize by combining lending and underwriting and the inefficiencies resulting from a bank's inability to certify issue quality to the market when the bank is suspected of harboring conflicts of interest. Our data should shed some light on this trade-off and the merits of arguments for Glass–Steagall reform.

We start with a brief history of the movement of commercial banks into the securities business in the 1920s. We then evaluate the traditional conflict-of-interest argument that bank securities affiliates could—and did—systematically fool the (naive) public investor. We do so by examining how securities underwritten by commercial-bank securities affiliates fared in comparison to ex ante similar securities underwritten by independent investment banks. Section II details our first battery of tests. We find no evidence that commercial banks systematically fooled the public securities markets. Instead, there is some evidence that the markets may have rationally discounted for potential conflicts among the bank affiliates. In Section III, we describe how the underwriting activities of the bank securities affiliates would compare with the activities of investment banks if, indeed, the market discounted certain types of affiliate issues. Our evidence on affiliate activities is consistent with the markets and the affiliates adapting to the potential for conflicts. In Section IV, we discuss the implications of the results for the importance of informational scope economies between lending and underwriting and consider alternative interpretations of the evidence. Section V concludes with policy implications and suggestions for future research.

I. The Movement of Commercial Banks into the Securities Business During the 1920s

According to W. Nelson Peach (1941), the government issues of Liberty bonds during World War I awakened public interest in securities markets. During the

---

[5] The conflict-of-interest issue has been central in the recent Congressional debates on financial regulation reform: "The idea behind the compromise [legislation, offered by Representative John Dingell and supported by both the securities and banking industries, is that special SEC] ... filings would be required when banks lend money to a corporate client and underwrite that client's securities within the same three-month period" (*New York Times*, September 26, 1991, p. C9).

sustained economic growth of the 1920s, many firms approached the capital markets for the first time, and the capital markets grew rapidly (see Carosso, 1970). With the growth of the equity and bond markets during this period, commercial banks began to lose some of their traditional lending business to the public markets. The banks' concerns about "disintermediation" in the 1920s parallel those heard in the 1970s and 1980s. Assessing the transformation of commercial banks in the 1920s into "financial emporiums," White (1984: 102) concludes, "... banks' new financial services were not begun as part of a speculative lark ... [but] represented a move by these firms to offset the decline of their traditional business ...."

While state-chartered institutions in many states could engage in a variety of financial services without organizing affiliates, national banks had to overcome more legal hurdles to diversify their product offerings (Peach 1941: 44–51). The National Banking Act of 1864 did not permit banks to handle common stocks. Many banks had active bond departments, but court decisions in the late nineteenth and early twentieth centuries cast doubt on the legal status of these operations (see White 1984).[6]

To avoid such impediments, national banks and some trusts incorporated affiliates under state corporate charters. These affiliates "... carried on types of business which were either expressly prohibited by statute or which the courts had declared to be *ultra vires* ..." (Peach 1941: 51). The Union Trust Company of Detroit, for example, incorporated an affiliate named the Union Commerce Investment Company under a Delaware charter. The Delaware charter permitted the company to do almost anything "except solemnize marriages and hold religious ceremonies" (U.S. Senate 1934: 4776). There were no minimum capital regulations, and some affiliates were quite small (see e.g. Peach 1941: 81). Many affiliates operated from the same premises as the parent bank. Since they generally shared the same name, affiliates enjoyed the "full benefit of the goodwill of their parent banks" (Peach 1941: 52).

The 1920s saw a dramatic increase in the extent of bank and trust involvement in nonbank activities, either directly or through affiliates. As Table 1 shows, the number of national banks operating securities affiliates rose from 10 in 1922 to a peak of 114 in 1931. The number of banks engaged in the securities business through their bond departments doubled from 62 to 123 during this period. Table 2 compares relative market shares and underwriting activities of commercial bank affiliates and investment banks for the decade of the 1920s. The table, however, does not reveal the rapid growth of bond originations by bank securities affiliates during the period: the affiliates' market share of bond originations more than tripled between the middle and late 1920's (U.S. Senate 1931: 299).

---

[6] In 1927 the McFadden Act, best known for its effective prohibition of interstate branching, explicitly permitted national banks to buy and sell debt instruments directly through their bond departments.

Table 1. Number of National Banks, State Banks, and Affiliates of National and State Banks Engaged in the Securities Business, 1922–1933

Year	National banks		State banks		Total
	Directly engaged in securities business	Operating security affiliates	Directly engaged in securities business	Operating security affiliates	
1922	62	10	197	8	277
1923	78	17	210	9	314
1924	97	26	236	13	372
1925	112	33	254	14	413
1926	128	45	274	17	464
1927	121	60	290	22	493
1928	150	69	310	32	561
1929	151	84	308	48	591
1930	126	105	260	75	566
1931	123	114	230	58	525
1932	109	104	209	53	475
1933	102	76	169	32	379

Source: Peach (1941: 83).

Table 2. Number and Dollar Volume of U.S. Industrial Securities Issued During the First Quarters of 1921–1929, by Type of Security and by Type of Underwriter

Type of security	Affiliates		Investment banks	
	Number of issues	Dollar volume (millions)	Number of issues	Dollar volume (millions)
Bonds	133	$798.6	329	$999.7
	(28.8)	(44.4)	(71.2)	(55.6)
	[81.6]	[70.8]	[48.2]	[60.6]
Preferred stock	19	$181.1	179	$316.9
	(9.6)	(36.4)	(90.4)	(63.6)
	[11.7]	[16.1]	[26.3]	[19.2]
Common stock	11	$147.6	174	$332.7
	(5.9)	(30.7)	(94.1)	(69.3)
	[6.8]	[13.1]	[25.5]	[20.2]
Total for all securities	163	$1,127.3	682	$1,649.3
	(19.3)	(40.6)	(80.7)	(59.4)
	[100]	[100]	[100]	[100]

Notes: Numbers in parentheses give percentages of market share; numbers in brackets are percentages of house activities.

Source: Compiled from the monthly "New Capital Flotations" section of the *Commercial and Financial Chronicle*.

Table 3. Initial Rating of All Industrial Bonds Issued During the First Quarters of 1921–1929, Annually by Type of Underwriter

Year	Number (percentage)					
	Affiliate-underwritten bonds			Investment-bank-underwritten bonds		
	Investment grade	Rated below investment grade	Unrated	Investment grade	Rated below investment grade	Unrated
1921	10(83.3)	0(0.0)	2(16.7)	22(71.0)	5(16.1)	4(12.9)
1922	8(57.1)	5(35.7)	1(7.1)	25(55.6)	10(22.2)	10(22.2)
1923	17(70.8)	3(12.5)	4(16.7)	29(69.1)	11(26.2)	2(4.8)
1924	4(40.0)	3(30.0)	3(30.0)	15(50.0)	8(26.7)	7(23.3)
1925	5(45.5)	1(9.1)	5(45.5)	18(42.9)	7(16.7)	17(40.5)
1926	6(33.3)	3(16.7)	9(50.0)	10(30.3)	11(33.3)	12(36.4)
1927	12(60.0)	2(10.0)	6(30.0)	14(38.9)	14(38.9)	8(22.2)
1928	7(46.7)	3(20.0)	5(33.3)	13(33.3)	12(30.8)	14(35.9)
1929	4(44.4)	3(33.3)	2(22.2)	10(32.3)	14(45.2)	7(22.6)
Total:	73(54.9)	25(18.8)	35(26.3)	156(47.4)	92(28.0)	81(24.6)

Notes: Bonds which have a Moody's rating of Baa and above or a Poor's rating of B** and above are classified investment grade. Bonds which have a Moody's rating of Ba and below or a Poor's rating of B* and below are classified as being rated below investment grade.

Sources: Compiled from the monthly "New Capital Flotations" section of the *Commercial and Financial Chronicle*, *Moody's*, and *Poor's*.

Table 3 describes the initial "quality" of issues in each year as defined by the initial rating category.[7] For both types of houses, average bond quality fell from the early to the late 1920s, but overall the affiliates originated higher-"quality" bonds, an interesting fact that we return to later.

The Glass–Steagall Act of 1933 put an end to the trend toward "universal" banking by prohibiting the involvement of commercial banks in the securities business. The 1921–1933 period affords a fertile research area because independent investment banks and commercial banks could compete on a relatively level playing field. Entry (and exit) in the financial sector was common and much less regulated by governmental bodies than it is today. In our study, we compare the activities of commercial banks, trusts, and their affiliates (we will use the term "affiliates" to describe all three) with those of specialized investment banking houses while they were engaged in direct competition in a dynamically

---

[7] The categories were based on initial ratings by Moody's or Poor's, and consisted of issues rated investment grade (Baa and above), rated below investment grade (Baa and below), and unrated by either Moody's or Poor's.

evolving market. We now turn to our first set of tests, which concern the relative performance of the securities underwritten by the affiliates and independent investment banks.

II. Did Commercial Bank Affiliates Systematically Fool the Public?

A. Conflicts of interest and the relative performance of securities underwritten by affiliates

Conflicts of interest may arise when a bank combines lending and deposit-taking with underwriting. If a firm has an adverse shock without the public realizing it, for example, a commercial bank may have an incentive to underwrite public issues on behalf of the firm and use the proceeds to repay earlier bank loans made to the firm. It has also been argued that, unlike an investment bank, a commercial bank has easy access to a large number of unsophisticated depositors.[8] Conflicts of interest thus may give banks both the incentive and the ability to defraud naive public investors by misrepresenting the quality of issue they underwrite.

If, as alleged in the Pecora committee hearings, commercial banks succeeded in systematically fooling naive investors into investing in low-quality securities, the securities underwritten by the affiliates would have performed "poorly." Securities underwritten by affiliates would have underperformed, on average, ex ante similar securities underwritten by the investment banks. Also, since information asymmetries between insiders (the underwriter and the firm's management) and the outside public may be largest for the low-quality and lesser-known firms, the potential for taking advantage of "naive" investors would be greatest for such firms. The "naive-investor" hypothesis thus implies that the inferior performance of the bank-affiliate-underwritten issues would have been most pronounced for low-quality issues about which there is little public information.

B. Data collection and sources

First, we identify commercial banks engaged in investment banking prior to Glass–Steagall. The *National Securities Dealers of North America* (February 1929) contains an extensive list of firms involved in investment banking activities and notes the firms' affiliations. Since this listing of affiliations is not complete, we

---

[8] During congressional debate on financial regulation in 1932, Senator Robert Bulkley stated: "The banker ought to be regarded as the financial confidant and mentor of his depositors.... Obviously, the banker who has nothing to sell to his depositors is much better qualified to advise disinterestedly and to regard diligently the safety of depositors than the banker who uses the list of depositors in his savings department to distribute circulars concerning the advantages of this, that or the other investment" (*Congressional Record*, 10 May 1932, p. 9912).

also look for underwriters with some form of the words "national," "bank," or "trust" in their names. We then determine from *Moody's Banking Manual* whether they have a bank charter. Finally, we include firms identified as securities affiliates in other sources: Carosso (1970), Peach (1941), H. H. Preston and A. R. Findlay (1930a, b), White (1986), and the *Commercial and Financial Chronicle*. Our search resulted in a list of just over 160 commercial banks or trusts engaged in investment banking, although only 64 of these are lead underwriters or syndicate managers in our sample.[9]

Our data on security issues are constructed from the monthly "New Capital Flotations" section of the *Commercial and Financial Chronicle* (CFC). The CFC provides a comprehensive listing of all new security issues for each month. It groups the individual issues by type of security (e.g. long bonds, short bonds, equity) and by sector (e.g. railroads, public utilities, governments), and each entry contains information on issue size, the coupon or price, the implied yield to maturity, and the underwriter(s). The lead underwriter or syndicate manager is listed first, if more than one firm is involved. Each issue for which a commercial bank, trust, or their securities affiliate is the lead underwriter or syndicate manager is included as an "affiliate-underwritten issue" in our sample. Rather than attempting to collect information on every issue during the decade of the 1920s, we limit our sample to issues in the first quarters of the years 1921–1929.[10]

Next, we construct our measure of bond quality. *Moody's Manuals* and *Poor's Manuals* provide annual ratings for many securities. The descriptions of the ratings given by Moody's and Poor's suggest three broad quality categories: investment grade (Baa and above), rated below investment grade (Ba and below), and unrated by either Moody's or Poor's.[11] The unrated category, with some exceptions, consists of small relatively unknown companies.

Finally, we construct measures of bond performance. Unfortunately, consistent and reliable price data are available for very few issues.[12] The only

---

[9] Some of the houses we classify as investment banks, such as J. P. Morgan and Brown Brothers Harriman, did perform deposit-taking and lending services for large clients even though they did not organize themselves as commercial banks in the 1920s. Both J. P. Morgan and Brown Brothers Harriman, however, chose to adopt commercial bank charters after the Glass–Steagall Act (see Carosso 1970: 372–4; Ron Chernow, 1991). Former partners of each organization broke away to form independent investment banks after 1933. Since the securities originated by these houses performed exceptionally well over the period, classifying such firms as bank affiliates would only strengthen our results.

[10] We did not find any evidence of a seasonal pattern in securities issuance which would render the first quarter unrepresentative of the whole year.

[11] If Moody's omits a rating due to "little public interest" or "insufficient information" we turn to Poor's.

[12] The larger and higher-rated issues tend to have more price data available, but many of the smaller issues appear to have been infrequently traded. As we will discuss, information on what bondholders received after a company defaults is scant, so it is difficult to construct a consistent measure of returns.

widely reported and consistent measure of performance we could find was the status of the bond—whether it was performing, called, retired at maturity, or in default.[13] We gather these data on all bonds in our sample until 1940 from *Moody's, Poor's, Fitch's Bond Book, The National Monthly Corporation Bond Summary*, and the *Fisher Manual of Valuable and Worthless Securities*.[14]

C. The matched-security method

We first perform a *matched-security test*: we match the bonds originated by bank affiliates in the first quarters of 1921–1929 with bonds issued by investment banks and compare their subsequent performance. Our focus is on bonds with maturities of at least five years ("long bonds" in the CFC) issued by industrial corporations during 1921–1929. We employ a number of criteria to find as close a match as possible to each commercial-bank-affiliate-originated issue. The following are the necessary conditions used to select a match from the issues originated by the investment banks. The issue must:

1. have the same initial Moody's or Poor's rating,
2. be in the same cohort (defined as being issued within plus or minus six months),
3. be of roughly the same maturity and have similar repayment provisions (e.g. serial bonds and sinking fund bonds),[15]
4. be within roughly the same size category (e.g. over $5 million,[16] between $1 million and $5 million, and under $1 million),
5. be an industrial bond (so railroad, public utility, and foreign-government bonds are excluded),[17]

---

[13] We consider a bond to be in default if it defaults on interest or principal payments. Following Arthur S. Dewing (1953: 1175–82), voluntary extensions of a bond involving no interest or principle reduction are not considered defaults.

[14] In earlier versions of the paper, we used rating changes over time as a performance measure, but this metric adds little to a default analysis.

[15] The most common maturity is ten years, and most bonds have some sinking fund or serial repayment provision.

[16] Due to the small number of large issues, the "over $5 million" category sometimes involves matches of very different sizes.

[17] We exclude these classes of issues from the present study for a number of reasons. The Reconstruction Finance Corporation made significant loans to the railroad industry and was accused of "playing favorites" in bailing out specific investment houses which had large stakes in railroads (James Olson 1977). Dramatic changes in the regulation (and in some cases ownership) of public utilities, on both the local and federal levels, took place during the 1930s, following the collapse of the Insull empire. Although foreign-government bonds received much attention in the Pecora hearings, they pose particular problems for our method. Except for four countries which had relatively few issues outstanding, all others defaulted on either all or none of their bonds (see Ilse Mintz 1951; Barry Eichengreen and Richard Portes 1989). Matching across countries would make performance measures extremely sensitive to the choice of country for an otherwise comparable issue.

6. have the same conversion provision (e.g. convertible into preferred or common, although few bonds in the sample had such provisions).

If the issue is unrated by Moody's and Poor's, then necessary condition 1 is replaced by:

1a. be unrated by Moody's and Poor's and
1b. have an initial yield within 50 basis points, plus or minus, of the initial yield on the affiliate-underwritten bond.[18]

In many cases, a number of bonds fit the necessary conditions for matching the affiliate-underwritten bond. In these cases, attempts were made to tighten the criteria to improve the match. Whenever possible, for example, we tried to match the collateralization status (e.g. first mortgages with first mortgages).[19] In addition, we chose the bond closest in issue date to the affiliate-underwritten bond if all of the other criteria were satisfied. Our matching procedure thus attempts to control for economy-wide factors both at time of issue and over the life of the bond, the yield curve, firm or project size, sector-specific shocks, and ex ante quality differences as perceived by the market.[20] We matched 121 corporate industrial bonds originated by the commercial banks and their affiliates in the first quarters of 1921–1929.[21]

D. Results of the matched-security test

For the sample of 121 matched pairs of industrial bonds, Table 4 shows that, at the end of every year after 1924, there are fewer cumulative defaults among affiliate-originated issues. The majority of the defaults occur between the beginning of

[18] Even though 50 basis points was the largest difference allowed, most of the bonds were much closer in yields. The mean yield of 6.15 for the 34 matched unrated affiliate-issued bonds is exactly equal to the mean yield of the corresponding investment-bank bonds.

[19] Since the vast majority of industrial bonds issued in the 1920s were secured, we were able to match the collateralization status in most of the sample.

[20] By using rating as a matching criterion, we are assuming that the Moody's and Poor's rating is an accurate proxy for public information about the security. To check this assumption, we regressed the initial yield reported in the CFC (which is an alternative summary measure of ex ante public information) for all the bonds in the first quarters of 1921–1929 against indicators for bond ratings and indicators for years to adjust for changes in interest rates over time. Compared to a Ba-rated bond, a Baa-rated bond yields 0.28 less, an A-rated bond yields 0.7 less, an Aa-rated bond yields 1.2 less, and an Aaa-rated bond yields 1.64 less. Each of the coefficients is highly significant. In addition, we examined the yields on the rated bonds in the matched sample and found no statistical difference in mean or median yields between affiliates and investment banks.

[21] We identified a total of 133 affiliate-underwritten industrial bond issues in the first quarters of 1921–1929. We have only 121 matched bond pairs because a dozen of the affiliate-underwritten bonds issues could not be matched using our necessary conditions (typically due to an unusual combination of size and rating) and are excluded from the matched sample. Only one of these affiliate-underwritten bonds subsequently defaulted (see footnote 28 for more details).

Table 4. Performance of Matched Sample of 121 Pairs of Industrial Bonds Issued During 1921–1929, by Type of Underwriter, 1921–1940

Year	Number (percentage)					
	Affiliate-underwritten bonds			Investment-bank-underwritten bonds		
	Retired	Outstanding	Default	Retired	Outstanding	Default
1921	0(0.0)	8(100.0)	0(0.0)	0(0.0)	9(100.0)	0(0.0)
1922	0(0.0)	20(95.2)	1(4.7)	0(0.0)	25(100.0)	0(0.0)
1923	2(4.6)	41(93.2)	1(2.3)	1(2.2)	45(97.8)	0(0.0)
1924	4(7.6)	47(88.7)	2(3.8)	2(3.7)	51(94.4)	1(1.9)
1925	6(9.4)	56(87.5)	2(3.1)	6(9.1)	58(87.9)	2(3.0)
1926	8(9.9)	71(87.7)	2(2.5)	10(11.4)	74(84.1)	4(4.6)
1927	13(13.0)	84(84.0)	3(3.0)	13(12.6)	84(81.6)	6(5.8)
1928	24(21.4)	84(75.0)	4(3.6)	23(19.7)	87(74.4)	7(6.0)
1929	32(26.5)	84(69.4)	5(4.1)	29(24.0)	85(70.3)	7(5.8)
1930	40(33.1)	76(62.8)	5(4.1)	30(24.8)	80(66.1)	11(9.1)
1931	42(34.7)	71(58.7)	8(6.6)	32(26.5)	69(57.0)	20(16.5)
1932	43(35.5)	60(49.6)	18(14.9)	37(30.6)	56(46.3)	28(23.1)
1933	45(37.2)	55(45.5)	21(17.4)	38(31.4)	49(40.5)	34(28.1)
1934	51(42.1)	45(37.2)	25(20.7)	44(36.4)	39(32.2)	38(31.4)
1935	59(48.8)	36(29.8)	26(21.5)	56(46.3)	27(22.3)	38(31.4)
1936	71(58.7)	23(19.0)	27(22.3)	66(54.6)	16(13.2)	39(32.2)
1937	77(63.6)	16(13.2)	28(23.1)	72(59.5)	10(8.3)	39(32.2)
1938	79(65.3)	14(11.6)	28(23.1)	75(62.0)	7(5.8)	39(32.2)
1939	81(66.9)	12(9.9)	28(23.1)	78(64.5)	4(3.3)	39(32.2)
1940	81(66.9)	12(9.9)	28(23.1)	79(65.3)	3(2.5)	39(32.2)

Notes: A bond is "retired" if the issue has been repaid in full at maturity or called before maturity; a bond is in "default" if the issue has missed a payment of principal or interest.

Source: Moody's, Poor's, Fitch's Bond Book, Commercial and Financial Chronicle, and National Monthly Corporation Bond Summary.

1931 and the end of 1934: 20 (or 71 percent of) affiliate-underwritten defaults and 27 (or 69 percent of) investment-bank-underwritten defaults occur during these four years. By the end of our sample period in 1940, 39 (or 32 percent) of the investment-bank issues default, whereas only 28 (or 23 percent of) the affiliate-underwritten issues default. Investment-bank-underwritten issues thus experience roughly 40-percent more defaults than do affiliate-underwritten issues.

When we compare default performance not by number of issues, but by dollar volume of the issues, the relative performance difference is even more pronounced.[22] (Given the size differences that can occur in matching issues

---

[22] A table detailing this comparison is available from the authors upon request.

larger than $5 million, however, the frequency data in Table 4 are perhaps a more appropriate performance measure for our method.) In terms of dollar volumes, approximately 28 percent ($127 million) of investment-bank-underwritten issues default by 1940 but only 11 percent ($79 million) of affiliate-underwritten issues do. Comparing these dollar volume results with the results in Table 4, we see that the defaults were primarily among the smaller issues.[23]

We also examine how the bonds performed in each year of the life of the bonds.[24] This method of tabulating adjusts for the age of bonds (see Paul Asquith et al. 1989). The investment-bank-underwritten issues default earlier in their lives than affiliate-underwritten issues. By the end of the seventh year of issue, for example, 30 of the 39 (77 percent) investment-bank issues have defaulted, but only 15 of the 28 (53 percent) affiliate issues have.

To examine the relative performance of the matched issues taking into account both the number of defaults and the timing of the defaults, we perform a log-rank test (see J. Kalbfleisch and R. Prentice 1980). This test compares the survival curves (or mortality rates) of the two groups of bonds. We define the life of a defaulted bond as the period from issue date to the date of default. A retired issue is treated the same way as a bond that is outstanding at the end of our observation period; thus, it is assumed to have survived until the end of 1940.[25] For the whole matched sample, the first row of Table 5 reports that the survival rate of affiliate-underwritten bonds is higher than the investment-bank-underwritten issues at the 10 percent significance level.

To investigate the importance of initial bond quality and time trends, we split the sample and rerun the log-rank test. If the matched sample of bonds is subdivided into bonds rated investment grade at issue and those which are non-investment grade (including both the unrated bonds and those rated below investment grade), we find a statistically significant difference at the 5 percent level for non-investment-grade bonds but not for bonds rated investment grade. The bank affiliates thus appear to do particularly well for the lower-rated and

[23] Because the largest affiliate-underwritten issues are much bigger than the largest investment-bank-underwritten issues, the volume figures must be interpreted with caution. To check that this does not drive the differences in default rates, we compared the 22 largest affiliate and investment-bank issues, where most of the size discrepancy exists. Both have four defaults by the end of 1940. The difference is in the 99 smallest issues where there are 24 and 35 defaults, respectively. There is no statistical difference in means or medians between affiliate and investment-bank issue sizes in this subsample of 99. (We chose a breakpoint of 99 rather than 100 simply because there were multiple issues of the same size as the 100th issue.)

[24] An "aging" analysis table is available from the authors upon request.

[25] The rationale is that investors could have bought securities with the repaid principal and been as well off as if the bonds had never been retired. Of course, this assumes that the cost of accepting potentially lower reinvestment rates is small.

Table 5. Results of the Log Rank Survival Analysis for the Matched Sample of 121 Pairs of Industrial Bonds Issued During 1921–1929

Sample	Affiliates		Investment banks		χ^2
	Actual defaults	Predicted defaults	Actual defaults	Predicted defaults	p value
All bonds ($n = 242$)	28	34.72	39	32.28	2.70 [0.100]
Non-investment grade ($n = 110$)	12	18.97	23	16.03	5.59 [0.018]
Investment grade ($n = 132$)	16	16.72	16	16.28	0.01 [0.92]
Issued 1923–1929 ($n = 196$)	22	29.56	35	27.44	4.02 [0.045]
Issued 1921–1922 ($n = 46$)	6	4.77	4	5.23	0.61 [0.435]

Notes: Subsamples are formed by initial rating and by year of issue. The log-rank test (chi-square) compares the number of defaults and the predicted number if the defaults were distributed equally across the two types of underwriters over time.

unrated issues.[26] In addition, to check for time effects, we split the sample into those bonds issued in the early phase of bank entry into underwriting (1921–1922), which includes a sharp macroeconomic contraction, and those issued in the later phase (1923–1929). Affiliate-underwritten issues in the later phase have a better survival rate (statistically significant at the 5 percent level), but there is no statistical difference in survival for the small sample of bonds issued in the early phase.

Although consistent data on the payments to bondholders when a firm defaults are difficult to obtain, we examined the defaults in this sample more closely to determine the returns to bondholders. Table 6 contains the results for the subsample of defaults on which we could obtain information. First, on average, bondholders of investment-bank-underwritten issues obtained cash or securities worth roughly half of face value when the default was resolved.[27] Bondholders of affiliate-underwritten issues obtained about 40 percent of face value, but the difference is not statistically significant. Second, affiliate defaults appear to have been resolved somewhat quicker with a mean time of resolution of 2.4 years compared to a mean time of 2.8 years

[26] Within the category of initially non-investment-grade bonds, we have the following performances: for the bonds rated below investment grade, three affiliate bonds versus six investment-bank bonds default; for the unrated bonds, nine affiliate bonds versus 17 investment-bank bonds default.

[27] This is defined as the value of the old bond or the package of securities obtained in exchange when the court finally approves the settlement or reorganization plan. In some cases, the securities prices used for valuing the resolution were prices more than one year after the approval date.

for investment banks, but again the difference is not statistically significant. Third, affiliate-underwritten defaults have disproportionately fewer liquidations and more security exchanges. Since we do not have data on all of the default resolutions, we must be cautious in drawing strong conclusions from Table 6.

To summarize, the results from the matched-sample test show that affiliate-underwritten issues defaulted statistically significantly less often than ex ante similar investment-bank-underwritten issues.[28] The differences in default rates are greatest for the non-investment-grade issues. Clearly, this refutes the naive-investor hypothesis, which would suggest significantly higher default rates among affiliate-originated bonds, especially for low-quality issues. Affiliates do not seem to have systematically fooled the public.[29] Before developing further hypotheses to explain the results from the matched-sample test, we now examine their robustness.

E. Logit default-prediction model

Our matching procedure may raise two concerns. First, it could involve a selection bias, and that bias may be driving the results. Second, we may be ignoring relevant data; that is, there are many investment-bank-underwritten issues brought out in the first quarters of 1921–1929 that we do not consider. While we believe that a matched-sample approach is a robust way of analyzing situations for which no clear theory exists to guide regression specifications, we undertake a more "efficient" test of relative underwriting performance using a logit default-prediction model.

The sample for the logit includes long-term industrial bonds underwritten by both affiliates and investment banks during the first quarters of 1921–1929 (thus we add a large number of investment-bank bonds to the matched-sample [see

[28] Recall that there were 12 issues we could not match (see footnote 21). Of these, seven were rated investment grade. These could not be matched because of their high rating and size (e.g. a $50 million issue by Anaconda Copper and a $20 million issue by Standard Oil of New Jersey). The remaining five issues are under $1 million and rated below investment grade. Of the 12, only one $900,000 issue defaulted (and we could not find performance information on one $500,000 issue). Thus, loosening the matching criteria to include these bonds would not change our results.

[29] A referee has pointed out that issuing junior claims such as equity might be attractive for an unscrupulous affiliate trying to enrich itself at the public's expense. To investigate this, we expanded the search for common stock issues by affiliates to all four quarters from 1921 to 1929 since there were so few in the first quarter (see Table 2). We found prices for 15 of the affiliate-underwritten stocks on the Center for Research in Security Prices (CRSP) tapes (which begin in December 1925) and used prices from the *Bond Quotation Record* for those issued earlier. We measure the return on these issues relative to the return on the portfolio of stocks listed on the CRSP tape in the firm's size decile and the S&P industrial stock index. The affiliate-underwritten stocks had superior performance at each of the intervals we checked (3-, 5-, and 10-year horizons from issue, the market troughs in 1932, 1935, and 1940), although the differences are not statistically different from zero. While the sample is small, the results for common stock issues corroborate our findings for bonds.

Table 6. Resolution of Default for the Defaulting Bonds in the Matched Sample of 121 Pairs of Industrial Bonds Issued During 1921–1929, by Type of Underwriter

Underwriter	Variable	How the default was resolved				
		Bondholders paid in full	Bond exchanged for new bond[a]	Bond exchanged for bond with lower face value or earnings-contingent securities[b]	Firm liquidated and bondholders paid partially[c]	Average for the samples
Affiliates	Number of defaults resolved (percentage of defaults)	3 (11.1)	11 (40.7)	8 (29.6)	5 (18.5)	—
	Value received on resolution[d]	100	43.6	18.4	39.6	41.1
	Years from default to resolution[e]	2	2	4.3	0.8	2.4

Investment banks	Number of defaults resolved (percentage of defaults)	3	8	11	13	—
		(8.5)	(22.9)	(31.4)	(37.1)	
	Value received on resolution[d]	100	55.8	34.9	49.6	50.8
	Years from default to resolution[e]	3	2.5	3.6	2.1	2.8

[a] This requires that there be no impairment to the amount of the principal or its security.

[b] The bond was generally replaced by a bond with the same security but lower face value. In some cases, securities junior to the original bond (e.g. debentures [only for secured bonds], income bonds [which have interest payments contingent upon current earnings], preferred stock or common stock) were offered in compensation.

[c] The firm was liquidated, and bondholders received less than the full value of principal and interest.

[d] The value is expressed as a percentage of face value. This value is calculated either from (i) a market price for the old bond immediately after the resolution was approved by the courts or (ii) the price of the securities offered in exchange as close after the resolution as possible. The values are available for only 32 of the 39 investment bank defaults and 24 of the 28 affiliate defaults.

[e] The time from the date of default to the date that the court gives final approval to the resolution plan.

Note: Information on resolution is available for only 35 of the 39 investment-bank defaults and 27 of the 28 affiliate defaults.

Sources: Moody's, Poor's, Fitch's Bond Book, Commercial and Financial Chronicle, National Monthly Corporation Bond Summary, National Monthly Stock Summary, and Fisher Manual of Valuable and Worthless Securities.

Table 7. Estimates for Logit Default Prediction for the Sample of All Industrial Bonds Issued During the First Quarters of 1921–1929

Independent variable	(i)	(ii)	(iii)
Unrated indicator (1 if unrated)	0.594	1.006	1.451
	(1.853)	(2.795)	(3.339)
Rated below investment grade indicator (1 if rated below investment grade)	0.250	0.414	0.297
	(0.909)	(1.364)	(0.795)
Affiliate indicator (1 if affiliate)	−0.565	−0.108	0.343
	(−2.061)	(−0.312)	(0.840)
(Affiliate) × (unrated) interaction	—	−1.801	−2.284
		(−2.340)	(−2.404)
(Affiliate) × (rated below investment grade) interaction	—	−0.563	−0.940
		(−0.864)	(−1.262)
Debt/total assets	—	—	0.916
			(0.408)
χ^2 for likelihood-ratio test that affiliate and interaction terms are jointly zero:	—	10.85	8.02
[p-value]:		[0.013]	[0.046]
Number of observations:	413	413	305
χ^2 for the regression:	29.65	36.04	28.83
[p value]:	[0.013]	[0.005]	[0.036]

Notes: The dependent variable, DEFAULT, equals 1 if the bond defaults, 0 otherwise, and has mean equal to 0.28. One-digit SIC industry and year indicators are included in the regression but have been omitted from the table. The numbers in parentheses below each coefficient estimate are t statistics.

Table 2] and discard investment-bank matches from outside the first quarter). We gathered data on the bonds and the firms from the sources we described above for the matched-sample test. The logit analysis examines whether the type of underwriter affects the likelihood of default, controlling for a variety of security and firm characteristics. It thus serves as a robustness check of the results from the matched security test. Since we do not derive the default prediction equation from an explicit model, in Table 7 we report a number of specifications. We include indicator variables for one-digit industry SIC code and the year of issue but do not report their coefficient estimates.[30]

Column (i) in Table 7 shows that, controlling for initial rating, affiliate-underwritten issues are less likely to default than are the investment-bank-underwritten issues, and the coefficient is statistically significant at the 5 percent

[30] We also tried including firm age, size of issue, indicators for collateralization, and indicators for the stated purpose of issue, but none of these variables was statistically significant. The results for the affiliate variables did not change, and thus we do not report these regressions.

level. For the mean issue in our sample, the coefficient estimates imply that underwriting by an affiliate reduces the probability of default by 0.11. To gauge the magnitude of the "affiliate" effect, this probability is approximately equal to the difference in probability of default between an investment-grade bond and an unrated bond in this sample. The effect is thus economically as well as statistically significant.

To identify the impact of underwriter type on issues of different quality rating, we include interaction terms which indicate whether an affiliate underwrites a bond rated below investment grade or an unrated bond. The coefficients are reported in column (ii). The coefficient estimates for the interaction terms indicate that the unrated affiliate-underwritten bonds defaulted far less often than unrated bonds underwritten by investment banks. A similar but smaller default-performance advantage for the issues underwritten by affiliates also obtains for the bonds rated below investment grade. In specification (ii), the affiliate indicator individually is no longer statistically significant, but this may be due to its high correlation with the interaction terms. We use a likelihood-ratio test to test whether the affiliate indicator and interaction variables are jointly statistically significant, and they are at roughly the 1 percent significance level. Finally, in column (iii) we include the ratio of debt (including the new bond issue) to total assets in the year of issuance. Although we lose a quarter of the observations, the same qualitative results emerge. In summary, the results from the matched-sample test are confirmed by the logit default prediction: affiliate-underwritten issues defaulted less frequently, and the difference in default performance is most pronounced for the lowest-quality issues. We now describe a hypothesis which might explain this finding.

III. Rational Adaptation to the Potential for Conflicts of Interest

A. An example of discounting for "rogue" banks

A rational-expectations analysis of conflicts of interest offers predictions which contrast with those of the simple naive-investor hypothesis and which are consistent with the above results. While rational investors may not possess the information the commercial-bank affiliate uses to gauge a firm's quality, they understand its motives. Investors realize that some affiliates may be less forthcoming than independent investment banks in communicating information about issue quality, due to possible conflicts of interest. They will be most wary when there is little public information about an issue, as in the case of small issues by little-known firms, which form the bulk of our unrated sample.

When information asymmetry and conflicts of interest are potentially important, suspicious investors rationally "tax" the issues underwritten by affiliates by
applying a "lemons-market" discount to their issues. This may account for the
difference in performance between affiliate and investment-bank offerings, and
the increasing difference as quality deteriorates. The following example makes
the point clear.

Assume that securities which have a true quality of Caa always default and
repay nothing in default; securities of true quality B default with probability
0.2 and repay half of the principal in default (and thus have an expected payout of 0.9 per dollar invested); and securities of true quality Ba do not default.
Let the market (and rating agencies) have rational expectations that one in ten
affiliates are "rogues" who succumb to conflicts of interest and misrepresent
securities of quality Caa as being Ba. The remaining nine banks underwrite
only Ba securities. Because the true quality is the affiliates' private information and the market cannot distinguish who the rogues are, they know the
expected payout from each dollar invested in the bond is $(9/10) \times 1 + (1/10) \times
0 = 0.9$. This is equivalent to the expected payout from each dollar invested
in a bond which is truly B. Investors and rating agencies will then treat all
Ba bonds issued by bank affiliates as B-rated, thus applying a "lemons" discount to nine out of ten affiliate-underwritten bonds. If the performance of
affiliate-underwritten bonds is compared with ex ante similar (B-rated bonds)
underwritten by investment banks, we should find ex post that more investment-
bank-underwritten bonds default (20 percent) than do affiliate-underwritten
bonds (10 percent), but pay more in default (50 percent vs. 0 percent). An identical argument can be made when bonds are matched on price (or yields) rather
than ratings.[31]

The low predictive power of ratings and yields for the subsequent performance of affiliate issues (but their high predictive power for the investment-bank
issues) is consistent with theories of the effect of apparent conflicts on an underwriter's ability to certify (e.g. Vincent Crawford and Joel Sobel, 1982; Rajan,
1992). For the matched sample, 16 of the 66 affiliate bonds rated investment
grade default (24 percent), compared to three of the 21 bonds rated below
investment grade (14 percent), and nine of the 34 unrated issues (26 percent).

---

[31] For the market to apply a lemons-market discount it is sufficient that the underwriter lack credibility as a certifier. Conflicts of interest are only one reason (though perhaps the most important
one) why the affiliates may have had lower credibility than independent investment banks. Another
potential reason is that many affiliates were more recent entrants than the investment banks into
underwriting and therefore had not built sufficient reputations of integrity. Also, we can interpret the
naive-investor hypothesis in this framework, namely, that the public market systematically under-
estimated the share of rogue affiliates. If the public did so, we would expect to find a higher default
rate for the affiliates—which is contrary to our findings. Our results are consistent with the investing
public's expectation about the market share of rogue affiliates that turned out to be either correct or
a bit too pessimistic.

The differences in default rates are not statistically significant. In contrast, the initial ratings and yields appear to be good predictors of default for the investment-bank-underwritten issues. For the matched issues underwritten by the investment banks, the default rate rises as the initial rating falls: 24 percent of the investment-grade bonds, 29 percent of the bonds rated below investment grade, and 50 percent of the unrated issues default. The difference in the default rates across the different grades of investment-bank-underwritten bonds is statistically significant at the 5 percent level. For the sample of all investment-bank-underwritten bonds issued in the first quarters of 1921–1929, the default rates are 25 percent, 34 percent, and 46 percent, respectively, and the differences are statistically significant at the 1 percent level. These results suggest that, relative to investment banks, affiliates were less able to certify quality for "information-intensive" issues to the rating agencies and the market.[32] We now discuss how this rational adaptation would affect the activities of the affiliates.

B. Implications of rational adaptation for the underwriting activities of the affiliates

The imposition of a "lemons" discount on certain affiliate-underwritten issues impairs the ability of bank affiliates to bring these issues to market. This is especially true for small, relatively lesser-known bank affiliates without much reputational or equity capital. Furthermore, the discount would tend to be larger for junior securities and information-sensitive securities issued by small, young, relatively unknown firms. Relative to independent investment banks with similar capital, we would expect small affiliates to underwrite more senior securities issued by older, larger, and less risky firms. Large affiliates of relatively well-known banks, however, have substantial reputations to offset the suspicion that they would succumb to conflicts. Their issues are less likely to be subject to discounts than the issues underwritten by small affiliates. If so, we expect less difference between the underwriting activities of large well-known affiliates and investment banks and large differences between the underwriting activities of small, little-known affiliates and investment banks. The counterpart of the public markets rationally adapting to the bank affiliates' conflicts of interest is that

[32] There are a number of possible reasons why firms might choose affiliates to underwrite their "information-intensive" securities despite being subject to the "discounts." First, White (1986) has documented diversification benefits for the banks combining underwriting and lending in the 1920's. Affiliates thus may have been able to charge lower underwriting fees to firms because underwriting would have helped hedge the rest of their operations. Second, affiliates may have been trying to build their credibility in this segment of the market during the 1920's, so they may have decided to invest in reputation by charging relatively low underwriting fees for these deals. Third, these firms may not have been able to convince independent investment banks to underwrite securities for them.

the affiliates themselves should adapt their underwriting activities to the market discount.[33]

C. The matched-underwriter test

The rational-adaptation hypothesis not only suggests that affiliates will differ from investment banks in their underwriting activities, but also that the difference will depend on the size of the underwriter's reputational and equity capital. There is no easy way to measure either reputational or equity capital. We will use the size of issues brought to market by the underwriter as a proxy for both aspects of capital. Our rationale is that only underwriters with large implicit (reputational) and explicit (equity) capital can provide the insurance and credibility that large issues require. We therefore use the median size of issue underwritten during the first quarter of 1921–1929 as a measure of the underwritter's capital.[34]

We divide underwriters into three groups on this basis. Because there are far fewer affiliate issues in our sample, we pick break points that ensure approximately equal affiliate issues in each group. A natural division is into underwriters with median issue size greater than $5 million, whom we call "large," those with median issue size less than $1 million whom we call "small," and those in the middle who are labeled "medium." Table 8 shows that there are nine large affiliates and investment banks, who account for 46 and 61 issues, respectively, in the first quarters of 1921–1929. Thirty-five small affiliate underwriters account for 52 issues, and 177 small investment banks account for 280 issues. Thus, the large underwriters also tend to underwrite more often. We now examine the activities of these underwriters in the first quarters of 1921–1929.

D. Results of the matched-underwriter test

Table 8 shows that the affiliates, in general, underwrite larger issues. The median issue size for all affiliate issues (not shown in the table) is $1.75 million, while the median issue size for all investment-bank issues is $1.005 million. The medians are different at the 1 percent level of significance. In our sample, large firms

---

[33] Another way to reduce the size of the potential discount is for affiliates to co-underwrite with credible investment banks. Prior to the Securities Acts of 1933 and the Securities Exchange Act of 1934, it appears that the burden of investigating and certifying the issue fell primarily upon the lead underwriter and not the syndicate (see Moore 1934: 479). It is not clear whether co-underwriters had enough influence over the lead underwriter's decisions for them to add credibility to the offering. Furthermore, the fixed costs of employing an additional underwriter (who also acquires information about the firm) are likely to be high. Multiple underwriters thus may have been a feasible way to attempt to reduce the lemons discount for large issues but not for small issues.

[34] We also tried an alternative proxy of the number of issues underwritten by a house. It results in a very similar classification of the underwriting houses and does not qualitatively alter the results. Neither measure, however, would be a good proxy for capital if some houses take on more risk by underwriting larger issues or more issues with the same amount of (unobserved) capital.

Table 8. Comparison of the Issuing Activities of Affiliates and Investment Banks by Size Class, for the Sample of All Industrial Bonds, Preferred Stock, and Common Stock Issued in the First Quarters of 1921–1929

Underwriter	Variable	Large underwriters[a]	Medium underwriters[b]	Small underwriters[c]	All underwriters
Affiliates	Number of underwriters	9	20	35	64
	Number of issues	61	50	52	163
	Mean size of issue ($thousand)	15,567.86	2,863.36	663.36	6,915.93
	Median firm age at issue[d]	22	17	23	21.5
Investment banks	Number of underwriters	9	143	177	329
	Number of issues	46	355	280	681
	Mean size of issues ($thousand)	11,496.80	2,778.69	476.98	5,055.73
	Median firm age at issue[d]	11	16	14	15

[a] Large underwriter: median issue size originated during the first quarters of 1921–1929 is greater than $5,000,000.
[b] Medium underwriter: median issue size originated during the first quarters of 1921–1929 is between $5,000,000 and $1,000,000.
[c] Small underwriter: median issue size originated during the first quarters of 1921–1929 is below $1,000,000.
[d] Firm age is defined as the number of years between the issue date and the date the industrial firm was founded.

Sources: Commercial and Financial Chronicle, Moody's, Poor's, and Fitch's.

(as measured by the size of book assets), in general, make large issues.[35] The table thus suggests that affiliates tend to underwrite larger firms. The median age (defined as the years from founding to issue date) of firms brought to market by the investment banks is 15, while the median age for affiliates is 21.5. Again these differences are significant at the 1-percent level. When the sample is partitioned into the three size classes, the age difference is statistically significant for only the small-underwriters subsample.

Table 2 shows that, on average for the decade of the 1920's, affiliates underwrote fewer common-stock and preferred issues than did the investment banks. More interesting patterns arise when we look at the different underwriter subgroups. Table 9 shows little economic or statistical difference between the mix of securities underwritten by the large affiliates and the mix underwritten by large investment banks. There is, however, a significant difference between the mix of securities underwritten by small affiliates and small investment banks. Small investment banks underwrite a greater fraction of junior securities than

[35] We have data on book assets for only a subset of the industrial firms in our sample. The correlation between book assets and size for firms for which we have the data is 0.7, so using issue size as a proxy for firm size seems reasonable.

Table 9. Comparison of the Types of Securities Issued by Large and Small Affiliates and Investment Banks During the First Quarters of 1921–1929

Underwriter	Number of issues (percentage)			
	Bonds	Preferred stock	Common stock	Total
Large underwriters:[a]				
Affiliates	42	11	8	61
	(68.9)	(18.0)	(13.1)	(100.0)
Investment banks	29	10	7	46
	(63.0)	(21.7)	(15.2)	(100.0)
		$\chi^2_{[2]} = 0.4,$	$p = 0.819$	
Small underwriters:[b]				
Affiliates	44	7	1	52
	(84.6)	(13.5)	(1.9)	(100.0)
Investment banks	137	75	69	281
	(48.8)	(26.7)	(24.6)	(100.0)
		$\chi^2_{[2]} = 24.4,$	$p < 0.001$	

[a] Large underwriter: median issue size originated during the first quarters of 1921–1929 is greater than $5,000,000 (see Table 8).

[b] Small underwriter: median issue originated during the first quarters of 1921–1929 is below $1,000,000 (see Table 8).

Note: The chi-square statistic reported is the Pearson's chi-square for the hypothesis that affiliate and investment-bank rows are from the same distribution.

do the large investment banks. By contrast, small affiliates underwrite far fewer junior securities than do large affiliates.[36] Together, Tables 8 and 9 suggest that affiliates underwrite larger, older firms and generally concentrate more on senior securities like debt than do the investment banks. The difference between affiliates and investment banks is the greatest for the small-underwriters group.

E. Logit analysis

We must be cautious in drawing conclusions from the unconditional correlations presented in Tables 8 and 9. If equity is issued only by younger firms, for example, the fact that investment banks underwrite equity could result in their underwriting younger firms. A more satisfying test of the hypotheses thus would involve conditional correlations. We obtain these by performing a logit analysis where the dependent variable is 1 if an issue is underwritten by an affiliate and

[36] The difference between the kinds of securities that affiliates and investment banks issue in the medium group is similar to that in the small group.

Table 10. Estimates for Logit Analysis Predicting Whether an Affiliate Underwrites an Issue, for the Sample of All Industrial Bonds, Preferred Stock, and Common Stock Issued in the First Quarters of 1921–1929

Independent variable	(i)	(ii)	(iii)	(iv)[a]
Log of issue amount (thousands)	0.286	0.335	0.315	0.429
	(3.378)	(3.140)	(3.184)	(3.782)
Indicator is 1 if issue of common	−1.594	−1.576	−2.901	−1.516
stock	(−4.189)	(−3.759)	(−4.338)	(−3.658)
Indicator is 1 if issue of preferred	−1.215	−1.051	−1.413	−1.314
stock	(−3.913)	(−3.167)	(−3.567)	(−3.153)
Log of firm age in years	0.223	0.252	0.137	0.192
	(2.385)	(2.315)	(1.275)	(1.766)
Indicator is 1 if firm is listed		0.127	—	—
on an exchange		(0.443)		
Ratio of debt to total assets			−1.025	—
at time of issue			(−1.082)	
Indicator is 1 if small underwriter				0.265
does the issue				(0.359)
Indicator is 1 if issue of common				−1.249
stock by small underwriter				(−1.119)
Indicator is 1 if issue of preferred				0.880
shares by small underwriter				(1.414)
(Log of firm age) × (indicator if				0.090
small underwriter) interaction				(0.397)
Number of observations:	651	545	520	651
χ^2 for the regression:	76.01	65.53	62.76	83.96
[p value]:	0.0000	0.0000	0.0000	0.0000

[a] The chi-square statistic for the likelihood-ratio test that the small underwriter and interaction terms are jointly zero is 7.96, which has a p value of 0.09.

Notes: The dependent variable, which has a mean of 0.20, is 1 if an affiliate is the lead underwriter for the issue and 0 if the lead underwriter is an investment bank. One-digit SIC industry and year indicators are included in the regression but have been omitted from the table. Numbers in parentheses are t statistics. A small underwriter is defined as having a median issue size originated during the first quarters of 1921–1929 below $1 million (see Table 8).

0 if underwritten by an investment bank. Another way to think about these regressions is that a firm chooses between an affiliate and an investment-bank underwriter based on its own characteristics and the kind of security it wants to issue. If the rational-adaptation hypothesis is valid, the firms know the discount that public capital markets will impose on issues under-written by affiliates lacking credibility. By a revealed-preference argument, the coefficients on firm and issue characteristics reveal the relative competencies of the two types of underwriters. The results are in Table 10.

The coefficients in column (i) indicate that affiliates are more likely to under-write larger, older firms and debt rather than junior securities like equity and preferred stock. The coefficient estimates for these variables are statistically and economically significant. A standard-deviation increase in the log of issue size increases the probability of the firm choosing an affiliate by 0.05. A standard-deviation increase in the log of the firm's age increases the probability of the firm choosing an affiliate by 0.04. A stock issue has a 0.21 lower probability than a bond issue to be underwritten by an affiliate. A preferred issue has a 0.16 lower probability than a bond issue to be underwritten by an affiliate. In specification (ii), we include an indicator which is 1 if the firm is listed on an exchange, and in (iii) we include the ratio of debt to total assets for the firm. A listed firm is more likely to prefer an affiliate, while a highly leveraged (and therefore more risky firm) is less likely to prefer an affiliate. The coeffi-cients on these two variables, however, are not measured precisely. In column (iv) we report coefficients when we interact the explanatory variables with an indicator if the underwriter is small. Except on the dimension of whether the issue is a preferred share, the difference in the activities of affiliates and invest-ment banks is accentuated in the case of small underwriters, and the affiliate and interaction terms as a group are statistically significant at the 10 percent level.

IV. Alternative Interpretations and Further Implications of the Results

A. The role of bank–borrower relationships

An alternative explanation of our result that the affiliate-underwritten issues default less frequently is that they were subject to a (largely unanticipated) factor which did not affect the investment-bank-underwritten issues. Perhaps firms that were clients of affiliates enjoyed stronger ties to their banks and so had better access to credit during the Depression. This relationship thus may have helped affiliate client firms avoid default.[37] In the 1920's, the expectation of a business-cycle downturn as prolonged and severe as the Great Depression was undoubtedly quite small. The ratings and initial yield thus (rationally) would have involved only a negligible adjustment for the "Great Depression" insurance provided by a close relationship with a commercial bank.

---

[37] Between the second quarter of 1932 and the first quarter of 1935, for example, the total issuance of bond, preferred-stock, and common-stock finance dwindled to nearly zero (*Moody's Bank-ing and Finance Manual*, 1939). The Reconstruction Finance Corporation made large loans to (and investments in) banks and other enterprises during this period (see U.S. Treasury, 1959).

If indeed banking relationships during the unanticipated Depression were valuable, affiliate-underwritten issues should outperform investment-bank-underwritten issues during the Depression years, but not before.[38] Although most of the performance differences occur in the 1930's, there were differences even before the onset of the Great Depression: by the end of 1929, in our matched sample seven investment-bank-underwritten bonds default compared with five defaults for the bonds underwritten by affiliates. While we should be cautious about drawing strong conclusions, because the difference is small (though the 40-percent difference in default rates is the same as that in the Depression subperiod 1930–1940) and not statistically significant, it is suggestive that unanticipated benefits from banking relationships may not be the entire explanation.

Banking relationships also could provide an alternative explanation of our result that affiliates underwrite relatively less equity than investment banks. If a banking relationship lowers the costs of financial distress, then ceteris paribus, firms with such a relationship may have been able to rely more heavily on debt finance than firms without it. The relative paucity of equity issues underwritten by affiliates thus may be driven by low demand from affiliate client firms rather than adverse selection. In our sample, however, the ratio of debt to total assets for affiliate client firms immediately after their bond issue is slightly lower than for the firms that use investment banks (0.296 vs. 0.306). This evidence does not suggest that affiliate client firms have higher debt capacities. The affiliate client firms, however, do make fewer equity issues during the 1920's; for the matched sample, 22 firms using an affiliate to underwrite their debt also issued common or preferred stock, whereas 30 firms using an investment bank to underwrite their debt did so. The difference in these numbers is too small to account for the large differences in equity issuances between affiliates and investment banks discussed in the previous section.

We also compare the identity of the underwriter for the equity issues with the underwriter for the bond issues. Of the 16 firms in the matched sample that use an affiliate for their bond issue *and* issue equity through an underwriter,[39] 11 (69 percent) use a different underwriter for the equity issue. Of the 18 firms that use an investment bank to underwrite a bond *and* issue equity through an underwriter, only eight (44 percent) use a different underwriter for their

---

[38] It is also possible to argue that a firm which depended extensively on a bank relationship may have been worse off during the (unanticipated) turmoil in the 1930's. First, the banking crises between 1930 and 1933 may have reduced the ability of banks to provide credit. Second, the Glass–Steagall Act of 1933 restricted the areas of interaction between banks and firms, thus reducing the benefit to banks of maintaining relationships and, perhaps, reducing their incentive to provide credit. This argument would suggest that banking relationships might have lowered the ex post relative performance of affiliate-underwritten issues.

[39] The rest undertook rights offerings.

equity issue. Firms using an affiliate for their debt issues thus switch to a new underwriter for their equity issuances more often than do investment-bank client firms.[40] Although the number of observations here is small, this evidence supports our interpretation that the affiliates appear to lack a comparative advantage in underwriting equity.

B. Informational scope economies from combining lending and underwriting

A prominent argument in the current debates about Glass–Steagall repeal concerns scope economies in information access and processing.[41] Since firms typically have had bank loans before they issue public securities, banks may have firm-specific information which would give them an advantage over investment banks in underwriting more "information-intensive" securities, in other words, junior securities of younger, smaller, and less well-known firms. Universal banking thus could particularly benefit small and young firms, providing them greater access to the public securities markets than they otherwise would have had.

We find, however, that commercial banks were relatively inactive in this segment of the market. We must be cautious in concluding from this evidence that the informational scope economies realized by affiliates were small relative to the cost of discounts imposed by a market concerned about conflicts. First, banks may have been more conservative due to potential reputational spillovers from their underwriting to their banking business (note that national banks had double liability and no deposit insurance prior to 1933).[42] The significance of this factor is difficult to measure, but the fact that the largest affiliates seem immune to these spillovers is troublesome for this theory (see Tables 9 and 10). Second, affiliates may have underwritten older and larger firms simply because those were firms with which they had preexisting relationships, which formed the basis for informational scope economies. If this is the case, then the benefits to smaller and younger firms from Glass–Steagall repeal may not be large. Third, commercial banks, with their prior experience in loan analysis, may have had more in-house expertise for evaluating debt contracts rather than equity. While this hypothesis is not directly testable, we do not find a tendency for affiliates

---

[40] All of the affiliate client firms that switched underwriters chose an investment bank, not another affiliate, for the equity issue. In all but two cases, the investment-bank client firms switched to another investment bank.

[41] There are a variety of other scope-economies arguments that our data do not address. There may be, for instance, economies in combining deposit-taking with the distribution of securities to savers. Also, as White (1986) has found, there may be diversification advantages to a bank combining the two activities.

[42] Also, the affiliates' natural securities distribution clientele—depositors—may have been more riskaverse and so less disposed toward buying risky, lowquality, junior claims than the wealthier and more sophisticated individuals with whom the investment banks typically dealt.

to "learn" about equities over time, that is, the affiliates' share of the equity issuance market declined somewhat during the 1920's.[43]

V. Conclusion

Our results are not consistent with the popular belief that "... bank affiliates had underwritten and sold unsound and speculative securities, [and] published deliberately misleading prospectuses ..." (Melanie Fein 1986: A-5). Not only did bank affiliates underwrite higher-quality issues, but also we find that the affiliate-underwritten issues performed better than comparable issues underwritten by independent investment banks. The superior affiliate performance is most pronounced among the lower-rated and more "information-intensive" issues.

Our study indicates that the focus of legislative action on protecting the investing public from the effects of conflicts of interest has been misplaced. Allowing commercial and investment banking to take place under one roof did not lead to widespread defrauding of investors. Indeed, our results suggest that the public markets and rating agencies were aware of the potential for conflicts (or weak reputations) of the affiliates and imposed a "lemons market" discount on information-intensive securities underwritten by the affiliates. The affiliates appear to have responded to the market's concerns by shying away from information-intensive securities and, instead, underwriting primarily more senior securities and securities of older, larger, and better-known firms than did the investment banks.

While our account of the market's adaptation to the potential for conflicts addresses the policy issue of protecting investors, it also raises questions about the efficiency of underwriting in an universal banking system (see the theoretical arguments made by Crawford and Sobel [1982] and Rajan [1992]). For large, well-known firms, our study suggests that both affiliates and investment banks can efficiently provide underwriting services. For smaller, lesser-known firms, the discount the market imposes on affiliate-underwritten issues suggests that the affiliates may suffer from a lack of credibility. Ceteris paribus, affiliates thus would be at a disadvantage vis-à-vis investment banks in competing for their business. If small firms freely choose their underwriters in a competitive market, the fact that some of them choose affiliates suggests that affiliates may have some other cost advantages in underwriting—such as diversification

---

[43] If affiliates did enjoy substantial economies in information-gathering, we would expect them to realize these economies over time by developing expertise in equities and expanding their equity underwriting as the 1920's progressed. Between 1921 and 1927, affiliates underwrote between zero and three common stock issues each year, rising to seven in 1928 and 11 in 1929 when the overall number of equity issues roughly quadrupled. As a share of the total number of industrial common-stock issues, however, their share fell from 5.2 percent during 1921–1925 to 3.7 percent during 1926–1929. This contrasts with their increasing share of bond originations over the same period.

benefits (White 1986)—which they pass on to the client firm. On the other hand, in circumstances where commercial banks have monopoly power over the smaller, lesser-known firms, some of these firms might be induced to use an affiliate when an investment bank would be a more credible, hence more efficient, underwriter. A way of testing these alternatives is to compare the underwriting fees charged to the smaller, lesser-known firms by affiliates with the fees charged to similar clients by investment banks. A finding that the affiliates' fees in these cases are lower would make the case for Glass–Steagall repeal even more convincing.

The affiliates' credibility problem could be mitigated in two ways. First, banks could be permitted to hold equity in the firms they underwrite. Through their equity stake, banks could signal to the market their beliefs about the firm's prospects (Hayne Leland and David Pyle 1977; Rajan 1992).[44] Second, the higher disclosure standards and other changes in the regulation of securities markets since the period we study may have increased the credibility of underwriters (see Carol Simon 1989). Whether these changes are sufficient to enable affiliates to overcome concerns about conflicts of interest in underwriting risky, lesser-known firms awaits examination of more recent data. A study of the foray by investment banks in the late 1980's into a form of universal banking, in which they made bridge loans to firms they were advising and underwriting, could illuminate this issue.

An important question our study raises but does not answer concerns the political considerations behind Glass–Steagall. If the economic rationales given in favor of the Act were not supported by the evidence, why was it passed? Were the alleged abuses simply an excuse for legislators in the 1930's to pursue other goals?

References

Ang, J. S., and Richardson, T. (1993). "The underwriting experience of commercial bank affiliates prior to the Glass–Steagall Act: A re-examination of evidence for passage of the act." Mimeo, University of Florida.

Asquith, P., Mullins, D., and Wolff, E. (1989). "Original issue high yield bonds: Ageing analysis of defaults, exchanges, and calls." *Journal of Finance*, 44(4): 923–52.

Benston, G. J. (1990). *The Separation of Commercial and Investment Banking*. Oxford: Oxford Univ. Press.

Bond quotation record. New York, various issues, 1921–1930.

---

[44] The ability to own equity would not only improve the credibility of the commercial bank's underwriting, but would also align the bank's interests with those of the client firm, thereby mitigating the distortions caused by a potential bank monopoly.

Carosso, V. P. (1970). *Investment Banking in America: A History*. Cambridge, MA: Harvard Univ. Press.

Chernow, R. (1991). *The House of Morgan*. New York: Simon & Schuster.

Commercial and Financial Chronicle. New York, various issues, 1921–1940.

Crawford, V., and Sobel, J. (1982). "Strategic information transmission." *Econometrica*, 50(6): 1431–51.

Dewing, A. S. (1953). *The Financial Policy of Corporations* (5th ed., 2 vols.). New York: Ronald.

Edwards, G. W. (1942). "The myth of the security affiliate." *Journal of the American Statistical Association*, 37: 225–32.

Eichengreen, B., and Portes, R. (1989). "After the deluge: Default, negotiation, and readjustment during the interwar years," in B. Eichengreen and R. Portes (eds.), *The International Debt Crisis in Historical Perspective* (Cambridge, MA: MIT Press), 14–47.

Fein, M. (1986). "The separation of banking and commerce in American banking history." Appendix A to the *Statement by Paul Volcker* before the Subcommittee on Commerce, Consumer and Monetary Affairs of the United States House of Representatives, pp. A1–A13.

Fisher manual of valuable and worthless securities, Vols. 1–10. New York: Fisher, 1927–1945.

Fitch's bond book. New York: Fitch, 1921–1929.

Kalbfleisch, J., and Prentice, R. (1980). *The Statistical Analysis of Failure Time Data*. New York: Wiley.

Leland, H., and Pyle, D. (1977). "Informational asymmetries, financial structure, and financial intermediation." *Journal of Finance*, 32(2): 371–87.

Macey, J., and Miller, G. (1992). *Banking Law and Regulation*. Boston: Little, Brown.

Mintz, I. (1951). *Deterioration in the Quality of Foreign Bonds Issued in the United States, 1920–1930*. New York: National Bureau of Economic Research.

Moody's Manuals: Industrial, Public utility, Government and municipalities, and Banking and financial. New York: Moody's, various volumes, 1921–1941.

Moore, T. (1934). "Security affiliate versus private investment banker—A study in security organizations." *Harvard Business Review*, 12: 478–84.

National Monthly Corporation Bond Summary. New York: National Quotation Bureau, various volumes, 1921–1941.

National Monthly Stock Summary. New York: National Quotation Bureau, various volumes, 1921–1941.

National Securities Dealers of North America (NSDNA). New York: Siebert, February 1929.

Olson, J. (1977). *Herbert Hoover and the Reconstruction Finance Corporation*. Ames, IA: Iowa State Univ. Press.

Peach, W. N. (1941). *The Security Affiliates of National Banks*. Baltimore, MD: Johns Hopkins University Press.

Poor's Industrial Section and Ratings Manuals. New York: Poor's, 1921–1941.

Preston, H. H., and Findlay, A. R. (1930a). "Investment affiliates thrive." *American Bankers Association Journal*, 22: 1027–8, 1075.

—— (1930b). "Era favors investment affiliates." *American Bankers Association Journal*, 22: 1153–4, 1191–2.

Rajan, R. G. (1992). "A theory of the costs and benefits of universal banking." Center for Research in Security Prices. Working Paper No. 346, University of Chicago.

Simon, C. (1989). "The effect of the 1933 securities Act on investor information and the performance of new issues." *American Economic Review*, 79(3): 295–318.

U.S. Senate, Committee on Banking and Currency (1931). 71st Congress, 3rd Session. *Operation of the National and Federal Reserve Systems: Hearings on S.R. 71*. Washington, DC: U.S. Government Printing Office.

—— (1933–1934). 72nd Congress, 2nd Session and 73rd Congress, 2nd Session. *Stock exchange practices: Hearings on S.R. 84 and S.R. 56 and S.R. 97*. Washington, DC: U.S. Government Printing Office.

U.S. Treasury (1959). *Final Report on the Reconstruction Finance Corporation*. Washington, DC: U.S. Government Printing Office.

White, E. (1983). *The Regulation and Reform of the American Banking System*. Princeton, NJ: Princeton University Press.

—— (1984). "Banking innovation in the 1920's: The growth of national banks' financial services." *Business and Economic History*, 13: 92–104.

—— (1986). "Before the Glass–Steagall Act: An analysis of the investment banking activities of national banks." *Explorations in Economic History*, 23(1): 33–55.

Wigmore, B. (1985). *The Crash and its Aftermath: A History of Securities Markets in the United States, 1929–1933*. Westport, CT: Greenwood.

14

Optimal Design of Bank Bailouts:
The Case of Transition Economies

Philippe Aghion, Patrick Bolton, and Steven Fries

1. Introduction

In most recent banking crises bank regulators have been caught off their guard and have been forced to respond to the crisis in a hurry without the support of an institutional or legal framework designed to deal with bank failures. Unfortunately most bank regulations (and in particular the BIS regulations) are concerned with the ex ante problem of how to avoid bank failures, and few rules have been devised on how to deal with bank failures when they occur.

This situation is in sharp contrast with the non-financial sector, where a detailed and elaborate bankruptcy law governs the process of liquidation or reorganization of financially distressed firms. In the case of banks it is generally up to the regulators to decide how to deal with an insolvent bank, and regulators have by and large too much discretion and little guidance on how best to restructure or liquidate an insolvent bank. When faced with a banking crisis regulators are often forced to improvise or imitate the hastily improvised solutions adopted by other regulators in some past crisis.

In this chapter we address the question of how to design a bankruptcy institution for banks that would serve a similar purpose as the existing bankruptcy law for non-financial firms. Because of the specific nature of banking activities and because of deposit insurance it is not suitable to simply apply the existing

This is a revised version of "Financial Restructuring in Transition Economies", CentER Discussion Paper No. 96111, Center for Economic Research, University of Tilburg, The Netherlands. This paper was first presented at the EBRD Conference on "Policy Studies to Promote Private Sector Development"; the International Conference on "The Theory of the Firm and China's Economic Reform" held at Beijing, China, in September 1996; and the LACEA Meetings at Bogota, Colombia, in October 1996. We thank Patricia Armendariz de Hinestrosa, Sudipto Bhattacharya, John Boyd, Janet Mitchell, Nick Stern and Harald Uhlig, as well as seminar participants of the IMF and the World Bank research workshops, and conference participants of the William Davidson Institute Conference on "Financial Sectors in Transition" for very helpful comments. The research reported in this paper is part of a wide EBRD research project on "Private Sector Development". We are grateful to the EBRD for financial and intellectual support.

bankruptcy law to banks. A special bankruptcy institution designed for banks is required. Such an institution would in all likelihood be as elaborate as current bankruptcy law and it is far beyond the scope of this chapter, let alone the capabilities of the authors, to outline such an institution in all its details. The more modest aim here is to outline a framework which could serve as a basis for the design of such an institution.

Most policy discussions of bank bailouts are concerned with regulatory forbearance and public confidence in the banking sector, with the supporters of bailouts emphasizing the dangers of a confidence crisis and the opponents emphasizing the moral hazard problems created by excessively soft bank bailouts. We shall take for granted that deposits must be insured and we shall sidestep the forbearance question by assuming that regulators can commit to an optimally designed bank bailout scheme.[1] Our focus will be on how to design the scheme optimally given that regulators can commit to the scheme.

The main questions we shall be dealing with are the following: When should a failing bank be bailed out? And if a bailout is desirable, how should the bank be bailed out? We shall be concerned with both the incentive effects of bailout policies on bank managers and the cost implications of the bailout for the government. In other words, the objective is to design a bailout scheme which preserves bank managers' investment and reporting incentives, while keeping the bailout bill as small as possible.

A common response of regulators in recent financial crises (e.g. in Norway, Mexico or Japan) has been to inject new funds (unconditionally) into distressed banks by purchasing preferred stock or subordinated bonds. The size of these injections has been massive (of the order of several percentage points of GDP).[2] With the benefit of hindsight one may question both the rescue method and the size of the rescue. These capital injections have had the advantage of buying precious time and breathing space for regulators but they did not address the underlying non-performing loans problem.

To address this problem it is essential to give banks adequate incentives to liquidate bad loans. Following Mitchell [1995], we argue in this chapter that bank managers' incentives to misreport the extent of their banks' loan losses is a major source of inefficiency leading generally to inefficiently low liquidation of bad loans, and, thus, to a magnified banking crisis down the road. We show how the form of an efficient bank bailout scheme is to a large extent determined by how it mitigates or overcomes bank managers' incentives to hide loan losses.

[1] The forbearance problem is somewhat tangential to the issues addressed in this chapter. While we believe that this problem is of real concern we think that it is best to address this question separately.

[2] The latest rescue package set up by the Japanese authorities this year, of the order of $ 102bn, represents about 2.5 percent of GDP (see the *Financial Times* of February 28, 1998). The overall bailout cost of the Mexican banking sector as disclosed to parliament by President Zedillo was estimated to be 14.5 percent of GDP (see the *Financial Times* of April 20, 1998).

Once it is recognized that bank managers can delay insolvency by hiding the extent of their banks' loan losses and that they may refrain from liquidating bad loans in an attempt to hide loan losses, it should be clear that strict bank closure rules requiring the closure of any insolvent bank may be counterproductive. Such rules may simply induce bank managers to hide the size of their banks' loan losses for as long as they can. Such behavior can result in huge misallocations of investments as well as massive bank failures.

Thus, this paper analyzes the effects of various bank bailout rules on both ex ante incentives to lend and ex post incentives to disclose the size of the non-performing loans problem. The basic set-up considered here includes three type of agents: firms, banks and a regulator. Firms and banks are controlled by their managers who derive private benefits from their continued operations and the main source of discipline on their behavior is the possibility of dismissal associated with insolvency. The regulator's objectives are to induce efficient ex ante investments, avoid the dead-weight cost associated with excessive bank recapitalizations, and promote the efficient restructuring or liquidation of firms which have defaulted on their blank loans.

Banks are assumed to have private information about the quality of their loan portfolios and the continuation values of firms in default. The regulator only knows the probability distribution over the fraction of non-performing loans across banks in the economy, therefore facing an *adverse selection* problem in the design of a bank recapitalization policy.

Our analysis leads to a number of interesting results. First, a tough recapitalization policy in which bank managers are always dismissed results—as already suggested—in the bank managers rolling over bad loans in order to conceal the extent of their banks' loan losses and therefore in the *softening* of the firms' budget constraints (see Mitchell [1995]). Vice-versa, a soft approach to recapitalization (in which the manager of a failing bank is not dismissed) encourages bank managers to take an overly tough approach to the liquidation of firms, while exaggerating their banks' recapitalization requirements.

However, and this is the second main conclusion of the paper, the socially efficient outcome can generally be achieved through a soft bailout policy combined with the carving out of bad loans at a suitable *non-linear transfer price*. In other words, our analysis suggests that the recapitalization of insolvent banks should be performed by buying out non-performing loans rather than through capital injections by buying subordinated bonds. Our key insight here is that a *non-linear* transfer price mechanism for bad loans can be used to combat effectively the adverse selection problem, and in particular to avoid over-reporting of non-performing loans by the healthier banks at the time of the bailout.

The existing theoretical literature on financial restructuring and bank recapitalization in transition economies comprises only a handful of papers. We have already referred to Mitchell [1995]—the most closely related paper to ours and the first to model bank restructuring. It sets up a formal model of a bank restructuring where banks must incur a (convex) cost of effort to avoid asset dissipation by firms. That paper also emphasizes the problem that in case of bank managers suffering in some way when their banks get into trouble they will roll over loans in default in order to postpone facing the cost of financial distress. However, Mitchell develops a different formal set-up and considers different policy options.

Also taking a moral hazard approach to bank restructuring, Berglof and Roland [1995] argue that ex ante recapitalizations of banks by governments can limit the extent to which banks will take on additional risky loans and then gamble for resurrection.

These studies do not provide a complete characterization of all possible bailout schemes and of the optimality of different bailout policies under different circumstances. While moral hazard considerations (and in particular the problem of excessive risk-taking in the choice of banks' portfolios) are reasonably well understood and arise in transition and developed market economies alike, informational asymmetries of the kind emphasized in the present paper are more likely to be relevant in the context of transition economies where the institutions for evaluating and disclosing the credit-worthiness of both firms and banks are inherently weak.

Two other related papers are Suarez [1995] and Povel [1997]. The former studies bank closure rules and bank recapitalization in a dynamic complete information model. Given the informational assumptions stressed therein it is not entirely surprising that Suarez finds that the closure of insolvent banks has good ex ante incentive properties. The latter paper deals with bankruptcy of non-financial firms but emphasizes a similar tension between ex ante incentives to avoid bankruptcy and ex post incentives to file for bankruptcy in a timely fashion.

The remainder of the present paper is organized as follows. Section 2 sets out the basic model, specifying the objectives and constraints of firms, banks and the regulator. Section 3 compares a "tough" and a "soft" bank recapitalization policy taken in isolation. Section 4 derives necessary and sufficient conditions for the existence of an efficient "non-linear transfer scheme" used for the carving out of bad loans. Finally, section 5 provides a brief summary of the main lessons of our analysis.

2. The Model

The model builds on Bolton and Scharfstein [1990] by enlarging their framework to allow for three types of agents: firms, banks and a regulator. We consider each in turn.

2.1 Firms

For simplicity, we assume that all firms are run by self-interested managers. Be they state-owned or privatized firms, shareholders do not play a significant governance role; rather the focus is on bank debt as a disciplining device. A firm is represented by an asset, which yields a random return. In the first period, the return is either high, $\pi > 0$, or low (equal to zero). The probability of receiving a high return is $p \in (0, 1)$. This probability could be controlled by the firm manager's actions, but we shall take it to be exogenously given. In the second period, the firm also has a random continuation value, which is the discounted stream of future returns.

Each firm has an outstanding stock of bank debt and, for simplicity, no other liabilities. This stock of debt imposes a repayment obligation on the firm of $D \in [0, \pi]$. When a firm defaults, its bank can either liquidate the firm, making the firm manager redundant, or it can allow the firm to continue. The certain liquidation value is L. The continuation value, $\tilde{v}$, is either high, $v > 0$, or low (equal to zero), with $v > L > 0$. The probability of a high continuation value is $(1 - \beta)$, with $\beta \in (0, 1)$. In the event of default, the continuation value can be costlessly observed.

For simplicity, we shall assume that the *private* continuation value of firm managers is sufficiently large that they will always honor their debt repayment obligations if they can. This assumption rules out strategic defaults by firms.[3]

2.2 Banks

As with firms, we assume that self-interested managers run banks. On the asset side of their balance sheets, banks have a portfolio of loans to firms, each of which has a scheduled debt service payment of D. As specified above, each firm may default on its loan with probability $(1 - p)$. In the event of a default, and in the absence of strategic behavior by bank managers, the bank liquidates the firm with probability β and obtains L. The alternative to liquidation is firm continuation with a realized return v. If all firms have independently and identically distributed returns and each bank holds a large and well diversified portfolio of loans, then each bank has approximately a fraction $(1 - p)$ of non-performing loans.

On the liability side of their balance sheets, banks issue deposits in the amount d to fund each loan. Thus, the net worth of a bank (per loan) is

$$W = (1 - p)[\beta L + (1 - \beta)v] + pD - d. \tag{1}$$

---

[3] It is possible to extend the model to allow for strategic defaults. The results obtained in this extension are qualitatively similar to those reported here.

For a bank to have a positive net worth, the weighted average payoff from non-performing and performing loans must thus exceed the value of deposits issued to fund the representative loans.

The fact that banks do fail in reality suggests that they cannot build completely diversified portfolios and that they are exposed to aggregate shocks. To introduce the possibility of bank failures we shall suppose that firms' returns are correlated to some extent so that the fraction of performing loans is a random variable which takes on a range of values, $p_1 > p_2 > p_3 > p_4 > 0$, with respective (positive) probabilities, $\mu_1, \mu_2, \mu_3, \mu_4$. We denote the expected fraction of performing loans to be $p = \sum_{i=1}^{4} \mu_i p_i$. A bank's realized net worth under each realization is then given by equation (2), but p_i ($i = 1, \ldots, 4$) now substitutes for p. Thus, under the four possible outcomes p_i, a bank's realized net worth is equal to

$$W_i = (1 - p_i)[\beta L + (1 - \beta)v] + p_i D - d, \tag{2}$$

where we assume that

$$W_4 < W_3 < W_2 = 0 < W_1. \tag{3}$$

That is, only banks in states $i = 1, 2$ are solvent while banks in states $i = 3, 4$ are insolvent. As will become clear in section 3, we need at least four different states of nature in order to compare alternative bank bailout policies.

We shall also suppose that bank managers can exert effort ex ante to reduce the probability of a bank failure. That is, by being more diligent in evaluating the distribution of firms' first period cash flows and in structuring efficient loan portfolios they can reduce the likelihood that a large fraction of projects will fail. For simplicity, a bank manager's decision to exert effort is an all-or-nothing choice, $e \in \{0, 1\}$. The cost to the bank manager of exerting this effort is $c(e)$, where $c(0) = 0$ and $c(1) = c$. We assume that when $e = 1$ the probability distribution $\mu_i(1)$ (first-order) stochastically dominates the probability distribution $\mu_i(0)$ when $e = 0$:

$$\sum_{i=1}^{j} \mu_i(1) > \sum_{i=1}^{j} \mu_i(0) \quad \text{for all } j = 1, 2, 3. \tag{4}$$

Finally, to simplify notation, we let $\phi_i = (1 - p_i)\beta$ denote the fraction of liquidated loans. We obviously have $\phi_1 < \phi_2 < \phi_3 < \phi_4$.

When a firm defaults, the manager of its bank must decide whether to allow the firm to continue or to seek its liquidation. We assume that the sale of the firm's assets can be observed costlessly so that the liquidation decision is observable and verifiable. However, loan continuation and write-down decisions are entirely at the discretion of the bank manager and cannot be verified. In other words, unless a non-performing loan is actually liquidated it is not possible to verify whether the loan is performing or not. This limited verification of the bank manangers' behavior in turn allows for strategic behavior on their part.

For example, bank managers may want to inefficiently refinance bad loans in order to hide (or understate) the overall extent of their non-performing loans problem. This seems to be a wide-spread banking practice, particularly in transition economies, but also in developing and industrialized market economies. Similarly, when a bank is to be bailed out, the bank manager may want to overstate the proportion of non-performing loans in order to elicit a larger recapitalization from the government. The core analysis of this paper centers around these two forms of strategic behavior by bank managers.

A bank manager's objective function involves a monetary and a private benefit component. The monetary component is the sum of a fixed salary (which we normalize to zero) and, in the case of a high-powered incentive scheme, a share of the bank's (reported) net worth, say equal to b. The private benefit component reflects the facts that bank managers like power, and that they, as firm managers, would rather retain their job than be fired. In addition, the objective function includes the cost of effort, if any, that is exerted in managing a bank's loan portfolio.

Formally, we can express a bank manager's objective function as

$$U_B = b \max(0, \hat{W}_i) + \tilde{B}[1 + \max(0, W_i + R)] - c(e); \qquad (5)$$

where $\tilde{B} = B$ if the bank manager retains her position and $\tilde{B} = 0$ if the bank manager is fired, with $B > 0$ being the unit private benefit of running a bank of size one; $\hat{W}_i$ is the reported net worth of the bank (absent recapitalization) and W_i is the true net worth; any additional resources accruing to the bank in the first period, in particular as a result of recapitalization, is given by R.

To keep the analysis simple, we shall assume that a bank manager has only a low-powered incentive scheme (i.e. $b = 0$), and therefore, that

$$U_B = \tilde{B}[1 + \max(0, W_i + R)] - c(e). \qquad (6)$$

The analysis can be extended straightforwardly to consider the effects of high-powered incentive schemes. The main effect of such schemes is to create even stronger incentives to hide bad loans, but to mitigate incentives to overstate losses.

2.3 The regulator

The regulator's decision problem is to form a policy toward the recapitalization of banks with announced negative net worth. A constraint on this policy is that any bank which declares its net worth as negative must receive a recapitalization to bring its declared net worth back to zero. In other words, in our model all depositors are fully insured.[4] Our results and analysis do not critically hinge on this assumption. If only a fraction of deposits, $\hat{d} < d$, is insured our analysis would be unchanged when d is replaced by $\hat{d}$.[5]

The regulator's problem is then to design a bank bailout policy (i) to maximize the expected social return of the underlying assets of firms, (ii) to induce maximum effort of bank managers in the ex ante evaluation of firms' returns, and (iii) to minimize the cost associated with the excessive recapitalization of banks.

With full information about the true net worth of banks, the regulator would avoid excessive recapitalizations, and the corresponding dead-weigth loss, by simply transferring $-W_i$ to those banks in states $i = 3, 4$ in the first period. It would also maximize bank managers' incentives by committing to dismiss them whenever a bank is insolvent.

The regulator's problem is made difficult, however, because it does not generally know the first period net worth of banks. So if the government wants to guarantee that all banks reach at least a minimum reported net worth of zero, it must be prepared to bailout banks up to an amount of $-W_4$, the worst possible net worth. Since the government does not know the net worth of banks, their managers may be able to get away with claiming to be in the worst possible state. Such misrepresentation by all bank managers would lead to excessive recapitalizations with an ex ante dead-weight loss of

$$\lambda[\mu_1(W_1 - W_4) + \mu_2(W_2 - W_4) + \mu_3(W_3 - W_4)] = \lambda E. \tag{7}$$

Of course, the government has the option to limit the size of recapitalizations to an amount less than $-W_4$, but then it exposes itself to the possibility of inadequate recapitalization of those banks in the worst state of nature.

The expected social return of the underlying assets of firms is given by their expected first period cash flows, $\bar{p}(e)\pi$ (where $\bar{p}(e) = \sum_{i=1}^{4} \mu_i(e)p_i$), plus their expected continuation values in each state,

$$\Omega_i = p_i(1 - \beta)v + (1 - p_i)\{\min[1 - \beta), (1 - \hat{\beta}_i)]v + \hat{\beta}_i L\}. \tag{8}$$

That is, for the proportion p_i of firms with high cash flows the expected continuation value is $(1-\beta)v$, since these firms will never be liquidated. For the proportion

---

[4] Banks must have fully insured deposits for two basic reasons: First, the failure of a large institution may adversely impact other banks in the system through the payment system and the inter-bank market, which can precipitate a generalized loss of confidence. Second, depositors in a large bank may effectively exert political pressure for deposit guarantees. In addition, banks are de facto perceived by depositors as being fully backed by the government.

[5] However, under partial deposit insurance new issues must be addressed, such as the behavior of uninsured depositors. These issues are undoubtedly important but they are somewhat orthogonal to our analysis.

$(1 - p_i)$ of firms with low cash flows the firm managers are forced to default and the average continuation values per loan are $\min[(1 - \beta), (1 - \hat{\beta}_i)]v + \hat{\beta}_i L$; here $\hat{\beta}_i$ denotes the fraction of defaulting loans the bank manager chooses to liquidate in each state $i = 1, \ldots, 4$.

Formally, the regulator's objective function can be summarized in the following expression:

$$U_G = \bar{p}(e)\pi + \sum_{i=1}^{4} \mu_i \Omega_i - \lambda E - c(e). \tag{9}$$

Thus, in our model social efficiency requires fulfillment of three conditions: First, a firm should be liquidated if, and only if, its liquidation value exceeds its continuation value $\tilde{v} \in \{0, v\}$; that is, $\hat{\beta}_i$ should be equal to β for states $i = 1, \ldots, 4$. Second, only those banks with truly negative net worth should be recapitalized; that is, E should be equal to zero. Third, bank managers should exert effort in managing their banks' loan portfolios provided that

$$\bar{p}(1)\pi - \bar{p}(0)\pi + \sum_{i=1}^{4} [\mu_i(1) - \mu_i(0)]\Omega_i > c. \tag{10}$$

We assume that this condition is satisfied, in other words that the ex ante evaluation of firms' returns by bank managers is socially efficient.

Throughout the remainder of the paper we make the (realistic) assumption that the liquidation value, L, is greater than a firm manager's private benefit from the firm's continued operation. In other words, it is socially efficient to liquidate a firm whenever the bank's continuation value of the project is zero, even though the firm manager always prefers not to liquidate. This assumption introduces an ex post inefficiency when firms which are able to service their current debt obligations but have a low continuation value remain in operation because of the private benefits derived by their managers. While first-best social efficiency would require that these firms be liquidated in the first period, this inefficiency is independent of the form of bank recapitalizations and is thus not a factor in evaluating the government's policy alternatives.

3. Tough Versus Soft Recapitalization Policy

The regulator's problem is to design a bank recapitalization policy that maximizes its objective (social efficiency) subject to the constraint of limited knowledge of banks' true net worth in the first period. Since the banks are managerially controlled, one possible condition to impose with a recapitalization relates to the dismissal of the bank manager. In particular, how tough or soft should the government be toward the manager of a bank in the event of its recapitalization.

Again, start with the benchmark case where the net worth of banks is known to the government in the first period. The optimal bailout policy is then straight-forward: restore the net worth of banks in states $i = 3, 4$ to zero after allowing for the expected recovery of non-performing loans, and dismiss their managers if these recoveries deviate from expectations. This policy satisfies two of the three conditions for first-best efficiency. In particular, it guarantees both that only those banks with truly negative net worth are recapitalized and that firms in default are liquidated if, and only if, their liquidation value exceeds their continuation value. Satisfaction of the third condition for first-best efficiency, the ex ante evaluation of firms' returns and the structuring of efficient loans portfolios, depends on the incentives faced by bank managers.

Such a policy would clearly have perverse effects when the regulator must rely on bank managers' reports to learn about the first period net worth of banks. We illustrate these perverse effects in this section by considering two extreme bailout policies that are often discussed in practice: On the one hand, a *"tough"* *recapitalization policy* (subsection 3.1), which results in the liquidation of a bank that is found insolvent and the ensuing dismissal of its manager. On the other hand, a *"soft" recapitalization policy* (subsection 3.2), which maintains an insolv-ent bank's manager in control and fully bails out the bank. We also consider an *"in-between" policy* (subsection 3.3), which involves the liquidation of an insolv-ent bank and the dismissal of its manager only in the worst state of nature, $i = 4$; whereas any bank in state $i = 3$ is fully bailed out by the government, leaving the bank managers in control.

3.1 A "tough" recapitalization policy

Consider first the case of a "tough" bailout policy in which the manager of a bank which reports a negative net worth is dismissed. The manager of a bank which realized p_1 or p_2 has no incentive to manipulate either the accounts of the bank or the decisions to liquidate firms, or to write down their loans. However, a bank would be insolvent if either p_3 or p_4 were realized. With such outcomes, its manager will act as if $p_k = p_2$ has occurred in order not to be fired. Since the liquidation of firms is verifiable, the bank manager will pretend that $p_k = p_2$ by liquidating a fraction ϕ_2 of firms in the bank's portfolio, where ϕ_2 is defined as the fraction of liquidated loans in the portfolio of a bank with realized p_2 (i.e., $\phi_2 = (1 - p_2)\beta$).

In other words, the bank manager will liquidate a fraction $\hat{\beta}_k$ of defaulting firms, such that

$$(1 - p_k)\hat{\beta}_k = \phi_2 = (1 - p_2)\beta. \tag{11}$$

Therefore, the proportion of defaulted loans that are actually liquidated by the bank manager in states $k = 3, 4$ is less than the socially efficient proportion (i.e. $\hat{\beta}_k < \beta$). The incentive of bank managers to maintain the appearance of bank solvency under a tough bailout policy, thus leads to a softening of debt as a disciplining device on firms and thereby a softening of firms' budget constraints. More formally, a tough bailout policy leads to an ex ante payoff of

$$U_G = \bar{p}(e)\pi + \sum_{i=1}^{2} \mu_i(e)\{p_i(1-\beta)v + (1-p_i)[(1-\beta)v + \beta L]\}$$

$$+ \sum_{i=3}^{4} \mu_i(e)\{p_i(1-\beta)v + (1-p_i)[(1-\beta)v + \hat{\beta}_i L]\} - c(e), \quad (12)$$

where, from equation (11), $\hat{\beta}_i < \beta$ for $i = 3, 4$. A tough bailout policy thus leads to an insufficient number of firm liquidations. The loss in social surplus due to the softness of banks on firms in default is the foregone liquidation value of those firms which are continued even though they have a zero continuation value.[6]

Introducing the possibility of strategic defaults by firms would amplify the loss in social surplus due to banks hiding the extent of their non-performing loans. More precisely, suppose that the private continuation value of firm managers is such that they would choose not to default strategically if the probability of liquidation in case of default is β, but might decide to default if they anticipate a lower probability of liquidation by banks. Then, not only will the number of firm liquidations be less than is socially optimal but there will also be a further build-up of non-performing loans in banks' portfolios.[7]

There is, however, no dead-weight cost due to excessive recapitalizations under a tough bailout policy. Indeed, no bank recapitalizations take place under this rule because no bank managers will declare their institutions insolvent.

Whether bank managers are induced to exert effort in managing loan portfolios under this policy depends here only on the private benefits derived from this activity. In particular, a bank manager will exert such effort under a tough policy

[6] The loss in social surplus also includes the misallocation of funds which could have been directed to better investments. An important limitation of our model is that it is not set up to account for that cost.

[7] For example, suppose that the private continuation value of firm managers is random, equal to V with probability $(1 - \varepsilon)$ and to zero with probability ε. Assuming that

$$\beta[1 - p_2(1-\varepsilon)]V < D < \beta V,$$

we then leave it to the reader to verify that in the case of a solvent bank (i.e., in states $i = 1, 2$), the pair of strategies ($\hat{\beta}_i = \beta$, strategic default with probability ε) is the unique Nash equilibrium. In the case of a bank in state $i = 4$, there exists a Nash equilibrium involving a higher probability of strategic default, namely with the pair of strategies ($\hat{\beta}_4 < \beta$, strategic default with probability one), where $\hat{\beta}_4$ satisfies

$$[1 - p_4(1-1)]\hat{\beta}_4 = \phi_2 = [1 - p_2(1-\varepsilon)]\beta.$$

only if

$$E[U_B(1)] = \sum_{i=1}^{4} \mu_i(1)B[1 + \max(0, W_i)] - c$$

$$> E[U_B(0)] = \sum_{i=1}^{4} \mu_i(0)B[1 + \max(0, W_i)],$$

or, equivalently,

$$[\mu_1(1) - \mu_1(0)]BW_1 > c. \tag{13}$$

Note that no bank manager is ever dismissed in equilibrium under this policy because of the costless ability to misrepresent a bank's net worth, and that R equals zero. Note also that bank managers receive private benefits in all states of nature. The value of private benefits equals B in all states of nature except in state $i = 1$, when the value of private benefits equals $B(1 + W_1)$. The expected value of private benefits thus rises with managerial effort to the extent that this effort raises the probability that state $i = 1$ will occur.

3.2 A "soft" recapitalization policy

Under a "soft" policy toward the recapitalization of banks, a bank manager is immune from dismissal, regardless of reported net worth of the bank. This approach creates an incentive for bank managers to overstate their banks' problem loans so as to increase the amount of recapitalization. Bank managers can easily overstate the extent of their anticipated loan losses by taking excessively high charges.[8] The change in bank managers' utility from reporting the worst possible net worth, W_4, instead of the true net worth, W_i, is always positive and equal to

$$\Delta U_b = B(W_i - W_4). \tag{14}$$

One benefit of soft bailouts, however, is that they restore bank managers incentives to impose financial discipline on the firms they lend to. Indeed, without a hard budget constraint, their incentive is to liquidate every defaulted loan if, and only if, the continuation value is less than the liquidation value. Thus, with a soft recapitalization policy, bank managers harden the budget constraint on firm managers.

---

[8] Note that by taking charges banks only bring forward in their books anticipated loan losses. They do not report actual loan losses. Unless reported anticipated loan losses turn into actual losses for banks, writing down loans is just "cheap talk" and bank managers have every incentive to exaggerate the size of anticipated loan losses if it results in larger recapitalizations.

The social payoff achieved through a soft bailout policy is

$$U_G = \bar{p}(e)\pi + \sum_{i=1}^{4} \mu_i(e)\{p_i(1-\beta)v + (1-p_i)[(1-\beta)v + \beta L]\}$$

$$- \lambda[\mu_1(e)(W_1 - W_4) + \mu_2(e)(W_2 - W_4) + \mu_3(e)(W_3 - W_4)] - c(e). \quad (15)$$

There are thus at least two social costs of a soft bailout policy: One is the dead-weight cost from excessive recapitalizations.[9] The second is an inadequate incentive for bank managers to exert effort in evaluating investment returns of firms and in structuring efficient loan portfolios. As with the tough recapitalization rule, the only incentive for bank managers to exert such effort under a soft rule arises from the associated private benefits.

More specifically, under this soft recapitalization policy, note that the government recapitalization of a bank equals the net worth of that bank in the worst state of nature. A bank manager would thus exert effort only if

$$\sum_{i=1}^{3} [\mu_i(1) - \mu_i(0)]B[\max(0, W_i) - W_4] > c. \quad (16)$$

Now, since

$$- \sum_{i=1}^{3} [\mu_i(1) - \mu_i(0)] = \mu_4(1) - \mu_4(0),$$

this incentive constraint is equaivalent to

$$[\mu_1(1) - \mu_1(0)]BW_1 + [\mu_4(1) - \mu_4(0)]BW_4 > c. \quad (17)$$

Comparing equations (13) and (17) reveals that whenever $\mu_4(1) - \mu_4(0) < 0$, the incentive-compatibility constraint on managerial effort is less tight under a tough than under a soft recapitalization policy provided that $|W_4|$ is not too large.

The reason that a tough policy is not necessarily more effort-inducing than a soft policy is that under a soft bailout policy the benefit of overstating loan losses is an increasing function of the extent of the overstatement. It may thus not always be a good idea for the government to minimize the scope for ex post overstatement of the bad loans problem (i.e. by implementing a tough bailout policy) because this may sometimes have adverse ex ante incentive effects.

We summarize our discussion so far in the proposition below.

PROPOSITION 1. *(a) Ex post efficiency: When μ_4 is close to one, that is, when the banking system as a whole is known by the government to be in crisis, a soft bailout*

---

[9] In practice, this cost is reduced somewhat since by purchasing preferred stock or taking a stake in a bank, the regulatory authorities obtain a cut in all future profits of that bank. It is not clear, however, that regulators are able to fully recover excessively generous recapitalizations.

policy dominates though bailout. However, when $(\mu_1 + \mu_2)$ *is sufficiently close to one, that is, when the banking system is basically sound, tough bailout dominates soft bailout.*

(b) Ex ante incentives: *A tough bailout policy will generally provide stronger ex ante incentives than a soft bailout policy, except when* $|W_4|$ *is large.*

While tough (soft) bailout policies dominate ex post when the banking system is known by the government to be basically sound (in deep crisis), the comparison between these two extremes becomes less clear cut in intermediate situations. For example, when μ_3 is close to one, then the excessive recapitalization of banks in state $i = 3$ and the excessive liquidation of firms by those banks under soft bailout policy must be weighted against the insufficient liquidations by banks in states $i = 3, 4$ under tough policy. The balance depends upon the dead-weight loss parameter λ, and upon the cost of excessive liquidation $(v - L)$.

3.3 An "in-between" policy

Now consider a less extreme approach toward the recapitalization of banks, under which dismissal of a bank manager depends on the amount of required recapitalization. Specifically, if a bank reported that p_3 has occurred, the bank would be recapitalized without its manager being dismissed. But if a bank manager reports p_4, the bank would be liquidated and its manager dismissed. In other words, a bank manager would be held accountable only for an extremely poor outcome.

Under this policy, banks in states $i = 1, 2$ will seek to increase their size by attracting excessive recapitalizations while banks in state $i = 4$ hide the true extent of their insolvency problem. Banks in state $i = 3$, however, accurately reveal their net worth and take efficient liquidation decisions. Thus, although such an "in-between" bailout policy combines inefficiencies present in the two extreme policies, it involves a smaller dead-weight cost from excessive recapitalizations than under soft bailout and less under-liquidations of defaulted firms than under a tough policy.

In terms of ex ante incentives, this policy may provide worse incentives for bank managers. Under this in-between recapitalization policy a bank manager would exert effort only if

$$\sum_{i=1}^{2}[\mu_i(1) - \mu_i(0)]B(W_i - W_3) > c. \tag{18}$$

A comparison of equations (18) and (16) readily reveals that the incentive-compatibility constraint on managerial effort is less tight under an in-between than under a soft recapitalization policy. Whether the incentive-compatibility constraint is less tight than under a tough policy depends again on the amount of the recapitalization a bank receives. As before, the reason that a tough policy is not necessarily less tight is because recapitalizations yield private benefits which increase with the size of the overstatement of loans losses.

Our discussion in this section can be summarized by the following.

PROPOSITION 2. *(a) Ex post efficiency: When μ_3 is close to one, an in-between bailout policy dominates both tough and soft bailout policies from an ex post efficiency viewpoint.*

(b) Ex ante incentives: *An in-between bailout policy will provide less effort incentives than a tough bailout policy, except when $|W_3|$ is sufficiently large.*

While an in-between policy may under certain circumstances reduce the ex post dead-weight cost of the recapitalization of banks and the cost of excessive continuation of defaulted firms, other policies may perform as well or better both from an ex post and an ex ante point of view. Such an alternative is explored in the next section.

4. Bank Recapitalizations Conditional on Firm Liquidations

Since one observable and verifiable action of bank managers is the liquidation of defaulted firms, this parameter can provide a possible condition for the regulator's policy toward the recapitalization of banks. The purpose of this section is to examine whether the regulator can use this parameter to achieve its overall objective of first-best social efficiency and, if so, under what circumstances.

We shall show that it is possible to use this action of bank managers as a conditioning parameter for recapitalizations in order to achieve two of the three criteria for first-best social efficiency. These criteria are the efficient liquidation of firms in default (i.e. $\hat{\beta}_i = \beta$ for $i = 1, \ldots, 4$), and the absence of excessive bank recapitalizations. A complementary policy, however, may be required to provide a sufficiently strong incentive for bank managers to exert effort in the ex ante evaluation of firms' returns.

A key issue in the design of a bank recapitalization policy which is conditional on the liquidation of defaulted firms is the relationship between the liquidation of firms by a bank and the amount, if any, of its recapitalization. Consider first a simple linear transfer scheme under which the government pays a fixed amount t for any loan to a firm which is liquidated by the bank manager (with proceeds L). To achieve a zero net worth for banks in the worst state of nature, $i = 4$, the transfer amount t must raise the true net worth of such a bank to break-even:

$$\phi_4(L + t) + (1 - p_4)(1 - \beta)v + p_4 D = d. \tag{19}$$

However, this recapitalization policy would be too generous for those insolvent banks in state $i = 3$, increasing their net worth beyond zero. Banks with positive net worth, moreover, would be encouraged to participate in the scheme even though they are not in need of recapitalizations.

Excessive recapitalizations can be eliminated, however, if the government introduces a non-linear transfer scheme. Suppose that the government sets a low transfer amount, t_L, for loans to firms in default which are liquidated, up to a threshold $\overline{m} \geq \phi_2$ of a bank's portfolio. And that beyond that threshold transfers per liquidated loan are increased to $t_H > t_L$. We can then establish the following.

PROPOSITION 3. *There exists an $\overline{m} \geq \phi_2$ such that the above two-part transfer scheme $(t_H, t_L, \overline{m})$ implements a policy that leads to the efficient liquidation of firms in default (i.e. $\hat{\beta}_i = \beta$ for $i = 1, \ldots, 4$), and that recapitalizes only those banks which are truly insolvent if, and only if,*

$$p_4 D + (1 - p_4)(1 - \beta)v + (\phi_4 - \phi_2)v + \phi_2 L \geq d. \tag{20}$$

Proof. Without loss of generality we can assume $D > v$.

First, in order to avoid excessive liquidation of non-performing loans by bank managers, the high transfer price, t_H, cannot be larger than the minimum possible recovery on a defaulted loan, v. With $t_H > (v - L)$, managers of all banks would have an incentive to engage in excessive liquidation since doing so would increase their recoveries on non-performing loans, including the per-loan transfer from the government. So we must have $t_H \leq (v - L)$. Without loss of generality, we restrict the analysis to two-part transfer schemes such that $t_H = (v - L)$.

Now, it is sufficient to show that the low transfer, t_L, and the cut-off level, $\overline{m}$, can be chosen so as to deter solvent banks in state $i = 2$ (and *a fortiori* those in state $i = 1$) from participating in the scheme. This requires that the pair $(t_L, \overline{m})$ satisfies the condition

$$(\phi_2 - \overline{m})v + \overline{m}(L + t_L) \leq \phi_2 L. \tag{21}$$

The LHS of equation (21) is the payoff that a bank in state $i = 2$ would receive by participating in the government's recapitalization scheme; the RHS is the bank's revenue from remaining outside the scheme and from liquidating those non-performing loans which have a zero continuation value. One set of parameter values for which this condition is satisfied is $t_L = 0$ and $\overline{m} = \phi_2$.

It is also sufficient to show that the two-part transfer scheme $(t_H = v - L, t_L = 0, \overline{m} = \phi_2)$ succeeds in fully recapitalizing insolvent banks in states $i = 3, 4$. Consider in particular a bank in state $i = 4$, the worst possible state. The realized net worth of such a bank under this recapitalization scheme which links government transfers to a bank's liquidation of firms in default, is

$$p_4 D + (1 - p_4)(1 - \beta)v + (\phi_4 - \phi_2)v + \phi_2 L - d. \tag{22}$$

From equation (22), it is clear that condition (20) must hold in order for a bank in state $i = 4$ to be fully recapitalized. This condition is therefore sufficient to ensure full recapitalization of insolvent banks, and to avoid both excessive liquidation of non-performing loans and excessive recapitalization of solvent banks.

To complete the proof, we must show that condition (20) is also necessary. This requires showing that the conditions cannot be relaxed by allowing a more generous two-part transfer scheme with $t_L > 0$.

Suppose we take $t_L > 0$, and still have $t_H = (v - L)$. The necessary condition on t_L and $\overline{m}$ for banks in state $i = 4$ to be fully recapitalized becomes

$$p_4 D + (1 - p_4)(1 - \beta)v + (\phi_4 - \overline{m})v + \overline{m}(L + t_L) \geq d. \tag{23}$$

In choosing the optimal t_L and $\overline{m}$, the government seeks to ease the above constraint, while discouraging solvent banks from participating in the scheme. In other words, the government is to choose $(t_L, \overline{m})$ so as to

$$\max[(\phi_4 - m)v + m(L + t_L)] \tag{24}$$

$$\text{s.t. } (\phi_2 - m)v + m(L + t_L) \leq \phi_2 L.$$

At the optimum the incentive constraint for a bank in state $i = 2$ is binding, so that the above problem simplifies to

$$\max_m[(\phi_4 - \phi_2)v + mL + (\phi_2 - m)L], \tag{25}$$

for which there is no unique maximum. Setting $t_L = 0$ and $\overline{m} = \phi_2$ thus involves no loss of generality, provided that condition (23) is satisfied. With $t_L = 0$ and $\overline{m} = \phi_2$, this is nothing but condition (20).

This establishes that condition (20) is both necessary and sufficient, and therefore completes the proof.   Q.E.D

Whenever condition (20) is satisfied, a bank bailout policy which is conditional on the liquidation of firms in default can meet two of the requirements for first-best social efficiency. Efficient liquidation decisions by bank managers and no excessive recapitalization of banks by the government. Moreover, this result obtains regardless of the government's knowledge (or beliefs), $\mu_i(e)$, about the state of the overall banking system. In particular, it dominates the tough, soft and in-between policies considered in the previous section, none of which would achieve these requirements for first-best efficiency, except perhaps on a negligible (measure-zero) subset of parameter values for $\mu_i(e)$. If condition (20) is not satisifed, this conditional recapitalization policy would lead to excessive recapitalization of solvent banks in state $i = 2$ (and/or of insolvent banks in state $i = 3$), with the associated dead-weigth cost. In which case, a tough bailout policy may sometimes dominate, in particular if $(\mu_1 + \mu_2)$ is close to one.[10]

The analysis of this section thus shows that conditioning the recapitalization of banks on an observable and verifiable action of bank managers can increase the ex post efficiency of bank bailouts and, under certain circumstances, meet the two requirements for ex post efficiency.

As for ex ante effort incentives, it turns out that the tough recapitalization policy analyzed in section 3 and the more complicated conditional recapitalization developed in this section provide bank managers with precisely the same incentives to exert effort. It is straightforward to show that the incentive-compatibility constraint for a bank manager to exert effort under the conditional bank recapitalization policy simplifies to

$$[\mu_1(1) - \mu_1(0)]BW_1 > c, \tag{26}$$

which is the same as under the tough recapitalization policy (see equation (13)). This equivalence arises because, the expected value of private benefits rises with managerial effort only to the extent that this effort raises the probability that state $i = 1$ will occur, since bank managers receive exactly B in all other states of nature.

That our conditional recapitalization scheme provides the same ex ante effort incentives as a tough bailout policy, should come as no surprise. Both policies give bank managers the option of distorting their ex post reports about loan losses (i.e. about β_i), although our conditional scheme is designed in such a way that bank managers are *indifferent* between distorting (and announcing state $i = 2$) and not distorting. This in turn explains why ex ante effort incentives are the same under the two policies, even though our scheme avoids the ex post inefficiencies induced by a tough bailout policy. Our scheme should thus be seen as a strict improvement over a tough recapitalization policy.

To conclude this section, we point to a limitation of our findings and to a possible further extension. The analysis shows that by reducing the incentive of bank managers to exaggerate the extent of their banks' bad loans, a suitably designed conditional recapitalization scheme in which government transfers to insolvent banks are linked to their liquidation of firms in default can achieve some of the first-best social efficiency conditions. However, in somewhat more complex circumstances, these efficiency gains could be lost. For example, if we allow for heterogeneity in the quality of non-performing loans (such as differences in the liquidation values of each loan) and if the exact quality of bad

---

[10] Another potential problem with this non-linear transfer scheme is that it may create incentives for solvent banks to sell their bad loans to insolvent banks. To prevent such profitable arbitrage from taking place the regulator would need to monitor the secondary market for loans and scrutinize more closely net purchasing banks.

loans were the private information of bank managers, then the two-part transfer scheme considered above would fail to deliver first-best efficiency because there would no longer be a simple relationship between the proportion of liquidated loans in a bank's portfolio and its true net worth. Characterizing a more sophisticated non-linear transfer scheme that would "solve" this problem, and more generally deriving the conditions under which such a scheme can dominate some simpler schemes (such as those analyzed in section 3) is left for further research.

5. Conclusion

The main lessons emerging from our analysis are first that recapitalizations should be made explicitly conditional on the liquidation of non-performing loans. Ideally, recapitalizations should not take the form of purchases of preferred stock or subordinated bonds. Of course, it may not be practical or feasible to set up such a conditional scheme at short notice following the outbreak of a banking crisis. This is why we advocate the institution of a bankruptcy procedure for banks in anticipation of future banking crises. We believe that, just as with non-financial firms, the establishment of such an institution can go a long way in resolving in an orderly and efficient way most banking crises.

The model in this paper is, of course, highly stylized and can only serve as a framework to organize our analysis of bank bailouts. While it does cover most important incentive aspects raised by bank failures and bailouts it does so only in a highly simplified way. Much additional work is required to design a proper bankruptcy institution for banks, but we hope that this paper can serve as a first step in this direction.

References

Berglof, E., and Roland, G. (1995). "Bank restructuring and soft budget constraints in financial transition." CEPR Discussion Paper No. 1250. Centre for Economic Policy Research, London.

Bolton, P., and Scharfstein, D. S. (1990). "A Theory of predation based on agency problems in financial contracting." *American Economic Review*, 80(1): 93–106.

Mitchell, J. (1995). "Cancelling, transferring or repaying bad debts: Cleaning banks' balance sheets in economies in transition." Mimeo, Cornell University, Ithaca, NY.

Povel, P. (1997). "Optimal 'soft' or 'tough' bankruptcy procedures." Financial Markets Group Discussion Paper No. 240, London School of Economics.

Suarez, J. (1995). "Closure rules and the prudential regulation of banks." Mimeo, Centro di Economia Monetaria e Finanziaria, Università Commerciale Luigi Bocconi, Milano, Italy.

Regulation of Financial Intermediaries: A Discussion

Xavier Freixas and Anthony M. Santomero

1. Introduction

Recently, the theory of banking regulation has undergone important changes. This has been the consequence of a number of compounding effects that have been occurring in the financial sector. First among these is on-going financial innovation, which has caused a virtual revolution in both financial instruments and markets. As a result, the markets and institutions that must be regulated have changed substantially over time. At the same time, regulation has evolved, as the regulators have learned the lessons from the recent spat of banking crises. As a consequence of these experiences, regulation has become more sophisticated, with the introduction of capital requirements and more complex restrictions on operating procedures.

At the same time, a second force of change has emerged in academic circles where a new paradigm central to our understanding of both financial markets and the regulation of these markets has been developing. Asymmetric information theory, a setting in which economic agents are presumed to operate in a world of incomplete and, at times, biased information has developed. In our view, this framework is perfect to adapt to the issues central to the theory of banking. The insights that this theory offers have had a profound effect on our view of regulation. In this chapter, we review the impact of imperfect information on our understanding of why financial markets exist, how they operate, and how best to regulate them. In the first part of this chapter (Section 2), we start by identifying the market failures that are specific to the banking industry. Namely, we will consider first the types of imperfections characteristic

The views expressed here are those of the authors and do not necessarily reflect those of the Federal Reserve System. Financial support from DGESIC (PB-1057) is acknowledged.

of financial markets, then turn to the justification of financial intermediaries, so as to provide a better understanding of what are the main market failures in the financial industry. This will allow us to draw a coherent view of the role of regulation in the financial intermediation industry. The benefits from constructing this overall perspective will be derived from showing how apparently disconnected regulatory measures, such as capital requirements, law and finance or the Glass–Steagall Act are interwoven.

The second part of this chapter (Section 3) considers the design of regulation as well as its impact, and reviews the working of the main regulatory instruments, as well as the effects they had on the banks' behavior.

2. Market Failure in the Banking Industry

2.1 Financial intermediation and banking regulation

Contemporary banking theory offers a rigorous perspective on financial market structure and the role played by banking institutions. It argues that financial intermediaries emerge endogenously to solve financial market imperfections that spring from various types of asymmetric information problems. These institutions arise to exploit such market information imperfections for economic gain. In other words, financial institutions begin where the conditions for the application of the Modigliani–Miller theorem ends.

Regulation is the rational response of the government to these new market failures. A lack of response would result in either financial institutions excessive risk taking or in the growth and development of monopoly power, which is a natural economic outcome of such market circumstances.

With this perspective, banking regulation is ultimately justified by an appeal to the existence of market failure, without which such regulation would be unnecessary and Pareto optimality in the allocation of resources would obtain. However, there is an additional level of complexity when one considers banking regulation. Its mere existence changes the nature of the information problem because the regulator itself is an interested party. This alters the information environment in an important way, and makes the attainment of Pareto efficiency more difficult (Stiglitz 1994).

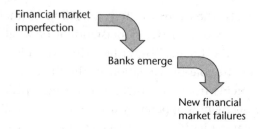

Figure 1.

In our view, therefore, one cannot discuss banking, its existence, its regulation, or the effect of such regulation, in a world without financial imperfections. In fact, in order to study banking regulation, one must start, as Bhattacharya et al. (1998) do, by examining why financial intermediaries exist in the first place, and follow all the implications from there. This is the perspective we adopt hereafter.

2.2 The reasons for intermediation

In contemporary theory, the question of why financial intermediaries exist has received several answers, which can be seen as complementary in nature. Contrary to the earlier work of Fama (1980), which argued that banks exist because of the economies of scope between transferring claims on property and offering investment opportunities, and other earlier transactions cost approaches recounted in Santomero (1984), most modern theories assume some form of information imperfection in the financial markets that permits the emergence of an intermediary sector.

Four alternative theories have developed to explain why banks exist in response to these financial market imperfections. Each has an alternative role for the banking firm.

1. *Screening of potential borrowers.* The first justification offered for the emergence of a banking institution suggests that banks screen potential clients ex ante on behalf of their depositors. They do so either because they are better at screening such potential customers than the average investor (Grossman and Stiglitz 1980), or because they are merely the delegated monitor of proposals, on behalf of a large number of interested parties (Campbell and Kracaw 1980). In the same vein, Ramakrishnan and Thakor (1983) establish the existence

of economies of scale in the screening process that are due to asymmetric information. The creation of banks, which are akin to coalitions of firms, could, therefore, alleviate the adverse selection problem.

2. *Monitoring customers' actions and efforts.* Monitoring theory is closely related to the previous rationale, but focuses more on the monitoring of borrowers' actions *after* loan approval. Models here have concentrated on the actual use of borrowed funds (Boot and Thakor 1993), effort involved (Allen and Gale 1998*b*) and ex post outcome revelation (Diamond 1984; Gale and Hellwig 1985).

3. *Providing liquidity risk insurance.* The next justification, offered by Diamond and Dybvig (1983), suggests that agents face uncertainty on the timing of their consumption. They are better off in a banking contract that allows for some ex ante insurance than buying financial securities. While such entities might prove unstable, as McCulloch and Huston (1986) suggests, the rationale proves quite robust and in fact dates back to the late nineteenth century.

4. *Creating a safe asset.* According to Gorton and Pennacchi (1990, 1993), banks may also emerge as an optimal security design. Bank deposits provide an investment in a safe asset, which is not affected by information in the financial markets, and is a feasible, efficient asset in optimal portfolio decisions.

Each of these theories offers justification for the emergency of an intermediary sector. Yet, existence is only a portion of the problem. Optimality requires that the market provides banks with the right incentives, that is, Pareto optimal incentives, to screen, monitor, invest, and produce a well-diversified safe deposit. This issue is often summarized by the question "who monitors the monitor?" It is only if the right incentives for banks to monitor firms exist that an efficient banking system will emerge. This is because, with incorrect incentives, market failures will occur in the absence of regulation of individual banks and the banking system as a whole. Such failures reduce social welfare and real economic activity, as Gertler (1988) adequately reviews. In addition, self-fulfilling bank runs may occur and lead to either ex ante or ex post dominated asset allocation. The fundamental issues here are closely associated with the contributions of Diamond and Dybvig (1983) and Calomiris and Khan (1991).

2.3 Market failures in the financial industry

Economics has enumerated several negative effects of market failure in the financial sector. These negative impacts may result from the breakdown of either the laissez-faire financial sector without intermediaries and/or an unregulated banking sector. Their importance has direct relevance to the need for regulation and the beneficial impact of effective deployment of government resources to reduce such losses. In addition, some have argued that further beneficial social effects may accrue to optimally engineering resource allocation within the financial sector. These benefits, of course, can only derive from the value weighting of winners and losers associated with any proposed non-Pareto improving regulation. Here, we briefly survey the three types of alleged market failures that are addressed by the regulation of the banking sector.

2.3.1 Monetary liquidity costs

In contemporary financial systems, aggregate liquidity is the responsibility of the central bank. It was this justification that first led them to have a monopoly over money creation (Friedman and Schwartz 1963). If the central bank is responsible for the assurance of sufficient liquidity, part of its responsibility must undoubtedly include overseeing the money markets and, therefore, the regulation of financial intermediaries. Essentially this is the logic behind the systemic stability role delegated to central banks throughout developed markets, for example, Federal Reserve, Bank of England, and the European Central Bank.

The central banks' oversight of the financial sector is derived from the intermediary sector's role in the asset transformation listed above. Banks have illiquid assets and allegedly liquid liabilities. Transformation is dependent upon prudent asset allocation and the expectation of trading within the sector. In addition, both assets and liabilities specify a nominal monetary return (nominal contracting). This payments system structure is an efficient approach to providing the transfer of property claims. Only Fama (1980) disagrees, with his assertion that bank deposits are private contracts with different levels of risk. To most others, bank deposits are money, and efficient consumption allocation is dependent upon a liquid and efficient operating financial structure.

2.3.2 The cost of bank failure

A bank failure generates negative externalities for two reasons. It destroys specific capital and it may lead to further contagion losses in the system.

On the one hand, a bank closure reduces economic welfare because there is a loss of the relationship with the bank's clients and the specific knowledge of management and risk preferences (as illustrated by Slovin et al. 1999 for the cost of the Continental Illinois failure). On the other hand, the costs of such closures are more acute, because the failure may spread throughout the banking system, amplifying the negative effects on unrelated intermediaries.

The very justifications of financial intermediation point out the high risk of contagion. In the screening and monitoring justifications, a bank failure may signal a weakness in bank assets in general (Gorton 1988; Chari and Jagannathan 1988). In addition, if systemic, it may cause depositors to question the entire system as it questions the incentives of any bank to adequately monitor its borrowers. If banks are seen as lacking incentives to monitor, they will engage in fraudulent operations and excessive risk taking (Campbell and Kracaw 1980). In such a case, a bank failure may lead depositors in other banks to run the bank and withdraw their deposits, at a high liquidation cost, in spite of the soundness of the affected secondary bank. In any case, if one bank fails, this may produce a perfectly rational (Bayesian) updating of the assessment of any other bank risk and a generalized withdrawal of deposits. If safe assets are presumed to be a central reason for banking firms' value and existence, such a bank failure would deprive the banking system itself of its rationale. Hence, for all four reasons for intermediation, contagion, or domino effects are likely and detrimental to economic welfare and prove detrimental to the potential outcome of an errant system.

Yet, it is traditionally accepted that contagion may occur both because of a change in depositors' expectations on bank returns and because their financial interdependence resulting from the net of reciprocal claims that are generated by the interbank borrowing, the payment system and OTC derivatives. Consequently, a bank failure may affect both the real and the perceived stability of the banking system. This is often referred to as the inherent instability of the financial system. As a consequence, social welfare is intimately involved with the regulatory environment and the way in which a bank crisis is handled. It may or may not trigger a domino effect on the rest of the banking system.

2.3.3 Enhancing efficiency

Independent of the features that are specific to the banking industry, the standard market failures that affect any other industry must also be taken into consideration. In particular, the inefficiency created by market power is relevant here as well. The complexity, though, is that market power may have been generated by the very regulatory measures that are designed to cope with concerns over liquidity and bankruptcy risk.

The efficient operation of the financial sector depends critically upon confidence that financial markets and institutions operate according to rules and procedures that are fair, transparent, and place the interests of customers first. This confidence is a public good. It increases the flow through financial markets and the effectiveness with which financial markets allocate resources across time and space. But this public good may be underproduced, because the private returns to firms that adhere to strict codes of conduct are likely to be less than the social returns. Unethical firms may be able to free ride on the reputation established by ethical firms and take advantage of the relative ignorance of clients in order to boost profits. The primary efficiency rationale for conduct of business and conflict of interest rules is to correct this perverse incentive.

Finally, financial markets provide critical information that helps to coordinate decentralized decisions throughout the economy (Santomero and Babbel 1997). Better access to high quality information by participants on a timely basis will allow financial markets to provide better pricing signals and to allocate resources more efficiently. This applies not only to information regarding issuers of financial instruments, but also to financial institutions themselves and the products they sell. Disclosure standards thus also serve to improve overall economic efficiency as well as a consumer protection rationale.

Efficiency would also be enhanced if regulators were required to justify each new regulation with a careful assessment of its costs and benefits. This requirement is an obligation of Britain's new Financial Services Authority. It should be a fundamental part of the regulatory process everywhere.

2.4 Other social objectives

Governments are often tempted to exploit the central role played by the financial sector in modern economies in order to achieve other social purposes. Budget constrained governments frequently use the banking system as a source of off-budget finance to fund initiatives for which they chose not to raise taxes or borrow. Over time this politically connected lending can have a devastating impact on the efficiency and safety and soundness of the financial system. We have learned this from the experience of many central and eastern European countries and the recent Asian banking crisis (Santomero 1997, 1998). Nonetheless, regulation is frequently used for this purpose.

The housing sector is often favored by government intervention in the financial sector. For example, the United States has chartered financial institutions with special regulatory privileges that specialize in housing finance. It has also promoted home ownership by extending implicit government guarantees to securities backed by housing mortgages and by allowing homeowners to deduct mortgage interest on their income taxes. In addition, until its interest rate ceilings were eliminated, the United States favored housing lenders by allowing them to pay their depositors a slightly higher interest rate than banks could pay their depositors, a policy that had the effect of enhancing the funds made available to finance housing.

Governments also channel credit to favored uses in other ways. Most countries subsidize financing for exports, sometimes through special guarantees, insurance, or through special discount facilities at the central bank. They also implement special programs to develop credit lines to fund small businesses. Many countries also require their financial institutions to lend to certain regions or sectors. Since the enactment of the Community Reinvestment Act in 1977, the United States has required its commercial banks and savings institutions to serve the credit needs of low-income areas.

The United States has also used regulation to achieve the social objective of preventing large concentrations of political and economic power within the financial sector, especially among banks. Until recently, the United States has restricted the ability of banking organizations to expand across state lines. And, until the end of 1999, restrictions continued limiting bank participation in non-banking activities.

Finally, many members of the Organization of Economic Cooperation and Development have imposed reporting requirements on banks and some other financial institutions in an effort to combat money laundering associated with the drug trade and organized crime. In the United States, for example, banks are required to report all currency transactions of $10,000 or more. Currently, Congress is considering even more stringent reporting requirements that have raised serious concerns about violations of privacy rights. Similarly the new Financial Services Authority in the United Kingdom (Davies 1998) has adopted the objective of "preventing … financial businesses being used for the purposes of financial crime."

2.5 The equilibrium level of effective regulation

By focusing on the optimal regulatory mechanism to cope with a specific market imperfection, we may fall prey to a naive view of the world: powerful regulators act in the best interest of society, and the regulated banks will submissively abide by the regulation. In fact, a more realistic view should be one in which regulation is an economic game with each agent developing its own strategy given its own objectives. Not only is it natural to assume that the regulators pursue their own objective in a world where their powers are limited by the legal framework, but it is also crucial to take into account that banks will react to regulation by developing new strategies, like introducing new financial innovations. Kane's now well-known "regulatory dialectic" and "regulatory captive" models captures this dynamic, as does Kroszner's political economy view of regulatory motivation (Kane 1995; Kroszner 1997).

We have attempted to describe these complex relationships between the welfare maximizing principal, the regulator (its agent), and the regulated agent (the banks) in Figure 2. Adding this perspective to the real life dynamics of regulation will introduce a series of important limitations to the likely outcome of regulation.

The first box in Figure 2 recalls the different options regarding the choice of a type of regulation. While in the banking industry, the main bulk of regulation stems from public regulation, some areas are left to the industry itself which establishes the standards to be applied. For instance, the level of training for a bank officer could be completely unregulated or established by the industry itself.

The second box describes the choice regarding how many regulators will implement the policy chosen, and their respective mandates. Whether because of institutional constraints or in order to enhance their efficiency, the overall regulatory problem has been delegated to different agencies. These agencies, for example, a central bank, may have incentives to focus on one dimension (say financial stability) rather than on another that may also be relevant to the public interest (e.g. the efficiency and competitiveness of the banking industry).

Once this structure of regulatory power is set, the regulatory agency incentives have to be considered, as illustrated in the third box. Even if we consider the case of effective public regulation, regulators may view their role, consciously or unconsciously, as one of a defender of the regulated

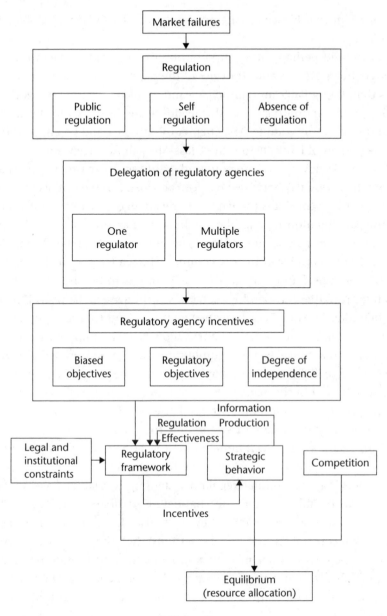

Figure 2.

industry's best interests. In addition, the letter of the law, as well as existing institutional structures may be manipulated to affect the impact of regulation on interested parties, or at least to change the focus of specific aspects of it. This leads to a new kind of second-best problem. More generally, the problem that is faced is the one of the regulatory agency's objective function.

Fourth, and perhaps most importantly, the regulatory framework will change the incentives and strategies of the regulated sector. This is a feedback that the regulator must anticipate and should factor into its regulatory design. Two important cases of this feedback are illustrated in the articles reproduced in this volume. The chapter by Kroszner and Rajan, considers the incentives of banks before the Glass–Steagall Act. They show that, in spite of banks having incentives to underwrite equity in order to pay back loans which would otherwise have been at a loss, this did not occur. A second paper also considers the feedback the change in banks strategies has on the banking industry equilibrium. In particular, the issue arises in connection with the disclosure of loan losses by banks. As argued by Aghion et al. (1999, reproduced in this volume), since a bank is always able to renew a non-performing loan, the regulator has to be careful not to set too high penalties for loan losses, because otherwise all banks will renew all their loans, possibly creating an even higher cost for the economy.

Finally, competition among banks, subject to the imposed regulatory constraint, may have "general equilibrium" effects that may differ from the ones expected at the individual level. If so, the sought after goal may not be achieved in the aggregate, even if regulation is well-meaning and fosters preferred firm-level incentives. For example, restrictions on credit allocation may favor certain sectors but the regulation may so tax the banking sector as to make it non-competitive and ineffective in providing needed resources to the target sector of the economy.

In choosing the optimal regulatory design, regulators have to face the overall equilibrium and the channeling of financial resources that will ultimately emerge. Yet, they will also have to consider both their own constraints and the limitations that they are facing when they compete with other markets and regulators, either internationally (as well illustrated by the euromarket developments) or even nationally when the boundaries of the different agencies attributions are sufficiently close.

Figure 2 attempts to capture this aggregate dynamic by offering a schematic representation of the impact of both market failures and regulation on the financial sector. It proves less than simple, with considerable indirect impacts of both the disease (market failure) and the cure (regulation).

3. Regulatory Design and its Impact

3.1 The safety net

Since bank failures appear to have strong externalities in terms of liquidity, bankruptcy costs, and asset destruction, an important part of banking regulation is designed to prevent bank failures or, at least, to limit their effects. This is referred to as "the safety net" that surrounds the banking system and protects bank customers. How extensive this safety net should be is still a matter of debate, among economists and politicians alike. In some countries, for example, France or Japan, allowing a bank to fail and its unsecured creditors to suffer the consequences of the bank decisions is deemed unacceptable. In others, for example, the United States and New Zealand, it is an event anticipated in regulation.

From a theoretical perspective, the safety net is generally justified as a mechanism to protect small, uninformed economic agents. Yet, the safety net may be extended further, to other financial stakeholders in order to avoid the undesirable externalities of a bank's bankruptcy enumerated above. Although some elements of the safety net, like deposit insurance are explicit and duly regulated, others, such as Lender of Last Resort intervention, are implicit and difficult to assess.

Nonetheless, in all cases the existence of the safety net has externalities on the firms' risk taking, altering the choice calculus by changing the state-dependent returns and fostering high-risk activity. Ultimately, in the case of a bail-out, taxpayers bear the cost of this incorrect risk weighting. It is the cost of creating a safety net, which may have desirable aggregate and structural stability effects. The appropriate height of the safety net will involve a weighing of these costs of its assistance against the benefits of the implied financial stability it brings. Evaluation of any one part of the safety net also involves consideration of the costs and benefits of each type of safety net enhancement. It is to this that we now turn.

3.1.1 Deposit insurance

Deposit insurance is a way to limit bank fragility. If the deposit insurance scheme is credible, the issue of bank runs in the Diamond–Dybvig setting is solved. However, since banks' creditors are their customers, the protection is usually justified by an appeal to those who are not well informed. Still, the extent and form of this portion of the safety net varies from one country to another. This raises several issues for the banking industry (Santomero and Trester 1997; Freixas and Rochet 1997).

The method to protect these liability holders is best understood if we recall that the rights the bank acquires by accepting an insured deposit in the presence of deposit insurance include a put option written by the Deposit Insurance Agency (Merton 1977), or, to be more precise, a callable put option (Acharya and Dreyfus 1988). The value of this right to the bank is monotonic in volatility and maximized at the maximum level of risk. Thus, bank risk taking behavior is altered, and if it is not fully observable, deposit insurance will lead to excessive risk absorption.

The price of such an option should depend on the level of risk (volatility of the underlying), as well as the ex ante capital ratio of the insured entity (which determined the strike price). It follows directly that flat or uniform deposit insurance pricing will lead to subsidizing risky banks at the expense of safe institutions. However, given the information environment, it is difficult to establish whether deposit insurance is fairly priced, and the extent of the distortion in resource allocation associated with the subsidy or tax on individual institutions. Given the opaque nature of assets on bank balance sheets, some of the determinants of the correct option value will be private information. This point leads some to conclude that it is impossible to obtain fair deposit insurance pricing (Chan et al. 1992).

This feature of the actuarial problem has led to a more global normative approach of banks regulation. Design mechanisms have shifted from relating a financial institution deposit insurance premium to its level of instantaneous risk to one in which sufficient capital is required to ensure that the government's option is reasonably far "out of the money" (Giammarino et al. 1993; Freixas and Gabillon 1999).

3.1.2 Capital requirements

The above logic has led to considerable interest in optimal capital regulation (Santomero 1991). However, the task of imposing an appropriate capital standard to justify the fixed or variable insurance premium is little easier than setting up a risk-related deposit insurance scheme. Theoretically, Sharpe (1978) illustrated the isomorphic nature of the two issues, and Koehn and Santomero (1980) and Kim and Santomero (1998) outline the instantaneously optimal risk-weighted capital ratios. The contribution of Rochet (1992, reproduced in this volume) provides the most consistent model of the feedback of capital requirement regulation on the banks portfolio choice. He remarks that limited liability implies that the distribution of returns has to follow a truncated distribution, and using this distribution shows, first, that capital requirements on each assets may induce the bank to select an inefficient portfolio; second, he proves that the absence of a minimum capital requirement, independent of the bank's portfolio, may induce the bank to become risk lover when the returns it obtains are low, as its profit function is convex as a consequence of its limited liability.

The Basel Accord of 1988 obviously falls far short of these optimal structures. However, this should not be a surprise. With real-time variations in bank risk-taking, and uncertain volatilities associated with given credit and/or market risk positions, most have concluded that optimal capital regulation is infeasible. While advances have been proposed, and are currently under review (by the Basel committee) little hope is offered that such remedies can or will address the imperfect information and moral hazard problems associated with any feasible bank capital regulation regime.

This has led to three different attempts to address the issue of appropriate capital. The first, associated with Kuester and O'Brien (1990) and Kupiec and O'Brien (1997) suggests that the banking firm be required to self-disclose its appropriate level of capital, based upon its more exact knowledge of the market and credit risk contained in its portfolio. The firm will, then, be held to this pre-commitment level on an ex post basis. If capital proves to be insufficient for observed volatility, ex post the regulators will impose a pecuniary penalty for violation. While this approach had immediate appeal, its implementation has proved no easier than earlier regulations surrounding risk-based capital requirements. While experiments have been conducted, a workable solution has proved illusory and the approach has been all but abandoned.

Interest then turned to a change in regulation that would require that banks fulfill a specified part of their capital requirement with subordinated debt, as a mechanism to increase market discipline. Subordinated debt, as a junior claim, serves as a buffer against losses by the deposit insurer (Benston and Kaufman 1997; Benston et al. 1989). Subordinated debt has some of the characteristics of patient money, because it typically has a maturity greater than one year and cannot be redeemed quickly during a crisis. Subordinated creditors have strong incentives to monitor bank risk taking and impose discipline. They are exposed to all downside risk that exceeds shareholder equity, but their potential gain on the upside is contractually limited. In contrast to shareholders that may choose higher points on the risk-return frontier, subordinated creditors, like the deposit insurer, generally prefer safer portfolios and are likely to penalize banks that take significant risks.

The market discipline of traded subordinated debt is a much quicker and more precise way of controlling bank risk than regulatory measures. A falling price of subordinated debt can alert other creditors about the condition of the bank or actions of the managers, creating a broad market reaction. Moreover, market prices are more forward looking than regulatory examinations and may provide regulators with valuable information on the market's perception of the risk taken by institutions (Horvitz 1983; Calomiris and Litan 2000).

When bank risk increases unexpectedly, banks may not have to pay higher rates or face possible quantity discipline until their subordinated debt matures. For this reason, subordinated debt proposals generally require that the bank stagger the maturities of debt issue so that a modest proportion matures each quarter. In this way, market discipline through price and quantity sanctions may be effective and informative, but sufficiently limited in magnitude to provide time for crisis resolution or orderly termination.

Critics of subordinated debt requirements emphasize that subordinated debt holders face the same informational asymmetry problems that the deposit insurer faces, but without the authority to conduct detailed examination (Kane 1995). They also question whether secondary markets in subordinated debt would be deep enough to provide reliable price signals. They, therefore, prefer to de-emphasize the market's role in risk-containment in favor of further advances in self-regulation.

Their cause has recently received increased credibility with the new BIS proposal for the use of internal models to set capital standards, along with existing rating agencies (BIS 1998). While there is much interest in the approach, its capitulation to the asymmetric information problem leaves some regulators unsatisfied. Not atypically, they would prefer *both* own model capital standards and significant regulatory oversight as part of any new system of capital regulation. In the end, they believe the regulator or central bank will still be performing the role of liquidity facility. They, therefore, have an obligation to maintain an appropriate level of oversight and comfort in the prudence of management's positions ex ante.

3.1.3 Lender of Last Resort

The term Lender of Last Resort (LOLR) refers to liquidity facilities that are open to banks. The classical theory argues that this function is reserved for lending to illiquid but solvent institutions, using good collateral and at a premium price. In fact, the reality of the use of the term Lender of Last Resort in many cases is quite different, although politically justified (see Freixas et al. 2000*b*). This is because although the LOLR facilities are supposed to solve a failure in the market provision for liquidity, banks in financial distress have often used them as a method to obtain a rescue package. This is the case because it is, at times, nearly impossible to distinguish ex ante (and even occasionally ex post) whether a loan is to solve an illiquidity problem being experienced by the institution or a solvency problem. Nevertheless, in a well-developed financial market, the Central Bank provides the necessary liquidity to such institutions even though this is only a minor part of their activity.

The provision of liquidity to the banking system as a whole is quite a relevant issue, since, as we have seen, there is an inherent instability of the banking sector directly related to the justification of banks. Not only are banks confronted with informational asymmetries but they also have to deal with illiquid assets and liquid liabilities. The provision of liquidity to the banking system will be an essential task, therefore, in order to maintain banking stability.

Central Banks may provide liquidity to banks through different channels. The classical justification of the LOLR dates from the nineteenth century and is based on the presumption that the money market may fail to allocate liquidity to solvent banks that require it. Therefore, it was not clear whether the LOLR was designed for monetary stability reasons, or for financial stability ones. Today's perspective is quite different because the money market provides liquidity to any solvent institution (Goodfriend and King 1988).

3.1.4 Bail-out policy and bank closure

Whether they act under cover, or use the LOLR alibi to perform a rescue operation, the central bank bail-out policy does exist (Goodhart and Schoenmaker 1993; Santomero and Hoffman 1999). It is characterized, first, by the fact that "too large to fail" banks are systematically rescued (see Hughes and Mester 1993); second, by the fact that the bail-out policy is never announced ex ante (constructive ambiguity), which is justified by the idea that free riding will be limited. These bailout operations are the result of the concern of the central bank for the externalities created by a bank's failure. Although there has been a general trend towards limiting the rescue packages, it is not credible that rescue packages will be denied to insolvent banks whose bankruptcy would have a large negative externalities. Freixas (1999) has recently examined the cost–benefit analysis of bail-outs and emphasizes the need to take the social cost of bail-outs into consideration. Even then, he concludes that it will be worth rescuing "too large to fail" institutions and using a mixed strategy to decide on the smaller institutions who have complied with regulatory requirements.

The concern about the externalities of a bank bankruptcy, however, tends to ignore the fact that the costs of bank externalities are the result of bankruptcy resolution legislation. As such, they are, at least partially, endogenous to the regulatory environment. Consequently, any attempt to establish a regulatory regime, which minimizes bankruptcy cost, must include consideration of the mechanism for orderly liquidation. Yet, the closure of financial institutions is a rather involved issue for three interrelated reasons. First, the regulator is constrained by the existing national bankruptcy code. Second, it is constrained by enacted banking regulation, and third, it is constrained by the information available at the time of the liquidation decision. Finally, and above all, the regulator may maximize its own objective function which may not coincide with welfare maximization.

The discrepancy between the regulators objectives and the efficient decisions has been discussed at length, but a crystal clear illustration is provided by Kane (1990) which establishes the costs implied by the excessively generous bail-out policy followed after the Saving and Loans crisis. Boot and Thakor (1993) provide a theoretical argument that justifies forbearance: Since a bank closure damages a regulator's reputation, in a reputational equilibrium regulators will always tend to implement excessively lenient bank closure policy that will be.

Mailath and Mester (1994) emphasize the fact that the regulators' objective function may be a restriction to regulation policy. This is indeed the case as a regulators thread has to be credible and, therefore, a bank will never be penalized for his past breaches of regulation if the penalty worsens the regulator outcome.

Repullo (2000) has illustrated the second point, regarding the limits set by enacted banking regulation, by examining how the delegation of the rights to close or rescue a bank could be made more efficient by making different parties responsible for the decision in different circumstances. The central bank could determine the closure point when the amount withdrawn by depositors in the first period is small and the deposit insurance agency in cases of potential large withdrawals and bank runs.

The information constraint faced by the regulatory body in charge of the liquidation–continuation decision (labeled "information production" in Figure 2) is modeled in a simple elegant way in Aghion et al. (1999, this volume). They argue that banks have the option to roll over loans that would have to be written off and in this way hide the real extent of their losses. In this case, they show that if the regulator is excessively tough and systematically liquidates banks in financial distress, the banks will react by hiding their losses. The optimal scheme is only obtained when the regulator is willing to bail out the insolvent bank in some cases.

However, the effect of these operations is to increase the safety net, thus covering uninsured depositors. As a consequence, it causes excessive risk-taking. The creditors that should be in charge of limiting the banks risk by exerting market discipline implying larger interest rates for the uninsured liabilities and, in particular, subordinated debt have no incentive to monitor the bank's risk. Calomiris and Kahn (1991) model clarified this point.

Nevertheless, no matter how negative the effects of the bail-out mechanism may be, it is clear that the existence of such a mechanism is essential in order to solve systemic risk crises. As we have mentioned, in the absence of any rescue procedure, the existence of interbank credit, with unsecured interbank market and a payment system, which is in general an efficient way to cope with liquidity shocks, may create a contagion channel that could trigger a systemic crises out of an individual bank bankruptcy (Allen and Gale 1998a; Freixas et al. 2000a).

We are, at the end, left in a world of second best, where perfect regulation is infeasible and spillover from necessary regulatory tools has deleterious effects on the equilibrium character of the system.

References

Acharya, S., and Dreyfus, J. F. (1988). "Optimal bank reorganization policies and the pricing of federal deposit insurance." *Journal of Finance*, 44(5): 1.314–34.
Aghion, P., Bolton, P., and Fries, S. (1999). "Optimal design of bank bailouts: The case of transition economies." *Journal of Institutional Theoretical Economics*, 155: 51–70.
Allen, F., and Gale, D. (1998a). "Financial contagion." *Journal of Political Economy*, forthcoming Bank for International Settlements, 2000; "Reducing Foreign Exchange Settlement Risk: A Progress Report." Basel, July.
Bagehot, W. (1873). *Lombard Street: A Description of the Money Market*. London: H. S. King.

Benston, G. J., Brumbaugh, D., Guttentag, J., Herring, R., Kaufman, G., Litan, R., and Scott, K. (1989). *Blueprint for Restructuring America's Financial Institutions.* Washington D.C.: The Brookings Institution.

——, and Kaufman, G. G. (1998). "Deposit insurance reform in the FDIC. Improvement act: The experience to date." Economic Perspectives, Federal Reserve Bank of Chicago.

Berger, A. N., Hancock, D., and Marquardt, J. C. (1996). "A framework for analyzing efficiency, risks, costs, and innovations in the payments systems." *Journal of Money, Credit & Banking,* 28: 696–732.

Bhattacharya, S., Boot, A., and Thakor, A. (1998). "The economics of bank regulation." *Journal of Money, Credit & Banking,* 30(4): 745–70.

Boot, A. W. A., and Schmeits, A. (2000). "Market discipline and incentive problems in conglomerate firms with applications to banking." *Journal of Financial Intermediation.*

——, and Thakor, A. (1993). "Self interested bank regulation." *American Economic Review,* 83(2): 206–12.

——, and —— (1993). "Security design." *Journal of Finance,* 48(4): 1349–78.

Bordo, M. D. (1986). "The lender of last resort: Alternative views and historical experience." *Federal Reserve Bank of Richmond Economic Review,* 76(1): 18–29.

Calomiris, C. (1998). "The IMF's imprudent role as lender of last resort." *The Cato Journal,* 17(3).

——, and Kahn, C. M. (1991). "The role of demandable debt in structuring optimal banking arrangements." *American Economic Review,* 81(3): 497–513.

——, and —— (1996). "The efficiency of self-regulated payment systems: Learning from the suffolk system." *Journal of Money, Credit & Banking,* 28(2): 766–97.

——, and Litan, R. (2000). "Financial regulation in a global marketplace." Litan and Santomero (eds.), *Brookings Wharton Papers,* 283–340.

Campbell, T., and Kracaw, W. A. (1980). "Information production, market signalling, and the theory of financial intermediation." *Journal of Finance,* 35: 863–82.

Chan, Y. S., Greenbaum, S. I., and Thakor, A. V. (1992). "Is fairly priced deposit insurance possible?" *Journal of Finance,* 47: 227–45.

Chari, V. V., and Jagannathan, R. (1988). "Banking panics, information and rational expectations equilibrium." *Journal of Finance,* 43(3): 749–61.

Chung, E. J., and Santomero, A. M. (1992). "Evidence in support of broader bank powers." *Financial Markets, Institutions and Instruments* (formerly Salomon Brothers Monograph series in Finance and Economics).

Davies, H. (1998). "Why regulate?" Henry Thornton Lecture, City University Business School, November 4.

Diamond, D. W. (1984). "Financial intermediation and delegated monitoring." *Review of Economic Studies,* 51: 393–414.

——, and Dybvig, P. (1983). "Bank runs, deposit insurance, and liquidity." *Journal of Political Economy,* 91(3): 401–9.

Di Noia, C., and di Giorgio, G. (1999). "Should banking supervision and monetary policy tasks be given to different agencies?" CONSOB and Universitá la Sapienza.

Fama, E. (1980). "Banking in the theory of finance." *Journal of Monetary Economics*, 6(1): 39–57.

Flannery, M. (1996). "Financial crises, payment system problems, and discount window lending." *Journal of Money, Credit & Banking*, 28: 804–24.

Freixas, X. (1999). "Optimal bail-out, conditionality and constructive ambiguity." Financial Market Group Discussion Paper 237, London School of Economics.

——, and Rochet, J. C. (1997). *Microeconomics of Banking.* Cambridge and London: MIT Press.

——, and Gabillon, E. (1999). "Optimal regulation of a fully insured deposit banking system." *Journal of Regulatory Economics*, 16(2): 111–34.

——, Parigi, B., and Rochet, J. C. (2000a). "Systemic risk, interbank relations and liquidity provision by the central bank." *Journal of Money, Credit & Banking*, 32(3, part 2): 611–38.

——, Giannini, C., Hoggarth, G., and Soussa, F. (2000b). "The lender of last resort: A review of the literature." *Journal of Financial Services Research*, 18(1): 63–87.

Friedman, M., and Schwartz, A. (1963). *A Monetary History of the United States: 1867–1960.*

Gale, D., and Hellwig, M. (1985). "Incentive-compatible debt contracts: The one-period problem." *Review of Economic Studies*, 52: 647–63.

Gertler, M. (1988). "Financial structure and aggregate economic activity: An overview." *Journal of Money, Credit & Banking*, 20(3): 559–88.

Giammarino, R. M., Lewis, T. R., and Sappington, D. (1993). "An incentive approach to banking regulation." *Journal of Finance*, 48: 1.523–42.

Goodhart, C. A. E., and Schoenmaker, D. (1995). "Should the functions of monetary policy and bank supervision be separated?" *Oxford Economic Papers*, 39: 75–89.

——, and —— (1993). "Institutional separation between supervisory and monetary agencies," in F. Bruni (comp.), *Prudential Regulation, Supervision and Monetary Policy.* Milan, Universita Bocconi.

Goodfriend, M., and King, R. (1988). "Financial deregulation, monetary policy and central banking," in W. Haraf and R. M. Kushmeider (eds.), *Restructuring Banking and Financial Services in America.* AEI Studies, 481 (Lanham MD: UPA).

Gorton, G. (1988). "Banking panics and business cycles." *Oxford Economic Papers*, 40: 751–78.

Gorton, G., and Pennacchi, G. (1990). "Financial intermediaries and liquidity creation." *Journal of Finance*, 45: 49–71.

——, and Pennacchi, G. (1993). "Security baskets and index-linked securities." *Journal of Business*, 66(1): 1–27.

——, and Winton, A. (1999). "Liquidity provision, the cost of bank capital, and the macroeconomy." Mimeo, University of Minnesota.

Grossman, S. J., and Stiglitz, J. (1980). "On the impossibility of informationally efficient markets." *American Economic Review*, 70: 393–408.

Holmstrom, B., and Tirole, J. (1997). "Financial intermediation, loanable funds and the real sector." *Quarterly Journal of Economics*, 112: 663–91.

Horvitz, P. (1983). "Deposit insurance after deregulation." Proceedings of the 9th Annual Conference of the Federal Home Loan Bank of San Francisco, December.

Huang, H., and Xu, C. (1998). *Financial Institutions, Financial Contagion and Financial Crises.* IMF and London School of Economics.

Hughes, J., and Mester, L. (1993). "A quality and risk adjusted cost function for banks: Evidence on the too big to fail doctrine." *Journal of Productivity Analysis*, 4(3): 293–315.

Kane, E. J. (1990). "Principal–agents problems in S&L salvage." *Journal of Finance*, 45(3): 755–64.

—— (1995). "Three paradigms for the role of capitalization requirements in insured financial institutions." *Journal of Banking & Finance*, 19: 431–59.

Kim, D., and Santomero, A. M. (1998). "Risk in banking and capital regulation." *Journal of Finance*, 43(5): 1219–33.

Koehn, M., and Santomero, A. M. (1980). "Regulation of bank capital and portfolio risk." *Journal of Finance*, 35(5): 1235–44.

Kroszner, R. S. (1997). "The political economy of banking and financial regulation in the United States," in Von Furstenberg and M. George (eds.), *The Banking and Financial Structure in the NAFTA Countries and Chile* (Boston; Dordrecht and London: Kluwer Academic), 200–12.

——, and Rajan, R. (1993). "Is the Glass–Steagall act justified?" *American Economic Review*, 845(4): 810–32.

Kupiec, P. H., and O'Brien, J. M. (1997). "The pre-commitment approach: using incentives to set market risk capital requirements." [Working Paper] Board of Governors of the Federal Reserve System, Finance and Economics Discussion Paper Series: 1997/14. p. 52. March.

Kuester, K. A., and O'Brien, J. M. (1990). "Market based deposit insurance premiums." Proceedings of the Conference on Bank Structure and Competition, Federal Reserve Bank of Chicago, pp. 62–95.

Lóránth, G. (1999). "Financial conglomerates: Innovations, scope-expansion and incentives." Universities London and Libre of Bruxelles.

Mailath, G., and Mester, L. (1994). "A positive analysis of bank closure." *Journal of Financial Intermediation*, 3(3): 272–99.

McCulloch, and Huston, J. (1986). "Bank regulation and deposit insurance." *Journal of Business*, 59(1): 79–85.

Merton, R. (1977). "An analytic derivation of the cost of deposit insurance and loan guarantees." *Journal of Banking and Finance*, 1: 3–11.

Miron, J. (1986). "Financial panics, the seasonality of the nominal interest rate, and the founding of the Fed." *American Economic Review*, 76(1): 125–40.

Ramakrishnan, R. T. S., and Thakor, A. (1983). "Information reliability and a theory of financial intermediation." *Review of Economic Studies*, 51: 415–32.

Repullo, R. (2000). "Who should act as lender of last resort? An incomplete contracts model." *Journal of Money, Credit & Banking*, 32 (3, part 2), 580–605.

Rochet, J. C. (1992). "Capital requirements and the behaviour of commercial banks." *European Economic Review*, 36: 1137–78.

——, and Tirole, J. (1996). "Interbank lending and systemic risk." *Journal of Money, Credit & Banking*, 28: 733–62.

Santomero, A. M. (1984). "Modeling the banking firm." *Journal of Money, Credit & Banking*, 16: 576–602.

—— (1991). "The bank capital issue," in M. Fratianni, C. Wihlborg, and T. D. Willett (eds.), *Financial Regulation and Monetary Arrangements after 1992*, Economic Analysis Series, Vol. 204 (Amsterdam; London; New York, and Tokyo: North Holland). (distributed in the U.S. and Canada by Elsevier Science, New York), 61–77.

—— (1997). "Effective financial intermediation," K. B. Staking, (ed.), *Policy-Based Finance and Alternatives: East Asian Lessons for Latin America and the Caribbean* (Inter-American Development Bank).

——, and Babbel, D. (1997). *Financial Markets, Instruments and Institutions*. Irwin Publications.

——, and Trester, J. (1997). "Structuring deposit insurance for a United Europe." *European Financial Management*.

—— (1998). "The regulatory and public policy agenda for effective intermediation in post soviet economies," in J. Doukas, V. Murinde, and C. Wihlborg, (eds.), *Financial Sector Reform and Privitization in Transition Economies* (7) (Amsterdam: Elsevier Science Publishers B. V.), 153–75.

——, and Hoffman, P. (1999). "Problem bank resolution: Evaluating the options," in B. E. Gup (ed.), *International Banking Crises, Large Scale Failures, Massive Government Interventions* (Greenwood Publishing), edited by Benton E. Gup, Quorum Books.

Sharpe, W. F. (1978). "Bank capital adequacy, deposit insurance, and security values." *Journal of Financial and Quantitative Analysis*, 13: 701–18.

Slovin, M. B., Sushka, M. E., and Polonchek, J. A. "An analysis of contagion and competitive effects at commercial banks." *Journal of Financial Economics*, 54(2): 197–225.

Stiglitz, J. E. (1994). "The role of the state in financial markets," in *Proceedings of World Bank Annual Conference on Development Economics*. Washington, D.C.: World Bank.

Part V

Financial Contracting and
Interbank Competition

15

Reputation and Discretion in Financial Contracting

Arnoud W. A. Boot, Stuart I. Greenbaum, and Anjan V. Thakor

> "My Word Is My Bond"
> —Lintel: London Stock Exchange

This chapter explains why financial contracts often allow participants a measure of discretion as to whether to honor or repudiate them. An example is the "comfort letter" used by a parent company to assure the subsidiary's lenders that the parent will support it in financial distress. The British High Court recently ruled that comfort letters represent nothing more than a moral commitment (see *American Banker*, 6 June 1989), thereby reversing an earlier ruling by a lower court (see René Sacasas 1989). Another example is the "highly confident" letter with which the investment banker promises to provide credit, but the promise is typically not legally enforceable. Other examples of such contracts are discussed in Section III.

Contracts that allow such discretion often give rise to what are called "illusory promises" in that they impose no legal obligation on the promisor. This lack of enforceability is central to the discretionary contract that we analyze. Our principal objective is to explain why such contracts exist in circumstances where legally binding contracts, called definite or enforceable, are neither technically nor economically infeasible. The class of contracts we focus on are guarantees that promise a state-contingent future payment in exchange for a payment made at

We gratefully acknowledge financial support from the Garn Institute of Finance at the University of Utah. For their helpful comments, we thank Steven Buser, William Emmons, Michael Fishman, Charles Kahn, Michael Metzger, George Pennacchi, John Persons, Edward Prescott, Jeremy Stein, René Stulz, workshop participants at the Board of Governors of the Federal Reserve System, Columbia University, University of Illinois, Indiana University, Rice University, Ohio State University, Hong Kong University of Science and Technology, Washington University of St. Louis, and participants at the 1992 American Economic Association Meeting, the 1991 Conference on Monetary Theory and Financial Intermediation at the Federal Reserve Bank of Minneapolis, and the August 1992 Conference on the Operation and Regulation of Financial Intermediaries and Financial Markets at the Stockholm School of Economics. The authors alone are responsible for remaining errors.

the outset. The future payment may be cash or a credit extension on pre-specified terms.

Our explanation for discretion rests on considerations of flexibility and reputation. Consider guarantees issued by a financial institution possessing both reputational and financial capital, but with only the latter reflected on its balance sheet. The reputational capital reflects the market's beliefs about the likelihood that the institution will honor its guarantees. The better the institution's reputation, the more the market should be willing to pay for its guarantees. If the institution writes an enforceable guarantee, it is legally bound. Thus, if a claim eventuates, the institution will honor it to the full extent of its financial capital. On the other hand, the institution can repudiate a discretionary contract with legal impunity. Thus, the institution has two choices. It can either augment its reputational capital by honoring the claim and accepting the nondissipative write-down of its financial capital, or it can conserve its financial capital by repudiating the claim and accepting a dissipative charge against its reputational capital. The discretionary contract therefore provides the institution with additional degrees of freedom in managing its assets. It liquefies reputational capital and also facilitates reputation enhancement.

The use of contractual discretion to manage jointly financial and reputational capital is illustrated by the recent experience of Robeco, a Dutch investment group that manages share, bond, and property funds. Most Robeco funds tacitly guarantee fund prices. For example, for 11 years prior to September 1990, Robeco bought back shares of its real-estate fund, Rodamco, at net asset value from any investor wishing to sell. In September 1990, however, following a dumping of Rodamco shares, Robeco suspended this policy, a move that could be interpreted as sacrificing reputational capital in order to conserve financial capital. We quote (emphasis ours):

Trading is scheduled to resume today in Rodamco, the large Dutch property investment fund which stunned the Amsterdam bourse on Monday with the news that it was suspending its traditional policy of buying back shares when asked to do so by investors.
Analysts say a substantial fall in share price is inevitable ... [and] Rodamco's move—
which came as a shock despite provisions in its statutes which allow for a reversal of policy—
had also caused a dent in confidence in its owner, the Rotterdam-based Robeco Group, Europe's biggest independent fund manager.

[*Financial Times*, September 26, 1990, p. 32]

This interplay between financial and reputational capital is central to the discretionary contracts we analyze. These are incomplete contracts in that they fail to legally bind in at least some states, thereby leaving residual discretion with the contracting parties. Since discretion in incomplete contracts takes many forms, ours is but one among a variety of possible explanations. One strand of the literature explains missing contingencies in incomplete contracts with the observation that future state-contingent outcomes may be too complex to permit precise contracting over all outcomes at reasonable cost (Oliver Williamson 1975; Oliver Hart and John Moore 1988; Gillian Hadfield 1990). Thus, the contract specifies a sharing rule that pools across subsets of future states of nature. Bengt Holmstrom and Paul Milgrom (1991) explain the absence of contingencies in incentive contracts by suggesting that a contract that bases an agent's compensation on readily monitored, well-specified contingencies may not be used because it could distract the agent from poorly monitored but potentially more productive tasks. Franklin Allen and Douglas Gale (1992) suggest that contingencies that are only indirectly observable through noisy manipulable signals may be optimally excluded from a contract. A second strand of the literature shows that discretion may be useful in deterring moral hazard (see Richard Craswell and John Calfee 1986; Boot and Thakor 1992).[1] A third strand is the literature on implicit contracting (Clive Bull 1987), which argues that incentive-compatible implicit contracts might be chosen if explicit ones are unenforceable in some states.[2]

Rather than explaining missing contingencies or imprecision in contract terms, we explain why unenforceable contracts may be optimal. We consider contractual obligations linked to state contingencies and assume that these are to be fulfilled by an agent, X, whose "type" is a priori unknown to the counterparty, Y. If all state contingencies were mutually and costlessly verifiable, the contract would precisely stipulate each party's obligation in each state. However, we assume that X privately observes some states, so that Y has a coarser partitioning of the state space. The question of discretion versus enforceability is whether the contract (legally) mandates that X satisfy the contractually stipulated obligation in each state *discernible to Y* (we call this an *enforceable contract*), or whether the contract permits X to repudiate the obligation with legal impunity in one or more states in which X has finer information (we call this a *discretionary contract*). The advantage of the discretionary contract is that it allows X to achieve a superior matching of the contractual obligation to the realized state. The disadvantage of the discretionary contract is that X may exploit its informational advantage by misrepresenting the state realization to Y's detriment. The incentive for X not to misrepresent is rooted in the potential gain from developing a reputation. Without this reputation-development incentive, there would be no role for a discretionary contract, because it would never be honored.

The principal contributions of our analysis are threefold. First, we establish conditions under which contractual discretion is preferred, even when greater

---

[1] The moral-hazard explanation seems relevant in explaining the government's refusal to guarantee explicitly bank deposits in excess of $100,000 per account, and also in explaining the vagueness of conditions precedent to access to lender-of-last-resort facilities. These ambiguities may encourage greater care in bank asset selection (see Gerald Corrigan 1989).

[2] The implicit-contracting literature addresses different issues. For example, Costas Aziardis (1975) uses implicit contracts to explain risk-sharing, whereas George Akerlof (1982) addresses partial gift exchange between employees and firms.

enforceability is feasible. Second, we develop a link between contract choice and reputation. In the reputation literature (e.g. Kose John and David Nachman, 1985), the contract between the uninformed party and the party attempting to develop a reputation typically is exogenously specified, and reputational incentives for settling the contract are analyzed. We show that reputational incentives are sensitive to contract choice, and we endogenize the choice of contract on that basis. Third, contrary to the presumption of legal doctrine, we show that there *is* a difference between the discretionary contract and the "no contract" alternative. In particular, even though a discretionary contract lacks legal enforceability, it is preferable to having no contract in that it establishes a reputation mechanism. The public observability of the discretionary promise and its honoring (breaching) affects reputation.

The rest of the paper is organized in four sections. Section I describes the model and the legal and economic environments. Section II contains the analysis, Section III discusses applications, and Section IV presents conclusions.

I. The Model

Consider an intermediary, X (the guarantor), who promises a state-contingent future payment to Y (the guaranteed) in exchange for a fee paid at the outset. We will first rationalize such a contract.

A. An Example of how the guarantee contract can be endogenized

Suppose that at time $t = 0$, a potential borrower Y anticipates that it will have the opportunity to invest in a project at $t = 1$ with a random return to be realized at $t = 2$. The return is $S_j > 0$ with probability ξ_j and zero with probability $1 - \xi_j$. The borrower, Y, can choose either a low-risk (ℓ) or a high-risk (h) project (i.e., $j \in \{\ell, h\}$, with $\infty > S_h > S_\ell > 0$ and $0 < \xi_h < \xi_\ell < 1$). Suppose the low-risk project is socially optimal, in the sense that $\xi_\ell S_\ell > \xi_h S_h$. Each project requires a one-dollar investment which is to be funded with a bank loan. Let X be a bank that cannot observe project choices, and *ex post* can only observe whether or not the borrower's project succeeds (but *not* the realized project payoff). At $t = 0$, the $t = 1$ spot risk-free interest factor (1 plus the interest rate) is a random variable $\tilde{R} \in \{\underline{R}, \overline{R}\}$, where $\overline{R} > \underline{R} > 1$. All agents are risk-neutral. The loan market is perfectly competitive in the sense that lenders earn zero expected profits on loans, and can avail themselves of an infinitely elastic supply of deposits at the spot risk-free interest rate.

If X anticipates that Y will choose project ℓ, then the competitive interest factor (i.e. one that yields the bank zero expected profit) charged for the $1 spot loan will be $\tilde{R}[\xi_\ell]^{-1} \in \{\underline{R}[\xi_\ell]^{-1}, \overline{R}[\xi_\ell]^{-1}\}$, and if X anticipates that Y will choose project h, the interest factor charged will be $\tilde{R}[\xi_h]^{-1} \in \{\underline{R}[\xi_h]^{-1}, \overline{R}[\xi_h]^{-1}\}$. We then have the following result.

LEMMA 1. *If*

$$\underline{R} < [\xi_\ell S_\ell - \xi_h S_h] \xi_\ell [\xi_\ell - \xi_h]^{-1} < \overline{R}$$

then there is a Nash equilibrium in which Y chooses project ℓ if $\tilde{R} = \underline{R}$ and project h if $\tilde{R} = \overline{R}$, and the competitive bank charges an interest factor of $\underline{R}[\xi_\ell]^{-1}$ if $\tilde{R} = \underline{R}$ and $\overline{R}[\xi_h]^{-1}$ if $\tilde{R} = \overline{R}$. There is no Nash equilibrium in which Y chooses project ℓ if $\tilde{R} = \overline{R}$.

(See Appendix for the proof.)

Note that, given the parametric restriction stated in Lemma 1, the bank will never price the loan under the assumption that Y will choose project ℓ when the spot interest rate is high. That is, Y chooses h when $\tilde{R} = \overline{R}$, regardless of whether X anticipates a choice of h or ℓ in the pricing of the loan. The social cost of Y investing in the socially suboptimal (high-risk) project is

$$P = [\xi_\ell S_\ell - \xi_h S_h] > 0.$$

This cost is avoidable if Y were to purchase a loan commitment from X at $t = 0$ that would permit Y to borrow \$1 from X at $t = 1$ at a fixed interest factor of $R_0 = [\xi_\ell S_\ell - \xi_h S_h][\xi_\ell - \xi_h]^{-1}\xi_\ell$. Now Y will choose project ℓ regardless of the spot borrowing rate at $t = 1$, although the commitment will be exercised only if $\tilde{R} = \overline{R}$. At $t = 0$, X will charge Y a fee to recoup the expected loss from future lending to Y at $R_0 < \overline{R}$ in the high-interest-rate state.

Thus far we have implicitly assumed that X will honor its commitment to lend to Y at R_0 if Y wishes to borrow. If the loan-commitment contract is legally enforceable, it will bind X. However, if the contract is discretionary, X may choose to renege even if it is financially able to satisfy the claim. The price (fee) that Y is willing to pay X for such a commitment will increase with X's reputation for honoring discretionary contracts.

B. Legal environment and contracting options

Michael Metzger and Michael Phillips (1990) note a trend toward reduced specificity/completeness in contract terms with a consequent increase in contractual discretion. Contracts can be thought of as lying in a precision continuum, with illusory and definite promises as endpoints.

Illusory promise

In the legal literature, an illusory promise is defined as "an expression cloaked in promissory terms, but which, upon closer examination, reveals that the promisor has committed himself not at all" (John Calamari and Joseph Perillo 1977: 159),

Arnoud W. A. Boot et al.

and as "words in promissory form that promise nothing; they do not purport to put any limitation on the freedom of the alleged promisor, but leave his future action subject to his own future will, just as it would have been had he said no words at all" (Arthur Corbin 1952: 211).

For present purposes, it is sufficient to note that illusory promises are unenforceable in the sense that there is no legal remedy for breach. A related notion is that of *indefiniteness*. A contract is called too indefinite to enforce if identifying an appropriate breach for remedy is impossible because the contract terms make it difficult to determine what the promisee is supposed to receive. Both illusory promises and indefinite contracts are extreme manifestations of contractual incompleteness. Incomplete contracts leave discretion with a guarantor in unspecified contingencies; illusory promises and promises that fail for indefiniteness leave discretion in too many contingencies.[3]

Definite promises

These are commitments that are legally enforceable. The enforceable contract in our model is a definite promise. It is also a complete contract in the sense that it clearly spells out the obligations of the parties based on contingencies observable by a court.[4]

Transacting parties in our model thus have three choices: (i) no contract at all, (ii) a discretionary contract (illusory promise), or (iii) an enforceable (definite) contract.

C. Information reusability, discretion, and reputation

The incentive for X to honor a discretionary contract will depend on considerations of reputational and financial capital. Suppose that X's financial capability evolves stochastically and X is privately informed about the probability distribution that determines this capability (i.e. its type). Moreover, suppose that X has a multiperiod planning horizon and produces a variety of information (e.g., market demand conditions and branch-specific information) in order to price its guarantees. Then X's information is potentially *reusable*, intertemporally and/or cross-sectionally (see Yuk-Shee Chan et al. 1986). Thus, the information

---

[3] Not all incomplete contracts are unenforceable, only those that are "too incomplete." It is easy to envision a more general variant of our model that includes an additional state in which the discretionary contract is legally enforceable. In such a setting, the contract can be thought of as a collection of promises, one for each contingency, some of which will be definite and enforceable and (if the contract is incomplete) others of which will be illusory or completely absent. The generalization does not affect our results qualitatively; details are available from the authors upon request.

[4] Our definition of a complete contract is one that specifies obligations in all contingencies observable by a court (see Ian Ayres and Robert Gertner 1992). However, our definite contract is not a "complete contingent contract" which specifies obligations in contingencies observable only to (at least one of) the parties and not to a court.

that X possesses regarding Y is idiosyncratic to a particular *class* of customers that Y belongs to, and not to Y exclusively. Then, even if X does not contract with Y in the future, it can benefit from information reusability (i.e. enjoy a lower future information-production cost) in dealing with another customer like Y.

The realization of a state in which X is financially impaired makes it more costly for X to satisfy Y's claim because X may be forced to liquidate information-sensitive assets. This may result in a loss of reusable information (e.g. information available in bank branches that may need to be liquidated), or X may incur costs in selling inherently illiquid assets. Note that reusable information is just one example of an asset that may be damaged as a result of financial distress. In addition, information reusability reinforces reputational rents by providing higher profits to a longer-lived X.

The likelihood that X will enjoy these rents depends on its ability to meet its contractual obligation, which in turn depends on its financial capital. Since the financial capital evolves randomly, misfortune alone could threaten X's rents. This is where a discretionary contract can help. Since X is not legally bound, it can repudiate a claim whenever honoring it is too costly; and because X is privately informed about the expected evolution of its financial capability (its type), an improved reputation can enhance future fee income and thus provide an incentive for honoring even discretionary guarantees. Without uncertainty as to X's type, however, there would be no reputational concerns, and discretionary guarantees would not be in evidence because they would be repudiated whenever possible. Reputational concerns confront X with a trade-off in the state in which it is financially capable of honoring the guarantee. Honoring the guarantee reduces financial capital but increases reputation, whereas repudiating has the opposite effects.

D. Types of contracts and information structure

We begin by describing the sequence of moves and the available contracting options. Consider four points in time, $t = 0, 1, 2,$ and 3, and hence three periods: period one ($t = 0$ to $t = 1$), period two ($t = 1$ to $t = 2$), and period three ($t = 2$ to $t = 3$). At the start of each period (i.e. at $t = 0, 1,$ and 2), X and Y can enter into an enforceable or a discretionary contract, or no contract at all. Formally, this is a game in which the informed agent, X, moves first by offering Y a contract, and then Y (the uninformed agent) reacts by either accepting or rejecting the offered contract. If accepted, X incurs an information-production cost, and one period hence Y may submit a claim against X's financial capital. At the end of each period, the claim is exercised with probability q.

If a claim is made under an enforceable contract and X refuses to honor the claim, we assume that a court of law will force liquidation of enough of X's assets to satisfy the claim. Since X's financial capital is not mutually verifiable, such forced liquidation will result in X surrendering more by refusing to honor a claim than it would by honoring it in states in which it is financially able. This ensures that X will always honor an enforceable contract when it is financially capable of doing so.[5] With a discretionary contract, there is no legal enforcement, and X chooses whether or not to honor the contract in states where it has private information. Thus, X moves first and last in this game, and X's strategies involve the choice of contract and whether or not to honor a claim if one eventuates.

It is interesting to compare the discretionary contract with the "no contract" option. Neither is legally enforceable, but there is a key distinction between the two. Discretionary promises are publicly observable and often involve formal documents. By contrast, the no-contract alternative may include less formal (unwritten and unwitnessed) promises which would be difficult for outsiders to monitor (i.e. they would not inform outsiders about the guarantor's behavior). Consequently, the performance (breach) of a discretionary contract will affect the guarantor's reputation, whereas the no-contract alternative lacks analogous reputational implications. The importance of the discretionary contract then stems from the role that these publicly observable formal documents play in reputation-formation. Because of the reputation mechanism, the discretionary contract becomes a viable alternative to an enforceable contract. It will therefore dominate the no-contract alternative because, as indicated in Subsection I-A, there are social and private gains to contracting.

We turn now to the information structure. The guarantor, X, can be either of two types. Let $i \in \{L, H\}$ be X's type where L and H differ in the probability distributions that determine the evolution of their financial capital. Both start out at $t = 0$ with capital $K_0 > 0$. In each period, capital is perturbed by a random shock. We make the following simplifying assumptions. The capital of a high-quality intermediary (type H) increases in each period with probability p_H, while for type L this probability is p_L with $1 > p_H > p_L > 0$. In any period in which capital increases, X is financially sound and is capable of honoring its guarantee. With probability $1 - p_i$, X is financially impaired. We assume that, conditional on being financially impaired, there is a probability η that X is in a low-resource state in which it can satisfy Y's claim only at a dissipative cost arising from the liquidation of information-sensitive assets ("weak impairment"), and with probability $1 - \eta$, X is insolvent and will be terminated ("strong impairment"). Termination is a state in which X is left with no assets or information-reusability advantage. Even if X were allowed to continue, it would be no better off than a

---

[5] Even if forced liquidation resulted in X suffering the same cost from not honoring the contract as it does from honoring it, X would be indifferent, and it would adopt the equilibrium choice of honoring the claim. With the standard remedy for breach of an enforceable contract—expectation damages—X will never prefer default if it is able to pay. This result will be reinforced if X sustains legal and other expenses upon breach of contract.

Table 1. Description of States

State	Probability of occurrence	Description
N	$[1 - q]\{1 - [1 - \eta][1 - p_i]\}$	No claim and no termination
C_S	$q p_i$	Claim, X financially sound (only privately known)
C_I	$\eta q[1 - p_i]$	Claim, X in low-resource state (only privately known)
T	$[1 - \eta][1 - p_i]$	X terminated, claim or no claim

de novo guarantor. Note that $1 - p_L > 1 - p_H$ implies that, in any period, a low-quality guarantor faces both a higher probability of incurring dissipative costs in satisfying Y's claim and a higher probability of insolvency.[6]

The guarantor, X, is privately informed about its type. The commonly known prior belief of all agents other than X is that X is of type H with probability $\gamma \in (0, 1)$. Also, while strong impairment (i.e. termination) is publicly observable and X always knows its financial state, the market cannot distinguish between the financially sound state and the low-resource (weak-impairment) state (i.e. X is then privately informed about its financial condition).

Table 1 lists the four relevant states in each period. In state N there is no claim under the guarantee, and X is not terminated. In state C_S, there is a claim, but X alone knows that it is financially sound. The assumption that X is privately informed about this state is crucial because it means that one cannot write a contract contingent on X's financial condition. In state C_I, there is a claim, but X knows privately that this is a low-resource state (i.e., Y cannot distinguish C_I from C_S). Note that, in state C_I, X would be compelled to honor the enforceable contract, but not the discretionary contract. Finally, in state T, X is terminated, and all claims are repudiated.

E. Reputation and fee structure

Let ψ_t be the probability assigned by the market at time t that X is of type H (i.e. the reputation of X). At $t = 0$, $\psi_0 = \gamma$, and thereafter ψ_t evolves in accord with the Bayesian posteriors formed by the market as it observes X's behavior. Let $f_t^j \equiv f^j(\psi_t)$ be the fee charged by X for a guarantee $j \in \{E, D\}$, where E stands for enforceable and D stands for discretionary. A guarantee is written to cover a contingency one period hence. Therefore, a guarantee made at time t can require a payment only at $t + 1$. Assume that the fee f_t^j is equal to the expected

---

[6] This is the simplest way to specify the intertemporal evolution of financial capital. It captures the notion that a type-H guarantor is more likely to be able to honor its commitments. Note that we could have chosen a more complicated formulation such that X's ability to honor claims in a specific period would depend on past actions and claims. This would have added substantial parametric complexity without obvious benefits.

value of the payment to be made by X under the guarantee, given Y's beliefs as represented by ψ_t. In the loan commitment, for example, the fee is equal to the present value of the interest rate subsidy under the commitment. Note that f_t^j does not compensate a type-H guarantor for the negative externality generated by type-L agents, nor does it compensate for the information-production cost. Thus, the type-H guarantor's participation constraint is violated if f_t^j is all that it receives.

We assume that adding a premium $\phi_t^j = \phi_t^j(\psi_t)$ satisfies the type-H guarantor's participation constraint. The reusability of information is captured by assuming that the information-production cost for a preexisting intermediary is $\underline{V}$, which is strictly less than $\overline{V}$, the cost for a de novo intermediary. If, however, the surviving intermediary is forced to honor a claim in the low-resource state, its information-production cost will be V^* in the next period, with $\underline{V} < V^* < \overline{V}$. This assumption captures the notion that a guarantor incurs a dissipative cost when it satisfies a claim in the low-resource state.

The premium that X can charge over the guarantee fee is anchored by the amount required for a new intermediary to participate. That is, $\phi_t^j = \phi_t^j(\gamma)$. A new intermediary charges $f_t^j(\gamma) + \phi_t^j(\gamma)$ so that its participation constraint holds tightly. An established intermediary, depending upon its reputation, can charge more. Moreover, the established intermediary enjoys a lower information-production cost, so that it earns a net rent relative to a new entrant.

II. Analysis of Equilibrium

The question is whether X and Y would choose a discretionary contract, given the availability of an enforceable one. Since X faces a potentially different Y in each period, we focus on single-period contracts and ensure that Y's utility in any period is invariant to the choice of contract in that period. Thus, Y is indifferent to contract choice. Because of the usual endgame problem, only enforceable contracts will be used at $t = 2$.

A. Conjectured equilibrium strategies and intuition

In Table 2, we summarize the conjectured equilibrium strategies of X with a discretionary contract at $t = 0$ and enforceable contracts at $t = 1$ and $t = 2$. In each period, the conjectured equilibrium contract has both types H and L offering the same contract.

A key feature of this conjectured equilibrium is that the type-H guarantor prefers a discretionary contract at $t = 0$. Discretion permits X to preserve information reusability, even in the impaired state, C_I. The disadvantage of the

State	Probability		X's strategy with respect to honoring contracts			
	H	L	Discretionary contract at $t=0$		Enforceable contract at $t=1,2$	
			H	L	H	L
N	$[1-q]$ $\times\{1-[1-\eta][1-p_H]\}$	$[1-q]\{1-[1-\eta]\}$ $\times[1-p_L]\}$	—	—	—	—
C_S	qp_H	qp_L	Honor	Default	Honor	Honor
C_I	$\eta q[1-p_H]$	$\eta q[1-p_L]$	Default	Default	Honor	Honor
T	$[1-\eta][1-p_H]$	$[1-\eta][1-p_L]$ (default)	Terminate (default)	Terminate (default)	Terminate (default)	Terminate

discretionary contract is that it permits type-L guarantors to default in the good state, C_S, and since Y will take this into account in deciding what it is willing to pay for the guarantee, the discretionary contract will amplify the negative externality type-L guarantors impose on guarantors of type H. This follows because the contract-honoring strategies of types H and L are identical with an enforceable contract; the only difference is that type-H guarantors have a lower probability of realizing the termination state, T. With a discretionary contract, however, there also is an additional behavioral difference between the types since type-H guarantors would not default in state C_S whereas type-L guarantors would. This externality, imposed by L with a discretionary contract, means that type-H guarantors will offer such a contract only if the expected incremental future surplus obtainable with a discretionary contract compensates for the externality. Recall that neither type can honor the contract in state T.

To see why type L defaults on a discretionary contract in state C_S at $t=1$ when type H does not, let us first examine H's incentive to honor the contract in C_S at $t=1$. By honoring the contract, H can distinguish itself from L who never honors a discretionary contract in states $\{C_S, C_I\}$. The consequent reputational enhancement permits H to earn more on the second-period enforceable contract. Observe that this gain is also available to L, should it decide to mimic H and honor the contract in state C_S. Therefore, in a model with only two periods, the incentives for honoring the contract at the end of the first period (when there is only one period left) would be identical for both types. This is why three periods are necessary. For any state realization at $t=2$ that does not involve termination, a guarantor that honored a discretionary contract at $t=1$ is able to earn more on its third-period guarantee. This reputational benefit is unavailable if termination occurs at $t=2$. At $t=1$, H assigns a lower probability to facing termination at $t=2$ than does L. Hence, the benefit of developing a reputation by honoring a discretionary guarantee at $t=1$ is greater for H, and L behaves more myopically at $t=1$.

This reasoning also explains why, absent a fourth period ($t = 3$ to $t = 4$), the second-period contract (offered at $t = 1$) as well as the third-period contract must be enforceable in the equilibrium we consider. To see this, suppose (counterfactually) that a discretionary contract is negotiated at $t = 1$. Then, at $t = 2$, since there is only one more contracting period left, both H and L face the same honoring incentives, and they will both honor or both renege. Now, both types honoring the discretionary contract at $t = 2$ cannot be part of an equilibrium because the reputational gain from honoring the discretionary contract is greater (for either type) at $t = 1$ than at $t = 2$, and L reneged on the discretionary contract at $t = 1$. Hence, L would surely renege on a discretionary contract at $t = 2$. However, this applies to H as well, because both types face the same trade-off with only one period remaining. Thus, a discretionary contract cannot be sold (at a positive price) at $t = 1$. The only way that such a contract can be sold at $t = 1$ is if exogenous parameters are such that *both* types honor it at $t = 1$ and $t = 2$. This case is of no interest to us because it involves qualitatively identical reputational consequences for discretionary and enforceable contracts.

B. Analysis and results

We begin by analyzing enforceable and discretionary contracts without reputational considerations.

LEMMA 2. *Ignoring second- and third-period payoffs, and given the conjectured equilibrium strategies in Table 2, the cost of the negative externality created by a type-L guarantor is greater in the first period with a discretionary contract than with an enforceable one.*

Proof. With the conjectured equilibrium strategies, the guarantee fees are

$$f_0^D = q\gamma p_H M \tag{1}$$

$$f_0^E = q\{\gamma[p_H + \eta[1 - p_H]] + [1 - \gamma][p_L + \eta[1 - p_L]]\}M \tag{2}$$

and $f_0^D < f_0^E$. At $t = 0$, H assesses the expected transfer to Y on the first-period guarantee as L_0^j, where $j \in \{D, E\}$, and

$$L_0^D = q p_H M \tag{3}$$

$$L_0^E = q\{p_H + \eta[1 - p_H]\}M. \tag{4}$$

From (1), (2), (3), and (4) it follows that

$$f_0^D - L_0^D < f_0^E - L_0^E < 0. \tag{5}$$

Thus, the presence of a type-L guarantor imposes a strictly larger first-period externality on H with a discretionary contract than with an enforceable contract. The actual difference in externality is even greater since Y faces a social cost P (see Section I-A) if the guarantee is not honored (which is more likely with a discretionary contract).

Let $\psi_t^j(H|\Omega_t)$ be the probability that Y attaches at time t to X being of type H, where the first-period guarantee was $j \in \{D, E\}$ and the information set of Y is Ω_t. The second- and third-period guarantees are assumed to be enforceable. For sequential rationality (David Kreps and Robert Wilson 1982a), Y revises its beliefs in accordance with Bayes' rule following an equilibrium action. The set Ω_0 contains Y's prior beliefs regarding X's type (i.e., $\psi_0^j(H|\Omega_0) = \gamma$ for $j \in \{D, E\}$.[7] At each time $t \in \{1, 2\}$, Y updates its beliefs in the states $\{C_S, C_I\}$ based on X's behavior. Let n_t, denote "no claim and no termination," whereas h_t denotes "honor" and d_t denotes "default" in the states $\{C_S, C_I\}$ at time $t \in \{1, 2\}$.

Thus, for example, $\psi_2^D(H|h_1, n_2)$ denotes the probability that Y attaches at time 2 to X being of type H, where the first-period guarantee was discretionary but was honored (i.e. h_1) and in the second period no claim eventuated and X's random shock to capital did not force termination. In the Appendix we provide explicit expressions for all $\psi_t^j(H|\Omega_t)$. We can now examine the reputational gains from honoring enforceable and discretionary contracts.

LEMMA 3. *Honoring a discretionary contract at $t = 1$ leads to a strictly greater increase in reputation than honoring an enforceable contract.*

Proof.

$$\psi_1^D(H|h_1) > \psi_1^E(H|h_1), \quad \text{while} \quad \psi_0^D(H|\Omega_0) = \psi_0^E(H|\Omega_0) = \gamma.$$

This result shows that a discretionary contract enables a type-H guarantor to enhance its reputation more than would be possible with an enforceable contract. We now explore this issue further.

LEMMA 4. *Suppose that the first-period contract is discretionary and state C_S occurs at $t = 1$. Then, given the conjectured equilibrium strategies, the effect of adopting strategy h on the expected reputation of X at $t = 2$ is strictly greater if X is of type H than if X is of type L. The impact on the (expected) reputation at $t = 1$ is identical across types.*

Proof. The second part of the lemma is obvious; honoring or defaulting leads to $\psi_1^D(H|h_1)$ and $\psi_1^D(H|d_1)$, respectively, for both H and L. The effect on third-period reputation is only relevant if X remains in business. The expected improvement

---

[7] In the specification of beliefs we have fixed the contract choice. The derivation of the Bayesian perfect Nash equilibrium in the ensuing analysis is more general and allows X to choose between discretionary and enforceable contracts. This is a strategic choice, which may affect Y's beliefs.

in a type-H guarantor's third-period reputation from honoring the discretionary contract (versus defaulting on it) at $t = 1$ is

$$K(\text{H}) = [1 - q]\{1 - [1 - \eta][1 - p_{\text{H}}]\}\psi_2^{\text{D}}(\text{H}|h_1, n_2)$$
$$+ q\{p_{\text{H}} + \eta[1 - p_{\text{H}}]\}\psi_2^{\text{D}}(\text{H}|h_1, h_2)$$
$$- \{[1 - q]\{1 - [1 - \eta][1 - p_{\text{H}}]\}\psi_2^{\text{D}}(\text{H}|d_1, n_2)$$
$$+ q\{p_{\text{H}} + \eta[1 - p_{\text{H}}]\}\psi_2^{\text{D}}(\text{H}|d_1, h_2)\}. \tag{6}$$

The corresponding expression for L is

$$K(\text{L}) = [1 - q]\{1 - [1 - \eta][1 - p_{\text{L}}]\}\psi_2^{\text{D}}(\text{H}|h_1, n_2)$$
$$+ q\{p_{\text{L}} + \eta[1 - p_{\text{L}}]\}\psi_2^{\text{D}}(\text{H}|h_1, h_2)$$
$$- \{[1 - q](1 - [1 - \eta][1 - p_{\text{L}}]\}\psi_2^{\text{D}}(\text{H}|d_1, n_2)$$
$$+ q\{p_{\text{L}} + \eta[1 - p_{\text{L}}]\}\psi_2^{\text{D}}(\text{H}|d_1, h_2)\}. \tag{7}$$

Compare (6) and (7) to see that $K(\text{L}) < K(\text{H})$.

For the first of our two major results, we assume that X is locked into the contract choices stipulated in the conjectured equilibrium.

PROPOSITION 1. *Given the contract choices stipulated in Table 2, there exists a set of parameter values for which the conjectured strategies are incentive-compatible [see the parameter restrictions (A11)–(A13) in the Appendix].*

(See the Appendix for the proof.)

To show that a discretionary contract is preferred in the first period, it is sufficient to identify conditions such that Y weakly prefers a discretionary contract in that period, and a type-H guarantor strictly prefers discretion. The reason for only considering the first period for Y is that contracts in the second and third periods are enforceable, and all future reputational rents accrue to X, so that Y's second- and third-period payoffs are independent of the first-period contract choice. We now have our final result.

PROPOSITION 2. *(i) The strategies stated in Table 2 and the Bayesian beliefs stated in the Appendix constitute a Bayesian perfect Nash equilibrium provided that the parametric conditions (A11)–(A13) hold. In this equilibrium, both H and L choose a discretionary contract in the first period. (ii) Holding Y's net payoffs fixed in each period, a type-H guarantor strictly prefers a discretionary contract in the first period over an enforceable contract, provided that the rents from information reusability exceed some lower bound.*

(See the Appendix for the proof.)

There is another Bayesian perfect Nash equilibrium in pure strategies, one in which both types choose an enforceable contract at $t = 0$. Part (ii) of Proposition 2 shows that H strictly prefers the stated equilibrium if there are sufficient rents from information reusability.

The equilibrium in Proposition 2 has a variety of interesting implications. First, defaults are more common with discretionary guarantees than with enforceable ones offered by a given guarantor. Second, the prices of discretionary guarantees are less than those of enforceable guarantees offered by the same guarantor. Third, across guarantors, prices for discretionary guarantees need not be lower than those for enforceable guarantees. This is because the likelihood of default on a discretionary guarantee provided by a guarantor with a good reputation may not be greater than the likelihood of default on an enforceable guarantee of another with a poorer reputation. Fourth, the price of a guarantee increases in the reputation of the guarantor, and the difference in prices for a given guarantee across guarantors is greater for a discretionary guarantee than for an enforceable one.

We have chosen to focus on parameter values such that a type-H guarantor honors a discretionary contract in state C_S, and type L does not. The general result is that type H always has a greater incentive than type L to honor a discretionary contract.

C. Interpretation

A discretionary contract is more costly to H than an enforceable one in the absence of reputational considerations because H is pooled with L, who always repudiates a discretionary contract. This cost is offset by two benefits of the discretionary contract. First, H is allowed to repudiate a discretionary contract in financially impaired states. This preserves financial capital and prevents the loss of reusable information. Second, because a discretionary contract leads to equilibrium behavior that makes guarantors more distinguishable, it enables H to develop a reputation more effectively. Thus, discretion aids reputation enhancement by facilitating the separation of high and low types.[8] Note also that Y will not purchase a discretionary contract if $\psi_0 = 0$. Thus, discretionary contracts are predictably the stock-in-trade of institutions with reputational capital at the outset.

---

[8] As in other reputation models (e.g. Kreps and Wilson, 1982b; Paul Milgrom and John Roberts 1982), the possibility of ex ante separation of types through signaling has been suppressed in our analysis. It is possible that X could signal its type through an appropriately crafted fee structure that permits intertemporal adjustments that allow the bank to break even across the three periods, but not necessarily in each period. However, given the possibility of a new Y in each period, such fee structures are precluded. Other more complicated schemes are likely to involve *dissipative* signaling and may lead to a greater loss in welfare than that in our reputation-based model.

III. Examples

A. Highly confident letters

Highly confident letters are sold by banks to those concerned with demonstrating their ability to borrow, typically for the purpose of persuading a potential seller of assets of the seriousness of a purchase offer. The highly confident letter is an illusory promise. However, consistent with our theory, customers are willing to pay for these illusory promises. Consider the following quote:

> In February of 1985, Black had a better idea—Drexel would write a letter to advise the banks it was "highly confident" it could raise the money for Icahn. There was nothing legally binding about this letter; it was an expression of faith in Milken's ability to raise a fortune for this Drexel client from Drexel's other clients. But because Milken was known to be a maniac about keeping his promises, the simple fact of his involvement might give the commercial bankers all the courage they needed....
>   Drexel's president [Fred Joseph] agreed that the lack of a legal commitment made the letter an interesting experiment—if it worked, great; if not, nothing significant was lost.
>   [Jesse Kornbluth 1992: 64]

The illusory nature of the promise embedded in the highly confident letter was illustrated by the October 1989 proposed buyout of UAL. Citicorp and Chase Manhattan Corp. jointly agreed to commit $3 billion to the buyout and further indicated they were "highly confident" that they could provide an additional $4.2 billion from other lenders. The two banks were paid combined fees of $8 million for the commitments. The deal fell through, however, when other banks withdrew after initial indications of interest (see *Wall Street Journal*, October 16, 1989: A1).

B. Holding-company cross-guarantees

Holding companies often provide "comfort letters" to assure creditors of their subsidiaries that they would come to their assistance in distress. Enforceable cross-guarantees are avoided, presumably because they reduce the holding company's flexibility in managing financial impairment and could also jeopardize the legal separation among the holding-company entities. Our theory explains why comfort letters (as opposed to implicit promises or no promises) are widely used, even though they are merely illusory promises.

C. Mutual-fund contracts

Managers of investment funds, such as the Dutch property investment fund described earlier, commonly provide publicly observable discretionary guarantees. Although its price-support promise was illusory, Robeco redeemed shares at net asset value. However, consistent with our theory, when confronted with a dumping of its shares, Robeco chose to violate its commitment rather than face financial impairment. This interplay between reputational and financial capital would not have been possible with an enforceable contract.[9]

Price support also has been provided by U.S. mutual-fund managers. For example, in 1989 Integrated Resources, Inc. defaulted on nearly $1 billion of commercial paper, and in March 1990 Mortgage & Realty Trust defaulted on $167 million of commercial paper. Rather than see their investors lose money, money-fund managers on both occasions voluntarily absorbed the losses by buying the defaulted paper at par from the money funds under their management (see *Wall Street Journal*, October 22, 1990: C1). Clearly, there was no legal obligation to do so; these actions were motivated by the desire to sustain investors' beliefs—explicitly engendered through marketing efforts—that the money-fund share price would not fall below $1.[10]

D. The loan commitment

Bank loan commitments are notable for their "general nervous" or "material adverse change" clauses. These permit the commitment to be voided at the sole discretion of the guarantor, conditional on material deterioration in the financial condition of the commitment owner. Material deterioration is typically left undefined, and there is rarely any provision for third-party adjudication of disputes. Bank discretion is therefore triggered in all states short of the borrower's unambiguous financial health or stability, and the bank's commitment then becomes an illusory promise. Thus, the loan commitment does not provide the guarantor unbounded discretion, and our model should be viewed as being applicable to loan commitments in states in which the borrower's financial condition is ambiguous.

Clearly, the loan commitment need not be designed as an illusory promise. The covenants in loan contracts are typically well specified, and the standby letter of credit, a companion contract to the loan commitment, incorporates no analogous lack of enforceability. The discretion–reputation nexus developed here thus provides a novel perspective on the design of loan commitments.

---

[9] The information available on the Robeco case strongly suggests that the company's strategies were driven by reputational considerations. According to the *Financial Times* of October 2, 1990 (p. 30), "In the wake of the Rodamco about-face on share buying, Ronald van de Krol finds the Dutch property fund's owner busily reassuring shareholders that its share and bond funds will remain open-ended.

[10] "Money funds are designed to keep a stable share price, typically $1. Many investors assume the $1 share price is guaranteed, and that money funds are as safe as a bank certificate of deposit or checking account. However, fund managers fear that as the economy weakens, more commercial paper defaults lie ahead; and next time it happens, fund managers may not be able to eat the loss" (*Wall Street Journal*, October 22, 1990: C1).

E. Other examples in financial contracting

The investment banker's "firm commitment" underwriting contract has greater enforceability than a "best efforts" contract under which no commitment about the issue price, or even success in floating the issue, is provided. Success in raising capital with the latter contract should, according to our model, have a greater positive effect on the underwriter's reputation.

Price-stabilization promises for new bond and equity issues during the issuance period can be viewed as illusory promises as well. As with mutual funds, underwriters may choose to support new issues to enhance reputational capital.

F. Nonfinancial applications

Although our analysis focuses on financial contracts, we believe it to have wider applicability, in particular to all situations involving illiquid reputational capital. For example, our theory suggests that firms may offer employment contracts that provide managerial discretion both in terms of the rewards for superior performance and the conditions under which employees may be terminated. That is, employment contracts often contain illusory promises that enable firms to avoid binding commitments and also facilitate the development of the firm's reputation. Note that since firms within the same industry can be expected to have different reputations, the discretionary components of employment contracts offered in an industry should display heterogeneity. Even within the firm, the manager often has discretion over the tasks assigned to subordinates, so that there are reputational effects associated with intrafirm task allocations. However, since the optimal amount of discretion will depend on the nature of the tasks, intrafirm heterogeneity in the discretion given to supervisors can be expected as well.

IV. Conclusion

We have shown that discretionary guarantees can be desirable. Contractual discretion offers two advantages. First, the guarantor can repudiate a claim in a state in which reputational capital is optimally sacrificed in order to preserve financial capital and reusable information. This substitution can promote efficiency because the (dissipative) sacrifice of reputation preserves the reusability of information which may be lost if the guarantor is compelled to honor a claim in a financially impaired state. Second, the discretionary contract fosters reputation enhancement, thereby increasing future fee income.

The theory also provides a new perspective on reputation models which typically take the contract as given and then examine incentives for reputation development. We have shown that discretion expands the potential for reputation development; thus, better agents have an incentive to choose discretionary contracts. Moreover, the discretionary contract provides a mechanism for the transmission of information necessary for reputation development. Thus, even though legally unenforceable, the discretionary contract is superior to having no explicit promise.

The empirical predictions of our theory are as follows. (i) The better the guarantor's reputation, the greater is its incentive to write discretionary contracts. The reason is that, with an exemplary reputation, the fees that a better (type-H) guarantor receives for discretionary contracts are only minimally affected by the negative externality imposed by the lesser (type-L) guarantor. (ii) Prices of discretionary guarantees will be lower than for otherwise similar enforceable guarantees written by the same guarantor. (iii) Since a discretionary guarantee of a highly reputed guarantor can be more valuable than an enforceable guarantee of a less-reputable guarantor, prices of discretionary guarantees need not be less than those for enforceable guarantees (across guarantors with different reputations). (iv) The better a guarantor's reputation, the higher will be the price of any guarantee.[11]

Our theory predicts a link between guarantor reputation and the prices of guarantees, and also predicts that the difference between prices for a *given* guarantee across intermediaries with disparate reputations is greater for a discretionary guarantee than for an enforceable one. Moreover, since the choice of contract depends on the nature of the transaction as well as the reputation of the guarantor, our theory has the distinctive feature of predicting diversity among contracts within a firm and across firms within a given industry.

APPENDIX

Derivation of Bayesian beliefs

We do not include the termination state T in the specification of Bayesian beliefs. In the expressions below, $S_i = \{1 - [1 - \eta][1 - p_i]\}$ is the "survival probability" of type i. Thus, we have

$$\psi_1^D(H|h_1) = \psi_2^D(H|h_1, n_2) = \psi_2^D(H|h_1, h_2) = 1$$

$$\psi_1^D(H|n_1) = \psi^E(H|n_1) = \gamma S_H[\gamma S_H + (1 - \gamma)S_L]^{-1}$$

$$\psi_2^D(H|n_1, n_2) = \psi_1^E(H|n_1, n_2) = \gamma S_H^2[\gamma S_H^2 + (1 - \gamma)S_L^2]^{-1}$$

---

[11] It should be possible to test some of these predicitions. For example, measures of underwriter reputation among investment bankers are available (see Samuel Hayes 1971; Richard Carter and Steven Manaster 1990).

$$\psi_1^D(H|d_1) = \gamma\eta(1-p_H)\{\gamma\eta(1-p_H) + (1-\gamma)[p_L + \eta(1-p_L)]\}^{-1}$$

$$\psi_2^D(H|d_1, n_2) = \gamma\eta(1-p_H)S_H\{\gamma\eta(1-p_H)S_H + (1-\gamma)[p_L + \eta(1-p_L)]S_L\}^{-1}$$

$$\psi_2^D(H|d_1, h_2) = \gamma\eta(1-p_H)[p_H + \eta(1-p_H)]\{\gamma\eta(1-p_H)[p_H + \eta(1-p_H)]$$
$$+ (1-\gamma)[p_L + \eta(1-p_L)][p_L + \eta(1-p_L)]\}^{-1}$$

$$\psi_2^D(H|n_1, h_2) = \psi_2^E(H|n_1, h_2) = \gamma S_H[p_H + \eta(1-p_H)]$$
$$\times \{\gamma S_H[p_H + \eta(1-p_H)] + (1-\gamma)S_L[p_L + \eta(1-p_L)]\}^{-1}$$

$$\psi_1^E(H|h_1) = \gamma[p_H + \eta(1-p_H)]\{\gamma[p_H + \eta(1-p_H)] + (1-\gamma)[p_L + \eta(1-p_L)]\}^{-1}$$

$$\psi_2^E(H|h_1, n_2) = \gamma[p_H + \eta(1-p_H)]S_H\{\gamma[p_H + \eta(1-p_H)]S_H + (1-\gamma)$$
$$\times [p_L + \eta(1-p_L)]S_L\}^{-1}$$

$$\psi_2^E(H|h_1, h_2) = \gamma[p_H + \eta(1-p_H)]^2\{\gamma[p_H + \eta(1-p_H)]^2 + (1-\gamma)$$
$$\times [p_L + \eta(1-p_L)]^2\}^{-1}$$

Proof of Lemma 1. We will prove that this is a Nash equilibrium by first establishing that the bank's pricing policy is a best response to the borrower's project choice and that the borrower's project choice is a best response to the bank's pricing policy. The parametric condition stated is identical to

$$\xi_\ell[S_\ell - \underline{R}/\xi_\ell] > \xi_h[S_h - \underline{R}/\xi_\ell] \tag{A1}$$

$$\xi_\ell[S_\ell - \overline{R}/\xi_\ell] < \xi_h[S_h - \overline{R}/\xi_\ell] \tag{A2}$$

Note that (A1) and (A2) imply that, *given* the bank's (equilibrium) pricing policy, the borrower will not deviate from its choice of ℓ if $\tilde{R} = \underline{R}$ and its choice of h if $\tilde{R} = \overline{R}$. The only out-of-equilibrium move for the borrower is to take no loan at all, but then it is strictly worse off than in the equilibrium. Thus, the borrower's project choice is a best response to the bank's pricing policy for each realization of the spot rate. Now, from (A1), we know that a bank that lends at $\underline{R}/\xi_\ell$, when $\tilde{R} = \underline{R}$, induces the borrower to choose project ℓ. Given this pricing policy, the (perfectly competitive) bank makes zero expected profit. If it were to choose a higher interest rate, it would lose the borrower to a competing bank (which gives the bank no greater profit than its equilibrium profit), and a lower interest rate would yield an expected loss. From (A2) it follows that if $\tilde{R} = \overline{R}$, the bank makes a loss by pricing the loan under the presumption that a borrower chooses project ℓ; the bank must assume a project choice h and price the loan at $\overline{R}/\xi_h$ to earn zero expected profit. A higher interest rate would cause the borrower to go to a competing bank. Thus, the bank's (equilibrium) pricing policy is a best response to the borrower's project choice for each realization of the spot rate.

Proof of Proposition 1. We adopt the usual approach and solve the model backwards, starting with $t = 2$ (the beginning of the third period). At $t = 2$, agent X with reputation ψ_2^D can charge the following fee for the guarantee:

$$f_2^E\left(\psi_2^D\right) = q\left\{\psi_2^D[p_H + \eta(1 - p_H)] + \left(1 - \psi_2^D\right)[p_L + \eta(1 - p_L)]\right\}M. \tag{A3}$$

A new intermediary with a reputation of $\psi_2^D = \gamma$ charges a premium of

$$\phi_2^E(\gamma) = q\{p_H + \eta(1 - p_H)\}M - f_2^E(\gamma) + \overline{V} \tag{A4}$$

where $q\{p_H + \eta(1 - P_H)\}M$ is the expected liability on the guarantee for a type H, $f_2^E(\gamma)$ is the guarantee fee, and $\overline{V}$ is the information-production cost. The price (i.e. total compensation) $f_2^E(\gamma) + \phi_2^E(\gamma)$ is such that the participation constraint for a de novo intermediary is just satisfied. We let the price that X can charge be anchored by the amount required for a new intermediary to participate. An intermediary of type H with reputation ψ_2^D receives a premium of

$$\phi_2^E\left(\psi_2^D\right) = \phi_2^E(\gamma) + \left(\psi_2^D - \gamma\right)(p_H - p_L)(1 - \eta)qP. \tag{A5}$$

The total compensation, $f_2^E\left(\psi_2^D\right) + \phi_2^E\left(\psi_2^D\right)$, reflects three sources of rents. First, it receives a higher guarantee fee, $f_2^E\left(\psi_2^D\right)$ (if $\psi_2^D > \gamma$). Second, it can extract rents because the expected value of the social loss P faced by Y is strictly lower if Y contracts with an established guarantor (with $\psi_2^D > \gamma$) instead of a de novo X. This rent to the type-H guarantor is

$$\left(\psi_2^D - \gamma\right)(p_H - p_L)(1 - \eta)qP.$$

Third, X earns rents on information reusability. Define $F_i(\psi_t)$ as the net rent earned in the period following t by a type $i \in \{L, H\}$ with reputation ψ_t. If H enters the third period with a reputation of ψ_2^D, he earns a *net* rent of

$$F_H\left(\psi_2^D\right) = f_2^E\left(\psi_2^D\right) + \phi_2^E\left(\psi_2^D\right) - \tilde{V} - q\{p_H + \eta(1 - p_H)\}M \tag{A6}$$

with $\tilde{V}$ equal to $\underline{V}$ or V^*, depending on the prior state realization. Substituting (A5) in (A6), and taking into account (A3) and (A4), yields

$$F_H\left(\psi_2^D\right) = \left(\psi_2^D - \gamma\right)(p_H - p_L)(1 - \eta)q(M + P) + \overline{V} - \tilde{V}. \tag{A7}$$

Similarly, for L we have

$$F_L\left(\psi_2^D\right) = \left(\psi_2^D - \gamma\right)(p_H - p_L)(1 - \eta)q(M + P) + \overline{V} - \tilde{V} + q(p_H - p_L)(1 - \eta)M. \tag{A8}$$

We now analyze the second-period solution. Using steps similar to those for the third period, we can write

$$F_H\left(\psi_1^D\right) = \left(\psi_1^D - \gamma\right)(p_H - p_L)(1 - \eta)q(M + P) + \overline{V} - \underline{V} \tag{A9}$$

$$F_L\left(\psi_1^D\right)=\left(\psi_1^D-\gamma\right)(p_H-p_L)(1-\eta)q(M+P)+\overline{V}-\underline{V}+q(p_H-p_L)(1-\eta)M. \quad \text{(A10)}$$

(Note that the discretionary first-period contract preserves full benefits of information reusability.)

We now show that if state C_S is realized at the end of the first period, H will honor the discretionary first-period contract and L will not. H will honor the contract at $t=1$ if the loss of financial capital from doing so, M, is less than the future gains of honoring, which is the excess of expected future rents from honoring over the expected future rents if it defaults. Thus, H honors the contract if

$$M < F_H\left(\psi_1^D(H|h_1)\right) + qp_HF_H\left(\psi_2^D(H|h_1,h_2),\underline{V}\right)$$

$$+ \eta q(1-p_H)F_H\left(\psi_2^D(H|h_1,h_2),V^*\right) + (1-q)[1-(1-\eta)(1-p_H)]F_H$$

$$\times \left(\psi_2^D(H|h_1,n_2)\right) - F_H\left(\psi_1^D(H|d_1)\right) - qp_HF_H\left(\psi_2^D(H|d_1,h_2),\underline{V}\right)$$

$$- \eta q(1-p_H)F_H\left(\psi_2^D(H|d_1,h_2),V^*\right)$$

$$- (1-q)[1-(1-\eta)(1-p_H)]F_H\left(\psi_2^D(H|d_1,n_2)\right). \quad \text{(A11)}$$

Similarly, L will choose to default in state C_S if

$$M > F_L\left(\psi_1^D(H|h_1)\right) + qp_LF_L\left(\psi_2^D(H|h_1,h_2),\underline{V}\right) + \eta q(1-p_L)F_L\left(\psi_2^D(H|h_1,h_2),V^*\right)$$

$$+ (1-q)[1-(1-\eta)(1-p_L)]F_L(\psi_2^D(H|h_1,n_2)) - F_L\left(\psi_1^D(H|d_1)\right)$$

$$- qp_LF_L\left(\psi_2^D(H|d_1,h_2),\underline{V}\right) - \eta q(1-p_L)F_L\left(\psi_2^D(H|d_1,h_2),V^*\right)$$

$$- (1-q)[1-(1-\eta)(1-p_L)]F_L\left(\psi_2^D(H|d_1,n_2)\right). \quad \text{(A12)}$$

Substituting (A7)–(A10) into (A11) and (A12) allows us to write the following expressions:

$$M < (p_H-p_L)(1-\eta)q(M+D)$$

$$\times \left\{\left[\psi_1^D(H|h_1)\right] - \psi_1^D(H|d_1)\right] + q[p_H+\eta(1-p_H)]$$

$$\times \left[\psi_2^D(H|h_1,h_2) - \psi_2^D(H|d_1,h_2)\right]$$

$$+[1-(1-\eta)(1-p_H)]\left[\psi_2^D(H|h_1,n_2) - \psi_2^D(H|d_1,n_2)\right]\right\} \quad \text{(A13)}$$

and

$$M > (p_H-p_L)(1-\eta)q(M+D)\left\{\left[\psi_1^D(H|h_1) - \psi_1^D(H|d_1)\right]\right.$$

$$+ q[p_L+\eta(1-p_L)]\left[\psi_2^D(H|h_1,h_2) - \psi_2^D(H|d_1,h_2)\right]$$

$$\left.+[1-(1-\eta)(1-p_L)]\left[\psi_2^D(H|h_1,n_2) - \psi_2^D(H|d_1,n_2)\right]\right\}. \quad \text{(A14)}$$

The right-hand side (RHS) in (A13) exceeds the RHS in (A14). It follows immediately that for any set of parameters there exists a range of values of M for which both inequalities hold.

We also have to show that both H and L will choose to default in the state C_I at $t = 1$. Recall that a decision to honor the discretionary contract in that state will lead to *partial* loss of information reusability in the next period. This enhances the benefit of not honoring by $V^* - \underline{V}$. To sustain the conjectured strategies, we now require that

$$M + V^* - \underline{V} > \text{RHS of (A13)} \qquad \text{(A15)}$$

and

$$M + V^* - \underline{V} > \text{RHS of (A14).} \qquad \text{(A16)}$$

Obviously, given (A14), (A16) is satisfied. It is easy to see that (A15) is compatible with (A13), and that for all values of $V^* - \underline{V}$ there exist values of M that satisfy (A13)–(A15).

Proof of Proposition 2. First, we will verify the conjectured equilibrium strategies conditioned on a discretionary contract in the first period. Two actions are possible: honor or default. In the conjectured equilibrium, both are observed. Given that (A13) and (A14) hold, it is straightforward to verify that, depending on type, X will honor or default on the first-period contract in state C_S according to the conjectures in Table 2 (i.e. compute the Bayesian posteriors and compare the intertemporal payoff to X; see also the proof of Proposition 1). Given that (A15) holds, the same is true for X's strategies in state C_I. In state T, X's choice of strategy is fixed (i.e. X is terminated and thus defaults). X's choice of strategy in the second and third period is fixed as well (the contracts in those periods are enforceable).

We will now verify the choice of first-period contract. The choice between an enforceable and a discretionary contract is *strategic*. Given the conjectured equilibrium, a choice of an enforceable contract at $t = 0$ is an out-of-equilibrium move. No other out-of-equilibrium moves exist. Define $\mu(\text{H}|\text{E})$ as the market's belief (i.e. the probability that the defector is type H given the out-of-equilibrium move E [choosing an enforceable contract]). It follows that for $\mu(\text{H}|\text{E})$ sufficiently small, neither type will defect. Take, for instance, $\mu(\text{H}|\text{E}) = 0$; then ψ_1^E (defection) $= \psi_2^E$(defection) $= 0$, and contracting would produce negative rents. This proves that the conjectured equilibrium is a Bayesian perfect Nash equilibrium. The alternative equilibrium involves both L and H choosing an enforceable contract in the first period. The strategies for $t = 2$ and $t = 3$ are those specified in Table 2. Choosing a discretionary contract is now an out-of-equilibrium move; but with the belief $\mu(\text{H}|\text{D}) = 0$, this equilibrium can be sustained.

Recall that a benefit of a discretionary contract is that it preserves full reusability of information in state C_I (i.e. it preserves the rents $V^* - \underline{V}$ that would be lost with the enforceable contract). Thus, the Bayesian perfect Nash equilibrium stated in this proposition is preferred by H if these rents are sufficiently large (details available from the authors upon request).

References

Akerlof, George, A. (1982). "Labor contracts as partial gift exchange." *Quarterly Journal of Economics*, 97: 543–69.

Allen, F., and Gale, D. (1992). "Measurement distortion and missing contingencies in optimal contracts." *Economic Theory*, 2: 1–26.

Ayres, I., and Gertner, R. (1992). "Strategic contractual inefficiency and the optimal choice of legal rules." *Yale Law Journal*, 101: 729–74.

Aziardis, C. (1975). "Implicit contracts and unemployment equilibria." *Journal of Political Economy*, 83: 1183–202.

Boot, A. W. A., and Thakor, A. V. (1992). "Ambiguity and moral hazard." Working paper, Indiana University, August.

Bull, C. (1987). "The existence of self-enforcing implicit contracts." *Quarterly Journal of Economics*, 102: 147–59.

Calamari, J. D., and Perillo, J. M. (1977). *The Law of Contracts* (2nd ed.). St. Paul, MN: West.

Carter, R., and Manaster, S. (1990). "Initial public offerings and underwriter reputation." *Journal of Finance*, 45: 1045–67.

Chan, Y.-S., Greenbaum, S. I., and Thakor, A. V. (1986). "Information reusability, competition and bank asset quality." *Journal of Banking and Finance*, 10: 243–53.

Corbin, A. L. (1952). *Corbin on contracts: A comprehensive treatise on the rules of contract law.* St. Paul, MN: West.

Corrigan, E. G. (1990). "Reforming the U.S. financial system: An international perspective." *Quarterly Review of the Federal Reserve Bank of New York*, 15: 1–14.

Craswell, R., and Calfee, J. E. (1986). "Deterrence and uncertain legal standards." *Journal of Law, Economics, and Organization*, 2: 279–302.

Hadfield, G. K. (1990). "Problematic relations: Franchising and the law of incomplete contracts." *Stanford Law Review*, 42: 927–92.

Hart, O., and Moore, J. (1988). "Incomplete contracts and renegotiation." *Econometrica*, 55: 755–85.

Hayes, S. (1971). "Investment banking: Power structure in flux." *Harvard Business Review*, 49: 136–52.

Holmström, B., and Milgrom, P. (1991). "Multi-task principal agent problems: Incentive contracts, asset ownership, and job design." *Journal of Law, Economics, and Organization*, 7: 24–52.

John, K., and Nachman, D. (1985). "Risky debt, investment incentives, and reputation in a sequential equilibrium." *Journal of Finance*, 40: 863–78.

Kornbluth, J. (1992). *Highly Confident: The True Story of the Crime and Punishment of Michael Milken.* New York: Morrow.

Kreps, D. M., and Wilson, R. (1982*a*). "Sequential equilibria." *Econometrica*, 50: 863–94.

——, and —— (1982*b*). "Reputation and imperfect information." *Journal of Economic Theory*, 27: 253–79.

Metzger, M. B., and Phillips, M. J. (1990). "Promissory Estoppel and reliance on illusory promises." *Southwestern Law Journal*, 44: 841–903.

Milgrom, P. R., and Roberts, J. (1982). "Predation, reputation, and entry deterrence." *Journal of Economic Theory*, 27: 280–312.

Sacasas, R. (1989). "The comfort letter trap: Parent companies beware." *Banking Law Journal*, 106: 173–82.

Williamson, O. (1975). *Markets and Hierarchies: Analysis and Anti-Trust Implications: A Study in the Economics of Internal Organization.* New York: Free Press.

16

The Effect of Credit Market Competition on Lending Relationships

Mitchell A. Petersen and Raghuram G. Rajan

Is it possible for firms facing competitive credit markets to form strong ties to particular creditors? Does the benefit to a firm of forming such relationships diminish when credit markets get more competitive? There is a theoretical reason for believing that credit market competition may be inimical to the formation of mutually beneficial relationships between firms and specific creditors. When a firm is young or distressed, the potential for future cash flows from its projects may be high, while the actual cash it generates is low. When evaluating the creditworthiness of the firm, a creditor should take into account the stream of future profits the firm may generate. When the credit market is competitive and creditors cannot hold equity claims, the lender cannot expect to share in the future surplus of the firm. She is constrained to break even on a period-by-period basis because she would drive away business if she charged a rate above the competitive one. Since uncertainty about a firm's prospects is high when the firm is young or distressed, creditors in a competitive market may be forced to charge a high interest rate until the uncertainty is resolved. This can be extremely distortionary to the firm's incentives and may, in fact, result in the firm not receiving credit at all. A monopolistic creditor, on the other hand, shares in the future surplus generated by the firm through the future rents she is able to extract.

We thank Alan Berger, Judith Chevalier, Constance Dunham, Mark Flannery, Michael Gibson, Anne Grøn, Oliver Hart, Steven Kaplan, Robert McDonald, George Pennacchi, Canice Prendergast, Rafael Repullo, Ivo Welch, Lawrence White, and John Wolken for valuable comments on a previous draft. We are again grateful to John Wolken for making a special effort to provide us with some of the data. The editor, Andrei Shleifer, and two anonymous referees made suggestions that improved the chapter significantly. We also thank workshop participants at Brigham Young University, the University of California at Los Angeles, Carnegie Mellon University, the Center for Economic Policy Research Conference on Financial Regulation at Toulouse, the Conference on Industrial Organization and Finance at San Sebastian, the University of Chicago, Columbia University, the Federal Reserve Board, the Federal Reserve Banks of Atlanta and Minneapolis, Harvard Business School, Indiana University, London School of Economics, Massachusetts Institute of Technology, Northwestern University, Southern Methodist University, Stanford University, Virginia Polytechnical Institute, the University of Wisconsin, and the Utah Winter Finance Conference for their insights.

She can backload interest payments over time, subsidizing the firm when young or distressed and extracting rents later. Consequently, she may be more willing to offer credit than a similarly placed lender in a competitive market. In other words, credit market competition imposes constraints on the ability of the firm and creditor to intertemporally share surplus. This makes lending relationships less valuable to a firm because it cannot expect to get help when most in need.

The argument that relationships and competition are incompatible recurs in other subdisciplines in economics.[1] For instance, labor economists claim that a firm is more reluctant to invest in training workers in a competitive labor market unless they post a bond, since workers can threaten to quit and demand a competitive salary once they are trained [Becker 1975]. While there is anecdotal evidence in the financial press suggesting that this kind of phenomenon is a reality, there is little formal supporting evidence in the academic literature.[2] This is partly because periods of increased competition are, in general, also accompanied by other changes that may make relationships less valuable. It is thus difficult to disentangle the effects. For example, Hoshi, Kashyap, and Scharfstein [1990] document that high quality Japanese firms moved away from their banks when the domestic bond markets were liberalized. This movement may reflect the adverse effects of competition on relationships. Alternatively, this movement may simply reflect a reshuffling of borrowing by firms that previously did not have access to public markets. The ideal test would examine the effects of competition on relationships in a situation where firms are not simultaneously faced with a change in the sources of capital available to them.

In this chapter we focus our analysis on small businesses in the United States. Such firms concentrate their external borrowing from banks (see Petersen and Rajan [1994]), and therefore the confounding effect of the portfolio choice problem discussed above is minor. In different regions of the country, the degree of

---

[1] The basic argument dates back, at least, to Schumpeter who proposed that a monopolistic economy offers better incentives for innovation because an inventor can recoup her investment in R&D through future rents. Mayer [1988] introduces this problem to the finance literature discussing the general inability of firms and creditors to commit to a mutually beneficial course of action. Fischer [1990] models the problem posed by competitive credit markets formally and suggests that a way for a firm to commit to sharing future rents with the bank is to give the latter an informational monopoly. Rajan [1992] argues that even the bank's information monopoly may be insufficient to bind the firm when competition comes from arm's-length markets.

[2] *The Economist* [November 13, 1993: 84] describes the problem as follows:

... banks remain unable to charge prices that reflect the high risks of lending to small companies. Startups are especially risky; not only do plenty of them fail, but those that succeed tend to exploit their success by refinancing their debt more cheaply .... One big British bank reckons that to make a profit today it would have to double interest margins on its loans, from an average of three percentage points over the base rate. That might provoke the government to intervene.

So banks are looking for other ways to boost returns from borrowers that succeed. Some, such as Midland, would like to take small equity stakes. Others talk of introducing a clause into loan agreements that would give the bank a one-off fee if a borrower wanted to refinance its debt. Customers are understandably unkeen.

competition between banks varies, partly because of restrictions on bank entry and branching, and partly because there is only so much banking business a local market can support. Thus, we can isolate the effects of competition on relationships in this sample.

In the next section we present a simple model that highlights the distinction between competitive and concentrated credit markets. In Section II we describe the data and the empirical tests. We find that significantly more young firms obtain external financing in concentrated markets than in competitive markets. Underlying differences in firm quality across markets do not appear to explain the differential access to capital. As the theory suggests, creditors smooth interest rates intertemporally in more concentrated markets, which may explain why they are able to provide more finance. We conclude in Section III with policy implications and suggestions for future research.

I. The Model

A. Agents and investment opportunities

Assume a risk-neutral world where there are two types of agents looking for finance: good entrepreneurs and bad entrepreneurs. At date 0, good entrepreneurs can choose either a safe project or a risky project. A safe project pays out S_1 at date 1 when amount I_0 is invested in it. Furthermore, when the project concludes, the good entrepreneur will be able to invest I_{1S} in another safe project that returns S_2. Alternatively, if the good entrepreneur chooses to gamble at date 0, he can invest I_0 in the risky project. At date 1, the risky project may succeed and pay out R_1 with probability p, or it may fail and pay 0 with probability $(1 - p)$. If it succeeds, he can invest I_{1R} in a safe project that pays R_2 at date 2. In contrast to good entrepreneurs, the projects of bad entrepreneurs are doomed to fail and return nothing at date 1.[3]

We also make the following assumptions:

$$S_2 + S_1 - I_{1S} - I_0 > 0; \tag{A.1}$$

$$p(R_2 + R_1 - I_{1R}) - I_0 < 0; \tag{A.2}$$

$$pR_2 = S_2 > pI_{1R} = I_{1S}; \tag{A.3}$$

$$I_{1S} > R_1 > S_1. \tag{A.4}$$

A.1 is simply that the safe project has positive net present value (NPV) in this risk-neutral world, while A.2 implies that the risky project has negative

---

[3] Bad entrepreneurs are the incompetent, the lazy, and the dishonest in the population of potential entrepreneurs. The incompetent invest in the wrong projects and consequently waste the investment; the lazy do not put in effort and see their investment wither away; and the dishonest steal the money or extract excessive private benefits from the firm.

NPV. A.3 implies that the future positive NPV project has the same expected returns and investment, regardless of whether the safe or risky project is chosen at date 0. Finally, A.4 implies that the revenue from the date 0 project is insufficient to finance the project at date 1.

B. Finance

Financial institutions are the only source of external finance in this market. For simplicity, we call these institutions banks. Agents know whether they are good or bad entrepreneurs. At date 0, banks only know that a fraction θ of the agents that demand finance are good entrepreneurs. Thus, θ is a measure of the ex ante credit quality of the agents. A number of studies suggest that a lending bank learns a lot about the kind of entrepreneur it is dealing with over the course of its relationship with the entrepreneur (for example, see the evidence in Lummer and McConnell [1989] and Petersen and Rajan [1994]). Therefore, we assume that at date 1 the bank becomes fully informed about the kind of agent with whom it is dealing. We also assume that for regulatory reasons banks can only hold debt claims, that is, contracts which require a fixed repayment by the borrower.[4] Due to the difficulty of describing investments or the character of the entrepreneur to courts, contracts cannot be made contingent on the project taken or the type of agent.[5] Finally, the bank can charge a rate such that its expected return on loans is M. M is a measure of the market power the bank has. In this risk-neutral world where the risk-free rate is zero, we get perfect competition in the credit market when M equals 1, while a bank has market power when M is greater than 1. For simplicity, we assume that [6]

$$S_2/I_{1S} > M \geq 1. \tag{A.5}$$

The borrowing process is as follows. The agent (the good or bad entrepreneur) goes to a bank and indicates how much he wants to borrow and for what maturity. The bank responds by quoting an interest rate that will give it an expected return less than or equal to M. If no interest rate gives the bank an expected return greater than or equal to its cost of funds (= 1), it turns down the loan. In what follows, we determine how the quality of firms getting financed, and the amount they pay for credit over time, varies with the bank's market power.

---

[4] In a more detailed model, we could motivate debt as a way of extracting cash from entrepreneurs, as, for example, in Hart and Moore [1989], or the optimal contract in a costly state verification setting as in Diamond [1984].

[5] See Myers [1977] and Hart and Moore [1989] for a discussion of the difficulties in writing such contingent contracts.

[6] The first inequality in A.5 limits the number of cases we have to examine and does not change the qualitative implications. In a more detailed model, M could be the outcome of a bargaining game.

C. Solving the model

This problem is a straightforward application of Diamond [1989] and Stiglitz and Weiss [1981].[7] At date 0, good entrepreneurs cannot distinguish themselves from bad ones. Therefore, they can borrow only at a rate that compensates the bank for possible losses if the entrepreneur turns out to be bad. The higher interest rate can distort the entrepreneur's incentives and persuade him to choose the risky project. Thus, adverse selection can cause moral hazard which in turn can lead to credit rationing.

To see this, first note that good entrepreneurs will try to reduce their own cost of borrowing by asking for terms that help expose the bad entrepreneurs. A bad entrepreneur will have no choice but to ask for the same terms at date 0. Since bad entrepreneurs have no new projects at date 1, the bank will not give them new money unless it has contracted to do so. Knowing this, good entrepreneurs will borrow as little as possible at date 0, so they can take advantage of the lower rate at date 1 when the bad entrepreneurs have been exposed. Therefore, a good entrepreneur will seek to borrow only I_0 at date 0. Without loss of generality, we assume that he proposes to repay amount D_1 at date 1, after which he will contract a new loan for any subsequent project.[8]

If the good entrepreneur chooses the safe project at date 0, at date 1 he must borrow

$$I_{1S} - (S_1 - D_1). \tag{1}$$

He can now borrow at the risk-free full-information rate M.[9] If the good entrepreneur chooses the safe project at date 0, he expects

$$\max[S_2 - M(I_{1S} - (S_1 - D_1)), 0]. \tag{2}$$

Similarly, his expected profit if he chooses the risky project is

$$\max\{p_1\{R_2 - M[I_{1R} - (R_1 - D_1)]\}, 0\}. \tag{3}$$

Using assumptions A.3, A.4, and A.5, the good entrepreneur strictly prefers the safe project if

$$(S_1 - pR_1)/(1 - p) \geq D_1. \tag{4}$$

[7] Our model is functionally identical to Becker [1975]. Our competitive credit market is his general training. Our concentrated credit market is his specific training.

[8] In other words, the firm borrows short term each period. Clearly, the firm could borrow at date 0 and spread repayments between date 1 and date 2. Since the discount rate is 0, this has no effect in the model and is omitted for simplicity. Of course, we allow for the fact that the good entrepreneur may not have enough cash to repay the loan at date 1.

[9] Note that the bank has no incentive to forgive debt (as long as expected cash flows are enough to meet the contracted repayments) at date 1, since there is no moral hazard or adverse selection problem at date 1.

For the bank to lend at date 0, two conditions must be satisfied. First, the loan must be structured so that the good entrepreneur has the incentive to take the safe project. This is inequality (4). In addition, the bank must expect to recover its date 0 investment I_0. Taking into account the profit it can make by charging the maximum interest rate on loans made at date 1, this implies that the bank will lend only if

$$D_1 \geq \frac{I_0}{\theta M} - \frac{M-1}{M}(I_{1S} - S_1). \tag{5}$$

Using (4) and (5), only entrepreneurs with credit quality greater than

$$\theta^c(M) = \frac{I_0(1-p)}{M(S_1 - pR_1) + (M-1)(I_{1S} - S_1)(1-p)} \tag{6}$$

will get financed.

Result 1. As the market power M of the bank increases, firms with lower credit quality obtain finance.

The intuition is straightforward. As the market power of the bank increases, it can extract a larger share of the future surplus generated by the firm. This implicit equity stake in the firm enables it to set a lower interest rate for the initial project (compared with a more competitive situation). The surplus extracted in the future does not affect the firm's choice between projects (see equation(4)), but the lower initial rate D_1 gives the firm an incentive to take the safe project. Consequently, firms of lower quality can be profitably financed.

The interest rate charged for funds lent at date 1 is M. But at date 0, the face value demanded, D_1 is bounded by

$$\min\left[\frac{I_0 M}{\theta}, \frac{S_1 - pR_1}{1-p}\right] \geq D_1 \geq \frac{I_0}{\theta M} - \frac{M-1}{M}(I_{1S} - S_1). \tag{7}$$

The first argument of the minimum function is the limit set on the interest rate by the bank's market power, while the second is the limit set by moral hazard. The term after the second inequality is the bank's individual rationality condition. For the lowest quality firm financed by the bank with market power M, the binding upper limit on the interest rate is moral hazard. The lower binding constraint is the bank's individual rationality condition which depends on M. Therefore,

Result 2. The initial interest rate contracted by the lowest quality firm financed by a bank with market power M is lower than it would be if such a firm were to be financed by a bank with market power M', where $M > M'$.

Finally, let t be the ratio of the face value charged per dollar lent at date 1 to the face value charged per dollar lent at date 0. This is the ratio of gross interest rates. Then for any initial credit quality θ and banks with market power M and M', where $M > M'$,

$$t(M) \geq t(M'). \tag{8}$$

In a population of firms where θ has positive density everywhere on $[0,1]$,

$$\text{Average}(t(M)) \geq \text{Average}(t(M')). \tag{9}$$

Result 3. On average, the relative decline in demanded repayments as the firm gets older is lower when the bank has more market power.

D. Caveats: Contractual remedies

Our main point, similar to Townsend [1992] and Gertler [1992], is that multiperiod state-contingent contracts allow for more efficient contracting than single or multiperiod fixed payoff contracts. In the environment we analyze, back-loaded state-contingent interest payments are less distortionary than front-loaded fixed interest payments. A creditor with market power can convert the latter into the former, which is why efficiency increases with creditor market power. There are obvious caveats.

We have abstracted from a variety of contracts that could commit the firm to sharing surplus with the lender, even in a competitive environment. For example, we have assumed that regulators do not allow creditors to hold equity claims. However, equity contracts may not be feasible even if allowed, since dividend payments are voluntary. Diamond [1984] and Hart and Moore [1989] specify environments where a firm's management will never voluntarily part with cash. One way to force management to pay out cash in these environments is through debt contracts. Another way that we emphasize above is for a supplier to have market power in an essential input (credit) which enables it to extract cash from the firm. Thus, the implicit equity stake that market power confers may be feasible even when explicit equity stakes are not.

The reader may wonder why long-term debt contracts between the firm and the bank in the competitive environment cannot replicate the same payments over time as those determined by market power. The reason, quite simply, is that the payments due on the long-term debt do not—and cannot—vary with the project taken. The share of the surplus the bank gets by virtue of its market power does, however, vary. The firm has to pay more to the bank if the risky (but ex post profitable) project succeeds. This reduces the owner's incentive to shift risk.[10] This also explains why contracts that require a high initial payment, and then commit the bank to relending at a lower-than-competitive rate will not work. These contracts have the effect of making the firm's payments conditional on the risky project succeeding lower and thus increase the firm's incentive to shift risk.

---

[10] This is because the rent on the funds lent conditional on the risky project succeeding is $(M-1)[I_{1R} - (R_1 - D_1)]$ which using A.1 and A.2 is easily shown to exceed the rent on the funds lent for continuing the safe project $(M-1)[I_{1S} - (S_1 - D_1)]$. This result holds much more generally. All we need for it to go through is that the bank receive a larger amount from projects which have higher NPV (net present value). This would happen if the firm expands and directs more business toward the bank, or if the bank uses its bargaining power to extract some of the additional NPV for itself.

Within the class of debt contracts, however, complicated bonding contracts could commit the firm to sharing surplus. For example, the entrepreneur could commit to asking the bank for a loan at date 1 (giving it a "first-right-of-refusal") at a predetermined high rate.[11] There may be practical difficulties in enforcing such a contract, primarily because the successful firm in a competitive credit market can easily find ways of borrowing without violating the letter of the "first-right-of-refusal" contract. For instance, the entrepreneur could take out a personal loan from another source, collateralized by the shares of the firm, or sell equity and use the proceeds to repay the high-priced loan. A contract ruling out such contingencies would be costly to write and difficult to enforce. Another problem is that having bonded the entrepreneur, the bank has no incentive to offer good service. Finally, it is possible that a populist legal system may refuse to enforce contracts which appear (ex post) to be extortionary. Thus, bilateral opportunism or political realities may make these contracts impractical.

We have also abstracted from the distortions to the firm's investment incentives created by the bank's market power. Even if these are large, Results 1, 2, and 3 will continue to hold as long as the bank can contractually dispose of its ability to extract future rents, as for example, by signing a loan commitment contract. The contract would need a "material adverse change" clause allowing the bank to deny credit to bad entrepreneurs. While such contracts are observed, opportunism may again make them impractical.

In summary, the theory is ambiguous on whether the problem we have described can be effectively contracted around, though casual empiricism (see note 2) suggests it cannot. The test of whether it is important, however, must be an empirical one.

II. Data and Empirical Investigation

A. Sample description

The data in this study are obtained from the National Survey of Small Business Finances. The survey was conducted in 1988–1989 under the guidance of the Board of Governors of the Federal Reserve System and the U.S. Small Business Administration. It targeted nonfinancial, nonfarm small businesses that were in operation as of December 1987. Financial data were collected only for the last fiscal year. The firms in the survey are small—fewer than 500 employees. The sample was stratified by census region (Northeast, North Central, South, and West), urban/rural location (whether the firm was located in a MSA), and by

---

[11] The bank cannot commit to lending at date 1, else the bad entrepreneurs waste even more money. Furthermore, a loan commitment contracted at a high rate will not work as the firm can always decide not to take it down.

employment size (less than 50 employees, 50–100 employees, more than 100 employees). The stratification was done to ensure that large and rural firms were represented in the sample. The response rate was 70 to 80 percent, depending upon the section of the questionnaire considered.[12]

There are 3404 firms in the sample, of which 1875 are corporations (including S corporations) and 1529 are partnerships or sole proprietorships. In the overall sample, the mean firm size in terms of book assets is $1.05 million; the median size is $130,000. The firms have mean sales of $2.6 million and median sales of $300,000. These companies are also fairly young, having spent a median of ten years under their current ownership. In comparison, firms in the largest decile of NYSE stocks have been listed for a median of at least 33 years. Nearly 90 percent of these firms are owner managed, 12 percent are owned by women, and 7 percent by minorities. Over 19 percent of the sample consists of firms in the hotel and restaurant business. Another 13 percent are in building and construction, 7 percent manufacture intermediate products like chemicals, and 7 percent perform communication, electric, gas, and sanitary services.

On average, firms in the sample have a debt-to-asset ratio of 0.33. Of the debt, approximately 80 percent is from institutions, while the rest consists of loans from the owners (in the case of partnerships or corporations) and the owner's family. Banks account for 80 percent of the institutional lending, and nonbank financial institutions about 15 percent.[13] On average, trade credit financing is 10 percent of total assets, or about a third of the size of debt.

B. Sources of market power

In order to proceed further, we must determine proxies for the bank's market power. Note that nothing in our analysis requires the market power to be present ex ante. One possibility then is that the bank obtains market power ex post from the private information it obtains about the firm during the course of the lending relationship. The problem with this kind of local monopoly is that it would dissipate as the firm gets older and better known by the credit market. A second problem is that firms who find it hard to get credit are likely to offer their banks a local monopoly, making the choice endogenous. Finally, it is empirically hard

---

[12] Firms involved in the agriculture, forestry, and fishing industry; finance and insurance underwriting; or real estate investment trusts were excluded from the survey. Firms were initially sent a series of work sheets that listed the financial information which was going to be collected by the questionnaire. The work sheets were followed up by a telephone interview.

[13] We classify commercial banks, savings and loans associations, saving banks, and credit unions as banks. Finance companies, insurance companies, brokerage or mutual fund companies, leasing companies and mortgage banks are classified as nonbank financial institutions. We also have loans made by nonfinancial firms. The remaining loans consist of venture capitalist loans (surprisingly few), loans from government agencies, and otherwise unclassified loans.

to quantify the extent of information asymmetries about the firm between the inside lender and the outside credit market.

Another source of market power is the spatial distribution of banks in the local market. Banks that are physically closer to the firm have lower costs of monitoring and transacting with the firm. These costs may be especially significant because the firms in our sample are small. If other banks are relatively far, close banks have considerable market power. The concentration of banks in the local geographical market is likely to be a proxy for how far competing lenders are likely to be from one other, and consequently how much market power any single lender has. Another way to think about this is that the search costs to a firm of finding a replacement lender who has the ability to deal with its specific needs are likely to be high when the local market has few lenders.

In what follows, we use the concentration of lenders in the local market as a measure of the lender's market power. Implicit in the analysis that follows is the following assumption. Variations between local markets in the market power banks have because of their concentration in the local markets is much larger than variations between local markets in the amount of "homemade" market power that firms voluntarily offer banks by giving them an information monopoly. If this were not true, our tests would be biased against finding any effect of spatial concentration on lending.

From the FDIC Summary of Deposit data, the SBA survey obtained the Herfindahl index of commercial bank deposit concentration for the county or Metropolitan Statistical Area where the firm is headquartered. The survey, however, reported only a broad categorization of competition in the local credit market. The survey reports whether the Herfindahl index is less than 0.1, between 0.1 and 0.18, or greater than 0.18. We refer to the first category as the most competitive credit market, and the last category as the most concentrated credit market.

In what follows, we take the concentration of the market for deposits to be a proxy for the concentration of the market for credit. This would be a good approximation if the firms in our sample largely borrow from local markets because of the prohibitive informational and transactional costs of going outside. While there is evidence in prior work (see Hannan [1991]) of this, we have independent confirmation that credit markets for small firms are local.[14] The firms in our sample report the distance to their primary financial institution. Over half the firms are within two miles of their primary institution. Ninety percent of the firms are within fifteen miles of their primary institution.

If the Herfindahl index for deposits is a good proxy for competition in the loan market, we would expect to find greater solicitation of new business by financial

---

[14] Hannan provides evidence that the market for bank commercial loans is local in nature; specifying which market the firm is in helps explain the rate charged. The unit of describing markets in his study is the Metropolitan Statistical Area. In our study, the unit can be either the Metropolitan Statistical Area or the county.

institutions in more competitive markets. For firms less than ten years old, 32 percent of the firms in the most competitive market have been approached by at least one financial institution seeking new business in the past year. Only 26 percent of the firms in the least competitive market were solicited. The difference in solicitation rates is marginally significant at the 13 percent level. The difference in solicitation rates is greater, both economically and statistically, for the older firms. For firms that are more than ten years old, the solicitation rates are 31 percent in the most concentrated market and 46 percent in the most competitive market. This difference (statistically significant at the 1 percent level) is, therefore, greatest for older firms where the model argues that competition is most destructive to relationships.

Solicitation of new financial business from the firms in this sample is once again a local phenomenon. Of the firms that were solicited for new business, over half report that the soliciting financial institution is within three miles of the firm. All this suggests that the Herfindahl index of deposits is a good measure of credit market competition. Before examining the data, it may be useful to restate our empirical predictions in terms of this proxy.

C. Empirical implications

The empirical predictions of the model are the following.

a. Provided that the distribution of firm qualities is similar in all markets and provided that in at least one market some firms do not obtain finance, relatively more firms should be able to obtain credit from financial institutions in areas where credit markets are more concentrated. Furthermore, the average quality of firms obtaining finance should be lower as the credit market becomes more concentrated.

b. Credit should be cheaper for the lowest quality firms in a concentrated credit market than if similar firms were to obtain credit in a more competitive market.

c. The cost of credit should fall faster as a firm ages in a competitive credit market than if it ages in a concentrated market.

D. Credit market competition and firm quality

The theory makes strong predictions about how borrowing will vary with firm age and market concentration. The sample we have is a cross section. However, by examining firms of different ages, we can make inferences about how borrowing changes over a firm's life.[15] The first prediction is that if the quality distribution

---

[15] We are assuming stationarity of the survival process so that we can indeed draw correct inferences about changes in borrowing and interest rates with age from a cross-sectional sample. This assumption is not required when we test differences across markets holding age constant.

of firms applying for credit is the same in the different markets, firms of lower average quality (and, consequently, relatively more firms) will be financed in more concentrated markets. We first describe the differences in quality of all the firms in the different markets in Table 1. Thus, this table is based on both those firms that borrow from institutional sources and those that do not.

We divide the data into two subsamples: firms younger than the median age of ten years and firms older than the median age. There are 296 firms in the most competitive credit markets and 2037 in the most concentrated markets. Firms in the two markets are approximately the same size as measured by the book value of total assets, with the median size of young firms being $102,000 and $103,000. There is greater disparity between the mean size of young firms ($863,000 in competitive markets and $569,000 in concentrated ones), but the difference is not statistically significant. Firms in the middle category (Herfindahl index between 0.10 and 0.18) are larger but not statistically so.

The young firms in the more competitive credit markets are somewhat more profitable. The ratio of gross profits (revenues less cost of goods sold) to assets is 2.78 in the competitive market and 1.88 in the most concentrated markets. The medians differ in similar ways. Moving on to operating profit ratios, again firms in the most competitive market are more profitable (a mean ratio of 1.14 versus 0.63), although the difference is no longer statistically different. The median ratios are even closer (0.17 versus 0.15). The rates of sales growth do not differ much across the markets (see Table 1).

A firm's access to capital may depend upon the tangibility or the liquidity of its assets. The industry the firm is in should be a good proxy for this. As is typical for small firms, a significant fraction of our sample are in the retail trade and services industry. However, over 10 percent of the firms are in construction and another 10 percent of the firms are in manufacturing. The distribution of firms across industries is very similar in the most concentrated and the most competitive markets (see Figure 1). The most competitive markets have relatively fewer firms in services and somewhat more in wholesale trade, but the fractions of firms in the other industries are roughly equal across markets. In sum, the quality of firms in the most competitive market appears as good as if not better than the quality of firms in the most concentrated market. Our results should be biased—if at all—toward finding more institutional financing in competitive areas.[16]

---

[16] When we consider only firms that have obtained institutional financing, the differences seem to widen. The mean size of such firms in most competitive markets is almost twice the size of such firms in the most concentrated markets ($1,444,327 in competitive markets and $768,868 in concentrated markets) and the difference is significant at the 5 percent level. The medians are also different, $170,000 versus $149,000, and this difference is significant at the 10 percent level. The mean operating profit-to-asset ratio is higher in the competitive market (0.58 versus 0.42), while the mean sales growth is also somewhat higher (0.34 versus 0.30) despite the fact that the firms in the competitive credit market are larger.

Table 1. Summary Statistics for Firms Classified by Age and Credit Market Concentration

Firm characteristics	Young firms			Old firms		
	Most competitive	Middle market	Most concentrated	Most competitive	Middle market	Most concentrated
Firm solicited by financial institution during the year (1 = yes)	0.32[10]	0.32	0.26	0.46[1]	0.39	0.31
	0.00	0.00	0.00	0.00	0.00	0.00
	(0.46)	(0.47)	(0.44)	(0.50)	(0.49)	(0.46)
	166	488	966	112	516	972
Firm size (in $1000s) Book value of assets	863	1074	569	1296	1692	1171
	102	108	103	151	207	155
	(3247)	(7188)	(1836)	(2722)	(5379)	(3062)
	179	517	1010	117	554	1027
Gross profits Assets	2.78[1]	2.18	1.88	2.39[1]	1.95	1.79
	1.61[1]	1.24	1.06	1.36[1]	1.66	0.97
	(2.96)	(2.46)	(2.21)	(2.76)	(2.31)	(2.21)
	170	491	965	114	520	973
Operating profits Assests	1.14	1.05	0.63	0.61	0.62	0.64
	0.17	0.18	0.15	0.23[10]	0.14	0.13
	(4.84)	(5.74)	(2.49)	(1.19)	(1.93)	(2.88)
	170	491	965	114	520	973
Sales growth (1986–1987)	0.30	0.32	0.31	0.15	0.15	0.14
	0.09	0.10	0.08	0.04	0.05	0.03
	(0.98)	(0.92)	(0.91)	(0.63)	(0.68)	(0.58)
	140	435	843	109	495	934
Number of instits. from which firm borrows	1.35	1.40	1.37	1.28[1]	1.36	1.43
	1.00	1.00	1.00	1.00	1.00	1.00
	(0.59)	(0.62)	(0.62)	(0.51)	(0.65)	(0.69)
	99	291	655	71	323	624
Longest business relation with financial institution (in years)	4.10[1]	4.66	4.75	16.37	16.42	17.42
	4.00	4.00	4.00	15.00	15.00	15.00
	(3.09)	(2.93)	(2.95)	(9.81)	(10.60)	(11.05)
	179	517	1010	117	554	1027

The SBA survey classifies the Metropolitan Statistical Area or county where the firm is headquartered into three categories on the basis of the commerical bank deposit Herfindahl index of the area. The most competitive markets are those with a value of the Herfindahl index of less than 0.10. The most concentrated markets are those with a Herfindahl index of more than 0.18. The middle market is those markets where the Herfindahl index is between 0.10 and 0.18. Young firms are ten years old (the median age) or less. Old firms are more than ten years old. We report the mean, the median, the standard deviation, and the number of observations in each cell.

For each variable we tested the equality of the means in the most concentrated and most competitive markets. We tested the equality of the medians in the most concentrated and most competitive markets using the Wilcoxon Bank-Sum test. Both tests were done separately for young and old firms. Differences in the means and median is noted for significance levels of 10 percent ([10]), 5 perecent ([5]), and 1 percent ([1]).

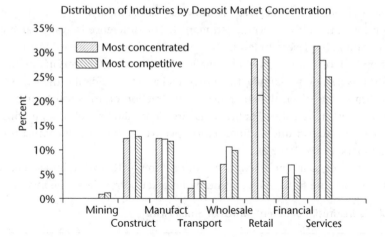

Figure 1. Firms are classified by their one-digit SIC code. We graphed the percent of firms in each industry for each of the deposit market concentrations: most competitive (Herfindahl index less than 0.10), most concentrated (Herfindahl index greater than 0.18), and the middle market.

Finally, it is useful to ask whether the concentration of credit markets is correlated with the region of the country. This is important to ensure that we do not pick up the effects of a regional shock in what follows. A cross tabulation of the region in which the firm is located (Northeast, North Central, South, and West) and the level of competition in the local credit market (we do not report this in a table) indicates that firms in the southern and western regions are underrepresented in the most competitive market and overrepresented in the most concentrated markets. However, the magnitude of these differences is small. The correlations between the Herfindahl index and each of the four region dummies ranges from −0.12 to 0.15.

E. Credit market competition and the availability of finance

The theory in the previous section suggests that young firms are more likely to receive institutional finance in a concentrated credit market than in a competitive one. Among the youngest half of our sample (firms that are less than ten years old), the firms in the most concentrated market are more likely to obtain capital from institutional sources. Sixty-five percent of the firms in the most concentrated market have institutional debt compared with only 55 percent of firms in the most competitive market, with the difference being significant at the 1 percent level. Ten-year-old firms may not be considered young. As Table 2 demonstrates, the difference in institutional financing is most extreme among firms that are four years old or less. Forty-eight percent of such firms in the

most competitive market have institutional debt compared with 65 percent of
the firms in the most concentrated market. The difference is again statistically
significant at the 1 percent level. The potential effects of a survival bias (see subsection II.H) on our results will be smallest for the youngest firms in our sample.
Yet in this part of our sample, the differential access to capital is the largest.

As firms grow older, the difference in the fraction of firms being financed in
the two markets vanishes. For firms that are older than ten years, approximately
61 percent use institutional finance, irrespective of the state of competition in
credit markets (see Table 2).

The difference in the fraction of young firms with institutional debt does
not arise because firms in a concentrated market borrow less. The institutional

Table 2. Institutional Indebtedness of Small Firms

Firm age (in years)	Most competitive market		Middle market		Most concentrated market	
	Firms with instit. debt	Debt/ assets	Firms with instit. debt	Debt/ assets	Firms with instit. debt	Debt/ assets
	Percent number	Mean std. dev.	Percent number	Mean std. dev.	Percent number	Mean std. dev.
≤ 2	0.47	0.49	0.49	0.44	0.65	0.46
	12	(0.36)	55	(0.46)	147	(0.38)
3–4	0.49	0.44	0.60	0.39	0.65	0.43
	20	(0.35)	60	(0.49)	141	(0.30)
5–6	0.65	0.28	0.55	0.43	0.68	0.39
	17	(0.26)	64	(0.56)	131	(0.36)
7–8	0.69	0.19	0.63	0.38	0.64	0.43
	20	(0.18)	50	(0.40)	125	(0.43)
9–10	0.57	0.32	0.60	0.34	0.65	0.40
	17	(0.45)	65	(0.32)	117	(0.34)
11–13	0.70	0.32	0.57	0.45	0.66	0.38
	19	(0.22)	60	(0.37)	142	(0.58)
14–17	0.59	0.44	0.64	0.38	0.62	0.33
	13	(0.64)	75	(0.48)	146	(0.28)
18–22	0.75	0.38	0.61	0.27	0.67	0.34
	15	(0.30)	75	(0.22)	126	(0.28)
23–31	0.63	0.96	0.55	0.29	0.61	0.33
	17	(0.84)	62	(0.24)	123	(0.27)
Greater than 32	0.33	0.24	0.57	0.30	0.47	0.25
	7	(0.14)	54	(0.28)	87	(0.24)

Firms are classified by the concentration of the credit markets where the firm is located and by the age of
the firm. Firm age is years since acquired by the present owners. The SBA survey classifies the Metropolitan
Statistical Area or county where the firm is headquartered into three categories on the basis of the commercial
bank deposit. Herfindahl index of the area. The most competitive market has a Herfindahl index of less than
0.10, and the most concentrated market has a Herfindahl index of more than 0.18. The debt-to-asset ratio
includes only debt from institutions in the numerator. Loans from owners and family are not included.

debt-to-assets ratio for young firms that have institutional debt is slightly higher in concentrated markets: 0.42 compared with 0.35. For firms older than ten years, the numbers are reversed. The institutional debt-to-asset ratio is 0.43 in the most competitive market and only 0.35 in the most concentrated market. As firms get older in the concentrated market, they borrow smaller amounts from these outside sources and rely more on equity and internal funds. This is consistent with our model. If borrowers in such markets are offered lower-than-competitive rates when young, this subsidy must be made up by charging them a higher-than-competitive rate when old. This will encourage them, at the margin, to substitute away from external borrowing when old.

In our discussion so far, we have implicitly assumed that the amount of institutional debt used is the amount of debt available to the firm. Such an assumption is, perhaps, defensible for the youngest firms that may have few internal sources of funds and many lucrative investment opportunities. For older firms it is less clear whether the amount of institutional debt is supply constrained (creditors do not want to lend more) or demand constrained (borrowers prefer internal sources). That older firms borrow less in concentrated markets does not necessarily indicate that these firms are more supply constrained. In order to explore this issue further, we turn to a better measure of credit availability.

F. An alternative measure of credit availability

If financial institutions limit the credit extended to a firm, the firm will borrow from more expensive noninstitutional sources as long as the returns from its investments exceed the cost of funds from those sources. Correcting for investment opportunities, the amount of expensive borrowing should be a measure of how much the firm is rationed by the (cheaper) institutional sources—provided that the following conditions hold. First, the marginal cost of borrowing from the noninstitutional source must exceed the marginal cost of available institutional credit. If it did not, the firm would turn to noninstitutional sources of credit first. Second, the cost of borrowing from the noninstitutional source should be relatively similar for firms within an identifiable class.

Most of the firms in our sample are offered trade credit—short-term financing that some suppliers provide with their goods and services. As reported in Table 3, the median firm in all three kinds of markets obtains 90 percent of its purchases on credit. Another measure of the firm's use of trade credit is its Days Payable Outstanding (DPO), which is defined as 365 times the firm's accounts payables divided by its cost of goods sold. The median firm's DPO is about fifteen days across the markets. We have data on the percentage of discounts for early payment which are taken by each firm. In general, discounts for early payment are substantial and are meant to encourage the firm to pay on time. For example, firms in the retail business refer to terms as the 10-2-30 rule. This is a discount of

Table 3. Trade Credit Usage Across Credit Markets with Differing
Degrees of Competition

	Median (Number of obs.)		
	Most competitive market	Middle market	Most concentrated market
Fraction of purchases offered on credit	0.90 (231)	0.90 (818)	0.90 (1597)
Days payable outstanding (DPO)	15.83 (160)	16.22 (594)	14.58 (1232)
Fraction of firms taking less than 10 percent of the discounts	0.33	0.29	0.19
Fraction of firms taking more than 90 percent of their discounts	0.50	0.52	0.59

The most competitive market has a Herfindahl index of less than 0.10, and the most concentrated market has a Herfindahl index of more than 0.18. Days payable outstanding is 365 × Accounts Payable/Cost of Goods Sold.

2 percent if the bill is paid within 10 days and the full amount if paid in 30 days. A firm that passes up the discount and pays the bill when due pays an annualized rate of 44.6 percent, far higher than the highest interest rate charged to firms in our sample.[17]

Previous work indicates that discount terms are not specific to a firm, but are common practice throughout the industry [Elliehausen and Wolken 1992; Petersen and Rajan 1994]. Furthermore, although the decision to offer trade credit depends upon the firm's quality, the decision by trade creditors to offer early payment discounts does not. Approximately 33 percent of trade credits are accompanied by early payment discounts. This number does not vary with firm size or firm age. As these discounts and penalties are substantial and are

[17] Clearly, the annualized rate is not that high if firms are allowed to stretch repayments beyond the due date. Conversely, it may be much higher if firms miss the discount but pay before the due date. Since the stated terms in an industry may differ from actual industry practice, Petersen and Rajan [1994] construct empirical measures of the actual period for which firms can borrow if they do not avail themselves of discounts. To estimate the potential stretch available to trade credit borrowers, they calculate the differences in the DPO between firms that regularly take the early payment discounts and those that do not. For each industry they determine the median DPO for firms that take less than 10 percent of the discounts they are offered and the median DPO for firms that take more than 90 percent of the discounts offered. The difference between these two numbers is an estimate of how long firms that do not take discounts stretch out their payments. For the retail industry it is 8.9 days. Based on the standard terms, firms that do not take the discount are paying an additional 2 percent for 8.9 days of credit, which translates to an annualized interest rate of 123 percent.

industry- not firm-specific, the fraction of trade discounts not taken is a good proxy for he costly noninstitutional credit source.[18]

By this measure, fewer firms appear to be credit constrained in concentrated markets than in competitive markets (see Table 3). Only 19 percent of firms in concentrated markets take fewer than 10 percent of offered discounts, compared with 29 percent in the middle market and 33 percent in the most competitive market. Conversely, over 59 percent of firms in the most concentrated market take more than 90 percent of offered discounts, compared with 52 percent in the middle market and 50 percent in the most competitive market.

Clearly, these monotonic relationships are only suggestive since they do not control for firm quality or other factors that may be correlated with credit market concentration. To test the robustness of these results, we regress the percentage of trade discounts taken against measures of the firm's investment opportunities, its cash flow, measures of the strength of its lending relationships, and the state of competition in credit markets. Firms that take a larger percentage of their early payment discounts should be less credit constrained. We include three measures of the firm's investment opportunities. Investment opportunities may depend on the firm's size—the book value of its assets—and the log of the firm's age (younger firms may have better opportunities). Since investment opportunities depend on the industry the firm is in, seven industry dummies are included as explanatory variables. Clearly, all these variables may also proxy for the credit quality of the firm.

The firm's internal cash flow is accounted for by including income after interest normalized by the firm's book value of assets. We include a dummy for whether the firms is a corporation or not, because credit rationing should be greater for firms with limited liability. An owner-managed firm has a greater incentive to take on risky projects if it has limited liability. Petersen and Rajan [1994] find that the strength of relationships between firms and financial institutions is an important determinant of whether firms rely on trade credit financing. This is why we include the measures of relationships: the log of the length of the longest relationship the firm has had with a financial institution, the fraction of borrowing that comes from institutions that provide at least one significant financial service to the firm, and the number of institutions that account for more than 10 percent of the firm's borrowing.

Finally, we include an indicator if the firm is in the most concentrated credit market. If availability does not depend on the concentration of the credit market, the coefficient for this term should be zero.

---

[18] Why do trade creditors lend when financial institutions are reluctant to lend? Trade creditors may have a better ability to dispose of the collateral, greater incentives related to the margins they make on the product they are selling, greater leverage over the firm because of their ability to cut off supplies, or greater information about the firm (see Mian and Smith [1992]). Trade credit is presumably very expensive because firms are not in the business of lending, though this merits further research.

The dependent variable in the regression should be the desired fraction of early payment discounts that the firm would like to take. Firms that are rationed by financial institutions will choose to borrow from trade creditors at the rates implicit in forgoing the early payment discount. In fact, they may wish to borrow more than is offered through their trade credits. Thus, the desired percentage may be less than zero. Since firms cannot take less than 0 or more than 100 percent of the early payment discounts, the observed dependent variable is censored at 0 and 100 percent. In our sample, 60 percent of the firms are censored at 0 or 100. Estimating the model with ordinary least squares ignores this censoring, and consequently, estimates will be biased toward zero. We, therefore, estimate a tobit regression with two-sided limits.

In Table 4 we examine the determinants of the percent of offered discounts taken by the firm. The estimates in column I indicate that the investment and cash flow variables have the predicted sign. Older and larger firms have fewer investment opportunities and so can take more trade discounts by paying on time. If age and size proxy for credit quality, this result suggests that higher quality firms are less likely to be credit rationed. Profitable firms have more internal cash so they are less likely to use trade credit as a means of long-term borrowing. Again, this may be a proxy for quality. Finally, because of their limited liability, corporations are more likely to take risky projects, which explains why they are more likely to be rationed.

The relationship variables also have the predicted signs. A long relationship with a financial institution increases the percentage of discounts taken, even holding the age of the firm constant. Borrowing a greater fraction from lenders who provide the firm services has a similar effect, although this effect is not statistically significant. Borrowing from multiple institutions makes relationships more diffused and increase the degree to which the firm is credit constrained.

The degree of concentration in financial markets enters in an economically and statistically significant way. Firms in the most concentrated market take 17 percentage points more trade credit discounts than do firms in most competitive credit markets ($t = 2.9$). This coefficient is 40 percent of the standard deviation of the percentage of discounts taken. In other words, after controlling for observable measures of credit demand and creditworthiness, we find that firms in the most concentrated credit market are the least credit rationed.

An alternative explanation for our results is that credit constraints are less binding in small towns. Information about small businesses and their managers may be more available, or the pressure to repay debts may be greater, in rural areas. This should make credit rationing less severe. The correlation between our measure of credit market concentration and whether the firm is in a Metropolitan Statistical Area (MSA) is 0.44. The estimated coefficient for the indicator variable for MSA in column I of Table IV is less than half that for the concentration indicator ($\beta = 7.4$) and statistically small ($t = 1.4$). However, when we drop the

Table 4. Credit Availability and the Role of Credit Market Competition

Independent variable	I	II	III	IV
Firm characteristics				
Log (book value of assets)	7.21^1	7.26^1	7.10^1	7.13^1
	(1.70)	(1.70)	(1.79)	(1.79)
Operating profits/book assets	5.88^5	5.95^5	5.22^{10}	5.35^{10}
	(2.79)	(2.80)	(2.82)	(2.84)
Firm is a corporation (0,1)	−8.96	−9.10	-10.84^{10}	-10.54^{10}
	(5.88)	(5.89)	(6.24)	(6.24)
Log firm age (in years)	8.69^1	8.74^1	10.19^1	10.39^1
	(3.35)	(3.35)	(3.73)	(3.73)
Firm is located in an MSA	−7.44	−6.93	−4.32	−4.97
	(5.45)	(5.47)	(5.75)	(5.78)
Sales growth (1986–1987)			4.40	4.41
			(3.86)	(3.86)
Firm is located in a unit banking state		9.36		
		(9.94)		
Relationship characteristics				
Log (length in years of longest relationship)	18.64^1	18.42^1	19.70^1	19.64^1
	(3.84)	(3.85)	(4.05)	(4.05)
Debt from financial service provider (percent)	2.54	2.11	3.37	3.51
	(5.74)	(5.75)	(6.03)	(6.03)
Number of institutions from which firm borrows	-11.62^1	-11.56^1	-11.40^1	-11.35^1
	(3.16)	(3.16)	(3.33)	(3.33)
Financial market concentration				
Herfindahl > 0.18 (0, 1)	16.54^1	17.21^1	16.87^1	19.05^1
	(5.66)	(5.70)	(5.98)	(6.30)
Herfindahl < 0.10 (0, 1)				11.48
				(10.35)
Number of observations	1459	1459	1339	1339
− Log likelihood	4120.1	4119.7	3743.0	3742.4

The dependent variable is the percentage of offered early payment discounts taken by the firm. The coefficient estimates are from a tobit regression with two-sided censoring. Fifteen percent of the observations are censored at 0 percent; 45 percent of the observations are censored at 100 percent. Standard errors are in parentheses. The regression also includes seven industry dummies, three region dummies, and a constant.
[1] Coefficient is significant at the 1 percent level.
[5] Coefficient is significant at the 5 percent level.
[10] Coefficient is significant at the 10 percent level.

indicator for SMSA from the estimation, the coefficient on the concentration indicator increases from 16.5 to 19.7. Thus, the rural/urban divide has some effect in the predicted direction, but this does not account for the influence of concentration.

Another possibility is that the Herfindahl index is correlated with whether the firm is located in a state with a unit banking law. These states may have been especially affected by regional shocks—for instance, to the oil or natural resources industries—which in turn may have affected the entire regional economy.[19] Thus, firms in competitive markets may be credit constrained not because the markets are competitive, but because they are in states affected by adverse regional shocks. The empirical facts, however, are not consistent with this alternative hypothesis. First, if the firms in competitive markets have been affected by regional shocks, then their profitability and sales should be affected by the shock. As is apparent in Table 1, the firms in competitive markets have profit-to-assets ratios that are at least as large as if not larger than the firms in the most concentrated markets. Sales growth for firms in the most concentrated market is the same as sales growth for firms in the most competitive market. Thus, sales and profits of firms in these markets do not reflect adverse shocks.

A more direct test of this hypothesis is to control for the banking laws of the state in which each firm is located. This is done in the second column of Table 4. Firms in unit banking states are less credit constrained ($\beta = 9.3$), although this coefficient is not statistically different from zero ($t = 0.9$). More importantly, including a control for firms in unit banking states has only a marginal effect on the coefficient of the indicator variable for concentration. This coefficient actually rises from 16.5 to 17.2. Given the low correlation between the firm being located in a unit banking state and it being located in the most concentrated market ($\rho = -0.07$), this finding is not surprising.[20]

The evidence presented so far suggests that controlling for the observable measures of quality, firms in more concentrated credit markets are less credit constrained. The remaining portion of this section adds additional controls to the model to test the robustness of this finding and the accuracy of our assumptions. First, we have assumed that the firm's investment opportunities do not differ systematically with the concentration of the credit markets. The potential problem is that firms in more competitive credit markets may have greater investment opportunities and thus take fewer early payment discounts. As an additional control for investment opportunities, we include the firm's sales growth, since intuitively firms with higher sales growth should also have more investment opportunities. The data, however, do not indicate that concentration proxies for differences in investment opportunities. The coefficient on the firm's sales growth is small and has the wrong sign. Firms with higher sales growth are slightly less credit constrained. In addition, the effect on the concentration coefficient is small. The coefficient on the Herfindahl index rises from 16.5 to 16.9 (see Table 4, column III).

---

[19] As of June 1986, five unit banking states remained: Colorado, Kansas, Montana, North Dakota, and Wyoming. Texas was a unit banking state until 1985.

[20] Some states limit branch banking without having unit banking laws. If we expand our indicator variable to include states with limits on branching, the banking law coefficient rises from 9.4 to 12.9. The coefficient on the Herfindahl index, however, is unchanged.

An alternative way of correcting for differences in industry profits, investment opportunities, and terms of trade credit in the industry is to include more detailed industry dummies. Instead of the seven industry dummies—representing one-digit SIC codes—we include indicators for all two-digit SIC industries that account for more than 1 percent of the sample. We lose a number of degrees of freedom, and the concentration coefficient falls slightly to 14.5 (estimates not reported in the table) but is still statistically significant ($t = 2.5$).

The model in the previous section argues that the greater the lender's market power, the less credit constrained the borrower will be. So far, we have focused on the differences between the most concentrated market and the other markets. But as Table 2 indicates, there seems to be a monotonic increase in the fraction of firms getting credit as we move across the three broad ranges for the Herfindahl. To test the monotonicity of this relationship in the trade credit regression, we add an additional dummy variable for the firms in the most competitive market. These estimates are reported in column IV of Table 4.

According to the model, the coefficient on the most competitive market dummy should be negative since these firms should be more credit constrained than the intermediate market that is the base. Instead, the coefficient is positive. However, the coefficient is not statistically different from zero ($t = 1.1$). Since our controls for relationships, such as the relationship length, depend upon the concentration of the credit market, we may be double counting. Interestingly, when we drop the relationship variable, the coefficient on the most competitive market drops to 3.7 ($t = 0.4$). Thus, we cannot distinguish the most competitive market from the middle market, although we can distinguish the most concentrated market from the other two.

Our inability to distinguish the estimates may be because the difference in credit availability between markets diminishes as firms become older and more established. Unfortunately, the data are not discriminating enough for us to detect this phenomenon in the trade credit regressions. When we include both dummy variable for different levels of credit market competition and interactions with the firm's age (estimates not reported), the standard errors grow dramatically. However, we report means and medians of the percent of early payment discounts taken by firms in different markets in Table 5. As expected from the model, we find that for young firms (age less than the median), the median discount taken is related to the concentration of the market. The difference in medians is 10 percent higher in the middle market than in the most competitive market, and 30 percent higher in the most concentrated market than in the middle market. For the old firms, these differences vanish. The means follow a similar pattern, and unlike the medians, the differences in means are statistically significant. [21]

---

[21] While Table 5 suggests that the structure of the credit market does influence the availability of credit to firms, it does not suggest that the difference in availability across market structure is

Table 5. Percent of Early Payment Discounts Taken Classified by Firm Age and Credit Market Competition

Firm characteristics	Most competitive	Middle market	Most concentrated
Firm age ≤ 10 years	53.4[5]	54.7	63.0
	50.0	60.0	90.0
	(44.6)	(44.6)	(41.5)
	93	290	593
Firm age > 10 years	68.4[10]	67.2	76.6
	100.0	95.0	100.0
	(41.7)	(41.5)	(35.9)
	69	331	640

We tested the equality of the mean percent of early payment discounts taken in the most concentrated and most competitive markets. The test is done separately for young (firms less than or equal to ten years old) and old firms (firms greater than ten years old). Differences in the means are noted for significance levels of 10 percent ([10]), 5 percent ([5]), 1 percent ([1]).

To summarize, we find that the amount firms borrow from financial institutions tends to increase with the concentration of the credit markets. When we examine a measure of availability of institutional finance rather than actual usage, we find that young firms appear less constrained in more concentrated markets. Regression estimates suggest that firms in the most, concentrated market appear to be significantly less credit constrained than firms in the other two markets. The evidence is largely consistent with the theory proposed in Section I. However, to establish that the greater availability is because lenders in concentrated credit markets intertemporally smooth interest rates, we now turn to analyze interest rates.

G. Cost of capital differences in competitive and concentrated markets

Our model suggests that in markets where lenders have market power, they should charge a lower-than-competitive interest rate early in a firm's life, when problems of moral hazard and adverse selection are large. Later, they will compensate by demanding an interest rate above the competitive rate. For this reason, we expect the interest rate to fall more rapidly in competitive markets.

substantially different for young and old firms as our model would indicate. As we see from Table 2, much of the difference in debt levels across markets is for firms four years of less in age. In a concentrated market, the median (mean) discount taken by such firms is 75 (60). In a competitive market, the median (mean) discount taken by such firms is 50 (52). So the difference in medians is 25, and the difference in means is 8. In comparison, consider firms older than fifteen years. In a concentrated market the median (mean) discount taken by such firms is 100 (78.5). In a competitive market the median (mean) discount taken by such firms is 100 (78.3). So the difference in medians is 0, and the difference in means is 0.2. While we have increased the power of the test (and the economic difference) by taking more extreme groupings, the difference in availability across market structure for young and old firms is still not statistically significant.

To test these predictions, we examine a subset of 1277 firms for which we have the interest rate charged on the firm's most recent loan. This is described in Table 6. The average interest rate is calculated for both the young (age less than ten years) and old firms in the most concentrated and most competitive markets. Young firms pay higher average rates than old firms, but the pace at which the rate declines is larger in the most competitive market. In the most concentrated market the young firms pay 34 basis points more than old firms ($t = 2.17$); however, in the most competitive market this difference is 86 basis points. Notice that the interest rate starts higher in the competitive market and ends lower. This result is inconsistent with the argument that market concentration is a proxy for town size and the associated access to information. If this were true, rates should be uniformly lower in the concentrated market, not just for the youngest firms.

These results are only suggestive. We have made no adjustment for observable firm quality. According to the model in the previous section, lenders will lend money, on average, to lower quality firms in the more concentrated markets. Thus, the above difference in rates between young firms in competitive and concentrated markets may understate the difference we should expect to find once we control for observable measures of quality.

To control for other factors that affect the interest rate a firm pays and to test the robustness of our findings, we estimate the loan rate as a function of the log of the firm's age and controls for observable firm and loan characteristics. In the regression results below we use the prime rate to control for changes in the underlying cost of capital. The prime rate includes both the risk-free rate as well as a default premium for the bank's best customers. Since these small businesses are not the bank's best customers, they pay an additional default

Table 6. Borrowing Costs Across Market Structures

	Young firms (Age ≤ 10 years)	Old firms (Age > 10 years)
Most competitive market	11.50	10.64
(Herfindahl < 0.10)	(2.31)	(2.19)
	59	48
Most concentrated market	11.38	11.04
(Herfindahl > 0.18)	(2.34)	(2.36)
	477	403

The SBA survey classifies the Metropolitan Statistical Area or county where the firm is headquartered into three categories on the basis of the commercial bank deposit Herfindahl index of the area. The most competitive markets are those with a value of the Herfindahl index of less than 0.10. The most concentrated markets are those with a Herfindahl index of more than 0.18. Young firms are ten years old (the median age) or less. Old firms are more than ten years old. We report the mean interest rate, the standard deviation, and the number of observations in each cell.

premium. We control for aggregate variations in this premium by including the difference between yield on corporate bonds rated BAA and the yield on ten-year government bonds. We also include a term premium, defined as the yield on a government bond of the same maturity as the loan minus the treasury bill yield, to account for interest rate differences across different loan maturities. For floating rate loans this variable is set to zero.

To control for variation in the loan rate due to the characteristics of the loan, we include dummies for whether it is a floating rate loan, for the kind of collateral offered, and for the type of lender making the loan. To control for variation in the loan rate due to the characteristics of the firm, we include the firm's size (book value of assets), dummies for the firm's industry, and whether the firm is incorporated. We also include the relationship variables used by Petersen and Rajan [1994].

Since we expect firm age to have a different effect in competitive and concentrated markets, we estimate different age intercepts and slopes for each level of market concentration. The intercept measures the difference between a loan in the most concentrated and in the most competitive market, when the firm is new. As Table 7 shows, firms in the most concentrated market start out at an interest rate that is 129 basis points lower than in the most competitive market. Interests rates drop as the firm grows older, consistent with Diamond's [1989] notion that survival is a signal about the true quality of the borrower. The rate at which the loan rates drop, however, differs significantly across markets. The coefficient on age is over four times larger in the most competitive markets (Herfindahl index < 0.10) than in the most concentrated markets (Herfindahl index > 0.18). As a firm ages from new to the median age of ten years, its interest rate drops by 167 basis points in a competitive market. The interest rate drops only 36 basis points for firms in the most concentrated markets (see Figure 2). In addition to being large in magnitudes, the difference in the slopes is also statistically significant ($t = 2.0$). The fact that the slope of interest rates with age is flatter in concentrated markets is a direct implication of our model.[22]

While it is interesting that interest rates start out lower for firms in the most concentrated area, it is not necessarily a prediction of our theory. Our theory only suggests that new firms of the *lowest quality* should obtain a lower loan rate in a concentrated market, it has nothing to say about the rate charged to the *average* new firm. The average loan rate in the concentrated market will be affected by both a higher markup charged to higher quality new firms ($M > 1$),

---

[22] The results indicate that as compared with firms in the most competitive market, firms in the most concentrated market pay lower interest rates when young and higher rates when old. One way to verify that this finding is not a result of our functional form is to examine the raw data. The evidence in Table 6 confirms our intuition. Another way to check our results is to graph the residuals by age for both the most concentrated and the most competitive markets. When we do this, we find no evidence of misspecification.

Table 7. The Evolution of Borrowing Costs Across Market Structures

Independent variable	I	II	III
Credit market conditions			
Herfindahl greater than 0.18 (0,1)	-1.285^{10}		-1.347^{10}
	(0.686)		(0.690)
Herfindahl between 0.10 and 0.18 (0,1)	-1.704^5		-1.759^5
	(0.721)		(0.724)
Log of firm age if Herfindahl is greater than 0.18	-0.154^{10}		-0.153^{10}
	(0.088)		(0.088)
Log of firm age if Herfindahl is between 0.10 and 0.18	-0.135		-0.134
	(0.127)		(0.127)
Log of firm age if Herfindahl is less than 0.10	-0.725^1		-0.732^1
	(0.273)		(0.273)
Log of firm age if firm is in an MSA		-0.240^5	
		(0.112)	
Log of firm age if firm is not in an MSA		-0.154^{10}	
		(0.090)	
Interest rate variables			
Floating rate loan (0,1)	-0.477^5	-0.459^5	-0.479^5
	(0.187)	(0.188)	(0.187)
Prime rate	0.278^1	0.272^1	0.277^1
	(0.032)	(0.032)	(0.032)
Term structure spread	0.011	0.014	0.010
	(0.084)	(0.085)	(0.084)
Default spread	0.357^5	0.364^5	0.352^5
	(0.153)	(0.153)	(0.153)
Firm characteristics			
Log (book value of assets)	-0.295^1	-0.301^1	-0.295^1
	(0.048)	(0.048)	(0.048)
Total debt/book assets	-0.011	-0.024	-0.003
	(0.147)	(0.148)	(0.148)
Firm is a corporation	-0.158	-0.173	-0.159
	(0.145)	(0.145)	(0.145)
Number of banks from which firm borrows	0.379^1	0.378^1	0.377^1
	(0.088)	(0.088)	(0.088)
Firm is in an MSA	-0.021	0.074	-0.031
	(0.138)	(0.343)	(0.139)
Firm is in a unit banking state			-0.213
			(0.244)
Loan is from a bank (0,1)	0.100	0.140	0.107
	(0.193)	(0.192)	(0.193)
Loan is from a nonfinancial firm (0,1)	-1.148^1	-1.140^1	-1.144^1
	(0.367)	(0.367)	(0.367)
Number of observations	1277	1277	1277
Adjusted R^2	0.160	0.154	0.159

The rate quoted on the firm's most recent loan is the dependent variable. The regression also includes seven industry dummies, three regional dummies, six dummy variables for the type of assets with which the loan is collateralized, and an intercept. The prime rate is the rate at the time the loan was made. The term structure spread is the difference between the ten-year government bond yield and the three-month T-bill yield at the time the loan was made. The default spread is the difference between the BAA corporate bond yield and the ten-year government bond yield at the time the loan was made.

[1] Coefficient is significant at the 1 percent level.
[5] Coefficient is significant at the 5 percent level.
[10] Coefficient is significant at the 10 percent level.

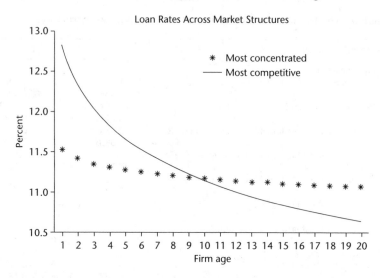

Figure 2. The loan rates are based on estimates from Table 7. All variables, expect the firm's age and the market type (most competitive versus most concentrated) were set equal to the sample means. The average loan rate is this sample is 11.1 percent.

which will tend to raise the average interest rate, and lower than competitive rates charged to low quality young firms, which will reduce it. The average effect depends on the distribution of firms. This may explain why the intercept is not monotonic, being even lower for firms in markets of intermediate concentration than in the most concentrated area (-1.70 and -1.29). But the slope coefficient in the intermediate market is not statistically or economically different from that for the most concentrated area (-0.135 versus -0.154).

As discussed in subsection II.F, market concentration is correlated with the urban/rural location of the firm. As further evidence that concentration is not a proxy for the location of the firm, we reestimate our rate regressions allowing the slopes to differ for firms in urban and rural locations rather than for firms in concentrated and competitive markets. Based on the results in the second column of Table 7, the rural/urban difference does not drive the results on concentration. The interest rate charged does fall with age, however, and the rate of decline is very similar in rural and in urban markets. For firms in an MSA the coefficient on age is -0.240; for rural firms the coefficient is -0.154. The difference is not statistically significant ($t = 0.6$). Instead of market concentration being a proxy for the location of the firm (urban versus rural), the location of the firm is a proxy for market concentration.

Finally, we test for the effect of state banking laws on the rate. The inclusion of an indicator for unit banking states has little effect on the coefficient on age or the intercept in any of the markets (see Table 7, column III). Our results appear to be robust; controlling for other firm and loan factors, the loan rates in the concentrated market start lower but do not fall as much with firm age as loan rates in the competitive market (see Figure 2).

H. Survivorship biases in different credit markets

Interest rates slope downward with firm age because good entrepreneurs survive while bad entrepreneurs go under. It is, however, important for us to ask whether differences in the survival rate of bad entrepreneurs across markets could be responsible for the differences in estimated slopes across markets.

We assume in the model that bad types are all weeded out after one period. This ensures that the quality of surviving firms at date 1 is the same in all markets, even though lower quality firms are started in the concentrated market. An alternative possibility is that the greater availability of finance for low quality firms could make the attrition rate lower for bad firms in concentrated markets. Yet another possibility is that competition in the product markets may be fiercer in areas with competitive loan markets. Under the assumption that age proxies for unobservable elements of firm quality, we would find that demand interest rates fall less with firm age in concentrated markets.

Clearly, unobservable quality should be correlated with observable proxies for quality. Table 1 provides little evidence that surviving old firms in concentrated credit markets are of lower quality. The mean and median firm size and growth rates for old firms (firms greater than ten years) is about the same in both competitive and concentrated markets, through median profits—but not mean profits—are larger in the competitive markets. It is possible that most low-quality firms have been weeded out in all markets by the time firms are ten years old. If differences in attrition rates are to explain the relative slopes of the interest rate with age, much of the difference in attrition rates should occur when firms are very young (because we have empirically documented a much steeper decline in interest rates with firm age for very young firms in competitive areas). We subdivide young firms into the very young (age less than five years) and the not so young (age greater than five but less than ten years). If differential attrition takes place when firms are very young, the not so young firms should look much healthier in the competitive market. The evidence (not reported in table) does not support this. The not so young firms in the middle market dominate or tie with similar firms in competitive markets on all four dimensions of quality (median size, gross profits, net profits, and sales growth). The not so young firms in the concentrated market are the same size as those in competitive markets and have higher net profits but lower gross profits and sales growth. None of these differences are significant at standard levels.[23] Interestingly, size, which is the variable least likely

---

[23] As might be expected given the similar distribution of industries across markets, industry adjustments do not affect these results. When we subtract the median value of sales growth for all firms

to be mismeasured, is approximately the same at $121,000 across the markets. While we hesitate to dismiss differential survivorship as an explanation for the different slopes, we do not find evidence supporting it. Note, however, that it would not explain the differences in intercepts or the differences in availability.

III. Discussion

Young firms in concentrated markets receive more institutional finance than do similar firms in competitive markets. As firms get old, the difference in the relative firms borrowing from institutions disappears. Young firms who get institutional loans are more indebted in concentrated markets than in competitive markets, but this pattern reverses for older firms. Creditors seem to smooth interest rates over the life cycle of the firm in a concentrated market, charging a lower-than-competitive one when the firm is young and a higher-than-competitive rate when the firm is old. We now discuss possible interpretations of this result.

The results do not arise because firms in concentrated credit markets are very different from firms in competitive credit markets, since they persist even after we correct for the obvious firm and industry characteristics (see Tables 4 and 7). In fact, the sample of all firms in the different markets does not look very different (Table 1). One possible explanation of our results is that banks in concentrated markets misprice their loans. But our results require them to be inconsistent in their mispricing, being excessively eager to lend to young, little-known firms and excessively cautions in lending to older, established firms. While we cannot rule out this possibility, it is hard to think of plausible assumptions that would lead to such behavior. It is also possible that concentration is a proxy for other factors. It may be easier for small firms in rural markets to get credit, simply because lenders have better information about borrowers in a small community where news, and gossip, travel fast. The problem with this explanation is simply that ease of information acquisition cannot be the whole story, or else firms in concentrated markets would enjoy uniformly lower rates independent of age. In addition, the results are not altered when we control directly for whether the firm is located in a rural area.

We think the most plausible explanation is the theoretical one provided in Section I. Creditors in concentrated markets have an assurance of obtaining future surplus from the firm and consequently accept lower returns up front. This enables many more firms to be financed before the nominal interest rate rises to the point where the possibility of moral hazard forces the lender to cut off credit. Of course, banks in concentrated markets lend with the expectation

---

having the same two-digit SIC code from the sales growth number and then find means and medians across markets, the differences (or the lack of them) are qualitatively similar. This is true for net profits and gross profits also. We adjust the assets by dividing them by the median in the industry. Again the results are qualitatively similar.

that they will recover the initial subsidy via higher interest rates in the future. This explains why the surviving, older firms in concentrated markets pay higher nominal rates than surviving older firms in competitive markets. Finally, the natural response of older firms who have few investment opportunities and are faced with higher interest rates is to use less external finance. This would explain why older firms in concentrated markets rely on internal opposed to institutional finance.

There is a legitimate concern about whether our findings are applicable to larger enterprises. The economic forces we have identified, however, are not special to small enterprises. While the main source of competition for a bank in the sample we examine is other banks, competition to fulfill the financing requirements of larger firms comes from arm's-length sources like the commercial paper, equity, and bond markets. The relative cost of borrowing from banks rather than from markets is likely to be high for large, reputable firms (see Diamond [1991] and Rajan [1992]). It is even less likely that banks will be able to retain the business of successful firms when competition is from arm's-length markets than when competition is from other banks. Therefore, a natural consequence of the opening up of arm's-length credit markets is that lending relationships deteriorate, young firms are more liquidity constrained, and banks are less willing to help their clients in financial distress.[24]

It is, however, easy to draw the wrong welfare implication from these findings. The absence of credit-market competition is only one way firms and creditors can share future surplus, and it is not costless. The higher interest rate paid by successful survivor firms in concentrated markets can be distortionary and force them to reduce their reliance on external funds. This may affect their investment and reduce their rate of growth. There are contractual ways of ensuring bilateral commitment between lender and borrower that may be less costly. For example, in addition to lending, the creditor could take an equity stake in the young or distressed firm.[25] While an equity claim would give the lender a share in the future surplus generated by the firm, explicit contracts (as opposed to implicit

---

[24] The evidence from the Japanese liberalizations seems to support this view. Hoshi, Kashyap, and Scharfstein [1990] find that firms with relatively high growth and high Tobin's q reduced their bank ties to borrow from the markets. This suggests that the relatively high-quality firms left the banks to borrow from the markets. Furthermore, *The Economist* reports that while banks write initially eager to lend to small firms to replace the business lost to the markets, they were now charging them an exorbitant rate "thus hitting the firms that borrowed at the wrong moment, and crimping their plans for new investment" [October 27, 1990: 74].

[25] That the sale of an equity stake to the lender helps a firm share surplus with it in times of distress has been put forward as one explanation of how the German universal banking system evolved. According to this view, the current stakes of German banks in large German firms are not part of a carefully planned strategy, but a historic accident. The German banks acquired their stakes when they helped ailing German firms out in the 1920s and 1930s. [*The Economist*, November 16, 1991: 102].

contracts enforced by the environment) have the added advantage of being voluntary so that firms whose incentives would be excessively distorted by sharing future surplus would not enter into them.

Of course, it may not always be possible to promote relationships via contracts. Equity contracts may not commit entrepreneurs to a credible payout policy. Creditors may not want to hold equity because it makes then "soft" when dealing with errant borrowers (see Dewatripont and Tirole [1992]). Owners may be reluctant to give the bank equity because they may fear too much bank interference. A bank may be less inclined to monitor the firm on behalf of, and act in the interest of, other fixed claim holders (like employees and other creditors) if it also holds equity claims. A political concern is that banks may effectively bypass antitrust laws if they build substantial equity holdings in similar companies. Clearly, it is an empirical matter whether these costs outweigh the benefits from stronger relationships, and our study has nothing to say about this.

It is interesting to speculate on the policy implications if the only way to promote relationships is by restricting credit-market competition. In the early stage of country's economic growth when there are comparatively few established firms, the availability of finance is most important. It may be least inefficient to restrict interbank competition in order to achieve this.[26] But as many firms become established, the distortionary price for credit becomes a more important source of inefficiency. At this point, regulation and introducing more interbank competition, as well as opening up arm's-length markets may make the most economic sense.[27] Clearly, the period before an anticipated liberalization will be troubled as relationships break down before the benefits of competition kick in. But this may be unavoidable for an economy that wants to optimize the trade-off between the availability and the price of credit.

The general point the chapter makes is that competition and long-term relationships are not necessarily compatible, whether the markets being analyzed are labor or capital markets. Reformers in relationship-based economies are not always right (as suggested by Mayer [1988]) if they think that adding a dose of

---

[26] Governments do actively restrain competition in the financial sectors in the early stages of a country's growth, though these restraints tend to take on a life of their own. Macrae [1990] has an entertaining description of the operation of the old government-sponsored bank cartels. Meerschwam [1991] describes the product market segmentation in lending implemented by the Meiji Restoration in 1868. Subsequent to the attempts to introduce more competition during the U.S. Occupation after World War II, government guidance reasserted itself through the Ministry of Finance and the Bank of Japan. He argues that until the opening up of the bond markets, "specialized financial institutions, operating in well-defined product markets . . . limited financing alternatives for the various corporations. In addition, a lack of price differentiation among products reduced the incentive for participants to break these relationships."

[27] This discussion presupposes that governments have a choice in deciding when to deregulate their financial systems. For some countries like Japan, the decision has been partly forced because large companies went offshore to tap Euromarkets (see Meerschwam [1991: 135]). In other countries the wealthy vested interests set up by cartelization will successfully oppose liberalization.

competition to their systems will necessarily make it better off. Conversely, it may be equally wrong to expect firm–creditor or firm–worker relationships to be as strong or as valuable in the competitive U.S. markets as in the cartelized markets elsewhere.

References

Becker, G. S. (1975). *Human Capital.* New York: Columbia Univ. Press.

Dewatripont, M., and Tirole, J. (1992). "A theory of debt and equity: Diversity of securities and manager-shareholder congruence." C.E.P.R. Working Paper.

Diamond, D. (1984). "Financial intermediation and delegated monitoring." *Review of Economic Studies,* LI: 393–414.

——(1989). "Reputation acquisition in debt markets." *Journal of Political Economy,* XCVII: 828–61.

——(1991). "Debt maturity structure and liquidity risk." *Quarterly Jounral of Economics,* CVI: 709–38.

Elliehausen, G., and Wolken, J. (1992). "The use of trade credit by small businesses." Board of Governors of the Federal Reserve System.

Fischer, K. (1990). "Hausbankbeziehungen als Instrument der Bindungzwischen Banken und Unternehmen." Ph.D. Thesis, Universität Bonn.

Gertler, M. (1992). "Financial capacity and output fluctuations in an economy with multi-period financial relationships." *Review of Economic Studies,* LIX: 455–72.

Hannan, T. (1991). "Bank commercial loan markets and the role of market structure: Evidence from surveys of commercial lending." *Journal of Banking and Finance,* XV: 133–49.

Hart, O., and Moore, J. (1989). "Default and renegotiation: A dynamic model of debt." Massachusetts Institute of Technology Working Paper.

Hoshi, T., Kashyap, A., and Scharfstein, D. (1990). "Bank monitoring and investment: Evidence from the changing structure of Japanese corporate banking relationships," in R. Glenn Hubbard (ed.), *Asymmetric Information, Corporate Finance and Investment* (Chicago, IL: University of Chicago Press).

Lummer, S., and McConnell, J. (1989). "Further evidence on the bank lending process and the capital market response to bank loan agreements." *Journal of Financial Economics,* XXV: 99–122.

Macrae, N. (1990). "Sweaty brows, slippery fingers." *The Economist,* September 8: 21–4.

Mayer, C. (1988). "New issues in corporate finance." *European Economic Review,* XXXII: 1167–89.

Meerschwam, D. (1991). *Financial Boundaries: Global Capital, National Deregulation and Financial Services Firms.* Cambridge, MA: Harvard Business School Press.

Mian, S., and Smith, C. (1992). "Accounts receivable management policy: Theory and evidence." *Journal of Finance,* XLVII: 169–200.

Myers, S. (1977). "Determinants of corporate borrowing." *Journal of Financial Economics*, V: 147–75.

Petersen, M., and Rajan, R. (1994). "The benefits of lending relationships: Evidence from small business data." *Journal of Finance*, XLIX: 3–37.

Rajan, R. (1992). "Insiders and outsiders: The choice between informed and arm's length debt." *Journal of Finance*, XLVII: 1367–400.

Stiglitz, J., and Weiss, A. (1981). "Credit rationing in markets with imperfect information." *American Economic Review*, LXXI: 393–410.

Townsend, R. (1982). "Optimal multiperiod contracts and the gain from enduring relationships." *Journal of Political Economy*, XC: 1166–86.

17

Long-term Contracts, Short-term Investment, and Monitoring

Ernst-Ludwig von Thadden

I. Introduction

An important question in the literature on corporate finance in the recent years has been whether the dependence on outside finance can force firms to undertake inefficient amounts of investment. Little work has been done, however, on the impact of outside finance on the quality of investment. The present chapter studies this issue in the context of a question which has attracted considerable attention in the financial press and in the economic policy debate: can the dependence on outside finance lead a firm to undertake inefficient myopic investment?[1] To do this, the chapter studies a dynamic model of financial contracting that allows one to characterize the choice of a firm's investment horizon. It points to information asymmetries as responsible for investment myopia, discusses the costs and benefits of monitoring as a reaction to it, and characterizes the optimal dynamic debt structure for unmonitored, as well as for monitored finance.

According to standard financial theory, the market sees through the corporate veil and encourages the choice of efficient projects. In response to this, an important recent literature has developed more explicit theories of financial contracts and their role for the behaviour of imperfectly informed and strategically acting economic agents.[2] This chapter builds on this literature and analyses the problem of optimal financial contracting for a firm that wants to raise capital for a risky long-term investment project. The framework used to study the

I wish to thank Martin Hellwig for his advice and for helpful discussions. I have benefited from discussions and comments by Bernard Bensaid, Erik Berglöf, Helmut Bester, Marco DaRin, Mathias Dewatripont, Ian Jewitt, Colin Mayer, John Moore, and Raghu Rajan. Financial support by Studienstiftung des Deutschen Volkes and Schweizerischer Nationalfonds is gratefully acknowledged.

[1] Examples for authors expressing serious economic policy concern are Porter (1992) and Jacobs (1993). Porter (1992), e.g. concludes that institutional investors in the U.S. are "trapped in a system that undermines the long-term earning power of the American companies."

[2] See, e.g. Hart (1993).

issue is a simple two-period contracting model, complicated by the interplay of hidden-characteristics and hidden-action problems on the side of the firm. More specifically, the probability distribution of project returns is assumed to depend on the intrinsic quality of the project, as well as on the investment horizon and effort chosen by the firm, all not freely observable. If a bad first-period result makes it optimal for uniformed outsiders to terminate the project, the firm, in response, may find it optimal to engage in short-term investments which are overall dominated, but make early liquidation less likely.

This model of myopia is similar in spirit to work by Narayanan (1985) and Stein (1989).[3] Both of these papers show how managers can boost short-term earnings through hidden actions at the expense of long-term earnings. Ignoring contractual issues, they identify short-termism as a Nash equilibrium resulting from signal jamming by managers who respond to performance pay or stock market reactions. While this approach is interesting in general, Darrough (1987) has pointed out that the equilibrium found by Narayanan vanishes if the share-holders of the company provide an appropriate incentive scheme. Furthermore, Jeon (1991) has shown that the behaviour identified by Stein can at most be transient and will not prevail in steady state, if stock prices take into account that the manager is behaving strategically.[4]

The contract approach developed here allows for an explicit consideration of the agency costs of outside finance in the implementation of long-term investment. As is well known from the work of Townsend (1982), Fudenberg, Holmström, and Milgrom (1990) and Rey and Salanié (1990, 1992), in long-term relationships under asymmetric information, sequences of short-term con-tracts typically can implement strictly less than long-term contracts. Therefore, the present chapter considers comprehensive long-term contracts to exclude a possible in-built short-term bias of short-term contracting.

Since short-run results are informative about the firm's quality, long-term con-tracts will optimally use this signal. This has several implications for the structure of optimal contracts, which go beyond the results obtained in static contracting problems by, e.g. Gale and Hellwig (1985) and Innes (1990). Most importantly, it is possible, and necessary, to distinguish between long-term debt (where funds are committed for both periods) and short-term debt. With short-term debt, funds are only committed for one period, and the firm obtains continuation finance if and only if it has produced good short-run results. Furthermore, in certain parameter constellations the firm receives some compensation, or keeps

---

[3] A similar point to that of Narayanan (1985) and Stein (1989) is made by Dewatripont and Maskin (1995). However, the thrust of their paper is different, since they are concerned with the problem of committing to terminate a financial relationship ex post in order to deter bad risks ex ante.

[4] For a very good survey of this and other contributions to the myopia problem, see Bohlin (1991).

some of its funds, although it does not repay its first-period debt and does not obtain continuation finance.[5] On the other hand, it turns out that for long-term debt the temporal structure of debt repayments matter: in some instances, standard long-term debt (see, e.g. Gale and Hellwing (1985)) will be optimal; in others, repayment is optimally made in two instalments.

Due to the imperfection of the signal given by short-term results, short-term debt has a cost: to terminate good projects too early. If, despite this cost, short-term debt is optimal, the analysis identifies three reasons why the optimal contract can induce short-term investment. First, note that the above cost of short-term debt is lower for short-term than for long-term investment. Therefore, it is possible that short-term investment would be preferred even if the firm could commit to project choice (Proposition 1). On the other hand, if conditioning on short-run results is not costly for long-term projects under commitment, the firm would like to commit itself to long-term investment. However, since project choice is private information, this may not be incentive-compatible (Proposition 2). And third, it may be the case that, although it would be ex ante preferred by both parties, committing funds for two periods is not credible, since termination following bad short-run results will ex post be in everybody's interest. In anticipation of this renegotiation, the firm can find it ex ante optimal to invest short-term (Proposition 4).

In all three cases, short-term investment results from lack of information. This suggests that the problem may be overcome by having the investors monitor the firm. As Diamond (1984) has argued, an important function of financial intermediaries is precisely to take on this role. If information gathering is costly and the information obtained private, there is an incentive to centralize this activity in one person's hands. In this sense, intermediaries may act as "delegated monitors" of investment projects to collect information and at the same time economize on overall monitoring costs.

The implications of monitoring for the problem of short-term investment are investigated in Section IV. Monitoring has the advantage of resolving the ambiguity of what has caused bad short-run results, and therefore allows to implement the efficient continuation decision. Potentially, this should eliminate the firm's moral hazard problem with respect to investment choice: if it knows that early failure will not be mistaken for bad quality, it should choose the superior long-term strategy. However, the positive effect of monitoring on investment choice is limited by the fact that the monitor must be given incentives to indeed provide continuation finance if the firm is good. This implies that she must be

---

[5] This feature may be interpreted as a deviation from absolute priority in bankruptcy proceedings. As described by Franks and Torous (1989), senior creditors in Chapter 11 negotiations often (18 out of their sample of 27) concede part of the value of the bankrupt firm to stockholders, although their own claims have not been fully satisfied. I am grateful to a referee for pointing this interpretation out of me.

given a certain share of long-run returns following early bad results, which again conflict with the firm's incentives to choose long-term investment.

However, it turns out that monitoring contracts can indeed be structured such that the conflicting objectives are reconciled and long-term investment is implemented (Proposition 5). Such contracts are long-term financial agreements which give a certain amount of discretion to the investor, without leaving the firm unprotected. Their main feature is a clause that the monitoring investor can unilaterally terminate funding if the project fails early on; if she continues, however, she must do so at terms pre-specified in the original contract. Hence, optimal contracts resemble debt contracts coupled with a credit line arrangement, an arrangement which is, in fact, widely used in bank-firm lending relationships.

As discussed in more detail in Section IV, optimal monitoring contracts have another interesting property. Since they can be shown to be interim efficient, they are strongly renegotiation-proof (Proposition 7). This provides a new perspective on some important recent research on bank–firm relationships (Rajan (1992), Sharpe (1990), and subsequent research), which works with the assumption that long-term contracting possibilities with respect to the terms of refinancing are limited. Under this, and the further assumption that informed lenders capture the surplus in contract continuations, Rajan (1992) analyses the relationship between informational efficiency and ex post opportunism of lenders. A tradeoff between these two effects then translates into a tradeoff between informed and "arm's length" finance.[6] The present paper shows that opportunism by informed lenders can also be controlled by making more efficient use of long-term contracting possibilities. This yields a more optimistic view of long-term lending relationships.

The remainder of this chapter is organized as follows. Section II sets out the model. Section III characterizes optimal contracts without monitoring, and Section IV considers the monitoring option. Section V provides a brief conclusion. Three proofs are in the Appendix.

II. The Model

Consider a risk-neutral firm that seeks to raise outside finance for a sequence of two investment projects, one today ($t = 1$) and one in the future ($t = 2$). Each investment requires a fixed amount $I_t, t = 1, 2$, and generates stochastic returns one period later. Market interest rates are certain and normalized to zero.

At the time of the initial investment the management of the firm must take two decisions which influence the distributions of all future returns. One decision is an initial effort $e \in \{0, \lambda\}$ which determines—and for simplicity of notation is

---

[6] In von Thadden (1992), I discuss the hold-up problem in some more detail and introduce the possibility of ex-post competition to mitigate it.

taken to be equal to—the probability that the firm will be of "good quality".[7] If $e = 0$, the firm will certainly be bad; if $e = \lambda, 0 < \lambda < 1$, the firm is good with probability λ and bad with probability $1 - \lambda$. A bad firm's return on both investments is zero with certainty, a good firm's returns are described below.

Effort is assumed to be costly. If it chooses $e = \lambda$, the firm bears non-pecuniary cost $E > 0$, while zero effort is costless.

If the firm chooses to exert effort ($e = \lambda$), it also must decide about its "investment horizon", a decision which can take two values and which influences its return distribution if the firm is good. The firm can choose a short-term horizon, $h = s$, which yields relatively high expected returns in the short run (i.e. in $t = 2$), but relatively low returns in $t = 3$. Alternatively, for the choice $h = l$, the distribution of short-term returns is first-order stochastically dominated by that of $h = s$, but the distribution of long-term returns dominates that of $h = s$. More specifically, conditional on being good and on the choice h, the firm's returns in period $t, t = 2, 3$, are stochastically independent and given by

$$\tilde{x}_t^h = \begin{cases} 0, & \text{with probability } 1 - p_t^h, \\ X_t, & \text{with probability } p_t^h, \end{cases} \tag{1}$$

where

$$p_1^s > p_1^l \quad \text{and} \quad p_2^s < p_2^l, \tag{2}$$
$$p_1^l X_1 + p_2^l X_2 > p_1^s X_1 + p_2^s X_2, \tag{3}$$
$$p_2^s X_2 - I_2 \geq 0. \tag{4}$$

By (3), the long-term project yields higher overall expected profits than the short-time project. Yet, by (2), in the first period the short-term project has a higher success probability, and, given (1), a higher expected return. By (4), the short-term project is worth while continuing in the second period, provided the firm is known to be good. Allowing for $p_2^s X_2 - I_2 < 0$, which would effectively reduce the short-term project to one period, would not change the results.

The above assumptions imply that if first-period returns are positive, the firm is revealed to be good. To simplify the analysis, I assume that if the firm has exerted effort ($e = \lambda$) and first-period returns are zero, neither the firm not the outside investors know whether this is due to bad luck with a good project or to bad quality.[8] Furthermore, while the incidence of investment and the returns from

---

[7] Think of effort that goes into the development of the firm's internal structure, the exploration of profitable marketing possibilities, the motivation and training of employees, etc.

[8] Hence, information at the time of reinvestment is symmetric, if investors do not monitor the firm. The assumption is mainly made to simplify the analysis (although it could also be justified on behavioural grounds, see, e.g. Kahneman et al. (1982)). If the firm knows its type in $t = 2$, the analysis would still be possible, but would require additional self-selection constraints for the provision of continuation finance. The definition of total surplus from contracting, (8), would change (see footnote 14), but the qualitative results of the analysis would continue to hold.

the projects are assumed to be costlessly observable by the firm and outsiders in both periods, the firm's decisions e and h cannot be observed by outsiders. E, λ and the distributions of $\tilde{x}_t^h$ are common knowledge. This informational structure reflects the observation that it is often relatively easy to obtain information about a company's results, but usually much more difficult to discern the real reasons for possible weak results.

Additionally, as in Diamond (1984), investors have the option to put up an amount K to monitor the firm's quality. This generates new information, but entails an extra cost. The tradeoff resulting from this option will be analysed in Section IV. This section and the next will consider contracts without monitoring.

Without monitoring, only first-period returns are informative about the return distribution of the second project. Therefore, for all participants the stochastic structure of project returns is given by the following simple event tree. Under the choice $e = 0$, all returns are zero with certainty. With $e = \lambda$ and given the choice of h, the first project yields a return $\tilde{x}_1 = X_1$ with probability $q_1^h := \lambda p_1^h$. Given $\tilde{x}_1 = X_1$, the second has a success probability of $q_{x_2}^h := p_2^h$, while the success probability following $\tilde{x}_1 = 0$ is

$$q_{02}^h := \frac{\lambda(1 - p_1^h)p_2^h}{1 - \lambda p_1^h}. \tag{5}$$

In this situation, contracts between the firm and investors will optimally make the terms of continuation finance contingent on first-period results. This, however, may bias the firm's project choice inefficiently towards the short-term project. As discussed in the Introduction, the optimal response to this will in general be to contract long-term in order to assure the firm about the terms of continuation finance already at the time of project choice and thus to provide better incentives. It is therefore necessary to consider long-term contracts. The question whether the parties find it in their joint interest to stick to the contract later on (renegotiation-proofness), will be considered in the course of the analysis in Sections III and IV. Furthermore, contracts are assumed to be complete in the sense that all observable variables are verifiable and can be contracted upon. Hence, returns and whether investment has occurred can be verified by outsiders, but effort e and the horizon h not.

If the firm obtains funding, a contract $\mathscr{C}$ between firm and investors must specify the following variables: a loan L_1 from the investors to the firm in $t = 1$, effort e, an action h, net payments $R_1(\tilde{x}_1)$ from the firm to the investors in $t = 2$, the decision whether to continue the project in $t = 2$, and repayments $R_2(\tilde{x}_1, \tilde{x}_2)$ by the firm in $t = 3$. For the continuation decision define

$$Y(\tilde{x}_1) := \begin{cases} 0 & \text{if the project is terminated,} \\ 1 & \text{if it is continued.} \end{cases}$$

The expected payoff to the firm from a contract $\mathscr{C} = (L_1, e, h, Y, R_1, R_2)$ is

$$P(\mathscr{C}) = L_1 - I_1 \frac{e}{\lambda} E + ep_1^h (X_1 + Y(X_1)) \left[p_2^h(x_2 - R_2(X_1, X_2)) - (1 - p_2^h) R_2(X_1, 0) - I_2 \right]$$
$$- R_1(X_1)) + e(1 - p_1^h)(Y(0)) \left[p_2^h(X_2 - R_2(0, X_2)) - (1 - p_2^h) R_2(0, 0) - I_2 \right]$$
$$- R_1(0)) - (1 - e)(R_1(0) + Y(0)R_2(0, 0) + I_2)), \tag{6}$$

and the expected payoff to investors

$$\Pi(\mathscr{C}) = - L_1 + ep_1^h \left(R_1(X_1) + Y(X_1) \left[p_2^h R_2(X_1, X_2) + (1 - p_2^h) R_2(X_t, 0) \right] \right)$$
$$+ e(1 - p_1^h) \left(R_1(0) + Y(0) \left[p_2^h R_2(0, X_2) + \left(1 - p_2^h \right) R_2(0, 0) \right] \right)$$
$$+ (1 - e)(R_1(0) + Y(0)R_2(0, 0)). \tag{7}$$

Adding (6) and (7) yields the total surplus from contract $\mathscr{C}$,

$$S(\mathscr{C}) = ep_1^h (X_1 + Y(X_1))(p_2^h X_2 - I_2))$$
$$+ Y(0)(e(1 - p_1^h)p_2^h X_2 - (1 - ep_1^h)I_2) - I_1 - \frac{e}{\lambda} E. \tag{8}$$

At the contracting stage, investors are assumed to be competitive and ready to provide funds, as long as they break even on the investment. An optimal contract without monitoring then maximizes P subject to the following constraints:[9]

$$L_t \geq I_t, \tag{9}$$

$$R_1(\tilde{x}_1) \leq L_1 - I_1 + \tilde{x}_1 - Y(\tilde{x}_1)I_2, \tag{10}$$

$$R_2(\tilde{x}_1, \tilde{x}_2) \leq L_1 - I_1 + \tilde{x}_1 - R_1(\tilde{x}_1) + \tilde{x}_2 - I_2, \tag{11}$$

$$\Pi(\mathscr{C}) \geq 0, \tag{12}$$

$$P(\mathscr{C}) \geq 0, \tag{13}$$

$$P(L_1, e, h, R_1, R_2) \geq P(L_1, e', h, R_1, R_2), \quad e' \neq e, \tag{14}$$

$$P(L_t, e, h, R_1, R_2) \geq P(L_1, e, h', R_1, R_2), \quad h' \neq h, \tag{15}$$

for all realizations of $\tilde{x}_1, \tilde{x}_2$. Here, (10)–(11) are the physical feasibility constraints of the firm's repayment obligation, (12) and (13) are the investors' and the firm's participation constraints, respectively, (14) the incentive compatibility constraint of effort choice, and (15) the incentive compatibility constraint of project choice.[10] Contracts satisfying (9)–(15) will be called admissible.

---

[9] It is easy to see that the investor's participation constraint, (12) will be biding. Hence, maximizing P is equivalent to maximizing S.

[10] This formulation assumes that any initial transfers $L_1 - I_1 > 0$ are not consumed between $t = 1$ and $t = 2$, but are available for continuation finance. The analysis would hold also if this were not the case, by appropriately redesigning the state-contingent payments $R_1(\tilde{x}_t^h)$.

III. Contracts without Monitoring

By Assumption (4), $p_2^h X_2 \geq I_2$ for both types of project. Therefore, by (8), optimal contracts have $Y(X_1)=1$, regardless of project choice.[11] This means that optimally the firm is refinanced after good results in the short run.

If a contract has $Y(0) = 1$, funds for both periods are committed already in $t = 1$, and the project is continued regardless of first-period results. Under a contract with $Y(0) = 0$, first-period results have a screening function. Funds are provided only for the first project, and continuation finance is given if and only if the firm has been successful. Hence, contracts with $Y(0) = 0$ resemble short-term debt, and contracts with $Y(0) = 1$ resemble long-term debt.

By (8), the only direct determinants of total surplus now are effort choice, e, project choice, h, and the continuation/termination decision after bad short-run results, $Y(0)$. All other variables redistribute returns between time periods and contracting parties. Hence, for an unrestricted maximization of (8), with $e = \lambda$ fixed, only four different outcomes would be relevant: short-term of long-term investment horizon with contingent or non-contingent continuation. The corresponding values of total surplus are

$$S^{lt} = \lambda p_1^l (X_1 + p_2^l X_2 - I_2) - I_1 - E \quad \text{for } h = l \text{ and termination after } \tilde{x}_1^h = 0,$$

$$S^{lc} = \lambda (p_1^l X_1 + p_2^l X_2) - I_1 - I_2 - E \quad \text{for } h = l \text{ and continuation after } \tilde{x}_1^h = 0,$$

$$S^{st} = \lambda p_1^s (X_1 + p_2^s X_2 - I_2) - I_1 - E \quad \text{for } h = s \text{ and termination after } \tilde{x}_1^h = 0.$$

Note that short-term investment with non-contingent continuation is always strictly dominated by long-term investment with non-contingent continuation. Contracts with $e = 0$ are precisely those with no lending and investment. The observations that follow will analyse what contracts with $e = \lambda$ can be implemented.

LEMMA 1. *If*

$$S^{lc} \geq 0, \tag{16}$$

then there is an admissible contract with $e = \lambda, h = l, Y(0) = 1,$ *and* $\Pi = 0$.

Proof. Consider contracts with $L_1 = I_1 + I_2, R_1(X_1) = r_1 > 0, R_1(0) = R_2(0,0) = R_2(X_1,0) = 0, R_2(0,X_2) = R_2(X_1,X_2) = r_2 \geq 0$. Then the firm's expected profits are

$$\lambda \left(p_1^l (X_1 - r_1) + p_2^l (X_2 - r_2) \right) - E.$$

If $\lambda p_1^l X_1 \geq I_1 + I_2$, let $r_2 = 0$, and r_1 be given by $\Pi = \lambda p_1^l r_1 - I_1 - I_2 = 0$. Then (9)–(13) hold. Incentive compatibility of project choice, (15), requires

$$p_1^l (X_1 - r_1) + p_2^l X_2 \geq p_1^s (X_1 - r_1) + p_2^s X_2,$$

---

[11] By (8), setting $Y(X_1) = 1$ maximizes S. For any given admissible contract with $Y(X_i) = 0$ this change does not affect admissibility.

which is true by (2) and (3). Incentive compatibility of effort choice, (14), holds by (16), because with no effort the firm makes zero expected profits under the given contract.

If $\lambda p_1^l X_1 < I_1 + I_2$, let $r_1 = X_1$ and r_2 be given by $\Pi = \lambda(p_1^l X_1 + p_2^l r_2) - I_1 - I_2 = 0$. The argument is as before. ∥

Lemma 1 states that if the total surplus from the long-term project under non-contingent continuation, S^{lc}, is non-negative, it is always possible to implement this outcome through a long-term debt contract. This contract rewards long-term returns, by using short-term returns as a prior source of repayment to the investors ("taxing the short run"). The point is to let the firm reap as little of short-term returns as is compatible with the investors' zero-profit constraint, in order to make deviations to the short-term project unattractive.

Such a contract can often, but not always, be designed as *standard* long-term debt (see Gale and Hellwig (1985))—i.e. a contract that requires no interim repayment and a final repayment of min $(\tilde{x}_1 + \tilde{x}_2, R)$ for a fixed number R. The problem with standard long-term debt is that it induces the firm to put excessive weight on the upper tail of the distribution of total returns $\tilde{x}_1 + \tilde{x}_2$. This conflicts with the incentive compatibility of $h = l$ if the overall repayment obligation R satisfies $\max(X_1 + X_2) < R < X_1 + X_2$ and if $p_1^s p_2^s > p_1^l p_2^l$. In this case the firm makes a profit if and only if $\tilde{x}_1 + \tilde{x}_2 = X_1 + X_2$ and this event is more likely under short-term investment. Therefore, standard long-term debt would induce the firm to privately change the project's risk structure, which is a variant of the standard agency cost of debt (Jensen and Meckling (1976)). Long-term debt with repayment in two instalments as described in the proof of Lemma 1 eliminates this problem.

LEMMA 2. *If*

$$S^{st} \geq 0, \tag{17}$$

then there is an admissible contract with $e = \lambda$, $h = s$, $Y(0) = 0$, and $\Pi = 0$.

Proof. Let $A \in \mathbb{R}$ be given by $\lambda p_1^s (A + p_2^s X_2 - I_2) = I_1$. Then it is easily verified that the contract with $L_1 = I_1$, $R_1(X_1) = A - I_2$, $R_1(0) = R_2(X_1), 0 = 0$, and $R_2(X_1, X_2) = X_2$ satisfies (9)–(15). ∥

S^{st} is the total surplus from the short-term project under contingent continuation. By Lemma 2, this outcome can be implemented by short-term debt as long as its surplus is non-negative. The contract example in the proof of the lemma does the opposite of the one considered for Lemma 1. In this example (which is extreme, others can be easily given) all long-run returns are "taxed away" ($R_2(X_1, X_2) = X_2$) and redistributed toward the short run ($R_1(X_1) = A - I_2$).

If $A < I_2$—which is the case if the short-term project is profitable in the long run, I_1 small, and λ large—then this intertemporal redistribution takes the form of a second loan to the firm in case of early success, with overall repayment in $t = 3$. If $A > I_2$, the firm repays $A - I_2$ as a first instalment, finances the second investment out of the first period profits, and the remaining debt is rolled over to $t = 3$.

Lemma 1 and 2 show that incentive compatibility is not a binding constraint for implementing $h = l$ with long-term debt or $h = s$ with short-term debt. The next lemma shows that it is binding for the implementation of $h = l$ with short-term debt.

LEMMA 3. *Suppose that*

$$s^{lt} \geq 0. \tag{18}$$

There is an admissible contract with $e = \lambda, h = l$, and $Y(0) = 0$ if and only if

$$s^{lt} \geq \frac{p_1^s p_2^s - p_1^l p_2^l}{\lambda p_1^s p_1^l (p_2^l - p_2^s)} E. \tag{19}$$

This contract can be chosen such that (14) *binds and* $\Pi = 0$.

Proof. In the Appendix. ‖

The left-hand side of (18) and (19) is the total surplus from the long-term project under contingent continuation. For this outcome to be implementable, it is in general not sufficient that its surplus is non-negative; if $p_1^s p_2^s > p_1^l p_2^l$, surplus must be strictly positive, with the lower bound given by (19). This is because in this case the incentive compatibility problem is hardest: the firm must be induced to choose the project with the high probability of early failure, knowing that in case of early failure it will be liquidated. The way an optimal contract can achieve this is to punish early success ($R_1(X_1) = X_1$) and reward late success ($R_2(X_1, X_2)$ small), as in the case of Lemma 1. However, in general this is not sufficient: since in order to be able to reap the reward for late success the firm must live until then, the firm also considers the probability of joint success in both periods. It turns out that if $p_1^s p_2^s > p_1^l p_2^l$, the above punishment/reward scheme is too weak to make the choice of $h = l$ incentive compatible. In this case, as an additional carrot, early failure must be rewarded—i.e. the firm must receive a payment if the project is liquidated. Instead of such a "compensation payment" the contract can, of course, equivalently specify an initial transfer $L_1 - I_1$ from the investors, which the firm is allowed to keep in case of bankruptcy. As pointed out in the Introduction, this feature of the optimal contract then resembles a violation of "absolute priority" in bankruptcy (see Franks and Torous (1989)). However, such a compensation conflicts with the firm's incentive to provide effort ex ante.

By (19), these objectives cannot be reconciled if the private cost of effort is too high.[12]

The above observations allow a classification of what outcomes will optimally be implemented. Lemma 1 and 2 imply:

PROPOSITION 1. *If*

$$S^{st} > \max(S^{lt}, S^{lc}), \tag{20}$$

any optimal contract without monitoring induces short-term investment and terminates funding after $\tilde{x}_1 = 0$. If

$$S^{lc} > \max(S^{lt}, S^{st}), \tag{21}$$

any optional contract without monitoring induces long-term investment and provides unconditional continuation finance.

Conditions (20) and (21) define what would be optimal if the choice of the investment horizon were contractible.[13] Hence, Proposition 1 states that if (20) or (21) hold, incentive compatibility is not binding.

Ceteris paribus, (21) will typically be satisfied if the probability of good firms, λ, is relatively large, so that long-term debt—which subsidizes bad firms for both periods—is not too costly. If λ is smaller—the case of interest for the discussion of short-termist behaviour—it is optimal to use the first project to sort out bad firms. Such screening enables the parties to eliminate "type II errors", namely the error to continue bad projects. But it also imposes the cost of "type I errors", namely to eliminate good projects. The likelihood of type I errors, however, which is $\lambda(1 - p_1^h)$, is smaller for the short-term project. Hence, using short-run returns as a screening device imposes a cost which is higher for the long-term project than for the short-term project. If (20) holds, the future gains from the long-term project are not sufficient to make up for these higher costs, and total surplus is maximized by short-term investment and contingent continuation.[14]

Given the informational structure, the outcomes described in Proposition 1 are first-best. However, incentive-compatibility problems may force the parties to contract short-term debt and choose short-term investment, although the future gains from the long-term project are large as compared to the costs of

---

[12] To see what is at work here, suppose effort provision is not an issue ($E = 0$). Then a simple way to solve the incentive problem of investment choice is to let the entrepreneur sell the firm to the investors and work for them for a flat wage. Now the entrepreneur does not care about the structure of investment returns and everything can be implemented by difference. If effort is an issue, this is not possible.

[13] Note that optimal contracts will in general not be unique, because of the possibility of offsetting state-contingent transfers. Existence follows if the admissible set is not empty, which is the case iff the maximum total surplus (left-hand side of (20) or (21)) is non-negative.

[14] The fact that total surplus can be maximized by short-term investment results from the assumption that the firm's type is not known in $t = 2$. If the type were known (to the firm or the investor), total surplus would be $\lambda(p_1^h X_1 + p_2^h X_2 - I_2) - I_1 - E$, which is always maximized by $h = 1$ (see Section IV).

type 1 errors. Lemma 3 implies:

PROPOSITION 2. *Suppose that*

$$S^{lt} > S^{st} > S^{lc}. \tag{22}$$

*Then any optimal contract without monitoring terminates funding after $\tilde{x}_1 = 0$. If (19)
holds, optimal contracts induce long-term investment; if (19) does not hold, short-term
investment.*

Proof. It is easily checked that short-term investment is incentive compatible
whenever long-term investment is not. The proposition therefore follows from
Lemma 3.   ∥

Proposition 2 characterizes the constellations in which incentive problems render long-term investment infeasible, although it would be surplus-maximizing.[15]
These are constellations where λ is so small as to make long-term debt (unconditional continuation) unattractive, the long-term project is highly profitable in
the long run, but the probability of two consecutive successes for the long-term
project, $p_1^l p_2^l$, is not high enough to make the long-run reward worth the effort.
In this situation there is no incentive scheme that would prevent the firm firm
secretly shifting the risk of failure from the short run to the long run. Hence, any
optimal contract implements short-term investment.

Propositions 1 and 2 show what allocations can be implemented by long-term
contracts, if the contracts are executed in $t = 2$ as specified in $t = 1$. Yet, the
contracts will not be executed as specified if the contracting parties are free to
renegotiate in $t = 2$ and if they both gain from doing so. For contingencies in
which this is the case, the contracting parties must anticipate at the contracting stage that inefficient actions stipulated by the contract will be renegotiated
ex post. In general, the restriction to contracts that are robust against renegotiation restricts the set of implementable outcomes (see, e.g. Bolton (1990),
Dewatripont and Maskin (1990)). For the parameter constellations (20)–(22),
however, it is easy to see that the optimal contracts of Propositions 1 and 2
are indeed renegotiation-proof.

PROPOSITION 3. *In the parameter constellations (20), (21), or (22), the contracts
identified in Propositions 1 and 2 are renegotiation-proof.*

---

[15] Here is an example of the impact of condition (19): Let

$$I_1 = 10, \quad X_1 = 30, \quad I_2 = 70, \quad X_2 = 100,$$
$$p_1^s = 0.7, \quad p_1^l = 0.4, \quad p_2^s = 0.7, \quad p_2^l = 1, \quad \lambda = 0.7.$$

Then total surplus, gross of effort, for the different contractual options are $S^{lt} + E = 6.8$, $S^s t + E = 4.7$,
and $S^{lc} + E = -1.6$. (19) is equivalent to $E \leq 2.67$. Hence, if $2.67 < E < 4.7$, the short-term project is
implemented; if $E > 4.7$, there is no admissible contract.

Proof. Note that, by assumption, information is symmetric in $t = 2$. If $\tilde{x}_1^h = X_1$ continuation is ex post efficient for both project choices, just as every optimal contract species. If $\tilde{x}_1^h = 0$, continuation is ex post efficient if and only if

$$q_{02}^h X_2 \geq I_2, \tag{23}$$

where q_{02}^h is the second-period success probability, given the choice h, $e = \lambda$, and first-period failure, as defined in (5). Simple algebra shows that (23) is equivalent to

$$\lambda \left(p_1^h X_1 + p_2^h X_2 \right) - I_2 \geq \lambda p_1^h (X_1 + p_2^h X_2 - I_2), \tag{24}$$

which is exactly the optimality criterion of Proposition 1 and 2. ‖

Hence, for the parameter constellations (20)–(22) the continuation/termination, decision which is optimal ex ante is optimal ex post. This may look trivial. However, renegotiation-proofness is a binding constraint in the one parameter constellation not covered by Propositions 1 and 2:

$$S^{lt} > S^{lc} > S^{st}. \tag{25}$$

If (25) holds, as in the case of (22), total surplus is maximized by long-term investment with contingent continuation, but the order of the other two outcomes is reversed. As before, if (19) holds, the surplus maximizing outcome can be implemented through short-term debt, which is ex post efficient as shown above. However, if (19) does not hold—i.e. if long-term investment is not incentive-compatible under short-term debt—the next best outcome, long-term investment with unconditional continuation, is not ex post efficient. By the first inequality of (25) and the equivalence of (23) and (24), both contracting parties are strictly better off if the firm stops the project after $\tilde{x}_t^l = 0$ and is compensated for this. Because the parties will anticipate this, the initial contract can be assumed right away to specify short-term investment. Therefore, if the parties cannot commit not to renegotiate, the analogue of Proposition 2 holds also for the case of (25).

PROPOSITION 4. *Suppose that (25) holds. Then any renegotiation-proof optimal contract without monitoring terminates funding after $\tilde{x}_t = 0$. If (19) holds, these contracts induce long-term investment, otherwise short-term investment.*

Proof. Suppose (19) does not hold. Then $h = l, Y(0) = 0$ is not incentive compatible. By the above argument, $h = l, Y(0) = 1$, is not renegotiation-proof. By (25) and (4)

$$p_1^s (X_1 + p_2^s X_2 - I_2) \geq p_1^s X_1 + p_2^s X_2 - I_2/\lambda,$$

which implies that $h=s, Y(0)=0$ is renegotiation-proof. Incentive-compatibility follows as in Proposition 2. ‖

This completes the characterization of contracts without monitoring.

IV. Monitoring

This section considers contracts in which investors make use of the monitoring option available to them. I make the following standard assumptions. First, monitoring takes place during the production process, i.e. the decision to monitor the firm must be made in $t = 1$. Hence, when contracting with the firm in $t = 1$, an investor has to decide whether to incur the extra cost K and monitor the firm, or not to monitor at all.[16] Second, the fact that an investor monitors is verifiable.[17] Third, monitoring is perfect: when an investor puts up the monitoring cost, she learns the firm's quality with certainty. And fourth, monitoring is private: the monitoring investor learns the firm's quality and nobody else.

Diamond (1984) has shown that, if the results of monitoring are not publicly observable, the individual character of information acquisition creates an incentive to concentrate the task of monitoring in one hand. This "delegated monitor", who collects funds from many investors and finances and monitors many firms, reduces total monitoring costs because the concentration of funding avoids the duplication of monitoring activity otherwise necessary.

In general, the strategic interaction between investors, delegated monitor, and firms can be quite complex.[18] Here, in order to focus on the costs and benefits of monitoring, I simply assume that there are investors, for brevity called banks, who have the funds necessary to finance and monitor the project on their own.

In Diamond (1984), the direct advantage of monitoring is that it eliminates the need for costly ex-post repayment enforcements under asymmetric information. In the present context, monitoring potentially has two other beneficial effects. First, an informed investor can make continuation finance contingent on the firm's quality, regardless of the realization of $\tilde{x}_1^h$ (ex-post efficiency). And second, anticipating this, the firm can invest long-term because short-term performance, $\tilde{x}_1^h$, does not provide new information about the firm's quality (ex-ante efficiency). Formally, potential total surplus from monitored finance therefore is

$$S^M = \lambda(p_1^l X_1 + p_2^l X_2 - I_2) - I_t - E - K. \tag{26}$$

For S^M to be realized, the firm must invest long-term, and the investment must be liquidated if and only if the firm is bad. However, neither the investment horizon nor the firm's quality are publicly observable. In particular, the bank has an informational monopoly at the refinancing stage. If this allows the bank

---

[16] The assumption describes a situation in which the investor learns about the firm over time ("relationship investment"). See Lummer and McConnell (1989) for empirical evidence on information acquisition in bank lending.

[17] If the bank cannot commit to monitoring, additional incentives have to be provided (see footnote 20 below). See Admati, Pfleiderer, and Zechner (1994) for an analysis of incentives to monitor in a stock market setting, and Rajan and Winton (1993) for a lending context.

[18] For an analysis of the strategic aspects of delegated monitoring, see Yanelle (1989). Hellwig (1991) provides a general discussion of monitoring and intermediation.

to extract rents in the event $\tilde{x}_1^h = 0$ and if this is anticipated by the firm, this may have negative consequences for ex-ante efficiency.[19] Hence, monitoring contracts must be designed such as to minimize these distortions. This makes the contracting problem under monitoring more complex than in the unmonitored case, because not only must the firm be given the right incentives for effort taking and project choice, but also the bank must be given the incentive to take the efficient continuation/liquidation decision.[20]

To understand the complication introduced by the additional incentive problem, note that optimal monitoring contracts must solve two conflicting moral hazard problems. On the other hand, if $\tilde{x}_1^h = 0$, the bank must have the incentive to provide continuation finance if and only if the firm is good. This implies that the bank's return from providing continuation finance to good firms after $\tilde{x}_1^h = 0$ must be high enough. On the other hand, in order for the firm to choose long-term investment, the firm should be "rewarded" for the outcome $\tilde{x}_1^h = 0, \tilde{x}_2^h = X_2$ and "punished" for $\tilde{x}_1^h = X_1$. But the larger the reward for $\tilde{x}_1^h = 0, \tilde{x}_2^h = X_2$, the smaller the bank's return from providing continuation finance to good firms after $\tilde{x}_1^h = 0$, which conflicts with the bank's incentives.

The above consideration shows that there is a potential conflict between the efficiency of continuation finance and that of project choice. However, the next proposition shows that it is possible to reconcile the friction between these two goals by designing monitoring contracts appropriately. The following type of contract, denoted $\mathscr{C}_M = \mathscr{C}_M(r_1, r_2, r_3, c, T)$, will achieve this.

$\mathscr{C}_M$: Choose numbers $T \geq 0, r_1 \leq T + X_1 - I_2, r_2 \leq T + X_1 - I_2 - r_1 + X_2, c \geq 0, r_3 \leq T + X_2$. In $t = 1$ the bank puts up K to monitor the firm, provides the amount, $I_1 + T$, and the firm invests I_1, chooses effort $e = \lambda$ and investment $h = l$. If $\tilde{x}_1 = X_1$, the firm makes a net repayment (net of receiving I_2) of r_1, continues the project, and repays 0 if $\tilde{x}_2 = 0$, and r_2 if $\tilde{x}_2 = X_2$, in $t = 3$. If $\tilde{x}_1 = 0$, the bank pays the firm c. Furthermore, the bank has the unilateral right to stop the project. If the project is continued, the bank provides $I_2 - c$, and the firm repays 0 if $\tilde{x}_2 = 0$, and r_3 if $\tilde{x}_2 = X_2$, in $t = 3$.

Before discussing this contract in some more detail, I state the main result of this section.

[19] This is a concern of much of the recent literature on relationship banking (see, e.g. Fischer (1990), Sharpe (1990), Rajan (1992), von Thadden (1992), and the discussion below).

[20] If the fact that monitoring occurs is not verifiable, the contract must also make sure that the bank indeed monitors. For the contract $\mathscr{C}_M$, defined below, the relevant additional incentive constraint is (ICM)

$$\lambda(1 - p_1^l)(p_2^l r_3 - I_2 + c) - \max(0, q_{02}^l r_3 - I_2 + c) \geq K,$$

the left-hand side of which is the bank's expected rent on its private information. However, the larger this rent, the weaker the firm's incentive to choose $h = l$. Hence, providing incentives to monitor to the bank renders the firm's incentive problem more severe. This in turn may necessitate additional contractual arrangements (as, e.g. in Rajan and Winton (1993)).

PROPOSITION 5. *If $S^M \geq 0$, there is a monitoring contract of type $\mathcal{C}_M$ which is feasible and yields an expected profit of S_M to the firm.*

Proof. In the Appendix.   ‖

If we focus on parameter constellations in which unmonitored finance yields short-term investment, an immediate consequence of Proposition 5 is

PROPOSITION 6. *Suppose that*

$$K/\lambda < \left(1 - p_s^l\right)\left(p_2^s X_2 - I_2\right)\left(p_1^l X_1 + p_2^l X_2 - p_1^s X_1 - p_2^s X_2\right). \tag{27}$$

Then, whenever unmonitored finance yields short-term investment, there is a monitoring contract of type $\mathcal{C}_M$ which is strictly superior and implements long-term investment.

As discussed above, if unmonitored finance yields short-term investment, two inefficiencies are present. First, good or projects are terminated because only an insufficient signal about quality is available, and second, for fear of early project termination the firm chooses the short-term investment project. The right-hand side of (27) is the sum of the two corresponding costs. The left-hand side is the cost, per average firm, of monitoring. Hence, (27) is just the statement that $S^M > S^{st}$. Since under both types of contracts the firm appropriates all the surplus, the monitoring contract is chosen.

Contracts of type $\mathcal{C}_M$ solve the problem of containing the bank's informational monopoly at the refinancing stage by fixing a menu of contract continuations from which the bank must choose. To solve the conflict between the efficiency of continuation finance and that of project choice, the contract exploits the commitment value of conditioning transfers on the outcome $\tilde{x}_1^l = 0$. As in the case of unmonitored finance (Lemma 3), a positive transfer c ("consolation") in this contingency may be necessary, which directly improves the firm's incentives to choose $h = l$. Furthermore, since c must be paid to the firm anyhow, it reduces the reward r_3 needed to induce the bank to provide continuation finance efficiently: the larger c, the less the bank needs to top it up for continuation. Hence, increasing c relaxes the incentive constraint of project choice, as well as the bank's incentive constraint.

Optimal contracts therefore are essentially long-term debt contracts with three special features. First, repayment is in two instalments. Second, projects that fail early on can get some compensation, depending on parameter values. And third, there is a convenant that the bank can unilaterally terminate funding if the project fails early on; if the bank continues, however, it must do so at prespecified terms. This last feature can be interpreted as a credit-line agreement, a financial instrument which is common in bank–firm lending relationships, not only for smaller companies.

The above analysis assumes that the contract is carried out as written, and in particular that there is no renegotiation if the bank declares termination of funding after $\tilde{x}_1^l = 0$. However, an important recent literature on bank–firm relationships has focused precisely on the problem of renegotiation of loan promises by informed lenders in long-term financial relationships (see, in particular, Fischer (1990), or Rajan (1992)). The argument there is roughly as follows.

Suppose that the blank, after observing $\tilde{x}_1^l = 0$, threatens to terminate funding even for good firms, unless the firm agrees to contract terms which are more favourable to the bank. If $q_{02}^l X_2 < I_2$, as, for example, in the case of Propositions 2 and 4, an uninformed outsider observing $\tilde{x}_1^l = 0$ will under no circumstances refinance the firm.[21] Hence, the bank has some bargaining power in this situation. If one assumes, as in Diamond (1984), that the bank is large and well-diversified and the firm is small, the bank can even be expected to be able to appropriate a substantial part of the surplus from project continuation. If the firm, however, anticipates at the project selection stage that it will not earn long-term profits following early project failure, it has similar incentives for short-term investment in $t = 1$ as in the unmonitored case, which in turn destroys some of the benefits of monitored lending.

In the light of this reasoning, it is useful to analyse the potential for renegotiating the $\mathscr{C}_M$—contracts considered in Propositions 5 and 6.

This analysis is facilitated by the observation that a renegotiation in the event $\tilde{x}_1^l = 0$ is an example of a principal–agent relationship with an informed principal, as analysed by Maskin and Tirole (1992) in greater generality. In $t = 2$, the firm can be viewed as an agent who is uninformed about the prospects of continuation finance.[22] On the other hand, the bank is the informed principal who proposes continuation contracts. If the agent rejects the principal's proposal, the old continuation contract defined by $\mathscr{C}_M$ remains in force; if the agent accepts the proposal, this replaces the old contract.

As is well known, this type of negotiation under asymmetric information usually admits several perfect Bayesian equilibria. Maskin and Tirole (1992), therefore, have proposed to call the original contract *weakly renegotiation-proof* if its prescribed continuation is one of the equilibrium outcomes of the negotiation game between principal and agent; the original contract is called *strongly renegotiation-proof* if it is weakly renegotiation-proof and if there is no equilibrium of the negotiation game in which it is replaced by another contract.

---

[21] This is because an outside offer on average attracts all bad firms (who do not get an offer from the inside bank) and at best all good firms, depending on the bargaining between the firm and the inside investor. Hence, the best mix of applicants the outsider can expect to attract is the underlying mix of the whole population ($\lambda : 1 - \lambda$), which looses money by assumption.

[22] Remember that, by assumption, the firm does not know its type in $t = 2$. Hence, the bank knows more about the firm's prospects than the firm. Allowing for the firm to know its type in $t = 2$ would not change the analysis.

As has been pointed out by Gale and Hellwig (1989), weakly renegotiation-proof contracts have the fundamental conceptual difficulty that their value to the contracting parties at the time of contracting is ambiguous. However, as the next proposition shows the optimal monitoring contract in the situation considered here is in fact even strongly renegotiation-proof, under one unproblematic, and obvious, additional assumption. This assumption is that the bank at the renegotiation stage does not propose to replace the original contract by a continuation contract which yields the same expected payoffs to everybody. An example for such a contract is a contract which is the same as the old one, but in which the bank makes an additional transfer of $\hat{T}$ to the firm in $t = 2$, and the firm makes an additional repayment of $\hat{T}$ to the bank in every state in $t = 3$. Formally, such a continuation contract is different from the original contract, but its acceptance or rejection is a matter of indifference to both contracting parties.[23] Under this assumption, we have the following

PROPOSITION 7. *The optimal monitoring contract is strongly renegotiation-proof.*

Proof. In the Appendix.   ‖

Proposition 7 reflects the no-trade logic (Milgrom and Stokey (1982)) invoked by Maskin and Tirole (1992). Since the original contract is interim efficient—the project is continued if and only if the project is good—any proposal to change the contract is perceived as disadvantageous by the firm and therefore rejected. It is important to realize that such a rejection does not leave the firm in a contractual vacuum or at the mercy of its bank, as is implicitly assumed in some of the recent literature on relationship banking, but that the bank is bound by the contract which it was wise enough to sign before it acquired its inside information.

V. Conclusion

The analysis of this chapter has identified several sources of potential short-term biases of investment in a comprehensive dynamic contracting model and has studied the potential of monitoring to overcome these biases. It suggests that a bias towards an inefficient choice of investment structure cannot be eliminated even under complete long-term contracting between firms and investors, as long as the investors do not actively engage in information acquisition about the firm's activities. This provides a dynamic perspective on Diamond's (1984) general analysis of monitoring in financial markets.

It also provides a new perspective on the more macroeconomic debate of short-termism. In his international study of comparative corporate finance,

---

[23] In particular, such contract renegotiations do not give rise to the argument of Gale and Hellwig (1989), because the ex-ante value of the contract remains unchanged.

Mayer (1988) argues that "what underlies the short-term concern is the lack of commitment of market investors". This position has sometimes been challenged with the question of "why, if these long-term relationships are so valuable, firms do not develop them with lenders" (Mankiw (1988)). The present chapter has taken Mankiw's (1988) critique seriously and developed a model with unrestricted long-term contracting possibilities. In this perspective, the main determinant of inefficient short-termism then is not the lack of long-term financial relationships, but the ability, or lack thereof, to provide low-cost monitoring services within such relationships.

APPENDIX

Proof of Lemma 3. To abbreviate, let for any contract $\mathscr{C}$

$$T = L_1 - I_1,$$
$$B_0 = X_1 + T - R_2(X_1, 0) - R_1(x_1) - I_2,$$
$$B_1 = X_1 + X_2 + T - R_2(X_1, X_2) - R_1(X_1) - I_2.$$

B_0 is the total return to the firm if it succeeds in the first, but not in the second period, and B_1 is the total return if it succeeds in both periods. For the long-term project under contingent continuation, the incentive compatibility constraint of effort choice, (14), then is

$$\lambda p_1^l p_2^l B_1 + \lambda p_1^l (1 - p_2^l) B_0 + (1 - \lambda p_1^l)(T - R_1(0)) \geq E, \qquad (ICE)$$

the incentive compatibility constraint of project choice, (15), is

$$(p_1^s p_2^s - p_1^l p_2^l) B_1 + \left(p_1^s(1 - p_2^s) - p_1^l(1 - p_2^l) \right) B_0 \leq (p_1^s - p_1^l)(T - R_1(0)), \quad (ICP)$$

and the participation constraint for the investor

$$\lambda p_1^l p_2^l B_1 + \lambda p_1^l (1 - p_2^l) B_0 + (1 - \lambda p_1^l)(T - R_1(0)) - E \leq S^{lt}. \qquad (PCI)$$

(1) For the sufficiency part, one easily checks that it is possible to choose $T, R_1(0), R_1(X_1), R_2(X_1, 0), R_2(X_1, X_2)$ satisfying (10)–(11) such that

$$T - R_1(0) = S^{lt}, \qquad (A1)$$

$$B_0 = 0, \qquad (A2)$$

$$p_1^l p_2^l B_1 = p_1^l (T - R_1(0)) + E/\lambda. \qquad (A3)$$

For this choice, *(ICE)* and *(PCI)* hold with equality and, by (19),

$$(p_1^s p_2^s - p_1^l p_2^l)B_1 + (p_1^s(1 - p_2^s) - p_1^l(1 - p_2^l))B_0$$

$$= (p_1^s p_2^s - p_1^l p_2^l)\frac{1}{p_1^l p_2^l}(p_1^l(T - R_1(0)) + E/\lambda)$$

$$\lesseqqgtr (p_1^s - p_1^l)(T - R_1(0)),$$

which is *(ICP)*.

(2) For the "only if" part consider a contract with $h = l$ and $Y(0) = 0$ satisfying *(ICE)* and *(PCI)*. Adding *(ICE)* and *(PCI)* yields

$$T - R_1(0) \le S^{lt}. \tag{A4}$$

Assume (19) does not hold. In particular, $p_1^s p_2^s > p_1^l p_2^l$. Then

$$(p_1^s p_2^s - p_1^l p_2^l)B_1 + \left(p_1^s(1 - p_2^s) - p_1^l(1 - p_2^l)\right)B_0$$

$$\ge \frac{1}{p_2^l}(p_1^s p_2^s - p_1^l p_2^l)\left[T - R_1(0) + \frac{E}{\lambda p_1^l} - (1 - p_2^l)B_0\right] + \left(p_1^s(1 - p_2^s) - p_1^l(1 - p_2^l)\right)B_0$$

$$= \left(\frac{p_1^s}{p_2^l}(p_2^s - p_2^l) + p_1^s - p_1^l\right)(T - R_1(0)) + \frac{1}{p_2^l}\left[(p_1^s p_2^s - p_1^l p_2^l)\frac{E}{\lambda p_1^l} + p_1^s(p_2^l - p_2^s)B_0\right]$$

$$\ge \frac{1}{p_2^l}\left[p_1^s(p_2^l - p_2^s)(E - S^{lt}) + (p_1^s p_2^s - p_1^l p_2^l)\frac{E}{\lambda p_1^l}\right]$$

$$+ \frac{p_1^s}{p_2^l}(p_2^l - p_2^s)B_0 + (p_1^s - p_1^l)(T - R_1(0))$$

$$\ge \frac{1}{\lambda p_1^l p_2^l}\left[(\lambda p_1^l p_2^l(p_2^l - p_2^s) + p_1^s p_2^s - p_1^l p_2^l)E - \lambda p_1^l p_1^s(p_2^l - p_2^s)S^{lt}\right]$$

$$+ (p_1^s - p_1^l)(T - R_1(0)),$$

where the first inequality comes from *(ICE)*, the second from (A4), and the third from the fact that $B_0 \ge 0$. If (19) does not hold, the last line of the above expression is strictly larger than $(p_1^s - p_1^l)(T - R_1(0))$, hence, *(ICP)* does not hold. ‖

Proof of Proposition. Consider a contract of type $\mathscr{C}_M$ with $T = 0$. With this contract, the firm obtains an expected payoff of

$$\lambda p_1^l(X_1 - r_1 - I_2 + p_2^l(X_2 - r_2)) + \lambda(1 - p_1^l)p_2^l(X_2 - r_3) + (1 - \lambda)c - E, \tag{A5}$$

and the bank's participation constraint is

$$\lambda p_1^l(r_1 + p_2^l r_2) + \lambda(1 - p_1^l)(p_2^l r_3 - I_2) - (I - \lambda)c - I_1 - k \ge 0. \tag{PCB}$$

Efficiency of the continuation decision requires

$$p_2^l r_2 \geq I_2 - c. \tag{EC}$$

Incentive compatibility of the firm's project and effort choices require, respectively:

$$p_1^l(X_1 - r_1 - I_2 + p_2^l(X_2 - r_2)) + (I - p_1^l)p_2^l(X_2 - r_3) \tag{ICP}$$
$$\geq p_1^s(X_1 - r_1 - I_2 + p_2^s(X_2 - r_2)) + (I - p_1^s)p_2^s(X_2 - r_3),$$
$$p_1^l(X_1 - r_1 - I_2 + p_2^l(X_2 - r_2)) + (I - p_1^l)p_2^l(X_2 - r_3) \geq c + E/\lambda. \tag{ICE}$$

Suppose first that $\lambda p_1^l(X_1 + p_2^l X_2 - I_2) \leq I_1 + K$. In this case, setting $r_1 = X_1 - I_2$, $r_2 = X_2$, $c = 0$, and r_3 such that (PCB) binds, satisfies (EC), (ICP), and (ICE). Since $S^M \geq 0$, (A5) is non-negative.

Suppose now that $\lambda p_1^l(X_1 + p_2^l X_2 - I_2) > I_1 + K$. Set, for any $c < I_2$,

$$p_2^l r_3 = I_2 - c.$$

Then (ICP) is equivalent to

$$p_2^l(p_1^l p_2^l - p_1^s p_2^s)(X_2 - r_2) + ((1 - p_1^l)p_2^l - (1 - p_1^s)p_2^s)(p_2^l X_2 - I_2 + c)$$
$$\geq p_2^l(p_1^s - p_1^l)(X_1 - I_2 - r_1), \tag{A6}$$

and (ICE) is equivalent to

$$p_1^l(X_1 - r_1 - p_2^l r_2) + p_2^l X_2 - I_2 \geq p_1^l c + E/\lambda. \tag{A7}$$

It is straightforward to verify that there are r_1, r_2, $c < I_2$ such that (PCB), (A6) and (A7) are compatible.

Setting

$$T = \lambda p_1^l(r_1 + p_2^l r_2) + \lambda(1 - p_1^l)(p_2^l r_3 - I_2) - (I - \lambda)c - I_1 - K,$$

then yields a contract on which the bank makes zero expected profits. Because $c < I_2$, the bank chooses to continue finance if and only if the firm is good. ‖

Proof of Proposition. The proof adopts the framework of Maskin and Tirole (1992). Suppose $\tilde{x}_1^l = 0$ is realized. An *outcome* of the lending relationship following $\tilde{x}_1^l = 0$ is a 4-tuple $\mu = (Y_2, T_2, R_f, R_s)$, where

$$Y_2 = \begin{cases} 0 & \text{if no continuation,} \\ 1 & \text{if continuation, loan } I_2 - c, \end{cases}$$

$T_2 \geq -(1 - Y_2)c - T$ is a transfer from the bank to the firm in $t = 2, R_f \leq T + T_2$ is a payment from the firm if the continuation project is unsuccessful, and $R_s \leq T + T_2 + X_2$ a payment from the firm if it is successful.

Denote by $V^h(\mu)$ the payoff to the bank from an outcome μ if the firm's quality is bad, by $V^R(\mu)$ the payoff if the quality is good. Analogously, let $U^i(\mu), i = b, g$, denote the firm's payoff. If we denote $\pi^b = 0$ and $\pi^E = p_2^l$, then for $i = b, g$

$$V^i(\mu) = Y_2[\pi^i R_2 + (1 - \pi^i)R_f - I_2 + c] - T_2$$

$$U^i(\mu) = Y_2[\pi^t(X_2 - R_s) - (1 - \pi^t)R_f - c] + T_2.$$

A (continuation) *contract* is a pair of outcomes (μ^b, μ^s), from which the bank is allowed to choose depending on its information. The existing contract, signed in $t = 1$, is (μ_0^b, μ_0^g), where

$$\mu_0^b = (0, 0, 0, 0)$$

$$\mu_0^g = (1, 0, 0, r_3).$$

By construction, (μ_0^b, μ_0^g) is *incentive compatible* (for the bank), i.e.

$$V^h(\mu_0^b) \geq V^b(\mu_0^g)$$

and

$$V^R(\mu_0^g) \geq V^g(\mu_0^b).$$

It is straightforward to show that (μ_0^b, μ_0^g) is *interim efficient with respect to prior beliefs*, i.e. that there is no other incentive compatible contract (μ^b, μ^g) for which (i) $V^i(\mu^i) \geq V^i(\mu_0)$ for $i = b, g$ with one inequality being strict, and (ii) $(1 - \lambda)U^b(\mu^b) + \lambda U^g(\mu^g) \geq \lambda(p_2^l(X_2 - r_3) - c)$. Given the assumption that no payoff-identical contracts are proposed in the renegotiation, the proposition now follows directly from Proposition 9 in Maskin and Tirole (1992). ∥

References

Admati, A., Pfleiderer, P., and Zechner, J. (1994). "Large shareholder activism, risk sharing, and financial market equilibrium." *Journal of Political Economy*, 102: 1097–130.

Bohlin, E. (1991). "Managerial incentives for myopic investments — A review of some recent models." Mimeo, Chalmers University of Technology, Göteborg.

Bolton, P. (1990). "Renegotiation and the dynamics of contract design." *European Economic Review*, 34: 303–10.

Darrough, M. N. (1987). "Managerial incentives for short-term results: A comment." *Journal of Finance*, 42: 1097–102.

Dewatripont, M., and Maskin, E. (1990). "Contract renegotiation in models of asymmetric information." *European Economic Review*, 34: 311–21.

—— (1995). "Credit and efficiency in centralized and decentralized economies." *Review of Economic Studies*, 62: 541–55.

Diamond, D. W. (1984). "Financial intermediation and delegated monitoring." *Review of Economic Studies*, 51: 393–414.

Fischer, K. (1990). "Hausbankbezjehungen als Instrument der Bindung zwischen Banken und Unternehmen." Ph.D. Dissertation, Universität Bonn.

Franks, J., and Torous, W. N. (1989). "An empirical investigation of U.S. firms in reorganization." *Journal of Finance*, 44: 747–69.

Fudenberg, D., Holmstrom, B., and Milgrom, P. (1990). "Short-term contracts and long-term agency relationships." *Journal of Economic Theory*, 51: 1–31.

Gale, D., and Hellwig, M. (1985). "Incentive-compatible debt contracts: The one-period problem." *Review of Economic Studies*, 52: 647–63.

—— (1989). "Repudiation and renegotiation: The case of sovereign debt." *International Economic Review*, 30: 3–31.

Hart, O. D. (1993). "Theories of optimal capital structure: The managerial discretion perspective," in Blair (ed.), *The Deal Decade. What Takeovers and Leveraged Buyouts Mean for Corporate Governance* (Washington, D.C.: The Brookings Institution), 19–53.

Hellwig, M. (1991). "Banking, financial intermediation and corporate finance," in A. Giovannini and C. Mayer (eds.), *European Financial Integration* (Cambridge: Cambridge Univ. Press), 35–63.

Innes, R. D. (1990). "Limited liability and incentive contracting with ex-ante action choices." *Journal of Economic Theory*, 52: 45–67.

Jacobs, M. T. (1993). *Short-Term America*. Cambridge, Mass.: Harvard Business School Press.

Jensen, M. C., and Meckling, W. H. (1976). "Theory of the firm: Managerial behavior, agency costs and ownership structure." *Journal of Financial Economics*, 3: 305–60.

Jeon, S. (1991). "Managerial myopia is only transient in 'rational' markets." Mimeo, Yale University.

Kahneman, D., Slovic, P., and Tversky, A. (1982). *Judgement under Uncertainty: Heuristics and Biases*. Cambridge: Cambridge Univ. Press.

Lummer, S., and McConnell, J. (1989). "Further evidence of the bank lending process and the reaction of the capital market to bank loan agreements." *Journal of Financial Economics*, 25: 99–122.

Mankiw, G. (1988). "Comment." *European Economic Review*, 32: 1183–6.

Maskin, E., and Tirole, J. (1992). "The principal–agent relationship with an informed principal, II: Common values." *Econometrica*, 60: 1–42.

Mayer, C. (1988). "New issues in corporate finance." *European Economic Review*, 32: 1167–83.

Milgrom, P., and Stokey, N. (1982). "Information, trade, and common knowledge." *Journal of Economic Theory*, 26: 17–27.

Narayanan, M. P. (1985). "Managerial incentives for short-term results." *Journal of Finance*, 40: 1469–84.

Porter, M. (ed.) (1992). *Capital Choices: Changing the Way America Invests in Industry*. Washington, D.C.: Council on Competitiveness.

Rajan, R. (1992). "Insiders and outsiders: The choice between informed and arm's length debt." *Journal of Finance*, 47: 1367–400.

——, and Winton, A. (1993). "Covenants and collateral as incentives to monitor." Mimeo, GSB Chicago.

Rey, P., and Salanié, B. (1990). "Long-term, short-term and renegotiation: On the value of commitment in contracting." *Econometrica*, 58: 597–619.

——, and —— (1992). "Long-term, short-term and renegotiation: On the value of commitment with asymmetric information." Mimeo, ENSAE.

Sharpe, S. A. (1990). "Asymmetric information, bank lending, and implicit contracts: A stylized model of customer relationships." *Journal of Finance*, 45: 1069–87.

Stein, J. C. (1989). "Efficient capital markets, inefficient firms: A model of myopic corporate behavior." *Quarterly Journal of Economics*, 104: 655–69.

von Thadden, E. (1992). "The commitment of finance, duplicated monitoring, and the investment horizon." Mimeo, Universität Basel.

Townsend, R. (1982). "Optimal multiperiod contracts and the gain from enduring relationships under private information." *Journal of Political Economy*, 90: 1166–86.

Yanelle, M.-O. (1989). "On the theory of intermediation." Ph.D. Dissertation, Universität Bonn.

18

Competition among Financial Intermediaries When Diversification Matters

Andrew Winton

1. Introduction

Many models of financial intermediaries (e.g. Diamond 1984; Ramakrishnan and Thakot 1984) imply that these institutions have substantial scale economies linked to improved diversification. History provides some support for this view. For example, in the period leading up to the Great Depression, the U.S., which restricted most banks to a single state, had higher bank failure rates than Canada, which had large, nationwide banks; within the U.S., larger banks were less likely to fail than smaller banks (Calomiris 1993). Some have used this to argue that, if regulators would only leave intermediaries alone, free entry and competitive would quickly lead to the dominance of several large, diversified, competitive intermediaries, laying to rest concerns about safety and collusion alike.

A closer look at the historical record suggests that this conclusion may be too sanguine. Consider the experience of Australia, Canada, and Scotland, where the formation of intermediaries was relatively unrestricted. In each case, one sees high initial entry, slow consolidation through failure and merger, and a strong tendency to collusion among the survivors, even when these numbered a dozen or more. Once consolidation occurred, these systems seem to have been almost immune to entry by new institutions. By contrast, the more fragmented banking system of the late nineteenth and early twentieth century U.S. did allow significant entry, and entry was greatest in those states that had formal deposit insurance. What forces account for these patterns, and what are the implications of these forces for bank regulation?

This chapter originally formed chapter Four of my Ph.D. dissertation, which was supported by a Unisys Fellowship. Since then, I have benefited from a research grant from the Banking Research Center at Northwestern University. I thank David Besanko, Susan Chaplinsky, Mike Fishman, Thomas Gehrig, Stuart Greenbaum, Laurie Hodrick. Rich Kihlstrom, Raghu Rajan, Anjan Thakor, Anne Villamil, and Asher Wolinsky, along with the members of the Penn Shadow Theory Workshop and participants at the *Journal of Financial Intermediation* Symposium on the Reform of Financial Institutions and Markets. All mistakes remain my responsibility.

In this chapter, I suggest that these patterns can be explained by looking more closely at how diversification affects competition among financial intermediaries. Suppose that, because of fixed costs in providing financial services to a given sector or group, larger intermediaries ("banks") are potentially better diversified than smaller ones, and that diversification improves the quality of the service the bank provides to investors. Furthermore, suppose that the bank funds itself with debt-like contracts, as do many intermediaries, such as banks, finance companies, and insurers. These features—common to many models of financial intermediation, such as delegated monitoring or insurance—have several implications for bank competition.

The link between size and diversification implies that the more investors use a given bank, the better off the investors are. This adoption externality makes investor beliefs self-fulfilling: if all believe a bank is small, hence risky and not worth investing in few investors will go to that bank, and it will in fact be small, hence risky and not worth investing in. If a bank wants to establish a reputation for being large, diversified, and thus well worth investing in, it must first get large: i.e. it must attract more investors. The only short-run tool at the bank's disposal is the "stated rate" (principal plus interest) that it offers investors. By raising this rate, it can offer a higher expected return to any investors already planning to use the bank; seeing this, marginal investors at other banks will now choose this bank, making the bank larger and better diversified, and further improving investors' expected return.

However, raising its stated rate is costly to the bank for two reasons. First, even without a change in size, the higher stated rate clearly decreases bank profits. Second, if the bank's size does increase, then, even for a fixed stated rate, improved diversification increases the bank's expected payments to each investor: debtholders benefit from reduced risk. As a result, if the bank's initial profit margins are not too high, it may prefer not to try to increase its market share. This is a form of the Myers (1977) underinvestment or "debt overhang" problem, where new business that reduces overall risk may not be chosen because it benefits debtholders at the expense of shareholders. This debt overhang effect weakens rate competition among banks, promoting collusion.

This apparent contradiction—banks may not wish to increase size despite economies of scale from diversification—is rooted in the adoption externality already mentioned. Although a larger, better diversified bank can give investors a better expected return while offering a lower stated rate than smaller, riskier rivals, getting investors to accept the lower stated rate relies on the bank having a reputation for being larger and better-diversified. To get this reputation, the bank must attract and maintain a larger market share for some period of time, which is costly. The less transparent the bank's situation and the less stable the banking system, the longer the bank will have to maintain a large market share in order to change its reputation, making the *eventual* improvement in profits less attractive relative to the immediate costs.

To see how this affects the evolution of intermediary structure, first consider a market where banks are not yet well established, either because intermediation is new or because market growth is high. In such a setting, it is unlikely that investor beliefs will have coordinated on any particular bank, so banks that enter split up the market. Here, the reverse of the debt overhang effect suggests that many banks will enter: for any given stated rate, banks have higher expected profit margins as they are smaller. Indeed, there is a tendency for the maximum number of (barely viable) banks to enter.

As time goes on, many of these small, risky banks will eventually fail. Investor beliefs are likely to focus on the survivors, giving them an incumbency advantage over new entrants: if, all else equal, investors expect incumbents to have a larger market share and thus greater diversification, any given stated rate from an incumbent offers investors a higher expected total return than the same rate from a new entrant. Thus, investor beliefs become a barrier to entry. The debt overhang cost of expanding through rate competition may make collusion among the incumbent banks feasible even when their numbers are somewhat large.

Now consider the problem of regulators maximizing social welfare. Encouraging free entry in the early stages of financial intermediation may lead to many inefficiently small intermediaries, with high rates of failure and ensuing costs. However, although restricting initial entry should help focus investors on a relatively small number of large (hence safer) intermediaries, this makes collusion more likely. Furthermore, as time passes, investor beliefs are likely to focus more and more on the incumbents, making it hard for "de novo" entrants to mount a credible threat even if regulators later drop entry restrictions. If banks in other jurisdictions are already well diversified, these institutions might be able to enter—if investors in the "domestic" region are sufficiently aware of these "foreign" banks' safety, and if the foreign banks can overcome the usual informational, cultural, and political difficulties of operating in a different region. In fact, as discussed in Section 7, it was the arrival of large foreign banks that finally broke the oligopoly of Britain's large "clearing banks" in the 1960s.

As an alternative, regulators can insure investors; by reducing investors' concern for the risk and thus the size of banks, such insurance weakens the advantage of incumbents, enhancing entry and competition. Indeed, the introduction of deposit insurance in Canada in 1967 seems to have had these effects (see Section 7). However, as U.S. experience shows, entry may be excessive, especially if guarantee fees are fixed regardless for some time, to prevent initial fragmentation; also, upon lifting such restrictions, they may not wish to fully insure investors, so that investors still give some preference to large incumbents.

These results rely critically on the assumptions that greater size is required for better diversification, that investors find it costly to coordinate their actions, and that investor beliefs are slow to change. These are most likely to apply in settings where information problems loom large, increasing the cost of risk-sharing agreements among institutions, coordination among investors, and credible disclosure of institutions' risk levels to investors. Thus, both historically and currently, the model's conclusions should apply most strongly to intermediation in developing economies, where such market imperfections are likely to play a greater role.

My analysis is related to several recent papers that explore competition among banks when diversification plays a role. Using the delegated monitoring paradigm of Diamond (1984), Yanelle (1989, 1997) explores the impact of different contracting structures, while Winton (1995) focuses on the role of bank capital and the choice between competitive and monopolistic regimes. Yosha (1997) examines efficient industry structure for risk-sharing intermediaries as a function of the size of the economy. Matutes and Vives (1996) examine spatial competition between two banks in the presence of transportation costs and find that deposit insurance increases rate competition and bank failure risk. Gehrig (1995) shows that spatial rent-seeking causes excessive entry. In Besanko and Thakor (1993), insured banks that diversify forfeit gains from risk shifting but increase their odds of surviving to collect informational rents from lending relationships; free entry diminishes these rents and encourages risk shifting. My work differs from these papers by focusing on how investor beliefs interact with bank competition, entry, and the impact of regulation to influence intermediary industrial structure.

A second related line of research examines the influence of adoption externalities on firm competition. Katz and Shapiro (1995) show that, if customer utility increases with the supplier's market share, then supplier incentives to provide compatible products are less than social incentives, and this may result in inefficient fragmentation. Farrell and Saloner (1986) show that adoption externalities can prevent users from switching to a new product even if it is innately superior, because users are worse off of they are the only ones to use the new product. My chapter resembles these papers in showing how adoption externalities can lead to inefficient fragmentation or excessive incumbency power. However, because the firms on which I focus are intermediaries whose "product" is a debt contract, increased market share has an immediate negative impact on firm profits; this strengthens the fragmentation result in new markets and undermines competition in mature markets.

The rest of the chapter is organized as follows. Section 2 motivates and sets out the basic framework. Section 3 examines investor beliefs and equilibrium outcomes when multiple banks compete in a static setting. Sections 4 and 5 extend the analysis to a dynamic setting, where banks interact repeatedly and market shares in the present may influence investor beliefs and behavior in the future. Section 6 examines regulatory issues. Section 7 discusses historical evidence that is consistent with the paper's implications, and Section 8 concludes.

2. Basic Model and Assumptions

A. General considerations

Four key modeling features are required for my analysis: (i) financial intermediaries provide a service that improves with diversification, (ii) diversification tends to increase with intermediary size, (iii) intermediaries optimally issue debt or debt-like contracts to investors, and (iv) large numbers of investors cannot coordinate their actions. Before going through the model's specifics, I discuss the motivation for these more general features.

Financial intermediation improves with diversification. In several models of financial intermediation there is a cost linked to intermediary risk, and a better diversified intermediary has less risk and thus lower costs. In models of insurance or liquidity provision, investors are risk averse and face same risk which the intermediary can pool and diversify on their behalf. In models of delegated investment monitoring or evaluation, the possibility of bad outcomes allows the intermediary to hide proceeds (if these are costly to verify) or to claim that bad luck rather than lack of effort led to the bad outcomes (if effort is unobservable); an intermediary with better diversified investments has less chance of very bad outcomes, reducing associated costs.[1] Real intermediaries may perform several of these functions: e.g. commercial banks provide liquidity and evaluate and monitor loans, and life insurers provide insurance and evaluate and monitor privately placed bonds and commercial mortgages.

Diversification tends to increase with intermediary size. If there are fixed costs to monitoring or evaluating an individual borrower, delegation to one or a few intermediaries avoids costly duplication of effort. By the same token, a larger intermediary can serve more borrowers, and so be better diversified, at lower cost. The same applies to diversifying across types of borrowers when there are fixed costs to developing skills to deal with each type of borrower, and to diversifying across customers in an insurance setting when there are fixed costs to providing insurance to a single customer or type of customer.

---

[1] For liquidity provision, see Diamond and Dybvig (1983), Chari and Jagannathan (1988), Jacklin and Bhattarcharya (1988), and Gorton and Pennacchi (1990); for delegated investment evaluation, see Campbell and Kracaw (1980), Ramakrishnan and Thakor (1984), and Boyd and Prescott (1986); references for delegated investment monitoring are given below. For further references and discussion, see Bhattacharya and Thakor (1993).

Of course, if intermediaries can credibly share information with ease, they can cheaply share risks among themselves without excessive agency problems, allowing diversification without an increase in scale. In reality, risk-sharing techniques such as loan sales and syndications among banks and reinsurance contracting among insurers do involve some costs and agency problems, but their existence suggests that my model's results apply most strongly to times and places where the technology for credibly sharing information among intermediaries is least developed, and vice versa.

A related issue is that, to the extent an intermediary has some choice over how and where it expands (in terms of asset risk in particular), the degree to which size improves diversification can be partly under the institution's control and is likely to be partly unobservable. As I argue is Section 5, this actually strengthens my model's results: a small and risky bank has the least incentive to expand in a more diversified manner, especially since it will take to convince the investors that the bank is both expanding and choosing the less risky strategy.

Finally, there may be diseconomies of scale (e.g. from managing larger numbers of employees and managers), so that intermediary performance eventually begins to deteriorate with size. As I argue at the end of Section 3, this does not change my model's qualitative results so long as there is significant range of bank sizes over which diversification is valuable. There is evidence that larger banks are indeed safer. In addition to U.S. experience in the nineteenth and early twentieth centuries, failure rates in Australia, Canada, Scotland, and England did decrease substantially once banks had consolidated (see references in Section 7). Thus, it seems reasonable to assume that diversification through size does add value over a significant range.

Intermediaries optimally issue debt-like contracts to investors. This follows under a variety of assumptions. If intermediary returns are costly to verify, debt is optimal because it minimizes the situations in which investors must verify the intermediary's true return. If the intermediary's effort invested in monitoring or evaluating risks is unobservable, debt is optimal among a wide class of contracts as a means of inducing effort (Innes 1990). Finally, debt is the least risky limited-liability contract, which may make it attractive to risk-averse investors. Empirically, many intermediaries are highly leverages: in the U.S., banks, finance companies, and life insurance all have average leverage ratios of roughly 90 percent or more (see the Federal Reserve's *Flow of Funds*).

Investors find it very costly to coordinate their actions. This seems especially reasonable for intermediaries with large numbers of small individual investors. Even institutional investors find coordinated action difficult when they are present in numbers: for example, most public corporate debt is held by institutional investors, yet debt renegotiations outside bankruptcy are rarer when more debt is public, hence diffusely held (Gilson et al. 1990).

B. Specific assumptions

Although the features just listed can be found in many models of intermediation, for purposes of exposition I use delegated monitoring with costly state verification. What follows is a streamlined form of this model that incorporates imperfect diversification.[2]

A continuum of identical risk-neutral investors are endowed with a generic good; the total sum of their endowments is N. Investors can consume their endowment or invest it elsewhere. There is also a continuum of entrepreneurs endowed with projects that requires funding: each entrepreneur's project requires the endowments of K investors and returns a random amount of generic consumption good at the end of the period. For simplicity, assume that the total mass of entrepreneurs greatly exceeds N/K; then investors have relative market power and entrepreneurs only receive their reservation return.[3]

Investors can only observe ("monitor") a project's return at effort cost C. Since an unmonitored entrepreneur has incentive to misrepresent returns (so as to pay investors less and pocket any difference), optimal investment contracts specify the reported returns and associated payments that lead to monitoring so as to minimize investors' expected monitoring costs. Williamson (1986) shows that the optimal symmetric investment contract is debt, but this leads to duplication of monitoring efforts. Let $\underline{v}$ be the maximum of investors' utility from either consuming their endowment or directly in entrepreneurs' projects. For simplicity, I abstract from how this "autarky" return depends on the distribution of project returns. Alternatively, one can assume consumption dominates direct investment.

As an alternative, investors can invest in an intermediary ("bank"), which given the investors debt contracts and invests their endowments in the projects of many entrepreneurs. Banks are run by risk-neutral agents with a reservation return of zero. Since the bank is the only monitor of each project it invests in, the per-unit cost of monitoring each entrepreneur is reduced to C/K. Of course, investors must now monitor the bank, but if project returns are imperfectly correlated, the per-unit risk of monitoring a sufficiently diversified bank can be

---

[2] The seminal work in this area of Diamond (1984) and Williamson (1986) assumes that perfect diversification is possible. The more realistic case of imperfect diversification has been explored by Winton (1995) and Yanelle (1997), who analyze finite environments, and Krasa and Villamil (1992), who analyze the case where project risk has a systematic component.

[3] Winton (1995) considers a setting where the supply of entrepreneurs is endogenous, and banks must compete for borrowers as well as investors. Because borrowers' probabilities of getting loans depend on how many deposits their bank has raised, *borrower* beliefs must be modeled, and investors and borrowers from beliefs based on banks' lending *and* deposit rates. Nevertheless, the current chapter's thrust would be unchanged: coordination is even more important under two-sided competition, so coordination problems and fragmentation would be even more likely in a young banking system, and borrower and investor beliefs would be even more likely to give incumbents an advantage in a mature system.

reduced significantly. I assume that a sufficiently diversified bank can indeed offer investors a return in excess of $\underline{v}$.

Within a period, the sequence of events is as follows. First, banks publicly and simultaneously offer stated rates to investors, after which investors simultaneously choose where to invest their funds. Once banks have raised funds, they invest in entrepreneurs' projects as already described. At the end of the period, entrepreneurs report their returns, which banks monitor as specified by contract. After receiving payments from entrepreneurs, banks report their portfolio returns to investors; if the per-unit return is less than the bank's states rate D, the bank's investors monitor. Payments are made to investors as per contract, all agents consume, and the period ends.

Denote the asset portfolio return of a bank of size n (i.e. a bank with mass n of investors) as $\tilde{X}_n$. If K_μ is the expected project cash flow net of an entrepreneur's reservation return, and the bank funds n/K entrepreneurs, then $E[\tilde{X}_n]$ is $n\mu$.[4] The precise distribution $G_n(x)$ of $\tilde{X}_n$ depends on the correlation between entrepreneurs' projects, which I abstract from. However, so long as different projects are not perfectly correlated, the risk of the per-unit portfolio return $\tilde{X}_n/n$ decreases in the sense of Rothschild and Stigliz (1970) as n increases; that is, bigger banks are better diversified.[5] The distribution of the per unit return $H_n(\cdot)$ is defined by $H_n(x/n) = G_n(x)$. Finally, let c be the bank's expected cost of monitoring per unit invested, i.e. c equals C/K times the probability with which the bank monitors each entrepreneur.

If the bank issues each investor debt with "stated rate" (principal plus interest) D, each investor receives cash payments equal to $\min\{D, \tilde{X}_n/n\}$, and must monitor the bank whenever $\tilde{X}_n/n$ is less than D. Letting $r(n, D)$ be an investor's *expected* cash payment, and integrating by parts, an investor's expected return $v(n, D)$ is

$$v(n, D) = r(n, D) - C \cdot H_n(D) = D - \int_0^D H_n(x)\, dx - C \cdot H_n(D). \qquad (2.1)$$

Similarly, the bank's expected profits $\pi(n, D)$ are given by

$$\pi(n, D) = n \cdot [\mu - c - r(n, D)], \qquad (2.2)$$

---

[4] I am abstracting from credit rationing, which occurs if lending at a rate that gives entrepreneurs their reservation return is dominated by lending at a lower rate and reducing verification costs. See Williamson (1986) and Winton (1995) for analysis of intermediation's effect on credit rationing.

[5] While some might argue that most of the gains from diversification of independent risks are achieved with relatively small numbers of different projects, there may be sectoral and systematic components leading to significant cross-correlations between groups of projects. This could be explicitly modeled by assuming that groups of entrepreneurs of some measure ε form communities or sectors, and then specifying a correlation structure across such groups.

and the bank's average profit margin $m(n, D)$ is

$$m(n, D) = \frac{\pi(n, D)}{n} = \mu - c - r(n, D). \tag{2.3}$$

The next lemma establishes some useful features of investor returns and bank profits.

LEMMA 2.1 (Effects of Bank Size and Stated Rate on Investor Returns and Bank Profits).

   (i) *All else equal, an increase in a bank's stated rate D increases an investor's expected payment $r(n, D)$, increases an investor's expected monitoring costs, and decreases expected bank profits $\pi(n, D)$ and profit margin $m(n, D)$.*

  (ii) *All else equal, an increase in bank size n increases an investor's expected payment $r(n, D)$ and decreases expected bank profit margin $m(n, D)$. If bank asset returns are normally distributed, an investor's expected monitoring cost decreases if the stated rate D is less than the mean per-unit asset return μ, and increases if D is greater than μ.*

The proof of this and other results is in the Appendix. The effects of a change in stated rate are intuitive: the expected payment to investors rises, hurting bank profits and margins, but the bank is more likely to default, increasing investor's expected monitoring costs. The effects of a change in bank size follow from the impact of improved diversification. Since debt payments are a concave function of bank asset returns, reducing the per-investor risk of asset returns increases investors' expected returns: the density of returns "tightens" about its mean μ, reducing expected shortfalls on the debt (Rothschild and Stiglitz 1970). This in turn hurts the bank's expected profits margin. However, although the expected payment to each investor rises, the probability of default need not decrease: indeed, if the stated rate D is above the mean return μ, tightening the density about μ may make default more likely.

In much of what follows, I impose two simplifying assumptions on the behavior of expected investor monitoring costs.

ASSUMPTION 1. *Suppose a bank of size n offers stated rate D such that investor expected return $v(n, D)$ exceeds $\underline{v}$ and expected bank profits $\pi(n, D)$ are nonnegative. Then the bank's chance of default declines with size (i.e., $\partial H_n(D)/\partial n < 0$).*

This implies that larger banks always *potentially* dominate smaller banks.[6] This assumption seems generally plausible in the context of delegated monitoring. For example, if bank returns are roughly normally distributed, Lemma 2.1(ii)

---

  [6] To see this, consider two banks, one of size n, the other of size $n' > n$. By Lemma 2.1(ii), $r(n, D) < r(n', D)$, and, so long as $v(n, D) \geq \underline{v}$, $C \cdot H_n(D) > C \cdot H_n(D)$. By lowering its rate to a level D' at which $r(n', D') = r(n, D)$, the large bank reduces investor monitoring costs further; thus investors are better off, while the large bank's margin is the same as the smaller banks'.

implies that the bank's chance of default increases with diversification only if the stated rate D exceeds the mean return μ; this implies that the bank defaults more than the time, which seems unlikely to be a general characteristic of viable banks. Nevertheless, small banks may have to offer rates in excess of μ, and there may be other unmodeled diseconomies of scale, so I consider the effects of weakening this assumption at the end of Section 3.

ASSUMPTION 2. *Suppose a bank of size n offers stated rate D such that expected bank Profits $\pi(n, D)$ are nonnegative. Then investors' expected return $v(n, D)$ rises with D (i.e. $\partial v(n, D)/\partial D > 0$).*

Assumption 2 says that, if the stated rate D is low enough to allow a bank of size n to earn positive profits, increasing D increases an investor's expected payment $r(n, D)$ more than it increases the investor's expected monitoring costs $C \cdot H_n(D)$. Suppose the distribution of bank asset returns has the monotone hazard rate property, as do many common distributions. Then Assumption 2 holds so long as monitoring costs C are not too high; otherwise, investor returns $v(n, D)$ are first increasing, then decreasing, in D.[7] As discussed at the end of Section 3, the main effect of weakening this assumption is to weaken rate competition among banks.

For any bank size n, define $D_0(n)$ as the stated rate that sets expected bank profits equal to zero, so that $r(n, D_0(n)) = \mu - c$. Since $r(n, 0)$ is 0, $r(n, \infty)$ is μ, and $r(\cdot)$ increases in D, $D_0(n)$ always exists and is unique; also since $r(\cdot)$ increases in n, $D_0(n)$ is decreasing in n. Similarly, for any n, define $\underline{D}(n)$ as the lowest stated rate D for which investor's expected return $v(n, D)$ equals $\underline{v}$. Assumption 1 (chance of default falls with size) guarantees that $\underline{D}(n)$ is decreasing in n with steeper downward slope than $D_0(n)$.[8]

Since I assume that banking is viable and larger banks can dominate smaller ones, $\underline{D}(N)$ must be less than $D_0(N)$. It seems reasonable to suppose that very small banks are not sufficiently diversified to be preferable to direct lending, so that $\underline{D}(0)$ is strictly greater than $D_0(0)$; this assumption is not essential to my results, but it simplifies analysis. Under this assumption, define $\underline{n}$ as the unique size for which $\underline{D}(n)$ and $D_0(n)$ are equal; $\underline{n}$ is the minimum size a bank must achieve to offer both itself and its investors returns better than autarky.

Figure 1 shows a numerical example of $\underline{D}(\cdot)$ and $D_0(\cdot)$. In this example, total market size N is 10. Bank asset returns are normally distributed with mean $\mu = 1.1$ and variance $0.0008 + (0.0012/n)$, so some risk is undiversifiable (a bank of size 10 has returns with 3 percent standard deviation). Investors have "autarkic" return 1.03, their cost of monitoring the bank C is 0.10, and the bank's, cost

---

[7] $\partial v(n, D)/\partial D = 1 - H_n(D) - C \cdot h_n(D)$. If the hazard rate $h_n(D)/[1 - H_n(D)]$ increases in D, $\partial v(n, D)/\partial D > 0$ for low D and switches sign at most once. The uniform, normal, and gamma distributions and their truncated versions all have this property (Barlow and Proschan 1975).

[8] Winton (1990) shows that $\underline{D}(n)$ has these same basic properties in a model where intermediaries provide insurance, so that $v(n, D) = E[\mu(\min\{D, \tilde{X}_n/n\})]$ for some concave u.

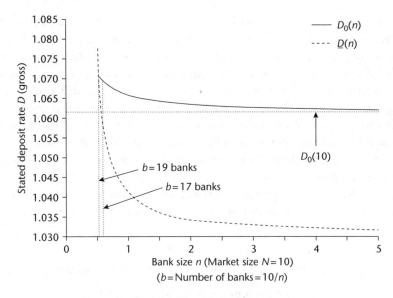

Figure 1. Bank and investor reservation rates.

per unit of assets c is 0.04. In this example, minimum viable bank size $\underline{n}$ is approximately 5.2 percent of total market size.

3. Rate Competition among Banks in a Static Setting

This section examines competition in a single-period setting, which establishes the key themes of the chapter and serves as a building block for the multiperiod analysis in Section 4. After examining how investors react to bank rates, I look at bank competition in two settings: a relatively new system where no banks are well established, and a mature system where some banks are well established. As argued below, these two settings have very different implications for which investor beliefs are plausible, affecting how investors react to bank rates and thus how banks compete with one another. At the end of the section I discuss some alternative investor beliefs, especially with regard to weakening Assumptions 1 and 2 from the previous section. Throughout, my analysis assumes that equilibrium must be subgame perfect: starting from any possible sequence of events through a point in time, the subsequent behavior of banks and investors satisfies "best response" (is a Nash equilibrium).

A. Investor behavior

For the moment, suppose the number of banks is fixed at b, either through regulatory fiat or historical accident; later, b will be endogenized under free entry. Solving for equilibrium through backward induction, the first question is how investors behave when faced with rates $\{D_i\}_{i=1}^b$, where D_i is bank i's stated rate. Subgame perfection requires that, for *any* such set of rates, each investor chooses a bank that maximizes her expected return. This expected return depends not only on her bank's rate, which she can observe ex ante, but on the bank's size, which depends on how many investors choose to use that bank. Thus, an investor's actions depend on the relationship between the stated rates banks offer and the share of the market each bank is expected to attract. Of course, in equilibrium, investor's beliefs must be consistent with their eventual behavior; i.e. if a bank is expected to have a certain market share, this must be the bank's share in equilibrium.

Let $n_i(D_1, \ldots, D_b)$ be investors' expectation of bank i's size, given rates $(D_1, \ldots, D_b)$. From the preceding discussion, a set of beliefs $\{n_1, \ldots, n_b\}$ is consistent with equilibrium if

$$v(n_i(\cdot), D_i) = v(n_j(\cdot), D_j) \geq v(n_k(\cdot), D_k) \quad \text{for all } i, j, k \quad \text{such that} \quad (3.1)$$

$$n_i(\cdot) > 0, n_j(\cdot) > 0, \quad \text{and} \quad n_k(\cdot) = 0,$$

$$v(n_i(\cdot), D_i) \geq \underline{v} \quad \text{for all } i \quad \text{such that} \quad n_i(\cdot) \geq 0, \quad \text{and} \quad (3.2)$$

$$\sum_{i=1}^b n_i(\cdot) \leq N, \text{ with equality whenever } v_i(n_i(\cdot), D_i) > \underline{v} \quad \text{for some } i. \quad (3.3)$$

Condition (3.1) says that individual investors must be indifferent among banks with positive market shares (otherwise, they would not be maximizing their expected returns), but they may strictly dislike banks that no one uses; (3.2) requires that, if a bank has positive market share, investors prefer that bank over autarky; finally, (3.3) assures that beliefs are consistent with market clearing.

A given set of bank rates may permit several sets of beliefs that are consistent with equilibrium. For example, as long as bank i's rate D_i is not too much lower than other bank rates, setting i's size to N and all other bank sizes to 0 is an equilibrium; this could be permuted, or several banks could have nonzero sizes, etc. However, in the current setting, some of these beliefs are more plausible than others.

Consider rates $\{D_i\}_{i=1}^b$ and an associated set of beliefs about bank sizes $\{n_i\}_{i=1}^b$. Suppose bank 1 increases its rate from D_1 to $D_1 + \varepsilon$. So long as $v(n_1, D)$ is increasing in D for D between D_1 and $D + \varepsilon$ any investors planning to use bank 1 would now be strictly better off, so they should still plan to use bank 1—and investors on the margin at other banks would now prefer to go to bank 1 as well. Indeed, by Assumption 1, $v(n, D)$ increases in n, so the resulting increase in bank 1's size would make investors there even better off. Thus, it seems reasonable that expected bank size $n_i(\cdot)$ should be weakly increasing in bank i's own rate D_i so long as $\partial v(n_i, D)/\partial D$ is positive at $D = D_i$.

By Assumption 2, this condition holds whenever a bank earns positive profits. It follows that the only way for a profitable bank to increase its market share is to raise its rate. However, this does not necessarily imply that the bank that posts the highest stated rate has the largest market share. If one bank is expected to be larger, hence more diversified, then its stated rate can be lower than those of other banks and still give investors a higher expected return; indeed, I analyze beliefs of this sort in Section 3.C below. Instead, the assumption that beliefs are "increasing" simply says that a profitable bank does not hurt its market share by raising its rate.

This leaves open the question of whether investors think that, all else equal, some banks will be bigger and better diversified. The answer depends on the nature of the banking market. In a new banking system, or one in which the market is growing so fast that banks' current investor bases are small relative to the volume of new investors, investors have no basis for believing that banks are different from one another. Since coordination among investors is prohibitively costly, the only plausible beliefs are that any two banks offering the same rate will have the same market share. By contrast, if some banks are well established, it seems reasonable that investors would think that these incumbent banks are likely to have larger share at any given rate than a new bank would; i.e. past market shares are a guide to future sizes.

In either case, given how investors react to the bank rates that they see, banks set their rates in a Nash equilibrium: i.e. each bank i must choose its rate D_i to maximize its profits $\pi(n_i(D_1, \ldots, D_b), D_i)$, taking the other banks' rates as given. I now explore each setting in turn.

B. Bank competition in a young banking system

Suppose that the banking system is young and no banks are well established. As just noted, coordination problems suggest that any two banks with the same stated rate will have same market share. Although it is always possible for investors to have the self-fulfilling belief that, regardless of rate, no bank is viable, for simplicity, I assume beliefs are as "optimistic" as possible.[9] Specifically, suppose b' banks have the highest rate D, and that, if these b' banks split the market, investors' expected return exceeds $\underline{v}$ (so $D \geq \underline{D}(N/b')$); then I assume that these banks do indeed split the market ($n_i(\cdot) = N/b'$ for these banks). Otherwise, if D is less than $\underline{D}(N/b')$), investors do not use banks ($n_i(\cdot) \equiv 0$).

Now consider a candidate equilibrium in which all b banks offer the same rate D. If banks are to be viable, D must weakly exceed $\underline{D}(N/b)$. D must also be no more than $D_0(N/b)$; otherwise, bank profits would be negative, and any one

---

[9] Autarky is always an equilibrium because, to be viable, a bank's size must be at least $\underline{n}$: if investors believe that no bank will have investors, then no bank can profitably offer a rate that tempts any one investor to come, making these beliefs self-fulfilling. See also footnote 19 in Section 6.

bank would benefit by lowering its rate and dropping out of competition. Notice that, given the absence of search of switching costs (see Section 5), a bank that raises its stated rate captures the whole market: increasing its rate makes it more attractive to investors even if its share does not increase, and, as more investors choose the bank, the resulting increase in n increases their expected return even further, while the drop in their market share hurts expected returns offered by competitors. Thus, each bank must compare the profits from increasing its rate and thus its market share with its candidate equilibrium profits $\pi(N/b, D)$.

From Lemma 2.1, bank profits $\pi(n, D)$ decrease in D, and the bank's profit margin $m(n, D)$ decreases in n. Also, $\partial \pi / \partial n$ equals $m(n, D) - n \cdot \partial r / \partial n$, so, all else equal, if its profit margin is not too large, a bank's expected profits decline with an increase in size. Intuitively, diversification's negative impact on the bank's overall profit margin (the debt overhang effect) outweighs the advantage of earning profits on the marginal investor. However, by assumption, if the bank's profits are nonnegative, investors' expected return in increasing in D, and the only way to increase share is to raise D, which is unprofitable. This leads to the next result.

PROPOSITION 3.1 (Equilibrium in a New Banking System with b Active Banks.)

(i) *Let $\underline{b}$ be the greatest integer less than or equal to $N/\underline{n}$. Then in a new banking system with $b \leq \underline{b}$ banks, there are equilibria in which the banks all offer the same rate D and share the market equally. No equilibrium exists with more than $\underline{b}$ banks having positive market shares.*

(ii) *In these equilibria, the bank's stated rate D can be anywhere in the interval $[D^*(N/b), D_0(N/b)]$, where $D^*(n)$ is the smallest rate such that (a) $D^* \geq \underline{D}(n)$ and (b) $\pi(n, D) \geq \pi(N, D)$ for all $D \geq D^*$. It follows that $\underline{D}(N/b) \leq D^*(N/b) \leq \max\{D_0(N), \underline{D}(N/b)\}$.*

(iii) *If $\partial^2 r(n, D)/\partial n \partial D > 0$, (ii) describes all equilibrium rates. One case where this condition holds is when $\tilde{X}_n/n$ is normally distributed and the rate D is below the mean per-unit asset return μ.*[10]

Thus, whenever b banks can viably share the market, there are equilibria in which they do so. If the condition in part (iii) holds, the most profitable of these equilibria has a bank rate of $D^*(N/b)$; this condition requires that the impact of an increase in a bank's stated rate on an investor's expected payments is greater the more diversified is the bank. Figure 2 graphs the relationship between D^* and n for the numerical example already given.

Here and throughout the chapter, I require that any collusion among banks must be consistent with subgame perfection; that is, collusion (tacit or explicit) must be self-enforcing. Since there are many subgame perfect equilibria with b active banks, a group of b banks may collude by picking the most profitable of

---

[10] More generally, $\partial r(n, D)/\partial D$ equal $1 - H_n(D)$: this increases with n if $H_n(D)$ decreases in n.

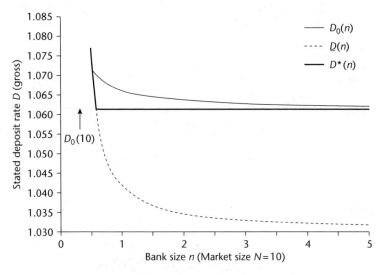

Figure 2. Minimum static collusive rates $D^*(n)$.

these equilibria, i.e., a rate $D^*(N/b)$. Indeed, unless banks merge or can credibly make side payments to compensate some banks for being less active, this is the best b banks can do in this static setting. In a symmetric equilibrium, industry-wide profits equal profit margin times the total market's size N, so the profit margin $m(N/b, D^*(N/b))$ serves to measure the static potential for collusion.[11]

PROPOSITION 3.2. *Define the (static) collusive profit margin as $m^*(n) = m(n, D^*(n))$.* (i) *If $D^*(n) = \underline{D}(n)$, $m^*(n)$ increases with n.* (ii) *If $D^*(n) > \underline{D}(n)$, $m^*(n)$ decreases with n if $\partial\pi(n, D^*(n))\partial n/ \leq 0$.*

When $D^*(n) = \underline{D}(n)$, banks can capture investor surplus in its entirety; by the assumptions of the model, this surplus increases with bank size. This case is likely to hold when the number of banks is close to the maximum viable number $\underline{b}$: here, diversification effects are strongest, so profits are most likely to decrease with bank size, reducing bank's incentive to compete for market share. As the number of banks falls below $\underline{b}$, banks are larger, reducing the marginal impact of diversification and thus the debt overhang effect. Eventually, debt overhang effects are small enough that $D^*(n)$ is above $\underline{D}(n)$; i.e. rates must be higher and margins smaller before debt overhang offsets the benefits to increasing market share.

---

[11] Requiring that collusion be self-enforcing follows the industrial organization literature (see Tirole 1988) and seems consistent with the historical examples of bank collusion discussed in Section 7. The use of merger to increase collusion and market power is discussed in Section 5. Contractual arrangements with side payments among banks would require costly ex post verification and might well be illegal.

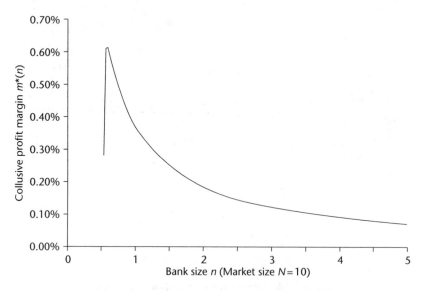

Figure 3. Maximum static collusive margins $m^*(n)$.

Thus, although there is generally a range of bank sizes bounded below by $\underline{n}$ for which collusive margins increase with bank size (and thus decrease with the number of banks), once banks are sufficiently large, collusive margins may begin to decrease with size. Figure 3 illustrates this for the numerical example: here, $m^*(n)$ peaks at $n = 0.59$, or $b = 17$ banks. However, as shown in the next section, if banks interact repeatedly, smaller numbers of banks may be able to do better than $m^*(n)$.

Until now, the analysis has assumed that the number of banks is fixed exogenously. When banks are not yet well established this assumption makes sense only if regulators explicitly fix the number of bank charters granted. The next result clarifies which equilibria remain when free entry is allowed and the number of banks is determined endogenously.

COROLLARY 3.3 (Equilibrium in a New Banking System with Free Entry). *Suppose any number of banks can freely enter the market and offer rates to investors. An equilibrium with $b \leq \underline{b}$ banks is possible if and only if $D_0(N) \leq \underline{D}(N/(b+1))$; if this holds, the equilibrium rate D can be anywhere in the interval between $\max\{D_0(N), \underline{D}(N/b)\}$ and $\min\{D_0(N/b), \underline{D}(N/(b+1))\}$. This interval always exists for the maximum number $\underline{b}$ of viable banks.*

The intuition here is that entry is always profitable if one of two conditions holds: either banks post rates that make splitting the market with one more bank both profitable and feasible, or banks post rates such that capturing the market with a slightly higher rate yields positive profits. A free-entry equilibrium with b banks is possible if and only if neither condition holds, but one or both hold if $D_0(N)$ exceeds $\underline{D}(N/(b+1))$, which is likely for few banks (small b). As b increases, $\underline{D}(N/(b+1))$ increases, so it is more likely that an interval of free entry equilibria exists; this becomes a certainty when b reaches the maximum number of viable banks $\underline{b}$. Thus, under symmetric beliefs, free entry tends to lead to a more fragmented banking system.

This can be seen in Figure 1. Here, $D_0(N)$ exceeds $\underline{D}(n)$ when n is 0.59 or greater (b is 17 or less); thus, no equilibrium with 16 or fewer banks is possible when entry is allowed. However, free-entry equilibria do exist with 17 or more banks.

Free entry complicates collusion among banks in several ways. First, Corollary 3.3 clearly shows that the potential for collusion is diminished by free entry (even if b banks wanted to collude at a rate below that permitted in Corollary 3.3, they could not possibly bribe all potential entrants to say away). Also, since the number of active banks is now endogenous, banks that want to collude may not know who all their potential "partners" are, making it difficult to coordinate on the correct equilibrium rate, and large numbers of potential entrants make it difficult for banks to coordinate on the number of banks b that leads to most the profitable equilibrium in Corollary 3.3.

To summarize, when the banking system is young and investor beliefs have not settled on a group of incumbent banks, banks have some ability to earn "collusive" profits if entry is limited. If free entry is allowed, there is a tendency for the banking system to fragment and for collusion to break down, reflecting both investors' and banks' inability to coordinate their beliefs and actions.

C. Bank competition in a mature banking system

Suppose now that banks have existed for some time and market growth has slowed. In such a setting, it seems plausible that, *all else equal*, investors will use a bank's past market share as an indication of other investors' likelihood of using that bank at present: since larger banks are better for investors, investors want to coordinate their choices among multiple banks with the same stated rate, and past market share is a cheap coordinating device. As I now show, this creates incumbency power.

First, suppose a group of banks has dominated the market recently. Investors believe these "incumbent" banks will continue to dominate unless an entrant offers a rate that would make investors better off if the entrant got the same market share that incumbents would otherwise have. Effectively, as long as they offer the highest rate, incumbent banks continue to dominate the market, splitting it symmetrically; however, if an entrant offers the highest rate, it will dominate. These beliefs give minimal preference to incumbents over entrants, which seems consistent with a setting where the incumbents have only lately arrived at dominance and investors are still on the lookout for better alternatives.

COROLLARY 3.4 (Entry When Incumbents Have Just Achieved Dominance). *Suppose a group of b incumbents have recently gained dominance in the market (so $b \leq \underline{b}$), but additional banks can freely enter and offer rates to investors. Under the beliefs just described, an equilibrium with the b incumbent banks splitting the market is always possible; the equilibrium rate D can be anywhere in the interval between $max\{D_0(N), \underline{D}(N/b)\}$ and $D_0(N/b)$, which always exists.*

Corollary 3.4 shows that even this slight advantage of incumbency allows incumbents to maintain market dominance, preventing fragmentation. In a new market, investors have no way to coordinate their choice of institutions, so an entrant can further split the market by offering the prevailing rate; the reduction in bank size increases bank risk and increases expected profits margins, giving the entrant positive profits. By contrast, under beliefs with the slight incumbency advantage described here, investors coordinate on the incumbents unless an entrant offers a higher rate, ruling out the entry strategy of profiting through further fragmentation.

The longer the incumbent banks have dominated the market, the more skepticism investors may display about the viability of entrants. One way in which this should manifest itself is that, in order to attract any investors at all, an entrant must post a rate D that offers investors an attractive expected return even if the entrant's size n is *smaller* than those that the incumbents would otherwise have.[12] Not surprisingly, such beliefs further reduce entry's potential to restrict collusion.

At an extreme, suppose that the incumbents have dominated the market so long that no investor will go to an entrant unless she would be better off even as the entrant's only customer. Thus, the entrant's rate must be at least $\underline{D}(0)$ in order to attract investors, which leads to the next results.

COROLLARY 3.5 (Entry When Incumbents Are Well Established). *Suppose a group of $b(\leq \underline{b})$ banks has dominated the market for a long time, but additional banks can freely enter and offer rates to investors.*

  (i) *Under the beliefs just described, an equilibrium with the b incumbent banks splitting the market is always possible.*
 (ii) *The set of possible equilibrium rates is the same as given in Proposition 3.1, so that the collusive profit margin is as given in Corollary 3.2.*

Since the minimum viable bank size $\underline{n}$ exceeds zero, a bank offering a rate of $\underline{D}(0)$ or more loses money if its size remains zero, and any increase in scale

---

[12] This can be viewed as a reduced form of a search model: early on, with fluid numbers of banks, more investors find it worthwhile to incur (small) search costs and check out the competition. As time goes on and the same group of banks are effectively the only players in town, investors find search less attractive, so fewer search and notice entrants' rate offers.

simply increases its expected losses at this rate.[13] Thus, entry is ruled out, and the b incumbents can achieve the collusive profit margin $m^*(N/b)$.

Note that any incumbency advantage makes it easier for banks to collude, since at least there is now a set of banks that are obvious partners. Although the number of incumbents may not be that which maximizes total industry profits, the difficulties in merging discussed in Section 5 suggest that, in the short run, the number of incumbents will be determined by historical accident.

In summary, if investors use past market shares as a coordinating device, incumbents have an advantage over new entrants; to the extent investor beliefs become more "focused" on the incumbents over time, this advantage increases. In the limit, the treat of entry evaporates.[14]

D. Alternative belief specifications

The analysis thus far suggests that, in a young banking system, free entry should cause excessive fragmentation, while in a mature system, free entry may not prevent well-established incumbents from earning collusive profits. I have assumed that (i) a bank's market share is always weakly increasing in its stated rate, and (ii) for a given rate D, investors are always better off the bigger the bank; however, as I now discuss, these assumptions can be weakened without changing the qualitative results.

Assuming that a bank's market share is weakly increasing in its stated rate is based on Assumption 2, which says that, if a bank raises its rate and its market share doesn't change, its investors are better of. This might not always be true. First, in the delegated monitoring model, if the stated rate D is high enough, investor's expected returns (net of monitoring costs) may decrease in D. Second, in a more general model, bank of the same size might vary in asset quality; if quality is not publicly observed, investors might view a sufficiently high rate as a sign the bank's assets are of worse quality.[15]

Even if sufficiently high rates are unattractive to investors, most of my qualitative results are unaffected. Such beliefs may rule out high-rate, low-profit

---

[13] Even if $\underline{n}$ were zero, so that a bank could offer a rate $\underline{D}(0)$ and earn positive profits, attracting a large share of the market at this rate might be unprofitable, since the increase in size would entail much greater diversification and a substantial drop in the bank's expected profit margin.

[14] For simplicity, I focus on situations where investors assume that all the incumbent banks are roughly equal, but beliefs can also support different incumbent banks splitting the market unequally. In these equilibria, the larger bank offers a lower stated rate and has higher expected profit margin (and thus profits) than its smaller rival; the larger bank's reputation for being bigger gives it an advantage.

[15] On practical grounds, it seems unlikely that lower rates are *always* viewed as better: such beliefs would lead to a "race to the bottom," with each bank competing to offer the lowest viable rate (and earn monopoly profits). There is no empirical evidence of such extreme behavior; indeed, evidence suggests that, to the extent banks use deposit rates to compete for market share, they raise them (for example, see Smith 1984, on the events leading to the banking panic of 1907).

equilibria, since a bank that lowers its rate may be able to improve investor returns and so profitably increase its size, but this does not rule out the possibility of low-rate, high-profit equilibria. Indeed, so long as the rate at which investor returns start decreasing in D is above $D^*(\cdot)$ as defined in Proposition 3.1, the maximum degree of collusion would be unaffected. Free entry would still fragment a new banking system, since this results from the investors' coordination problem and the debt overhang effect of increased size and diversification. Similarly, in a mature system, investor beliefs should still favor well-established incumbents, restricting entry.

However, it is also possible that an increase in bank size at a given stated rate may not always benefit investors. One case was discussed in Section 2: if the stated rate is sufficiently high, an increase in size and diversification increases the chance of default, so higher expected monitoring costs may offset the increase in expected payments on investors' debt contracts. Also, in a more general model, there may be other diseconomies of scale. For example, as per Cerasi and Daltung (1996), there are probably limits to how many borrowers an individual can monitor, so larger banks must have more monitors, which in turn increases free riding and other agency costs. To the extent marginal benefits to diversification tail off as a bank becomes larger, such diseconomies could eventually offset diversification benefits.

Such organizational diseconomies might prevent a bank from capturing the whole market, either because monitoring quality would be too low to attract investors or because monitoring costs would be too high to be profitable. It would now be easier for large and small banks to coexist. Still, so long as diversification economies dominated over some range, the qualitative trust of the paper would be unchanged: debt overhang would still undermine banks' desire to expand to the optimal size; entry would still excessively fragment a young banking system, and incumbents in a mature system would gain power by becoming the focus of investors beliefs.

The same is true if the stated rate is so high that an increase in diversification increases the probability of bank default. Indeed, this may reinforce the excessive fragmentation of a young banking system, since the stated rate is most likely to be high when banks are small. If an expansion at current rate levels or higher is unattractive to investors, the many small banks may be completely unable to increase their size through rate competition, even though it is quite possible that this structure is dominated by one with larger banks and lower stated rates.

4. A Simple Model of Dynamic Competition and Collusion

Although the static model is suggestive, banks typically exist and compete over extended horizons. Since current market shares may effect future investor beliefs, this may give banks incentive to try to capture larger market shares even at a current loss so as to gain a dominant position in the future. To address this issue, this section presents a simple model of dynamic competition. It turns out that so long as investor beliefs do not assign full dominance (a la Corollary 3.5) to incumbents too quickly, a dynamic setting can actually increase the potential for collusion among banks. Then, in Section 5, I discuss some additional considerations that suggest that the pattern discussed in the static setting—fragmentation in a young banking system, collusion in a mature one—is likely to hold.

Suppose investors and banks live forever and maximize the discounted sum of period returns, with a common discount factor δ between 0 and 1. (This implicitly ignores the fact that failed banks may be unable to resume business, which is discussed in Section 5.) For simplicity, assume that single-period contracts are still used. Equilibria must be subgame perfect.

Since there is no cost of switching between banks in subsequent periods, investors will choose banks on the basis of the expected return each bank offers in the current period. However, the arguments of Section 3.C suggest that investors will use available information on past market shares to conjecture how likely other investors are to use each bank in the current period.

Following that discussion, suppose that a bank or group of banks have just achieved positive market share, becoming "incumbents". At first, these banks should gain only the slight advantage used in Corollary 3.4: faced with a rate offer form an "entrant" (a bank that did not have positive share in the previous period), investors go to that bank only if its return dominates that of the incumbents under the assumption that it would have similar share to theirs. However, if the incumbents maintain their dominance over a longer period, their advantage should grow, eventually reaching that used in Corollary 3.5: to gain share, an "entrant" has to offer a rate that is more attractive than the incumbents even if the entrant has only one investor. Although the transition between these two extremes of incumbency advantage might well be gradual, I model it in the following simple way: if a group of banks has dominated for no more than T periods, they have only the slight incumbency advantage of Corollary 3.4; after T periods have passed, this switches to the strong incumbency advantage of Corollary 3.5. Also, for simplicity, I will assume that the best expected return a bank of size zero can offer investors is $\underline{v}$, so that, once a bank or group of banks are well established as incumbents, no entry is possible. These simplifying assumptions ease analysis without affecting the qualitative nature of the results.

Suppose first that only b banks are competing, entry being ruled out either because they have dominated the market for over T periods or by regulatory fiat. If the banks maintain some collusive rate D period after period, each bank's discounted profits are $(1-\delta)^{-1} \cdot \pi(N/b, D)$. If collusion is to be self-enforcing, this discounted value must exceed the discounted profits from a bank's alternative strategy of raising its rate, capturing the market, maintaining dominance in the face of any retaliation, and eventually reaping the benefits of investor beliefs that strongly favor it over all potential rivals. Under this alternative strategy, the bank's expected discounted profits are just under $\pi(N, D) + \delta \cdot \Pi^1$, where Π^1 is the expected discounted value of a bank's profits when it has just become the sole incumbent.

Suppose the bank does capture the market and maintains dominance for another $T - 1$ periods. Investor beliefs now favor it so strongly that from now on it is immune to entry and can pay the minimum stated rate $\underline{D}(N)$, earning profits $\pi(N, \underline{D}(N)) \equiv \pi_{max}$ in every period thereafter; by Assumption 1, π_{max} is the largest single-period profit a bank can earn. However, during the $T - 1$ periods before investor beliefs become so focused, other banks may try to capture the market so that *they* can become the incumbents. Given its initial slight incumbency advantage, the bank can always block such entry by offering the same rate as its rivals; however, since rivals are willing to lose money now in order to earn future monopoply profits, blocking involves a current loss. This leads directly to the following result.

LEMMA 4.1 (The Value of Sole Incumbency). *Suppose that a bank has just become the only incumbent in the previous period. Then, assuming that investor expected returns $v(N, D)$ increase in the stated rate D for a sufficient range above $D_0(N)$, the value of incumbency is*

$$\Pi^1 = \frac{\delta^{T-1}}{1 - \delta^T} \cdot \pi_{max}, \tag{4.1}$$

where π_{max} equals the maximum per period profit $\pi(N, \underline{D}(N))$. Π^1 is increasing in the discount factor δ and decreasing in the number of periods T required to become unchallenged monopolist.

The requirement that investors' expected returns $v(N, D)$ increase in D for rates above $D_0(N)$ (the rate at which the incumbent breaks even) guarantees that rivals can pose a credible threat even at rates that lead to current losses. By contrast, if $v(N, D)$ reached a maximum at $D_0(N)$, the incumbent could block its rivals by offering $D_0(N)$ for $T - 1$ more periods, and Π^1 would now equal $[\delta^{T-1}/(1 - \delta)] \cdot \pi_{max}$. As noted is Section 3, once investors' expected returns begin to decrease in the stated rate, it is harder for competition to discipline incumbents, increasing the advantage and value incumbency.

PROPOSITION 4.2. (Collusion in a Dynamic Setting).

(i) *With b well-established incumbent banks, a stated rate of D can be supported as a repeated equilibrium if and only if*

$$\pi(N, D) + \delta \cdot \Pi^1 \leq (1 - \delta)^{-1} \cdot \pi(N/b, D), \tag{4.2}$$

or, equivalently,

$$\frac{\delta^T}{(1 - \delta^T)} \cdot \pi_{\max} \le [\pi(N/b, D) - \pi(N, D)] + \frac{\delta}{1 - \delta} \cdot \pi(N/b, D). \qquad (4.3)$$

(ii) *For any time T until a new incumbent becomes well established, a sufficiently small discount factor δ guarantees that any rate above $D^*(N/b)$ as defined in Proposition 3.1 can be supported as a collusive equilibrium.*

(iii) *If the discount factor δ is greater than $1 - b^{-1} \cdot m(N/b, D)/m(N, D)$, or $D^*(N/b)$ equal $\underline{D}(N/b)$, then sufficiently long T guarantees that any rate D above $\underline{D}(N/b)$ can be supported as a collusive equilibrium. Otherwise, a sufficiently long T guarantees that any rate above $D^*(N/b)$ can be supported as a collusive equilibrium.*

As (4.3) shows, the would-be monopolist weighs the discounted value of eventually becoming well established as sole incumbent against two factors: the gain or loss in current profits from trying to capture the market (the first term on the right-hand side) and the discounted value of foregone collusive profits (the second term on the right-hand side). If the collusive rate exceeds $D^*(N/b)$, capturing the market involves a current loss, so a low discount rate means that any future considerations of monopoly profits $\pi_{\max}$ are so far removed as to be negligible; the same is true if the time required to become well established is relatively long. Indeed, if the time to become well established is long enough, and the discount rate is not too low, collusive rates below $D^*(N/b)$ may be possible; although capturing the market gives a current profit, the discounted value of foregone collusive profits is higher still, and the monopoly profits from capturing the market are long delayed. This is analogous to the familiar "Folk Theorem" for repeated Bertrand competition. However, here the discount factor must exceed $1 - b^{-1} \cdot m(N/b, D)/m(N, D)$; because profit margins decline with size, this lower bound is smaller then $1 - b^{-1}$, the limit in the standard Bertrand competition model. Once again, the debt overhang effect makes collusion easier to support, especially for larger numbers of (smaller) banks.

The upshot is that, even in dynamic setting where higher market share today translates into a competitive advantages tomorrow, once some banks have become well established, it is quite possible that they will collude and maintain their current shares rather than compete more aggressively for additional advantage. Indeed, the possibilities for collusion may be enhanced: rates below $D^*(N/b)$ are not equilibria in a single-period setting, but may be supportable here. Collusion of some sort is most likely if the time to become well established T is not too short.

Now consider the case of young banking system with no well established banks. From Corollary 3.3, any attempt to earn positive profits in the present is likely to attract entry, resulting in a fragmented market. Even if fewer than $\underline{b}$ banks try to set rates so high that they would lose money, they are unlikely to prevent entry: with more banks at the same rate, profit margins will be higher and possibly positive. Thus, as in the static analysis, entry is likely to be maximal.

Maximal entry suggests that bank profits will not be too high, since even the minimum viable stated rate $\underline{D}(\underline{n})$ is close to the breakeven point $D_0(\underline{n})$. Nevertheless, even though collusion may have little scope, banks may still prefer to keep things as they are rather than compete aggressively to try and capture the entire market. This is because capturing the market is most expensive for a small bank: the initial rate D is likely to exceed $D_0(N)$, so that the bank actually suffers large losses if it expands. Intuitively, the increase in diversification is greatest for small banks, making their "debt overhang" cost of expansion largest as well. Furthermore, if D exceeds the mean bank asset return μ, then the argument from the end of Section 3 suggests that a small bank may be unable to capture the market even if it is willing to bear the cost: larger size may increase the bank's chance of default, making it less attractive to investors.

5. Additional Considerations for Dynamic Competition

To simplify analysis, I have omitted several complications. I now discuss those that seem especially relevant to dynamic competition: the effect of a bank's default on investors' subsequent beliefs; a less rigid link between bank size and risk; the role of bank capital; investor switching costs; and mergers as an alternative means of expansion. These concerns tend to reinforce the prediction that young banking systems are excessively fragmented, while mature systems are stable and prone to collusion.

The impact of a bank's default on investor beliefs. The analysis in Section 4 assumes that, if a bank defaults in one period, it reopens for business in the next period with no harm done. In reality, such a default might well make investors skeptical about the reorganized bank's viability, and the bank's initial owners are likely to have lost much or all of their stake in any future profits the bank might earn. Moving to the other extreme, assume that the owner of a bank that defaults loses any financial interest in the bank, and that the bank itself now becomes an "entrant." These assumptions reduce the effective discount factor: a bank of size n and rate D survives with probability $1 - H_n(D)$, so the current value of profits $\pi(\cdot)$ next period is only $[1 - H_n(D)] \cdot \delta \cdot \pi(\cdot)$. The lower effective discount factor means that future profits weigh less heavily on the bank's current decisions, moving the situation closer to that analyzed in Section 3.[16]

---

[16] There are some additional complications for bank's choice between colluding or deviating to become sole incumbent: deviating increases market share, which generally decreases a bank's chance of default, but it also requires a higher rate and so a higher default probability for $T-1$ periods. Thus, it is ambiguous whether deviating or not deviating has the higher effective discount factor.

A bank's failure also means that there are fewer incumbents, giving survivors greater market power. Thus, even if the bank system is initially fragmented, as time passes and some banks fail, their more fortunate rivals will gain in market share and diversification, becoming safer and thus placing greater weight on future profits when choosing between collusion and deviation.

Bank size and risk. Although my analysis assumes that an increase in bank size leads to a fixed increase in diversification, real banks do have some control over their industry and geographic concentrations. Also, investors may have difficulty observing the bank's asset mix in a clear and timely fashion; public reports on asset concentrations are infrequent and lagged, and typically show only broad asset groupings. To model these points simply, suppose banks can choose high- or low-risk asset strategies, where for any size the low-risk strategy has the same mean return as the high-risk strategy, but is less risky (better diversified) in the sense of Rothschild and Stiglitz (1970). Also, first suppose that strategies can be changed anew each period and that the choice is unobservable.

If banks do not care about the future (their discount rate δ is zero), they will choose the high-risk strategy: for any stated rate, increasing risk decreases expected payments per investor $r(n, D)$, increasing expected bank profits. Expecting such "risk shifting," investors will demand a higher stated rate. Ex post, banks will not profit from risk shifting, but ex ante, they cannot commit to abstain from it.

If banks do care about the future (δ exceeds zero), increasing risk today reduces the odds of surviving to capture future profits, so sufficiently high future profits deter risk shifting, as in Marcus (1984) and Besanko and Thakor (1993). The bank's relative credibility can have a self-fulfilling effect on its decision. If investors believe the bank will choose the high-risk strategy, they will demand a higher stated rate; by reducing the bank's profit margins and increasing its chance of failure, this increases current debt overhang and decreases future profits' relative importance, making the high-risk strategy relatively more attractive to the bank. Conversely, if investors believe the bank will choose the low-risk strategy more attractive.

An important caveat is that the low-risk expansion strategy involves choosing and monitoring borrowers that differ more by region or sector, so that the bank must have expertise in a number of different areas. Since such expertise takes time to build and manage, it may not be possible for a bank to expand too rapidly without following a more risky strategy: either specialized and undiversified, or diversified but poorly chosen and worse in a first-order stochastic dominance sense.

Risk-shifting incentives, credibility with investors, and difficulties with rapid expansion are most likely to weigh against the low-risk strategy in a new or rapidly growing system. Since banks are likely to be small and risky, they must pay higher stated rates, making the high-risk strategy relatively more attractive.

Also, a bank that wishes to diversify well and build a reputation for doing so will have to pay excessively high rates until investors gradually learn the bank's actual risk profile. Finally, small banks have few relationships or assets in place to constrain their choice and thus have both greater opportunity to choose a high-risk expansion strategy and greater cost to developing the expertise necessary for a low-risk strategy. Conversely, in a mature system, surviving banks are likely to be larger and safer, have well-established reputations and incumbency power, and have more existing business to constrain risk taking, all of which should encourage collusion and a low-risk strategy.

Bank capital and leverage. Although I do not model bank equity capital explicitly, model is consistent with banks having a constant cost of equity capital and keeping the ratio of equity to total assets fixed as they expand. However, equity capital is likely to have increasing cost due to increased agency problems between bank management and outside shareholders (Besanko and Kanatas 1996); indeed, larger banks are generally more highly levered, suggesting a trade-off between diversification and leverage. One might argue that, by offering a higher rate, a bank can always expand its market share profitably, the reduction in profit margin caused by better diversification being offset by the increase in margin caused by higher leverage.

However, this argument ignores the impact of higher leverage on investors' expected returns. As shown in Winton (1995), if an increase in bank size is to make investors better off, their gains from diversification must outweigh their losses from increased bank leverage; and even if the change is attractive to investors, lowering the deposit rate is unlikely to attract them in the first place. Thus, the bank may still find such an increase in size unattractive. Conversely, if the expansion is not in investors' interest, they will not respond. Thus, in a young system, coordination problems may still cause the formation of many underdiversified banks that cannot profitably increase market share.[17] As time passes, surviving banks can increase their equity capital through retained earnings rather than costly external finance, and stronger capital reinforces their advantage over entrants.

Switching costs. Search or switching costs would tend to reinforce this chapter's results. Early on, investors would face even more difficulty in coordinating on a few banks; later, unless the economy was growing rapidly and new investors were flooding the market, banks would find it harder to increase market share via rate competition. Indeed, this chapter's focus on beliefs and their evolution over time motivates switching costs that are psychological rather than physical.

---

[17] Even if capital protects debtholders in a fragmented banking system, bank equity will be very risky, which will be costly if shareholders are risk averse or must monitor bank managers. Comparing concentrated Canadian banking system with the fragmented American system during 1920–80, Bordo et al. (1995*b*) find evidence of such costs.

Expansion via merger. Given the costs of rate competition for market share, expansion through merger may well be more attractive. However, if the merged entity is to lower its rate and reap gains from improved diversification, investors must anticipate that it will retain the merged banks' market shares and choose a low-risk strategy. This suggests that mergers are most likely to occur after enough time has elapsed so that incumbent banks have amassed some advantage in terms of investor beliefs. The pace of mergers will also be slower to the extent there are costs of integrating different banks or investors require time to fully digest the permanence of increased market share.

6. Regulatory Issues

Suppose regulators want to maximize social welfare in this setting. After discussing social objective in somewhat more detail, I analyze the efficacy of two instruments regulators are likely to have at their disposal: entry restrictions and government insurance for investors.[18] By themselves, entry restrictions reduce excessive fragmentation, but also enhance incumbency power, but may lead to excessive entry and fragmentation. However, under some circumstances, a judicious mix of temporary entry restrictions and government insurance can achieve good results.

A. Social objectives

Fragmentation. Absent diseconomies of scale, the model implies that larger banks always potentially dominate smaller ones: as per footnote 6, being better diversified, larger banks can guarantee investors the same expected payments with lower stated rates, typically reducing monitoring costs as well. As else equal, a single bank should be optimal, and concentration preferred to fragmentation.

Collusion. If they are few in number, banks may collude. In the basic model, this may actually be attractive: the sum of all agents' utilities is maximized by minimizing total monitoring costs (total consumption is constant); since lower stated rates reduce monitoring costs, a single bank with a stated rate of $\underline{D}(N)$ is optimal. This can easily be achieved by offering one banking license and forbidding entry.

However, this stark result ignores many likely complications. Concern for fairness or the populist pressures of a democracy (Roe 1997) may make regulators place more weight on the welfare of the many investors dead-weight costs: in my model regulators must monitor each bank whenever its transfers are below their

---

[18] If regulators could optimally choose both the number of banks and their prices (rates), the first-best could easily be attained. Such precision seems unlikely in practice: especially when it comes to pricing, regulation is slow to adapt to changes in the precise level of risk, monitoring costs etc.

maximum level. Also, in richer models, collusion or monopoly cause distortions: for example, if the supply of entrepreneurs is endogenous (Winton 1995) or firm investment scale is not fixed (Rajan 1992), a monopoly bank's pricing can cause underinvestment, harming welfare; if there is separation between ownership and control, collusion may increase managerial slack at all investors' expense.

Thus, from a social viewpoint, allowing the banking system to evolve naturally may lead to two types of inefficiency: early on, there will be excessive fragmentation and risk; once the market has matured, costly collusion is likely. I now turn to the question of what regulators can do about this.

B. Entry restrictions

Since fragmentation is socially costly, an obvious solution is to restrict the number of entrants into a young banking system, reducing coordination problems and hastening the formation of a few well-diversified banks. The downside is that these banks immediately become incumbents, gaining an advantage over later entrants; furthermore, bureaucratic rigidities may lead to delays in removing the restrictions, and the longer restrictions are in place, the more heavily investor beliefs will focus on the incumbents, increasing their advantage. Thus, entry restrictions hasten both concentration and collusion.

In banks in other jurisdictions are well diversified, regulators can reduce incumbency advantage by allowing entry be these "foreign" banks: facing less debt overhang, such banks have greater incentive to expand at any given rate. However, informational problems in assessing "foreign" banks may reduce the banks' credibility with investors; even if cheap disclosure is possible, cultural distrust or outright xenophobia may interfere. Such issues will pay into the hands of special interest groups (e.g. domestic bankers) that wish to prevent entry; a case in point is that of the European Union, many of whose member countries delayed financial integration to let domestic institutions "bulk up."

C. Government guarantees or insurance

Another way to weaken incumbency advantage is to insure investors against bank default, funding the insurance either with premia from banks or with general tax levies. With full insurance, investors no longer care about bank size and risk; since they receive their bank's stated rate for sure, they will choose the bank or banks with the highest stated rate, regardless of incumbency status. Thus, insurance makes the banking market more "contestable" in the sense of Baumol et al. (1986).[19]

[19] Insurance may have other advantages: ruling out "pessimistic" beliefs that lead to autarky (Diamond and Dybvig 1983), improving the liquidity of deposits (Gorton and Pennacchi 1990), and delegating bank monitoring from investors to regulators (Emmons 1993). On the other hand,

Although it is unlikely that regulators can quickly and precisely assess bank risk (see footnote 18), consider this as a benchmark. If investors were fully insured and insurance correctly priced, a bank of size n and rate D would pay a per-dollar premium $\phi(n, D) = D - r(n, D)$, giving it profits of $n \cdot [\mu - c - D]$.[20] Since fully insured investors do not care about bank size, an entrant offering the same rate as incumbents could attract some investors, and entry would be attractive unless bank profits were zero; i.e., $D = \mu - c$. Thus, if regulators initially restricted entry, then lifted restrictions and offered full deposit insurance, the threat of entry would force the few incumbent banks to keep rates at $\mu - c$.

In practice, risk-based premia are likely to be rigid and imprecise; for example, those mandated by FDICIA vary much less across risk classes than do credit spreads on bonds of different credit ratings. At the other extreme, suppose investors are fully insured and banks pay a flat premium ϕ per depositor; now bank profits are $\pi(n, D) - n\phi$, and profits margins are $\mu - c - r(n, D) - \phi$. Since investors care only about stated rates, and $r(n, D)$ increases with n, and additional bank can always offer the same rate as others and profitably split the market. Absent entry restrictions, fragmentation will be extreme: unless the premium ϕ is so high that banks cannot be profitable at any size, banks will be as small as possible (in the absence of fixed costs of operation, each bank would have only one borrower). This is a variant of the well-known result that flat rate deposit insurance encourages risk shifting: investors do not care about bank size and diversification, and new banks profit from being smaller and riskier.

Under full flat-rate insurance, temporary entry restrictions will not prevent fragmentation; banks have incentive to enter even if incumbents are earning zero profits. However, if insurance is not full or there are costs and delays in processing investors' claims, investors care somewhat about perceived bank size and risk. Nevertheless, it is still easier for entrants to threaten incumbents than in the uninsured case: even if investors think an entrant will be small, size matters less to investors, so they will switch to the entrant for a lower premium over incumbents' rates. In this less extreme case, a policy of restricting entry, allowing incumbents to gain some advantage in investor beliefs, and then removing entry barriers may lead to a system of relatively few banks posting almost competitive rates.

The upshot is that government insurance does reduce incumbency advantage, but since it can be perfectly priced in a timely fashion, it increases the system's

---

there may be costs of transferring funds to investors, and, as monitors, regulators are unlikely to be free from agency problems or error. Since my focus is on the effects of government insurance on bank competition. I ignore any net improvement in social welfare from improved liquidity, reduced monitoring costs etc.

[20] To prevent risk shifting, the premium should be collected after banks set lending rates and terms. However, if collected before banks invest, aggregate investment is reduced: if collected afterwards, monitoring costs must be incurred. My discussion abstracts from these issues.

tendency toward fragmentation. This suggests that regulators may prefer a system with less than full insurance, combined with temporary entry restrictions aimed at preventing initial fragmentation. However, if regulators are not totally selfless and regulatory capture is a concern, entry restrictions may be continued indefinitely at the behest of the incumbents, leading to the collusive outcome already discussed.

7. Historical Evidence

As suggested in the introduction, historical evidence from Australia, Canada, Britain, and the U.S. is consistent with the model's predictions. I now summarize and discuss this evidence.

Australia. In the second half of the nineteenth century, Australia's relatively unregulated and rapidly growing economy saw the number of "regular" (trading) banks increase from 8 in 1850 to 23 by 1892, with even greater increases in the numbers of building societies and savings and land banks. During the 1891–3 depression, many building societies and savings and land banks failed, and 13 of the regular banks suspended and underwent "reconstruction." After the crisis, the regular banks began to merge, their number dropping by half through 1920 (Dowd 1992); they became more conservative, emphasizing "short-term self-liquidating investments in place of longer, more speculative ones" (Dowd 1972: 72); and they were now "able to maintain agreements on deposit rates and foreign exchange rates and margins, and there was no longer any effective competition except for advances" (Dowd 1992: 72).

Canada. Although Canada had only 37 banks when separate provinces first united in 1867, by 1874, this had grown to 51 banks (Neufeld 1972). Figure 4 shows that the number of banks slowly fell to 10 by 1932, much of the consolidation occurring initially through failure, then increasingly through merger. Up to 1920, losses to depositors were similar to those in the much more fragmented U.S. system (Bordo et al. 1995a), but once the Canadian system had consolidated, it became quite stable; there were no failures after 1923, even during the Great Depression. Incumbents were almost immune from entry— from 1912 to 1967, only one new bank formed—and began to collude on loan and deposit rates. This collusive behavior came out in the 1964 Porter Commission report, which helped motivate the introduction of compulsory flat-rate deposit insurance in 1967. After this, "near-banks" (who could join the insurance scheme) became more competitive (Bordo et al. 1995b), and two new banks were formed in 1968–9 (Neufeld 1972), suggesting that the incumbents' advantage was greatly weakened. Indeed, Shaffer (1993) finds little evidence of collusive behavior during the subsequent period.

Britain. Scotland's well-known free-banking regime had 36 banks in 1825; this fell to 17 by 1850 and 8 by 1913, with merger accounting for most of the

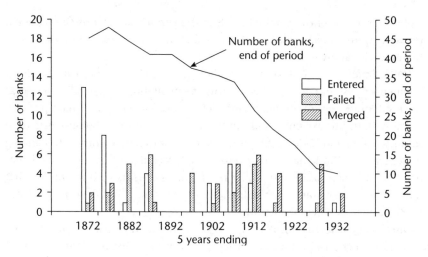

Figure 4. Entry and exit in Canadian banking, 1868–1932.
Source: Neufeld (1972).

consolidations after 1850 (Collins 1988: 52–3). By 1850, banks were able to support collusion (Checkland 1975: 391–2 and 486).

The banking system in England was initially far more fragmented due to regulatory restrictions, with 650 banks in 1825. Limits on the number of partners per bank were lifted in 1826, and limited liability became generally available in 1862. Consolidation took some time to occur: the number of banks fell to 358 in 1875, and 164 in 1990 (Collins 1988: 52), while the 10 largest banks held 33 percent of all deposits in 1870, 46 percent in 1990, and 97 percent in 1920 (Capie and Rodrik-Bali 1982: 287–8). Collusion began on some accounts in the 1860s and became total by 1920 (Griffiths 1973: 6–7). The banking system was quite stable by the turn of the century (Capie 1995).[21]

Consistent with the result that mature systems without explicit guarantees should endogenously create large barriers to entry, the British banking system seems to have been virtually immune to entry from the late nineteenth century until the late 1950s, when "foreign banks and domestic merchant banks, drawing on the growing pool of Euro-dollars, stepped up their intervention in the domestic market place" (Sheppard 1971: 17). When entry did arrive, it came in the form of large money center banks from other countries rather than de novo banks, consistent with the notion that well-established, well-diversified rivals would suffer less of a disadvantage in competing for investor funds. In

---

[21] The relatively unregulated evolution of property and casualty insurance in nineteenth century Britain also displays initial risky fragmentation and slow consolidation (Jenkins 1984, and Cockerel and Green 1994). Insurers established a stable cartel by the early 20th century (Sheppard 1971: 13–17).

addition, the new entrants raised funds in the Euromarkets, whose institutional investors were probably more sophisticated (and perhaps less culturally biased) than individual investors.

United States.   As is well known, regulation in the U.S. produced an extremely fragmented system. However, while this fragmentation is generally viewed as the result of restrictions on branching, deposit insurance seems to have played a roll as well. In study of entry and exit in U.S. banking during the early twentieth century, Flood and Kwan (1995) find evidence of excessive entry into banking in general, and find that such "overbanking" was highest in those states that had (flat rate) deposit insurance programs. This is consists with the notion that fragmented systems are most vulnerable to entry and that deposit insurance further undercuts incumbency advantage.

Discussion.   The historical evidence is in many ways consistent with the model's predictions. In those countries with relatively little regulation (banking in Australia, Canada, and Scotland, insurance in Britain), initial fragmentation and high rates of failure are followed by slow consolidation, first through failure, then increasingly through merger. Even without explicit restrictions, consolidation is linked to increased stability, difficulty of entry, and conclusion (Australia, Britain, and Canada). The U.S. experience shows the converse, with a fragmented system inviting continued entry and risk. In an already concentrated system, deposit insurance weakens incumbency power, but need not fragment the market (Canada); by contrast, in a fragmented system, it makes fragmentation oven worse (U.S).

Although organizational diseconomies of scale might also lead to the formation of many small intermediaries, with slow consolidation keeping step with technological progress, the path of intermediation in the countries just discussed seems to owe as much to the maturity and growth prospects of the intermediary sector as to technological progress per se. this is particularly true of late nineteenth-century Australia and Canada; for example, the Australian banks were able to operate large networks of over 100 branches (Dowd 1992), but the economy was in a high growth phase, which would tend to make market shares more fluid entry easier. The same applies to Canada, where the economy and bank asset as a share of GNP grew rapidly until roughly 1910 (Neufeld 1972: Chart 3:1, 56).

8. Conclusion

Existing theories of financial intermediation imply increasing returns to scale linked to diversification. This suggest a simply policy prescription for regulators: the banking sector should be left relatively unrestricted, which should in turn lead to an equilibrium with a few large, well-diversified, and competitive banks.

However, the actual pattern of unrestricted banking sector evaluation in many countries is at odds with this prediction: high initial entry is followed first by slow consolidation through failure and merger and than by a strong tendency to collusion among survivors.

I develop a model that illuminates this pattern. I show that, in unregulated settings where intermediaries are new or the market is growing rapidly, there should be substantial entry, with many risky intermediaries coexisting: investors cannot coordinate their actions, and debt overhang makes the cost of capturing market share through rate competition highest when the potential for diversification is greatest. Over time, banks will fail, and survivors will again an incumbency advantage simply by becoming the focus of investors beliefs. Unless intermediaries in other jurisdiction are both well diversified and able to overcome the obstacles to penetrating a foreign market, these incumbents will become relatively immune to entry. This suggests a greater tendency towards collusion in mature banking systems than in other industries with similar concentration: investor beliefs make the market less "contestable" in general, and the debt overhang effect may further reduce competition.

From the regulatory view, these result suggest a trade off between fragmentation and collusion. Barriers to entry enhance collusion as well as stability, while government insurance for investors makes the market more contestable but may encourage excessive entry. As a result, regulators may wish to combine less than full insurance with temporary entry restrictions.

The model's results should apply most strongly in situations where gains to additional diversification are large and informational asymmetries both among intermediaries and between intermediaries and investors are especially costly to resolve. At the present day, these concerns seem to be of decreasing importance in the U.S. and other developed economies, where loan sales and credit derivatives are becoming more efficient and investors are able to obtain more timely and detailed information about intermediaries and their exposures. Nevertheless, to the extent some information asymmetries remain, the role of investor beliefs modeled here will continue to have some relevance, particularly for intermediaries that deal with (relatively unsophisticated) individual investors. Moreover, these concerns should be of critical importance to regulators in developing areas such as Latin America and Eastern Europe, where financial systems are younger and information problems greater.

APPENDIX

Proof of Lemma 2.1.

(i) This follows immediately from (2.1) through (2.3) and the fact that expected monitoring costs are $H_n(D)$. For future reference, note that $\partial r / \partial D = 1 - H_n(D)$.

(ii) An increase in n increases bank diversification, reducing the risk of $\tilde{X}_n/n$ in the sense of Rothschild and Stiglitz (1970); it follows from condition (7) in Rothschild and Stiglitz that

$$\frac{\partial}{\partial n} \int_0^D H_n(x)\, dx < 0, \tag{A.1}$$

which implies that $\partial r/\partial n > 0$. Thus $\partial m/\partial n = -\partial r/\partial n < 0$. Finally, if returns are normally distributed, an increase in n reduces the variance σ_n of $\tilde{X}_n/n$; if D is below μ, $H_n(D)$ falls, while if D is above μ, it rises.   Q.E.D.

Proof of Proposition 3.1. Suppose the banks' rate is $D \in [D_0(N), D_0(N/b)]$. If $D < \underline{D}(N/b)$, investors prefer autarky, so such rates can be ignored. Similarly, with more than $\underline{b}$ banks offering the same rate, investors do not believe the banks are viable. Otherwise, each bank receives market share N/b and nonnegative profits. Deviation to a lower rate causes the bank to have zero market share and profits, while deviation to a higher rate leads to a bank of size N with non-positive profits since its rate is greater than or equal to $D_0(N)$. Since $\pi(\cdot)/n$ is decreasing in n, $\pi(N/b, D_0(N)) > 0$; so long as $D_0(N) \geq \underline{D}(N/b)$, by continuity there is some range of rates below $D_0(N)$ for which it does not pay to raise one's rate and capture the market.

If $D^*(N/b) = \underline{D}(N/b)$, all feasible and profitable rates are equilibria. Otherwise, $\pi(N/b, D^*) = \pi(N, D^*)$. Since $\partial \pi/\partial D = -n \cdot \partial r/\partial D$, so long as $\partial^2 r/\partial n \partial D > 0$, $\pi(N/b, D) < \pi(N, D)$ for all $D < D^*(N/b)$, so these lower rates cannot be equilibria.   Q.E.D.

Proof of Proposition 3.2.

(i) If $D^*(n) = \underline{D}(n)$, then the collusive profit margin is $\mu - c - r(n, \underline{D}(n))$. $dm^*(n)/d(n) = -\partial r/\partial n - (\partial r/\partial D)[d\underline{D}(n)/dn]$. By the Implicit Function Theorem, $d\underline{D}(n)/dn = -(\partial v/\partial n)/(\partial v/\partial D)$; since $\partial v/\partial n = \partial r/\partial n - C \cdot \partial H_n(D)/\partial n > \partial r/\partial n (\partial H_n(D)/\partial n < 0$ by assumption), and $\partial v/\partial D = \partial r/\partial D - C \cdot h_n(D) < \partial r/\partial D$, $d\underline{D}(n)/dn < -(\partial r(n, D)/\partial n)/(\partial r(n, D)/\partial D) < 0$, and $dm^*(n)/dn$ is positive.

(ii) Now, $dm^*/dn = -\partial r/\partial n - (\partial r/\partial D)(dD^*(n)/dn)$. $D^*(n) > \underline{D}(n)$, so $\pi(n, D^*(n)) = \pi(N, D^*(n))$ and $\partial \pi(n, D^*)/\partial D \geq \partial \pi(N, D^*)/\partial D$ (otherwise, $D^* - \varepsilon$ would be an equilibrium rate, contradicting the definition of D^*). Applying the Implicit Function Theorem to the first condition, $dD^*/dn = -[\partial \pi(n, D^*)/\partial n]/[(\partial \pi(n, D^*)/\partial D) - (\partial \pi(N, D^*)/\partial D)]$. Since the denominator is positive, $\partial \pi(n, D^*)/\partial n$ negative implies dD^*/dn positive and $dm^*(n)/dn$ negative.   Q.E.D.

Proof of Corollary 3.3. If b banks are earning non-negative profits at some rate $D, \underline{D}(N/b) \leq D \leq D_0(N/b) < D_0(N/(b+1))$; an entrant that also sets its rate to D can profitably and feasibly split the market if and only if $D > \underline{D}(N/(b+1))$. If the entrant sets its rate to $D + \varepsilon$ (where ε is small and positive), it captures the entire market; this is profitable if and only if $D < D_0(N)$. This accounts for the end points of the set of possible equilibria which resist entry; the interval will be empty if and only if $D_0(N) > \underline{D}(N/(b+1))$. Since this interval is contained within the interval specified in Proposition 3.1, these are in fact equilibria. By definition $\underline{b} \leq N/\underline{n}$, but $\underline{b} + 1 > N/\underline{n}$, so $\underline{D}(N/(\underline{b}+1)) > D_0(N/(\underline{b}+1)) > D_0(N)$, proving the last part of the corollary. Q.E.D.

Proof of Corollary 3.4. Suppose an entrant posts the same rate as the incumbents; then it gets no share, and profits are zero. The only way to profitably enter is to offer a higher rate and take the entire market, which requires that $D > \underline{D}(N/b)$; such entry will not be profitable if $D > D_0(N)$. Thus, the incumbents can profitably share the market and prevent entry if $D > \max\{D_0(N), \underline{D}(N/b)\}$ and $D < D_0(N/b)$; since this is a subset of the equilibria in Proposition 3.1, it is also a subgame perfect equilibrium among the b incumbents. Q.E.D.

Proof of Corollary 3.5. As outlined in the text, entry cannot be feasible and profitable under these beliefs. Thus, the banks can support any equilibrium from Proposition 3.1. Part (ii) follows immediately. Q.E.D.

Proof of Lemma 4.1. Once the bank becomes well-established as sole incumbent, its discounted profits are $(1 - \delta)^{-1} \cdot \pi_{max}$. During the $T - 1$ periods preceding this, rivals will be willing to pay up to some rate D_R to try to get sole incumbency (the value of getting sole incumbency is static, so the rivals' rate D_R is constant), so the incumbent gets $\pi(N, D_R)$ in each of those periods. Thus

$$\Pi^I = \frac{1 - \delta^{T-1}}{1 - \delta} \cdot \pi(N, D_R) + \frac{\delta^{T-1}}{1 - \delta} \cdot \pi_{max}. \tag{A.2}$$

Any rival would be willing to lose up to $\delta \cdot \Pi^I$ to gain sole incumbency, so $\pi(N, D_R) = -\delta \cdot \Pi^I$. Substituting for $\pi(N, D_R)$ in (A.2) leads to (4.1) in the text. The effects of change in δ and T are immediate. Q.E.D.

Proof of Proposition 4.2.

(i) If a bank captures the market today at a rate just above D, it gets just less than $\pi(N, D)$ this period, and becomes sole incumbent next period, which is worth $\delta \cdot \Pi^I$ today; this equals the left-hand side of (4.2). The left-hand side of (4.2) is the value of the candidate collusive equilibrium. If capturing the market today is not worthwhile, it is not worthwhile later, either (nothing has changed), so this condition is necessary and sufficient. To get (4.3), subtract $\pi(N, D)$ from both sides, rewrite $(1 - \delta)^{-1}$ as $1 + [\delta/(1 - \delta)]$, and substitute for Π^I.

(ii) As $\delta \to 0$, (4.3) approaches $0 \leq \pi(N, D) - \pi(N/b, D)$, which is the defining condition for $D^*(N/b)$ in Proposition 3.1.

(iii) As T becomes large, the LHS of (4.3) approaches zero, while the RHS is unchanged. If D exceeds $D^*(N/b)$, then the first term on the RHS of (4.3) is nonnegative (by the definition of $D^*(N/b)$), so (4.3) holds for T sufficiently large. If D is less than $D^*(N/b)$, the RHS of (4.3) is positive if and only if $1 - \delta < \pi(N/b, D)/\pi(N, D)$. Using $\pi(n, D) = n \cdot m(n, D)$, this is the same as $\delta > 1 - b^{-1} \cdot m(N/b, D)/m(N, D)$, so if this holds and T is sufficiently large, (4.3) holds. Q.E.D.

References

Barlow, R., and Proschan, F. (1975). *Statistical Theory of Reliability and Life Testing*. New York: Holt, Rinehart & Winston.

Baumol, W., Panzar, J., and Willig, R. (1986). "On the theory of perfectly contestable markets," in J. Stiglitz and F. Mathewson (eds.), *New Developments in the Analysis of Market Structure* (Cambridge, Mass: MIT Press) pp. 339–65.

Besanko, D., and Thakor, A. (1993). "Relationship banking, deposit insurance, and portfolio choice," in C. Mayer and X. Vives (eds.), *Capital Markets and Financial Intermediation* (Cambridge: Cambridge Univ. Press), 292–319.

Bhattacharya, S., and Thakor, A. (1993). "Contemporary banking theory." *J. Finan. Intermediation*, 3: 2–50.

Bordo, M., Redish, A., and Rockoff, H. (1995*a*). "A comparison of the stability and efficiency of the Canadian and American banking systems, 1870–1925." NBER Historical Paper No. 67.

——, ——, and ——(1995*b*). "A comparison of the stability and efficiency of the Canadian and American banking systems in the twentieth century: Stability v. efficiency?" in M. Bordo and R. Sylla (eds.), *Anglo-American Financial Systems: Institutions and Markets in the Twentieth Century* (New York: Irwin Professional Publishing), 11–40.

Boyd, J., and Prescott, E. (1986). "Financial intermediary coalitions." *J. Econ. Theory*, 38: 211–32.

Calomiris, C. (1993). "Regulation, industrial structure, and instability in U.S. banking: An historical perspective," in M. Klausner and L. White (eds.), *Structural Change in Banking* (Homewood, IL: Business One Irwin), 19–116.

Campbell, T., and Kracaw, W. (1980). "Information production, market signalling, and the theory of financial intermediation." *J. Finance* 35: 863–82.

Capie, F. (1995). "Prudent and stable (but inefficient?): Commercial banks in Britain, 1890–1940," in M. Bordo and R. Sylla (eds.), *Anglo-American Financial Systems: Institutions and Markets in the Twentieth Century* (New York: Irwin Professional Publishing), 41–64.

——, and Rodrik-Bali, G.(1982). "Concentration in British banking, 1870–1920." *Business History*, 24: 280–92.

Cerasi, V., and Daltung, S. (1995). "The optimal size of a bank: Costs and benefits of diversification." Working Paper, Sveriges Riksbank.

Chari, V., and Jagannathan, R. (1988). "Banking panics, information, and rational expectations equilibrium." *J. Finance* 43: 749–61.

Checkland, S. (1975). *Scottish Banking: A History, 1695–1973*. London: Collins.

Cockerell, H., and Green, E. (1994). *The British Insurance Business: A Guide to its History and Records*. Sheffield: Sheffield Academic Press.

Collins, M. (1988). *Money and Banking in the UK: A History*. London: Routledge.

Diamond, D. (1984). "Financial intermediation and delegated monitoring." *Rev. Econ. Stud.*, 51: 393–414.

——, and Dybvig, P. (1983). "Bank runs, deposit insurance and liquidity." *J. Polit. Economy*, 91: 401–19.

Dowd, K. (1992). "Free banking in Australia," in K. Dowd (ed.), *The Experience of Free Banking* (London: Routledge), 48–78.

Emmons, W. (1993). "Deposit insurance and last-resort lending as delegated monitoring: A theory of bank safety nets." Working Paper, Dartmouth College.

Farrell, J., and Saloner, G. (1986). "Installed base and compatibility: Innovation, product preannouncements, and predation." *Am. Econ. Rev.*, 76: 940–55.

Flood, M., and Kwan, S. (1995). "The boom and bust phenomenon and U.S. bank failure experience, 1914–1929." Working Paper, Concordia University.

Gehrig, T. (1995). "Excessive risk and banking regulation." Working Paper, University of Basel.

Gilson, S., John, K., and Lang, L. (1990). "An empirical study of private reorganization of firms in default." *J. Finan. Econ.*, 27: 315–53.

Gorton, G., and Pennacchi, G. (1990). "Financial intermediaries and liquidity creation." *J. Finance*, 45: 49–71.

Griffiths, B. (1973). "The development of restrictive practices in the U.K. monetary system." *Manchester Sch. Econ. Soc. Stud.*, 41: 3–18.

Innes, R. (1990). "Limited liability and incentive contracting with ex-ante action choices." *J. Econ. Theory*, 52: 45–67.

Jacklin, C., and Bhattacharya, S. (1988). "Distinguishing panics and information-based bank runs: Welfare and policy implications." *J. Polit. Econ.*, 96: 568–92.

Jenkins, D. (1984). "The practice of insurance against fire, 1750–1840, and historical research," in O. Westall (ed.), *The Historian and the Business of Insurance* (Manchester: Manchester Univ. Press), 9–38.

Katz, M., and Shapiro, C. (1985). "Network externalities, competition, and compatibility." *Am. Econ. Rev.*, 75: 424–40.

Krasa, S., and Villamil, A. (1992). "A theory of optimal bank size." *Oxford Econ. Pap.*, 44: 725–49.

Marcus, A. (1984). "Deregulation and bank financial policy." *J. Banking Finance*, 8: 557–65.

Matutes, C., and Vives, X. (1996). "Competition for deposits, fragility, and insurance." *J. Finan. Intermediation*, 5: 184–216.

Myers, S. (1997). "Determinants of corporate borrowing." *J. Finan. Econ.*, 5: 147–75.

Neufeld, E. (1972). *The Financial System of Canada.* New York: St. Martin's Press.

Rajan, R. (1992). "Insiders and outsiders: The choice between informed and arm's-length debt." *J. Finance*, 47: 1367–400.

Ramakrishnan, R., and Thakor, A. (1984). "Information reliability and a theory of financial intermediation." *Rev. Econ. Stud.*, 51: 415–32.

Roe, M. (1997). "Backlash." Center for Law and Economic Studies Working Paper No. 127, Columbia University.

Rothschild, M., and Stigliltz, J. (1970). "Increasing risk: I. A definition." *J. Econ. Theory*, 2: 225–43.

Shaffer, S. (1993). "A test of competition in Canadian banking." *J. Money, Credit, Banking*, 25(1): 49–61.

Sheppard, D. (1971). *The Growth and Role of UK Financial Institutions, 1880–1962.* London: Methuen.

Smith, B. (1984). "Private information, deposit interest rates, and the 'stability' of the banking system." *J. Monet. Econ.*, 14: 293–317.

Tirole, J. (1988). *The Theory of Industrial Organization.* Cambridge, Mass: MIT Press.

Williamson, S. (1986). "Costly monitoring, financial intermediation, and equilibrium credit rationing." *J. Monet. Econ.*, 18: 159–79.

Winton, A. (1990). "Three essays on information, contracting, and financial intermediation." Ph.D. dissertation, University of Pennsylvania.

—— (1995). "Delegated monitoring and bank sturcture in a finite economy." *J. Finan. Intermediation*, 4: 158–87.

Yanelle, M. (1989). "The strategic analysis of intermediation." *Eur. Econ. Rev.*, 33: 294–301.

—— (1997). "Banking competition and market efficiency." *Rev. Econ. Stud.*, 64: 215–39.

Yosha, O. (1997). "Diversification and competition: Financial intermediation in a large Cournot–Walras economy." *J. Econ. Theory*, 75: 64–88.

Financial Contracting and Interbank Competition: A Discussion

Andrew Winton

Many financial institutions connect borrowers and investors, not by brokering transactions between the two groups, but rather by entering into contracts with each group separately. Indeed, although the growth of securities markets is often seen as superseding such contractual intermediation, it would be more accurate to say that the mix of contractual forms is changing, with "equity-financed" institutions like mutual funds and defined-contribution pension funds increasing in importance relative to "debt-financed" institutions such as commercial banks and insurance firms. It follows that understanding how contracting issues influence relations between financial institutions and their customers is critical to the theory of intermediation.

Perhaps the most salient example of this contracting view is the delegated monitoring model of financial intermediation. The basic idea of this model is that problems of asymmetric information and moral hazard between borrowers and investors lead to a role for costly monitoring; concentrating a borrower's funding with a small number of institutions improves the institutions' incentives to monitor on behalf of their own investors and reduces duplication of effort and free rider problems.[1] Despite these potential gains, a delegated monitor must overcome potential agency problems between itself and its own investors. Thus, in the delegated monitoring view of financial intermediaries, there will be contracting problems both between the institution and the firms that it funds and between the institutions and the investors that fund it, and these concerns will affect both institutional structure and competition among institutions.

This paradigm leads to several types of questions. The first, and most fundamental, is whether potential gains from delegated monitoring are

---

[1] Note that the notion of delegated monitoring may be extended more broadly to any situation where an institution must select financial assets on behalf of investors using specialized skills or information that the investors do not possess.

in fact feasible once the agency problem between the institution and the investors that fund it is taken into account. This is the focus of Part I of this volume, "Monitoring of and by Banks"; seminal papers here include Diamond (1984) and Boyd and Prescott (1986), which are both included in Part II, and Ramakrishnan and Thakor (1984). By contrast, the four chapters in the current section (Part V) deal with a second, more applied set of questions: What are the precise mechanics of delegated monitoring, and how do these interact with relationships between institutions and borrowers and with competition between institutions?

Von Thadden (1995) (Chapter Seventeen) focuses on the nature of contracting between an institution and the firms that it funds. Here, key issues are the way in which an institution's role as a delegated monitor affects this contracting problem, and the resulting tradeoffs between monitored finance from an institution and relatively unmonitored "arm's-length" finance from diffuse investors. This chapter was one of first in what is now a large literature on the optimal structure and mix of monitored and unmonitored finance.

Whereas Von Thadden looks at contracting when a monitoring institution operates in isolation, in reality, such institutions often compete with one another for borrowers. Although competition might seem to be unequivocally good news for borrowers, Petersen and Rajan (1995) (Chapter Sixteen) show that there may be costs as well: Increased competition may undermine an institution's incentive to build relationships with borrowers based on implicit contracting. This has led to a large empirical literature examining the pros and cons of increased bank competition for loans.

In focusing exclusively on the "investment" side of intermediation, both Von Thadden and Petersen and Rajan implicitly assume complete separation between the institution's funding structure and the structure of its investments in firms. Since a key insight of the delegated monitoring model is that investors' concerns will influence the structure of financial institutions, another key focus for research is the interaction between an institution's investment and funding sides.

This is the focus of another chapter in this part, Boot, Greenbaum, and Thakor (1993) (Chapter Fifteen). Noting that additional capital can be costly to obtain, especially when an institution is suffering financial difficulties, they examine the impact that this has on the contracts financial institutions write with their customers, especially with would-be borrowers. As they show, using contracts that are deliberately ambiguous can allow an institution to substitute reputational capital for financial capital. Subsequent work has expanded on this by illuminating other ways in which an institution's funding structure may have spillover effects on the types of contracts it uses on its investment side. This in turn links to some of the funding issues raised in Parts III and IV of this volume, "Liquidity" and "Bank Runs and Financial Crises."

A final insight of the delegated monitoring model is that diversification can be useful to financial institutions not only by reducing investor risk per se, but also by reducing the cost of controlling the agency problem between institutions and investors. Nevertheless, in the final chapter in this part, Winton (1997) (Chapter Eighteen) shows that diversification may have costs as well as benefits for investors: When size and diversification go hand in hand, increased diversification can induce pricing collusion among institutions. Winton (1997) also points to the importance of adoption externalities in the evolution of industry structure. If no institution has established a reputation for being well diversified, a fragmented structure is likely to develop due to coordination problems among investors. As the industry consolidates over time and institutions become better diversified, their increased size and diversification can become a barrier to entry, making it easier for them to collude. Subsequent work has expanded on this by looking at how diversification interacts with monitoring skill and performance in influencing institution structure and competition.

In what follows, I examine each of these topics in more detail, giving a fuller sense of the four chapters just mentioned and related work. I then conclude with a few thoughts for what remains to be done. A more extended treatment of these and other issues in intermediation can be found in Gorton and Winton (2003).

1. Monitored Finance versus Arm's-length Finance

As noted earlier, the delegated monitoring literature identifies clear benefits to having a single institution monitor borrowers on behalf of dispersed investors. Nevertheless, many firms choose to borrow from public markets, relying on the dispersed investors directly. Thus, there must be some pros and cons to the choice between monitored finance and diffuse "arm's-length" finance. Moreover, although the initial work on delegated monitoring produced fairly simple financing structures, in reality, bank loans and other forms of monitored finance are fairly complex contracts.

The research discussed in this section examines how monitored finance and arm's-length finance lead to different contractual structures and inter-action between the firm and its investor(s), which then gives some insight into the pros and cons of these two funding modes. Not surprisingly, monitored finance typically permits a richer array of contracts and inter-action than does arm's-length finance. It follows that the main cost of arm's-length finance is that investors make uninformed, hence inefficient, decisions about letting a firm continue or be terminated; this in turn can exacerbate moral hazard on the firm's part. Costs of monitored finance include the direct cost of monitoring and indirect costs induced by the monitor's information advantage over other outside investors.

In Von Thadden (1995), an entrepreneur seeks funding. He must then invest in effort that improves his firm's return distribution, and simultan-eously choose between "short-term" and "long-term" projects. If the effort is successful, then the short-term project produces lower overall expected returns, but it is more likely to generate a positive interim return than the long-term project. If effort is not successful, the firm is bad and will produce no returns regardless. At the time of the interim return, the firm requires a fixed amount of additional investment if it is to continue; if it is not continued, the firm yields only the interim return.

The model makes three critical informational assumptions. First, the entrepreneur's effort and project choices are not freely observable to out-siders, but interim returns are freely observable. Second, neither the entrepreneur nor outside investors freely observes whether or not the entrepreneur's effort has been successful—that is, whether the firm is good or bad. Third, at a fixed cost, an outside investor can learn the firm's quality (whether it is good or bad). Such "monitoring" is assumed to be contractible.[2]

Given this setting, in the absence of monitoring, the interim return serves as a public signal of the project's profitability. If this return is not sufficiently high, it is efficient to terminate the project. Von Thadden

---

[2] Modeling monitoring as an ongoing process fits well with the empirical evidence of Lummer and McConnell (1989), who find that stock market investors glean more information from revisions to existing loan terms than from initial lending decisions. On the other hand, Lummer and McConnell study publicly traded firms, where a bank's initial information advantage may be small; for firms that are not publicly-traded (start-ups, small firms), initial screening as in Boyd and Prescott (1986) may be just as important as subsequent monitoring.

then explores how this affects arm's-length contracting between the entrepreneur and investors.

The model's assumptions imply that, even though long-term projects are efficient conditional on the firm being good, it may be optimal to choose the short-term project and terminate the firm if it has a poor interim return. Intuitively, neither the entrepreneur nor the investors knows for sure whether poor interim returns are caused by temporary bad luck or by an innately bad project. Because a good long-term project has a higher chance of producing poor interim returns than does a good short-term project, choosing the long-term project might lead to too much termination of truly good firms. In this case, short-term debt-like financing is best: investors will refuse to renew the debt when the interim return is poor, and the entrepreneur will choose the short-term project so as to minimize the chance of being terminated.

Conversely, if effort is more likely to be successful and the long-term project's chance of poor interim returns is not too high, the long-term project is optimal and can easily be implemented through long-term financing, under which the firm is never liquidated. Nevertheless, there are cases where the long-term project is ex ante optimal yet the firm should be liquidated if its interim return is poor. This occurs when the chance that initial effort is successful is very low, so that a poor interim return is a strong signal of an unsuccessful firm. In this case, short-term financing is optimal, yet it may lead to excessive "myopia"—the entrepreneur chooses the short-term project even though it is not efficient.

Now suppose that, for some cost, an institution ("bank") can observe whether or not the firm's initial effort has been successful. Given this new information, the long-term project is, in principle, now optimal—the firm can be liquidated if unsuccessful, and continued otherwise, regardless of its interim return. So long as the cost of monitoring is not too high relative to the chance that initial effort is successful, it is in fact optimal to engage in such monitoring. The contract that implements this first-best outcome is a long-term contract that gives the "bank" total control over project continuation but requires that the bank compensate the entrepreneur whenever the interim return is poor, even if the project is then liquidated.

Before I discuss the importance of Von Thadden's results, it is useful to compare them with those of Rajan (1992). As in Von Thadden's model, an entrepreneur needs funding and chooses effort that increases his firm's probability of success, and an interim signal of the firm's chance of eventual success is available to some agents. Terminating the project at the interim date yields positive liquidation value, analogous to Von Thadden's assumption that interim termination avoids additional costly investment. Unlike Von Thadden, only debt contracts are permitted. Also, the entrepreneur's effort choice is completely unobservable to investors, whereas the interim signal can be observed both by the entrepreneur and by an institutional investor ("bank") that holds a significant claim on the firm and monitors. Rajan assumes that free rider problems prevent diffuse arm's-length debt holders from observing this signal.

In this setting, arm's-length debt might as well be "long-term," that is, maturing when the firm's project is completed; having no new information at the interim date, investors would always roll over shorter-term debt without any change in terms. Having limited liability and residual claimant status, the entrepreneur always prefers to continue and have *some* chance of eventual success rather than liquidate and get no residual payment for sure; thus, the firm is never liquidated. Furthermore, because some of the benefits of initial effort accrue to investors by reducing the default risk they face, the entrepreneur under-invests in effort—a variant on the debt overhang problem of Myers (1977).

By contrast, bank finance obtained from a single large investor that does monitor may meaningfully have a short maturity, since the bank can condition its rollover decision on the project's eventual chance of success. This leads to efficient interim liquidation decisions. Nevertheless, short-term bank finance can also cause problems. Even if continuation is efficient, by threatening to refuse to renew the loan the bank can precipitate renegotiation of the loan's terms. If the bank's bargaining power is too high, it appropriates so much of the surplus from continuation that the entrepreneur's incentive to under-invest in effort is worse than under arm's-length finance, potentially overwhelming the benefits of more efficient liquidation decisions. The upshot is that short-term bank debt may be dominated by unmonitored arm's-length debt if banks have too much bargaining power.

One source of this bargaining power is that the incumbent ("inside") bank has private information about the firm that outside banks lack. Rajan shows that this information advantage generates endogenous bargaining power. Outside banks know they can only get the borrower's business if the inside bank does not want it, and this "Winner's Curse" generates monopoly rents for the inside bank. These rents are greater as the borrower's credit quality is worse.

The contrast between Rajan's and Von Thadden's results has its roots in the informational and contractual settings that they use. Rajan's setting—the entrepreneur knows more than outside investors, the firm's project is well understood, moral hazard revolves around a simple continuation/liquidation decision—corresponds to that of a firm in an established, well-understood industry. Limiting contracts to debt implicitly focuses on settings where costly state verification concerns are so high that equity contracts are prohibitively expensive,[3] and public information about the firm's interim status is assumed to be lacking; both assumptions fit the situations of firms in developing economies and small to medium-sized firms in developed economies.

Nevertheless, firms in new industries or industries facing sudden change often face high strategic uncertainty, so that even insiders are not immediately sure whether their choices have been successful. Moreover, in developed economies, interim returns are reasonably easy to observe, enabling firms in these situations to make use of equity finance, either privately (through venture capital) or publicly (through organized equity markets). Von Thadden's analysis captures these features. Indeed, in his model, monitoring is preferred in a setting that corresponds closely to organized venture capital: The firm has a high chance of being completely unsuccessful, it has a high chance of producing poor interims even if it is going to be successful in the long run, the value of interim liquidation is more in terms of avoiding inefficient subsequent investment rather than providing interim liquidation value per se, and the monitoring investor is better informed than the entrepreneur in terms of underlying success.

It follows that the optimal contract looks more like venture capital finance than a bank loan: The monitoring investor has full control, and the entrepreneur may get compensation even when interim returns are poor. In Rajan's model, this would only undermine the entrepreneur's initial effort choice; it is optimal in Von Thadden's model because the entrepreneur must be compensated for choosing the long-term project, which though efficient has a high chance of producing poor interim returns.

Subsequent research has extended these papers in several ways. One focus has been the nature of the control provided by the monitoring institution. For example, Burkart et al. (1997) and Pagano and Röell (1998) apply Rajan's notion that monitoring can create costs through excessive

---

[3] For work on how costly state verification favors debt over equity finance, see Gale and Hellwig (1985) and Boyd and Smith (1999).

control to the theory of optimal firm ownership structure. Berlin et al. (1996) show that, despite being in a position to implement first-best firm decisions, an informed bank may instead collude with its distressed borrower so as to exploit arm's-length investors; under some circumstances, this argues against allowing banks to hold much equity in the firms they lend to. Repullo and Suarez (1998) examine how similar issues affect a firm's optimal mix of arm's-length and monitored debt. Manove and Padilla (1999) extend Von Thadden's notion that the monitoring institution may in some respects be better informed than the borrower to the case of clear-sighted bankers financing overly optimistic entrepreneurs.

Another focus of continuing research is how investment structure affects the institution's own incentives to monitor. Both Rajan and Von Thadden sidestep this issue: Rajan assumes that monitoring is costless so long as the lender has an ongoing relationship with the borrower, and Von Thadden assumes that monitoring effort is contractible, albeit the information gained from this effort is not. Rajan and Winton (1995) address this issue and find that giving the lender short-term senior debt may actually undermine its monitoring incentives; long-term debt with covenants or unsecured short-term debt with the right to later secure collateral may be better because they force the lender to monitor in order to safeguard its position. In situations where a firm with poor interim results sometimes legitimately needs additional investment, Longhofer and Santos (2000) show that seniority may enhance an institution's monitoring incentives; if it is senior it will be more willing to invest additional funds in the firm, so it captures more of the benefit from being better-informed about whether or not the additional investment is really needed.

Thus, Von Thadden's (1995) work can be seen as one of the first steps towards a greater understanding of what monitored finance looks like and how it compares with unmonitored arm's-length finance. The precise details depend very heavily on the informational setting—both what is observable to different parties and what they can verify and so contract upon. Nevertheless, several themes are repeated. Arm's-length finance tends to be simpler and make "noisier" decisions than monitored finance. Even if monitored finance is better-informed than arm's-length finance, however, the monitoring bank may "misuse" its information. The need to minimize such misuse while still giving the bank incentive to monitor and use information appropriately helps to explain many of the contractual features that we see in practice.

2. Competition and Bank–Borrower Relationships

As mentioned above, one potential benefit of monitored finance is that the monitoring institution can act in a better-informed, hence more flexible, fashion than diffuse arm's-length investors. Although the papers just discussed have focused on how this affects explicit contracting, a number of papers have explored how long-term relationships between banks and borrowers can lead to improved outcomes through implicit contracting supported by the banks' concern for maintaining reputation or future rents. To the extent that future rents or quasi-rents are critical for maintaining beneficial relationships, this suggests that increased competition among banks may actually be harmful. In this section, I discuss research in this area.

Early models of how long-term relationships allow for implicit contracting between banks and borrowers include Haubrich (1989) and Boot et al. (1993). Haubrich shows that, rather than incur the cost of verifying borrower earnings every time they are reported as bad, a sufficiently patient bank can simply perform statistical tests on reports over time and penalize the borrower if too many reports are bad. This arrangement can be incentive compatible even if the reports are not verifiable in a court of law. Thus, relationship banking allows cost savings through implicit contracting. As discussed in the next section, Boot et al. (1993) show that implicit contracting supported by a bank's concern for its reputation can allow the bank valuable flexibility, the benefit of which can be passed on to the borrower through lower costs. Finally, a body of empirical work supports the idea that long-term bank relationships expand borrowers' access to credit: See, for example, Hoshi, Kashyap, and Stein (1990), Petersen and Rajan (1994), Berger and Udell (1995), and Elsas and Krahnen (1998).

Whereas the papers just discussed focus on how repeated interaction and reputation can help maintain valuable implicit contracts between banks and borrowers, Petersen and Rajan (1995) suggest that bank rents from market power can also help maintain implicit contracts. In their model, banks do not initially know which borrowers are good and which are bad, but they do learn this over time as firms establish track records. Firms can also unobservably choose projects with higher risk but lower returns, and their incentive to do so increases in the interest rate they are charged. If banks compete for loans, the rates they charge new firms will reflect average credit quality, which may in turn be so high that even good firms choose risky projects, which in turn may lead to credit rationing (as per Stiglitz and Weiss, 1981). By contrast, if banks have some market power, then they can charge a lower rate on new firms, knowing that they can make up any losses by earning monopoly rents on good firms in the future. This, in turn, reduces risk-shifting incentives and thus credit rationing for new firms.

Petersen and Rajan test their theory by regressing the rates that small businesses pay on their loans against a number of controls for firm risk and the Herfindahl index of the local banking market. Consistent with their theory, in highly concentrated banking markets, young firms are more likely to receive bank finance, and the rate of interest that firms pay declines more slowly over time than in less concentrated banking markets. This allows banks in more concentrated markets to earn rents on surviving firms.

Subsequent empirical work has found more evidence of such effects. For example, Fischer (2000) finds that German firms in more concentrated banking markets are less credit-constrained and transfer more information to their lender; also, banks provide more liquidity if they have received such information. Bonaccorsi di Patti and Dell'Ariccia (2001) examine the impact of local bank concentration on rates of firm creation in Italy. They find that more concentrated banking markets have lower rates of firm creation on average, but the opposite is true in industries with low fixed assets, which they argue proxies for high asymmetric information. At a "macro" level, Cetorelli and Gambera (2001) examine how cross-country differences in banking sector concentration affects different industries' growth rates. They find that more concentrated banking sectors lower average growth rates, but do increase the growth rates of industries that have very high external finance needs.

Thus, implicit contracting does seem to be an important force in bank–borrower relationships. Petersen and Rajan (1995) show that monopoly rents can help maintain such implicit contracts. Nevertheless, as in Rajan (1992), monopoly rents can also cause costly distortions. The work of Bonaccorsi di Patti and Dell'Ariccia (2001) and Cetorelli and Gambera (2001) suggests that the net impact varies across industries, with some gaining and some losing.

3. Interaction between the Institution's Funding Structure and its Monitoring Role

Most of the papers discussed in the previous two sections implicitly assume complete separation between a institution's investment activities and the financing it receives from investors: A monitoring institution is assumed to perform its role so as to maximize the value of its investment, without any concern for how the investment structure it chooses affects and is affected by its own financing. In reality, this seems implausible. Just as a borrower may be tempted to misuse financing obtained from others, an institution depends on "other people's money" which it may be tempted to misuse, so its financing structure may in part be aimed at controlling this agency problem. Just as financing structure may distort a nonfinancial firm's investment choices, financing structure may influence the firms an institution lends to and the lending terms that it chooses.[4] The papers discussed in this section examine three related channels through which this can occur: Through the use of demandable claims as a way of disciplining an institution, through an institution's need to provide liquidity to its customers, and through an institution's need to conserve costly equity capital.

Fama and Jensen (1983) were among the first to suggest that the need to control intermediary agency problems causes some financial institutions (mutual savings banks and insurers) to give their investors claims that are wholly or partly payable on demand. The same idea was formally modeled and applied to commercial banks by Calomiris and Kahn (1991) and Flannery (1994), but only recently have researchers (Jean-Baptiste 1999; Diamond and Rajan 2001) addressed the full interaction between an institution's investment structure, its funding structure, and its incentives to monitor and control its borrowers.

The Diamond and Rajan paper is also noteworthy because it combines the need for short-term funding as a disciplinary device with the need that the institution's investors have for liquidity (see Part III). In the simplest version of their model, investors' own random needs for liquidity are completely diversifiable, and making the institution's liabilities demandable serves chiefly as a means for disciplining it through the threat of a run. If instead such liquidity needs are not perfectly diversifiable, there may be a spillover from an institution's role as a liquidity provider to its role as a monitor of borrowers; as in Chari and Jagannathan (1988), runs may incorrectly be triggered by investor liquidity needs. In Diamond and

---

[4] The early work on delegated monitoring certainly touches on this point, but because monitoring is assumed either to take the form of ex ante screening or contractible ex post verification, the institution's ex ante financing structure completely solves the problem without any dynamic ex post interaction between the institution and its investors.

Rajan (2000), outside equity capital is shown to be useful in reducing the incidence of such liquidity shocks.

Outside equity is a costly financing source, however, so the institution may be better off changing the structure of its investments.[5] Diamond and Rajan (2000) show that capital-constrained institutions may structure their loans in a more conservative fashion, and Winton (2003) shows that the threat of liquidity needs will lead institutions to favor debt investments over equity investments.

One of the chapters in this part of the current volume (Chapter Fifteen), Boot et al. (1993), examines yet another way in which costly capital affects the contracts an institution enters into. Most papers on such contracting assume that some eventualities simply cannot be contracted upon; e.g. the interim signal of the borrower's situation in Rajan (1992), or the monitoring institution's knowledge of the borrower's project type in von Thadden (1995). While this is undoubtedly true, in many cases, institutions' contracts often *deliberately* leave out contingencies which are easy to contract on. Boot et al. show that this may be valuable because it allows institutions to choose between using financial capital and using reputational capital.

The basic idea is quite simple: suppose that an institution sells financial guarantees to borrowers, and that over time it gains valuable information about borrowers that other institutions can only acquire at a cost. Since a defaulting institution cannot honor its guarantees, the price of guarantees will reflect the perceived default risk of the institution—its reputation. If the guarantees it sells are strictly enforceable, the institution will have to honor them even in circumstances where its own capital is limited and it must access costly additional financing or perhaps even default. By contrast, if the institution sells a discretionary guarantee which is not legally enforceable, then it can choose between honoring the guarantee and thus enhancing its reputation, or reneging on the guarantee, hurting its reputation but saving costly financial capital. Since weaker institutions are more likely to face capital shortfalls in the future, it is more costly for them to honor such discretionary commitments, and thus the reputation-enhancing effect of honoring a discretionary contract is in fact self-sustaining.

---

[5] For example, building on Jensen and Meckling (1976) and Besanko and Kanatas (1996), Diamond and Rajan (2000) analyze the agency problem between outside shareholders and bank insiders. Other costs of equity include information asymmetries that make equity costly to issue and costly to hold; see Bolton and Freixas (2000) and Gorton and Winton (2000).

As Boot et al. note, this simple idea has applications to a number of contracts used by financial institutions. Loan commitments often have a "material adverse change" clause, which allows the institution to renege on the commitment if anything "materially adverse" happens to the would-be borrower. Nevertheless, such commitments are used to back commercial paper issuance, where the commitment is unlikely to be used *unless* something materially adverse has occurred, and they are in fact sometimes honored in such circumstances. "Highly confident" letters perform a similar function in financing acquisitions, and "comfort letters" from holding companies perform a similar function in obtaining financing for subsidiaries. Managers of money market mutual funds have often compensated investors for losses on the funds' holdings, even though in principle such losses should be passed through to the fund shareholders. In all cases, the discretionary promise to honor some commitment enables the institution to honor the commitment in normal conditions when capital is relatively plentiful, and to renege on it in abnormal conditions when capital is relatively scarce and honoring the commitment would be especially costly.

The upshot is that interaction between an institution's funding and investment activities suggests a number of institutional features: Prevalence of short-term or demandable funding, a tendency towards conservatism in the investments of capital- or liquidity-constrained institutions, and the use of implicit rather than explicit guarantees. While these predictions seem in accordance with the stylized facts, empirical work on the detailed predictions of these models remains a fertile field for further research.[6]

4. Diversification and Intermediary Competition

All of the theoretical papers I have mentioned thus far are "single-loan" models: Either a single loan and its risk serve as shorthand for the overall risk of the institution's portfolio, or else the bank holds a perfectly diversified portfolio of loans with independent and identically distributed

---

[6] One exception is the copious body of work on "credit crunches"—the notion that capital-constrained institutions cut back on lending. Nevertheless, this work has tended to focus on the link between a bank's overall loan growth and capital level rather than looking at detailed bank–borrower interaction; see the discussion and references in Gorton and Winton (2003). An exception is Hubbard et al. (2002), who find that, all else equal, borrowers that lack access to public funding markets pay higher rates if their bank has weaker capital levels.

returns. In reality, loan returns are not independent and institutions are not perfectly diversified. Nevertheless, institutions' degree of diversification is an important factor for their customers. Investors may value diversification in and of itself, and diversification may also reduce the cost of overcoming the agency problem between investors and institution. Borrowers may value diversification because a better-diversified institution may be less likely to find itself in financial distress, when its own financial constraints may interfere with implicit guarantees to maintain borrowers' access to funds.

The papers discussed here focus on two aspects of diversification. The first is the notion that bigger institutions are better-diversified, hence more efficient, than smaller ones. The second is the notion that diversification is a matter of strategic choice rather than size alone, and that benefits of specialization may outweigh those of diversification. The papers that follow suggest that both the goal of achieving efficient diversification and the choice between diversification and specialization are more complex than the first generation of delegated monitoring models suggested.

At first glance, it might seem that the potential benefits of diversification should cause unregulated banking systems to quickly become dominated by a few well-diversified and competitive banks. In fact, the history of such systems tends to show a different pattern. Initially, the system is quite fragmented; over time, consolidation occurs through failure and merger, culminating in a stable system dominated by a few large banks that behave collusively and are almost immune to entry. This suggests a need for a closer look at the dynamics of competition between institutions when their performance improves with size and diversification.

Yanelle (1989, 1997) and Winton (1995) examine this issue in the context of the delegated monitoring model. They find that, in general, competitive outcomes are not as well defined as in the case of normal firms; because institutions compete for both borrowers and investors simultaneously, borrower beliefs about which institution investors will use and vice versa are critical in determining the equilibrium size and structure of institutions. A further complication is that such "adoption" externalities are present even on one side of the market; that is, because the size of an institution influences its diversification and thus customer welfare, and this size depends on how many customers choose to use that institution, customer beliefs about which institution other customers will use have a big impact on competitive outcomes.

The last chapter in this part of the current volume, Winton (1997) (Chapter Eighteen), uses this adoption externality to motivate the stylized pattern of intermediary formation and competition discussed earlier. In a streamlined version of the delegated monitoring model of Williamson (1986), institutions compete for investors, to whom they issue debt. Compared to smaller institutions, larger institutions are better diversified, so they are better able to make payments on their debt and can avoid agency problems vis-à-vis investors at lower cost. Thus, for any given promised debt rate, investors would prefer to go to a larger institution; indeed, they would be willing to accept a somewhat lower promised rate if they could be sure that the institution would be larger.

The problem is that if a given institution lowers its rate, it is unlikely to attract more investors. If instead it raises its rate and investors do respond, the institution's increase in size and diversification actually lowers its expected profits *per investor*. If such profits are already close to zero, further expansion tends to hurt total profits, whereas reductions in size increase these profits. All else equal, this tends to encourage entry.

It follows that if investors have no basis other than an institution's promised rate on which to base their expectations of the institution's size, the equilibrium structure of the intermediary sector is one of extreme fragmentation. Over time, some institutions will fail and investors will begin to use an institution's past size as an indication of how many investors it is likely to attract in the future, all else equal. It follows that investors believe a surviving institution will be larger (hence better diversified) than a de novo entrant with the same promised rate, and so survivors can gain market share with lower promised rates (hence higher profit margins) than entrants. In time, a relatively small number of incumbent institutions will dominate the industry and price collusively without fear of entry.

Common assumptions of these and other papers on diversification by institutions are that monitoring expertise is not hampered by diversification and that diversification is a simple function of size.[7] In reality, monitoring may involve sector-specific expertise, so diversifying into unrelated sectors may entail worse monitoring performance; also, an institution can choose to expand in a few related areas or many different areas, so the degree of diversification is not a passive function of size. Both of these ideas have been the subject of recent research.

---

[7] See also Gehrig (1995), Matutes and Vives (1996), and Yosha (1997).

With regard to the pitfalls of diversifying into new areas, Marquez (1997), Dell'Arricia (1998), Gehrig (1998), Shaffer (1998), and Dell'Arricia et al. (1999) all model how a bank entering a sector with several established banks faces increased adverse selection in its pool of borrowers (the "Winner's Curse"); Shaffer also provides empirical evidence. Boot and Thakor (2000) analyze a bank's decision to invest in sector-specific expertise in a model where "relationship" (monitored) loans require such expertise whereas "transactional" (arm's-length) loans do not. They find that increased competition among banks tends to increase the number of relationship loans that they make while reducing their overall investment in specialized expertise; increased competition from the capital market has the opposite effect. Hauswald and Marquez (2000) model this notion of specialization with the ideas from the Winner's Curse papers just mentioned and find that increased competition from other banks makes banks refocus their investment in expertise: they invest more in their core area of expertise, and less in "peripheral" areas.

While the papers just mentioned look only at the impact of diversification and specialization on average loan performance, these also have an impact on the risk of a bank's loan portfolio. Besanko and Thakor (1993) examine this issue in the context of deposit insured banks; as interbank competition increases, banks are less likely to diversify in order to capture future informational rents of the sort analyzed in Rajan (1992). Winton (2000) shows that, although diversification may reduce the chance of bank failure and improve monitoring incentives, the skewed nature of bank loan returns means that diversification may actually increase the chance of bank failure and harm monitoring incentives, particularly when the monitoring advantage of specialized banks is high or when bank loans have very low or very high risk. As a result, increased interbank competition can either increase or decrease incentives to diversify.

Thus, research on bank diversification suggests that the paradigm of the early work on delegated monitoring—perfectly diversified financial institutions competing perfectly—is overly simplistic. Work on competition among institutions suggests that the path to diversification through size may not be straightforward and may eventually result in an overly collusive system. Moreover, work on the potential benefits of specialization questions the notion that diversification should be the only goal for institutions that monitor borrowers.

5. Conclusions

What remains to be done? Of the areas surveyed here, the most well explored are the first two: Contracting between institutions and borrowers in the absence of interaction with the institution's funding structure, and the impact of bank competition on implicit bank–borrower relationships. In both areas, further research is likely to be empirical, making use of increasingly available data on the details (loan amounts and rates, other funding sources, etc.) of bank–borrower interaction in an expanding number of economies.

A richer area for further research is the third that I discussed, namely how the institution's monitoring and contracting incentives are affected by its funding structure, and how monitoring concerns interact with the institution's role as an investment vehicle that provides diversification or liquidity for its investors. In addition, as loans and other monitored contracts are increasingly securitized and "equity-financed" institutions like mutual funds capture an increasing share of investors' dollars, a key issue is how explicit contract structures and implicit reputational concerns à la Boot et al. (1993) interact to guarantee institutions' monitoring incentives. Again, the increasing availability of detailed data on institution structure in a growing number of economies makes empirical work on these issues especially attractive.

Finally, with regard to diversification and competition, although there has been a great deal of recent work on the effects of specialization and diversification on an institution's average performance, much more remains to be done on how these decisions affect an institution's portfolio risk and how this in turn interacts with institutions' funding structure. Despite the increasing use of and debate over practical ways of measuring institutions' risk by both managers and regulators, this debate has generally treated risk as a variable unaffected by contract structure, monitoring ability, and monitoring incentives; thus, this last topic of research is quite timely.

References

Berger, A. N., and Udell, G. (1995). "Relationship lending and lines of credit in small firm finance." *Journal of Business*, 68: 351–82.

Berlin, M., John, K., and Saunders, A. (1996). "Bank equity stakes in borrowing firms and financial distress." *Review of Financial Studies*, 9: 889–919.

Besanko, D., and Kanatas, G. (1996). "The regulation of bank capital: Do capital standards promote bank safety?" *Journal of Financial Intermediation*, 5: 160–83.

——, and Thakor, A. (1993). "Relationship banking, deposit insurance, and portfolio choice," in C. Mayer and X. Vives (eds.), *Capital Markets and Financial Intermediation* (Cambridge: Cambridge Univ. Press), 292–319.

Bolton, P., and Freixas, X. (2000). "A dilution cost approach to financial intermediation." *Journal of Political Economy*, 108: 324–51.

Bonaccorsi di Patti, E., and Dell"Ariccia, G. (2001). "Bank competition and firm creation." Working Paper, Bank of Italy Research Department.

Boot, A., and Thakor, A. (2000). "Can relationship banking survive competition?" *Journal of Finance*, 55: 679–713.

——, Greenbaum, S., and Thakor, A. (1993). "Reputation and discretion in financial contracting." *American Economic Review*, 83: 1165–83.

Boyd, J., and Prescott, E. (1986). "Financial intermediary coalitions." *Journal of Economic Theory*, 38: 211–32.

——, and Smith, B. (1999). "The use of debt and equity in optimal financial contracts." *Journal of Financial Intermediation*, 8: 270–316.

Burkart, M., Gromb, D., and Panunzi, F. (1997). "Large Shareholders, monitoring, and the value of the firm." *Quarterly Journal of Economics*, 112: 693–728.

Calomiris, C., and Kahn, C. (1991). "The role of demandable debt in structuring optimal banking arrangements." *American Economic Review*, 81: 497–513.

Cetorelli, N., and Gambera, M. (2001). "Banking market structure, financial dependence and growth: International evidence from industry data." *Journal of Finance*, 56: 617–48.

Chari, V. V., and Jagannathan, R. (1988). "Banking panics, information, and rational expectations equilibrium." *Journal of Finance*, 43: 749–61.

Dell'Ariccia, G. (1998). "Asymmetric information and the structure of the banking industry." Working Paper, International Monetary Fund.

——, Friedman, E., and Marquez, R. (1999). "Adverse selection as a barrier to entry in the banking industry." *RAND Journal of Economics*, 30: 515–34.

Diamond, D. (1984). "Financial intermediation and delegated monitoring." *Review of Economic Studies*, 51: 393–414.

——, and Rajan, R. (2000). "A theory of bank capital." *Journal of Finance*, 55: 2431–65.

——, and —— (2001). "Liquidity risk, liquidity creation, and financial fragility: A theory of banking." *Journal of Political Economy*, 109: 287–327.

Elsas, R., and Krahnen, J. P. (1998). "Is relationship lending special? Evidence from credit-file data in Germany." *Journal of Banking and Finance*, 22: 1283–316.

Fama, E., and Jensen, M. (1983). "Agency problems and residual claims." *Journal of Law and Economics*, 26: 327–49.

Fischer, K.-H. (2000). "Acquisition of information in loan markets and bank market power—an empirical investigation." Working Paper, J. W. Goethe University.

Flannery, M. (1994). "Debt maturity and the deadweight cost of leverage: Optimally financing banking firms." *American Economic Review*, 84: 320–31.

Gale, D., and Hellwig, M. (1985). "Incentive compatible debt contracts: The one period problem." *Review of Economic Studies*, 52: 647–63.

Gehrig, T. (1995). ' "Excessive Risk" and Banking Regulation." Working Paper, University of Basel.

—— (1998). "Screening, cross–border banking, and the allocation of credit." Working Paper, University of Freiburg.

Gorton, G., and Winton, A. (2000). "Liquidity provision, the cost of bank capital, and the macroeconomy." Institute for Financial Studies Working Paper 9806, University of Minnesota.

——, and —— (2003). "Financial intermediation." In G. Constantinides, M. Harris, and R. Stulz (eds.), *Handbooks in the Economics of Finance, Volume 1A* (Amsterdam, Elsevier), 429–550.

Haubrich, J. (1989). "Financial intermediation, delegated monitoring, and long-term relationships." *Journal of Banking and Finance*, 13: 9–20.

Hauswald, R., and Marquez, R. (2000). "Relationship banking, loan specialization, and competition." Working Paper, Indiana University.

Hoshi, T., Kashyap, A., and Scharfstein, D. (1990). "The role of banks in reducing the costs of financial distress in Japan." *Journal of Financial Economics*, 27: 67–88.

Hubbard, R. G., Kuttner, K., and Palia, D. (2002). "Are there 'Bank Effects' in borrower's costs of funds? Evidence from a matched sample of borrowers and banks." *Journal of Business*, 75: 559–81.

Jean-Baptiste, E. (1999). "Demand deposits as an incentive mechanism." Working Paper, Wharton School, University of Pennsylvania.

Jensen, M., and Meckling, W. (1976). "Theory of the firm: Managerial Behavior, agency costs and ownership structure." *Journal of Financial Economics*, 3: 305–60.

Longhofer, S., and Santos, J. (2000). "The importance of bank seniority for relationship lending." *Journal of Financial Intermediation*, 9: 57–89.

Lummer, S., and McConnell, J. (1989). "Further evidence on the bank lending process and the capital-market-response to bank loan agreements." *Journal of Financial Economics*, 25: 99–122.

Manove, M., and Padilla, A. J. (1999). "Banking (conservatively) with optimists." *RAND Journal of Economics*, 30: 324–50.

Marquez, R. (1997). "Lending capacity and adverse selection in the banking industry." Working Paper, Massachusetts Institute of Technology.

Matutes, C., and Vives, X. (1996). "Competition for deposits, fragility, and insurance." *Journal of Financial Intermediation*, 5: 184–216.

Myers, S. (1977). "Determinants of corporate borrowing." *Journal of Financial Economics*, 5: 147–75.

Pagano, M., and Röell, A. (1998). "The choice of stock ownership structure: agency costs, monitoring, and the decision to go public." *Quarterly Journal of Economics*, 113: 187–225.

Petersen, M., and Rajan, R. (1994). "The benefits of lending relationships: Evidence from small business data." *Journal of Finance*, 49: 3–37.

——, and —— (1995). "The effect of credit market competition on lending relationships." *Quarterly Journal of Economics*, 110: 407–43.

Rajan, R. (1992). "Insiders and outsiders: The choice between informed and arm's-length debt." *Journal of Finance*, 47: 1367–400.

——, and Winton, A. (1995). "Covenants and collateral as incentives to monitor." *Journal of Finance*, 50: 1113–46.

Ramakrishnan, R., and Thakor, A. (1984). "Information reliability and a theory of financial intermediation." *Review of Economic Studies*, 51: 415–32.

Repullo, R., and Suarez, J. (1998). "Monitoring, liquidation, and security design." *Review of Financial Studies*, 11: 163–87.

Shaffer, S. (1998). "The winner's curse in banking." *Journal of Financial Intermediation*, 7: 359–92.

Stiglitz, J., and Weiss, A. (1981). "Credit Rationing in markets with imperfect information." *American Economic Review*, 71: 393–410.

von Thadden, E.-L. (1995). "Long-term contracts, short-term investment and monitoring." *Review of Economic Studies*, 62: 557–75.

Williamson, S. (1986). "Costly monitoring, financial intermediation, and equilibrium credit rationing." *Journal of Monetary Economics*, 18: 159–79.

Winton, A. (1995). "Delegated monitoring and bank structure in a finite economy." *Journal of Financial Intermediation*, 4: 158–87.

—— (1997). "Competition among financial intermediaries when diversification matters." *Journal of Financial Intermediation*, 6: 307–46.

—— (2000). "Don't put all your eggs in one basket? Diversification and specialization in lending." Working Paper, University of Minnesota.

—— (2003). "Institutional liquidity needs and the structure of monitored finance." *Review of Financial Studies*, 16: 1273–1313.

Yanelle, M.-O. (1989). "The strategic analysis of intermediation." *European Economic Review*, 33: 294–301.

—— (1997). "Banking competition and market efficiency." *Review of Economic Studies*, 64: 215–39.

Yosha, O. (1997). "Diversification and competition: Financial intermediation in a large Cournot–Walras economy." *Journal of Economic Theory*, 75: 64–88.

Part VI

Comparative Financial Systems

19

Credit and Efficiency in Centralized and Decentralized Economies

Mathias Dewatripont and Eric Maskin

1. Introduction

We investigate how the degree to which credit markets are centralized affects efficiency when there is asymmetric information. Specifically, we argue that decentralization of credit may promote efficient project selection when creditors are not fully informed ex ante about project quality.

Our starting point is the idea that, although an entrepreneur (project manager) may have a relatively good idea of her project's quality from the outset, creditors acquire this information only later on, by which time the criteria for profitability may have changed. Thus, a poor project (one whose completion time is too long to be profitable ex ante) may nevertheless be financed, since a creditor cannot distinguish it at the time from a good (quick) project. Moreover, the project my not be terminated even after the creditor has discovered its quality, if significant sunk costs have already been incurred. If the threat of termination deterred entrepreneurs from undertaking poor projects in the first place, creditors would wish to commit ex ante not to refinance them. But, sunk costs may well render this threat incredible: ex post, both creditor and entrepreneur could be better off carrying on with the project, i.e. refinancing it.

How can decentralization help in such circumstances? We conceive of a decentralized credit market as one in which ownership of capital is diffuse, so that the capital needed to refinance a poor projects may be available but not in the hands of the initial creditor. This creditor, we assume, can monitor the project and thereby enhance its value. However, monitoring is not observable to subsequent creditors. Consequently, the initial creditor's incentive to monitor is blunted (relative to a centralized market where he owned all the capital) because he cannot fully appropriate the marginal return from doing so. With incentives reduced, he

We thank Patrick Bolton, Jeremy Edwards, Ian Jewitt, Charles Kahn, Janos Kornai, Colin Mayer, John McMillan, John Moore, Yingyi Qian, Gérard Roland, David Scharfstein, and Chenggang Xu for useful comments. This research was supported by the NSF, and by the Belgian Government under PAJ grant No. 26.

will monitor less than under centralization, which in turn reduces the value of the project and therefore the profitability of refinancing. That is, refinancing is less likely than in a centralized market; the threat to terminate a project is more credible.[1] Entrepreneurs are thereby induced not to undertake poor projects in the first place, and this enhances efficiency.[2]

Decentralization tends to deter projects that drag on too long, but for similar reasons may also discourage profitable projects that are slow to pay off. That is, the same features that strengthen commitments to terminate poor projects foster an over-emphasis on short-term profit opportunities.

To see this, suppose that the slow-and-quick-project model we have sketched is enriched so that not only poor projects but also highly profitable projects require long-term financing. Poor (i.e. inept) entrepreneurs are stuck with poor projects, but good (i.e. capable) entrepreneurs have a choice about whether their project is to be long-term and highly profitable or short-term and only moderately profitable. Finally, suppose that the degree of decentralization in the credit market is determined *endogenously*. That is, owners of capital can come together and *choose* whether to form a few big "banks" or a lot of small banks.

In such a model *multiple equilibria* (and, hence *coordination problems*) may well arise. If, in equilibrium, banks are small, even good entrepreneurs will have trouble getting continued financing for long-term projects for the reasons mentioned above. Thus they will choose the short-term option. But given that they do so, it will pay banks to be small (a single big bank would be overrun with unprofitable long-term projects from poor entrepreneurs). Thus, an equilibrium with only short-term projects and small banks exists.

But another equilibrium is also possible, one in which all banks are big. With a profusion of big banks, good entrepreneurs can get long-term financing and so choose highly lucrative projects. The profits from these projects outweigh the losses that banks incur from poor projects (which because of adverse selection are also financed). Such a "long-term" equilibrium can, in fact, be shown to Pareto-dominate the "short-term" equilibrium.

We believe that our framework may be relevant for two widely discussed issues: the "soft budget constraint" problem of centrally planned economies and the contrast in financing practices and investment horizons between economies of the "Anglo-Saxon" and "Japanese–German" modes.

---

[1] Lack of commitment in centralized settings has been the focus of the *ratchet effect* literature. (See, for example, Freixas *et al.* (1985), Laffont and Tirole (1988), and Schaffer (1989)). What remains unsettled in this particular literature, however, is why lack of commitment should pertain particularly to centralization. Our chapter attempts an answer to that question.

[2] As in Stiglitz and Weiss (1981), creditors face an adverse selection problem. In the Stiglitz–Weiss model, credit rationing is a way to deal with this problem and improve the mix of projects being financed. In our setting, by contrast, it is the threat of termination that serves as the device for screening out poor projects.

Kornai (1979, 1980) has emphasized that the absence of bankruptcy threats in socialist economies resulted in the proliferation of inefficient enterprises. Firms realized that their losses would be covered by the state, and so operated quite independently of profit considerations. The pervasiveness of these soft budget constraints under socialism is widely acknowledged, and attempts to harden them are central features of several recent proposals for reform in eastern Europe.

But although the consequences of soft budget constraints have been intensively investigated, the same is not true of their causes. Most explanations have focused on political constraints, such as the need to avoid unemployment or socially costly relocation. While not denying the importance of such constraints, we wish to suggest that *economic* factors may also be relevant. Specifically, the slow-and-quick-project model outlined above (and presented in detail in Sections 2 and 3) offers an explanation of soft budget constraints in which "softness" arises from the profitability of refinancing poor projects. Indeed, in our framework, softness is the "normal" state of affairs; the pertinent question is how, in some circumstances (e.g. a decentralized credit market), budget constraints can be hardened.[3]

We can also apply the framework to explain differences between Anglo-Saxon (U.S. and U.K.) and German–Japanese corporate finance. Several economists have noted that large German or Japanese firms have been more likely to obtain financing from banks than their American or British counterparts (which have relied more on equity or bonds for external finance). Moreover, these banking relationships have typically had a long-term structure in which banks assumed an active monitoring role. (See Aoki (1990), Baliga and Polak (1994), Corbett (1987), Edwards and Fischer (1994),[4] Mayer and Alexander (1989) and Hoshi, Kashyap and Scharfstein (1988, 1989).) Most important from our standpoint, the Anglo-Saxon/German–Japanese financial contrast seems to be marked by differences in project length. Specifically, German and Japanese corporations have seemed less prone to "short-termism" (see, for example, Corbett (1987) and *The Economist* (1990)).

Although highly stylized, the enriched model sketched above, is consistent with these differences. The "long-term" equilibrium accords with German–Japanese experience, and the "short-term" equilibrium with that of the U.S. and U.K.

We proceed as follows. In Section 2, we present a very simple (in some respects, over-simplified) model and show how credit decentralization can improve efficiency. We then discuss several alternative specifications that lead to the same

---

[3] Qian and Xu (1991) and Qian (1994) have used this approach to show how soft budget constraints both interfere with innovation and can contribute to the endemic shortages that plague socialism.

[4] Edwards and Fischer (1994) note, however, that the reliance on external finance among German banks has not been so great as commonly supposed.

conclusions. In particular, we argue that the contrast between centralization and decentralization is only heightened if we suppose, following one tradition, that the central financing authority maximizes social surplus rather than profit.

Section 2 distinguishes decentralization from centralization rather crudely by identifying the former with two creditors and the latter with one. In Sections 3 and 4 we turn to a richer model in which the market structure is determined endogenously. Section 3 establishes that the main qualitative conclusions of Section 2 carry over to a framework in which market structure is determined endogenously. Finally, Section 4 introduces profitable long-run projects as an additional option for good entrepreneurs and shows that there can be two (Pareto-ranked) equilibria marked by different average project lengths.

2. Decentralization as a Commitment Device

a. The model

There are three periods, one entrepreneur, and either one or two creditors (banks). Contracting between the entrepreneur and a bank occurs in period 0, and projects are carried out in periods 1 and 2. If a project remains incomplete at the end of period 1, the entrepreneur and bank can renegotiate the terms of the contract to their mutual advantage.

The entrepreneur's project can be either good (g) or poor (p). A good project is completed after one period; a poor project requires two periods for completion. (We identify the quality of a project with that of its entrepreneur; thus, we shall refer to good and poor entrepreneurs.) The project generates an observable (and verifiable) monetary return only at its completion. Whether good or poor, it requires one unit of capital per period (all returns, capital inputs, and payoffs are denominated in money).

The entrepreneur has no capital herself and so has to obtain financing from the bank(s). Banks have capital but cannot initially distinguish between good and poor projects. Let α be the prior probability that the project is good. All parties are risk neutral, i.e. they maximize expected profit.

For the time being we will assign no bargaining power to the entrepreneur (we will relax this assumption in Section 3). Thus, in negotiating financial terms, a bank can make a take-it-or-leave-it offer to the entrepreneur and thereby extract the entire observable return. The entrepreneur is limited to unobservable private benefits such as the perquisites she can command, the enhancement of her human capital and reputation, or what she can divert from the project into her own pocket.

Let E_g be a good entrepreneur's private benefit. E_t is a poor entrepreneur's benefit when her project is terminated after the first period, whereas E_p is her benefit from a completed project. We assume that $E_p \geq E_t$. This inequality makes sense if we imagine that the entrepreneur can extract more from a project the longer it continues. It would also follow from a more elaborate model in which her reputation is enhanced if the project is completed. In any case, it must hold in any model in which poor projects are ever refinanced (provided that the entrepreneur always has the option of quitting after the first period).[5] We allow for the possibility that any of E_g, E_t, and E_p may be negative,[6] which could occur, for example, if private benefits include the cost of effort that the entrepreneur must incur to set the project up.

Consider centralization first. In this case, there is a single bank B endowed with two units of capital. In period 0, the entrepreneur E (whose type is private information) turns up and requests financing (i.e. a loan of one unit of capital). B makes a take-it-or-leave-it contract offer in which the repayment terms depend on the observable return and when it is realized (because E has no endowment, the repayment cannot exceed the observable return[7]). Assume that a good project generates observable return $R_g > 1$, which, given its bargaining power, B can fully extract (provided that $E_g \geq 0$; if $E_g < 0$, B can extract only $R_g + E_g$ because E will require an inducement $-E_g$ to undertake the project).

If the project is poor, B obtains nothing unless he agrees to refinancing at the beginning of period 2, i.e. agrees to loan another unit of capital[8] (since the observable return is zero at the end of the first period). Moreover, we assume that regardless of the first period agreement, B cannot commit himself not to refinance (or, rather, that any such commitment can be renegotiated). If refinanced, the poor project's observable return at the end of the second period is a random variable $\tilde{R}_p$, whose realization is either 0 or $\overline{R}_p$, where $0 < \overline{R}_p$. (We could allow R_g to be a random variable as well, but this would not matter in view of the parties' risk neutrality.) One can interpret $\tilde{R}_p$ as the liquidation or resale value of the completed project. We suppose that, in addition to its role as lender, B serves to *monitor* the project.[9] This is modeled by assuming that, through his efforts, B can influence the distribution of $\tilde{R}_p$.[10] Assume that B learns E's type at the beginning of period 1. If E is poor, B can expend *monitoring effort* $a \in [0, 1]$ to raise the expectation of $\tilde{R}_p$. Specifically, let a be the probability of $\overline{R}_p$. As a rises, so does the cost of B's efforts. Let $\psi(a)$ denote this cost, with $\psi' > 0$, $\psi'' > 0$, $\psi(0) = \psi'(0) = 0$,

---

[5] And it is precisely the problem created by refinancing poor projects that is of interest to us.

[6] As we shall see, in fact, the major case of interest for our purposes is where $E_t < 0$ and $E_p > 0$.

[7] This is not necessarily true if the private return is known to be positive and bounded away from zero. But as long as B is uncertain about the value of this private return, he will not be able to extract it fully.

[8] Here we are assuming for convenience that E cannot contribute any of what she may have saved from the first loan to reduce the size of the second.

[9] In the 1990 version of this paper, we assumed that, instead of monitoring, B acquires information about the project that it can use to affect the distribution of $\tilde{R}_p$.

[10] We could also assume that monitoring affects the realization of R_g. Because such monitoring would play no role in our analysis, however, we do not consider it.

Table 1. Payoff's under Centralization

	Good project (assuming $E_g > 0$)	Poor project without refinancing	Poor project with refinancing
Entrepreneur	E_g	E_t	E_p
Bank	$R_g - 1$	-1	$\Pi_p^* - 2$

and $\psi'(1) = \infty$. These assumptions ensure an optimal effort level $a^* \in (0, 1)$ such that $\overline{R}_p = \psi'(a^*)$ and, given its bargaining power, an expected return for B (gross of its capital investment) of $\Pi_p^* \equiv a^* \overline{R}_p - \psi(a^*)$.

To summarize, the payoffs (net of the cost of capital) of the entrepreneur and bank under centralization are displayed in Table 1.

Under decentralization, the model is much the same as above, but now assume that there are two banks, B_1 and B_2, each with only one unit of capital. The entrepreneur presents herself to B_1 in at the beginning of period 1 (we will postpone the issue of competition between banks until Section 3). If she turns out to be good, the analysis is as above. The same is true if she is poor but not refinanced. If, however, she is to be refinanced, she must turn to B_2, since by then B_1 has no capital left.[11] Suppose that any monitoring that B_1 has done in period 1 is unobservable to B_2.

For the sake of comparability, we assign B_2 no bargaining power so that, as in the case of centralization, B_1 can make take-it-or-leave-it offers. The problem for B_1 is to convince B_2 to loan a second unit of capital in exchange of a share of $\tilde{R}_p$. The higher B_2's expectation of B_1's monitoring effort in period 1, the smaller this share can be. We claim that equilibrium monitoring effort is less than a^* (the effort level under centralization), despite the fact that endowing B_1 with all the bargaining power maximizes his incentive to monitor. To see this, let $\hat{a}$ be B_2's assessment of the expected level of B_1's monitoring activity. Then, to induce B_2 to participate, the repayment he receives must be $1/\hat{a}$ if $\tilde{R}_p = \overline{R}_p$. This means that B_1 chooses a to maximize

$$a(\overline{R}_p - 1/\hat{a}) - \psi(a),$$

i.e. to satisfy $\overline{R}_p - 1/\hat{a} = \psi'(a)$.[12] Now, in equilibrium, $\hat{a}$ must be correct, so that if a^{**} is the equilibrium effort level, a^{**} satisfies $\overline{R}_p = \psi'(a^{**}) + 1/a^{**}$.[13] Clearly, a^{**}

---

[11] Actually, all that is needed for our purposes is that B_1 should not be willing or able to undertake all the refinancing itself. Indeed, even if B_1 had more than 1 unit of capital left, B_2 would still have to be brought in if B_1 were sufficiently risk averse.

[12] This first-order condition is valid provided that $\overline{R}_p \geqq 1/\hat{a}$. Otherwise, the maximizing choice of a is $a = 0$.

[13] If there is no solution to this equation, then $a^{**} = 0$ (see footnote 12). If there are several solutions, choose the one that maximizes $a(\overline{R}_p - 1/a) - \psi(a)$, in order to rule out inefficiencies due simply to coordination failure.

Table 2. Payoff's under Decentralization

	Good project (if $E_g > 0$)	Poor project with no refinancing	Poor project with refinancing
E	E_g	E_t	E_p
B_1	$R_g - 1$	-1	$\Pi_p^{**} - 2$
B_2	0	0	0

is less than a^* (because B_1 concedes part of the marginal return from monitoring to B_2). Therefore, $\Pi_p^{**} \equiv a^{**}\overline{R}_p - \psi(a^{**})$ is less than Π_p^*.

Recapping we exhibit the (net) equilibrium payoffs under decentralization in Table 2.

We are interested in comparing the (perfect Bayesian) equilibria under centralization and decentralization, and, especially, in investigating how these two alternatives fare in deterring poor entrepreneurs. For these purposes, it makes sense to suppose that poor projects generate negative "social surplus" ($\Pi_p^* + E_p < 2$),[14] that good projects have positive surplus ($R_g + E_g > 1$), and that poor entrepreneurs are deterred only by termination[15] ($E_t < 0 < E_p$). We shall (briefly) consider the other cases after Proposition 1 and in Section 3. (Not surprisingly, centralization and decentralization perform very similarly in most of those other cases.)

PROPOSITION 1. *Assume that $E_p > 0 > E_r$. Under either centralization or decentralization, there exists a unique equilibrium. For parameter values such that some financing is undertaken in equilibrium, a necessary and sufficient condition for project selection to differ in the two equilibria is $\Pi_p^* > 1 > \Pi_p^{**}$. If this condition holds, only a good project is financed under decentralization (the socially efficient outcome); both good and poor projects are financed (and the latter refinanced) under centralization.*[16]

---

[14] Even if $\Pi_p^* + E_p > 2$, a poor project may not necessarily be desirable. In view of the unobservability of the entrepreneurs' private return, she cannot be made to compensate the centralized creditor for its negative profit $\Pi_p^* - 2$. Thus the project's desirability will depend on the creditor's and entrepreneur's relative weights in the social welfare function. However, if $\Pi_p^* + E_p < 2$, then a slow project is unambiguously inefficient.

[15] Poor entrepreneurs might be threatened by legal sanctions (e.g. the threat of being thrown in jail), which could have a deterrent effect. However, if these entrepreneurs are needed for the completion of the project in the second period, such threats may not be very credible.

[16] As modeled, negotiation between the entrepreneur and the bank can occur only after period 1 has elapsed, i.e., after one unit of capital has already been sunk. Let us consider what would happen if regeneration were also permitted *before* the capital is sunk (but after the initial financing contract has been signed). In that case, the bank could propose returning the first period's capital unused in exchange for a fee of $E_p + \varepsilon$. A poor entrepreneur would accept this deal, whereas a good entrepreneur would not (provided that $E_p + \varepsilon < E_g$). Moreover, given our assumption that $\Pi_p^* + E_p - 2 < 0$, the bank would be better off. To rule out such a peculiar outcome, we can suppose that, in addition to good and poor projects, there is a third type that is so dreadful that refinancing is never desirable but for which the entrepreneur's payoff is positive if financed for even one period. Let us suppose that, with high

Sketch of Proof 1. If $\Pi_p^* < 1$, then it is inefficient to refinance a poor project under centralization (and *a fortiori* under decentralization). Thus, a poor entrepreneur will not seek financing (since $E_t < 0$), and so only a good project is financed under both centralization and decentralization. If $\Pi_p^{**} > 1$, then once even a poor project is started, parties will end up refinancing it under decentralization (and *a fortiori* under centralization). Because $E_p > 0$, we conclude that a poor entrepreneur will gain by getting funded and so, under both decentralization and centralization, both types of projects will be financed.[17] Finally, if $\Pi_p^{**} < 1 < \Pi_p^*$, refinancing is efficient under centralization but not under decentralization. Hence, a poor project will be funded in the former case but not the latter.

Hence, either centralization and decentralization lead to the same project selection in equilibrium,[18] or else decentralization is strictly better, i.e. it selects efficiently whereas centralization is subject to a soft budget constraint.

We have been assuming that $E_t < 0 < E_p$. If $E_t > 0$, then termination does not deter a poor entrepreneur from seeking financing, and both poor and good projects are financed under either centralization or decentralization (although that is not to say that the two systems are equally efficient; see footnote 17). If $E_p < 0$, then only good projects are financed under either system.

b. *Alternative specifications*

We have modeled the initial project selection as a problem of adverse selection and refinancing as one of moral hazard, but these imperfections can readily be switched around. Specifically, suppose that instead of project length being given exogenously, E can affect it through (unobservable) effort. Under centralization, B could reward the entrepreneur for early completion, but such a reward might make financing unattractive from B's perspective. The advantage of decentralization would be to induce E to complete early without having to reward her; the threat of termination would be inducement enough. Such an alternative model

---

probability, the quality of such a project is detected by the bank before the capital is sunk. Nevertheless if the probability is less one, dreadful entrepreneurs will still seek financing. Therefore, the bank will thwart its detection mechanism and seriously interfere with efficiency if it offers the above deal.

[17] This relies on our assumption that some financing is undertaken in equilibrium. If this assumption is violated, then it is possible that no projects are financed under either system, or even that both are financed under centralization and neither under decentralization. The latter possibility is an artefact, however, of the crude way we have modelled decentralization. If the market structure is determined endogenously (as in the model of Section 3), this particular discrepancy between centralization and decentralization disappears.

[18] But not necessarily the same degree of efficiency. If $\Pi_p^{**} > 1$, both centralization and decentralization select the same projects, but the former if more efficient, since $\Pi_p^* > \Pi_p^{**}$. However, this discrepancy derives from our over-simplified model of decentralization (see footnote 16). In the more satisfactory model of Section 3, centralization and decentralization are equally efficient in the case where they make the same project selection.

should yield qualitatively very similar results. Undoubtedly, both specifications are relevant in reality.

By the same token, B_2's informational disadvantage has been formally expressed as a problem of moral hazard but could alternatively be derived from adverse selection and *collusion* between E and B_t. Let us, for example, drop B_1's effort from the model (so that $\tilde{R}_p$'s distribution becomes exogenous) but also abandon the assumption that $\tilde{R}_p$'s realization is verifiable. Interpret B_1's informational advantage as the ability to prove to a court that $\tilde{R}_p = \overline{R}_p$, if that equality holds. As in models of hierarchies (Tirole (1986); Kofman and Lawarrée (1993)), collusion between two parties who share some information may prevent a third party without access to that information from sharing the benefits. Here it would be in B_1's and E's joint interest to agree to conceal the evidence that $\tilde{R}_p = \overline{R}_p$ (putting aside the unresolved theoretical issue of how such an agreement would be enforced) in order to prevent B_2 from extracting some of the return. Hence decentralization, by giving rise to collusion, reduces the incentive to refinance poor projects, as in subsection *a*.

In our model, it is the non-transferability of information that makes multi-creditor financial arrangements problematic. But there is a related (yet informal)[19] idea from the finance literature that would serve our purposes just as well: the principle that renegotiation becomes more difficult to coordinate the more parties are involved. From this standpoint, having two creditors reduces the chances of refinancing because getting them to agree to it is harder.

We have endowed the creditors in both the centralized and decentralized models with the same objective expected profit maximization. But ever since Lange and Lerner it has been common practice to have the centre in planned economy models maximize expected *social surplus*. To do so here would, in fact, only aggravate the inefficiency of centralization. To see this, recall the centralization's shortcoming is that it promotes "too much" refinancing. Now if, at the beginning of period 2, the creditor takes into account total social surplus rather than just its own profit (see footnote 14, however, for why social surplus is not unambiguously the bet measure of efficiency in this model), the criterion for refinancing would become $E_p + \Pi_p^* > 1$, i.e. it would be more relaxed than before and so refinancing would occur even more readily.

3. Equilibrium in a Decentralized Credit Market

The contracting model of the previous section is rather "microeconomic" in nature, involving a single entrepreneur and at most two creditors. For the case of centralization, assuming only a single creditor seems quite reasonable; in many

---

[19] See Bolton and Scharfstein (1994) and Hart and Moore (1995) for two recent contributions that build upon this insight.

centralized economies, the state has been the only significant lender. However, to equate decentralization with the existence of two banks is fairly heroic (or foolhardy). Moreover, our model leaves out two ingredients that are important features of decentralized credit markets, namely, competition among creditors and the endogenous determination of the market structure.

Thus in this section, we enrich the previous model of decentralization by assuming that there is an indefinitely large population of (identical) investors, each endowed with a small amount of capital. Thus, as in the introduction, a decentralized market is one with *diffuse ownership*, in the sense that there are many small investors. Investors, however, are allowed to *join forces* at the beginning of period 1, to form banks. Each bank has capital equal to the sum of its investors' endowments and should be viewed as a *cooperative*, i.e. as managed jointly with all members having access to the information acquired when monitoring a project. (Actually, given our risk-neutrality assumption, we could alternatively assume that joining forces entails setting up a lottery that gives each participant a chance to receive *all* the capital.) But the transfer of information across banks is assumed to be impossible.

We assume that there is a population n of entrepreneurs, each drawn independently from a distribution in which there is a probability α of being good. Although n should be thought of as large, the indefinite supply of capital (which we may suppose takes the form of a liquid asset with interest rate normalized to zero) ensures that every project can in principle be financed. Operationally, this will have the effect of driving creditors' profits to zero through competition (i.e. the entrepreneur will now retain some of the observable return herself).

As for centralization, we modify the model of subsection 2a only by adopting the above assumption of n entrepreneurs and by supposing that the single creditor has enough capital to accommodate them all. The earlier analysis of equilibrium in the centralized case clearly carries over completely.

As modelled, centralization differs from decentralization in two respects: ownership of capital and transferability of information. It is this combination of attributes that generates our results. Of course, we are idealizing the quality of the flow of information within a centralized hierarchy, and our perspective is quite "un-Hayekian" in that respect. Still this flow, however imperfect, is likely to be better than the transferability of information between separate (and competing) hierarchies (e.g. rival banks).

The timing of our modified decentralization model is al follows. At the beginning of period 1, investors can join forces to form banks (in equilibrium, not all investors need do so). An investor can contribute his capital to a bank of any "size" he chooses (because all creditors are identical and there are indefinitely many of them, he will be able to find sufficiently many other like-minded investors in equilibrium to actually form the bank). At the same time, each bank/creditor offers a set of contracts (a contract is the same as in Section 2). Entrepreneurs then choose among contracts. If more than one entrepreneur chooses the same contract, then there has to be rationing (see below). If after period 1 some projects are not yet complete, existing or new creditors can offer refinancing contracts. The affected entrepreneurs then choose among these contracts (again, possibly with some rationing).

Because everyone is risk neutral, there is no advantage to diversification *per se*, and so in equilibrium the largest creditor that need form is one with two units of capital. We shall refer to creditors with one and two units of capital[20] as small and large creditors, respectively.

Notice that what we are referring to as a bank's "size" is more accurately thought of as the bank's *liquidity*—how much of its assets are available to be loaned out—which may bear little relation to its literal size, i.e. *total* assets. Thus, the terms "small" and "large" creditor might more properly be relabeled "illiquid" and "liquid" creditor. (From this perspectives, soft budget constraints arise in a centralized economy because the centre is too liquid, e.g. it can print money to refinance projects.)

A small creditor must invest all its capital in a single project if it is to do any financing in period 1. In this case the refinancing problem is the same as in subsection 2a.

A big creditor has two choices: it can fund a single project and keep its second unit of capital liquid, or it can finance two projects, thus sinking all its capital. Such a creditor is, respectively, denoted *diversified* or *undiversified* (the usage here is not quite standard because, as noted, ordinary diversification plays no role). A poor entrepreneur financed by a diversified creditor knows that its chance of being refinanced is the same as in the centralized model of subsection 2a. When the creditor is undiversified, however, refinancing possibilities depend on its *mix* of projects. Indeed, a poor entrepreneur financed by such a creditor is in the same situation, if the creditor's other project is also slow, as though financed by a small creditor. In this sense, lack of diversification is a *substitute* for being small. However, it is not a perfect substitute because the poor entrepreneur *can* obtain refinancing if the other project is good. (The creditor can use the return on the good project either to refinance the poor one directly or—if this return is realized too late—as collateral against a loan from another bank.)

As we have mentioned, entrepreneurs have to be rationed if more than one chooses the same financing contract. By a *rationing scheme* we mean a rule that, for any set of contracts that could be offered, specifies, for each contract in the set and each entrepreneur, the probability that the contract is assigned this entrepreneur. For our purposes, many different schemes would do. For

---

[20] Notice that it is of no value and possibly actually harmful to have strictly between one and two units of capital. To prevent refinancing from occurring, it is better to have one unit. And if refinancing *does* occur, it is better to have two.

concreteness, we concentrate on the following simple scheme:

The Rationing Scheme:[21] All entrepreneurs of a given type are first allocated uniformly over the set of their favourite contracts (this reflects the attempt by an entrepreneur to choose the best contract for herself); if there are fewer entrepreneurs of a given type than favourite contracts, the entrepreneurs are allocated at random to these contracts. If only one entrepreneur is allocated to a given contract, she is *assigned* to that contract with probability one. If more than one is allocated, each has an equal chance of being assigned. At the end of this round, the procedure is repeated with all entrepreneurs and contracts not yet assigned. The process continues iteratively until either the supply of unassigned entrepreneurs or that of desirable contracts (those that are preferred to no contract at all) is exhausted.

Instead of modelling entrepreneurs' behaviour explicitly, we shall subsume it within the rationing scheme (which is applied both after the period 1 and period 2 contracts are offered). We can thus define equilibrium in terms of creditors' behaviour alone.[22]

Equilibrium. An equilibrium is a configuration of creditors, each creditor's set of period 1 contracts (possibly empty), and each creditor's refinancing strategy (the period 2 contracts it offers as a function of what happened in the first period) such that, given the rationing scheme,

  (i) each creditor earns non-negative expected profit on each of its contracts (whether first or second period) given other creditors' contracts and their refinancing strategies;
 (ii) there is no other set of contracts that a creditor could offer and no other refinancing strategy that, given others' behaviour, would earn higher expected profit;
(iii) there is no group of inactive investors (i.e. investors who do not already form a bank) who could come together to become a creditor with a set of contracts and a refinancing strategy that, given the behaviour of the already existing creditors, makes strictly positive expected profit.

We will focus on pure-strategy equilibria (where, moreover, all creditors of a given size offer the same contracts).

---

[21] We ignore the issue of strategic behaviour on the part of entrepreneurs, i.e. the possibility that an entrepreneur will choose a less favoured contract because she has a better chances of being assigned it. However, with enough uncertainty about who the other entrepreneurs are, etc., such behaviour would not be optimal in any case.

[22] Actually, it is investors, rather than creditors, who are the basic decision-making units. We find it too cumbersome, however, to define equilibrium in terms of investor behaviour. Whichever way one does it, the "natural" notion of equilibrium is not entirely clear. This is because if an investor contemplates joining a bank of a given size he must compare the corresponding payoff with what he would get if he joined some other bank. But what is he to suppose happens to the first bank if he does not join it? (The answer may well be relevant to his payoff.) That it finds a replacement for him? That it does not form at all? Implicity, our definition of equilibrium adopts the former hypothesis.

As in Section 2, we are interested in comparing equilibria under centralization and decentralization. Once again, the interesting case (i.e. the case where there is a significant difference) is $E_p > 0 > E_t$, and so we shall stick to this assumption. We shall also continue to assume that $E_g + R_g > 1$ (good projects are efficient), and, that $E_p + \Pi_p^* < 2$, i.e. poor projects are inefficient (but see the discussion of equilibrium efficiency after Proposition 3, where this is relaxed).

When $\Pi_p^* > 1 > \Pi_p^{**}$, we have seen that the centralized outcome entails inefficient project selection: both good and poor projects are financed. According to the simple model of Section 2, decentralization hardens the budget constraint and induces an efficient outcome in which only good projects are funded. We now observe that the same conclusion obtains for more elaborate model (Proposition 2 shows that an equilibrium with this hardening feature exists, and Proposition 3 demonstrates that it is essentially unique). Basically, this is because creditors would like to avoid financing poor projects. Hence, whether or not there is competition among them, they will extract all the observable surplus from such projects. And so, even in this more elaborate model, the condition $\Pi_p^* > 1 > \Pi_p^{**}$ continues to imply that refinancing will occur with big creditors but not small.

PROPOSITION 2. *Suppose $\Pi_p^* > 1 > \Pi_p^{**}$. There exists an equilibrium in which each of $n+1$ or more small (one-unit) creditors offers a first-period contract that just breaks even on good entrepreneurs. No big creditors (two or more units) offer first-period contracts.*

Proof. Each of these small creditors earns zero profit because it breaks even on good entrepreneurs and does not attract poor entrepreneurs (since they cannot be refinanced). Moreover, none of these creditors could make positive profit by deviating because any contract that earned positive profit on good entrepreneurs would not (in view of the rationing scheme) be allocated any of them since there are enough other small creditors (that is, at least n) offering more favourable terms to accommodate all good entrepreneurs. Finally, no new creditor can enter and make positive profit: it cannot make money on good entrepreneurs for the reason just given, and if it attracted poor entrepreneurs (which would require that it consist of two or more units since $\Pi_p^* > 1 > \Pi_p^{**}$), it would lose money on them since $\Pi_p^* < 2$. ∥

PROPOSITION 3. *If $\Pi_p^* > 1 > \Pi_p^{**}$, then the only equilibrium is that described in Proposition 2.*[23]

Proof. We first show that there cannot be an equilibrium in which a big creditor offers any first-period contracts. If there were such contracts in equilibrium, then there would be one to which a poor entrepreneur is assigned with positive

---

[23] Actually, Proposition 2 describes a *multiplicity* of equilibria in which the number of active creditors can vary as long as it exceeds $n + 1$. However, this sort of non-uniqueness is clearly not essential.

probability. (A poor entrepreneur can earn a positive return only from big creditors, contracts because, since $\Pi_p^* > 1 > \Pi_p^{**}$, only these are refinanced. Indeed, if
such a contract is refinanced, the entrepreneur's return is certainly positive. This
will be the case when the big creditor is diversified, but also when undiversified
provided that the other project financed is good. Thus, it cannot be the case that
every big creditor contract is assigned only good entrepreneurs.) Of the contracts
that are assigned poor entrepreneurs with positive probability, let c^0 be the one
that gives poor entrepreneurs the best terms. Contract c^0 earns a negative return
on poor entrepreneurs (since $\Pi_p^* < 2$), and so, in order to earn a non-negative
return over all, it must earn a strictly positive return on good entrepreneurs and
be assigned them with positive probability. Suppose that a group of investors
who are inactive in equilibrium come together as a small creditor and offer a
contract c^{00} with slightly more favourable terms for good entrepreneurs than c^0
(i.e. the contract c^{00} slightly "undercuts" c^0). This contract c^{00} must be assigned
good entrepreneurs. But because it is not refinanced (since $\Pi_p^{**} < 1$) it will not be
assigned poor entrepreneurs. Therefore, it makes positive profit overall, a contradiction. We conclude that big creditors cannot offer first-period contracts in
equilibrium.

We next observe that the only contract that is accepted with positive probability in equilibrium is the break-even contract for good entrepreneurs. A contract
that offered more favourable terms to good entrepreneurs would lose money, and
a less favourable contract would make positive profit and so induce entry
and slight undercutting as above.

Finally, there must be at least $n+1$ small creditors offering the break-even contract in equilibrium. Otherwise, a small creditor could enter and offer a contract
that, if assigned to a good entrepreneur, would make a profit (and also would be
preferred by the entrepreneur to no contract at all). Because there are fewer than
n other small creditors, there would be a positive probability that not all good
entrepreneurs could find financing elsewhere and therefore would be assigned
this contract. ∥

The proof of Proposition 3 is somewhat involved, but the idea that underlies
it is very simple: If $\Pi_p^* > 1 > \Pi_p^{**}$, then small creditors have the advantage over
their big counterparts of not attracting poor entrepreneurs. Thus they are more
efficient and so, in equilibrium with free entry, drive the big creditors out of the
market.

We have been considering the case in which $E_p + \Pi_p^* < 2$. If instead this inequality goes the other way (but all other inequalities remain the same, in particular
$\Pi_p^* < 2$), then, according to the criterion of social surplus, slow projects are
efficient (see footnote 14, however, for why social surplus may not be the right
criterion). Nonetheless, Propositions 2 and 3 continue to hold. That is, only
good projects are financed under decentralization. This follows because creditors

ignore the entrepreneurs' private benefits in deciding whether or not to fund a project, and suggests that there may be an excessive tendency in decentralized credit markets to focus on short-term (i.e. one-period) projects (because banks are too illiquid to make efficient loans). For a less ambiguous illustration of this tendency (one that does not rely on this questionable measure of efficiency), see the next section.

In the case $\Pi_p^* > 1 > \Pi_p^{**}$, the market outcome reproduces the features of the decentralized model of subsection 2a. When $\Pi_p^{**} > 1$, matters are more complicated because both types of entrepreneurs will be financed regardless of the size of creditors. A potential problem of non-existence of equilibrium may arise if a creditor is able to affect its mix of entrepreneurs (the relative probabilities of good and poor entrepreneurs choosing its contracts) sharply by slightly changing the terms it offers. Such a problem is similar to those arising in insurance models à la Rothschild–Stiglitz (1976) and Wilson (1997). To avoid all this, we introduce the following mild assumption:

ASSUMPTION A. *Slow entrepreneurs have an (arbitrarily) small probability of completing their projects in one period.*

This assumption limits the effect that improving the terms offered to good entrepreneurs has on a creditor's mix of entrepreneurs; any improvement will be attractive to poor as well as to good entrepreneurs. Assumption A enables us to derive the following result:

PROPOSITION 4. *Let $\Pi_p^{**} > 1$, Under Assumption A, there is a unique equilibrium (where uniqueness is qualified the same way as in Proposition 3) in which (i) only big creditors are active in the market, and (ii) at least $n + 1$ of them offer contracts that break even on average across good and poor projects and that extract the entire observable return from poor projects.*

Proof. We will show that the behaviour described constitutes an equilibrium. Uniqueness can be established as in the proof of Proposition 3. Clearly, it is not optimal to leave any observable return to poor entrepreneurs: a creditor would only improve its mix of entrepreneurs by lowering the return offered to poor ones. Under Assumption A, however, a creditor cannot improve its mix by offering better terms to good entrepreneurs, since such improvement would attract all the poor entrepreneurs as well. Therefore, if at least n other big creditors offer break-even contracts as described in the proposition, a big creditor can do no better than to follow suit.

As for small creditors, they cannot avoid attracting poor as well as good entrepreneurs since $\Pi_p^{**} > 1$. However, they are less efficient in monitoring poor projects than are big creditors. Thus if the latter creditors break even, the former lose money. ‖

Thus, in this model, a decentralized market leads to efficient creditor liquidity. When neither large nor small creditors can commit not to refinance poor entrepreneurs, large creditors are more efficient because they have the incentive to provide monitoring. Therefore, they drive small creditors out of the market.

4. Decentralization and Short-Termism

We now introduce a third project: a two-period but *very profitable* undertaking denoted by the subscript v. This project requires one unit of capital per period and generates a return $R_v > 2$ after two periods. For simplicity, we suppose that R_v is deterministic and does not require monitoring. A good entrepreneur can choose between a good or very profitable project (poor entrepreneurs are stuck with poor projects), but her choice is unobservable.[24] Moreover, poor and very profitable projects are indistinguishable to creditors at the end of period 1.[25] A good entrepreneur's private benefit from a very profitable project is E_t (if the project is terminated after one period) or E_v (if the project is completed). We adopt the natural assumption that $E_v \geqq E_p$.

The timing is much the same as that of Section 3. But we now must insert the choice between good any very profitable contracts, which we assume is made at the same time as creditors offer contracts. A creditor's monitoring intensity depends on its beliefs in period 1 about project quality. Specifically, a large creditor will expend effort $a^*(\alpha')$ such that $(1-\alpha')\overline{R}_p = \psi'(a^*(\alpha'))$ if it believes that α' is the probability, the project is very profitable and $1-\alpha'$ is the probability it is poor. Note that if $\alpha' = 0$, the model reduces to that of Section 3. Hence $a^*(0) = a^*$, and the financial return (gross of capital) is Π_p^*. Similarly, for a small creditor, we define $a^{**}(\alpha')$, and obtain $a^{**}(0) = a^{**}$, which generates gross financial return Π_p^{**}. Refinancing decisions clearly also depend on α'. Pessimistic beliefs (i.e. low values of α') lead to *short-termism* — i.e. the choice of good over very profitable projects — because good entrepreneurs forecast that long-term projects will not be refinanced:

PROPOSITION 5. *If $\Pi_p^{**} < 1$ there exists an equilibrium in which only small creditors are active and only good projects are chosen.*[26]

---

[24] We thank Ian Jewitt for suggesting that we replace our earlier adverse selection treatment of very profitable long-run projects with the current moral hazard formulation.

[25] To simplify analysis, however, we suppose that these projects *are* distinguishable at the end of period 2.

[26] As the model stands, this result depends to some extent on the timing. If good entrepreneurs choose projects *before* creditors move, nothing is changed since the entrepreneurs' decisions are unobservable anyway. But if the creditors move first, then a group of investors might form a bank so big that good entrepreneurs are encouraged to choose very profitable projects. Still, the bank may have to be very big indeed — big enough to accommodate a large fraction of all entrepreneurs — otherwise, a good entrepreneur may face too high a risk of not being assigned to one of this bank's contracts if she chooses the very good project. Thus, if there are reasonable limits on creditor size/liquidity, our results should not be very sensitive to timing after all.

Proof. Suppose that $n + 1$ or more small creditors are active (and no other creditors are) and offer the contract that breaks even on good projects. Suppose, furthermore, that creditors believe that, if a project has to be refinanced, then with high probability it is poor. Under these circumstances, all good entrepreneurs will choose good projects, since $\Pi_p^{**} < 1$ and the creditors' pessimistic beliefs together imply that two-period projects will not be refinanced. Hence the creditors' beliefs are justified. Now, a small creditor clearly cannot do better than break even. Suppose then that a big creditor enters. It will attract *all* the poor entrepreneurs and only its share of good projects. But since the former are unprofitable ($\Pi_p^* < 2$), the creditor will lose money on average. ‖

The equilibrium of Proposition 5 can be highly inefficient. As in Section 2, let α be the fraction of entrepreneurs who are good. Notice that the Proposition 5 equilibrium exists no matter how close α is to 1. However if R_v is big, then, for α near 1, it is clearly better from a social standpoint to put up with poor projects for the sake of the very good ones. Indeed, for big enough R_v, there exists another and more efficient equilibrium, provided that α is sufficiently near 1. If $E_v = E_g$, the precise condition we require for existence of this other equilibrium is

$$\alpha R_v + (1 - \alpha)a^*(\alpha)\overline{R}_p - \psi(\alpha^*(\alpha)) - 2 > \alpha(R_g - 1). \qquad (*)$$

Condition $(*)$ implies that if all good entrepreneurs choose very profitable projects, big creditors can offer them better terms than on good projects, while still breaking even. In such a case, creditors' *optimistic* expectations are self-fulfilling.

PROPOSITION 6. *Suppose that $\Pi_p^{**} < 1$, $E_v = E_g$, and $(*)$ is satisfied. Then there exists an equilibrium in which only big creditors form and all good entrepreneurs select very profitable projects.*

Proof. Suppose that there are at least $n + 1$ big creditors and each offers the contract $\hat{c}$, which gives the entrepreneurs nothing (except her private return) if the project turns out to be poor, T_v if the project is very profitable, and T_g if the project is good where

$$\alpha(R_v - T_v) + (1 - \alpha)a^*(\alpha)\overline{R}_p - \psi(a^*(\alpha)) - 2 = 0 \qquad (1)$$

and

$$R_g - 1 - T_g = 0. \qquad (2)$$

From (1), $\hat{c}$ just breaks even if creditors' beliefs that all good entrepreneurs choose very profitable projects are correct. Now, good entrepreneurs will choose these projects provided that

$$E_v + T_v > E_g + T_g. \qquad (3)$$

From (1) and (2) and because $E_v = E_g$, (3) can be rewritten as

$$\alpha R_v + (1 - \alpha)\Pi_p^* - 2 > \alpha(R_g - 1), \qquad (4)$$

which is just (∗). Hence, good entrepreneurs will select very profitable projects as claimed. The arguments that no big creditor can do better by deviating and that any creditor can profit from entering are the same as in the proof of Proposition 4. ‖

Propositions 5 and 6 imply that the same economy may end up in two quite different equilibria. In the equilibrium of Proposition 5, creditors are small and projects are short-term. In that of Proposition 6, creditors are big and projects are long-term. Note that, even ignoring entrepreneurs' private benefits, (∗) implies that the latter equilibrium is more efficient. Including the private benefits only aggravates the discrepancy (it would entail adding $(1 - \alpha)E_p$ to the left-hand side of (∗)). Indeed, the equilibrium of Proposition 6 Pareto-dominates that of Proposition 5.

To conclude, let us note that Proposition 5 and 6 have some connection with those of von Thadden (1995). Von Thadden argues that a commitment not to refinance projects may be an optimal screening device for creditors facing an adverse selection problem, even though it can induce short-termism on the part of good entrepreneurs. Although the set of technological opportunities available to entrepreneurs and the initial asymmetry of information in his paper are similar to those in our model, von Thadden takes a different perspective, since he does not explicitly address ex post incentives to refinance or the role of creditor liquidity. Rather, he concentrates on a one-creditor problem. In this model, bank finance can reduce short-termism thanks to economies of scale (à la Diamond (1984)), which make direct inspection of project types profitable.

References

Aoki, M. (1990). "Toward an economic model of the Japanese firm." *Journal of Economic Literature*, 28: 1–27.

Baliga, S., and Polak, B. (1994). "Credit markets and efficiency." Mimeo.

Corbett, J. (1987). "International perspectives on financing: Evidence from Japan." *Oxford Review of Economic Policy*, 3: 30–55.

Diamond, D. (1984). "Financial intermediation and delegated monitoring." *Review of Economic Studies*, 51: 393–414.

The Economist (1990). "Punters or proprietors?: A survey of capitalism." May 5–11.

Edwards, J., and Fischer, K. (1994). *Banks, Finance and Investment in Germany.* Cambridge: Cambridge Univ. Press.

Freixas, X., Guésnerie, R., and Tirole, J. (1985). "Planning under incomplete information and the ratchet effect." *Review of Economic Studies*, 52: 173–92.

Hoshi, T., Kashyap, A., and Scharfstein, D. (1988). "Corporate structure, liquidity, and investment: Evidence from Japanese industrial groups." Mimeo.

——, ——, and —— (1989). "Bank monitoring and investment: Evidence from the changing structure of Japanese corporate banking relationships." Mimeo.

Kofman, F., and Lawaree, J. (1989). "Collusion in hierarchical agency." Mimeo.

Kornai, J. (1979). "Resource-Constrained versus Demand-Constrained Systems." *Econometrica*, 47: 801–19.

—— (1980). *The Economics of Shortage*. New York: North-Holland.

Laffont, J. J., and Tirole, J. (1988). "The dynamics of incentive contracts." *Econometrica*, 56: 1153–75.

Mayer, C., and Alexander, I. (1990). "Banks and securities markets: Corporate financing in Germany and the UK." Mimeo.

Qian, Y. (1994). "A theory of shortage in socialist economies based on the soft budget constraint." *American Economic Review*, 84: 145–56.

——, and Xu, C. (1991). "Innovation and financial constraints in centralized and decentralized economies." Mimeo, London School of Economics.

Rothschild, M., and Stiglitz, J. (1976). "Equilibrium in competitive insurance markets: An essay on the economics of imperfect information." *Quarterly Journal of Economics*, 90: 629–49.

Schaffer, M. (1989), "The Credible-commitment problem in the center–enterprise relationship." *Journal of Comparative Economics*, 13: 359–82.

Stiglitz, J., and Weiss, A. (1981). "Credit rationing in markets with imperfect information." *American Economic Review*, 71: 393–410.

Tirole, J. (1986). "Hierarchies and bureaucracies: On the role of collusion in organizations." *Journal of Law, Economics and Organizations*, 2: 181–214.

von Thadden, E. L. (1995). "Bank finance and long-term investment." *Review of Economic Studies*, 62: 557–75.

Wilson, C. (1977). "A model of insurance markets with incomplete information." *Journal of Economic Theory*, 16: 167–207.

20

Proprietary Information, Financial Intermediation, and Research Incentives

Sudipto Bhattacharya and Gabriella Chiesa

I. Introduction

In their examination of corporate financial policy, Bhattacharya and Ritter (1983) introduced an equilibrium model of proprietary information and its disclosure in financial markets. In equilibrium, a firm with superior private knowledge, having a higher Poisson intensity of invention in a research and development (R&D) race, is induced to disclose part of its knowledge as a signal. The benefit of the signal is that the financing for the R&D can be obtained at lower cost. The cost of the signal arises from the fact that the information disclosed benefits the firm's product market competitors.

In this chapter, we consider a scenario in which technological knowledge revealed to a firm's financier(s) need not also flow to its R&D and product market competitors. Thus, while proprietary knowledge exists, whether it is revealed to other competing firms is determined endogenously by self-interested financiers. Whether this information is revealed at the interim stage of an R&D contest depends on the financing process; we consider two possibilities; bilateral bank–borrower ties and multilateral (multifirm and multibank) lending relationships. At the outset of the R&D contest, competing firms may find it efficient ex ante to share their knowledge at the interim stage of the contest. However, since at the interim stage firms will be in different positions in the race to the finish, knowledge sharing may be impossible to enforce unless done by financiers acting in their own interest. Of course, firms will anticipate whether interim-stage knowledge sharing will occur, and this will affect their ex ante incentives to invest in R&D. We analyze the implications of these tradeoffs, vis-à-vis interim

Bhattacharya gratefully acknowledges research support, past and present, from the Institut d'Analisi Economica, Barcelona and IRES, Université Catholique de Louvain. Both authors acknowledge financial and/or research support from the Innocenzo Gasparini Institute for Economic Research at Milan, including a Senior Fellowship for the first author over the 1992/3 academic year. Gabriella Chiesa acknowledges support from CNR and MURST. We thank Guy Laroque for helpful comments on content and exposition.

knowledge spillover and ex ante research incentives, for the ex ante equilibrium choice between bilateral and multilateral financing mechanisms.

Our model is articulated in three stages: (i) ex ante financing choice with monitorable investment and privately observed research expenditures by firms, (ii) interim knowledge acquisition and its possible disclosure across firms, and (iii) postinvention payoffs for firms and lenders. We allow lenders to offer either long-term debt contracts or short-term debt, which must be refinanced at the interim (knowledge acquisition) stage. We do so because firms' incentives to make privately observed R&D investments are often superior under such short-term financing. In addition, we show that a multi-lateral lender may also help coordinate product market collusion across its borrowers in the event of multiple cost-reducing inventions by these firms.[1] If such postinvention collusion is coordinated in favor of the firm with the best research knowledge at the interim stage, then firms' ex ante incentives for R&D investments will also improve.[2]

Our model contributes to two areas of research. The first is the literature on bank monitoring and information acquisition in long-term bank-borrower relationships. Diamond (1984) examined the prudential monitoring of ex post cash flow and diversification of risk across borrowers by financial intermediaries. Since then, others have examined how banks acquire borrower-specific information through time and the implications of this for equilibrium loan contracts, rent-extraction from borrowers by banks, and the nature and optimality of borrowers' investment decisions (see Dewatripont and Maskin 1995; Garella 1995; Pagano and Japelli 1993; Rajan 1992; Sharpe 1990; and von Thadden 1995). Our work extends this research to proprietary information environments in which the private value of research knowledge to a firm is reduced by the revelation of this knowledge to the firm's competitors.

A complementary approach to the choice of financing in these environments is pursued in Yosha (1995), who models firms' choices between bilateral and multilateral (public information) financing at the interim stage following their acquisition of proprietary knowledge. The informed firms' preference for bilateral versus multilateral financing depends on the perception its competitors have about its type since these perceptions shape the competitors' actions and their impact on the informed firm's profit. The analysis exploits the tension between an exogenous cost of disclosing information to a large number of lenders in a public financial market and an endogenous cost faced with bilateral financing because its competitors may believe that the firm's choice of bilateral

---

[1] Hence, multilateral financing may also serve as a partial substitute for knowledge licensing contracts as in Bhattacharya et al. (1992).

[2] Thus, our approach provides the foundations for a theory of comparative financial systems based on bilateral financing without knowledge sharing of postinvention collusion, public financing with knowledge sharing but no product market collusion, and strategic multilateral institutional financing with *both*.

financing means that it has something to conceal, and hence react accordingly. In equilibrium, the higher quality firms (those with more to lose with disclosure) choose bilateral financing. The cost differential between bilateral and multilateral financing prevents competitors from unambiguously inferring that these firms are hiding information.

The second line of research pertinent to our paper is that on knowledge-licensing contracts in the context of R&D races or contests. The work of Bhattacharya et al. (1992), for example, assumes that the courts can verify knowledge voluntarily disclosed by a successful leading firm to its competitors in an R&D contest. Hence, such interim knowledge can be licensed for a fee. By contrast, we assume that licensing fees are infeasible, owing to information nonverifiability problems. Thus multilateral financing may serve as a precommitment mechanism for knowledge sharing among competing firms, when such sharing is ex ante efficient but not interim incentive compatible for the competing firms.

Our model should be viewed as primarily normative, suggesting that knowledge sharing among competing firms may be predicated on the manner in which these firms are financed. However, there is some empirical support for our thesis that lenders or other stakeholders may help borrowers cooperate in sharing information. Hellwig (1991) cites evidence that German and Austrian banks in an earlier era facilitated product market collusion among their multiple borrowing firms through the coordination of production and investment decisions. Our model suggests an analogous role for lenders under multilateral financing from the ex ante perspective of borrowers, even though disclosure of one borrower's proprietary knowledge to another by a lender might be viewed (if proven) as a violation of the lenders' fiduciary duty.

More recently, Sako's (1995) research on suppliers' associations in the Japanese automobile industry provides evidence that these affiliate suppliers value inter-firm learning about technology or knowledge spillover among themselves (rather than from the coordinating large assembler firm which often owns some of their equity) as the main advantage of association membership. She also finds that suppliers outside these associate relationships, in which the large assembler firms rarely hold an equity stake, invest relatively more in duplicative R&D. The latter finding is also consistent with our result regarding firms' R&D incentives under bilateral financing of different firms by different lenders.[3]

Our model also provides an alternative framework for studying comparative financial systems. Dewatripont and Maskin (1995) have emphasized the differential ability of centralized financial markets with multiple smaller investors to gather information about their borrowers. They analyze the implications for

[3] Firms in suppliers' association typically have several different equity owners other than the assembler firm whose "club" they belong to. Hence, the role of the assembler firm in coordinating interim knowledge disclosure among its suppliers is more complex than in our model here.

"short- termism" on investment decisions in decentralized credit markets, versus "soft-budget constraints" regarding further interim investment under centralized institutional financing. In contrast, Allen (1993) has suggested that information about firms' prospects is better analyzed and aggregated in decentralized stock markets containing many informed investors and having a publicly observable price mechanism.

Our approach sidesteps these debates about the a priori advantage of one institutional mechanism for financing over another in the processing of information about firms. We suggest instead that the financiers' incentives for information disclosure, and hence interfirm knowledge spillover, would differ according to the institutional arrangements for financing. These differences will have implications for the incentives of borrowers to invest in R&D.

The chapter is organized as follows. The basic model is outlined in Section II. Tradeoffs vis-à-vis knowledge disclosure and research incentives, under bilateral and multilateral financing with long-term debt, are analyzed in Section III. Section IV extends the analysis to include short-term debt and interim refinancing. In Section V we discuss other extensions, such as interim investments and postinvention collusion among the borrower firms. Section VI concludes.

II. The Model

A. The setting

We consider an economy in which two banks compete to provide risky loans[4] to firms engaged in an R&D contest for cost-reducing inventions in the product market. For simplicity, we assume that there are only two such rivals in each of many industries. Each bank monitors the investments of its borrowers who obtain financing at the ex ante stage, and in the process banks are assumed to acquire the knowledge generated by their borrowers' research at the interim stage. These banks also diversity across borrowers in many industries to guarantee an almost certain rate of return to their depositors who thus need not monitor.

We consider two alternative institutional arrangements as equilibrium outcomes for financing with qualitatively different bank-borrower linkages. Under bilateral financing, each bank in equilibrium finances only one of the rivals in each industry. Under multilateral financing, the ex ante equilibrium is such that bank takes its symmetric (half) share in the financing of both the rivals; this may also be thought of as a metaphor for a public financial market.[5] The two

---

[4] Given the dichotomous payoffs of an R&D contest, with the lower outcome being zero, conventional distinctions between debt and equity financing are irrelevant for the model we develop below.

[5] With multiple (countably infinite number of) industries, an alternative multilateral financing equilibrium would have each bank lending to both borrowers in different industries, such as the first

banks are assumed to be contract-setting (price and quantity) competitors in the loan market, each facing an infinitely elastic deposit supply curve at a rate of interest $d = 0$.[6]

The R&D investment opportunity faced by each of the two borrowing firms requires an observable investment of capital I, and an externally unobservable expenditure C, at date $t = 0$, where C is a privately observed effort choice by the firm's manager. The R&D project delivers a payoff at the final date, $t = 2$, which is either 0 or $V > 0$. The firms are Betrand competitors in the product market, so that the R&D payoff is V if and only if there is one invention only, in which case the inventor earns the rent V, limit pricing at its rival's cost. In the event of no invention as well as of inventions by both firms, the private payoff to a firm from R&D is zero. Since product market competition is unrestrained by knowledge-licensing contracts.[7]

The R&D project consists of two stages. In the first stage, firm i, $i = 1, 2$, undertaking the projects, invests cash, I, at date $t = 0$. The R&D project delivers an interim result, r, at the end of the first stage, date $t = 1$. Firm i's interim result, r_i, can be either $r_i = k$, in which interim knowledge relevant to the R&D project is produced, or $r_i = 0$, in which no interim knowledge is produced by firm i. The probability of $r_i = k$ is S if firm i also expends the effort cost C at date $t = 0$, and is zero if firm i chooses not to expend C, where $0 < S \leq 1$. At the second stage, firm i uses the interim research knowledge it has acquired (and not necessarily produced) as an input in its R&D process for a patentable invention at $i = 2$. This interim knowledge input, $\underline{r}_i$, can be either k or 0. If $\underline{r}_i = k$, then firm i faces probability P of inventing at the final date $t = 2$. If $\underline{r}_i = 0$, then firm i's probability of inventing at the second stage is Q, satisfying $0 \leq Q < P \leq 1$.

In principle, firm i's input at the second stage, $\underline{r}_i$, can equal k in two possible ways. Because firm i has been successful at the first stage, or alternatively because firm i has obtained knowledge k by having its competitor's result. $r_i = k$, $j \neq i$, disclosed. Clearly, at date $t = 1$ a firm j whose interim results is $r_i = k$ will not wish to disclose its knowledge to its competitor whose result is $r_i = 0$, $j \neq i$, since by so doing firm j reduces its probability of sole invention from $P(1 - Q)$ to $P(1 - P)$, and $P > Q$. Nevertheless, both firms may wish to precommit at date $t = 0$ to knowledge sharing at date $t = 1$. The potential benefit to firm j, $j = 1, 2$, of precommiting at the outset arises from the possible occurrence of the state in which firm j fails at the first stage of R&D and firm i succeeds. Then the probability that firm j is the sole inventor at the final stage under no

bank in odd-numbered industries and the second in even-numbered ones. This outcome results in the same knowledge disclosure decisions as in our multilateral financing equilibrium.

[6] See Bhattacharya (1982), Yanelle (1989), and Matutes and Vives (1992) for issues that arise when banks compete strategically for finitely elastic deposit supplies.

[7] See Bhattacharya et al. (1992) for an analysis of the case where knowledge-licensing contracts across firms are feasible.

knowledge sharing is $Q(1-P)$, whereas given knowledge sharing, it increases to $P(1-P)$. We prove below that in a first-best world firms would precommit to knowledge sharing when $P \leq \frac{1}{2}$, even when they cannot restrain their product market competition if both firms invent at the final stage.

B. The first-best outcome

Consider a first-best (full-information) world where firms can precommit at date $t = 0$, to (i) invest effort cost C, and (ii) have a disclosure rule for date $t = 1$. Because of ex ante competition between the two banks in the lending market, it would be in both firms, interest to choose the disclosure rule that maximizes the aggregated ex ante expected values of their R&D projects.

Under a regime of no information disclosure, the interim knowledge available to firm $i, i = 1, 2$, at the second stage of the R&D project is $\underline{r}_i = r_i \in \{0, k\}$, the interim knowledge that firm i has produced at the first stage of the R&D. Therefore, V_{ND}, the ex ante expected present value of each R&D project with no knowledge disclosure is given by

$$V_{ND} = S[P(1-P)S + P(1-Q)(1-S)]V$$
$$+ (1-S)\{Q(1-P)S + Q(1-Q)(1-S)\}V. \tag{1}$$

The expression in the square brackets in Eq. (1) is the probability of sole invention by a firm conditional upon having produced interim knowledge at the first stage, and the expression in the curly brackets is the corresponding conditional probability when the firm has not succeeded in acquiring interim knowledge.

Under a regime of information disclosure or knowledge sharing, the interim knowledge available at the second stage of the R&D project to firm 1 and firm 2 is $\underline{r}_1 = \underline{r}_2 = \max(r_1, r_2)$, where the $\max(r_1, r_2) = 0$ if and only if both the firms have failed at the first stage of research. Hence, the ex ante expected value of the R&D project under interim knowledge disclosure, V_D, is given by:

$$V_D = S[P(1-P)(1-S) + P(1-P)S]V + (1-S)\{Q(1-Q)(1-S) + P(1-P)S\}V. \tag{2}$$

The expression in square brackets in (2) is the probability of sole invention by either firm conditional upon its success at the first stage of R&D, given that its knowledge will be disclosed to its competitor. The expressions in curly brackets in (2) is the probability of sole invention by each firm conditional upon its failure at the first state of R&D, and the possible receipt of knowledge from its successful competitor. Lemma 1 characterizes the circumstances in which a policy of interim knowledge disclosure across rivalrous firms maximizes both firms' ex ante probability of sole invention in their R&D contest.

LEMMA 1. *If $P \leq \frac{1}{2}$, then knowledge disclosure across rivals at the interim stage is optimal ex ante. The expected present values of both R&D projects are maximized by having the firm that has produced interim knowledge disclose it to its competitor, and having the competitor reciprocate when the situation is reversed.*

Proof. Information disclosure is optimal if and only if

$$V_D \geq V_{ND},$$

which is true, using Eqs. (1) and (2), if

$$S(1-S)[2P(1-P) - P(1-Q) - Q(1-P)] \geq 0$$

or,

$$(P-Q) \geq 2P(P-Q),$$

which is equivalent to the condition

$$P \leq \tfrac{1}{2}. \quad \text{Q.E.D.}$$

C. Feasible contracts

In our model, the set of contracts that can be enforced is restricted because (i) the entrepreneurs' effort choices, C or 0, are not monitorable by outsiders, and (ii) disclosure of interim knowledge cannot be committed to or licensed. In this informationally constrained environment, we seek an optimal financing arrangement that maximizes the ex ante expected values of the R&D projects of borrowers. We shall consider two possible financing arrangements arising in ex ante equilibrium: bilateral financing, BF, and multilateral financing, MF. With BF, each firm borrows only from its private bank: under MF, each firm borrows from both of the banks. Within each regime, financing is with debt contracts for which the maturity can be either the final date $t = 2$ (long-term debt), or the interim date $t = 1$ (short-term debt) which is followed by (possible) refinancing up to $t = 2$. These financing arrangements differ in the incentives they provide lenders for interim knowledge sharing across borrowers, as well as the ex ante incentives they provide borrowers to incur privately observed costs for research. For tractability, we specialize the problem by making the following assumptions:

(i) The interim expected value of the R&D project of a firm without interim knowledge, $r = 0$, is negative in net present value:

$$V[Q(1-Q)] < I. \tag{A1}$$

(ii) Provide a firm invests C at date $t = 0$, its R&D project has positive ex ante net present value with or without interim sharing of knowledge, when interfirm knowledge disclosure is value maximizing, $P \leq \frac{1}{2}$, and without interim sharing of knowledge otherwise, when $\frac{1}{2} \leq P \leq 1$:

$$\min[V_D, V_{ND}] = V_{ND} \geq (I + C), \quad \text{when } 0 \leq P \leq \frac{1}{2} \qquad \text{(A2)}$$

and

$$\max[V_D, V_{ND}] = V_{ND} \geq (I + C), \quad \text{when } \frac{1}{2} < P \leq 1. \qquad \text{(A2')}$$

(iii) For a knowledgeable firm at the interim stage to have a probability of invention P, the entrepreneur of the firm must remain in charge until

$$t = 2. \qquad \text{(A3)}$$

(iv) Interim knowledge obtained by a bank can be disclosed to a firm if and only if the recipient had borrowed from the bank during the first stage of its R&D project, at

$$t = 0. \qquad \text{(A4)}$$

Assumption (A3) implies that enforcing bankruptcy of borrowers at the interim stage is costly for their banks. Assumption (A4) implies that bank j cannot disclose the interim knowledge produced by its borrower to that of another bank $i, j \neq j$, at date $t = 1$. In particular, (A4) prevents the bank threatening to force it successful borrower to disclose his knowledge to a product–market competitor. Hence, the refinancing game at the interim stage only involves the one-sided threat of a bank's successful borrower obtaining refinancing from the other bank at the cost of knowledge disclosure to his competitor. With long-term debt contracts, a bank could only benefit from selling its borrower's knowledge to the borrower of another bank, and this is infeasible.

We now characterize the circumstances in which bilateral or multilateral financing arrangements arise as the preferred ex ante equilibrium in the game between banks and borrowers involving loan contract offers by banks and accept/reject choices by borrowers. We do so by initially allowing only long-term debt contracts in Section III, and then consider short-term debt, and its interim refinancing, in Section IV.

III. Long-Term Debt Contracts

In the first subsection we prove that multilateral financing with long-term debt implements the first-best disclosure rule and hence, absent entrepreneurs' incentive problems, it maximizes the expected present value of the R&D projects for both the borrowing firms. We then focus on each borrower's incentive to incur C, which is privately observed and noncontractible.

A. Multilateral financing

Under multilateral financing, both banks bid to finance parts of the investment requirement of each borrower. To simplify, we assume that each bank finances half of the required cash outlay, I. Competition implies that both banks offer the same financing terms and earn zero profit. Let $(\frac{1}{2})R$ be the contractual repayment due at date $t = 2$ to a bank. Where $R < V$ given assumption (A2) and ex ante interbank competition. The probability that an entrepreneur will repay his debt maturing at $t = 2$ equals the probability that he will be the sole inventor at $t = 2$. Suppose a borrower has been successful at the first stage, whereas his competitor has failed. Given knowledge disclosure to its failed rival, the probability that a successful firm $i, i = 1, 2$, is the sole inventor and hence is solvent is $P(1 - P)$. Consequently, the expected payoff to a bank under information disclosure, π_D, when at least one of its borrowers has succeeded, is given by:

$$\pi_D = 2[P(1 - P)(R/2)]. \tag{3}$$

With no information disclosure from a successful to an unsuccessful borrower at the interim stage, the successful borrower repays his debt at $t = 2$ when he is the sole inventor, an event with probability $P(1 - Q)$, whereas the unsuccessful borrower is solvent with probability $Q(1 - P)$. The expected payoff to both the banks under no information disclosure, from a successful and unsuccessful borrower combination, π_{ND}, is therefore

$$\pi_{ND} = [P(1 - Q) + Q(1 - P)](R/2). \tag{4}$$

Thus, each bank finds it optimal to share interim ($t = 1$) knowledge across its borrowers if and only if

$$\pi_D \geq \pi_{ND},$$

or, using Eqs. (3) and (4),

$$2P(1 - P) \geq P(1 - Q) + Q(1 - P),$$

which is true if and only if

$$P \leq \tfrac{1}{2}.$$

Hence, under multilateral financing with long-term debt, the lenders' interim criterion for knowledge sharing across borrowers coincides with the first-best disclosure rule, derived in Lemma 1 above. Consequently, the expected present value of the R&D projects is the $\max(V_D, V_{ND})$.

Since the credit market is competitive, if $P \leq \frac{1}{2}$, information will be disclosed at date $t = 1$, and the gross repayment due at $t = 2$, R, will satisfy

$$R[SP(1-P) + (1-S)[P(1-P)S + Q(1-Q)(1-S)]] = I. \tag{5}$$

Because in equilibrium banks obtain zero ex ante expected profit, the ex ante expected payoff to the borrower, $Z_0(MFL)$, is

$$Z_0(MFL) = V_D - I. \tag{6}$$

The borrower's interim expected payoff conditional upon success at the first stage of R&D, $Z(S)$, is

$$Z(S) = (V - R)P(1 - P), \tag{7}$$

and the borrower's interim expected payoff conditional upon failure, $Z(F)$, is

$$Z(F) = (V - R)[P(1 - P)S + Q(1 - Q)(1 - S)], \tag{8}$$

where R is given by Eq. (5).

The difference between the borrower's conditional expected payoffs in (7) and (8) is crucial in providing the borrowing firms incentives to invest C. We label this difference the Reward to Research Effort. These expressions are summarized in Table 1 below. The expression for $[Z(S) - Z(F)]_{MFL}$ has been obtained by substituting from Eq. (5) into (7) and (8), and noting that

$$[Z(S) - Z(F)]_{MFL} = (L/S)[V_D - I - Z(F)]$$
$$= (V_D - I)[K/(L + SK)], \tag{9}$$

where K and L are as in Table 1 (Eqs. (15a) and (15b)).

If $P > \frac{1}{2}$, and we replace Assumption (A2) by

$$\max(V_D, V_{ND}) = V_{ND} \geq (I + C), \tag{A2'}$$

then the borrower's interim knowledge will not be shared at $t = 1$. The expected value of each R&D project therefore equals $V_{ND} = \max(V_D, V_{ND})$, and the promised repayment R that provides the banks zero ex ante expected profit solves

$$R[S[P(1-P) + (1-S)P(1-Q)] + (1-S)[Q(1-P)S + Q(1-Q)(1-S)]] = I, \tag{10}$$

where $R < V$, by (A2'). The ex-ante expected payoff to the borrower, $Z_0(MFL)$, is then

$$Z_0(MFL) - V_{ND} - I. \tag{11}$$

Table 1. Borrowers Ex Ante Surplus and Reward to Research Effort with Long-Term Debt

Financing	Multilateral		Bilateral
	$0 \leq P \leq \frac{1}{2}$	$1 \geq P > \frac{1}{2}$	All P
Ex ante surplus	$Z_0(\text{MFL})$		$Z_0(\text{BFL})$
	$V_D - I$	$V_{ND} - I$	$V_{ND} - I$
Reward to Research Effort	$[Z(S) - Z(F)]_{\text{MFL}}$		$[Z(S) - Z(F)]_{\text{BFL}}$
	$\dfrac{(V_D - I)K}{(L + SK)}$	$\dfrac{(V_{ND} - I)A}{(B + SA)}$	$\dfrac{(V_{ND} - I)A}{(B + SA)}$,

$$\text{where } k = (1 - S)[P(1 - P) - Q(1 - Q)] \tag{15a}$$
$$L = [P(1 - P)S + Q(1 - Q)(1 - S)] \tag{15b}$$
$$A = [P - Q[S(1 - P) + (1 - S)(1 - Q)] \tag{16a}$$
$$B = Q[S(1 - P) + (1 - S)(1 - Q)] \tag{16b}$$

The borrower's expected profits conditional upon success and failure, respectively, are

$$Z(S) = (V - R)[P(1 - Q)(1 - S) + P(1 - P)S] \tag{12}$$

$$Z(F) = (V - R)[Q(1 - P)S + Q(1 - Q)(1 - S)], \tag{13}$$

where R is given by (10). The difference between the conditional expected payoffs to the successful and failed borrowers under multilateral financing with long-term debt, when $P > \frac{1}{2}$, can thus be written, using Eqs. (10), (12), and (13) as

$$[Z(S) - Z(F)]_{\text{MFL}} = (V_{ND} - I)[A/(B + SA)], \tag{14}$$

where A and B are defined in Table 1 (Eqs. (16a) and (16b)).

B. Bilateral financing

Under bilateral financing with long-term debt, there is no value of P for which a bank or a borrower has an incentive to disclose the outcome. Consequently, regardless of P, the ex ante expected value of each R&D project equals V_{ND}. The ex ante expected payoff to the borrower, $Z_0(\text{BFL})$, and the Reward to Research Effort, $[Z(S) - Z(F)]_{\text{BFL}}$, are summarized in Table 1. These are the same expressions as the ones derived above for the multilateral financing regime when banks do not share interim research knowledge across their common borrowers (when $P > \frac{1}{2}$), but these formulas are now valid for all $P \in (0, 1)$.

We now turn to the question of incentives for borrowers to incur C. In the process, we shall show that the equilibrium choice of financing regimes, in ex ante

competition among banks for borrowers, crucially depends on the importance
of such incentives at the initial stage.

C. Research incentives and choice of financing regimes

Table 1 including Eqs. (15a), (15b), (16a), and (16b), indicates the crucial differences between the bilateral and multilateral financing regimes when $P \leq \frac{1}{2}$.
When interim disclosure of R&D knowledge across borrowers is ex ante optimal,
multilateral (bilateral) financing does (not) lead to such disclosure, resulting in
higher (lower) ex ante surplus for borrowers. However, the incentives to incur
C can be lower for borrowers under multilateral financing. This is the case, for
example, as the probability of success in first-stage research, S, tends to unity for
any $(P - Q)$ difference. Equation (15a) reveals that $K \to 0$ as $S \to 1$, but (16a)
shows that $A \neq 0$ when $S = 1$, so that Reward to Research Effort tends to
zero under multilateral financing as $S \to 1$, but not under bilateral financing.
The intuition is that, with the interim knowledge disclosure anticipated from
its rival under the multilateral financing regime, each firm is induced to free
ride on its rival's R&D, in contrast to bilateral financing, which has no interim
knowledge sharing. However, a situation in which only one of the two firms
incurs C is incompatible with equilibrium multilateral financing. A borrower
that incurs C in this case would be lured away by a competitive zero-profit
bilateral financing offer from either bank because it could then incur C without having to share the resulting knowledge. We make the following additional
assumption:

(v) Sufficient incentives to incur C always exist under bilateral financing with
no knowledge sharing, so that

$$S[Z(S) - Z(F)]_{\mathrm{BFL}} = \left[\frac{(V_{\mathrm{ND}} - I)SA}{(B + SA)} \right] \geq C. \qquad (A5)$$

We can now state the key result of this section on long-term debt financing.

PROPOSITION 1.

(a) *When $P > \frac{1}{2}$, bilateral and multilateral long-term debt are equivalent; both
regimes lead to no interim disclosure of knowledge across rival borrowing firms,
and provide borrowers incentives to incur C.*
(b) *When $P \leq \frac{1}{2}$, multilateral financing leads to disclosure of interim research knowledge across borrowers, but bilateral financing does not result in such disclosure,
even though it is ex ante optimal (as is no disclosure when $P > \frac{1}{2}$).*
(c) *When $P \leq \frac{1}{2}$, there exists $S^* \in (0, 1)$ such that for $S > S^*$ only bilateral financing
provides adequate incentives for R&D effort. Hence, for $S > S^*$, the bilateral*

financing regime arises as the ex ante equilibrium choice of the institutional arrangement for financing.

Proof. Parts (a) and (b) have already been proved in the text above, as summarized in Table 1. To prove that (c), note first that each borrowing firm would incur C under multilateral financing if and only if:

$$S[Z(S) - Z(F)]_{\text{MFL}} = \left[\frac{(V_D - I)SK}{(L + SK)} \right] \geq C > 0.$$

But using (15a) and (15b) in Table 1, there exists $0 < S^* < 1$ such that the inequality above cannot be satisfied for $S > S^*$. Hence, using assumption (A5), the proposition is proved.   Q.E.D.

Proposition 1 summarizes the key tradeoffs in the equilibrium choice of financing arrangement. When interim knowledge disclosure across rivals in an R&D contest improves their ex ante probability of sole invention, and free riding problems related to these rivals' incentives to make privately observed investments in R&D are not too severe, multilateral financing arrangements would arise in equilibrium. Otherwise, bilateral financing with no interim disclosure of R&D knowledge arises in equilibrium.[8]

IV. Short-Term Debt Contracts

If there are incentive (moral hazard) problems present when $C > 0$, there is scope for shortening debt maturity. Debt that matures at $t = 1$ implies recontracting at the date when the outcomes of the first stage of research are realized. It is possible that firms' expected payoffs conditional upon first-stage success and failure, and hence the Reward to Research Effort, may be enhanced by the use of short-term debt. In this section we characterize loan market equilibria when banks can offer short-term debt contracts at $t = 0$, which must be refinanced, if possible, at $t = 1$.

A. Multilateral financing

At the initial date, $t = 0$, each bank lends (by symmetry) amounts equaling at least $1/2$ to either firm as short-term debt, in return for repayments due of $R_1/2$, at the interim date, $t = 1$. We refer to a borrower who has succeeded (failed) at the first-stage of R&D as an S-type (F-type) borrower. The game at $t = 1$, when

---

[8] A purely public financing mechanism may lead to interim knowledge disclosure across rivals even when that is not ex ante optimal, i.e. when $P > \frac{1}{2}$, if the privacy of knowledge gathered by many financiers simply cannot be protected. Then, for $P > \frac{1}{2}$ bilateral financing would be chosen in equilibrium.

the repayment of the first period loan, R_1, is due proceeds as follows:

(i) Bank 1 offers an S-type (F-type) borrows a refinancing contract—a loan of size R_1—with repayment $\tau_S(\tau_F)$ due at $t = 2$. Bank 2 offers analogous refinancing contracts with repayments due of τ_S' and τ_F', respectively.

(ii) If the $\min(\tau_S, \tau_S') > V$, then the S-type borrower defaults. If $\tau_S \neq \tau_S'$ and if the $\min(\tau_S, \tau_S') \leq V$, then the S-type accepts the loan offer with the lower repayment demand. If $\tau_S = \tau_S' \leq V$, then the S-type borrower refinances $(\frac{1}{2})R_1$ from each of the to banks. The F-type borrower makes a similar choice, and in calculating his payoff he anticipates whether the interim knowledge of the other borrower will or will not be disclosed to him (depending upon the state of the other borrower).

(iii) Given the contracts offered by the banks $i, i = 1, 2$, and given the borrowers' choices of refinancing offers, each bank i chooses whether or not to disclose the interim knowledge produced by a successful borrower to a failed borrower.

We characterize below the first-period debt contract, i.e., the size of the loan granted at $t = 0$ and the repayment due at $t = 1$. R_1, so that (a) in the equilibrium of the game above interim research knowledge is shared across borrowers if and only if $P \leq \frac{1}{2}$, and (b) banks earn zero expected profit ex ante.

Consider first an equilibrium of the refinancing game outlined above when $0 < P \leq \frac{1}{2}$, in which R_1 satisfies:

$$VQ(1 - Q) < I < R_1 < VP(1 - P). \tag{17}$$

We shall prove that, given the outcome of the refinancing game at $t = 1$, the R_1 that gives banks zero expected profit ex ante satisfies (17). Let the interim state realization be (S, F) at date $t = 1$; one borrower has succeeded at the first stage of R&D and the other has failed. Let banks offer the refinancing contract $\tau_F' = \tau_F = \tau_S' = \tau_S = \tau$, satisfying

$$P(1 - P)\tau = R_1, \tag{18}$$

where $\tau < V$, given the inequality in (17) above. Then both firms borrow $(\frac{1}{2})R_1$ from each bank, and a bank chooses to disclose the interim knowledge of one borrower to the other if and only if:

$$(\tfrac{1}{2})P(1 - P)\tau + (\tfrac{1}{2})P(1 - P)\tau \geq (\tfrac{1}{2})P(1 - Q)\tau + (\tfrac{1}{2})Q(1 - P)\tau. \tag{19}$$

The left-hand side of (19) is the bank's expected payoff under disclosure when each borrowers is the sole inventor at $t = 2$ (the probability of each borrower being the sole inventor is $P(1 - P)$); the right-hand side of (19) is the bank's expected payoff conditional upon no knowledge disclosure, so that the successful borrower is the sole inventor at $t = 2$ and hence is solvent with probability $P(1 - Q)$, and the failed borrower is the sole inventor and hence τ with probability $Q(1 - P)$.

By Lemma 1, when $P \leq \frac{1}{2}$ inequality (19) is satisfied, so that knowledge sharing is the bank's optimal choice given the loan offers defined by (18) and given the entrepreneurs' choices of borrowing. Analogous reasoning in the cases where the realized (knowledge) state of the two borrowers at $t = 1$ is either (S, S) or (F, F), leads us to the following result.

LEMMA 2. *Let $P \leq \frac{1}{2}$ and assume (A1), (A2), and (A3), as given in Section II. Then, in the short-term debt refinancing game at $t = 1$, the unique (subgame perfect Nash) equilibrium outcome is as follows:*

(a) *If the interim knowledge state is (S, S), i.e., both borrowers have succeeded in their first-stage research, then $\tau_S = \tau_S' = \tau < V$, where τ satisfies (18).*

(b) *If the interim knowledge state is (F, F) i.e., both borrowers have failed in their first-state research, then $\tau_F = \tau_F' > V$, and both borrowers default on their first-period loan.*

(c) *If the interim knowledge state across the two borrowers is (S, F) or (F, S), i.e. only one of the two borrowers has succeeded in first-stage research, then knowledges is shared across the two borrowers, who are refinanced with $\tau_S = \tau_S' = \tau_F = \tau_F' = \tau < V$, where τ satisfies (18).*

(d) *Furthermore, in the ex ante contract-setting (Bertrand) competition between the two banks, the (Nash) equilibrium repayment amount on the first-period loan, R_1, satisfies (17).*

Proof. Part (a) is obvious given interim ($t = 1$) interbank competition. To prove part (b), notice that a first-period repayment of $R_1 < I$ cannot provide the lending bank with nonnegative expected profit ex ante, and (A1) implies that a repayment $R_1 \geq I$, cannot be refinanced from either bank when the interim knowledge state is (F, F).

To prove part (c), first note that the contract given above is the only subgame perfect equilibrium with interim interbank competition if the banks' optimal policy in stage (iii) of the refinancing game is to share the knowledge of the S-type borrower with the F-type borrower. To establish that this is the only possible outcome, we must show that a subgame perfect Nash equilibrium without knowledge sharing by the banks at stage (iii) of the refinancing game cannot arise. This is accomplished in Appendix A.

Finally, to establish part (d), note that R_1 must yield banks zero ex ante expected profit, i.e., given parts (a), (b), and (c) above,

$$R_1[1 - (1 - S)^2] + V[(1 - S)^2 Q(1 - Q)] = I, \tag{20}$$

so that, given (A1) and (A2), R_1 satisfies (17).   Q.E.D.

Lemma 2 has important implication for the relative performance of multilateral financing with short-term debt versus that with long-term debt, with respect to borrowers' Reward to Research Effort. The reason is that with short-term debt when the interim knowledge state is (F, F), both borrowers are bankrupt and hence obtain zero payoffs, whereas they would have earned positive expected payoffs with long-term debt financing (the option value). Correspondingly given R_1, the short-term debt repayment, and τ, the repayment of refinanced short-term debt, S-type borrowers obtain strictly higher conditional expected payoffs with short-term debt financing. Before summarizing these results, we consider the case when $P > \frac{1}{2}$, so that interim knowledge disclosure across borrowers is not first-best, and examine the refinancing game at $t = 1$ across the banks and their borrowers. Assuming $Q < \frac{1}{2}$, so that the probability if sole invention is not maximized by having two F-type borrowers, we have the following result.

LEMMA 3. *Let $P > \frac{1}{2} > Q$, and assume (A1), (A2'), and (A3) are satisfied. Then R_1 will satisfy:*

$$V[P(1 - Q)] > R_1 \geq max\{V[2P(1 - P) \cdot Q(1 - P)], V[Q(1 - Q)]\}. \qquad (21)$$

As a result, in the refinancing game at $t - 1$, the unique set of subgame perfect equilibrium outcomes is as follows:

(a) *If the interim knowledge state is (F, F), i.e. both borrowers have failed in their first-stage research, then $\tau_F = \tau'_F > V$ and the failed borrowers are forced to default on their first-period loans.*

(b) *If the interim knowledge state is (S, F), or (F, S), i.e. only one of the two borrowers has succeeded in first-stage research, then (i) interim research knowledge is not shared across the borrowers, (ii) $\tau_F = \tau'_F > V$ so that the failed F-type borrower defaults, and (iii) the S-type borrower is refinanced with promised repayment $\tau_S = \tau'_S = \tau < V$ at $t = 2$, satisfying*

$$P(1 - Q)\tau = R_1 \qquad (22)$$

and each bank lends $R_1/2$ to each borrower at $t = 1$.

(c) *If the interim knowledge state is (S, S), so that both the borrowers have succeeded in their first-stage research, only one of the two borrowers is declared in default, and the banks set τ for refinancing the other borrower to satisfy*

$$P(1 - Q)\tau = R_1 \qquad (22)$$

under interim competition.[9]

---

[9] The repayment demanded of the borrower put into default is $\tau_S = \tau'_S > V$, since $VP(1 - P) < R_1$, and the defaulted borrower's success probability drops to Q by (A3). The renegotiation is at least weakly Pareto-improving for banks and borrowers.

(d) *Given parts (a), (b), and (c) above, the ex ante expected net profit of each bank is set equal to zero when each bank lends to each borrower the amount $I'/2$, where I' satisfies the equation*

$$I \leq I' = S\left[(1 - S)R_1 + \frac{S}{2}\{R_1 + Q(1 - P)V\}\right]$$
$$+ (1 - S)[SVQ(1 - P) + (1 - S)VQ(1 - Q)], \tag{23}$$

in accordance with the equilibrium characterized in parts (a), (b), and (c) above. A solution to (23) satisfying (21) exixts, and the excess lending $(I' - I)$ if any is assumed to be consumed by the borrowers ex ante, at $t - 0$.

Outline of Proof. The complete proof of Lemma 3 is lengthy and tedious, and hence it is relegated to Appendix B which is available from the authors on request. Here we sketch the proof.

The crucial problem the bank lenders now face is that of avoiding opportunistic disclosure of an S-type borrower's interim research knowledge to an F-type borrower by one of them, at $t = 1$ when the short-term debt must be refinanced. Such knowledge revelation is undesirable from the (first-best) perspective of ex ante surplus maximization, since $P > \frac{1}{2}$, by Lemma 1. To preclude such disclosure, R_1 must be set sufficiently high, so that

$$\left(\tfrac{1}{2}\right)[R_1 + VQ(1 - P)] \geq VP(1 - P). \tag{21a}$$

The left-hand side of (21a) represents a bank's payoff from the equilibrium strategies, as spelled out above. The right-hand side of (21a) represents a bank's payoff from deviating by repaying the first-period loan of the F-type borrower from the other bank of amount $\frac{1}{2}R_1$, using the repayment of its first-period loan to the S-type, and then transferring the S-type borrower's interim research knowledge to the captured F-type at stage (iii) of the refinancing game, in return for promised repayment of V at $t - 2$, which is subgame perfect given the deviation.

The proof of part (a) of the lemma is obvious, and analogous to that of part (b) of Lemma 2. Given the argument following inequality (21a) above, which makes use of Assumption (A3), part (b) of Lemma 3 follows from interim competition for the successful S-type borrower between the two banks, given the first inequality in (21).

The proof of part (c) of Lemma 3 involves the observation that, for the short-term debt contract, the required repayment R_1 (satisfying (21)) exceeds $VP(1-P)$, so that at least one of the knowledgeable borrowers would be declared bankrupt. Declaring only one to be bankrupt is optimal, given assumption (A3), since it improves the probability of sole invention by the two borrowers taken together.

Thus, one of the two S-type borrowers, chosen randomly, is declared bankrupt and the other is refinanced competitively.

Finally the proof of part (d) of the Lemma and the inequality in (23), follow from ex ante (Bertrand) competition between the two bank lenders.

Given Lemmas 2 and 3 above, the ex ante expected net surpluses of the borrowers under multilateral short-term debt financing are

$$Z_0(\text{MFS}) = [V_D - I], \quad \text{when } P \le \tfrac{1}{2} \tag{24}$$

and

$$Z_0(\text{MFS}) = [V_{ND} - I] - \frac{S^2}{2}[P(1 - Q) + Q(1 - P) - 2P(1 - P)]V,$$

$$\text{when } P > \frac{1}{2}. \tag{25}$$

Analogously, the expressions for Reward to Research Effort, $[Z(S) - Z(F)]_{\text{MFS}}$, are now given by

$$[Z(S) - Z(F)]_{\text{MFS}} = \left[\frac{(V_D - I)(1 - S)}{(2S - S^2)}\right] \tag{26}$$

when $P \le \tfrac{1}{2}$, and when $P > \tfrac{1}{2}$ by

$$[Z(S) - Z(F)]_{\text{MFS}} = Z(S)$$

$$= \left[\left(1 - S + \frac{S}{2}\right)P(1 - Q)(V - \tau)\right], \tag{27}$$

where τ satisfies (22), and R_1 satisfies (23) and (21) as well.

Equation (26) has been obtained by using Lemma 2, which implies that

$$[Z(S) - Z(F)]_{\text{MFS}} = [(V - \tau)P(1 - P)](1 - S).$$

where τ satisfies Eq. (18) and R_1 satisfies (20), and V_D is given by (2). Notice that (26) implies that Reward to Research Effort under multilateral financing is greater with short-term than with long-term debt, for $P \le \tfrac{1}{2}$, since

$$[Z(S) - Z(F)]_{\text{MFS}} = (V_D - I) \Big/ \left[S + \frac{S}{(1 - S)}\right] \tag{26'}$$

and $[S/(1 - S)]$ is strictly less than the corresponding term L/K of Eqs. (15a) and (15b) in Table 1, for long-term debt.

However, when $P > \tfrac{1}{2}$, multilateral financing need not provide greater Reward to Research Effort for borrowers with short-term debt than with long-term debt, since the equilibrium loan contract in Lemma 3 implies that some successful borrowers in the (S, S) state, as well as failed F-type borrowers, obtain zero expected payoffs.[10] We can examine this issue further, using (27), (22), (23), and (21). Under some conditions, derived in Appendix B, (23) is satisfied with $I' = I$ whereas (21) is strict inequality and hence, using (22) and (27) also, we have[11]

$$[Z(S) - Z(F)]_{MFS} = \frac{1}{S}\{V_{ND} - I\} + \frac{S}{2}\left[P(1 - Q) + Q(1 - P) - 2P(1 - P)\right]V. \quad (27')$$

The curly-bracketed term in (27') reflects the fact that, with short-term debt financing, all F-type borrowers at the first stage are forced into bankruptcy. The square-bracketed term further reflects the fact that, with optimal refinancing of the multilateral short-term debt contract, in the state (S, S) at $t = 1$ when both borrowers have succeeded in their first-stage research, only one of the two borrowers is allowed to continue, which is optimal when $P > \frac{1}{2}$. The expression for Reward to Research Effort in (27') clearly exceeds that for multilateral financing with long-term debt, given in Table 1 including (16a) and (16b). Hence, short-term debt financing again improves borrowers' incentives to incur the cost C.[12]

B. Bilateral financing

As with multilateral financing, for each borrower the short-term debt from his original lender matures at $t = 1$ with R_1 due, but only the unique lender of each borrower is now aware of his interim knowledge. Hence, the refinancing game among the two borrowers and the two banks at $t = 1$ is now one of incomplete information; a new lender is convinced of the knowledge of the erstwhile borrower of another bank if and only if the latter reveals it. Furthermore, given (A3), the probability of invention in the event of success at the first stage of R&D is P if and only if the entrepreneur is kept in control at the second stage.

Suppose that $R_1 > VQ(1 - Q)$. Then, conditional on failure of the first stage of R&D, the borrower has no outside option, i.e. he cannot get refinancing from bank other than the one from which he borrowed in the first period. Since the probability of invention of a nonknowledgeable firm is Q no matter who is

---

[10] The resulting expected surplus for lenders is remitted to borrowers in the form of the excess lending $(I' - I)$ over and above that required for the initial investment I.

[11] Sufficient conditions for (27') to hold, derived in Appendix B, are that either (i) $Q \geq 2(1 - P)$, which implies that $VQ(1 - Q)$ drives the R_1 solution satisfying (21), or (ii) $Q < 2(1 - P)$ and $[S(1 - S)(2P - 1)(P - Q)]V \geq [V_{ND} - I]$, which imply that inequality (21) is strict, and (23) is satisfied with $I' - I$. Condition (ii) requires that the net surplus from R&D is not too high, and it may not hold for P in a neighborhood of $P > \frac{1}{2}$.

[12] As we noted earlier in footnote 8, our analysis is predicated on a strategic view of financiers' behavior under multilateral financing. If one thinks of multilateral financing instead as simply being decentralized public financing, then interim knowledge disclosure across borrowers may take place even when $P > \frac{1}{2}$, and that is likely to reduce the Reward for Research Effort under such financing.

in control, a failed F-type borrower of either bank is always forced into a zero expected payoff situation at $t = 1$, so that $Z(F) = 0$.

The payoff to the borrower in the event of success at the first stage of R&D is the outcome of bilateral bargaining at $t = 1$ with the bank he borrowed from in the first period, with an outside option for the borrower. The bilateral bargaining element comes from the fact that, as noted above, the entrepreneur being in control is crucial for the probability of invention to be $P > Q$ (by Assumption (A3)), and this implies that a surplus can be generated by having the entrepreneur in control at the second stage of R&D relative to the entrepreneur being removed (declared bankrupt). The value of this surplus is given by:

$$ES = [VP(1 - Q)(1 - S) + VP(1 - P)S] - [VQ(1 - Q)(1 - S) + VQ(1 - P)S]$$
$$= V(P - Q)[(1 - Q)(1 - S) + S(1 - P)]. \tag{28}$$

The outside option feature derives from the fact that a successful borrower can seek refinancing of R_1 at $t = 1$ from the other bank. Due to the infeasibility of knowledge licensing, contracting can only take place after a successful borrower seeking refinancing from the other bank reveals his success at the first stage of R&D. Moreover, once such information has been disclosed, the other bank will find it optimal to inform its failed borrower, since it can always refuse to refinance the knowledgeable erstwhile borrower of its competing bank. Consequently, the expected value of the R&D project of a successful borrower seeking refinancing from the other bank is $VP(1 - P)$, independent of whether his competitor succeeded or failed at the first stage of R&D. Hence, the S-type borrower succeeds in refinancing from the other bank if and only if:

$$VP(1 - P) \geq R_1. \tag{29}$$

The value of the outside option of the successful S-type borrower is then the $\max[VP(1 - P) - R_1, 0]$, and therefore the $t = 1$ expected payoff to the successful S-type borrower, $Z(S)$, is given by

$$Z(S) = \max[\mu ES, \max[VP(1 - P) - R_1, 0]], \tag{30a}$$

where $0 \leq \mu \leq 1$ is the fraction of the surplus ES (see (28)) accruing to the borrower. Assume that the bank has all the bargaining power, i.e., $\mu = 0$. Then the $t = 1$ expected payoff to the successful borrower equals the value of his outside option, i.e.

$$Z(S) = \max[VP(1 - P) - R_1, 0]. \tag{30b}$$

Ex ante Bertrand competition among banks implies that R_1 must satisfy, for the equilibrium loan amount I', at date $t = 0$.

$$(1 - S)\,[VQ(1 - P)S + VQ(1 - Q)(1 - S)]$$
$$+ S\,[[VP(1 - P)S + VP(1 - Q)(1 - S)] - Z(S)] = I' \geq I, \tag{31}$$

which can be expressed, when $I' = I$, as

$$[V_{ND} - I] = SZ(S), \tag{31'}$$

where $Z(S)$ satisfies (30b) and $VP(1 - P) > R_1$.

Let $P \leq \frac{1}{2}$, then $[\dot{V}_{ND} - I] > 0$ by (A2), and an R_1 that solves (31') exists and satisfies $VQ(1 - Q) < R_1 < VP(1 - P)$ if $[V_{ND} - I]$ is not too large, i.e. if $[V_{ND} - I] < s\,[VP(1 - P) - VQ(1 - Q)]$, where $P(1 - P) > Q(1 - Q)$, because $Q < P \leq \frac{1}{2}$. The value of the outside option of the S-type borrower is then indeed positive, whereas the value of the outside option of the F-type borrower is zero. The borrower's ex ante surplus is therefore given by

$$Z_0(\text{BFS}) = (V_{ND} - I) \tag{32}$$

and the Reward to Research Effort is given by

$$[Z(S) - Z(F)]_{\text{BFS}} = VP(1 - P) - R_1 - \frac{1}{S}\,[V_{ND} - I]. \tag{33}$$

On comparing (32) and (33) with the corresponding quantities in Table 1 for bilateral financing with long-term debt, we see that while short-term debt financing leaves the ex ante surplus of borrowers unchanged, it improves the Reward to Research Effort.

If $P > \frac{1}{2}$, then there are two ranges of values of P that are relevant. If P is sufficiently close to $\frac{1}{2}$, then the same conclusion as above applies. If P is sufficiently higher than $\frac{1}{2}$, i.e., $VP(1 - P)$ is sufficiently small, then the value of the outside option of the S-type borrower, and hence his expected interim payoff, is zero. This in turn implies $I' > I$ in (31), and research incentives are destroyed. In essence, when $P > \frac{1}{2}$ and short-term debt is used, the possibility of disclosure of the knowledge of the successful borrower of Bank 1 to the failed borrower of Bank 2 erodes the desirable incentive properties of bilateral financing. The derivations in the two subsections above are summarizes in Table 2.

C. Comparison of financing regimes and equilibrium choices

On comparing Tables 1 and 2, and taking into account the results summarized in Proposition 1 above, we can now state the full result for our comparison of

Table 2. Borrowers Ex Ante Surplus and Reward to Research Effort with Short-Term Debt

Financing	Multilateral		Bilateral
	$0 \leq P \leq \frac{1}{2}$	$1 \geq P > \frac{1}{2}$	All P
Ex ante surplus	$Z_0(MFS)$		$Z_0(BFS)$
	$V_D - I$	$\left[\begin{array}{c} V_{ND} - I + \\ \dfrac{S^2}{2} \left\{ \begin{array}{c} P(1-Q) + \\ Q(1-P) - 2P(1-P) \end{array} \right\} V \end{array} \right]$	$V_{ND} - I$
Reward to Research Effort	$[Z(S) - Z(F)]_{MFS}$		$[Z(S) - Z(F)]_{BFS}$
	$\left[d \dfrac{(V_D - I)(I - S)}{(2S - S^2)} \right]$	$\left[\begin{array}{c} \dfrac{1}{S}(V_{ND} - I) + \\ \dfrac{S}{2} \left\{ \begin{array}{c} P(1-Q) + Q(1-P) \\ -2P(1-P) \end{array} \right\} V \end{array} \right]^a$	$\dfrac{1}{S}(V_{ND} - I),$ or zero[b]

[a] Under conditions described in footnote 11 and derived in Appendix B.
[b] See discussion in Section IV.B in text.

alternative institutional arrangements for the financing of R&D intensive firms. These comparisons take into account multilateral and bilateral financing, as well as optimal security design between long-term and short-term debt, the latter with refinancing and renegotiation at $t = 1$.

PROPOSITION 2. *Assume* (A1), (A2), (A2'), (A3), (A4), *and* (A5) *as above are satisfied. Then the ex ante equilibrium choice of financing regimes is as follows:*

(i) *If $P \leq \frac{1}{2}$ and $0 < S \leq S^*$, then the equilibrium choice is multilateral financing, with long- or short-term debt, where S^* is characterized in the proof of Proposition 1.*

(ii) *If $P \leq \frac{1}{2}$, and $S^* < S \leq S^{**}$, where S^{**} satisfies*

$$\left[\frac{S^{**}(V_D - I)(1 - S^{**})}{2S^{**} - S^{**2}} \right] = C, \tag{34}$$

where C is the privately chosen (effort) cost of first-stage research, the multilateral financing with short-term debt prevails in ex ante equilibrium.

(iii) *If $P \leq \frac{1}{2}$, and $S^{**} < S \leq 1$, then bilateral financing with long- or short-term debt prevails in ex ante equilibrium.*[13]

---

[13] If Assumption (A5), on the viability of bilateral financing with long-term debt, is not satisfied for S sufficiently close to 1, bilateral financing with short-term debt may still provide borrowers with adequate incentives to incur the first-stage research cost C. Since (by Table (1)) it provides greater incentives for costly research.

(iv) *If $P > \frac{1}{2}$, and the assumptions behind (27') are met, as detailed in footnote 11 and Appendix B, then multilateral financing with short-term debt prevails in ex ante equilibrium.*[14]

Proof. Straightforward, on comparing Tables 1 and 2.   Q.E.D.

The major difference between Propositions 1 and 2 lies in the fact that multilateral financing with short-term debt increases ex ante surplus and Reward-to-Research-Effort, particularly when $P > \frac{1}{2}$. This arises from the strategic use made of short-term debt contracts by multilateral lenders to increase ex ante surplus and Reward to Research Effort. These strategies go beyond implementing optimal nondisclosure of interim research knowledge across a successful and a failed borrower at the interim stage, when $P > \frac{1}{2}$. They further involve eliminating one of two knowledgeable firms at the interim stage from carrying out further R&D with its knowledge. Such a collusive role (from an ex ante point of view) for multilateral bank lenders distinguishes multilateral financing in our model from straightforward public (debt) financing with earlier no information acquisition about borrowers over time, and/or no strategic refinancing renegotiations at the interim stage, at date $t = 1$. In the following section, we consider the idea that multilateral lenders can facilitate collusion in the post-invention product market among two borrowers who are R&D rivals and are both successful in the second stage of their R&D projects.

V. Extensions

We have thus far assumed that the R&D project requires capital only at the initial stage, and also that the new technology requires no investment in order to be implemented. In this section we discuss the implications of relaxing these assumptions.

If further investment is required to complete the project and the efficient continuation decision is contingent upon the R&D outcomes of the two firms, then the basic tradeoff determining the equilibrium choice between the two financing regimes will be reinforced. To see this, suppose a second cash outlay, I_2, is required at $t = 1$. Further, a firm that is successful in first-stage R&D should always invest I_2 and complete the project, but a firm that is unsuccessful should do so only if the competitor has also failed, i.e.

$$I_2 < VQ(1 - Q). \tag{35}$$

[14] If the characterization of borrowers' research incentives in Eq. (27') does not hold, and research incentives under multilateral short-term financing are inadequate, then multilateral or bilateral financing with long-term debt will prevail.

We assume that I_2 should not be invested if the competitor's R&D outcome is not known, i.e.

$$I_2 > V[SQ(1-P) + (1-S)Q(1-Q)], \tag{36}$$

given no knowledge sharing across the borrowing firms. With knowledge sharing in multilateral finance, both projects will be continued when either firm has succeeded and $P \leq \frac{1}{2}$. But with an absence of knowledge sharing in bilateral finance, only the successful firm(s) at the first stage will invest I_2. Moreover, when both firms fail in the first stage of R&D, projects will be continued under multilateral financing (with complete information at the interim stage) but not under bilateral financing. The reason is that truthfully revealing their borrowers' R&D outcomes cannot be an equilibrium for banks. If bank i truthfully reveals that its borrower has failed, bank j is better off announcing that its borrower has succeeded, since by so doing it maximizes the probability of its borrower being the sole inventor. As a result, under bilateral financing the ex ante surplus will further decline below that under multibilateral financing. But under bilateral financing the borrower who failed at the first stage gets nothing since he will discontinue the project. Consequently, the result that bilateral financing provides better incentives to engage in first-stage research (when $P \leq \frac{1}{2}$) is reinforced.

Finally, consider the possibility that an invention at $t = 2$ requires some capital, I_3, to introduce it to the produce market. Now, with inventions by both firms, the product-market rent V can be captured if and only if one of the two inventors invests I_3. In a world of complete contract, firms would maximize expected profits by signing an agreement whereby: (a) in case of joint invention only one firm invests I_3 and enters the market, and (b) the firm that acquires acknowledge at the interim stage discloses its knowledge to its competitor. Since collusion prevents rent dissipation in the postinvention product market, information disclosure is now first-best optimal (since $P > Q$) regardless of P, in contrast to Lemma 1. In such a world, the firms' incentives to invest in first-stage research could be further enhanced by ensuring that, in the case of interim knowledge disclosure, the interim knowledge provider is chosen to be the one that enjoys the postinvention rent.

Because of contract incompleteness, such an agreement is unenforceable. However, multilateral finance provides a mechanism to implement the (constrained) efficient solution. Since no rent is dissipated in product market competition, lenders maximize their overall expected repayments by maximizing the probability if invention. Product market collusion will occur because banks that lend to firms in the same industry have the incentive to coordinate and finance market entry of only one of two inventors.

Let the interest rate at which firms can obtain financing of I_3 from their lenders at the market-entry stage be preset contractually, and let it equal the safe rate of interest. Then there will be no further scope for competition in providing financing at date $t = 2$, and lenders will earn the same payoff irrespective of which inventor receives the loan of I_3. Lenders can then credibly commit ex ante to finance entry only by the interim-knowledge provider in the event of multiple inventions.

In contrast, under bilateral finance, the privacy of interim knowledge is preserved, and hence some of the ex ante surplus is lost, now even when $P > \frac{1}{2}$. Moreover, in the event of multiple inventions, each lender will wish that its own borrower is the sole market entrant. Collusion occurs only if lenders can commit ex ante to a randomized strategy for permitting product-market entry. However, this strategy is now independent of the outcome of the first-stage knowledge of their borrowers. Hence, the relative advantage of bilateral finance in motivating first-stage research, when $P \leq \frac{1}{2}$, will be reduced. This issue, as well as the possibility of repeated lender–borrower interactions creating even greater incentives for R&D and information sharing, deserves further study.

VI. Concluding Remarks

This chapter has expected the idea that financiers may act as facilitators of knowledge sharing in environments where a market for such proprietary information cannot exist. We have considered informational environments where: (i) a firm's knowledge is proprietary, in the sense that disclosure to competitors in product markets can reduce the private value of such knowledge, (ii) a lender in the process of monitoring learns its borrowers' interim research knowledge, and (iii) a market for selling such proprietary information is made infeasible by legal nonverifiability of such knowledge. In such an environment, knowledge transfer among firms through a common lender is shown to be a partial substitute for explicit contractual mechanisms.

We have focused on the comparative allocational properties of bilateral and multilateral financing, allowing for both long- and short-term debt. We have shown that with multilateral financing (i) information sharing among firms takes place if and only if it is in the lenders' interest, and that this coincides with the first-best criterion, and (ii) a collusive mechanism may be structured so that in equilibrium only one firm among multiple inventors enters the product market. However, the prospect of disclosure of proprietary knowledge to a borrower's competitor creates a free-rider problem regarding a firm's incentive to invest in R&D. This problem does not arise under bilateral financing (especially with long-term debt), because the privacy of proprietary knowledge is always preserved. Hence, when incentive problems are very important, multilateral financing may be replaced by bilateral financing.

Finally, we have shown that with multilateral and possibly also bilateral financing, incentives to make privately observed investments in R&D are enhanced by recontracting possibilities at the stage new information is acquired, and this amounts to issuing short-term debt. Indeed, the use of short-term debt with multilateral financing may lead to efficient elimination of at least one of the firms engaged in R&D, thus reducing duplication; the evidence in Sako (1995) supports this thesis.

The main contribution of our chapter is that it shows how the choice of financing source can serve as a precommitment device for pursuing ex ante efficient (but not necessarily ex post incentive compatible) strategies in knowledge-intensive environments. The implications of this general idea for a theory of comparative financial systems, and their implications for equilibrium knowledge sharing (and thus growth), should be pursued further in future research.

APPENDIX A

LEMMA 2. *Multilateral financing with short-term debt when* $P \leq \frac{1}{2}$.

Proof. We show here that given that R_1 satisfies (17), an equilibrium in (S, F) necessarily involves information sharing among borrowers. Suppose counterfactually that no information sharing is an equilibrium. Then, we must have the following:

(i) banks' offers are:

$$\tau_F' = \tau_F > V, \tag{A1}$$

and

$$\tau_S' = \tau_S = \tau,$$

satisfying

$$P(1 - Q)\tau = R_1 \tag{A2}$$

and

(ii) bank $j \neq i$, offering τ_F' and τ_S' is the optimal to bank i offering τ_F, τ_S, where τ_F', τ_S', τ_F, and τ_S are defined by (A1) and (A2).

Given the loan refinancing offers in (A1) and (A2), the successful entrepreneur refinances $(\frac{1}{2})R_1$ from each bank. The F-type borrower defaults on his first-period debt, losing control at the second stage, thereby leaving no scope for banks to share information across borrowers. Bank i's, $i = 1, 2$ payoff with the combination of strategies defined by (A1), (A2), π, is then

$$\pi = (\tfrac{1}{2})R_t + (\tfrac{1}{2})Q(1 - P)V. \tag{A3}$$

We now show that condition (ii) fails to hold. Given bank i's offers τ_F and τ_S. bank $j \neq i$ is better off by offering

$$\tau_F' = V \tag{A4}$$

and

$$\tau_S' > \tau_S. \tag{A5}$$

Given bank j's offer $\{(A4), (A5)\}$, the S-type borrower repays $(\frac{1}{2})R_1$ to bank j by borrowing from bank i, whereas the F-type borrower repays $(\frac{1}{2})R_1$ to bank i by borrowing from bank j. Because bank j, the deviant, has no more claims on the R&D project of the S-type, it finds it optimal to disclose the interim knowledge to the (originally) F-type borrower. By so doing it raises the value of its claim on the F-type's project to $VP(1 - P) > VQ(1 - P)$. The expected payoff to bank j deviating, π_d, is then:

$$\pi_d = [P(1 - P)V], \tag{A6}$$

which is profitable. i.e., $\pi_d > \pi$, comparing across (A6) and (A3), since

$$V[2P(1 - P) - Q(1 - P)] > R_1, \tag{A7}$$

given that R_1 satisfies inequality (17), and $p > Q$. Hence, an equilibrium in (S, F) cannot be one where information is not shared across borrowers.   Q.E.D.

References

Allen, F. (1993). "Stock markets and resource allocation," in C. Mayer and X. Vives (eds.), *Capital Markets and Financial Intermediation* (Cambridge: Cambridge Univ. Press), 81–107.

Bhattacharya, S. (1982). "Aspects of monetary and banking theory and moral hazard." *J. Finance*, 37: 371–84.

——, Glazer, J., and Sappington, D. (1992). "Licensing and the sharing of knowledge in research joint ventures." *J. Econ. Theory*, 56: 43–69.

——, and Ritter, J. (1983). "Innovation and communication signaling with partial disclosure." *Rev. Econ. Stud.*, 50: 331–46.

——, and Thakor, A. V. (1993). "Contemporary banking theory." *J. Finan. Intermed.*, 3: 2–50.

Dewatripont, M., and Maskin, E. (1995). "Credit and efficiency in centralized versus decentralized markets." *Rev. Econ. Stud.*, forthcoming.

Diamond, D. W. (1984). "Financial intermediation and delegated monitoring." *Rev. Econ. Stud.*, 51: 393–414.

Garella, P. (1995). "Informational rents in interbank competition." *Rev. Econ.*, forthcoming.

Hellwig, M. (1991). "Banking financial intermediation and corporate finance," in A. Giovannini and C. Mayer (eds.), *European Financial Integration* (Cambridge: Cambridge Univ. Press), 35–63.

Matutes, C., and Vives, X. (1992). "Competition for deposits, risk of failure, and regulation in banking." Working paper 18. European Science Foundation Network in Financial Markets.

Pagano, M., and Japelli, T. (1993). "Information sharing in the consumer credit market." *J. Finance*, 48: 1693–718.

Rajan, R. G. (1992). "Insiders and outsiders: The choice between informed and arm's-length debt." *J. Finance*, 47: 1367–400.

Sako, M. (1995). "Suppliers' associations in the Japanese automobile industry: Collective action for technology diffusion." *Cambridge J. Econ.*

Sharpe, S. (1990). "Asymmetric information, bank lending and implicit contracts: A stylized model of customer relationships." *J. Finance*, 45: 1069–87.

von Thadden, E. L. (1995). "Bank finance and long-term investment." *Rev. Econ. Stud.*

Yanelle, M. O. (1989). "The strategic analysis of intermediation." *European Econ. Rev.*, 33: 294–304.

Yosha, O. (1995). "Disclosure costs and the choice of financing source." *J. Finan. Intermed.*, 4: 3–20.

21

Financial System Architecture

Arnoud W. A. Boot and Anjan V. Thakor

A primary function of the financial system is to facilitate the transfer of resources from savers ("surplus units") to those who need funds ("deficit units"). In a well-designed financial system, resources are efficiently allocated. The question we address is, what is the configuration of such a financial system? In particular, we examine why bank lending and capital market financing coexist and the factors—such as regulation and the stage of economic development—that determine which dominates.

These issues are important for many of the current policy debates regarding the structuring of financial system. How do banks and capital markets emerge and evolve? What services should be provided by banks and what services by the capital market? How is the resolution of informational problems related to how the financial system is configured?

These questions are particularly interesting in the context of Eastern European countries. In the financial systems that are currently in place there are interim arrangements to facilitate transition to systems with lesser emphasis on the central planning of capital allocation [Checchi (1993)]. Although reform discussions have focused largely on the creation of financial markets [Mendelson and Peake (1993)], the more spectacular initial developments are likely to be in banking. For example, privately owned commercial banks were uncommon in Communist

A. V. Thakor would like to thank the Edward J. Frey Chair in Banking and Finance for financial support. A. W. A. Boot thanks the Olin program in Law and Economics at Cornell University for its hospitality during part of the research on this article. The authors would also like to thank Todd Milbourn, Kathleen Petrie, and Anjolein Schmeits for excellent research assistance, and seminar participants at the University of Michigan, Indiana University, University of Amsterdam, Erasmus University, Rotterdam (the Netherlands), University of Minnesota, the JFI Symposium on Market Microstructure and the Design of Financial Systems at Northwestern University (May 1995), the Nordic Finance Symposium at Vendsnu, Norway (February 1995), Queen's University, Cornell University, the London School of Economics, the Stockholm School of Economics, the University of Goteborg (Sweden), McGill University (Canada), and participants at the CEPR meetings in St. Sebastian, Spain (April 1994), and Gerzensee, Switzerland (July 1994), and the American Finance Association meeting, San Francisco (January 1996) for helpful comments. The authors are particularly indebted to Ed Kane, Sudipto Bhattacharya, Paolo Fulghieri, Neil Wallace, Mike Stutzer, and Franklin Allen for helpful suggestions.

Europe until recently. Since then, however, banks have evolved rapidly [Perotti (1993) and Van Wijnbergen (1994)]. These developments point to a key aspect of financial system architecture: the determination of the roles of the banking system and the financial market.

Despite its importance, the research on this topic is still only emerging. Allen (1993) provides a qualitative assessment and sketches a preliminary framework for analysis. That article links financial system design to the complexity of decision making within firms seeking capital and provides a perspective on the disparate evolutions of financial markets in Europe and the United States. Bhattacharya and Chiesa (1995), Dewatripont and Maskin (1995), von Thadden (1995), and Yosha (1995) examine the comparative allocational efficiencies of "centralized" (bank-oriented) credit markets versus "decentralized" (market-oriented) credit markets. Somewhat different approaches are taken by Allen and Gale (1995, forthcoming) who suggest that bank-oriented systems provide better intertemporal risk sharing, whereas market-oriented systems provide better cross-sectional risk sharing, and Sabani (1992) who argues that market-dominated economies will restructure financially distressed borrowers less than bank-dominated economies.

These contributions notwithstanding, there are unanswered questions. For example, how is the informativeness of market prices affected by financial system design? If unfettered by regulation, what determines the design of the financial system? And how does this design affect the borrower's choice of financing source? Does financial system design have real effects?

This article is a modest first attempt to address these issues. We explain how financial institutions and markets from and evolve when economic agents are free to choose the way organize themselves. Rather than taking the roles of institutions and markets as given and then asking how borrowers make their choice or financing source [e.g. Berlin and Mester (1992); Besanko and Kanatas (1993); Diamond (1991); and Chemmanur and Fulghieri (1994)], we start with assumptions about primitives—endowments and informational frictions—and endogenize the roles of banks and financial markets. The distinction we make between a bank and a market is that agents within a bank can cooperate and coordinate their actions, whereas agents in a market compete;[1] we assume nothing more about what banks and markets do.

We begin by positing three types of informational problems: (i) incomplete information about future projects that is of relevance for firm valuation and real investment decisions within firms, (ii) postlending (asset substitution) more hazard that can affect payoffs to creditors, and (iii) uncertainty about whether postlending moral hazard will be encountered. Part of the primitives

---

[1] Perhaps an even more basic distinction is that agents can be anonymous in a market but not in institution. This may be a way to rationalize the possibility of coordination within a bank and the lack of it in an anonymous, competitive market setting.

are economic agents who specialize in resolving these informational problems, with each individual agent being atomistic in impact. Our first major result is that problem (i) is most efficiently resolved in an "uncoordinated" market setting where individual agents compete with each other, and problems (ii) and (iii) are most efficiently resolved through coordinated action by agents coalescing to form a bank. The scope of banking vis-à-vis the financial market is thereby determined endogenously in an unregulated economy in which the financial markets is characterized by many agents and a rational expectations equilibrium price formation process that noisily aggregates information contained in the order flows for securities. A key attribute of the financial market, and one that delineates its role from that of a bank, is that there is valuable information feedback from the equilibrium market prices of securities to the real decisions of firms that impact those market prices.[2] This information loop provides a propagation mechanism by which the effects of financial market trading are felt in the real sector. Bank financing does not have such an information loop. Hence, real decisions are not impacted by the information contained in bank credit contracts. However, banks are shown to be superior in resolving asset substitution moral hazard. Thus, in choosing between banks and financial markets, one trades off the improvement in real decisions due to feedback from market price against a more efficient attenuation of moral hazard.

The relative levels of credit allocated by banks and the financial market depend on the efficacy of the bank's monitoring and the "development" (i.e. sophistication or level of financial innovation) of the financial market. We let the latter be reflected in the information acquisition cost for those who wish to become informed. We show that the cost of information acquisition affects the informativeness of equilibrium security prices, and therefore the relative scopes of banks and the financial market in credit allocation. In describing these scopes, our article explains:

- why banks emerge even when every agent in a bank could trade on his own in the market;
- why financial markets develop even when there are no restrictions on bank's activities;
- why a financial market equilibrium in which prices convey information can exist only if prices do not have too much or too little informativeness;[3]

---

[2] Allen (1993) suggests that an important role of the stock market is to provide decision-makers in firms with information they would not otherwise have possessed. Holmström and Tirole (1993) examine the role of the stock market as a monitor of managerial performance. They show that a firm's stock price incorporates performance information that cannot be gleaned from the firm's current or future profit data, and that this information is useful in structuring managerial incentives.

[3] This is in contrast to the existing literature in which the value of information acquisition is non-decreasing the noisiness of the process by which information is aggregated [e.g. Grossman and Stiglitz (1980)].

- why borrowers prefer either the financial markets or banks based on differences in observable borrower attributes; [4]
- how financial market trading affects firm's real decisions;
- how the state of development of the financial market can impact the borrower's choice of financing source.

The rest of the article is organized as follows. Section 1 contains a description of the basic model. Section 2 analyzes the formation of banks and the financial market. Further analysis is contained in Sections 3 and 4. Section 5 examines model robustness issues. Section 6 explores the implications of the analysis for financial system design. Section 7 concludes. All proofs are in the Appendix.

1. The Basic Model

1.1 Production possibilities for firms

1.1.1 Preferences and types of projects

There is universal risk neutrality, and the riskless interest rate is zero. The economy consists of firms each with a project that needs a \$1 investment. As shown in Figure 1, each firm has a stochastic investment opportunity set that contains two projects: good and bad. The contractible end-of-period return for the good project has a probability distribution with a two-point support: with probability η the end-of-period return will be $Y > 0$, and with probability $1 - \eta$ it will be 0. The contractible end-of-period return for a bad project will be 0 with probability 1, but this project offers the borrowing firm's manager a noncontractible private rent, N, from investing in the project [see, e.g. O'Hara (1993)]. Let $\eta Y > N$, so that the borrower prefers the good project with self-financing.

1.1.2 Project availability and payoff enhancement possibility

Project availability is stochastic. With probability $\theta \in (\underline{\theta}, \overline{\theta}) \subset (0, 1)$, the firm finds itself in the "low flexibility" (LF) state in which it has only the good project available. With probability $1 - \theta$, the firm finds itself in the "high flexibility" (HF) state and has both the good and the bad projects available.

We assume that the firm can possibly enhance the return of the good project at a private cost of $K = \overline{K} > 0$, where $K \in \{0, \overline{K}\}$. This investment is unobservable to outsiders, and it enhances the project return by $\alpha \in (0, 1)$, conditional

---

[4] Since banks resolve moral hazard in our model, the bank's decision to grant a loan does not trigger an abnormally positive reaction in the borrower's stock price as found empirically by James (1987), Lummer and McConnell (1989), and Shockley and Thakor (1996, forthcoming). Of course, if our model were to be altered to introduce uncertainty about whether the borrower would have a project available, then the bank's decision to grant a loan would signal good news. See Boot and Thakor (1996, forthcoming) for such an approach.

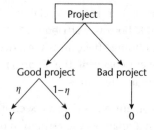

Figure 1. A schematic of the types of projects (without payoff enhancement) and contractible returns.

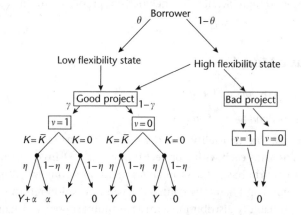

Figure 2. A schematic of the types of projects (with payoff enhancement) and contractible returns.

on a favorable realization of an "environmental" or "market" random variable $v \in \{0, 1\}$,[5] with $\Pr(v = 1) = \gamma \in (0, 1)$ as the probability that the a priori uninformed assign to the event that $v = 1$. Let $\alpha > \overline{K}$. Note that v is specific to each firm rather than being an economywide variable. Thus, if $v = 1$ and the firm invests $K = \overline{K}$, then the good project pays off $Y + \alpha$ with probability η and α with probability $1 - \eta$. If a borrower invests $K = 0$, then the good project's return is Y with probability η and 0 with probability $1 - \eta$, regardless of v. If a borrower invests either $K = \overline{K}$ or $K = 0$ in a bad project, the contractible project return is 0 with probability 1, regardless of v. Thus, the improvement in the project return depends on borrower-specific investments as well as the realization of exogenous uncertainties like market demand (see Figure 2).

We assume that the realization of v can only be observed by those who become informed at a cost; we will say more about this later. For now, it suffices that the borrower cannot observe v, but believes that $\Pr(v = 1) = \gamma$. This belief is common

---

[5] It does not matter much if we assume that K is observable to outsiders. With K unobservable, the firm underinvests relative to first best, whereas with K observable, there is no underinvestment.

knowledge. If the borrower is uninformed about v, an investment $K = \overline{K} > 0$ is suboptimal. That is, we assume $\gamma\alpha - \overline{K} < 0$, where $\gamma\alpha$ is the expected project enhancement if the borrower is uninformed about v. We assume $\eta > \gamma$ and that

$$\gamma\alpha < \overline{K} < \eta\alpha. \tag{1}$$

Further, we assume that exogenous parameter values are such that there exists an interest factor (one plus the interest rate) $r^0 < 1$ satisfying $\eta[Y + \alpha - r^0] - \overline{K} = N$.

Given this, the firm prefers the bad project with external financing if the interest factor exceeds r^0, and it prefers the good project with external financing if the interest factor is less than r^0. Since $r^0 < 1$ and we had earlier assumed that $\eta Y > N$, the firm always prefers the good project with self-financing and the bad project with external financing. From the lender's standpoint, therefore, there is asset-substitution moral hazard only in the HF state. We view the parameter θ as the commonly known prior probability assigned by the market to the event that a randomly selected borrower will be in the LF state and hence pose no moral hazard. Each potential borrower is characterized by its observable $\theta \in (\underline{\theta}, \overline{\theta})$. Let H be the cumulative distribution function over the cross-section of θs.

1.2 *Types of securities*

We limit financiers to debt contracts. This is primarily because bank lending is typically done through debt contracts, and we want to have comparability between the bank and capital market financing cases. Thus, the capital market financing in our model is through bonds. Of course, information acquisition in bond markets is probably smaller than that in the stock market. It is therefore important to note that our analysis understates the information acquisition benefits of financial markets, but is qualitatively unaffected if debt is replaced by equity (see Section 5).

1.3 *Sequence of events in lender–borrower interaction*

The firm first makes an irreversible decision about whether to borrow from a bank or the financial market. At this stage the only information that it has is about its θ, and this information is common knowledge.[6] Subsequently, the firm learns whether it is in the LF or the HF state, and after this v is realized and learned by those who choose to become informed about it. The lender (either the bank

---

[6] We assume that the firm commits to a financing choice at the outset to avoid the situation in which financial market investors produce information about a firm that ends up borrowing from a bank. Although in equilibrium each firm's choice of financing source is unambiguously linked to its θ, and this θ is commonly known at the outset. What we wish to avoid is the firm learning about v from its market price (which is based on investors erroneously believing that the firm will borrow in the financial market) and then borrowing from a bank.

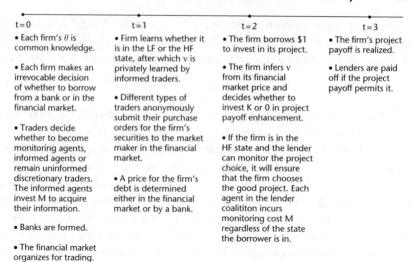

t = 0	t = 1	t = 2	t = 3
• Each firm's θ is common knowledge.	• Firm learns whether it is in the LF or the HF state, after which v is privately learned by informed traders.	• The firm borrows \$1 to invest in its project.	• The firm's project payoff is realized.
• Each firm makes an irrevocable decision of whether to borrow from a bank or in the financial market.	• Different types of traders anonymously submit their purchase orders for the firm's securities to the market maker in the financial market.	• The firm infers v from its financial market price and decides whether to invest K or 0 in project payoff enhancement.	• Lenders are paid off if the project payoff permits it.
• Traders decide whether to become monitoring agents, informed agents or remain uninformed discretionary traders. The informed agents invest M to acquire their information.	• A price for the firm's debt is determined either in the financial market or by a bank.	• If the firm is in the HF state and the lender can monitor the project choice, it will ensure that the firm chooses the good project. Each agent in the lender coalititon incurs monitoring cost M regardless of the state the borrower is in.	
• Banks are formed.			
• The financial market organizes for trading.			

Figure 3. A description of the sequence of events in the economy.

or the financial market) offers a price of credit that the firm can either accept or respond to with a take-it-or-leave-it counteroffer. Moreover, based on the lender's actions (the offered credit price or the market demand for the firm's security in the financial market), the firm makes its inference about the realization of v. Next, the firm makes its initial choice of project if it is in the HF state; in the LF state, this choice is trivially the good project in the event that the firm had initially chosen the bad project. If the lender can observe this initial choice and monitor, it can force a change to the good project in the event that the firm had initially chosen the bad project. This leads to the firm's final project choice decision and its investment of \$1 in the project. Moreover, at this time the firm also makes its decision regarding investing $K \in \{0, \overline{K}\}$ for project payoff enhancement (see Figure 3).

1.4 Types of agents in the economy

The structure for the financial market is as follows.[7] There are two types of investors/traders in the market: liquidity traders and discretionary agents. The aggregate asset demand, ℓ, of the liquidity traders is random and exogenously specified by the continuously differentiable probability density function $f(\ell) = A - (A^2\ell)/2$, where A is a positive constant. Thus, the support of $f(\ell)$ is $[0, 2/A]$. A discretionary agent can become an "informed" or a "monitoring" agent at a finite cost $M > 0$. This investment M either generates a signal that

---

[7] This structure is similar to that in Boot and Thakor (1993a), but richer in that agents can also choose to monitor an there is information feedback from the financial market to the firm.

perfectly reveals the v for the firm in question or enables the agent to monitor the firm's investment choice between the good and the bad project. The discretionary agent must decide before investing M whether she wishes to be an informed agent and receive the signal or become a monitoring agent. If the discretionary agent does not invest M, she can be an uninformed discretionary trader who can either invest in the capital market or in bank deposits.

We will first focus on agents who become informed about v. Each submits a demand order d_I. Let us conjecture that the equilibrium strategy of an informed trader is to set $d_I = 1$ if the signal says $v = 1$ and $d_I = 0$ if the signal says $v = 0$; we will validate this conjecture later. Each trader is very small but of $\epsilon > 0$ Lebesgue measure on the real line. We will focus on the limiting case in which $\epsilon \to 0$ so that each trader is atomistic, and all traders lie in a continuum. Let Ω be the (Lebesgue) measure of informed traders, with each submitting a demand of 0 or 1. The total informed demand is therefore $D_I = \Omega d_I$.

Liquidity traders' demand is not information driven and is based on exogenous factors outside the model. All demand orders are submitted to a market maker, and informed and liquidity traders are observationally identical to the market maker. Thus, the market marker observes only the total demand, $D = D_I + \ell$, and not its individual components, D_I and ℓ. The supply of the (debt) security is fixed at $1. We assume that there is a sufficient number of "professional" market makers, so that the market is competitive. The market maker receives all the orders for a given security and takes the position in the security required to clear the market at a price that yields her zero expected profit, conditional on the information in the order flow. Thus, the market maker takes a long position in the security if supply exceeds demand and a short position if demand exceeds supply. The debt security in question is a bond issued at par, and the price set by the market maker is the bond's coupon rate (or interest rate).

If the discretionary agent becomes a monitoring agent, she has the ability to monitor the borrower and detect its choice of the bad project; allowing this detection to be noisy is inconsequential. However, since each agent is atomistic, the borrower cannot be prevented from choosing the bad project unless a sufficiently large measure of monitoring agents is involved.[8] We assume that the minimum measure of monitoring agents needed to deter the borrower is $\Lambda^* < 1$. Moreover, while the discretionary agent decides at the outset whether to be an informed trader or a monitoring agent, the actual expense, M, of a monitoring agent, is not

---

[8] The idea is that an individual bondholder who has purchased a $100 bond as part of a $50 million IBM bond issue can do little to influence the firm's project choice. However, collectively—as with bank lending—the bondholders who purchased all of IBM's bonds could dictate a lot. Even when a borrower is solvent, "large block" creditors (either coalitions of bondholders who own significant portions of the firm's public bonds or institutional lenders like banks) can influence specific aspects of a firm's investment policy for reasons related to the borrower's desire to maintain a good relationship with the lender and retain operating flexibility when temporary negative shocks to cash flows elevate the risk of covenant violations.

incurred until after a loan has been extended to the borrower, whereas the outlay of $M > 0$ by an informed trader occurs prior to her placing her order for the security. The distinguishes information acquisition from postlending monitoring. For later use, we assume

$$\bar{\theta}[1 + \Lambda^* M] - 1 < 0. \tag{2}$$

This ensures that lending without monitoring and information acquisition is unprofitable, even if the promised interest rate is grossed up to compensate for anticipated monitoring expenses. To understand Equation (2) intuitively, note that the following two conditions are sufficient (but not necessary) to obtain Equation (2): (i) $\bar{\theta}\eta Y < 1$, which implies that an unmonitored project has a negative net present value (NPV), and (ii) $\eta Y > 1 + \Lambda^* M$, which implies that a monitored project has a positive NPV.

2. The Emergence of Banks and the Capital Market

2.1 Definitions of markets, institutions, and the overall equilibrium

A *financial market* is a collection of traders who all compete to buy debt securities offered by borrowing firms, and where the equilibrium security price is determined through a Walrasian market clearing condition enforced by a market maker. A *bank* is a collection of traders who coalesce to from an institution, provide deposit funding, and coordinate their actions with respect to the borrower. In an interior equilibrium, discretionary agents must be indifferent between becoming informed traders, monitoring agents, or uninformed discretionary traders/depositors.[9] Since the expected equilibrium profit from being an uninformed discretionary trader/depositor is zero, informed traders and monitoring agents must also earn zero expected profit in equilibrium.

2.2 Discretionary agents' choices

Consider discretionary agents who have chosen to become informed traders. Each now stands ready to receive a signal about v. They must decide whether to compete with others in the market in bidding for a debt security or coalesce into a bank and coordinate their actions.

LEMMA 1. *Those who invest M to become informed traders will prefer to compete with each other as financial market traders rather than become bankers.*

The monitoring agents must make a similar choice.

---

[9] We will assume throughout that the costs of becoming informed and monitoring agents are such that an interior equilibrium obtains. It is possible, however, that if these costs are sufficiently high, all traders may strictly prefer to remain uninformed and the measures of informed and monitoring agents are zero.

LEMMA 2. *Those who invest M to become monitoring agents will prefer to coalesce to form a bank and coordinate their actions in monitoring the borrower. Moreover, the measure of monitoring agents in the bank will be exactly Λ^*, the minimum needed to deter the firm from choosing the bad project.*

Given Lemma 1, we see that the financial market will consist of informed traders and liquidity traders. While the informed traders' demand is endogenously determined and the liquidity traders' demand is exogenous, it is possible that their total demand is not equal to 1, the available supply of the security. We assume that some of the uninformed discretionary traders in the market form coalitions called "market makers," each of whom is forced by competition to earn zero expected profit and "correct" the demand-supply imbalance by taking an appropriate position in the security. Moreover, given Lemma 2, the equilibrium measure of monitoring agents equals $\Lambda^* < 1$. Thus, some uninformed discretionary traders join the bank as nonmonitoring depositors and provide the remaining funding, $1 - \Lambda^*$. Combining Lemmas 1 and 2 yields the next observation.

PROPOSITION 1. *In equilibrium, the financial market consists of informed traders, uninformed discretionary traders, and liquidity traders. The informed traders are the only ones who learn v, and their trades have the potential to convey this information. The financial market is ineffective, however, in deterring borrowers from investing in the bad project when they have the choice. In equilibrium, banks consist of monitoring agents and uninformed discretionary agents who act as nonmonitoring depositors. The bank specializes in deterring borrowers from investing in bad projects, but it learns nothing about v.*

The intuition is as follows. If the informed agents were to form a bank, they could try to communicate information about v to the borrower. This information communication may be either truthful or not. With truthful communication, the borrower invests $\overline{K}$ whenever optimal. However, once the borrower learns v, it has no incentive to compensate the bank for its information acquisition cost. It can make a "take it or leave it" offer to the bank that merely yields the bank a zero expected profit on the loan itself. Since M is a sunk cost, the bank will find it in its own interest to accept the offer, thereby violating the ex ante participation constraints of informed agents. If communication is not truthful, then this problem is exacerbated, as the borrower remains uninformed about v and thus chooses $K = 0$.[10] On the other hand, if the informed agents compete as traders in the financial market, each can recover his information acquisition cost because the presence of liquidity traders makes prices noisy and sustains the ex post trading profits of those with privileged information.

---

[10] We find the case involving no truthful revelation of information to be the most realistic. It also rules out trivial alternative resolutions, for example, a borrower hiring an agent to produce information about v.

But if the monitoring agents decide to trade in the financial market as well, they face a coordination failure. Since a certain mass of them must choose too monitor in order to be effective, each monitoring agent must rely on sufficiently many others to monitor as well. But since each agent is arbitrarily small, this arrangement is beset with a free-rider problem in that there is at least one Nash equilibrium in which no agent monitors in the financial market. An effective way to resolve this problem is to form a coalition of monitoring agents whose measure is precisely Λ^*. These monitoring agents can observe each other's actions costlessly and thus implement a coordinated monitoring strategy. This endogenously gives rise to a financial intermediary, as in Ramakrishnan and Thakor (1984). Each monitoring agent contributes his $1 endowment for lending and an additional M for monitoring, so that these agents supply Λ^* of loanable funds and Λ^*M of monitoring resources; the remaining $1 - \Lambda^*$ of loanable funds is collected from nonmonitoring discretionary depositors.[11] The endogenously emerging role of banks as monitors is reminiscent of the role of banks in Diamond (1984). However, whereas the banks in Diamond's model monitor ex post cash flows, the banks here monitor ex ante project choices.

The role of banks that we have characterized is consistent with the key qualitative asset transformation functions served by real-world depository institutions [see Bhattacharya and Thakor (1993)]. For example, depository institutions that make loans and monitor borrowers to influence credit risk look very much like the banks in our model. Specifically, our banks are mutuals owned by their depositors. The nonmonitoring depositors are "pure" financiers, whereas the monitoring depositors are both depositors and loan officers since they monitor borrowers. This is akin to real-world mutual depository institutions in which there are depositors who are not involved in the management of the mutual and managers who hold ownership stakes by virtue of their deposits.

3. The Analysis and Equilibrium Definition

3.1 Determination of interest rates

3.1.1 Banking lending

The bank monitors the borrower's choice of project but does not learn v. Thus, there is no information feedback about v from the bank to the borrower, and by Equation (1) the borrower cannot be induced to invest $K = \overline{K}$. The competitive

---

[11] Our modeling of the impact of agents in the information production and monitoring cases is symmetric in the sense that, in both cases, individual agents are viewed as (almost) atomistic in their impact. In the financial market equilibrium, it will turn out that there must be sufficiently many informed traders for the security price to be influenced by their trades. And in the banking equilibrium, there must be sufficiently many monitoring agents to deter asset-substitution moral hazard.

bank's loan interest rate is set to yield an expected profit of zero. Thus, the loan interest factor (one plus the interest rate) r_B solves $\eta r_B = 1 + \Lambda^* M$, or

$$r_B = \frac{1 + \Lambda^* M}{\eta}. \tag{3}$$

Note that in deriving Equation (3) we have allowed the bank to recoup its monitoring cost. The reason is as follows. The bank's monitoring cost (M times the measure of monitoring agents) is incurred in the postlending stage, and at this stage it is in the bank's best interest to monitor. This is because the lack of bank monitoring means that the borrower will invest in the good project only with probability θ; recall that the realization of whether the borrower has access to a bad project is privately observed by the borrower that precludes realization-contingent monitoring. The bank's expected profit on the loan (if it does not monitor) is

$$\theta \eta \frac{[1 + \Lambda^* M]}{\eta} - 1 = \theta[1 + \Lambda^* M] - 1 < 0$$

by Equation (2). Thus, when the competitive bank quotes a price prior to making the loan, its quoted price must include the monitoring cost $\Lambda^* M$ in order to satisfy the bank's participation constraint.

3.1 2 *Financial market funding*

As will become apparent later, informed traders submit orders for the security only when their signal reveals that $\nu = 1$. The market maker observes the total order flow and has to decide whether total demand is such that the borrower will be induced to invest $\overline{K}$ in improving the project. From Equation (1), we know that this investment is socially efficient (first best) only when the probability that $\nu = 1$ is sufficiently high, that is, when $\Pr(\nu = 1|D)\alpha > \overline{K}$, where $\Pr(\nu = 1|D)$ is the posterior probability that the borrower (or the market maker) assigns to the event $\nu = 1$.[12] Of course, a borrower will be induced to invest only if

$$\Pr(\nu = 1|D)\eta\alpha > \overline{K}. \tag{4}$$

Note that Equation (4) is more stringent than the social efficiency condition, because a borrower with a good project benefits from investing $\overline{K}$ only if the project succeeds, even though the improvement, α, occurs in both the successful and unsuccessful state if $\nu = 1$ is realized. The reason is that $\alpha < 1$, so that all of it accrues to the lender (investors in the bond) if the unsuccessful state is realized. This distorts the borrower's decision further away from the first best (attainable with self-financing). This is the usual underinvestment moral hazard or debt overhang problem.

---

[12] Total demand will convey no information about ν if $\Omega = 0$ in equilibrium.

We now define $D_{\min}$ as the minimum total demand to induce the borrower to invest $\overline{K}$ in improving the project. That is (see Equation (4)),

$$\Pr(v = 1D_{\min})\eta\alpha = \overline{K}. \tag{5}$$

Since $\Pr(v = 1|D)$ is monotonically increasing in D (we will verify this), we have

$$\Pr(v = 1|D)\eta\alpha > \overline{K} \quad \text{for } D > D_{\min}.$$

Therefore, for $D > D_{\min}$, the borrower invests in project improvement. The best decision rule, given the observability problem about v (second best), would be to choose the cutoff D^* such that $\Pr(v = 1|D^*)\alpha = \overline{K}$. The decision rule of investing only when $D > D_{\min}$ is therefore more distortionary. We will later verify that the $D_{\min}$ defined in Equation (5) exists.

In Figure 4 we describe the inference process underlying the information feedback that occurs in the financial market. With the help of this figure, we can derive the interest rates that are set in the financial market. Henceforth, we consider the limiting case in which an individual trader's measure $\epsilon = 0$, that is, each trader is atomistic. Where appropriate, we will point out what happens if ϵ is small but positive. Let $r(D)$ be the equilibrium interest factor as a function of the realized demand D. First, for $D \in [0, D_{\min}]$, we have $K = 0$. Thus, $r(D) = r_{\max}$,

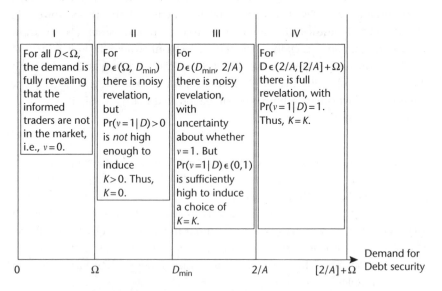

Figure 4. A schematic of financial market realizations of
security demand and inferences.

where $\theta \eta r_{max} + [1 - \theta] \times 0 = 1$. Thus,

$$r_{max} = \frac{1}{\theta \eta}. \tag{6}$$

Note that in deriving Equation (6), we have used the result that the financial market does not monitor borrowers. Next, for $D\epsilon(D_{min}, 2/A)$, we have $K = \overline{K}$ and $\Pr(v = 1|D) > \overline{K}/\eta\alpha$. Thus (see Equation (4)), $r(D) = \hat{r}(D)$, where $\theta\{\Pr(v = 1|D)[\eta\hat{r}(D) + [1 - \eta]\alpha] + [1 - \Pr(v = 1|D)][\eta\hat{r}(D)]\} = 1$, or

$$\hat{r}(D) = \frac{1 - \theta \Pr(v = 1|D)\,[1 - \eta]\,\alpha}{\theta \eta} \tag{7}$$

Finally, for $D \in \left[\frac{2}{A}, \frac{2}{A} + \Omega\right]$, we have $K = \hat{K}$ and $\Pr(v = 1|D) = 1$. Thus, $r(D) = r_{min}$, where

$$\theta\{\eta r_{min} + [1 - \eta]\,\alpha\} = 1, \quad \text{or}$$

$$r_{min} = \frac{1 - \theta\,[1 - \eta]\,\alpha}{\theta \eta}. \tag{8}$$

3.2 Definition of equilibrium in the financial market

A noisy rational expectations Nash equilibrium is:

(i) a measure of informed traders, Ω^*, such that the expected profit of each informed trader is zero (and the first derivative of this expected profit with respect to Ω is negative at Ω^*) when each informed trader takes as given the equilibrium strategies of the other potentially informed traders and the liquidity traders, and all other participants, including banks and borrowing firms, but assumes that the impact of his own trade on the price is negligible;

(ii) an aggregate security demand from informed and uninformed liquidity traders equal to
$$D^*(v, \ell) = \Omega^* d_I(v) + \ell;$$

(iii) a market-clearing interest factor $r(D)$, which is determined by the market maker in such a way that the supply and demand for the debt security are equated, and the expected net gain to the a priori uninformed market maker is zero, conditional on the information contained in the order flow; and

(iv) an investment choice K by each borrowing firm that it conditional on the information contained in the demand for its debt security and is made to maximize the firm's net expected profit, taking as given the equilibrium strategies of all other participants.

It is intuitive that the equilibrium expected profit of each informed trader is zero [see also Boot and Thakor (1993a)]. This would be sufficient if we could guarantee that the expected profit of an informed trader was monotonically decreasing in Ω. However, this is not necessarily true here because an increase in Ω exerts two opposing influences on the expected profit of the informed. On the one hand, we have the usual effect that an increase in Ω makes the equilibrium price reflect more of the information possessed by the informed and hence reduces their expected profit. But on the other hand, the increased price informativeness also makes it more likely that the borrower will choose $K = \overline{K}$ when the informed are in the market. This increases the expected profit of the informed as Ω increases. Hence, for an Ω to qualify as the equilibrium measure of informed, it must also be true that, taking both these effects into account, a small increase in Ω reduces the expected profit of an informed trader below zero.

Note that our modeling of markets and institutions is symmetric from the standpoint of competitive structure. Each bank's expected profit is zero in equilibrium, and each informed trader earns a zero expected profit in equilibrium, net of the information acquisition cost.

4. Further Analysis

4.1 Derivation of $D_{\min}$

We wish to ensure that $D_{\min}$ is in the interior of its feasible range. By Bayes's rule we know that

$$
\begin{aligned}
\Pr(v = 1|D) &= \frac{f(D - \Omega)\gamma}{f(D - \Omega)\gamma + f(D)[1 - \gamma]} \\
&= \frac{\gamma[A - B\{D - \Omega\}]}{\gamma[A - B\{D - \Omega\}] + [1 - \gamma][A - BD]},
\end{aligned} \tag{9}
$$

when $B \equiv A^2/2$. Note that $\partial \Pr(v = 1|D)/\partial D > 0$. We now substitute the above expression in Equation (4). Writing $S \equiv \overline{K}/\eta\alpha$ yields (note that $S > \gamma$)

$$
D^*_{\min} \equiv D^*_{\min}(\Omega) = \frac{A}{B} - \frac{[1 - S]\gamma\Omega}{[S - \gamma]}. \tag{10}
$$

The solution for $D^*_{\min}$ stated in Equation (10) exists if and only if $D_{\min} \geq \Omega$. Otherwise $D_{\min} = \Omega$, and interval II in Figure 4 vanishes. Thus, the desired cutoff demand level, $D_{\min}$, is

$$
D_{\min} = \Omega \vee D^*_{\min}, \tag{11}
$$

where $\vee$ is the max operator. Thus, the minimum total demand for the security that will induce the borrower to invest is $D^*_{\min}$ (the value of demand such that the expected payoff enhancement to the borrower exactly equals $\overline{K}$, the investment in payoff enhancement) unless $D^*_{\min}$ is less than Ω, the measure of informed agents. In this case, the minimum total demand to induce an investment of $\overline{K}$ must be Ω, since any $D < \Omega$ leads to $\Pr(v = 1|D) = 0$.

4.2 Determination of equilibrium measure of informed traders

If we assume that $D_{\min} = D^*_{\min}$ (see Equation (11)), then the expected profits of the informed, for a given Ω, can be expressed as:

$$V = -M + \theta \eta \gamma \int_{D_{\min} - \Omega}^{[2/A] - \Omega} \{\hat{r}(\Omega + \ell) - r_{\min}\} f(\ell) \, d\ell, \tag{12}$$

where we have $D = \Omega + \ell$ in the range over which the integration in Equation (12) is performed. The limits of the integration arise from the fact that it is only when D goes from $D_{\min}$ to $2/A$ that the borrower chooses the value-enhancing investment $\overline{K}$ and revelation is noisy (so that the informed can profit). In this range, the informed are in the market (i.e. they know that $v = 1$) and the total demand D is sufficiently revealing so that $r_{\min}$ is the break-even interest factor on the firm's bond. What the firm is being charged is $\hat{r}(\Omega + \ell)$, which is the equilibrium interest factor determined in the financial market. The informed profit because $\hat{r}(\Omega + \ell) > r_{\min}$. We now have the following result.

PROPOSITION 2. *The lowest value of Ω such that the expected profit of each informed trader is zero is given by*

$$\Omega_1 = \sqrt{M/X}, \tag{13}$$

where $X \equiv \theta \gamma \alpha [1 - \eta][1 - \gamma]\{A^2 \gamma \Gamma_1 [1 - \gamma + \gamma \Gamma_1] + \dfrac{A^2 \gamma (1 - \gamma)}{2} \ln(\Gamma_2)\}$

$$\Gamma_1 \equiv \frac{[1 - \{\overline{K}/\eta\alpha\}]}{[\{\overline{K}/\eta\alpha\} - \gamma]}$$

$$\Gamma_2 \equiv \frac{[\{K/\eta\alpha\} - \gamma]}{[1 - \gamma]}.$$

Moreover, $\partial V / \partial \Omega > 0$ at $\Omega = \Omega_1$.

According to the definition of the equilibrium, Ω^* has to be such that each informed trader earns an expected profit of zero. Ω_1 satisfies this requirement. However, because $\partial V / \partial \Omega_1 > 0$, it must be the case that Ω_1 is not the equilibrium measure of informed traders. At $\Omega = \Omega_1$, the increased informativeness of prices due to the presence of more informed traders increases the expected profit of each informed trader. For an equilibrium to exist, the function V must slope down at some point and become zero again, as shown in Figure 5. That is, we have multiple solutions in Ω to the equation $V(\Omega) = 0$, and Ω^* is the larger of

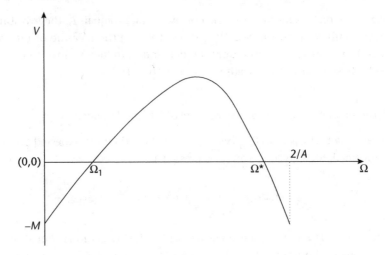

Figure 5. A graph of the expected profit of an informed trader as a function of the measure of informed traders.

the two Ωs satisfying this equation. This situation arises here because, unlike the usual setting, informed traders here both compete with and complement each other.

If $\epsilon > 0$, then it is transparent that the larger of the two Ωs satisfying $V(\Omega) = 0$ is the unique equilibrium, assuming that $\Omega > 0$.[13] This is because at $\Omega = \Omega_1$, an additional individual trader can make a positive expected profit from becoming informed since $\partial V(\Omega)/\partial\Omega/|_{\Omega=\Omega_1} > 0$, that is, $V(\Omega_1 + \epsilon) > 0$ for $\epsilon > 0$. Thus, Ω_1 cannot be an equilibrium with traders of arbitrarily small but positive measure. It is only at the limit itself, when $\epsilon = 0$, that we have multiple equilibria—both values of Ω for which $V(\Omega) = 0$ are possible equilibria under a somewhat less restrictive definition of equilibrium.[14] The reason why Ω_1 is an equilibrium in this case is that no additional trader would individually decide to enter the market when $\Omega = \Omega_1$ since his zero measure fails to increase Ω and this keeps V at zero. Because we view this economy as only the limiting case of an economy with small but positive measure agents, we will henceforth focus only on the larger of the two Ωs for which $V(\Omega) = 0$.

We have assumed thus far that $D_{\min} = D^*_{\min}$, and with this we obtain a solution Ω_1 to $V(\Omega) = 0$ such that $\partial V/\partial\Omega > 0$ at $\Omega = \Omega_1$. As will be shown, increasing Ω above Ω_1 to Ω^* will switch $D_{\min}$ in Equation (11) to $D_{\min} = \Omega^*$. Like

---

[13] If the equilibrium $\Omega > 0$, then it must be at least as great as Ω_1 because $V(\Omega) < 0 \; \forall \; \Omega < \Omega_1$. Note that $\Omega = 0$ is always a candidate for equilibrium; it does not pay any agent of small measure ($\epsilon < \Omega_1$) to become informed if $\Omega = 0$.

[14] Strictly speaking, according to our definition of equilibrium, Ω_1 is not an equilibrium. But our discussion here serves to clarify the reason why in our equilibrium definition we imposed the restriction $\partial V/\partial\Omega < 0$ on the equilibrium Ω. We thank Neil Wallace for discussing this with us.

Equation (12), the expected profit to the informed can now be written as[15]

$$V = -M + \theta\eta\gamma \int_0^{[2/A]-\Omega} \{\hat{r}(\Omega + \ell) - r_{min}\}f(\ell)\,d\ell. \qquad (14)$$

We now have our next result.

PROPOSITION 3. *There is a set of exogenous parameter values for which the equilibrium measure of informed traders, Ω^*, is the solution to*

$$V(\Omega^*) = -M + \theta\gamma\alpha[1 - \eta][1 - \gamma]\{1 - A\gamma\Omega^* + [\Omega^* + (\Omega^*)^2 J(\Omega^*)]\} = 0, \qquad (15)$$

where

$$J(\Omega^*) \equiv \frac{A^2\gamma}{2} - \frac{A^2}{4} + \frac{A^2\gamma\,[1-\gamma]}{2}\left\{\ell n\frac{A\Omega^*\gamma/2}{1 - [A\Omega^*(1-\gamma/2])}\right\}.$$

Moreover, $D^*_{min}(\Omega) < \Omega^*$ at $\Omega = \Omega^*$, so that $D_{min} = \Omega^*$ (see Equation (11)).

We can now examine some interesting properties of the financial market equilibrium.

PROPOSITION 4. *The equilibrium measure of informed traders is positive only if, for a given M, θ is sufficiently high, or, for a given θ, M is sufficiently low.*

This proposition is intuitive. When the moral hazard problem is severe (the observable θ is low), a potentially informed trader anticipates that even her superior information about v does not reduce the high probability that she will invest in a firm that chooses a bad project and imposes a loss on her. This reduces her incentive to become informed at a cost. If θ is sufficiently low, no potentially informed trader may choose to acquire costly information. Similarly, for a given θ, an increase in M reduces the expected profit of an informed trader, and a sufficiently high M will cause a breakdown of the market for information. This also highlights another interesting result, which is stated below.

PROPOSITION 5. *The expected profit of an informed trader is always maximized at some $\Omega > 0$.*

In Boot and Thakor (1993a), for example, the expected profit of an informed trader is always maximized at $\Omega = 0$, that is, when there are no other informed traders in the market. This is never true here since a borrower with a good project always eschews its investment in project improvement if it knows there is nothing to be learned from market prices. Given this, it does not pay for any investor

---

[15] In Figure 5, Equation (12), and Equation (14) we have implicitly assumed that $\Omega < 2/A$. It is easy to see why this holds. Note that if $\Omega \geq 2/A$, where $2/A$ is the maximum realization of liquidity demand, then there are only two possibilities: (i) $D < 2/A$, in which case the market maker infers that the probability is 1 that the informed traders are not in the market, and (ii) $D \geq 2/A$, in which case the market maker infers that the probability is 1 that the informed traders are in the market. In both cases, prices are fully revealing and the informed can earn no profit on their information. Hence, $\Omega \geq 2/A$ cannot be the equilibrium measure of informed traders.

to become informed. Thus, as Figure 5 shows, an informed trader earns a higher expected profit when there is a positive measure of informed traders in the market and the borrower views the market price as an information communicator. This means that if the V function were to have a maximum value that was negative,[16] then no one will choose to become informed in equilibrium (i.e. the equilibrium $\Omega = 0$). Another way of saying this is that an investor will become informed only if she believes there will be a sufficiently large number of others who will also choose to become informed.

4.3 The borrower's choice of financing source

The borrower's expected utility is the expected return net of its borrowing cost. If a borrower chooses the financial market, its borrowing cost depends on the anticipated informativeness of the market price of its debt. We have shown that the equilibrium measure of informed traders is Ω^* and that $D_{\min} = \Omega^*$ is the appropriate aggregate demand cutoff [see Equation (11)] and Proposition 3]. Therefore, whenever the informed discover $v = 1$ and are in the market, the borrower will find that $D \geq D_{\min}$, and hence will choose $K = \overline{K}$. But it is possible that the borrower will choose $\overline{K}$ even when the informed have discovered $v = 0$ and do not bid for the firm's debt since $\ell \geq D_{\min}$ is possible.

The expected return of the borrower from financial market borrowing is given by

$$E(R^F) = \theta\{\gamma E(R^F|v = 1) + [1 - \gamma]E(R^F|v = 0)\} + [1 - \theta]N, \tag{16}$$

where $E(R^F)$ is the unconditional expected return and $E(R^F|v)$ is the expected return conditional on the realization of v. To understand Equation (16), recall that the borrower invests in the good project with financial market funding only if it is locked into that project (this happens with probability θ), and invests in the bad project whenever it has a choice (this happens with probability $1 - \theta$). Note that

$$E(R^F|v = 1) = \int_0^{[2/A] - \Omega^*} \{\eta[Y + \alpha - \hat{r}^*(D = \ell + \Omega^*)] - \overline{K}\}f(\ell)\,d\ell$$

$$+ \int_{[2/A] - \Omega^*}^{2/A} \{\eta[Y + \alpha - r_{\min}] - \overline{K}\}f(\ell)\,d\ell \tag{17}$$

and

$$E(R^F|v = 0) = \int_0^{\Omega^*} \{\eta[Y - r_{\max}]\}f(\ell)\,d\ell + \int_{\Omega^*}^{2/A} \{\eta[Y - \hat{r}^*(D = \ell)] - \overline{K}\}f(\ell)\,d\ell, \tag{18}$$

---

[16] At $\Omega = 0$, it is always the case that $V < 0$.

where
$$\hat{r}^*(\ell) = \frac{1 - \theta \Pr(v = 1|D)[1 - \eta]\alpha}{\theta \eta} \tag{19}$$

and
$$\Pr(v = 1|D) = \frac{\gamma\{A - B[D - \Omega^*]\}}{\gamma\{A - B[D - \Omega^*]\} + [1 - \gamma]\{A - BD\}}. \tag{20}$$

Next, we turn to bank financing. The cost of bank borrowing is given by Equation (3). Thus, the expected return for the borrower is given by

$$E(R^B) = \eta Y - E(r_B) = \eta Y - 1 - \Lambda^* M, \tag{21}$$

since interbank competition ensures that $E(r_B) = 1 + \Lambda^* M$. The borrower's choice of financing source is determined by comparing $E(R^F)$ and $E(R^B)$. This gives us the following result.

PROPOSITION 6. *There exists a cutoff value of θ, say $\hat{\theta}$ (assumed to be in the interior of $[\underline{\theta}, \overline{\theta}]$), such that there is a Nash equilibrium in which borrowers with observable $\theta \leq \hat{\theta}$ choose bank financing and borrowers with observable $\theta > \hat{\theta}$ choose financial market financing. Moreover, $\hat{\theta}$ is increasing in M.*

Figure 6 shows how the net return for a borrower changes as a function of its observable quality θ. It is intuitive that borrowers with lower observable quality prefer bank financing. Banks specialize in attenuating asset-substitution moral hazard, so the borrower does not suffer a loss in utility with bank financing as this problem worsens. That is, the borrower's expected return with bank financing is invariant to θ. On the other hand, the benefit of financial market financing to the borrower is increasing in θ. The reasons are twofold. First, the expected profit of an informed trader is increasing in θ [see Equation (14)], so that the higher the θ, the larger is the equilibrium measure of the set of informed traders for the debt security sold by the borrower. This means that the equilibrium interest factor reflects more of the information possessed by the informed traders and is consequently lower on average. Second, the "moral hazard premium" paid by borrowers in the financial market is decreasing in θ.

Numerical simulations of the model (details available upon request) illustrate that $\hat{\theta}$ increases as M increases. The intuition is clear. An increase in M reduces the expected profit of an informed trader ceteris paribus. This causes a reduction in Ω^*, leading to a decline in the value of financial market financing for the borrower. If the increase in M refers only to an increase in the information acquisition cost, but not in the monitoring cost, then it is transparent that bank financing will become more attractive, leading to a larger set of observable quality levels choosing bank financing. What our numerical analysis shows is that bank financing becomes more attractive with an increase in M even when this increase applies equally to the costs of information acquisition and monitoring.

We next consider the implication of permitting only noisy monitoring by the bank. Suppose that, conditional on being in the state in which the borrower has

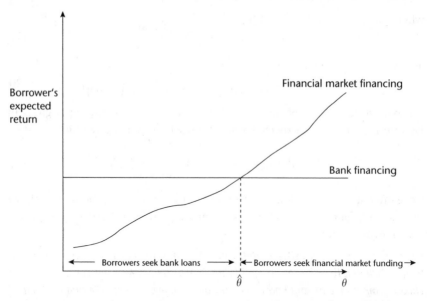

Figure 6. A graph of the expected returns of a borrower as a function of the borrower's observable quality. Borrowers with observable qualities below threshold $\hat{\theta}$ choose bank financing and those with observable qualities above threshold $\hat{\theta}$ choose financial market financing.

a choice of project, the bank can enforce the choice of good project only with probability $\xi \in (0, 1)$. We then have the following result.

PROPOSITION 7. *If the bank can prevent the choice of the bad project only with probability $\xi \in (0, 1)$, there exists a θ^0 (assumed to be in the interior of $[\underline{\theta}, \overline{\theta}]$) such that there is a Nash equilibrium in which borrowers with observable $\theta \leq \theta^0$ prefer bank financing and borrowers with observable $\theta > \theta^0$ prefer financial market financing. Moreover, the value of bank financing to the borrower is increasing in θ, and $\theta^0 < \hat{\theta}$.*

Thus, we see that while noise in the monitoring technology reduces the value of bank financing to the borrower ceteris paribus ($\theta^0 < \hat{\theta}$), we still encounter the earlier result that borrowers with relatively high θs access the financial market and borrowers with relatively low θs approach banks.[17] One noteworthy difference that noisy monitoring makes is that it causes the borrower's net expected payoff with bank financing to be increasing in θ, rather than being invariant to θ. The intuition is that the higher the θ, the lower is the probability that the noise in its monitoring technology will obstruct the bank's ability to deter selection of the bad project, and hence the lower is the bank's loan interest factor. There is a fairly large literature on the borrower's choice of financing source that we do not discuss here. [For example, Diamond (1991); Berlin and Mester (1992);

---

[17] Of course, the limit of $\xi \to 0$ involves the financial market dominating banks for all θ.

Hirshleifer and Suh (1992); Rajan (1992); Wilson (1994); and Thakor and Wilson (1995). See Bhattacharya and Thakor (1993) for a review.] Unlike that literature, we endogenize banks and the financial market. Moreover, our result here is novel in that it links the borrower's choice to its observable quality in a moral hazard setting and predicates this link on the cost of information acquisition in the financial market.

5. Model Robustness and Extensions

In this section we indicate how our model could be generalized along some important dimensions: the possibility of eliminating noise traders, the use of equity rather than debt in the financial market, information aggregation involving traders with information, the simultaneous use of bank and financial market funding, and the impact of institutional sellers. Our conclusion is that the analysis can be extended in all of these directions without qualitatively altering its results.

5.1 *Elimination of noise traders and introduction of equity*

The liquidity traders in our model are "noise" traders in the sense that they make expected losses from trading. Indeed, their losses enable the informed traders to earn the profits that justify their investment in information. While this is a standard assumption in market microstructure models, one may find the presence of noise traders in our analysis somewhat awkward. In particular, why wouldn't these traders invest exclusively in securities that are immune to adverse selection concerns? Why don't they deal with banks rather than the financial market?

Clearly, in any model in which agents potentially acquire private information at a cost, there must be sufficient noise in equilibrium prices to make it privately optimal for agents to become informed. However, it is unnecessary for the agents who provide the noise to sustain trading losses. We could assume instead that it is the issuing firm that loses through the systematic underpricing of its security. The liquidity traders could then break even. This would be in the spirit of Rock's (1986) IPO underpricing model. We will show shortly that this approach is consistent with our model.

Consider now the use of debt contracts in our analysis. From an information acquisition standpoint, equity is clearly better than debt to examine in a financial market context. We will also show that using equity instead of debt does not change our conclusions. To deal with this and the liquidity traders issue, we consider a simplified version of our model, an example.

Example 1: Data: Suppose $\theta = 1, \gamma = 0.4$, and $\eta = 1$. Let S represent the equity ownership share the firm must surrender to outside shareholders to raise the $1 investment it needs. There are uninformed discretionary traders who can choose to become informed above v at a cost of $M = 0.24\alpha[Y + 0.5\alpha]^{-1}$, and there are liquidity traders whose demand equals $\ell \in \{0, 1/2\}$, with $\Pr(\ell = 0) = 0.6$. and $\Pr(\ell = 1/2) = 0.4$. The prior probability distribution of v is $\Pr(v = 1) = 0.4$, and $\Pr(v = 0) = 0.6$. Assume that $\alpha > 2\overline{K}$ and $\gamma\alpha < \overline{K}$, and that $\overline{K}$ is an unobserved private investment by the firm.

Analysis: We conjecture that $\Omega = 1/2$. Informed traders will submit a purchase order only when $v = 1$. Note that $\alpha > 2\overline{K}$ ensure that the firm invests $\overline{K}$ whenever $D \geq 1/2$. Since the available supply of equity for outsiders to buy is $1, there are only three relevant states:

  (i) $v = 1$ and $\ell = 1/2$, so that the total demand from the liquidity traders and informed traders is $1. In this case $\Pr(v = 1|D = 1) = 1$, and the uninformed discretionary traders buy 0.

  (ii) $v = 1$ and $\ell = 0$ or $v = 0$ and $\ell = 1/2$, so that the total demand D from liquidity traders and informed traders is $1/2. The UDTs buy $1/2 worth of equity. Using Bayes's rule, the posterior probability assessment that the firm has that the informed traders have observed $v = 1$ can be determined as

$$\Pr(v = 1|D = 1/2)$$
$$= \frac{\Pr(D = 1/2|v = 1)\Pr(v = 1)}{\Pr(D = 1/2|v = 1)\Pr(v = 1) + \Pr(D = 1/2|v = 0)\Pr(v = 0)}$$
$$= \frac{0.24}{0.48} = \frac{1}{2}. \tag{22}$$

  (iii) $v = 0$ and $\ell = 0$, so that the total demand D from liquidity traders and informed traders equals $0, and $\Pr(v = 1|D = 0) = 0$. The uninformed discretionary traders buy $1 of equity.

Table 1 summarizes the ownership fractions outsiders obtain in the three different states. It can be verified that these ownership fractions are such that

  (i) the uninformed discretionary traders earn zero expected profit;
  (ii) the liquidity traders earn zero expected profit;
  (iii) the informed traders earn positive expected profits on their trades, but zero expected profits when their information production costs M are taken into account;
  (iv) the firm prefers to underprice $D = 1$;
  (v) $\Omega = 1/2$ in equilibrium.

A proof of this is available upon request. Thus, our analysis is robust with respect to using equity instead of debt and ensuring that liquidity traders break even on average.

Table 1. Outside Investor's Ownership Fractions for Different Loan Demand Realizations

Description	Realized total demand		
	$D = \$1$	$D = \$1/2$	$D = \$0$
Inference of market maker	$v = 1$ and $\ell = 1/2$	$v = 0$ and $\ell = 1/2$ or $v = 1$ and $\ell = 0$	$v = 0$ and $\ell = 0$
$S_{\text{Fairly Priced}}(D)$	$[Y + \alpha]^{-1}$	$[Y + 0.5\alpha]^{-1}$	Y^{-1}
$S_{\text{Underpricing}}(D)$	$[Y + 1.25\alpha]\{[Y = 0.5\alpha]$ $\times [Y + \alpha]\}^{-1} > [Y + \alpha]^{-1}$	$[Y + 0.5\alpha]^{-1}$	Y^{-1}

5.2 Information aggregation

Although we have assumed in our analysis that all informed traders obtain the same information, it is clear that information aggregation is an important element of the intuition behind our story. Without aggregation of heterogeneous signals in the financial market, we must rely solely on the inability of banks to internalize any benefits from information acquisition in order to obtain the sharp dichotomy of functions across banks and the financial market that is described in Proposition 1. Moreover, one might wonder why entrepreneurs can't directly acquire information about v, a single piece of information. That is, in order to simplify, our analysis ignores an important advantage of financial markets, namely to aggregate payoff-relevant information when it is widely dispersed in the economy and difficult to purchase directly.

In what follows, we provide a simple extension of our model that illustrates how financial markets may aggregate diverse information and how the desirability for such aggregation can further diminish the role of banks as pure information sellers.

Example 2: Data: Suppose $\theta = 1, \gamma = 0.25$, and $\eta = 1$. There are two distinct signals, $x \in \{0, 1\}$ and $y \in \{0, 1\}$, that are conditionally uncorrelated, that provide information about v. In particular,

$$\Pr(x = 0) = \Pr(y = 0) = 0.5;$$

$$\Pr(v = 1) = 0.25, \Pr(v = 1|x = 1) = \Pr(v = 1|y = 1) = 0.5;$$

$$\Pr(v = 1|x = 1, y = 1) = 1; \quad \text{and}$$

$$\Pr(v = 1|x = 1, y = 0) = \Pr(v = 1|x = 0, y = 1)$$
$$= \Pr(v = 1|x = 0, y = 0) = 0.$$

There are liquidity traders whose demand $\ell \in \{0, 1/2\}$, with $\Pr(\ell = 0) = \Pr(\ell = 1/2) = 0.5$. Let S represent the equity ownership share the firm must surrender to outside shareholders to raise the \$1 investment it needs. There are uninformed discretionary traders who can choose to become informed about either x or y, but not both, at a cost $M = 0.0625\alpha\,[Y + 0.5\alpha]^{-1}$.

Analysis: For simplicity, we will assume that the firm's equity is fairly priced and therefore the liquidity traders make losses on average. Let the measure of those who invest to learn x be Ω_x and the measure of those who invest to learn y be Ω_y. We conjecture that $\Omega_x = \Omega_y = \frac{1}{4}$, and that each group of informed traders will submit a purchase order only when the signal for that group takes a value of 1.

There are now five relevant states, each distinguished by a different realization of total demand from the liquidity traders, those who are informed about x and those who are informed about y. Let D represent the total demand from these three groups. As usual, the market maker cannot distinguish the individual components of total demand, the price of the equity is set at its expected value conditional on the information contained in D, and the uninformed discretionary traders purchase equity in the amount needed to clear the market. Thus, $D \in \left\{0, \frac{1}{4}, \frac{1}{2}, \frac{3}{4}, 1\right\}$. These five states arise as follows.

(i) $D = 0$: This arises only when $x = 0, y = 0$, and $\ell = 0$. The market maker unambiguously infers $v = 0$. The probability of this state is 0.125.

(ii) $D = 1/4$: This arises if $\ell = 0, x = 0, y = 1$ or $\ell = 0, x = 1, y = 0$. The market maker unambiguously infers $v = 0$. The probability of this state is 0.25.

(iii) $D = 1/2$: This arises if $x = 1, y = 1, \ell = 0$ or $x = 0, y = 0, \ell = 1/2$. In this state, v could be either 0 or 1. The probability of this state is 0.25.

(iv) $D = 3/4$: This arises if $x = 1, y = 1, \ell = 1/2$ or $x = 0, y = 1, \ell = 1/2$. The market maker unambiguously infers that $v = 0$. The probability of this state is 0.25.

(v) $D = 1$: This arises only if $x = 1, y = 1, \ell = 1/2$. The market maker unambiguously infers $v = 1$. The probability of this state is 0.125.

In states (i), (ii), and (iv), $S(D) = 1/Y$. In state (iii), $S(D) = [Y + 0.5\alpha]^{-1}$. In state (v), $S(D) = [Y + \alpha]^{-1}$. It is now straightforward to verify that the expected profit of each group of informed traders, per unit measure of informed traders, is exactly equal to $0.0625\alpha\,[Y + 0.5\alpha]^{-1}$, which is M. This verifies our conjecture that $\Omega_x = \Omega_y = 1/4$.

5.3 Direct information elicitation mechanisms

A natural question that arises in the context of our analysis is why it is not possible to directly elicit the private information possessed by informed traders rather than have it indirectly revealed (noisily) through the equilibrium market price. In particular, one could think of informed traders coalescing to form a bank and selling information directly to the firm.

While this seems reasonable, it is plagued by the potential lack of credibility of the information that is communicated. The problem exists at two levels: within the bank, and between the bank and the firm. Consider the more important intrabank problem first. When there are multiple agents engaged in information production, a free-rider problem arises with unobservable individual inputs in information production since each agent bears the fall cost of his input and only shares in the collective output. Ramakrishnan and Thakor (1984) show that this problem can completely vitiate any risk-sharing gains from coalescing; they therefore examine the benefit of intermediation (coalition formation) when individual agents can costlessly monitor each other's inputs.

Their model has n agents in the intermediary, each producing information about a distinct firm, so that the free-rider problem arises not from information aggregation but from each agent's payoff being a prorata share of the pooled payoff that represents the intermediary's compensation. Without costless internal monitoring, the agents within the intermediary cannot overcome their own free-riding incentives.

Information aggregation exacerbates this problem. This can be seen most readily within the context of Example 2, as well as more generally. In the context of the example, suppose that the bank consists of two groups of informed agents, one group specializing in x and the other in y. Each group provides $0.5 to the bank to enable it to lend $1 to the firm. For simplicity, assume that there are no intragroup incentive problems and that members of each group can function as a single entity; we make this assumption to focus on intergroup incentive problems. The bank is competitive and is paid a fee that compensates it for the information acquisition costs of the two groups. Let the measure of each group be 1, so that each group is paid M for its information acquisition.

Consider now the marginal benefit of becoming informed for each group within the bank, assuming that the bank always truthfully reports the information it receives from the two groups to the firm and that it gives each group M plus its prorata share of the output accruing to the bank under its equity contract with the firm. Now, if a particular group produces information, its expected profit (assuming that the other group will also produce information) is zero, since the bank is competitively compensated, and in turn it seeks to just satisfy each group's reservation constraint.

On the other hand, if a particular group decides to always report 0 without producing information, then its expected profit (regardless of what the other group does) is M, since the firm does not make the value-enhancing decision. Similarly, if the group (say the x group) unconditionally reports a signal value of 1, its expected profit (assuming that the other group produces information and truthfully (reports) can be shown to be less than M, since now this group bears some of the cost associated with the firm making a value-enhancing decision when it should not.

Thus, each group's dominant strategy is to report 0 without producing information. In particular, it is not a Nash equilibrium for each group to invest in information acquisition, given the interbank contracting technology of giving each group M plus its prorata share of the output accruing to the bank under its equity contract with the firm. Although mechanisms may be found to restore incentive compatibility in information acquisition within the bank, these are unlikely to be costless.

One such costly mechanism would be for the firm to offer the bank a higher expected payoff when the output is $Y + \alpha$ than when it is Y; this would reduce each group's incentive to unconditionally report 0. If the firm's net payoff enhancement is sufficiently large relative to M, then perhaps each group within the bank can be "bribed" to report truthfully. What is interesting is that the ability of such a mechanism to restore incentive compatibility is weakened as we increase the number of signals that are being aggregated. To see this, suppose there are three signals that are being aggregated. To see this, suppose there are three signals, x, y, and z in Example 2, with $\Pr(v = 1|x = 1, \, y = 1, \, z = 0 \text{ or } 1) = \Pr(v = 1|x = 0 \text{ or } 1, \, y = 1, \, z = 1) = \Pr(v = 1|x = 1, \, y = 0 \text{ or } 1, \, z = 1) = 1$ and $\Pr(v = 1|0 \text{ for any two or more of } x, \, y, \text{ and } z) = 0$. Now, incentive compatibility will be more difficult to achieve because the strategy of unconditionally reporting 0 has become less costly to each group, conditional on the other two groups producing information and reporting truthfully. More generally, the intuition is that as we increase the number of signals being aggregated, each group's signal becomes less pivotal in its impact on the group's share of the output. Thus, misreporting incentives are strengthened with greater aggregation.

The second problem we alluded to earlier was between the bank and the firm. Even apart from the groups within the bank free riding on each other's inputs, the bank's incentive to generate costly and reliable information and truthfully report it may be weak. Firms may attempt to deal with this by appealing to the revelation principle and designing incentive contracts that link the bank's fees to performance in a way that achieves incentive compatibility. For example, the firm could sell the bank a call option with its payoff on the exercise date dependent on the realization of v; the exercise of this option would reveal information about v. However, there are three difficulties with such mechanisms. First, the firm would need to ensure that the option is not resold by the bank, or else the vexing problem of dealing with the coalitional incentive compatibility constraints associated with traded contracts arises.[18] Second, if there are multiple signals that the bank reports to the firm for aggregation, then applying the revelation principle becomes particularly complex as multiple nontraded options must

---

[18] See Jacklin (1987) for an analysis of this in the context of traded deposit claims.

be offered. Third, suppose one interprets "noise" as agents/banks that mistakenly think they can acquire information, that is, these intermediaries mistakenly buy and exercise options that are valuable if and only if information is acquired. In such a world, the market solution—which requires only the knowledge of the probability distribution of noise—is superior to revelation schemes that require knowledge of the agent type, that is, whether the signal sender in the scheme can indeed acquire the relevant signal. This problem too is exacerbated as one increases the number of signals being aggregated.

Thus the very reason that financial markets have a role for aggregating heterogeneous information puts financial intermediaries at a disadvantage in performing the same task.

Is our theory then at odds with the existence of institutions that sell information?[19] While it is true that bond rating agencies and investment advisory firms sell information about corporations, the credibility of such information sellers and consequently the demand for their services depends on their reputation in possessing the requisite information-processing skills and providing reliable information. To the extent that this reputational mechanism is not perfect, institutional information sales will at best substitute only partially for the direct acquisition of information about v by an informed trader. Thus, the presence of institutional information sellers could diminish the marginal profit from becoming informed, but will not eliminate it entirely. In particular, the preceding analysis suggests that institutional information sellers are likely to be viable only when relatively few pieces of information must be aggregated to provide a relevant set of information, whereas market-based information dissemination is likely to predominate when numerous pieces of information must be aggregated.

5.4 *Simultaneous access to bank loans and financial market funding*

While in our formulation a firm either chooses bank financing or chooses to fund itself in the financial market, we could envision firms lying along a continuum with sole bank or financial market funding as the polar extremes. This generalized version would allow firms to optimally balance the benefits of bank monitoring and financial market information aggregation. Such "mixed" financing would be useful in a variety of contexts. For example, Diamond (1993) shows that a mix of private and public debt can improve investment efficiency.

If asset-substitution moral hazard is severe (low θ), a firm is likely to choose considerable bank funding to induce sufficient monitoring. The relatively small amount of funding raised in the financial market would provide some information aggregation benefits, although these would not be large because the measure

---

[19] Ramakrishnan and Thakor (1984), Millon and Thakor (1985), Allen (1990), Kane and Marks (1990), and Fishman and Hagerty (1995) are examples of articles that rationalize institutions that sell financial information.

of informed traders (Ω) would be rather small in response to the low funding level. A high-θ borrower is likely to borrow considerably more in the financial market since its low monitoring demand necessitates only a small amount of bank funding to mitigate asset-substitution moral hazard. Thus, this firm can better exploit the information aggregation benefits of financial markets.

This formulation generalizes our results but does not alter them qualitatively.

6. Implications for Financial System Architecture

Our discussion in this section, which focuses on just a subset of the issues in financial system architecture, is organized in four parts. First, we examine the likely starting point for a "free-market" financial system. That is, if an economy is making a transition from being centrally planned to being in a free-market mode, what is likely to be the initial configuration of its financial system? Second, we examine the potential impact of financial innovation on borrowers' financing source choices and on real investment decisions. Third, we examine the implications of large ("block") financial market traders who are nonatomistic. Finally, we discuss what the analysis suggests for overall financial system design.

6.1 *The starting point of a new financial system*

In a new financial system—one previously managed by a central planner—the historical absence of profit-motivated banks or financial market traders implies possibly severe informational frictions pertaining to potential borrowers. In particular, asset-substitution moral hazard is likely to be rampant. Consequently, borrowers will have lower observable qualities (θs) on average. This enhances the value of bank financing for two reasons. First, borrowers face a large "moral hazard premium" in the financial market. Second, lower θs reduce the value of the informed traders' information, thereby weakening information acquisition incentives. Moreover, the expected lack of sophistication of financial market traders in such an economy connotes a higher cost to them of acquiring relevant borrower-specific information (i.e. M is higher). This leads to a lower Ω^* at the outset than at the later stages of development of a financial market. Both these effects—lower Ω^* and higher M—generate a relatively high $\hat{\theta}$. Consequently, bank financing dominates a financial system during its infancy.

As the financial system evolves, successful borrowers will develop credit reputations that will ameliorate moral hazard and improve the average θ of the borrower pool [Diamond (1991)]. More borrowers will migrate to the financial market and traders will become more familiar with firms, leading to a lower M and a higher Ω^*. Thus, even a financial system that begins as a bank-dominated system will evolve to a system in which banks lose market share to the financial market.

6.2 *Financial market sophistication*

Greater sophistication in a financial market is often manifested in lower friction in informational flows. There are many ways in which such lower friction is achieved. One is through security design innovations that stimulate greater informed trading and improve liquidity [Back (1993) and Boot and Thakor (1993a)].[20] Another is through improved information transmission mechanisms that permit investors to acquire information at a lower cost. An example is the emergence of information-gathering agencies (e.g. Dun and Bradstreet) that provide lower-cost access to information. We shall focus on this latter characterization of financial market sophistication and assume that it lowers the cost of learning about v. The effect of a lower information acquisition cost is to increase Ω^*, ceteris paribus. And an increase in Ω^* reduces the borrower's expected cost of funding in the capital market. Nothing changes for bank financing as long as the monitoring cost remains unchanged. Hence, $\hat{\theta}$ decreases and increased financial sophistication of this type results in banks losing market share to the capital market. This is consistent with recent financial history—the greatest shift in corporate borrowing from banks to the capital market has occured in the United States, which has also led the world in financial market sophistication and efficiency. For a formal analysis of these issues, see Boot and Thakor (1996, forthcoming).

6.3 *Large financial market traders*

We have assumed that each financial market trader is atomistic. But what if individual traders were allowed to a mass "block" holdings of bonds? This would have two potentially important effects. First, if a trader who acquired information about v were to be endowed with sufficient investible wealth to submit a demand with positive measure, then such a large demand would noiselessly reveal the trader's superior information to the market maker and lead to a perfectly revealing price. To avoid the Grossman and Stiglitz (1980) paradox, we could provide the informed trader an opportunity to break up her trade into many smaller units, each of which would mimic the trade of atomistic trader. Alternatively, we could permit liquidity traders to also submit block orders. Either case would change the financial market equilibrium, but is unlikely to alter out principal conclusions.

[20] A somewhat more subtle way in which security design can resolve informational problems in a dynamic setting is through contractual discretion that stimulates reputation development [see Boot, et al. (1993)].

More interesting, however, is the second effect. If monitoring agents were nonatomistic, an individual monitoring agent could be of measure Λ^*, which would trivially resolve the free-rider problem associated with capital market monitoring. Our model predicts that such larger traders would diminish the importance of banks and decrease $\hat{\theta}$. This is roughly consistent with the stylized facts in the United States in that the emergence of institutional investors (like CALPERS and TIAA-CREF) as active players in monitoring firms has coincided with a decline in banks' lending to corporations.

6.4 *Tentative thoughts on financial system design*

Our analysis predicts that an optimal financial system will configure itself skewed toward bank financing if borrowers have relatively poor credit reputations (a higher moral hazard propensity) and toward capital market financing if borrowers have relatively good credit reputations, but can improve real decisions based on the information conveyed by market prices. Moreover, capital market financing is more valuable for those borrowers who attach a high value to information regarding v.

Do these observations have anything to say about how a financial system will evolve if left to its own machinations? Our analysis provides some indications. In particular, our earlier observations on emerging financial systems suggest that the welfare relevance of financial markets should grow through time as the financial system develops. However, financial market growth will come at the expense of commercial banks. This implies that some institutional resistance from existing banks should be expected as financial markets grow in prominence. But unless the actions of banks are coordinated—in contrast to our assumption that competitive banks do not coordinate—it is unlikely that financial market growth can be retarded. Thus, it is possible that a critical factor in the development of the financial market is the fragmentation of the banking industry, which in turn may depend on the number of banks in the industry.

7. Conclusion

We have rationalized the coexistence of banks and financial markets based on assumptions about primitives—endowments, types of agents, and informational constraints. Banks arise as coalitions of agents who coordinate their actions to resolve asset-substitution moral hazard. The financial market arises to permit noncolluding agents to compete, and this facilitates the transmission of valuable information about market conditions with a concomitant impact on firm's real decisions. We find that borrowers who pose relatively onerous asset-substitution moral hazards prefer bank financing, and borrowers who pose less serious moral hazards go directly to the capital market. Moreover, increased financial market sophistication diminishes bank's market share.

The predictions of our theory match up with cross-sectional differences across industries. For example, our theory predicts that firms in industries. For example, our theory predicts that firms in industries with substantial state verification use financial markets, while firms in industries that require a lot of monitoring use banks. An example of this is the choice of venture capital versus financial market funding. Borrowers who have few tangible assets to offer as collateral pose particularly onerous moral hazards [see, e.g. Boot, Thakor and Udell (1991)] and require a lot of monitoring. We do find that such borrowers tend to seek financing from venture capitalists who specialize in monitoring. In the other hand, firms that rely on more complex technologies have more to gain from the feedback role of market prices and should prefer financial market funding. The evidence on cross-sectional financing patterns in the United States (e.g. the recent explosion of biotech and computer technology firms' IPOs) seems consistent with this. Allen (1993) comprehensively discusses the consistency of this aspect of our model with the cross-sectional and intertemporal evidence on global financing patterns. For example, Allen points out that stock market-based financial systems have been associated with nineteenth-century U.K., which was the first country to go through the Industrial Revolution, when managerial decision making ostensibly increased in complexity. Similarly, Mayer (1988) points out that between 1970 and 1985, companies in France, Germany, Japan, and the U.K. relied primarily on retained earnings and bank loans to finance investment, in contrast to U.S. firms that raised significant amounts in the bond markets. Allen (1993) suggests a possible explanation for this that is consistent with our model. He provides evidence that significantly more firms are covered by financial analysts in the United States than in these other countries, so that stock prices in U.S. financial markets are likely to reflect much more information of relevance to managers.

Recently, Carey (1995) provided empirical evidence that is supportive of our analysis. He found that informational asymmetries are not an important factor in bank loan contracting with large borrowers, but moral hazard is. He concludes from his evidence that bank loans are special primarily because of their moral hazard attenuation implications.

Our article has scratched only the surface of financial system design. There are other significant unresolved issues. Foremost is understanding how regulatory policies, aimed principally at banking scope, affect the financial system, particularly when one considers not only incentive problems between banks on the one hand and depositors and regulators on the other, but also between regulators and taxpayers [see Boot and Thakor (1993b) and Kane (1989, 1990)]. Such an exercise may point to potentially interesting multiperiod extensions of the analysis, creating a role for reputational rents and their interaction with regulation.

APPENDIX

Proof of Lemma 1. Suppose, counterfactually, that traders whose combined measure integrates to 1, including a strictly positive measure of traders each having invested M to learn about v, coalesce to form a bank that can lend \$1 to the same borrower. Suppose first that information communication is truthful. Then, once the borrower learns v, it will find it optimal to offer to pay the bank $\{\theta^{-1} - [1 - \eta]\alpha\}\{\eta\}^{-1} + t$ if $v = 1$ and $[1 + /\eta\theta] + t$ if $v = 0$, where t is an arbitrarily small positive scalar approaching zero. This will be a "take it or leave it" offer. At these interest factors, each bank makes an expected profit of t on the loan itself, thereby incurring a net expected loss because of its inability to recoup its information acquisition cost (M times the measure of informed traders in the bank). Of course, if information communication is not truthful, the borrower does not invest in $\overline{K}$. Thus, informed traders do not form a bank.

If these traders choose to trade independently in the capital market, however, they compete with each other. The presence of liquidity traders means that the equilibrium security price will not always fully reflect all of the informed trader's information. This noise in prices is sufficient to enable each informed trader to recoup M.   ∎

Proof of Lemma 2. Suppose, counterfactually, that the monitoring agents trade in the capital market. Since actions in the capital market are uncoordinated, we may view the measure of monitoring agents as being greater or less than Λ^*. We show below, however, that agents must believe that it is either 0 or Λ^*. If it is believed to be less than Λ^*, then it must be zero in a Nash equilibrium since each agent recognizes that her investment in monitoring is useless due to the assumption that any measure less than Λ^* leads to ineffective monitoring. If it is conjectured to be greater than Λ^*, then there is a free-rider problem in that any agent can arbitrarily choose to not monitor without affecting the efficacy of monitoring. If the measure is believed to be precisely Λ^*, then the assumption that each agent is atomistic implies that the dominant strategy of each agent is not to monitor. The reason is as follows. If the set of monitoring agents is Z (with measure Λ^*), then if agent $i \in Z$ believes that no other agent $j \in Z$ will monitor, i's best response is to not monitor either. If agent $i \in Z$ believes that all other agents $j \in Z$ will monitor, then once again her best response is not to monitor since agents i's measure is zero, and her lack of monitoring does not affect the measure of those who monitor. (This proof clarifies that if each agent had measure $\epsilon > 0$, we would obtain two Nash equilibria, one in which all agents in Z monitor and one in which none of them do.) Thus, monitoring agents will not trade in the financial market.

Monitoring agents will form a bank, however, since exactly Λ^* monitoring agents can coalesce and invite measure $1 - \Lambda^*$ of discretionary uninformed agents to join as nonmonitoring depositors. Given that monitoring inputs of individual agents are costlessly observed within the bank, the free-rider problem is trivially resolved. When it comes to contracting with the borrower, the bank can charge an interest factor $\{1 + \Lambda^* M\}\eta^{-1}$ and thus recoup the cost of monitoring, $\Lambda^* M$, since lending without monitoring is unprofitable [see Equation (2)]. Given the competitive environment, no higher or lower rate is feasible. ∎

Proof of Proposition 1. Follows readily from Lemmas 1 and 2. ∎

Proof of Proposition 2. Using Equations (7) and (8) and simplifying, we can write

$$\hat{r}(\Omega + \ell) - r_{min} = \frac{\alpha[1 - \eta]}{\eta} \left\{ \frac{[1 - \gamma]\{A - B[\Omega + \ell]\}}{\gamma[A - B\ell] + [1 - \gamma][A - B\{\Omega + \ell\}]} \right\}.$$

Substituting the above in Equation (12) and simplifying yields

$$V = -M + \theta\gamma\alpha[1 - \eta][1 - \gamma]$$

$$\times \int_{D_{min} - \Omega}^{[2/A] - \Omega} \left\{ \frac{B^2\ell^2 + [B^2\Omega - 2AB]\ell + A^2 - AB\Omega}{-B\ell + A - B\Omega[1 - \gamma]} \right\} d\ell. \tag{A1}$$

Tedious algebra enables one to simplify Equation (A1) and express it as

$$V = -M + X\Omega^2. \tag{A2}$$

Ω_1 is obtained by setting $V = 0$ in Equation (A2) and choosing the positive root. This leads to Equation (13). Tedious algebra shows that $\partial V/\partial\Omega > 0$ at $\Omega = \Omega_1$. ∎

Proof of Proposition 3. We substitute Equations (7) and (8) in Equation (14) and simplify. With some tedious algebra, this leads to Equation (15). Note that since $\Omega < 2/A$, We have $A\Omega\gamma/2 < 1 - \{A\Omega[1 - \gamma]/2\}$, so that $\ell n\left([A\Omega\gamma/2]/(1 - [A\Omega\{1 - \gamma\}/2])\right)$ is negative. Although signing $\partial V/\partial\Omega$ analytically does not seem possible, we have verified through numerical analysis that there exist sets of exogenous parameter values for which $\partial V/\partial\Omega < 0$ for some $\Omega > \Omega_1$ and that V cuts the x axis only once at Ω^* for all $\Omega > \Omega_1$. The numerical analysis also helps to verify that $D^*_{min}(\Omega^*)$ defined in Equation (10) is less than Ω^*. ∎

Proof of Proposition 4. The proof follows immediately from Equation (15). For any $M > 0$, V becomes negative at $\theta = 0$ independently of Ω^*. Similarly, for given θ, V becomes negative if M is sufficiently high, once again for any $\Omega^* \geq 0$. ∎

Proof of Proposition 5. From Proposition 1 we know that $\partial V/\partial\Omega > 0$ at $\Omega = \Omega_1 > 0$. Hence, an increase in Ω beyond Ω_1 can increase an informed trader's expected profit. ∎

Proof of Proposition 6. The proof follows immediately from comparing Equation (16) and (21). $E(R^B)$ is independent of θ and $E(R^F)$ increasing in θ. Moreover, $E(R^B) > E(R^F) = 0$ at $\theta = 0$ and $E(R^F) > E(R^B)$ at $\theta = 1$. Thus, given continuity of $E(R^F)$ in θ, $\exists\,\theta \in [\underline{\theta},\overline{\theta}] \subset (0,1) \exists\, a\, \hat{\theta} \in (\underline{\theta},\overline{\theta})$ can be found to satisfy $E(R^F) > E(R^B)\,\forall\theta > \hat{\theta}$ and $E(R^F) \leq E(R^B)\,\forall\theta \leq \hat{\theta}$. ∎

Proof of Proposition 7. With noisy monitoring, the zero expected profit interest factor charged by the bank, r_B^0, satisfies

$$r_B^0\eta[\theta + \{1 - \theta\}\xi] = 1 + \Lambda^*M,$$

which yields

$$r_B^0 = \frac{1 + \Lambda^*M}{\eta[\theta + \{1 - \theta\}\xi]}. \tag{A3}$$

The borrower's net payoff from bank financing is,

$$E(R_0^B) = [\theta + \{1 - \theta\}\xi]\eta[Y - r_B^0] + [1 - \theta][1 - \xi]N. \tag{A4}$$

Substituting Equation (A3) in Equation (A4) and using the fact that $\eta Y > N$, we see that $\partial E(R_0^B)/\partial\theta > 0$. Moreover, comparing Equation (21) and Equation (A4) also shows that $E(R_0^B) < E(R^B)$ for every $\theta \in [\underline{\theta},\overline{\theta}]$.

To show that there exists a cutoff θ^0, note that $E(R^F) = 0$ at $\theta = 0$ [see Equation (16)], and by Proposition 5 and the fact that $E(R_0^B) < E(R^B)\,\forall\theta$, we know that $E(R^F) > E(R_0^B)$ at $\theta = \overline{\theta}$. Thus, continuity of $E(R^F)$ and $E(R_0^B)$ in θ guarantees that $E(R_0^B) = E(R^F)$ for an interior $\theta > 0$ sufficiently small (assuming that $\underline{\theta}$ is small enough). This then establishes that $\exists\,\theta^0 \in (\underline{\theta},\overline{\theta}) \ni E(R^F) > E(R_0^B)\,\forall\theta > \theta^0$ and $E(R^F) \leq E(R_0^B)\,\forall\theta \leq \theta^0$. The result that $\theta^0 < \hat{\theta}$ follows from the result that $E(R_0^B) < E(R^B)\,\forall\theta \in [\underline{\theta},\overline{\theta}]$. ∎

References

Allen, F., (1990). "The market for information and the origin of financial intermediation." *Journal of Financial Intermediation*, 1: 3–30.

——, (1993). "Stock markets and resource allocation," in C. Mayer and X. Vives (eds.), *Capital Markets and Financial Intermediation* (Cambridge: Cambridge Univ. Press).

Allen, F., and Gale, D. (1995). "A welfare comparison of the German and U.S. financial systems." *European Economic Review*, 39: 179–209.

——, and —— "Financial markets, intermediaries and intertemporal smoothing." *Journal of Political Economy*.

Back, K. (1993). "Asymmetric information and options." *Review of Financial Studies*, 6: 435–72.

Berlin, M., and Mester, L. (1992). "Debt covenants and renegotiation." *Journal of Financial Intermediation*, 2: 95–133.

Besanko, D., and Kanatas, G. (1993). "Credit market equilibrium with bank monitoring and moral hazard." *Review of Financial Studies*, 6: 213–32.

Bhattacharya, S., and Chiesa, G. (1995). "Financial intermediation with proprietary information." *Journal of Financial Intermediation*, 4: 328–57.

——, and Thakor, A. V. (1993). "Contemporary banking theory." *Journal of Financial Intermediation*, 3: 2–50.

Boot, A. W., Greenbaum, S. I., and Thakor, A. V. (1993). "Reputation and discretion in financial contracting." *American Economic Review*, 83: 1165–83.

——, and Thakor, A. V. (1993a). "Security design." *Journal of Finance*, 48: 1394–78.

——, and —— (1993b). "Self-interested bank regulation." *American Economic Review*, 83: 206–12.

——, and —— (1996). "Banking scope and financial innovation." Working paper, University of Michigan and Tinbergen Institute/University of Amsterdam, presented at the Western Finance Association Meeting, Sunriver, Oregon, June; *Review of Financial Studies*.

——, ——, and Udell, G. F. (1991). "Secured lending and default risk: Equilibrium analysis and monetary policy implication." *Economic Journal*, 101: 458–72.

Carey, M. (1995). "Some evidence on the nature of information problems in debt contracting and financial intermediation." Manuscript, Board of Governors of the Federal Reserve System, December.

Checchi, D. (1993). "Creation of financial markets in (previously) centrally planned economies." *Journal of Banking and Finance*, 17: 819–47.

Chemmanur, T. J., and Fulghieri, P. (1994). "Reputation, renegotiation, and the choice between bank loans and publicly traded debt." *Review of Financial Studies*, 7: 475–506.

Dewatripont, M., and Maskin, E. (1995). "Credit and efficiency in centralized versus decentralized markets." *Review of Economic Studies*, 62: 541–55.

Diamond, D. (1984). "Financial intermediation and delegated monitoring." *Review of Economic Studies*, 51: 393–414.

—— (1991). "Monitoring and reputation: The choice between bank loans and privately placed debt." *Journal of Political Economy*, 99: 688–721.

Diamond, D. (1993). "Seniority and maturity of debt contracts." *Journal of Financial Economics*, 33: 341–68.

Fishman, M. J., and Hagerty, K. M. (1995). "The incentive to sell financial market information." *Journal of Financial Intermediation*, 4: 95–115.

Grossman, S. J., and Stiglitz, J. E. (1980). "On the impossibility of informationally efficient markets." *American Economics Review*, 70: 393–408.

Hirshleifer, D., and Suh, Y. (1992). "Risk, managerial effort and project choice." *Journal of Financial Intermediation*, 2: 308–45.

Holmström, B., and Tirole, J. (1993). "Market liquidity and performance monitoring." *Journal of Political Economy*, 101: 678–709.

Jacklin, C. (1987). "Demand deposits, trading restrictions, and risk sharing," in E. C. Prescott and N. Wallace (eds.), *Contractual Arangements for International Trade* (Minneapolis: University of Minnesota Press), 26–47.

James, C. (1987). "Some evidence on the uniqueness of bank loans." *Journal of Financial Economics*, 19: 217–35.

Kane, A., and Mars, S. G. (1990). "The delivery of market timing services: Newsletters versus market timing funds." *Journal of Financial Intermediation*, 1: 150–66.

Kane, E. J. (1989). "Changing incentive facing financial-services regulation." *Journal of Financial Services Research*, 2: 263–72.

—— (1990). "Principal–agent problems in S & L salvage." *Journal of Finance*, 45: 755–64.

Lummer, S. L., and McConnell, J. J. (1989). "Further evidence on the bank lending process and the capital market response to bank loan agreements." *Journal of Financial Economics*, 25: 99–122.

Mayer, C. (1988). "New issues in corporate finance." *European Economic Review*, 32: 1167–88.

Mendelson, M., and Peake, J. W. (1993). "Equity markets in economics in transition." *Journal of Banking and Finance*, 17: 913–29.

Millon, M., and Thakor, A. V. (1985). "Moral hazard and information sharing: A model of financial information gathering agencies." *Journal of Finance*, 40: 1403–22.

O'Hara, M. (1993). "Real bills revisited: Market value accounting and loan maturity." *Journal of Financial Intermediation*, 3: 51–76.

Perotti, E. C. (1993). "Bank lending in transition economies." *Journal of Banking and Finance*, 17: 1021–32.

Rajan, R. (1992). "Insiders and outsiders: The choice between informed and arm's length debt." *Journal of Finance*, 47: 1267–400.

Ramakrishnan, R. T. S., and Thakor, A. V. (1984). "Information reliability and a theory of financial intermediation." *Review of Economic Studies*, 51: 415–32.

Rock, K. (1986). "Why new issues are underpriced." *Journal of Financial Economics*, 15: 187–212.

Sabani, L. (1992). "Market oriented versus bank oriented financial systems: Incomplete contracts and long term commitments." Unpublished manuscript, Universita' di Roma "La Sapienza" Dipartimento di Economia Pubblica and Trinity College, Cambridge, September.

Shockley, R., and Thakor, A. V. (1996). "The structure of loan commitment contracts: Data, theory, and tests." Working paper, Indiana University and University of Michigan, September; *Journal of Money, Credit and Banking*, forthcoming.

Thakor, A. V., and Wilson, P. (1995). "Capital requirements, loan renegotiation and the borrower's Choice of financing source." *Journal of Banking and Finance*, 19: 693–712.

Van Wijnbergen, S. (1994). "The role of banks in corporate restructuring: The Polish example." Working Paper, CEPR, London, November.

von Thadden, E. L. (1995). "Long-term contracts, short-term investment and monitoring." *Review of Economic Studies*, 62: 557–75.

Wilson, P. (1994). "Public ownership, delegated project selection and corporate financial policy." Working paper, Indiana University, February.

Yosha, O. (1995). "Information disclosure costs and the choice of financing source." *Journal of Financial Intermediation*, 4: 3–20.

22

Financial Markets, Intermediaries, and Intertemporal Smoothing

Franklin Allen and Douglas Gale

I. Introduction

In the early 1970s, most industrialized countries were adversely affected by a sharp rise in oil prices. This "oil shock" had a dramatic effect on the value of U.S. firms. As illustrated in Figure 1, the real value of shares listed on the New York Stock Exchange fell by almost half compared to their value at the peak in 1972. This collapse in share prices had a severe negative impact on the wealth of any investor whose portfolio contained a significant amount of stocks. Any investor who was forced to liquidate stocks after market prices fell would have suffered from lower consumption over the remainder of his or her life. Retirees in particular might have been affected in this way.

In Germany, where savings are mostly placed with intermediaries such as banks and insurance companies and assets are not marked to the market, the effect was rather different. Since their claims on intermediaries were fixed in nominal terms, these individuals did not suffer a fall in wealth as their counterparts in the United States and would not have been forced to reduce their consumption. Somehow the German financial system was able to smooth the oil price shock rather than pass it on to investors.

In the 1980s the situation was reversed. The economies of most industrialized countries performed relatively well. In the United States, the stock market boomed, as shown in Figure 1. Investors who held stocks were able to achieve higher than expected returns and could use these returns to finance a higher level of consumption. The dissaving generation in Germany did less well, by

We are grateful to seminar participants at Indiana University; the Federal Reserve Banks of Cleveland, Philadelphia, and Richmond; the University of Pennsylvania; the University of Toulouse; Virginia Polytechnic Institute; Gerald Faulhaber; and particularly to the editor, Lars Hansen, and an anonymous referee for helpful comments. Financial support from the National Science Foundation and the Wharton Financial Institutions Center is gratefully acknowledged.

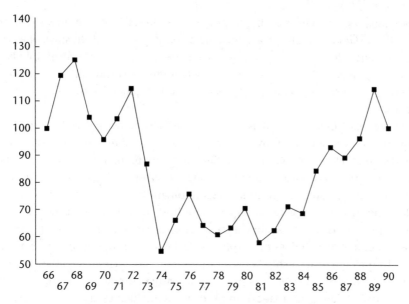

Figure 1. Variation of real U.S. stock prices, 1966–90
(NYSE index, constant dollars, 1966=100).

comparison. Since Germans' savings were placed with intermediaries, such as banks, on which they held fixed claims there was no windfall gain for them.

The effect of the "oil shock" on the U.S. market is an example of what is usually considered a nondiversifiable risk. The shock causes highly correlated changes in most asset values, so investors cannot avoid the risk by holding a diversified portfolio. Nonetheless, these episodes illustrate that the risks borne by individuals in two countries may be very different, even though the countries are subjected to similar shocks. This raises the interesting question of whether and how different financial systems can cope with this sort of risk.

Traditional financial theory has little to say about hedging nondiversifiable risks. It assumes that the set of assets is given and focuses on the efficient sharing of these risks through exchange. For example, the standard diversification argument requires individuals to exchange assets so that each individual holds a relatively small amount of any one risk. Risks will also be traded so that more risk-averse people bear less of the risk than people who are less risk-averse. These strategies do not eliminate macroeconomic shocks, which affect all assets in a similar way. We call this kind of risk sharing *cross-sectional risk sharing* because it is achieved through exchanges of risk among individuals at a given point in time.

Departing from the traditional approach, this chapter focuses on the *intertemporal smoothing* of risk. Risks that cannot be diversified at a given point in time can nevertheless be averaged over time in a way that reduces their impact on individual welfare. One hedging strategy for nondiversifiable risks in *intergenerational risk sharing*, which spreads the risks associated with a given stock of assets across generations with heterogeneous experiences. Another strategy involves *asset accumulation* in order to reduce fluctuations in consumption over time. Both of these strategies are examples of the intertemporal smoothing of asset returns.

In standard financial models with fixed asset supplies and a single period, it is usually argued that somebody must bear the nondiversifiable risk. Such models implicitly overlook possibilities for intertemporal smoothing. At the other extreme, in an ideal, Arrow-Debreu world, cross-sectional risk sharing and intertemporal smoothing are undertaken automatically because markets are complete and there is complete participation in those markets. Neither the standard financial models, which assume a fixed set of assets, nor the idealized Arrow-Debreu model, which does not explicitly deal with institutions, provides much insight into the relationship between the structure of a country's financial system and the stock of assets accumulated. In particular, they do not tell us how a country's reliance on financial markets or intermediaries affects its ability to smooth asset returns by changing its dynamic accumulation path.

The purpose of this chapter is to consider the consequences of intertemporal smoothing for welfare and for positive issues such as asset pricing in a model with incomplete markets. In practice, markets may not be complete in the Arrow-Debreu sense for as wide variety of reasons, including moral hazard, adverse selection, transaction costs, and incomplete participation. For simplicity we consider an economy with an overlapping generations structure, which results in incomplete participation. This is tractable paradigm for the analysis of intertemporal smoothing and captures many of the features common to a wide range of models of market incompleteness.

Our analysis is related to a number of strands of the literature. First, Scheinkman (1980), McCallum (1987), and others have shown that incorporating a long-lived asset rules out the possibility of overaccumulation. These papers are not concerned with risk. In contrast, our chapter analyzes how the risk arising from the dividend stream of long-lived assets is not eliminated by financial markets but can be eliminated by an intermediary. Second, Qi (1994) extends the Diamond and Dybvig (1983) model to an overlapping generations context. In his model there is no aggregate risk and no role for intertemporal smoothing. Flughieri and Rovelli (1994) and Bhattacharya and Padilla (1996) also compare the performance of markets and intermediaries in achieving an efficient intertemporal allocation of resources in an overlapping generations model. There is again aggregate uncertainty in their models, and they do not consider intertemporal smoothing. Third, Gordon and Varian (1998) consider how governments can implement policies such as social security to allow intergenerational risk sharing in the context of a model with a single asset. They do not consider market allocations and asset pricing or the role of intermediation, which are the focus of the present chapter.

In Section II, we describe a standard overlapping generations (OLG) model with two assets, a risky asset in fixed supply and a safe asset that can be accumulated over time. In Section III, we show that under certain conditions the safe asset is never held in the market equilibrium; in fact, it is dominated by the risky asset. Then we show, in Section IV, that intertemporal smoothing can lead to a higher level of average expected utility than is possible in the market equilibrium. Section V shows that the market equilibrium is in fact ex ante Pareto inefficient: there exist allocations with intertemporal smoothing that make all generations better off ex ante compared to the market equilibrium. We suggest that intertemporal smoothing could be implemented by a long-lived intermediary. In Section VI, we show that this mechanism is fragile and the competition from financial markets can lead to disintermediation, which causes the smoothing mechanism to unravel. Section VII contains concluding remarks. Formal proofs are contained in the Appendix.

II. The Model

As a vehicle for the analysis of intertemporal risk smoothing, we use a standard, infinite-horizon, OLG model. Time is divided into a countable number of dates $t = 1, 2, \ldots$, and a new generation is born at each date t. Each generation consists of an equal number of identical agents, so there is no loss of generality in treating each generation as though it consists of a single representative agent. There is an initial old generation lives for two periods.

There is a single good available for consumption in each period, and an agent born at date t has an endowment of e units of the good when young and nothing when old.

There are two types of assets, safe asset and a risky asset, which are held to provide for future consumption. The supply of the risky asset is normalized to unity and is initially owned by the old generation. The risky asset lasts forever and pays a dividend of y_t units of the consumption good at each date t. The only exogenous uncertainty in this economy comes from the stochastic process y_t. We assume that y_t is independently and identically distributed (i.i.d.) and nonnegative, with a positive and finite expectation and variance.

The safe asset is represented by a storage technology, which converts one unit of the consumption good at date t into a unit of consumption at date $t+1$. None of the safe asset is owned by the initial old generation, so $s_0 = 0$.

Agents choose their investments maximize their von Neumann–Morgenstern expected utility. Their risk preferences are represented by the additive utility function

$$U(c_1, c_2) = u(c_1) + v(c_2),$$

where c_i is the agent's consumption in the ith period of life. The functions $u(\cdot)$ and $v(\cdot)$ satisfy the usual properties: both are twice continuously differentiable, increasing, and strictly concave.

The special features of this model are chosen for the sake of simplicity. In particular, the OLG structure is a metaphor for all the other sources of market incompleteness that may arise in practice. Extensions are discussed below.

III. Market Equilibrium

Let $x_t \geq 0$ denote the amount of the risky asset and $s_t \geq 0$ the amount of the safe asset held by the young generation at date t. For simplicity, we do not allow short sales, but nothing is changed in equilibrium if short sales are allowed, as we explain at the end of the section. The agent's first-period budget constraint restricts the sum of his first-period consumption and the value of his portfolio to be equal to his first-period endowment:

$$c_{1t} + s_t + p_t x_t = e,$$

where p_t is the price of the risky asset at date t. The second-period budget constraint restricts his second-period consumption to be equal to the portfolio's liquidation value *plus* the dividend on the risky asset:

$$c_{2t+1} = s_t + p_{t+1} x_t + y_{t+1} x_t.$$

At every date the agents know the present and past values of asset returns. In other words, the (common) information set is $y^t \equiv \{y_1, \ldots, y_t\}$. Since an agent's decision can at most depend on the information available to him, his choice of (x_t, s_t) is a function of y^t; that is, it is adapted to the stochastic process $\{y_t\}$. Asset prices and consumption satisfy the same condition since they are functions of the agent's portfolio decisions. At each date the representative agent chooses his portfolio to maximize his expected utility, conditional on the available information and subject to the period budget constraints.

An *equilibrium* consists of a sequence of portfolio $\{(s_t, x_t)\}$ and prices $\{p_t\}$, adapted to the stochastic process $\{y_t\}$ and satisfying the following conditions. First, at each date t, the portfolio $(s_t, x_t) \geq 0$ chosen by the representative young agent solves the problem

$$\max \quad E_t \left[u(c_{1t}) + v(c_{2t+1}) \right]$$
$$\text{subject to} \quad c_{1t} + p_t + s_t = e,$$
$$c_{2t+1} = s_t + (y_{t+1} + p_{t+1}) x_t.$$

Second, the market for the risky asset must clear; that is, $x_t = 1$ for every date t. In what follows, we focus our attention on *Markov* equilibria, that is, equilibria with the property that the endogenous variables (p_t, s_t, x_t) are functions of the contemporaneous shock y_t. A Markov equilibrium is said to be *stationary* if this functional relationship is time-invariant: $(p_t, s_t, x_t) = f(y_t)$, for all t.

Although the safe asset would seem to be a useful hedge against the uncertainty generated by the risky asset, it turns out that this is not the case. Since the returns to the risky asset are assumed to be i.i.d., the representative young agent in a stationary Markov equilibrium solves the same decision problem at each date, regardless of the state in which he is born; and since the old supply the risky asset inelastically, the equilibrium price is constant and nonstochastic. The net return from holding the risky asset in such an equilibrium is $r_t = y_{t+1} + p_{t+1} - p_t = y_{t+1}$, and since y_{t+1} is nonnegative and sometimes positive, the safe asset is clearly dominated and will never be held in equilibrium.

PROPOSITION 1. *There exists a stationary Markov equilibrium* $\{(p_t, s_t, x_t)\}$ *in which the price of the risky asset is a constant* $p_t = p$ *and the demand for the safe asset is* $s_t = 0$ *at every date* t *if* $\sup u'(\cdot) > \inf v'(\cdot)$.

The assumption that $\sup u'(\cdot) > \inf v'(\cdot)$ is needed to ensure that there exists a positive rate of return at which the representative young agent wants to transfer wealth from the first to the second period of his life. Otherwise, there is no (constant) asset price at which the young agent is willing to hold the risky asset and a stationary equilibrium cannot exist.

To illustrate the operation of the market equilibrium, consider the following example:

$$U(c_1, c_2) = \ln(c_1) + \ln(c_2),$$

$$e = 1,$$

$$y_t = \begin{cases} 0 & \text{with probability } 0.5 \\ 1 & \text{with probability } 0.5. \end{cases}$$

For this case it can be shown that the stationary equilibrium price is $p_t = 0.5$ and the allocation of consumption in equilibrium is as follows:

y_t	c_{1t}	c_{2t}
0	0.5	0.5
1	0.5	1.5

The levels of expected utility attained are $E[v(c_{21})] = -0.14$ for the initial generation and $E[U(c_{1t}, c_{2t+1})] = -0.84$ for each subsequent generation. The long-run average expected utility is therefore also -0.84.

In this example the risky asset is very attractive. It can be bought in youth for 0.5 and sold for the same amount in old age; it also pays nonnegative dividends, which are 1 half of the time. Since the risky asset is so attractive, investors sacrifice consumption in youth in order to be able to consume in old age. They consume only 0.5 in youth but in old age consume 0.5 or 1.5 with equal probability, or 1 on average.

It has been assumed so far that no short sales are slowed. This assumption can be dropped at no cost, however, since the equilibrium allocations would be exactly the same if short sales were allowed. The existence of a representative agent and the fact that net asset holdings must be nonnegative in equilibrium together ensure that no short sales can actually take place in equilibrium, even if they were allowed. Furthermore, market clearing requires $x_t = 1$, so the short-sale constraint is never binding for the risky asset. The short-sale constraint $s_t \geq 0$ for the safe asset may be binding in equilibrium. If it is, then we need to introduce a price $q_t < 1$ for claims to the safe asset in order for the market to clear at zero net supply.

The model can also be extended to allow for (random) endowments (e_{1t}, e_{2t}) in both periods of an agent's life. In this case, the safe asset may sometimes be used in equilibrium. However, it is always true that $s_t = 0$ with positive probability in a stationary Markov equilibrium. Furthermore, by restricting the distribution of e_{1t}, we can ensure that the conclusion of proposition 1 continues to hold. In any case, financial markets do not eliminate the risk created by random fluctuations in endowments and asset returns. Similarly, if the return on the safe asset is positive or it is possible that $y_t < 0$, the yield on the risky asset will no longer be uniformly higher then the yield on the safe asset and some of the safe asset may be held in equilibrium. Again, however, financial markets will not eliminate risk. In the next section, we shall see that there exist feasible allocations in which risk is almost entirely eliminated in the long run.

IV. Intertemporal Smoothing

In a stationary Markov equilibrium, the safe is not used to hedge against the uncertainty of the risky asset's return. However, in an infinite-horizon economy, almost all of the risk can be eliminated through a program of accumulating buffer stocks of the risk-free asset. This is simply an application of a well-known theorem of Schechtman (1976). He considered the problem of an individual who has a risky income ω_t and wants to maximize the expected value of his long-run average utility:

$$E\left[\lim_{T \to \infty} T^{-1} \sum_{1}^{T} u(c_t)\right].$$

The individual cannot borrow but is able to self-insure by investing in a safe asset (storage technology). Consider the following policy: at each date t, the individual, who has accumulated savings s_{t-1}, consumes $E\omega_t$ if this is feasible and $\omega_t + s_{t-1}$ otherwise. Then the individual's savings at date t will be

$$s_t = \max\{\omega_t + s_{t-1} - E\omega_t, 0\}.$$

Let $M_T \equiv \#\{t \leq T | s_t = 0\}$ be the (random) number of periods that this process spends at the boundary in the first T periods. The renewal theorem tells us that if the random variables $\{\omega_t\}$ are i.i.d., then with probability one, M_T/T converges to zero as T approaches infinity. Since the individual's consumption is less than $E\omega_t$ only when $s_t = 0$, this implies that his consumption is equal to $E\omega_t$ for all but a negligible fraction of the time, and his long-run average utility converge to $u(E\omega_t)$ almost surely.

The same policy works in the present framework. Suppose that a planner wants to maximize the long-run average of the expected utilities of the different generations. To this end, the planner accumulates part of the economy's total endowment using the storage technology. Let s_t denote the accumulated savings at the end of date t and let $\omega_t \equiv e + y_t$ denote the total endowment of the economy at date t. Then by following the policy of setting

$$s_t = \max\{\omega_t + s_{t-1} - E\omega_t, 0\},$$

we can provide the two generations at each date with a total consumption equal to $\bar{\omega} \equiv E\omega_t$ in almost every period, with probability one. The planner will divide the consumption between the two generations in a way that maximizes the typical generation's utility. If we let

$$(c_1(w), c_2(w)) \equiv \underset{c_1+c_2=w}{\operatorname{argmax}} u(c_1) + v(c_2)$$

and put $U^*(w) \equiv u(c_1(w)) + v(c_2(w))$, then we have shown that the planner can achieve

$$E\left[\lim_{T\to\infty} T^{-1} \sum_{1}^{T} u(c_1(\min\{\bar{\omega}, \omega_t + s_{t-1}\})) + v(c_2(\min\{\bar{\omega}, \omega_{t+1} + s_t\}))\right] = U^*(\bar{\omega}).$$

PROPOSITION 2. *There exists a feasible policy $\{s_t\}$ that ensures with probability one that all but a negligible fraction of generations are able to achieve the expected utility level $U^*(\bar{\omega})$.*

The utility level $U^*(\bar{\omega})$ is at least as great as the level achieved in the market equilibrium on average. In fact, this must be true for any feasible allocation in which the long-run average consumption levels of the old and young are well defined. Let $\{(c_{1t}, c_{2t})\}$ be a feasible consumption process and suppose that

$$\bar{c}_i \equiv \lim_{T \to \infty} T^{-1} \sum_{1}^{T} c_{it}$$

is well defined. Then, by concavity,

$$E \left[\lim_{T \to \infty} T^{-1} \sum_{1}^{T} [u(c_{1t}) + v(c_{2t+1})] \right]$$

$$\leq E \left[u \left(\lim_{T \to \infty} T^{-1} \sum_{1}^{T} c_{1t} \right) + v \left(\lim_{T \to \infty} T^{-1} \sum_{1}^{T} c_{2t+1} \right) \right]$$

$$= E[u(\bar{c}_1) + v(\bar{c}_2)]$$

$$\leq u(E\bar{c}_1) + v(E\bar{c}_2).$$

Now, we have assumed that $\{(c_{1t}, c_{2t})\}$ is feasible, so with probability one,

$$T^{-1} \sum_{1}^{T} (c_{1t} + c_{2t}) \leq T^{-1} \sum_{1}^{T} \omega_t \to \bar{\omega}.$$

From this it follows that $E\bar{c}_1 + E\bar{c}_2 \leq \bar{\omega}$, which in turn implies that $u(E\bar{c}_1) + v(E\bar{c}_2) \leq U^*(\bar{\omega})$. From this we conclude that

$$E \left[\lim_{T \to \infty} T^{-1} \sum_{1}^{T} [u(c_{1t}) + v(c_{2t+1})] \right] \leq U^*(\bar{\omega}).$$

The inequality will be strict when $\{(c_{1t}, c_{2t})\}$ corresponds to the market allocation, since the agents' risk preferences are strictly concave in old age and the variance of y_t is strictly positive. This result can be summarized as follows.

PROPOSITION 3. *For any feasible allocation* $\{(c_{1t}, c_{2t}, s_t)\}$ *for which long-run average consumptions are well defined,*

$$E \left[\lim_{T \to \infty} T^{-1} \sum_{1}^{T} [u(c_{1t}) + v(c_{2t+1})] \right] \leq U^*(\bar{\omega}),$$

and the inequality is strict if $\{(c_{1t}, c_{2t}, s_t)\}$ *is the market equilibrium allocation.*

In the example from the previous section, $\bar{\omega} = 1.5$, and the additive logarithmic utility function implies that the long-run average expected utility is maximized by setting $c_1(w) = c_2(w) = \bar{\omega}/2 = 0.75$. In this case, $U^*(\bar{\omega}) = -0.58$, which compares favorably with the long-run average expected utility in the market equilibrium $E[U(c_{1t}, c_{2t+1})] = -0.84$.

Propositions 2 and 3 extend immediately to the case in which there are both random endowments (e_{1t}, e_{2t+1}) and random asset returns y_t, as long as we assume that the aggregate endowments $\omega_t \equiv e_{1t} + e_{2t} + y_t$ are i.i.d.

V. Ex Ante Efficiency and the Genesis of Intertemporal Smoothing

In the preceding section, we saw that a long-lived agent, or a planner who maximized the long-run average of expected utility, might behave very differently from the successive generations in the OLG model, who maximized their own expected utility over a two-period horizon. The former would have an incentive to accumulate large stocks of the safe asset in order to provide insurance against rate of return risk, whereas the latter have no incentive to hold the safe asset at all in a stationary Markov equilibrium.

This raises the question of whether there is some sort of market failure, some form of inefficiency, in the equilibrium described in proposition 1. Before we can answer this question, we have to be more precise about how we define the welfare of an individual agent. There are two salient definitions. The first identifies the individual's welfare with his expected utility $E\left[U(c_{1t}, c_{2t+1})|y^t\right]$, *conditional on the information that is available when he is born.* In effect, it treats the "same" individual born at two different information sets as two different individuals. The second definition identifies the individual's welfare with his *unconditional* expected utility $E\left[U(c_{1t}, c_{2t+1})\right]$, implicitly assuming that there is only one individual born at any date, regardless of the information available at that date.

Correspondingly, there are two notions of Pareto efficiency, ex ante and ex post, depending on whether or not we take into account the state in which an agent is born. A feasible allocation is *ex post efficient* if it is impossible to increase the ex post expected utility, $E\left[U(c_{1t}, c_{2t+1})|y^t\right]$, of some generations without reducing the ex post expected utility of other generations. On the other hand, a feasible allocation is *ex ante efficient* if it is impossible to increase the ex ante expected utility, $E\left[U(c_{1t}, c_{2t+1})\right]$, of some generations without reducing the ex ante expected utility of other generations. We consider efficiency initially using the ex ante notion and then using the ex post notion.

It is easy to see that a market equilibrium allocation will not be ex ante efficient in general, because agents are not allowed to trade before they are born. Hence, all traders are undertaken by an agent after the state in which he is born has been revealed. In other words, the birth state y^t is a "preexisting condition," against which an agent cannot insure. However, a planner could provide such insurance by making appropriate transfers between the old and the young at each date. Thus, even without making use of the storage technology, the planner could achieve a Pareto improvement from the ex ante point of view. However, the expected utility of the typical generation will be even higher if intergenerational smoothing is carried out, accumulating reserves of the safe asset and using them to smooth fluctuations in consumption. Intergenerational risk sharing by means of transfers between the old and young at each date does not remove the aggregate uncertainty caused by the randomness of the aggregate endowment. Intertemporal smoothing eliminates this uncertainty, at no cost in terms of long-run average consumption.

Although it is easy to see that intertemporal smoothing can increase long-run average expected utility, some care must be taken about the way in which intertemporal smoothing is introduced in order to ensure that *each* generation is better off ex ante compared to the equilibrium allocation. Consider the policy described in Section IV. Under that policy, $c_{1t} + c_{2t} = \bar{\omega}$ when $\omega_t + s_t \geq \bar{\omega}$ and $c_{1t} + c_{2t} = \omega_t + s_t$ otherwise. In the market equilibrium, $c_{1t} + c_{2t} = e + y_t$ in all periods. Since $s_0 = 0$, it follows that if the intertemporal smoothing scheme were implemented at the first date, either the initial old generation or the initial young generation or both would be worse off in an ex ante sense compared to the market allocation. A similar argument applies in subsequent periods. In order to achieve an ex ante Pareto improvement, intertemporal smoothing has to be introduced in two stages. The first stage achieves an increase in expected utility by means of intergenerational risk sharing (transfers), which allows the planner to accumulate some of the endowment in the form of reserves of the safe asset without making any generation worse off. Once reserves are sufficiently large, it is possible to switch to a policy if intertemporal smoothing and make every generation better off ex ante than it would be with intergenerational risk sharing alone.

To see how the first stage is implemented, consider some necessary conditions for ex ante efficiency. If the equilibrium is ex ante efficient, it must be impossible to make both generations at date t better off by reallocating consumption at that date. That means that the equilibrium consumption allocation (c_{1t}, c_{2t}) must solve the maximization problem

$$\max \quad E\left[\lambda u(c_{1t}) + (1 - \lambda)v(c_{2t})\right]$$
$$\text{subject to} \quad c_{1t} + c_{2t} = \omega_t \equiv e + y_t,$$

for some constant $0 \leq \lambda \leq 1$. A necessary condition for this to be true is that $u'(c_{1t})/v'(c_{2t}) = $ constant with probability one. In the market equilibrium, $c_1 t = e - p_t$ is nonstochastic, whereas $c_{2t} = p_t + y_t$ is stochastic; so the necessary condition for ex ante Pareto efficiency cannot be satisfied and the market equilibrium is ex ante inefficient. In fact, it is possible to find an ex ante Pareto-preferred allocation by making stationary transfers contingent on the contemporaneous asset returns. Let $\tau(y_t)$ be the transfer from young to old at period t when the asset returns is y_t, and define the new consumption allocation by putting

$\hat{c}_{1t} = c_{1t} - \tau(y_t)$ and $\hat{c}_{2t} = c_{2t} - \tau(y_t)$. For an appropriate specification of the transfer function $\tau(\cdot)$.

$$E\left[v(\hat{c}_{2t})\right] > E[(c_{2t})]$$

and

$$E\left[u(\hat{c}_{1t}) + v(\hat{c}_{2t+1})\right] > E[u(c_{1t}) + v(c_{2t+1})]$$

for every date t. By continuity, the same will be true if we reduce the consumption of the young at each date by a constant amount $\eta > 0$ and add this amount to the stock of the safe asset, so that by period t we have accumulated $s_t = \eta t$. Hence with intergenerational transfers, an arbitrarily large level of reserves can be built in preparation for switching to the intertemporal smoothing program.

Let S denote the target level of reserves accumulated in the first stage and let T denote the end of the first stage; that is, choose T so that $s_T = S$. To show that a Pareto-improving scheme with intertemporal smoothing can be implemented, the following lemma is needed.

LEMMA 1. *For any $\epsilon > 0$, there is a level of initial reserves S sufficiently large that, when the intertemporal smoothing plan starts at date T, the probability of $s_t = 0$ at any $t \geq T$ is less than ϵ.*

In the short run, this is obvious because it will take some time to run down the reserves to zero. In the longer run, it is not so obvious that the probability of running out of reserves is uniformly small at all future dates. The lemma follows from the fact that reserves follow a "random walk" when $s_t > 0$ and are expected to increase when $s_t = 0$. This means that reserves are expected to increase, on average, without limit under the intertemporal smoothing policy. Even though the event $s_t = 0$ will occur infinitely often, the probability that it happens at any fixed date t is becoming vanishingly small as t approaches infinity.

The fact that the probability of the event $s_t = 0$ is bounded by ϵ for each future generation means that the ex ante expected utility of any generation living after date T is at least $(1 - \epsilon)U^*(\bar{\omega})$, which is greater than the equilibrium ex ante expected utility $E[U(c_{1t}, c_{2t+1})]$ for ϵ small. Thus generations $t \geq T$ will prefer the intertemporal smoothing plan ex ante to their market allocation. There is a problem with the generation born at date $T - 1$ since this generation does not get the full benefit of intergenerational risk sharing but has its second-period consumption reduced on average. To compensate this generation, we make a one-time transfer out of the reserves. With this adjustment, every generation is ex ante better off.

Furthermore, since the first stage with intergenerational sharing is finite in length, the analysis in Section IV shows that the long-run average expected utility will converge to $U^*(\bar{\omega})$. All this can be summarized in the following result.

PROPOSITION 4. *The market equilibrium allocation is ex ante Pareto-inefficient. There exists an attainable allocation with intertemporal smoothing that provides every generation with higher ex ante expected utility and achieves the long-run average expected utility* $U^*(\bar{\omega})$.

The existence of an allocation that ex ante improves welfare for all generations compared to the market equilibrium can be illustrated in the context of the numerical example used above. In the initial stage, the market allocation is altered by intergenerational transfers:

$$\tau y_t = \begin{cases} 0.1125 & \text{if } y_t = 0 \\ -0.275 & \text{if } y_t = 1. \end{cases}$$

When $y_t = 0$, the old receive a transfer of 0.1125 from the young; when $y_t = 1$, the young receive a transfer of 0.275 from the old. These transfers ensure that the expected utility of the initial generation is greater than the market equilibrium level of -0.84. They also allow an addition to reserves of 0.028 to be extracted each period from each generation except the initial one, while still leaving them slightly better off than the market allocation.

To see how the second stage operates, consider the effect on the ex ante expected utilities of the generations around date T if intertemporal smoothing were implemented at date T and there were no reserves at that date, as shown in Table 1. We assume that the generation $T - 1$ simply receives the market allocation when it is young. The generation born at date $T + 1$ is clearly better off than in the equilibrium, but generation $T - 1$ and T are worse off. If there were positive reserves at date T, $s_t > 0$, the generations born after T would be even better off. For the generation born at $T - 1$, a transfer of 0.21 in their youth at date $T - 1$ would be sufficient to make them better off than in the market equilibrium. For the generation born at date T, a transfer of 0.03 would be sufficient. Hence the total reserves at the time of the transition must be at least 0.24. Remember that the initial generation and generation $T - 1$ do not help build reserves; this implies that the initial stage must last at least six periods, so $T = 7$.

Table 1.

Generation born at	c_{1t}	c_{2t+1}	$E[c_{1t}, c_{2t+1})]$
$T - 1$	0.5	0.5 with prob. 0.5	-1.18
		0.75 with prob. 0.5	
T	0.75 with prob. 0.05	0.5 with prob. 0.25	-0.88
	0.75 with prob. 0.5	0.75 with prob. 0.75	
$T + 1$	0.5 with prob. 0.25	0.5 with prob. 0.25	-0.78
	0.75 with prob. 0.75	0.75 with prob. 0.75	

Comparing the paths of utility in this ex ante Pareto-superior allocation with that in the market equilibrium, we can see that the first six generations in this example have slightly higher utility, but all subsequent generations are significantly better off. The long-run average expected utility is -0.58, compared to -0.84 in the market equilibrium. Note also that the average expected utility is also significantly greater than what can be achieved with intergenerational transfers alone. The consumption allocation that maximizes long-run average expected utility through intergenerational transfers with no accumulation of reserves is

$$
c_{it} = \begin{cases} 0.5 & \text{with probability } 0.5 \\ 1.0 & \text{with probability } 0.5 \end{cases}
$$

for $i = 1, 2$, which gives expected utility $E[U(c_{1t}, c_{2t+1})] = -0.69$.

At the start of the section it was pointed that there exist two notions of efficiency depending on whether we take into account the state in which an agent is born. Ex ante efficiency, which proposition 4 focused on, takes the expectations of utility across all possible states. An alternative view is ex post efficiency in which an individual's welfare is conditional on the information available when he is born. The discussion of lemma 1 provides insights into ex post expected utility in the model in which intertemporal smoothing is adopted. Aggregate consumption is $\bar{\omega}$ if and only if $s_t > 0$ and $Pr[s_t = 0] \to 0$ as t approaches infinity. Hence, ex post expected utility will converge to $U^*(\bar{\omega})$ in probability as t approaches infinity. In other words, except when reserves are low, the ex post expected utility of each generation will be $U^*(\bar{\omega})$, which is higher than in the market equilibrium. As t becomes large, the probability that reserves will be low and that a generation will be worse off ex post than in the market equilibrium becomes vanishingly small. In fact, in the long run, all but a negligible fraction of generations can be made better off ex post.

We have so far studied the existence of allocations that allow the introduction of intertemporal smoothing *and* an ex ante Pareto improvement over the market allocation, without specifying the institutional framework that implements them. The existence of such allocations suggests a story of how intertemporal smoothing by intermediaries might come into existence. Given the opportunity to make individuals better off, some institution will try to exploit that opportunity and capture part of the surplus. One possibility is that a long-lived intermediary is set up to provide insurance against uncertain returns by averaging high and low returns over time. Such an intermediary could hold all the assets and offer a deposit contract to each generation. Initially, the intermediary offers intergenerational insurance. Later on, after accumulating large reserves, the intermediary can offer almost all generations a constant return on deposits, independently of the actual returns.

Some degree of market power will be required to ensure that individuals participate in this scheme, as we shall see in the next section. This marker power may arise naturally or it may be the result of government intervention. For example, the government may give the intermediary an exclusive license in order to achieve an ex ante Pareto improvement.

Of course, we do not suggest that intertemporal smoothing would always occur in this way, merely that the introduction of intertemporal smoothing is consistent with market incentives.

VI. Competition between Intermediaries and Financial Markets

A commonly heard argument is that financial markets are desirable because of the risk-sharing opportunities they provide. It is well known that this is correct as far as cross-sectional risk-sharing opportunities are concerned, but the results of the preceding sections suggest that this argument ignores the possibilities for intertemporal risk smoothing. We have shown in the context of a simple OLG model that an intermediated financial system can make every generation better off than it would be with financial markets alone. Note that, in this interpretation, financial markets and intermediaries are not simply veils thrown over a fixed set as assets. They actually determine, in conjunction with other factors, the set of assets accumulated by the agents in the economy. By adopting one or another set of institutions, the economy is placed on a different trajectory, with important implications for risk smoothing.

A natural question that arises is whether it is possible to combine the cross-sectional risk-sharing advantages of financial markets with the intertemporal risk-smoothing advantages of an intermediated system. There is a significant obstacle in the path of trying to combine the two types of systems. Risk sharing of the kind discussed in the last few sections implies some form of arbitrage opportunity. Taking advantage of arbitrage opportunities is rational for the individual, but is undermines the insurance offered by the intermediary. For this reason, an open financial system may not be able to provide imtertemporal risk smoothing, although it provides a tremendous variety of financial instruments.

One way to illustrate the effect of competition from financial markets is to consider the effect of opening up a relatively small, closed, and intermediated financial system to global financial markets. Initially, the small country's financial system is monopolized by a cartel of banks that engage in intertemporal smoothing without the threat of competition. After opening the small country's financial system, the banks now face the constraint that individuals can opt out and invest in global markets instead. The assumption that the country is small relative to the rest of the world implies that prices in the global market are not market are not affected by the financial system of the small country or its investor's decision to participate in the risk-sharing mechanism provided by the intermediary.

Let $\{(p_t, s_t, x_t)\}$ be the equilibrium in the global market and let $\{(c'_{1t}, c'_{2t}, s'_t)\}$ be the optimal allocation implemented in the small country. The global equilibrium represents a benchmark for the welfare of investors in the absence of a long-lived intermediary, as well as an outside option for the individuals when the intermediary is in operation. We assume that all investors in the small country make use of the intermediary. Since the intermediary can always replicate the investment opportunities available through the market, there is no loss of generality in this assumption.

Disintermediation can take several forms, depending on whether investors are able to make side trades while taking advantage of the intermediary. We assume that the intermediary can enforce exclusivity, which means that an agent who wants to trade in the market is unable to make use of the intermediary at all. This assumption makes disintermediation less attractive and hence produces a weaker constraint on the intermediary's problem of designing a risk-smoothing scheme. We can show that even this weak constraint on the intermediary is sufficient to rule out any welfare improvement from intertemporal risk smoothing. Alternative (stronger) specifications of the disintermediation constraint would only strengthen this result.

The *disintermediation constraint*, which ensures that people do not abandon the small country's risk-sharing mechanism once they have access to global markets, can be stated as follows: for any history $y^t = (y_1, \ldots, y_t)$, the allocation $\{(c'_{1t}, c'_{2t}, c'_t)\}$ satisfies

$$E\left[u(c'_{1t}) + v(c'_{2t})|y^t\right] \geq \max_{(x,s)\geq 0} E\left[u(e - p_t) + v(x(y_t + s))|y^t\right].$$

The expression on the right is the maximum expected utility an agent born at date t could obtain from trading on the open market. The expression on the left is the expected utility offered by the risk-sharing mechanisms. The crucial point is that both expressions are conditioned on all the information available at date t. An agent makes his decision whether to join the risk-sharing mechanism after he has observed y^t.

The possibility of disintermediation implies that an intermediated financial system in a small open country does not allow any improvement in expected utility over that obtained by investors in global financial markets. To prove this result, we need two additional assumptions. The first rules out the possibility of a welfare-increasing Ponzi scheme: we assume that there exists a constant K such that if $U(c_{1t}, c_{2t+1}) \geq U(e, 0)$, then $c_{1t} \geq -K$ and $c_{2t+1} \geq -K$ with probability one. Since the utility level $U(e, 0)$ is always attainable, an agent's expected utility must be at least this high in equilibrium, which means that his consumption will be bounded below with probability one. The second assumption is purely technical: we assume that the random asset return y_t assumes a finite number of values. Under these assumptions we can show that the equilibrium allocation is ex post Pareto-efficient, and so there is no feasible allocation that makes any generation better off without making some generation worse off ex post. The disintermediation constraint requires each generation to be at least as well off ex post as it was under the equilibrium allocation and hence no better off.

PROPOSITION 5. *If the allocation* $\{(c'_{1t}, c'_{2t}, s'_t)\}$ *is feasible and satisfies the disintermediation constraint, then each agent is ex post no better off under* $\{(c'_{1t}, c'_{2t}, s'_t)\}$ *than he would be in the market equilibrium* $\{(p_t, s_t, x_t)\}$.

To understand proposition 5, it is helpful to think about the policy described in proposition 2. That policy provides the two generations at each date with a total consumption equal to the lesser of $\bar{\omega}$ and the sum of the actual return and the reserves held by the intermediary, so that the total amount consumed each period is

$$c'_{1t} + c'_{2t} = \min\{\bar{\omega}, y_t + s'_{t-1} + e\}.$$

If the reserves held by the intermediary endowment are very low (close to zero), the expected utility of an agent must be lower than in the market equilibrium. In comparison with the equilibrium allocation, he loses the high returns from the risky asset when $y_t > \bar{\omega}$ and still suffers the probability of loss when $y_t > \bar{\omega}$. So any generation will be better off only if it inherits a large reserve from the previous generation. This will be true most of the time, but occasionally a generation will be born when reserves are low, and that generation will be worse off ex post. If that generation can opt out of the risk-sharing mechanism, the whole scheme will break down, leaving us in the situation described by proposition 5.

To see this in the context of the numerical example, suppose that reserves are at zero at date T^*. If intermediation is initiated or continued and intertemporal smoothing were implemented, the allocation of consumption would be as shown in Table 1 in the previous section with $T = T^*$. The young generation (born at T^*) would obtain $E[U(c_{1T^*}, c_{2T^*+1})] = -0.88$. However, with markets they obtain the usual market allocation, which gives $E[U(c_{1T^*}, c_{2T^*+1})] = -0.84$. Hence when there are no reserves, the young generation will prefer the competitive market allocation and will defect if given the opportunity. This is why some monopoly power is important in establishing and maintaining intermediation as discussed in the previous section. Building up the reserves necessary to start intertemporal smoothing requires intergenerational transfers initially. Across to competitive financial markets ensures that this type of insurance will not be feasible. Any allocation of consumption offered by an intermediary must match the market and give the young generation $E[U(c_{1T^*}, c_{2T^*+1})] = -0.84$. This means that an intermediary cannot improve on the market.

Proposition 4 implies that ex ante expected utility will be higher for all generations in an intermediated economy than in an economy with financial markets only. Incomplete financial markets do not allow intertemporal smoothing, but intermediaries in principle can, provided that investors do not have ready access to financial markets. This suggests that economies that are intermediary-based may be worse off by allowing access to financial markets. As discussed below, this result may have important policy implications for European Union and other regions considering liberalizing access to global financial markets.

VII. Concluding Remarks

Our formal analysis has focused on a simple overlapping generations model. This benchmark is meant to illustrate the absence of intertemporal smoothing that can result from incomplete markets and to show how an intermediated financial system can eliminate the resulting inefficiencies. It is important to stress that the overlapping generations structure is chosen because of its tractability. We believe that there are many other types of incompleteness that lead to the absence of intertemporal smoothing.

In our model, investors have a short time horizon; this means that they do not self-insure. Individuals live more than two "periods," but whether self-insurance can realistically be achieved in a single individual's lifetime is questionable. In the first place, the number of independent shocks may be small. We can think of the Great Depression as being on shock and the boom of the 1950s and 1960s as another. With this interpretation, the number of periods each generation lives through is small. In addition, there are life cycle considerations that may prevent households from self-insuring. For example, the desire to purchase a house and provide an education for their children means that many households do not start saving for retirement until fairly late in life. For both these reasons, the possibilities for self-insurance may be limited.

Finally, note that incomplete market participation will not be a problem when agents have a bequest motive that causes successive generations to act like a single infinitely lived individual. There is some evidence that in the general population, bequest motives and risk sharing within extended families are limited (see Altonji, Hayashi, and Kotlikoff [1992], Hayashi, Altonji, and Kotlikoff [1996], and the references cited therein.) The issue here is whether the wealthy, who own most of the capital, have a sufficient bequest motive for intertemporal smoothing not to be a problem. Altonji et al. (1992) point out that wealthy individuals are underrepresented in the data sets most commonly studied in this area, and we are unaware of any evidence regarding this group specifically.

In the Introduction, we used the comparison of Germany and the United States to suggest that different financial systems deal with nondiversifiable risk in different ways. The model shows that it is theoretically possible for an intermediated financial system to achieve a higher level of welfare than a market-based system. It is tempting, then, to compare the U.S. and German financial systems in the light of this example. It is often suggested that German banks hold high levels of hidden reserves, which they rely on when asset returns are low. Even if this form of intertemporal smoothing is limited by comparison with the theoretical schemes considered above, it may nonetheless be an improvement over competitive financial markets in terms of reducing nondiversifiable risk. Thus the German financial system, with its reliance on financial intermediaries, may have some advantages over the United States, which relies more on financial markets.

Given this interpretation, proposition 5 has important policy implications. It suggests that opening the German financial system to foreign competition — for example, by creating a single European market in financial services — could threaten intertemporal smoothing and make Germans worse off in the long run. Of course, risk sharing is not the only consideration in the choice of optimal financial systems. Other important issues are discussed in Allen and Gale (1995).

APPENDIX

A. Proof of Proposition 1. Suppose that $(s_t, x_t) = (0, 1)$ for ever t. Then the necessary and sufficient conditions for the optimality of this portfolio are

$$u'(e - p_t)p_t = E_t \left[v'(p_t + y_t)(p_t + y_t) \right],$$
$$u'(e - p_t) \geq E_t \left[v'(p_t + y_t) \right].$$

If these conditions are satisfied with $p_t = p_{t+1} = p$, then $\{(s_t, x_t, p_t)\}$ is a stationary Markov equilibrium. If we substitute $p_t = p_{t+1} = p$ in the first-order conditions, it is clear that the first condition implies the second. Hence, we need only to fine a solution to the equation

$$u'(e - p) = E \left[\frac{v'(p + y_t)(p + y_t)}{p} \right] \leq E \left[v'(p + y_t) \right] E \left[\frac{p + y_t}{p} \right].$$

Since $u'(\cdot), v'(\cdot) > 0$, the left-hand side is clearly less than the right when p is sufficiently small. On the other hand, for p sufficiently large, the right-hand side must exceed the left; otherwise, taking the limit as $p \to \infty$ noting that $E[(p + y_t)/p] \to 1$, we have $\sup u'(\cdot) \leq \inf v'(\cdot)$, a contradiction. Thus, for some intermediate value of p, the first-order condition must be satisfied, and this value of p is the equilibrium asset price.   Q.E.D.

B. *Proof of Lemma* 1. Recall that $s_{t+1} = \max\{0, s_t + \omega_t - \bar{\omega}\}$, so that $E[s_{t+1}|s_t] \le s_t$. Define $f(s) = 1/(s+1) \in [0,1]$ for any $s \ge 0$. Then

$$E[f(s_{t+1})|s_t] \ge f(E[s_{t+1}|s_t])$$
$$\ge f(s_t)$$

since f is convex and decreasing. With $F_t \equiv f(s_t)$, $\{F_t\}$ is a bounded supermartingale. So by the martingale convergence theorem, $F_t \to F_\infty$ almost surely as $t \to \infty$. Since ω_t has positive variance, it is clear that $F_\infty = 0$, almost surely. Convergence almost surely implies convergence in measure, so for any $\epsilon > 0$, there is a finite T such that

$$\Pr[F_t < \epsilon] > 1 - \epsilon \quad \forall t > T.$$

Suppose that we want to start the intertemporal smoothing plan at date T when the reserves have grown to $s_T = S$. We have shown that for any $\epsilon > 0$ there is a $T' > T$ such the $\Pr[s_t = 0] < \epsilon$ for all $t > T'$. Keeping ϵ and T fixed, we see that when S is made sufficiently large, the probability that $s_t = 0$ for any $T \le t \le T'$ can be made less than ϵ. Then we have shown that for any $\epsilon > 0$ there is a level of initial reserves S sufficiently large that when the intertemporal smoothing plan starts at date T, the probability of $s_t = 0$ at any $t \ge T$ is less than ϵ as required. Q.E.D.

C. *Proof of Proposition* 5. Index the values of y_t by $s = 1, \ldots, S$ and let $c_1 \in R$ and $c_2 \in R^s$. Then we can write the expected utility of an agent who consumes c_1 in the first period and c_{2s} in the second period if state s occurs as $u(c_1) + V(c_2)$, where $V(c_2) \equiv \sum_{s=1}^{S} \pi_s v(c_{2s})$. Let $C \subset R \times R^s$ be a compact set such that $c \in C$ implies that

$$u'(c_1) \ge \sum_{s=1}^{S} \pi_s v'(c_{2s}),$$

and for any $c \in C$, let

$$\Delta(c) = \{\delta \in R \times R^s | u(c_1 + \delta_1) + V(c_2 + \delta_2) \ge u(c_1) + V(c_2)\}.$$

From the concavity of $u(\cdot)$ and $v(\cdot)$ and the gradient inequality, it follows that

$$u'(c_1)\delta_1 + \sum_{s=1}^{S} \pi_s v'(c_{2s})\delta_{2s} \ge 0.$$

Then $c \in C$ implies that $\max \delta_{2s} \ge -\delta_1$. We now prove a slightly stronger result.

LEMMA 2. *For any $\epsilon > 0$, $c \in C$, and $\delta \in \Delta(c)$, there exists $\lambda > 1$ such that $\delta_1 \leq -\epsilon$, implies that max $\delta_{2s} \geq \lambda\delta_1$.*

Proof. The lemma is proved by contradiction. Suppose that, contrary to what we want to prove, for some $\epsilon > 0$ and any $\lambda > 1$, we can find $c \in C$ and $\delta \in \Delta(c)$, such that $\delta_1 \leq -\epsilon$, and max $\delta_{2s} < \lambda\delta_1$. Then we can find a sequence (c^k, δ^k) such that, for each k, $c^k \in C$, and $\delta^k \in \delta(c^k)$, $\delta_1^k \leq -\epsilon$, and

$$\lim_{k\to\infty} \frac{\max_s \delta_{2s}^k}{|\delta_1^k|} = 1.$$

The set C is compact, so there exists a convergent subsequence of $\{c^k\}$. Since u and v are concave, there is no loss of generality in assuming that $\delta_1^k = -\epsilon$. Then $\{\delta^k\}$ is bounded above; $\delta^k \in \Delta(c^k)$ implies that it is bounded below as well, so $\{\delta^k\}$ has a convergent subsequence as well. There is no loss of generality, then, in taking $\{(c^k, \delta^k)\}$ to be a convergent sequence with a limit (c^0, δ^0), say. By continuity,

$$u'(c_1^0) \geq \sum_s \pi_s v'(c_{2s}^0),$$

$$u(c_1^0 + \delta_1^0) + V(c_2^0 + \delta_2^0) \geq u(c_1^0) + V(c_2^0),$$

and max $\delta_{2s}^0 = -\delta_1^0$. However, the second inequality and the strict concavity of u and v imply that

$$u'(c_1^0)\delta_1^0 + \sum_{s=1}^{S} \pi_s v'(c_{2s}^0)\delta_{2s}^0 > 0,$$

which contradicts the other two relations. This completes the proof of the lemma.   Q.E.D.

Now, turning to the proof of proposition 5, let $\{(c_{1t}, c_{2t}, s_t)\}$ denote the equilibrium allocation and let $\{(c_{1t}', c_{2t}', s_t')\}$ denote another feasible allocation that satisfies the disintermediation constraint. Suppose to begin with that $s_t = s_t' = 0$ for every date t. Let $\delta_t \equiv (c_{1t}', c_{2t+1}') - (c_{1t}, c_{2t+1})$ denote the difference in generation t's consumption in the two allocations. The equilibrium allocation satisfies

$$u'(c_{1t}) \geq E[v'(c_{2t+1})|y^t], \quad (c_{1t}, c_{2t+1}) \geq 0, \quad c_{1t} \leq e, \quad c_{2t} \leq e + y_t.$$

The first inequality is the first-order condition, the second holds by assumption, and the last two follow from the budget constraints and the fact that $p_t = p_{t+1}$. If we define C as

$$C = \{(c_1, c_2) \in \mathbf{R} \times \mathbf{R}_+^S | u'(c_1) \geq E[v'(c_2)], c_1 \leq e, c_2 \geq e + \max y_s\},$$

then it is clear that $(c_{1t}, c_{2t+1}) \in C$ for every t. Furthermore, $\delta_t \in \Delta(c_{1t}, c_{2t+1})$ for each t. Hence, the conditions of the lemma are satisfied.

Suppose that, contrary to what we want to prove, some generation is ex post better off under the alternative allocation than it would be in equilibrium. Without loss of generality, we can assume that generation 1 is better off. Since the initial generation is no worse off and there is no possible gain from using the storage technology, the improvement in generation 1's welfare must come from a transfer from generation 2, which implies that in some state(s), $\delta_{12} < 0$. Since generation 2 is ex post no worse off, there must be some state in which $\delta_{22} \geq -\lambda\delta_{12}$ for some $\lambda > 1$. The increase in generation 2's second-period consumption can come only from a reduction in generation 3's first-period consumption, and since $\delta_{13} = -\delta_{22} \geq \delta_{12}$, our lemma implies that $\delta_{23} \geq -\lambda\delta_{13} \geq -\lambda^2\delta_{12}$ in some state(s). Continuing in this way, we can find a sequence of states $(y_1, y_2, \ldots)$ such that, at each date t, generation t reduces its first-period consumption by $-\lambda^{t-1}\delta_{12}$ and increases its second-period consumption by at least $\lambda^t\delta_{12}$. Since $\lambda > 1$, this will become infeasible in finite time.

Now suppose that there may be changes in the holding of the safe asset. Other things being equal, an increase in storage will have the effect of reducing the first-period consumption and increasing the second-period consumption of a given generation by the same amount, but will not reduce the ratio λ in the inequalities above. The preceding argument will continue to hold, with δ_{2t+1} interpreted as the transfer of consumption between generations $t + 1$ and t. Again, there is no feasible sequence of transfer that will make some generation better off ex post without making some other generation(s) worse off.   Q.E.D.

References

Allen, F., and Gale, D. (1995). "A welfare comparison of intermediaries and financial markets in Germany and the U.S." *European Econ. Rev.*, 39: 179–209.

Altonji, J. G., Hayashi, F., and Kotlikoff, L. J. (1992). "Is the extended family altruistically linked? Direct tests using micro data." *A.E.R.*, 82: 1177–98.

Bhattacharya, S., and Padilla, A.J. (1996). "Dynamic banking: A reconsideration." *Rev. Financial Studies*, 9: 1003–32.

Diamond, D. W., and Dybvig, P. H. (1983). "Bank runs, deposit insurance, and liquidity." *J.P.E.*, 91: 401–19.

Fulghieri, P., and Rovelli, R. (1994). "Capital markets, financial intermediaries, and the supply of liquidity in a dynamic economy." Manuscript, Milan: Innocenzo Gasparini Inst. Econ. Res., April 1994.

Gordon, R. H., and Varian, H. R. (1988). "Intergenerational risk sharing." *J. Public Econ.*, 37: 185–202.

Hayashi, F., Altonji, J. G., and Kotlikoff, L. J. (1996). "Risk sharing between and within families." *Econometrica*, 64: 261–94.

McCallum, B. T. (1987). "The optimal inflation rate in an overlapping-generations economy with land," in W. A. Barnett and K. J. Singleton (eds.), *New Approaches to Monetary Economics* (Cambridge: Cambridge Univ. Press).

Qi, J. (1976). "Bank liquidity and stability in an overlapping generations model." *Rev. Financial Studies*, 7: 389–417.

Schechtman, J. (1976). "An income fluctuation problem." *J. Econ. Theory*, 12: 218–41.

Scheinkman, J. A. (1980). "Notes on asset trading in an overlapping generations economy." Manuscript. Chicago: Univ. Chicago, Dept. Econ., July.

Comparative Financial Systems: A Discussion

Franklin Allen and Douglas Gale

1. What is a Financial System?

The purpose of a financial system is to channel funds from agents with surpluses to agents with deficits. In the traditional literature there have been two approaches to analyzing this process. The first is to consider how agents interact through financial markets. The second looks at the operation of financial intermediaries such as banks and insurance companies. Fifty years ago, the financial system could be neatly bifurcated in this way. Rich households and large firms used the equity and bond markets, while less wealthy households and medium and small firms used banks, insurance companies, and other financial institutions. Table 1, for example, shows the ownership of corporate equities in 1950. Households owned over 90 percent. By 2000 it can be seen that the situation had changed dramatically. By then households held less than 40 percent, non-bank intermediaries, primarily pension funds and mutual funds, held over 40 percent. This change illustrates why it is no longer possible to consider the role of financial markets and financial institutions separately. Rather than intermediating directly between households and firms, financial institutions have increasingly come to intermediate between households and markets, on the one hand, and between firms and markets, on the other. This makes it necessary to consider the financial system as an irreducible whole.

The notion that a financial system transfers resources between households and firms is, of course, a simplification. Governments usually play a significant role in the financial system. They are major borrowers, particularly during times of war, recession, or when large infrastructure projects are being undertaken. They sometimes also save significant amounts of funds. For example, when countries such as Norway and many Middle Eastern States have access to large amounts of natural resources (oil), the government may acquire large trust funds on behalf of the population.

Table 1. Holdings of Corporate Equities in the United States (in percent)

Sector	1950	1970	1990	2000
Private pension funds	0.8	8.0	16.8	12.9
State and local pension funds	0.0	1.2	7.6	10.3
Life insurance companies	1.5	1.7	2.3	5.4
Other insurance companies	1.8	1.6	2.3	1.1
Mutual funds	2.0	4.7	6.6	19.0
Closed-end funds	1.1	0.5	0.5	0.3
Bank personal trusts	0.0	10.4	5.4	1.9
Foreign sector	2.0	3.2	6.9	8.9
Household sector	90.2	68.0	51.0	39.1
Other	0.6	0.6	0.7	1.2
Total equities outstanding (billions of dollars)	142.7	841.4	3542.6	19047.1

Source: Federal Reserve Board "Flow of Funds," www.bog.frb.fed.us. Figures are for the end of period except for 2000, where the figures are for the third quarter.

In addition to their roles as borrowers or savers, governments usually play a number of other important roles. Central banks typically issue fiat money and are extensively involved in the payments system. Financial systems with unregulated markets and intermediaries, such as the United States in the late nineteenth century, often experience financial crises (Gorton 1988; Calomiris and Gorton 1991). The desire to eliminate these crises led many governments to intervene in a significant way in the financial system. Central banks or some other regulatory authority are charged with regulating the banking system and other intermediaries, such as insurance companies. So in most countries governments play an important role in the operation of financial systems. This intervention means that the political system, which determines the government and its policies, is also relevant for the financial system.

There are some historical instances where financial markets and institutions have operated in the absence of a well-defined legal system, relying instead on reputation and other implicit mechanisms. However, in most financial systems the law plays an important role. It determines what kinds of contracts are feasible, what kinds of governance mechanisms can be used for corporations, the restrictions that can be placed on securities and so forth. Hence, the legal system is an important component of a financial system.

A financial system is much more than all of this, however. An important prerequisite of the ability to write contracts and enforce rights of various kinds is a system of accounting. In addition to allowing contracts to be written, an accounting system allows investors to value a company more easily and to assess how much it would be prudent to lend to it. Accounting information is only one type of information (albeit the most important) required by financial systems. The incentives to generate and disseminate information are crucial features of a financial system.

Without significant amounts of human capital it will not be possible for any of these components of a financial system to operate effectively. Well-trained lawyers, accountants and financial professionals such as bankers are crucial for an effective financial system, as the experience of Eastern Europe demonstrates.

The literature on comparative financial systems is at an early stage. Our survey builds on previous overviews by Allen (1993), Allen and Gale (1995), and Thakor (1996). These overviews have focused on two sets of issues.

1. Normative: How effective are different types of financial system at various functions?
2. Positive: What drives the evolution of the financial system?

The first set of issues is considered in Sections 2–6, which focus on issues of investment and saving, growth, risk sharing, information provision, and corporate governance, respectively. Section 7 considers the influence of law and politics on the financial system while Section 8 looks at the role financial crises have had in shaping the financial system. Section 9 contains concluding remarks.

2. Investment and Saving

One of the primary purposes of the financial system is to allow savings to be invested in firms. In a series of important papers, Mayer (1988, 1990) documents how firms obtained funds and financed investment in a number of different countries. Table 2 shows the results from the most recent set of studies, based on data from 1970 to 1989, using Mayer's methodology. The figures use data obtained from sources-and-uses-of-funds statements. For France, the data are from Bertero (1994), while for the United States, United Kingdom, Japan, and Germany they are from Corbett and Jenkinson (1996). It can be seen that internal finance is by far the most important source of funds in all countries. Bank finance is moderately important in most countries and particularly important in Japan

Table 2. Unweighted Average Gross Financing of Nonfinancial
Enterprises 1970–89 (percent of total)

	U.S.	U.K.	Japan	France	Germany
Internal	91.3	97.3	69.3	60.6	80.6
Bank finance	16.6	19.5	30.5	40.6	11
Bonds	17.1	3.5	4.7	1.3	−0.6
New equity	−8.8	−10.4	3.7	6	0.9
Trade credit	−3.7	−1.4	−8.1	−2.8	−1.9
Capital transfers	−	2.5	−	1.9	8.5
Other	−3.8	−2.9	−0.1	−6.5	1.5
Statistical adjustment	−8.7	−8	0	2.5	0

Source: Bertero (1994) and Corbett and Jenkinson (1996).

and France. Bond finance is only important in the United States and equity finance is either unimportant or negative (i.e. shares are being repurchased in aggregate) in all countries. Mayer's studies and those using his methodology have had an important impact because they have raised the question of how important financial markets are in terms of providing funds for investment. It seems that, at least in the aggregate, equity markets are unimportant while bond markets are important only in the United States. These findings contrast strongly with the emphasis on equity and bond markets in the traditional finance literature. Bank finance is important in all countries, but not as important as internal finance.

Another perspective on how the financial system operates is obtained by looking at savings and the holding of financial assets. Table 3 shows the relative importance of banks and markets in the United States, United Kingdom, Japan, France, and Germany. It can be seen that the United States is at one extreme and Germany at the other. In the United States, banks are relatively unimportant: the ratio of assets to GDP is only 53 percent, about one-third the German ratio of 152 percent. On the other hand, the U.S. ratio of equity market capitalization to GDP is 82 percent, three times the German ratio of 24 percent. Japan and the United Kingdom are interesting intermediate cases where banks and markets are both important. In France, banks are important and markets less so. The United States and the United Kingdom are often referred to as market-based systems while Germany, Japan, and France are often referred to as bank-based systems. Table 4 shows the total portfolio allocation of assets ultimately owned by the household sector. In the United States and the United Kingdom, equity is a much more important component of

Table 3. An International Comparison of Banks and Markets in 1993 (all figures in billions of dollars)

	GDP	Banking assets (BA)	BA/GDP (%)	Equity market capitalization (EMC)	EMC/GDP (%)
U.S.	$6,301	$3,319	53	$5,136	82
U.K.	$824	$2,131	259	$1,152	140
Japan	$4,242	$6,374	150	$2,999	71
France	$1,261	$1,904	151	$457	36
Germany	$1,924	$2,919	152	$464	24

Source: Based on Table 1 of Barth et al. (1997).

Table 4. Total Gross Financial Assets Ultimately Owned by the Household Sector

Country	$ billion	Value relative to GDP	% held directly by households	% held by pension funds (public and private)	% held by insurance companies	% held in mutual funds etc.
U.S.	20,815	3.00	58	17	13	10
U.K.	3,107	2.97	40	24	27	7
Japan	12,936	2.71	71	10	16	3
France	2,689	1.90	62	2	17	19
Germany	2,900	1.46	67	4	20	5

Note: Aggregation of direct asset holdings, pension fund assets, assets of insurance companies, and assets in mutual funds and other collective investment schemes at the end of 1994.

Source: Miles (1996: table 4, p. 21).

household assets than in Japan, Germany, and France. For cash and cash equivalents (which includes bank accounts), the reverse is true.

Tables 3 and 4 provide an interesting contrast to Table 2. One would expect that, in the long run, household portfolios would reflect the financing patterns of firms. Since internal finance accrues to equity holders, one might expect that equity would be much more important in Japan, France, and Germany. There are, of course, differences in the data sets underlying the different tables. For example, household portfolios consist of financial assets and exclude privately held firms, whereas the sources-and-uses-of-funds data include all firms. Nevertheless, it seems unlikely that these differences could cause such huge discrepancies. It is puzzling that these different ways of viewing the financial system produce such radically different results.[1]

Another puzzle concerning internal versus external finance is the difference between the developed world and emerging countries. Although it is true for the United States, United Kingdom, Japan, France, Germany, and for most other developed countries that internal finance dominates external finance, this is not the case for emerging countries. Singh and Hamid (1992) and Singh (1995) show that, for a range of emerging economies, external finance is more important than internal finance. Moreover, equity is the most important financing instrument and dominates debt. This difference between the industrialized nations and the emerging countries has so far received little attention.

There is a large theoretical literature on the operation of and rationale for internal capital markets. Internal capital markets differ from external capital markets because of asymmetric information, investment incentives, asset specificity, control rights, transaction costs or incomplete markets (see, e.g. Williamson 1975; Grossman and Hart 1986; Gertner et al. 1994; Stein 1997; Allen and Gale 2000a: chapters 11 and 12). There has also been considerable debate on the relationship between liquidity and investment (see, e.g. Fazzari et al. 1988; Hoshi et al. 1991; Whited 1992; Kaplan and Zingales 1997; Lamont 1997; Shin and Stulz 1998).

Internal capital markets are an extreme case in which the allocation of resources is achieved entirely within the firm. The other extreme is arm's length (external) finance. An intermediate case is a long-term relationship finance, say, between a firm and an investment bank. Much of the debate on comparative financial systems has associated arm's length finance with market-based systems like the United States and the United Kingdom and relationship finance with bank-based systems like Japan, France, and Germany. The extensive use of the main bank system in Japan and the hausbank system in Germany means that long-lived relationships between large firms and banks are commonplace. In the United States, large firms have much more limited long-term relationships with banks.

---

[1] There is no widely accepted resolution to this puzzle. However, Hackethal and Schmidt (1999) argue that it results from an apparently innocuous assumption in the methodology used in the studies based on sources and uses of funds. This is that the proceeds from new bank finance are first used to repay old loans and then are used for funding investment. It is similar for other sources of funds such as bonds and equity. The only exception is internal finance where there is nothing to be repaid. This distorts the measurement of the sources of finance toward internal finance and makes it seem more important than it is. When they correct for this distortion they find figures more in line with the portfolio data here.

There is a growing literature that analyzes the advantages and disadvantages of relationships in banking (for theoretical analyses see Diamond 1991; Boot et al. 1993; von Thadden 1995; Yosha 1995; Dinç 1996; Aoki and Dinç 1997; for empirical analyses see Berger and Udell 1992; Petersen and Rajan 1994, 1995; Berlin and Mester 1997, 1998; Elsas and Krahnen 1998; Boot and Thakor 2000).

It is often argued that long-term relationships promote cooperative behavior. Stiglitz and Weiss (1983) have argued, in the context of credit markets with incomplete information, that inefficiencies associated with adverse selection, and moral hazard are mitigated if lenders can threaten borrowers with punishment in the event of default or poor performance. For example, a firm that defaults on a bank loan may be refused credit in the future. However, such arguments are undermined by the possibility of renegotiation.

In analyzing the optimal use of threats, it is assumed that the lender can commit itself to a particular course of action in advance. From a purely economic perspective, the assumption of commitment is problematical. Although it is optimal to threaten to terminate the availability of credit in advance, once the borrower has defaulted, the first loan becomes a "sunk cost." As such, it should not affect future decisions. If the firm has another project which offers positive net present value, there exists an incentive-compatible contract that finances the project and makes the borrower and the lender both better off. In that case, it would be irrational not to take advantage of this opportunity. Thus, we should expect that the lender will continue to extend credit, even if the borrower defaults.

Renegotiation thus creates a time-consistency problem. The threat to terminate credit creates good incentives for the borrower to avoid the risk of default. Termination of credit is not Pareto-efficient ex post, but the incentive effect makes both parties better off. However, if the borrower anticipates that the lender will not carry out the threat in practice, the incentive effect disappears. Although the lender's behavior is now ex post optimal, both parties may be worse off ex ante.

The time inconsistency of commitments that are optimal ex ante and sub-optimal ex post is typical in contracting problems. The contract commits one to certain courses of action in order to influence the behavior of the other party. Then once that party's behavior has been determined, the benefit of the commitment disappears and there is now an incentive to depart from it. Whatever agreements have been entered into are subject to revision because both parties can typically be made better off by "renegotiating" the original agreement. The possibility of renegotiation puts additional restrictions on the kind of contract or agreement that is feasible (we are referring here to the contract or agreement as executed, rather than the contract as originally written or conceived) and, to that extent, tends to reduce the welfare of both parties ex ante. Anything that gives the parties a greater power to commit themselves to the terms of the contract will, conversely, be welfare-enhancing.

Dewatripont and Maskin (1995) (included as Chapter Nineteen in this part) have suggested that financial markets have an advantage over financial intermediaries in maintaining commitments to refuse further funding. If the firm obtains its funding from the bond market, then, in the event that it needs additional investment, it will have to go back to the bond market. Because the bonds are widely held, however, the firm will find it difficult to renegotiate with the bond holders. Apart from the transaction costs involved in negotiating with a large number of bond holders, there is a free-rider problem. Each bond holder would like to maintain his original claim over the returns to the project, while allowing the others to renegotiate their claims in order to finance the additional investment. The free-rider problem, which is often thought of as the curse of cooperative enterprises, turns out to be a virtue in disguise when it comes to maintaining commitments.

From a theoretical point of view, there are many ways of maintaining a commitment. Financial institutions may develop a valuable reputation for maintaining commitments. In any one case, it is worth incurring the small cost of a sub-optimal action in order to maintain the value of the reputation. Incomplete information about the borrower's type may lead to a similar outcome. If default causes the institution to change its beliefs about the defaulter's type, then it may be optimal to refuse to deal with a firm after it has defaulted. Institutional strategies such as delegating decisions to agents who are given no discretion to renegotiate may also be an effective commitment device.

Several authors (Huberman and Kahn 1988; Hart and Moore 1988; Gale 1991; Allen and Gale 2000a: chapter 10) have argued that, under certain circumstances, renegotiation is welfare-improving. In that case, the Dewatripont–Maskin argument is turned on its head. Intermediaries that establish long-term relationships with clients may have an advantage over financial markets precisely because it is easier for them to renegotiate contracts.

The crucial assumption is that contracts are incomplete. Because of the high transaction costs of writing complete contracts, some potentially Pareto-improving contingencies are left out of contracts and securities. This incompleteness of contracts may make renegotiation desirable. The missing contingencies can be replaced by contract adjustments that are negotiated by the parties ex post, after they observe the realization of variables on which the contingencies would have been based. The incomplete contract determines the status quo for the ex post bargaining game (i.e. renegotiation) that determines the final outcome.

An important question in this whole area is "How important are these relationships empirically?" Here there does not seem to be a lot of evidence. As far as the importance of renegotiation in the sense of Dewatripont and Maskin (1995), the work of Asquith et al. (1994) suggests that little renegotiation occurs in the case of financially distressed firms. Conventional wisdom holds that banks are so well secured that they can and do "pull the plug" as soon as a borrower becomes distressed, leaving the unsecured creditors and other claimants holding the bag.

Petersen and Rajan (1994) suggest that firms that have a longer relationship with a bank do have greater access to credit, controlling for a number of features of the borrowers' history. It is not clear from their work exactly what lies behind the value of the relationship. For example, the increased access to credit could be an incentive device or it could be the result of greater information or the relationship itself could make the borrower more credit worthy. Berger and Udell (1992) find that banks smooth loan rates in response to interest rate shocks. Petersen and Rajan (1995) and Berlin and Mester (1997) find that smoothing occurs as a firm's credit risk changes. Berlin and Mester (1998) find that loan rate smoothing is associated with lower bank profits. They argue that this suggests the smoothing does not arise as part of an optimal relationship.

This section has pointed to a number of issues for future research.

- What is the relationship between the sources of funds for investment, as revealed by Mayer (1988, 1990), and the portfolio choices of investors and institutions? The answer to this question may shed some light on the relative importance of external and internal finance.
- Why are financing patterns so different in developing and developed economies?
- Is renegotiation important and is it a good thing or a bad thing?

- Do long-term relationships constitute an important advantage of bank-based systems over market-based systems?

3. Growth and Financial Structure

The relationship between the growth rate of an economy and its financial structure is a long-debated issue. On the one hand, Bagehot (1873) and Hicks (1969) argue that the UK's financial system played an important role in the Industrial Revolution. On the other hand, Robinson (1952) suggests that the causation goes the other way and that the financial system developed as a result of economic growth. In his survey of development economics, Stern (1989) does not even mention finance (not even under 'omitted topics'). Levine (1997) provides an excellent overview of the literature on economic growth and financial development.

In a pioneering study using cross-country data, Goldsmith (1969) found a relationship between growth and financial development. However, his study was based on limited data and did not control in a satisfactory way for other factors affecting growth. In a series of studies King and Levine (1993a–c) consider data for eighty countries over the period 1960–89 and carefully control for other factors affecting growth. They find a strong relationship between growth and financial development and also find evidence that the level of financial development is a good predictor of future economic growth. In an innovative study Rajan and Zingales (1998) use data from the United States to find which industries rely on external finance and investigate whether these industries grow faster in countries with better developed financial systems. They find a positive correlation between growth rates and financial development, suggesting that finance is important for growth. Demirgüç-Kunt and Maksimovic (1996) consider firm-level data from thirty countries and argue that access to stock markets leads to faster growth. In an influential contribution, McKinnon (1973) did case studies of Argentina, Brazil, Chile, Germany, Korea, Indonesia, and Taiwan in the period after the Second World War. His conclusion from these cases is that better financial systems support faster economic growth. Taken together these studies provide considerable support for a relationship between finance and growth.

A large number of theoretical studies consider the growth–finance relationship. Hicks (1969) and Bencivenga et al. (1995) argue that the liquidity provided by capital markets was key in allowing growth in the U.K. Industrial Revolution. Many of the products produced early in the Industrial Revolution had been invented some time before but lack of long-term finance delayed their manufacture. Liquid capital markets allowed the projects to be financed by savers with short time horizons and/or uncertain liquidity needs. Similarly, Bencivenga and Smith (1991) argue that intermediaries may be able to enhance liquidity, while at the same time funding long-lived projects. Greenwood and Jovanovic (1990) point out that intermediaries that can effectively process information about entrepreneurs and projects can induce a higher rate of growth. King and Levine (1993c) suggest that intermediaries can also do a better job of choosing innovations. Another avenue for increasing growth is the higher expected returns that can be achieved if risk is reduced through diversification (Saint-Paul 1982). Boyd and Smith (1996, 1998) suggest that banks are important at low levels of development while markets become more important as income rises. Rajan and Zingales (1999) suggest that banks are less dependent than markets on the legal system. Hence, banks can do better when the legal system is weak and markets do better when the legal system is more developed.

Another important element of the debate concerns the relative contributions of banks and financial markets in spurring growth. This debate was originally conducted in the context of German and United Kingdom growth in the late nineteenth and early twentieth centuries. Gerschenkron (1962) argues that the bank-based system in Germany allowed a closer relationship between bankers providing the finance and industrial firms than was possible in the market-based system in the United Kingdom. Goldsmith (1969) pointed out that although manufacturing industry grew much faster in Germany than the United Kingdom in the late nineteenth and early twentieth centuries the overall growth rates were fairly similar. More recently, Levine (2000) uses a broad database covering 48 countries over the period 1980–95. He finds that the distinction between bank- and market-based systems is not an interesting one for explaining the finance–growth nexus. Rather, elements of a country's legal environment and the quality of its financial services are most important for fostering general economic growth. In contrast, in a study of thirty-six countries from 1980 to 1995, Tadesse (2000) does find a difference between bank- and market-based financial systems. For underdeveloped financial sectors, bank-based systems outperform market-based systems, while for developed financial sectors market-based systems outperform bank-based systems. Levine and

Zervos (1998) show that higher stock market liquidity or greater bank development lead to higher growth, irrespective of the development of the other. There is some evidence that financial markets and banks are complements rather substitutes. Demirguç-Kunt and Maksimovic (1998) show that more developed stock markets tend to be associated with increased use of bank finance in developing countries.

There is a large theoretical literature on the relative merits of bank- and market-based systems. Many of these papers are covered in the other sections of this survey. Here we focus on the contributions concerned with innovation and growth. Bhattacharya and Chiesa (1995) (included as Chapter Twenty in this part) consider a model of R&D incentives and financing. Two regimes are considered. Under multilateral financing, each bank lends to each firm and finances only part of its project. This can be thought of as a metaphor for a financial market. The lenders learn the value of each firm's R&D at the interim stage after R&D has been undertaken but before production takes place. The lenders can share the information among the firms and will do so if it is in their interest. Bhattacharya and Chiesa show that their incentives to do this correspond to maximizing the aggregate value of the firms' R&D projects. Also, a collusive agreement can be structured so that only one firm actually produces at the production stage. However, this collusion creates a free-rider problem and reduces incentives to undertake the R&D at the first stage. If this incentive problem is severe enough, bilateral financing may be preferable. Under this arrangement, each firm is financed by one bank and there is no scope for information sharing. As a result, each firm's R&D information remains proprietary.

A related model is developed by Yosha (1995). In his model, firms differ in the quality of proprietary information at the interim stage. He focuses on the signalling effect of choosing bilateral versus multilateral financing. With multilateral financing in a public financial market, the proprietary information must be disclosed. With bilateral financing, the information does not have to be revealed. In equilibrium, firms with high quality proprietary information use bilateral financing. Product market competitors deduce this relationship and take appropriate actions to offset it.

Allen and Gale (1999, 2000a: chapter 13) ask whether financial markets or banks are better at providing finance for projects where there is diversity of opinion, for example, in the development of new technologies. Diversity of opinion arises from differences in prior beliefs, rather than differences in information. The advantage of financial markets is that they allow people with similar views to join together to finance projects.

This will be optimal provided the costs necessary for each investor to form an opinion before investment decisions are made are sufficiently low. Finance can be provided by the market even when there is great diversity of opinion among investors. Intermediated finance involves delegating the financing decision to a manager who expends the cost necessary to form an opinion. There is an agency problem in that the manager may not have the same prior as the investor. This type of delegation turns out to be optimal when the costs of forming an opinion are high and there is likely to be considerable agreement in any case. The analysis suggests that market-based systems will lead to more innovation than bank-based systems.

There are a number of important open questions about the relationship between growth and financial structure.

- There appears to be a wide range of empirical evidence that growth and financial structure are positively correlated. There is little agreement as to the direction of causation and the channels by which each influences the other.
- The empirical evidence on the effectiveness of bank-based and market-based systems is mixed.

In both cases, we are a long way from being able to make welfare-based recommendations.

4. Risk Sharing

One of the most important functions of the financial system is to share risk and it is often argued that financial markets are well suited to achieve this aim. However, market-based financial systems can actually create risk through changes in asset values. Table 4 illustrates the degree of exposure to this kind of risk. It shows the differences in total assets ultimately owned by households, including both directly and indirectly owned assets, in five countries. In the United States, only 19 percent is held in the form of cash and cash equivalents which includes bank deposits. A significant proportion, 31 percent, is held in the form of relatively safe, fixed-income assets, including domestic and foreign bonds, loans, and mortgages. The largest proportion, 46 percent, is held in risky assets, including domestic and foreign equity and real estate. The United Kingdom is similar with slightly more in cash and cash equivalents at 24 percent, significantly less in fixed income assets at 13 percent and substantially more in risky equity and real estate assets at 52 percent. In both countries households are exposed to substantial amounts of risk through their holdings of assets.

At the other extreme, households in Japan are shielded from risk because of the composition of the portfolio of assets they ultimately hold. In Japan, 52 percent of assets are held in cash and cash equivalents, 19 percent are held in fixed income assets, and only 13 percent are held in risky equity and real estate. Although not quite as safe as in Japan, households' asset holdings in France and Germany are much safer than in the United States and the United Kingdom. Cash and cash equivalents are lower than Japan at 38 percent and 36 percent, respectively, while fixed-income assets are substantially higher at 33 percent and 40 percent, respectively. The amount of risky assets is comparable to Japan, 16 percent for both countries.

It can be seen from these statistics that the proportions of risky assets held by households in the United States and the United Kingdom are much higher than in Japan, France, and Germany. This does not necessarily mean that the absolute amount of risk borne by households is greater because the amount invested in financial assets could be greater in the latter countries. Figure 1 shows the gross financial assets ultimately owned by the household sector in the five countries in 1994. In the United States, the value of financial assets relative to GDP is the highest at 3 but the United Kingdom and Japan are broadly similar. To normalize for the size of each country's GDP, Figure 2 reports financial assets as a percentage of GDP. France and Germany have a significantly lower amount of financial assets with ratios less than 2 for Germany and 1.5 for France. Combining the results illustrated in Table 4 and Figures 1 and 2 shows that taking into account the amount of wealth held in financial assets increases the differences in the amount of risk borne by households in the different countries, rather than reduces it. Not only do households hold much higher proportions in risky securities in the United States and the

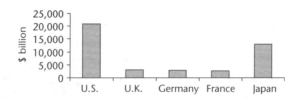

Figure 1. Total gross financial assets ultimately owned by the household sector.

Source: Miles (1996: table 4, p. 21).

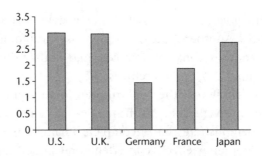

Figure 2. Total gross financial assets ultimately owned by the household sector—ratio value relative to GDP.

Source: Miles (1996: table 4, p. 21).

United Kingdom, they also hold more financial assets, particularly relative to France and Germany.

How can one explain these differences in the amount of risk households are apparently exposed to in different financial systems? Standard financial theory suggests that the main purpose of financial markets is to improve risk sharing. Financial markets in the United States and the United Kingdom are more developed by most measures than in Japan and France and much more developed than in Germany. How can it be that households are exposed to more risk in the United States and the United Kingdom than in Japan, France, and Germany?

Allen and Gale (1997, 2000a: chapter 6) (included as Chapter Twenty-two in this part) have provided a resolution to this paradox. They point out that traditional financial theory has little to say about hedging non-diversifiable risks. It assumes that the set of assets is given and theory focuses on the efficient sharing of these risks through exchange. For example, the standard diversification argument requires individuals to exchange assets so that each investor holds a relatively small amount of any one risk. Risks will also be traded so that more risk-averse people bear less risk than people who are less risk-averse. This kind of risk sharing is termed cross-sectional risk sharing, because it is achieved through exchanges of risk among individuals at a given point in time. However, importantly, these strategies do not eliminate macroeconomic shocks that affect all assets in a similar way.

Departing from the traditional approach, Allen and Gale focus on the intertemporal smoothing of risks that cannot be diversified at a given point in time. They argue that such risks can be averaged over time in a way that reduces their impact on individual welfare. One hedging strategy for non-diversifiable risks is intergenerational risk sharing. This spreads the risks

associated with a given stock of assets across generations with heterogeneous experiences. Another strategy involves asset accumulation in order
to reduce fluctuations in consumption over time. Both are examples of the
intertemporal smoothing of asset returns.

Allen and Gale show that the opportunities for engaging in intertemporal smoothing are very different in market- and bank-based financial
systems. They demonstrate that incomplete financial markets, on the
one hand, may not allow effective intertemporal smoothing. Long-lived
financial institutions, such as banks, on the other hand, can achieve
intertemporal smoothing, as long as they are not subject to substantial
competition from financial markets. In fact, competition from financial
markets can lead to disintermediation and the unraveling of intertemporal
smoothing provided by long-lived institutions. In good times, individuals
would rather opt out of the banking system and invest in the market, thus
avoiding the accumulation of reserves from which they may not benefit.
Therefore, in the long run, intertemporal smoothing by banks is not viable
in the presence of direct competition from markets.

This theory provides a framework for thinking about the role of risk
management in different financial systems. In bank-based systems, such as
those in Japan, France, and Germany, risk management could be achieved
through intertemporal smoothing, in which financial intermediaries eliminate risk by accumulating low risk, liquid assets. Cross-sectional risk
sharing through markets is less important, and the importance of other
forms of risk management is reduced correspondingly.

In market-based financial systems, on the other hand, intertemporal
smoothing by intermediaries is ruled out by competition from financial
markets. Here, cross-sectional risk sharing becomes correspondingly more
important. As a result, individuals and institutions acting on their behalf
need to trade and manage risk in a very different way. They need to ensure
that those who are most tolerant of risk end up bearing most of the risk.
The Allen–Gale theory thus predicts that as financial systems become more
market-oriented, risk management through the use of derivatives and
other similar techniques will become more important. The theory is thus
consistent with the fact that these particular forms of risk management
are much more important in the United States and the United Kingdom
than they are in less market-oriented economies such as Japan, France,
and Germany.

The Allen–Gale theory points to clear opportunities for improving welfare through intertemporal risk sharing when markets are incomplete, but

it leaves open the question of whether financial institutions will have the right incentives to offer this kind of risk sharing. In fact, there is as yet no adequate theory of long-lived financial institutions. In some cases, we can obviate this gap in the theory by assuming that competitive institutions maximize the welfare of their depositors. However, when depositors are heterogeneous as, for example, in an overlapping generations economy, this device breaks down. One of the important questions posed by the behavior of financial institutions in different countries is, what is the objective function of a financial institution? At the moment, we do not know.

The risks associated with holding stocks, bonds, and other financial assets are only some of the risks that individuals face. There are many other risks, such as the risk of unemployment, illness, changes in the value of one's home, and changes in the value of one's human capital, to name a few. Despite the enormous pace of financial innovation in the 1980s and 1990s, there are very few ways in which these risks can be shared. Shiller (1993) has argued that there is scope for creating securities for hedging risks such as changes in the value of real estate, or changes in the level of national, regional, or occupational incomes. However, in many cases there are good reasons why such markets do not exist. These include moral hazard, adverse selection, and transaction costs. In many cases, these market failures have led to government intervention. For example, governments in most countries are heavily involved in the provision of unemployment insurance, health care, disability insurance, and so forth. Thus, the public sector plays an important role in the sharing of risks. The tax system itself can also be thought of as a risk-sharing vehicle. The fact that gains can be set against losses and so forth also helps to share risks.

Perhaps one of the most important areas in which the government intervenes to share risks is the public provision of pensions. Because of problems of adverse selection and moral hazard, the market for annuities is inefficient. This market failure provides a rationale for government provision of pensions. Other reasons include the fact that agents cannot trade before they are born and hence cannot insure against "accidents of birth." This "market failure" and the resulting overlapping generations structure means that a Pareto improvement can be achieved with a pay as you go public pension system. In addition to the public provision of pensions, many countries provide tax advantages for private pensions.

In practice, the extent to which countries provide public pensions differs substantially (see Davis 1992, 1996 for an account and Miles 1996 for asset holdings or Allen and Gale 2000*a*: chapter 3, for a summary of both). For example, in the United Kingdom public pensions are rather meagre. The basic component is small. There is also an earnings-related component to supplement the basic rate. However, it is possible to contract out of this earnings-related part and replace it with a private pension scheme. As a result of the limited public pension scheme, private pensions are popular in the United Kingdom. The contributions and asset returns are untaxed and only the benefits are taxed. Coverage is high with 50 percent of the work force participating in company schemes. The proportion of assets ultimately owned by the household sector and held by public and private pension funds is 24 percent. Over 75 percent of these assets are equities. Clearly, the importance of private pensions in the United Kingdom has contributed to the growth of the stock market there.

In Germany, the structure of pensions is quite different. The social security system provides pensions to all workers. These state pensions are linked to average earnings during working life. The replacement ratio is high. In addition to the public pension system, there is also an extensive private pension system. Private plans are usually defined-benefit and provide a flat benefit. Inflation indexing is mandatory. One special feature of German pensions is how they are taxed at the corporate level. Pensions funded by book reserves are given special advantages. Firms are allowed discretionary use of the funds accumulated on the firm's balance sheet, free of tax. As a result, very few funds in Germany are invested in anything other than book reserves of the firm. In addition, benefits booked this way are insured by the Pension Guarantee Association. Very few assets are held by pension funds. Just 4 percent of household assets are held by public and private pension funds. For those funds which are held externally, there are guidelines on how they can be invested. There are maximum limits of 20 percent in equity, 5 percent in property, and 4 percent in foreign securities. Equities in fact only constitute 6.6 percent of pension assets. Bonds represent 42.8 percent and loans and mortgages are 29.5 percent. The lack of externally invested funds in private pension funds contributes to the relatively small size of the German stock market.

Finally, no discussion of risk sharing would be complete without including the role of the insurance industry. The property and casualty part of the industry allows many everyday risks such as property damage and theft, accidents and so forth to be shared. The life insurance part of the industry provides not only life insurance but also long-term savings vehicles, which in some countries are tax-advantaged. The fact that premiums are paid in advance and that the life insurance industry provides savings vehicles means that insurance companies are usually holders of a significant proportion of a country's financial assets. The degree of regulation and the way in which the industry operates vary significantly across countries. The United Kingdom and Germany again illustrate the range of possibilities.

In the United Kingdom, the insurance industry is fairly lightly regulated. It is not dominated by a few large players and is quite competitive. Like the pension funds, insurance companies represent a large proportion, 27 percent, of household assets. They also invest significantly in equities, with 59.8 percent of their assets being in this form. The insurance industry in Germany is more regulated. The Insurance Supervisory Office requires funds be invested according to the requirements of security, profitability, mixing, and spreading, with liquidity assured at all times. More than 80 percent of the insurance companies' assets are placed with the banks. Although insurance companies can invest in equities, this type of investment plays a very small role in their portfolios. An important feature of the German insurance industry is the legal requirement that life insurance be separate from other forms of insurance. The supervisory authority has extended this requirement to other insurance lines. As a result, insurance tends to be offered by groups with many consolidated subsidiaries. The assets held by insurance companies represent 20 percent of household assets. The proportion of these investments in bonds is 66.3 percent while only 12.6 percent are in equities.

As this section indicates, there are many different institutions for sharing risk in a modern economy. When we think about the financial system as encompassing all of these different risk sharing mechanisms, a number of new questions are suggested.

- How important are different types of risk sharing (e.g. cross-sectional versus intertemporal risk sharing)?
- How do different mechanisms for sharing risk interact? For example, what is the interaction between the public provision of pensions and the development of the capital markets.

5. Information Provision

The acquisition and use of information to allocate resources efficiently is one of the most important functions of a financial system. In market-based systems, such as the United States, the large number of publicly listed firms, together with extensive disclosure requirements, means that a great deal of information about firms' activities is released. In addition to this publicly available information, there are many analysts working for mutual funds, pension funds, and other intermediaries who gather private information. The empirical evidence on efficient markets suggests that much of this information is reflected in stock prices. On the other hand, in some countries with bank-based systems, such as Germany and other continental European countries, relatively few companies are listed and accounting disclosure requirements are limited, so very little information is publicly available. In addition, the number of analysts who follow stocks is small, so only limited private information is incorporated into stock prices. Although the financial markets have more information available in market-based financial systems like the United States than in bank-based systems like Germany the reverse is true for intermediaries. The greater prevalence of long-term relationships in bank-based systems means that the banks are able to acquire considerable amounts of information about the firms they lend to, more than is released to the market. This can be used to allocate resources more efficiently.

Corresponding to these two perspectives are two traditional approaches to the role of information in financial systems. The first comes from the general equilibrium and rational expectations literatures on the role of prices in resource allocation. The second comes from the interme- diation literature and is concerned with the role of banks as delegated monitors. We consider each in turn. Based on the first approach, it is some- times argued that since market-based financial systems have many more prices that are publicly observed they allocate resources better than bank- based systems. Similarly based on the second approach it is sometimes argued that bank-based systems do better. As will be seen these simplistic arguments ignore many important factors.

5.1 Prices and Information

The standard neoclassical view of prices, which originated with Adam Smith's "invisible hand," is that they are indicators of scarcity and value. The modern version of this theory is captured in the Arrow–Debreu– Mackenzie (ADM) model and the fundamental theorems of welfare eco- nomics. If markets are complete and certain other restrictions are satisfied, markets allow a Pareto-efficient allocation of resources.

The neoclassical theory of resource allocation, which culminated in the ADM theory, was initially developed under the assumption of *certainty*. Under these conditions, decision-making is relatively simple. How firms should make investment decisions to maximize their value is the subject of capital budgeting. Over the years, it has become a mainstay of the curriculum in most business schools. It has been expounded in numerous textbooks. Current examples in wide use are Brealey and Myers (2000) and Ross et al. (2001). According to the methodology outlined in these books, managers first need to derive the stream of cash flows that will accrue to shareholders over time, including the initial cost of the investment. This is done using various types of information. Projections based on accounting data generated within the firm usually play an important part. Once the cash flows have been calculated, they are discounted at the opportunity cost of capital for each period to give the net present value (NPV). NPV is obviously maximized by accepting positive NPV projects and rejecting negative NPV projects. There are a number of other capital budgeting methods such as internal rate of return (IRR) and profitability index (PI) which are widely used and are equivalent to NPV if correctly applied. We will focus on NPV below.

The discount rates that should be used are found from the term structure of interest rates. Since there is no uncertainty, markets are complete if every agent can borrow and lend at these rates. Then there is unanimous agreement among the shareholders about the optimal policy for the firm. Shareholders should simply tell the managers to follow the NPV rule (or an equivalent). If all managers follow this rule, the allocation of resources within the economy will be Pareto-efficient. Furthermore, the actual mechanics of decentralizing decisions from shareholders to managers are particularly simple. The information that shareholders need to convey to managers is minimal. The shareholders do not need to tell the managers anything except "Maximize NPV." In particular, they do not need to tell the managers their preferences or the discount rates that should be used. The managers can observe the term structure of interest rates themselves.

The assumption of certainty on which this whole theory is based is, of course, unrealistic. However, all the important elements of the theory carry through with *uncertainty* provided markets are complete. In other words, provided there are markets at the initial date for all goods and services contingent on every possible state of nature, the introduction of uncertainty has no effect as far as firms are concerned. A firm buys all its inputs and sells all its outputs on a contingent basis, before any uncertainty is resolved. Consequently, the firm's profits and market value are known for sure at the initial date when all decisions are made.

In the case of certainty the main informational role of financial markets is to provide the term structure of interest rates. Stock markets are informationally redundant since the value of the firm can easily be calculated from the prices of inputs and outputs and interest rates. Since both market- and bank-based financial systems have a term structure of interest rates that can be publicly observed by all agents, there is essentially no difference between them. The fact that bank-based systems do not have stock market prices available is of no consequence for resource allocation. A similar argument can be made in the case where there is uncertainty and markets are complete.

The glaring weakness of this argument is that, in practice, markets are not complete. How can firms make decisions in this case? Corporate finance textbook expositions of capital budgeting techniques suggest a simple method of calculating the effect of an investment decision on the value of the firm in this situation. The stream of certain cash flows is replaced with a stream of *expected* cash flows and the present value is calculated using a discount rate from an asset pricing model estimated from historical price data. The model that is typically used is the capital asset pricing model (CAPM). In order to calculate the discount rate using the CAPM, it is necessary to have historical data from the stock market on the covariance of returns for the firm's stock with the market portfolio (a value weighted portfolio consisting of all the stocks in the market). It is possible to show that if firms adopt this method, there will be an efficient allocation of resources in a stock-market economy provided some firms are listed in every industry (see, e.g. Allen and Gale 2000a: chapter 7). Thus, a stock market provides the information that is necessary for efficient decentralization. Stock market prices provide information in the sense that they allow the asset pricing model to be estimated. They are no longer redundant.

Even though the CAPM is based on very special assumptions and has limited empirical support, this result revives the argument that market-based financial systems are superior to bank-based systems because of the availability of stock-price information. If the financial system is bank-based, it would appear that this kind of decentralization is not possible. However, Allen and Gale (2000a: chapter 7) suggest that if the institutional structure is similar to the United States in the nineteenth century or some European economies in the twentieth century, decentralization will still be possible in an intermediated economy. Suppose finance is provided by intermediaries such as banks and insurance companies. There is a stock exchange, but only the intermediaries are listed. They make loans to firms and have equity investments in them. Since the intermediaries are listed and hold equity in all the firms in the economy, a portfolio consisting of the intermediaries is like the market portfolio in a full stock market economy. Provided firms can use accounting data to calculate the returns on a firm they will then be able to calculate the covariance with the market and hence be able to use the CAPM to find a discount rate. In this case, bank-based systems will not be at a disadvantage compared to market-based systems in terms of the information available to allocate resources.

In the frameworks discussed so far, information is public. An important issue in the literature has been the process by which private information becomes reflected in prices; in other words, their role as aggregators of information. One of the questions that received considerable attention in the 1960s and 1970s is the extent to which stock markets are informationally efficient and reflect all the available information. The notion implicit in much of this research is that if stock prices are informationally efficient, they would provide a good mechanism for allocating investment resources. This view is well exposited by Fama (1976: 133) who wrote:

An efficient capital market is an important component of a capitalist system. In such a system, the ideal is a market where prices are accurate signals for capital allocation. That is, when firms issue securities to finance their activities they can expect to get 'fair' prices, and when investors choose among the securities that represent ownership of firms' activities, they can do so under the assumption they are paying 'fair' prices. In short, if the capital market is to function smoothly in allocating resources, prices of securities must be good indicators of value.

Extensive evidence was provided during the 1960s and 1970s that markets are efficient in the sense that investors pay "fair" prices and it is not possible to make excess returns above the reward for bearing risk using information that is publicly available. This is termed *semi-strong form efficiency*. There was some evidence that even using apparently private information, it is not possible to make excess returns. This is termed *strong-form efficiency*. More recently studies have been less supportive. For surveys of the empirical literature on efficient markets see Fama (1970, 1991) and Hawawini and Keim (1995).

Grossman (1976) developed a theoretical model based on rational expectations to show how private signals obtained by investors could become incorporated in prices, so that apparently private information became public. If an investor has favorable information, she will buy the security and bid up its price while if she has unfavorable information she will sell and bid down the price. Grossman was able to show that, under certain conditions, prices aggregate all the economically relevant private information. This result provides a theoretical underpinning for the notion of prices as aggregators of information and led to a large literature on information revelation, including Grossman and Stiglitz (1976, 1980), Hellwig (1980), and Diamond and Verrecchia (1981). For surveys, see Grossman (1981) and Admati (1989).

An important point, which is often disregarded in discussions of financial systems, is that informational efficiency and welfare (Pareto) efficiency are different things (see, e.g. Dow and Gorton 1997; Allen and Gale 2000a: chapter 7). In special cases, full revelation of information through market prices or in some other way can lead to the first best, as the above quote from Fama suggests. In other words, informational efficiency is equivalent to Pareto-efficiency. However, this need not be true in general. For example, in order to reveal information, prices have to fluctuate with changes in underlying information; but price fluctuations themselves are costly to the extent that they impose risk of uninsured changes in wealth on investors. There is therefore a trade-off between allocative efficiency and risk sharing. This is similar to the point made by Hirshleifer (1971) that the public release of information can destroy valuable risk sharing opportunities.

There is a large literature on the welfare analysis of rational expectations models. Allen (1983) and Laffont (1985) showed that more information could make people worse off because the added price volatility increases consumption variability. Jacklin and Bhattacharya (1988) showed that bank deposits can be more desirable than equity mutual funds for similar reasons. Much of this literature is concerned with the desirability of allowing insider trading. One view is that insider trading involves the informed benefiting at the expense of the uninformed. Another view is that insider trading is desirable because it leads to prices being more informative, which improves the allocation of investment. For a variety of positions on and analyses of insider trading see Glosten (1989), Manove (1989), Ausubel (1990), Fishman and Hagerty (1992), Leland (1992), Bernhardt et al. (1995), and Bhattacharya and Nicodano (1995).

Another set of papers analyzes what happens when one group of traders is simply better informed than another, either because they have paid to acquire information or because they are endowed with superior information. Bernardo and Judd (1997) analyze a version of the Grossman and Stiglitz (1980) model with pure exchange using numerical techniques and show that everybody would be better off without information. Dow and Rahi (1997) analyze a parametric model with investment in productive assets by firms. They are able to derive closed-form solutions for all agents' utilities and this allows a nice characterization of the trade-off between risk-sharing and investment.

A third strand of the literature takes a security-design approach to analyze the relationship between incomplete markets and information revelation. This literature has identified three effects of security design on welfare when agents are asymmetrically informed: spanning, adverse selection, and insurance destruction (i.e. the Hirshleifer effect). In general, welfare improves with spanning and is reduced with adverse selection and insurance destruction. Taking the number of assets as given, Rahi (1995) finds that it is constrained Pareto-efficient to issue information-free securities as a way to minimize the adverse selection problem. Marín and Rahi (1999) generalize the analysis of the previous paper and show that under certain conditions its main conclusion is reversed. In particular, they identify conditions on the primitives of the economy for which it is Pareto-efficient to issue "speculative securities." These are securities whose payoff explicitly depends on private information sunspots (i.e. a random shock unrelated to endowments and preferences about which some agents have private information). Finally, Marín and Rahi (2000) consider the effect of endogenizing the number of assets in this type of model and build a theory of (endogenous) market incompleteness. They find that, under certain conditions, the introduction of a new security makes all agents worse off because it provides new information that destroys insurance opportunities. In the last two chapters, the incorporation of asymmetric information, sunspots, and the reduction of the number of tradable securities inject noise into the price system so that less information is revealed and, consequently, fewer insurance opportunities are destroyed.

A number of papers consider the feedback role of stock prices in providing incentives when there is an agency problem between shareholders and managers. Diamond and Verrecchia (1982) and Holmstrom and Tirole (1993) consider how compensation contracts can be conditioned on stock prices to give incentives to make an effort. Dow and Gorton (1997) consider how good investment incentives can be provided to managers when stock prices contain information managers do not have.

The trade-off between allocative efficiency and risk sharing has important implications for the structure of financial systems. Although there may be allocational advantages, the mere existence of more price data from stock markets in the United States may not be a decisive point in favor of a market-oriented system. In financial systems like Germany's, few companies are publicly quoted and little information is revealed by the companies that are. This lack of information, which may be bad from the point of view of efficient decision-making, may be a good thing from the point of view of risk sharing. There is no theoretical presumption that more information leads to a better outcome, even if that information is useful for productive efficiency. This suggests that countries such as Germany and France, where accounting information about companies is not freely available and few analysts follow companies, are not necessarily at a disadvantage compared to countries such as the United States and the United Kingdom, where the reverse is true. Allocative efficiency is offset by the fact that investors bear a lot of risk.

5.2 Delegated monitoring and banks

One of the arguments that is often put forward in favor of bank-based systems is that banks form long-term relationships with firms and thus allow various informational problems to be solved. In Japan, this is called the main bank system while in Germany it is called the hausbank system. The problem that is of particular interest here is that borrowers must take some action to make proper use of the funds they have borrowed. This action could be the level of effort or choice of project from among various different risky alternatives. The borrower can always claim that a low outcome is due to bad luck rather than from not taking the correct action. Lenders cannot observe the borrower's action unless he pays a fixed cost to monitor the borrower. In a financial market with many lenders, there is a free-rider problem. Each lender is small, so it is not worth paying the fixed cost. Everybody would like to free-ride, leaving it to someone else to bear the monitoring cost. As a result, no monitoring will be done.

A possible solution is to hire a single monitor to check what the borrower is doing. The problem then becomes one of monitoring the monitor, to make sure she actually monitors the borrowers. Diamond (1984) develops a model of delegated monitoring to solve this problem. Intermediaries have a diversified portfolio of projects for which they provide finance. They precommit to monitor borrowers by promising lenders a fixed return. If the intermediary does not monitor, then it will be unable to pay the promised return to lenders. Diamond's model thus illustrates how intermediaries and, in particular, banks have an incentive to act as a delegated monitor and produce the information necessary for an efficient allocation of resources.

Boot and Thakor (1997a) (included as Chapter Twenty-one in this part) develop a model of financial system architecture that builds on this view of banks as delegated monitors. They assume there are three types of information problem. The first is that there is incomplete information about the future projects a firm has available to it. Outside investors can gather information about this type of information. The second problem is that lenders cannot observe whether borrowers invest the funds in a risky or safe project. The third problem is the likelihood that borrowers will have the opportunity to invest in a risky project. Boot and Thakor are able to show that the first problem can best be solved by a financial market and the second and third problems can best be solved by intermediaries. They argue that banks will predominate in an emerging financial system, while the informational advantages of markets may allow them to develop in a mature financial system.

Boot and Thakor (1997b) compare various aspects of different financial systems. The important characteristic of financial markets in their models is that prices reveal information. This is what differentiates financial markets from financial institutions. They show that financial innovation occurs more often in a system where commercial and investment banking are separated than in a system with universal banking.

Subrahmanyam and Titman (1997) are also interested in the development of financial systems. In their theory, stock markets are characterized by information revealing prices. There can be interesting interactions between information that is acquired fortuitously by investors and information that is paid for. Similarly to Pagano (1993), they show that, with a fixed cost for investors to participate in primary equity markets, there may exist multiple equilibria, specifically, a high participation equilibrium with many new issues and a low participation equilibrium with few new issues.

5.3 Open questions

Although there has been considerable theoretical work on the relationship between information provision and the form of the financial system, relatively little empirical work has been done in this area. In particular, a number of questions remain unanswered.

- Is the information available in bank-based systems sufficient to enable firms to correctly assess the risk return trade-off?
- What is the nature of the trade-off between allocative efficiency and risk sharing in practice?

6. Corporate Governance

In most countries, including the United States, the United Kingdom, Japan, and France, managers of corporations are ultimately responsible to the shareholders. However, the details of corporation law differ across countries. The common origins of company law in the United States and the United Kingdom have led to a similar structure. In both countries, managers have a fiduciary duty, that is, they have a strong legal requirement to act in the interests of shareholders. The official channel through which shareholders influence company affairs is the board of directors, elected by the shareholders, typically on the basis of one share, one vote. The board of directors is a mixture of outside and inside directors, the latter being the top executives in the firm. The role of management is to implement the policies determined by the board. Shareholders have very little say beyond electing directors. For example, it is the directors who decide their own compensation without any input from shareholders. A committee of outside directors determines the senior management's compensation. Except in unusual circumstances, such as a proxy fight, the outside directors are nominated by the incumbent management and thus typically owe their allegiance to the CEO. Table 5 shows the total number of directors for a typical sample of large firms in each of the countries. For the United States, and the United Kingdom, and Japan, the number of outside directors is given in parentheses. The size of boards is roughly the same in the United States and the United Kingdom, usually around 10–15 people. In the United States, a majority are typically from outside the firm; in the United Kingdom, a minority are from outside the firm.

Japan resembles the United States in terms of the legal form of corporations because of the heavy influence of the United States Occupation Forces on the legal system and the structure of institutions after the Second World War. Some important differences do exist, however. In the past,

Table 5. Number of Members on Boards of Directors

U.S.[1]		U.K.[1]		Japan[1]		France[1]		Germany[2]	
Ford	15 (10)	Glaxo	16 (7)	Toyota	60 (1)	Saint Gobain	16	Hoechst	21 11
IBM	14 (11)	Hanson	19 (8)	Hitachi	36 (3)	AGF	19 (5)	BASF	28 10
Exxon	12 (9)	Guinness	10 (6)	Matsushita	37 (6)	Usinor Sacilor	21 (5)	Robert Bosch	20 11
Mobil	16 (10)	British Airways	10 (6)	Nissan	49 (5)	Alcatel Alsthom	15	Krupp	22 7
Philip Morris	16 (4)	Allied Domecq	12 (4)	Toshiba	40 (3)	Elf Aquitaine	11	Bayer	22 11
RJR Nabisco	9 (6)	Grand Metropolitan	14 (1)	Honda	37 (3)	Renault	18	Daimler-Benz	20 8
Texaco	13 (11)	BTR	10 (4)	Sony	41 (6)	Thomson	8	Volkswagen	20 7
Johnson & Johnson	14 (12)	Associated British Foods	7 (1)	NEC	42 (5)			Thyssen	23 27
GAP	11 (8)	British Steel	8 (0)	Fujitsu	36 (7)			Siemens	20 15
				Mitsubishi Electric	37 (3)				
				Mitsubishi Motors	43 (4)				
				Mitsubishi Heavy Industries	43 (3)				
				Nippon Steel	53 (1)				
				Mazda	45 (8)				
				Nippon Oil	22 (0)				

Notes: 1. Figures in parentheses: U.S., outside directors; U.K., non-executive (outside) directors; Japan, outside directors (including cross directorships); France, directors from the government.

2. For Germany the first column represents the members of the Supervisory Board and the second is the members of the Management Board.

Source: Institute of Fiscal and Monetary Policy (1996: Chart III-3-3, p. 69).

nonfinancial corporations faced elaborate restrictions that prevented them from establishing holding companies. The rights of Japanese shareholders are in theory greater than those of shareholders in the United States and the United Kingdom. For example, in Japan it is easier for shareholders to nominate and elect directors. Also management remuneration must be decided at general meetings of shareholders. Despite these differences in shareholders' rights, the structure of Japanese boards is such that share-holders do not in fact have much influence. It can be seen from Table 5 that Japanese boards are much larger than those of other countries. There are a handful of outside directors, but they have very little influence. The overwhelming majority of directors are from inside the company and they include many people in addition to the most senior members of management. The nominations of individuals for positions as a director are essentially controlled by the company's CEO. This together with the unwieldy size of the board and its composition means CEOs hold tremen-dous power. As long as the financial position of a Japanese corporation is sound, the CEO and those closest to him control the company's affairs.

Germany has a very different type of governance structure than the United States, the United Kingdom, or Japan. The system of *co-determination*, which has a long history, arose in the late nineteenth century from an attempt to overcome the contradiction between the real-ity of industrialization and liberal ideas about the self-determination and the rights of individuals (Pistor 1996). Currently the most important legislation governing it is the Co-determination Act (*Mitbestimmungsge-setz*) of 1976. This generally applies to companies with more than 2,000 employees.

Firms to which it applies have two boards, the supervisory board and the management board. The supervisory board is the controlling body. As outlined in Schneider-Lenné (1992) and Prowse (1995), one-half of the representatives are elected by shareholders and the other half by the employees. The shareholders' general meeting elects the shareholder representatives. Two-thirds of the employee representatives work for the company, while the other third are trade union representatives. The super-visory board elects a chairman and deputy chairman from its members. The chairman is usually from the shareholder side, while the deputy chair-man is from the employee side. In the event of a tie in the voting of the supervisory board, the chairman has a casting vote. It is in this sense that shareholders have ultimate control. However, members of the supervisory board legally represent the interests of the company as a whole and not just the groups they represent. It can be seen from Table 5 that supervisory boards have typically just over twenty members and so are slightly bigger than boards in the United States and the United Kingdom but smaller than those in Japan. The management board is appointed by the supervisory board. Nobody can be a member of both boards and cross-company board memberships are restricted. The management board is responsible for the operation of the company while the supervisory board supervises the management board's activities. Table 5 shows that the management board is usually fairly small, smaller than the supervisory board and the boards in other countries.

The German system provides an interesting contrast to the Anglo-American and Japanese systems. It is often argued that the dual board system better represents outside shareholders and ensures management must take account of their views. In addition, employees' views are also represented and their bias is presumably to ensure the long run viability of the firm.

France has a system that contains elements of both the Anglo-American and the German systems. Firms can choose between two types of boards of director. The first type, which is more common, is single-tiered as in the Anglo-American system. The board elects the *président directeur-général* (PDG) who is like a CEO but more powerful. He or she has the sole right to 'represent' the company and is the only person who can delegate this power. Single-tiered boards mostly consist of outside directors who are shareholders and representatives from financial institutions with which the firm has transactional relationships. As in the Anglo-American model, the board determines business policies, which are then carried out by the PDG and management.

The second type of board has two tiers, as in Germany. The *conseil de surveillance* is like the German supervisory board except that employees do not have the right to representation. However, one unique feature of the French system which makes it more akin to the German one is that with single- and double-tiered boards workers' representatives have the right to attend board meetings as observers in all companies with at least fifty employees. The *conseil de surveillance* appoints the *directoire* who have responsibility for the management of the company. One of the members of the *directoire* is designated *président de directoire* by the others.

It can be seen from Table 5 that the size of boards in France is roughly similar to the United States. Complete or partial government ownership of corporations is more prevalent than in other countries and as Table 5 indicates in some cases this translates into government representation on boards (figures in parentheses are directors from the government).

In addition to having different legal structures for the firm, the countries also place differing restrictions on the holding of shares by financial institutions and nonfinancial corporations. Table 6 summarizes these. These restrictions have had important implications for the countries' patterns of share ownership, which are shown in Table 7.

Restrictions on institutional holdings of shares are one area where the United States differs significantly from the United Kingdom. In the United States, the Glass–Steagall Act used to prevent banks from holding equity stakes in companies except in unusual circumstances, such as when the firm has gone bankrupt. Insurance companies are regulated by state laws. The most significant regulations are those of New York State, which affect a large proportion of companies not only because many companies are based there but also because other states tend to follow their lead. Historically, New York regulations prevented insurers from holding any equity. However, in more recent times, life insurance companies have been able to hold a limited amount of equity. Mutual and pension funds are also restricted in the amount of any single stock they can own to ensure diversification. It can be seen from Table 7 that these regulations have meant that the pattern of share ownership in the United States is significantly different from the pattern in other countries. Only a small amount of equity, 6 percent, is held by financial institutions, whereas in the other countries the average holding is 29 percent. Instead, the proportion owned by individuals is much higher than elsewhere and the proportion owned by mutual and pension funds is higher than in Japan, Germany, and France. The main restriction on the holding of shares by nonfinancial corporations in other firms is the requirement that this does not restrict competition in any way. The US's 14 percent ownership of shares by nonfinancial corporations is much lower than in Japan, Germany, and France, but is comparable to the UK's.

It can be seen from Table 6 that the United Kingdom has far fewer formal regulations than the United States does. Banks can hold equity if they wish and need only obtain permission from the Bank of England to purchase large blocks of equity. Insurance companies are only limited by the (self-imposed) need to diversify. With regard to holdings of nonfinancial corporations, the only limitation is that firms must not mutually hold each other's shares to prevent a transfer of control. The relative lack of regulation creates different ownership patterns. Compared to the United States, financial institutions hold more and individuals less. Compared to Japan,

Germany, and France, the holding of shares by nonfinancial corporations is much less and the holdings of pension funds much greater.

As Tables 6 and 7 indicate, Japan, Germany, and France are all somewhat similar in terms of the regulatory restrictions on holding shares and the patterns of ownership. In all three countries, banks can hold the equity of companies. There are regulations on the proportions of the equity of firms that banks can hold in Japan. In Germany and France there are restrictions on holdings of equity relative to bank capital. As mentioned above, holding companies were traditionally not permitted in Japan. In Germany and France there are limitations on the percentages of firms that can be owned. Complex interactions of holding companies occur in both Germany and France. Van Hulle (1998) contains an account of European holding groups. In Japan, the interactions in terms of crossholdings are relatively simple.

In their seminal book, Berle and Means (1932) argued that, in practice, managers pursued their own interests rather than the interests of shareholders. The contractual aspect of the firm together with the problem highlighted by Berle and Means led to the development of the agency approach to corporate governance by, among others, Coase (1937), Jensen and Meckling (1976), Fama and Jensen (1983a, b), and Hart (1995). Excellent surveys are contained in Shleifer and Vishny (1997) and Becht et al. (2001). Vives (2000) contains a number of recent papers that provide good coverage of the literature. The main focus of the agency approach is the question:

How can shareholders ensure that managers pursue their interests.

The literature describes a number of corporate governance mechanisms that encourage managers to act in the interests of the shareholders.

6.1 The board of directors

The board of directors is, in theory at least, the first mechanism shareholders have to control managers and ensure the company is run in their interest. As discussed above, the way that boards are chosen and structured differs significantly across countries. Although the structure of boards is different across countries, the limited empirical evidence available suggests that they are equally effective (or ineffective) at disciplining management. Mace (1971), Weisbach (1988), and Jensen (1989) document the weakness of U.S. boards in disciplining managers. Bhagat and Black (1998) survey the

Table 6. Regulations on Shareholding of Financial Institutions and Nonfinancial Corporations

	U.S.	U.K.	Japan	France	Germany
Banks	Banks: Cannot hold shares of other corporations (Glass-Steagall Act) Bank holding companies: Holdings are limited to a maximum of 5% of the shares of nonfinancial corporations Trusts: Holdings are limited to a maximum of 10% of the fund's assets in any one company's shares	No special regulations on holdings. However, in the case of large volume acquisitions of shares, advance permission of the bank of England is required. A report to the Bank of England is required when exposure (all claims including shares invested) exceeds 10% of a bank's total capital. (See note 1)	Under Article 11 of the Anti-Monopoly Law, holdings are limited to 5% of the total number of issued shares of a domestic company	The holding of shares of any single nonfinancial corporation is limited to a maximum of 15% of the bank's capital. Total holdings of all shares cannot exceed 60% of all the bank's capital	Holdings greater than 10% are permitted, but only up to the value of the bank's capital (See note 1)
Life insurance companies	Varies by state. For instance, under New York State Law (which applies to 60% of all insurance companies), investments must be less than 20% of assets or a maximum of 50% of surpluses. Holdings of the shares of any single company are limited to 2% of total assets	Voluntary self-limitation of holding of stock in any single company (normally 2.5% of assets), for the purpose of portfolio diversification. A maximum (normally 5% of assets) is imposed on the amount of stock in any single company which a pension fund or insurance company can hold on its own	Under the Anti-Monopoly Law, holdings are limited to a maximum of 10% of the total number of issued shares of any single company		Holding of shares up to 20% of total assets is permitted
Other insurance companies	Prohibition on holding a non-insurance company in its entirety	Same as above	Same as above		No regulations
Mutual funds	Tax penalty imposed on holdings in excess of 10% of the stock of any single company.	Under laws regulating financial services holding of stock for the purpose of controlling a company is prohibited	No regulations		No regulations

	Pension funds	Other
	Under the Employee Retirement Income Securities Act, investment diversification is required. Holdings in excess of 10% of the pension fund's own stock are prohibited	Holding of stock which results in restricting competition is prohibited
	Same as for insurance companies	Under "The City Code on Takeovers and Mergers," the mutual holding of shares the purpose of which is to prevent the transfer of control of stock is prohibited
		Establishment of holding companies is prohibited (Article 9 of the Anti-Monopoly Law). A subsidiary whose parent company owns more than half of its stock cannot hold stock in its parent company (Commercial Code Article 211 [2])
		When one company controls another through shareholdings the controlled company has no voting rights with respect to the controlling company's stock (Commercial Code, Article 241 [3])
		A corporation which engages in nonfinancial business and has capital assets worth at least 10 billion yen, or net assets worth at least 30 billion yen, is prohibited from holding shares in domestic companies exceeding the value of its capital or net assets, whichever is greater (Anti-Monopoly Law, Article 9 [2]) (See note 2)
	A company can hold a maximum of 10% of the total number of issued shares of another company Subsidiaries can also hold up to 10% of the stock of parent companies but cannot vote	A subsidiary whose parent company owns more than half of its stock cannot hold stock in its parent company Mutual holding of shares is possible, but voting rights are limited to 25% of all voting rights, even when a company owns more than 25% of the stock of another company. Establishment of holding companies is permitted (in the case of pure holding companies and management holding companies)
	No regulations	

Notes: 1. The United Kingdom and Germany are scheduled to make modifications to their regulations as EU integration progresses.

2. Japan is scheduled to make changes to its laws on holding companies as part of the "Big Bang" reform of its financial system.

Source: Institute of Fiscal and Monetary Policy (1996: Chart III-2-3, p. 60).

Table 7. Comparison of Shareholders by Sector (percent of total)

	Individuals	Pension funds etc.	Financial institutions	Nonfinancial corporations	Public sector	Foreign individuals and institutions	Other
U.S.	50	20	5	14	0	5	6
U.K.	20	31	30	3	4	12	
Japan	23		41	25	1	4	6
France	34		23	21	2	20	
Germany	17		22	42	5	14	

Notes: Data are for 1990 except for France which are for 1992.

Source: Prowse (1995: Table 2, p. 13) for United States and Institute of Fiscal and Monetary Policy (1996: Chart III-2-1, p. 59) for the other countries.

literature on the relationship between board composition and firm performance. The evidence indicates that boards with a majority of independent directors do not perform better than firms without such boards. However, it does seem that having a moderate number of inside directors is associated with greater profitability. Kaplan (1994*a*, *b*) has conducted studies of the relationship between management turnover and various performance measures in Japan, Germany, and the United States. His findings indicate a similar relationship in each of the countries. Kang and Shivdasani (1995) confirm these results for Japan and also provide evidence on the effectiveness of different types of governance mechanisms. Among other things, they find that the presence of outside directors on the board has no effect on the sensitivity of top executive turnover to either earnings or stock-price performance. In contrast, concentrated equity ownership and ties to a main bank do have a positive effect. For Germany, Franks and Mayer (1997) find a strong relationship between poorly performing companies and turnover on management boards but not with turnover on supervisory boards. Gibson (1999) considers the relationship between CEO turnover and firm performance in eight emerging countries. The results are fairly similar to those obtained in studies of the United States.

6.2 Executive compensation

An additional method of ensuring that managers pursue the interests of shareholders is to structure compensation appropriately. Diamond and Verrecchia (1982), Holmstrom and Tirole (1993), and Dow and Gorton (1997) have developed models where compensation is conditioned on the firm's stock price and this reflects information gathered by analysts. Stock prices are not the only contingency that can be used to motivate managers. Accounting based performance measures are also frequently used. Managers who perform extremely well may be bid away at higher compensation levels to other companies. The managerial labor market thus also plays an important part in providing incentives to managers. There has been some debate about the optimal sensitivity of executive compensation to stock price in practice. Jensen and Murphy (1990) confirm previous findings of a positive relationship between executive pay and performance in the United States and estimate CEO compensation varies by about $3 for every $1,000 change in firm value. They suggest that this figure is much too small. Haubrich (1994) has calibrated an appropriately designed principal agent model which takes into account risk aversion and argues that a small sensitivity is optimal for reasonable parameter values. For other countries, the number of empirical studies is small. Kaplan (1994*a,b*) considers the sensitivity of pay and dismissal to performance in Germany and Japan. He finds that they are similar to the United States in this respect.

6.3 The market for corporate control

Manne (1965) has argued that an active market for corporate control is essential for the efficient operation of capitalist economies. It allows able management teams to gain control of large amounts of resources in a small amount of time. Inefficient managers are removed and replaced with people who are better able to do the job. The existence of a market for corporate control also provides one means of disciplining managers. If a firm is pursuing policies which do not maximize shareholders' wealth it can be taken over and the managers replaced.

The market for corporate control can operate through proxy contests, friendly mergers and hostile takeovers. Recent theoretical analyses of proxy fights, which throw some light on why they do not work well, are contained in Bhattacharya (1997), Yilmaz (1997), and Maug (1998).

Friendly mergers occur when both firms agree that combining them would be value creating. Friendly mergers and takeovers occur in all countries and account for most of the transaction volume that occurs. Prowse (1995) reports that in the United States, friendly transactions constituted 82.2 percent of transactions, in the United Kingdom 62.9 percent and in the rest of Europe 90.4 percent.

The third way in which the market for corporate control can operate is through hostile takeovers. This mechanism is potentially very important in ensuring an efficient allocation of resources in the way Manne (1965) suggested. However, Grossman and Hart (1980) have pointed to a problem with the operation of this mechanism of corporate governance. Existing shareholders will have a strong incentive to free ride on raiders who plan to increase the value of the firm. On the one hand, if the price offered by the raider is below the price that the new policies will justify and the shareholder believes the offer will succeed, then there is no point in tendering. However, in that case the offer will not succeed. On the other hand, if the raider offers a price above the current value and the shareholder believes that the offer will not succeed, then it will be worth tendering his shares. But then the offer will succeed. In both cases, the shareholder's beliefs are inconsistent with equilibrium. The only equilibrium is one in which the raider's offer price is equal to the price the new policies will justify. In that case, the raider's profit will be zero, before allowing for any costs incurred in undertaking the bid. If these costs are included, the profit will be negative and there will be no incentive to attempt a takeover.

A number of solutions to the free-rider problem have been suggested. Grossman and Hart's (1980) solution is that corporate charters should be structured so that raiders can dilute minority shareholders' interests after the takeover occurs. This means the raider can offer a price below the post-takeover value of the firm to him and the bid still succeeds. Existing shareholders will know that if they retain their shares the raider will dilute their interest. Shleifer and Vishny (1986) pointed out that if the raider can acquire a block of stock before attempting a takeover at the low pre-takeover price there will be a profit on this block even if all the remaining shares are purchased at the full price justified by the raider's plans. Burkart (1995) shows that it is privately optimal for a large shareholder to overbid and this can lead to possible losses and inefficiencies.

In addition to the Grossman and Hart free rider-problem, there are a number of other problems with the operation of the market for corporate control. One is that once a takeover bid is announced other raiders will realize it is an attractive target and will bid. This will mean it is not possible for the initial firm to recoup any fixed costs from identifying the target in the first place. The third problem in the operation of the market for corporate control is the possibility of management entrenchment. Managers may be incompetent and want to prevent a takeover to preserve their jobs.

Despite all these problems, hostile takeovers do occur fairly frequently in the United States and the United Kingdom. Prowse (1995) points out that in the United States almost 10 percent of companies that belonged to the Fortune 500 in 1980 have since been acquired in a transaction that was hostile or started off as hostile. For the United Kingdom, Franks and Mayer (1992) report that there were thirty-five successful hostile bids made over 2 years in the mid-1980s. This is much higher than in Germany, France, or Japan. In Germany, Franks and Mayer (1998) report that there have only been three hostile takeovers between 1945 and 1994 and analyze them. Franks and Mayer (1997) document a substantial market in share stakes but their analysis suggests such sales do not perform a disciplinary function. In Japan, Kester (1991) argues that there have been no hostile takeovers among large firms in that period. In France, hostile takeovers were also rare until recently.

Why do these differences in the number of hostile takeovers between the United States and the United Kingdom and other countries exist? A standard explanation for the difference in the occurrence of takeovers across countries is the prevalence of cross shareholdings in Japan and the structure of holding companies and cross shareholdings in Germany and France that make it difficult to acquire the necessary number of shares.

Another important issue is the extent to which the market for corporate control leads to an improvement in efficiency in the way Manne's (1965) argument suggests it should. There have been numerous empirical studies of takeovers in an attempt to understand whether they create value. Jensen (1993) estimates the total increase in the stock market value of target firms in the United States from 1976 to 1990 as $750 billion. In contrast, it seems that the increase in value for bidding firms was zero and possibly even negative. Overall, the stock market data suggests that total value (i.e. the sum of the targets' values and bidding firms' values) did increase significantly. There is an issue of whether this was caused by the mergers and takeovers or was simply a reflection of a previous undervaluation in the stock market. Another possibility, suggested by Shleifer and Summers (1988), is that gains from takeovers may be the result of violating implicit contracts with workers and other suppliers.

A number of studies have attempted to use accounting data to identify the reason why the value of the targets increased. For example, Ravenscraft and Scherer (1987) and Herman and Lowenstein (1988) have found little evidence that operating performance improves after takeovers. Franks and Mayer (1996) found for a sample of U.K. firms that hostile takeover targets did not underperform before acquisition, but were subject to the redeployment of assets afterwards. There are some studies, such as Kaplan (1989), Bhagat et al. (1990), Kaplan and Weisbach (1991), and Healy et al. (1992, 1997), which do find changes and improvements in operations that can at least partially explain takeover premia, so the evidence is mixed.

6.4 Concentrated holdings and monitoring by financial institutions

Stiglitz (1985) has argued that one of the most important ways that value maximization by firms can be ensured is through concentrated ownership of the firm's shares. Shleifer and Vishny (1986), Huddart (1993), and Admati et al. (1994) all model equity financed firms which have one large shareholder and a fringe of smaller ones. In all these models, more wealth commitment by owners increases monitoring and firm performance. Shleifer and Vishny find that firm value increases with the large shareholder's holding but this need not be true. In Huddart (1993) and Admati et al. (1994) the reverse can occur because the large shareholder is risk averse.

A number of recent theoretical analyses have reconsidered important aspects of concentrated ownership. Burkart et al. (1997) consider the costs and benefits of monitoring by large shareholders. They show that such monitoring may restrict the misuse of resources ex post, but may also blunt ex ante managerial initiative. There is a trade-off between control and initiative. Bolton and von Thadden (1998a, b) develop a framework to analyze the trade-off between liquidity and control. Large blocks result in incentives to monitor but also lead to a lack of liquidity. Pagano and Röell (1998) consider the trade-off between public and private ownership and monitoring. With private ownership there is monitoring because of shareholder concentration but no liquidity. Going public is costly and public ownership results in less monitoring but greater liquidity.

The importance of equity ownership by financial institutions in Japan and Germany, shown in Table 7, and the lack of a market for corporate control in these countries have led to the suggestion that the agency problem in these countries is solved by financial institutions acting as outside monitors for large corporations. In Japan, this system of monitoring is known as the main bank system. The characteristics of this system are the long-term relationship between a bank and its client firm, the holding of both debt and equity by the bank, and the active intervention of the bank should its client become financially distressed. It has been widely argued that this main bank relationship ensures the bank acts as delegated monitor and helps to overcome the agency problem between managers and the firm. Hoshi et al. (1990*a*,*b*, 1993) provide evidence that the main bank system helps firms by easing liquidity constraints and reduces agency costs. They also document that firms reduced their bank ties in the 1980s as access to the bond market became easier. In contrast to Hoshi et al., Hayashi (1997) finds no evidence that main bank ties ease liquidity constraints. He suggests their results are probably due to the poor quality of their capital stock estimate. Kang and Shivdasani (1997) find that companies restructure to a greater extent in response to adverse circumstances the greater the ownership of the main bank. Aoki and Patrick (1994) contains a number of studies suggesting that until recently the effectiveness of the main bank system has been high. A dissenting view is contained in a paper by Ramseyer (1994) who suggests that the traditional emphasis in the literature on the importance of this system in achieving effective corporate governance is too strong. He argues that, if the system really worked in the way described, explicit contracts should be used much more than they are in practice. Overall, the main bank system appears important in times of financial distress, but less important when a firm is doing well.

In Germany, the data on concentration of ownership probably understate the significance of the banks' effective position. The reason is that many bank customers keep their shares "on deposit" at banks and allow banks to exercise proxies on their behalf. As a result banks control a higher proportion of voting equity and have more representation on boards of large industrial enterprises than their direct holdings suggest. A 1978 Monopoly Commission study found that, of the top 100 corporations, banks controlled the votes of nearly 40 percent of the equity and were represented on two-thirds of the boards. German banks thus tend to have very close ties with industry and form long-run relationships with firms. This is the *hausbank* system. A number of studies have provided evidence on the effectiveness of the outside monitoring of German banks. Elston (1993) finds firms with strong ties to a bank are not as likely to be liquidity-constrained as firms with weaker ties. Cable (1985) and Gorton and Schmid (2000) find evidence that firms with a higher proportion of equity controlled by banks have better performance. This evidence is consistent with the hypothesis that bank involvement helps the performance of firms, but it is also consistent with the hypothesis that banks are good at picking winners.

A number of issues concerning the effectiveness of banks as outside monitors arise in the case of Japan and Germany. The first is that banks are themselves subject to the same agency problems as firms. Charkham (1994: 36) points out that, in effect, the big three banks essentially control themselves: "At general meetings in recent years, Deutsche Bank held voting rights for 47.2 percent of its shares, Dresdner for 59.25 percent and Commerzbank for 30.29 percent." In addition, other large shareholders are often widely held themselves. Schreyögg and Steinman (1981) compare a sample of 300 large German firms according to whether there is concentration in terms of direct ownership or ultimate ownership taking into account the holding company structure. They find that in terms of ultimate ownership there is significantly less concentration.

An early critic of the view that banks provide effective monitoring of firms in Germany was Hellwig (1991). Hellwig argued that close relationships between banks and firms involved costs as well as benefits for the firm. Banks acquire private information about the firm, which they can use to extract rents. Using historical sources, he argued that firms have an incentive to seek autonomy from banks as quickly as possible. In more recent work, Hellwig (1998) argues that intermediaries and firms are often involved in a collusive relationship whose aim is to limit the power of outsiders. In this model, firms and intermediaries cooperate to share control, and not necessarily to promote effective management of the firm.

In an important book, Edwards and Fischer (1994) have argued that in Germany the corporate governance role of banks has been overemphasized in the literature. They provide a variety of evidence that banks do not have the degree of influence as lenders, shareholders, or voters of proxies that is usually supposed. For example, they find that the number of votes controlled in a company is only weakly related to the number of representatives the bank has on the supervisory board. Wenger and Kaserer (1998) point to the examples of Metallgesellschaft and Daimler-Benz as extreme examples of the failure of the German corporate governance system.

6.5 Debt

An important strand of the corporate governance literature has focused on the role of debt as a means of disciplining managers. Grossman and Hart (1982) were the first to argue that managers could precommit to work hard by using debt rather than equity. Similarly, Jensen's (1986) free cash flow theory suggested that debt could be used to prevent managers from squandering resources. In the late 1980s and early 1990s it was widely argued that leveraged buyouts (LBOs) whereby managers or other groups purchased firms using a large proportion of debt financing were a response to agency problems. However, debt can have undesirable as well as desirable effects on managers' behavior. Jensen and Meckling (1976) pointed out managers have an incentive to take risks and may even accept projects that destroy value if significant amounts of debt are used. Myers (1977) pointed to the debt overhang problem where firms may forego good projects if they have significant debt outstanding. The reason is that for a firm facing financial distress a large part of the returns to a good project go to bondholders.

Perhaps the most important weakness of the argument that debt is important for ensuring managerial discipline in corporations is the fact that retained earnings are the most important source of finance for corporations, as Table 6 indicates. In most countries, debt is much less important than retained earnings. Typically, large corporations can service their debt without difficulty, that is, without constraining their operations or investment plans. Taggart (1985) has found that during the post-war period, long-term debt constituted about 35 percent of the market value of large U.S. corporations, with most of the remainder being made up of equity. Although such firms have issued relatively little new equity, the significant level of internal finance through retained earnings has ensured outside equity is (indirectly) the most important financing instrument.

6.6 Product market competition

It has been argued (see, e.g. Alchian 1950; Stigler 1958) that competition in product markets is a very powerful force for solving the agency problem between owners and managers. If the managers of a firm waste or consume large amounts of resources, the firm will be unable to compete and will go bankrupt. There is little doubt that competition, particularly internationally, is a powerful force in ensuring effective corporate governance.

Competition between different organizational forms may be helpful in limiting efficiency losses. If a family-owned business has the sole objective of maximizing share value, it may force all the corporations in that industry to do the same thing. Hart (1983) develops a model based on this idea. Unobservable effort leads to "managerial slack." Using the assumption that managers are infinitely risk averse at a particular level of income,

Hart is able to show that aggregate output is lower and price is higher than in the first best, where every action is contractible. Scharfstein (1988) shows that if the manager's marginal utility of income is strictly positive, increased competition can increase rather than reduce managerial slack. Schmidt (1997) addresses a related question in a model without hidden information. He observes that increased competition may threaten the survival of a firm by forcing it into bankruptcy and asks what effect this may have on managerial slack. As in Scharfstein (1988), he demonstrates that increased competition does not necessarily reduce managerial slack.

Allen and Gale (2000b) depart from the agency approach and argue that motivating managers is not the main problem in the modern corporation. They view the top management of firms as being "entrepreneurial" in that they choose the direction of the firm and assign crucial tasks to subordinates. Shareholders' concern is not whether managers work hard but whether they have the "right stuff." If product markets are competitive, then good firms can push out bad firms and capture the market. This contrasts with the standard story in which companies with underperforming managements are taken over by corporate raiders.

6.7 Discussion

The literature on corporate governance is vast, but much work remains to be done in this area. In our view, the focus on agency problems that dominates the literature is unnecessarily narrow. Many important issues remain to be explored.

- When is separation of ownership and control optimal? Burkart et al. (1997) and Allen and Gale (2000a: chapter 11) have identified some special circumstances where separation is desirable. How robust is this result?
- What are the alternatives to modeling the firm as a profit maximizing entity? In countries such as Germany, the governance mechanism explicitly incorporates workers. In practice, stakeholders other than shareholders play an important role in other countries too. How should the firm be modeled in such cases? Aoki (1984a, b, 1988, 1992) and Allen and Gale (2000a: chapter 12) have made a start in this direction.

7. Law, Politics, and Finance

In an important contribution, Roe (1994) argues that political factors play a crucial role in the development of the legal and regulatory system and, hence, the structure of corporate governance in different countries. In particular, he argues that the United States chose to have a financial system where the power of financial institutions such as banks and insurance companies is very limited. As a result, they cannot play a significant role in corporate governance. In Germany and Japan, a different political climate allows financial institutions to become more deeply involved in corporate governance.

Political factors are important, without a doubt, but there is a question about the extent of their importance. Allen (1995) argues that the United Kingdom presents an interesting contrast to the United States. It has a similar separation of ownership and control in corporations, but very different financial institutions. In particular, the banking system is concentrated and, although the Bank of England has wide powers of intervention, there are few explicit restrictions on the activities that banks may undertake, as Table 6 indicates. Nevertheless, banks have chosen not to become involved in corporate governance. Similarly, insurance companies have not been barred from playing an important governance role, but have chosen not to do so. If banks and insurance companies in the United Kingdom chose not to become involved in corporate governance, the same might have been true in the United States even if they had the legal freedom to do so. This comparison is difficult to reconcile with the idea that it is politics and legal and regulatory constraints that is the sole determinant of differences in corporate governance across countries.

In an influential set of papers, La Porta et al. have developed an approach to comparative financial systems based on legal systems. They consider two basic issues. The first is the extent to which legal systems differ in the protection afforded to shareholders and creditors in different countries. The second is the impact that this has on corporations' financing, governance, payout and other policies. La Porta et al. (1998) examine how laws protecting investors differ across forty-nine countries. They identify two legal traditions for commercial law. The first is the common law tradition, which originated in England. The second is the civil law tradition. There are three branches of the civil law tradition, French, German, and Scandinavian. Through a variety of means, such as conquest, imperialism, and imitation, the English, French, and German systems have spread around the world. In general, La Porta et al. (1998) find that civil law systems give investors weaker legal rights than do common law systems. Common law countries give both shareholders and creditors the strongest protection. The quality of enforcement of legal rules is highest in Scandinavian and German civil-law countries, next highest in common-law countries and weakest in French civil-law countries. Given these differences in rights and enforcement, La Porta et al. (1998) investigate whether there are substitute mechanisms for corporate governance. One example is "bright-line" rules that specify mandatory dividends. They find that only French civil-law countries have these. Another example is ownership concentration. It turns out that there is a negative correlation between the extent of minority shareholder protection and concentrated equity ownership. The implication is that the easiest way to prevent abuse of minority shareholders when legal protection is poor is to hold large blocks of stock.

La Porta et al. (1997) consider the relationship between the form of finance and the legal system. They find a relationship between investor protection and the importance of capital markets. Countries with stronger rights for shareholders and creditors have broader and deeper capital markets. French civil-law countries have the weakest rights, the worst enforcement, and the least developed capital markets. La Porta et al. (1999) consider the incidence of widely held corporations in twenty-seven wealthy economies. They find that with the exception of countries such as the United States and the United Kingdom, where minority investors are well protected, corporations are not widely held but instead are controlled by families or the State. Another exception is Germany, where banks play a significant role in the governance of some large corporations through their ownership of shares. La Porta et al. (2000a) consider the relationship between payout policies and investor protection in thirty-three countries. They distinguish between an "outcome model" where minority holders are able to pressure insiders to pay dividends and a "substitute model" where firms develop a reputation for paying out dividends. They find that firms in common law countries, which usually have better investment protection, pay more dividends than firms in civil-law countries. This is interpreted as support for the outcome model. La Porta et al. (2000b) describe the differences in laws and enforcement across forty-nine countries, discuss the possible origins of these differences, and consider their consequences and potential strategies for corporate governance reform.

Rajan and Zingales (2000) argue that political factors are more important in determining the financial structure of a country than the origin of the legal system. They document the relative sizes of capital markets through the twentieth century. Contrary to the received wisdom, they find that continental European countries, such as France, Belgium, and Germany, have had large capital markets in certain periods. When measured by the ratio of capitalization to GDP, they were not that much different in size from those in the United Kingdom and bigger than those in the United States. The modern view that capital markets are not important for these countries is true for the period after the Second World War, but was not true at the start of the century. In recent years, markets have regained their importance in countries such as France and are moving in that direction in countries such as Germany. Rajan and Zingales argue that understanding this reversal requires an analysis of political factors, including the openness of the country to outside influences and the centralization of the political system.

Another important legal aspect of comparative financial systems is the form of the bankruptcy code. The literature compares the bankruptcy codes in use in different countries and suggests reforms of these codes. One broad category of procedures comprises liquidations through cash auctions to the highest bidder, like the US Chapter 7 procedure. Another comprises structured auctions, like the court-supervised reorganizations in the US Chapter 11. Rajan and Zingales (1995) report that all the countries in their sample have cash auctions, while those with developed financial markets like Canada and the United States have structured auctions. Stromberg (2000) finds that, in practice, cash auctions in Sweden work very like reorganization procedures.

In practice, there is considerable evidence of deviations from absolute priority in bankruptcy (see Eberhart et al. 1990; Weiss 1990; Franks and Torous 1994; Betker 1995). Brown (1989), Bergman and Callen (1991), and Gertner and Scharfstein (1991) provide arguments for deviations from absolute priority. Berkovitch et al. (1998) and Berkovitch and Israel (1999) have argued that deviations from absolute priority can lead to efficient ex ante decisions.

Bebchuk (1988), Aghion et al. (1992), and Shleifer and Vishny (1992) have argued that inefficiencies are likely to arise from transaction costs and illiquidity in cash auctions. Pulvino (1998, 1999) provides some evidence that market liquidity leads to low-value users ending up in control. Bebchuk (1988) suggested an ingenious scheme of options to overcome the liquidity problems and different valuations by security holders. Aghion et al. (1992) suggest a development of this type of plan that allows managers to remain in control when they are the highest valued claimants in the view of the residual claimants.

The intersection of law, finance, and politics contains many interesting topics for further research.

- Historically, financial activity has often taken place without an effective legal system or with a legal system that did not play an important role (see, e.g. Greif 2000). Understanding the operation of such systems is an important complement to understanding the role of the law.
- Even in countries with sophisticated legal systems, reputations and implicit contracts play an important role. Gaining a fuller understanding of the operation of these mechanisms is important (see, e.g. Diamond 1991; Allen and Gale 2000*a*: chapter 15).
- More important than the details of bankruptcy codes and the design of optimal liquidation procedures is the relationship between bankruptcy codes and growth. Bankruptcy codes that impose penalties on default will discourage risk taking while leniency leads to moral hazard. Understanding this trade-off is important (see, e.g. Santos 1997).

8. Financial Crises

In addition to the legal system and political factors, Allen and Gale (2000*a*) have argued that financial crises have had a significant impact on the historical development of financial systems. Prior to the twentieth century, banking crises, currency crises, and stock market crashes occurred frequently in Europe and the United States. These crises were generally regarded as a bad thing. Over time one of the most important roles of central banks came to be to eliminate panics and ensure financial stability. The Bank of England played an especially important role in the development of effective stabilization policies in the eighteenth and nineteenth centuries. By the end of the nineteenth century, banking panics had been eliminated in Europe. The last true panic in England was the Overend, Gurney & Company Crisis of 1866.

The United States took a different tack. Alexander Hamilton had been impressed by the example of the Bank of England and this led to the setting up of the First Bank of the United States and subsequently the Second Bank of the United States. However, after Andrew Jackson vetoed the renewal of the Second Bank's charter, the United States ceased to have any form of central bank in 1836. It also had many crises during the nineteenth and early twentieth centuries. During the crisis of 1907, a French banker commented that the United States was a "great financial nuisance." The comment reflects the fact that crises had to a large extent been eliminated in Europe and it seemed as though the United States was suffering gratuitous crises that could have been prevented by setting up a central bank.

The Federal Reserve System was eventually established in 1914. In the beginning it had a decentralized structure, which meant that even this development was not very effective in eliminating crises. In fact, major banking panics continued to occur until the reforms enacted after the crisis of 1933. At that point, the Federal Reserve was given broader powers and this together with the introduction of deposit insurance finally led to the elimination of periodic banking crises. Bordo (2000) contains an overview of the historical literature on crises.

The tight regulations that were imposed on banks in the United States and other countries in response to the experience of the Great Depression meant that for the period between 1945 and the early 1970s there were no banking crises. The structure of the Bretton Woods fixed exchange rate system meant that there were currency crises when a country's macroeconomic policies were inconsistent with its exchange rate. Following the collapse of the Bretton Woods agreement in the early 1970s and the deregulation that followed in many countries financial crises re-emerged. Lindgren et al. (1996) find that about three-fourths of the IMF's member countries suffered some form of banking crisis between 1980 and 1996. In many of these crises, panics in the traditional sense were avoided either by central bank intervention or by explicit or implicit government guarantees. In an important study Kaminsky and Reinhart (1999) found that the advent of financial liberalization in many economies in the 1980s has led to "twin" banking and currency crises. Historical evidence provided by Bordo and Eichengreen (2000) suggests that twin crises both in recent decades and prior to the First World War have been fairly similar in a number of respects. In particular in both periods crises were particularly disruptive in terms of the depth of ensuing recessions. The recent experience with crises has meant that the susceptibility of different types of financial systems to crises has become one of the most important areas of comparative financial systems.

Although many crises have occurred in emerging economies, many have also occurred in developed countries. Recent deregulation has often been associated with monetary expansion and lending booms and apparent bubbles in real estate and stocks. The subsequent bursting of these bubbles has led to financial crises. The idea that the amount of money and credit available is an important factor in the determination of asset prices is not new. In his description of historic bubbles, Kindleberger (1978: 54) emphasizes the role of this factor: "Speculative manias gather speed through expansion of money and credit or perhaps, in some cases, get started because of an initial expansion of money and credit."

Perhaps the best-known recent example of this type of phenomenon is the dramatic rise in real estate and stock prices that occurred in Japan in the late 1980s and their subsequent collapse in the 1990s. Financial liberalization throughout the 1980s and the desire to support the U.S. dollar in the latter part of the decade led to an expansion in credit. During most of the 1980s, asset prices rose steadily, eventually reaching very high levels. For example, the Nikkei 225 index was around 10,000 in 1985. On December 19, 1989 it reached a peak of 38,916. A new Governor of the Bank of Japan, less concerned with supporting the U.S. dollar and more concerned with fighting inflation, tightened monetary policy and this led to a sharp increase in interest rates in early 1990 (see Frankel 1993; Tschoegl 1993). The bubble burst. The Nikkei 225 fell sharply during the first part of the year and by October 1, 1990 it had sunk to 20,222. Real estate prices followed a similar pattern. The next few years were marked by defaults and retrenchment in the financial system. The real economy was adversely affected by the aftermath of the bubble and growth rates during the 1990s have mostly been slightly positive or negative, in contrast to most of the post war period when they were much higher.

Similar events occurred in Norway, Finland and Sweden in the 1980s (see Heiskanen 1993; Drees and Pazarbasioglu 1995). In Norway, the ratio of bank loans to nominal GDP went from 40 percent in 1984 to 68 percent in 1988. Asset prices soared while investment and consumption also increased significantly. The collapse in oil prices helped burst the bubble and caused the most severe banking crisis and recession since the war. In Finland, an expansionary budget in 1987 resulted in massive credit expansion. The ratio of bank loans to nominal GDP increased from 55 percent in 1984 to 90 percent in 1990. Housing prices rose by a total of 68 percent in 1987 and 1988. In 1989 the central bank increased interest rates and imposed reserve requirements to moderate credit expansion. In 1990 and 1991 the economic situation was exacerbated by a fall in trade with the Soviet Union. Asset prices collapsed, banks had to be supported by the government and GDP shrank by 7 percent. In Sweden, a steady credit expansion through the late 1980s led to a property boom. In the fall of 1990 credit was tightened and interest rates rose. In 1991, a number of banks had severe difficulties because of lending based on inflated asset values. The government had to intervene and a severe recession followed.

Mexico provides a dramatic illustration of an emerging economy affected by this type of problem. In the early 1990s, the banks were privatized and a financial liberalization occurred. Perhaps most significantly, reserve requirements were eliminated. Mishkin (1997) documents how bank credit to private nonfinancial enterprises went from a level of around 10 percent of GDP in the late 1980s to 40 percent of GDP in 1994. The stock market rose significantly during the early 1990s. In 1994, the Colosio assassination and the uprising in Chiapas triggered the collapse of the bubble. The prices of stocks and other assets fell and banking and foreign exchange crises occurred. These were followed by a severe recession.

These examples suggest a relationship between the occurrence of significant rises in asset prices or *positive* bubbles and monetary and credit policy. They also illustrate that the collapse in the bubble can lead to severe problems because the fall in asset prices leads to strains on the banking sector. Banks holding real estate and stocks with falling prices (or with loans to the owners of these assets) often come under severe pressure from withdrawals because their liabilities are fixed. This forces them to call in loans and liquidate their assets which in turn appears to exacerbate the problem of falling asset prices. In other words, there may be *negative* asset price bubbles as well as positive ones. These negative bubbles, in which asset prices fall too far, can damage the banking system and unnecessarily exacerbate problems in the real economy. Just as monetary and credit policy can cause positive price bubbles, monetary policy may also have a role to play in preventing asset prices from falling too far. In the Scandinavian and Mexican examples, discussed above, asset prices quickly rebounded and the spillovers to the real economy were relatively short-lived. In Japan, asset prices did not rebound and the real economy has been much less robust.

8.1 Theories of banking crises

There are two traditional views of banking panics. One is that they are *random events*, unrelated to changes in the real economy. The classical form of this view suggests that panics are the result of "mob psychology" or "mass hysteria" (see, e.g. Kindleberger 1978). The modern version, developed by Diamond and Dybvig (1983) and others, is that bank runs are self-fulfilling prophecies. Given the assumption of first-come, first-served and costly liquidation of some assets there are multiple equilibria. If everyone believes that a banking panic is about to occur, it is optimal for each individual to try to withdraw her funds. Since each bank has insufficient liquid assets to meet all of its commitments, it will have to liquidate some of its assets at a loss. Given first-come, first-served, those depositors who withdraw initially will receive more than those who wait. On the one hand, anticipating this, all depositors have an incentive to withdraw immediately. On the other hand, if no one believes a banking panic is about to occur, only those with immediate needs for liquidity will withdraw their funds. Assuming that banks have sufficient liquid assets to meet these legitimate demands, there will be no panic. Which of these two equilibria occurs depends on extraneous variables or "sunspots." Although "sunspots" have no effect on the real data of the economy, they affect depositors' beliefs in a way that turns out to be self-fulfilling. (Postlewaite and Vives 1987 have shown how runs can be generated in a model with a unique equilibrium.)

An alternative to the "sunspot" view is that banking panics are a natural outgrowth of the *business cycle*. An economic downturn will reduce the value of bank assets, raising the possibility that banks are unable to meet their commitments. If depositors receive information about an impending downturn in the cycle, they will anticipate financial difficulties in the banking sector and try to withdraw their funds. This attempt will precipitate the crisis. According to this interpretation, panics are not random events but a response to unfolding economic circumstances.

A number of authors have developed models of banking panics caused by aggregate risk. Wallace (1988, 1990), Chari (1989), and Champ et al. (1996) extend Diamond and Dybvig (1983) by assuming the fraction of the population requiring liquidity is random. Chari and Jagannathan (1988), Jacklin and Bhattacharya (1988), Hellwig (1994), and Alonso (1996) introduce aggregate uncertainty which can be interpreted as business cycle risk. Chari and Jagannathan (1988) focus on a signal extraction problem where part of the population observes a signal about future returns. Others must then try to deduce from observed withdrawals whether an unfavorable signal was received by this group or whether liquidity needs happen to be high. Chari and Jagannathan are able to show panics occur not only when the outlook is poor but also when liquidity needs turn out to be high.

Jacklin and Bhattacharya (1988) also consider a model where some depositors receive an interim signal about risk. They show that the optimality of bank deposits compared to equities depends on the characteristics of the risky investment.

Hellwig (1994) considers a model where the reinvestment rate is random and shows that the risk should be born both by early and late withdrawers. Alonso (1996) demonstrates using numerical examples that contracts where runs occur may be better than contracts which ensure runs do not occur because they improve risk sharing.

Building on the empirical work of Gorton (1988) and Calomiris and Gorton (1991) that nineteenth-century banking crises were predicted by leading economic indicators, Allen and Gale (1998) develop a model that is consistent with the business cycle view of the origins of banking panics. In their model, crises can improve risk sharing but they also involve deadweight costs if they cause projects to be prematurely liquidated. A central bank can avoid these deadweight costs and implement an optimal allocation of resources through an appropriate monetary policy. By creating fiat money and lending it to banks, the central bank can prevent the inefficient liquidation of investments while at the same time allowing optimal sharing of risks.

8.2 Theories of currency crises and twin crises

The large movements in exchange rates that occurred in many East Asian countries in 1997 have revived interest in the topic of currency crises. In many of the early models of currency crises, such as Krugman (1979), currency crises occur because of inconsistent and unsustainable government policies (see Flood and Marion 1998 for a survey of the literature on currency crises). These models were designed to explain the problems experienced by a number of Latin American countries in the 1970s and early 1980s. In the recent East Asian crises, by contrast, many of the countries which experienced problems had pursued macroeconomic policies that were consistent and sustainable. This characteristic of the recent crises has prompted a re-examination of theoretical models of currency crises.

The other characteristic of the South East Asian crises that has received considerable attention is that the banking systems of these countries also experienced crises. Kaminsky and Reinhart (1999) have investigated the relationship between banking crises and currency crises. They find that in the 1970s, when financial systems were highly regulated in many countries, currency crises were not accompanied by banking crises. However, after the financial liberalization that occurred during the 1980s, currency crises and banking crises became intertwined. The usual sequence of events is that initial problems in the banking sector are followed by a currency crisis and this in turn exacerbates and deepens the banking crisis. Although banking crises typically precede currency crises, the common cause of both is usually a fall in asset values due to a recession or a weak economy. Often the fall is part of a boom-bust cycle that follows financial liberalization. It appears to be rare that banking and currency crises occur when economic fundamentals are sound.

Despite the apparent interrelationship between currency crises and banking crises in recent episodes, the literatures on the two topics have for the most part developed separately. Important exceptions are Chang and Velasco (1998, 2000). The first paper develops a model of currency and banking crises based on the Diamond and Dybvig (1983) model of bank runs. Chang and Velasco introduce money as an argument in the utility function. A central bank controls the ratio of currency to consumption. Different exchange rate regimes correspond to different rules for regulating the currency–consumption ratio. There is no aggregate uncertainty in these models: Banking and currency crises are "sunspot" phenomena. In other words, there are at least two equilibria, a "good" equilibrium in which early consumers receive the proceeds from short-term assets and late consumers receive the proceeds from long-term assets and a "bad" equilibrium in which everybody believes a crisis will occur and these beliefs are self-fulfilling. Chang and Velasco (2000) shows that the existence of the bad equilibrium depends on the exchange rate regime in force. In some regimes, only the good equilibrium exists; in other regimes there exists a bad equilibrium in addition to the good equilibrium. The selection of the good or the bad equilibrium is not modeled. In Chang and Velasco (1998) a similar model is used to consider recent crises in emerging markets. Again there is no aggregate uncertainty and crises are sunspot phenomena.

A number of other papers have focused on the possibility of multiple equilibria. These include Flood and Garber (1984), Obstfeld (1986, 1994), and Calvo (1988). In these models governments are unable to commit to policies and this lack of commitment can give rise to multiple equilibria, at least one of which is a self-fulfilling crisis. Again, the selection of equilibrium is problematic. An exception is Morris and Shin (1998) who show that traders' lack of common knowledge about the state of the economy can lead to a unique equilibrium selection.

Corsetti et al. (1999) have developed a model of twin crises designed to explain the Asian meltdown in 1997. The basic reason that twin crises occur in their framework is because of moral hazard arising from government guarantees. Foreigners are willing to lend for unprofitable projects against the promise of future government bailouts. When the project payoffs turn out to be low there will be a banking crisis. The prospect of the government using seigniorage to finance the bailouts leads to the prospect of inflation and so the currency also collapses.

Kaminsky and Reinhart's (1999) finding that crises are related to economic fundamentals is consistent with work on U.S. financial crises in the nineteenth and early twentieth centuries. Gorton (1988) and Calomiris and Gorton (1991) argue that the evidence is consistent with the hypothesis that banking crises are an essential part of the business cycle rather than a sunspot phenomenon. Allen and Gale (2000c) extend the model of Allen and Gale (1998) to consider twin crises. A model is developed where the "twin" crises result from low asset returns. Large movements in exchange rates are desirable to the extent that they allow better risk sharing between a country's bank depositors and the international bond market.

8.3 Bubbles and crises

As the historical summary at the beginning of the section indicated, crises often follow apparent bubbles in asset prices. Allen and Gale (2000d) provide a theory of bubbles and ensuing crises based on the existence of an agency problem. Many investors in real estate and stock markets obtain their investment funds from external sources. If the ultimate providers of funds are unable to observe the characteristics of the investment, there is a classic risk shifting problem. Risk shifting increases the return to investment in the assets and causes investors to bid up the asset price above its fundamental value. A crucial determinant of asset prices is the amount of credit that is provided for speculative investment. Financial liberalization, by expanding the volume of credit for speculative investments, can interact with the agency problem and lead to a bubble in asset prices.

An alternative theory of financial crises has been suggested by McKinnon and Pill (1997) and Krugman (1998). They suggest that government guarantees are the fundamental cause of crises. Because deposits are guaranteed by the government, banks are not subject to the usual discipline of the market. This allows banks to engage in speculative investment, which bids up asset prices and creates a bubble that eventually bursts. It can be argued that while government guarantees can certainly exacerbate the situation, they are neither necessary nor sufficient for the occurrence of a crisis. Many crises occurred when there was no prospect of a government guarantee for banks. The United States in the late 1920s and early 1930s witnessed a dramatic rise in asset prices and a subsequent crisis when no government guarantees existed. The United States in the 1950s and 1960s provides an example where government guarantees of the banking system existed but no crisis occurred.

8.4 Contagion and financial fragility

The prevalence of financial crises has led many to conclude that the financial sector is unusually susceptible to shocks. One theory is that small shocks can have a large impact. A shock that initially affects only a particular region or sector or perhaps even a few institutions can spread by contagion to the rest of the financial sector and then infect the larger economy. There are a number of different types of contagion that have been suggested in the literature. The first is contagion through interlinkages between banks and financial institutions. The second is contagion of currency crises. The third is contagion through financial markets. De Bandt and Hartmann (2000) contains a survey of this literature.

Banks are linked in several ways including payments systems and interbank markets. These linkages can lead to a problem of contagion. We start by considering models of payment system contagion. Building on a locational model of payment systems developed by McAndrews and Roberds (1995), Freixas and Parigi (1998) have considered contagion in net and gross payment systems. In a net payment system banks extend credit to each other within the day and at the end of the day settle their net position. This exposes banks to the possibility of contagion if the failure of one institution triggers a chain reaction. In a gross system, transactions are settled on a one-to-one basis with central bank money. There is no risk of contagion but banks have to hold large reserve balances. A net payment system is preferred when the probability of banks having low returns is small, the opportunity cost of holding central bank money reserves is high, and the proportion of consumers that have to consume at another location is high. Freixas et al. (1999) use this model to examine the conditions under which gridlock occurs. They show that there can be gridlock when the depositors in one bank withdraw their funds, anticipating that other banks cannot meet their netting obligations if all their depositors have also withdrawn their funds. Rochet and Tirole (1996*a*) consider the role of the too-big-to-fail policy in preventing contagion.

Allen and Gale (2000*e*) focus on a channel of contagion that arises from the overlapping claims that different regions or sectors of the banking system have on one another through interbank markets. When one region suffers a banking crisis, the other regions suffer a loss because their claims on the troubled region fall in value. If this spillover effect is strong enough, it can cause a crisis in the adjacent regions. In extreme cases, the crisis passes from region to region and becomes a contagion. Aghion et al. (1999) also consider a model of contagion through interbank markets. In their model there are multiple equilibria. In one equilibrium, there are self-confirming beliefs that a bank failure is an idiosyncratic event and in the other there are self-fulfilling beliefs that a bank failure signals a global shortage of liquidity. Lagunoff and Schreft (2001) study the spread of crises in a probabilistic model. Financial linkages are modeled by assuming that each project requires two participants and each participant requires two projects. When the probability that one's partner will withdraw becomes too large, all participants simultaneously withdraw and this is interpreted as a financial crisis. Van Rijckeghem and Weber (2000) document linkages through banking centers empirically. Rochet and Tirole (1996*b*) use monitoring as a means of triggering correlated crises: if one bank fails, it is assumed that other banks have not been properly monitored and a general collapse occurs.

There is a growing literature on contagious currency crises. Masson (1999) provides a good overview of the basic issues. He distinguishes between "monsoonal" effects, spillovers, and pure contagion. Monsoonal effects occur when there are major economic shifts in industrial countries that impact emerging economies. Spillovers occur when there are links between regions. Pure contagion is when there is a change in expectations that is not related to fundamentals and is associated with multiple equilibria. Eichengreen et al. (1996) and Glick and Rose (1999) provide evidence that trade linkages are important factors in the spread of many currency crises.

There are a number of papers that consider contagion through financial markets. King and Wadwhani (1990) considered a situation where information is correlated between markets. Price changes in one market are perceived to have implications for asset values in other markets. Calvo (1999) and Yuan (2000) consider correlated liquidity shocks as a channel for contagion. When some investors need to obtain cash to, for example, meet a margin call they may liquidate in a number of markets so the shock is spread. Kodres and Pritsker (2000) use a multi-asset rational expectations model to show how macroeconomic risk factors and country-specific asymmetric information can combine to produce contagion. Kyle and Xiong (2000) present a model of contagion in financial markets due to the existence of a wealth effect.

The notion of financial fragility is closely related to that of contagion. When a financial system is fragile a small shock can have a big effect. The shock may be spread by contagion. A financial crisis may rage out of control and bring down the entire economic edifice. The memory of the Great Depression and earlier crises is still with us and it powerfully reinforces belief in financial fragility. Financial multipliers are modeled by Kiyotaki and Moore (1997). In their model, the impact of illiquidity at one link in the credit chain travels down the chain and has a big impact. Chari and Kehoe (2000) show that herding behavior can cause a small information shock to have a large effect on capital flows.

8.5 Discussion

The literature on financial crises is still at an early stage. Many important questions remain.

- Conventional wisdom holds that financial crises are undesirable and should be eliminated. However, the theoretical underpinnings of this idea are sparse. It is not entirely clear what the market failure is. Allen and Gale (2000f), for example, show that in some cases crises are constrained efficient.
- What exactly is the link between the financial sector and the real sector? Why do financial crises have such quick and important effects on real activity?
- What precisely is the role of the central bank with regard to crises and what should its policy be?

9. Concluding Remarks

The field of comparative financial systems is relatively new. Despite its youth, there is already a large literature, as this survey demonstrates. The transformation of the formerly communist economies in Eastern

Europe, the development of a single economy in the European Union, and the continuing process of globalization of financial markets underline the importance of this field. Much work remains to be done before the advantages and disadvantages of rival financial systems are fully understood.

References

Admati, A. (1989). "Information in financial markets: The rational expectations approach," in S. Bhattacharya and G. M. Constantinides (eds.), *Financial Markets and Incomplete Information: Frontiers of Modern Financial Theory*, Volume 2 (Totowa, NJ: Rowman and Littlefield), 139–52.

——, Pfleiderer, P., and Zechner, J. (1994). "Large shareholder activism, risk sharing, and financial market equilibrium." *Journal of Political Economy*, 102: 1097–130.

Aghion, P., Bolton, P., and Dewatripont, M. (1999). "Contagious bank failures." Working Paper, Princeton University.

——, Hart, O., and Moore, J. (1992). "The economics of bankruptcy reform." *Journal of Law and Economics*, 8: 523–46.

Alchian, A. (1950). "Uncertainty, evolution, and economic theory." *Journal of Political Economy*, 58: 211–21.

Allen, F. (1983). "A Normative analysis of informational efficiency in markets for risky assets." Mimeo, Nuffield College, Oxford.

—— (1993). "Stock markets and resource allocation," in C. Mayer and X. Vives (eds.), *Capital Markets and Financial Intermediation* (Cambridge: Cambridge Univ. Press).

—— (1995). "Book review of *Strong Managers, Weak Owners* by M. Roe, Princeton University Press." *Journal of Economic Literature*, 33: 1994–6.

Allen, F., and Gale, D. (1995). "A welfare comparison of intermediaries and financial markets in Germany and the U.S." *European Economic Review*, 39: 179–209.

——, and —— (1997). "Financial markets, intermediaries, and intertemporal smoothing." *Journal of Political Economy*, 105: 523–46.

——, and —— (1998). "Optimal financial crises." *Journal of Finance*, 53: 1245–84.

——, and —— (1999). "Diversity of opinion and the financing of new technologies." *Journal of Financial Intermediation*, 8: 68–89.

——, and —— (2000*a*). *Comparing Financial Systems*. Cambridge, MA: MIT Press.

——, and —— (2000*b*). "Corporate governance and competition," in Vives (ed.), *Corporate Governance: Theoretical and Empirical Perspectives* (Cambridge: Cambridge Univ. Press).

——, and —— (2000*c*). "Optimal currency crises." *Carnegie Rochester Series on Public Policy*, 53: 177–230.

Allen, F., and Gale, D. (2000*d*). "Bubbles and crises." *Economic Journal*, 110: 236–55.

——, and —— (2000*e*). "Financial contagion." *Journal of Political Economy*, 108: 1–33.

——, and —— (2000*f*). "Banking and markets." Working Paper 00-44, Wharton Financial Institutions Center.

Alonso, I. (1996)."On Avoiding Bank Runs." *Journal of Monetary Economics*, 37: 73–87.

Aoki, M. (1984*a*). *The Co-operative Game Theory of the Firm*. Oxford: Oxford Univ. Press.

—— (1984*b*). "Shareholders' non-unanimity on investment financing: Banks vs. individual investors," in M. Aoki (ed.), *The Economic Analysis of the Japanese Firm* (Amsterdam: North-Holland).

—— (1988). *Information, Incentives, and Bargaining in the Japanese Economy*. New York: Cambridge Univ. Press.

—— (1992). "Decentralization–Centralization in Japanese organization: A duality principle," in Shumpei Kumon and Henry Rosovsky (eds.), *The Political Economy of Japan, Volume 3: Cultural and Social Dynamics* (Stanford: Stanford University Press): 142–69.

——, and Patrick, H. (eds.) (1994). *The Japanese Main Bank System: Its Relevancy for Developing and Transforming Economies*. New York: Oxford Univ. Press, 592–633.

——, and Dinç, S. (1997). "Relational financing as an institution and its viability under competition." CEPR Publication No. 488, Stanford University.

Asquith, P., Gertner, R., and Scharfstein, D. (1994). "Anatomy of financial distress: An examination of junk-bond issuers." *Quarterly Journal of Economics*, 109: 625–58.

Ausubel, L. M. (1990). "Insider trading in a rational expectations economy." *American Economic Review*, 80: 759–76.

Bagehot, W. (1873). *Lombard Street*. Homewood, IL: Irwin (1962 edition).

Bebchuk, A. (1988). "A new approach to corporate reorganizations." *Harvard Law Review*, 101: 775–804.

Becht, M., Bolton, P., and Röell, A. (2001). "Corporate governance and control," in G. Constantinides, M. Harris, and R. Stulz (eds.), *Handbook of the Economics of Finance* (Amsterdam, The Netherlands: North Holland).

Bencivenga, V., and Smith, B. (1991). "Financial intermediation and endogenous growth." *Review of Economic Studies*, 58(2): 195–209.

——, Smith, B., and Starr, R. (1995). "Transactions costs, technological choice, and endogenous growth." *Journal of Economic Theory*, 67(1): 53–177.

Berger, A., and Udell, G. (1992). "Some evidence on the empirical significance of credit rationing." *Journal of Political Economy*, 100: 291–9.

Bergman, Y., and Callen, J. (1991). "Opportunistic underinvestment in debt renegotiation and capital structure." *Journal of Financial Economics*, 29: 137–71.

Berkovitch, E., and Israel, R. (1999) "Optimal bankruptcy laws across different economic systems." *Review of Financial Studies*, 12: 347–77.

——, and Zender, J. (1998). "The design of bankruptcy law: A case for management bias in bankruptcy reorganizations." *Journal of Financial and Quantitative Analysis*, 33: 441–64.

Berle, A., and Means, G. (1932). *The Modern Corporation and Private Property*. Chicago, IL: Commerce Clearing House, Inc.

Berlin, M., and Mester, L. (1997a). "Why is the banking sector shrinking? Core deposits and relationship lending." Working Paper 96-18/R, Federal Reserve Bank of Philadelphia.

——, and —— (1998). "On the profitability and cost of relationship lending." *Journal of Banking and Finance*, 22: 873–97.

Bernardo, A. E., and Judd, K. L. (1997). "Efficiency of asset markets with asymmetric information." Working Paper, UCLA.

Bernhardt, D., Hollifield, B., and Hughson, E. (1995). "Investment and insider trading." *Review of Financial Studies*, 8: 501–43.

Bertero, E. (1994). "The banking system, financial markets, and capital structure: Some new evidence from France." *Oxford Review of Economic Policy*, 10: 68–78.

Betker, B. (1995). "Management's incentives, equity's bargaining power and deviations from absolute priority in Chapter 11 bankruptcies." *Journal of Business*, 68: 161–83.

Bhagat, S., and Black, B. (1998). "The uncertain relationship between board composition and firm performance," in K. Hopt, M. Roe, and E. Wymeersch (eds.), *Corporate Governance: The State of the Art and Emerging Research* (New York: Oxford Univ. Press).

——, Shleifer, A., and Vishny, R. (1990). "Hostile takeovers in the 1980s: The return to corporate specialization." *Brookings Papers on Economic Activity: Microeconomics*, Special Issue: 1–72.

Bhattacharya, S., and Chiesa, G. (1995). "Financial intermediation with proprietary information." *Journal of Financial Intermediation*, 4: 328–57.

——, and Nicodano, G. (1995). "Insider trading, investment, and welfare: A perturbation analysis." Working Paper, London School of Economics.

Bhattacharya, U. (1997). "Communication costs, information acquisition, and voting decisions in proxy contests." *Review of Financial Studies*, 10: 1065–97.

Bolton, P., and von Thadden, E. (1998a). "Blocks, liquidity, and corporate control." *Journal of Finance*, 53: 1–25.

——, and —— (1998b). "Liquidity and control: A dynamic theory of corporate ownership structure." *Journal of Institutional and Theoretical Economics*, 154: 177–223.

Boot, A., Greenbaum, S., and Thakor, A. (1993). "Reputation and discretion in financial contracting." *American Economic Review*, 83: 1165–83.

——, and Thakor, A. (1997a). "Financial system architecture." *Review of Financial Studies*, 10: 693–733.

——, and —— (1997b). "Banking scope and financial innovation," *Review of Financial Studies*, 10: 1099–131.

——, and —— (2000). "Can relationship banking survive competition?" *Journal of Finance*, 55: 679–713.

Bordo, M. (2000). "The globalization of international financial markets: What can history teach us." Working Paper, Sveriges Riksbank, Stockholm.

——, and Eichengreen, B. (2000). "Is the crisis problem growing more severe." Working Paper, Sveriges Riksbank, Stockholm.

Boyd, J., and Smith, B. (1996). "The co-evolution of the real and financial sectors in the growth process." *World Bank Economic Review*, 10(2): 371–96.

——, and —— (1998). "The evolution of debt and equity markets in economic development." *Economic Theory*, 12(3): 519–60.

Brown, D. (1989). "Claimholder incentive conflicts in reorganization: The role of bankruptcy law." *Review of Financial Studies*, 2: 109–23.

Brealey, R., and Myers, S. (2000). *Principles of Corporate Finance*, 6th edn. New York: McGraw Hill Irwin.

Burkart, M. (1995). "Initial shareholdings and overbidding in takeover contests." *Journal of Finance*, 50: 1491–515.

——, Gromb, D., and Panunzi, F. (1997). "Large shareholders, monitoring, and the value of the firm." *Quarterly Journal of Economics*, 112: 693–728.

Cable, J. (1985). "Capital market information and industrial performance." *Economic Journal*, 95: 118–32.

Calomiris, C., and Gorton, G. (1991). "The origins of banking panics, models, facts, and bank regulation," in R. G. Hubbard (ed.), *Financial Markets and Financial Crises* (Chicago, IL: University of Chicago Press).

Calvo, G. (1988). "Servicing the public debt: The role of expectations." *American Economic Review*, 78: 1411–28.

—— (1999). "Contagion in emerging markets: When Wall Street is a carrier." Unpublished Manuscript, University of Maryland.

Champ, B., Smith, B., and Williamson, S. (1996). "Currency elasticity and banking panics: Theory and evidence." *Canadian Journal of Economics*, 29: 828–64.

Chang, R., and Velasco, A. (1998). "Financial crises in emerging markets: A canonical model." Working Paper, New York University.

——, and —— (2000). "Financial fragility and the exchange rate regime." *Journal of Economic Theory*, 92: 1–34.

Chari, V. (1989). "Banking without deposit insurance or bank panics: Lessons from a model of the U.S. National Banking System," *Federal Reserve Bank of Minneapolis Quarterly Review* 13 (Summer): 3–19.

——, and Jagannathan, R. (1988). "Banking panics, information, and rational expectations equilibrium." *Journal of Finance*, 43: 749–60.

——, and Kehoe, P. (2000). Financial crises as herds." Working Paper, Federal Reserve Bank of Minneapolis.

Charkham, J. (1994). *Keeping Good Company: A Study of Corporate Governance in Five Countries*. Oxford: Clarendon Press.

Coase, R. (1937). "The nature of the firm." *Economica*, 4: 386–405.

Corbett, J., and Jenkinson, T. (1996). "The financing of industry, 1970–1989: An international comparison." *Journal of the Japanese & International Economies*, 10: 71–96.

Davis, E. P. (1992). "The development of pension funds in the major industrial countries." in J. Mortensen (ed.), *The Future of Pensions in the European Community* (London: Brassey's), 107–31.

—— (1996). "An international comparison of the financing of occupational pensions," in Z. Bodie, O. Mitchell, and J. Turner (eds.), *Securing Employer-Based Pensions: An International Perspective* (Philadelphia, PA: University of Pennsylvania Press), 244–81.

De Bandt, O., and Hartmann, P. (2000). "Systemic risk: A survey." Working Paper No. 35, European Central Bank.

Demirgüç-Kunt, A., and Maksimovic, V. (1996). "Stock market development and financing choices of firms." *World Bank Economic Review*, 10(2): 341–70.

——, and —— (1998). "Law, finance, and firm growth." *Journal of Finance*, 53(6): 2107–37.

Dewatripont, M., and Maskin, E. (1995). "Credit and efficiency in centralized and decentralized economies." *Review of Economic Studies*, 62: 541–55.

Diamond, D. (1984). "Financial intermediation and delegated monitoring." *Review of Economic Studies*, 51: 393–414.

—— (1991). "Monitoring and reputation: The choice between bank loans and directly placed debt." *Journal of Political Economy*, 99: 689–721.

——, and Dybvig, P. (1983). "Bank runs, deposit insurance, and liquidity." *Journal of Political Economy*, 91: 401–19.

——, and Verrecchia, R. (1981). "Information aggregation in a noisy rational expectations economy." *Journal of Financial Economics*, 9: 221–35.

——, and —— (1982). "Optimal managerial contracts and equilibrium security prices." *Journal of Finance*, 37: 275–87.

Dinç, S. (1996). "Bank competition, relationship banking and path dependence." Ph.D. Dissertation, Stanford University.

Dow, J., and Gorton, G. (1997). "Stock market efficiency and economic efficiency: Is there a connection?" *Journal of Finance*, 52: 1087–129.

——, and Rahi, R. (1997). "Informed trading, investment, and welfare." European University Institute Working Paper 97/3.

Drees, B., and Pazarbasioglu, C. (1995). "The Nordic banking crises: Pitfalls in financial liberalization?" International Monetary Fund Working Paper 95/61.

Eberhart, A., Moore, W., and Roenfeldt, R., (1990). "Security pricing and deviations from the absolute priority rule in banktruptcy proceedings." *Journal of Finance*, 45: 1457–69.

Edwards, J., and Fischer, K. (1994). *Banks, Finance and Investment in Germany.* Cambridge: Cambridge Univ. Press.

Eichengreen, B., Rose, A., and Wyplocz, C. (1996). "Contagious currency crises: First tests." *Scandinavian Journal of Economics*, 98: 463–84.

Elsas, R., and Krahnen, J. (1998). "Is relationship lending special? Evidence from credit-file data in Germany." *Journal of Banking and Finance* 22: 1283–316.

Elston, J. (1993). "Firm ownership structure and investment: Theory and evidence from German panel data." Unpublished Manuscript.

Fama, E.F. (1970). "Efficient capital markets: A review of theory and empirical work." *Journal of Finance,* 35: 383–417.

—— (1976). *Foundations of Finance.* New York: Basic Books.

—— (1991). "Efficient capital markets, II." *Journal of Finance,* 46: 1575–617.

——, and Jensen, M. (1983a). "Separation of ownership and control." *Journal of Law and Economics,* 26: 301–25.

——, and —— (1983b). "Agency problems and residuals claims." *Journal of Law and Economics,* 26: 327–49.

Fazzari, S., Hubbard, R. G., and Petersen, B. (1988). "Financing constraints and corporate investment." *Brookings Papers on Economic Activity,* 141–95.

Fishman, M., and Hagerty, K. (1992). "Insider trading and the efficiency of stock prices." *Rand Journal of Economics,* 23: 106–22.

Flood, R., and Garber, P. (1984). "Gold monetization and gold discipline." *Journal of Political Economy,* 92: 90–107.

——, and Marion, N. (1998). "Perspectives on the recent currency crisis literature." Working Paper 98/130, Research Department, International Monetary Fund.

Frankel, J. (1993). "The Japanese financial system and the cost of capital," in S. Takagi (ed.), *Japanese Capital Markets: New Developments in Regulations and Institutions,* (Oxford: Blackwell), 21–77.

Franks, J., and Mayer, C. (1992). "Corporate control: A synthesis of the international evidence." IFA Working Paper No. 165-92, London Business School, London.

——, and —— (1996) "Hostile takeovers and the correction of managerial failure." *Journal of Financial Economics,* 40: 163–81.

——, and —— (1997). "Ownership, control and the performance of German corporations." Working Paper, London Business School.

——, and —— (1998). "Bank control, takeovers and corporate governance in Germany." *Journal of Banking and Finance,* 22: 1385–403.

——, and Torous, W. (1994). "A comparison of financial recontracting in distressed exchanges and Chapter 11 reorganizations." *Journal of Financial Economics,* 35: 349–70.

Freixas, X., and Parigi, B. (1998). "Contagion and efficiency in gross and net interbank payment systems." *Journal of Financial Intermediation,* 7(1): 3–31.

——, and Rochet (2000). "Systemic risk, interbank relations and liquidity provision by the central bank." *Journal of Money, Credit, and Banking,* 32(3): 611–38.

Gale, D. (1991). "Optimal risk sharing through renegotiation of simple contracts." *Journal of Financial Intermediation,* 1: 283–306.

Gerschenkron, A. (1962). *Economic Backwardness in Historical Perspective.* Cambridge, MA: Harvard University Press.

Gertner, R., and Scharfstein, D. (1991). "A theory of workouts and the effects of reorganization law." *Journal of Finance,* 46: 1189–222.

——, and Stein, J. (1994). "Internal versus external capital markets." *Quarterly Journal of Economics,* 109: 1211–30.

Gibson, M. (1999). "Is corporate governance ineffective in emerging markets?" Working Paper, Board of Governors of the Federal Reserve System, Washington, D.C.

Glick, R., and Rose, A. (1999). "Contagion and trade: Why are currency crises regional?" in P. Agénor, M. Miller, D. Vines, and A. Weber (eds.), *The Asian Financial Crisis: Causes, Contagion and Consequences*, Chapter 9 (Cambridge: Cambridge Univ. Press).

Glosten, L. (1989). "Insider trading, liquidity, and the role of the monopolist specialist." *Journal of Business*, 62: 211–35.

Goldsmith, R. (1969). *Financial Structure and Development*. New Haven, CT: Yale Univ. Press.

Gorton, G. (1988). "Banking panics and business cycles." *Oxford Economic Papers*, 40: 751–81.

——, and Schmid, F. (2000). "Universal banking and the performance of German firms." *Journal of Financial Economics*, 58: 29–80.

Greenwood, J., and Jovanovic, B. (1990). *Journal of Political Economy* 98: 1076–107.

Greif, A. (2000). "The fundamental problem of exchnage: A research agenda in historical insitutional analysis." *European Review of Economic History*, 4: 251–84.

Grossman, S. (1976). "On the efficiency of competitive stock markets where traders have diverse information." *Journal of Finance*, 31: 573–85.

—— (1981). "An introduction to the theory of rational expectations under asymmetric information." *Review of Economic Studies*, 48: 541–9.

——, and Hart, O. (1980). "Takeover bids, the free-rider problem, and the theory of the corporation." *Bell Journal of Economics*, 11: 42–64.

——, and —— (1982). "Corporate financial structure and managerial incentives," in J. McCall (ed.), *The Economics of Information and Uncertainty* (Chicago, IL: University of Chicago Press).

——, and —— (1986). "The costs and benefits of ownership." *Journal of Political Economy*, 94: 691–719.

——, and Stiglitz, J. (1976). "Information and competitive price systems." *American Economic Review*, 66: 246–53.

——, and —— (1980). "On the impossibility of informationally efficient markets." *American Economic Review*, 70: 393–408.

Hackethal, A., and Schmidt, R. (1999). "Financing patterns: Measurement concepts and empirical results." Working Paper, University of Frankfurt.

Hart, O. (1983). "The Market mechanism as an incentive scheme." *Bell Journal of Economics*, 14: 366–82.

—— (1995). *Firms, Contracts and Financial Structure*. Oxford: Clarendon Press.

——, and J. Moore (1988). "Incomplete contracts and renegotiation," *Econometrica*, 56: 755–85.

Haubrich, J. (1994). "Risk aversion, performance pay, and the principal–agent problem." *Journal of Political Economy*, 102: 258–76.

Hawawini, G., and Keim, D. (1995). "On the predictability of common stock returns: World-wide evidence," in R. A. Jarrow, V. Maksimovic, and W. T. Ziemba (eds.),

Handbooks in Operations Research and Management Science, Volume 9: Finance (Amsterdam: North Holland), 497–544.

Hayashi, F. (1997). "The main bank system and corporate investment: An empirical reassessment." NBER Working Paper 6172, Cambridge, MA.

Healy, P., Palepu, K., and Ruback, R. (1992). "Does corporate performance improve after mergers?" *Journal of Financial Economics*, 31: 135–75.

——, ——, and —— "Which takeovers are profitable? Strategic or financial?" *Sloan Management Review* (Summer) 45–57.

Heiskanen, R. (1993). "The banking crisis in the Nordic countries." *Kansallis Economic Review*, 2: 13–19.

Hellwig, M. (1980). "On the aggregation of information in competitive markets." *Journal of Economic Theory*, 22: 477–98.

—— (1991). "Banking, financial intermediation and corporate Finance," in A. Giovannini and C. Mayer (eds.), *European Financial Integration* (New York: Cambridge Univ. Press), 35–63.

—— (1994). "Liquidity provision, banking, and the allocation of interest rate risk." *European Economic Review*, 38: 1363–89.

—— (1998). "Banks, markets, and the allocation of risks in an economy." *Journal of Institutional and Theoretical Economics*, 54: 328–45.

Herman, E., and Lowenstein, L. (1988). "The efficiency effects of hostile Takeovers," in J. Coffee, Jr., L. Lowenstein, and S. Rose-Ackerman (eds.), *Knights, Raiders, and Targets: the Impact of the Hostile Takeover* (New York: Oxford Univ. Press).

Hicks, J. (1969). *A Theory of Economic History*. Oxford: Clarendon Press.

Hirshleifer, J. (1971). "The private and social value of information and the reward to inventive activity." *American Economic Review*, 61: 561–74.

Holmström, B., and Tirole, J. (1993). "Market liquidity and performance monitoring." *Journal of Political Economy*, 101: 678–709.

Hoshi, T., Kashyap, A., and Scharfstein, D. (1990*a*). "Bank monitoring and investment: Evidence from the changing structure of Japanese corporate banking relationships," in R. G. Hubbard (ed.), *Asymmetric Information, Corporate Finance and Investment* (Chicago, IL: Chicago Univ. Press).

——, ——, and —— (1990*b*) "The role of banks in reducing the costs of financial distress in Japan." *Journal of Financial Economics*, 27: 67–8.

——, ——, and —— (1991). "Corporate structure, liquidity and investment: Evidence from Japanese industrial groups." *Quarterly Journal of Economics*, 106: 33–60

——, ——, and —— (1993). "The choice between public and private debt: An analysis of post-deregulation corporate finance in Japan." National Bureau of Economic Research Working Paper 4421, Cambridge, MA.

Huberman, G., and Kahn, C. (1988). "Limited contract enforcement and strategic renegotiation." *American Economic Review*, 78: 471–84.

Huddart, S. (1993). "The effect of a large shareholder on corporate value." *Management Science*, 39: 1407–21.

Jacklin, C., and Bhattacharya, S. (1988). "Distinguishing panics and information-based bank runs: Welfare and policy implications." *Journal of Political Economy*, 96: 568–92.

Jensen, M. (1986). "Agency costs of free cash flow, corporate finance, and takeovers." *American Economic Review*, 76: 323–9.

—— (1989). "The eclipse of the public corporation." *Harvard Business Review* 67: 60–70.

—— (1993). "The modern industrial revolution, exit, and the failure of internal control systems." *Journal of Finance* 48: 831–80.

——, and Meckling, W. (1976). "Theory of the firm: Managerial behavior, agency costs and ownership structure." *Journal of Financial Economics*, 3: 305–60.

——, and Murphy, K. (1990). "Performance pay and top-management incentives." *Journal of Political Economy*, 98: 225–64.

Kaminsky, G., and Reinhart, C. (1999). "On the impossibility of informationally efficient markets." *American Economic Review*, 80: 393–408.

Kang, J., and Shivdasani, A. (1995). "Firm performance, corporate governance, and top executive turnover in Japan." *Journal of Financial Economics*, 38: 29–58.

——, and —— (1997). "Corporate restructuring during performance declines in Japan." *Journal of Financial Economics*, 46: 29–65.

Kaplan, S. (1989). "The effects of management buyouts on operating performance and value." *Journal of Financial Economics*, 24: 581–618.

—— (1994a). "Top executives, turnover, and firm performance in Germany." *Journal of Law, Economics, and Organization*, 10: 142–59.

—— (1994b). "Top executive rewards and firm performance: A comparison of Japan and the United States." *Journal of Political Economy*, 102: 510–46.

——, and Weisbach, M. (1991). "The Success of Acquisitions: Evidence from Divestitures," *Journal of Finance* 47: 107–38.

——, and Zingales, L. (1997). "Do investment-cash flow sensitivities provide useful measures of financing constraints?" *Quarterly Journal of Economics*, 112: 169–215.

Kester, C. (1991). *Japanese Takeovers: The Global Contest for Corporate Control*. Boston, MA: Harvard Business School Press.

Kindleberger, C. (1978). *Manias, Panics, and Crashes: A History of Financial Crises*. New York: Basic Books.

King, M., and Wadhwani, S. (1990). "Transmission of volatility between stock markets." *Review of Financial Studies* 3(1): 5–33.

King, R., and Levins, R. (1993a). "Financial intermediation and economic development," in C. Mayer and X. Vives (eds.), *Financial Intermediation in the Construction of Europe* (London: Center for Economic Policy Research).

——, and —— (1993b). "Finance and growth: Schumpeter might be right." *Quarterly Journal of Economics*, 108(3): 717–38.

——, and —— (1993c). "Finance, entrepreneurship, and growth: Theory and evidence." *Journal of Monetary Economics*, 32(3): 513–42.

Kiyotaki, N., and Moore, J. (1997). "Credit chains." *Journal of Political Economy*, 105: 211–48.

Kodres L., and Pritsker, M. (2000). "A rational expectations model of financial contagion." Working Paper, International Monetary Fund. *Journal of Finance*, forthcoming.

Krugman, P. (1979). "A model of balance of payments crises." *Journal of Money, Credit, and Banking*, 311–25.

——(1998). 'Bubble, boom, crash: Theoretical notes on Asia's crisis." Working Paper, Cambridge, MA: MIT.

Kyle, A., and Xiong, W. (1999). "Contagion as a wealth effect of financial intermediaries." Working Paper, Duke University.

Laffont, J. (1985). "On the welfare analysis of rational expectations equilibria with asymmetric information." *Econometrica*, 53: 1–29.

Lagunoff, R., and Schreft, S. (2001). "A model of financial fragility." *Journal of Economic Theory*, 99: 220–64.

Lamont, O. (1997). "Cash flow and investment: Evidence from internal capital markets." *Journal of Finance*, 52: 83–109.

La Porta, R., Lopez-de-Silanes, F., and Shleifer, A. (1999). "Corporate ownership around the world." *Journal of Finance*, 54: 471–517.

——, ——, ——, and Vishny, R. (1997). "Legal determinants of external finance." *Journal of Finance*, 52: 1131–50.

——, ——, ——, and —— (1998). "Law and finance." *Journal of Political Economy*, 106: 1113–55.

——, ——, ——, and —— (2000a). "Agency problems and dividend policies around the world." *Journal of Finance*, 55: 1–33.

——, ——, ——, and —— (2000b). "Investor protection and corporate governance." *Journal of Financial Economics*, 58: 3–27.

Leland, H. (1992). "Insider trading: Should it be prohibited?" *Journal of Political Economy*, 100: 859–87.

Levine, R. (1997). "Financial development and economic growth: Views and agenda." *Journal of Economic Literature*, 35: 688–726.

——(2000). "Bank-based or market-based financial systems: Which is better?" Working Paper, Carlsson School, University of Minnesota.

——, and Zervos, S. (1998). "Stock markets, banks and economic growth." *American Economic Review*, 88(3): 537–58.

Lindgren, C., Garcia, G., and Saal, M. (1996). *Bank Soundness and Macroeconomic Policy*. Washington, DC: International Monetary Fund.

Mace, M. (1971). *Directors, Myth and Reality*. Boston, MA: Harvard Business School Press.

Manne, H. (1965). "Mergers and the market for corporate control." *Journal of Political Economy*, 73: 110–20.

Manove, M. (1989). "The Harm from insider trading and informed speculation." *Quarterly Journal of Economics*, 104: 823–45.

Marín, J., and Rahi, R. (1999). "Speculative securities." *Economic Theory* 14: 653–68.

——, and —— (2000). "Information revelation and market incompleteness." *Review of Economic Studies*, 67: 455–81.

Masson, P. (1999). "Contagion: Monsoonal effects, spillovers and jumps between multiple equilibria," in P. Agénor, M. Miller, D. Vines, and A. Weber (eds.), *The Asian Financial Crisis: Causes, Contagion and Consequences*, Chapter 8 (Cambridge: Cambridge Univ. Press).

Maug, E. (1998). "How effective is shareholder voting? Information aggregation and conflict resolution in corporate voting contests." Working Paper, Duke University.

Mayer, C. (1988). "New issues in corporate finance." *European Economic Review*, 32: 1167–88.

—— (1990). "Financial systems, corporate finance, and economic development," in R. G. Hubbard (ed.), *Asymmetric Information, Corporate Finance and Investment* (Chicago, IL: University of Chicago Press).

McAndrews, J., and Roberds, W. (1995). "Banks, payments and coordination." *Journal of Financial Intermediation*, 4(4): 305–27.

McKinnon, R. (1973). *Money and Capital in Economic Development*. Washington, DC: Brookings Institution.

——, and Pill, H. (1997), "Credible economic liberalizations and overborrowing." *American Economic Review*, 87: 189–203.

Miles, D. (1996). "The future of savings and wealth accumulation: Differences within the developed economies." Global Securities Research & Economics Group, Merrill Lynch, London.

Mishkin, F. (1997). "Understanding financial crises: A developing country perspective." *Annual World Bank Conference on Development Economics 1996*. Washington, DC: The International Bank for Reconstruction and Development, 29–61.

Morris, S., and Shin, H. (1998). "Unique equilibrium in a model of self-fulfilling currency attacks." *American Economic Review*, 88: 587–97.

Myers, S. (1977). "Determinants of corporate borrowing." *Journal of Financial Economics*, 5: 147–75.

Obstfeld, M. (1986). "Rational and self-fulfilling balance of payments crises." *American Economic Review*, 76: 72–81.

—— (1994). "Risk-taking, global diversification, and growth." *American Economic Review*, 84(5): 10–29.

Pagano, M. (1993). "The flotation of companies on the stock market: A coordination failure model." *European Economic Review*, 37: 1101–25.

——, and A. Röell (1998). "The choice of stock ownership structure: Agency costs, monitoring and the decision to go public." *Quarterly Journal of Economics*, 113: 187–225.

Pistor, K. (1996). "Co-determination in Germany: A socio-political model with governance externalities," in *Conference on Employees and Corporate Governance*, Columbia Law School, November 22.

Petersen, M., and Rajan, R. (1994). "The benefits of lending relationships: Evidence from small business data." *Journal of Finance*, 49: 3–37.

Petersen, M., and Rajan, R. (1995)."The effect of credit market competition on lending relationships." *Quarterly Journal of Economics,* 110: 407–43.

Postlewaite, A., and Vives, X. (1987). "Bank runs as an equilibrium phenomenon." *Journal of Political Economy,* 95: 485–91.

Prowse, S. (1995). "Corporate governance in an international perspective: A survey of corporate control mechanisms among large firms in the U.S., U.K., Japan and Germany." *Financial Markets, Institutions and Instruments* 4: 1–63.

Pulvino, T. (1998). "Do asset fire-sales exist? An empirical investigation of commercial aircraft transactions." *Journal of Finance,* 53: 939–78.

—— (1999). "Effects of bankruptcy court protection on asset sales." *Journal of Financial Economics,* 52: 151–86.

Rahi, R. (1995). "Optimal incomplete markets with asymmetric information." *Journal of Economic Theory,* 65: 171–97.

Rajan, R., and Zingales, L. (1995). "What do we know about capital structure? Some evidence from international data." *Journal of Finance* 50(5): 1421–60.

——, and ——(1998). "Financial dependence and growth." *American Economic Review,* 88: 559–86.

——, and —— (1999). "Financial systems, industrial structure and growth." Working Paper, University of Chicago.

——, and —— (2000). "The great reversals: The politics of financial development in the 20th century." Working Paper, University of Chicago.

Ramseyer, J. M. (1994). "Explicit reasons for implicit contracts: The legal logic to the Japanese main bank system," in M. Aoki and H. Patrick (eds.), *The Japanese Main Bank System: Its Relevancy for Developing and Transforming Economies* (New York: Oxford Univ. Press).

Ravenscraft, D., and Scherer, F. (1987). *Mergers, Selloffs and Economic Efficiency.* Washington, DC: Brookings Institution.

Robinson, J. (1952). "The generalization of the general theory," in *The Rate of Interest, and Other Essays,* London: Macmillan, 67–142.

Rochet, J., and Tirole, J. (1996a). "Interbank lending and systemic risk," *Journal of Money, Credit, and Banking,* 28: 733–62.

——, and —— (1996b). "Controlling risk in payment systems." *Journal of Money, Credit, and Banking,* 28: 832–62.

Roe, M. (1994). *Strong Managers, Weak Owners.* Princeton, NJ: Princeton Univ. Press.

Ross, R., Westerfield, and Jaffe, J. (2001). *Corporate Finance,* 6th edn. New York: McGraw Hill Irwin.

Saint-Paul, G. (1982). "Technological choice, financial markets and economic development." *European Economic Review,* 36(4): 763–81.

Santos, J. (1997). "Financial innovations with endogenous risk." Working Paper, University of Chicago.

Scharfstein, D. (1988). "Product market competition and managerial slack." *The RAND Journal of Economics,* 19: 147–55.

Schmidt, K. (1997). "Managerial incentives and product market competition." *Review of Economic Studies*, 64: 191–214.

Schneider-Lenné, E. (1992). "Corporate control in Germany." *Oxford Review of Economic Policy*, 8: 11–23.

Schreyögg, G., and Steinmann, H. (1981). "Zur Trennung von Eigentum und Verfügungsgewalt—Eine Empirische Analyse der Beteiligungsverhältnisse in Deutschen Grossunternehman." *Zeitschrift fur Betriebswirtschaft*, 51: 533–56.

Shiller, R. (1993). *Macro Markets: Creating Institutions for Managing Society's Largest Economic Risks*. Oxford: Clarendon Press.

Shin, H., and Stulz, R. M. (1998). "Are internal capital markets efficient?" *Quarterly Journal of Economics*, 113: 531–52.

Shleifer, A., and Summers, L. (1988). "Breach of trust in hostile takeovers," in A. Auerbach (ed.), *Corporate Takeovers: Causes and Consequences* (Chicago, IL: University of Chicago Press), 33–56.

——, and Vishny, R. (1986). "Large shareholders and corporate control." *Journal of Political Economy*, 94: 461–88.

——, and —— (1992). "Liquidation values and debt capacity: A market equilibrium approach." *Journal of Finance*, 52: 1343–66.

——, and —— (1997). "A survey of corporate governance." *Journal of Finance*, 52: 737–83.

Singh, A. (1995). "Corporate financial patterns in industrializing economies: A comparative international study." International Finance Corporation, Technical Paper 2, Washington, DC.

——, and Hamid, J. (1992). "Corporate financial structures in developing countries." International Finance Corporation, Technical Paper 1, Washington, DC.

Stein, J. (1997). "Internal capital markets and the competition for corporate resources." *Journal of Finance*, 52: 111–33.

Stern, N. (1989). "The economics of development: A survey." *Economic Journal*, 99: 597–685.

Stigler, G. (1958). "The economies of scale." *Journal of Law and Economics* 1: 54–71.

Stiglitz, J. (1985). "Credit markets and the control of capital." *Journal of Money, Credit, and Banking*, 17: 133–52.

——, and Weiss, A. (1983). "Incentive effects of terminations: Applications to the credit and labor markets." *American Economic Review*, 73: 912–27.

Stromberg, P. (2000). "Conflicts of interest and market illiquidity in bankruptcy auctions: Theory and tests." *Journal of Finance*, 55: 2641–92.

Subrahmanyam, A., and Titman, S. (1997). "Information, resource allocation, and the development of financial Markets." Working Paper, UCLA, *Journal of Finance*, forthcoming.

Tadassee, S. (2000). "Financial architecture and economic performance: International evidence." Working Paper, University of South Carolina.

Taggart, R. (1985). "Secular patterns in the financing of U.S. corporations," in B. Friedman (ed.), *Corporate Capital Structure in the United States* (Chicago, IL: University of Chicago Press).

Thakor, A. (1996), "The design of financial systems: An overview." *Journal of Banking and Finance*, 20: 917–48.

Tschoegl, A. (1993). "Modeling the behaviour of Japanese stock indexes," in S. Takagi (ed.), *Japanese Capital Markets: New Developments in Regulations and Institutions* (Oxford: Blackwell), 371–400.

Van Hulle, C. (1998). "On the nature of European holding groups." *International Review of Law and Economics*, 18: 255–77.

Van Rijckeghem, C., and Weder, B. (2000). "Spillovers through banking centers: A panel data analysis." IMF Working Paper WP/00/88, Washington DC: International Monetary Fund.

Vives, X. (ed.) (2000). *Corporate Governance: Theoretical and Empirical Perspectives.* Cambridge: Cambridge Univ. Press.

von Thadden, E. (1995). "Long-term contracts, short-term investment and monitoring." *Review of Economic Studies*, 62: 557–75.

Wallace, N. (1988). "Another attempt to explain an illiquid banking system: The Diamond and Dybvig model with sequential service taken seriously." *Federal Reserve Bank of Minneapolis Quarterly Review*, 12 (Fall): 3–16.

—— (1990). "A banking model in which partial suspension is best." *Federal Reserve Bank of Minneapolis Quarterly Review*, 14 (Fall): 11–23.

Weisbach, M. (1988). "Outside directors and CEO turnover." *Journal of Financial Economics*, 20: 431–60.

Weiss, L. (1990). "Bankruptcy resolution: Direct costs and violation of priority of claims." *Journal of Financial Economics*, 27: 285–314.

Wenger, E., and Kaserer, C. (1998). "The German system of corporate governance—A model which should not be imitated," in S. Black and M. Moersch (eds.), *Competition and Convergence in Financial Markets—The German and Anglo-American Models* (Amsterdam: North-Holland Elsevier Science, Amsterdam), 41–78.

Whited, T. (1992). "Debt, liquidity constraints, and corporate investment: Evidence from panel data." *Journal of Finance*, 47: 1425–70.

Williamson, O. (1975). *Markets and Hierarchies: Analysis and Antitrust Implications.* New York: Collier Macmillan.

Yilmaz, B. (1997). "Strategic voting and proxy contests." Working Paper, University of Pennsylvania.

Yosha, O. (1995). "Information disclosure costs and the choice of financing source." *Journal of Financial Intermediation*, 4: 3–20.

Yuan, K. (2000). "Asymmetric price movements and borrowing constraints: A rational expectations equilibrium model of crisis, contagion, and confusion." Mimeo, Department of Economics, MIT.

Part VII

Credit Markets, Intermediation, and the Macroeconomy

23

Financial Intermediation, Loanable Funds, and the Real Sector

Bengt Holmström and Jean Tirole

I. Introduction

During the late 1980s and early 1990s several OECD countries appeared to be suffering from a credit crunch. Higher interest rates reduced cash flows and pushed down asset prices, weakening the balance sheets of firms. Loan losses and lower asset prices (particularly in real estate) ate significantly into the equity of the banking sector, causing banks to pull back on their lending and to increase interest rate spreads. The credit crunch hit small, collateral-poor firms the hardest. Larger firms were less affected as they could either renegotiate their loans or go directly to the commercial paper or bond markets.

Scandinavia seems to have been most severely hit by the credit crunch. The banking sectors of Sweden, Norway, and Finland all had to be rescued by their governments at a very high price.[1] Yet, it is the U.S. experience that has received the closest empirical scrutiny. A lot of work has gone into characterizing, identifying, and measuring the effects of the alleged credit crunch. While the exact role of the credit crunch in the 1990–1991 recession remains unclear, there are several pieces of evidence that point to a material influence.

First, bank lending experienced a significant and prolonged decline, which from a historical perspective appears rather exceptional (see Friedman and Kuttner [1993]). Second, and most relevant to this chapter, the 1990–1991 change in bank lending within states can be rather well explained by the 1989 capital–asset ratio of a state's banking sector, suggesting that the equity value of the banking sector did affect lending.[2] The sharp decline in lending in the Northeast, where real estate markets experienced the biggest drop, is particularly

We are grateful to Olivier Blanchard, Sonja Daltung, and Marco Pagano for helpful comments and to the National Science Foundation for financial support.

[1] Vihriala [1996] contains a summary account of the Finnish experience.

[2] For an extensive survey of the empirical work on the role of bank capital on the growth of lending, see Sharpe [1995].

telling. Third, there is plenty of evidence to indicate a "flight-to-quality" in lending, defined by Gilchrist et al. [1994] as a decline in the share of credit flowing to borrowers with high agency costs (proxied by small firms). Gertler and Gilchrist [1994] offer the first such evidence, which later studies have confirmed. As indirect evidence one can point to the many studies that show that investment in financially stressed firms is more sensitive to cash flow (see subsection IIIB in Gilchrist et al. [1994]). Also, inventories and production in small firms (which presumably have the weakest balance sheets) contract the most when money is tight [Gertler and Gilchrist 1994].

The final, and most controversial, evidence on credit crunches comes from interest rate spreads. There is a significant empirical problem: because of a possible flight to quality, interest rate spreads across different periods are not comparable. The selection effect tends to reduce the observed differential (see Bernanke [1993] for a further discussion). This may explain why the findings with respect to interest rate spreads are less consistent. Friedman and Kuttner [1993] find that the commercial paper-Treasury bill spread reacts positively both to tighter money and to reductions in the capital-asset ratio of banks. However, Miron, Romer and Weil [1994] find little supportive evidence when one goes farther back in time.[3]

The purpose of this chapter is to construct a simple equilibrium model of credit that can reproduce some of the stylized facts reported above and thereby shed light on the role of different kinds of capital constraints. In the model a firm's net worth determines its debt capacity. Firms that take on too much debt in relation to equity will not have a sufficient stake in the financial outcome and will therefore not behave diligently. Assuming that investment projects are of fixed size, only firms with sufficiently high net worth will be able to finance investments directly. Firms with low net worth have to turn to financial intermediaries, who can reduce the demand for collateral by monitoring more intensively.[4] Thus, monitoring is a partial substitute for collateral. However, all firms cannot be monitored in equilibrium, because intermediaries, like firms, must invest some of their own capital in a project in order to be credible monitors. In the market for monitoring, the equilibrium interest premium paid on monitoring capital is then determined by the relative amounts of aggregate firm and aggregate intermediary capital.

We are primarily interested in the effects that reductions in different types of capital have on investment, interest rates, and the forms of financing. The novelty in our analysis is that we study how these choices are influenced by the

---

[3] Vihriala [1996] reports that in Finland the bank interest rate spread (between lending and funding) correlated positively with tightness of money.

[4] Since our model is a principal-agent model, it cannot distinguish between different monitoring institutions. In subsection III.3 we discuss in some depth two equivalent interpretations of monitoring: intermediation and certification.

financial status of intermediaries as well as of firms. Since our model incorporates both demand factors (changes in collateral) and supply factors (changes in intermediary capital), we can identify a separate "balance sheet channel" and a "lending channel," a distinction that previously has only been discussed in the empirical literature (see Bernanke [1993]).

Our model features behavior that is broadly consistent with the earlier reported evidence: firms with substantial net worth can rely on cheaper, less information-intensive (asset-backed) finance; highly leveraged firms demand more information-intensive finance (monitoring); when monitoring capital decreases, capital-poor firms are the first to get squeezed; and credit crunches increase the interest rate spread between intermediated debt and market debt. However, note that if both intermediary capital and firm capital contract, as they appear to have done in the recent recession, then the sign of the change in the interest rate spread depends crucially on the change in the relative amounts of capital.

We also find that if we allow intermediaries to vary the intensity of monitoring, then an increase in monitoring capital relative to firm capital leads to lending that involves more intensive monitoring. This is consistent with the recent Scandinavian experience, where banks have begun to invest in more information-intensive lending technologies in the wake of reduced firm collateral.

Another implication of our model is that intermediaries must satisfy market-determined capital adequacy ratios. Interestingly, these capital adequacy ratios are procyclical, suggesting a possible rationale for looser banking norms in recessions.

Our model builds on the previous literature on capital-constrained lending, borrowing extensively from its insights.[5] The papers most closely related to ours are by Hoshi, Kashyap, and Scharfstein [1992] and Repullo and Suarez [1995], who employ the same basic moral hazard model as we do to analyze how the firm's net worth determines its choice between direct and indirect financing, and by Diamond [1991], who studies this choice as a function of the firm's reputation for repaying debt (its reputation capital). However, in neither paper are intermediaries capital constrained, which is the main feature we are interested in. The paper by Besanko and Kanatas [1993] is related in that it investigates the choice of financing and monitoring intensity in an equilibrium model like ours. However, collateral plays no role in their model. Intermediary capital is plentiful, and the firms finance part of their investment

---

[5] See Jaffee and Russell [1976], Stiglitz and Weiss [1981], and Bester and Hellwig [1987] on credit rationing; Bester [1985, 1987], Diamond [1991], and Hoshi, Kashyap, and Scharfstein [1992] on capital-constrained borrowing; Diamond [1984] and Besanko and Kanatas [1993] on intermediation; and Holmstrom and Weiss [1985], Williamson [1987], Bernanke and Gertler [1989], and Kiyotaki and Moore [1993] on agency costs that amplify the business cycle.

from uninformed capital in order not to be monitored too carefully by intermediaries.[6]

The next section describes the basic model, which features fixed-size investment projects. The equilibrium of this model is analyzed in Section III. Section IV moves on to a model with variable investment size, in order to avoid some of the technical complications that stem from fixed-size investment. The variable investment model is highly tractable and delivers preliminary answers to most of the questions raised above. Several variations of it are discussed to illustrate its versatility. Section V concludes with caveats and some future research directions.

II. The Basic Model

The model has three types of agents: firms, intermediaries, and investors. There are two periods. In the first period financial contracts are signed, and investment decisions made. In the second period investment returns are realized, and claims are settled. All parties are risk neutral and protected by limited liability so that no one can end up with a negative cash position.

II.1 The real sector

There is a continuum of firms. All firms have access to the same technology; the only difference among them is that they start out with different amounts of capital A. For simplicity, we assume that all initial capital is cash. More generally, it could be any type of asset that can be pledged as collateral with first-period market value A.[7] The distribution of assets across firms is described by the cumulative distribution function $G(A)$, indicating the fraction of firms with assets less than A. The aggregate amount of firm capital is $K_f = \int A \, dG(A)$.

In the basic version of the model, each firm has one economically viable project or idea. It costs $I > 0$ (in period 1) to undertake a project. If $A < I$, a firm needs at least $I - A$ in external funds to be able to invest. In period 2 the investment generates a verifiable, financial return equaling either 0 (failure) or R (success).

Firms are run by entrepreneurs, who in the absence of proper incentives or outside monitoring may deliberately reduce the probability of success in order to enjoy a private benefit. We formalize this moral hazard problem by assuming that the entrepreneur can privately choose between three versions of the project as described in Figure 1.

---

[6] In an independent work Cantillo [1994] develops an equilibrium model with limited intermediary capital, which is used to address many of the same questions as we do. Cantillo's model is one with costly state verification, but the conclusions are rather similar to ours.

[7] To the extent that the first-period value of collateral depends on the market interest rate, this distinction between cash and real collateral becomes important.

Project	Good	Bad (low private benefit)	Bad (high private benefit)
Private benefit	0	b	B
Probability of success	p_H	p_L	p_L

Figure 1.

We assume that

$$\Delta p = p_H - p_L > 0.$$

Furthermore, in the relevant range of the rate of return on investor capital, denoted by γ, only the good project is economically viable; that is,

$$p_H R - \gamma I > 0 > p_L R - \gamma I + B. \qquad (1)$$

We introduce two levels of shirking (two bad projects) in order to have a sufficiently rich way of modeling monitoring (see below). Private benefits are ordered $B > b > 0$ and can, of course, be interpreted alternatively as opportunity costs from managing the project diligently. Note that either level of shirking produces the same probability of success. This has the convenient implication that the entrepreneur will prefer the high private benefit project (B-project) over the low private benefit project (b-project) irrespectively of the financial contract.

II.2 The financial sector

The financial sector consists of many intermediaries. The function of intermediaries is to monitor firms and thereby alleviate the moral hazard problem. In practice, monitoring takes many forms: inspection of a firm's potential cash flow, its balance sheet position, its management, and so on. Often monitoring merely amounts to verifying that the firm conforms with covenants of the financial contract, such as a minimum solvency ratio or a minimum cash balance. In the case of bank lending, covenants are particularly common and extensive. The intent of covenants is to reduce the firm's opportunity cost of being diligent. With that in mind, we assume that the monitor can prevent a firm from undertaking the B-project. This reduces the firm's opportunity cost of being diligent from B to b.

A key element in our story is the assumption that monitoring is privately costly; the intermediary will have to pay a nonverifiable amount $c > 0$ in order to eliminate the B-project. Thus, intermediaries also face a potential moral hazard problem. While we assume that each intermediary has the physical capacity to monitor an arbitrary number of firms, the moral hazard problem puts a limit on the actual amount of monitoring that will take place. Moral hazard forces inter- mediaries to inject some of their own capital into the firms that they monitor, making the aggregate amount of intermediary (or "informed") capital K_m one of the important constraints on aggregate investment.

It turns out that the exact distribution of assets among intermediaries is irrel- evant if we assume that all projects financed by an intermediary are perfectly correlated and that the capital of each intermediary is sufficiently large relative to the scale of a project (allowing us to ignore integer problems).[8] In practice, projects may be correlated because intermediaries have an incentive to choose them so, or because of macroeconomic shocks. Nevertheless, assuming perfect correlation is obviously unrealistic. We make this assumption only because we know that, without some degree of correlation, intermediaries would not need to put up any capital (see Diamond [1984] and the concluding section for further discussion). While perfect correlation is an extreme case, it greatly simplifies the analysis.

II.3 Investors

Individual investors are small. We will often refer to them as uninformed investors, to distinguish them from intermediaries, who monitor the firms that they invest in. Uninformed investors demand an expected rate of return γ. We sometimes assume that γ is exogenously given (there is an infinite supply of out- side investment opportunities that return γ) and sometimes that the aggregate amount of uninformed capital invested in firms is determined by a standard, increasing supply function $S(\gamma)$. The determination of the equilibrium rate of return on intermediary capital, β, will be described momentarily.

We assume that firms cannot monitor other firms, perhaps because they have insufficient capital to be credible monitors (see below) or because they do not have the informational expertise. Therefore, firms with excess capital will have to invest their surplus cash in the open market, earning the uninformed rate of return γ.

III. Fixed Investment Scale

In this section the investment scale I is fixed.

---

[8] One way to model perfect correlation is to let θ, distributed uniformly on $[0, 1]$, represent an intermediary specific random disturbance, such that if $\theta < p_L$, all the intermediary's projects succeed, if $\theta \geq p_H$, all of its projects fail and if $p_L \leq \theta < p_H$, its projects succeed if and only if they are good. With this formulation one can let the θ's vary arbitrarily across intermediaries without affecting the analysis.

III.1 Direct finance

We start by analyzing the possibility of financing a project without intermediation, that is, by using *direct finance*. Consider a firm that borrows only from uninformed investors, treated here as a single party. A contract specifies how much each side should invest and how much it should be paid as a function of the project outcome. It is easy to see that *one* optimal contract will have the following simple structure: (i) the firm invests all its funds A, while the uninformed investors put up the balance $I - A$; (ii) neither party is paid anything if the investment fails; (iii) if the project succeeds, the firm is paid $R_f > 0$, and the investors are paid $R_u > 0$, where

$$R_f + R_u = R.$$

Given (1), a necessary condition for direct finance is that the firm prefers to be diligent:

$$p_H R_f \geq p_L R_f + B.$$

Direct finance, therefore, requires that the firm be paid at least

$$R_f \geq B/\Delta p. \tag{IC$_f$}$$

This leaves at most $R_u = R - B/\Delta p$ to compensate investors, so the maximum expected income that can be promised investors without destroying the firm's incentives, call it the *pledgeable expected income*, is $p_H[R - B/\Delta p]$. The pledgeable expected income cannot be less than $\gamma[I - A]$, the market value of the funds supplied by the uninformed investors. Therefore, a necessary and sufficient condition for the firm to have access to direct finance is

$$\gamma[I - A] \leq p_H[R - (B/\Delta p)].$$

Defining

$$\overline{A}(\gamma) = I - p_H/\gamma[R - (B/\Delta p)], \tag{2}$$

we conclude that only firms with $A \geq \overline{A}(\gamma)$ can invest using direct finance.[9]

In principle, $\overline{A}(\gamma)$ could be negative, in which case firms could invest without own capital. We rule out this uninteresting case by assuming that the external opportunities for investors are such that

$$p_H R - \gamma I < -p_H B/\Delta P. \tag{3}$$

---

[9] Firms with $A \geq \overline{A}(\gamma)$ are indifferent between investing the surplus $A - \overline{A}(\gamma)$ in the firm or in the market for uninformed capital.

Condition (3) simply states that the total surplus from a project is less than the minimum share a firm must be paid to behave diligently. To get external financing, therefore, total surplus must be redistributed. But given limited liability, the only way a firm can transfer some of the surplus back to investors is by investing its own capital. Capital-poor firms will be unable to invest, because they do not have the means to redistribute surplus.

It follows that in this model, as in most models with liquidity constraints, efficiency is not defined by total surplus maximization. Therefore, while it is true that aggregate surplus (and investment) could be increased by reallocating funds from uninformed investors to firms that are capital constrained, such transfers are not Pareto improving. There are no externalities in this model that the firm and the investor cannot internalize just as effectively as a social planner facing the same informational constraints.

III.2 Indirect finance

An intermediary that monitors can help a capital-constrained firm to invest. Monitoring reduces the firm's opportunity cost of being diligent (by eliminating the high benefit B-project), allowing more external capital to be raised. Some of the external funds will be provided by the intermediary itself, and some by outside investors. Thus, in the case of indirect finance, there are three parties to the financial contract: the firm, the intermediary, and the uninformed investors.

It is easy to see that an optimal three-party contract takes a form analogous to the two-party contract discussed earlier: in case the project fails, no one is paid anything; in case the project succeeds, the payoff R is divided up so that

$$R_f + R_u + R_m = R,$$

where R_m denotes the intermediary's share and R_f and R_u denote the firm's and the investors' shares as before.

Suppose that the intermediary monitors. Since monitoring eliminates the high benefit project (the B-project), the firm is left to choose between the good project and the low benefit project (the b-project). The firm's incentive constraint is now

$$R_f \geq b/\Delta p. \tag{IC_f}$$

We may assume that $R_f < B/\Delta p$, else the firm would behave without monitoring. In order for the intermediary to monitor, we must have

$$R_m \geq c/\Delta p. \tag{IC_m}$$

The two incentive constraints (IC_f) and (IC_m) imply minimum returns for the firm and the intermediary, respectively. The pledgeable expected income, again defined as the maximum expected income that can be promised to uninformed investors without destroying incentives, is then

$$p_H [R - (b + c)/\Delta p].\qquad (4)$$

Note that condition (IC_m) implies that $p_H R_m - c > 0$, so monitors earn a positive net return in the second period. Competition will reduce this surplus by forcing monitors to contribute to the firm's investment in the first period. For the moment, assume that monitoring capital is scarce so that intermediaries make a strictly positive profit. We will later derive the condition under which this assumption holds. Intermediary capital is then entirely invested in he monitoring of projects. Let I_m be the amount of capital that an intermediary invests in a firm that it monitors. The rate of return on intermediary capital is then

$$\beta = p_H R_m / I_m.$$

Since monitoring is costly, β must exceed γ. Consequently, firms prefer (whenever possible) uninformed capital to informed capital. However, since the incentive constraint (IC_m) requires that the intermediary be paid at least $R_m = c/\Delta p$, it will contribute at least

$$I_m(\beta) = p_H c/(\Delta p)\beta$$

to each firm that it monitors. In fact, all firms that are monitored will demand precisely this minimum level of informed capital. More would be excessively costly, and less would be inconsistent with proper incentives for the monitor. However, note that it is not the capital put into the firm that provides the intermediary an incentive to monitor. The incentive is provided by the return R_m. The required investment $I_m(\beta)$ merely regulates the rate of return on the intermediary's capital so that the market for informed capital clears. (We can take either I_m or β as the equilibrating variable, since the relationship between the two is monotone.)

Uninformed investors must supply the balance $I_u = I - A - I_m(\beta)$, whenever this amount is positive. A necessary and sufficient condition for a firm to be financed therefore is

$$\gamma [I - A - I_m(\beta)] \leq p_H [R - (b + c)/\Delta p].$$

We can rewrite this condition as

$$A \geq \underline{A}(\gamma, \beta) = I - I_m(\beta) - p_H/\gamma [R - (b + c)/\Delta p].\qquad (5)$$

A firm with less than $\underline{A}(\gamma, \beta)$ in initial assets cannot convince uninformed investors to supply enough capital for the project. Could the firm still invest by demanding more than $I_m(\beta)$ in informed capital? That does not work either, because for each additional dollar of informed capital, the pledgeable expected income will be reduced by β. Since β exceeds γ, the total amount of capital that the firm can raise does not increase. This argument just restates the it is optimal for a firm to demand the minimum amount of informed capital.

It follows from (4) and (5) that $\underline{A}(\gamma, \beta)$ increases in both β and γ. As one would expect, it becomes more difficult to get financing when either the market rate of return γ or the monitoring rate of return β increases. If for some combination of interest rates $\underline{A}(\gamma, \beta) > \overline{A}\gamma$, the price of monitoring is too high, and there will be no demand for monitoring. The rate β has to come down. However, β must be high enough to make the intermediary prefer monitoring to investing its capital in the open market, where it would earn at return γ. The minimum acceptable rate of return $\underline{\beta}$ is determined by the condition,

$$p_H c / \Delta p - c = \gamma I_m(\beta) = \gamma p_H c / \Delta p \beta,$$

which translates into

$$\beta = p_H \gamma / p_L > \gamma.$$

If $\underline{A}(\gamma, \underline{\beta}) > \overline{A}\gamma$ there is no demand for informed capital even at the lowest rate of return acceptable to the monitor; the monitoring technology is too costly to be socially useful. Naturally, we want to rule out this case. A little algebra yields the following necessary and sufficient condition for monitoring to be socially valuable: $c\Delta p < p_H[B - b]$. This condition is met for a small enough c, since $B > b$.[10]

III.3 Certification versus intermediation

The preceding analysis shows that firms fall into three categories according to their demand for informed capital. At one extreme are the well-capitalized firms with $A > \overline{A}(\gamma)$. These firms can finance their investment directly and demand no informed capital. At the other extreme are the poorly capitalized firms with $A < \underline{A}(\gamma, \beta)$. These firms cannot invest at all. In between, we have firms with $\underline{A}(\gamma, \beta) \le A < \overline{A}(\gamma)$. These firms can invest, but only with the help of monitoring.

---

[10] If $b + c < B$, monitoring would allow a firm to raise more uninformed capital than without monitoring; see (4). Therefore, there could be an equilibrium with monitoring even if intermediaries possessed no own capital. Since intermediaries earn a positive profit in that case, and since we have assumed that there is no constraint on how many firms an intermediary can technically monitor, such an equilibrium would feature rationing of intermediaries analogous to rationing in efficiency wage models. However, with any amount of intermediary capital, those without capital could not be active. For the benefit of Section IV we assume that $b + c < B$, ruling out intermediation without capital.

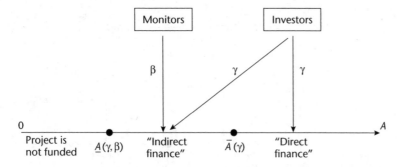

Figure 2. Certification.

The typical firm in the monitoring category finances its investment with a mixture of informed and uninformed capital.[11] We can interpret mixed financing in one of two ways. As we have described the investment process so far, the uninformed are independent investors as illustrated in Figure 2. They invest directly in the firm, but only after the monitor has taken a large enough financial interest in the firm that the investors can be assured that the firm will behave diligently. In this interpretation the monitor resembles a venture capitalist, a lead investment bank, or any other sophisticated investor whose stake in the borrower *certifies* that the borrower is sound, allowing the firm to go to less informed investors for additional capital.[12] A related example is that of a bank providing a loan guarantee, or originating a secured loan.

An alternative interpretation of our model views the monitor as an *intermediary* such as a commercial bank. In this interpretation investors deposit their money with the bank, which invests the deposits, along with its own funds, in the firms that it monitors (see Figure 3). One can check that the optimal, incentive-compatible intermediary arrangement is equivalent to the certification arrangement we have described.[13]

[11] If there are firms for which $A < \overline{A}(\gamma)$, but $A + I_m(\beta) > I$, these firms only demand informed capital and invest their excess funds in the market for uninformed capital.

[12] There is a large literature on certification by venture capitalist; see, for instance, Barry et al. [1990] and Megginson and Weiss [1991] and references therein. For evidence that the participation of sophisticated investors can substantially enhance the ability to attract external capital, see Emerick and White [1992].

[13] Intermediation can always duplicate the outcome of certification, which consists of writing an isolated contract for each funded project. One may wonder whether intermediation could not do strictly better than certification by "cross-pledging" the returns on the various projects that the intermediary funds. That this is not the case can be seen from the optimal contract under intermediation. Because of perfect correlation if one project fails and another succeeds, it must be the case that the intermediary did not monitor the former. Because harshest punishments are always optimal when a deviation is detected, the intermediary must then receive 0. This implies that the optimal strategy for the intermediary is either to monitor all projects or to monitor none, and that therefore intermediation does not improve on certification.

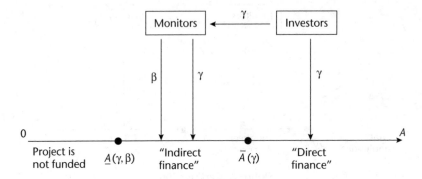

Figure 3. Intermediation.

The amount of uninformed capital that an intermediary can attract will depend on how much equity it has as well as on the rates of return in the market for informed and uninformed capital. The intermediation case makes clear that investors will demand that intermediaries meet solvency conditions that put a lower bound on the ratio of their equity to total capital. For reasons of tractability, we will only analyze solvency conditions in the variable investment model (Section IV).

III.4 Equilibrium in the credit market

Since each firm demands the minimum amount of informed capital $I_m(\beta)$, the aggregate demand for informed capital is $D_m(\gamma,\beta) = [G(\overline{A}(\gamma)) - G(\underline{A}(\gamma,\beta))]I_m(\beta)$. Assuming that there is no excess supply of informed capital at the minimum acceptable rate of return $\underline{\beta}$,[14] an equilibrium in the monitoring market obtains when β satisfies

$$K_m = D_m(\gamma, \beta) = [G(\overline{A}(\gamma)) - G(\underline{A}(\gamma,\beta))]I_m(\beta). \qquad (6)$$

The demand for informed capital D_m is decreasing in β because $I_m(\beta)$ is decreasing and $\underline{A}(\gamma,\beta)$ is increasing in β. Therefore, for each γ there is a unique β that clears the market for informed capital. The effect of γ on D_m is ambiguous, however. A higher γ increases both $\overline{A}\gamma$ and $\underline{A}(\gamma,\beta)$, and then it depends on the distribution function G whether aggregate demand increases or decreases with γ.

Equation (6) fully describes the equilibrium if the rate of return γ demanded by the uninformed is exogenous. If γ is endogenous, that is, if the supply of uninformed capital $S(\gamma)$ is imperfectly elastic, one must add an equilibrium condition

---

[14] The less interesting case of excess informed capital occurs when (6) is an inequality for $\beta = \underline{\beta}$. We will not discuss that case.

for uninformed capital. Let

$$D_u(\gamma, \beta) = \int_{\underline{A}(\gamma,\beta)}^{\overline{A}(\gamma)} [I - A - I_m(\beta)] \, dG(A) + \int_{\overline{A}(\gamma)}^{\infty} [I - A] \, dG(A) \qquad (7)$$

denote the demand for uniformed capital.[15] The demand D_u is decreasing in γ. On the one hand, firms with assets just above $\underline{A}(\gamma,\beta)$ are squeezed out by an increase in γ. On the other hand, firms with assets just above $\overline{A}(\gamma)$ move from direct to indirect finance, which uses less uninformed capital (since $I_m > 0$). Both effects reduce the demand for uninformed capital. By contrast, an increase in β has an ambiguous effect on D_u because there are two opposing effects. Firms with assets just above $\underline{A}(\gamma, \beta)$ drop out, which reduces the demand for uninformed capital, while firms relying on intermediation, now demand more uninformed capital, since intermediaries have to invest less per firm ($I_m(\beta)$ decreases with β).

The market for uninformed capital clears when

$$D_u(\gamma, \beta) = S(\gamma). \qquad (8)$$

For each β there is a unique γ that solves (8).[16]

Instead of using (6) and (8) to determine β and γ, we can replace (8) with the following condition, obtained by substituting (6) into (8):

$$\int_{\underline{A}(\gamma,\beta)}^{\infty} (I - A) \, dG(A) = S(\gamma) + K_m. \qquad (9)$$

Equation (9) equates the firms' aggregate demand for capital (the left-hand side) with the total supply of external capital.

III.5 Changes in the supply of capital

Our main interest is with the effects that changes in asset values and capital supply have on the equilibrium outcome. Unfortunately, the fact that neither D_u nor D_m is monotone limits what we can say about the behavior of interest rates. The problem stems from our assumption that the investment size is fixed, which

[15] In this demand function we have netted out the capital that firms with $I_m + A > I$ or $I > A$ will reinvest in the market.

[16] The reader familiar with Yanelle's [1989] analysis might be concerned that an intermediary could raise deposit rates enough to attract all deposits, and having obtained a monopoly, control the interest rates on loans. However, Yanelle, who uses Diamond's [1984] model with perfect diversification, rules out agency problems. In our model the intermediary's ability to attract deposits is limited by its own capital. So long as informed capital is not too concentrated, each intermediary will take β and γ as approximately given.

creates discontinuities in individual firm demands and makes the distribution function $G(A)$ play a critical role. Rather than trying to circumvent these problems by introducing specific assumptions about G, we will in this section restrict attention to the behavior of investment in response to changes in the supply of capital. The next section will look at the behavior of interest rates in a variant of the model that is analytically more tractable.

We consider three types of capital tightening, corresponding to the three forms of capital in the model. In a *credit crunch* the supply of intermediary capital K_m is reduced. In a *collateral squeeze* aggregate firm capital $K_f = \int A dG(A)$ is reduced. Moreover, we assume that the reduction affects firms in proportion to their assets. In a *savings squeeze* the savings function $S(\gamma)$ shifts inward.

PROPOSITION 1. *In either type of capital squeeze, aggregate investment will go down, and $\underline{A}(\gamma,\beta)$ will increase. Consequently, poorly capitalized firms will be the first to lose their financing in a capital squeeze.*

Proof of Proposition 1. If all capital were supplied inelastically, this result would be immediate, since a firm with more assets can always do as well as a firm with fewer assets. The one detail to check is that a reduction in firm or intermediary capital is not offset by an increase in uninformed capital.

Suppose, hypothetically, that $\underline{A}(\gamma,\beta)$ goes down with any kind of capital squeeze. A reduction in $\underline{A}$ is equivalent to an increase in aggregate investment. Since an increase in investment must be funded by uninformed capital, S would have to go up (see equation (9)), implying an increase in the interest rate γ. As uninformed capital becomes more expensive, fewer firms have access to direct finance; $\overline{A}(\gamma)$ goes up as seen from equation (2). With $\underline{A}$ reduced and $\overline{A}$ increased, intermediation spans a strictly larger set of firms. Each firm must therefore receive less informed capital (I_m decreases; see equation (6)), implying that (β) is pushed up. As informed and uninformed capital both have become more expensive, $\underline{A}(\gamma,\beta)$ cannot go down (see equation (5)), contradicting the initial hypothesis.   Q.E.D.

Proposition 1 implies that at least one of the interest rates, (β) or γ, must go up when there is a capital squeeze. If both went down, equation (5) would imply that $\underline{A}$ goes down. If uninformed capital is supplied inelastically, so that γ is exogenous, then β must increase. But in general we cannot rule out the possibility that one of the two interest rates decreases. For instance, in a credit crunch, as $\underline{A}$ and $\overline{A}$ move up, I_m could be pushed above its original level, implying a decrease in β. It all depends on the shape of the distribution function G. Similar ambiguities about interest rate effects can arise in the other cases as well.

Another corollary of Proposition 1 is that the equilibrium in the fixed investment model must be unique. If there were two different equilibria, Proposition 1 implies that $\underline{A}$ would have to be the same in both. But then $\overline{A}$ must also be the same, else both β and γ would be lower in one of the equilibria, which, as we just noted, is impossible.

Since all forms of capital tightening result in the same outcome, namely that capital-poor firms lose their financing, the effect will be all the stronger when the tightening occurs on all three fronts. While simple, this conclusion is quite robust, which is reassuring given the strong empirical evidence that small firms are more highly leveraged and bear the brunt of a capital squeeze. The conclusion is reinforced by considering changes in R or in p_H. In a recession it is natural to assume that both R and p_H decrease as well. Following the logic of the proof of Proposition 1, it is easy to see that either change will again cause an increase in $\underline{A}(\gamma, \beta)$, that is, in capital poor firms being squeezed out first.

One may argue that in the real world small firms are abandoned because of scale economies in monitoring. In a credit crunch, banks will have to sort out the good risks from the bad, and small firms will not be worth the fixed cost of getting informed. On the surface, our model does not seem to have scale economies. But in fact it does, with much the same effect as just described. A large firm that is monitored has to pay the same absolute amount for monitoring as a small firm, so per unit of net worth, which is the relevant measure here, monitoring costs do decrease with size.

IV. Variable Investment Scale

For the reminder of the chapter we switch to a model with a variable level of investment in order to avoid the problem with discontinuities in individual demand for capital. We assume that investments can be undertaken at any scale I. All benefits and costs are proportional to I (the private benefits are $B(I) = BI$, respectively, $b(I) = bI$, the cost of monitoring is $c(I) = cI$, and the return from a successful investment is $R(I) = RI$. Thus, the investment technology is constant returns to scale. The probabilities of success remain as before equal to p_H or p_L depending on the firm's action.

IV.1 The firm's program

Given the rates of return β and γ, a firm that holds initial assets A_0 will choose its overall level of investment I, its own capital contribution A, and the variables R_f, R_m, R_u, I_m, I_u to solve program A_0:

maximize $U(A_0) = p_H RI - p_H R_m - p_H R_u + \gamma(A_0 - A)$
subject to

(i) $A \leq A_0$,
(ii) $A + I_m + I_u \geq I$,
(iii) $p_H R_m \geq \beta I_m$,
(iv) $p_H R_u \geq \gamma I_u$,

(v) $R_m \geq cI/\Delta p$,

(vi) $R_f \geq bI/\Delta p$, and

(vii) $R_f + R_m + R_u \leq RI$.

In setting up the program in this way, we are assuming that it is desirable to employ an intermediary and, as in Section III, that informed capital is scarce. We will return to check that this is indeed the case in equilibrium.

Divide through all equations in Program A_0 by the firm's level of assets A_0. This yields a program in which all choice variables are scaled by A_0 and all the parameters are independent of A_0. Consequently, an optimal solution takes the form, $R_f = \tilde{R}_f A_0$, $R_m = \tilde{R}_m A_0$, and so on, where the variables with a tilde solve the program with $A_0 = 1$. In other words, firms with different levels of assets use the same optimal policy scaled by their assets. This feature greatly simplifies the aggregate analysis.

It is evident from our previous discussion that in equilibrium all constraints will bind. The firm will invest all its assets; it will be paid just enough to be diligent; the intermediary will be paid just enough to have an incentive to monitor; the intermediary will be required to invest to the point where its return on capital is β; and the investors will invest to the point where the pledgeable expected return equals the market return γ. This way the firm maximizes the leverage and return on its own assets. To find the maximum level of investment, substitute equalities (i) and (iii)–(vii) into (ii) to get

$$A_0 + \frac{I p_H c}{\beta \Delta p} + I\left(\frac{p_H}{\gamma}\right)\left[R - \left(\frac{b+c}{\Delta p}\right)\right] \geq I. \tag{10}$$

We see that the highest sustainable level of investment is

$$I(A_0) = A_0/A_1(\gamma, \beta), \tag{11}$$

where the denominator

$$A_1(\gamma, \beta) \doteq 1 - \frac{p_H c}{\beta \Delta p} - \left(\frac{p_H}{\gamma}\right)\left[R - \left(\frac{b+c}{\Delta p}\right)\right] \tag{12}$$

represents the amount of firm capital needed to undertake an investment of unit size ($I = 1$). Clearly, $A_1(\gamma, \beta) < 1$, reflecting the fact that the firm can lever its own capital; the lower is $A_1(\gamma, \beta)$, the higher the leverage. In equilibrium, rates of return must also be such that $A_1(\gamma, \beta) > 0$, else the firm would want to invest without limit.

Substituting equalities (i)–(vii) into the objective function gives the firm's maximum payoff:

$$U(A_0) = p_H bI(A_0)/\Delta p. \tag{13}$$

The net value of leverage to the firm is

$$[p_H b/(\Delta p A_1(\gamma, \beta)) - \gamma] A_0. \tag{14}$$

Assuming that monitoring is valuable, the term in brackets is positive.[17] It represents the difference between the internal and the external rate of return on firm
capital. As in most models with liquidity constraints, the internal rate of return
exceeds the market rate, in our case, because a dollar inside the firm is worth the
market rate plus the incentive effect.

IV.2 Equilibrium in the capital markets

Because firms choose the same optimal policy per unit of own capital, an equilibrium is easily found by aggregating across firms. Let K_f be the aggregate amount
of firm capital, K_m the aggregate amount of informed capital, and K_u the aggregate supply of uninformed capital. The first two are fixed, while the third, K_u, is
determined so that the demand for uninformed capital (the sum of the pledgeable expected returns of individual firms, discounted by γ) equals the supply $S(\gamma)$.
Let $\gamma = \gamma(K_u)$ be the inverse supply function. The equilibrium in the market for
uninformed capital obtains when

$$p_H(K_f + K_m + K_u)[R - (b + c)/\Delta p] = (\gamma)(K_u)K_u. \tag{15}$$

The equilibrium rates of return in the two capital markets are

$$\gamma = p_H K[R - (b + c)/\Delta p]/K_u, \tag{16}$$

$$\beta = p_H cK/(\Delta p)K_m, \tag{17}$$

where $K = K_f + K_m + K_u$ is the total amount of capital invested.

Figure 4 provides a graph of how K_u is determined. As can be seen from Figure 4,
in order for investment to be finite, the equilibrium value of γ must be such
that it exceeds the pledgeable expected income $p_H[R - (b + c)/\Delta p]$ (per unit of
investment).

Equations (16) and (17) show that the equilibrium rates of return on firm and
intermediary capital depend in the obvious way on the relative scarcity of these
two forms of capital. However, equation (15) shows that the aggregate level of
investment only depends on the sum of firm and intermediary capital. This
is a consequence of our assumption that firm and intermediary capital are in
fixed supply; only uninformed capital responds to changes in the rate of return.
If firms had more than one type of investment opportunity, the optimal choice
would generally depend on the relative costs of capital, and consequently, overall

---

[17] It is easy to give a condition for monitoring to be of value. If a firm tried to finance investment
without monitoring, the optimal solution would be the same as with monitoring, but with the
substitutions $c = 0$ and $b = B$. Comparing monitoring with no monitoring, evaluated at the lowest
acceptable rate of return $\beta = \underline{\beta}(= p_H\gamma/p_L)$, one finds that monitoring will be preferred to direct
finance whenever $c(p_H\gamma - p_L)/\Delta p < (B - b)/B$. Taking γ as exogenous, this condition is satisfied for
small enough c.

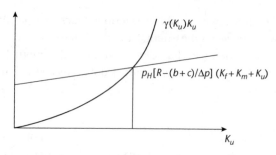

Figure 4.

investment would be sensitive to the relative supplies of firm and intermediary capital. Subsection IV.4 will illustrate a variation on this theme.

IV.3 Changes in the supply of capital

In addition to analyzing the effect that changes in the supply of capital have on interest rates and investment, we will also consider the effect these changes have on the solvency ratios of firms and intermediaries. Each firm's solvency ratio equals the aggregate solvency ratio, which is defined by $r_f = K_f/K$. Likewise, an intermediary's solvency ration is defined by $r_m = K_m/(K_m + K_u)$.[18]

PROPOSITION 2.

    A. A decrease in K_m(credit crunch)
        (i) decreases γ, (ii) increases β,
        (iii) decreases r_m, (iv) increases r_f.
    B. A decrease in K_f (collateral squeeze)
        (i) decreases γ, (ii) decreases β,
        (iii) increases r_m, (iv) decreases r_f.
    C. An inward shift in $S(γ)$ (savings squeeze)
        (i) increases γ, (ii) decreases β,
        (iii) increases r_m, (iv) increases r_f.
In all cases investment (K) and the supply of uninformed capital (K_u) decline.

These results follow directly from (15)–(17). To illustrate, in a credit crunch, when intermediary capital contracts, less uninformed capital can be attracted, lowering K_u and γ. Dividing equation (15) through by K_u shows that K_m/K_u must decrease, since k_f/K_u increases and γ goes down. The contraction in uninformed capital is less than proportional to the contraction in K_m. Consequently, informed capital will be relatively scarcer than before which increases β and lowers r_m. Since both informed and uninformed capital contracts, the solvency ratio r_f of firms will increase.

---

[18] Here we are adopting the interpretation that investors invest in firms via an intermediary.

As an illustration, lets us see how the predictions of Proposition 2 match up with the Scandinavian experience of the late 1980s and early 1990s. A recession, of course, hits all our capital variables as well as some of the parameters, such as the probability of success (p_H) or the payoff R, so it may be imprudent to compare our results with reality. On the other hand, if reality looked very different from our simple predictions, it would be disquieting.

Arguably, the Scandinavian recession started as a credit crunch. Banks were overextended and had to rein in on lending.[19] The gap between lending and deposit rates widened at this stage, which is in line with the increase in β and decrease in γ. Overall investment dropped by more than the reduction in bank lending as banks forced firms to consolidate their battered balance sheets (improve solvency); this is consistent with A(iv).

A related empirical counterpart to r_f is the leverage provided by a dollar's worth of collateral. We know of no systematic evidence, but anecdotal reports from Scandinavia indicate that at the height of the 1980s boom, a dollar of collateral brought in about a dollar and a half of loans. Currently, that ratio averages 70 cents per dollar of collateral. Again, this is consistent with A(iv).

The solvency of the banks dropped dramatically and recovered only with government support and a monetary ease. Even though r_m should go down according to A(iii), this result cannot be directly matched with the evidence, since regulatory rules clearly governed the behavior of banks. Nevertheless, our analysis may have some bearing on the ongoing debate about the regulation of capital ratios. Should these ratios vary with the business cycle and, if so, how? Our model suggests one reason why capital adequacy ratios should be procyclical. In a recession, intermediaries will have the right incentives with a lower share of own capital, because interest rates, and hence contingent payoffs, are higher.[20]

Needless to say, there are numerous other aspects to consider when discussing the regulation of solvency. Our model gives no reason for regulating solvency ratios in the first place, since the market will provide the proper level of discipline. Indeed, if one adds solvency constraints to the model, the aggregate level of

---

[19] It appears that the Scandinavian credit crunches were a consequence of the deregulation of credit markets, which first caused them to overheat and then collapse [Vihriala 1996]. Regulatory reforms have been implicated in other credit crunches as well. For example, the big 1996 credit crunch in the United States started when ceilings on CD rates were imposed (see Wojnilower [1966]). More recently, the 1990 reclassification of many private placements, from investment grade to speculative grade, produced a sharp decrease in lending by life insurance companies. In 1991 gross insurance holdings of nonfinancial corporations below investment grade, fell by 53 percent (while those of investment grade fell by 6 percent; see Carey et al. [1993]). In his review of recent empirical work on the credit crunch, Sharpe [1995] concludes that the current evidence does not pin the decline in lending on any particular change in capital regulation but that there is other evidence (especially for New England) that suggests a close link.

[20] In an unconventional interpretation of government subsidies, one can see them as a way to permit countercyclical solvency ratios.

investment and welfare will go down if the constraints bind. But if one views government as a representative of investors, as in Dewatripont and Tirole [1994], then our results on solvency ratios can be interpreted normatively.

Incidentally, our dual interpretation of monitoring illustrates rather nicely one dilemma with regulating capital adequacy. The market equilibrium is the same whether investors invest directly in firms (certification) or indirectly (intermediation). In the former case, the monitor offers an implicit guarantee to the investors, while in the latter case the guarantee is more explicit (there is a contract between the parties). The investors—and this is the crucial point—do not care about which form the guarantee takes. All they care about is whether the monitor holds a sufficient contingent interest in the project. Solvency ratios alone do not capture the effectives guarantee provided. Indeed, the solvency ratio of a certifier that does not intermediate is by definition equal to 1, but that no assurance for proper monitoring.

IV.4 Endogenous monitoring

So far, we have kept monitoring intensity fixed. The logic of the model suggests that monitoring intensity should vary in response to changes in aggregate as well as individual levels of capital. There is an obvious way to model varying monitoring intensity: let the opportunity cost b be a continuous rather than discrete variable. In accordance with our earlier interpretation of monitoring, one can imagine that the firm has a continuum of alternative bad projects, distinguished by differing levels of private benefit b. Monitoring at the intensity level c eliminates all bad projects with a private benefit higher than $b(c)$, say, where c represents the cost of monitoring and $b(c)$ the functional relationship between monitoring intensity and the firm's opportunity cost for being diligent.

With this apparatus let us first revisit the fixed investment model. In that model all firms that were monitored demanded the same amount of informed capital because the monitor had to be paid a minimum return. It is evident, however, that if firms could choose to reduce the intensity of monitoring, all but the most poorly capitalized firms would do so. Any firm for which $A > \underline{A}(\gamma, \beta)$ can reduce its cost of capital by letting b increase. A higher b implies a lower c. This relaxes the intermediary's incentive-compatibility constraint (IC_m) and with it the amount that the intermediary has to be paid, R_m, and the amount the intermediary has to invest, I_m. The firm replaces the loss in intermediary capital with cheaper uninformed capital for a net gain.

In this variation the relationship between the intensity of monitoring and the level of firm assets is continuously rather than discretely declining. More interestingly, the model implies that the intensity of monitoring is positively related to the amount of capital that the intermediary has to put up. Intermediaries that monitor more intensively are required to have a higher solvency ratio. This seems consistent with casual evidence. Commercial banks do not monitor very intensively, which partly explains why they can leverage their capital so extensively. By contrast venture capitalists hold a much larger stake in the projects they finance because their participation in overseeing management is much more intense.

In the variable investment model with endogenous monitoring, all firms would be monitored at the same level of intensity (because the choice of b in Program A_0 is independent of A_0). However, this level would vary with the relative amounts of intermediary and firm capital. Using (11)–(13), we see that a firm would choose b to minimize $A_1(\gamma, \beta)/b$, the amount of own assets per unit of private benefit. It is immediate, by revealed preference, that b increases in response to an increase in β (keeping γ exogenous). Therefore, when informed capital gets scarcer, the response is to shift toward less intensive monitoring. Conversely, when informed capital gets more abundant relative to firm capital, the most efficient use of informed capital requires that it be employed for more intensive monitoring.

When monitoring is endogenous, aggregate investment will depend not just on the sum of firm and monitoring capital as in equation (15), but also on the relative amounts of each. In particular, an extra dollar of informed capital will expand investment by more than an extra dollar of firm capital because an increase in monitoring capital leads to more intensive monitoring, which in turn allows firms to increase their leverage (without a change in monitoring, equation (15) tells us that the transfer would have no investment effect). As before, transferring a dollar from investors to intermediaries would not be Pareto improving. But for a government preoccupied with the level of economic activity, this suggests a reason why it may be more efficient to subsidize intermediaries than to subsidize firms. (Of course, a second reason is that, unlike in our model, the government typically has little knowledge of which firms are worthy of support. Using intermediation utilizes information more effectively.)

Another variation in which aggregate investment will depend on the relative amounts of firm and intermediary capital is worth brief mention.

Suppose that investment is continuous, but subject to decreasing returns to scale. Let $R(I)$ denote a firm's gross profit in case of success, with $R' > 0, R'' < 0, R'(0) = \infty, R'(\infty) = 0$. For given expected rates of return β and γ, a firm's net utility $U(I)$ is still equal to the expected net profit, $p_H R(I) - \gamma I$, minus the extra cost of using intermediary capital, $(\beta - \gamma)I_m$, or

$$U(I) = p_H R(I) - \gamma I - (\beta - \gamma/\beta)(p_H c/\Delta p)I.$$

$U(I)$ is maximized at some investment I^*. A firm's utility therefore depends on its asset level only through its borrowing capacity. The latter is obtained by replacing

"*RI*" by "*R(I)*" in the derivation of equation (11). Incentive compatibility for the firm requires that $1 \leq I(A_0)$, where $I(A_0)$ is given by

$$\Delta p \left[R(I) - \frac{cI}{\Delta p} - \frac{\gamma}{p_H} \left[I - \frac{p_H cI}{\beta \Delta p} \right] - A_0 \right] = bI.$$

The investment capacity $I(A_0)$ is an increasing and concave function of assets A_0. Firms with assets A_0 such that $I(A_0) > I^*$ bunch at investment level I^* while the others are credit constrained.

In this version the investment-over-assets multiplier is a decreasing function of assets; that is, firms with more assets will have a higher solvency ratio r_f. For this reason, it is evident that the distribution of capital across firms, as well as between firms and intermediaries, influences aggregate investment, unlike in the constant returns to scale case analyzed in subsection IV.1. Whether firms with more capital will be more adversely affected by a reduction in intermediary capital depends on the shape of $R(I)$. There are two conflicting effects: lower leverage makes large firms less sensitive, while lower marginal returns make them more sensitive to a rise in β.

V. Concluding Remarks

We have offered this analysis as a first step toward understanding the role played by the distribution of capital across differently informed sources of capital. In our model the borrowing capacity of both firms and intermediaries is limited so that a redistribution of wealth across firms and intermediaries impacts investment, monitoring, and interest rates. All types of capital tightening—a credit crunch, a collateral squeeze, and a savings squeeze—hit poorly capitalized firms the hardest, and as Proposition 2 shows, each such shock has a distinguishable impact on interest rates, monitoring intensity, the solvency of intermediaries and the firms' leverage.

The models we have worked with are simple, and the exercises we have been through should be seen as experiments with prototype models that will be useful to future efforts to understand how information and ideas get matched through a financial network featuring different levels and kinds of expertise, and how such a financial network reacts to real or monetary shocks. The fact that our models are able to reproduce some of the stylized facts associated with capital crunches is encouraging. Also, the general methodology seems quite tractable.

We have been careful not to get ahead of ourselves on policy matters; the models are too primitive for that. Nevertheless, it is legitimate to let pilot studies suggest new avenues for thinking about policy issues. In this regard, we find the logic behind procyclical solvency ratios of interest for the regulatory debate.

In a desire to get a first cut at the relative shifts in capital and its implications for monitoring and investment, we have made several unpalatable assumptions.

We wish to point out some limitations of our modeling that deserve particular attention.

In our analysis we took the supply of firm and intermediary capital as exogenous and performed comparative statics exercises on each one of them independently. A proper investigation of the transmission mechanism of real and monetary shocks must take into account the feedback from interest rates to capital values. This will require an explicitly dynamic model, for instance, along the lines of Kiyotaki and Moore [1993]. Preliminary investigations suggest that this route is interesting and tractable.

To keep matters simple, we have stayed away from modeling features that would enable us to identify monitoring with alternative forms of institutions. Our intermediary could be a bank, an equity holder, a venture capitalist, or any other monitor. To the extent one wants to explain the emergence of and evaluate the relative role of these institutions, one has to bring in other ingredients (presumably control-related considerations) into the model. However, for a preliminary macroeconomic analysis, organizational refinements of this kind may not be of first-order importance.

Another caveat concerns our assumption that the intermediary's projects are perfectly correlated. As we explained, there is nothing realistic about this assumption. It is just a way of avoiding the extreme (and equally unrealistic) conclusion that all intermediation can be carried out without own capital. We see the issue of diversification, the degree of leverage, and the intensity of monitoring as closely linked, complementary choice variables that deserve more careful study in the future.

Our final, and most important, caveat concerns the role of own capital. It seems to make sense only in an entrepreneurial model. But most intermediaries (including firms) are of course not run by entrepreneurs. So how is one to interpret our model? First, let us note that most agency models in finance suffer from the same criticism, though here the critique may have more bite, because we are highlighting the role of own capital. One interpretation is that the manager and the owners of the intermediary have formed such close ties that for practical purposes they can be treated as a single entrepreneur—not a very convincing story, and logically hollow in that it leaves open the question why new capital providers cannot join this close-knit team, obviating the need for external funds (going along this route would require introducing some adverse selection, say). Another interpretation, and the one we favor, is that management enjoys a continuing stream of private benefits (which in our analysis is normalized to zero for convenience), which is proportional to the funds under its management. Thus, committing funds to a project in which the funds may get lost has incentive consequences much like those in the original model. We have explored this variation, which leads to somewhat different expressions for incentive compatibility, necessary levels of assets and so on, but the fundamental insights and the character of the analysis do not change. Yet, it is evident that a fuller understanding of how intermediaries allocate capital will require a much richer managerial model.

In closing, we emphasize the broader research agenda associated with the introduction of scarce loanable funds. Limited intermediary capital is a necessary ingredient in the study of credit crunches and cyclical solvency ratios. But it also ought to be the key to a better understanding of other issues such as the propagation of monetary policy through the banking system. Accordingly, we hope that future theoretical research will put greater emphasis on loanable funds.

References

Barry, C., Muscarella, C., Peavy, J., and Vetsuypens, M. (1990). "The role of venture capital in the creation of public companies." *Journal of Financial Economics*, XXVII: 447–71.

Bernanke, B. (1993). "Credit in the macroeconomy." Federal Reserve Bank of New York, *Quarterly Review*, XVIII: 50–70.

——, and Gertler, M. (1989). "Agency costs, net worth and business fluctuations." *American Economic Review*, LXXIX: 14–31.

Besanko, D., and Kanatas, G. (1993). "Credit market equilibrium with bank monitoring and moral hazard." *Review of Financial Studies*, VI: 213–32.

Bester, H. (1985). "Screening vs. Rationing in credit markets with imperfect information." *American Economic Review*, LXXV: 850–55.

—— (1987). "The role of collateral in credit markets with imperfect information." *European Economic Review*, XXXI: 887–99.

——, and Hellwig, M. (1987). "Moral hazard and equilibrium credit rationing: an overview of the issues," in G. Bambers and K. Spremann (eds.), *Agency Theory, Information and Incentives* (Germany: Springer Verlag).

Cantillo, M. (1994). "A theory of corporate capital structure." Draft. Department of Economics, Stanford University.

Carey, M., Prowse, S., Rea, J., and Udell, G. (1993). "Recent developments in the market for privately placed debt." *Federal Reserve Bulletin*, LXXIX: 77–92.

Dewatripont, M., and Tirole, J. (1994). *The Prudential Regulation of Banks*. Cambridge, MA: MIT Press.

Diamond, D. (1984). "Financial intermediation and delegated monitoring." *Review of Economic Studies*, LI: 393–414.

—— (1991). "Monitoring and reputation: The choice between bank loans and directly placed debt." *Journal of Political Economy*, XCIX: 689–721.

Emereck, D., and White, W. (1992). "The case for private placements: How sophisticated investment adds value to corporate debt issuers." *Journal of Applied Corporate Finance*, V: 83–91.

Friedman, B., and Kuttler, K. (1993). "Economic activity and the short-term credit markets: An analysis of prices and quantities." *Brookings Papers on Economic Activity* 193–266.

Gertler, M., and Gilchrist, S. (1994). "Monetary policy, business cycles, and the behavior of small manufacturing firms." *Quarterly Journal of Economics*, CIX: 309–40.

Gilchrist, S., Bernanke, B., and Gertler, M. (1994). "The financial acceleration and the flight to quality." WP 94–18, Board of Governors of the Federal Reserve System, Washington, DC.

Holmström, B., and Weiss, L. (1985). "Managerial incentives, investment and aggregate implications." *Review of Economic Studies*, LII: 403–26.

Hoshi, T., Kashyap, A., and Scharfstein, D. (1992). "The choice between public and private debt: An examination of post-regulation corporate financing in Japan." MIT working paper.

Jaffee, D., and Russell, T. (1976). "Imperfect information, uncertainty, and credit rationing." *Quarterly Journal of Economics*, XC: 651–66.

Kiyotaki, N., and Moore, J. (1993). "Credit cycles." Mimeo, London School of Economics.

Megginson, W., and Weiss, K. (1991). "Venture capitalist certification in initial public offerings." *Journal of Finance*, XLVI: 879–903.

Miron, J., Romer, C., and Weil, D. (1994). "Historical perspectives on the monetary transmission mechanism," in G. Mankiw (ed.), *Monetary Policy* (Chicago, IL: The University of Chicago Press).

Repullo, R., and Suarez, J. (1995). "Credit markets and real economic activity: A model of financial intermediation." DP 203 CEPR, London.

Sharpe, S. (1995). "Bank capitalization, regulation, and the credit crunch: A critical review of the research findings." DP 95–20, Finance and Economics Discussion Series, Board of Governors of the Federal Reserve System, Washington, DC.

Stiglitz, J., and Weiss, A. (1981). "Credit rationing in markets with imperfect information." *American Economic Review*, LXXI: 393–410.

Vihriala, V. (1996). "Theoretical aspects of the Finnish credit cycle." Bank of Finland Discussion Paper 8.

Williamson, S. (1987). "Financial intermediation, business failures, and real business cycles." *Journal of Political Economy*, XCV: 1196–216.

Wojnilower, A. (1980). "The central role of credit crunches in recent financial history." *Brookings Papers on Economic Activity*, 277–326.

Yanelle, M.O. (1989). "The strategic analysis of intermediation." *European Economic Review*, XXXIII: 294–324.

24

Credit Cycles

Nobuhiro Kiyotaki and John Hardman-Moore

I. Introduction

This chapter is a theoretical study into how credit constraints interact with aggregate economic activity over the business cycle. In particular, for an economy in which credit limits are endogenously determined, we investigate how relatively small, temporary shocks to technology or income distribution might generate large, persistent fluctuations in output and asset prices. Also we ask whether sector-specific shocks can be contagious, in the sense that their effects spill over to other sectors and get amplified through time.

For this purpose, we construct a model of a dynamic economy in which credit constraints arise naturally because lenders cannot force borrowers to repay their debts unless the debts are secured.[1] In such an economy, durable assets such as land, buildings, and machinery play a dual role: not only are they factors of production, but they also serve as collateral for loans. Borrowers' credit limits are affected by the prices of the collateralized assets. And at the same time, these prices are affected by the size of the credit limits. The dynamic interaction between credit limits and asset prices turns out to be a powerful transmission mechanism by which the effects of shocks persist, amplify, and spread out.

The transmission mechanism works as follows. Consider an economy in which land is used to secure loans as well as to produce output, and the total supply of land is fixed. Some firms are credit constrained, and are highly levered in that they have borrowed heavily against the value of their landholding, which are their major asset. Other firms are not credit constrained. Suppose that in some

We are indebted to many colleagues and seminar participants. In particular we would like to thank Rao Aiyagari, Fernando Alvarez, John Carlson, Terry Fitzgerald, Mark Gertler, Edward Green, Oliver Hart, Frank Heinemann, Ellen McGrattan, François Ortalo-Magné, and Edward Prescott for their thoughtful comments and help. Financial assistance is acknowledged from the U.S. National Science Foundation, the U.K. Economic and Social Research Council, and Financial Markets Group at the London School of Economics. We are also grateful to the Research Department of the Federal Reserve Bank of Minneapolis for its hospitality and support. However, our views are not necessarily those of the bank of the Federal Reserve System.

[1] The specific model of debt we use is a simple variant of the model in Hart and Moore (1994).

period t the firms experience a temporary productivity shock that reduces their net worth. Being unable to borrow more, the credit-constrained firms are forced to cut back on their investment expenditure, including investment in land. This hurts then in the next period: they earn less revenue, their net worth falls, and, again because of credit constraints, they reduce investment. The knock-on effects continue, with the results that the temporary shock in period t reduces the constrained firms' demand for land not only in period t but also in periods $t + 1, t + 2, \ldots$. For the market to clear in each of these periods, the demand for land by the unconstrained firms has to increase, which requires that their opportunity cost, or use cost, of holding land must fall. Given that these firms are unconstrained, their user cost in each period is simply the difference between that period's land price and the discounted value of the land price in the following period. This anticipated decline in user costs in periods $t, t + 1, t + 2, \ldots$ is reflected by a fall in the land price in period t—since price equals the discounted value of future user costs.

The fall in land price in period t has a significant impact on the behavior of the constrained firms. They suffer a capital loss on their landholding, which, because of the high leverage, causes their net worth to drop considerably. As a result, the firms have to make yet deeper cuts in their investment in land. There is an intertemporal multiplier process: the shock to the constrained firms' net worth in period t causes them to cut their demand for land in period t and in subsequent periods; for market equilibrium to be restored, the unconstrained firms' use cost of land is thus anticipated to fall in each of these periods, which leads to a fall in the land price in period t; and this reduces the constrained firms' net worth in period t still further. Persistence and amplification reinforce each other. The process is summarized in Figure 1.

In fact, two kinds of multiplier process are exhibited in Figure 1, and it is useful to distinguish between them. One is a within-period, or static, multiplier. Consider the left-hand column of Figure 1, marked "date t" (ignore any arrows to and from the future). The productivity shock reduces the net worth of the constrained firms, and forces them to cut back their demand for land; the user cost falls to clear the market; and the land price drops by the same amount (keeping the future constant), which lowers the value of the firm's existing landholdings, and reduces their net worth still further. But this simple intuition misses the much more powerful intertemporal, or dynamic, multiplier. The future is not constant. As the arrows to the right of the date t column in Figure 1 indicate, the overall drop in the land price is the cumulative fall in present and future user costs, stemming from the persistent reductions in the constrained firms' net worth and land demand, which are in turn exacerbated by the fall in land price and net worth in period t.

We find that in our basic model, presented in Section II, the effect of this dynamic multiplier on land price exceeds that of the static multiplier by a factor

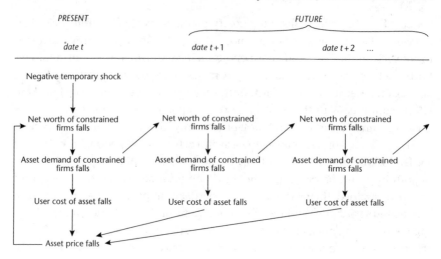

Figure 1.

equal to the inverse of the net real rate of interest. For our basic model, in percentage terms, the change in land price is of the same order of magnitude as the temporary productivity shock, and the change in land usage exceeds the shock. In the absence of the dynamic multiplier, these changes would be much smaller: the percentage change in price would only be of the order of the shock times the interest rate (i.e. the price would experience only a tiny blip if the length of the period is not long).

A feature of equilibrium is that the marginal productivity of the constrained firms is higher than that of the unconstrained firms—not surprisingly, given that the constrained firms cannot borrow as much as they want. Consequently, and shift in land usage from the constrained to the unconstrained firms leads to a first-order decline in aggregate output. Aggregate productivity, measured by average output per unit of land, also declines, not because there are variations in the underlying technologies (aside from the initial shock), but rather because the change in land use has a compositional effect.[2]

Our full model is in Section III of the chapter. There are two substantive changes to the basic model of Section II. First, we introduce another asset, which, unlike land, depreciates but can be reproduced. We suppose that the asset has no resale value and so cannot be used to secure loans. This reduces leverage, and hence weakens the contemporaneous effects of a shock. However, there is greater persistence. We also show that if collateralized land is smaller component of input, then, in relative terms, land prices respond to a shock more than quantities.

---

[2] This may shed light on why the aggregate Solow residual fluctuates so much over the business cycle.

The second change we make to the basic model is that investment is lumpy at the level of the individual firm. Specifically, we suppose that in any period, only a fraction of firms are in a position to invest. This means that only a fraction of the credit-constrained firms currently borrow up to their credit limits; the rest have to await an investment opportunity before reacting to a shock. The economy thus adjusts more slowly: contemporaneous effects are smaller, but, in contrast to the basic model, the response can build up over time. Moreover, such an economy can exhibit damped oscillations: recessions lead to booms, and booms lead to recessions. Investment in the reproducible asset moves with output and land price. And, in simulations, we find that the land price leads the fluctuations in output.

A simple way to understand why the economy cycles is to use the analogy of a predator–prey model.[3] The predators correspond to the debts of the credit-constrained firms, and the prey correspond to their landholdings. On the one hand, a rise in these firms' landholdings means that they have more net worth with which to borrow: the prey feed the predators. On the other hand, a high level of debt erodes the firms' available funds and curtails their investment in land: the predators kill off their prey. Our model is actually richer than this because, in addition to the debts and landholdings of the credit-constrained firms, we have a third variable, the price of land, which is forward-looking and causes the economy to react much more to a shock.[4]

In Section IV we extend the basic model of Section II so that it has more sectors, to see to what extent shocks spill over through the (common) land market. Suppose the credit-constrained firms in one sector suffer a productivity shock. We show that, given high leverage, the indirect effects of the fall in land price dwarf the direct effect of the shock, and so there is significant comovement across sectors.

In Section V we relate our chapter to the literature and make some final remarks.

From the start of the next section, it will be seen that, in the interests of streamlining the model, we have chosen to make certain unorthodox assumptions about preferences and technologies. To confirm the robustness of our findings, in the Appendix we present an overlapping generations model that is entirely orthodox, except that all borrowing has to be secured. Arguably, this provides a better framework for quantitative analysis; and the model can be used to show how

---

[3] For example, image populations of deer and wolves. If the deer population rises, the wolves that feed on them also multiply. However, as the wolves grow in number, they kill off the deer. Eventually, the deer population falls, which means that fewer wolves can survive. But with fewer wolves, the deer population can in time start to grow again; and so on. That is, away from the steady state, the two populations oscillate. For some interesting economic applications of the predator–prey model, see Das (1993).

[4] The classic predator–prey model is entirely backward-looking. That literature focuses mainly on nonlinear limit cycles, whereas we shall be concerned with characterizing the equilibrium path that converges back to the steady state.

fluctuations in the interest rate sere to exacerbate the multiplier effects identified in the text.

II. The Basic Model: Amplification and Persistence

Consider a discrete-time economy with two goods, a durable asset and a non-durable commodity. It is helpful to think of the durable asset as land, which does not depreciate and has fixed total supply of $\overline{K}$. The nondurable commodity may be though of as fruit, which grows on land but cannot be stored. There is a continuum of infinitely lived agents. Some are farmers and some are gatherers, with population sizes one and m, respectively. Both farmers and gatherers produce and eat fruit. They are risk neutral: at date t, the expected utilities of a farmer and a gatherer are

$$E_t\left(\sum_{s=0}^{\infty}\beta^s x_{t+s}\right) \quad \text{and} \quad E_t\left(\sum_{s=0}^{\infty}\beta'^s x'_{t+s}\right), \tag{1}$$

where x_{t+s} and x'_{t+s} are their respective consumptions of fruit at data $t + s$, and E_t denotes expectations formed at data t. The discount factors β and β' both lie strictly between zero and one; and we make the following assumption.

ASSUMPTION 1. $\beta < \beta'$.

We shall see later that Assumption 1 ensures that in equilibrium farmers will not want to postpone production, because they are relatively impatient.

At each data t there is a competitive spot market in which land is exchanged for fruit at a price of q_t. (Throughout, fruit is taken as the numeraire). The only other market is a one-period credit market in which one unit of fruit at data t is exchanged for a claim to R_t units of fruit at data $t + 1$. We shall see that in equilibrium the farmers borrow form the gatherers, and the rate of interest always equals the gatherers' constant rate of time preference; that is, $R_t \equiv 1/\beta' = R$, say.

Both farmers and gatherers take one period to produce fruit from land, but the farmers differ from the gatherers in their production technologies. We begin with the farmers since they play the central role in the model. Consider any particular farmer. He or she as a constant returns to scale production function:

$$y_{t+1} = F(k_t) \equiv (a + c)k_t, \tag{2}$$

where k_t is the land used at data t, and y_{t+1} is the output of fruit at data $t + 1$. Only ak_t of this output is tradable in the market, however. The rest, ck_t, is bruised and cannot be transported, but can be consumed by the farmer. We introduce non-tradable output in order to avoid the situation in which the farmer continually postpones consumption. The ratio $a/(a+c)$ may be thought of as a technological upper bound on his savings rate, which we take to be less than β; that is, we make the following assumption.

ASSUMPTION 2.

$$c > \left(\frac{1}{\beta} - 1\right) a.$$

This inequality is weak assumption, insofar as β is close to one. We shall see later that Assumption 2 ensures that in equilibrium the farmer will not want to consume more than the bruised fruit: the overall return from farming, $a + c$, is high enough that all his tradable output is used for investment.[5]

There are two further critical assumptions we make about farming. First, we assume that each farmer's technology is idiosyncratic in the sense that, once his production has started at data t with land k_t, only he has skill necessary for the land to bear fruit at data $t + 1$. That is, if the farmer were to withdraw his labor between dates t and $t + 1$, there would be no fruit output at date $t + 1$; there would be only the land k_t. Second, we assume that a farmer always has the freedom to withdraw his labor; he cannot precommit to work. In the language of Hart and Moore (1994), the farmer's human capital is inalienable.

The upshot of these two assumptions is that if a farmer has a lot of debt, he may find it advantageous to threaten his creditors by withdrawing his labor and repudiating his debt contract. Creditors protect themselves from the threat of repudiation by collateralizing the farmer's land. However, because the land yields no fruit without the farmers's labor, the liquidation value (the outside value) of the land is less than what the land would earn under his control (the inside value). Thus, following a repudiation, it is efficient for the farmer to bribe his creditors into letting him keep the land. In effect, he can renegotiate a smaller loan. The division of surplus in this renegotiation process is moot, but Hart and Moore given an argument to show that the farmer may be also negotiate the debt down to the liquidation value of the land.[6] Creditors know of this possibility in

---

[5] Notice that we have made two unorthodox modeling choices: we have assumed that agents have linear preferences but different discount factors; and we have in effect assumed that farmers can save only a fraction of their output. Both assumptions can be dispensed with. In the Appendix we lay out an overlapping generations model in which agents have common concave preferences, and face conventional saving/consumption decisions.

In the text we have taken the shortcut of assuming nonidentical linear preferences and a technologically determined savings rate for the farmers, so that they operate at corner solutions rather than at interior optima. We think that this helps to focus attention on the fact that agents face a *sequence* of cash flow constraints, which is the crucial difference between our framework and Arrow-Debreu.

[6] The case we have in mind in one in which the liquidation (outside) value is greater than the *share* of the continuation (inside) value that creditors would get if the liquidation option were not available to them—albeit that the liquidation value is less than the *total* continuation value. In this case, the creditors' "outside option" (the option to liquidate) is binding, which pins down the division of surplus in the renegotiation process. For a discussion of the noncooperative foundation of the so-called outside option principle, see Osborne and Rubinstein (1990, sec. 3.12). See the appendix to Hart and Moore (1994) for specific details of the debt renegotiation game.

advance, and so take care never to allow the size of the debt (grow of interest) to exceed the value of the collateral.[7] Specifically, if date t the farmer has land k_t, then he can borrow b_t in total, as long as the repayment does not exceed the market value of his land a data $t + 1$:

$$Rb_t \leq q_{t+1}k_t. \tag{3}$$

Note that there is no aggregate uncertainty in our model (aside from an initial unanticipated shock), and so, given rational expectations, agents have perfect foresight of future land prices.[8]

The farmer can expand his scale of production by investing in more land. Consider a farmer who holds k_{t-1} land at the end of date $t - 1$, and has incurred a total debt of b_{t-1}. At date t he harvests ak_{t-1} tradable fruit, which, together with a new loan b_t, is available to cover the cost of buying new land, to repay the accumulated debt Rb_{t-1} (which includes interest), and to meet any additional consumption $x_t - ck_{t-1}$ (over and above the automatic consumption of non-tradable output ck_{t-1}). The farmer's flow-of-funds constraint is thus

$$q_t(k_t - k_{t-1}) + Rb_{t-1} + x_t - ck_{t-1} = ak_{t-1} + b_t. \tag{4}$$

We turn now to the gatherers. Each gatherer has an identical production function that exhibits decreasing returns to slace: per unit of population, an input of

---

[7] An alternative, somewhat starker, form of moral hazard would be to assume that the farmers can steal the fruit crop at data $t + 1$ (see Hart and Moore 1989, 1996). In our basic model, this simple diversion assumption leads to the same borrowing constraint: creditors must never allow a farmer's debt obligation to rise above the value of his land; otherwise he will simply abscond, leaving the land behind but taking all the fruit with him. We have chosen not to tell the story this way because in our full model given in Section III there are specific trees growing on the land, which are valuable to the farmer but not to outsiders. Were stealing fruit the only moral hazard problem, the farmer would be able to collateralize his trees as well as his land (since, if he absconded, he would have to leave the trees behind). We are interested in investigating the role of an uncollateralized asset (trees), so we want the farmer to be able to put up only his land as security.

[8] Readers may wonder why farmers cannot find some other way to raise capital, e.g. by issuing equity. Unfortunately, given the specific nature of a farmer's technology, and the fact that he can withdraw his labor, equity holders could not be assured that they would receive a dividend. Debt contracts secured on the farmer's land are the only financial instrument investors can rely on. The same considerations rule out partnerships between farmers, or larger farming cooperatives.

Longer-term debt contracts also offer no additional source of capital, insofar as the farmer can repudiate and renegotiate at any time during the life of a contract. To avoid repudiation and renegotiation, creditors have to ensure that the value of their outstanding loan never exceeds the current liquidation value of the land, i.e. that (3) holds at all time. This means that any credible long-term debt contract can be mimicked by a sequence of short-term debt contracts.

It is worth remarking that if land were rented rather than purchased, this would not change production or allocation along the perfect-foresight equilibrium path of the economy (although the economy would react differently to unanticipated aggregate shocks). We choose to rule out a rental market for land because in our full model in Section III farmers plant trees on land, and each farmers's trees are specific to him. If land were rented period by period, then a farmer would be at the mercy of the landlords who own the land on which his specific trees are growing. Given that, along the equilibrium path, the farmer can buy just as much land as he can rent, he is better off purchasing the land outright, so as to avoid being held up by landlords.

k'_t land at date t yields y'_{t+1} tradable fruit at date $t + 1$, according to

$$y'_{t+1} = G(k'_t), \quad \text{where } G' > 0, G'' < 0, G'(0) > aR > G'\left(\frac{\overline{K}}{m}\right). \tag{5}$$

(The last two inequalities in [5] are included to ensure that both farmers and gatherers are producing in the neighborhood of the steady-state equilibrium.) Gatherers' production does not require any specific skill; nor do they produce any nontradable output. As a result, no gatherer is credit constrained. A gatherer's budget constraint at date t is

$$q_t(k'_t - k'_{t-1}) + Rb'_{t-1} + x'_t = G(k'_{t-1}) + b'_t, \tag{6}$$

where x'_t is consumption at date t, Rb'_{t-1} is debt repayment, and b'_t in new debt. In equilibrium, b'_{t-1} and b'_t are actually negative, reflecting the fact that gatherers are creditors to the farmers.

Market equilibrium is defined as a sequence of land prices and allocations of land, debt, and consumption of farmrs and gatherers, $\{q_t, k_t, k'_t, b_t, b'_t, x_t, x'_t\}$, such that each farmer chooses $\{k_t, b_t, x_t\}$ to maximize the expected discounted utility (1) subject to the production function (2), the borrowing constraint (3), and the flow-of-funds constraint (4); each gatherer chooses $\{k'_t, b'_t, x'_t\}$ to maximize the expected discounted utility (1) subject to the production function (5) and the budget constraint (6); and the markets for land, fruit, and debt clear.

To characterize equilibrium, we first examine the farmers' behavior. We claim that, in the neighborhood of the steady state, farmers prefer to borrow up to the maximum and invest in land, consuming no more than their current output of nontradable fruit. In other words, at each data t a farmer's optimal choice of $\{k_t, b_t, x_t\}$ satisfies $x_t = ck_{t-1}$ in (4), and the borrowing constraint (3) is binding. That is, $b_t = q_{t+1}k_t/R$ and

$$k_t = \frac{1}{q_t - 1/R(q_{t+1})}[(a + q_t)k_{t-1} - Rb_{t-1}]. \tag{7}$$

The term $(a + q_t)k_{t-1} - Rb_{t-1}$ is the farmer's net worth at the beginning of date t; that is, the value of his tradable output and land held from the previous period, net of debt repayment. In effect, (7) says that the farmer uses all his net worth to finance the difference between the price of land, q_t, and the amount he can borrow against each unit of land, q_{t+1}/R. This difference, $q_t - (q_{t+1}/R) = u_t$ say, can be thought of as the down payment required to purchase a unit of land.

To prove our claim, consider the farmer's marginal unit of tradable fruit at date t. He can invest it in $1/u_t$ land, which yields c/u_t nontradable fruit and a/u_t tradable fruit date $t + 1$. The nontradable fruit is consumed; and the tradable fruit is reinvested. This in turn yields $(a/u_t)(c/u_{t+1})$ nontradable fruit and $(a/u_t)(a/u_t + 1)$ tradable fruit at date $t + 2$; and so on. Now we appeal to the principle of unimprovability, which says that we need consider only single deviations at date t to show that this investment strategy is optimal.[9] There are two alternatives open to the farmer at date t. Either he can save the marginal unit—equivalently, reduce his current borrowing by one—and use the return R to commence a strategy of maximum levered investment from date $t+1$ onward. Or he can simply consume the marginal unit. His choice boils down to choosing one of the following consumption paths:

$$\text{invest:} \quad 0, \quad \frac{c}{u_t}, \quad \frac{a}{u_t}\frac{c}{u_{t+1}}, \quad \frac{a}{u_t}\frac{a}{u_{t+1}}\frac{c}{u_{t+2}}, \cdots \tag{8a}$$

$$\text{save:} \quad 0, \quad 0, \quad R\frac{c}{u_{t+1}}, \quad R\frac{a}{u_{t+1}}\frac{c}{u_{t+2}}, \cdots \tag{8b}$$

$$\text{consume:} \quad 1, \quad 0, \quad 0, \quad 0, \cdots \tag{8c}$$

at dates $t, t+1, t+2, t+3, \ldots$, respectively. To complete the proof, we need to confirm that, given the farmer's discount factor β, consumption path (8a) offers a strictly higher utility than (8b) or (8c), in the neighborhood of the steady state. We shall be in a position to show this once we have found the steady-state value of u_t in (13a) below.

Since the optimal k_t and b_t are linear in k_{t-1} and b_{t-1}, we can aggregate across farmers to find the equation of motion of the aggregate landholding and borrowing, K_t and B_t say, of the farming sector:

$$K_t = \frac{1}{u_t}[(a+q_t)K_{t-1} - RB_{t-1}], \tag{9}$$

$$B_t = \frac{1}{R}q_{t+1}K_t. \tag{10}$$

Notice from (9) that if, example, present and future land prices, q_t and q_{t+1} were to rise by 1 percent (so that u_t also rises by 1 percent), then the farmers' demand for land at date t would also rise—provided that leverage is sufficient that debt repayments RB_{t-1} exceed current output aK_{t-1}, which will be true in equilibrium. The usual notion that a higher land price q_t reduces the farmers' demand is more than offset by the facts that (i) they can borrow more hen q_{t+1} is higher, and (ii) their net worth increases as q_t rises. Even though the required down payment, u_t, per unit of land rises proportionately with q_t and q_{t+1}, the farmers' net worth is increasing more than proportionately with q_t because of the leverage effect of the outstanding debt.

Next we examine the gatherers' behavior. A gatherer is not credit constrained, and so his or her demand for land is determined at the point at which the present

---

[9] On the principle of unimprovability, see, e.g. proposition 4 in app. 2 of Kreps (1990).

value of the marginal product of land is equal to the opportunity cost, or cost, of holding land, $q_t - (q_{t+1}/R) = u_t$:

$$\frac{1}{R}G'(k_t') = u_t. \tag{11}$$

Notice the dual role played by u_t in the model: not only is it the gatherers' opportunity cost of holding a unit of land, but it also happens to be the required down payment per unit of land held by the farmers.[10]

Finally, we consider market clearing. Since all the gatherers have identical production functions, their aggregate demand for land equals k_t' times their population m. The sum of the aggregate demands for land by the farmers and gatherers is equal to the total supply; that is, $K_t + mk_t' = \overline{K}$. Thus, from (11), we obtain the land market equilibrium condition

$$u_t = q_t - \frac{1}{R}q_{t+1} = u(K_t), \quad \text{where } u(K) \equiv \frac{1}{R}G'\left[\frac{1}{m}(\overline{K} - K)\right]. \tag{12}$$

The function $u(\cdot)$ is increasing: if the farmers' demand for land, K_t, goes up, then in order for the land market to clear, the gatherers' demand has to be choked off by a rise in the user cost, u_t. Given that the gatherers have linear preferences and are not credit constrained, in equilibrium they must be indifferent about any path of consumption and debt (or credit); and so the interest rate equals their rate of time preference ($R = 1/\beta'$). Moreover, given (12), the markets for fruit and credit are in equilibrium by Walras' law.

We restrict attention to perfect-foresight equilibria in which without unanticipated shocks, the expectations of future variables realize themselves. For a given level of farmers' landholding and debt at the previous date, K_{t-1} and B_{t-1}, an equilibrium from date t onward is characterized by the path of land price, farmers' landholding, and debt, $\{(q_{t+s}, K_{t+s}, B_{t+s})|s \geq 0\}$, satisfying equations (9), (10), and (12) at dates $t, t+1, t+2, \dots$. We also rule out exploding bubbles in the land price by making the following assumption.

ASSUMPTION 3. $\lim_{s \to \infty} E_t(R^{-s}q_{t+s}) = 0$.

Given Assumption 3, it turns out that there is a locally unique perfect-foresight equilibrium path starting from initial values K_{t-1} and B_{t-1} in the neighborhood of the steady state.

---

[10] We say "happens to be" because a borrowing constraint different from (3) would yield different expressions for k_t and K_t in (7) and (9). For example, we might suppose that, out of equilibrium, if a farmer were to repudiate his debt contract and the renegotiation of a new contract with his creditors were to break down, then there would be a (proportional) transactions cost τ associated with disposing of his land. That is, the liquidation value would be multiplied by $1 - \tau$. The borrowing constraint (3) would become $Rb_t \leq (1-\tau)q_{t+1}k_t$, and the denominator on the right-hand sides of (7) and (9) would read $q_t - [(1 - \tau)q_{t+1}/R]$. Although the analysis of the model would then be slightly different, its behavior would be similar.

Before we turn to dynamics, it is useful to look at the steady-state equilibrium. From equations (9), (10), and (12), it is easily shown that there is a unique steady state, (q^*, K^*, B^*), with associated steady-state user cost u^*, where

$$\frac{R-1}{R}q^* = u^* = a, \tag{13a}$$

$$\frac{1}{R}G'\left[\frac{1}{m}(\overline{K}-K^*)\right] = u^*, \tag{13b}$$

$$B^* = \frac{a}{R-1}K^*. \tag{13c}$$

In the steady state, the farmers' tradable output, aK^*, is just enough to cover the interest on their debt, $(R-1)B^*$. Equivalently, the required down payment per unit of land, u^*, equals the farmers' productivity of tradable output, a. As a result, farms neither expand nor shrink.[11]

We are now in a position to compare consumption paths (8a), (8b), and (8c). In the steady state, the user cost equals a; and so, given the farmer's discount factor β, investment gives him discounted utility $\beta c/(1-\beta)a$, saving gives $R\beta^2 c/(1-\beta)a$, and consumption gives one. By Assumption 1, investment strictly dominates saving; and by Assumption 2, investment strictly dominates consumption. This completes the proof of our earlier claim about farmers' optimal behavior in the neighborhood of the steady state.

Figure 2 provides a useful summary of the economy. On the horizontal axis, farmers' demand for land is measured form the left, gatherers' demand for the right, and the sum of the two equals total supply $\overline{K}$. On the vertical axes are the marginal products of land. The farmers' marginal product of land equals $a+c$, indicated by the line AC^*E^0. The gatherers' marginal product is shown by the line DE^0E^*; it falls with their land usage. If there were no debt enforcement problem so that there were no credit constraints, then the first-best allocation would be at the point $E^0 = (K^0, a+c)$, at which the marginal products of the farmers and the gatherers would be equalized. The land price would be $q^0 = (a+c)/(R-1)$, the discounted gross return from farming. In our credit-constrained economy, the steady-state equilibrium is at the point $E^* = (K^*, aR)$, where the marginal product of the farmers, $a+c$, exceeds the marginal product of the gatherers, $G'[(\overline{K}-K^*)/m] = aR$. (Assumptions 1 and 2 tell us that $aR < a/\beta < a+c$.) That is, relative to the first-best, in the credit-constrained equilibrium too little land is used by the farmers.

The area under the solid line, AC^*E^*D, is the steady-state output, Y^* say, of fruit per period. The triangular shaded area $C^*E^*E^0$ is the output loss relative to

---

[11] Appealing to assumption 1, one can show that there is no steady-state equilibrium in which the farmers' credit constraints are not binding. (We are grateful to Frank Heinemann for pointing out to us that such an equilibrium can exist if $\beta = \beta'$.) The model in the Appendix has no such equilibrium either, even though the farmers and the gatherers have identical preferences.

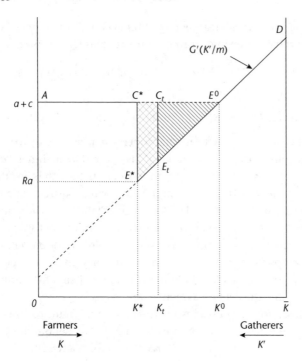

Figure 2.

the first-best. It is important to observe that, in the neighborhood of the steady state, aggregate output, Y_{t+1} say, at some date $t+1$ is an increasing function of the farmers' landholding, K_t, at date t. In fact, around K^*, a rise in K_t causes a first-order increase in Y_{t+1}: the area under the solid line in Figure 2 changes by the trapezoid $E^*C^*C_tE_t$.[12]

To understand the dynamics of the economy, we find it helpful to consider the response to an unexpected impulse. Suppose at date $t-1$ the economy is in the steady state: $K_{t-1} = K^*$ and $B_{t-1} = B^*$. There is then an unexpected shock to productivity: both the farmers' and the gatherers' fruit harvests at the start of date t are $1 + \Delta$ times their expected levels. (For exposition, we take Δ to be positive.) However, the shock is known to be temporary. The farmers' and gatherers' production technologies between dates t and $t+1$ (and thereafter) return to (2) and (5), respectively.[13]

---

[12] This would not be true in the first-best near K^0, where the change in area would be only triangle: a second-order change in output. (In fact we shall argue at the end of this section that in the first-best K_t does not respond at all to an unanticipated, temporary output shock at date t, since land demands are entirely determined by current and future prices, which do not change.)

[13] Our analysis of a farmer's borrowing constraint (3) presupposed a deterministic environment. To allow for the possibility of an unexpected shock, we assume that a farmer's labor supply decision is made *between* periods, before the shock is realized. That is, it is too late for a farmer to repudiate

Combining the market-clearing condition (12) with the farmers' demand for land (9) and their borrowing constraint (10) at dates $t, t+1, t+2, \ldots$, we obtain

$$u(K_t)K_t = (a + \Delta a + q_t - q^*)K^* \quad \text{(date } t) \tag{14a}$$

and

$$u(K_{t+s})K_{t+s} = aK_{t+s-1} \quad \text{for } s \geq 1 \quad \text{(dates } t+1, t+2, \ldots). \tag{14b}$$

Equations (14) say that at each date the farmers can hold land up to the point K at which the required down payment, $u(K)K$, is covered by their net worth. Notice that in (14b), at each date $t+s(s \geq 1)$, the farmers' net worth is just their current output of tradable fruit, aK_{t+s-1}: from the borrowing constraint at date $t+s-1$, the value of the farmers' land at date $t+s$ is exactly offset by the amount of debt outstanding. In (14a), however, we see that the farmers' net worth at date t—just after the shock hits—is more than simply their current output, $(1 + \Delta)aK^*$, because q_t jumps in response to the shock and they enjoy unexpected capital gains, $(q_t - q^*)K^*$, on their landholdings (the value of land held from date $t-1$ is now q_tK^*, while the debt repayment is $RB^* = q^*K^*$).

To find closed-form expressions for the new equilibrium path, we take Δ to be small and linearize around the steady state. Let $\hat{X}_t$ denote the proportional change, $(X_t - X^*)/X^*$, in a variable X_t relative to its steady-state value X^*. Then, using the fact that $(R-1)q^*/R = u^* = a$, we obtain from equations (14)

$$\left(1 + \frac{1}{\eta}\right)\hat{K}_t = \Delta + \frac{R}{R-1}\hat{q}_t \quad \text{(date } t) \tag{15a}$$

and

$$\left(1 + \frac{1}{\eta}\right)\hat{K}_{t+s} = \hat{K}_{t+s-1} \quad \text{for } s \geq 1 \quad \text{(dates } t+1, t+2, \ldots), \tag{15b}$$

where $\eta > 0$ denotes the elasticity of the residual supply of land to the farmers with respect to the user cost at the steady state.[14]

The right-hand side of (15a) divides the change in the farmers' net worth at date t into two components: the direct effect of the productivity shock, Δ; and the indirect effect of the capital gain arising from the unexpected rise in price, $\hat{q}_t$. Crucially, the impact of $\hat{q}_t$ is scaled up by the factor $R/(R-1)$ because of leverage: the farmers' steady-state net worth equals aK^*; and so, ceteris paribus, a 1 percent rise in q_t increases their net worth by $q^*K^*/aK^* = R/(R-1)$ percent.

his debt contract after the shock because by then he has input his labor. Of course, we are relying here on the fact that the shock is a genuine surprise, and that the debt contract is not contingent; for further discussion, see Section V.

[14] That is,

$$\frac{1}{\eta} = \frac{d\log u(K)}{d\log K}\bigg|_{K=K^*} = -\frac{d\log G'(k')}{d\log k'}\bigg|_{k'=(1/m)(\bar{K}-K^*)} \times \frac{K^*}{\bar{K}-K^*},$$

which is the elasticity of the gatherers' marginal product of land times the ratio of the farmers' to the gatherers' landholdings in the steady state. Given our assumption that $G'' < 0$, η is positive.

The factor $1 + (1/\eta)$ on the left-hand sides of (15) reflects the fact that as the farmers' land demand rises, the user cost must rise for the market to clear; and this in turn partially chokes off the increase in the farmers' demand. The key point to note from (15b) is that, except for the limit case of a perfectly inelastic supply ($\eta = 0$), the effect of a shock persists into the future. The reason is that the farmers' ability to invest at each date $t + s$ is determined by how much down payment they can afford from their net worth at that date, which in turn is historically determined by their level of production at the previous date $t + s - 1$.

It remains to find out the size of the initial change in the farmers' landholdings, $\hat{K}_t$, which, from (15a), is jointly determined with the change in land price, $\hat{q}_t$. Now Assumption 3 together with (12) tells us that the land price q_t is the discounted sum of future user costs, $u_{t+s} = u(K_{t+s})$, $s \geq 0$. Linearizing around the steady state and then substituting from (15b), we obtain

$$\hat{q}_t = \frac{1}{\eta} \frac{R-1}{R} \sum_{s=0}^{\infty} R^{-s} \hat{K}_{t+s} = \frac{1}{\eta} \frac{R-1}{R} \frac{1}{1 - (1/R)\eta/(1+\eta)} \hat{K}_t. \tag{16}$$

The multiplier $\{1 - [\eta/R(1+\eta)]\}^{-1}$ in (16) captures the effects of persistence in the farmers' landholdings and has a dramatic effect on the sizes of $\hat{q}_t$ and $\hat{K}_t$. Solve (15a) and (16) to find $\hat{q}_t$ and $\hat{K}_t$ in terms of the size of the shock Δ:

$$\hat{q}_t = \frac{1}{\eta} \Delta, \tag{17}$$

$$\hat{K}_t = \frac{1}{1 + (1/\eta)} \left(1 + \frac{R}{R-1} \frac{1}{\eta} \right) \Delta. \tag{18}$$

Equation (17) tells us that, in percentage terms, the effect on the land price at date t is of the same order of magnitude as the *temporary* productivity shock! As a result, the effect of the shock on the farmers' landholdings at date t is large: the multiplier in (18) exceeds unity, and can do so by a sizable margin, thanks to the factor $R/(R-1)$. In terms of (15a), the indirect effect of $\hat{q}_t$, scaled up by the leverage factor $R/(R-1)$, is easily enough to ensure that the overall effect on $\hat{K}_t$ is more than one-for-one.[15,16]

---

[15] The direct effect of the productivity shock Δ is less than one-for-one because a rise in user cost u_t chokes it off. Notice that for inelastic supply ($\eta < 1$), the indirect effect is particularly marked. We know from (17) that a 1 percent productivity shock leads to a more than 1 percent increase in land price. However, the effects are shorter-lived: from (15b) we see that the decay factor is $\eta/(1+\eta) < 1/2$. Conversely, for elastic supply the indirect effect is less marked, and the impact on land price is less than proportional; however, there is more persistence. In the limit, as $\eta \to \infty$, there is no indirect effect: a 1 percent productivity shock leads to a 1 percent change in the farmers' landholdings, and there is no change in land price; but there is complete persistence.

[16] Because of the larger multiplier effects, the nonlinear equilibrium system comprising (14) and the land price equation

$$q_t = \sum_{s=0}^{\infty} R^{-s} u(K_{t+s})$$

Recall the distinction we drew in the Introduction between the static and dynamic multipliers. Imagine, hypothetically, that there were no dynamic multiplier. That is, suppose q_{t+1} were artificially pegged at the steady-state level q^*. Equation (15a) would remain unchanged. However, the right-hand side of (16) would contain only the first term of the summation—the term relating to the change in user cost at date t—so that the multiplier $\{1 - [\eta/R(1 + \eta)]\}^{-1}$ would disappear. Combining the modified equation, $\hat{q}_t = [(R-1)/\eta R]\hat{K}_t$, with (15a), we solve for $\hat{q}_t$ and $\hat{K}_t$:

$$\hat{q}_t|_{q_{t+1}=q^*} = \frac{R-1}{R}\frac{1}{\eta}\Delta,$$

$$\hat{K}_t|_{q_{t+1}=q^*} = \Delta.$$

These are the changes in the land price and the farmers' landholdings that can be traced to the static multiplier alone. Subtracting (17') from (17), we find that the additional movement in land price attributable to the dynamic multiplier is $1/(R - 1)$ times the movement due to the static multiplier. And a comparison of (18) with (18') shows that the dynamic multiplier has a similarly large proportional effect on the farmers' landholdings.[17]

As we saw in Figure 2, aggregate fruit output—the combined harvest of the farmers and gatherers—moves together with the farmers landholdings, since the farmers' marginal product is higher than the gatherers'. It is straightforward to show that at each date t the proportional change in aggregate output, $\hat{Y}_{t+s}$, is given by

$$\hat{Y}_{t+s} = \frac{a + c - Ra}{a + c}\frac{(a + c)K^*}{Y^*}\hat{K}^*_{t+s-1} \quad \text{for } s \geq 1. \tag{19}$$

The term $(a + c - Ra)/(a + c)$ reflects the difference between the farmers' productivity (equal to $a + c$) and the gatherers' productivity (equal to Ra in the steady state). The ratio $(a + c)K^*/Y^*$ is the share of the farmers' output. If aggregate productivity were measured by $Y_{t+s}/\overline{K}$, it would be persistently above its steady-state level, even though there are no positive productivity shocks after date t.

---

can have multiple dynamic equilibria, even though the linearized system (15), (16) has a unique equilibrium. Solving (14b) as $K_{t+s} = \phi(K_{t+s-1})$ or $K_{t+s} = \phi^s(K_t)$, we can combine (14a) and the equation above to obtain

$$u(K_t)K_t - (a + \Delta a)K^* - \sum_{s=0}^{\infty} R^{-s}[u(\phi^s(K_t)) - a]K^* = 0.$$

This can have a solution K_t outside a neighborhood of K^*. (This can be true *even when there is no shock* $[\Delta = 0]$.) In particular, if $Ru(0) < a$, then there is another solution K_t that is considerably less than K^*. Intuitively, if the farmers' future landholdings are expected to be small, then currently the land price will be low, the farmers will have little net worth, and they will be unable to borrow much to buy land—which in turn justifies the expectation that their future landholdings will be small. Eventually, the economy returns to the unique steady state.

[17] A less artificial way to get $q_{t+1} = q^*$ would be to have a second, *negative*, productivity shock, $-\Delta$, at date $t + 1$ (anticipated at date t). That is to say, the static multiplier has the same effect as two equal but opposite shocks hitting the economy in succession.

The explanation lies in a composition effect: there is a persistent change in land *usage* between farmers and gatherers, which is reflected in increased aggregate output.

One interesting issue is how the economy would respond to other kinds of shock. In particular, suppose that instead of a temporary productivity shock at date t, the economy experiences an unanticipated, one-time reduction in the value of debt obligations. This debt reduction has the same qualitative effect as the temporary productivity increase (expect that there is no increase in output at the initial date). Quantitatively, however, since the outstanding debt of the farmers is $R/(R-1)$ times their output of tradable fruit (in the steady state, $RB^*/aK^* = R/[R-1]$), a reduction of only $(R-1)/R$ percent in the value of their debt obligations is enough to generate the same effects as a 1 percent temporary productivity shock.[18]

To close this section, let us ask what would happen in the first-best economy, where there are no credit constraints. Consider the effect of the same unanticipated, temporary productivity shock Δ at date t. Aggregate output Y_t would rise by the factor Δ. But there would be *no effect* on the land price q_t or the land usage K_t; they would stay at q^0 and K^0. Nor would there be any change to future prices and production. The point is that in the first-best economy, all agents are unconstrained in the credit market, and prices and production are unaffected by changes to net worth. This is in marked contrast to what we have seen happens in the credit-constrained economy, where q_t and K_t (and hence Y_{t+1}) increase significantly, and these increases persist into the future.

III. The Full Model: Investment and Cycles

The basic model of Section II has a number of limitations. The only "investment" occurs in land itself; and although land changes hands between farmers and gatherers, aggregate investment is automatically zero because the total land supply is fixed. Also, the impulse response of the economy to a shock is arguably too dramatic and short-lived (especially when the residual supply of land to the farmers is inelastic). The reason is that the leverage effect is so strong: in the steady state the farmers' debt/asset ratio is $1/R$, which is unreasonably of the model hides certain important dynamics.

In this section we extend the basic model to overcome these limitations. There are two substantive changes. First, we introduce reproducible capital, trees, into the farmers' production function. A farmer plants fruit in his land to grow trees,

---

[18] Although our model does not have money, so we cannot analyze monetary policy per se, one possible monetary transmission mechanism would be through the redistribution of wealth between debtors and creditors, as emphasized by Fisher (1933) and Tobin (1980). If debt contracts were uncontingent and nominal, and if an unexpected increase in the money supply increased the nominal price level, then it would reduce the real burden of outstanding debt.

which later yield fruit. Land does not depreciate, but trees do. As the farmer must replenish his stock of trees by planting more fruit, the planted fruit can be thought of as investment. We shall see that aggregate investment is always positive, and fluctuates together with aggregate output and land price. Trees are assumed to be specific to the farmer who planted them, and so, we shall argue, cannot be used as collateral—unlike the land on which they are grown. Farmers' debt/asset ratios are thus reduced, which weakens the leverage effect. The contemporaneous response of the economy to a shock is less dramatic, but there is more persistence. We further show that the presence of the uncollateralized trees causes there to be greater movement in land price, relative to quantities.

The second substantive change we make to the model of Section II is that in each period only a fraction of the farmers have an investment opportunity. The other farmers are unable to invest, and instead use their revenues partially to pay off their debts. Ex post, then, farmers are heterogeneous. The probabilistic investment assumption simply captures the idea that, at the level of the individual enterprise, investment in fixed assets is typically occasional and lumpy.[19] Since it is no longer the case that all farmers are borrowing up to their credit limits, in aggregate the value of the farmers' debt repayments is strictly smaller than the value of their collateralized asset, land. We shall see that this uncoupling of the farmers' aggregate borrowing from their aggregate landholdings allows for rich dynamic interactions among q_t, K_t, and B_t, and can lead to cycles.

To understand the specifics of the model, consider a particular farmer. We say that his land is *cultivated* if he has trees growing on it. If he works on k_{t-1} units of cultivated land at date $t - 1$, he will produce ak_{t-1} tradable fruit and ck_{t-1} nontradable fruit at date t—just as in Section II. A fraction $1 - \lambda$ of the trees are assumed to die by date t, and so this part of the land is no longer cultivated. This does not mean that the land cannot be used; it may be used by gatherers, or it may be cultivated again, possibly by another farmer.

In order to increase his holding of cultivated land at date t from λk_{t-1}, to k_t, the farmer must plant $\phi(k_t - \lambda k_{t-1})$ fruit, as well as acquire $k_t - k_{t-1}$ more land.[20] However, we assume that a new investment opportunity to plant fruit arises only with probability π. With probability $1 - \pi$, the farmer is unable to invest, so the scale of his operations is limited to λk_{t-1} and (in equilibrium) he sells off the $(1 - \lambda)k_{t-1}$ uncultivated land. We assume that the arrival of investment opportunities

---

[19] For empirical evidence on this, see, e.g. Doms and Dunn (1994). Investment by individual firms may be lumpy because of fixed costs—an idea that clearly warrants a full analysis. However, in the interests of keeping our aggregate model simple, we rely on the assumption of a probabilistic investment opportunity.

[20] Formally, the farmers have a one-period Leontief Production function. There are two inputs, land and trees, in 1 : 1 fixed proportion. There are four outputs: land, trees, tradable fruit, and nontradable fruit, in fixed proportions $1 : \lambda : a : c$. In addition, the farmers have an instantaneous technology for growing trees: ϕ fruit make one tree.

is independent both across farmers and through time (hence, because there is a continuum of farmers, there is no aggregate uncertainty).[21]

We make three assumptions about the parameters. In Assumption 4, the tradable output is at least enough to replant the depreciated trees.

ASSUMPTION 4. $a > (1 - \lambda)\phi$.

In Assumption 5, the arrival rate of an investment opportunity is not too small.

ASSUMPTION 5. $\pi > 1 - (1/R)$.

Finally, Assumption 2' strengthens Assumption 2.

ASSUMPTION 2'.

$$c > \frac{1 - \beta R\lambda(1 - \pi)}{\beta R \left[\lambda\pi + (1 - \lambda)(1 - R + \pi R)\right]} \left(\frac{1}{\beta - 1}\right)(a + \lambda\phi).$$

Notice that Assumptions 5 and 2' are both weak assumptions, given that β and R are typically close to one.

We suppose that each farmer grows his own specific trees, and only he has the skill necessary for them to bear fruit (the other farmers do not know how to prune them). This means that, a farmer having sunk the cost (in terms of fruit) of growing trees, there is a wedge between the inside value to him of his cultivated land and the outside value of the land to everyone else. Also, we continue to assume that a farmer's specific human capital is inalienable: he cannot precommit to tending his trees. And so, from the argument given earlier, we deduce that creditors will be unwilling to lend beyond the limit in (3). That is, only land can serve as collateral.

The rest of the model is exactly the same as in Section II. To sum up, we have made two changes to the basic model. First, the farmer's flow-of-funds constraint (4) now includes the investment in trees, $\phi(k_t - \lambda k_{t-1})$:

$$q_t(k_t - k_{t-1}) + \phi(k_t - \lambda k_{t-1}) + Rb_{t-1} + x_t - ck_{t-1} = ak_{t-1} + b_t. \qquad (20)$$

Second, at each date t, with probability $1 - \pi$, a farmer may now face the additional technological constraint $k_t \leq \lambda k_{t-1}$.

It is worth observing that, at the risk of laboring the exposition, we could have made these changes one at a time. We could have introduced trees into the model without introducing heterogeneity ($\phi > 0$, $\pi = 1$). Equally, we could have introduced heterogeneity into the model without introducing trees ($\pi < 1$, $\phi = 0$). Later we shall isolate the particular contributions that π and ϕ make to the dynamics of the model.

---

[21] An alternative, possibly more natural, specification of the depreciation process is that the *entire stock* of trees of an individual farmer dies with probability $1 - \lambda$, and survives with probability λ. (For example, there may be a storm or a disease.) These shocks are independent across farmers and through time, and are also independent of the arrival of investment opportunities. In aggregate, this alternative specification leads to the same equilibrium paths as the model in the text.

To characterize equilibrium, we need to examine the farmers' behavior. Start with a farmer who can invest at date t. We claim that he will choose to borrow up to the maximum and invest in land, consuming no more than his current output of nontradable fruit. Specifically, we claim that, in the neighborhood of the steady-state equilibrium, by Assumption 1 it is strictly better for the farmer to invest than to save, and by Assumption 2' it is strictly better for him to invest than to consume. (For a proof of these claims, see n. 22 below.) That is, the credit constraint (3) is binding, and $x_t = ck_{t-1}$; so it follows from (20) that

$$k_t = \frac{1}{\phi + q_t - 1/R(q_{t+1})} \left[(a + q_t + \lambda_\phi)k_{t-1} - Rb_{t-1} \right] \qquad (21)$$

The term is brackets is the farmer's net worth, which, as we define it, includes the replacement cost of the λk_{t-1} trees inherited from date $t-1$. (The liquidation value of his assets would exclude the $\lambda \phi k_{t-1}$ term since the trees have no public value.) The investing farmer uses his net worth to finance the difference between the unit cost of investment, $\phi + q_t$, and the amount he can borrow against a unit of land, q_{t+1}/R.

Next consider a farmer who cannot invest at date t. We claim that he will choose not to divest, that is, he will set

$$k_t = \lambda k_{t-1}; \qquad (22)$$

and, by Assumption 2', he will use his tradable output, ak_{t-1}, together with his receipts from land sales, $q_t(1 - \lambda)k_{t-1}$, to pay off his debt rather than consume more than the bruised fruit ck_{t-1}.[22,23]

---

[22] To prove these claims, we again appeal to the principle of unimprovability and consider only single deviations at date t. At the start of any subsequent date—after harvest, but before we know whether there is an investment opportunity at that date—let $V(L, T)$ denote a farmer's steady-state expected discounted utility, where L denotes the liquidation (i.e. public) value of his assets, and T denotes his tree holding. Since trees die at the rate $1 - \lambda$, we deduce that he must have cultivated T/λ land at the previous date, and will thus have a harvest of aT/λ tradable fruit and cT/λ nontradable fruit. The liquidation value L comprises the tradable fruit harvest, together with the value of the land (without trees), net of debt repayments. Assuming that from date $t + 1$ onward the farmer uses the strategy given in the text, we can solve for $V(L, T)$ from the Bellman equation

$$V(L, T) \equiv \frac{cT}{\lambda} + \beta \pi V \left(a \frac{L + \phi T}{\phi + u^*}, \lambda \frac{L + \phi T}{\phi + u^*} \right) + \beta(1 - \pi)V(RL + aT - Ru^*T, \lambda T),$$

where u^* is the steady-state user cost of land (see [25a] below). The value function $V(L, T)$ takes the linear form $L\alpha_L + T\alpha_T$, where the constants α_L and α_T are found by the method of undermined coefficients. Now consider the farmer's choices at date t. On the one hand, suppose that he has an investment opportunity. If he uses his marginal unit of tradable fruit as a down payment for investment, then he gains an expected discounted utility $[\beta a/(\phi + u^*)]\alpha_L + [\beta \lambda/(\phi + u^*)]\alpha_T$. If he saves, he gains $\beta R\alpha_L$. If he consumes, he gains one. It can be shown that, by Assumption 1, investment strictly dominates saving; and, by Assumption 2', investment strictly dominates consumption. On the other hand, suppose that the farmer cannot invest at date t. Then he will strictly prefer to save rather than to consume his marginal unit of tradable fruit if $\beta R\alpha_L > 1$. It can be shown that this also in implied by Assumption 2'. Divestment is not optimal, since, inter alia, the farmer would waste his trees.

[23] Note that a noninvesting farmer's new level of indebtedness is given by $Rb_{t-1} - ak_{t-1} - q_t(1 - \lambda)k_{t-1}$. We need to show that the farmer *can* borrow this much. With Assumption 5, it is

Expressions (21) and (22) have the great virtue that they are linear in k_{t-1} and b_{t-1}. Hence we can aggregate across farmers and appeal to the law of large numbers to derive the equations of motion for the farmers' aggregate landholding and borrowing, K_t and B_t, without having to keep track of the distribution of the individual farmers' k_t's and b_t's. Since the population of farmers is unity, with a fraction π investing and a fraction $1 - \pi$ not investing, we have

$$
\begin{aligned}
K_t =& (1 - \pi)\lambda K_{t-1} \\
&+ \frac{\pi}{\phi + q_t - \frac{1}{R}q_{t+1}}[(a + q_t + \lambda\phi)K_{t-1} - RB_{t-1}].
\end{aligned} \tag{23}
$$

And since no farmer consumes more than his nontradable output, we deduce from the flow-of-funds constraint (20) that

$$
B_t = RB_{t-1} + q_t(K_t - K_{t-1}) + \phi(K_t - \lambda K_{t-1}) - aK_{t-1}. \tag{24}
$$

Notice that (23) and (24) generalize (9) and (10) to the case in which $\phi > 0$ and $\pi < 1$.

The land market-clearing condition for the user cost $u_t = q_t - (q_{t+1}/R)$, equation (12), is unchanged. Thus, for predetermined levels of the farmers' landholding and debt, at the previous date, K_{t-1} and B_{t-1}, an equilibrium from date t onward is characterized by the path of land price, farmers' landholding, and debt, $\{(q_{t+s}, K_{t+s}, B_{t+s})|s \geq 0\}$, satisfying (12), (23), and (24) at dates $t, t+1, t+2, \dots$. These equations constitute a first-order nonlinear system. There is a unique steady state, (q^*, K^*, B^*), with associated steady-state user cost u^*, where

$$
\frac{R-1}{R}q^* = u^* = \frac{\pi a - (1 - \lambda)(1 - R + \pi R)\phi}{\lambda\pi + (1 - \lambda)(1 - R + \pi R)}, \tag{25a}
$$

$$
\frac{1}{R}G'\left[\frac{1}{m}(\bar{K} - K^*)\right] = u^*, \tag{25b}
$$

$$
B^* = \frac{1}{R-1}(a - \phi + \lambda\phi)K^*. \tag{25c}
$$

Assumptions 4 and 5 ensure that these steady-state values are positive.

straightforward to confirm that, in the neighborhood of the steady-state equilibrium, the borrowing constraint (3) is always strictly satisfied. This is equivalent to saying that the farmer's landholding after he has been forced to shrink it back (the right-hand side of [22]) is strictly less than what it would have been had he been able to invest (the right-hand side of [21]). In fact, if by chance an individual farmer has a long history of no opportunity to invest, he may eventually become a net creditor (i.e. his b_t may become negative)—whereas his landholding is always positive and is declining geometrically at the rate λ.

To examine the dynamics, we linearize around the steady state.[24]

We continue to assume Assumption 3, to rule out exploding bubbles in the land price. It can be shown that one eigenvalue equals $R > 1$, which corresponds to an explosive path; and that the other two eigenvalues will be stable and complex if

$$\eta^- < \eta < \eta^+,$$

where

$$\eta^+, \eta^- \equiv R(1 - \pi)\theta$$

$$\times \left[\frac{\sqrt{\lambda^2 \pi + \lambda(1 - \lambda)(1 - R + \pi R)} \pm \sqrt{\lambda^2 \pi - (1 - \lambda)^2}}{1 - \lambda R(1 - \pi)} \right]^2$$

and $\theta \equiv u^*(\phi + u^*)$, the steady-state ratio of the user cost of land to the farmers' required down payment per unit of investment. (Note that $0 < \theta < 1$. In Section II, θ was unity.) From now on, we assume that the condition above holds. The argument of the first square root is positive by Assumption 5; and the argument of the second square root will be positive insofar as λ is close to one. If π is not too close to zero or one, then there is little difficulty in meeting the condition.

We take the land price to be a jump variables so that the vectors $(q_{t+s}, K_{t+s}, B_{t+s})'$, $s = 0, 1, \ldots$, lie on a two-dimensional stable manifold. For the linear approximation, this stable manifold, expressed in terms of proportional deviations from the steady state, is a plane

$$\hat{q}_{t+s} = \mu_K \hat{K}_{t+s} - \mu_B \hat{B}_{t+s}, \tag{26}$$

where $\mu_k > 0$ and $\mu_B > 0$.[25] Within the stable manifold, the system exhibits damped oscillations, and decays at the rate

$$1 - \sqrt{\frac{\lambda R(1 - \pi)}{1 + \dfrac{\theta}{\eta}(1 - \lambda + \lambda\pi)}}. \tag{27}$$

The intuition for why the system cycles can best be understood by using (26) to reduce the dimensionality of the linearized system from three to two:

$$\begin{pmatrix} \hat{K}_{t+s} \\ \hat{B}_{t+s} \end{pmatrix} = \begin{pmatrix} + & - \\ + & ? \end{pmatrix} \begin{pmatrix} \hat{K}_{t+s-1} \\ \hat{B}_{t+s-1} \end{pmatrix} \quad \text{for } s \geq 1. \tag{28}$$

---

[24] For details of what follows, see the appendix of Kiyotaki and Moore (1995).

[25] Specifically,

$$\mu_k = \frac{\pi(\phi + q^*)}{\eta(1 - \lambda + \lambda\pi)(\phi + u^*)} \quad \text{and} \quad \mu_B = \frac{\pi B^*}{\eta(1 - \lambda + \lambda\pi)(\phi + u^*)K^*}.$$

For $s = 0$, (26) generalizes (16) from Section II; here $\hat{B}_t$ enters separately from $\hat{K}_t$, because in aggregate the farmers' debt repayment is no longer tied to the value of their landholdings. Notice that, on the stable manifold, $\hat{q}_{t+s}$ is an increasing function of $\hat{K}_{t+1}$ and a deceasing function of $\hat{B}_{t+s}$.

From the sign pattern of the reduced-from transition matrix in (28), we see that our model is closely related to the predator–prey model discussed in the Introduction.[26] The farmers' debts B_{t+s-1} play the role of predator, and their landholdings K_{t+s-1} act as prey. A rise in $\overline{K}_{t+s-1}$ means that farmers inherit more land at date $t+s$, which enables them to borrow more ($\partial B_{t+s}/\partial K_{t+s-1} > 0$). However, a rise in B_{t+s-1} implies that farmers have a greater debt overhang at date $t+s$, which restricts their ability to expand ($\partial K_{t+s}/\partial B_{t+s-1} < 0$). As the simulations below will demonstrate, this type of system tends to exhibit not only large but also persistent oscillations when hit by a shock.[27]

As in Section II, consider the impact of a small, unanticipated, temporary productivity shock Δ at date t. Prior to date t, the economy is in the steady state: $K_{t-1} = K^*$ and $B_{t-1} = B^*$. Using (26) with $s = 0$, we can solve simultaneously for $\hat{q}_t$, $\hat{K}_t$, and $\hat{B}_t$ to obtain

$$\hat{q}_t = \frac{1}{\eta} \frac{\lambda\pi + (1-\lambda)(1-R+\pi R)}{1 - \lambda + \lambda\pi} \frac{a}{a+\lambda\phi}\Delta \qquad (29)$$

and

$$\hat{K}_t = \frac{1}{1 + (\theta/\eta)(1 - \lambda + \lambda\pi)} \left(1 + \frac{R}{R-1} \frac{\pi}{1 - \lambda + \lambda\pi} \frac{\theta}{\eta}\right) \qquad (30)$$
$$\times [\lambda\pi + (1-\lambda)(1-R+\pi R)] \frac{a}{a+\lambda\phi}\Delta.^{28}$$

Much of the discussion of the basic model in Section II carries over.

In percentage terms, the impact on the land price, given by (29), is of the same order of magnitude as the temporary shock Δ. And the impact on the farmers' landholdings (and hence on aggregate fruit output) is large. The multiplier in (30) can be significant because of the leverage effect: a 1 percent rise in land price increases the farmers' aggregate net worth by $[R/(R-1)][\pi/(1 - \lambda + \lambda\pi)]\theta$ percent. This is not as large as in Section II, but still can be considerably larger than unity.

---

[26] The expression for this matrix can be found in the appendix of Kiyotaki and Moore (1995).

[27] While we are concerned here with how the model behaves in the neighborhood of the steady state, it should be borne in mind that predator–prey models typically have interesting global properties, such as limit cycles. We have not investigated the nonlinear dynamics of our model, although the simulations we report below pertain to the full non-linear model, not to the linear approximation.

A difference between (28) and a classic predatory–prey model is that one of the diagonal entries of the transition matrix in (28) may be negative: the partial effect of B_{t+s-1} on B_{t+s} is ambiguous, because the direct positive effect of rolling over debt from date $t+s-1$ may be dominated by indirect negative effects. These indirect effects come through the negative impact an increase in B_{t+s-1} has on farmers' net worth at date $t+s$—and hence on their land demand and the land price. Also, there is no counterpart to the forward-looking land price in the classic predator–prey model, which is backward-looking.

[28] The expression for $\hat{B}_t$ is given in the appendix of Kiyotaki and Moore (1995). Notice that (29) and (30) generalize (17) and (18) from Section II to the case in which $\phi > 0$ and $\pi < 1$.

Let us consider the roles of π and ϕ in turn. From (29) and (30), the contemporaneous responses are dampened by π—understandably, given that not all the farmers can immediately adjust their investment at date t to respond to the shock. However, after date t, when other farmers have investment opportunities, the effects of the shock can continue to build up. See the simulations below. (This is in contrast to Section II, where decay starts immediately.) Moreover, the effects last longer: from (27), the decay rate is smaller when π is smaller, as long as trees are not too costly.[29]

From (29) and (30), the contemporaneous responses are dampened also by ϕ, because the farmers' net worth at date t includes the value of the trees inherited from date $t - 1$, and so there is less leverage. However, the effects are more persistent: from (27), the decay rate is a decreasing function of ϕ. The reason is that ϕ reduces the choking-off effect at all dates $t + s, s \geq 0$: the required down payment per unit of land comprises the user cost u_{t+s} *and* the cost of trees, and so the farmers' land demand is less sensitive to a rise in u_{t+s}. (It is tantamount to an increase in the elasticity of the residual supply of land to the farmers from η to η/θ.) Greater persistence in turn means that a given shock to land usage at date t has a bigger impact on the land price: from (29) and (30), the ratio $\hat{q}_t/\hat{K}_t$ increases with ϕ. In other words, ϕ shifts the action from quantities to asset prices.[30]

Simulations

A number of questions remain concerning the cyclical response the economy. What is the periodicity of the cycle? Following a shock, do prices and quantities continue to build up? If so, in what order do they peak? Which are lead and lag indicators? What are the cumulative movements over the first and second halves of the cycle? Although analytical answers to these questions could be provided (with increasing difficulty), it is more sensible at this point to turn to numerical simulations. Note that, with shooting methods, our simulations pertain to the full *nonlinear* model.[31]

---

[29] The decay rate is smaller when π is smaller if and only if

$$ a > \left[1 + (R - 1)(1 - \lambda) \left(\frac{1 - \pi}{\pi} \right)^2 \right] (1 - \lambda)\phi, $$

which is a slightly stronger condition than Assumption 4.

[30] For further analysis of the model with $\phi > 0$ and $\pi = 1$, see Kiyotaki and Moore (1995, sec. 4). For this special case, there is geometric decay, as in the basic model: the condition at the top of p. 234 does not hold.

[31] The algorithm is first to use (12), (23), and (24) to solve for (K_t, b_t, q_{t+1}) as a function of (K_{t-1}, B_{t-1}, q_t). Then we iterate to give the mapping from q_t to q_{t+T}. Finally, we find the value of q_t such that $q_{t+T} = q^*$ for large T. We are thus able to confirm that the linear approximations are reasonably accurate. See Kiyotaki and Moore (1995, sec. 5) for details.

We select parameter values that might accord with a quarterly model: $R = 1.01$, equivalent to a 4 percent annual real interest rate; $\lambda = .975$, equivalent to a 10 percent annual depreciation rate of trees; and $u(K) \equiv K - v$, where the intercept v is set to make η, the elasticity of the residual supply of land to farmers, equal to 10 percent in the steady state. Normalizing $a = 1$, we choose $\overline{K}$ so that, in the steady, the farmers use two-thirds of the total land stock. Let $\pi = 0.1$; that is, the average interval between investments for a farmer is 2.5 years.

Define the aggregate debt/asset ration as $B_t/[(q_t + \phi)K_t]$ for the entire farming sector; and define the marginal debt/asset ratio as $q_{t+1}/[R(q_t + \phi)]$, for a farmer who is investing in period t. We set $\phi = 20$, so that the steady-state values of these debt/asset ratios are 63 percent and 71 percent, respectively.

Consider an unanticipated, temporary productivity shock $\Delta = 0.01$ in period 1. That is, there is a 1 percent increase in quarterly output of all the farmers and gatherers. Prior to the shock, the economy is in the steady state. In Figure 3 we present the simulation results for q_t/q^*, K_t/K^*, and B_t/B^*—the ratios of the land price, the farmers' aggregate landholding, and their aggregate debt to their respective steady-state values.

The contemporaneous effect of the shock is to increase the land price by 0.37 percent, and the farmers' landholding and debt by 0.10 percent and 0.13 percent. A 0.37 percent increase in the land price may not appear large, but it is much larger than it would be in a standard competitive model without credit

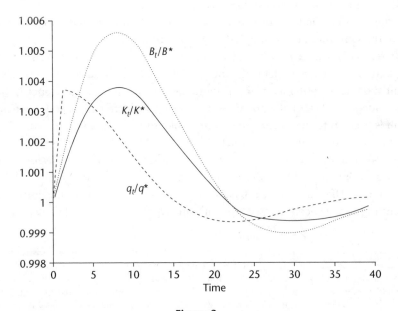

Figure 3.

constraints.[32] The effects on the farmers' landholding and debt build up thereafter. By period 7 they peak, at 0.37 percent and 0.55 percent. The length of the
cycle is about 40 periods, or 10 years. Land price peaks at the time of the shock;
that is, land price leads by seven quarters.

The movement in aggregate fruit output depends on the size of parameter c.[33]
We set $c = 1$, so the maximum savings rate of an individual farmer is 50 percent. Output is 1 percent higher than the steady state in period 1: this is simply
the direct effect of the productivity shock. The sum of the increases in output
between period 2 and the midpoint of the cycle (period 22) is 1.79 percent, which
exceeds the direct effect in period 1. The sum of the decreases in output over the
second half of the cycle is 0.35 percent.

In section 5 of Kiyotaki and Moore (1995), we report on simulations for other
parameter values. In particular, we find that a lower π or a higher ϕ leads to
smaller contemporaneous effects, more persistence, longer cycles, and more
volatility in prices relative to quantities.

IV. Spillovers

As the model is constructed, there cannot be any positive spillovers between the
farming and gathering sectors, since their combined land usage must always sum
to $\overline{K}$. In order to study spillover effects, we make an extension to the basic model
of Section II so that it has two farming sectors, 1 and 2.

Suppose that there are different types of fruit. Gatherers make regular fruit,
with the same production function as before. Farmers, however, produce slightly
differentiated fruit. The farming technology is very similar to that in Section II.
In sector $i = 1$ or 2, a farmer with land k_{it-1} at date $t-1$ produces $a_i k_{it-1}$ tradable
fruit at date t, together with $c_i k_{it-1}$ nontradable fruit. The only difference is that
the tradable fruit is peculiar to that sector. The only difference is that the tradable
fruit is peculiar to that sector. The nontradable fruit is equivalent to regular fruit
in consumption value to the farmer.

We assume that consuming a bundle comprising x_{1t} fruit from sector 1 and
x_{2t} fruit from sector 2 is equivalent to consuming x_t regular fruit, where $x_t^{1-\epsilon} =
x_{1t}^{1-\epsilon} + x_{2t}^{1-\epsilon}$. The parameter $\epsilon > 0$ is the inverse of the elasticity of substitution in
consumption between the two types of fruit. We take ϵ to be small: any positive

---

[32] Recall that in a standard competitive model, the period 1 land price would not increase at all,
because the shock does not affect the future. Alternatively, one might consider the possibility that,
although the shock is announced in period 1, it will not happen until period 2—in which case the
period 1 land price would increase only in the order of the net real interest rate, 0.01 percent.

[33] The parameter c has no effect on the dynamics of q_t, K_t, and B_t as long as it satisfies
Assumption 2'.

value will pin down the size of each farming sector in equilibrium, and ensure that neither sector disappears.[34]

Let regular fruit be the numeraire good. Then at date t, the competitive price, p_{it} say, of fruit from farming sector i is equal to the marginal rate of substitution:

$$p_{it} = (a_i K_{it-1})^{-\epsilon} \left[(a_1 K_{1t-1})^{1-\epsilon} + (a_2 K_{2t-1})^{1-\epsilon} \right]^{\epsilon/(1-\epsilon)} \quad \text{for } i = 1, 2, \qquad (31)$$

where K_{it-1} denotes the aggregate landholding of the farmers in sector i at date $t - 1$.

As in (9), the aggregate landholding of the farmers in sector i at date t is given by

$$K_{it} = \frac{1}{q_t - \frac{1}{R} q_{t+1}} [(a_i p_{it} + q_t) K_{it-1} - R B_{it-1}] \quad \text{for } i = 1, 2, \qquad (32)$$

where B_{it-1} denotes their aggregate debt at date $t - 1$. (The only substantive difference between [32] and [9] is that the tradable fruit output $a_i K_{it-1}$ is priced at p_{it} rather than at unity.) And as in (10), the aggregate debt of the farmers in sector i at date t is given by

$$B_{it} = \frac{1}{R} q_{t+1} K_{it} \quad \text{for } i = 1, 2. \qquad (33)$$

The land market equilibrium condition is the same as (12), except that the farmers' landholdings from the two sectors are added together:

$$q_t - \frac{1}{R} q_{t+1} = u(K_{1t} + K_{2t}). \qquad (34)$$

For given levels of K_{it-1} and B_{it-1}, $i = 1, 2$, an equilibrium from date t onward is characterized by a sequence $\{(q_{t+s}, p_{it+s}, K_{it+s}, B_{it+s}) | s \geq 0, i = 1, 2\}$ satisfying equations (31), (32), (33), and (34) at dates $t, t+1, t+2, \ldots$.[35]

Let us consider the impulse response to a sector-specific technology shock. Suppose that the economy is in the steady state at date $t - 1$, and, for simplicity, suppose that $a_1 = a_2 = a$. As the two farming sectors are symmetric, the steady state is described by (13) with $K_1^* = K_2^* = K^*/2$ and $B_1^* = B_2^* = B^*/2$. At the start of date t there is an unanticipated, temporary increase in the output of *sector 1 only*: the harvest of the farmers in sector 1 is $1 + \Delta$ times the expected levels.

---

[34] If the products of the two farming sectors were perfect substitutes ($\epsilon = 0$), then the sector with the higher productivity would eventually take over the whole market—unless $a_1 = a_2$, in which case the sizes of the sectors would be indeterminate.

[35] We continue to make Assumptions 1 and 3 and a suitably modified version of Assumption 2:

$$c_i > 2^{\epsilon/(1-\epsilon)} \left(\frac{1}{\beta} - 1 \right) a_i \quad \text{for } i = 1, 2.$$

(The factor $2^{\epsilon/(1-\epsilon)}$ here is the steady-state value of p_{it}, in the symmetric case $a_1 = a_2$.)

We can follow the argument of Section II to show that, for a small shock Δ, the proportional changes in the land price, $\hat{q}_t$, and the farmers' combined land-holdings, $\hat{K}_{1t} + \hat{K}_{2t}$, are half those given by (17) and (18), respectively—simply because only half of the farmers experience the shock.

Our main concern is to see how the effects of the sector-specific shock are divided across the sectors:

$$\hat{K}_{1t} = \left[1 + \frac{1}{2(R-1)(1+\eta)} - \frac{\epsilon}{2} \right] \Delta \tag{35a}$$

and

$$\hat{K}_{2t} = \left[\frac{1}{2(R-1)(1+\eta)} + \frac{\epsilon}{2} \right] \Delta. \tag{35b}$$

The first term in the brackets in (35a) is the direct impact of the productivity shock on the farmers in sector 1. However, given R close to one, this first term is dwarfed by the second term, the indirect effect on the farmers' land demand arising from the change in their net worth caused by the jump in the land price. But this indirect benefit is enjoyed by the farmers in the other sector: (35b) is almost as large as (35a). in other words, because all the farmers hold land, the immediate spillover effect is significantly positive. (The $\epsilon/2$ terms in [35] represent demand linkage: expansion in sector 1 is partially offset by a fall in product price p_{1t}, which boosts sector 2's demand and product price p_{2t}.)

Thereafter, the changes in the farmers' landholdings in each of the sectors follow the two-sector analogue of (15b): for $s \geq 1$,

$$\begin{pmatrix} \hat{K}_{1t+s} \\ \hat{K}_{2t+s} \end{pmatrix} = \begin{pmatrix} 1 - \dfrac{1}{2(1+\eta)} - \dfrac{\epsilon}{2} & -\dfrac{1}{2(1+\eta)} + \dfrac{\epsilon}{2} \\ -\dfrac{1}{2(1+\eta)} + \dfrac{\epsilon}{2} & 1 - \dfrac{1}{2(1+\eta)} - \dfrac{\epsilon}{2} \end{pmatrix} \begin{pmatrix} \hat{K}_{1t+s-1} \\ \hat{K}_{2t+s-1} \end{pmatrix}. \tag{36}$$

Here the $-1/2(1+\eta)$ terms reflect the choking-off effect we identified in Section II. That is, an increase in the demand for land by either farming sector causes the market-clearing user cost of land to rise, which partially chokes off demand in both sectors. This leads to a negative spillover between sectors after date t: for small ϵ (negligible demand linkage), the off-diagonal entries in the transition matrix in (36) are negative. Crucially, however, the diagonal entries are positive—reflecting the fact that an increase in the landholdings of a farming sector at date $t + s - 1$ increases those farmers' net worth, and hence their land demand, at date $t + s$. Overall, the implication of (36) is that the initial increases $\hat{K}_{1t}$ and $\hat{K}_{2t}$ persist; and the two sectors comove after a shock, at least for a time.[36]

---

[36] The eigenvalues of the transition matrix in (36) are $\eta/(1+\eta)$ and $1 - \epsilon$, which both lie between zero and one.

V. Related Literature and Final Remarks

The ideas in this chapter can be traced at least as far back as Veblen (1904, chap. 5), who described the positive interactions between asset prices and collateralized borrowing. Since the theoretical literature on financial structure and aggregate economic activity is vast, it would be unwise to attempt to review it here. We have picked out for discussion two papers that directly relate to out ideas.[37]

Bernanke and Gertler (1989) construct an overlapping generations model in which financial market imperfections cause temporary shocks in net worth to be amplified and to persist.[38] All agents earn a wage when young, which they then invest for their old age. Some agents—entrepreneurs—have access to projects, which require outside finance over and above the inside finance their own labor income provides. Because project returns can be verified only at a cost, financial contracts are imperfect, and so only a limited number of the better projects are funded. The projects that do go ahead provide employment for the next generation of young agents. In this economy, a positive technology shock both increases the labor demanded by the entrepreneurs who have been funded, and allows for more projects to be undertaken. Moreover, the accompanying rise in wage improves the financial position of the next generation of entrepreneurs, so more of their projects will be funded too, they will subsequently demand more labor, and so on.

Aside from matters of modeling strategy,[39] our model adds quite a kick to the Bernanke and Gertler story. At business cycle frequencies, a major channel for shocks to net worth is through changes in the values of firms' assets or liabilities. Asset prices reflect future market conditions. When the effects of a shock persist (as they do in Bernanke and Gertler), the cumulative impact on asset prices, and hence on net worth at the time of the shock, can be significant. This positive feedback through asset prices, and the associated intertemporal multiplier process, are the key innovations in our paper.

The two-way feedback between borrowing limits and the price of assets connects with the paper by Shleifer and Vishny (1992) on debt capacity. They argue that when a firm in financial distress liquidates assets, the natural purchasers are other firms in the same industry. But if one firm is experiencing hard times, it is likely that other firms in the industry will be too, and so demand for liquidated assets will be lower. The concomitant fall in asset price exacerbates the problem by lowering the debt capacity of all the firms. The essentially static nature of

---

[37] For more on related papers, see Kiyotaki and Moore (1995). Gertler (1988) has written an excellent survey that not only identifies and clarifies the broader issues, but also provides an account of the historical developments.

[38] Greenwald and Stiglitz have pursued a similar line of inquiry; see, e.g., their 1993 paper.

[39] We think that a model of debt that is based on control over assets, rather than on the cost of verifying project returns, is mover compelling (and considerably simpler, especially when extended to more than two periods; see Gertler [1992]). For a comparison of these two approaches, see the appendix to chap. 5 of Hart (1995).

this argument—which is akin to the static multiplier process we identified in the Introduction—misses the more important dynamic multiplier process, and the crucial interplay between amplification and persistence.[40]

There is some empirical evidence to support the view that investment decisions are not solely determined by the net present value of new projects, but are also affected by an investing firm's balance sheet position and the value of its collateralized assets (see, e.g. Fazzari, Hubbard, and Petersen 1988; Evans and Jovanovic 1989; Hoshi, Kashyap, and Scharfstein 1991; Hubbard and Kashyap 1992; Whited 1992; Gertler and Gilchirst 1994; Holtz-Eakin, Joulfaian, and Rosen 1994; Gilchirst and Himmelberg 1995; Black, de Meza, and Jeffreys 1996). At the aggregate level, a number of studies have highlighted the importance of credit constraints in explaining fluctuations in activity; see in particular Bernanke (1983), Eckstein and Sinai (1986), and Friedman (1986).

The pressing next step in the research is to construct a fully fledged stochastic model, in which a shock is not a zero probability event and is rationally anticipated. In the chapter we constructed a model of a dynamic economy that, at the aggregate level, is deterministic; and we then hit the economy with an unexpected temporary shock. Although this approach succeeds in keeping the analysis tractable, it skirts around some central issues. The key question is, To what extent can *contingent* debt contracts be written? There are a number of explanations for why it may be impossible to condition debt repayments on idiosyncratic shocks. For example, such shocks may not be observable to outsiders, such as the courts (see Hart and Moore 1996).[41] However, it is less clear why the terms of a contract cannot be made sensitive to aggregate events, such as movements in the price of land or in the interest rate. This is a difficult matter to resolve.

Let us turn to less thorny issues. A weakness of our model is that it provides no analysis of who becomes credit constrained, and when. We merely rely on the assumption that different agents have different technologies. One can instead assume that all agents have access to a common, concave technology, but differ in their levels of accumulated wealth. Ortalo-Magné (1996)

---

[40] A similar remark can be made with regard to the two-period multiple equilibrium models of Kashyap, Scharfstein, and Weil (1990) and Lamout (1995).

We should mention two other papers that relate to ours. Stein (1995) analyzes trading in the housing market and shows that, because of leverage, an increase in the price of housing can increase net worth by more than the required down payment, leading to an increase in the demand for houses. That is, as in our model, asset demand schedules can slope upward. Although Stein's model is not dynamic, his paper provides an interesting explanation for the observed correlation between price and trading volume in the housing market.

Scheinkman and Weiss (1986) construct a dynamic general equilibrium model in which a durable, nonproduced asset serves as a means for precautionary saving. In their model, only the net positions of agents matter: there are no leverage effects. By contrast, in our model the asset provides security for borrowing. And because an agent needs the asset in order to produce, he holds a levered position— which make his net worth very vulnerable to changes in the asset price.

[41] Even if financial contracts can be written contingent on idiosyncratic shocks, it may not be efficient to diversify risk fully, for standard moral hazard reasons.

constructs a life cycle model of farming and agricultural land prices. Farmers borrow against the landholdings, and are most likely to face borrowing constraints when they are young and relatively poor. As they save and accumulate assets, they become unconstrained.[42]

Finally, it would be interesting to relax the assumption that, the supply side, the credit market is anonymous. In the chapter we have implicitly taken the position that debt contracts can be free traded by creditors—because the value of a debt contract equals the value of the collateral, land, which is priced in a market. However, the identity of the creditor may matter. A particular creditor may have additional information about, or leverage over, a particular borrower, which enables the creditor or lend more. Such debt contracts are unlikely to be tradable at full value. Once anonymity is dropped, the net worth of creditors, and the value of their collateral, start to matter. The interaction between asset markets and credit market that we have highlighted in this chapter will be even richer if both sides of the credit market are affected by changes in the price of their collateralized assets.

APPENDIX

This appendix sketches an overlapping generations version of the basic model of Section II. The main purpose is to show that our two unorthodox modeling choices—the assumption that agents have linear preferences but different discount factors, and the assumption that a fraction of the farmers output is nontradable—can both be dispensed with in an overlapping generations framework.

Consider an economy in which agents die with probability $1 - \sigma$ between one date and the next, and survive with probability σ. Death is independent across agents (there is no aggregate uncertainty), and independent of an agent's age, technology, or net worth. The total population has measure $1 + m$, and comprises farmers and gatherers in ratio $1 : m$. At each date, new farmers and gatherers are born, with populations $1 - \sigma$ and $(1 - \sigma)m$. Newborns are endowed with a small amount, e, of fruit per unit of population.

All fruit is tradable. At each date t, agent maximize the expected discounted utility of fruit consumption, x_{t+s}, conditional on surviving to date $t + s$:

$$E_t \left[\sum_{s=0}^{\infty} (\beta\sigma)^s \ln x_{t+s} \right],$$

---

[42] Firms may well go through similar kinds of life cycles. An alternative to the overlapping generations framework would be to assume that agents face a stochastic technology, as in Scheinkman and Weiss (1986).

where $\beta \in (0, 1)$ is their common discount factor, and $\ln x$, the natural logarithm of x, is their common utility function.

Farmers and gatherers differ only in their technologies. If a farmer invests in $k_t l$ and at date t and survives to date $t + 1$, then, unless he withdraws his labor, the produces ak_t fruit. By contrast, a gatherer cannot withdraw his labor during production: if he invests in k_t' land at date t and survives to $t + 1$, then he produces $G(k_t')$ fruit, per unit of population, where $G' > 0, G'' < 0$, and $G'(0) > a > \sigma a > G'(\overline{K}/m)$. (These last inequalities ensure that in the neighborhood of the steady state, both farmers and gatherers produce.) If an agent dies, there is no fruit output, but the land regions. In what follows, we ignore unanticipated productivity shocks, and just consider perfect-foresight paths.

There is no bequest motive, and so all agents will choose to mortgage their land fully at each date t, by borrowing up to the collateral value. That is, they pay only the down payment

$$u_t = q_t - \frac{1}{R_t} q_{t+1} \qquad (A1)$$

on land, where R_t is the gross rate of interest on debt.

In addition, gatherers may choose to borrow against some or all of their fruit output, since they cannot threaten to withdraw their labor. To this end, an individual gatherer may issue an "annuity" contract: in return for borrowing one unit of fruit at date t, he promises to repay R_t/σ fruit at date $t + 1$ if he survives until then. (The only constraint here is that no gatherer can issue more annuities than can be repaid out of his date $t + 1$ fruit output, $G(k_t')$. In the neighborhood of the steady state, this constraint does not bind.) A wealthy (old) gatherer may choose to *buy* annuities; that is, pay one unit of fruit at date t in order to receive R_t/σ fruit at date $t + 1$ if he survives. Because there is no aggregate uncertainty, the fraction of gatherers who survive is exactly σ; and so, through pooling, no one need be exposed to anyone else's risk.

Farmers cannot precommit not to withdraw their labor, and so cannot credibly issue annuities. Moreover, they will not choose to buy annuities, provided that the return on farming is greater:

$$\frac{1}{u_t} a > \frac{1}{\sigma} R_t. \qquad (A2)$$

We shall show later that (A2) holds in the neighborhood of the steady state.

Since a fraction $1 - \sigma$ of the farmers die between dates $t - 1$ and t, since all land is mortgaged, and since no farmer buys annuities, the net worth the farmers alive at date t equals the surviving farmers' output $\sigma a K_{t-1}$ where K_{t-1} is the aggregate landholding of farmers at the end of date $t - 1$) plus the newborn farmers' endowment $(1 - \sigma)e$. Given logarithmic references, farmers spend a fixed proportion, $1 - \beta\sigma$, of their net worth on consumption. The rest is used as a down payment on land:

$$K_t = \frac{1}{u_t}\beta\sigma[\sigma a K_{t-1} + (1 - \sigma)e]. \tag{A3}$$

Gatherers also spend a fixed proportion $1 - \beta\sigma$ of their net worth on consumption. Aggregating across farmers and gatherers, we can equate consumption demand at date t to total fruit output, Y_t:

$$(1 - \beta\sigma)(Y_t + q_t\overline{K} + mV_t) = Y_t, \tag{A4}$$

where the term in the second set of parentheses is the aggregate net worth of the current population, and V_t is the net worth of a gatherer's technology:

$$V_t = \frac{\sigma}{R_t}G(k_t') - u_t k_t' + \frac{\sigma}{R_t}V_{t+1}. \tag{A5}$$

Here k_t' equates the marginal return on gathering to that on annuities:

$$\frac{1}{u_t}G'(k_t') = \frac{1}{\sigma}R_t. \tag{A6}$$

The land market clears:

$$K_t + mk_t' = \overline{K}. \tag{A7}$$

Total fruit output comprises the output of the surviving farmers and gatherers, plus the endowment of the newborn:

$$Y_t = \sigma a K_{t-1} + \sigma m G\left[\frac{1}{m}(\overline{K} - K_{t-1})\right] + (1 + m)(1 + \sigma)e. \tag{A8}$$

In a stable equilibrium, equations (A1) and (A3)–(A8) hold at each date t, subject to condition (A2), and the expected discounted values of q_{t+1s} and V_{t+s} converge to zero as s tends to infinity.

Denote steady-state values with an asterisk. It is straightforward to show the following proposition.

PROPOSITION. *For small e, there is a unique steady-state equilibrium in which the farmers' credit constraints are binding.*[43] *The equilibrium R^* lies strictly between $1/\beta$ and $1/\beta\sigma$.*

To confirm that condition (A2) is satisfied, notice from (A3) that if the size of the farming sector is to say constant in the steady state, then u^* must equal approximately $\beta\sigma^2 a$ (for small e). Thus, in the neighborhood of the steady state, (A2) reduces to $R^* < 1/\beta\sigma$.

---

[43] There is no steady-state equilibrium in which the farmers' credit constraints are not binding.

There are two important points to observe. First, an individual farmer grows if he survives, because his savings rate times his return on land, $\beta\sigma a$, exceeds the down payment, u^*. However, in aggregate the net worth of the farming sector does not grow because as rich old farmers die they are replaced by poor young ones.

Second, $R^* > 1/\beta$ implies that the return on annuities, R^*/σ, exceeds the effective rate of time preference, $1/\beta\sigma$. Hence a gatherer chooses an upward-sloping path of lifetime consumption, which is the source of loan-able funds in the economy.

Details of how this overlapping generations economy responds to an unanticipated shock can be obtained from the authors. In particular, the model can be used to see how the rate of interest interacts with asset prices and output. We find that a temporary increase in productivity causes the current interest rate to fall, which raises the land price and increases output *more* than in, say, an open economy where the interest rate is constant.[44]

References

Bernanke, B. S. (1983). "Nonmonetary effects of the financial crisis in propagation of the Great Depression." *A.E.R.*, 73: 257–76.

——, and Gertler, M. (1989). "Agency costs, net worth, and business fluctuations." *A.E.R.*, 79: 14–31.

Black, J., de Meza, D., and Jeffreys, D. (1996). "House price, the supply of collateral and the enterprise economy." *Econ. J.*, 106: 60–75.

Das, S. P. (1993). *New Perspectives on Business cycles: An Analysis of Inequality and Heterogeneity.* Aldershot, U.K.: Elgar.

Doms, M., and Dunne, T. (1994). "Capital adjustment patterns in manufacturing plants." Working paper. Washington: U.S. Census Bureau, Center Econ. Studies.

Eckstien, O., and Sinai, A. (1986). "The mechanisms of the business cycle in the Postwar Era" in Robert J. Gordon (ed.), *The American Business Cycle: Continuity and Change* (Chicago: University of Chicago Press (for NBER)).

Evans, D. S., and Jovanovic, B. (1989). "An estimated model of entrepreneurial choice under liquidity constraints." *J.P.E.*, 97: 808–27.

Fazzari, S. M., Hubbard, R. G., and Petersen, B. C. (1988). "Financing constraints and corporate investment." *Brookings Papers Econ. Activity*, no. 1, pp. 141–95.

Fisher, I. (1933). "The debt–deflation theory of great depressions." *Econometrica*, 1: 337–57.

Friedman, B. M. (1986). "Money, credit, and interest rates in the business cycles," in R. J. Gordon (ed.), *The American Business Cycle: Continuity and Change* (Chicago: University of Chicago Press (for NBER)).

---

[44] This is assuming that future interest rates are not too sensitive to changes in current conditions.

Gertler, M. (1988). "Financial structure and aggregate economic activity: An overview." *J. Money, Credit and Banking*, 20(3, pt. 2): 559–88.

—— (1992). "Financial capacity and output fluctuations in an economy with multi-period financial relationships." *Rev. Econ. Studies*, 59: 455–72.

——, and Gilchrist, S. (1994). "Monetary policy, business cycles, and the behavior of small manufacturing firms." *Q.J.E.*, 109: 309–40.

Gilchrist, S., and Himmelberg, C. P. (1995). "Evidence on the role of cash flow for investment." *J. Monetary Econ.*, 36: 541–72.

Greenwald, B., and Stiglitz, J. E. (1998). "Financial market imperfections and business cycles." *Q.J.E.*, 108: 77–114.

Hart, O. (1995). *Contracts, and Financial Structure*. Oxford: Oxford Univ. Press.

——, and Moore, J. (1989). "Default and renegotiation: A dynamic model of debt." Discussion paper. Edinburgh: Univ. Edinburgh. Rev. manuscript. Cambridge, MA.: Harvard Univ., Dept. Econ., 1996.

——, (1994). "A theory of debt based on the inalienability of human capital." *Q.J.E.*, 109: 841–79.

Holtz-Eakin, D., Joulfaian, D., and Rosen, H. S. (1994). "Sticking it out: Entrepreneurial survival and liquidity constraints." *J.P.E.*, 102: 53–75.

Hoshi, T., Kashyap, A. K., and Scharfstein, D. (1991). "Corporate structure, liquidity. and investment: Evidence from Japanese industrial groups." *Q.J.E.*, 106: 33–60.

Hubbard, R. G., and Kashyap, A. K. (1992). "International net worth and the investment process: an application to U.S. agriculture." *J.P.E.*, 100: 506–34.

Kashyap, A. K., Scharfstein, D., and Weil, D. (1990). "The high price of land and the low cost of capital: Theory and evidence from Japan." Manuscript. Cambridge: Massachusetts Inst. Tech.

Kiyotaki, N., and Moore, J. (1995). "Credit cycles." Discussion Paper no.TE/95/255. London: London School Econ., Suntory-Toyota Internat. Centre Econ. and Related Disciplines, 1995; Working Paper no.5083. Cambridge. MA: NBER, April 1995.

Kreps, D. M. (1990). *A Course in Microeconomic Theory*. New York: Harvester Wheatsheaf.

Lamont, O. (1995). "Corporate-debt overhang and macroeconomic expectations." *A.E.R.*, 55: 1106–17.

Ortalo-Magné, F. (1996). "Asset price fluctuations in a lifecycle economy: Do collateral constraints matter?" Discussion Paper no. 234. London: London School Econ., Financial Markets Group, March.

Osborne, M. J., and Rubinstein, A. (1990). *Bargaining and Markets*. San Diego: Academic Press.

Scheinkman, J. A., and Weiss, L. (1986). "Borrowing constraints and aggregate economic activity." *Econometrica*, 54: 23–45.

Shleifer, A., and Vishny, R. W. (1992). "Liquidation values and debt capacity: A market equilibrium approach." *J. Finance*, 47: 1343–66.

Stein, J. C. (1995). "Prices and trading volume in the housing market: A model with down-payment effects." *Q.J.E.*, 110: 379–406.

Tobin, J. (1980). *Asset Accumulation and Economic Activity: Reflections on Contemporary Macroeconomic Theory*. Chicago: University of Chicago Press.

Veblen, T. (1904). *The Theory of Business Enterprise*. New York: Scribner.

Whited, T. M. (1992). "Debt liquidity constraints, and corporate investment: Evidence from panel data." *J. Finance*, 47: 1425–60.

25

Endogenous Cycles in a Stiglitz–Weiss Economy

Javier Suarez and Oren Sussman

1. Introduction

Economic research in recent years has revitalized the idea that financial factors should play a central role in business-cycle theory.[1] On the one hand, there exists a growing body of empirical work showing that financial imperfections affect real economic decisions[2] in a way which varies systematically along the business-cycle. On the other hand, theoretical work—Bernanke and Gertler [2] and more recently Kiyotaki and Moore[20]—shows how transitory shocks are *propagated* via imperfections in financial markets. The novel contribution of this chapter is the modeling of an endogenuous *reversion mechanism*, such that the economy may converge to a two-period equilibrium cycle. The model is kept deliberately simple so as to allow a transparent exposition of the mechanism. Indeed, the model is a dynamic extension of the well-known Stiglitz–Weiss [24] (henceforth SW) model of lending under moral hazard.[3]

Let it be clear that we view the reversion mechanism as a complement to the propagation mechanism. Obviously, it takes both to produce a complete theory of business fluctuations. But further, we use our model to clarify some theoretical issues. First, it is often argued that financial imperfection provide a crucial amplification effect that can solve the "small shocks, large cycles" puzzle

This work was initiated during the 1994 European Summer Symposium in Financial Markets at the Gerzensee Studienzentrum. Earlier versions of this chapter were presented at the CEPR Conference on Macroeconomics and Finance in Gerzensee, 16–20 January 1996, and the V "Tor Vergata" Financial Conference in Rome, 28–29 November 1996. We thank Martin Hellwig, Bengt Holmstorm, and John Moore for extremely helpful comments and suggestions.

[1] Fisher [10] gives one of the first coherent statements; see King [19]. For many years, however, it was ignored: it is not quoted by Patinkin [22], the authoritative handbook of the 1950's and 1960's.

[2] Usually, this literature shows that liquidity effects economic decisions, in contrast to the prediction of the Modigliani–Miller theorem where only net-present value matters. See Bernanke et al. [3] for an up-to-date survey.

[3] SW also contains a, maybe better known, adverse-selection section.

(see Bernanke *et al.* [3]). In our model the amplification effect is dramatic: the variance of external shocks is zero while output fluctuations may still be sizable.

Secondly, in both Bernanke and Gertler [2] and Kiyotaki and Moore [20] the external shock is not anticipated in advance. Hence, agents do not hedge in precaution. It seems, however, that agents who fail to foresee a repeated shock do not have rational expectations. That raises the concern that irrationality is an indispensable ingredient within such a theory. We show that this is not the case. In our model the whole sequence of future prices is rationally (and perfectly) foreseen. Moreover, contracts are "complete" and all relevant information (future prices included) is internalized. To the best of our knowledge our example is the first clear-cut demonstration of a cycle generated solely by financial imperfections, without any modification of the rationality assumption.

More to the point, the issue at hand is that of "indexation." Consider, again, Kiyotaki and Moore [20].[4] The external shock operators *via* a price decline that decreases the value of collateral and, hence, borrowing capacity. It is well known that in that case insurance can easily be provided by price indexation.[5] Since such indexation is mutually beneficial, assuming it away is hard to justify.[6] In our model, the economy slumps due to endogenous reversion and that happens despite the fact that contracts are optimally designed on the basis of a perfect foresight of future prices. It follows that financial factors can affect business fluctuations even without assuming indexation away.

And finally, we use our model in order to clarify the role of a potential stabilizing policy: its existence and welfare evaluation. (Note that it is full rationality and completeness of contracts which open the way for the welfare analysis.) We start the analysis of this part by demonstrating that there exists a stabilizing policy, which can be interpreted as an ordinary demand policy. Then, we show that when costs and benefits are aggregated, the policy produces a net positive surplus. But, unfortunately, the surplus cannot be lump-sum redistributed so as to generate a Pareto-dominating allocation. The reason is that lump-sum transfers do not exist in our model: because rents and liquidity matter, and reallocation of wealth affects real economic decisions.

---

[4] The problem goes back to Fisher [10]. In his view, the Great Depression was a result of money-price deflation that increased the real value of corporate debt, drained capital out of the corporate sector, which caused an adverse supply effect. But the initial effect can be indexed away to the mutual benefit of lenders and borrowers. Note that Fisher's explanation has two ingredients: lack of indexation and financial imperfections (which create the link between corporate wealth and supply). We show that the second effect is sufficient for a business-cycle theory. Needless to say, the first ingredient is extremely problematic. It may have been one of the reasons that prevented a serious consideration of Fisher's theory for so long.

[5] Indexation is assumed away for the shock period only. All subsequent price dynamics is indexed.

[6] We believe our model can be used in order to defend the Kiyotaki–Moore model against such criticism: had their economy slumped due to endogenous reversion, there would have been no need to assume indexation away.

As noted, our model is, essentially, a dynamic extension of the SW model with overlapping two-period projects. Hence, external finance generates excessive risk taking (i.e. above first-best probability of failure).[7] Entrepreneurs face a downward sloping demand schedule so that prices fall when quantities boom. So here our story follows:[8] boom production leads to low prices, which generates low liquidity and increases external finance. That leads to excessive risk taking and a high rate of failure—a bust. When quantities decreases, price increases, liquidity flows in and the moral-hazard problem is mitigated. Low levels of risk taking will expand the industry, and it all stars over again.[9]

It is important to stress that our model is "clean" in the sense that it contains no unusual ingredient that drives the result. As mentioned above, contracts are fully endogenized. The asymmetric information structure is a simple textbook moral-hazard problem. The basic story about the relation between external finance and risk taking comes from SW. The extension of project duration to more than one period is just an ordinary (and realistic) feature of capital theory. Preferences are standard and display risk neutrality in the *numeraire* good. In addition, we take a precautionary measure in order to assure that our result is properly interpreted: we prove formally (in Appendix A), that output quickly converges to a stationary level once the moral hazard is removed. Hence, the cycle results from the financial imperfection.

We have already made clear that the primary goal of this chapter is theoretical. Obviously, it does not produce realistic time series. Yet, it is not without empirical value. A salient feature of the business cycle is that it is usually accompanied by a "credit cycle:" profits tend to decline towards the peak of the cycle, and the "liquidity crunch" leads the economy into the bust.[10] The essence of this story is captured in our model: it is the high quantities of the boom which depress prices and create the liquidity shortage that increases the propensity to default that ends in a bust.

It is also noteworthy that our model can, in principle, be calibrated. The main behavioral relationship—the inverse relation between liquidity and default risk—is observable and can be estimated. Indeed, Holtz-Eakin et al. [17] examine the wealth effect of an "exogenous" windfall (bequest) on the probability of survival of individual entrepreneurs. They find a significant positive effect which is consistent with our modeling. Needless to say there is, still, much more to be done before the model is ripe for calibration.

---

[7] After SW, the words risk and probability of failure are used interchangeably.

[8] Some elements of this story can be found in Sussman [25].

[9] There is some similarity with the cobweb model, but, with differences in two major respects: first, rationality of expectation, and second, the cobweb model is a partial equilibrium model. Nevertheless, the general equilibrium characteristics of our model are too primitive to be emphasized.

[10] See Gertler and Gilchrist [11], Kashyap et al. [18] and Bernanke et al. [3]

There are two other branches of the literature which deserve to be mentioned. Boldrin and Woodford [6] survey the general equilibrium theory on endogenous fluctuations (*a la* Day [8] or Grandmont [12]). They argue that although endogenous cycles are compatible with complete markets, some "friction" (financial or other) is probably needed in order to get empirically relevant results. A step in that direction is taken by Woodford [26] (see also Bewley [4] and Scheinkman and Weiss [23]). In his model equilibrium dynamics may be chaotic, but financial structure is crude and exogenously determined. Secondly, there is a growing literature, mostly of a static nature, on more realistic features of financial structure and aggregate economic activity. Many emphasize the role of the banking system, and describe mechanisms by which aggregate economic activity may be affected by changes in the cost of financial intermediation or by the level of banks' capitalization.[11] Some authors have stressed the role of bankruptcy costs (Greenwald and Stiglitz [14]). Others still have remarked on the role different financial instruments (i.e. debt and equity) play in the "transmission mechanism" (see [14] or King [19]).

The chapter is organized as follows. Section 2 presents the model. Section 3 analyzes the contract problem and shows the relationship between liquidity and risk taking. Section 4 derives the aggregate supply and defines a market equilibrium. Section 5 discusses the existence and stability of equilibrium cycles. A welfare analysis of the stabilizing policy is provided in Section 6. Section 7 contains some concluding remarks.

2. The Model

Consider an infinite horizon, discrete time ($t = 0, 1, \ldots$) economy with two goods. One is a *numeraire* good which is used for both consumption and investment, the other is a perishable staple good which is used for consumption only. We call it *coffee*.[12] At each date there is a perfectly competitive spot market in which coffee is exchanged for the numeraire good at a price p_t.

There are two types of agents in our economy: entrepreneurs (who grow coffee) and consumers-lenders (who consume coffee and provide external finance to the entrepreneurs). Consumers are identical and live forever. They consume both the numeraire and coffee and they are risk-neutral in terms of the numeraire good:

$$E_t \left\{ \sum_{s=0}^{\infty} \left(\frac{1}{1+r} \right)^s [x_{t+s} + u(c_{t+s})] \right\} . \tag{1}$$

---

[11] See Bernanke [1], Bolton and Freixas [7], Blum and Hellwig [5], Holmström and Tirole [16].
[12] We use this name to hint that the coffee sector may be interpreted as a small open economy which is highly dependent on the production of a single staple good.

x_{t+s} and c_{t+s} are the consumption of the numeraire and coffee, respectively, at date $t + s$; $u(c)$ is an increasing and concave utility function: the constant $r > 0$ is the rate of time preference; E_t denotes expectations formed at date t. Let a_t denote the amout of (period t) external finance they supply; and let $\tilde{R}_t$ be the gross (random) rate of return per unit of finance extended at period t (to be determined by the contract problem below). Then, the consumers' budget constraint is

$$x_t + p_t c_t + a_t = e + \tilde{R}_{t-1} a_{t-1}. \tag{2}$$

Suppose that consumers' endowments are such that the solution to their problem is always interior.[13] Their behavior is characterized by two simple behavioral functions: (i) a time-invariant perfectly elastic supply of lending at the expected gross rate of return $1 + r$ (namely, r is the riskless rate), and (ii) a time-invariant downward sloping demand for coffee, $D(p_t)$, which will only depend on the spot price of coffee at each period. The one-period indirect utility function of the consumers can be written as

$$U(p_t),$$

where, by Roy's Identity,

$$U'(p_t) = -D(p_t). \tag{3}$$

At each period a measure one continuum of entrepreneurs is born, each of which lives for three periods. They consume no coffee themselves, and have linear preferences in the numeraire good; their rate of time preference, r, is the same as the consumers'. (Hence, given that r is the riskless rate, entrepreneurs are indifferent about the timings of consumption.) Entrepreneurs have exclusive access to the production technology of coffee: each is endowed with a single, indivisible, project that can be activated by investing one unit of the numeraire good. Once invested, this amount is sunk.

Once activated (at the entrepreneurs' first period of life), a project has two production periods. In the first period it yields $Y > 0$ units of coffee deterministically. In the second period it yields Y units of coffee in case of "success" and zero in case of "failure." The probability of success is π. Returns in the second period of production are independent across projects, which means that there is no aggregate uncertainty in the economy. Both the entrepreneur, his project and the capital invested perish, simultaneously, after the second production period. It may be useful to think of failure as a random event which destroys capital after the first production period.

An entrepreneur can affect the probability of "success," π, through the amount of "effort" he puts into the project. We denote the disutility of effort (evaluated at the second production period, in terms of the numeraire) by $\psi(\pi)$, and

---

[13] It is sufficient to assume that the endowment e is large enough to cover the entrepreneurs' financing requirements at each date.

assume

$$\psi(0) = 0, \quad \psi' \geqslant 0, \quad \psi'' > 0, \quad \psi''' \geqslant 0, \quad \psi'(0) = 0, \quad \psi'(1) = +\infty. \quad (4)$$

Hence, increasing the probability of success entails a sacrifice of entrepreneurial utility (at an increasing rate). The last two assumptions are made to guarantee that the entrepreneurs' problem has an interior solution. The assumption about the third derivative guarantees that the solution is a continuous function of the relevant prices (see below).

Entrepreneurs are born penniless, and have to borrow in order to activate their project. Note, however, that the $t - 1$ born entrepreneur has a deterministic cash flow of $p_t Y$, in the first production period, which is not affected by the agency problem. This source of "liquidity" plays a crucial role in the analysis below.

We assume that effort is not observable by the consumers. It is therefore impossible to write contracts contingent upon the amount of effort the entrepreneur puts into his project. A certain level of effort can be implemented only by making it incentive compatible with the entrepreneur's self interest. Crucially, we impose no other constraint on the problem, and allow entrepreneurs and financiers to use any observable information they wish so as to minimize the agency problem.

It is worth mentioning that our story is, in essence, the same as in SW.[14] The crucial assumption is that the $(t - 1$ born) entrepreneur may increase his second-period income (net of the disutility of effort), $p_{t+1}Y - \psi(\pi)$, by increasing the risk of failure. As we show below, the outcome is the same as in SW: when investment is externally financed, entrepreneurs tend to take an excess risk of failure. We differ from SW in that we split net income into an observable (pecuniary) part and a non-observable (non-pecuniary) part. That is done in order to make effort unobservable ex post, so that the contract is resilient to a De Meza and Webb [9] sort of criticism. Also, we have to continuum of failure probabailities rather than two ("risky" and "safe" in SW), but that is done, mainly, for analytical convenience.

3. The Contract Problem

In this section we solve the contract problem. It is convenient to consider the problem of the generation born at $t - 1$ so that t is the first production period and $t + 1$ the second production period.

To establish a benchmark, consider the first-best, full-information problem. In the case, the interests of the entrepreneur and the financier are aligned: to maximize the project's net present value and to activate it if such value is positive.

---

[14] In the moral-hazard section of this chapter.

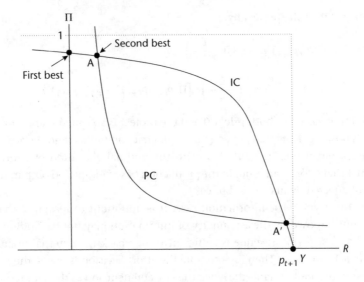

Figure 1. The contract problem.

Hence

$$\underset{\pi}{\text{Maximize}} -1 + \left(\frac{1}{1+r}\right) \cdot p_t Y + \left(\frac{1}{1+r}\right)^2 [\pi p_{t+1} Y - \psi(\pi)]. \qquad (5)$$

The first-order condition of this problem is

$$p_{t+1} Y = \psi'(\pi), \qquad (6)$$

which has an ordinary production-theory interpretation. Effort is an input; to find its optimal amount one should equate the value of its marginal product to its marginal cost.

We plot, in Figure 1, a rotated (by 90°, counter clock-wise) ψ' curve with its origin at the point $(p_{t+1}Y, 0)$. For reasons to become clear below, we call it the IC curve.[15] It follows from Eq. (6) that the first-best level of effort is at the intersection of the IC curve with the vertical axis (see Figure 1). Obviously, when the price of second-period output increases, the value of the marginal product of effort increases as well and the input of effort should be increased. We refer to this as the *profitability* effect.

To check whether activating the project is profitable at all, denote the solution of (5) by the function

$$\pi = \overline{\Pi}(p_{t+1}), \quad \text{where } \overline{\Pi}' > 0, \qquad (7)$$

---

[15] The shape of the IC curve is determined by the assumptions in (4).

and the value of the project by

$$\bar{v}(p_t, p_{t+1}) \equiv -1 + \left(\frac{1}{1+r}\right) \cdot p_t Y$$

$$+ \left(\frac{1}{1+r}\right)^2 \{\bar{\Pi}(p_{t+1})p_{t+1}Y - \psi[\bar{\Pi}(p_{t+1})]\}, \tag{8}$$

which is increasing in both prices. Then the project is activated if and only if its value is positive. Note that p_t has a pure rent effect on profits (and the activation decision), but it does not interfere with the optimal allocation of effort. The reason is that effort is an input in the production of second-period output; hence, it is not affected by first-period prices.

Now the asymmetric-information case. It is important to recognize that the constraint imposed by the asymmetry of information may not be binding. Suppose that first-period revenue is sufficient to pay back the external financiers, namely $p_t Y \geqslant (1+r)$. Then, by the time the effort decision is made, the project is already internally financed. Hence the entrepreneur solves the same problem as in (5) and inserts the first-best level of effort into the project.

Consider next the case where first-period income is not sufficient to pay back the financiers, namely $p_t Y < (1+r)$. The problem is how to guarantee the required repayment to the financiers with a minimal decrease in the entrepreneur's welfare. A contract should be designed which is contingent upon all relevant, observable information, i.e. the success or failure of the project in the second production period. A feasible contract is a repayment, $R \in [0, p_{t+1}Y]$ in case of success, and zero in case of failure. Technically, the optimal contract maximizes the entrepreneur's welfare (9), subject to an incentive compatibility constraint (IC)—Eq. (10)—and participation constraints (PC) for both the financier and the entrepreneur—Eq. (11) and (12), respectively:

$$\underset{\pi,R}{\text{Maximize}} \left(\frac{1}{1+r}\right)^2 [\pi(p_{t+1}Y - R) - \psi(\pi)] \tag{9}$$

subject to:

$$\pi \in \arg\max_\pi \left(\frac{1}{1+r}\right)^2 [\pi(p_{t+1}Y - R) - \psi(\pi)], \tag{10}$$

$$\left(\frac{1}{1+r}\right) \cdot p_t Y + \left(\frac{1}{1+r}\right)^2 \pi R \geqslant 1, \tag{11}$$

$$\left(\frac{1}{1+r}\right)^2 [\pi(p_{t+1}Y - R) - \psi(\pi)] \geqslant 0. \tag{12}$$

By standard considerations one can show that the constraint in (12) is not binding. It follows that the feasibility set is defined by Eq. (10) and (11) only. First, consider the first-order condition of Eq. (10):

$$p_{t+1}Y - R = \psi'(\pi). \tag{13}$$

Hence, for any repayment R, the incentive-compatible level of effort can be found with the aid of the IC curve of Figure 1: just measure R on the horizontal axis and find π on the curve. Next, consider the financier's participation constraint (11). The (R, π) combinations that satisfy this constraint lie above the PC curve, which is given by

$$\left(\frac{1}{1+r}\right) \cdot p_t Y + \left(\frac{1}{1+r}\right)^2 \pi R = 1. \tag{14}$$

That is the rectangular hyperbola in Figure 1. Hence, the feasibility set is defined by the arc of the IC curve between points A and A'. It is easy to see that moving leftwards, and closer to the first-best point, would increase the value of the objective (9).[16] Hence, point A, where (11) holds with equality, is the second-best, optimal contract.

It is obvious that the IC and PC curves may not intersect at all, in which case the feasibility set defined by constraints (10)–(12) is empty. In that case no funds can be obtained by the entrepreneur. Let the boundary of the set of activation prices be given by the $p_{t+1} = f(p_t)$ function, defined by the tangency of the IC and PC curves. Then, the project is activated if prices are above f, and is not activated if prices fall below f. It is easy to see that f is downward sloping.

Hence, the optimal contract is characterized by three "regimes": internal finance, external finance and no activation as follows:

$$\pi_t = \Pi(p_t, p_{t+1}) = \begin{cases} \overline{\Pi}(p_{t+1}) & \text{if } p_t > (r+1)/Y \\ \text{"point } A\text{"} & \text{if } p_t < (1+r)/Y \text{ and } p_{t+1} > f(p_t). \\ 0 & \text{if } p_{t+1} < f(p_t) \end{cases} \tag{15}$$

Let us summarize the solution with the aid of Figure 2, where the three regimes are clearly visible.

   (i) Internal finance: this regime is effective when p_t is sufficiently high for the project to be financed out of the first-period deterministic income. Higher first-period prices will increase rents but will have no effect on the allocation of effort as it is already at the first-best level. Hence, the Π function is flat with respect to p_t (see Figure 2).
  (ii) External finance: this regime is effective for interim p_t's such that the project cannot be internally financed, but is still activated. It is clear from Figure 1 that effort is *below* the first-best level. Further $\Pi_1 > 0$: as p_t increases, effort increases *continuously*[17] and approaches its first-best level. The reason is straightforward: p_t is a source of liquidity which allows

---

[16] To prove this claim diagrammatically notice that the area below the IC and right of R represents the value of the objective multiplied by $(1+r)^2$.

[17] Within the external finance regime continuity is guaranteed by $\psi''' > 0$ (see Figure 1); continuity is preserved at the switch from the external to the internal finance regime: as p_t approaches $(1+r)/Y$ (from below) the PC curve collapses to the axes and effort approaches the first best level.

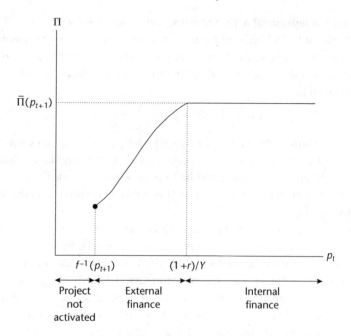

Figure 2. The three regimes.

the entrepreneur to mitigate the distortionary effect of external finance. Hence, the Π function is upward sloping with respect to p_t (see Figure 2). The crucial difference between this regime and the one above is in the presence of this *liquidity* effect: whether first-period income has a pure-rent or an allocational effect. Note also that $\Pi_2 > 0$ (see Figure 1), thus, since $\overline{\Pi}' > 0$ as well, the whole curve in Figure 2 shifts upwards when p_{t+1} increases.

(iii) No activation: this regime is effective when p_t is very low. Financial requirements are so high that incentive-compatible effort falls to a level at which financiers cannot get the market return on their funds. Finance is not supplied, the project is not activated, and effort jumps *discontinuously* to zero.[18]

For the sake of the welfare analysis in Section 6, we define

$$v(p_t, p_{t+1}) \equiv -1 + \left(\frac{1}{1+r}\right) p_t Y$$

$$+ \left(\frac{1}{1+r}\right)^2 \{\Pi(p_t, p_{t+1}) p_{t+1} Y - \psi[\Pi(p_t, p_{t+1})]\}, \qquad (16)$$

---

[18] When the IC and the PC curves are tangent π is still strictly positive.

which represents the present value of entrepreneurial profits, provided the project is activated at all.[19] It is easy to check that the two partial derivatives of (16) are positive.

4. Aggregate Supply and Market Equilibrium

Credit rationing is a possibility in our model. Intuitively, suppose that prices are p_t and $p_{t+1} = f(p_t)$ such that the IC and the PC curves are just tangent. These prices are demand determined and some ($t-1$ born) entrepreneurs do not participate in the market. Now what would happen if they participated? Prices would fall further below, which would drive *all* entrepreneurs into the no activation regime. Hence the credit rationing. We focus, below, on no-rationing equilibria because they are simpler to analyze and sufficient to illustrate the functioning of the reversion mechanism in which we are interested.

Suppose there exist an equilibrium with no rationing at any point on the equilibrium path. (We provide a condition that guarantees the existence of such an equilibrium at the end of this section.) Hence all entrepreneurs participate in the market, and the market-clearing condition in period $t+1$ is simply

$$[1 + \Pi(p_t, p_{t+1})]Y = D(p_{t+1}). \tag{17}$$

Note that the $t+1$ supply is made up of the output of all the t born entrepreneurs who are producing for the first time, and the successful $t-1$ born entrepreneurs who are producing for the second time.

Equation (17) defines a first-order difference equation in prices. Denote it by

$$p_{t+1} = g(p_t).$$

The function g has two properties which are essential to our analysis. First, if projects are internally financed, i.e., $p_t \geqslant (1+r)/Y$, then the market-clearing condition is

$$[1 + \overline{\Pi}(p_{t+1})]Y = D(p_{t+1}). \tag{18}$$

The solution of (18) in terms of p_{t+1} is unique. Denote it by $\bar{p}$. It follows that, for $p_t \geqslant (1+r)/Y$, p_{t+1} equals $\bar{p}$ as Figure 3 shows. Intuitively, projects are internally financed, so that higher period t prices create additional rents, but rents do not affect effort, so the next period price does not change in response.

On the other hand, if $p_t < (1+r)/Y$, g is downward sloping

$$g'(p_t) = -\frac{\Pi_1}{\Pi_2 - D'} < 0. \tag{19}$$

---

[19] Equation (14) is obviously valid for the internal finance regime, but also for the external finance regime. To see the latter, one can use the fact that the financier's participation constraint (11) is binding to rewrite (9).

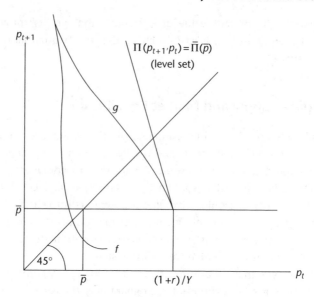

Figure 3. The difference equation.

Notice that g is continuous at point $(1+r)/Y$ (see Figure 3 again) due to the corresponding continuity of Π. As for the magnitude of g' (to the left of $(1+r)/Y$), note that the more responsive demand is to changes in prices, the flatter the curve is. It is useful to describe two limiting cases:

(i) Inelastic demand. As $D' \to 0$, g approaches the level set defined by $\Pi(p_t, p_{t+1}) = \overline{\Pi}(\overline{p})$. Using (13) and (14) one can verify that this level set is linear with a (downward) slope of $-(1+r)/\pi < -1$.

(ii) Perfectly elastic demand. If $D' \to -\infty$, g will be flat and equal to $\overline{p}$.

Thus, for intermediate values of D', the g function lies anywhere in the triangle below the above mentioned level set, and the horizontal line $p_{t+1} = \overline{p}$. So, it turns out, the slope of g *may* be greater than one (in absolute value).

Having discussed the law of motion, let us look at the initial conditions. Suppose that at $t = 0$ there is a measure one continuum of entrepreneurs (born at $t = -1$) who have only one production period left. Given their wealth, they choose an effort level π_0 such that the initial price, p_1, is determined by

$$(1 + \pi_0)Y = D(p_1).$$

Since there exist a one-to-one mapping from the wealth of the initial generation to p_1,[20] we consider the initial price p_1 as a given data for our economy.

---

[20] Namely: for any initial price p_1 there exists a level of initial wealth, $g^{-1}(p_1)Y$, such that π_0 is a rational choice for a perfectly-foreseen p_1.

We can now state a sufficient condition for a no-rationing equilibrium. Obviously, any pair of consecutive prices (p_t, p_{t+1}) should lie above the graph of the f function. So consider the case where g and f intersect like in Figure 3; if the point $(\bar{p}, \bar{p})$ lies above f, then whenever p_t exceeds $(1+r)/Y$, the following p_{t+1} and the whole continuation equilibrium sequence will be above f; if, in addition, the initial point is above f the equilibrium path will have no rationing at any point. Hence, a sufficient condition for a no-rationing equilibrium is

$$\bar{p} > f(\bar{p}), \quad \text{and} \quad p_1 \geq \bar{p}. \tag{20}$$

That condition (20) can be satisfied at all is clear from the fact that if the demand D became larger the graph of g would shift upwards and to the right, whereas the graph of f would remain unchanged. Hence, for some demand schedules this sufficient condition can be satisfied.

Before we continue, let us just point out that the downward sloping segment of g captures the basic intuition of our model. When the period t price of coffee increases, entrepreneurs are more liquid. They are thus less dependent on external finance, which gives them an incentive to increase π. That increases the quantity supplied next period and decreases prices. So next period entrepreneurs would be less liquid. Hence, a cobweb sort of dynamics appears and cycles may be generated.

5. Dynamics, Steady States, and Cycles

Denote the stationary point of g by p^*. Then, given an initial price p_1, three types of equilibria can emerge

   (i) If the point $[(1+r)/Y, \bar{p}]$ lies to the left of the 45° line then $p^* = \bar{p}$. The system would converge to its stationary point at $t = 3$, the latest.
  (ii) If the point $[(1+r)/Y, \bar{p}]$ lies to the right of the 45° line then $p^* > \bar{p}$. If $|g'(p^*)| < 1$, the system would converge[21] to p^* with short run oscillations which would die out, eventually.
 (iii) If $p^* > \bar{p}$ (like in the previous case), but the system cannot converge to its stationary point (say) because $|g'(p^*)| > 1$, then the system would converge (after a finite number of periods) to a (two-period) periodic equilibrium as in Figure 4. The only exception is when the initial price happens to equal p^*. Since the high price is associated with a contraction of supply we call it the "bust price." By the same logic, we call the other price the "boom price." Note that entrepreneurs live through both a boom and a bust, but they face different sequences of the two prices depending on

---

[21] At least from a neighborhood of p^*.

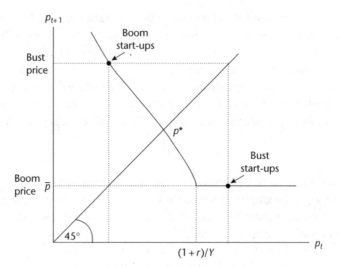

Figure 4. Endogenous cycles.

whether they start to produce in a boom ("boom start-ups") or in a bust ("bust start-ups").

A few points are in place here. The stationary cycle may not be unique. But all stationary cycles have a periodicity of two.[22] Further, the whole equilibrium path is uniquely determined by the g function and the initial condition. If there are many stationary cycles, the initial price will determine to which of these the system will converge. Our story involves no element of multiplicity of equilibria. Note also that the system cannot "jump" to p^* by means of saddle path convergence because of the tight correspondence between initial prices and initial wealth as discussed above.

It is obvious that without the informational problem, the system would quickly converge to the stationary price $\bar{p}$.[23] That reflects some fundamental differences in the way a moral-hazard economy operates, relative to the full-information one. As already emphasized, rents have no allocational role in the full-information economy. In that case p_{t+1} is not affected at all by p_t, and can "freely" jump to $\bar{p}$. The whole dynamic relation between p_t and p_{t+1} results from the mechanics of the contract and the agency problem. Without that mechanism cycles are not generated. In fact one should be more careful about that argument: the discussion above already assumes (via the restriction on the location of f) that the demand for coffee is high enough so that all entrepreneurs get sufficiently high rents and participate in the market. What would happen

---

[22] It is well-known that it takes a non-monotonic (first-order) difference equation to produce higher order cycles, see Grandmont [13].

[23] As indicated, a non-negative net present value condition should be satisfied. It is easy to see that condition (20) ensures that.

in the full information case if demand is not high enough to assure positive net present value under full participation? Can the dynamics of partial entry generate cyclical prices? The answer is no. In Appendix A we explore partial entry dynamics with a binding "zero profit" condition $\bar{v}(p_t, p_{t+1}) = 0$, and prove that this equilibrium has a unique saddle path convergence to a stationary point. (Note that in this case, unlike in the asymmetric information case entrepreneurs are indifferent between participating in the market and staying out of it.) Hence, a full-information economy will not oscillate even without the restrictions imposed on the location of the demand schedule. This property gives extra power to our claim that moral hazard is the very ingredient that generates cycles in our model.

It is obvious that the economy is more cyclical the steeper is the g function. Looking again at Eq. (18) we can relate its slope to the liquidity and the profitability effects mentioned above (in relation to Figure 2). g is steeper the stronger is the liquidity effect Π_1, and the weaker is the profitability effect Π_2. That a strong liquidity effect contributes to cyclicality is in line with the main thrust of the paper: entrepreneurs depend more on external finance, and effort is reduced further away from the first best. Note, however, that a weak profitability effect contributes to cyclicality. To understand why, consider an entrepreneur who starts to produce in the bust (see Figure 4). Obviously he is little liquid and may be tempted to choose a low level of effort. But then, he anticipates that other entrepreneurs will do the same, generating high second period prices which will bring about high profits. This will push him in the direction of a higher level of effort. The more effort he puts, the lower are next period prices, the flatter is the g function, and the smaller is the magnitude of output fluctuations.

So flows of wealth in and out of the entrepreneurial sector keep on fueling the cycle. A boom leads to a bust and the bust to a boom. Importantly, no constraints on rationality, either via expectations formation or sub-optimal contracting are imposed. In particularly, we do not assume indexation away: all contracts written from period one onwards make use of all available information, including the future price of coffee. But this sort of indexation does not provide insurance and it does not smooth entrepreneurs' income. We may think about it in the following way: since the state of the world (i.e., the initial p_1) is already realized when an entrepreneur is born, insurance markets are closed by a standard Hirshleifer [15] argument. On the other hand, our theory depends on some initial, maybe just a little deviation, from the stationary price p^*. We build no theory to explain the initial discrepancy, but we show that the cycle can persist even as we get arbitrarily further away from period one.[24]

---

[24] Unlike in Kiyotaki and Moore [20] where the cycles dies out, eventually, and it takes an additional "unanticipated" shock to start it all over again.

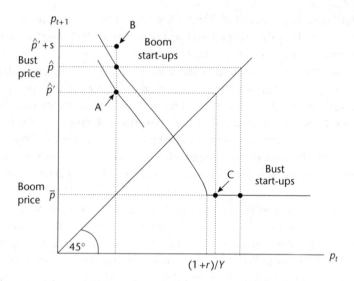

Figure 5. Stabilization policy.

6. Stabilization: Welfare Analysis

Now to the policy issue: can a stabilizing policy be implemented, and could such a policy be justified on the basis of some welfare accounting? We focus on the case in which the economy is at the periodic equilibrium as in Figure 4, with alternating "boom" (low) and "bust" (high) prices, $\bar{p}$ and $\hat{p}$ respectively (see Figure 5). Obviously, entrepreneurs who start up production in the bust (when prices are high) put the first-best amount of effort into their projects. Hence, there is no point in trying to improve on them. But those who start up in the boom (when prices are low) are excessive risk-takers. Getting them closer to the first-best level of effort would require enhancing the liquidity or the profitability of their projects by means of a subsidy. Suppose that is done by an expansionary demand policy in the bust, just like in an old-fashioned macroeconomics textbook.

Consider a perfectly foreseeable policy that allocates a subsidy s per unit of output to old boom start-up entrepreneurs, in a bust period.[25] Note that the policy is discriminating: entrepreneurs who start producing in the bust do not get the subsidy. To see the effect of the subsidy, use the implicit function theorem on the market-clearing condition for the bust price

$$[1 + \Pi(\bar{p}, \hat{p} + s)]Y - D(\hat{p}) = 0,$$

---

[25] A policy giving a subsidy per unit of first period output or per investment project to each generation of boom start-ups has an identical impact.

in order to set

$$-1 < \frac{\partial \hat{p}}{\partial s} = -\frac{\Pi_2 Y}{\Pi_2 Y - D'(\hat{p})} < 0. \tag{21}$$

Consider the boom start-ups and assume, for the moment, that they face the same boom price, $\bar{p}$, as before. The subsidy drives these entrepreneurs closer to the first-best level of effort. Hence, bust quantities are expanded (see the broken line in Figure 5); the market-price of coffee—as seen by coffee buyers and bust start-ups (who do not get the subsidy)—falls to $\hat{p}'$. Since the price falls by less than the subsidy (see (21)), the price, as seen by the boom start-ups increases to $\hat{p}' + s$. Note that if the subsidy is not too big, the lower bust price will not affect the effort of the bust start-ups, who are already at the first best. Hence, the boom price, $\hat{p}$, is indeed unaffected. It follows that the price combination observed by the boom start-ups is given by point B, while the price combination observed by the bust start-ups is given by point C. But then, the market (i.e. buyers) price combination is given by point A. Obviously, the amplitude of boom–bust market prices is decreased by the policy: from $(\bar{p}, \hat{p})$ to $(\bar{p}, \hat{p}')$. Since market prices are monotonic in quantities the policy is, indeed, unambiguously stabilizing.

It is obvious that the bust start-ups are hurt by the policy: they face a lower price when starting-up and the same price when old. Obviously, boom start-ups gain by the policy. Also, coffee buyers gain by facing a lower price in the bust. To see whether the benefits exceed the losses, let us add-up both (they are easy to evaluate in terms of the numeraire); the whole computation is done for a bust period

$$W = (1+r)^2 \cdot v(\bar{p}, \hat{p} + s) + (1+r) \cdot \bar{v}(\hat{p}, \bar{p}) + U(\hat{p}) - s\Pi(\bar{p}, \hat{P} + s)Y.$$

W adds up the (properly capitalized) values of the projects of the boom and bust start-ups, the utility of the consumers, and the cost of the subsidy to the taxpayers.

Differentiating W with respect to s and evaluating at $s = 0$, we get

$$\frac{\partial W}{\partial s} = (1+r)^2 \cdot \frac{\partial v}{\partial \hat{p}} \left(1 + \frac{\partial \hat{p}}{\partial s} \right) + (1+r) \cdot \frac{\partial \bar{v}}{\partial \hat{p}} \cdot \frac{\partial \hat{p}}{\partial s} + U'(\hat{p}) \cdot \frac{\partial \hat{p}}{\partial s} - \Pi(\bar{p}, \hat{p} + s)Y.$$

(See Appendix B for the derivatives in this and the next equation.) For brevity, denote $\partial/\hat{p}/\partial s$ by $-\lambda$ (recalling that $0 < \lambda < 1$ by Eq. (21)), $\Pi(\bar{p}, \hat{p})$ by $\hat{\pi}$, and the repayment obligation of the boom start-ups by $\hat{R}$. Then, using Eq. (3), (8), (16), and $D(\hat{p}) = (1 + \hat{\Pi})Y$, we can write

$$\frac{\partial W}{\partial s} = \hat{\pi} \left(Y - \frac{\partial \hat{R}}{\partial \hat{p}} \right) (1 - \lambda) - Y\lambda + (1 + \hat{\pi})Y\lambda - \hat{\pi}Y = -\hat{\pi} \frac{\partial \hat{R}}{\partial \hat{p}} (1 - \lambda),$$

where $\partial \hat{R}/\partial \hat{p}$ can be computed using (13) and (14). Note that if $\hat{R}$ were zero (as it is for the bust start-ups), the above derivative would equal zero; this confirms our intuition that there is no room for a subsidy like s in a boom. If $\hat{R}$ is positive (as it is for the boom born generation), then $\partial \hat{R}/\partial \hat{p} < 0$ and the aggregate welfare measure can be improved by choosing a positive s. Intuitively, unlike other agents, the marginal value of income for the entrepreneurs who start to produce in a boom is higher than one, since, in addition to the direct distributive effect, increasing their income has an allocational effect, that pushes them closer to the first best. Thus, when they obtain additional rents by means of the subsidy, they generate added value in excess of the taxpayers' loss.

From this result, it is tempting to say that Pareto improvements could be achieved by compensating the losers by lump-sum taxation. But this is not true. In a world where rents have a role in providing incentives, lump-sum taxes are not neutral. Consumers and bust start-ups could be lump-sum taxed without affecting their marginal decisions.[26] But if the boom start-up entrepreneurs were lump-sum taxed for compensation purposes (say, out of their first-period revenue) that would undo the allocational effect of the subsidy.[27]

Hence, the question of whether cycles as those described in this model should be stabilized has no clear answer. Stabilization polices are desirable according to a policy criterion which is weaker than Pareto optimality.

7. Concluding Remarks

As noted above, our modeling gives priority to analytical transparency rather than to realism. Since we model a pure reversion mechanism the system (while in a stationary cycle) reverts each period to its previous state: from boom to bust and vice versa, one period after another. Of course, this is an incomplete description of the fluctuations observed in the real world, as captured by macroeconomic time series.

There is no reason why the reversion and the propagation mechanisms cannot be combined, within a single model, in order to generate equilibria with realistic time-series properties. Namely, after a reversion period the propagation mechanism takes over for several periods and the system grows out of the recession. At a certain point it reverts back to a bust and it all starts over again. It is unlikely, however, that such a combined model can preserve the simplicity and transparency that characterizes the current one. Our experience with related models (work in progress) shows that important properties may vanish: the equilibrium path may not be unique, the dynamic system may be of a higher order,

---

[26] It is immediate to check that the consumers' gain from the subsidy does not suffice to compensate for both its direct cost to the taxpayers and the losses caused to the bust start-ups.

[27] Strictly speaking, entrepreneurs cannot be lump-sum taxed in the second period. Since they have zero wealth in case of failure, any tax is necessarily state contingent, and can be avoided in probability by excessive risk taking. Hence, it is not neutral.

numerical procedures may have to replace analytical arguments. Also, getting a more realistic financial structure may require to depart from complete contracts, thus undermining one of the main points we make. We have thus chosen, in this chapter, to put down the bare bones of the theoretical skeleton and prove some basic results. Hopefully, that would provide better foundations for future, more empirically motivated, work.

Meanwhile, it is useful to point out that even in its crude form our model can provide some insight into an important policy question. It is sometimes argued that insufficient indexation, especially in the banking sector is the source of financial instability. The remedy would be to make banks' assets and liabilities more responsive to market conditions, either through indexation or via securitization. It is argued that by the mere replacement of banks by mutual funds, much of the problem can be resolved.[28] Our analysis does not support that sort of an argument. Rather, it shows that even after contracts are made responsive to any relevant market price, "financial instability" is still a basic fact of life: an inherent feature of a competitive market economy subject to moral hazard.

APPENDIX A

Existence and uniqueness of a saddle-path in the full-information economy

This appendix analyzes first-best full-information dynamics. We prove that the system converges, within at most one period, to an equilibrium with stationary prices and stationary *total* output. It has been shown in the text that the optimal choice of π by the entrepreneurs facing prices (p_t, p_{t+1}) is $\overline{\Pi}(p_{t+1})$ and the associated net present value of the project is $\overline{v}(p_t, p_{t+1})$. Investment is feasible if and only if $\overline{v}(p_t, p_{t+1}) \geqslant 0$. In fact, when $\overline{v}(p_t, p_{t+1}) = 0$ entrepreneurs are indifferent between investing and not investing, and we may have a situation where only a fraction $q_t < 1$ of the entrepreneurs who can start up production at t activate their projects at $t - 1$. Allowing for that possibility, the dynamics of the system can be described by the market-clearing condition

$$[q_{t+1} + q_t\overline{\Pi}(p_{t+1})]Y = D(p_{t+1}),\tag{A1}$$

and the free-entry condition

$$\overline{v}(p_t, p_{t+1}) \begin{cases} > 0 & \text{and} \quad q_t + 1 \\ = 0 & \text{and} \quad q_t \in [0, 1] \\ < 0 & \text{and} \quad q_t = 0. \end{cases}\tag{A2}$$

---

[28] See Mankiw [21] for an argument along these lines, though more in the context of liquidity provision and bank-runs.

Notice that $\bar{v}(p_t, p_{t+1}) = 0$ defines a first-order difference equation in p_t with

$$dp_{t+1}/dp_t = (1+r)/\overline{\Pi}(p_{t+1}) < -1. \tag{A3}$$

It intersects with the horizontal axis at $p_t = (1+r)/Y$. Denote the stationary point of this difference equation by $\tilde{p}$ and recall that $\bar{p}$ was defined by $[1 + \overline{\Pi}(\bar{p})]Y = D(\bar{p})$. Clearly, if $\bar{p} \geqslant \tilde{p}$ then $\bar{p}$ is the stationary equilibrium with $q_t = 1$ for all t and, as shown in the text, the system converges to this steady state immediately.[29] If $\bar{p} < \tilde{p}$ the stationary price is $\tilde{p}$ and the stationary q_t is the value $\tilde{q}$ which satisfies $[1 + \overline{\Pi}(\tilde{p})]\tilde{q}Y = D(\tilde{p})$. We now show that convergence to the stationary price $\tilde{p}$ (within, at most, one period) is the unique equilibrium in the system. The proof is done in two steps.

Step 1: Existence of an equilibrium convergent to $\tilde{p}$. Let q_0 and π_0 represent the initial conditions of the system in terms of the fraction and effort decision of the entrepreneurs who start up production at $t = 0$ and whose projects are activated. Consider the following two cases:

(i) $q_0\pi_0 \in [0, [1 + \overline{\Pi}(\tilde{p})]\tilde{q}]$. Then $p_t = \tilde{p}$ and $q_t = [1 + \overline{\Pi}(\tilde{p})]\tilde{q} - \overline{\Pi}(\tilde{p})q_{t-1}$ for $t = 1, 2, \ldots$ is an equilibrium of the system given by (A1) and (A2).

(ii) $q_0\pi_0 \in ([1 + \overline{\Pi}(\tilde{p})]\tilde{q}, 1]$. Then $p_1 < \tilde{p}$ and $p_t = \tilde{p}$ for $t = 2, 3, \ldots$, and $q_1 = 0$ and $q_t = [1 + \overline{\Pi}(\tilde{p})]\tilde{q} - \overline{\Pi}(\tilde{p})q_{t-1}$ for $t = 2, 3, \ldots$, where p_1 solves $q_0\pi_0 Y = D(p_1)$, is an equilibrium of the system given by (A1) and (A2).

Checking the previous assertions is immediate. Notice that in (ii) $\bar{v}(p_1, p_2) < \bar{v}(\tilde{p}, \tilde{p}) = 0$ since $p_1 < \tilde{p}$. Note also that in both (i) and (ii) the convergence of q_t to $\tilde{q}$ is asymptotic and non-monotonic. Note also that no agent cares about these oscillations in q, least of all entrepreneurs themselves who are on the zero profit condition (A1) along the whole process.

Step 2: Uniqueness. We now show that there are no oscillations in prices after $t = 2$. Suppose that there exists an equilibrium with such oscillations. Notice, first, we can rule out the possibility of having oscillations with $\bar{v}(p_t, p_{t+1}) = 0$ for all t since that dynamics is explosive according to (A3); two consecutive $\bar{v} > 0$ or $\bar{v} < 0$ periods can be also excluded. Thus, oscillations must involve either (a) periods of $\bar{v} > 0$ between periods of $\bar{v} \leqslant 0$ or (b) periods of $\bar{v} < 0$ between periods of $\bar{v} \geqslant 0$. Further, some of these *switching* periods must dampen the otherwise explosive oscillations. Suppose (a): the cycle is dampened at $t = s$ with $\bar{v}(p_s, p_{s+1}) > 0$, hence $q_s = 1$. Then, $p_{s-1} \leqslant p_{s+1} < p_s$. Using (A1), $D(p_{s+1}) > D(p_s)$ implies

$$q_{s+1} - q_{s-1}\overline{\Pi}(p_s) > 1 - \overline{\Pi}(p_{s+1}). \tag{A4}$$

---

[29] Actually, the demonstration in the text is for an initial value of $q_0 = 1$. But it extends immediately to other initial values, only that convergence will then take one period.

Similarly, as $D(p_{s-1}) \geqslant D(p_{s+1})$ and $\overline{\Pi}$ is increasing, $q_{s-1} - q_{s+1} \geqslant \overline{\Pi}(p_{s+1}) - q_{s-2}\overline{\Pi}(p_{s-1}) > 0$. Then,

$$q_{s+1} - q_{s-1}\overline{\Pi}(p_s) \leqslant q_{s+1} - q_{s+1}\overline{\Pi}(p_s). \tag{A5}$$

Using the property of $\overline{\Pi}$ again, we get

$$q_{s+1}[1 - \overline{\Pi}(p_s)] < 1 - \overline{\Pi}(p_{s+1}). \tag{A6}$$

Combining (A5) and (A6) we contradict (A4). A similar contradiction can be obtained for (b) where $\overline{v}(p_s, p_{s+1}) < 0$ and $p_s < p_{s+1} \leqslant p_{s-1}$.

From here we deduce that the saddle-path convergence to the stationary price described in Step 1 is the unique equilibrium of the system given by (A1) and (A2).

APPENDIX B

Derivatives used in the welfare analysis

The partial derivatives of the solution of the contract problem for the external finance regime are

$$\frac{\partial \pi}{\partial p_t} = \frac{(1+r)Y}{\pi \psi''(\pi) - R},$$

$$\frac{\partial \pi}{\partial p_{t+1}} = \frac{\pi Y}{\pi \psi''(\pi) - R},$$

$$\frac{\partial R}{\partial p_t} = \frac{\psi''(\pi)(1+r)Y}{\pi \psi''(\pi) - R},$$

$$\frac{\partial R}{\partial p_{t+1}} = \frac{RY}{\pi \psi''(\pi) - R}.$$

Notice that $\pi \psi''(\pi) - R > 0$ because of the relative slopes of the IC and PC curves at the optimum. The partial derivatives of Eq. (16) for the external finance regime are

$$\frac{\partial v}{\partial p_t} = -\frac{\Pi(p_t, p_{t+1})}{1+r} \frac{\partial R}{\partial p_t},$$

$$\frac{\partial v}{\partial v_{t+1}} = \frac{\Pi(p_t, p_{t+1})}{1+r}\left(Y - \frac{\partial R}{\partial p_{t+1}}\right).$$

References

Bernanke, B. (1983). "Non-monetary effects in the propagation of the Great Depression." *Amer. Econ. Rev.*, 73: 257–76.

——, and Gertler, M. (1989). "Agency costs, net worth, and business fluctuations." *Amer. Econ. Rev.*, 79: 14–31.

——, ——, and Gilchrist, S. (1996). "The financial accelerator and the flight to quality." *Rev. Econ. Statist.*, 78: 1–15.

Bewley, T. (1983). "Dynamic implications of the form of the budget constraint," in H. Sonnenschein (ed.), *Models of Economic Dynamics* (New York: Springer-Verlag).

Blum, J., and Hellwig, M. (1994). "The macroeconomic implications of capital adequacy requirements for banks." WWZ Discussion Paper No. 9416, University of Basel.

Boldrin, M., and Woodford, M. (1990). "Equilibrium models displaying endogenous fluctuations and chaos." *J. Monet. Econ.*, 25: 189–222.

Bolton, P., and Freixas, X. (1994). "Direct bond financing, financial intermediation and investment: an incomplete contract perspective." Unpublished manuscript, ECARE, Brussels.

Day, R. (1982). "Irregular growth cycles." *Amer. Econ. Rev.*, 72: 406–14.

De Meza, D., and Webb, D. C. (1987). "Too much investment: A problem of asymmetric information." *Quart. J. Econ.*, 102: 281–92.

Fisher, I. (1933). "The debt-deflation theory of Great Depressions." *Econometrica*, 1: 337–57.

Gertler, M., and Gilchrist, S. (1994). "Monetary policy, business cycles, and the behavior of small manufacturing firms." *Quart. J. Econ.*, 109: 309–40.

Grandmont, J. M. (1985). "On endogenous competitive business cycles." *Econometrica*, 53: 995–1046.

—— (1986). "Periodic and aperiodic behavior in discrete, one-dimensional, dynamical systems," in W. Hildenbrand and A. Mas-Collel (eds.), *Contributions to Mathematical Economics* (New York: North-Holland).

Greenwald, B. C., and Stiglitz, J. E. (1993). "Financial market imperfections and business cycle." *Quart. J. Econ.*, 108: 77–114.

Hirshleifer, J. (1971). "The private and social value of information and the reward to inventive activity." *Amer. Econ. Rev.*, 61: 561–74.

Holmström, B., and Tirole, J. (1994). "Financial intermediation, loanable funds and the real sector." Unpublished manuscript, Massachusetts Institute of Technology.

Holtz-Eakin, D., Joulfaian, D., and Rosen, H. (1994). "Sticking it out: Entrepreneurial survival and liquidity constraints." *J. Polit. Economy*, 102: 53–75.

Kashyap, A. K., Stein, J. C., and Wilcox, D. W. (1993). "Monetary policy and credit conditions: Evidence from the composition of external finance." *Amer. Econ. Rev.*, 83: 78–98.

King, M. (1994). "Debt deflation: Theory and evidence." *Eur. Econ. Rev.*, 38: 419–45.

Kiyotaki, N., and Moore, J. H. (1997). "Credit cycles." *J. Polit. Economy*, 105: 211–48.

Mankiw, N. G. (1993). "Discussion of 'Looting: The economic underworld of bankruptcy for profit'" by G. Akerlof and P. Romer, *Brookings Pap. Econ. Act.*, 2: 64–7.

Patinkin, D. (1965). *Money, Interest, and Prices* (New York: Harper & Row).

Scheinkman, J., and Weiss, L. (1986). "Borrowing constraints and aggregate economic activity." *Econometrica*, 54: 23–45.

Stiglitz, J., and Weiss, A. (1981). "Credit rationing in markets with imperfect information." *Amer. Econ. Rev.*, 71: 393–410.

Sussman, O. (1993). "On moral hazard and spontaneous fluctuations." Unpublished manuscript, Ben-Gurion University of the Negev.

Woodford, M. (1989). "Imperfect financial intermediation and complex dynamics," in W. A. Barnett, J. Geweke, and K. Shell (eds.), *Economic complexity: Chaos, Sunspot, Bubbles, and Nonlinearity* (Cambridge: Cambridge Univ. Press).

Credit Markets, Intermediation, and the Macroeconomy: A Discussion

Pietro Reichlin

1. The General Problem

The view that the "financial structure" and the performance of credit markets may be important to understand the macroeconomy dates back to Gurley and Shaw (1955) and it has been reconsidered in the last 20 years in a growing number of studies.[1] The common feature of these contributions is the idea that the way in which agents finance their activities, have access to financial markets and choose contractual arrangements is mostly relevant to understand the business cycle. For expositional convenience I will refer to this approach as the "financial structure approach" (FSA) to macroeconomics.[2]

From an empirical point of view, the FSA is based on a general critique of the predictive power of both Keynesian and monetarist macro-theories of the monetary transmission mechanism (the "money view"). This mechanism relies on the effect of changing interest rates on investment and consumer durable expenditure or, alternatively, on sizable wealth effects on consumption. Some empirical investigations have shown that both the interest rate channel and the wealth effects are either insignificant or at variance with a number of empirical regularities.[3] In contrast with (or as a supplement to) the money view, a number of studies have emphasized the role of bank credit to understand the effects of monetary policies[4] ("credit view"). This view is based on the assumptions that the monetary authority is able to control the volume of bank credit through bank reserves and that bank loans and securities are imperfect substitute for a large set of borrowers (namely, small firms and consumers). Hence,

---

[1] See the Gertler (1988) for an overview of some early contributions.

[2] I consider the search for rigorous microeconomic foundations and the assumption that agents have rational and forward-looking behavior a distinguished feature of this approach. For this reason I will not discuss the pioneering works of Minsky (1975) and Kindleberger (1978).

[3] Fazzari et al. (1988) and the Symposium on the Monetary Transmission Mechanism (1995).

[4] King (1986), Bernanke and Blinder (1988), and Bernanke and Gertler (1990).

a monetary contraction has a negative impact on investment and spending because of a fall in bank credit rather than as a consequence of interest rate movements. However, the credit view has been criticized for a number of reasons. Among these is the fact that, since banks can fund loans using different type of liabilities, monetary policy has a limited control of bank credit. Moreover, as the financial system evolves, the importance of non-bank intermediaries in supplying credit (even to small firms) seems to be increasing.[5]

In contrast with (or as a supplement to) these views, the FSA is offering a theory about the interaction between financial markets and business cycles largely independent of the behavior of Central Banks and the impact of monetary policy.

According to the FSA, standard neoclassical models are unable to explain the observed degree of macroeconomic volatility (well in excess of what these models can predict), to account for the propagation to the macro-economy of shocks originated in financial markets and to explain why financial markets may, in some cases, aggravate the consequences and the persistence of shocks originated in the real economy ("financial fragility" or "financial propagation"). The last issue has been particularly stressed within the FSA. Calomiris (1995) identifies four type of "financial propagators": (i) the cash-flow constraint, (ii) the balance-sheet constraint, (iii) the external supply-of-funds constraint (limitation on bank credit), and (iv) financial regulations that may magnify business cycles.

The cash-flow constraint arises when firms can raise funds more cheaply internally than externally and it implies an increasing sensitivity of investment to changes in firms' earnings. The balance-sheet constraint arises when firms with a high leverage (large amount of debt relative to assets) find it more difficult to get additional funds from outside investors. This circumstance gives rise to the definition of a firm's "debt capacity" (see below). Finally, the external supply of funds constraint arises when the monitoring activity of intermediaries (especially banks) leads to a fall in the costs of external finance. The general idea coming from the FSA is that these phenomena are all implying some amount of macroeconomic volatility and the extent of this volatility is a function of various agency costs associated to the implementation of contractual arrangements in the presence of imperfect information.

---

[5] Gertler and Gilchrist (1993).

Mishkin (1978) and Bernanke (1983) provide empirical support to the idea that financial, rather than monetary factors, played a dominant role in the Great Depression. In these papers, the term "financial factors" is a proxy for a bunch of variables, such as the availability of credit, the degree of indebtness of consumers and firms and some indicators of financial distress. These and other studies support Fisher's debt-deflation theory:[6] An initial business downturn and deflation causes an increase in firms' real debt inducing borrowers to reduce spending and implying a further downturn and deflation. More recent empirical investigations have emphasized the great sensitivity of investment to cash flow as a proof that firms' financial structure may be relevant to investment decisions, in violation of Modigliani–Miller theorem.[7]

From a more theoretical standpoint, the FSA has tried to develop dynamic aggregative models with financial market imperfections and rigorous microfoundations.

Some early contributions along these lines simply assume the existence of liquidity constraints and market incompleteness[8] (short sales constraints on securities, the inability to insure against all events). These contributions have emphasized at least two effects of financial market imperfections. One effect is the excess variability of aggregate output and individual consumption in response to exogenous disturbances. The other effect is the emergence of endogenous deterministic cycles in models where these cycles would be impossible with perfect financial markets. I turn to these two different theories in the next section.

2. Credit Constraints

In the last two decades, economists have tried to evaluate the macroeconomic consequences of removing the assumption that agents can completely insure themselves with respect to idiosyncratic risks (through a full set of Arrow–Debreu securities). Scheinkman and Weiss (1986) analyze an economy with two infinitely lived agents whose labor productivity is subject to idiosyncratic random disturbances. There is no aggregate uncertainty and agents have identical quasilinear utility in consumption and leisure. With a full set of Arrow–Debreu contingent claim markets the

---

[6] Fisher (1933).

[7] See Fazzari et al. (1988), Gertler and Gilchrist (1993), and Hubbard (1998).

[8] Bewley (1980), Scheinkman and Weiss (1986), Becker and Foias (1987), and Woodford (1988).

economy has a competitive equilibrium where individual consumption and leisure are constant across time and states. Hence, agents are able to eliminate fluctuations of individual labor and consumption levels and they can completely insure against productivity shocks. Complete markets essentially allow the less productive agent to get consumption goods in excess of his labor income from the more productive agent at any time. Subsequently, Scheinkman and Weiss remove the complete market assumption to impose that agents can transfer purchasing power across periods and states with a single durable asset. Agents cannot have a negative net asset position at any point in time. Hence, the ability of the less productive agent to exchange some his asset for the consumption good from the more productive agent is limited by the level of his net asset position at any point in time. Then, agents have a precautionary demand for savings, i.e. they accumulate assets when they are productive to provide for consumption during periods in which they have low productivity. In turn, precautionary asset demand generates aggregate output and relative price fluctuations. These variables may exhibit high-order serial correlation despite the fact that the exogenous disturbances follow a first-order Markovian process. Excessive output variability can be readily explained in the light of agents' precautionary asset accumulation. Agents who have been unproductive for some time periods have been decumulating their assets. Hence, when they suddenly switch to a high productive state, they have low non human wealth and they have to work harder to accumulate more assets. This behavior will push output up and prices down. As individual asset accumulation is proceeding along periods of high productivity, labor supply goes down along with output and prices are driven up.

Starting with Bewley (1986), it has been recognized that liquidity constraints, that is, the form of the budget constraints, have an important role in the characterization of the dynamic paths of output and prices. In particular, output and prices are more stable and smooth in a Ramsey model where agents are allowed to transfer purchasing power across times and states of nature as they like. On the other hand, in some cases liquidity constraints make the Ramsey model formally equivalent to an overlapping generations model. A typical feature of this model, which is shared by the Ramsey model with binding liquidity constraints, is that consumption and investment are highly sensitive to current disposable income and cash flows. Liquidity constrained agents in an infinite lived agents economy cannot freely transfer purchasing power between periods and they face a sequence of short-run budget constraints. This feature implies that the agents' actual behavior is "as if" their time horizon was much shorter than the time horizon of the whole economy. Hence, turnpike theorems cannot be applied and endogenous fluctuations can be obtained. Examples of fluctuations that have been provided in a deterministic setting with liquidity constraints (e.g. Becker and Foias 1987; Woodford 1988) rely on a strong income effect or a low substitutability between inputs in the production function.

Consider a standard deterministic growth model with a representative infinitely lived agent, maximizing a concave, time-separable utility function in consumption only. The transition path to a stationary state in this model is very simple. By the second welfare theorem, competitive equilibria of this model can be derived from the solution of the following problem:

$$\max \sum_{1}^{\infty} \beta^{t-1} u(c_t) \text{ s.t. :}$$

$$c_t + k_{t+1} \le f(k_t) + (1-\delta)k_t, \qquad k_t, c_t \ge 0, \quad k_0 > 0, \quad t = 0, 1, \ldots$$

where c and k denote per-capita consumption and capital, $f(\cdot)$ is a neoclassical constant returns to scale production function, $u(\cdot)$ is a concave utility function, $\beta \in (0,1)$ is the time-discount factor, and $\delta \in (0,1)$ a depreciation rate.

Using dynamic programming techniques, we can reduce the above problem to the problem of finding the sequence $\{k_t\}$ of capital stocks satisfying the following functional equation:

$$V(k_t) = \max_{k_{t+1}} \{u(f(k_t) - k_{t+1}) + \beta V(k_{t+1})\}$$

where $V(\cdot)$ is the value function.

It is a simple exercise to show that, when $f(\cdot)$ and $u(\cdot)$ are increasing and concave, the value function is also increasing and concave. Since the first-order condition for the above problem is:

$$u'(f(k_t) - k_{t+1}) = \beta V'(k_{t+1})$$

it follows that a rise in k_t for a given k_{t+1} implies a fall in marginal utility and, by the above equation, a fall in $V'(\cdot)$. Since $V(\cdot)$ is concave, we can claim that a rise in k_t implies a rise in k_{t+1}. Hence, this model can only produce monotonic transition paths.

Becker and Foias (1987) and Woodford (1986, 1988) show that monotonicity may break down when there is a constraint on the level of individual indebtness in a model with heterogeneous infinitely lived agents. In these models, some set of agents are more impatient than the remaining set of the population. It is well known that in this case the less impatient agents will end up consuming the entire amount of the available resources. With a borrowing constraint, we easily get equilibria where this agent owns the entire stock of capital and all remaining agents (the more impatient) have zero or negative assets.

This heterogeneity can be responsible for the emergence of endogenous cycles even in the simple one-dimensional optimal growth model. The intuition can be readily explained with the help of the following illustration. Consider a standard one-sector infinitely lived agents model with two consumers, 1 and 2, having the following preferences:

$$\sum_1^\infty \beta_j^{t-1} u\left(c_t^j\right), \quad \beta_j \in (0,1), \quad j = 1, 2.$$

The two consumer have the same utility function, but 2 is more impatient than 1, that is, $\beta_1 > \beta_2$. We assume that 2 cannot borrow in the capital market and, for simplicity, that 1 has no labor endowment.

Consider now the case in which the borrowing constraint for consumer 2 is binding in all periods and consumer 1 owns the entire capital stock (these two conditions must be verified eventually). Then, the budget constraints of the two agents at an equilibrium path of a competitive economy are respectively given by:

$$c_t^1 = k_t R_t - k_{t+1}, \qquad c_t^2 = w_t,$$

where R_t and w_t are the gross interest rate and the wage rate, respectively.
The first-order conditions for an optimal consumption path are:

$$u'\left(c_t^1\right) = \beta_1 R_{t+1} u'\left(c_{t+1}^1\right), \qquad u'\left(c_t^2\right) > \beta_2 R_{t+1} u'\left(c_{t+1}^2\right).$$

The first is the usual first-order condition for an unconstraint maximum of the agent's optimal consumption path (i.e. the marginal rate of substitution between today and tomorrow's consumption must be equal to the market interest rate), the second condition states that an unconstraint maximum cannot be reached since it would imply negative assets.

Now let $u(c) = \log c$. Then, we can easily compute agent 1 optimal capital accumulation path to find:

$$k_{t+1} = \beta_1 R_t k_t.$$

By zero profits and constant returns to scale, $R = f'(k)$ and we can write the above as:

$$k_{t+1} = \beta_1 f'(k_t)k_t.$$

This difference equation shows that concavity is not enough to have monotonic convergence to a steady state. If:

$$\partial(kf'(k))/\partial k = f'(k) + kf''(k) < 0$$

capital stock may be oscillating along an equilibrium path. Woodford (1988) shows conditions under which the deterministic dynamics may be chaotic.

3. Asymmetric Information

The models analyzed in the Section 2 do not attempt to derive credit constraints from more primitive economic considerations. For example, one may ask why a constrained borrower cannot succeed in obtaining a larger loan size at a higher interest rate in a competitive credit market. Early contributions toward a theory of credit constraints based on first principles are Jaffee and Russell (1976) and Stiglitz and Weiss (1981). These contributions are respectively based on the impossibility to enforce debt contracts (i.e. the existence of incentives to default) and adverse selection or moral hazard phenomena.

With non-enforceable debt contracts lenders may ration credit to increase the borrowers' incentive to repay their loans (a large loan size may make debt repayment "too costly"). In Stiglitz and Weiss (1981) credit rationing may result from a conflict of interest between borrowers and lenders over the choice of projects with different risks. A higher interest rate reduces the borrower's incentive to choose safe projects for a given limited liability standard debt contract. However, as pointed out by Bester (1985), credit rationing may not be a robust phenomenon even in these cases, provided lenders can use screening devices (such as collateral requirements) in addition to the interest rate, to sort out borrowers with different characteristics. In general, a problem with the early approaches to the microfoundations to credit rationing is that these models impose restrictions on the type of debt contracts that agents are allowed to exchange (sometimes a conflict of interest between borrowers and lenders over the choice of a project can be solved by replacing a debt contract with a profit sharing contract).

A more recent and growing literature has investigated the role of financial market imperfections in the macroeconomy using models where agents are allowed to select the best contractual arrangements. Within this alternative research agenda, one is facing the challenge to provide an extension of the existing theories of incentives and financial contracting to a general equilibrium framework where the relation between business cycle fluctuations and credit market frictions can be analyzed. This literature is based on two alternative type of assumptions. The first is imposing asymmetric information between lenders and borrowers. The second is assuming limited commitment with respect to the fulfillment of contractual obligations. In what follows I will discuss a selected number of recent contributions based on one or the other of these two alternative type of assumptions.

3.1 Financial propagators

Financial propagators (cash-flow and balance-sheet constraints) may be a product of optimal contractual arrangements set in financial markets characterized by asymmetric information. This is shown in a number of contributions based on the assumption that borrowers have private information about the characteristics of investment projects or about the actual realizations of uncertain investment returns.[9]

In Bernanke and Gertler (1990) entrepreneurs undertake a costly screening activity to assess the characteristic of a project. Since these characteristics are privately observed, lenders face an adverse selection problem in financing entrepreneurs' project. In Williamson (1987b) and Bernanke and Gertler (1989) lenders need to undertake costly monitoring and take actions inducing borrowers to reveal informations about investment returns. The theoretical underpinning of these two models is the costly state verification approach devised by Townsend (1979), Diamond (1984), and Williamson (1987a). Gertler (1992) has a model with

---

[9] Williamson (1987b), Farmer (1984), Mankiw (1986), Bernanke and Gertler (1989, 1990), Calomiris and Hubbard (1990), Gertler (1992), Holmström and Tirole (1997), and others.

a multi-period borrowing–lending relationship characterized by a moral hazard problem deriving from the assumption that the borrower can hide the realizations of his revenue in different contingencies. In this model agents are able to make their contracts contingent on a limited number of observable variables (inputs).

The optimal contracts that borrowers and lenders can exchange have a number of features consistent with observed regularities. Namely, borrowers may be credit constrained even if there is no ad hoc interest rate rigidity and the cost of borrowing may exceed the price of internal funds. Both of these phenomena imply the emergence of real costs associated to lending activity due to the borrowers' incentives to misreport project returns or characteristics ("agency costs"). These costs are endogenously derived and shown to be negatively related to the borrowers' wealth or balance sheet position. The idea is common to many models with moral hazard and adverse selection: The higher is the borrower's stake in a project (the entrepreneurs' endowment or the value of the collateral), the lower are the agency costs associated to optimal contracts. Since the borrower's stake in the project is likely to be procyclical, these papers are showing that imperfect financial markets may have a role in amplifying the business cycle.

The model by Holmström and Tirole (1997) is basically a variant of the Stiglitz and Weiss (1981) formulation of a lender–borrower relation with moral hazard, where borrowers have some unverifiable cost (benefit) from undertaking a specific investment project. This cost (benefit) creates a conflict of interests between entrepreneurs and outside investors.

The model can be used for several purposes. At the simplest level it can be used to derive the notion of "debt capacity", that is, the firm's level of leverage over which a loan should be denied in an optimal contractual arrangement. This notion is fundamental for producing some sort of credit rationing and financial fragility. To sketch the basic insights of Holmstrom and Tirole (1997), I provide a simplified version of their model.

An entrepreneur can choose among two projects $j \in \{H,L\}$ characterized by a linear technology with a random marginal product $\tilde{\alpha}$. The realizations of this random variable are $(\alpha, 0)$ (where $\alpha > 0$) and the two projects differ with respect to the probability of these realizations. Letting p^j be the probability that $\tilde{\alpha} = \alpha$, we have $p^H > p^L$. Project returns are verifiable and they require a perfectly divisible investment $k \in [0, +\infty)$.

Entrepreneurs have a fixed endowment $A > 0$ ("net worth") and the model incorporates the following moral hazard problem: If the entrepreneur chooses project H he has to take a non-contractible effort which gives him a disutility[10] $ek > 0$.

In order to undertake the project, an entrepreneur has to borrow an amount $B = k - A$. Now consider a (limited liability) loan contract $C = (B, R)$, where B is the size of the loan and R is the repayment per unit of loan in case of success. The entrepreneur's payoffs with contract C are:

$$\Pi^H(C) = p^H(\alpha k - RB) - ek,$$
$$\Pi^L(C) = p^L(\alpha k - RB).$$

The borrower chooses the "safe" project H iff $\Pi^H(C) \geq \Pi^L(C)$. Since $B = k - A$, this condition can be written as:

$$(\alpha - R)k + RA \geq ek/\Delta p, \tag{1}$$

where $\Delta p = p^H - p^L$. The above equation defines the incentive constraint that has to be satisfied by a contract C in order to induce the entrepreneur to choose the safe project.

Now suppose that the opportunity cost of lending any unit of capital is equal to $r \in (0, \alpha)$. Then, a lender will be willing to offer a contract C iff:

$$p^j R \geq r, \tag{2}$$

where $j = H$ or $j = L$ according to whether contract C is implementing the safe or the risky technology.

A contract is selected by maximizing the entrepreneur's payoff subject to an incentive constraint (the borrower chooses the technology for which the contract is designed) and to the lender's participation constraint. We call this an optimal contract and denote it with C^*. Since this contract maximizes the borrower's surplus, equation 2 must be satisfied with equality whatever is the project to be selected (whatever is j). It is assumed:

$$p^L \alpha < r, \qquad p^H \alpha > r + e, \qquad p^H \alpha < r + p^H e/\Delta p.$$

The first assumption insures that the risky project is not economically viable (if the lender is not loosing money, the borrower is always better off if he uses his cash for consumption instead of using it to implement

---

[10] Holmström and Tirole (1997) make the equivalent assumption that borrowers derive a private benefit from undertaking project L.

project L). The second inequality insures that the H project is economically viable and the entrepreneur's profits are increasing in k for any contract such that the lender breaks even and the third assumption insures that the incentive compatibility constraint 1 is binding for some big enough level of k (otherwise optimal investment would be unbounded). The reader can readily check that the optimal contract C^* under these assumptions is such that:

$$B^* = \sigma(r)A, \qquad R^* = r/p^H, \qquad k = (1 + \sigma(r))A,$$

where:

$$\sigma(r) = \frac{p^H\alpha - p^He/\Delta p}{r + p^He/\Delta p - p^H\alpha}.$$

The optimal loan size B^* is defined as the entrepreneur's "debt capacity" and $\sigma + 1$ can be defined as the "financial multiplier."

Claim 1 *Entrepreneurs can only invest (and borrow) up to a limit proportional to the value of their net worth.*

Since entrepreneurs' net worth is typically low in recessions, the above claim has the strong implication that investment spending tends to be highly procyclical, irrespective of relative price and interest rate movements.

3.2 Credit crunches

The model has the additional goal of deriving the equilibrium composition of firms' liabilities, the impact of banks liabilities on the degree of moral hazard and firms' investment activity.

Among the most important stylized facts characterizing financial crises is the existence of negative capital spillovers from the balance sheets of firms to those of intermediaries. Following a negative shock originated in asset markets, rising interest rates deteriorate firms' balance sheet, lowering asset values and increasing the bankruptcy rate. This will have a negative effect on banks' equity value and produce a fall in lending activity and a rise in interest rate spreads. This type of negative spillover (a "credit crunch") is likely to hit collateral-poor firms harder, as testified in a number of empirical investigations (see Gertler and Gilchrist 1994). The model by Holmström and Tirole (chapter Twenty-three) is an attempt to offer some theoretical support to these phenomena.

The optimal contract C^* that we have derived in Section 3.1 is considered as part of "direct finance" (uninformed investors). A second set of lenders is introduced to model intermediaries' lending activity or "indirect finance." These lenders are endowed with the ability to make costly monitoring on entrepreneurs and help a capital constrained firm to invest. At a cost $c > 0$ per unit of invested capital k, monitoring (or informed) lenders can "deter" borrowers from using the risky technology. Deterrence is attained by reducing entrepreneurs' payoff from adopting the risky technology (maybe because monitors have a limited power in enforcing a promise by the borrower to undertake this technology[11]). Namely, entrepreneurs pay $\tau > 0$ units of invested capital if and only if they choose technology L. For simplicity, I set $c = \tau$ (the lender can penalize the borrower's shirking behavior by charging him the full cost of monitoring) and $c < e$ (alternatively, the incentive problem would be trivial). A contract offered by an informed lender is $C^m = (B^m, R^m)$.

Now suppose that the entrepreneur is offered a pair of contracts (C, C^m) from uninformed and informed lenders, respectively. Payoffs with the H and L project respectively, evaluated with these contracts are:

$$\Pi^H(C, C^m) = p^H(\alpha k - RB - R^m B^m) - ek,$$
$$\Pi^L(C, C^m) = p^L(\alpha k - RB - R^m B^m) - ck,$$

where $k = A + B + B^m$.

We have to impose two constraints on contract C^m. The first is a non-negative profit constraint. It is assumed that total supply of informed capital, K^m, is relatively scarce at the given rate r and uninformed capital is in infinite supply. Then, letting r^m be the interest rate equilibrating supply and demand of informed capital, we have $r^m \geq r$ and, whereas uniformed lenders break even for $p^j R = r$, informed lenders break even for:

$$p^j R^m B^m = r^m B^m + ck, \tag{3}$$

The second constraint arises from the assumption that informed lenders may have an incentive to shirk on their monitoring activity, because the monitoring cost is not verifiable. Hence, monitoring will take place only if, by doing it, lenders are making at least as much money as by allowing borrowers to save on effort and select the risky technology. This condition implies the following incentive constraint:

$$R^m B^m \geq ck/\Delta p. \tag{4}$$

---

[11] Holmström and Tirole assume that there are two levels of shirking and that monitoring prevents borrowers from attaining a high private benefit.

Since $r^m \geq r$, $R^m > R$ and informed capital is more expensive than uninformed capital. Thus, borrowers will always profit from increasing their debt with uninformed lenders. However, this substitution is limited by the incentive constraint (under which the borrower selects the safe project[12]). When $B^m > 0$, the latter can be written as:

$$(\alpha - R)k + RA - (R^m - R)B^m \geq (e - c)k/\Delta p. \tag{5}$$

If we set $B^m = 0$ we are back to the situation described in the previous section. The incentive compatibility constraint is defined by equation 1 and investment k is bounded above by $(1 + \sigma(r))A$. The question is whether the borrower, by setting $B^m > 0$, is able to increase investment above this bound.

Notice that the informed lenders incentive compatibility constraint 4 must hold with equality at the optimal contract. This implies $r^m B^m = p^L ck/\Delta p$ by the break even condition 3. Using this to rewrite $\Pi^H(C, C^m)$ and 5, we get that, when $p^H \alpha > r + e + p^H c/\Delta p$ (the H project is economically viable for all $B^m > 0$), an optimal contract pair (B, B^m) implies:

$$k = (1 + \sigma(r))(A + B^m). \tag{6}$$

Claim 2 *Entrepreneurs can only invest up to a limit proportional to the value of their net worth plus the available informed capital.*

The above claim provides a rationale for the external supply of funds constraint as defined by Calomiris (1995). One can solve for the demand of uninformed capital and find that this is a decreasing function of r^m. In equilibrium this rate of return must be endogenized using the market clearing condition $B^m = K^m$. Hence, the equilibrium level of investment is $k(r) = (1 + \sigma(r))(A + K^m)$ and we can state the following:

Claim 3 (Credit crunch) *A unit fall in K^m generates a more than a unit fall of investment.*

To be sure, the above result is no more than a simple comparative statics exercise since the model is static and the determination of a number of important variables is left unexplained. However, Holmström and Tirole's contribution provides interesting suggestions on how to construct a theory of financial fragility where the balance sheets of borrowers and intermediaries are both taken into account.

---

[12] Recall that the risky technology is not economically viable ($p^L \alpha < r$).

3.3 Moral hazard and endogenous cycles

Like Holmström and Tirole (1997), Suarez and Sussman (1997) (chapter Twenty-five) have a model where borrowers can take unobservable actions affecting the probability of going bankrupt on investment projects with uncertain returns. However, in this paper liquidity effects may be responsible for an endogenous reversion mechanism, unlike Holmstrom and Tirole and the other papers that we have discussed so far, where financial fragility is responsible for the amplification of exogenous shocks.

We know that entrepreneurs' effort to implement "good" projects is an increasing function of the liquidity that the firms lose when their projects fail (or that could be seized by the lender). This is the mechanism whereby liquidity may have a role in amplifying shocks. More generally, agency costs are likely to be higher in recessions than in booms. The reason why Suarez and Sussman obtain endogenous cycles is that liquidity effects are assumed to be a function of relative price movements.

Suarez and Sussman consider an economy with two consumption goods, fruit and coffee. Coffee is produced using fruit with a given technology which is only accessible to one set of agents, called "borrowers." These are overlapping generations of agents living for three periods and having no endowment (of fruit) during their life. Fruit is a non-storable depreciating good available in fixed supply and owned by a complementary set of agents called "lenders."

Coffee comes out from indivisible projects such that one unit of fruit invested at any time t produces α units of coffee at time $t + 1$ (with certainty) and a random amount $\tilde{\alpha}$ of coffee at time $t+2$. This random variable is i.i.d. across borrowers and it takes two values only. Namely, $\tilde{\alpha} = \alpha$ with probability p and $\tilde{\alpha} = 0$ with probability $1 - p$.

Hence, the probability distribution of $\tilde{\alpha}$ can be characterized in terms of the single probability p. By the assumed moral hazard problem, borrowers' effort has a direct effect on this variable. In particular, I assume that the success probability p equals the borrower's effort and this has a disutility measured by $\psi(p)$. For simplicity, the disutility function $\psi(\cdot)$ is assumed to be twice differentiable, strictly increasing and strictly convex, with boundary conditions $\psi(0) = 0$, $\lim_{p \to 0} \psi'(p) = 0$, $\lim_{p \to 1} \psi'(p) = +\infty$.

In the model, agents can exchange a safe asset with one-period maturity yielding a gross interest rate R_t. There are no short sale constraints on this asset, but borrowers cannot invest in the indivisible project by selling this asset on the market. External funds to be invested in the indivisible project are obtained on a separate market by signing a loan contract $C_t = (I_{t+1}, \tilde{Z}_{t+2})$. This is defined below as a Pareto optimal contractual arrangement between borrowers and lenders.[13] For a unit loan size, C_t specifies a deterministic payment at time $t + 1$ and a stochastic payment (contingent on the realization of $\tilde{\alpha}$) at time $t + 2$. By limited liability, $\tilde{Z}_{t+2} = 0$ when $\tilde{\alpha} = 0$. I set $\tilde{Z}_{t+2} = Z_{t+2}$ when $\tilde{\alpha} = \alpha$.

Now let c and x denote consumption of fruit and coffee, fruit be the numeraire good and q the relative price of coffee. For simplicity, borrowers are risk neutral and consume fruit in the last two periods of their life only, whereas lenders have linear instantaneous utility over fruit consumption and a quasilinear instantaneous utility $c + v(x)$. The subjective discount rates are equal across agents.

When consumption choices are interior, the following conditions must hold:

$$R_t = 1/\beta \equiv R, \quad v'(x_t) = q_t, \quad \forall t.$$

Since lenders are risk neutral, they will sign contract C_t iff:

$$I_{t+1}/R + p_{t+2}Z_{t+2}/R^2 \geq 1. \tag{7}$$

Since borrowers are risk neutral and born with zero endowment, they never have an incentive to use some of their income to accumulate the safe asset. Then, a borrower born and investing in his technology at time $t - 1$ with contract $C_{t-1} = (I_t, Z_{t+1})$ has expected utility:

$$U^{t-1} = (q_t\alpha - I_t) + (1/R)p_{t+1}(q_{t+1}\alpha - Z_{t+1}) - (1/R)\psi(p_{t+1}).$$

C_{t-1} satisfies a limited liability and an incentive compatible constraint. The former constraint simply imposes an upper bound on repayments I_t, Z_{t+1} given by the borrower's revenues at time t and $t + 1$ respectively, that is:

$$I_t \leq q_t\alpha; \tag{8}$$

$$\tilde{Z}_{t+1} \leq q_{t+1}\tilde{\alpha}_{t+1}. \tag{9}$$

The incentive compatibility constraint arises from moral hazard. Since effort is not contractable, p_{t+1} is optimally selected by the borrower for

---

[13] Since this contract is derived from the maximization of the borrowers' surplus (just as in the last section), these agents have no incentive to go short on the safe asset.

the given contract C_{t-1}. This implies that $p_{t+1} = p(q_{t+1}, Z_{t+1})$, with $p(q, Z)$ defined by the first-order condition:

$$\psi'(p(q_{t+1}, Z_{t+1})) = q_{t+1}\alpha - Z_{t+1}. \tag{10}$$

An optimal contract maximizes the borrowers' expected utility subject to the limited liability constraints 8, 9, the incentive constraint 10, and the lenders' participation constraint 7. This contractual arrangement can be decentralized by assuming that lenders Bertrand compete with each other when setting the terms of the contract (I, Z). Evidently, the lenders participation constraint is always binding at the optimal contract. Then, dropping time subscripts, we can rewrite the borrowers' utility index as:

$$U = (q\alpha - R) + (1/R)p(q', Z)q'\alpha - (1/R)\psi(p(q', Z)),$$

where $q' = q_{t+1}$ if $q = q_t$. Using the incentive compatibility constraint 10, we get:

$$\partial U/\partial Z = -Z/\psi''(p). \tag{11}$$

Then, the optimal contract $C^* = (I^*, Z^*)$ has:

$$I^* = q\alpha, \qquad \psi'(p(q', Z^*)) = q'\alpha - Z^*$$

and:

$$Z^* = \begin{cases} R(R - q\alpha)/p(q', Z^*) \equiv Z(q, q') & \text{if } q\alpha < R, \\ 0 & \text{if } q\alpha \geq R. \end{cases}$$

Notice that $Z^* = 0$ characterizes the optimal contract even when the farmers' effort is contractible. Hence, when $q > R/\alpha$, C^* is a first best contract, otherwise the contract cannot implement the first best effort and p will be lower than in the first best case. I call this (low first period revenue with respect to the market interest rate) a case of financial distress.

Claim 4 *The optimal contract is such that the borrower pays the entire (deterministic) revenue to the lender in the first production period. In the second production period he pays a positive amount as a function of first and second period revenues in case of financial distress, otherwise he pays zero. Accordingly, the success probability depends on first and second period revenue in case of financial distress, otherwise it only depends on second period revenue.*

The intuition for this result hinges on the presence of two different constraints, the limited liability constraint 8 and the participation constraint 7. Since the incentive problem only arises in the second production periods (when lenders get payment Z), optimality requires that the borrowers are charged the lowest possible repayment in the second production period. This implies that they should substitute Z for I along the lender's participation constraint frontier 7. However, by limited liability, I cannot be greater than $q\alpha$ (the first period cash flow) and this value may imply a positive second period repayment Z along equation 7. Hence, second best contracts arise when first period cash flow (liquidity) is relatively low.

We define the "optimal probability" as $p^*_{t+1} = p(q_{t+1}, Z^*_{t+1})$ (the probability of a positive second period cash flow with an optimal contract). Assuming that there is a continuum of borrowers with size one, the law of large numbers implies that the total supply of coffee is equal to $(1 + p)\alpha$. For interior consumption choices, the equilibrium price of coffee at time $t + 1$ is:

$$\left(1 + p^*_{t+1}\right)\alpha = (v')^{-1}(q_{t+1}) \equiv x(q_{t+1}).$$

It is clear that, when $q_t \geq R/\alpha$, p^*_{t+1} only depends on q_{t+1} and market clearing does not generate any dynamics in prices. On the other hand, when $q_t < R/\alpha$, we have:

$$p^*_{t+1} = p\left(q_{t+1}, Z(q_t, q_{t+1})\right) \equiv \Pi(q_t, q_{t+1}).$$

Hence, when $q_t < R/\alpha$, market clearing can be written as:

$$\left(1 + \Pi(q_t, q_{t+1})\right)\alpha = x(q_{t+1}). \tag{12}$$

Recall that $Z(q, q')$ is decreasing in both arguments. Since $p(q', Z)$ is increasing in q' and decreasing in Z, it follows that $\Pi(q, q')$ is increasing in both arguments. We skip a detailed analysis of the circumstances in which equation 12 defines a proper dynamical system in q_t for all t (existence and stability of a steady state $q^* < R/\alpha$ are the usual assumptions to be used for this purpose). The main point to be emphasized is that, when such a dynamical system can be defined, this is always characterized by endogenous price (and output) fluctuations. In fact, notice that a rise in q_t implies a rise in the left-hand side of equation 12. Then, aggregate supply of coffee goes up and market clearing can only be restored by a fall in q_{t+1}, since this generates a rise in demand and a fall in supply.

Claim 5 *In case of financial distress the relation between two consecutive equilibrium relative prices q_t and q_{t+1} must be non-monotonic. A rise in borrowers' production generates excess supply and a price deflation, which in turn reduces their liquidity (cash flow). In this model, low liquidity aggravates the moral hazard problem by reducing the borrowers' incentives to improve the probability of a successful investment.*

4. Limited Commitment and Collateral

The models discussed in the previous section are based on the assumption that, because of asymmetric information, optimal contracts reflect high costs of monitoring income or effort and all agency costs arising from inducing truth-telling or adequate efforts by the borrowers.

It has been observed, though, that credit rationing (as well as incomplete diversification and insurance) also occurs in economic environments where the degree of asymmetric information about individual characteristics is relatively small.

Limited commitment and unenforceability of contracts is an alternative way to explain credit constraints and financial propagators. This explanation does not necessarily hinge on the existence of asymmetric information. The basic idea is that some portion of agents' assets and endowments are not seizable when they decide to go bankrupt. In this case, the most important incentive to repay a loan contract arises from the threat of being excluded from future trading in asset markets. If one assumes perfect information, a debt contract will be signed only if the borrower has no incentive to default. A contract such that the borrower derives at least the utility level that he could get if he were to default is said to be individually rational.

More generally, limited commitment and the unenforceability of contracts may arise from legal limits on how much a borrower can be punished in case of default, from the inability of outside agencies to learn about some critical characteristics of borrowers' investments and from the inalienability of human capital (see Hart and Moore 1989, 1994). In the last instance, it is assumed that the borrower has special (non-replaceable) skills that are involved in his investment project and the two parties cannot possibly write a contract preventing the borrower from quitting from the project, that is, withdrawing his human capital.

Recent papers have investigated the consequences on risk sharing and the possible emergence of credit rationing with no commitment.[14] In particular, Kehoe and Levine (1993), Kocherlakota (1996), and Alvarez and Jermann (2000) study the characteristics of efficient allocations when individual rationality constraints are explicitly taken into account. They show that perfect diversification of consumption risks across individuals may not be optimal and optimal portfolio allocations may be subject to solvency constraints prohibiting agents from holding large amounts of contingent debt. More general macroeconomic implications of these models are yet to be characterized. However, a reasonable conjecture is that these implications may be comparable with those obtained by Scheinkman and Weiss (1986), where incomplete consumption diversification and insurance is simply assumed.

The paper by Kiyotaki and Moore (1997) (henceforth KM) (chapter twenty-four) can be seen as a contribution within the limited commitment approach with some distinguished features. The paper is an attempt to rationalize Fisher's debt-deflation theory in a fully dynamic equilibrium model assuming that borrowers cannot precommit to repay their debts and that lenders are unable to appropriate the product of the borrowers' labor. However, KM assume that borrowers cannot be excluded from participating in any future asset trading when they decide to default. Incentives to repay a loan derive from the existence of collateralizable assets.

When studying optimal (individually rational) contracts with limited commitment, the existence of collateralizable assets may play a very important role. This is apparent from our discussion about the role of the borrower's net worth in enhancing his debt capacity and financial propagation. The latter may be especially strong since the value of collateral is typically low in situations of financial distress (for the borrower and, possibly, for the economy as a whole) and sometimes the borrower takes actions that reduce the value of seizable assets when his project is liquidated (the "outside value" of collateral may be lower than the "inside value").

In KM, the role of collateral is twofold. On one hand it determines the economy's aggregate output through its use in the production process. On the other hand it affects the equilibrium allocations as a binding credit limit on borrowers. Following a negative productivity shock, borrowers will cut back on their investment spending and decrease their demand of

---

[14] See Eaton and Gersovitz (1981), Allen (1983), Bulow and Rogoff (1989), Kehoe and Levine (1993), Kocherlakota (1996), and Alvarez and Jermann (2000).

collateral. This implies a fall in the price of collateral and a propagation of the effect of the initial shock across periods.

There are two critical assumptions in KM's paper:

1. the borrower has the option to repudiate his debt contract and, in case of repudiation, he keeps the product of his investment and loses the full value of his collateral;
2. borrowers and lenders have access to two different technologies, with the borrower's technology providing higher rates of return.

The first assumption is based on the idea that the borrower's human capital is inalienable. These agents can threaten to withdraw their labor and leave lenders with no more than the value of the collateral (i.e. the liquidation value of the investment project). In KM's formulation, this argument is used to state that, under suitable assumptions about the respective bargaining power of lenders and borrowers, repudiation will not be individually rational if and only if interest payments fall short of the collateral value. KM base their model on the theory of debt renegotiation developed by Hart and Moore (1994), where borrowers can threaten to repudiate a loan contract by withdrawing their (inalienable) human capital, leaving the lender with the options of liquidating the project or renegotiating the terms of the contract. However, in the model by Hart and Moore, the borrower has an exclusive and long term relationship with a single lender, whereas KM assume that borrowers can get new loan contracts, in each time period, from a large set of lenders and contractual relations are short-run and anonymous. Given these assumptions, one may ask what type of credit constraint (if any) would arise if, in violation of contract anonymity, defaulting firms were partially or totally excluded from the credit market (e.g. as in Kehoe and Levine 1993 and Alvarez and Jerman 2000).

The second assumption implies that the evolution of the price of collateral is determined by a no arbitrage condition between using savings for lending activity and using it on an inefficient investment project. This is a feature shared by any model with binding credit constraints (e.g. Woodford 1988).

Here I sketch a slightly modified version of KM model to clarify these issues. Consider an economy with two large sets of identical representative agents, farmers f and gatherers g, two goods, land k and fruits y, and two technologies, "farming" and "gathering." The technologies take one period to be productive and they employ land as the only input, with production functions given by:

$$y = f_j(k), \quad \text{with: } f_j(\cdot) > 0, \ f_j'(\cdot) \geq 0, \ f_j''(\cdot) \leq 0, \ (j = f, g).$$

Fruit cannot be stored and the total fixed supply of land is K. Prices are measured in units of fruit and the relative price of land is q. Both lenders and borrowers are born at time $t = 1$ and they live for an infinite number of discrete time periods $t = 1, 2, \ldots$.

Gatherers have no access to the farming technology, there is no stock market and agents can borrow and lend by trading an asset a (denominated in units of the consumption good) with one period maturity and a gross rate of interest R. Markets are competitive and anonymous.

Let $c^j (j = f, g)$ be agents' consumption. Then, agents' utility and their period-t budget constraint are given by:

$$U_j\left(c^j\right) = \sum_{t=1}^{\infty} \beta_j^{t-1} u_j\left(c_t^j\right),$$

$$c_t^j + a_{t+1}^j + q_t k_{t+1}^j = R_t a_t^j + f_j(k_t) + q_t k_t^j, \quad t = 1, 2, \ldots \tag{13}$$

where $\beta_j \in (0, 1)$ is the subjective gross time discount rate and u_j is assumed to be increasing and concave.

As in KM we assume now that loan contracts are fully collateralized. Then we have to impose the following short sales constraint:

$$a_{t+1}^j \geq -q_{t+1} k_{t+1}^j / R_{t+1}. \tag{14}$$

The above inequality establishes a lower bound on the ratio between an agent's net asset position and the amount of purchased land, i.e.:

$$\frac{a_{t+1} + q_t k_{t+1}}{k_{t+1}} \geq q_t - \frac{q_{t+1}}{R_{t+1}} \equiv d_{t+1},$$

where the right-hand side of this inequality is the (minimum) down payment required to purchase a unit of land.

An equilibrium is an allocation $\{c_t^j, k_t^j\}$ and a price sequence $\{R_t, q_t\}$ for $t = 1, 2, \ldots$ such that U_j is maximized over the choice variables $\{c_t^j, k_t^j, a_t^j\}$ under constraints 13, 14, $c_t^j \geq 0, k_t^j \geq 0$ and such that markets clear, that is:

$$\sum_j a_t^j = 0, \qquad \sum_j k_t^j = K, \qquad \sum_j c_t^j = \sum_j f_j(k_t^j).$$

Now define the gross rates of return on farmers and gatherers technology as:

$$\rho_t^j = \left(q_t + f_j'\left(k_t^j\right)\right)/q_{t-1} \quad j = f, g$$

and consider an equilibrium with positive consumption and capital. In this equilibrium we have $\rho_t^j \geq R_t$ for all t and, by the first-order conditions for utility maximization, there exists a sequence of non negative multipliers $\{\eta_t^j\}$ such that:

$$u_j'(c_t^j) = \beta_j R_{t+1} u_j'(c_{t+1}^j) + R_{t+1} \eta_t^j; \tag{15}$$

$$\eta_t^j = \left(q_t/f_j'(k_{t+1})\right) \left(\frac{\rho_{t+1}^j - R_{t+1}}{R_{t+1}}\right) \lambda_t^j. \tag{16}$$

When $\eta_t^j > 0$ we say that credit constraint 14 is binding, that is, agent j would like to invest in his technology more than he is allowed to at time t. In this case $R_{t+1} d_{t+1}^j = -q_{t+1} k_{t+1}^j$, $\rho_{t+1}^j > R_{t+1}$. Now suppose that there is an equilibrium where farmers' are credit constrained for all t. By the market clearing conditions the same constraint cannot be binding for gatherers and we get $\rho_t^f > R_t = \rho_t^g$ for all t, that is, the farmer's technology must dominate the gatherer's technology in returns.

Claim 6 *Agent j is credit constrained (would like to invest more than he is allowed to by the value of his collateral) at time t if and only if $\rho_{t+1}^j > R_{t+1}$. In equilibrium the technology of the credit constrained agents must dominate the technology of the non-credit-constrained agents in returns and the market interest rate equalizes the rate of return on the dominated technology.*

To construct some specific examples, assume that:

$$u_f(c) = \log c, \qquad u_g(c) = c, \qquad \beta_g \geq \beta_f, \qquad f_f(k) = \alpha k.$$

By the assumed preference relations, the farmer has a stronger desire for consumption smoothing. Notice that this is enough to rule out equilibria where the credit constraint is binding for gatherers. In fact, by the linearity of gatherers' utility function and equations 15, 16 we get:

$$\rho_{t+1}^g = R_{t+1}, \qquad R_{t+1} = 1/\beta_g \equiv R, \qquad \rho_{t+1}^g = R.$$

It follows that:

$$f_g'(k_t^g) = R q_{t-1} - q_t = R d_t, \quad t = 1, 2, \ldots$$

that is, the down payment required to purchase a unit of land equals the ratio between the gatherers' marginal product of capital and the gross interest rate. Since agents' demand for land is assumed to be positive in equilibrium, $\rho_t^f \geq R$ for all t and $d_t \leq \alpha/R$.

There are two type of equilibria. In the first best equilibrium allocation, where debt repayments can be fully enforced, we have:

$$d_t = f_g'\left(k_t^g\right)/R = \alpha/R.$$

Hence, the down payment is constant. The above equalities, together with the trasversality condition, imply that the first best equilibrium is a steady state with $k_t^f = k^*$, $q_t = q^*$ such that:

$$f_g'(K - k^*) = \alpha, \qquad q^* = \frac{\alpha}{R - 1}.$$

A first best equilibrium cannot hold in a credit constrained economy when $\beta^f < \beta_g = 1/R$. In fact, by logarithmic utility, the farmers' optimal portfolio allocation satisfies:

$$a_{t+1}^f + q^*k^* = \beta_f R\left(a_t^f + q^*k^*\right),$$

that is, $a_t^f \to -q^*k^*$ and 14 is violated in finite time with $\beta^f < \beta_g = 1/R$. Hence,

Claim 7 *When loans must be fully collateralized, we can only have a credit constrained equilibrium where the more impatient agents (farmers) are credit constrained and running the dominating technology.*

By first-order conditions 15, 16, farmers' budget constraint and logarithmic utility, one obtains:

$$k_{t+1}^f d_{t+1} = \beta_f \alpha k_t^f. \tag{17}$$

To simplify the notation let $k^f = k$ at equilibrium and recall the no arbitrage conditions:

$$d_t = f_g'\left(k_t^g\right)/R = f_g'(K - k_t)/R \equiv d(k_t).$$

Then, a credit constrained equilibrium can be defined as a sequence $\{k_t\}$ such that, for all $t = 1, 2, \ldots$:

$$d(k_{t+1})k_{t+1} = \beta_f \alpha k_t, \tag{18}$$

$$f_g'(K - k_{t+1}) \leq \alpha. \tag{19}$$

The former equation 18 combines farmers' optimal investing behavior with the no arbitrage condition and the latter equation 19 guarantees that the credit constraint is binding for all t.

Since $f_g'(\cdot) > 0$ and $f_g''(\cdot) \leq 0$, the map $h(k) = d(k)k$ is increasing and invertible in the interval $[0, K)$ and we can redefine equation 18 as a difference equation:

$$k_{t+1} = h^{-1}(\beta_f \alpha k_t) = \phi(k_t),$$

where $\phi'(k) > 0$, $\phi(0) = 0$. If $f_g'(K) < \beta_f R \alpha$, $\lim_{k \to 0} f_g'(k) = +\infty$, this difference equation has a steady state $k^o \in (0, k^*]$ such that $k^o < k^*$ iff $\beta_f < \beta_g$ and the equilibrium dynamics generated by the map $\phi(\cdot)$ is monotonic and convergent to k^o.

Since the benchmark equilibrium is the steady state k^* for all initial conditions k_1 and the credit constrained equilibrium converges to the steady state $k^o \leq k^*$ asymptotically for all $k_1 \neq k^o$, this proves that:

Claim 8 *A fully collateralized credit constraint generates more persistence of (unanticipated) exogenous shocks than in the benchmark equilibrium.*[15]

We are now in a position to compare the results of this model with Fisher's debt-deflation theory. Output growth in this model is driven by a reallocation of productive land from a relatively inefficient to a relatively efficient use. However, this reallocation is limited by the amount of expected down payment, $d_{t+1} = q_t - q_{t+1}/R$, that farmers have to submit to buy land. A re-examination of equation 18 shows that the higher is the expected down payment, the smaller is the amount of land that farmers can use for next period production. Now suppose that the economy is experiencing a deflation of land prices and that this deflation is large enough to imply a rise in the expected down payment. Then, farmers may not be able to buy enough land and the economy may fall into a recession. However, under the stated assumptions, the model has a stabilizing mechanism. In fact, by the no arbitrage condition between lending (at the rate R) and gathering (at the rate ρ^g), the fall in land prices and in the down payment d_{t+1} goes along with a fall in the marginal product for gathering, that is, a rise in the demand for land for gathering. This reallocation of land prevents land prices from falling by enough to destabilize the economy. Hence, the model can be used to show the persistence of the effects of unanticipated exogenous shocks on the economy (magnified by

---

[15] See the discussion in KM for more details.

the credit constraint), but it is not suitable for analyzing destabilization or cycles that may be arising endogenously from the economy.[16] In other words, the model does not explain why a growing and apparently healthy economy may suddenly fall into a recession in the absence of exogenous disturbances.

A more complicated version of the model is provided by KM to show that endogenous cycles may arise under special conditions (land producing capital goods, uncertainty about production outcomes). This proves that the interaction between the dynamics of interest rate payments and credit limits may produce a non monotonic time path of investment.

It is worth noticing that cycles may be obtained under a variety of alternative specifications of the KM's model. In fact, by previous works on the dynamics of models with (exogenous) credit constraints (e.g. Becker and Foias 1987; Woodford 1988) we know that endogenous cycles are a pervasive phenomenon in these models.[17] As an alternative example of a simple mechanism generating cycles in the KM model, consider the case in which, just like in Suarez and Sussman (1997), one adds a new produced good in the economy and agents' demand of this good is decreasing in its own price. In the appendix to this discussion it is shown that this modification is enough to generate cycles that would not be possible if debt repayments were fully enforceable.

5. Policy Implications

All models belonging to the FSA are based on established results from corporate finance and financial contracting. This literature offers many insights on when and how financial regulation should be implemented in a partial equilibrium setting and a review of these results is beyond the scope of my discussion. The appropriate policy questions to be raised here concern the role and the macroeconomic targets of fiscal and monetary policy.

Abstracting from the specific examples that we have been considering here, it can be argued that the FSA assigns a special role to redistributive policies such as taxes and transfers. Since the low borrowers' net worth

[16] Suarez and Sussman (1997) notice that KM have to rule out price indexation as a way to insure against unanticipated shocks.

[17] I have already mentioned that this is a consequence of the impossibility of transferring purchasing power across periods and the lack of some no arbitrage conditions.

and lack of liquidity is at the root of financial propagation, a natural policy instrument for avoiding financial crisis and excessive output variability is a transfer to borrowers or poorly capitalized intermediaries in case of financial distress. By the same arguments, it is very important for the Central Bank to stand ready to act as a lender of last resort to avoid bank runs and panics. However, these policies may be undermined by moral hazard problems unless they are used when shocks are unanticipated or when they are beyond the borrowers' control.

Traditional macroeconomic analysis is mainly concerned with the problem of controlling inflation and stabilizing output. Looking at the recent debates among macro economists one sees that fiscal policy and aggregate demand management is rarely seen as an effective mechanism to compensate for excessive output fluctuations. There seems to be a strong consensus among policy makers that the stability of the price level and the pre-determination of an inflation target should be the main objectives. The FSA suggests that this limited range for monetary policy may produce excessive output variability and that other policies should be considered.

In fact, whereas low inflation rates have been generally achieved in most countries, policy makers are increasingly concerned with recent and expected episodes of international financial crises as well as extreme asset price and exchange rate movements. The FSA provides empirical and theoretical ammunitions to the opinion that we should be strongly concerned with excessive asset price variability. Since the objective of a low inflation rate may sometime be in conflict with asset price stability, the question if monetary policy targets and instruments should be redefined is particularly challenging.[18] This is not to say that improving the financial structure and achieving price stability are always conflicting objectives. As noted by Mishkin (1996), price stability and low inflation may be important for avoiding financial crises, since these goals are instrumental for achieving a stable exchange rate and promoting international financial transactions.[19]

The question whether standard monetary policies may have a role in curbing financial propagation is still unsettled and a theoretical literature integrating monetary theory with the FSA is under way. Most of the contributions that we have discussed so far assume that money and nominal

[18] Empirical evaluations of the role of monetary policies along the lines of Fisher's debt-deflation theory have been provided by Mishkin (1978), Bernanke (1983), and Mishkin (1991), among others.

[19] Price stability may enable developing countries to increase the maturity of debt contracts and to denominate debts in domestic currency.

variables have no real effects on the economy and a consensus about the appropriate instruments and targets for monetary policy is still missing.

We have already mentioned that the FSA offers a theory of financial propagations quite independent of the way in which monetary aggregates (demand deposits and banks credit) are interacting with the real economy. In the words of Gertler and Gilchrist, this approach is "... about a propagation mechanism—a mechanism whereby credit market frictions may serve to amplify the impact of disturbances on borrower' spending decisions" (Gertler and Gilchrist 1993: 47). We have seen that, in some cases, financial propagations may arise from endogenous reversion mechanisms and the existence of initial external disturbances are not even required. In any case, when there is a demand for money (either as a mean for transactions or as a store of value), monetary shocks will affect borrower' spending by changing the real value of outstanding assets, redistributing wealth across borrowers and lenders, etc.

The idea that the FSA should be integrated with more standard monetary models so as to generate predictions about the effects of monetary policy is justified both from an empirical and a theoretical standpoint. It is well known that the importance of money has not diminished in well-developed financial institutions. By noticing that a sizable amount of demand deposits are held by financial businesses even in the present US economy, Lucas (1990) develops a model with a cash-in-advance constraint affecting security trading as well as consumption. The model explains the role of liquidity in asset pricing, the effectiveness of open market operations and it can be used to justify excessive stock market volatility. Less recent extentions of the cash-in-advance model to investment demand show that money may not be superneutral and inflation may have a negative effect on the long run capital stock.[20] The importance of money for financial transactions goes beyond the pure transaction motive when markets are incomplete. For instance, Gottardi (1994) shows that money non neutrality may emerge, even in the absence of transaction costs, in a multi-agents–multi-goods overlapping generations economy when markets are incomplete. In this model agents exchange nominal assets and monetary policy may affect assets payoffs by changing the level of money prices over time. Aiyagari and Gertler (1991) have a model with uninsurable individual consumption risks where, because of transaction costs, liquid assets have

----

[20] See Stockman (1981) and Abel (1985).

an edge over stocks in providing for precautionary savings (i.e. money may be used for self insurance). By using an overlapping generations model, Azariadis and Smith (1993) show that adverse selection in financial markets may reduce the rate of return at the inside-money steady state. Hence, an economy that would not generate monetary equilibria under full information may generate these equilibria in the asymmetric information case. The intuition behind this result is that the equilibrium credit rationing induced by adverse selection will force agents to save more than in the full information case and this will lower the autarkic interest rate.

These are just few examples of models where the existence of money can be associated to informational frictions and financial market imperfections. Future research will hopefully better qualify the best monetary instruments that policy makers should be using to reduce the amplitude of financial propagations.

We may say that the policy implications of some of the leading theoretical models presented in this discussion are not always comparable with current debates. For example, within the KM's model, policy actions cannot be advocated in the light of the economic consequences of investors' "irrational exuberance" (a point often raised by policymakers). In that model the price of land does not exceed the market fundamental (of gatherers and farmers technology) and there is no "excessive" asset price variability with respect to any alternative situation where the two conditions for inefficiency, gatherers' inability to run farmers' technology and borrowers limited commitment, cannot be removed. A policy intervention could only be justified under the condition that this is redistributing resources from credit unconstrained to credit constrained agents so as to reduce an inefficiency arising from the under-utilization of farmers' technology. This type of policy is not part of the standard tools of monetary and fiscal authorities. Suarez and Sussman's contribution is not offering simple policy prescriptions either. In their model agents are risk neutral and contractual arrangement are Pareto optimal. Hence, a policy stabilizing endogenous output fluctuations cannot be Pareto improving.[21]

The limited role for macroeconomic policy action within more theoretical contributions to the FSA sometime derives from the strategy of imposing contract optimality. The main motivation of this strategy is that financial propagation is shown to be compatible with situations

---

[21] The authors are discussing conditions under which this policy may increase an equal weights welfare function.

where agents are exploiting all mutually profitable opportunities, given the set of contracts that are allowed to exist by the assumed informational asymmetries or by limited commitment. However, one may ask whether these contracts are always decentralizable in competitive markets and if, by imposing decentralization, additional inefficiencies, more extensive propagation mechanisms and a wider role for the policymakers may emerge.[22]

6. Summary and Conclusions

The contributions which I have discussed so far offer two type of predictions about the effect of financial market imperfections on business fluctuations. The dominant prediction is that exogenous shocks tend to be more persistent and amplified by a financial propagation mechanism (as in Bernanke and Gertler 1989, 1990; Holmström and Tirole 1997; Kiyotaki and Moore 1997). An alternative prediction is that these market imperfections may be responsible for an endogenous reversion mechanism (as in Suarez and Sussman 1997; Kiyotaki and Moore 1997). The first prediction can be easily understood when we consider that moral hazard and agency costs are a decreasing function of firms' liquidity and collateralized assets. Most models predict that these variables are highly procyclical when endogenized in a general equilibrium framework. Hence, moral hazard and agency costs are more important in recessions rather than in booms. Suarez and Sussman show, however, that this may not be a valid prediction in a multi commodity economy, where, in some cases, relative price movements make firms' liquidity counter-cyclical. However, a counter-cyclical borrowers' net worth is at variance with empirical observations.

A model with asymmetric information between lenders and borrowers where moral hazard may be more important in booms rather than recessions for reasons that are independent from the cyclical behavior of borrowers' net worth is in Reichlin and Siconolfi (2000). This chapter analyzes the Pareto optimal contracts between lenders and borrowers by generalizing the Rothschild–Stiglitz pure adverse selection model to include moral hazard. Entrepreneurs with unequal "abilities" borrow to

---

[22] On the issue whether "constrained Pareto optima" can be interpreted as competitive equilibria and, more generally, on how general equilibrium analysis and welfare theorems can be extended to asymmetric information, see Townsend (1987), Prescott and Townsend (1984), Boyd and Prescott (1986), and Arnott and Stiglitz (1993).

finance alternative investment projects that differ in degree of risk and productivity and the endogenous distribution of projects is determined as a function of the amount of loanable funds, assuming that lenders have no information about borrowers' ability and technological choices. Embedding this framework in an overlapping generations economy it is shown that equilibria may be such that the average quality of the selected projects in equilibrium is high in recessions and low in booms. The key step in the paper is to relate the equilibrium contracts and the distribution of bad projects to the opportunity cost of lending (the risk free interest rate) and the amount of loanable funds. The proportion of bad projects is an increasing function of interest payments (loan rate times loan size) on good projects, that is, higher interest payments and limited liability make the moral hazard and adverse selection problems more important. A rise in the interest rate induces a price and a quantity effect on interest payments. The price effect increases the cost of borrowing (higher loan rate), while the quantity effect reduces the loan size. If the quantity effect dominates over the price effect, interest payments go down along with the proportion of bad projects. When the interest rate is determined by a market-clearing condition in the market for loans, a rise in loanable funds may have a negative effect on the loan rates and a positive effect on the average loan size. Hence, when the quantity effect dominates over the price effect, the proportion of bad projects may be procyclical.

All papers surveyed in this discussion offer important contributions to the understanding of macroeconomic fluctuations under plausible assumptions about the market structure. However, most of the models employed to address these issues may not be entirely suitable for a quantitative evaluation of the impact of market imperfections on business cycles. In some case these models are static (as Holmström and Tirole 1997) and in some case they assume that agents are short lived (as Bernanke and Gertler 1990; Suarez and Sussman 1997). Kiyotaki and Moore put more emphasis and effort in trying to construct a model that could be used to quantify their predictions (their model is fully dynamic and they assume long lived agents). The way in which the equilibrium loan contracts are specified may be criticized on the ground that the market mechanism assumed by KM imposes very little incentives to avoid strategic default (e.g. no information on borrowers' records can be exchanged across lenders) and that contracts have one period maturity. However, since the assumption that agents (consumers and entrepreneurs) are infinitely lived is essential for a quantitative evaluation of the importance of financial factors for business cycles, a drastic simplification of the contracting problem may be inevitable. Carlstrom and Fuerst (1997, 1998) offer an alternative computable general equilibrium analysis in the spirit of the FSA. As in KM, they assume infinitely lived agents and anonymous contractual relations between lenders and borrowers. However, the agency problem derives from the costly state verification model of Townsend (1979). In the first of these two papers it is shown that production of investment goods depends on two key variables: entrepreneurs' net worth and the price of new capital goods. Because of incentive problems, the price of capital exceeds production cost and, abstracting from the role of agents' net worth, the model is almost isomorphic to a model with costs of adjusting capital. This explains why, computing the effects of exogenous shocks, Carlston and Fuerst (1997) find more propagation and less amplification than in the standard Real Business Cycles model. In fact, a positive shock on agents' net worth increases the supply of new capital goods and drives down the price of capital. Since the response of agents' net worth to exogenous shocks is sluggish, aggregate fluctuations may loose amplitude and gain persistence.

Most models analyzed in this discussion take very little care in specifying financial market institutions. Most contributions assume Pareto optimal contractual arrangements. These may either take the form of a debt or an equity contract, according to the underlying assumptions about investors' information. In the models by Holmström and Tirole and Suarez and Sussman, we are allowed to interpret optimal contracts both as debt or as equity contracts, since investment realizations are either positive or zero. In the model by Kiyotaki and Moore, the existence of a stock market is explicitly ruled out, due to the assumption that a borrower cannot precommit to work on his project. This implies that these models cannot be used for comparing the extent of financial propagation in countries with different financial institutions and that policy implications are hard to address.

APPENDIX

Cycles in the Kiyotaki–Moore model

Here is a brief sketch of the model. Suppose that the farmer and the gatherer have technologies defined by the production functions $f_f(k)$ and $f_g(k)$. However, farmers produce coffee and gatherers produce fruit. For simplicity, I assume that coffee is only desired by the gatherer.

Individual consumption of fruit is still denoted by c^j ($j = f, g$) and gatherers consumption of coffee is denoted by x. The relative price of coffee (in units of fruit) is p. The gatherers' instantaneous utility is quasilinear, that is, $u_g(c, x) = c + v(x)$ ($v(\cdot)$ increasing and strictly concave and $v'(x) \to \infty$ as $x \to 0$). This assumption add to all the other features and assumptions that I made in the last section, with the proper adjustments.

The first-order conditions for utility maximization that we have already discussed in the previous version of the model need very little modifications. Since gatherers have quasilinear utility and they are not credit constrained:

$$R_t = 1/\beta_g \equiv R, \tag{20}$$

$$d_t = f_g'\left(k_t^g\right)/R \le p_t \alpha/R; \tag{21}$$

$$p_t = v'(x_t); \tag{22}$$

As for farmers, notice that the marginal product of capital on their own technology must be multiplied by the relative price of coffee. Since utility is logarithmic:

$$k_{t+1}^f d_{t+1} = \beta_f p_t \alpha k_t^f. \tag{23}$$

Here again the first best equilibrium (where loans need not be collateralized) is a steady state where $k^f = k^{**}$ and $q_t = q^{**}$ satisfy:

$$f_g'(K - k^{**}) = \alpha v'(\alpha k^{**}), \qquad q^{**} = \frac{\alpha v'(k^{**})}{R - 1}.$$

Now consider the case in which debt need to be fully collateralized and the credit constraint is binding. Letting $k^f = k$, $d(k) = f_g'(K - k)/R$ and rearranging conditions 20–23, we obtain that a sequence $\{k_t\}$ in a credit constrained equilibrium satisfies:

$$d(k_{t+1})k_{t+1} = \beta_f v'(\alpha k_t)\alpha k_t, \tag{24}$$

$$f_g'(K - k_{t+1}) \le v'(\alpha k_t)\alpha. \tag{25}$$

As usual, equation 24 combines farmers' optimal investing behavior with the gatherers no arbitrage condition and equation 25 guarantees that farmers' credit constraint is binding for all t.

Under the assumption $f_g'(K) < \beta_f R\alpha v'(0)$, $\lim_{k\to 0} f_g'(k) = +\infty$, the dynamical system defined by equation 24 generates a steady state $k^{oo} > 0$.

Now recall that $h(k) = d(k)k$ is increasing and invertible in the interval $[0, K)$ and redefine equation 24 as a difference equation:

$$k_{t+1} = h^{-1}(\beta_f \alpha k_t v'(\alpha k_t)) \equiv \phi(k_t),$$

where:

$$\phi'(k) = \frac{\beta_f \alpha}{h'(\cdot)} \left(v'(\alpha k) + \alpha k v''(\alpha k) \right).$$

Hence, the dynamics generated by the map $\phi(\cdot)$ may not be monotonic and convergent to k^o. In particular, non monotonicity may occur when the elasticity of the demand for coffee, $-x v''(x)/v'(x)$, is greater than one.

The possibility of an endogenous reversion mechanism in this version of the KM model is a consequence of the interaction between the credit constraint and the effect of a change in relative prices on farmers' liquidity. The binding credit constraint implies that investment depends on farmers' current income (liquidity) and farmers' liquidity is affected by the relative price of their output. During a boom high production generates a low relative price of coffee. This will eventually decrease farmers' liquidity and lead to a fall in investment.

References

Abel, A. B. (1985). "Dynamic behavior of capital accumulation in a cash-in-advance model." *Journal of Monetary Economics*, 16: 55–71.

Allen, F. (1983). "Credit rationing and payment incentives." *Review of Economic Studies*, 50: 639–46.

Aiyagari, R., and Gertler, M. (1991). "Asset returns with transaction costs and uninsured individual risk." *Journal of Monetary Economics*, 27: 311–31.

Alvarez, F., and Jermann, U. (2000). "Efficiency, equilibrium and asset pricing with the risk of default." *Econometrica*, 68: 775–98.

Arnott, R., and Stiglitz, J. (1993). "Equilibrium in competitive insurance markets with moral hazard." Mimeo., Boston College.

Azariadis, C. and Smith, B. (1993). "Adverse selection in the overlapping generations model: The case of pure exchange." *Journal of Economic Theory*, 60: 227–305.

Becker, R., and Foias, C. (1987). "A characterization of Ramsey equilibrium." *Journal of Economic Theory*, 41: 173–84.

Bernanke, B. (1983). "Nonmonetary effects of the financial crisis in propagation of the great depression." *American Economic Review*, 73: 257–76.

——, and Blinder, A. (1988). "Is it money, or credit, or both, or neither?" *American Economic Review*, 78: 435–9.

Bernanke, B., and Gertler, M. (1989). "Agency costs, net worth and business fluctuations." *American Economic Review*, 79: 14–31.

——, and —— (1990), "Financial fragility and economic performance." *Quarterly Journal of Economics*, 105: 87–114.

——, and —— (1995). "Inside the Black Box: The credit channel of monetary policy transmission." *Journal of Economic Perspectives*, 4: 27–48.

Bester, H. (1985). "Screening vs rationing in credit markets with imperfect information." *American Economic Review*, 57: 850–5.

Bewley, T. (1986). "Dynamic implications of the form of the budget constraint," in H. F. Sonnenschein (ed.), *Models of economic Dynamics* (New York: Springer-Verlag).

Boyd, J., and Prescott, E. (1986). "Financial intermediary-coalitions." *Journal of Economic Theory*, 38: 211–32.

Bulow, J., and Rogoff, K. (1989). "Sovereign debt: Is to forgive to forget?." *American Economic Review*, 79: 43–50.

Calomiris, C. (1995). "Financial fragility: Issues and policy implications." *Journal of Financial Services Research*, 9: 241–57.

——, and Hubbard, G. (1990). "Firm heterogeneity, internal finance and credit rationing." *Economic Journal*, 100: 90–104.

Carlstrom, C., and Fuerst, T. (1997). "Agency costs, net worth, and business fluctuations: A computable general equilibrium analysis." *American Economic Review*, 87: 893–910.

——, and —— (1998). "Agency costs and business cycles." *Economic Theory*, 12: 583–97.

Diamond, D. (1984). "Financial intermediation and delegated monitoring." *Review of Economic Studies*, 51: 393–414.

Eaton, J., and Gersovitz, M. (1981). "Debt with potential repudiation: Theoretical and empirical analysis." *Review of Economic Studies*, 48: 289–309.

Farmer, R. (1984). "New theory of aggregate supply." *America Economic Review*, 74: 920–30.

Fazzari, S., Hubbart, R. G., and Petersen, B. (1988). "Financing constraints and corporate investment." *Brooking Papers on Economic Activity*, 1: 141–95.

Fisher, I. (1933). "The debt-deflation theory of great depressions." *Econometrica*, 1: 337–57.

Gertler, M. (1988). "Financial structure and aggregate economic activity: An overview." *Journal of Money, Credit and Banking*, 20: 559–88.

—— (1992). "Financial capacity and output fluctuations in an economy with multi-period financial relationships." *Review of Economic Studies*, 59: 455–72.

——, and Gilchrist, S. (1993). "The role of credit market imperfections in the monetary transmission mechanism: Arguments and evidence." *Scandinavian Journal of Economics*, 95: 43–64.

——, and —— (1994). "Monetary policy, business cycles, and the behavior of small manufacturing firms." *Quarterly Journal of Economics*, 109: 309–40.

Gottardi, P. (1994). "On the non-neutrality of money with incomplete markets." *Journal of Economic Theory,* 62: 209–20.

Gurley, J., and Shaw, E. (1955). "Financial aspects of economic development." *American Economic Review,* 65: 515–38.

Hart, O., and Moore, J. (1989). "Default and renegotiation: A dynamic model of debt." MIT mimeo.

——, and —— (1994). "A theory of debt based on the inalienability of human capital." *Quarterly Journal of Economics,* 109: 841–79.

Holmström, B., and Tirole, J. (1997). "Financial intermediation, loanable funds and the real sector." *Quarterly Journal of Economics,* 112: 663–91.

Hubbard, G. (1998). "Capital-market imperfections and investment." *Journal of Economic Literature,* 36: 193–225.

Jaffee, D., and Russell, T. (1976). "Imperfect information, uncertainty and credit rationing." *Quarterly Journal of Economics,* 90: 651–66.

Kehoe, T., and Levine, D. (1993). "Debt-constrained asset markets." *Review of Economic Studies,* 60: 865–88.

——, and —— (2001). "Liquidity constrained asset markets versus debt constrained markets." *Econometrica,* 3: 575–98.

Kindleberger, C. (1978). *Manias, Panics and Crashes.* New York: Basic Books.

King, R. K. (1986). "Monetary transmission: Through bank loans or bank liabilities?" *Journal of Money, Credit, and Banking,* 18: 290–303.

Kocherlakota, N. (1996). "Implications of efficient risk sharing without commitment." *Review of Economic Studies,* 63: 595–609.

Kiyotaki, N., and Moore, J. (1997). "Credit cycles." *Journal of Political Economy,* 105: 211–48.

Lucas, R. E. (1990). "Liquidity and interest rates." *Journal of Economic Theory,* 50: 237–64.

Mankiw, N. G. (1986). "The allocation of credit and financial collapse." *Quarterly Journal of Economics,* 101: 455–70.

Minsky, H. (1975). *John Maynard Keynes.* New York: Columbia Univ. Press.

Mishkin, F. (1978). "The household balance sheet and the great depression." *Journal of Economic History,* 38: 918–37.

—— (1991). "Asymmetric information and financial crises: A historical perspective," in G. Hubbard (ed.), *Financial Markets and Financial Crises* (Chicago: University of Chicago Press), 69–108.

—— (1996). "Understanding financial crises: A developing country perspective." *Annual World Bank Conference on Development Economics,* 29–62.

Prescott, E., and Townsend, R. (1984). "Pareto optima and competitive equilibria with adverse selection and moral hazard." *Econometrica,* 52: 21–45.

Reichlin, P., and Siconolfi, P. (2000). "Optimal debt contracts and moral hazard along the business cycle." CEPR D.P. n. 2351, 2000 *Economic Theory* (forthcoming).

Scheinkman, J., and Weiss, L. (1986). "Borrowing constraints and aggregate economic activity." *Econometrica,* 45: 23–45.

Stiglitz, J., and Weiss, A. (1981). "Credit rationing in markets with imperfect information." *American Economic Review*, 71: 393–410.

Stockman, A. (1981). "Anticipated inflation and the capital stock in a cash-in-advance economy." *Journal of Monetary Economics*, 8: 387–93.

Suarez, J., and Sussman, O. (1997). "Endogenous Cycles in a Stiglitz–Weiss Economy." *Journal of Economic Theory*, 76: 47–71.

Symposium on The Monetary Transmission Mechanism (1995). *Journal of Economic Perspectives*, 4: 3–95.

Townsend, R. (1979). "Optimal contracts and competitive markets with costly state verification." *Journal of Economic Theory*, 21: 265–93.

—— (1987). "Arrow–Debreu programs as microfoundations to macroeconomics," in Bewley (ed.), *Advances in Economic Theory: Fifth World Congress* (Cambridge: Cambridge Univ. Press).

Williamson, S. (1987*a*). "Costly monitoring, loan contracts and equilibrium credit rationing." *Quarterly Journal of Economics*, 102: 135–45.

—— (1987*b*). "Financial intermediation, business failures and real business cycles." *Journal of Political Economy*, 95: 1196–216.

Woodford, M. (1986). "Stationary sunspot equilibria in a finance constrained economy'." *Journal of Economic Theory*, 40: 128–37.

—— (1988). "Imperfect financial intermediation and complex dynamics," in W. Barnett, J. Geweke, and K. Shell (eds.), *Economic Complexity: Chaos, Sunspots, Bubbles and Nonlinearity* (Cambridge: Cambridge Univ. Press).

INDEX